RBS player Jack Nicklaus, winner of 18 professional major championships.

Introduction

It is a privilege for RBS to once again present *The World of Professional Golf 2005*, the golf annual founded by the late Mark H. McCormack.

As an international company headquartered in Scotland, the home of golf, we have enjoyed a long association with the game. In the case of the R&A and the Open Championship that relationship now dates back over 100 years. More recently, we have deepened our involvement with golf in both the US and Europe.

The annual represents an excellent record of professional golf around the world. It is both informative and definitive; enjoy!

Sir Fred Goodwin
Group Chief Executive

The Royal Bank of Scotland Group

The Royal Bank of Scotland Group

Presents

The World of
Professional Golf
Founded by
Mark H. McCormack
2005

An IMG PUBLISHING Book

An IMG PUBLISHING Book
Editor: Bev Norwood
Contributors: Andy Farrell, Doug Ferguson, Donald (Doc) Giffin, Marino Parascenzo, Robert Sommers

First published 2005
© IMG Operations, Inc. 2005

Designed and produced by Davis Design

ISBN 1-878843-41-9

Printed and bound in the United States.

Contents

1   The Year In Retrospect   1

THE ROYAL BANK OF SCOTLAND PRESENTS
THE MAJOR CHAMPIONSHIPS
2   Masters Tournament   25
3   U.S. Open Championship   36
4   The Open Championship   51
5   PGA Championship   67

OTHER SIGNIFICANT EVENTS
6   The Players Championship   79
7   Ryder Cup   85
8   HSBC World Match Play   96

WORLDWIDE TOURS
9   American Tours   103
10 European Tours   167
11 Asia/Japan Tours   199
12 Australasian Tour   234
13 African Tours   240
14 Senior Tours   254
15 Women's Tours   300

APPENDIXES
Official World Golf Ranking   362
World's Winners of 2004   370
Multiple Winners of 2004   377
World Money List   378
World Money List Leaders   386
Career World Money List   387
Senior World Money List   388
Women's World Money List   391
U.S. PGA Tour   394
Special Events   462

Nationwide Tour   471
Canadian Tour   493
Tour de las Americas (South America)   503
PGA European Tour   512
Challenge Tour   561
Asian Tour   577
Japan Tour   596
Australasian Tour   618
African Tours   626
Champions Tour   646
European Seniors Tour   672
Japan Senior Tour   687
U.S. LPGA Tour   692
Ladies European Tour   713
Japan LPGA Tour   722
Australian Women's Tour   744
Nedbank Women's Tour of South Africa   747

Foreword
(Written in 1968)

It has long been my feeling that a sport as compelling as professional golf is deserving of a history, and by history I do not mean an account culled years later from the adjectives and enthusiasms of on-the-spot reports that have then sat in newspaper morgues for decades waiting for some patient drudge to paste them together and call them lore. Such works can be excellent when insight and perspective are added to the research, but this rarely happens. What I am talking about is a running history, a chronology written at the time, which would serve both as a record of the sport and as a commentary upon the sport in any given year — an annual, if you will....

When I embarked on this project two years ago (the first of these annuals was published in Great Britain in 1967), I was repeatedly told that such a compendium of world golf was impossible, that it would be years out of date before it could be assembled and published, that it would be hopelessly expensive to produce and that only the golf fanatic would want a copy anyway. In the last analysis, it was that final stipulation that spurred me on. There must be a lot of golf fanatics, I decided. I can't be the only one. And then one winter day I was sitting in Arnold Palmer's den in Latrobe, Pennsylvania, going through the usual motions of spreading papers around so that Arnold and I could discuss some business project, when Arnold happened to mention that he wanted to collect a copy of each new golf book that was published from now on, in order to build a golf library of his own. "It's really too bad that there isn't a book every year on the pro tour," he said. "Ah," I thought. "Another golf fanatic. That makes two of us." So I decided to do the book. And I have. And I hope you like it. If so, you can join Arnold and me as golf fanatics.

Mark H. McCormack
Cleveland, Ohio
January, 1968

Mark H. McCormack
1930 – 2003

In 1960, Mark Hume McCormack shook hands with a young golfer named Arnold Palmer. That historic handshake established a business that would evolve into today's IMG, the world's premier sports and lifestyle marketing and management company — representing hundreds of sports figures, entertainers, television properties, artists, musicians, writers, celebrities and prestigious organizations and events around the world. With just a handshake Mark McCormack had invented a global industry.

Sean McManus, President of CBS Sports, reflects, "I don't think it's an overstatement to say that like Henry Ford and Bill Gates, Mark McCormack literally created, fostered and led an entirely new worldwide industry. There was no sports marketing before Mark McCormack. Every athlete who's ever appeared in a commercial, or every right holder who sold their rights to anyone, owes a huge debt of gratitude to Mark McCormack."

Mark McCormack's philosophy was simple. "Be the best," he said. "Learn the business and expand by applying what you already know." This philosophy served him well, not only as an entrepreneur and CEO of IMG, but also as an author, a consultant and a confidant to a host of global leaders in the world of business, politics, finance, science, sports and entertainment.

He was among the most-honored entrepreneurs of his time. *Sports Illustrated* recognized him as "The Most Powerful Man in Sports." In 1999, ESPN's Sports Century listed him as one of the century's 10 "Most Influential People in the Business of Sport."

Golf Magazine called McCormack "the most powerful man in golf" and honored him along with Arnold Palmer, Gerald Ford, Dwight D. Eisenhower, Bob Hope and Ben Hogan as one of the 100 all-time "American Heroes of Golf." *Tennis* magazine and *Racquet* magazine named him "the most powerful man in tennis." Tennis legend Billie Jean King believes, "Mark McCormack was the king of sports marketing. He shaped the way all sports are marketed around the world. He was the first in the marketplace, and his influence on the world of sports, particularly his ability to combine athlete representation, property development and television broadcasting, will forever be the standard of the industry."

The London *Sunday Times* listed him as one of the 1000 people who influenced the 20th century. Alastair Cooke on the BBC said simply that "McCormack was the Oracle; the creator of the talent industry, the maker of people famous in their profession famous to the rest of the world and making for them a fortune in the process ... He took on as clients people already famous in their profession as golfer, opera singer, author, footballer, racing car driver, violinist — and from time to time if they needed special help, a prime minister, or even the Pope."

McCormack was honored posthumously by the Golf Writers Association of America with the 2004 William D. Richardson Award, the organization's highest honor, "Given to recognize an individual who has consistently made an outstanding contribution to golf."

Among McCormack's other honors were the 2001 PGA Distinguished Service Award, given to those who have helped perpetuate the values and ideals of the PGA of America. He was also named a Commander of the Royal Order of the Polar Star by the King of Sweden (the highest honor for a person living outside of Sweden) for his contribution to the Nobel Foundation.

Journalist Frank Deford states, "There have been what we love to call dynasties in every sport. IMG has been different. What this one brilliant man, Mark McCormack, created is the only dynasty ever over all sport."

Through IMG, Mark McCormack demonstrated the value of sports and lifestyle activities as effective corporate marketing tools, but more importantly, his lifelong dedication to his vocation — begun with just a simple handshake — brought enjoyment to millions of people worldwide who watch and cheer their heroes and heroines. That is his legacy.

1. The Year in Retrospect

He was the man to beat in every tournament he played, an imposing figure who was as relentless in the gym as he was on the golf course, a man so dialed into his game that he became a regular fixture on the leaderboard. No one ever counted him out. Four shots behind with four holes to play? No problem. He fired off four straight birdies and made the winner sweat the very last putt. Faced with a seven-shot deficit, he played the final nine holes in 29 for a stunning victory. He won a major championship by letting others make the mistakes, then burying them with perfect shots under the most stifling pressure. Give him the lead going into the final round and the only question was his margin of victory. There simply was no stopping him. By year's end, he had nine victories, the lowest scoring average and set a record for single-season earnings on the PGA Tour. He was No. 1 in the world, no argument.

In many respects, 2004 was no different from the previous five years in golf. Only the name changed.

Vijay means "victory" in his Hindi. Vijay Singh was all of that by churning out one of the greatest seasons in golf. Singh became only the sixth player to win at least nine times on the PGA Tour, equal to Paul Runyan in 1933 and Tiger Woods in 2000, but trailing Sam Snead (11 victories in 1950), Ben Hogan (13 victories in 1946, 10 victories in 1948) and Byron Nelson, whose 18 victories in 1945 might never be broken. He won his first Vardon Trophy and became golf's first $10 million man: $10.9 million on the PGA Tour, and $11.6 million to lead the World Money List. (See Appendixes for complete list.) Singh spent eight months chasing Tiger Woods, but had no rival at year's end.

Even more impressive is that Singh had a year for the ages at 41, a time when most players slide into the twilight of their careers. Singh hit his stride. "As the saying goes, 'Life starts at 40.' That's true for me," Singh said.

Truth is, his quest to supplant Tiger Woods at No. 1 in the world started at the end of 2003 when the PGA Tour revealed that Woods had won his fifth consecutive Player of the Year award. It was another controversial vote in Florida, this one without the hanging chads. Singh had won four times on the PGA Tour and ended Woods' five-year reign atop the money list. Woods had five victories and won the Vardon Trophy. Neither player won a major. Still, the Fijian must have wondered what else he had to do to get the recognition he felt he deserved. The plan was simple. He would have to leave no doubt who was the best player.

"I had something to prove this year, knowing last year it was so close," Singh said.

The year sure didn't start out that way. Singh sent a subtle message in the first tournament of the year, the winners-only Mercedes Championships at Kapalua. He finished second behind Stuart Appleby, but not until he birdied the final four holes, leaving a 100-foot eagle putt that would have forced a playoff on the edge of the cup.

After top 10s in the Sony Open in Hawaii and FBR Open in Phoenix, followed by his first victory of the year in the AT&T Pebble Beach National Pro-Am, Singh extended his streak to 12 consecutive top 10s and was approaching the modern-day record of 14 that Jack Nicklaus set in 1977. That ended at Torrey Pines, when Singh missed his only cut of the year at the Buick Invitational.

Still, no one had any premonition this would be Vijay's year, and his alone.

The focus was on the "Big Four" in golf — Singh, Woods, Ernie Els and a resurgent Phil Mickelson. Woods posted top 10s in his first three tournaments, then won the WGC - Accenture Match Play at La Costa for the second consecutive year, narrowly escaping the first round when John Rollins hit a sand wedge into the bunker on the 18th hole. That shot ultimately kept Woods from getting shut out on the PGA Tour this year. More on that later.

Els made it two straight playoff victories at the Sony Open, emerging from the spotlight cast on 14-year-old Michelle Wie to show that the Big Easy was ready to make another run at No. 1. Mickelson was coming off his worst season ever, but showed up at the Bob Hope Chrysler Classic looking fit and determined, and he won his first start of the year in a playoff. Along with Retief Goosen, they became central figures in golf for the first seven months of the year.

Mickelson had a chance to win the first seven tournaments he played. By the time he got to the Masters, the burden as the "best player to never win a major" was never more weighty. Mickelson seemed to relish the label. Augusta National member Billy Morris conducted the pre-tournament interview and lauded Mickelson's "beautiful" record at the Masters — no worse than seventh the last five years, third place each of the last three years. "But no wins," Mickelson quickly pointed out with that sneaky grin. Then he reached over and playfully tugged at the sleeve of the green jacket Morris wore and said, "I want one of these. Those are nice."

What followed was one of the most compelling Masters in its storied history. It started with the departure of the King — Arnold Palmer playing in his 50th consecutive and final Masters — and ended with a classic duel between Mickelson and Els, two men desperate to slip into a green jacket. Els holed an eagle putt on the par-five 13th hole that rocked Augusta National, then added a nifty up-and-down from behind the green on the par-five 15th that gave him a two-shot advantage. He did everything required of a Masters champion, and he had history on his side — not only his three majors, but Mickelson's lifetime of failure in them.

But Lefty finally got it right. He made a 15-foot birdie on the 12th, a two-putt birdie on the 13th, then struck a wedge that stopped a foot from the cup on No. 14 for three straight birdies to pull within one shot of the lead. The crucial shot was an eight iron on the par-three 16th hole, which does not set up well for some left-handers. The last time Mickelson was this close to a Masters title, he left his shot on the top shelf and took three putts. This time, his eight iron stopped 15 feet below the cup for an eagle and a share of the lead.

Els made two pars coming in and was on the practice green, bracing for a playoff, when he heard a roar that made him sick to his stomach. Mickelson put his approach to within 18 feet on the final hole and got a huge break when Chris DiMarco blasted out of a greenside bunker to just beyond his ball mark, allowing Mickelson to get a good read on the line. He took full advantage, the birdie putt swirling in the left side of the cup.

The final numbers were staggering: Mickelson birdied five of the final seven holes, shot 31 on the back nine, and had his first major championship. He nearly won the next two tournaments he played, the HP Classic of New Orleans and the Wachovia Championship. Surely, this would be the year Mickelson squeezed everything out of his awesome abilities.

Goosen changed all that with a miraculous short game at Shinnecock Hills, a classic course that the United States Golf Association ruined in its desperate attempt to protect par. With light rain and morning fog keeping the links-styled course on Long Island too soft for the USGA's liking, officials shut down the water and rolled the greens, which became a problem on the par-three seventh hole. Almost every ball that landed on the putting surface rolled off into a swale. About the only hope of making par was to purposely hit the ball in a bunker and try to get up-and-down.

The USGA realized it made a mistake early Sunday morning, then began syringing the greens after each twosome came through. But the rest of the brick-yard course was no picnic. Els, playing in the final group with Goosen, shot an 80. The average score was 78.7, the highest for a final round at the U.S. Open since 1972 at Pebble Beach. Bo Van Pelt took six putts on the fourth green and made eight. Twenty-eight players failed to break 80.

Goosen and Mickelson played a game with which no one else was familiar. The stoic South African was pure magic with the putter, making a 12-foot par putt on the 13th, a 25-foot bogey putt on the 14th, an eight-foot par putt on the 15th and a 12-footer for birdie on the 16th to tie Mickelson for the lead. It all turned on the 17th hole. Mickelson blasted out of the bunker to five feet, but ran the par putt some four feet by and missed that coming back to make double bogey. Goosen, playing in the group behind, saved par from the same bunker and finished with a 71 for a two-shot victory and his second U.S. Open title in four years.

Mickelson at least had his green jacket. Els was 0-for-2 in chances to win a major, but he looked like a shoo-in at Royal Troon when he went into the final round trailing American Todd Hamilton by one stroke.

Hamilton was the quintessential journeyman, having spent a dozen years toiling in remote outposts from Pakistan to Kuala Lumpur, winning four times on the Japan PGA Tour and getting through the PGA qualifying tournament for the first time as a 38-year-old father of three. Not many expected Hamilton to hang on in the final round, not with players like Els, Mickelson, Goosen and Woods close behind. "I'm sure there is no one in this room that would expect me — at least before the tournament started — to win," Hamilton said. "And probably not too many expect it to happen tomorrow. It may not. But I will definitely be trying."

He withstood every challenge, including a 12-foot birdie putt by Els on the final hole that would have given the South African his fourth major. Instead, they went to a playoff, and Hamilton was as steady as ever. Both made pars on the first and second holes, then Els missed the green long on the par-three 17th. The Big Easy missed a 10-foot par putt, giving Hamilton a one-shot lead going to the 18th. Hamilton came up short, but relied on his utility club again for a delicate bump-and-run that stopped two feet from the hole. When Els missed a 12-foot birdie putt from the same line he faced in regulation, Hamilton only had to tap in for par to claim the silver claret jug.

Singh, meanwhile, had gone AWOL in the first three majors.

He narrowly made the cut at the Masters, and only weekend rounds of 69 and 67 allowed him to sneak into the top 10. He was in contention at Shinnecock Hills until a 77 in the third round knocked him off the leaderboard. He was only two shots back going into the weekend at Royal Troon until his hopes again were derailed with a 76. Heading into the final three months of the season, it appeared the biggest threat to Woods' No. 1 ranking would come from Els.

Singh was never more disgusted with himself. He had hit the ball so pure at Royal Troon that he felt he should have won, instead of finishing 11 shots behind in a tie for 20th. He attributed everything to his putting, which had been his Achilles' heel throughout his career. Despite winning three times on tour, he decided to ditch his belly putter and return to a conventional size.

"The British Open was it," Singh said. "I think I averaged 34 putts there, and you can't win golf tournaments doing that. I came back home and decided, 'Hey, I'm going to try it out.' I worked every day at least an hour and a half a day, just putting with it and felt comfortable." He never could have imagined the dividends it would pay.

It started at the Buick Open in Grand Blanc, Michigan, where Singh had to withstand an incredible start to the final round by John Daly, which stoked the large gallery into a frenzy. A two-time major winner during a turbulent career, Daly is the people's choice, and a victory at the Buick Invitational in February was his first on U.S. soil in 10 years. He was having his most consistent year ever — no small task for Big John — and he started birdie-eagle-birdie-birdie at Warwick Hills Country Club to build a quick lead. Singh never blinked, eventually catching up to Daly, holding off a late charge from Woods, and winning his fourth PGA Tour title when Daly missed a four-foot par putt on the final hole.

Even then, Singh was only a leading candidate for Player of the Year. Mickelson had the Masters and was a combined three shots away from winning the other two majors. Els had two victories and three close calls in the majors. The PGA Championship at Whistling Straits in Wisconsin, the dream of Herb Kohler and the creation of Pete Dye, would determine who would be the star of 2004. Adding to the pressure for Singh was being drawn the first two rounds with Daly and Woods.

Despite his success, Singh had not fared well going up against Woods. The last two times they played together, Woods beat him in the final round of the 2003 WGC - American Express Championship and put five shots between them in the first five holes in the first round of the 2003 Tour Championship. And each time Singh closed in on No. 1 in the Official World Golf Ranking, Woods beat him in the next three tournaments they played. The first round of the PGA Championship set the tone for the week, and for the rest of the year.

As Woods soared to a 75, Singh quickly got himself into contention with amazing control of his long game, opening with rounds of 67 and

68 to join Justin Leonard atop the leaderboard. Woods turned in the most dramatic round of the day, but typical of his year, it was only to make the cut. Two shots over the cut line, Woods birdied three of his final six holes to extend his cut streak to 129 consecutive PGA Tour events. After three rounds, Singh had a one-shot lead over Leonard, and the Texan said what his peers had been thinking for some time.

"Vijay is an incredible player," Leonard said. "It's going to be a fun day. I get to go head-to-head with one of the best players in the world, if not the best player in the world."

By Sunday evening, there was no argument. Leonard had the Wanamaker Trophy in his grasp until his putter, normally the most reliable club in his bag, failed him miserably. Leonard missed six putts inside 12 feet on the back nine and still had a chance to win until his five iron on the 18th came up short and into the bunker. He made bogey to set up a three-man playoff among Leonard, Singh and Chris DiMarco. The only one who felt worse was Els, who took three putts from about 100 feet on the 18th hole and missed out on the playoff by one shot.

Singh made short work of the three-hole playoff, opting for driver on the 361-yard 10th hole and hitting it so perfectly that he had only a flip wedge to the green, setting up a six-foot birdie. It was his only birdie Sunday, but it carried him to his third major championship. Singh closed with a 76, the highest final round ever by a PGA champion and the highest by a winner in the final round of any major since Reg Whitcombe shot 78 and won the 1938 Open Championship at Royal St. George's.

"It looked ugly," Singh said. "But it's the prettiest one, I think."

It was beautiful for many reasons. The victory was his fifth of the year, making him the clear-cut favorite as the Player of the Year and closer than he had ever been to No. 1 in the world. Singh figured it might take him two or three years of great golf to supplant Woods atop the World Ranking. Suddenly, he was one tournament away.

The showdown came three weeks later outside Boston at the Deutsche Bank Championship, a tournament that benefits the Tiger Woods Foundation. But in the final round, as Woods made a charge at the lead, he let everything slip away with a three-putt on the 14th hole — the tournament, and ultimately, his No. 1 ranking. Singh closed him out for a three-shot victory, and for the first time in 264 weeks, dating to the 1999 PGA Championship, there was a new world No. 1.

"If I'm playing my best, I can beat anybody," Singh said. "I have never been one who is intimidated by Tiger."

TIGER WOODS

EVENT	POSITION
Mercedes Championships	T-4
Buick Invitational	T-10
Nissan Open	T-7
WGC - Accenture Match Play	1
Dubai Desert Classic	T-5
Bay Hill Invitational	T-46
The Players Championship	T-16

Masters Tournament	T-22
Wachovia Championship	T-3
EDS Byron Nelson Championship	T-4
Memorial Tournament	3
U.S. Open Championship	T-17
Cialis Western Open	T-7
The Open Championship	T-9
Buick Open	3
PGA Championship	T-24
WGC - NEC Invitational	T-2
Deutsche Bank Championship	T-2
WGC - American Express Championship	9
Tour Championship	2
Dunlop Phoenix	1
Target World Challenge	1

Woods was the consummate intimidator in golf for five years, but no more. Not many saw this kind of year coming, especially after he won the WGC - Accenture Match Play in February for his 40th career victory on the PGA Tour at just 28 years old. But he was not satisfied with how he was playing and decided to embark on a new round of swing changes.

Having split with longtime coach Butch Harmon, Woods enlisted the help of Hank Haney to rebuild a swing that would take pressure off his left knee (he had surgery in December 2002) and rely more on keeping the club on plane, instead of trying to match the speed of his lower and upper body. Not that he was willing to share this information with anyone. Woods was coy when asked about his changes, saying at the Memorial Tournament it was only minor adjustments. He was equally secretive about Haney, the longtime coach of his best friend on tour, Mark O'Meara. And if anyone got too close, caddie Steve Williams was there to take matters — or cameras, as the case may be — into his own hands.

At the Memorial, Williams purposely planted the golf bag in front of a CBS Sports camera designed to analyze swings. And at the U.S. Open, Williams kicked one camera out of a news photographer's hands because of an early click, and he went into the gallery to remove the camera from a fan in the final round. Little did he know the fan was an off-duty police officer.

Woods had his worst year on tour, but one most players would not mind having — 14 top-10s out of 19 tournaments, more than $5.3 million in earnings. Still, he lost 36-hole leads on consecutive weekends at the Wachovia Championship and the EDS Byron Nelson Championship, something he had not done in five years. And he finished the year by losing a share of the 54-hole lead in the Tour Championship at East Lake to Retief Goosen, something he had not done since the 2000 Tour Championship.

His spat with Harmon reached epidemic levels at the U.S. Open when Harmon, working as an analyst for the British cable network Sky Sports, said, "He's not working on the right things in his golf swing, although Tiger obviously thinks he is. For him to stand there in every one of his interviews and say, 'I'm close, I feel really good about what I'm doing,' I think he might be in a bit of denial."

Statistically, Woods was 182nd in driving accuracy and 47th in greens in regulation. He made progress as the year ended, however, winning the Dunlop Phoenix tournament in Japan by eight shots and then his Target World Challenge at Sherwood Country Club in California by two shots over Padraig Harrington. He extended his record on the PGA Tour to 133 consecutive tournaments without missing the 36-hole cut. And the year wasn't a total loss. He got married to Elin Nordegren on October 5 in Barbados, then sailed off in the Caribbean on his 150-foot yacht, *Privacy*. Still, Woods was glad to get 2004 behind him. "The entire year, I felt like I was defending myself after each and every round," he said. "I was getting frustrated with that." Asked what it would take to regain the No. 1 ranking, Woods said, "Win tournaments."

That's what Singh did better than anyone else in a year that closely resembled one of the best Woods has ever put together — not 2000, but 1999.

VIJAY SINGH

EVENT	POSITION
Mercedes Championships	2
Sony Open in Hawaii	T-10
FBR Open	T-3
AT&T Pebble Beach National Pro-Am	1
Buick Invitational	MC
Nissan Open	T-24
WGC - Accenture Match Play	T-17
Bay Hill Invitational	T-31
The Players Championship	T-13
Masters Tournament	T-6
Shell Houston Open	1
HP Classic of New Orleans	1
Wachovia Championship	T-10
EDS Byron Nelson Championship	T-59
Volvo PGA Championship	T-15
Memorial Tournament	T-24
Buick Classic	T-4
U.S. Open Championship	T-28
Cialis Western Open	T-17
John Deere Classic	T-4
The Open Championship	T-20
Buick Open	1
PGA Championship	1
WGC - NEC Invitational	T-32
Deutsche Bank Championship	1
Bell Canadian Open	1
84 Lumber Classic	1
Dunhill Links Championship	T-18
HSBC World Match Play	T-9
Funai Classic at Walt Disney World Resort	T-2
Chrysler Championship	1

Tour Championship	9
PGA Grand Slam	2
Office Depot Father-Son Challenge	T-9
Target World Challenge	T-8

Woods was battling David Duval for No. 1 in the world in 1999. He had won three times on the PGA Tour when he arrived at Medinah outside Chicago for the PGA Championship, winning by one stroke over Sergio Garcia and using the final major as a springboard to a great season. Woods went on to win five of his last six PGA Tour events, ending the season with four straight to reach eight wins and shatter the PGA Tour earnings record.

In 2004 Singh converted a good year (three victories) into a spectacular one in a span of three months. Starting with the Buick Open, he won six of eight tournaments, including three straight during his ascent to No. 1 in the World Ranking.

The most amazing was at the Bell Canadian Open, which offered another parallel to 1999. Then Woods won the WGC - American Express Championship in Spain by making a triple bogey on the 17th hole at Valderrama, still getting into a playoff, dealing with a vocal, partisan crowd, and beating local favorite Miguel Angel Jimenez after the Spaniard made a mess of the 18th hole in the playoff. Here Mike Weir played the part of Jimenez, only there was far more at stake. A Canadian had not won his national Open in 50 years, and this was the 100th anniversary of the Canadian Open, the third-oldest national championship in golf. The electricity at Glen Abbey was second only to the Masters. The gallery screamed every time Weir made contact, and he later said he had to pop his ears on the tee box because of the deafening noise. One can only imagine what it would have been like had he won.

In perhaps the most amazing feat of his year, Singh made two triple bogeys on the par-four 11th hole and still won the tournament. Of course, he had some help from Weir, who had a two-shot lead with three holes to play and stood over an eight-foot birdie putt on the 16th hole. The Canadian three-putted for bogey, then three times had putts to win. He missed them all, including a five-footer on the second extra hole. Singh finally wore him down, winning on the third playoff hole for his seventh victory of the year. It was his first week as the No. 1 golfer, and even though he felt like Public Enemy No. 1 in Canada, the 41-year-old Fijian sent a powerful message.

"You don't want to let that position go," Singh said. "The only way you can hang onto it is by playing better than the rest of the guys. I'm not going to back off."

Instead, he poured it on. His seventh victory of the year pushed him closer to Woods' PGA Tour record of $9.1 million, and when Singh won the 84 Lumber Classic the following week in routine fashion, he had had eight victories and started thinking about a 10-10 season — 10 victories, $10 million. He got part of that equation right. Singh outlasted everyone at Innisbrook to win the Chrysler Championship in the final full-field tournament of the year, giving him nine victories and surpassing $10 million.

All he needed was one more victory in the Tour Championship at East

Lake — he won the last time it was there in 2002 — to reach 10 victories. But the putter failed him, Singh shot 73 in the second round and never quite recovered. He had to settle for being one of only six players to have won nine times in one year, and a No. 1 ranking that he traveled farther than anyone to achieve.

And there was at least one perk.

"I really didn't have to wait for the vote," Singh said in New York on the day he was presented the Jack Nicklaus Trophy as the PGA Tour's Player of the Year. The tour doesn't disclose its vote totals, but it's hard to imagine any player selecting anyone but Singh.

The United States could have used him at the Ryder Cup. Despite playing a European team that had no major champions for the first time since 1981, it was no contest. The Americans bring stars. Europe brings a team. The only buzz all week at Oakland Hills came when U.S. captain Hal Sutton put Woods and Mickelson together for the first time, wanting to set the tone for the week. "I felt like history needed it. I felt like the fans needed it," Sutton said. "And most of all, I felt like Phil Mickelson and Tiger Woods needed it."

And yet, Europe got the most out of it. Colin Montgomerie and Padraig Harrington made birdies on the first four holes and never trailed in winning the opening fourball match, 2 and 1. It set the tone, all right. The Americans went 70 holes and nearly six hours before they led in any match the first day, and even then, they couldn't protect the lead. One of the most indelible images from the Ryder Cup was Mickelson hitting a three wood on the 18th hole that bounced off the out-of-bounds fence, as Woods tried to keep from cringing. They lost that foursome match, too, and Europe was off to its best start ever.

The lone U.S. star might have been Chris Riley until he went to sleep at the wheel — or at least wanted to. Riley teamed with Woods, his longtime friend from junior golf, and they scored a rousing fourball victory Saturday morning over Darren Clarke and Ian Poulter that gave the Americans a glimmer of hope. But when Riley was asked about going out in the afternoon, he told Sutton he was tired. Stunned, Sutton put Woods with Davis Love.

By the end of the day, the Europeans led 11-5 and were well on their way to an 18½-to-9½ victory, its largest margin of victory in the 77-year history. Montgomerie holed the putt that clinched victory for Europe, but its stars were many, starting with captain Bernhard Langer. Sergio Garcia and Lee Westwood each went unbeaten in five matches, as every European contributed at least one point.

"We had strength at the top, strength in the middle and strength at the end," Montgomerie said. "That's the first time I can say that. We had strength everywhere." It was the seventh time in the last 10 matches Europe had captured the cup, and there was no doubt who the underdogs were now.

"I don't know what it is," David Toms said. "But we've got to find the right formula." The task now falls to Tom Lehman, whom the PGA of America selected as U.S. captain for the 2006 Ryder Cup in Ireland.

Fred Funk, scorned by his peers when he ducked the Open Championship in Britain for the B.C. Open to earn Ryder Cup points, and Kenny Perry failed to earn a point for the Americans. But the scapegoat was Mickelson, who wasted a year's worth of goodwill with some peculiar decisions leading up to the first match.

The week before the Ryder Cup, Mickelson changed equipment from Titleist to Callaway. Then, after a nine-hour practice session early in the week at Oakland Hills, the Masters champion did not practice with the team on Wednesday. And if that wasn't enough, he played the adjacent North course at Oakland Hills on Thursday, practicing with Woods' Nike golf ball in private to prepare for their first-day partnership. When Mickelson played poorly in both matches Friday, Sutton benched him. "It's not going to cause us any grief in the morning because he's going to be cheering instead of playing," Sutton said.

The Ryder Cup was about the only thing that didn't go right for Lefty in 2004.

PHIL MICKELSON

EVENT	POSITION
Bob Hope Chrysler Classic	1
FBR Open	T-7
AT&T Pebble Beach National Pro-Am	3
Buick Invitational	T-4
WGC - Accenture Match Play	T-5
Ford Championship at Doral	T-24
The Players Championship	T-3
BellSouth Classic	10
Masters Tournament	1
HP Classic of New Orleans	T-2
Wachovia Championship	T-5
EDS Byron Nelson Championship	MC
Bank of America Colonial	T-35
Buick Classic	T-16
U.S. Open Championship	2
Barclays Scottish Open	MC
The Open Championship	3
PGA Championship	T-6
WGC - NEC Invitational	T-43
Bell Canadian Open	T-57
Michelin Championship at Las Vegas	WD
Chrysler Championship	MC
Tour Championship	T-19
PGA Grand Slam	1

After failing to make the Tour Championship for the first time, Mickelson waited until the calendar turned before getting started on his game, a symbolic move to put last year behind him. He looked leaner and more determined. And in a telling moment in his first start of the year at the Bob Hope Chrysler Classic, Mickelson backed off a three wood into a par-five hole and instead chose to lay up. He three-putted for bogey, but the point had been made. He was playing smarter, no longer willing to risk victory with reckless abandon.

He finished in the top 10 in 10 of his first 11 events, but established himself as the man to beat in the majors. Mickelson prefers to play the week before majors to get into a competitive frame of mind, but it was clear his mind was elsewhere. He tied for 10th at the BellSouth Classic the week before the Masters. He tied for 16th at the Buick Classic ahead of the U.S. Open. He missed the cut at the Barclays Scottish Open before heading to Royal Troon. And when the PGA Championship rolled around, Mickelson chose not to play the week before a U.S. major for the first time in five years. His planning was meticulous, taking eight hours for a practice round with coach Rick Smith, plotting where he could save a shot or two that would make the difference. By the end of the year, he was five shots away from a Grand Slam.

He was leading the U.S. Open when he stepped to the 17th tee on Sunday. By the time he walked off the green with a three-putt double bogey from five feet, he was two shots behind. The Open Championship in Britain was the only major where Mickelson had failed to finish in the top 10, but he pulled into the lead on the final nine Sunday at Royal Troon with conservative play and a few timely birdies.

Mickelson missed a four-foot par putt on the 13th hole, ending his streak of 49 holes without a bogey at Royal Troon, and he fell one stroke short of a playoff. He figured pars would be enough, only this time he was wrong. "The guys behind me were making birdies, and I wasn't," he said. Mickelson still had a chance at the PGA Championship with two holes to play, but he missed a 15-foot birdie putt on the 17th hole, then hit his approach into the bunker on the 18th and made bogey to finish two strokes out of the playoff. Still, his record in the majors showed that he finally figured them out — first, second, third and a tie for sixth.

"I feel like I'm really onto something good, and I'm looking forward to next year," Mickelson said. "I'm sorry we have such a long way to go."

ERNIE ELS

EVENT	POSITION
Mercedes Championships	T-21
Sony Open in Hawaii	1
Johnnie Walker Classic	T-10
Heineken Classic	1
Dubai Desert Classic	T-3
Bay Hill Invitational	MC
The Players Championship	T-26
Masters Tournament	2
MCI Heritage	T-3
EDS Byron Nelson Championship	T-7
Deutsche Bank - SAP Open	T-5
Volvo PGA Championship	7
Memorial Tournament	1
Buick Classic	T-16
U.S. Open Championship	T-9
Barclays Scottish Open	T-3
The Open Championship	2

The International	29
PGA Championship	T-4
WGC - NEC Invitational	T-65
Omega European Masters	7
WGC - American Express Championship	1
Dunhill Links Championship	T-7
HSBC World Match Play	1
Tour Championship	T-10
Nelson Mandela Invitational	1
Nedbank Golf Challenge	T-2

Els could only wonder what went wrong. Take away the majors, and he might not have any complaints about his season. He won five times around the world, repeating at the Sony Open, turning in a clutch putting performance at the Memorial that even impressed tournament host Jack Nicklaus, battling Thomas Bjorn in the cold rain at Mount Juliet Estate to win the WGC - American Express Championship in Ireland, and remained No. 3 in the world.

The Big Easy also won at Royal Melbourne despite squandering a nine-shot lead on the first nine in the final round, and in his biggest victory of the year, he won the HSBC World Match Play for a record sixth time, breaking the record held by Gary Player and Seve Ballesteros. He captured his second straight Order of Merit title on the PGA European Tour with a record €4,061,905. He was second on the PGA Tour money list with nearly $5.8 million, the closest anyone has come to winning the money title on both sides of the Atlantic.

But any great player measures his year by majors, and Els can only look back at one lost chance after another. "To be No. 1 in the world is one thing, but to win a major, that's what we all strive for. That's what we all want," the Big Easy said three weeks before the Masters.

Three times Els had putts on the final hole at a major that would have won (Open Championship) or at least got him into a playoff (Masters, PGA Championship). He missed them all. Els started the final round only two shots behind Goosen at the U.S. Open and playing with his South African friend in the final group, but made double bogey on the first hole and never quite recovered.

It is hard to say which one hurt the most, although evidence points to the first and last. Els wants to win the career Grand Slam, and the Masters and PGA Championship are what he needs. The toughest part about the Masters was having to listen for the outcome of Mickelson's putt from the practice green. "The split-second moment when you know it's over is a horrible feeling," Els said. "It mentally knocks the stuffing out of you a bit."

The PGA Championship knocked him silly, too. Els fought gamely in the final round, hitting a two iron into the wind to within two feet on the par-four, 518-yard 15th hole and adding another birdie on the 16th. Thinking he needed a birdie on the final hole, Els hit driver just through the fairway on the 18th, missed the green to the right, and three-putted from 100 feet. He had no idea that last putt from 10 feet would cost him a spot in the playoff.

"I'm three shots away from winning three majors. This close," Els said, pinching together his thumb and index finger. "This year, the hammer has been on my head, and I had to pick myself up every time. A lot of people would love to have my year. It's just the bloody results that hurt."

RETIEF GOOSEN

EVENT	POSITION
Mercedes Championships	T-4
Sony Open in Hawaii	T-10
Bob Hope Chrysler Classic	T-26
FBR Open	T-9
WGC - Accenture Match Play	T-33
Ford Championship at Doral	3
Bay Hill Invitational	MC
The Players Championship	MC
Masters Tournament	T-13
MCI Heritage	MC
Daily Telegraph Damovo British Masters	T-52
Deutsche Bank - SAP Open	T-9
Volvo PGA Championship	T-11
Memorial Tournament	T-8
U.S. Open Championship	1
Smurfit European Open	1
The Open Championship	T-7
WGC - NEC Invitational	DNS
BMW International Open	T-6
The Heritage	T-15
WGC - American Express Championship	T-6
Dunhill Links Championship	T-23
HSBC World Match Play	T-5
Chrysler Championship	T-20
Tour Championship	1
PGA Grand Slam	3
Nedbank Golf Challenge	1

Goosen had no complaints. He has emerged as one of the toughest players in golf, especially with the lead, but never quite gets the credit he deserves. His reputation got a huge lift at Shinnecock Hills with his second U.S. Open title, a case study in quiet determination as he closed with six consecutive one-putts to stay close to Mickelson, catch him on the 16th, and take advantage of Lefty's double bogey. Like Singh, Goosen was a late bloomer in 2004. The U.S. Open was his first victory of the year, but he soon looked unstoppable by winning his next start at the Smurfit European Open and contending at the Open Championship until a 73 in the final round.

The only thing that slowed the Goose was a jet ski. He took an awkward spill in Barbados during a holiday and wound up missing six weeks, which knocked him out of the PGA Championship. But he returned as strong as ever, and did the unthinkable at the Tour Championship at East Lake. First came a five iron from 195 yards in the rough on the 481-yard 16th hole that stopped three feet away for birdie. That led to a four-stroke victory over Woods, the first time in four years that Woods failed to win after leading through 54 holes.

For all the talk about the "Big Four" in golf, Goosen showed there was room for five. He was second on the Order of Merit in Europe to Els, and sixth on the PGA Tour money list despite playing only 16 tournaments. Goosen finished the year at No. 4 in the World Ranking.

"Tiger and Vijay and Ernie, they're probably in a different league with the amount of tournaments they've won and things like that," Goosen said. "I think I have to win a few more probably to get into that stature. They've been on tour here a little bit longer than me, and people know them a little bit better. I think a couple more years of good play, it might be a different story."

TODD HAMILTON

EVENT	POSITION
Sony Open in Hawaii	MC
AT&T Pebble Beach National Pro-Am	T-25
Buick Invitational	MC
Chrysler Classic of Tucson	T-40
Ford Championship at Doral	T-15
Honda Classic	1
Bay Hill Invitational	T-69
The Players Championship	T-58
Masters Tournament	40
MCI Heritage	MC
Shell Houston Open	MC
HP Classic of New Orleans	MC
Wachovia Championship	T-21
EDS Byron Nelson Championship	T-59
Bank of America Colonial	T-44
Memorial Tournament	T-33
Buick Classic	MC
U.S. Open Championship	MC
Cialis Western Open	MC
John Deere Classic	T-59
The Open Championship	1
The International	T-12
PGA Championship	T-37
WGC - NEC Invitational	T-21
Linde German Masters	T-84
84 Lumber Classic	T-53
WGC - American Express Championship	T-6
HSBC World Match Play	T-9
Tour Championship	28
Dunlop Phoenix	T-42
PGA Grand Slam	4
Nedbank Golf Challenge	8
Target World Challenge	T-15

Hamilton sure has a story to tell, and it's a whopper. An All-American at Oklahoma who never could get through PGA Tour qualifying, Hamilton embarked on a journey that took him through remote golf outposts in Asia. He was ready to give up on his career until winning the 1992 Asian Order of Merit. That got him to the Japan Tour, and he won four times in 2003 to finish third on the money list.

At age 38, Hamilton gave the U.S. PGA Tour one more try and earned his card with a tie for 16th in the qualifying tournament. It took him two months to cash in. Despite blowing a four-shot lead at the Honda Classic, he coolly sank a 10-foot birdie putt on the 17th hole at Mirasol to regain a share of the lead with Davis Love. And when a playoff looked imminent, Hamilton stuffed a seven iron to two feet for his first PGA Tour victory.

"There's probably a lot of people that might think this is a fluke," Hamilton said. "I would like to prove that to not be true. It may not happen next week. It may not happen this year. Hopefully, somewhere down the line, I can say, 'Hey, I won another one.'"

How about the Open Championship? Fast-forward four months to Royal Troon, and Hamilton was getting about as much respect as he did at the Honda Classic, somewhere between little and none. He was a fascinating story considering his global travels, but most figured his chances at the Open Championship were not much different from a guy named Ben Curtis last year at Royal St. George's. The leaderboard was chock-full of major champions. Curtis was playing in his first major championship, and no one paid attention to him until he seized the lead on the final nine, then emerged the winner when Thomas Bjorn took three shots to get out of a bunker on the 16th hole and made double bogey.

Hamilton had to earn this the hard way, playing the final two rounds — and then four playoff holes — with Els. He never was too far from the lead, overcoming Mickelson early on the last nine and holding off a dramatic bid from the Big Easy. In the process, Hamilton advanced the growing popularity of the hybrid clubs, using it to play a variety of chips from in front of the greens. The last one was the most crucial of all, the Shot of the Year, from 30 yards short of the cup on the 18th hole in the playoff to within two feet to save par and win the silver claret jug.

He had only one other top 10 on the PGA Tour, a tie for sixth in the WGC - American Express Championship. But he finished the year with over $3 million and was voted PGA Tour Rookie of the Year. "I always felt my game was decent," Hamilton said. "I felt if I could get out here and maybe contend, or have a couple good years, the Honda Classic would happen. But I never dreamed that I would win one tournament, let alone two tournaments, my first year as a rookie." Or that one of them would be the oldest championship in golf.

ANNIKA SORENSTAM

EVENT	POSITION
ANZ Ladies Masters	1
Safeway International	1
Kraft Nabisco Championship	T-13
Office Depot	1
Chick-Fil-A Charity Championship	T-10
Michelob Ultra Open at Kingsmill	T-8
Corning Classic	1
Kellogg-Keebler Classic	T-2
McDonald's LPGA Championship	1
Wegmans Rochester	T-7
U.S. Women's Open	2
Evian Masters	2
Weetabix Women's British Open	T-13
HP Open	1
John Q. Hammons Hotel Classic	1
Safeway Classic	T-4
Samsung World Championship	1
CJ Nine Bridges Classic	T-2
Mizuno Classic	1
ADT Championship	1

Singh didn't have the best year in golf, even with his nine victories. Annika Sorenstam could make a case for that. Despite playing a reduced schedule, she won 10 times around the world, eight times in 18 starts on the LPGA Tour, and captured her seventh major with a victory at the McDonald's LPGA Championship. But that was all part of a consolation prize considering what Sorenstam had hoped to achieve.

While other great players think it, the Swede had the audacity to state at the start of the year that her goal was to win all four majors. And why not? She had come within two shots of winning the LPGA Grand Slam the year before, during a season in which she was hounded with attention over her appearance in the Colonial. But she never had a chance, falling well behind at the Kraft Nabisco Championship and finishing in a tie for 13th. It was one of two times she finished out of the top 10 all year.

Sorenstam had to reassess her goals, focused on the majors, and captured the next one she played at DuPont Country Club, outlasting the field in a 36-hole Sunday brought on by rain. The signature shot was a 94-yard wedge from the adjacent fairway and over a row of 60-foot pines trees to within three feet on the par-five 16th that wrapped up her victory.

Sorenstam tied Laura Davies for winning the same tournament four years in a row at the Mizuno Classic in Japan. She ended the year with $2.54 million and 56 career victories, moving her past Betsy Rawls for fifth place on the LPGA Tour.

And hardly anyone noticed. Sorenstam, like Woods before her, simply was a victim of her own success. Her 10 victories in 2004 gave her 38 worldwide trophies in the last four years, an astounding rate of over nine per year.

"Everyone is talking about Vijay's year," Meg Mallon said. "She's done it for the last six years. My years on tour, I've seen great players, and Annika is one of them. But those great players always go through a down time. She hasn't done that. That's what is so exceptional about what she's done. That's why it makes it even more fun to beat her occasionally, because you know it doesn't happen very often."

Mallon beat her where it matters the most, at the biggest tournament in women's golf. Playing before a supportive home crowd in western Massachusetts, Mallon relied on a pure putting stroke at The Orchards to win her second U.S. Women's Open title by two shots over Sorenstam. Mallon closed with a 65, the lowest final round by a winner in the 59-year history of the Women's Open.

The other LPGA majors went to Grace Park at the Kraft Nabisco Championship and Karen Stupples of England at the Weetabix Women's British Open, who started the final round at Sunningdale with an eagle and a double eagle.

Cristie Kerr won three times on the LPGA Tour, but those looking for a young American star paid attention to a pair of teenagers — Paula Creamer, who earned her LPGA Tour card in December before taking her final exams in high school, and Wie. Both had a chance to win an LPGA Tour event, and they tied for 13th at the U.S. Women's Open. Other teenagers could be coming. Ai Miyazato, an 18-year-old who is spiking the television ratings in Japan, won five times and nearly knocked off Yuri Fudoh, with seven victories, atop the Japan LPGA Tour money list. And a 14-year-old, Ashleigh Simon, won the Acer Women's South African Open.

Wie did not win a trophy in 2004, although her performance was no less impressive. She received a sponsor's exemption to the PGA Tour's Sony Open at Waialae Country Club in Honolulu, played a practice round with Els (the Big Easy and the Big Wiesy), and opened with a respectable 72. Figuring that even par would make the cut, the 14-year-old shot a 68 in the second round with a clutch par on the 17th and an up-and-down from 40 yards short of the green for birdie on the par-five 18th.

It was the lowest score ever posted by a woman competing on a men's tour, only it proved to be one stroke short of making the cut. The amazing thing about Wie's expectations is that having made the birdie putt on the 18th, which she thought was for a weekend tee time, her reaction was not of a ninth grade girl who had made history, but of a prodigy who wondered when her tee time was Saturday and with whom she was playing.

"You guys have been looking for the next Tiger Woods," Jesper Parnevik said. "I think you found her."

By the end of the year, the next Tiger Woods turned out to be a 41-year-old who grew up in Fiji, honed his game while exiled to Borneo as a club professional, worked as a bouncer in Scotland to help pay the bills until he could make it in Europe, and was a PGA Tour Rookie of the Year at age 33. Singh's journey from a tiny country in the South Pacific to a two-time major champion already was an amazing story. His 2004 season made it the stuff of legend. Only this fantasy was grounded in the reality of hard work. Like so many other great players wherever they started or how far they traveled, Singh found success by digging it out of the dirt. Not surprisingly, he often drew comparisons to Ben Hogan.

"I never played golf with Ben Hogan, but I've played a lot of golf with Vijay the last year and a half," Nick Price said. "If Ben Hogan ever hit the ball as well as Vijay does week in and week out, I'd be amazed. I really would." Strong praise also came from the guy he replaced at the top. "He's had one of the great years," Woods said. "For him to play as much as he does and still maintain that edge, and as much as he practices, it's pretty impressive."

It was only fitting that a new world order belonged to a foreign-born player. For the first time in history, international players won more PGA Tour events (26) than the Americans (22). During one stretch from the Memorial in early June to the Open Championship in the middle of July, international players won six weeks in a row, and Singh wasn't among them. It was a reflection of how many players were coming to the United States to make a living, and perhaps it is time to treat winners on the PGA Tour and LPGA Tour like an Olympic medals table. In that regard, Americans won 22 PGA Tour titles, Fiji won nine and Australia won six.

The amazing thing about the half-dozen Australian winners was that the list did not include Robert Allenby or Peter Lonard, although Lonard made up for it by winning three straight weeks in Australia late in the year. No one was surprised that Adam Scott was a two-time winner, no victory greater than The Players Championship. Despite hitting a six iron into the water on the 18th hole while protecting a two-shot lead, Scott used a tip he received from Greg Norman earlier in the week to get up-and-down for bogey and become the youngest winner, at age 23, of the tournament regarded by some as the fifth major. Scott also won the Booz Allen Classic and ended the year at No. 11 in the World Ranking.

There were eight multiple winners on the PGA Tour — Singh, Els, Hamilton, Goosen, Mickelson, Scott, Sergio Garcia and Stewart Cink, who won the WGC - NEC Invitational at Firestone the week after Sutton made him a captain's pick for the Ryder Cup team.

There were 10 first-time winners, including two big surprises toward the end of the year. Andre Stolz was 217th on the money list until putting together four great rounds of 67-67-65-67 to win the Michelin Championship at Las Vegas. Two weeks later, 28-year-old rookie Ryan Palmer closed with a 62 in the Funai Classic at Disney to hold off Singh and win by two shots, finishing the year at No. 38 on the money list.

Chad Campbell won the Bay Hill Invitational by turning a four-shot deficit into a six-shot victory. More notable about Bay Hill was that Tiger Woods tied for 46th, his worst finish since he tied for 56th at Bay Hill in 1999, the week Steve Williams came on board as his caddie. Woods was trying to become the first player to win the same tournament five years in a row, and his struggles were another harbinger of the difficult road ahead.

Campbell, meanwhile, won for the second time in 10 starts and climbed into the top 10 in the World Ranking. The rest of the year was not nearly as promising, as the 30-year-old Texan missed the cut in three of the four majors. David Toms returned from wrist surgery to win the FedEx St. Jude Classic. Joey Sindelar, age 46, won for the first time in 14 years and 370 tournaments by beating a strong field at Quail Hollow in the Wachovia Championship.

Among regular PGA Tour victories, none generated more attention than

John Daly's. He had gone nine years since his last PGA Tour victory (1995 Open Championship at St. Andrews), and 10 years since his last official victory in the United States, at the 1994 BellSouth Classic. His roller-coaster career reached another level at Torrey Pines in the Buick Invitational, where the Wild Thing showed amazing control off the tee with a controlled cut shot. And he wound up winning with his soft touch around the green, one aspect of his game that rarely gets enough credit.

As usual, no one saw this victory coming. Only six months earlier, Daly learned his wife had been indicted on federal drug and gambling charges, just five days after she gave birth to his first son. His game was such a mess that he was No. 299 in the world. But he forged a one-shot lead going into the final round, and a large gallery that normally divides time between Woods and Mickelson threw its support behind Daly. Even in tough times, he remains the favorite of everyday people.

"One guy said, 'Put the cows in the barn.' I'm from Arkansas, and I'm still not sure what that means," Daly said. "I knew it was a compliment, so it was kind of cool." He wound up in a playoff with Luke Donald and Chris Riley, and Daly ended it with a magical shot. From 100 feet away in a bunker behind the green on the par-five 18th on the South Course, with a large pond beyond the flag, Daly blasted out to four inches for a tap-in birdie. Donald missed his six-foot birdie putt, and Riley's three-foot birdie horseshoed around the cup, giving Daly his first tour victory in 189 events.

"I never doubted I could win," he said.

Davis Love was the only player in the top 10 on the PGA Tour money list without a victory, earning just over $3 million. He had a chance to win the WGC - Accenture Match Play until he was let down by his putter, and then his emotions. A fan in the gallery kept saying, "No Love" as he stood over putts, and Love finally confronted him on the fifth hole and had him removed. By then, Woods was on his way to a 3-and-2 victory, which turned out to be his only title of the year on tour. For Love, it was the fourth time in the last six years he failed to win on the PGA Tour.

Jim Furyk failed to win for the first time in six years on tour, although it was another gritty effort. He had surgery on his left wrist in March and was expected to miss as many as six months. He returned two months later to defend his title in the U.S. Open, where he made the cut and tied for 48th.

For David Duval, it was a victory just showing up. Mired in a mystifying slump, Duval stayed away from competitive golf the first half of the year. He got married in March and moved to Denver, content to be at home with his wife and three children. Out of the blue, he decided to make his return at the U.S. Open, the most demanding test in golf.

Cheered around at every turn with a chorus of "Welcome back, David," he shot 83 for his worst score as a professional and never looked happier. "All in all, I would call it an enormous victory for me," Duval said. He played eight more times the rest of the year and made three cuts. Formerly No. 1 in the world, he was at No. 528 as the year ended and still facing a long road back.

One player who didn't win could still count 2004 as a success. Jay Haas turned 50 the previous December and was eligible for the Champions Tour, but decided to compete against the best with hopes of making the Ryder Cup team. He finished 12th in the standings, but became the second-oldest player in Ryder Cup history when Sutton made him a captain's pick.

Haas finished 27th on the PGA Tour money list to become the oldest player to qualify for the Tour Championship, and he shared the 54-hole lead with Woods at East Lake until they were beaten by Goosen. Even so, Haas is eligible for all four majors and sees no reason to play with guys his own age.

Haas also is driven by hopes of playing with his son, 22-year-old Bill, who finished his career at Wake Forest as the college Player of the Year and came close to earning his card through sponsor's exemptions. But that wasn't the best father-son story in golf. As Craig Stadler was cleaning up on the Champions Tour, his son, Kevin, was a two-time winner on the Nationwide Tour and earned his PGA Tour card for 2005. They won on the same day, Craig at the Bank of America Championship, Kevin at the Lake Erie Charity Classic.

Stadler won five times on the Champions Tour, including his second major at the JELD-WEN Tradition. He won the money title with $2.3 million and was voted Player of the Year by his peers. Hale Irwin enhanced his reputation as a hard-nosed competitor by winning his eighth Champions Tour major, capturing the Senior PGA Championship for the fourth time just a week before his 59th birthday. Two victories gave him 40 for his career on the 50-and-older circuit. Former Ryder Cup captain Mark James of England captured his first major at the Ford Senior Players Championship, while little-known Pete Oakley won the Senior British Open at Portrush. Peter Jacobsen won the biggest prize on the Champions Tour with a victory in the U.S. Senior Open.

Tom Watson won the Wendy's Champions Skins Game in Hawaii to start the season, but he failed to win a regular tournament for the first time since he joined the Champions Tour in 1999. It was a difficult year for Watson off the course, learning during the first round of the Masters that his longtime caddie, Bruce Edwards, had died of Lou Gehrig's disease. "He's not with us in body anymore, but I can tell you he's with us in spirit," Watson said. "He could make you laugh in the worst of times."

Europe's biggest moment of the year was winning the Ryder Cup. No European has won a major championship since Paul Lawrie in the 1999 Open Championship, the longest drought since a nine-year stretch from Tony Jacklin in 1970 to Seve Ballesteros in 1979. "We're not setting the world alight at the moment," said Padraig Harrington of Ireland, who rose to No. 6 in the world by the end of the year. "We don't have players winning majors. These things go in cycles."

But there were baby steps taken by some of the younger players. Justin Rose held the 36-hole lead at the Masters until he was derailed by an 81 in the third round. Paul Casey and Thomas Levet shared the first-round lead at the Open Championship. Lee Westwood turned his game around and finished fourth at Royal Troon, his best showing ever in a major. Ian Poulter won the season-ending Volvo Masters in a playoff over Sergio Garcia, although his finest moment was at the tailor. Poulter makes Jesper Parnevik's wardrobe look drab, especially his trousers made of the Union Jack that he wore at the Open Championship.

The most prolific winner in Europe was Miguel Angel Jimenez, who decided to be a happier soul on the golf course and laughed all the way to the bank. The 40-year-old Spaniard was noticeable because of his red, shaggy ponytail and his cigars, but his game got plenty of notice, too. Jimenez won four times on the 2004 schedule, adding his fifth victory of the year at the Hong Kong Open when the 2005 European Tour season began in December. His biggest victory was the BMW International, the final tournament for qualifying for the Ryder Cup. Jimenez began the year at No. 94 in the world, but climbed all the way to No. 12 when it ended.

Harrington was the highest-ranked European-born player on tour, winning the Linde German Masters for his only victory. Consistent as ever, the Irishman was second at the Deutsche Bank - SAP Open and tied for second at the Nissan Irish Open. He finished third on the Order of Merit with €1.8 million.

Among those who made the biggest moves were Graeme McDowell of Northern Ireland, who won the Telecom Italia Open and had three other finishes in the top three to go from No. 234 in the world to No. 55, and David Howell, who advanced from No. 111 to No. 43 despite not winning.

Howell had to settle for hitting the most pivotal shot in the Ryder Cup, a six iron that stopped eight feet away for birdie on the 17th hole that led to a fourball victory and swung momentum back in Europe's favor for good. Another Ryder Cup star was Luke Donald, who spent most of his time in America, but won twice in Europe to give Langer reason to pick him for the team. Donald won the Scandinavian Masters and the Omega European Masters.

The toughest year belonged to Colin Montgomerie. For seven years the best in Europe, his game was in a slow decline as he dropped out of the world's top 50 and saw his streak of majors played end at 49 when he did not qualify for the U.S. Open. The reason behind his drastic fall was a very public divorce from his wife, Eimear. The couple announced in late April they were splitting up after 14 years, and the divorce became final the week before the Ryder Cup.

Returning to his hometown, Troon, as a lonely figure in July, Montgomerie opened with rounds of 69-69 to give hope to the massive gallery cheering his every move at the Open, only to fall too far behind on the weekend. He had to rely on being a captain's pick for the first time in the Ryder Cup, but he delivered in a big way by going 3-1, raising his record to 19-8-5, and remaining unbeaten in singles. By year's end, he had fallen to No. 81 in the world.

"The primary cause was getting divorced, okay?" Montgomerie said. "Obviously, you don't have that emotion in your game, but when you are playing out in public, it's very, very difficult to concentrate on what one's doing. So that's why I've dropped 40 spots in the world, and I intend to get that back in a hurry."

He probably will have to barrel through a bunch of Aussies to get there. The Land Down Under proved to the most fertile foreign country to produce top players, with 11 among the top 80 in the world. The six winners on the PGA Tour included Craig Parry, who holed a six iron from the 18th fairway on the Blue Monster at Doral to win in a playoff over Scott Verplank at the Ford Championship. Lonard won the Australian Open and the Australian PGA, but he failed in his bid to become the first player to win his country's "triple crown" when he did not win the Australian Masters.

Shingo Katayama won twice on the Japan Tour and led the money list with ¥105 million. Shigeki Maruyama remained the top Japanese player in the United States, losing in a playoff to Mike Weir at the Nissan Open and tying for fourth in the U.S. Open. He was 23rd on the PGA Tour money list and No. 28 in the World Ranking, the only Japanese player among the top 50 in the world.

Korea's S.K. Ho (also known as Hur Suk-ho) was third on the Japan Tour but was overshadowed by a countryman playing in the United States, K.J. Choi, who placed third in the Masters and was ranked No. 25 in the world. Elsewhere, on the Asian Tour, the Thais were most prominent — Boonchu Ruangkit, Thongchai Jaidee, Thammanoon Srirot and Thaworn Wiratchant.

The best of the Thai golfers? That was a title Tiger kept.

The Royal Bank of Scotland Group

Presents

The Major Championships

Masters Tournament   25

U.S. Open Championship   36

The Open Championship   51

PGA Championship   67

2. Masters Tournament

Phil Mickelson was on the witness stand before the 2004 Masters Tournament, in the main chair in the press building at Augusta National Golf Club. The question was, why haven't you won a major yet? The answer was like trying to prove a negative, but Lefty gave it his best. "I don't know why I haven't broken through," Mickelson said. "I don't know why I haven't had things just go my way. I don't feel, if I were to win, like I would be a different player ... but I think that I might be looked at differently. I don't know if that's understandable or not."

It was most understandable. For some time now, Mickelson had been carrying the label "The Best Never To Have Won A Major." Unfortunately, the golfer brings it on himself by being good enough to be saddled with the highest expectations, and that certainly fit Mickelson, who caught the world's eye by winning the 1991 Northern Telecom Open on the PGA Tour while still an amateur and a college student.

It's impossible to tell exactly when the label was hung around his neck like the chains on Marley's Ghost in Charles Dickens' *A Christmas Carol*. The Masters would seem like his apple. He had finished third in the last three Masters and no worse than a tie for seventh in the past five. The big picture was grimmer. He was 0-for-46 in the major championships.

There was no telling whether the streak would end in this Masters until the final instant at the final hole, when that 18-foot putt rolled lazily down the slope and finally dropped. Mickelson rushed to his wife, Amy, and their three kids just off the 18th and said pretty much what people everywhere were probably saying: "Oh, my God!"

Compared to the major surgery the course had undergone in some recent years, Augusta National had just had a nip here and a tuck there before the 2004 Masters week was underway in Augusta, Georgia. The biggest change came at No. 11, the fearsome downhill par-four of 490 yards. It was a sterner test now, with 36 trees, 25 to 35 feet tall, having been installed at the right side of the fairway, to dissuade golfers from shading to the right to avoid the pond at the front-left of the green. No longer. Said Masters chairman Hootie Johnson, "It continues our longstanding emphasis of accuracy off the tee."

Tiger Woods hadn't won a major title in his last six tries — a veritable drought for him. He was going through a swing change and having trouble keeping the ball under his famous control. He had won once this year, at the WGC - Accenture Match Play late in February. Erratic play aside, he was the clear favorite in the Masters, and people kept reminding him of this quiet spell and offering all the usual tips.

"I get it all the time," Woods said. And his response? "Under my breath or to them?"

At all events, the universal feeling was that Tiger Woods soon would be winning his fourth Masters.

Others, of course, were under consideration, Northern Ireland's Darren Clarke was part of the rich United Nations at the Masters. There were

19 countries represented, including — as the precise Masters folks noted — the United States. It was, however, a barely recognizable Darren Clarke. Under a fitness program, he had trimmed down from 260 pounds to 220. Clarke stood out as a reminder that the Europeans, for some reason, used to dominate the Masters, winning 10 of the 17 from 1980 through 1996. The last European winner was Jose Maria Olazabal of Spain in 1999.

The Masters added to the international flavor by inviting Zhang Lian-wei, the first Chinese ever to play there. Zhang, age 38, had taken up golf when the game began to flourish in the 1980s as the Communist government began to approve the building of golf courses to attract outside business-men. Zhang was the first Chinese to win on the European Tour, and he even beat the formidable Ernie Els of South Africa in the 2003 Caltex Masters — a European co-sponsored event in Singapore — with a birdie on the final hole. "We felt it good for the game to extend a hand to the most populous nation in the world," said Johnson. Zhang launched his first Masters with a five-over-par 77 that included one birdie, two bogeys and two double bogeys.

Mickelson continued to get peppered with questions. For example, was this his year, finally? "I've entered this tournament the past few years believing that I had very good chances," he said. "This year, I certainly feel like I have a very good chance. I'm playing well enough to get into contention without having to do anything extraordinary."

The man just said his regular game ought to be good enough.

Mickelson had led off that pre-tournament interview Tuesday sitting next to Billy Morris, an Augusta National member and Media Committee member, who was clad in the requisite Masters green jacket. Mickelson leaned over, beaming, and tugged at Morris' sleeve. "I want one of these," he said. "Those are nice."

A few days later, he was sleeping in one.

Mickelson did not have an encouraging start, however. He shot a par 72 and was five strokes off the lead. It did little to justify his own confidence, much less excite the fans. "I thought I could have had a little bit better of a score," Mickelson said. "The pins were just so tough today." A particularly difficult hole position was at the 170-yard 16th, at least from where he put his tee shot. It was about 30 feet to the right of the hole. He four-putted for a double-bogey five. He was two under par coming to the 16th, and even par leaving. What bothered him more, though, were the birdies he couldn't get. "I played the par-fives well, but the only one I could birdie was No. 2," he said. He also birdied Nos. 7 and 10, and bogeyed No. 5. With his new under-control game, he hit 11 of 14 fairways and 13 of 18 greens.

This Masters opened with a strong international flavor, led by Justin Rose of England, who took the first-round lead with a five-under-par 67, two strokes in front of Americans Jay Haas and Chris DiMarco. Rain, and then darkness, forced the end of the round over into Friday, but by then the scoreboard showed Clarke in at 70, and Bernhard Langer of Germany, Colin Montgomerie of Scotland and Phillip Price of Wales in at 71, among the top eight players who had finished. Langer was a two-time Masters champion, and the veteran Montgomerie was still looking for a win of any kind in the United States.

When the first round was completed, those at 70 with Clarke were Els, Alex Cejka of Germany and American Chris Riley. Added to the group with 71s, tied for eighth place, were Olazabal and K.J. Choi of South Korea. Those tied for 15th place with Mickelson with 72s included former champion Sandy Lyle of Scotland, Sergio Garcia of Spain and Nick Price of Zimbabwe for a total of 12 non-Americans among the top 21 on the scoreboard.

Rose, now age 23, was a 17-year-old amateur who jolted the 1998 Open Championship at Royal Birkdale by pitching in at the last hole and finishing tied for fourth place. He then turned professional and missed the cut in 28 of his first 45 starts. He finally broke through in 2002, notching four international victories. He tied for 39th in the 2003 Masters, his first. The improvement showed. He hit 17 of 18 greens in regulation and had six birdies and one bogey. He launched his attack from the start, with two quick birdies, a 25-foot putt on No. 1 and two putts at the par-five No. 2. It seemed Rose never expected the lead, and it unsettled him. "My goal was to try and cruise this week and really enjoy it," Rose said. "Obviously, it's going to really test me now, the situation I'm in."

DiMarco posted his 69 with some flair — with a hole-in-one. He hit a six iron at the 180-yard No. 6, and while aces are strictly luck, he was deliberately firing right at the hole placement. "The way the pin was placed, I had no choice but to go right at it," he said. The ace, the fourth of his career, was the 16th in Masters history, but the first since 1996, and the first at No. 6 since Charles Coody's in 1972. It livened an otherwise routine day for DiMarco. He had a birdie at the 15th and parred all the rest.

Haas was the sentimental favorite, bar none. Haas, age 50, was Champions Tour material who was still playing the PGA Tour. He figured five top-seven finishes in 20 Masters armed him nicely for this one. "I think I've made all of the mistakes there are to make here, and I've hit it in all of the wrong places," he said. "So I know where not to go." He came to the 18th needing to save par for his best first-round Masters score. He coolly rolled in the 15-foot putt for his 69 and a share of second place.

Cejka tied for fourth place with the wildest 70 of the four on the scoreboard. He had two birdies and a bogey on the first nine, then opened the second nine with a double bogey, a bogey, a birdie, an eagle, finally a par at the 14th, then a birdie at the 15th.

Ernie Els got his 70 more quietly and with an outstanding par at the par-five 13th. His second shot nearly went into the creek, but left him a tough lie on a dry patch in front of the green. He chipped to eight feet and two-putted. "I'm happy with the way I played today," Els said, possibly recalling his start in 2003, which had been a 79.

The two surprise champions of 2003 had solid if modest starts to their first Masters. Ben Curtis, the unknown who came from Ohio to win Britain's Open Championship, shot 73, including a 125-yard nine iron for an eagle at the par-four seventh. Shaun Micheel, who won the PGA Championship, shot a one-birdie, one-bogey par 72. Said Micheel, "There's impending doom everywhere you go on the greens."

The first round had some fascinating hidden results, the kind that end up as just a score on the scoreboard or in the newspapers, but that hide a story. Take Choi, for example, with his 71. Here's how he did it: With four bogeys and five birdies, and four of those birdies were in a streak from the 12th. Triplett also shot 71, but after starting with a triple-bogey eight at No. 2 and a bogey at No. 3. He made five birdies the rest of the way. Vijay Singh, the No. 2 player in the world, shot 75, but he was a flawless two under par through the 14th. Then he made an eight at the par-five 15th and bogeyed the 17th and 18th. Amateur Brandt Snedeker, the U.S. Public Links champion and one of five amateurs in the field, shot a 73 that included birdieing the entire Amen Corner. He chipped in from 40 feet at the 11th, chipped in from 35 feet at the 12th, and two-putted from 35 feet at the par-five 13th. And then there were the wide-open big numbers, such as the 79 by Mike Weir, the highest first round ever by a defending champion. It didn't seem this Masters would have a repeat winner.

Attention, however, was focused on Woods. He started with one of those bad news-good news situations. The bad news was he shot 40 on the first nine. The good news was the last time he started with 40, he came back and won his first Masters by 12 strokes. That was in his memorable year of 1997. Whether he had even thought back to that time couldn't be ascertained. Woods was still four over par when darkness after the rain delay forced him off the course with four holes to play, and he declined to speak to reporters as he left Augusta National. "It doesn't mean anything in the scheme of things," said amateur Casey Wittenberg, who played in the group with Woods. "He had an off-day. Everybody has them." Woods returned Friday morning and completed a 75 that left him seven shots off the lead.

For all of the bright surroundings and excitement at Augusta, drama hung heavy over the start of this Masters. Tom Watson, before teeing off, was informed that his longtime caddie and friend, Bruce Edwards, who had struggled so mightily against Lou Gehrig's disease, had died that morning. Watson, a two-time Masters champion, shot 76 in deep sadness. "I think he's not with us in body anymore," Watson said. "But I can tell you he's with us in spirit."

There was also a bittersweet quality to this Masters. Arnold Palmer, age 74, a four-time champion, was starting his final Masters. He had "unretired" from his previous retirement from the tournament and had come back to make it an even 50 playings, this legend that former Masters chairman Jackson Stephens credited with making the Masters. Stephens had said that before Palmer started in the 1950s, they had to give tickets away to get a crowd. After Palmer, they couldn't meet the demand, and before long they had to limit the galleries. Said current chairman Hootie Johnson, "I guess Arnold has meant more to the Masters Tournament than anyone."

Palmer found himself battling the modern Augusta National, much longer these past few years than the course he and others won on. His will to conquer was still strong. "I'm trying to hit it too far," Palmer said, after shooting 84. He had eight bogeys, two double bogeys and no birdies. Even a vintage Palmer would be hard-pressed to come back from 84. "I hope we've got more than one more round to go," Palmer said, half in jest, half in prayer. "I'm tired, I'll admit. But I'll be all right tomorrow. And Saturday," he added with a wink, "I'll be better than that." The game was gone, but Arnie was still Arnie.

This was the first-round leaderboard:

Justin Rose	67	Jose Maria Olazabal	71
Jay Haas	69	Charles Howell	71
Chris DiMarco	69	Bernhard Langer	71
Chris Riley	70	K.J. Choi	71
Alex Cejka	70	Kirk Triplett	71
Ernie Els	70	Phillip Price	71
Darren Clarke	70	Colin Montgomerie	71

An era in the Masters came to an end with the second round. It wasn't unexpected, but it was bittersweet nonetheless. Arnold Palmer, who made the Masters what it is, who won it four times, shot a second 84 for a 168 total and of course missed the cut in his 50th and final playing. It was at the 1958 Masters that Arnie's Army was born. So many memories. "How are you, Arnold?" someone asked. "Use your imagination," Palmer said softly, "and you will understand the emotion."

It was the last of the four major championships to be played in his towering career. But he left them laughing. It seems he made a rest stop at the men's room near No. 13 and came out to find a snake in his path. He thought it was a poisonous water moccasin. Masters official Billy Payne grinned and said it was a rubber snake because Augusta National doesn't have snakes.

"Well," Palmer said, "if I had felt a little tired, I didn't then. I came up out of there and I was flying."

And then he wrote *finis* to his Masters career.

"I'm through," Palmer said. "I've had it. I'm done. Cooked. Washed up. Finished. Whatever you want to say."

All anybody wanted to say was, "Thanks, Arnie."

There was yet another bittersweet moment after the second round of this Masters. "I don't think I'm going to play again," said Jack Nicklaus, age 64. Winner of a record six green jackets, he was playing in his 44th Masters and shot 75-75–150 and missed the cut by two strokes. As he left the 18th green, awash in the cheers, he took his cap off and waved it in all directions. Would he return? "I don't think I'm going to play again," he said. "I'm just about done. I've had enough."

But the 2004 Masters rolled on and so did the chances of another European victory. England's Justin Rose shot 71 for a two-round total of 138, keeping his two-stroke lead, but this time over two European compatriots tied at 140 — Germany's Alex Cejka, who shot another 70, and the unsinkable Spaniard, Jose Maria Olazabal. This wasn't quite the same Olazabal who had won two Masters, but enough like him to post a 69. Next came South Korea's K.J. Choi (70) and the nearest American, none other than Phil Mickelson (69), tied at 141. There were nine international players among the top 21 after 36 holes.

The tough question to Rose was, do you think you can win from here? "I believe I can, yes," said Rose, playing in only his second Masters.

Rose didn't seem to be under pressure. "I wasn't paying any attention to the leaderboards today," he said. "I wanted to not put myself under pressure at all in terms of having to scramble for pars and get up and down."

And he was solid with 15 pars, two birdies and a bogey. For the 36 holes, he had hit 90 percent of the greens in regulation. But he could use some help with his putting. He needed 32 putts in each round.

This was the first time in the 68 years of the Masters that Europeans occupied the first three spots at the halfway point. Said Olazabal, the last to win it, in 1999, "It would have been nice to have another European win the tournament, that's for sure." Olazabal's 69 was fueled by an eagle at the par-five 13th. He hit a driver and a six iron to 36 feet and rolled in the putt. He more or less owns that hole. It was his third eagle there.

Cejka just missed a chance to take second place alone when he bogeyed the 18th in a roller-coaster round. He had five birdies and three bogeys and was happy to be back after an eight-year absence. He finished 44th in 1996. "The game has improved a little bit, I think mentally, especially," said Cejka, now age 34. "I've got more experience — 1996 was the first tournament in America, the first major. I was young. I was wild."

A more experienced Cejka and a sharper Olazabal increased the chances for a European to win, but overall, the odds in general for Europeans were dramatically reduced by a strange turn of events. Darren Clarke, thought to be a prime candidate for this Masters and who tied for fourth in the first round with a 70, ballooned to a one-birdie 79 in the second and missed the cut. Also gone in a huge swing was Colin Montgomerie, 71-80.

The day had enough twists and turns for an Agatha Christie mystery. Choi, for example — he tied for 15th in 2003 — blistered the first nine in a record-tying 30. "When I started out the day, I just thought, 'Let's have an easy day, a good start,'" Choi said. "But as I got going, I kept making birdies." He birdied Nos. 2, 3, 5, 7, 8 and 9. It's called momentum. Then he saw his wife between No. 9 and No. 10, and she told him she was praying for him. Was it a perverse cause-and-effect? Whatever it was, he hit a wall. He bogeyed the 10th, 11th and 12th — he was reeling — then bogeyed the 16th as well for a 40 on the birdie-free second nine. "I thought even par would be a good score," a relieved Choi said. "But finishing at two under, I feel very lucky."

Chris DiMarco, tied for second in the first round, was running hot on the first nine, shooting 33 with three straight birdies from the sixth. That got him to six under par and in a tie with Rose. Then came a killer at the 13th. "I hit one poor shot all day," DiMarco said, "and it wasn't even a shot. It was a chip shot, but it cost me two strokes." He had laid up and was trying to flip the ball across the water to the green, but got too delicate and dropped it in the water. That cost him a double-bogey seven. This came after he went 30 holes without a bogey. It shook him. He bogeyed the 14th and 16th as well, shot 73, and dropped to a tie for sixth with, among others, Fred Couples (69), Ernie Els (72) and Davis Love (67, with an eagle on a huge 50-foot putt at the 13th).

Tiger Woods stirred the faithful with a 69 that lifted him to a tie for 14th at even-par 144. He made two bogeys and a burst of birdies — at the 13th, 15th and 16th holes — that got the galleries going. Was he on his way? "I'm still here," Woods said. "I'm looking all right. I just hung in there."

Meanwhile, in the midst of all this, experienced Masters watchers noted that Phil Mickelson had shot 69 and had moved up on the leaderboard

— somewhere just under the lead. He tied for fourth with Choi at 141. On paper, it was a workaday 69 — a birdie and a bogey on the first nine for an even-par 36, and on the second nine, birdies at the 12th, 13th and 17th, that on a 30-foot putt. What the scorecard didn't show was the new Mickelson, where patience kept him from gambling on shots that used to get him big numbers. He had spoken of trying to save a half shot here and there. "I think where I've received that half a shot was the par-fives," he said. "Now, I haven't birdied very many. I think I was only one under yesterday, one under today, but where I'm seeing it [the patience] is I'm not making six or seven like I have in the past on the holes that you need to make birdie. I'm giving myself a chance to make four, and if not, I'm making five. It's those par-fives where I think I'm not giving the shots back."

For another example, the 12-foot birdie putt he missed at the 18th looked like a blown chance. "It was a defensive putt," Mickelson said. "I thought, boy, if I rolled it three or four feet by it would go all the way down the hill. Even though I wanted to make it, I was just trying to trickle it over the edge."

The 36-hole cut came at four-over-par 148 and took away, among others, defending champion Mike Weir, who bounced back from that opening 79 with a 70, but missed by one. Also gone was the historic Zhang Lian-wei, the first Chinese ever in the Masters, and only by a stroke (77-72–149). For the record, his first Masters included three birdies, one eagle, six bogeys and two double bogeys. "It was my dream to play here, and now it's my job to conquer the course in the future," Zhang said. Other victims: Adam Scott, the young Australian who won The Players Championship two weeks earlier, Open champion Ben Curtis and 2003 Masters playoff runner-up Len Mattiace, still recovering from skiing injuries suffered some five months earlier.

Of the five amateurs in the field, Casey Wittenberg and Brandt Snedeker made the cut, both on the number, at 148. Three other amateurs missed: Nick Flanagan, the U.S. Amateur champion, with 78-74–152; Gary Wolsten-holme, Britain's Amateur champion, 77-76–153, and for the unkindest cut of all, Nathan Smith, 25, the U.S. Mid-Amateur champion (78-72–150), whose joy and sorrow both came from playing with Arnold Palmer through two highly charged days. Rushing to leave the final stage to Palmer at the 18th, Smith hit his approach shot into a bunker, blasted poorly to 25 feet, and three-putted for a double bogey to miss the cut by two.

The leaderboard after 36 holes:

Justin Rose	71 - 138		Ernie Els	72 - 142
Jose Maria Olazabal	69 - 140		Charles Howell	71 - 142
Alex Cejka	70 - 140		Davis Love	67 - 142
K.J. Choi	70 - 141		Mark O'Meara	70 - 143
Phil Mickelson	69 - 141		Steve Flesch	67 - 143
Fred Couples	69 - 142		Jeff Sluman	70 - 143
Chris DiMarco	73 - 142			

Phil Mickelson was no stranger to the pressure of the third-round lead. On the PGA Tour he had won nine of the 13 times he led going into the final round. But the major championships were a different matter. He'd had a total of 17 top-10 finishes in the four majors, but never did he go into the final round with the lead. "I feel like I've had so many chances to win, I can't believe that I haven't been in the lead," Mickelson said. "That's interesting to me." Mickelson had even been in the final pairing a number of times going into the fourth round, but never as the leader. And now, in the 2004 Masters, there he was, tied with Chris DiMarco, his old friend, going into the final round.

DiMarco shot 68 and Mickelson another 69, and they were locked at six-under-par 210, and they were both seeking their first major title. But could they have done it without a group fold in front of them?

The international campaign took a setback. Justin Rose, leader through the first two rounds, shot 81 and fell to a tie for 20th place. The two players who had been tied for second place also dropped — Alex Cejka (78) to a tie for 16th and Jose Maria Olazabal (79) to a tie for 20th. Still, however, the top 25 included 12 international players.

The Europeans were hardly out of the running. Paul Casey of England, a Masters rookie, shot 68 and rose to third place, two strokes behind the leaders. And tied for fourth place at 213 were the durable two-time champion Bernhard Langer with a 69, K.J. Choi (72) and Ernie Els (71). Els got his opportunity thanks to a controversial ruling by an official who said Els was entitled to a free drop after hooking his drive into some fallen limbs well left of the fairway at the 11th. Els scrambled to an excellent bogey from there.

Unfairly or not, veteran golf observers were wondering whether Rose might throw a tantrum in anger and frustration, as he had done before in his young career. Not this time, although the Masters was over for him. "I'm still shell-shocked," Rose said after his 81. "Whether you believe me or not, I felt in a great frame of mind going out there." He got a sympathetic reception as he trudged up the 18th fairway. "It was a beautiful ovation," said an appreciative Rose. "It was a nice touch."

Cejka's big wound came at the 18th, where he blew to a triple-bogey seven. Olazabal's fall was more prolonged. He had one birdie and five bogeys, then double-bogeyed the 17th.

But yet another European entered the picture. Sweden's Fredrik Jacobson logged six birdies and stumbled to a bogey at the 18th for 67, the day's best score, and held eighth place. "Looking at tournaments in the past, I think this course and the British Open courses suit my game," Jacobson said. "There is less rough, and you can create shots more. I had to create shots around the green." In fact, he did a great job of it. He hit only 12 of the 18 greens in regulation, but he needed only 26 putts.

Casey got off to a shaky start. "I've put too much pressure on myself in the past," Casey said of his experience in the majors. "I've almost tried too hard." He had one bogey, that at the par-three No. 6. He birdied Nos. 3 and 5, however, and after the bogey, he birdied Nos. 7, 9 and 15. "In England, they're looking for another Masters champion," he said, thinking of Nick Faldo, Sandy Lyle and Ian Woosnam. "I would dearly love to fill that slot."

Kirk Triplett, who had opened with 71-74, turned in one of the wilder 69s the Masters has seen in some time — a six-birdie, three-bogey exercise in the art of the up-and-down that included birdies at Nos. 7, 8 and 9. He ended at two-under 214, four off the lead. He was asked whether he was an underdog going into the final round. Said Triplett, "I'm an underdog every time I tee it up."

Ireland's Padraig Harrington made a leap. He entered the third round in the nothing-to-lose category, 10 strokes out of the lead. He shot a one-bogey, five-birdie 68 to leap from a tie for 32nd to a tie for ninth, at 216 six shots back. It would be now or never. "If you're already last in the field, what's the worst you can do?" he said.

Stewart Cink also moved into the tie for ninth with a no-bogey 69, matching his all-time low in seven Masters. "Making no bogeys can take care of a lot of missed opportunities," he said.

Whatever chance Tiger Woods still had pretty much disappeared in another 75. That left him nine shots off the lead heading into the final round. The big blow came at the 13th, where he hit his drive into the trees and double-bogeyed. Then he bogeyed the 14th as well. He still gave himself hope. "Anything can happen," he said. "There's so much danger on that back nine, especially the holes that have been lengthened." And his game overall? "Frustrating," he said. "Because I'm so close to putting it together."

DiMarco, a good-natured man, was especially so after his 68. He had made a good save at the first, where his seven-iron approach just rolled off the back of the green and he putted back up to six inches. Then he birdied the second hole and was on his way to his second bogey-free round of the tournament. He solved the tricky 14th for his fourth and final birdie, holding an eight-iron shot against the wind from about 150 yards that trickled down to about three feet. "I was able to sneak that one in," he said. The conversation then turned to the pressure he would face in the final round. Did he have anything to prove?

"No, to tell the truth," DiMarco said. "I obviously want to win majors, certainly. I want to win more tournaments. But if it all ended tomorrow, I'd be happy with my career, the way I've played and what I've done and the success I've had."

And the pressure on Mickelson?

"He's going to have a lot of pressure on him, too, because he's going to try to get that monkey off there," DiMarco said. "Certainly I don't think he has anything to prove. I know that he hasn't won a major yet, but in my mind, he doesn't need to. He's had a pretty good career."

Mickelson, however, filled in the rest of the blanks. "I think you need to win a major to show the credibility that you can play in the toughest conditions," he said. He also had a bogey-free round, posting his second straight 69. Once again, he made just one birdie at a par-five hole, No. 8 this time, but he didn't waste any strokes trying to force birdies at the other three. "The pin was in a great spot to make birdie at No. 2," he said. "In past years, I felt like I have to birdie this hole. It's one of the few opportunities. But when I didn't birdie, it didn't bother me." His three birdies came on the first nine, at Nos. 3, 7 and 8.

The message for the fourth round came from Cink. "The leader is always capable of being caught," he said. "This is the Masters. This course brings nerves to the forefront like no other place in the whole world."

The third-round leaderboard:

Phil Mickelson	69 - 210		Fredrik Jacobson	67 - 215
Chris DiMarco	68 - 210		Stewart Cink	69 - 216
Paul Casey	68 - 212		Fred Couples	74 - 216
K.J. Choi	72 - 213		Jay Haas	72 - 216
Ernie Els	71 - 213		Padraig Harrington	68 - 216
Bernhard Langer	69 - 213		Davis Love	74 - 216
Kirk Triplett	69 - 214		Nick Price	71 - 216

Every good show has some warm-up acts, some people to go out and get the audience in a receptive mood. Not that the final round of the Masters needed any, but there they were anyway.

Bernhard Langer, age 46, was chasing his third green jacket until his approach shot to the 15th hole rolled back into the water and he double-bogeyed. He shot 72 for a three-under 285 total and tied for fourth place, six strokes behind. "I felt I could pull it off today," Langer said. "I just didn't play the back nine well enough."

Sergio Garcia, age 24 and winless in 46 consecutive PGA Tour events, tied Langer for fourth after entering the final round nine strokes off the pace. After a double bogey at the sixth, Garcia raced to eight under par for the last 12 holes for 66. "I just feel like I played well enough to win," Garcia said. "Unfortunately, I'm not going to." Still, it was his best showing in his six Masters.

Tiger Woods continued playing erratically and shot an up-and-down 71 for a 290 total and tied for 22nd, his worst finish in eight Masters as a professional. It was his seventh straight major championship without a win. "I'm not that far off with my game," he insisted.

There had been no holes-in-one at the Masters since 1996 until Chris DiMarco broke the dry spell at No. 6 in the first round. Now in the final round came two at the 16th, back-to-back. Padraig Harrington hit a seven iron, and right behind him Kirk Triplett hit a six iron. These made 17 aces in the 68 playings of the Masters, starting in 1934.

This Masters was destined to be a Phil-and-Ernie show for the final round, and Chris DiMarco was brushed off the stage. DiMarco had said that the pressure wouldn't matter, but somehow for someone who was so steady all week, he became very erratic. He birdied No. 2, then had three bogeys and a double bogey over the next five holes. He would shoot 76 and tie for sixth place, seven strokes behind. But there would be a curtain call for DiMarco. He would be the one who would show Mickelson the path to winning on the final green. Mickelson became only the fourth to win the Masters with a birdie on the final hole. Arnold Palmer did it in 1960, Sandy Lyle in 1988 and Mark O'Meara in 1998.

Mickelson entered the final round leading Els by three strokes. Ordinarily, that would be an encouraging cushion, but not at the Masters. While Mickelson was playing with DiMarco in the final pairing, Els was two groups in front with K.J. Choi.

Mickelson's three-shot lead was gone by the eighth hole. Actually, it disappeared in a three-hole stretch. Els had the lead. Same old Mickelson. They trotted along like two puppies tugging at the same stick. They matched each other shot for shot over the first five holes — par, birdie, bogey, par, bogey. Mickelson bogeyed the par-three No. 6. Els parred and closed to within two strokes. Els birdied No. 7, and Mickelson's lead was down to one.

Then came the dramatic turn. At the uphill par-five eighth, Els hit a driver, and from 212 yards hooked a five iron around the trees. When he arrived at the green, he understood the roar from the gallery. His ball was sitting five feet from the hole. He holed the putt for the eagle to take a one-stroke lead. Els held that one-stroke lead until the 12th, when Mickelson abandoned his new, prudent game and went for the throat. The nasty little 12th, with the Sunday hole placement beckoning to all who need a birdie and are foolhardy enough to go at it in that narrow place.

"I took a pretty aggressive line at that pin," Mickelson said. "Nobody goes after that pin." He fired an eight iron to 12 feet and got his birdie. "When the putt went in, that's when I thought I could make this happen," he said.

Els eagled the par-five 13th up ahead of him — his second eagle of the round. He hit a three wood off the tee, and from 205 yards fired a six iron to 10 feet. He was ahead by two strokes until Mickelson put a seven iron on the green and two-putted for birdie. Els' lead was down to one.

At the 14th, Mickelson fired a wedge shot from 146 yards to within inches of the hole and birdied to tie Els at seven under par. The irrepressible Els slipped in front again with a birdie at the 15th. Then Mickelson caught him at the par-three 16th, the hole he had four-putted for a double bogey in the first round. He put an eight iron to 15 feet and birdied. They were locked at eight under par. The break would come at the 18th.

Els drove into the fairway bunker on the 18th and had about the same shot as Sandy Lyle in 1988. And, like Lyle, he hit an exquisite long bunker shot that settled on the green within 14 feet of the hole. But he missed the birdie putt and finished with a five-under 67 and an eight-under 280 total.

Now the world awaited Mickelson and his moment of truth at the 18th. The bold Mickelson who went for the dangerous pin at the 12th gave way to the prudent new Mickelson. He hit a three wood off the tee to avoid the bunker and the trees, then lofted an eight iron to the right of the hole, about 18 feet above the flag.

Here, Mickelson got the last little piece of the grand prize. DiMarco hit a bunker shot that finished just a few inches beyond Mickelson's ball. DiMarco would be putting first. There's no better way to read a putt than to watch someone else's. "Chris' ball was hanging on that left lip, and when it got to the hole it just fell off," Mickelson said. "And my putt was almost on the identical line."

Mickelson's putt crept toward the hole, turned slightly to the right, paused indecisively for a breathtaking moment, and then fell in.

Els was deflated. "I gave it my best shot," he said. "I'm very disappointed now, but I'll get over this, no problem. But I'll have another shot. I'll have another shot."

When the ball dropped, Mickelson gave a big, clumsy leap, rushed to his family, scooped up daughter Amanda and said, "Can you believe daddy won?"

3. U.S. Open Championship

Positions changed quickly during the final round of the United States Open Championship. In the end the outcome settled into a duel between Retief Goosen, the 2001 champion, and Phil Mickelson, who in April had won the Masters Tournament. All the others played supporting roles in this dramatic championship that ended when Mickelson misplayed the 17th hole and handed the Open to Goosen, the calmest of men.

Paired with Ernie Els, a fellow South African, Goosen had stepped onto the first tee two strokes ahead of both Els and Mickelson, but on that opening hole Els had taken four strokes just to get his ball inside Goosen's, which lay 40 feet from the flagstick. Goosen holed for a birdie three; Els took a six and never recovered.

Goosen's reaction when the putt fell? No fist pumping so common in the modern game. Instead, behaving as if he were a relic of an earlier generation, he gave the impression he had *expected* to hole the putt.

Later in the day, when Mickelson whittled away at his formidable lead, Goosen's mood froze at placid.

Quiet, shy and aloof fairly well describes this man who had by then won two of the last four U.S. Opens, his first in 2001 at Southern Hills Country Club in Tulsa, Oklahoma, by beating Mark Brooks in a playoff, and his second simply by holding his composure while both Els and Mickelson wilted under the heat of championship golf at its highest level at Shinnecock Hills Golf Club in Southampton, New York.

Blond-haired, blue-eyed and broad-shouldered, Goosen stands just under six feet tall and weighs a solid 185 pounds. Always considered a first-class ball-striker, over the four days of the Open he combined precision irons with exceptional putting and, with his strong arms and legs, significant power. Over the four rounds, Goosen averaged 314 yards on his drives on the fifth and 16th, two par-five holes, not the best — Allenby averaged 316.5 and Els 316 — but not far from it.

His putting over those last nine holes touched on extraordinary. Official statistics say he one-putted seven of the last nine greens, but they're wrong. He one-putted just six. These statisticians insist that shots played from only an inch or so off a green are not putts. Of course they are, and so Goosen took two putts on the final hole, his first from just off the back of the green.

Goosen closed with a marvelous final round of 71, one over par. Only Australian Robert Allenby beat it with 70, a score that jumped him from a tie for 34th place at 54 holes into a tie for seventh at the end. Mickelson shot 71 as well, along with the ageless Jay Haas, who tied for ninth place. Goosen shot 276 for the 72 holes, four under par and lower than the winning scores of the two previous Opens at Shinnecock Hills during the modern era. Raymond Floyd won with 279 in 1986 and Corey Pavin with 280 in 1995. With a final score of 278, Mickelson outscored the previous winners as well.

Jeff Maggert took third place at 281, Mike Weir and Shigeki Maruyama tied at 284 for fourth place, and Fred Funk took sixth place at 285. Not yet fully recovered from an injury to his wrist, Jim Furyk, the 2003 champion, withered toward the end, shot 298, and tied for 48th place.

With his even-par 70, Allenby shot the low round of the day, a statistic that outraged some critics with short memories. In 1972, the first Open at Pebble Beach, a par-72 course, only Mason Rudolph broke par in the last round. He shot 70 and tied for 40th place. Jack Nicklaus, the winner, closed with 74, two over par, and won by three strokes even with a bogey six on the last hole. The Pebble Beach field turned in only 19 rounds under par. The 66 men who completed 72 holes at Shinnecock Hills showed 37 rounds under par, along with five others by those who missed the cut.

All that aside, without question Shinnecock Hills in 2004 must take its place among the more difficult courses of the modern era. It stands alongside Oakland Hills as it was set up for the 1951 championship, Olympic in 1955, Pebble Beach in 1972 and 1992 and, of course, Bethpage Black in 2002.

Nevertheless, Shinnecock Hills had turned into something more than a difficult course. It played brutally hard, especially in the last round. Hardly anyone complained during the first two rounds when the field turned in 33 scores in the 60s, but Shinnecock Hills began toughening in the third round when the course gave up only three sub-par scores, and then approached the impossible on the last day when only Appleby could even match par.

Essentially, the USGA miscalculated its options. Organizational dogma ruled that, given the choice, those who set up the course should err on the side of firm and fast. Err they did. Greens already fast grew faster still, leading to the shock of a gently tapped ball rolling yards past its target.

Greens mowed by machines at microscopically low settings, no rain to soften the ground and an overnight wind that turned them dry and hard created havoc. Some of what we saw that day couldn't really be called golf. Joakim Haeggman, a Swede who plays the European Tour, faced a fairly long putt from the back of the 10th green to a hole set close to the front. Struck a touch too forcefully, his ball eased past the hole, down a steep incline into a valley 20 yards below and a pitch shot away. Six strokes later he finished with a nine.

Shinnecock Hills' seventh hole approached unplayable. A beautifully designed par-three of 190 yards, it had been laid out in 1916 by Charles Blair Macdonald and modeled after the famous redan hole, the 14th at North Berwick, on the east coast of Scotland. A classic risk-reward teaser, its green sits diagonally to the shot, protected by a deep bunker usually set in line to the flagstick. Difficult enough in concept, the shaved green turned the seventh into a terror.

Of the first four men off the tee that Sunday morning, three of them scored six. Kevin Stadler, the son of Craig Stadler, faced a two-foot putt for a par three. Tapped just a touch off line, his ball caught the lip of the hole, spun away, and crept into the bunker.

Aware before play began that the redan could be troubling, Walter Driver, the chairman of the USGA's championship committee, repositioned the hole to the easiest, most accessible spot he could find. Even that wasn't enough. As tales of the early starters' miseries reached him, he ordered a short delay while Shinnecock's grounds crew syringed the green.

The gallery cheered.

Driver ordered the same treatment for every green once and continued periodic watering to the seventh. It helped.

That it had to be done upset not only the players but USGA officials as well, because over the years Shinnecock Hills had grown in stature and earned its place among the great courses of the American continent. Historically the club reaches back to the very beginnings of golf in the United States. Willie Davis, then the professional at the Royal Montreal Golf Club, laid out its first course in 1891, and its wooden-frame clubhouse, primitive compared to the baronial palaces common to any number of prominent clubs, is believed the first built specifically for a golf club in the United States.

It has an impeccable pedigree since it had been designed by Stanford White, perhaps the nation's most gifted architect of the late 19th and early 20th centuries. Among his works, he had designed the old *New York Herald* building, the Boston Public Library, the Washington Square Arch in New York and the second Madison Square Garden, the last of the series actually located at Madison Square in downtown Manhattan. He rebuilt the classic Rotunda at the University of Virginia as well. Originally done by Thomas Jefferson in 1819, the Rotunda collapsed when a frantic faculty member set off dynamite trying to put out a fire sweeping through adjoining buildings. That didn't help at all and, instead, damaged the Rotunda badly.

A dashing figure with his flame red hair, White had married Bessie Smith, whose family had founded the Long Island city of Smithtown. Married or not, he seduced an untold number of young showgirls in the private apartment he had built for himself above Madison Square Garden. During a musical revue on the Garden's Roof Garden, Harry Thaw, the husband of one of White's conquests, shot and killed him. After two trials and one escape from a mental home, Thaw won his release. The episode eventually became the subject of a book by E.L. Doctorow and the movie *The Girl in the Red Velvet Swing*.

White died at the age of 53, but at the time of the 2004 Open, his Shinnecock Hills clubhouse had lasted more than a century. A simple structure, worn over time, its stairway, pickled by spike marks, leads to a smallish lounge where a wooden image of a Shinnecock Indian brave hangs on a wall. Without heat or air conditioning, this is strictly a seasonal club; the flagsticks go into the holes in April and come out of the holes in November.

Its course is, nevertheless, a classic of golf design. Davis had laid out 12 simple holes at first, that later had been expanded to 18 by Willie Dunn, the winner of an informal U.S. Open in 1894. Later in the year, representatives of Shinnecock joined with others from The Country Club in Boston, Newport Golf Club in Rhode Island, St. Andrew's, also in New York, and the Chicago Golf Club and organized the United States Golf Association. Two years later, in 1986, the USGA awarded the Open to Shinnecock Hills.

That original course had become outdated by 1916. The club then commissioned Macdonald to create an entirely new design. By then Macdonald had built the National Golf Links of America on property that abuts Shinnecock Hills. The National became an instant success and is judged the country's first modern golf course. But by the late 1920s, Macdonald's redesign of

Shinnecock Hills became obsolete as well, prompting Shinnecock Hills to engage the firm of Toomey and Flynn to begin from scratch with a modern design.

Bill Flynn handled the design work while Howard Toomey took care of construction and finance. After studying Macdonald's work, Flynn had the wit to build around some of his holes and absorb them into his design. Thus the redan remained in place and, over time, won its place among the great holes of American golf.

Through the four days of the 2004 Open it ranked among the hardest of them all, although the fourth round, when it played so abnormally hard, skewed the final figures.

Goosen had no trouble at all, and in fact made his par every day, the only man among the top 10 scorers who played the seventh in even par over the four rounds. It cost Mickelson three strokes though, and he lost to Goosen by two. Yet, against the odds, he made his three in the fourth round.

Goosen opened with an even-par round of 70, which left him four strokes out of first place, a position shared by the three men who shot 66s. Once again a man in his 50s stood at the top of the first-round standings. A year earlier it had been 53-year-old Tom Watson at Olympia Fields in Chicago. Three years younger, 50-year-old Jay Haas shot 66 and shared first place with Shigeki Maruyama of Japan and Angel Cabrera of Argentina.

This had been a day of low scoring as 19 men broke par 70, a group that included Vijay Singh at 68 and Corey Pavin, one of the great maneuverers of the ball, at 67. Two months after winning the Masters Tournament, Mickelson shot 68 as well, along with Maggert, Steve Flesch, Stadler and Ben Curtis, winner of the 2003 Open Championship in Britain.

Among the strange happenings this day, Spencer Levin, a 20-year-old amateur from California, holed the 17th in one and finished with 69, along with Mike Weir and four others, and Miguel Angel Jimenez, who had tied for second place in 2000, took nine strokes to play the 11th, another trying par-three. His tee shot ran down a slope off the back and shot after shot failed to reach safe ground.

Despite his still sore wrist, Furyk shot a reasonable 72 and matched Tiger Woods, who looked not at all like the overpowering presence of the century's first few years.

Then there were Nick Faldo and David Duval, two dominating players of the past. No longer exempt, Faldo had gone through sectional qualifying to win his place, while Duval, who hadn't played a round of competitive golf in eight months, still held an exemption as the 2001 British champion.

After winning that championship, Duval had looked around and asked himself, "Is this all there is?", decided indeed it was, and walked away unfulfilled. Now he decided he wanted to play and filed his entry. Cheered on every tee and green, Duval showed none of the precision golf he had played three years earlier and shot 83; Faldo shot 81. The next day Duval cut his score to 81 and Faldo shot 70. Both men missed the 36-hole cut.

And while those two who had reached the top of the game stumbled around Shinnecock Hills, David Roesch shot 68, two strokes out of first place. Totally unknown, Roesch had not enjoyed a successful career. He normally played the Hooters Tour, a second level down from the PGA

Tour, and just weeks earlier had decided to give up the game. He changed his mind when he qualified for the Open. His success restored his sense of humor as well. Passing a scoreboard that showed him in first place at one stage, Roesch approached a rules official and asked if he could take a picture.

"I was thinking, just get me a picture of that and I'll go home right now," Roesch said.

His was not the only Cinderella story of opening day. Haas had shot his 66 playing in a group with 54-year-old Tom Kite, the 1992 Open champion, and 61-year-old Raymond Floyd, who had won at Shinnecock Hills in 1986 and held a membership there. Kite shot a workmanlike 72 and Floyd shot 75.

Playing forceful, attacking golf on a course that doesn't yield low scores easily, Haas opened with a pitch to three feet and birdied the first, missed the second green and bogeyed, then birdied both the fourth, with an eight iron to five feet, and the fifth, the shorter and easier of Shinnecock's two par-fives. He had bunkered his second but pitched out and holed from 18 feet for the four.

Out in two under par, Haas played a nine iron to 12 feet on the 11th, another teasing par-three, and birdied a hole that gave up only 26 others that day. Spencer Levin birdied it as well. A 20-year-old Stanford University student, Levin holed the 17th in one and had the distinction of playing the two par-threes on the home nine in three strokes. He beat Haas by one; Jay holed an improbable 40-footer and birdied the 17th. (Levin followed with a birdie two on the 17th the following day, then a three on Saturday, and finally a four on Sunday. In consecutive rounds he had played the 17th in one, two, three, four. Call Ripley.)

Haas, meantime, struggled with his driver throughout the day, hitting just eight of the 14 fairways on driving holes, but he played steady recoveries, and with four one-putt greens on each nine, his putting could hardly have been better.

When he finished, Haas said he had been driving the ball farther than ever and claimed, "That's all equipment. It gives me the feeling I can play these courses as well or better than I could 20 years ago. Just because I'm 50 years old shouldn't eliminate me from the equation."

Nor could Maruyama be eliminated because he had trouble speaking English and stood just 5-foot-7. He could, nevertheless, hit his driver with anyone, and he played the game well enough to be in position to win the 2002 Open Championship in Britain. Unfortunately for him, he shot 75 in the third round and tied for fifth. A joy to watch in the great events, Maruyama looked the world's happiest man; his smile outshined the sun. He teed off in the group immediately behind Haas, along with Chad Campbell, a 30-year-old Texan who had won the Bay Hill Invitational, and Tiger Woods, who at 28 had won everything.

Woods wasn't on his game this day. Missing fairways (he hit only five), missing half the greens, and not putting at the level that made him the game's most dangerous player, Woods shot a scrambling 72 with just one birdie. By scoring a four on the fifth, he showed he most likely had more shots in his arsenal than anyone in the game. His second shot trickled into a greenside bunker and lay close to the near edge and behind a sharp rise.

Taking an awkward stance with his left foot higher than his right, he drew back his sand wedge quite sharply and swing on a decidedly downward plane. The ball shot up, cleared the bunker's edge and rolled close enough to the hole to assure his birdie.

Maruyama, meanwhile, played textbook golf through the first nine, missed only the first and ninth fairways, hit every green except the ninth, and two-putted all but the ninth green, where he saved his par with his only one-putt of the first nine.

Coming in, he roused the gallery by holing a 45-foot putt on the dicey 10th and dipped two under par, added another birdie at the 11th, and still another at the 16th, the longer and tougher of the par-fives.

At the end of the day, Maruyama had parred 14 holes, birdied four, and escaped from this treacherous course without a bogey. Someone asked later if he might pop a bottle of champagne. Maruyama smiled.

By contrast, Cabrera rarely smiled. A bulky, powerful man who lumbered along with little to say, he showed he could play with finesse. Hitting fairways and hitting greens, Cabrera birdied four of the first eight holes and caught Haas and Maruyama. With a par four at the ninth he went out in 31, the best first nine of the round.

He had teed off at 1:40 p.m., grouped with Billy Mayfair and J.L. Lewis and with only two groups behind them. A layer of fog had hung over Shinnecock Hills since early morning, reviving memories of Pebble Beach in 2000, when both the first and second rounds carried over to the next day. Clouds began closing in throughout the afternoon and soon the rain fell. Play continued for a time, but then thunder rumbled and in the distance lightning flashed across the dull gray sky. At about 4:45 p.m., just after Cabrera finished the first nine, sirens sounded and play was suspended. Half the field still had holes to play, among them Fred Funk, three under par at that stage, just one stroke behind the leaders. The delay lasted until 6:55 p.m.

Back on the course, Cabrera ran off routine pars at the first three homeward holes, but now fog moved in, darkness came early, and the USGA suspended play once again. The 19 groups still on the course would finish their first round Friday morning, then begin their second.

The overnight delay caught Mickelson about to play the treacherous seventh, his 16th hole of the round, at two under par (he had started from the 10th tee). When he resumed the following morning, he took a bogey at the seventh but birdied the eighth and finished with 68.

Cabrera scrambled for his par at the 13th, but then he birdied the 14th. Five under par now, for a fleeting moment he led the Open. But he took a six at the 15th, not among Shinnecock's more difficult par-fours, and with those two lost strokes fell to three under. He rebounded quickly with another birdie at the 16th and moved back to four under.

Funk, meanwhile, lost all his three strokes and finished with 70, which left him in a tie with 1994 and 1997 Open champion Ernie Els, 2001 champion Retief Goosen, and a gang of others.

The first-round leaders:

Jay Haas	66	David Roesch	68
Shigeki Maruyama	66	Ben Curtis	68
Angel Cabrera	66	Skip Kendall	68
Corey Pavin	67	Kevin Stadler	68
Phil Mickelson	68	Steve Flesch	68
Jeff Maggert	68	Vijay Singh	68
Kris Cox	68		

With 36 holes behind them, Mickelson and Maruyama led with 134, six under par and one stroke ahead of Maggert at 135. Funk and Goosen followed with 136.

After finishing his first-round 68 early in the morning, Mickelson shot a bogey-free 66. Reversing Mickelson's rounds, Maruyama shot 68 in the second after opening with 66. Both Funk and Goosen shot 66 as well, along with Stephen Ames and Tim Herron, who played the kind of round that makes strong men weep. He had six pars, four bogeys and eight birdies, one short of half the holes. Altogether 21 men broke par, two more than in the first round, and 11 men came in under 140.

The weather had improved overnight. The sun beamed, the temperature climbed, and the wind blew with barely the strength to disturb the wispy, knee-high grasses bordering bridle-path fairways. The relative calm aside, the field groaned as well-played shots veered left or right on inverted-bowl greens and scurried either into the rough, downsloping chipping areas or perhaps tumbled into a bunker.

While Mickelson and Maruyama may have felt like preening, quite a few others hung within range. Els added a 67 to his opening 70 and Cabrera followed his 66 with a 71 for 137s, and both Singh, with 70, and Pavin, with 71, remained under par at 138.

With his 67, Maggert had played 15 rounds under 70 in his 14 Opens, more than anyone who had not won the championship. He had placed as high as fourth twice and finished in the top 10 in six Opens, the most of anyone over a 10-year period. (For those who question that record, Woods had placed among the top 10 in just three Opens since he entered his first, in 1995. Of course, he played amateur golf until he joined the professional tour late in 1996.) Now Maggert was at it again, just a stroke off the lead.

Still playing below his standard, Woods nevertheless wrenched a 69 from Shinnecock, which left him seven strokes behind Mickelson and Maruyama. Making up seven strokes in 36 holes would have been routine for Woods two years earlier, but his game showed little of his accustomed precision. His driver almost out of control, he flew shots into the right rough, the left rough, hit only seven fairways, slightly better than his first round, and just 10 of the 18 greens. You can't putt for birdies from bunkers.

Woods had birdied the fifth hole in the first round, and as he approached the fifth tee the following day, his 14th of the round, he hadn't made another in the 27 holes since. Then he birdied the fifth once again and immediately added another at the sixth. He made no more, although he one-putted his last five greens, mostly through deft work with his chipping clubs. At 141 he had tied David Roesch, who added 73 to his opening 68 and safely survived the 36-hole cut.

Through the truly superb golf he had played through 2002 and into early 2003, Woods had commanded the galleries, but now they belonged to Mickelson. And Friday turned out as Phil's day. Since he had teed off from the 10th tee with an afternoon starting time in the first round, he moved up to a morning time and first-tee start for the second round, again grouped with Paul Lawrie and Kirk Triplett.

Mickelson began with shaky driving, hitting only one of the first four fairways on driving holes, but after missing the fifth, he did not miss another throughout the round. Nor did he miss many greens — only the third, fifth and 17th — yet did not lose a stroke on any of them, unless we count his par five on the fifth, so reachable with the second shot.

Mickelson went out in 33 with birdies on both the first and eighth holes, then turned for home at four under par for 27 holes. Coming back he reached the 10th green with his approach, yet had to hole a putt of about six feet to save his four, and lost a chance for another birdie on the 11th, struggling to get down in two from eight feet on a slick and testy green.

Even so, he had fallen a stroke behind Cabrera. Two strokes ahead of Mickelson after the first round, Cabrera had started from the 10th tee 20 minutes behind Mickelson, birdied the 11th, moved to five under par, and for a short time took over first place. He lost that stroke by bogeying the 15th, took it back with another birdie at the 16th, then made a miserable six on the 18th, a par-four of 450 yards.

Cabrera pulled his drive into the heavy rough on the left, and instead of hacking out sideways to the fairway, he chose to risk a shot at the green. His ball fell short, his pitch over a bunker from a questionable lie scampered over the green into a bunker, and he took two putts. He was back to three under, trailing Mickelson.

While Cabrera struggled at the 18th, Mickelson gained ground. A 15-foot birdie putt fell at the 12th, dropping him to five under, and from there on in he played safe fairway-and-green golf, along the way picking up another birdie on the vulnerable 16th. With a 36-hole score of 136, he could do nothing but wait. And while he waited, Maruyama closed in.

Grouped with Woods once more, and again outplaying him, Maruyama at one stage dipped to seven under par, which would have taken over first place, but he mis-played the ninth, his final hole, and shot 68.

With his perpetual grin, Maruyama admitted, "I'm really surprising myself."

He certainly was. Opening with pars on the 10th and 11th, two dangerous holes, Maruyama pitched to five feet and birdied the 13th, at 370 yards Shinnecock's shortest and easiest par-four. He missed the fairway on the 14th but still saved par, but he needed three strokes to reach the green of the 16th, which gave up 93 birdies through 36 holes. Then he played his shot of the day.

From just off the back of the 17th, a 180-yard par-three, Maruyama played a little pitch-and-run that ran straight into the hole for a birdie two. When it dropped, his caddie gave him a high-five. A routine par four on the 18th, and Maruyama stood six under par for 27 holes, then opened the first nine with a par four, his 28th hole without a bogey.

He went no further. He bunkered his tee shot to the second and bogeyed, holed from five feet on the third and moved to six under par once again, and added another birdie at the fifth, where he flew an iron onto the green and got down in two for his four. Now he had gone to seven under and taken over first place. Of course he gave it away by mis-playing the ninth.

At 443 yards, the ninth didn't seem long to the modern tournament golfer, but the green sat high above the drive zone, and with the hole cut toward the front of the green, any attempt to attack the hole risked watching the ball roll back off into high fescue at the top of the grade.

Maruyama drove into the high fescue, gave it all he had with an iron, but moved his ball only into the shorter primary rough, barely reached the front of the green with his third, and held his breath as his ball rolled backward toward the high grass and left him a simple little chip. He nearly holed it, and of course parred and walked off sharing first place with Mickelson. They would play together the following day.

As Maruyama finished, Els had only a hole or two left of a rather strange round of his own. Beginning from the first tee in the afternoon shift, Els ran off four pars and then birdied the fifth, sixth, seventh and eighth and went out in 31, four under par. With nine more holes to play, he seemed primed to catch the co-leaders, but his edge apparently gone, Els played the second nine with eight pars and a bogey on the difficult 14th, perhaps Shinnecock's best par-four.

Meantime, had he continued to play as he had in the first round, Haas would have become the oldest U.S. Open champion by a matter of five years. Instead his game weakened and, still missing fairways and greens, Haas shot 74 and dropped into a tie for 12th, alongside Stadler, Sergio Garcia, Mayfair, who would hang around until the end, Ames and Pat Perez, who shot 67.

The 36-hole cut fell at 145. Tom Kite made it, but it caught a number of prominent players. Rich Beem, the 2002 PGA champion, missed by a stroke with 146, the Irishman Darren Clarke shot 147, and Thomas Bjorn, who had been so close to winning the 2003 British title, shot 148. Stewart Cink, another winner on the PGA Tour, shot 149, along with Stuart Appleby. Both Davis Love and Fred Couples played loose golf and missed the cut, Couples with 75-77–152, and Love with 76-75–151.

At 61, Raymond Floyd had probably played his last round of the Open. In recognition of his winning the 1986 Championship, the USGA extended a special exemption, and as usual, Floyd played solid golf, shooting two rounds of 75. This had been his 31st Open, and throughout his career he had never given less than his best.

The second-round leaders:

Phil Mickelson	66 - 134	Ernie Els	67 - 137
Shigeki Maruyama	68 - 134	Vijay Singh	70 - 138
Jeff Maggert	67 - 135	Corey Pavin	71 - 138
Fred Funk	66 - 136	Mike Weir	70 - 139
Retief Goosen	66 - 136	Trevor Immelman	70 - 139
Angel Cabrera	71 - 137		

After two days when the course surrendered 40 sub-par rounds, Shinnecock Hills suddenly turned mean in the third round. On a bright, sunshiny day with the wind blowing just a little stronger, it gave up only three rounds below 70. Tim Clark shot 66, Charles Howell shot 68, and Retief Goosen shot 69, good enough to move him two strokes ahead of the field at 205. Els and Mickelson shared second place at 207, and Funk and Maruyama tied for fourth at 208.

Looking back on his day, Goosen said Shinnecock had played like a real U.S. Open course. Asked how tough he rated the course after his even-par round of 70, Els said, "On a scale of 1 to 10, I would give it an 11."

Sub-par scores worked wonders. By whittling four strokes from par, Clark leaped 28 places into a tie for sixth, and Howell, who had barely made the cut, climbed from a tie for 57th into a tie for 13th.

Both Mickelson and Maruyama, who had shared the 36-hole lead at 134, had off days, along with Maggert, who had begun the day in third place but faded on the homeward nine. Maruyama and Maggert shot 74s, and Mickelson, damaged by the first nine, shot 73. Maruyama wrecked his round on the 18th.

Even with his troubles, Mickelson tied for second and Maruyama slipped to fourth with Funk, who shot 72 and lost no ground, but Maggert fell from third place into a tie for sixth, with Clark. Haas had captured the gallery's heart with his opening 66, but he slipped further back with a 76 that dropped him into a tie for 34th with his son, Bill, an amateur.

Tiger Woods continued his lusterless golf until the final hole. On his way to a 75 with only the 18th to play, Woods lofted a 100-yard wedge that caught the green, took two bounces, and before the eyes could focus, jumped into the hole. His eagle two had turned a 75 into a 73, and at 214 kept him within nine strokes of first place. On a frustrating day when he played two pitch shots to the 10th that rolled back down the hill almost to his feet, Woods broke par on only one other hole. He birdied the eighth, his third birdie in 54 holes. He had, however, eagled the 18th, but he had bogeyed eight holes and double-bogeyed the 10th.

Shinnecock's 10th runs level about 250 yards and then plunges sharply downhill to a deep valley before rising quickly to the green. It had hurt both Greg Norman and Ben Crenshaw in previous Opens, and now it cost Woods a six on a hole that measures 450 yards, just a drive and a pitch for the current group of tournament golfers.

With the hole cut teasingly close to the front edge, Woods tried a pitch shot that didn't carry far enough, then a running shot up the hill that didn't make it either. Both balls came back down the steep slope almost to his feet. His third attempt, played more aggressively, ran up the hill, onto the green and ran out of steam 35 feet past the hole. Two putts and he had double-bogeyed.

Mickelson's double-bogey five highlighted the controversy over the seventh hole, Shinnecock's redan, Macdonald's favorite design. He had built a similar hole on the National Links, and he added Shinnecock Hills' during his 1916 revision. The seventh green had the added disadvantage of tilting to the left. A shot just a little left of the flagstick often curled off the green into the sand. Tee shots played toward the back ran off and set up a dangerous chip. Maruyama, for example, played a nice tee shot that held the green but left him quite a long putt. When he stroked it, the ball seemed ready to stop near the hole, but slowly, very slowly, it ran off the back. He chipped on and holed the putt for a bogey four.

Mickelson's tee shot dived into the bunker, though, and he played a useful recovery that left him a sidehill putt of perhaps 12 feet. Played too softly, the putt turned before it reached the hole, and while he walked beside it, the ball eased down the slight slope and stopped perhaps 30 feet away. Mickelson missed and took his five. Chez Reavie, a 22-year-old amateur from Mesa, Arizona, claimed the day's only birdie and shot 71, one of the best scores of the day.

The fifth hole, the patsy of the course, gave up 120 birdies over the first two rounds, an average of 60 each round to the 155 players. In the third it gave up 41 birdies to the 66 player. Only the left-handed Steve Flesch birdied the 13th, at 370 yards the shortest of the 12 par-fours, and only Howell and Lee Janzen, twice the Open champion, birdied the 17th, another par-three.

This was a day when the usual statistics meant nothing. They show, for example, that Fred Funk hit only 10 greens, that Goosen and Els hit 11, and Mickelson and Maruyama nine. They don't show they actually hit more greens, but the ball simply wouldn't stay put.

Paired with Angel Cabrera, Goosen teed off at 2:30 p.m., two groups ahead of Mickelson and Maruyama, who, as the co-leaders, played last. As an example of how the course played, after a good drive into the first fairway, Goosen lofted a pitch that carried to the green with a little back-spin, then backed off. He putted on, then holed out for a par four. Earlier, Els had driven into the light rough along the left and played a running shot that reached the green, turned right, then drifted back into the fairway. He saved the four.

Goosen missed the second green once again (he had yet to hold that green) and dropped a shot, but he birdied the fifth and went back to four under par. By then, though, Maggert had birdied the second and caught both Mickelson and Maruyama at six under. Now the leaders had bunched, with Goosen two strokes behind and Els and Cabrera another stroke back. Soon Cabrera began running up bogeys, finished the day with 77, and dropped from the race.

Goosen, meanwhile, played steady golf through the rest of the first nine and made the turn at even-par 35. Now he played a precise pitch to the 10th that pulled up eight feet from the hole and ran it in for the three on a hole that yielded only seven birdies all day. On to the 11th, another test-ing par-three. Another precise seven iron caught the green, but he faced a difficult putt that would break sharply left. He read the putt exactly. His ball took the break, but it died less than one turn from falling.

Behind him, Els had made one of those 41 birdies on the fifth, but his eight iron into the seventh hit short but ran on, turned left, and tumbled into the bunker. He bogeyed and dropped back to three under par, a lot better than Vijay Singh, playing alongside him. Singh had gone into the Open with some confidence, but he was having a miserable day. He bogeyed the first three holes, went out in 38, came back in 39, shot 77, and played no further part in this Open.

Maggert was having problems as well. Briefly ahead following his birdies on the second and fifth, he played the rest of the holes in six over par, shot 74, yet fell only three places, from third into a tie for sixth with Clark.

Now Funk made a move. A fan favorite, he had passed his 48th birthday three days before the Open began, but he played with as much enthusiasm as anyone in the game.

Off to an ugly start, he bogeyed the first two holes, but birdied both the fourth and fifth, lost another along the way, and shot 36 going out. Once more he rebounded, played a terrific shot into the 11th that left him no more than a few feet from the hole and ran it in, and followed with another birdie at the 12th. One under par, smiling and having fun, he lost three more strokes, shot another 36, and with 72 actually held his position in fourth place.

Up ahead, Goosen had holed a six-foot putt and saved his par on the 12th, but he overshot the 13th green with a nine iron, played a loose chip to no closer than 20 feet and two-putted. He overshot the next green as well and missed a putt of four feet. Back to three under par. Quickly, though, he ran in a 25-foot putt and birdied the 15th, bunkered his approach to the 16th, but recovered nicely to six feet and birdied again. Five under once more, he had climbed past Funk and back into a tie with Mickelson, playing a hole behind him.

Goosen had a distinct chance to add a stroke when he played a stunning pitch that settled within five feet on the 18th, but the putt slipped past the hole. With the par four, he closed out the round and waited for the rest to finish.

Mickelson, meantime, was having no fun at all. After scratching out four consecutive pars on the second nine, he holed a 20-foot putt for a birdie on the tough 14th and moved ahead, but he bunkered his approach to the 16th and failed to birdie one of the more vulnerable holes. Still five under, he buried his tee shot in the left greenside bunker and bogeyed the 17th, then lipped out his second putt and bogeyed the 18th as well, shot 73, and fell into a tie for second place alongside Els.

Maruyama had hung on through the first nine, still five under as he headed for the 10th, lost strokes on the 11th and 13th, but picked up a birdie on the 16th. Then he butchered the 18th, flaying his ball from rough to rough to rough, taking a six on a par-four hole, and sinking three strokes behind the leader.

The third-round leaders:

Retief Goosen	69 - 205	Tim Clark	66 - 209
Ernie Els	70 - 207	Jeff Maggert	74 - 209
Phil Mickelson	73 - 207	Mike Weir	71 - 210
Fred Funk	72 - 208	Sergio Garcia	71 - 211
Shigeki Maruyama	74 - 208	Corey Pavin	73 - 211

Even though he finished with 78, Vijay Singh announced he had played Shinnecock Hills in par. Actually, using the field's average score as a guide, Singh had broken par. The surviving 66 of the game's leading players averaged over 78.727 strokes on a day when only one player shot par 70.

Goosen won with a score of 276, four strokes better than a nearly unreachable standard. Mickelson scored 278, the difference the result of two missed putts on the 71st green, where he needed five strokes to play a hole measuring less than 180 yards.

Third place at 281 went to Jeff Maggert, who went into the last round in a tie for sixth place, shot 72, yet passed Ernie Els, Fred Funk and Shigeki Maruyama.

Even though both Goosen and Mickelson had bettered both Raymond Floyd's winning 279 in 1986 and Corey Pavin's 280 of 1995, the two other Opens played over Shinnecock Hills in the modern era, seldom has a course played so harshly over the last two days. Only Australian Robert Allenby matched Shinnecock's par that day and leapfrogged from a tie for 34th place into a tie for seventh with Steve Flesch at 286.

Maggert picked up three places with his 72 and placed third, at 281, and Mike Weir slipped to 74 yet climbed from eighth into a tie for fourth with Maruyama. A contender throughout the first three rounds, Maruyama lived through a miserable day when nothing went right and shot 76.

Once a scoring machine, Tiger Woods closed with a 76 of his own and yet moved up from a tie for 19th to a tie for 17th. He had birdied only five of the 72 holes and eagled the 18th as he closed out his third round. Woods finished with 290, matching his highest Open score as a professional.

Perhaps no one suffered so badly as Ernie Els. Teeing off in the last pairing with Goosen, Els began the day two strokes off the lead, but made a double-bogey six on the first, where Goosen birdied, and played one of those rare rounds when he lost control of every part of his game. He missed fairways, couldn't hold his ball on most greens, parred just two holes on the first nine and five on the second, scored two over par on four others, went out in 41, came back in 39 and walked off with an ignoble 80. At 287, he dropped into a tie for ninth.

With Shinnecock Hills playing so severely, five players shot 79 and still advanced. Jim Furyk and Kris Cox began in a tie for 55th, but when they signed their scorecards they had moved into a tie for 48th. Casey Wittenberg, one of four amateurs who made the cut, Englishman Lee Westwood and Japanese golfer Hidemichi Tanaka moved from a tie for 43rd to a tie for 36th.

Despite scores of 82, Cliff Kresge climbed from a tie for 64th to a tie for 62nd, and Zach Johnson held onto his share of 48th place. Among the other 20 men in the 80s, Tom Kite, the 1992 Open champion, shot 84; Shaun Micheel, the 2003 PGA champion, shot 80; Craig Parry, the winner at Doral early in the season, shot 85; and Billy Mayfair shot 47 on the first nine, came back in 42, and saved shooting 90 by one stroke.

At the other end of the scale, both Goosen and Mickelson shot 71, and so did Jay Haas, who skipped from a tie for 34th place up to a tie for ninth. Only 11 men shot under 75.

Shinnecock Hills' greens intimidated most of the field. Often they barely tapped a putt and watched the ball roll endlessly. Aside from Joakim Haeggman's nine on the 10th, Chris Riley's chip from behind the first green turned back, rolled down the sloping ground, through the gallery, down a footpath and eventually settled in the grass. He scored seven.

Nothing matched the seventh, though. Difficult beyond reason, three of the first four men out that morning scored sixes. Kevin Stadler could have parred by holing from two feet, but his putt caught the lip of the hole, spun out, and began a creeping journey into the deep bunker on the left. He took three more to hole out. Mayfair had a similar experience. Like

Stadler's, his tee shot held the green and his 20-foot putt nearly stopped beside the hole. Instead it rolled ever so slowly until it caught a sharp slope and slid into the bunker as well. The other two, Kresge and J.J. Henry, each suffered a six.

At first the grounds crew syringed the green between each group, then eased off. Later in the day when the crew hurried out to spray again as Tiger Woods arrived, the fans booed, assuming special consideration. He did indeed par the hole. But pars helped him not at all. The championship was being settled behind him.

As the leaders filed off the first tee, the feeling persisted that, unlike when Mickelson and Els had thrown birdies at one another at the Masters, here we would see survival tactics. Shinnecock Hills simply wasn't giving up birdies. The sixth and 10th holes allowed one each, and the fourth and eighth just two.

Nevertheless, the Open did indeed end in gripping drama, with both Goosen and Mickelson dueling over the final few holes until Mickelson cracked.

Paired with Fred Funk and playing directly ahead of Goosen, Mickelson put himself under pressure from the start with a loose drive on the third that flew into tall fescue flattened by the gallery. His approach died short of the green and he bogeyed.

Two strokes behind at the start, he suddenly fell four strokes back when Goosen played the first hole as if he were in a one dollar Nassau with a couple of 10-handicappers. He drove the fairway, pitched a nine iron to the middle of the green, and, cool as ever, holed from 40 feet. Goosen was six under par now with Mickelson just two under and Els out of contention following his six on the opening hole.

Moving on to the second hole, Goosen flew his four-iron tee shot into a greenside bunker and dropped a stroke, and now Mickelson had an opening that could have cut a further stroke from Goosen's lead. Instead he three-putted the fifth, which had given up so many birdies, and did no better than a par five.

Both men passed the wicked seventh without damage, then Mickelson hit the eighth green, left his first putt dangerously short, yet holed for his par four while Goosen missed the green and bogeyed. He had yet to hit that green. One over par for the round, his lead had shrunk to one stroke, and that is how the first nine ended, with Goosen four under par for 63 holes and Mickelson three under.

Starting back, both men lost strokes at the 10th, Goosen now three under and Mickelson two under.

While they had struggled for the lead, Maruyama had lost his touch, went out in 39, played only slightly better coming in, and finished with a 76. While his score may have bruised his ego, he held onto a share of fourth place, where he had begun the day.

At the same time, Maggert had played erratic golf yet gave up little ground, and Funk had slipped from two under at the beginning to four over through the 14th. The game had been left to Goosen and Mickelson, with the gallery solidly behind Mickelson. The fans cheered every shot, groaned when a putt refused to fall, and all the while Mickelson kept smiling and playing shot after glorious shot.

Of course Goosen played glorious shots as well, especially his eight iron into the 11th within relatively easy birdie range. He ran his putt squarely into the center of the hole.

Moments later Mickelson overshot the 12th and bogeyed, falling to one under par. Goosen moved ahead by three strokes once again.

Safely past the 12th with a routine four, Goosen played one of the key holes of the championship. On the 13th, Shinnecock's shortest par-four, he pushed his drive so deep into the right rough that his next shot squirted into the gallery on the left. Now he played a marvelous pitch from matted grass and holed his putt. Still ahead by three.

Perhaps Goosen played an even more important putt on the 14th. Bunkered by his approach, he had left himself an awkward stance and a difficult fried egg lie, barely popped it out into shaggy grass and chipped 15 feet past the hole. Had he missed, he could have been badly hurt, because Mickelson had birdied the 13th and 15th and could pick up three strokes. Goosen, instead, holed the putt, his eighth one-putt green of the round. Still, Goosen lost two strokes to Mickelson and suddenly he and Mickelson were tied at three under par.

The tension continued building as Mickelson added another birdie on the 16th. At four under par for 70 holes, he led Goosen by one stroke.

The gallery loved it. Mickelson certainly seemed confident as he walked toward the 17th. Two more well-played holes and the Open could be his.

Goosen, though, wasn't through, and when he holed still another putt and birdied the 16th, he had caught up, both men now at four under par. The gallery sensed a playoff ahead.

Just as Goosen holed his birdie putt, up ahead Mickelson began unraveling. He had played his six iron too far left of the 17th green and into the bunker. With what must have seemed the whole world watching, Mickelson pitched eight feet right of the flagstick, played his first putt just left of the hole, then missed again coming back. Instead of going into the last hole tied, he had fallen two strokes behind Goosen.

That effectively ended the Open.

With a two-stroke lead, Goosen's approach to the 18th slipped just off the back edge, he took two putts for a change, and with a par four and a 72-hole score of 276, he had won his second U.S. Open Championship.

He had won in grand style and had beaten one of the game's premier golfers in what had developed into a tense two-man battle.

As Goosen stepped off the final green, his wife, Tracy, ran to him, they kissed, and she handed him their infant son, Leo. Goosen cradled him in his arms and strode away toward the scorer's enclave, still holding Leo. This was, after all, Father's Day.

4. The Open Championship

The Mississippi River rises in northern Minnesota, beginning as a trickle from Lake Itaska and gradually swelling into the Father of Waters as it flows nearly 4,000 miles to the Louisiana Delta, then disperses into the Gulf of Mexico.

Along its tortuous path it rolls past Oquawka, a small Illinois town of 1,500 residents perched on the river's eastern bank. Until Todd Hamilton won The Open Championship in 2004, Oquawka, had it been known of at all, had been known best as the final resting place of a circus elephant named Norma Jean.

Back in the early 1970s, the circus had come to Oquawka. When it shut down for the night, Norma Jean's keeper chained her to a stout tree in the town square. During the night an electrical storm moved in, lightning struck the tree, the bolt carried along the chain and killed Norma Jean as she stood. With no means of carting the animal away, the town simply buried her there and rolled a big headstone into place.

None of this had anything to do with Todd Hamilton except that he grew up in Oquawka. After he surprised just about everyone and outplayed both Ernie Els and Phil Mickelson, at the moment the two most dangerous players in the game, and won The Open, he hoped he had become as well known in his home town as Norma Jean. Well … maybe.

Hamilton shot 274, 10 under par, the same as Els, then beat Ernie by one stroke, 15 to 16, in a tense four-hole playoff over the first, second, 17th and 18th holes at Royal Troon, as tough a course as any on The Open rota.

It was a bitter loss for Els, but, in truth, he could blame only himself for losing. He squandered two strokes on the 10th, missed a makeable birdie putt on the 72nd hole that would have ended it there, then missed the 17th green and bogeyed in the playoff, a stroke that cost him dearly when Hamilton scraped out a final par four on the home hole, which made the difference.

This had been as hotly contested a final-round battle as any within recent memory, as first one man, then another moved ahead, then fell back. Someone counted 10 changes of leaders. At one time or another Hamilton, Els, Mickelson or Thomas Levet broke in front, but Hamilton became the last man standing in the twilight of that final electrifying day.

The stirring finish followed a Masters Tournament that went down to the last hole and a U.S. Open Championship that, for all realistic purposes, ended on the 71st. Els had been central in each of them, and gone through three disheartening losses. He had played his heart out at Augusta in April, turned in a final score of 67, the second lowest of the week, yet lost the Masters by one stroke to Mickelson, who birdied five of the last seven holes. Two months later, Ernie went into the last round of the U.S. Open a stroke behind Retief Goosen, yet played an abysmal round of 80 and fell like a stone.

At Troon once again he played a strong final eight holes in three under par and yet lost to Hamilton's steadier game. For the second time in The

Open, Els had played all four rounds in the 60s and yet lost. He did it first in 1993, yet tied for sixth, seven strokes behind Greg Norman.

Els had not been alone in losing to a player who no one had seriously considered until the championship's closing moments. Any of those four men could have won. Els could have won but failed through missed opportunities. Mickelson could have won, and so might have Levet, yet each man failed at the critical moment.

After an opening round of 73, which everyone felt had crippled his chances, Mickelson played uncannily steady golf through the next 54 holes. From the 17th hole of the first round until the 13th of the last, he did not lose a stroke — a string of 49 consecutive holes without a bogey — but with the championship at stake he missed the 13th green and took a five where he needed something better. With 275, he turned in a score one stroke too many and took third place.

Levet had gone into the final round two strokes behind Hamilton, the leader, passed him and moved into first place by scoring an eagle three on the fourth, lost three strokes over the final 14 holes, and dropped into a tie for fifth at 279 with Davis Love, five strokes behind Hamilton and Els.

Lee Westwood played the last 36 holes in 135 and claimed fourth place at 278, four strokes out of first place and three behind Mickelson. Two other pre-tournament favorites fell on hard times as well. Neither Colin Montgomerie nor Tiger Woods played his best golf. Monty started well, with two opening rounds of 69, but slipped to 72 in the third and closed with a grim 76 for a 286 total and a tie for 25th place. As for Woods, truthfully, he had never been in the chase at all despite a score of 68 in the third round. By then he had played Royal Troon in 70 and 71, then closed with 72. At 281 he tied Mike Weir for ninth.

Only Hamilton held his composure, played his own game, and made certain that anyone who wanted to win this old championship would have to beat him; he would not give in. He had come in with a plan, and he would not waver from it no matter that over the opening holes of the last round, Els seemed to tempt him into playing Ernie's game, not his own.

Perhaps he had studied previous Royal Troon championships or he simply knew his strengths and weaknesses. Whatever the reason, Hamilton looked at the bunkers and determined he would waste no strokes with over-ambitious tee shots. Instead of trying to find a path through them, he would lay up and rely on his approach shots and his short game. It certainly paid off. Over the four rounds, Hamilton played from only three bunkers.

Those bunkers — deep, steep-faced, and all over the place — had wrecked more than one career. Bobby Clampett had led the 1982 Open by seven strokes through five holes of the third round, but Royal Troon's sixth hole, then a par-five of 577 yards, ambushed him. He hooked his drive into one fairway bunker, pitched out into another, and after three more shots his ball landed in still another bunker. He scored an eight, played the round in 78, added 77 in the last, tied for 10th place, and was never heard from again until he climbed into the television booth.

Seven years later, Greg Norman had tied Wayne Grady and Mark Calcavecchia after the regulation 72 holes of the 1989 Open, birdied the first two holes of what was then the new system of four-hole playoffs, lost one stroke on the 17th, went all-out with a driver from the 18th tee and knocked his ball into a fairway bunker that, until then, had been considered unreachable. From the bunker he flew his second over the home green and out of bounds. Calcavecchia, meantime, had played a marvelous five iron to holing distance, birdied, and claimed the championship.

Hamilton wanted no part of those bunkers, and he obviously knew his game.

When he stood before the gallery assembled for the presentation, he was being compared to such unknown and surprising recent winners of the game's premier events as Ben Curtis, the 2003 Open champion, and Rich Beem and Shaun Micheel, winners of the 2002 and 2003 PGA Championships.

Actually, the comparison didn't fit. Theirs had been brief moments in the sunlight, then quick retreats. On the other hand, Hamilton's career had been a consistently successful and steady rise. He had earned his place in the Open field through his position among the top 50 in the Official World Golf Ranking in May, the deadline for exemptions, and his third-place standing on the 2003 Japan Tour money list.

He had made his first move toward a career in golf by persuading his high school principal to form a golf team, with Hamilton as the only member and his father as the team coach. Todd played well enough to win two Illinois State High School championships, attended the University of Oklahoma on a golf scholarship, and played so impressively he was named to three All-America teams. Then began his disheartening 17-year campaign to join the PGA Tour, a quest that finally succeeded in December of 2003. By then he had reached the age of 38, rather advanced for a rookie.

In the meantime, through that frustrating period, he played the Canadian Tour in 1988 and 1989, then headed to the Far East, where he won tournaments in Japan, Thailand, Korea and Singapore. Eventually he settled on playing most of his golf in Japan. Over his Asian period, he won 11 tournaments and made lots of money, but, nevertheless, he tired of long 14-hour flights from Tokyo to Dallas every month to see his wife and three children (he lived a few miles north of the city). He tried the PGA Tour's qualifying ritual once again, passed, and rather quickly let everyone know he had arrived.

During the PGA Tour's early-season 2004 swing through Florida, Hamilton won the Honda Classic by birdieing the last two holes and beating Love by one stroke. He birdied the last with a first-class pitch within four feet of the hole, a shot that not only won the tournament but proved to himself that he could play the shots he needed to play when he needed to play them. The lesson would certainly help him at Troon.

Of all the courses on The Open rota, Royal Troon is probably the least forgiving — always excepting Carnoustie as it was set up for the 1999 championship. The town of Troon is situated south of Glasgow, on Scotland's western coastline. The opening holes run along the beach of the Firth of Clyde, a wide waterway feeding Glasgow, a city once renowned as a major shipbuilding center. It is along this string of undemanding holes that the golfer must make his birdies, because once he passes the eighth, Troon's demands grow unrelenting.

Its ninth, 10th, 11th and 12th, all par-fours, can be more menacing than

Augusta National's Amen Corner, its 10th, 11th, 12th and 13th, two par-fours, a par-three and a par-five. There the golfer faces holes that at least offer beauty; Royal Troon's four-hole swing is hardly pretty, winding through deep, dense rough and impenetrable gorse. Beginning with the ninth, Royal Troon's holes measure 423 yards mostly downhill, 438 yards, the last of them decidedly uphill, 490 yards with a narrow margin of error for the drive and a green close to a stone wall separating the golf course from a railroad line, and 431 yards that turns in the opposite direction from the 11th.

The 11th stands among the most dangerous holes in the game. To reach the fairway, a substantial drive, played slightly uphill at an angle to the fairway's flow, must clear a thicket of prickly gorse bushes on the right and be careful not to reach another copse of gorse on the left, all the while being careful not to lose the shot over the wall and out of bounds. The 11th ranked as the most difficult par by far. The best players in the game averaged 4.41 strokes. It claimed 159 scores of five strokes or higher. Playing the innocent-looking 12th, the field averaged 4.31 strokes. It exacted 149 scores of five or higher.

This was a terrifying run of holes, but over the four days, Hamilton played them in even par with threes on the 11th and 12th and two fives on the 10th. Both Els and Mickelson played them in one over par, but Levet played them in three over.

When he won the 1962 Open, Arnold Palmer had taken one look at the 11th and, defying his swashbuckling style, determined to drive with a one iron, then thread a two iron down that narrow fairway to the green. The 11th that year played just five yards shorter than the 490 yards of 2004, and carried a par of five instead of four.

His strategy paid off. Over the four rounds Palmer scored one three, two fours and one five. His 276 won by a satisfactory six strokes over Kel Nagle, the Australian golfer who had beaten him by one stroke at St. Andrews in 1960. That had been Arnold's first attempt to win The Open, the step that jolted the old championship back to life and led to its station among the game's great occasions.

From the 13th onward, the holes turn back toward the clubhouse in an almost straight line, finishing with Royal Troon's longest par-four, the 483-yard 15th, followed by its shortest par-five, the 542-yard 16th, its longest par-three, the 222-yard 17th, and its 457-yard home hole, where out of bounds lies just three or four yards behind the green. It was there that Norman lost the 1989 Open and where in 2004 Darren Clarke over-clubbed his approach and made six where a shorter club could have saved him two strokes at least and perhaps a share of first place.

Along that last stretch leading to the clubhouse, the holes pass the Marine Hotel, which overlooks the home green. During the later stages of the Second World War, the pilot of a P-51 Mustang fighter plane looking for suitable ground for an emergency landing put down on Royal Troon's fourth hole, an occasion that of course attracted a few concerned citizens of the town. As he climbed from his cramped cockpit, the least concerned of them all, the pilot asked, rather calmly everyone thought, if he had just passed the Marine Hotel as his wheels touched down. Assured he had, he headed directly for the bar.

As a further aside, had Levet won he would have become the second Frenchman to cuddle the old claret jug, the championship trophy. Arnaud Massy had beaten the great J.H. Taylor by two strokes and won the 1907 Open at Hoylake. Four years later he tied Harry Vardon at Sandwich, but five strokes behind after 16 holes of the playoff, he played a marvelous shot about 15 feet from the hole of the 17th only to be outdone by Vardon, who put his shot inside him. Defeated, Massy simply conceded The Open to Vardon and walked away muttering, "I cannot play zis damned game."

While it does not rank among those courses that have seen the most Opens, Royal Troon had been the site of eight of them by 2004, the first in 1923 and the most recent in 1997. The Englishman Arthur Havers won the first, and then the South African putting wizard Bobby Locke won in 1950. Since Palmer in 1962, none but Americans had won The Open at Troon. Tom Weiskopf followed in 1973, then Tom Watson in 1982, Calcavecchia in 1989, Justin Leonard in 1997 and of course Hamilton.

A month before Watson's Open he had won the U.S. Open and joined Bobby Jones, Gene Sarazen, Ben Hogan and Lee Trevino as the only men to have held the two championships in the same year (Tiger Woods joined them in 2000). Jack Nicklaus had designs on doing it in 1962, but after beating Palmer in a playoff at Oakmont, he played loose golf at Royal Troon, shot 305, and trailed Palmer by 29 strokes.

Only history fanatics cared at all about this once the 2004 championship started at 6:30 on the Thursday morning. Almost from the start balls flew into holes at an alarming rate. Before most of the gallery had rubbed the sleep from their eyes, Ernie Els holed his wedge tee shot and scored a hole-in-one on the eighth, the Postage Stamp, a par-three of just 126 yards that had ruined many a man's game. Also:

Playing in the first group off the tee, Gary Evans holed a 227-yard five iron and double-eagled Royal Troon's 560-yard fourth hole.

Kenny Perry holed a 70-yard pitch and eagled the first.

K.J. Choi ripped a 235-yard five iron onto the fourth green and eagled.

And Rich Beem, who hadn't been heard from since he won the 2002 PGA Championship, reached the 601-yard sixth with his second shot, and where 24 years earlier Bobby Clampett had ended his career with an eight, Beem holed for an eagle three.

This had been a tough day for tough old Royal Troon. Besides Evans' double eagle, the field battered the course by taking 10 eagles, divided equally between the fourth and sixth holes, along with 410 birdies. Of the 156 men who played that day, the elite of the game, 39 broke Troon's rugged par of 71, about a quarter of the field, and 16 others matched it. By day's end, 25 men had turned in scores in the 60s. Some of their appetites for birdies approached gluttonous.

Paul Casey, a 26-year-old Englishman, birdied seven holes and tied Levet, a 37-year-old Frenchman, for first place with 66. Levet, Scot Alistair Forsyth, Micheel, Christian Cevaer, another Frenchman, and Englishmen Barry Lane and Westwood each birdied six holes. Fifteen others birdied five, among them the unlucky Thomas Bjorn, who nevertheless shot 74.

New Zealander Michael Campbell shot 67, and nine others tied at 68, a group that included Vijay Singh, who a month later would win the PGA Championship. Evans, Choi, Forsyth, Kenneth Ferrie and Stuart Wilson, the Amateur champion, shot 68s as well and tied for fourth place.

Bogeys on the 17th, the treacherous par-three, hurt both Choi and Evans, and in position to share first place, Forsyth lost strokes on both the closing holes.

Both Beem and Perry sped around the first nine in 31, five under par, but each man stuttered coming back and closed with 38s. At 69, they were among the 13 men tied for 13th place.

A year earlier Casey had opened with an 85 at Sandwich and, predictably, missed the cut, but he had risen to some prominence early in 2004 by joining six others in a tie for sixth at the Masters, a group that included Singh, Love, Nick Price and Fred Couples. Here, playing alongside Mickelson, who had won that Masters, Casey appeared the more polished player. His chipping and putting certainly outshone Mickelson's.

Casey's opening drive sliced the first fairway, he pitched inside 10 feet, holed the putt, and he was on his way. Two routine pars and then he birdied the fourth, not uncommon this day, played his tee shot to six feet and birdied the eighth, but then he lost a stroke on the ninth.

Out in 34, two under par, he moved on to the intimidating second nine, where most of the holes played into the wind. He began by missing the 10th green, but he brushed that loose shot aside and holed his chip for a birdie three, struck two well-played shots into the intimidating 11th and holed from 30 feet — two under par on a pair of holes that, together, surrendered only 23 birdies all day.

Four under par now, Casey bogeyed the 12th, but he holed a 30-foot putt on the 16th, at 542 yards Troon's shortest par-five, closed with another birdie on the 18th, came back in 32 and finished in 66.

Before deciding to play as a professional, Casey had built an impressive amateur record. He had won the English Amateur twice, represented Britain and Ireland in the World Amateur Team Championship, and played college golf in the United States at Arizona State University, Mickelson's school. Casey had, indeed, broken a few of Mickelson's college records.

Levet, who had teed off at 9:20 Thursday morning, 50 minutes behind Casey, had worked quite hard to win his place in this field. He played the home nine at Loch Lomond in 29 strokes the previous Sunday and won the Barclays Scottish Open, his entree into The Open. He was, of course, better known for having nearly won the 2002 Open. He and Els had tied with Steve Elkington and Stuart Appleby after 72 holes at Muirfield, and Levet and Els were still tied after the regulation four-hole playoff. Moving to sudden death, Els saved a par from a bunker beside the 18th green, Levet bogeyed, and Els won.

Where Casey had made his move on the home nine, Levet played his best golf going out. He reached the fourth green, the first of the par-five holes, with a well-played three wood and got down in two for his first birdie, lashed a two iron onto the fifth, a 210-yard par-three, then played two six irons to the seventh and holed from 45 feet.

Not through yet, Levet played an eight iron to the eighth and holed from 10 feet, his fourth birdie in eight holes. Out in 32, he lost a stroke at the 10th, missing the green with an eight iron, but he made up for it with birdies on both the 11th and 17th, not easy to do. He had come back in 34 and tied Casey.

While sizeable galleries followed most groups, none matched the esprit de corps of Colin Montgomerie's. Even though Colin had been born and grown up in England, he had come to Troon when his father became secretary of the Royal Troon Golf Club and had lived within a short distance of the club. For that, the Scots considered him one of their own. When he teed off just before nine o'clock, he took along the biggest gallery of the day, and when he finished, it seemed as if his followers had seen all they wanted to see and left. Then this vast horde marched down a road bordering Royal Troon's late holes, against the flow of spectators heading for refreshment stands and other facilities. Their trip suggested swimming against a rip tide.

By shaving Royal Troon's par by two strokes with his 69, Montgomerie had left his followers happy, though. With cries of "Go, Monty" urging him on, he played steady if not inspiring golf through the first nine while avoiding two potential incidents with the large crowds.

In the first, a group of protesters paraded along the beach alongside the early holes carrying banners supporting pensioners' rights. As Montgomerie stepped onto the second tee, a demonstrator's cell phone pierced the silence, a sound that in the past might have triggered a reaction but instead had no effect. Later, about to putt on the eighth, he heard a camera's "click" and stepped away. In both incidents, not only had he simply got on with his game, he had actually birdied the second hole.

Birdies on the fifth and sixth as well and Montgomerie had played the first nine in three under par. But as he made the turn and headed down the 10th, 11th and 12th, he looked as if his game had collapsed. A wild drive on the 10th followed by an eight iron down a bank over the green led to a six, and another loose drive on the 11th cost him a bogey five. Three strokes lost in two holes and Monty had fallen back to even par.

Feeling low as he approached the 12th tee, he perked up when the gallery exploded in cheers. It was just what he needed; he put his mistakes behind him.

"That rescued my round," he claimed later. "I think it enabled me to go on and break 70, so all credit to them."

Whatever the reason, Montgomerie immediately picked up one lost stroke with a stunning six iron to four feet on the 12th and another with a six iron to 20 feet on the 15th, the longest of the par-four holes. With those two putts, he had recovered two of the three strokes he had lost at the turn. Monty finished just three strokes off the lead.

The first-round leaders:

Paul Casey	66	Matthew Goggin	68
Thomas Levet	66	Kenneth Ferrie	68
Michael Campbell	67	Stuart Wilson (amateur)	68
Gary Evans	68	Vijay Singh	68
K.J. Choi	68	Marten Olander	68
Carl Pettersson	68	Alistair Forsyth	68

One day after racking up a bevy of birdies and shaving five strokes from par, Paul Casey played the ninth through the 13th in six over par, shot 77, and fell from a tie for first into the depths of 37th place, never to rise too far again. Of the others who stood high after the first round, Levet hung on to second place after a 70, Campbell added 71 and shared fifth place, but Evans shot 73 and dropped into a tie for 17th.

The 36-hole lead belonged to Skip Kendall, a shortish 5-foot-8, 150-pound American who had played the PGA Tour for 13 years and entered 310 tournaments without winning a single one. He had tied Mickelson in the Bob Hope Chrysler Classic early in the year and lost the playoff, tied for fifth in the Bank of America Colonial in May, but missed eight cuts in 18 starts.

Kendall had been known best, though, for having tried to cut a bagel a year earlier but along the way slicing off a chunk of his left index finger as well. He raced to a hospital with it, where surgeons made him whole again, and four weeks later he went back to the wars.

He had found his game this day, though. He had opened with 69 in the first round, then played Royal Troon in 66 strokes in the second and rose to the head of the class with a 36-hole score of 135, seven under par.

A 44-year-old Englishman, Barry Lane hadn't won a tournament in nine years until the Daily Telegraph British Masters early in May, but he added 68 to his opening 69 and shared third place with Korean golfer K.J. Choi, who played rounds of 68 and 69.

While his supporters rocked the heavens with their cheering, Montgomerie went around in another 69 and, at 138, tied Els, Singh, Campbell and Hamilton, whose 67 stood as the second lowest score of the round. The five of them shared fifth place.

A few others made their moves as well. Shrugging off his disappointing 73 of the opening round, Mickelson birdied four of the first six holes, matched Kendall's 66, and climbed into a tie for 10th place. Woods, meantime, shot 71, one stroke higher than his opening 70, yet still rose from a tie for 26th into a tie for 17th. He birdied just two holes and bogeyed two, all of them on the easier first nine.

Royal Troon obviously played harder than it had during the first round, partly because of the weather. Trouser legs flapped and the national ensigns flying above the massive grandstand snapped in the freshening breeze as golfers struggled to control shots played through crosswinds. While this was no gale, the wind whipped in with enough strength to cause grief.

Mike Weir, the left-handed Canadian who had won the Masters a year earlier, claimed he played a significant number of drawn shots going out because the wind blew right-to-left coming off the Clyde, and as many faded shots coming back, now fighting a left-to-right wind. (For most of the field, it was just the opposite.) Nevertheless, Weir shot 68 and jumped into the tie for 10th at 139.

The 36-hole cut, which fell at 145, three over par, pared the field down to 73 men from the original 156. Some great players of the past, seven former Open champions among them, would not finish the 72 holes. The victims included Ben Curtis, the surprise winner of 2003. Curtis had little of the command of shots he had shown in the milder weather of Sandwich a year earlier, shot 75-74, and at 149 missed qualifying by four strokes.

John Daly, Greg Norman, Tom Lehman, Nick Faldo, Paul Lawrie and Tom Weiskopf, all former champions, missed the cut. At the age of 61, Weiskopf had been the oldest man in the field.

Other victims included Jim Furyk, the 2003 U.S. Open champion, still not completely healed from an injured wrist, Jay Haas, the 50-year-old marvel, Padraig Harrington, Thomas Bjorn and Sergio Garcia.

Until his surprising 66, Kendall had given no indication he could play so well under Open tension, although he had done reasonably well a month earlier by tying for 17th place in the U.S. Open. Of course none of his earlier failures mattered when he birdied two of the first five holes. He made his first on the third hole, a 379-yard par-four with a stream cutting across the fairway 280 yards out.

Kendall missed the water, but his approach settled into a greenside bunker. No problem; he pitched into the hole for the three. Two holes later he played a stunning four iron to the par-three fifth that died no more than two feet from the hole.

He had gone out in 34, but Kendall played his best on the more testing second nine, even though he lost a stroke on the merciless 11th. He drove into an unplayable lie in the gorse, dropped behind the bush and played a four iron that missed the green to the left, chipped to four or five feet, and holed for a hard-won five. Striking back quickly, he played a seven iron into the 12th, not the easiest of holes, and birdied from 25 feet, played a six iron onto the 14th green and ran in another putt from 15 feet, then capped his round on the 16th, the last of the par-fives. After a two iron from the tee and a three-wood second that stopped just short of the green, Kendall read the line perfectly and holed a 50-footer for an eagle three.

Kendall had come home in 32, and even though he knew he led the field, he realized as well that with his 70, Levet had closed within a stroke of him. But Kendall didn't know that Levet had played five holes without knowing if he would be penalized two strokes for a rules infraction.

Levet had pulled his opening drive so far left it landed close to an ice cream truck parked behind metal fencing. Debating how to play his next shot, Levet saw a few marshals remove sections of the fence from his line of play while a referee, possibly distracted by another player's even wilder drive, stood by. Of course, allowing your line of play to be changed violated the Rules of Golf. Made aware of the circumstances, officials conferred with one another, and after Levet had played the fifth hole, they told him he had been excused.

None of this seemed to disturb Levet since he played solid golf throughout the first nine, hitting every fairway except the first, of course, and every green, yet gained only two strokes. He birdied only the second, where he holed from 30 feet, and the par-five fourth, where he pitched to 10 feet from a greenside bunker and holed once again.

He played not nearly so well on the inward nine, losing one stroke to par on the 12th, the second toughest hole. Levet's drive caught the fairway nicely enough, but he pulled his nine iron left of the green, played a poor chip, and took two more strokes to hole out. He parred the rest of the holes, came back in 36, and held on to second place.

Speaking of the potential penalty later in the day, Levet said that he led the field by two strokes at the time and "when you're leading the tournament, it (the penalty) doesn't matter," which seemed a strange comment. But then Levet wasn't your conventional golfer. "A golf shot is only a golf shot," he had said. "It can't change your life."

To back up his point, he told the story of the golfer who pitched to 10 feet, missed four putts, whacked his ball 120 yards back down the fairway, pitched on to 10 feet once again, and holed the putt for a 10.

"That was me," he crowed. "I can be very patient, but when I go over the top, I can be very ... smoky."

By the time Levet began emitting his smoke, Hamilton had already finished his less-than-surgically-precise 67. He hit only eight of the 14 fairways on driving holes and 11 of the 18 greens, and yet beat par by four strokes. He picked up two of them on the highly vulnerable seventh, even though he played what he termed a poor drive.

Playing a hole that others had nearly driven, Hamilton let his ball drift into the rough about 120 yards short of the green and flew his wedge out from the grass with no spin. The ball carried to the green, ran to the back and into the hole for an eagle two. Hamilton had already birdied the sixth, and now he had gone three under par.

Out in 33, he missed the 10th green and bogeyed, but reaching the 12th tee, he drove with what he called his hybrid club. Shaped somewhat like a small-headed wooden club but, as all modern woods, made of metal, the hybrid could be used for all sorts of shots. Hamilton used it as a driver, to play from fairways, and even for delicate shots around the green, such as running shots, so necessary for links golf. He would use it later to play the critical shot of the championship.

In its original form it had a loft of 17 degrees, the usual loft of a contemporary two iron, but by bending the hosel, Hamilton lowered the loft to 14 degrees, the rough equivalent of a tour player's three wood.

Whatever the club's pedigree, Hamilton drove into the rough once more, followed with a six-iron approach, and holed from 25 feet and birdied once again. Three more pars followed, and then, playing cautiously, he birdied the 16th. Even though the hole measured 542 yards, he drove with a six iron, laid up with a seven iron, pitched to eight feet, and ran in still another putt. Hamilton walked away with a score of 138 for the 36 holes, four under par.

The second-round leaders:

Skip Kendall	66 - 135	Vijay Singh	70 - 138
Thomas Levet	70 - 136	Todd Hamilton	67 - 138
Barry Lane	68 - 137	Ernie Els	69 - 138
K.J. Choi	69 - 137	Colin Montgomerie	69 - 138
Michael Campbell	71 - 138		

As quickly as he rose to the top, Kendall fell back with a loose third round of 75 that dropped him from first place into a tie for ninth at 210. With the reshuffling, the leaderboard took on a more predictable appearance. With one exception.

Three days earlier, when the championship began, no one could have expected Todd Hamilton to lead the field into the closing round — including Hamilton himself. Yet, there he stood in first place after a second successive round of 67 over an unforgiving course that had broken the hearts of so many of the game's great players.

Hamilton had played three rounds with a total score of 205, but his grip on first place hardly seemed secure, for just behind him lurked three of the game's more dangerous players. One stroke behind, at 206, Els threatened, and one behind Ernie, at 207, Mickelson prowled, along with Retief Goosen, the current U.S. Open champion, and Levet, who had been hanging around since the first day. Els, Mickelson and Goosen each shot 68, and Levet added 71 to his series of ascending scores.

Els need make up just one stroke, and the others only two on a player untried in the crucible of the game's most important competitions.

Tiger Woods had won quite a number of them, and when be raced around Royal Troon in 68 as well, he leaped 10 places into a tie for seventh, within four strokes of Hamilton. Had this been two years earlier it would have been reasonable to assume that with Woods only four strokes behind, all was lost. But eight major championships had passed since those days, and he no longer caused panic.

While Woods moved upward, Montgomerie headed downward with a dull 72, for the second consecutive day dropping a stroke on the 18th and prompting groans from his gallery. At 210, Monty had fallen into a tie for ninth, alongside Kendall and Weir, and a stroke behind Woods and Verplank.

Other 36-hole leaders toppled as well. Tied for fifth going into the third round, Campbell shot 74 and dropped from sight; Choi had 74 as well and skidded from a tie for third to a tie for 12th; and Singh, the best player in the game earlier in the year, stumbled around in 76 and fell from contention into oblivion.

As the day began, Royal Troon seemed ripe to be beaten. Off at 12:40, nearly three hours before the final pairing, Justin Leonard birdied the fifth, sixth, seventh and ninth and went out in 32; Shaun Micheel played the first five holes in three under par; Love birdied the first, second and fourth; and Woods birdied the first two holes and barely missed a putt for an eagle on the fourth.

But just as Kendall and Levet teed off at 3:30, the last group of the day, the weather turned foul. Rain clouds swept in, the wind freshened, and the temperature fell 10 degrees, from 64 to 54. A cold, piercing, wind-blown rain turned conditions miserable, a reminder of that Saturday two years earlier when Woods shot 81 at Muirfield and bettered Montgomerie by three strokes. Unlike Muirfield, though, the conditions didn't last. Before long the rain clouds dissipated, the wind calmed, the sun shone brightly and the temperature climbed again. Just another summer's day on the west coast of Scotland.

Making his run on the leaders, Woods, meanwhile, birdied four of the first seven holes, dropping him to five under par for 43 holes, and for a time revived memories of his magnificent streak from the PGA Championship of 1999 through the U.S. Open of 2002 when he won seven of the 11 major competitions he entered.

Grim-faced and focused only on the job at hand, Woods played irons from the first few tees and followed with the sort of deadly pitches that had set up so many birdies in the past. He did indeed birdie the first two holes, holing putts from 12 feet on the first and four feet on the second.

Two holes later he pulled out his driver for the first time and followed with a classic four iron onto the fourth green and two-putted from 45 feet.

Three under for the day, four under for the distance, he added another birdie at the seventh and turned for home five under for 45 holes.

He would go no further, and indeed lost a stroke on the 12th, then missed a makeable six-footer on the 17th that should count as another lost stroke. When Woods had been at his best, the hole seemed to jump in front of his ball, but no longer. Now it seemed to dodge it. The second nine had treated him especially cruelly. Against a par figure of 105, he had shot 107. Even more amazing, his first-round four on the 16th, a weak par-five, had been his only birdie over those 27 holes.

Nevertheless, he had pulled within four strokes of first place.

After his listless 72, though, Montgomerie showed no sign he could regain the ground he lost. Three strokes behind when he teed off, he finished five behind. Off to a promising start, he played two fine shots on the first but walked away with no better than a par four. Then his swing quickened, his drive to the third rolled into a bunker, and he bogeyed. After that, he struggled throughout the round, saving pars with steady putting after his approaches held only three greens on the outward nine and three more coming in.

He did, however, add comic relief on the 14th, a par-three of 178 yards. With his tee shot embedded in a bunker, Monty took a mighty swing, dug his ball out, and flew it onto the green. Then the fun began. He had swung so hard he lost his balance, fell backwards, and saved the indignity of a pratfall by maneuvering himself onto the bunker's back lip.

Again he closed as he had the previous day by missing the final green and taking another unsettling bogey five. He had, though, wrung about as much from this round as he could. Usually playing his approaches from the rough or the sand, he had one-putted 10 greens, only two for birdies, the others for pars. By now even Monty's most zealous supporters realized the game was up.

While Montgomerie fell back, Mickelson took another step toward contention with his 68, a score saved by a lucky incident on the 15th, at 483 yards Troon's longest par-four. Pushed by a left-to-right wind, Mickelson's drive drifted right and appeared to roll onto a paved road clearly marked out of bounds. But, luckily, his ball had hit a spectator and remained in play. Mickelson admitted later that, "there was nothing to stop it but that gentleman's leg.

"Did I thank him? Oh yeah."

By then Mickelson stood three under par, principally because of a blazing start, helped along by a career pitch to the first green. He pushed his opening drive so far left it nearly reached the 18th fairway but instead settled in heavy grass. From a shaggy lie, he flew his ball within eight feet of the hole and birdied. A short approach to the second, hardly more than a chip, set up another birdie, and then another at the seventh, at 405 yards among Royal Troon's shortest par-fours. A big drive followed once more by nothing more than a chip to four feet and Mickelson fell to five under par for 43 holes. He played the homeward nine in even par and climbed into a tie for third place.

In good position to match Woods' 2000 performance of winning both the U.S. Open and The Open, Retief Goosen played an up-and-down round with six birdies and three bogeys, and even though he shot 68, he headed directly to the practice range saying, "I have to sort out a few things. It doesn't matter how many majors you've won, it's never easy to deal with the last day."

Els matched Goosen's 68, but his score might have been better. After birdieing both the first and sixth, at 601 yards among the longest holes in championship golf, Ernie ran afoul of the eighth, the Postage Stamp, where he had holed in one two days earlier. His tee shot faded into the deep bunker right of the green and he bogeyed, his third different score in three rounds. He'd had a one on Thursday, a three on Friday and now a four on Saturday.

He bogeyed the 11th as well, but only through a stroke of good luck. Headed out of bounds, his ball caromed off the stone wall along the right defining the course boundary and into the gorse. With a clean shot although a bad lie, Els scrambled onto the green with his third and missed the par putt.

Recovering quickly, he birdied both the 13th and 15th, then played a first-rate three iron into the 16th that bored through the wind and set up a 30-foot eagle putt. The ball grazed the hole but wouldn't fall. A third birdie in four holes and Els had come back in 33 and finished just one stroke behind the nerveless Hamilton.

After his second consecutive 67, the best score of the third round, Hamilton claimed he felt comfortable playing what he called ugly golf, explaining:

"If you've got 200 yards, usually it's a five or maybe a six iron. Over here you can take a three or four iron and just run it onto the green. I call that ugly golf. I'm usually pretty good at ugly golf."

How he did it didn't matter much, although he did save six pars after missing greens. Starting with three scrambling fours, he reached the green of the 560-yard fourth with a drive and eight iron, and then got down in two putts for the first of his four birdies. Two holes later he ripped a 327-yard drive, tore into a two iron that settled short and left, wedged to 12 feet, and holed for another birdie.

Moving to the eighth, he birdied from 20 feet and scored his last birdie with a stunning six iron to three feet on the 14th, another par-three. He did not bogey a hole, and said later, "I've played so badly for so long, it's strange to sit here commenting on my golf. Usually when I'm commenting, it's to my wife and kids — and in an angry tone."

The third-round leaders:

Todd Hamilton	67 - 205	Tiger Woods	68 - 209
Ernie Els	68 - 206	Scott Verplank	70 - 209
Phil Mickelson	68 - 207	Mike Weir	71 - 210
Retief Goosen	68 - 207	Colin Montgomerie	72 - 210
Thomas Levet	71 - 207	Skip Kendall	75 - 210
Barry Lane	71 - 208		

Speaking to the press after the third round, Ernie Els suggested the rest of the field be wary of Todd Hamilton because, "He is a quality player who will take some beating."

Els knew first hand. He had been paired with Hamilton in Saturday's third round, and now would play alongside him again in the fourth as the last pairing of the day. In the end, Ernie's prophesy would bear out, because as the tension mounted, Hamilton clearly outplayed Els and denied him still another major championship, his third disappointment of the year.

When the day ended, The Open, as it had a year earlier, once again had been claimed by an uncelebrated American with no great record. Hamilton faced down not only the game's two best players in Els and Mickelson, but a strong supporting cast that included Goosen, Weir and, of course, Woods, who might have awakened from his slumber at any time. Each of them had shown they could maneuver around the great courses in any score at all. That Hamilton remained calm, kept his composure, and followed his plan may stand as his major accomplishment of the day, for he neither wavered nor rose to the bait, and in the end beat every one of them.

A brisk wind swept across Royal Troon in early morning, driving the temperature down and leading most players to wear warmer outfits. Els chose a gray sweater vest over a blue shirt and gray slacks, while Hamilton wore a white, long-sleeved sweater and olive-colored slacks. The dull weather not only sent the golfers searching through their wardrobes, it masked even a hint of the tension and drama that lay ahead. Within about 10 minutes after the leaders began teeing off, anything less than eagles drew yawns from the spoiled gallery.

Two strokes behind at the start, Levet holed a chip from behind the fourth green just before Lane, playing alongside him, holed a putt from 20 feet, both for eagle threes.

Just behind them, Mickelson holed a chip from 40 feet for another eagle, and not long before those heroics, Weir holed his pitch from a greenside bunker for a birdie two on the fifth.

Nor did it end there. Late in the day, Love holed a full-blooded six iron at the 18th for an eagle two, shot 67, which matched the lowest score of the day, and with 279 tied Levet in fifth place.

Golf like this held the promise of an exceptional day. Some men barely in contention made brief runs, then backed off. Spraying shots left and right, Woods birdied the fifth and sixth, but had no more to give and shot 72, his worst score of the week. Five strokes behind at the start, Weir birdied the first, holed from a bunker on the fifth, and birdied the sixth. Six under par by then, he, like Woods, lost ground the rest of the day, shot 71, and tied Woods for ninth place with 281.

Placid as ever, Goosen shot a lifeless 73 and tied Verplank in seventh place with 280. Montgomerie, after beginning with hope, ended in misery by scoring 76 and at 286 sinking to 25th place, 12 strokes behind Hamilton and Els.

Following his torrid beginning, Levet began losing strokes soon after his eagle three. Leading the field then at eight under par, he played the remaining 14 holes in three over, shot 72, and tied Love at 279. Nevertheless, no one had hung around the lead so consistently. He had shared first place after the first round, held second place alone after the second, tied for third after the third, and tied for fifth at the end.

Meanwhile, the championship came down to a struggle among Hamilton, Els and Mickelson.

Off the tee immediately before Els and Hamilton, Mickelson played the first three holes in par fours and followed with his eagle on the fourth.

Eight under now, he had tied Els and passed Hamilton, who had misplayed the first and fallen back. Fighting back, Hamilton birdied both the fourth and fifth, moving to nine under, the clear leader. Mickelson nearly drove the seventh, barely missed holing his chip, and birdied. At nine under, he had tied Hamilton and passed Els after Ernie bogeyed the fifth.

On and on they went, Els lost two strokes on the 10th by driving into such deep rough he had no hope of reaching the green with his second, but then he saved par on the 11th, a hole he should frame.

Once again his drive drifted into the gorse, but instead of falling to the ground as it had a day earlier, his ball hung suspended knee-high among the branches. Taking a roundhouse swing as if hitting baseballs to the outfield, Els hacked the ball loose and followed with a marvelous iron to within 12 feet of the hole. He ran the putt home for perhaps the most remarkable par of the week. It saved his skin because Hamilton birdied from about 10 feet, caught Mickelson at nine under, and left Els two strokes behind.

Then Mickelson committed his fatal error on the 13th and could not recover. Els birdied, but still couldn't catch Hamilton, who simply refused to give ground. Instead, once again he opened his lead to two strokes over both men by holing a chip from behind the 14th green. Hamilton was 10 under now while both Els and Mickelson stood at eight under.

The situation changed not at all as all three birdied the 16th, but then Els birdied the 17th, climbed within a stroke of Hamilton, and left Mickelson behind. One hole to go.

Understandably nervous now, Hamilton misplayed the home hole. He pushed his tee shot into high grass along the right, yanked his second across the fairway into more rough close to a restraining fence, took a drop, hit the green with his third, and missed his putt, leaving Els 10 feet from his second Open victory.

As the gallery hushed, Els either misread the line or played the shot too timidly. Whatever the reason, his ball ran right at the hole, but about three feet short it swerved too far left and glided past. Hamilton holed for his five, Ernie made his four, and they had tied at 274. Els had shot 68 and Hamilton 69. Together they had shot seven consecutive rounds in the 60s.

The four-hole playoff went down to the final stroke. Hamilton had played first on both the first and second holes, and since both had been halved, he still held the honor on the third, Royal Troon's long par-three 17th. Obviously tense, he paced back and forth along the tee before finally settling down and playing a first-class shot within about 15 feet of the hole.

With another pause while a big jet from Prestwick Airport thundered overhead, Els pulled his tee shot 20 feet left of the green. With no way to pitch his ball close to the hole on a green that fell away, he played a low chip that bounced against the upgrade, hopped onto the green, and settled 12 feet from the flagstick. He missed the putt, Hamilton made his three and held the championship in his hand.

Once again Hamilton botched the home hole. His drive squirted right and onto the spectator crosswalk marked as ground under repair. He dropped onto a more playable lie, then left his approach about 30 yards short of the green.

Els, meanwhile, played the hole perfectly once again: drive down the middle, pitch to about 12 feet. At this stage a par seemed certain to send the playoff to sudden death while a birdie would probably end with Els the champion.

Here Hamilton took out that hybrid club once again and stroked the ball with a putting motion. It rolled along the ground, up onto the green, then pulled up hole-high about two feet right of the hole.

Now it was up to Els.

Ernie missed his putt once again and stepped off the back of the green, arms folded across his chest, staring with a downcast, resigned expression as Hamilton holed his putt and claimed The Open Championship.

5. PGA Championship

On Monday after the PGA Championship, on a warm, breezy day beside Lake Michigan, three guests were playing Whistling Straits, one of golf's wonders of the world, but situated by a rural outpost of Wisconsin called Haven, more than an hour's drive north of Milwaukee. At the 10th hole, far up the fairway, one of the caddies said, "Come here, I want to show you something." He pointed to a patch in the ground, a filled-in divot hole. "That was Vijay's drive," he said. And just a short way ahead lay the 10th green. The 10th was an uphill par-four of 361 yards. It had been a stupendous and daring drive, flirting with a steep drop into the course's notorious sands on the left. From there Vijay Singh hit a wedge shot of 30 yards that set up the six-foot birdie putt that gave him the lead in the three-way playoff against Justin Leonard and Chris DiMarco and ultimately the championship. It was the end of one of the more stimulating weeks — to say the least — in the event's 86 years.

Classically speaking — in retrospect, in the most generous spirit of forgiveness, it was a playoff that never should have happened. It needn't have come to that. Singh went into the final round leading by one stroke but staggered home in four-over-par 76, the highest final-round score by a winner in the history of the championship. Singh led through the last three rounds, and in the final round he had not one birdie, but a double bogey and two bogeys. He got some last-second reprieves. Both Leonard and DiMarco failed to cash in their opportunities at the 18th hole. DiMarco had the less likely chance. He hit a splendid six iron to 15 feet and needed the birdie to win. He left it just short. Leonard needed just a par to win. He came up short with his approach shot and bogeyed, and so there was a three-way tie and a three-hole aggregate playoff. Singh's winning edge was the bold and magnificent birdie he made at the 10th hole.

Before the PGA Championship could begin, there was the requisite visit with Tiger Woods, a two-time PGA champion struggling with his game but still ranked No. 1 in the world. He had one victory for the year, the WGC - Accenture Match Play back in February, and more to the point, he had not won in his last nine major championships. Was he concerned? "No," Woods said. "You've just got to keep grinding and keep working at it, and give yourself a lot of opportunities. I think that's what Jack [Nicklaus] was able to do better than any other player in the history of our game. He gave himself a lot of chances. I gave myself some chances and just haven't won. It's a matter of keep putting yourself up there."

Butch Harmon, whom Woods dismissed as his coach, created a stir when he said Woods was in denial about his game. Woods brushed him off. He referred to a similar dry spell in 1998, when he was going through the changes Harmon put into his game. "This is very similar to that period," Woods said. "It feels very similar, and things are starting to come together. Have I ever second-guessed it? No. Because I knew that this is the direction I want to go in order to become better. I'm very excited about the prospects of that happening."

And that was about as close as he ever got to winning. He would tie for 24th place, six strokes behind.

The 86th PGA Championship, if nothing else, had the distinction of being played on an illusion. Whistling Straits was designed to look like a links course from the Irish or Scottish coast. It was covered with dunes and shaggy fescue grass. Looking far older than its six years, the golf course was totally contrived. Owner Herbert V. Kohler, president and CEO of the Kohler Co., wanted one of those links courses, and architect Pete Dye hauled in a Sahara of sand, about 170,000 truckloads, and spread it out on an ordinary stretch of coast. He heaped the sand in mounds here and there, like a child making sand castles, and ended up with about as close as man can come to making a links course. It was a par-72 of 7,597 yards, and even Dye didn't know how many bunkers there were. Maybe a thousand or more. Or maybe it was one huge bunker interrupted by stretches of grass. Judging from pre-championship predictions, the golfers would be playing on a wee corner of hell.

"I thought we were going to get close enough to smell Satan's breath," said television commentator Gary McCord. "Then I look up and it looks like they're playing in Hawaii."

In the first round, 21 players shot in the 60s, leading a total of 39 who broke par, and they were among the 60 who were at par or better out of a field of 155 competitors. Fittingly, it was an Irishman — Northern Ireland's Darren Clarke — who discovered the fangs were made of something else. He birdied the first four holes, made nine birdies overall and two bogeys, and took the first-round lead with a seven-under-par 65.

"I didn't think, after my practice round Sunday, that I would be able to shoot 65 today," Clarke said. "We got fortunate with the conditions this morning. The greens were holding and we were able to fire at the flags." That opening stretch did it all. At No. 1, Clarke hit a driver and wedge to 12 feet. At the par-five No. 2, a three-iron approach to the edge of the green and two putts; the par-three No. 3, an eight iron 18 feet, and at the par-four No. 4, a driver and nine iron to 12 feet. He hit into bunkers at Nos. 9 and 13 for his only two bogeys.

Part of the reason for the low scores was that the tees had been moved forward out of respect for the wind, and some hole positions were relatively easy. Woods shot 75 and noted, "It was a hell of a lot easier than it played during practice. I hit two iron, wedge on No. 18. In the practice round, I hit driver, three wood."

There was a different kind of pressure in the first round — peer pressure. Justin Leonard was paired with Clarke and South Korea's K.J. Choi and suddenly found himself in a bird-shooting gallery. Where Clarke opened with four straight birdies, Choi started with five. "About an hour into the round, I was lagging way behind," Leonard said. "Those guys were feeding off each other, and for me to get sucked into it on the second nine was a lot of fun."

Leonard was out in one under par and erupted into a burst of five birdies over seven holes. He hit a wedge to 12 feet at the 10th, and also birdied the 12th, 13th, 14th and 16th for a 66 to tie Ernie Els at 66, one behind Clarke. Choi made six birdies, giving the threesome 22 for the round. Choi didn't agree that the course was too easy. "No, no, no," he said. "It's tougher turning No. 8, and the back nine is tough. Every day there's a different wind, so it's very tough."

Ernie Els wasn't in the hot threesome, but he did his share of damage — seven birdies and a bogey for 66, one off the lead. He made real hay on the par-threes and par-fives — three birdies on each thanks to brilliant iron play. On the par-fives (he started on the second nine): No. 11, a lay-up out of the rough, a 110-yard pitch to seven feet; No. 16, driver, five iron missed to the right and a pitch to seven feet, and No. 2, a driver, six iron and two putts. At the par-threes: No. 12, an eight iron to three feet; No. 17, a seven iron and a cross-country 50-foot putt, and No. 3, a nine iron to five feet.

"The flags were accessible," Els said. "They didn't put them where they could put them, and I made some nice putts." But Els wasn't about to downplay Whistling Straits. "It's a very tough golf course," he said.

Others were inclined to agree that the course wasn't as easy as some thought, or at least to be cautious, and that included Phil Mickelson. He had a nice parlay going — first in the Masters, second in the U.S. Open and third in Britain's Open five weeks earlier, his last competitive round before the PGA. He shot 69 — a tie for 17th in the swollen field — and noted that his driving wasn't accurate enough, his irons were solid enough, and that he had let a lot of shots get away. Summing up, he said, "I didn't play the way I need to play if I'm going to win this championship." He had early encouragement, though. He birdied the first three holes, then had three birdies and two bogeys on the second nine.

Jay Haas, 50 but ageless, hadn't won since 1993, but there he was again, deep in the mix with a five-birdie 68, just three strokes off the lead. "Good play feeds that good attitude and vice versa," Haas said. "I'm just having the time of my life." There was more than good fun at stake for Haas. He was hoping for a good performance that could convince Hal Sutton, the captain, to pick him for the U.S. Ryder Cup team.

There was a Ryder Cup berth on Chris DiMarco's mind, too. "This week is worth double points, and if I have another finish like I did last week, it should give me enough points to where I'm fine," he said. He turned in a one-bogey 68, one of eight at that figure, and pronounced himself happy. "I just hit it down the middle and played some good, solid golf," he said. He also had an explanation for the generally good play. "They gave us a little bit today," he said. "They moved some tees up and we didn't have any two irons into the par-four holes like we did in the practice rounds."

Vijay Singh, after a six-birdie, one-bogey 67 that tied him for fourth, went a step further. "I think they kind of went a little too easy," he said. "All of the par-fives were playing downwind and you are hitting irons into the greens. But the other par-fours, where you didn't have to go into the wind, you could hit a decent drive and a six iron instead of hitting three irons and two irons. So that way, it was easier."

Vijay watchers, meanwhile, might have noticed a good omen. That 67 was his best start in 13 PGAs.

The first-round leaderboard:

Darren Clarke	65	K.J. Choi	68
Justin Leonard	66	Padraig Harrington	68
Ernie Els	66	Loren Roberts	68
Vijay Singh	67	Chris DiMarco	68
Scott Verplank	67	Tim Petrovic	68
Luke Donald	67	Stuart Appleby	68
Briny Baird	67	Stephen Ames	68
Jay Haas	68	Geoff Ogilvy	68

If Tiger Woods wasn't going to win a tournament this year — and at this early point it seemed he wasn't going to win this PGA Championship — then the focus was on whether he would make the cut. He had a remarkable run going. He had made 128 in succession. But with 75 in the first round at Whistling Straits, and with practically half the field breaking par, his chances were looking slim this time. He shot even par on the first nine. Woods ducked under the wire with three quick birdies on the second nine, at the 13th, 15th and 16th holes, to extend his streak. He shot 69 for an even-par 144 total, making the cut with one stroke to spare. The last time he missed the cut was in the 1998 AT&T Pebble Beach National Pro-Am, where he withdrew at four over after two rounds of the rain-shortened 54-hole tournament.

"I take pride in how I was playing," said Woods, now nine strokes out of the lead but not writing himself off. "I tee it up with the intent of giving it everything I've got. I don't leave anything on the golf course. I think that's one thing I'm most proud of is that I've never bagged it. I've never dogged it."

The star of the show Friday, apart from Woods, was the golf course itself. Whistling Straits quit whistling Friday and started biting back after the beating it took in the first round. "It played a couple hundred yards longer," said Bob Tway, after making the cut with a 70–141. "I don't think they were too happy with the 65s." Said Luke Donald (73–140), "This is a pretty tough course, and if the weather gets bad, you could have people not finishing. They did a good job of making it at least a couple shots harder today."

But maybe difficulty, like beauty, is in the eye of the beholder. Whistling Straits played fractionally easier in the second round, averaging 73.255 to Thursday's 73.340.

Speaking for the minority, Phil Mickelson (72–141) offered, "I thought it was awfully easy, actually," probably meaning his three-birdie 33 first nine (the second). But that probably was before his crash. He was six under coming to his 14th (the par-five No. 5). He started the hole with a ball in the water and finished it with three putts for a seven. Two bogeys coming in, then a birdie at the last hole left him six strokes off the lead going into the third round. "I certainly like the position, but it's got to stay difficult and the wind has got to stay up for me to stay within six shots," he said.

Justin Leonard, looking happier than he had in years, shot 69 to tie for the 36-hole lead with Vijay Singh, at nine-under-par 135. There was a smile on his face. But some wondered whether there was a little gloom inside. The PGA Championship had not been good to him. In 1997, he got overrun by Davis Love in his famous "rainbow" championship. But the 2002 PGA was the one that really hurt. It was all but in his hands, but he collapsed to 77 in the final round, and Rich Beem went on to win over Tiger Woods.

"I tend to learn more from failure than I do success," Leonard said. "However, I don't know how much I learned after that round." How much had he changed? It would be a critical question in two days. "That's a deep question," Leonard said. "I may need all night to think of that one."

If there were any doubts lingering from 2002, they didn't show on Leonard's card. Starting on the second nine, he logged five birdies of a good variety. For example, a 25-foot putt at No. 10, his first hole, then chipping to one foot at the 16th, then a wedge to eight feet at his 10th, and a wedge to two feet at his 14th (No. 5). "The pin positions were a little tougher," he said, "but the wind died down, so I think those two things almost offset each other."

Said Vijay Singh, "You don't have to be long to play this golf course. You've got to be in the fairway. Everyone hits the ball a good distance and the greens are running smoothly. If you hit the right shots, you can score around here." Following his own formula, he shot a six-birdie, two-bogey 68 to tie Leonard at 135.

Singh shook off a three-putt bogey at No. 1 and birdied all three par-fives — No. 2 for the second straight day, from eight feet, and No. 5 for the second day, on two putts from 20 feet, and then the 16th, with a five iron to the green and two putts from 25 feet. "The wind was blowing when we started off," he said, "and we saw Ernie go to 10 under, and so I thought, you've got to play some golf to get up there. I didn't want to move away from the lead too much. And then everybody started coming back to us. But I kept my head and I played well on the front nine, kept the ball in play."

Ernie Els shook up the field when he reached 10 under par with a birdie at the 10th, his fourth birdie through that stretch. He hit only five fairways, but shot 70 for a 136 total, tied with Briny Baird (69) and Darren Clarke (71) one stroke off the lead. "I've never been a stats man," Els said. "I've won the British Open hitting probably fewer fairways than that. So I was probably born in the rough."

Chris DiMarco had an erratic day. He had two birdies and two bogeys on the first nine. On the second nine, he missed birdies by inches at the 10th, 11th, 12th and 13th holes. But he eagled the par-four 14th, then bogeyed the 15th, and then birdied the 16th for 70 and a 138 total. "The front nine played really tough," he said, remarking on the wind. At No. 8, a par-five of 507 yards, "I smoked the drive, I smoked it right with a two iron, and I was still 45 feet short." He trailed Leonard and Singh by three strokes going into the third round.

Ireland's Padraig Harrington, who's usually in the thick of things, pulled back from the edge just in time. "I really struggled with my focus at the end of the front nine and into the back nine," Harrington said. "When you get low, energy-wise, it's hard to keep your mind on one thing. If it wasn't for those five or six holes, I would have been okay. It's nice when you do lose your focus to be able to get it back." After birdies at the first and seventh got him to six under par, Harrington bogeyed the eighth, birdied the 10th, then bogeyed the 11th, 12th and 15th. He got one stroke back with a birdie at the par-three 17th and finished at 71–139, four strokes off the lead.

Elsewhere, it was day of fascinating events.

Spain's Miguel Angel Jimenez, for example, was in line to miss the cut after his 76 in the first round. Then he birdied his first four holes and five of his first six, matched the week's low with 65, and made the cut with room to spare with his 141 total. Canada's Mike Weir, the 2003 Masters champion, was on his way to making the cut until he pulled his tee shot at the par-five 11th. It took him two strokes to get out of a bunker, and he finished with two putts for a triple-bogey eight for 73, and missed the cut by one stroke. The pain was even greater for Sergio Garcia. He missed a five-foot par putt at the 18th and also missed the cut by a stroke. And it was a double cut for Mark Calcavecchia. He was disqualified for signing an incorrect scorecard — he made four, not three, at No. 7 — but he would have missed the cut anyway.

Pain came in different forms for others. John Daly, after his opening 81, said he had to play some incredible golf to impress Ryder Cup captain Hal Sutton to make him a wild-card pick. The unfortunate Daly shot 76 and missed the cut by 12 strokes.

Sutton, the 1983 PGA champion, also missed the cut (74–147) and could devote himself to the Ryder Cup picks he would have to make by Monday, the day after the PGA. He gave no hints of his candidates. "I feel the same way I did at the beginning of the week. I'll bet you at the end of the day I'm still going to feel largely the same way." And he was depending on the PGA to fuel his candidates. "I've seen guys win major championships and it usually sparks them into playing better golf," Sutton said. "It elevates their way of thinking."

And perhaps the most disappointed man in the field, apart from Tiger Woods, was Jerry Kelly, a native son from Madison, Wisconsin, with large galleries following him. Kelly shot 77–153 and missed the cut. "It's Lake Michigan, but it might as well be an ocean," Kelly said. "I hit it awful. It's my first missed cut in a year. It's the one I didn't want to miss the most."

And so the second round closed with 43 golfers under par for 36 holes. This surprised Darren Clarke, among others. "If you had asked guys during the practice rounds," he said, "there's no way we expected so many guys under par."

The second-round leaderboard:

Justin Leonard	69 - 135	Chris DiMarco	70 - 138
Vijay Singh	68 - 135	Stephen Ames	71 - 139
Briny Baird	69 - 136	K.J. Choi	71 - 139
Darren Clarke	71 - 136	Padraig Harrington	71 - 139
Ernie Els	70 - 136	Chris Riley	70 - 139

Ernie Els was the winner of two U.S. Opens and one Open Championship, but despite his talent and many opportunities, had not been able to add the Masters and the PGA hardware to his trophy case. Now this PGA seemed to be slipping away too. Els started the day at eight under par, one stroke off the lead, and while all ahead of him were breaking par, he could only manage a lackluster 72 that left him four strokes behind the leader, Vijay Singh, going into the final round.

"I just couldn't get it quite on target today," Els said. "I struggled a little bit off the tee, and it cost me." One reason might have been his club selection. He bogeyed the 15th hole and was still one under par, but did a puzzling thing at the 18th, a tough par-four of 500 yards. He used an iron off the tee and never reached the fairway. He made a brilliant bogey, but a bogey nonetheless. And so his chances of winning this PGA suddenly got three shots harder. Els had a remarkable record in the major championships coming into this PGA — three victories and 18 other top-10 finishes. This year in particular was frustrating. In the Masters, Mickelson beat him by a stroke on the last hole. In the U.S. Open, he trailed Retief Goosen by two and shot 80 in the final round. And in Britain's Open, Todd Hamilton beat him in a playoff.

"I have to believe I still have a chance," Els said. "It's been an awkward year so far, but maybe it will go my way tomorrow."

But Singh, Justin Leonard and Phil Mickelson put tomorrow a lot farther away. Singh shot another 69 for a 12-under-par 204 total and led by one stroke over Leonard (70) and by four over a surging Mickelson, who shot his lowest score yet, 67, and that tied him for third place with Els, Stephen Ames (69), Darren Clarke (72) and Chris Riley (69).

"At least I have a chance," said Mickelson. "If I go play a solid round tomorrow — and I know I can shoot quite a few under par on this golf course — I should have an opportunity." He bogeyed only once, a three-putt at the par-five 11th that momentarily cooled a hot start. He birdied the first two holes, four of the first six, and added another at the ninth for an outward 31. He offset the bogey with a birdie at the par-five 16th. The jewel of his round was dropping a 50-foot putt for a birdie at the fifth after a poor bunker shot.

Someone wondered, for some reason, whether it was better to enter the final round trailing rather than leading. Mickelson stated the obvious with patience. "Well, you want to be in the lead," he said. "The only time I've led after 54 holes [in the majors] I was able to win, this year's Masters. It's much easier having a couple shots in hand than it is trying to chase."

Singh underlined a sunny day in which 38 of the 73 players who made the cut broke par on the supposed Beast by the Lake, which didn't help the ego of Herbert V. Kohler, the owner of Whistling Straits. "It was a lot harder than it looked today," said Singh, after a four-birdie 69. "I didn't play as well as yesterday, I didn't drive the ball as well, I didn't hit it as close. But I managed to score well." That must mean putting. At Nos. 6, 10, 13 and 16 he dropped putts of 20, eight, 15 and 15 feet, respectively.

Singh revealed how simple it is to get as good as he had become. First, he's practically anchored to the practice range. And then there was his putting. He had discarded the long "belly putter" and gone back to a conventional putter. Then he got some kind of putting device to practice his swing on, for perhaps two hours a day. That's about all there was to it.

Leonard missed tying Singh by a weak bunker shot at the 18th. It came up some 35 feet short, and he two-putted for a bogey and 70. He finished the third round at 205, one stroke behind Singh. "I felt I played pretty solid today," Leonard said. "I didn't play great. I missed a few fairways, but I hit some smart shots and gave myself some chances like I've done most of the week." He bogeyed No. 1 from a fairway bunker, then made four birdies from No. 5 through No. 12 on strong iron play. They came on putts of three, three, four and six feet. After a bogey at the 15th, he birdied the 16th from six feet and was tied with Singh at 12 under par going to the 18th. Then came the three-iron approach into a greenside bunker and the weak out, and they were separated by a shot.

Chris DiMarco, meanwhile, was pretty much back with the group just tagging along. Hardly anyone noticed him in his solitary pursuit of a place on the U.S. Ryder Cup team. His workaday 71 left him at 209, five strokes out of the lead. "It played tough out there," DiMarco said. "The pins were in some good positions. The green speed — I don't know if it's me, but if I had another foot on my putts I would have made about three or four more." He birdied Nos. 5, 6 and 12 and bogeyed Nos. 11 and 17 for 71 and a 209 total, five off the lead and in eighth place behind Singh.

"If I play to win tomorrow, I'll be fine," DiMarco said. "I'll start looking at the board with probably four or five to go. I'll start looking to see what I need to do. If I'm only two or three shots behind, I'm still going to try to be aggressive and make some birdies coming in and try to win the tournament."

The end came for Briny Baird at the dangerous 17th. Baird, winless since joining the PGA Tour in 1999, was high on the leaderboard with 67-69 in the first two rounds. He was only one stroke off the lead at the start of the third round. He was two under for the round through the 14th. He said he was nervous from the start. He made an innocent bogey at the 15th, and then maybe the nerves really kicked in. At the dangerous par-three 17th, perched on a manmade bluff with the steep drop to sand and thick fescue below on the left, he made the most grievous of sins. He hit it to the left, down there. It took him two shots to get up to the green and three putts to get down, for a triple-bogey six. "I could have been down there a lot longer," he said. Then he bogeyed the 18th for 41 on the last nine and a 75, dropping seven shots off the lead.

Darren Clarke also ran afoul of the 17th, but he could wisecrack at the minimal damage. "I hit as good of a shank as you can see," Clarke said. "It was one to be proud of." But he escaped with a bogey and shot 72 for a 208 total, four off the lead.

A second consecutive 69 Saturday left Tiger Woods feeling and looking a bit perkier, but he headed into the final round 11 strokes off the lead. "I'm definitely going to need some help from the guys not to run away from me," said Woods. There were some good signs to his game. Although he needed 30 putts, he had no three-putts, and he hit nine of the 14 driving fairways (64 percent) and hit a week-high 15 greens in regulation. But he still would be 0-for-10 in his last 10 majors and major-less for the second straight year.

There was this final note on the question to Mickelson, whether it's better to be leading or just behind after the third round: In the last seven tournaments in which Vijay Singh led or shared the lead through 54 holes, dating back to the 2002 Houston Open — he won.

The third-round leaderboard:

Vijay Singh	69 - 204	Darren Clarke	72 - 208
Justin Leonard	70 - 205	Ernie Els	72 - 208
Phil Mickelson	67 - 208	Chris DiMarco	71 - 209
Chris Riley	69 - 208	Brian Davis	69 - 210
Stephen Ames	69 - 208	Loren Roberts	70 - 210

Perhaps the final vindication for Whistling Straits and owner Herbert V. Kohler was the knowledge that in all of a final field of 73 on the last day of this PGA Championship, only two players shot in the 60s. Ireland's Paul McGinley shot 69–282 and tied for sixth place, two strokes out of the playoff. It was only his second finish in five PGAs, the other a tie for 22nd. Open champion Todd Hamilton shot 68–288, tied for 37th, and noted, "I think all the putts I missed on the first three days, I made today."

Vijay Singh wasn't wringing his hands over this PGA. "Let me make this clear," he'd said. "Majors are important to me. Probably not as important as to the other guys. I strive to win majors. But it's not the end of the world if I don't win a major. I mean, it's important, so don't get me wrong. It will be tense out there. I'm going to go out and try my hardest. I'm going to try to beat everybody in the field, and I'm in the best position right now to do that."

The question of being No. 1 in the world also came up, and this meant chasing Tiger Woods. "Right now, I am totally focused on what I'm doing," Singh said, "and I'm not really worried about the rankings."

So it was a totally businesslike Singh who set out on the final round seeking his second PGA and third major title. But something was wrong. Someone noted that the last player to lead a major going into the final round and then shoot 76 didn't win it. That would be Greg Norman, in the 1986 PGA at Inverness, where Bob Tway holed that electrifying bunker shot on the last hole to beat him.

Still, Singh did shoot four-over-par 76 in this one. It was the highest final round by a PGA champion. The all-time mark in a major championship was 78 by Reg Whitcombe when he won the 1938 Open at Royal St. George's.

The irony of the week was that five players out of the field of 73 went the entire last round without a birdie, and one of them was the champion. Justin Leonard had two birdies in his 75, Chris DiMarco three in his 71. Singh had one birdie all day, and he got it when it counted — in the playoff. Of course, Singh got something else right when he needed it — a shaky finish by Leonard, bogeying three of the last five holes in regulation and raising the ghost of his closing 77 in the 2002 PGA.

Others had their chances and failed, most notably Ernie Els. He reached the 18th hole in two shots, but three-putted for a bogey, 73 and a 281 total. The bogey cost him a spot in the playoff. He tied for fourth with Chris Riley (73), stretching the grandest close-but-no-cigar record in the modern game. Els, who owns three major titles, now had a career 23 top-10 finishes in majors and an astonishing four this year alone. He was second to Phil Mickelson in the Masters, tied for ninth behind Retief Goosen in the U.S. Open after 80 in the final round, and lost to Todd Hamilton in a four-hole playoff in the Open.

Mickelson closed with 74 and finished at 282, tying for sixth place. The biggest blow was a double-bogey five at No. 3. "Then I just struggled to make anything happen," Mickelson said. "I never really hit it well."

Tiger Woods-watchers were left to note that he closed with 73 and a 286 total, tying for 24th place. The summary for his game change in progress: His tee shots were erratic. In succession over the four rounds, he hit nine, five, nine and seven of the 14 driving fairways. Putts? He needed 32, 28, 30 and 29. He makes no secret that he lives for the majors. And now he was 0-for-10 since the 2002 U.S. Open.

DiMarco, paired with Els, teed off in the fourth from last group, a half hour before Singh and Leonard. He birdied the ninth after hitting a wedge shot to eight feet. He birdied the par-five 11th, laying up with a six iron and hitting a wedge to 15 feet. He birdied the par-three 12th as well, from two feet, and was 10 under par for the tournament. DiMarco had said he wouldn't look at the leaderboard until late in the round and so didn't know that behind him Leonard and Singh were struggling.

When did DiMarco know he had a chance to win?

"Not until I made the second putt for par at the 17th, really," DiMarco said. "Because I don't know what anybody's doing, and I just went bogey-bogey [at the 15th and 16th], and I finished at eight under. I don't know if that's going to be good enough. Once I made that par on 17 and hit my driver into the fairway on 18, and hit my six iron on the green, I looked at my caddie and said, 'That is good enough, for sure.' Those holes were playing brutal coming in." He had a 15-footer for birdie. He couldn't know it at the time, but it would have won for him. He left it a little short.

So DiMarco, who made up five shots on Singh and four on Leonard, logged his 71 and 280 total and watched the battle unfold out on the course.

Leonard had started the final round one stroke behind Singh. He tied Singh with a birdie at the third, then took a two-shot lead when Singh doubled-bogeyed the par-four fourth. They both bogeyed the seventh, and Leonard lost a shot when he bogeyed the 10th. He regained it then lost it with a birdie-bogey set at the 13th and 14th. And when Singh bogeyed the 15th, Leonard was two strokes ahead with three holes to play.

Leonard bogeyed the 16th, but he still led by one. It was still his championship to win. He needed a par at the 18th. From the fairway, all he had to do was hit the green and two-putt and he was a winner. He had 204 yards. He hit a five iron. "When I hit the shot, I thought I just ended the golf tournament," he said. Had he hit it fat or underclubbed himself? The ball came down just short in a grassy depression next to a greenside bunker. He chipped awkwardly, leaving himself a 10-foot putt to win. The putt slid by on the right side. He bogeyed, and the three were tied at eight-under 280. It was off to a three-way aggregate playoff.

And now Singh hit that towering drive far up into the 10th fairway, where he would leave a scar for visitors to see days later. Then the pitch to six feet and the putt for his only birdie of the day and a one-stroke lead. Leonard and DiMarco had parred. The next playoff hole was No. 17, the clinging 236-yard par-three. Singh hit a three-iron tee shot to five feet and two-putted, leaving the other two to match him with pars. The final playoff hole was the 18th. Singh hit a three wood off the tee and a nine wood to the green. DiMarco caught a bunker on the left, and Leonard barely reached the collar of the green. Neither came close to holing out the birdie needed to tie Singh, and he lagged up and dropped his par putt for the win.

Was this the ugliest win of Singh's career? Said Singh, "It's the prettiest."

The Royal Bank of Scotland Group

6. The Players Championship

Like many young Australian golfers, Adam Scott had Greg Norman for a hero. He admired Norman's power, his touch, his swing and his boldness, and — as youth are wont to do — he wanted to be like his idol. Although not to the point he had come to at the final hole of The Players Championship. Which is to say Scott was about to cross the line from champion to, well, someone unable to bring in the successful result. He'd had a four-shot lead during the final round, but it had melted away, and he looked like a loser for certain when, still leading by two strokes, he hooked a six-iron approach into the water at the 18th hole that last day. Folks grouped around the 18th green and their television sets probably were noting that Norman, unfortunately, was known to do that kind of thing in tight situations.

But it was Norman to the rescue. After taking a penalty drop, Scott faced a chip shot from a few yards off the 18th green, about 90 feet from the flag. Now he called on a shot Norman had just taught him.

"C'mon," Scott said, comforting his caddie, Alastair McLean, "it's just a chip and a putt." Would this have been false bravado? Maybe. But he made the delicate chip to 10 feet, holed the putt for a bogey five, and picked up the most prestigious title of his young career by one stroke over Ireland's Padraig Harrington. At age 23, Scott became the youngest Players champion. It was his second win on the PGA Tour, after the 2003 Deutsche Bank Championship the previous autumn, and his fifth victory worldwide in his short career.

Sometimes the dramatists have no heart. Norman himself was playing in The Players Championship, an event he had run away with in 1994, but this time he wasn't in the picture, except for his role with Scott. Norman couldn't get below par in any round and tied for 81st in the 83-man finish. Still, it can be said he had a hand in winning this one. The day before the tournament started, Butch Harmon, Scott's instructor (and formerly Norman's), asked Norman to help Scott with his chipping. Norman had Scott elevate the toe of his club more on the takeaway and accelerate more toward the bottom of the swing. That produced the first check that would stop the ball quickly on the green. Scott summoned the magic of that shot on three of his last holes in the final round — and nowhere to greater effect than at the 18th.

Scott is one of the new breed of young golfers expected to challenge Tiger Woods, and while he idolized Norman, he swung more like Woods. Harmon first saw Scott when he was a freshman at the University of Nevada at Las Vegas, at age 18, and noted then that it was a Woods-like swing. "That was the way he was born to swing," Harmon said.

He wasn't about to do a Norman on this one — in 1994, Norman shot a record total of 24-under-par 264 and won by four strokes — but he was in command most of the way. He shot rounds of 65, 72, 69 and 70 for a 276 total, 12 under par at the par-72 Tournament Players Club at Sawgrass in Ponte Vedra Beach, Florida, the home of the PGA Tour. The home too of this classy event which has now been staged for 31 years and has long been touted as the fifth major championship, although never fully accepted as such.

He was tied with Ernie Els for third place in the second round, but he was the solo leader the rest of the way, no small feat for a lad against the toughest all-professional field in golf. The event started as the Tournament Players Championship in 1974 and was played at different courses for the first three years, then moved to Sawgrass Country Club near here in 1977. In 1982 it got its current and permanent home, the Pete Dye-designed TPC at Sawgrass.

The favorite, as usual, was Tiger Woods, but he was in the process of trying to refine his swing and never caused a ripple. But he caused a stir when he shot 75 in the first round — with just 25 putts — and suddenly was in position to miss the cut after having made it 119 consecutive times. He got a strong dose of his problems right off the bat. Accuracy, and especially distance control, were what made him great. But at the wicked little par-three 17th, the infamous Fantasy Island sitting out in the lake all by itself, he hit his tee shot over the island and into the water beyond. He did well to get by with a bogey. He took the penalty drop, hit on, and one-putted for a bogey. In fact, he one-putted each of the last three holes or his score could have been even higher.

His play at the moment was part of a pattern. He had just come from his worst finish in five years at the Bay Hill Invitational, a tie for 46th. There was continuing speculation that he ought to go back to his swing guru, Harmon, with whom he had worked for some 12 years. Woods parted from Harmon about a year ago. But Woods brushed off the notion of returning. "I'd just like to not make as many bogeys, and made some more birdies," Woods said. "If I get in the red numbers [under par], I'll be all right."

He bounced back in the second round and made the cut with room to spare, but this wasn't Tiger Woods. He shot 75, 69, 68 and 73 and tied for 16th place at three-under 285. In his opening 75, he hit only six fairways in regulation and hit only six greens. It was his fourth consecutive round over par. The way he made the cut was pure Tiger. He eagled the 11th (his second hole) from 10 feet and birdied the 12th from 10 feet, and came in under the cut with two strokes to spare. He made that surge for the 69 and extended his record to 120 consecutive cuts made.

The streak began in 1998 after the AT&T Pebble Beach National Pro-Am, a tournament that was shortened to 54 holes by heavy rains, starting in February and finishing in August. Woods was four over par after two rounds and when play was resumed in August, Woods chose to withdraw, which was considered by the PGA Tour as a missed cut. His only true missed cut in 151 professional starts was in the 1997 Bell Canadian Open.

"I just go out there and grind it out," Woods said. "It doesn't change for me. The effort is the same if I'm shooting 82 or 62. I have the same type of focus on every shot. I treat every shot the same. I take pride in what I do on the golf course. I go out there and give it everything I have." If he wasn't playing like the old Tiger Woods, he sure was talking like him, and that comforted his fans, with the Masters coming up in two weeks.

Scott set the pace in the first round with a hot short game. He made six birdies from inside six feet, starting with a three-hole burst — a nine iron to four feet at No. 7, a four iron to three feet at the par-three No. 8 and a nine iron to six feet at No. 9. His only bogey came at the 15th, where he was bunkered. He stamped himself as the guy to beat when he flipped a nine iron to three feet at the 18th for the 65 and a one-stroke lead on Duffy Waldorf and Kevin Sutherland.

The greens became the issue of the day. Scott and Waldorf both played in the morning, when the greens were still a little moist and could hold shots. By the end of the day, they were fading fast. "The greens look like they're about to die," said Sutherland, who played in the afternoon. "They're brownish and shiny. They're about to turn blue."

Waldorf had a finish that was as wild as the Hawaiian-style shirts he always wears. He eagled the 16th from 15 feet, splashed his tee shot into the lake at the island par-three 17th and made five, then birdied the 18th from 10 feet. Sutherland solved the dangerous greens with a long putter that he had put in his bag just to steady it on his airline flight. He decided to give the long putter one last chance, and suddenly he was making just about everything from inside 12 feet.

The first round had its delicious oddities, although some weren't so tasty to the players. Tasty: There was Phil Mickelson (70), chipping in for birdie at the 17th with his left foot almost hanging out over the edge of the pilings by the lake. "If you play well, you can shoot well under par," Mickelson noted. "And if you don't, it eats you up." Not tasty: David Peoples did not hit into the water at the 10th and he needed just two putts, and still triple-bogeyed. Elsewhere in the tournament, John Daly had a bogey-free 69 — "That's not happened too many times to me out here" — and Retief Goosen made three double bogeys and shot 77.

In the second round, a former hockey player bulled his way into the picture. Jerry Kelly, like all hockey players, blessed with powerful forearms and swings, shot 66 to tie for the halfway lead with Kevin Sutherland, who shot 69. They were at nine-under 135, two strokes ahead of Ernie Els (69) and Adam Scott (72). Kelly had this other distinction: He had gone through 36 holes without a bogey. In the two rounds, he hit 23 of 28 fairways and 24 of 36 greens, and saved par 12 times.

Kelly was more than a performance chart in the second round. He made six birdies, including an up-and-down from a greenside bunker to start, and two-putted for another birdie at the next. He posted a miracle shot at No. 6, his 15th hole. He had missed the green, then from thick rough popped a bump-and-run shot from a downhill lie to about six feet. "That was a pretty hard shot, even for the armchair quarterbacks," Kelly said.

Sutherland had come to The Players after a three-week break. He had played six straight events. He had a tie for ninth in one and was 39th or worse in the other five. Another round in the 60s was a good sign that he could be on to something.

"I made about all the momentum putts today that I needed to make," said Sutherland, "and I'm hitting my irons well." Ah, but the driver. "If you want to be around late Sunday afternoon," he said, "you have to drive the ball in the fairway." And what's a momentum putt? Sutherland demonstrated at the 14th hole. He had driven into a bad lie in the rough and hacked out into a waste bunker. From there, he hit a low hook that came up short of the green, and finally he was looking at a 12-footer for bogey. And he made it. "There's bad bogeys and good bogeys — and that was a great bogey," Sutherland said. "For me, making that putt was like making a birdie putt, as far as momentum goes. When I walked off that green, I felt great."

Davis Love, the defending champion, also made the cut despite a chronic back problem that flared up and nearly forced him out. He had shot 77 in the first round, then got treatment in the fitness trailer Thursday afternoon. "I spent all afternoon trying to get where I could play today," he said. It got him through. He shot 68 in the second round and made the cut, and went on to tie for 33rd in the tournament.

Another former champion didn't make the cut, but he did find a new way to make a par. This was Fred Couples, who was on his way out in the second round, pretty disgusted with himself. At one hole Friday, he blasted weakly out of a greenside bunker and his ball came down in the rough. He slapped at the ball left-handed with the back of his wedge. The ball shot out of the rough and was headed for more trouble, but it hit the flagstick and dropped into the hole for a par. But it only helped a little. He shot 78 and was gone. Others gone with him included Lee Janzen, Stuart Appleby, David Toms, Ben Curtis and Mike Weir.

The cut was made at two-over 146, the highest on the PGA Tour so far in the year. The last time The Players cut was at two over was in 2002 when Craig Perks won. The cut left 83 players to finish the tournament, the highest number of competitors since 1994, when 85 made it. The figures were pushed up, of course, by the generally higher scoring. The average round for Thursday was 72.810, and on windier Friday, 73.548.

A hot sun baked out the wicked greens even more for the third round on Saturday, and Adam Scott retook the lead in a champion's fashion — with a burst of three straight birdies making the turn. Scott was two behind leaving the ninth hole, then birdied the 10th from 20 feet, two-putted the 11th, and stuck a wedge to four feet at the 12th. He was well on his way to a 69 and a two-stroke lead entering the final round. "I'm far from winning the event," Scott said. "There's a full leaderboard of the best players behind me."

In fact, there were 19 players within six shots of him — including Woods — and six shots is not a great number in a bad day at the TPC at Sawgrass. He could take some encouragement from the fact that he was the only one in the last five groups to break 70 on a course getting tougher and tougher as the sun continued to bake out the greens and capricious breezes made shot selection and shots themselves an iffy proposition.

Woods shot 68 and was at 212, six strokes behind, but he had squandered a chance to be in much closer contention. He birdied the 12th and 13th holes from short range, getting to six under par, and was closing in while the leaders were still on the practice range warming up. Then he had trouble at the 17th again, coming up short, but this time dry. His chip was short and he bogeyed. At the 18th, he was between clubs. He took his seven iron and then felt the wind shift just as he reached the top of his backswing. The ball soared three rows deep into the grandstand. He got a free drop on the other side of the hill and bogeyed again. A bogey-bogey finish is painful for anyone, but Woods insisted he was still in it at six strokes back.

"A lot of things can happen on the golf course," he said. "You can shoot low rounds and you can shoot high ones." This one was almost a very low one. He made eight birdies in the round — but also four bogeys. Maybe the eight birdies were more of a surprise than the four bogeys. He was driving it very well. He missed just two fairways. But he hit just nine greens in regulation and missed eight of the final 11. Given these figures, the 68 was remarkable.

Sometimes it takes a great break to win, and that great break was the really bad break that hit Kevin Sutherland. It was a gaffe by a rules official that might have cost him the tournament. It couldn't have come at a worse time. Sutherland, co-leader with Jerry Kelly coming into the third round, had been passed by Scott on that third birdie at the 12th. Sutherland was nine under and trailing by a stroke coming to the par-five 16th. He laid up with his second shot, 105 yards from the hole, with his ball just behind a divot. Worse, there was a patch of sand behind his ball. A rules official said he couldn't ground his club, since that would be improving his lie. Sutherland's shot suddenly became that much tougher. He had to hold his sand wedge above the ball at address rather than have the steadying influence of grounding it. He left the ball short of the green in thick grass. He chopped out to 25 feet and bogeyed. At the scorer's table later, he was informed that the official was wrong and that he could have grounded his club. Would that have made a difference?

"It would have made the shot quite a bit easier," Sutherland said. "It would have been nice to know then what I know now." The bogey gave him a 73 and tied him for second place going into the final round, two strokes behind Scott. There is no way to measure the impact of the bad ruling, but it's reasonable to assume it hurt his game.

Meanwhile, the tournament was heating up. Frank Lickliter, who lives there at the TPC at Sawgrass, closed with three birdies for a 68 and a share of second place with Sutherland. Vijay Singh got active with a 72, and Craig Parry, who had made the cut right on the number, shot an eight-under 64 that included two eagles and six birdies. The eagles came at both par-fives on the second nine — from five feet at the 11th hole and from 18 feet at the 16th. "Two eagles in one round is amazing," Parry marveled. "I normally have two eagles a year." Then he added, "Yesterday I didn't have a chance at all. Now I've got a chance for tomorrow." So did Paul Stankowski, who birdied his final four holes for a 66 that carried him right into the hunt, in the group three strokes off the pace.

And then there was the new Phil Mickelson, playing the throttled-back game that had already brought him the title at the Bob Hope Chrysler Classic. This was the prudent Mickelson: At the 18th, rather than try to force a shot out of the rough — it might have squirted left into the water or right into the grassy mounds — he opted to lay up short of the green. He ended up making his par from 10 feet. His 70 left him three shots behind Scott heading into the final round. "It's going to be a fun day for all the guys at the top," Mickelson said. "There are about 20 guys who have a shot — and I'm one of them."

England's Ian Poulter, on the other hand, had no shot. But Poulter, he of the many-colored hair, did manage to add a little chapter to the event's history with one of the strangest pars ever. Even stranger than Fred Couples' backhander out of the rough in the second round. At the No. 4 green, he had marked his ball then made a swipe at it to lift it, but it flew across the green and into the water beyond. Now he was looking at a two-stroke penalty for not finishing with the same ball he started with. His physical therapist, Kam Bhabra, came to his rescue. Bhabra stripped down to his underwear, jumped in and found the ball. Poulter, after identifying it as his, then proceeded to make par, and all things being equal, the difference was between his 74–288 and a tie for 33rd place, and a 290 and a tie for 53rd. "I wasn't going to go in," Poulter said. "I would have taken the two-stroke penalty. He'll be rewarded nicely." There was no report on what the reward was.

It was then Adam Scott's tournament to win or lose. He started the final round with a two-stroke lead, and he built that to four, and he would need it.

Some of the 20 players Mickelson said had a chance to win faded, including Mickelson himself. His putter acted up and he shot 71. Kenny Perry, who started tied for fourth, bogeyed three of the last five holes and fell short with a 71. Together with Mickelson and Lickliter (72), he tied for third, four strokes behind. The second biggest surprise of the tournament, after Padraig Harrington, was Ernie Els. He was also tied for fourth going into the final round, then blew to a 78 and plummeted to a tie for 26th.

So it seemed Scott had nothing to do but cruise on in. Suddenly, out of nowhere came Harrington. He started the day tied for 12th, five strokes behind Scott, and things got a lot worse before they got better. He had three bogeys and a birdie in the first five holes. Over the next 13 holes, he had six birdies and an eagle for a six-under 66 and an 11-under 277 total. He had played the brutal final nine in 30. Harrington posted his clubhouse lead and went to the practice range, there to make a couple of telephone calls and practice in case of a playoff. He didn't watch Scott's finish. "I wasn't going to sit there three or four holes following every shot," Harrington said. "That would be counterproductive. The one thing I always hate is watching golf in a current tournament because you see people do things, and you don't want to wish anyone bad."

Three times over the last four holes, Scott had to summon the chip shot that Greg Norman had given him. It saved him, and nowhere more dramatically than under the horrendous pressure at the 18th, where he had hit his second shot into the water. Later, he said he knew as soon as he hit that six iron that it was headed into the lake. "I chased it with my hands, flipped my hands over, and it was always going left," Scott said.

Then he had to summon the lesson from Norman. "He really changed my technique," Scott said, pressed for an explanation. His old way, he said, had the club going back inside, which shuts down the clubface and which then forced him to do the rest with his hands. "He got me keeping the loft on the club and letting my hands through," Scott said. "And I quieted everything down, got myself covering the ball a lot better, and hit more aggressive chips." The chip saved him down the last three holes, and most especially at the mighty 18th, where he escaped with a bogey for a 70, and the one stroke that he needed.

It was left to Scott to make a statement of intent. "You want to become a major champion and No. 1 in the world," Scott said. "I think Tiger has got that No. 1 spot locked down right now. I'm climbing up there."

7. Ryder Cup

Maybe David Toms put his finger on the answer to the European magic in the Ryder Cup. Maybe it was as simple as the feeling, "Oh, no, here we go again."

Months after the 35th playing of the Ryder Cup Matches, at Oakland Hills Country Club near Detroit, the question hung in the air, the greatest golf puzzle of its time. The Americans had more victories in the major championships among them, had greater names and stood higher in the World Ranking, and thus were favored. So how could the Europeans not only beat them but thoroughly wallop them? People could give the usual arguments — team chemistry, European togetherness, American overconfidence — but they might as well read tea leaves or the stars. Toms, who went 1-2-0 in this playing, just might have touched on the answer.

Maybe it started when the Americans' Friday punch, the pairing of Tiger Woods and Phil Mickelson, turned into a pillow fight. Maybe when they lost the first match on the first day, the other guys got that sinking feeling that it was happening all over again, and everyone went flat. The way Toms put it later: "When you're getting beat so bad, it's hard to sleep at night. Every day, you just don't quite feel up for the next day, like you should. You're not as confident as you should be." It seemed he was talking about a team that had gone flat.

Colin Montgomerie and Padraig Harrington beat Woods and Mickelson in the Friday morning four-ball (better-ball, as the Americans call it). Then American captain Hal Sutton stuck with them for the Friday afternoon foursomes (alternate shot) and this time it was Darren Clarke and Lee Westwood who beat them. One got the feeling that European captain Bernhard Langer would have liked to pass them around to give all of his guys a crack at them.

Could the answer possibly be that simple? Probably not. But does anyone have a better answer? Except for the obvious one — the Europeans can sure play this game.

Europe then rolled to an 18½-to-9½ victory, the Americans' worst loss in the 77-year history of the competition. And although the Americans haven't lost much in that span (their match record is 24-9-2 overall), it's the "modern" Ryder Cup that counts. That began in 1979 when the Great Britain-Ireland side was expanded to include all of Europe so that the matches could be competitive. So Europe is now 4-1 since 1995 and 6-3-1 since 1985.

For Americans looking for villains and for Europeans looking for heroes, look no further than the British bookmakers and Bernhard Langer. The bookmakers because they keep making the Americans the favorites and so it always looks like an upset, and Langer for the uncanny way in which he made his pairings and scheduled his players. It's almost as if he knew that Sutton would pair Woods and Mickelson and send them out first for that knockout. Sutton was criticized for this pairing on two points: First, that Woods and Mickelson did not mix, and if team golf is helped by good chemistry, there would be none here. Second, paired together they were worth one point at the most, but split up and paired with others, they could fetch two. And worst of all — this is conjecture, of course — they were potentially a three-point crash. If they got beat, they not only lost that point, they also would have lost the other two that each might have won if they had been split up. And as for chemistry, every one of the millions of television viewers around the world could see that Woods and Mickelson barely spoke in their two matches that first day and that Woods kept his distance.

The situation was fractured from the start when Mickelson missed two days with the U.S. team. He didn't practice with them on Wednesday because, he said, it's part of his routine not to practice on Wednesday before a major championship. He also missed practice with the team on Thursday. Sutton said he was across the road on Oakland Hills' North Course practicing with Tiger Woods' Nike brand of golf balls for the Friday foursomes, in which two players play one ball brand. Sutton said the team understood and took no umbrage to either absence.

A number of other forces were at play in the American camp. First, Woods was having — for him — a down year. He had won once, the WGC - Accenture Match Play in February. He had only flashes of his old self in stroke play. It was a year of frustration while he was remaking his swing. Mickelson was enjoying a very fine year. Having undergone some changes of his own, he finally broke through and won his first major title, the Masters, and he came close in the other three. But he switched from Titleist to Callaway golf clubs just two weeks before the Ryder Cup (and, for that matter, just over a month from the end of the PGA Tour season). He would start playing with the Callaway driver and two fairway woods and golf ball at the Ryder Cup. Many believe it takes longer than two weeks to adjust to new clubs. It seems Mickelson proved them right. He was hitting the ball all over the place. He had his worst Ryder Cup in five playings, going 1-3-0. Would a different pairing have helped? Sutton critics noted that David Toms was on the team, and he and Mickelson went 2-1-1 in 2002.

Others were more concerned about the "slump" Tiger Woods was in. Or "lull," as some would prefer. Did Langer see that as a key to the matches?

"I don't feel he's the key to the team," Langer said. "The team is 12 players. One player is not going to be the key. You can only play him five times, and even if he wins every point, that only gives him five points. They need 14½ to win the cup, so that explains it already. You need more than one player."

As for Langer as hero or villain? His pairings turned out to be brilliant and his order of play uncanny the way they matched up, and no more so than the one on opening day. First off, clearly, he divined that Sutton would not resist the temptation to open up with both of his big guns, sending out Woods and Mickelson to lead off the Ryder Cup in the Friday morning four-ball. Sutton explained later that the world wanted to see this pairing. At all events, Langer sent out Montgomerie, the great Ryder Cup fire horse, and Harrington. And the rout was on.

Monty set a Ryder Cup record, playing in his 29th consecutive match, and he marked this one by beating Woods and Mickelson a lot more easily than the 2-and-1 score. They opened with four straight birdies, and only two offsetting birdies by Woods held down the damage. And Montgomerie was now 13-2-3 in his last 18 Ryder Cup matches. "Psychologically, it was almost worth two points to us," he said. "I think it's important for the other guys to see us ahead early on."

Darren Clarke and Miguel Angel Jimenez were 3 up after five holes, 4 up at the turn, and raced to a 5-and-4 victory over Davis Love and Chad Campbell, who failed to win a hole. Then came Sergio Garcia, the young Spaniard. If Montgomerie was the heart of the European team, the lively Garcia was the spirit. He teamed with Lee Westwood, and they lost only two holes en route to swamping Toms and Jim Furyk, 5 and 4.

The only thing that kept the Americans from being swept in the morning was the halve that Stewart Cink and Chris Riley wrested from Luke Donald and Paul McGinley. Cink squared the match with a birdie at the 15th, and Riley preserved the halve with a six-foot putt for par at the 18th.

"I pulled him aside before he talked to anybody," Sutton said, "and I said, 'You understand one thing — you, Chris Riley, kept the Americans from getting skunked. Not Tiger Woods or Phil Mickelson. You, Chris Riley, kept that from happening.'"

"Hal said that half-point might be the difference come Sunday afternoon," Riley said. And then the question of team feelings came up, a reference to the famed European reputation for togetherness. "Our team is as tight as I've ever seen," Riley said. "I've seen a lot of team sports, and I feel like these guys are my brothers almost. I think they are my family." And it was a far more composed Riley than the one who started out. The question was on Ryder Cup pressure. Riley spoke of stepping out on the first tee. "My knees were about to buckle," he said.

Said Langer, "To have the biggest lead we've ever had after the first day is just incredible and awesome and fantastic." Montgomerie put it another way. Said Monty, "It's been a super morning."

And indeed it had. Europe was leading, 3½-½.

Things got only fractionally better for the Americans in the afternoon foursomes (or alternate shot). This time they won a full point, but lost the afternoon's play 3-1. The match everyone was watching was No. 3 — Woods and Mickelson again, this time against Darren Clarke and Lee Westwood — and at last it seemed the Dream Team had found its legs. With a birdie at the second hole followed by back-to-back European bogeys, they were 3 up through the fifth. The cavalry had arrived! Not quite. Their lead bled away, and they fell behind at the 11th. They scrambled back to all-square with a par at the 17th. Now came a chance for a win. Mickelson, with his new clubs, was on the tee. He hit a huge slice that ended up next to an out-of-bounds fence. The television camera zeroed in on Woods and his face said it all: What on earth was that? Now it was his turn. He had to take a penalty drop. The Europeans were struggling with the hole. Clarke was short with his approach shot, Westwood was weak with his chip, and they two-putted for a bogey five. But that bogey won the hole and the match. "I let it slide on 18 with a poor tee shot," Mickelson said. "And it basically cost us the match."

Earlier in the week, Mickelson defended his move to switch brands of golf clubs. "I could have waited until the end of next year," he said, "but

I felt that it was in my best interests and the best interests of the team that I do this now."

Best interests of the team? someone countered. Because there are some people questioning your timing and your commitment to the team. "Why?" Mickelson said. "Why would they question that? I've been looking forward to this event for a long time. I feel that I am most confident that my ability to score lowest is now." That didn't seem to be the case after play started. A sympathetic Westwood came to Mickelson's defense. "Everybody is entitled to make a bad swing once in a while," he said. "He just made it in a critical situation."

But Sutton, Mickelson's captain, wasn't that sympathetic. Later, someone asked him whether the change in clubs had contributed to Mickelson's problems. Sutton was as blunt as a sledgehammer. "We'll all be left scratching our heads on that," he said. "We'll all want answers on that. But the most important person that's going to have to wonder about that is going to be Phil Mickelson." And then he added, "It's not going to cause us any grief in the morning because he's going to be cheering instead of playing."

Big Lefty, the Masters champion, had just got benched, and he didn't know it yet. Sutton told the whole world before telling him.

Mickelson was a cheerleader, if a quiet one, on Saturday morning. He was tired. "Well, I didn't sleep," he said. "It was a brutal night. I think Hal and the team put a lot of faith in Tiger and me to play well — and I didn't. I looked at some of the pictures as we walked down the fairway, and boy, I was so tight. I was tighter than I played all year."

FIRST DAY
Morning Fourballs

Colin Montgomerie and Padraig Harrington (Europe) defeated Phil Mickelson and Tiger Woods (USA), 2 and 1.
Darren Clarke and Miguel Angel Jimenez (Europe) defeated Davis Love and Chad Campbell (USA), 5 and 4.
Paul McGinley and Luke Donald (Europe) halved with Chris Riley and Stewart Cink (USA).
Sergio Garcia and Lee Westwood (Europe) defeated David Toms and Jim Furyk (USA), 5 and 3.

TOTAL: Europe 3½, United States ½

Afternoon Foursomes

Chris DiMarco and Jay Haas (USA) defeated Miguel Angel Jimenez and Thomas Levet (Europe), 3 and 2.
Colin Montgomerie and Padraig Harrington (Europe) defeated Davis Love and Fred Funk (USA), 4 and 2.
Darren Clarke and Lee Westwood (Europe) defeated Phil Mickelson and Tiger Woods (USA), 1 up.
Sergio Garcia and Luke Donald (Europe) defeated Kenny Perry and Stewart Cink (USA), 2 and 1.

TOTAL: Europe 6½, United States 1½

At the end of Black Friday, American captain Hal Sutton met the media and said, "Well, we made history today." The European team, with that 6½-to-1½ performance, had taken the largest first-day lead of their history. Sutton might have been equal parts puzzled and angry, but it was more like one percent puzzled, the rest angry, and possibly the focus was on Mickelson — the Masters champion, second in the U.S. Open, third in the Open and tied for sixth in the PGA Championship. And possibly, if one could hear from a fly on the wall in the American enclave, maybe last in the hearts of his countrymen for changing brands of golf clubs so close to the big event.

Sutton's battlefield analysis: "My impression," he said, "is it looked like they [the Europeans] were trying to make something happen and we were trying to make sure we didn't have anything bad happen."

The Americans, facing that five-point deficit, held a bit of a revolution in the Saturday morning four-ball matches. In fact, it looked for a while like a reversal, for 3½ points. But then it got put down by another one of those inspired Langer pairings.

First, Sergio Garcia and Lee Westwood rallied for a halve against Chris DiMarco and Jay Haas, who held a 1-up lead until the 11th, when Garcia squared the match with a birdie. They halved in from there. Garcia got the halve in spectacular fashion. He had a 45-foot putt that had to go up and over a huge mound, then down toward the cup. The putt also had about 25 feet of break in it. It would seem he was hoping for a good lag putt, at best. He also was trying to give a good read to Westwood, who waited on the other side of the green. The ball made the big sweeping trip and then fell in the hole. They halved in bogeys.

"He said he was going to hit it over the hill and show me the line," Westwood said. "And then he knocked it over the hill, and about that far away I knew where not to hit it after that."

"You know, I think the wheels were coming off all four of us coming in," Haas said.

Then came a spark for the Americans.

Sutton had paired Woods with Chris Riley, a rookie, and they enjoyed a 4-and-3 romp over Darren Clarke and Ian Poulter. Woods and Riley had been pals in junior golf, but now, Riley said, "Getting paired with the best player in the world ... I pretty much free-wheeled it out there because I knew I was going to have a backup." Some security blanket. Riley made four birdies, all of them to win holes. His first was for a 2-up lead after Woods, smarting under an 0-2 record, made a statement of intent at the first hole. He crushed his drive over 300 yards, setting up a par for a 1-up lead. They never trailed.

Then came a bit of light comedy at the par-five second. Riley was off the back of the green in a tough lie. Woods was about 12 feet from the cup and Darren Clarke about 10. "You know what?" Riley said to Woods. "I'm going to hole it." And he almost did, chipping his ball into the slope to kill the momentum. It rolled to within a foot of the cup and earned him a hand slap from Woods, then a birdie.

The Langer surprise pairing put together rookies Paul Casey and David Howell in their first action. It seemed that Langer was willing to give up a point not to disturb other pairings. Langer insisted they weren't throwaways.

"I really deep down felt that they would be the surprise of the morning," he said. He didn't say so, but perhaps he reasoned it this way: First, he wanted all of his rookies to see some action before the singles. Next, he could split them up and pair each with a veteran, but that could cost two points. If he kept them together, and didn't disturb his other pairings, the most he could lose with them was one. Of course, there was always the chance they could win.

Langer was right about that. They edged into a 1-up lead over Jim Furyk and Chad Campbell, himself a rookie, on Howell's birdie at the sixth, and got to 2 up on Casey's birdie at the 10th. Then Furyk ran off three straight birdies from the 11th hole to give the Americans their first lead at the 13th. At the 15th, Howell hit his approach to three feet for a birdie to square it, and Campbell holed a 35-foot birdie putt at the 16th for a 1-up American lead. At the 17th, Howell faced both one of the toughest par-threes in the game and the prospect of losing. Unfazed, he fired his tee shot to five feet and then coolly sank the putt to square the match.

At the 18th, Howell took himself out of the hole with a poor tee shot, and Casey hit far to the right side of the green. The rookies were in danger of losing this one. Campbell was just short of the green and chose to chip through about six feet of fringe instead of putting. His chip raced eight feet past the hole and he bogeyed. Casey had looped his 40-footer close and summoned Howell. "Very rarely," Casey allowed, "do I get somebody else to help me look at the line on a two-footer." He holed it for the win. The American uprising had been put down. The rookies did it. Everything Langer touched was turning to gold.

"A little nerve-wracking, a little scary," Casey said. "We were nervous on the first tee. I think it's only justice, really. We really played our hearts out and we put up with a lot of noise out there. But it was great to finally get a break. We hung in there and I think we deserved it." How to play the nerve game with rookies? Said Casey, "We were told by Bernhard not to look at the board unless it's full of blue. But how do you know if it's full of blue unless you look at the board? So unfortunately, we knew what was going on." And finally, the sense of belonging. "The first Ryder Cup point — that's the main thing," Casey said. "You want to come through for your captain, and you've got to play your first match sometime. And to play a tough match and to come out on top is fantastic."

And there was every reason to believe that Langer had paired them as a throwaway gamble. "We were told yesterday that if we played, we probably wouldn't be playing with another rookie," Casey said. So Langer's bold move was a late-bloomer. As Howell put it, "You could see we were having a tough day as a team, so we were a little light at the end of the tunnel."

Montgomerie and Harrington were starting to look like an unbeatable pair, but that was until they ran into Stewart Cink and Davis Love in the Saturday morning four-ball. The Americans were in great shape, 3 up coming to the 15th tee. It seemed the match was about to be extended, what with Cink facing a curling 25-foot putt that didn't offer much hope for a birdie. But he rolled it in, and he and Love locked up a 3-and-2 win. But the American uprising was over. They won the morning four-ball, 2½ to 1½, but heading into the afternoon foursomes, Europe led by 8 to 4.

The Americans won just one of the afternoon matches, and interestingly enough, it was the Mickelson and Toms pairing, the one that worked so well in 2002. Mickelson, returning from the morning exile, and Toms had little trouble. Once they took the lead, they were never headed or square. They took the lead at the sixth, where Mickelson hit Toms' tee ball to nine feet and Toms holed it for a birdie. At the par-five 12th, Toms blasted out of a greenside bunker to eight inches for a conceded birdie, and at the par-three 13th, it was Mickelson's tee shot to 18 feet and Toms' birdie putt for a 3-up lead. It ended at the par-four 15th on Mickelson's chip to two feet, setting up Toms' winning par for a 4-and-3 win.

The Europeans led off in the first match with Clarke and Westwood breezing, 5 and 4, over Haas and DiMarco, who won just one hole and that with their only birdie. In a youth pairing, Garcia, the veteran at 24, took Donald, the 26-year-old rookie, under his wing in a 1-up win over Jim Furyk and Fred Funk, the latter seeing his first action. The Americans made it interesting toward the end. They left the 14th hole 3 down. They cut that to 2 down on Funk's birdie at the 15th, and then to 1 down with a birdie at the 17th off Furyk's tee shot to three feet. They halved the 18th for the European 1-up win.

Finally the day ended with an Irish party that also marked the peak of American frustration. But it was also marked by one of the stranger things to happen at a Ryder Cup. Sutton had found a winning combination in Tiger Woods and Chris Riley, and so stuck with it for the Saturday afternoon foursomes. But Riley begged off. "I've never played alternate shot," Riley said, "and to tell the truth, I'm really tired and I want to be fresh and ready to go tomorrow morning [in singles]."

Sutton, himself a veteran of four Ryder Cups (7-5-4), was stunned. "I told him, 'Look, a 42-year-old fat man in '99 [himself] went five straight matches, so I'm sure that a 30-year-old flatbelly that's hyper can go four, can't ya?'" Sutton said. Then Sutton thought the better of pressing the issue. "If he's tired and he just doesn't feel like it," Sutton said, "well then, I'm not sure he can help us as much as somebody who is really energetic about going out there." And so Sutton sent out Davis Love with Woods.

In that final foursomes match of the day, Woods and Love were leading but couldn't hold on against the Irish pair of Padraig Harrington and Paul McGinley. The Americans went to 2 up with an eagle at the par-five second on a flash of power. Love drove into the fairway and Woods hit the flagstick with the second shot, the ball stopping about six feet away and setting up the eagle. The Irish got a stroke back with a birdie at the fourth, then squared it at the eighth when Woods hit the second shot from the fairway to 50 feet, setting up a bogey. The Irish won Nos. 9, 11 and 13 on pars and came to the 15th with a chance to close out the match. McGinley fired his approach to just five feet from the hole, setting up the conceded birdie for the 4-and-3 win. McGinley and Harrington were greeted by a sea of countrymen, many wrapped in the flag.

"That scene around the 15th green when we finished, with all the Irish there, was something I'll always remember," McGinley said. And maybe so would Sutton and his team. The Europeans, now leading 11 to 5, were looking at a Sunday of singles that wasn't a mere formality, but it was close. And when the European performance came up at an interview, Sergio

Garcia took the opportunity to twit the media corps. "Believe it or not," he said, "there's people that can play golf outside the States."

SECOND DAY
Morning Fourballs

Sergio Garcia and Lee Westwood (Europe) halved with Jay Haas and Chris DiMarco (USA).
Tiger Woods and Chris Riley (USA) defeated Darren Clarke and Ian Poulter (Europe), 4 and 3.
Paul Casey and David Howell (Europe) defeated Jim Furyk and Chad Campbell (USA), 1 up.
Stewart Cink and Davis Love (USA) defeated Colin Montgomerie and Padraig Harrington (Europe), 3 and 2.

TOTAL: Europe 8, United States 4

Afternoon Foursomes

Darren Clarke and Lee Westwood (Europe) defeated Jay Haas and Chris DiMarco (USA), 5 and 4.
Phil Mickelson and David Toms (USA) defeated Miguel Angel Jimenez and Thomas Levet (Europe), 4 and 3.
Sergio Garcia and Luke Donald (Europe) defeated Jim Furyk and Fred Funk (USA), 1 up.
Padraig Harrington and Paul McGinley (Europe) defeated Davis Love and Tiger Woods (USA), 4 and 3.

TOTAL: Europe 11, United States 5

It was all over but the final counting.

U.S. captain Hal Sutton was discussing his singles order with the media, and he was about as relaxed and warm and open as a guy could be on the way to a wake. The Europeans were leading, 11 to 5, going into the final-day singles. They would need only three points to retain the Ryder Cup with a tie and 3½ points to win the match outright. Someone pointed out that his singles lineup had Tiger Woods leading off, Phil Mickelson second, Davis Love third, and so on down the list of the World Ranking.

"I'm proud of you," Sutton said, chuckling. "You noticed that." Someone else asked about this "front-loading." "How about a deficit of this order?" Sutton said. "That had a lot to do with it."

Said European captain Bernhard Langer at his conservative best, "We are obviously extremely happy where we are at the moment, but we still have another tough day."

The optimist could look at it this way: All the Americans needed to do to take this Ryder Cup was win nine of the 12 singles matches. And when the singles got under way Sunday morning, it seemed that's exactly where the Americans were heading. The scoreboard was awash in red, the color for the Americans, and the European blue just peeked out here and there. A grand counterattack was on.

The Americans ripped through the first two matches. Woods came up swinging and zipped past Paul Casey, 3 and 2, without losing a hole, to give the Americans the first point of the day. Woods set off the crowd at the par-five 12th, reaching the green in two shots and making the eagle. Jim Furyk followed with a 6-and-4 rout of David Howell, and the magical rookies of Saturday had been swept. Howell bogeyed his first two holes and won only one, the 11th, on Furyk's bogey. Furyk rebounded with a birdie at the 13th and an eagle at the 14th to end it.

Worse for the Europeans, the spirited Garcia, their young hero, was getting beaten by Mickelson. Neither was playing well. Mickelson was still finding the trees, but Garcia was in rough, trees, bunkers. In fact, he was bunkered on his first three holes, and at the par-four eighth, he was even hitting off a cart path, raising memories of Seve Ballesteros. And he was only 2 down. "A bit shaky on the front nine," Garcia said. "A couple holes there. But I really felt like I hit a lot of quality shots and made some nice putts when I had to." Then something clicked back into place. He birdied Nos. 9, 10 and 11 to edge into the lead. At the par-three 13th, he went 2 up on Mickelson's bogey and stayed there. The match ended when Mickelson, trying a desperate low, running hook at the 16th, caught the water instead. It was the pivotal match of the singles. Garcia, getting his first singles point in three Ryder Cups, won, 3 and 2. He had stopped the bleeding. Europe now led, 12-7.

The Americans would scrape up just 2½ more points. Darren Clarke rallied from 2 down with three holes to play to scrape out a halve with Davis Love. Clarke hit a magnificent approach to the 16th and holed the putt for a winning birdie and cut his deficit to one. He chipped in at the par-three 17th for a birdie to square the match, and they halved the 18th. In a display of sportsmanship at the 18th, Love declined to take advantage of the rules. His tee shot was in thick rough near a sprinkler head, and he might have improved his lie if he would take a free drop for relief. But Love declined, saying that the sprinkler head wouldn't interfere with the shot he was tying to hit. Instead of being able to go for the green, he had to be content with chopping the ball out with a wedge, and he and Clarke ended up halving the hole in bogeys.

Then Clarke and Love sat down side-by-side at the 18th and lit up cigars. Said Clarke, "It's tough when you're playing against a real good friend. And I'm smoking his cigars that he brought me up here this week."

Said Love, "He'll be needling me for two years about this."

The Americans then won two more matches. Chad Campbell took the lead at the third hole and ground out a 5-and-3 win over Luke Donald. Chris DiMarco never got the lead on Miguel Angel Jimenez until the 14th, and after Jimenez squared it at the 15th, DiMarco went ahead to stay at the 16th for a 1-up win. At 2-1-1 in his rookie year, he was the only American with a winning record. Tiger Woods also had two wins, but he had three losses.

All other things being equal, the first goal in the Ryder Cup is to retain it. In the event of a tie, the winning team gets to keep the trophy until the next time. It was Lee Westwood, playing against Kenny Perry, who clinched at least a tie. Perry was 2 up through the seventh, but Westwood slowly made his way back and finally took the lead for good with a par at the

15th. But Perry wasn't going to go quietly. At the 18th, he holed a 15-foot putt for his par four, leaving Westwood with the task of topping him for the win. And Westwood did. So the cup was safely in hand, although it would have to be shared unless a teammate dictated otherwise. And that teammate was in the script, bigger than life, and he was in the very next match.

The picture will go down in Ryder Cup annals — Colin Montgomerie, putter fallen at his feet, hands uplifted, a beaming smile on his face. He had just won the Ryder Cup.

The great dramatist in Bernhard Langer had come out. This was the man who paired rookies Paul Casey and David Howell in the four-ball Saturday, leaving them to sink or swim. And they won. And then Montgomerie — age 41, the oldest player on the European team, and his very own captain's pick. He scheduled Monty sixth in the singles, just about the spot where the Europeans should about wrap it up. And what better piece of theater than to let Monty win it? And he did.

Montgomerie was leading David Toms 1 up coming down the 18th fairway. From 185 yards out, he put a six iron on the back of the green. He lagged the putt down to about four feet, and then, with the whole world watching, he holed it, matching Toms' par. The ball dropped at 4:37 p.m. There was the Ryder Cup.

Monty, playing in his seventh Ryder Cup, found himself a hero once again. And he rejected the credit. "Personally, it means nothing, okay?" he insisted. "This is all about a team event. Personally, it means nothing to me. I've said that many times." This was the same Monty who earlier in the week was saying, "Dramatic, isn't it? But it always seems to happen to me, doesn't it?"

Langer laughed. No, he didn't put Montgomerie sixth so that he could win it. "I had no clue who would make the winning point," he said. "I was hoping we would make it even sooner."

"I didn't know I was in this team until half an hour before the selection was made," Montgomerie said. "But I knew Bernhard would get this team together and to play for each other, and that's what we did. That's what I'd like to thank Bernhard for, and also for picking me." Montgomerie had let it be known that he would like to be the Ryder Cup captain some day. "He's too young to be a captain," said Langer. "He needs to play. You agree, Monty? Come on, say the truth." And, of course, Monty didn't rule out the possibility that he would be on the European team in 2006, at age 43.

"There's plenty of time to be a captain, possibly," said Montgomerie, who went 3-1-0 in this Ryder Cup, running his career record to 19-8-5. "It's been a difficult time to get to this stage this particular year, and I'm only glad that Bernhard had some faith in me, and I'm only glad that I managed to perform half-decent and help the team cause. And if I can do that again, I'd be delighted to do that."

And so it was over and in the books — Europe 18½, U.S. 9½.

It was time for the post-mortems.

"I'm disappointed," said Love. "Tigers Woods, Phil Mickelson and Davis Love are supposed to play great and none of us did."

Thomas Levet, a rookie posting a 1-2-0 record after beating fellow rookie

Fred Funk in singles, spoke of European unity. "We are not individuals, we are a team," he said. "And it doesn't matter who hits it well, who plays bad. It's just a team. I didn't put a point on the board before today and I feel like I put 20 points on it." Montgomerie said the European secret was strength. "We had strength at the top this morning, we had strength in the middle, and we had strength at the bottom," he said. "That's the first time I could say that."

But weren't things bound to change? someone wondered. "They may not," said American rookie Kenny Perry. "We may just keep losing."

"The truth is, the Europeans were the best players this week," said Hal Sutton. "So I'm going to live with it. I'm going to move on. I'm going to hug my kid tomorrow and everything will be great."

Langer got the tough question: Was this the best European team ever? "That's a very difficult question to answer," Langer said. "It might as well be the best. But I certainly think we have far more depth than we ever had on the teams I played on. We could have come here with 18 or 20 guys and given the Americans a good show."

So the Europeans left Oakland Hills tied with the U.S. at 6-6-1 in the modern Ryder Cup, dating to 1979. But more to the point for the Americans, Europe left with a 4-1 record over the last five. And so the Americans returned to their homes beaten and swamped with questions, criticism and advice. By December, the PGA of America, which runs the American side, announced a new method of selecting the U.S. team for the 2006 Ryder Cup in Ireland. It's an involved thing that adjusts the points for various events and puts the emphasis on the Ryder Cup year itself instead of both years in between. And maybe one other crucial change will take place.

"I don't think we'll be the favorite next time," Phil Mickelson said. "No matter what the World Ranking says, I think we'll be the underdog. And hopefully, we'll play like they have."

THIRD DAY
Singles

Tiger Woods (USA) defeated Paul Casey (Europe), 3 and 2.
Sergio Garcia (Europe) defeated Phil Mickelson (USA), 3 and 2.
Darren Clarke (Europe) halved with Davis Love (USA).
Jim Furyk (USA) defeated David Howell (Europe), 6 and 4.
Lee Westwood (Europe) defeated Kenny Perry (USA), 1 up.
Colin Montgomerie (Europe) defeated David Toms (USA), 1 up.
Chad Campbell (USA) defeated Luke Donald (Europe), 5 and 3.
Chris DiMarco (USA) defeated Miguel Angel Jimenez (Europe), 1 up.
Thomas Levet (Europe) defeated Fred Funk (USA), 1 up.
Ian Poulter (Europe) defeated Chris Riley (USA), 3 and 2.
Padraig Harrington (Europe) defeated Jay Haas (USA), 1 up.
Paul McGinley (Europe) defeated Stewart Cink (USA), 3 and 2.

TOTAL: Europe 18½, United States 9½

8. HSBC World Match Play

Whether it is trying to defeat him over 36 holes of the West Course or try-ing to sell him a house, there is no greater competitor to face at Wentworth than Ernie Els. Take the estate agent who showed Els and his wife, Liezl, around properties on the Surrey estate six years ago. "As soon as we came through the gates of this one house I said to Liezl, 'Don't get too excited, but this is it.' I didn't want to tip off the estate agent, but that was the one. We've done a lot to the house since then, but it's really home now."

With daughter Samantha going to school locally and son Ben to follow suit, Wentworth has become the Els' principle residence, ahead of those in Orlando, Florida, the Bahamas and George, South Africa. Els said, "Away from South Africa, this is definitely the closest to being home, I would say. I've got a lot of friends over here and I truly feel a sense of support from the people in the crowd when I play here. I think it helps when you have a home in England. They can relate to that and I can relate to them."

Wentworth has become no stranger to celebrations of Els' golfing success and another fine old time was had when, on the day of his 35th birthday, he retained his HSBC World Match Play title. The win gave Els a hat-trick of victories for the second time and a total of six triumphs in all, taking him one ahead of the five collected by both Gary Player and Seve Ballesteros. "Gary has still got me with the majors, but it is nice to get one record off him," Els said.

A 2-and-1 victory over a sickly Lee Westwood in the final brought Els' record in the championship to 22 wins out of 26 matches. His first match was against Ballesteros in 1994 and he still reckons it is the best he has been involved in. "Seve was tough. It's a good job he is not still around," Els said. But Els won it and all of his first 11 before losing at the 36th hole to Vijay Singh in the 1997 final when he was attempting to win a fourth successive title. "I remember thinking about the record that day and it backfired on me," Els admitted. The result triggered a run of four defeats in five matches, including two to Westwood and one to his semi-final opponent, Padraig Harrington. Now he has won the last 10 matches. How does he keep doing it?

"You know, I am competitive," Els said. "I really don't like losing, believe me. I know exactly how Lee feels at the moment. That's not a good feeling to have, believe me. So that is really the driving force, to try and do whatever you can to win without being obsessed. You want to be competitive and take your game and say, 'Here I am, what are you going to do to beat me.'

"I think in many ways my first match this year was almost the most dif-ficult against Scott Drummond. I've never played him; if he gets hot, you never know what to expect. But the other players, I kind of know what to expect. I can apply pressure the same way they try and apply pressure to me, and that's the name of the game in match play. You need to keep firing away. You can't get despondent. In these kind of matches, over 36 holes, you've got all day. Look at Lee. At lunch he started getting a bit sick, which is to my benefit and negative to him.

"A lot of things can happen in a full day's golf. You have to keep your nerve all day. You have to be aggressive at times, but you have to be patient a lot more than in 18-hole matches. When you have 18-hole matches, you'll see some guys get lucky and beat guys that might be playing a little better."

From a certain perspective, Els played some of the best golf during 2004 but was not rewarded in the major championships. He was beaten by Phil Mickelson's birdie at the last hole to win the Masters Tournament. He played alongside countryman Retief Goosen in the final pairing on the last day of the U.S. Open Championship but crashed to an 80. He lost a four-hole playoff to Todd Hamilton for The Open Championship at Royal Troon and finished only one stroke outside the playoff won by Singh at the PGA Championship. To get so close but fail to add to his three major titles did not sit well with the South African at first.

But then Els went away and cleared his head. "It's history, I'm moving forward," he said to himself. When he returned he won the WGC American Express Championship at Mount Juliet and two weeks later claimed the HSBC World Match Play crown again. "Three weeks ago I was complaining about all kinds of stuff and now, you know, I've won twice in three weeks," Els said. "I'm definitely eating my words at the moment. It's turning out to be a great season. If I can keep up this standard, I'll have some good years to come. If I can keep going the way I'm going, I'll be fine."

For the 41st staging of the championship and the second under HSBC's sponsorship, the field was expanded to 16 players. The format had evolved so that there were 12 players, with the top four seeds getting a bye into the quarter-finals on Friday. For the finalists, it meant the most grueling week of the season, with eight rounds in four days. The compensation was £1 million to the winner. For the first time, a proportion of that also counted towards the European Tour's money list, which Els clinched for the second year in succession. There were also World Ranking points on offer, and while Els maintained his No. 2 spot, behind Singh but ahead of Tiger Woods, by reaching the final, Westwood moved back into the world's top 30.

It was the first time, however, that Els had been required to play on the opening Thursday. "I guess they want us to really work for our money this week," he said with a grin. "They've been good to me all of these years by seeding me, but why not play the whole field? It's good for television, it's good for the spectators. For that prize money, I think it is fine."

Although there were a couple of high-profile absentees — Woods and Mickelson — five of the top eight in the World Ranking were present along with three of the major champions, Goosen, Hamilton and Singh. The Fijian had just taken over from Woods as the world No. 1. He was seeded second here behind the defending champion, and an Els-Singh final would have been an intriguing prospect. "It would be great," Els said when asked about the possibility on the eve of the championship. "One and two in the world, I would love to see that happen. But," he added, "I wouldn't mind seeing him taken out before the final."

No one was seeing anyone play on Thursday morning as a storm delayed play for two and a half hours. In a week of wet weather, this was the wettest. It meant of the eight first-round matches, only one was to finish that day. It took a record performance by Goosen to get a result declared, as he dismissed Jeff Maggert 12 and 11, the biggest winning margin ever in the event.

Following his win at Shinnecock Hills, Goosen had injured his pelvis in a jet ski accident and, given the considerable surface water at Wentworth that day, he might have been powered by such a machine. Maggert, who won the 18-hole version of the Accenture Match Play at La Costa in its first year in 1999, qualified to play here for the first time by finishing third in the U.S. Open. But his recent golf had been restricted by the birth of his twins and he did not win a single hole.

Six bogeys in the first nine holes handed a 6-up lead to Goosen, whose first 18 holes amounted to an approximate round of 65. By that stage he was 10 up, matching the record lunchtime margin set by Tom Watson against Dale Hayes in 1978 and equaled by Mark O'Meara against Singh 20 years later.

At the short second hole, Goosen hit an eight iron to seven feet for his first birdie in the morning and then at the same hole in the afternoon hit the same club even closer, holing from four feet to go 11 up. When he holed a putt from off the green at the seventh he beat O'Meara's record 11-and-10 win over Singh. "I felt like I was going to win, it was just by how much," Goosen said. "Jeff was not at his best and I tried to stay focused in the afternoon."

Els faced the lowest ranked player in the field, the world No. 118, Scott Drummond. The 30-year-old from Shropshire, via Scottish parents, won the Volvo PGA Championship at Wentworth earlier in May to propel the European Tour rookie onto the global scene. In May, Drummond had stayed in an inexpensive hotel with his wife, Claire, and their then one-month-old baby, Kiera. This time they stayed next door, in five-star luxury. Drummond won the first hole, when Els bogeyed, and was either 1 or 2 up for the first 19 holes.

But at the second hole in the afternoon, Els holed from six feet to draw even, and then at the next, with Drummond in trouble, birdied again to take the lead. It was at the fourth that Els showed he would not lie down quietly. Drummond hit a fine five iron to two feet, but the South African, from short of the green, chipped in for a half in eagles. Els eased ahead but could not clinch the victory, and when darkness fell, it was conveniently at the 16th green, just a few steps from his home.

They required just one hole the following morning for Els to complete a 2-and-1 win. "Scott showed a lot of character and certainly made a match of it," Els said. "I'm just happy to get through." With spectators only just arriving at the course, there followed a succession of results. Angel Cabrera defeated Korea's K.J. Choi at the last hole, while Padraig Harrington beat Chris Riley, the only American Ryder Cup player present, 2 and 1. They had resumed at all-square with four holes to play, but at the 15th Harrington holed from 20 feet and Riley missed from 12.

"Whoever struck first was going to have a huge advantage," Harrington said. "Fortunately, it was me." The Irishman won the next hole and Riley succumbed at the 17th, where Mike Weir then went out of bounds to hand a 2-and-1 win to Thomas Levet, one of four members of the victorious European Ryder Cup playing in the championship. The other two also won, with Miguel Angel Jimenez beating Steve Flesch, 3 and 2, and Lee Westwood overcoming Hamilton, 4 and 3. This had been a tightly fought match on Thursday until late in the day, when the afternoon's watery sunshine had given way to rain once again, and Westwood had won three holes in a row.

Hamilton, in fact, had won the sixth and seventh of the second round to get back to all-square, but the eighth was halved with Westwood holing from 30 feet and Hamilton from 12 feet. "It felt like a win rather than a half for me, and that seemed to be the turning point," Westwood said. He immediately won the next three holes and finished the match swiftly the next morning.

For the winning European Ryder Cup captain, Bernhard Langer, to follow the example of his charges from Oakland Hills, the German had to beat Singh. The difference in their ages, 47 to 41, was not as marked as in their World Ranking, 86th to first. Langer had spent the time since the Ryder Cup talking about the victory with all those who wanted to ask him about it and plowing through the mountain of correspondence that had arrived at his office in Florida. He had not played for a month, when he had missed the cut, and had been unable to recapture his fine early season form following a wrist injury in mid-season.

Yet, by winning three holes in a row late on Thursday, Langer was 3 up. He lost the 26th but was still 2 up with 10 to play overnight. Singh won the 10th hole with a birdie but lost the next and saw Langer hole from over 35 feet at the 14th to return to 3 up. But as the gallery swelled as the players neared home, Singh almost pulled off a remarkable recovery. He birdied the next three holes and almost four in a row, but his putt for victory at the last, where he had been in the trees and then crashed into the greenside hospitality unit, just missed.

They returned to the 17th for the first extra hole, and despite its being a long par-five, it was Langer who found the green in two and won with a birdie four to a par five. "It reminded me of the old Bible story when little David beat Goliath," Langer said. "He was the hot favorite, but I played fairly well and I am always tremendously motivated."

There was to be no Els-Singh final, then, but Els himself had his hands full and in the quarter-finals only defeated Cabrera at the 36th hole. Els had not been at his best, admitting to snatching the club at the takeaway and trying to swing too hard as if he was still at St. Andrews, where he had played the previous week.

He twice went out of bounds on the 17th in the morning and was trailing again after 18 holes, but won the 17th in the afternoon and, although Cabrera almost chipped in at the last for an eagle, Els holed from nine feet for the match. "I wasn't playing all that well, but I started swinging the club as I wanted to in the afternoon and hit a lot of good shots down the stretch," he said. "It was a tough match, but it's good just to get through the opening rounds and be finding my rhythm."

His semi-final opponent, Harrington, was playing far better and shot 63 in the morning on the way to going 6 up after 19 holes on Levet. But then the Irishman suffered a grievous, all too literally and painfully. By the ninth in the afternoon, Levet had won three holes back and his par there put him only 2 down. But it was here that, playing a three iron from close to the trees on the left, Harrington smashed his thumb into a tree, which produced an agonizing reaction.

"Part of it was surprise because I couldn't believe I had hit the tree," Harrington said, "I thought I had plenty of room. It hurt, but the pain was not the problem. After I had it iced, it felt like I had a shovel in my hands rather than a club. After a while I realized I could not hit any full shots and just endeavored to get home whatever way I could." Twice he went out of bounds on the way home, at the 12th and the 16th, but the Irishman secured the win at the last hole.

Westwood was the next on the casualty list, although at this stage he was only reporting a cold as he followed his victory over the Open champion, Hamilton, with another over the U.S. Open champion, Goosen, 2 and 1. What was a tight match all morning suddenly opened up when Westwood won the 18th to go 3 up, and he held a comfortable advantage for much of the afternoon, although Goosen pulled two holes back at the 15th and 16th. "One of the keys to match play is not to panic," Westwood said. "It was a long day and I could do with a good night's sleep, but when I looked at the draw I knew I was going to have to go through the major champions."

Singh, of course, should have been Westwood's next challenge, but instead Langer and Jimenez were still battling away, their match having been delayed by the drama of Singh's exit on the extra hole in the morning. Langer continued to play fine golf, birdieing four of the first seven holes, but by then finding himself 1 down. Jimenez, by holing a full nine-iron shot, produced the first-ever eagle at the par-four seventh hole and was 3 up after an approximate 63 after the first round.

It was the same score when they resumed on Saturday morning with eight holes to play, but by winning the 14th and the 15th, Langer had got back to 1 down. When Jimenez pitched to four feet at the 17th to make a birdie and Langer missed from 11 feet, the German's magnificent run was over. Jimenez, with hardly time to savor the victory, immediately had to turn around and play Westwood in their semi-final.

Three times the Spaniard went ahead on the first nine, but perhaps fatigue was catching up with him, as Westwood won three holes in a row from the 15th to go 4 up. Jimenez won the 18th, but after another hurried lunch, Westwood won the first and the fourth. He was 5 up with eight to play, so there was no warning that it would be another classic Wentworth contest. Jimenez, at the age of 40, was enjoying the season of his career. His taste for cigars, Rioja wine and espresso coffees had helped him to four victories on the European Tour after a couple of unsuccessful years in the United States.

He birdied the 11th, eagled the 12th and birdied the 13th, so now he was only 2 down. A wedge to one foot at the 16th for another birdie piled the pressure on Westwood, who promptly missed for his three from six feet. Westwood's "no panic" approach was receiving the most severe test. He survived the 17th when they halved in pars and then found the green at the last with a three iron for a half in birdies that sealed his 1-up victory. Jimenez, after playing 44 holes in the day, could feel aggrieved. "I never gave up," he said. "It was a good effort to get it to the last. I've never played that many holes in a day before and I don't want to again."

"It wasn't like I was ever complacent," Westwood said. "I knew it wasn't all over. It was just a great game. There was a spell there, from the back nine in the morning, when I was 10 or 11 under for 19 holes. Then Miguel started winning holes, but it wasn't like I was giving him anything. I hit a lot of good shots down the stretch. Any time you win a match like that, it boosts your confidence."

Els had the easier time of it, defeating the injured Harrington, 5 and 4. The Irishman's demise was confirmed at the 14th of the afternoon round when he had a most inelegant stance in a bunker, could not keep his recovery on the green and missed a long putt for the half. Harrington had his right thumb bandaged and it was more the distraction than the pain that he found off-putting. "I couldn't put my thumb on the club in the morning," Harrington said. "I did in the afternoon, but it was awkward to say the least. It distracted me a number of times, but I didn't make enough putts and made too many mistakes. Ernie didn't make any."

He rarely does. Els played some fine golf, occasionally missing the odd tee shot on the right, but only because on the second nine of the West Course you cannot go right. But some of his approach shots were scintillating, and early in the piece it was the fact that he missed four putts from inside eight feet on the first six holes that was a minor source of irritation. He said he had not quite found the pace of the greens, but with an inevitability that confirms the absurdness of the game, he banged in a 30-footer at the seventh to go ahead for the first time. He threw away the 15th and the 16th with bogeys, but from 3 up at lunch, he was not troubled in the afternoon.

The odd hole was exchanged, but Harrington never got closer than 3 down and could not respond when Els went 4 up at the 11th by holing from 15 feet. Three victories used to be enough for Els to lift the trophy, but this year he had one more match to play. "Now I know what the other guys have had to go through," he said. "But it's worth it, isn't it? What we do for a living is like being in heaven." Playing for £1 million would certainly appear so. Of the financial reward, he said, "You put that thought right at the back of your mind while you're playing."

As for Westwood, his take on the game's biggest first prize was simply, "Yeah, I haven't really thought about it to be honest." Here was a final match between the imperturbable and the unflappable. Their two previous encounters had brought victories for Westwood, in the second round in 1998 by 2 and 1 and in the semi-finals of 2000, the year Westwood won the title at the 36th hole. Though the weather was at its least uncooperative of the week, this time it was not quite a classic.

After a week in which Els played 138 holes and Westwood 139 on such heavy going, it was hardly surprising neither player could produce their best. Els had six bogeys in the first 19 holes, which does not happen very often. "I was not at my best, but that doesn't matter in match play," Els said. "You can only get your nose in front of the guy you are playing." Westwood's cold, however, had turned into a chest infection and he struggled all day. "I slept terribly and felt awful all day," he said. "The main problem was the putting, bending over and trying to remain still over the ball. It felt like I had no balance and was moving all over the place."

There were some fine moments, however, such as at the fourth in the morning when the hole was halved in eagles. Els gave away the next two holes and, although he twice got back to even, Westwood holed from 12 feet for a birdie at the 16th. It was the last time Westwood was ahead. On the 17th tee he hooked his drive out of bounds, modern technology being his downfall. "I heard a camera phone go off," he said. "Phones are banned from the course and so are cameras, so I don't know why camera phones aren't banned."

In the afternoon it was Els who took command by birdieing the third hole with a six iron to eight feet and then chalking up his third eagle of the day with a five iron to 12 feet at the fourth. Westwood responded with a terrific tee shot at the short fifth, a five iron to three feet, but from there on Els did what he does so well in not giving anything away.

The Englishman, coughing and spluttering, lost the 10th when he went over the green, and the hourglass was running out of sand as the next four holes were halved. But Els three-putted the 15th, an error he was forced into by Westwood's fine six iron to three feet. Back to 1 down with three to play, Westwood immediately lost the 16th, and his drive and three wood, hit with all his remaining strength, at the 17th was the act of a desperate man. But he was on the green in two, while Els was in the rough short, right of the green.

He chipped to 20 feet and, after Westwood's eagle attempt just missed, Els rolled in the winning putt. His 96-year-old grandfather would have nodded appreciatively. "We spoke this morning and he was giving me some grief about my putting," Els said. "He was telling me to keep my head still, which is pretty basic; my wife could have told me that."

There had been so many cards that morning for his birthday "that it felt like Christmas." Now the party was only just beginning. "Really, I'm very grateful for what's happened here," Els said. "It's been wonderful. It's great to have the record. Six wins and I'm 35, so there is something to build on. But I don't want to get ahead of myself. It's just a wonderful feeling."

9. American Tours

Vijay Singh made two major changes to his game for 2004. First, he went from the long "belly" putter to the conventional one. Second, he quit worrying about Tiger Woods. That may be a little oversimplified, but that was the gist of it. The result: Player of the Year award, nine victories, nine other top-10 finishes, $10,905,166 in winnings, and — as some icing for that cake — the No. 1 ranking in the world. And this at the time when Tiger Woods was having what was for him an off-year — "only" one victory.

Some called it a kind of golf justice — the hardest working man in the game getting the top billing in the game. Singh is noted for his long, grueling, tunnel-vision hours on the practice tee, and it took until he was 41 to accomplish all this.

He became only the sixth player to win at least nine times, tying Paul Runyan of 1933 and Tiger Woods of 2000, but the records of Sam Snead (11), Ben Hogan (13) and Byron Nelson (18) were still safe.

If any one aspect of Singh gives insight to his year, it would be some representative comments he made at each of his nine victories. Accordingly:

No. 1 — AT&T Pebble Beach National Pro-Am in February: "I'm No. 2. I'm playing the best I can. I want to be No. 1 before I finish. But it's a hard feat to take Tiger off the top because he's playing well. If I keep playing like I'm doing now, I have a shot — maybe not this year, but in a year or two."

No. 2 — Shell Houston Open in April (his sixth top-10 finish in 11 starts): "I'd like to play this way all the time."

No. 3 — HP Classic of New Orleans the following week, early in May (when he thought he was out of it): "Just keep going, there is another nine to go … and all of a sudden everything changed."

No. 4 — Buick Open, August 1 (on thinking about becoming No. 1): "I put too much pressure on myself trying to get that spot in the beginning of the year … and maybe [I was] focusing on the wrong things. I'm really not worried about who is No. 1 now."

No. 5 — PGA Championship, August 14 (before the final round): "Majors are important to me. Probably not as important as to the other guys. I strive to win majors. But it's not the end of the world if I don't win a major."

No. 6 — Deutsche Bank Championship in September, when he replaced Tiger Woods as No. 1 in the world: "I never thought I would be sitting here — the best player in the world right now."

No. 7 — Bell Canadian Open, the next week (on beating native son Mike Weir): "I feel for Mike. That was the one person I didn't want to beat."

No. 8 — 84 Lumber Classic, in late September (on working hard): "I want to win, I want to play well, and it's a good habit."

No. 9 — Chrysler Championship, October 31: "The wins keep coming. It's good to see my name up there and see people worry about me instead of me worrying about others. It's a great feeling. I'm enjoying it. I love it. Come and get me."

Even all that couldn't overshadow the year Phil Mickelson had. Not that it approached Singh's for sheer magnitude, but that he finally got off that

0-for-46 count in major championships and won his first, the Masters. And with no little drama — shooting 31 on the final nine, coming from behind Ernie Els, and beating him by one stroke with a birdie on the 18th hole. It simply was one of the most gripping Masters of all time.

This was the new Phil Mickelson, somewhat overhauled. For one thing, he geared back on his aggressive game. Second, he went to hitting a low fade off the tee, the better to keep the ball in play. He was giving up a few yards on the drives to stay out of the trees and the long grass. He had served notice with that new game in his first start, the Bob Hope Chrysler Classic late in January, playing the last hole patiently, then winning in a playoff. These were his only two regular season victories, but he also won the PGA Grand Slam of Golf and had a terrific season in the majors — second in the U.S. Open, third in the Open Championship and tied for sixth in the PGA.

There were two other dominant figures in 2004, but not for the reasons they liked. Tiger Woods, who was replaced at No. 1 after a five-year reign, spent the year explaining how his new swing changes had just about come together. Golf's towering figure since joining the PGA Tour in 1996, he won only once on tour, and it was a match play event, the WGC - Accenture Match Play. The only stroke play events he won were the Dunlop Phoenix in Japan and his own Target World Challenge late in the year. Woods had what would be an outstanding year on the PGA Tour for anyone else — one win and 13 other top-10 finishes worth $5.4 million in 19 starts. By his own standards, however, it was not a Tiger Woods year. He did, however, extend his record of cuts made to 133, and he got married to Elin Nordegren in October.

Then there was Ernie Els. He could have won all four majors, but he was always getting zapped. First in the Masters, by Mickelson. Then in the U.S. Open, he was deep in contention until he blew to an 80 in the final round. In the Open Championship, he caught little-known Todd Hamilton, but got beaten in a playoff, and in the PGA Championship, he finished one stroke out of the playoff. Els had a great year — three victories on the Tour and won $5.7 million, and two victories outside the United States, but he was still talking to himself about those close calls in the majors.

The four majors were almost romances in themselves. First with Mickelson breaking through for his first. Then Retief Goosen, the silent South African, surviving the gruesome stretches of an overcooked Shinnecock Hills, one-putting his way to a two-stroke win over Mickelson for his second U.S. Open. Then the incredible Open Championship, with Hamilton, a veteran of golf everywhere but his native U.S., beating Els in a playoff. And finally Singh lurching to a final-round 76 in the PGA Championship, then getting the winning edge with his only birdie of the day in a playoff against Chris DiMarco and Justin Leonard.

The final high point of the season might have been the Ryder Cup, the great redeemer for all souls. Except the Americans, highly favored, suffered their worst loss ever, led by Mickelson and his switch — two weeks before the event — from Titleist to Callaway equipment.

The year ended with eight multiple winners — Mickelson, Singh, Els, Goosen, Hamilton, Adam Scott, Sergio Garcia and Stewart Cink. And there were 10 first-time winners.

U.S. PGA Tour

Mercedes Championships—$5,300,000
Winner: Stuart Appleby

The PGA Tour in the United States got off to a new season early in January with the Mercedes Championships, an exclusive gathering that welcomed 30 winners from 2003 to the fellowship of competition, riches and fun in the sun in Hawaii. Except someone forgot to impress this point on Stuart Appleby and Vijay Singh. They proceeded to make it their own private show. This was the Appleby-Singh Shootout, thank you. Others need not apply.

It would end with Appleby characterizing the entire tournament in his summation of the final round. "I really felt like it was up to Vijay to catch me," he said. "I wasn't going to let him have anything for free. I didn't make any mistakes. And unfortunately — to the benefit of me — he ran out of holes."

"I'm not disappointed in finishing second," Singh said. "I'm just disappointed in not winning."

To coin an expression, what a finish. Appleby led by five shots with five holes to play and withstood Singh's furious finish to win by one.

Appleby opened with a seven-under-par 66 at the par-73 Plantation Course at Kapalua and pronounced himself fit. "I liked the way I swung it, liked the way I rolled it," he said.

Appleby was one ahead of the new, trim Darren Clarke, who saluted his opening 67 as "My first competitive round without having any nicotine in my body." The burly Ulsterman had dropped both cigarettes and 30 pounds in a fitness program. And the eternally working Singh shot 68, using the medium-long "belly" putter, oddly enough, after practicing with a conventional putter. Then it turned into the two-man war.

In the second round, Appleby was up by four through the turn. Then over-ambition caught him up. He tried to drive the green at the 305-yard 14th, lost his ball in deep growth, suffered a penalty, but scrambled to a bogey five. Singh, meantime, was off on a rampage of seven straight birdies. It started with a 20-footer at the 12th. He converted short birdie putts at the next two holes, two-putted the par-five 15th, nailed the 16th from five feet, dropped another 20-footer at the 17th, and then tapped in a two-footer at the 18th after chipping brilliantly from near the grandstand. Said Singh, "I wasn't expecting all that." It got him the lead, his 64–132 against Appleby's 67–133.

It was Appleby's turn in the third round, with a 66 highlighted by a 55-foot putt at the seventh and a 10-footer at the 17th, and he was sitting at 20-under 199. Singh, at 69–201, had a chance to tie Appleby on a 15-foot birdie putt at the 17th, but he three-putted for a bogey. Appleby was going to be tough to catch. But Singh gave it a real go in the final round.

Appleby led by five strokes with five holes to play and turned cautious, challenging Singh to come get him if he wished. Singh wished, once he tamed a cranky putter that cost him two three-putts on the front nine. Appleby went six ahead of Singh with a birdie from above the hole at No. 4 and another from 25 feet at No. 7. Singh missed short birdie putts at the 12th and 13th, then caught fire. He birdied the 14th from 12 feet, the 15th from 10 and the 16th from 20. But then he ran out of steam and finished with a three-under 70. Appleby closed with a 71 for the 22-under 270 total and a one-stroke victory over Singh.

While they battled, other eyes were on two other powerhouses who weren't in the running. Ernie Els, the defending champion, labored to a tie for 21st. And Tiger Woods, by his standards playing a mish-mash of golf, was never in contention but birdied the last two holes to tie for fourth, seven back. "Nothing went right," Woods said. "I either hit great shots or horrific ones."

Sony Open in Hawaii—$4,800,000
Winner: Ernie Els

The Sony Open wasn't so much a golf tournament as a cultural statement. A field of 144 had assembled at Waialae Country Club at Honolulu, including three of the biggest names in the game — defending champion Ernie Els, who would win again, Vijay Singh and Davis Love. But they were the supporting cast. The week belonged to Michelle Wie, a 14-year-old schoolgirl and the latest in the novelty of females playing a PGA Tour event. She was the third in eight months and was believed to be the youngest player ever in a tour event. Wie, a ninth-grader at a nearby school, had received a sponsor's invitation to play.

Wie shot 72-68–140 and missed the 36-hole cut by a stroke. Observers were impressed, but noted that she had saved par on about half of her holes and that two of her birdies in the second round came from about 50 feet. "I think I learned that I can play here," Wie said. Even after she missed the cut, she continued to be the big news.

Meanwhile, back at the golf tournament …

"There was a such a high yesterday, trying to get her to the weekend," said Els, after the third round. "Today it was back to business." Was there a touch of sarcasm in there? Anyway, for Els, who sputtered the week before, "business" meant a four-under-par 66 that pulled him to within a stroke of Harrison Frazar's 66–196 lead after three rounds. Frazar, a seventh-year man without a victory, seemed oddly resigned to staying that way. This was the third time he would lead going into the final round. In Phoenix last year, Vijay Singh overran him with a 63. "I fully expect that to happen tomorrow, too," said Frazar.

Els had opened with a 67, four behind Carlos Franco's 63 in the first round, all of this going on while everyone was watching Wie. So hardly anyone noticed in the second round when winless Australian Steve Allan shot an eight-under 62 for a 129 total to lead Frazar (63) by a stroke and Els (64) by two. A 70-74 finish would drop Allan to a tie for 27th place.

Going into the final round, Frazar led Els by one and didn't go down without a fight. They battled away, both parring the first five holes. Frazar went from his one-stroke lead to a two-shot deficit late on the first nine.

He rallied with four straight birdies to tie Els, but then Els chipped in at the 13th. Finally, Els looked like a winner at the 15th, leading by two and facing a 30-foot birdie putt while Frazar was in heavy rough behind the green facing a bogey. But Frazar chipped beautifully and saved his par while Els three-putted for a bogey. Els' lead was down to one. Frazar caught him with a 20-foot birdie at the par-three 17th, and Els had to hole a 10-foot birdie putt at the 18th for a 65 to tie Frazar at 18-under 262. Els was now in a playoff for the Sony Open for the second straight year.

Els and Frazar parred the first playoff hole, No. 18. At the second, No. 10, Els had 10 feet from the fringe for a birdie. Frazar missed the green on the left and chipped weakly, 15 feet short, but he made the putt and tied Els again. At the third extra hole, the par-three 11th, Els had a 30-footer for birdie. He holed it. He was the first back-to-back Sony Open winner in 17 years.

"I had a one-shot lead and shot four under on a pretty tough golf course," Frazar said. "Most of the time, that's going to be good enough. I just got beat."

Said Big Easy, "Nothing comes easy."

Bob Hope Chrysler Classic—$4,500,000
Winner: Phil Mickelson

The Bob Hope Chrysler Classic was all about healing. First, there was Skip Kendall, age 39, winless in 293 career starts. He had to cure a slice — a real one. He was slicing a bagel one day last year, and the next thing he knew, doctors were reattaching a piece of his left index finger. Phil Mickelson, on the other hand, had to cure his entire game. It seems that over a year ago he decided to tinker with his swing and he hadn't been the same since. The miracles of modern medicine (Kendall) and self-determination (Mickelson) brought the two together to decide the Bob Hope Chrysler Classic in La Quinta, California, late in January.

"I'm not going to get hung up on winning," the winless Kendall said after tying for the first-round lead with a nine-under-par 63 at Palmer Course at PGA West, one of four courses used for the celebrated five-round event (the others being Indian Wells, La Quinta and Bermuda Dunes, all par 72s). "I think I have enough game to win," he said, no doubt warmed by the thoughts of his 25-foot birdie putts at Nos. 4 and 5, and the three wood and 30-foot putt for an eagle three at No. 6. The 63 tied him with Australian Mark Hensby, whose highest finish was a tie for ninth in 2001.

Mickelson, making his 2004 debut, had opened five strokes off the lead, but a 63 in the second round lifted him to within a stroke of Kenny Perry (66–130) and also showed that he had scrapped whatever changes had rendered him winless for the past 19 months. He had gone back to the game that got him his last two victories back in 2002 — the Chrysler Classic, ironically, and the Canon Greater Hartford Open. "I feel like I've driven the ball very well," Mickelson said, "and I feel much more confident from 134 yards in, which last year was a point of dissatisfaction." He did another thing. He resurrected the little-used one iron to deal with some narrow fairways off the tee.

Mickelson shot 64 in the third round and led by two, then 67 in the fourth and was tied with Kirk Triplett (63) at 262. Kendall (66) trailed them by three going into the final round. Triplett, bogey-free for four rounds, made some quick errors, leaving the final stage to Mickelson and Kendall.

In the final round, Kendall edged ahead on a short birdie putt at the 16th while Mickelson was bogeying the 15th. Kendall then missed the green and bogeyed the 17th. They both birdied the 18th, Mickelson for a 68, Kendall a 65, to tie at 30-under-par 330. The playoff started at the par-five 18th, and ended there. Both hit good drives. Both also missed the green and caught rough, Kendall on the left, Mickelson on the right, but much closer to the hole. Kendall chipped 20 feet short and missed his birdie putt. And Mickelson, the short-game master, chipped to three feet and rapped it in for the win. Mickelson was now 6-1 in playoffs, Kendall 0-3.

"I played my heart out," said Kendall, now winless in 294 starts. "It's hard to take, but I'm glad I was there."

Said Mickelson, "It's terrific. I can't wait to do it again."

Meanwhile, some interesting notes surfaced in the aftermath:

• Hensby, who tied for the first-round lead with a 63, missed the fourth-round cut.

• Robert Gamez shot 60 at Indian Wells in the third round, including a 27 on the first nine, tying the PGA Tour record.

• Like a pitcher who doesn't want to be reminded he has a no-hitter going, Triplett, co-leader after the fourth round, tried to wave off the fact that he hadn't made a bogey in the first four rounds. "You bring it up or you hear the commentator — 'The guy is a great this or a great that,'" he said, "and immediately he blows whatever they're saying he was." Jinx? In the fifth round, Triplett had four bogeys and a double bogey, and dropped to a tie for ninth.

• Perry scored a rare double in the fourth round — back-to-back eagles at PGA West's fifth and sixth, both par-fives. He shot 64, trailed by one, then closed with a 71 and finished fifth, four shots back.

FBR Open—$5,200,000
Winner: Jonathan Kaye

It's now called the FBR Open, after the new sponsor — Friedman, Billings, Ramsey Group, Inc. — but the galleries gave away the tournament. An announced crowd of 113,088 turned out Friday, and on Sunday another 90,768, a record for Super Bowl Sunday. For the week, 503,564 spectators were said to have been there. And the par-three 16th still had the loudest gallery in golf. It was the old Phoenix Open doing business as usual under a new name at the TPC of Scottsdale.

The cast was compelling. There was Phil Mickelson, just four days from his first victory in 19 months; the always dangerous Vijay Singh, defending champion; Chris DiMarco, the 2002 champion; gritty Scott Verplank, and then another name popped up — Jonathan Kaye, age 33, a 10th-year man out of Phoenix itself and probably the only man in professional golf interested in jalapeno farming. Kaye had two distinctions in golf. As an amateur, he beat Mickelson in the 1992 Ping Intercollegiate, and as a pro, he had the 2003 Buick Classic to his credit. In a word, he seemed out of place. He himself was extremely cautious after tying for the lead with DiMarco through the third round.

"I'm happy with my position going into tomorrow," Kaye said. "If I continue to do what I'm doing, we'll just see what happens."

The safe platitudes did nothing to call attention to him as he went about his business of trying to outlast some pretty tough customers. Which he did in the final round, shooting a four-under-par 67 for an 18-under 266 total and a two-stroke victory over DiMarco (69). Singh (66) rallied to tie Steve Flesch for third place, and Mickelson (72) slipped to seventh.

Overall, it was a good scramble. Verplank led the first round with a 63, one ahead of Mickelson (64) and two ahead of Kaye (65) and Mike Weir. Mickelson, still enjoying the return of his old game, led the second round with a 68–132, including an eagle at the par-five 13th off a 360-yard drive and a five iron to three feet. "I feel very comfortable with the way I'm playing," he said. Mickelson was one shot ahead of Kaye (68), Verplank (70) and Jeff Sluman (67).

Then it was DiMarco's turn to join the crowd. A 64 got him a share of the third-round lead with Kaye (66), both at 14-under 199. "I'm surprised the leaders didn't do more," DiMarco said. "I was expecting someone to go 15 or 16 under today." Singh came roaring into contention with a 63. "Just scraping slowly," he said. "Made a lot of good shots." Speaking of charges, Kaye made all five of his birdies on the second nine and just missed a 15-footer at the 18th for the solo lead.

Kaye's challengers fell away one at a time in the final round, but grudgingly. Mickelson started a stroke behind Kaye and DiMarco, then jumped to a two-shot lead with a birdie at the fifth. But he two-putted from four feet to bogey the par-three seventh. All three birdied the 13th, tying at 16 under. Then came the attrition. Kaye and DiMarco birdied the 14th, and Mickelson slipped two shots behind with a bogey. He would limp home, bogeying the last three holes.

Kaye and DiMarco had a matched set of birdies at the par-five 15th. Both laid up short of the water, wedged on, and two-putted from about 10 feet. Then came DiMarco's decisive errors. He bogeyed the next two holes — the par-three 16th from a bunker and the par-four 17th on two chips and two putts after nearly driving the green. Kaye, meanwhile, parred in. He had gone 194 starts before winning his first. He went only 12 until this one.

"This one," Kaye said, "feels a little better than the first one."

AT&T Pebble Beach National Pro-Am—$5,300,000
Winner: Vijay Singh

It became clear early on in the AT&T Pebble Beach National Pro-Am that Vijay Singh was paired with and against his most stubborn competitor — Vijay Singh. Despite the crowds and hoopla surrounding the old Bing Crosby Clambake on California's Monterey Peninsula, it was clear that Singh was playing all alone. There was some amazing golf coming from the man, and before he knew it, someone handed him a crystal trophy and told him he had won. This was early February, and if this was a sign of things to come in 2004, Singh might finally conquer that one more mountain, knocking Tiger Woods off the No. 1 perch in the Official World Golf Ranking and taking it over himself.

"I'm No. 2. I'm playing the best I can," Singh said. "I want to be No. 1 before I finish. But it's a hard feat to take Tiger off the top because he's playing well. If I keep playing like I'm doing now, I have a shot — maybe not this year, but in a year or two."

The sooner the better, the other guys were saying. Maybe he could let up and they could get some breathing room. Every time he seemed out of it, he found a way back in, leaving golfers and fans shaking their heads. Especially Phil Mickelson, he of the rejuvenated game, winner of the Bob Hope Chrysler Classic two weeks earlier. Take this stretch, for instance: In the third round, Mickelson led Singh by three through the turn. When Mickelson bogeyed the 17th, he was four behind. Singh had gone on one of his tears, birdieing five out of six holes.

"I'll have to play a great round tomorrow," said Mickelson. "I'll have to be six, seven, eight under." He needed to shoot 64, but shot 69 and finished third. Singh shot 67-68-68-69–272, 16 under par across the three par-72 courses — Spyglass Hill, Poppy Hills and Pebble Beach — and won by three over Jeff Maggert.

Singh had given no hint that he was going to overrun the field. Matt Kuchar and J.J. Henry, who faded after promising rookie seasons, shared the first-round lead on 65s. Singh was fourth, two behind. He was one behind Luke Donald after the second round and was tied for the lead through the third round with an admiring Arron Oberholser, a second-year player in contention for the first time on the PGA Tour. "The man snap-hooked his first three drives and made birdies," Oberholser would observe. "It's hard to compete with that."

Singh's traveling circus started on the first hole of his first round, at Poppy Hills. He made a great escape from the trees, but three-putted from four feet for a bogey. He also bogeyed No. 4. He escaped trees two other times: At the 10th, his only out was high up over an evergreen; he birdied. At the 16th, his escape shot ended within 10 feet of the hole; he birdied again.

At Pebble Beach in the third round, Singh bogeyed the first two holes, but two birdies got him back to even par at the turn — and three down to Mickelson. Then Singh went on his five-birdie spree, starting with an 18-footer at the 11th and ending with a 40-footer at the 16th. Mickelson, with a couple of bogeys, found himself four strokes behind.

In the final round, Singh was comparatively tame. He birdied the first three holes: No. 1 on a tap-in after hooking his tee shot into deep rough; No. 2 on a 10-footer after hooking his tee shot and then missing the green by 60 yards, and No. 3 on another 10-footer after missing the fairway to the left. He squeaked past trouble at the 17th, and then someone was handing him a trophy. The golfers had a better idea.

"I think we're about ready to take up a collection," said Scott McCarron, "and send him on a paid vacation."

Buick Invitational—$4,800,000
Winner: John Daly

It was easily the most popular win on the PGA Tour in years — John Daly, executing a paralyzing down-slope bunker shot from 100 feet away to within four inches, then tapping in for a birdie to end the three-man playoff to a thunderous ovation at the Buick Invitational in LaJolla, California. Daly, one of the most popular men on tour and certainly the most troubled, fighting his various demons, had dropped to 299th on the Official World Golf Ranking and had gone without a win for 189 events, since the 1995 British Open. That's eight years, six months and 22 days. And so it surprised no one that the big guy with an easy smile buried his face in his hands and cried.

"It's the greatest," Daly said. "I've had a lot of ups and downs. Geez, this is sweet."

He had burst on the scene as an unknown and ninth alternate who gripped-it-and-ripped-it for the 1991 PGA Championship. Then the troubles surfaced, most traceable to his drinking. His battle against his demons was public knowledge. He had played well only in occasional spurts. And now, actually threatening to win a tournament was out of character. Maybe even astonishing.

Going into the final round, Daly led by one over Stewart Cink — his first 54-hole lead in 10 years. And then he showed some frazzled nerves in those unfamiliar surroundings. He hooked his tee shot wildly on the second hole, hitting a cart path and tree. At the par-three third, he hit into a hazard, tried to hack the ball out and moved it only three feet, then blasted over the green and two-putted from 90 feet — a double bogey. Mickelson, meanwhile, ran off four straight birdies, then double-bogeyed the 12th. Tiger Woods, the defending champion, came within two strokes, then missed four fairways in a row and dropped two shots. While Daly was shooting a near-fatal 75, two guys didn't miss their opportunities. Luke Donald and Chris Riley both made clutch 15-footers for birdies at the 18th for 69s to tie Daly with 278 totals, 10 under par at Torrey Pines.

The playoff returned to the par-five 18th. Donald and Riley both laid up and pitched on for makeable birdie putts. Daly wasn't about to play it safe. After one of his huge drives, he told his caddie that if he was within 275 yards of the green, he was going for it. He had 262 yards left and went for it. His three wood hit the green and rolled into the right bunker, 100 feet from the pin, leaving him with a scary downhill blast, with water waiting just beyond the green. He could lose it all right here.

But Daly, for all of his size and strength, is also known for a delicate touch. He blasted exquisitely, yelling "Go! Go!" as the ball homed in on the cup. It stopped four inches away. Donald missed his six-footer, and Riley lipped out his five-footer, and Daly had his victory.

Daly had worked his way through the ranks at Torrey Pines — past Kevin Stadler (son of Craig), the first-round leader with 64; past Cink, the second-round leader, and then he held on in the face of the third-round leader — himself.

The pre-tournament favorite, of course, was Woods. He didn't really threaten. He tied for 10th, just two strokes away on the jammed leaderboard. Vijay Singh, the winner at Pebble Beach just the week before, was no worse than second choice, but he missed the cut for the first time after making it 25 straight times, and his pursuit of Jack Nicklaus' record of 14 consecutive top-10 finishes ended at 12. Maybe only one person noticed.

"This is the greatest victory," Daly said. "I won two majors. Nothing can take away from that. But I've never won a tournament that Tiger Woods has been in the field. That feels good."

Nissan Open—$4,800,000
Winner: Mike Weir

Mike Weir, the celebrated left-hander, had the truly unenviable record of going 0-for-5 when leading a tournament through 54 holes. He was about to get that monkey off his back in the Nissan Open in Pacific Palisades, California. He not only led through 54 holes, he had a huge seven-shot lead through No. 3 in the final round. Then, gruesomely, he was about to go 0-for-6. In a Greg Normanesque nightmare, Weir saw all seven shots melt away to zero by the 16th. Maybe it was for the best.

"It's probably better for me down the road that it happened this way," Weir said, meaning maybe having to pull himself together over the final two holes under such pressure would make him a better golfer. At any rate, Weir held on and polished off a wickedly tough par at the 18th while his tormentor, Shigeki Maruyama, bogeyed from the rain-soaked rough. Thus did Weir match his hero, Ben Hogan, in winning back-to-back Nissan Opens. Hogan did it in 1947-48 when it was the Los Angeles Open, stamping Riviera Country Club as "Hogan's Alley."

The debilitating stretch was a real nightmare. Weir led by seven with 15 holes to play. Then, in the mysterious way of golf, Weir went into idle while Maruyama charged. Weir's lead was five after nine holes, three after 10, two after 13, one after 15, and then at the par-three 16th, Maruyama holed a 10-foot putt for birdie and they were tied. The irony here was unbelievable. Last year, Weir was seven behind coming into the last round and caught Charles Howell and beat him in a playoff. Now Weir was seven ahead and was the one who got caught. Fortunately for him, history didn't make a complete duplicate this time — with him as victim.

Weir shot 66-64-66-71–267, 17 under par. He trailed Maruyama in the first round, tied him in the second, and led from there. John Daly peeked at the lead early on, then closed with a 67 and finished fourth. Tiger Woods, 0-for-6 as a professional at Riviera, didn't come close. It took a closing 64 to boost him to a tie for seventh.

Weir won with his putter. Or rather, with putting. Miffed at his putter, he used his sand wedge in the first round. He holed a 15-foot eagle putt with it on his first hole. He needed only 99 putts for the tournament, an average of under 25 per round. But it was a great chip that finally saved him.

It came at the final hole, when they were tied. The course was wet from heavy rains. Maruyama, a confessed poor wet weather player, drove into the right rough. His second shot was short, and his 50-yard chip shot raced past the pin. He had a tricky 12-foot downhill putt for par. Weir, meanwhile, had driven into the fairway and put his second on the bank above and left of the green. He had a downhill chip from thick kikuyu grass. He played it brilliantly, nearly holing it. When Maruyama missed his 12-footer for par, Weir tapped in for his par and the one-stroke victory.

The closing statements summed things up:

"You have to dig deep," Weir said. "I was able to do that."

Maruyama said his errant drive at the final hole was his biggest mistake of the week, and he blamed it on the rain and his dislike thereof. "I hate playing in the rain," he said. "I'm still not good at playing in rain. I am going to start practicing in the shower."

WGC - Accenture Match Play—$7,000,000
Winner: Tiger Woods

Tiger Woods was the scourge of match play as a kid. Literally, the enfant terrible. He had three straight U.S. Junior Amateur championships and three straight U.S. Amateurs in his bag, and a highway full of wreckage behind him. For some reason, once he reached the Ryder Cup, he wasn't terrible, much less enfant, but in the World Golf Championship Accenture Match Play Championship, he had found a home. He chalked up his second victory in a row, beating Davis Love 3 and 2 in the final.

Truth was, that week in February at the La Costa Resort in Carlsbad, California, it wasn't pretty but it was effective. Woods was still having trouble, but he made do.

"Today I did not drive the ball well," Woods said after the final. "I was struggling with my swing. My iron game was kind of erratic. I was trying to put the ball on the fat side of the green and I'd miss on the short side. The only thing I could really rely on was my short game and my putter. I had been putting beautifully the last three days and holing some putts. I knew that it was going to come down to that. It's certainly more difficult to win the way I did today."

Woods was knocking shots all over the place against Love in the 36-hole final, but he made eight putts of four to 17 feet, including the 12-footer for birdie at the 25th hole that gave him the lead for the first time. He took the 26th with a birdie from four feet and the 27th on a two-putt par, and he was 3 up to stay.

"In order to win matches, you've got to putt well," said Woods, after dropping four putts of 11 feet or more in beating Stephen Leaney in the semi-finals. "That's what it boils down to. The good old flat stick is a great equalizer."

Said Love, "He was missing fairways the first 18 holes, and I let him get away with it. I played pretty good. I just didn't have it on the greens." It didn't help that Love missed about six putts from 10 feet or less. It also didn't help that a spectator heckled him.

Love was 1 up after the first 18, and at the 20th hole (No. 2) the man began heckling him. He missed the green and eventually missed an 11-footer for par. He bogeyed, and Woods squared the match. The heckler continued until No. 5, when Love finally located him in the gallery and had him removed.

Love said Woods tried to settle him down. "He said, 'Take your time and get back into it,'" Love said. Woods has known hecklers, too. "You can block it out as many times as you can," he said, "but after a while you're going to snap." But Love didn't win another hole after the incident.

Woods' tightest match was the opener against John Rollins, a 1-up win. He then beat Trevor Immelman, Thomas Bjorn, Padraig Harrington and Stephen Leaney. Love went through Briny Baird, Fred Couples, Adam Scott, Phil Mickelson and Darren Clarke.

It wasn't a vintage Tiger Woods, not with that erratic game, but it was a tough and victorious one who loves match play. "It basically boils down to what my dad has always told me when it comes to match play," he said. "All you have to do is just be better than your opponent that day. That's it. All you have to do is win more holes than you lose. It's as simple as that."

Given that one-hole-at-a-time grind, match play is more severe than stroke play at wilting concentration and fraying nerves. "I think if we played match play every week, guys would be toast by 40," Woods said. "They'd be in a padded room drooling on themselves."

Chrysler Classic of Tucson—$3,000,000
Winner: Heath Slocum

In a battle of two players seeking their first win, Aaron Baddeley, a rising young Australian in his second year, three-putted only once in the 72 holes of the Chrysler Classic of Tucson. It couldn't have happened at a worse time — the 72nd hole. Heath Slocum, a struggling 30-year-old American, on the other hand, parred the 72nd hole. And that couldn't have come at a better time. He had worked and waited some four years, 77 tournaments and 73 holes for his first victory, and now he had it.

Slocum won a "battlefield promotion" to the PGA Tour in 2001, with three victories on the Nationwide Tour. But this was only after his career was set back for about three years by a case of ulcerative colitis. He could have done without the colitis, but then he learned from it, too. "It put things in perspective," Slocum said. "When I got back out there, I didn't want to give away any more opportunities."

Some memories burn. Slocum missed two chances to win in 2002. In Tucson, he led after 54 holes but managed only par golf in the final round and tied for sixth. In the WorldCom Classic, he led by a stroke with three holes to play, double-bogeyed the 16th, and finished second to Justin Leonard. The difference this time? "Coming down and just playing my game, and it worked out this time," he said.

At the decisive, water-guarded 18th, Slocum put his approach 15 feet from the cup. Baddeley left his 50 feet short, then missed his first putt by five feet. Then he missed that one too, and he had the fatal bogey. Slocum two-putted for his winning par.

On scores of 67-64-70-65–266 at the par-72 Omni Tucson National, Slocum was 14th in the first round behind Frank Lickliter, the defending champion, who streaked to a 63 and a two-shot lead. A fit of ambition cost Per-Ulrik Johansson a chance to join him. Johansson had eight birdies, an eagle and a bogey through the 17th. He took his three wood off the 18th tee, watered the shot, and double-bogeyed to join a group at 65. "I wanted to shoot 10 under," Johansson said. "I've never shot 27 on nine holes before, and it cost me two shots."

Lickliter lifted to a 73 in the rain-interrupted second round, and Slocum, with his 64, took over the lead for good. Slocum had just gone 36 holes without a bogey. Little wonder. He had hit 17 of 18 greens in each round.

Baddeley, meantime, was in 25th place in the first round, then 17th, then zoomed into a tie with Slocum with a 64 in the third round. "It's just being patient," Baddeley said. " ... my flow with the strokes was really great today."

They were in a tight match in the final round, neither able to pull away. Baddeley was dazzling with the putter early, getting three of his six birdies on putts of 26 to 28 feet. Finally, they came to the 18th all tied up. Then it was a five-footer that did Baddeley in.

If that was misfortune, consider John Daly. He needed some great play to get an invitation to the Masters. He had won the Buick Invitational two weeks earlier and was fourth in the Nissan Open a week ago, and now was aiming for a third-consecutive top-10 finish. Then came the 170-yard par-three No. 4 in the third round. His tee shot landed on the green but spun all the way back — past the pin, off the green and into the fronting pond. So did the next three. He finally got on and holed a 13-foot putt for a 10. He shot 76.

Ford Championship at Doral—$5,000,000
Winner: Craig Parry

Scott Verplank had hit a superb approach shot from the rough on the 18th hole in a playoff. He took his putter from his caddie and began walking toward the green where he would attempt a putt that could win the tournament. Then Craig Parry, the Popeye-armed Australian, hit his approach shot. Verplank watched the ball for a moment, then he handed the putter back to his caddie. He wouldn't be needing it. The noise of the crowd told him that Parry had just holed his shot. That ended the Ford Championship at Doral in Miami, Florida.

"I still haven't seen the ball go in the hole yet," Parry said later. "They replayed it about four times and I missed every one of them."

The title went to a man who started the tournament by almost missing his first-round tee time. Parry woke up just 15 minutes before his 7:54 start, grabbed any clothes in reach — black slacks, white shoes, blue belt — and shot a one-under-par 71.

"I guess he was supposed to win," a stunned Verplank said. "Now I know how Greg Norman feels."

Verplank, closing with a 67, tied Parry, who shot 68, at 17-under-par 271. They went on to the playoff on Doral's dangerous 18th hole, a par-four that doglegs to the left around water, where only Parry and 13 others had made par or better in each of the four rounds.

Verplank caught the right rough with his tee shot and hit the edge of the green with a difficult approach. "I was proud of it ..." Verplank would say. Parry had hit his drive 298 yards to the center of the fairway and had 176 yards left. He had a brief disagreement with his caddie, younger brother Glenn. Parry wanted to hit the five iron. Glenn said hit the six. Parry deferred to his brother and hit the six, and the eagle two ended all discussions and the tournament. He picked up the second PGA Tour victory of his career.

Parry, with a 71, trailed Chris Smith by six strokes in the first round, and with a 65 in the second round, was tied with Phil Mickelson and Todd Hamilton, one stroke behind Retief Goosen, who had a 135 total. Parry took the lead in the third round with a 67 for a 203 total, one ahead of Verplank and Gene Sauers.

"Anyone within eight shots can win," Parry insisted, a prudent prediction considering that 18 players started the final round within five strokes of the lead.

Parry bolted to birdies on four of his first eight holes. Then Verplank forced the playoff with three birdies on the second nine, only to set the stage for Parry's miracle shot. "It's amazing," Parry said. "I probably won't be able to put into words what actually happened." Verplank probably felt pretty much the same way.

Honda Classic—$5,000,000
Winner: Todd Hamilton

Todd Hamilton had the secret formula for overnight success. First, you have to have been a college All-American. Then you spend 17 years trying to get on the PGA Tour. Refusing to give up, you play the Nationwide Tour, Canadian Tour, Asian Tour, Japan Tour — and even win there four times last year alone. And you take eight cracks at the PGA Tour's qualifying tournament, and on the eighth try, you finally make it. Welcome, 38-year-old rookie.

Then Hamilton made himself right at home at the Honda Classic early in March at Mirasol at Palm Beach Gardens, Florida. Just when it seemed he had self-destructed under pressure from Davis Love down the final stretch, Hamilton braced himself and closed with two clutch birdies to chalk up his first victory.

"Until I got my tour card," Hamilton said, "I always doubted something like this would happen."

But Hamilton made it happen. First, he had to get past a Swedish player, Carl Pettersson, who shot 63 and 68, and led Mark Hensby by two strokes in the first round and Hamilton and Brad Faxon by three in the second round.

"I've never had a 36-hole lead," Pettersson said. "We'll see what happens." What happened was a 76-75 finish and a drop to a tie for 13th place. The 76 included the worst kind of triple bogey — a five-putt from 40 feet at the par-four 16th. "I hit the first one 15 feet past," the shocked Pettersson said. "And hit the next one four feet behind. A couple of misses, and before your know it, it's a seven."

Hamilton shot 68-66-68-74, a 12-under-par 276 total and a one-stroke win over Love. Then he realized he wasn't knocking around the world anymore: He was given a check for $900,000.

Hamilton's baptism as a PGA Tour golfer was complete when in the third round a television viewer called to accuse him of aligning his ball on the green after picking up his marker. A replay of the video tape showed he never even touched the ball. So Hamilton zipped past the falling Pettersson and took a four-stroke lead over another Swede, Fredrik Jacobson, into the final round. There, Hamilton almost lost it.

He blew most of his four-shot lead on the first nine. A bogey from a bunker, two more from missed greens, and he was leading by only one stroke when he made the turn. He did pull himself together to make two great par saves. At the 10th, his chip from a downhill lie to an uphill pin ended up as a tap-in. At the 12th, he chipped so poorly he didn't reach the green, and his next chip still left him six feet from the pin. But he made the putt for the par five. Then he three-putted the 13th, and this fourth bogey dropped him into a tie at 10 under par.

Once again, Hamilton pulled himself together. He was 50 feet from the pin at the 14th and made a seven-footer to save par. At the par-three 15th, he ended up in a collection area 80 feet from the pin, but chipped to three feet and made that. Then came the winning shots.

Love, three groups in front of Hamilton, was staying loose at the practice range. He had shot 69–277 and had the clubhouse lead. Hamilton trailed by one stroke with two tough holes to play. Then Hamilton birdied the 17th from 10 feet. They were tied. And at the 18th he fired an eight iron from 162 yards to four feet, and he holed that one, too. It was a 74 for the rookie, but it also was his first PGA Tour win.

"He finished like a true champion," Love said.

Said Hamilton, "There's probably a lot of other golfers who deserve it more, talent-wise, but I guarantee you no one will appreciate it more than I will."

Bay Hill Invitational—$5,000,000
Winner: Chad Campbell

It has to be a measure of a man's stature when something he doesn't do makes as much news as something he does. And so it was with Tiger Woods, when he didn't win the Bay Hill Invitational at Arnold Palmer's Bay Hill Club in Orlando, Florida.

Woods had won at Bay Hill for four consecutive years and was a heavy favorite to become the first ever to win the same event on the PGA Tour five times in a row. He opened the week on track, with a five-under-par 67, one stroke behind the three-way lead of Darren Clarke, Chad Campbell and Shigeki Maruyama.

"I just played well," Woods said. "I drove it well and controlled my irons. I have three more rounds to go. It doesn't happen very often, you get to do something no one has ever done before, and I've done it a few times so far in my career."

Then something slipped. He shot 74 in the second round and was nine shots off the lead. Woods would tie for 46th place, his worst finish in five years. It was only mid-March, but it seemed this was not the Tiger Woods who had been dominating golf. He hit 42 of 56 fairways, a good figure, but only 45 of 72 greens.

By the final stretch, things went the way Palmer would have loved. Chad Campbell, playing the role as Palmer once did, charged from a four-stroke deficit with 11 holes to play to win by an incredible six-stroke margin. Stuart Appleby, who led Campbell by four going into the final round, blew to a 76 while Campbell closed with a six-under 66 and an 18-under 270 total.

Maruyama was the early pacesetter. He tied for the first-round lead and led by two through the second with a par of 66s. He was leading Stuart Appleby, Clarke and Campbell by two strokes, but so pervasive was the presence of Woods that the attention was on him despite his 74. Maruyama was nine strokes ahead of Woods at this point and was asked whether he could stop Woods' bid for five in a row. Maruyama smiled and said, "Maybe eight shots from Tiger Woods after the third round, I would have a good chance."

Maruyama started the third round with a two-stroke lead, but it was gone by the time he reached the sixth tee. He shot 75. Clarke also had troubles. At the 13th, he visited sand and water and made a double bogey and shot 74. It may not have mattered. On a windy day, Appleby raced into the lead on four straight birdies, three from about 30 feet, on his way to a 66 for a four-stroke lead over Campbell, who made three bogeys over his last five holes and shot 70.

The fourth round was Campbell's — the last 11 holes of it, anyway. He was four behind Appleby with 11 to play. Campbell made up one shot at the eighth, holing a 10-footer for a birdie. Then came a two-shot swing on the ninth, where both players were in the trees. Campbell punched out with a five iron and the ball rolled to within 30 feet of the cup. He holed it for birdie. Appleby hit his shot into a bunker and bogeyed. Then he lost the lead on the 11th, going bunker-to-bunker for another bogey. And then he slipped behind for the first time in 27 holes when he three-putted the par-three 14th. Campbell birdied the 15th and had a two-stroke lead with three holes to play.

Said Palmer, master of the charge, "I never counted him out."

The Players Championship—$8,000,000
Winner: Adam Scott

See Chapter 6.

BellSouth Classic—$4,500,000
Winner: Zach Johnson

The BellSouth Classic was barely into the third round when the only question for fans was whether the champion had a "k" or an "h" at the end of his first name. It was an "h," as in Zach. The last name was Johnson, and despite some ill-timed caution down the stretch, the little-known rookie steadied himself and took the tournament by one stroke. But it nearly slipped through his hands.

Leading by three going into the final round, Johnson, the 2003 Player of the Year on the Nationwide Tour, rang up five birdies then settled back to make pars. Suddenly, he made four bogeys in five holes and his five-stroke lead was down to one.

"I was just trying to make pars," Johnson said. "There's a danger in that, but on this golf course, par is a good score." Not entirely. While Johnson was coasting on the Tournament Players Club at Sugarloaf, near Atlanta, and parred home to a par 72, Australian Mark Hensby, another former Nationwide Tour player, was racing to a 67.

Johnson started the tournament four shots out of the lead, behind Jose Maria Olazabal and Roger Tambellini, another Nationwide player, who shot 65s on a cold, windy day. Adam Scott, who hung on to win The Players Championship the previous week, shot 68. "I started playing nicely on the back," he said. "I'm pretty happy with that score." But not the next one. He shot 79 and missed the cut. Olazabal was encouraged by his 65, but cautious. At age 38, the two-time Masters champion had been struggling. In his first seven starts, he missed three cuts and withdrew once. "I've been going through a tough spell," he said. The bright moment ended abruptly. He shot 77 in the second round and finished 45th. Tambellini shot 78 but recovered enough to tie for 14th.

Johnson notched four birdies in his final six holes for a 66 and a nine-under 135 total, a two-stroke lead over Craig Bowden, Tim Petrovic and defending champion Ben Crane. "My putter has been pretty good," said Johnson, after a day of such rough weather that there were only 16 scores in the 60s. "With the temperature and the wind the way it is," said Petrovic, after a 70, "it wasn't hard to make three or four bogeys in a row."

Johnson clung jealously to the lead in the third round, with a 68–203 and a three-stroke margin over Australian Scott Hend, another rookie, and Ireland's Padraig Harrington, who keeps threatening. "It would be important to win on the U.S. Tour," Harrington said. "But I'm not putting pressure on myself to do it." Just as well. Harrington bogeyed the first two holes and double-bogeyed the third. After a birdie, he double-bogeyed again and was on his way to fourth place. The Johnson-Hensby drama took center stage in the final round.

"It was a roller coaster," Johnson said. "I don't even know what I shot." It was 72 — just enough and just in time. Johnson seemed to have it all locked up when a birdie at the par-five 10th gave him a five-stroke lead. But he three-putted for bogeys on the next two holes, then bogeyed the 14th and 15th. Then he settled down and parred the last three holes for his first win. A review of the numbers reveals the secret to the victory.

When he birdied the 10th, he had made all 55 of his putts from inside nine feet. Elsewhere in the statistics, he ranked 28th for the tournament in driving distance, 31st in driving accuracy, but more to the point, tied for first in hitting greens in regulation, at 76 percent, and third in putting, an average of 1.6 per hole.

Masters Tournament—$6,000,000
Winner: Phil Mickelson

See Chapter 2.

MCI Heritage—$4,800,000
Winner: Stewart Cink

Stewart Cink, on his way to scoring his third career victory, wrote the latest chapter on how a professional is supposed to act while awaiting a playoff, to wit: Clean out the locker, eat a cheeseburger with only half the bun, eat part of a turkey sandwich, make a few telephone calls, watch television (the tournament, that is), and whatnot.

"I had lots of time," Cink said. "I've never been in that situation before. I didn't know what to do."

The MCI Heritage at Harbour Town Golf Links in Hilton Head Island, South Carolina, had a scrambled start. Cameron Beckman, seeking his second PGA Tour victory, stepped out with a four-under-par 67 for a one-stroke lead in the first round. He enjoyed 12 one-putt greens, including a 38-footer. "I putted like a little kid today," he said. "It was a blast."

But putting never lasts, of course. Then 2003 Open champion Ben Curtis shot 66 in the second round for a one-stroke lead and didn't bother to putt on three holes. He holed out a fairway wedge for an eagle and chipped in twice for birdies. "Three zero putts," Curtis marveled. "I haven't had three zero putts in a month." The zero putts didn't last, either. Up stepped Ted Purdy, age 30, a rookie off the Nationwide Tour, looking for his first win. He poured in five birdies on the first nine and zipped to a six-under 65 for a four-shot lead over Heath Slocum through the third round.

Then it was the final round. Purdy was leading and playing the 10th hole about the time Cink wrapped up a blistering rally. Cink was a non-factor until then. He was in 51st place in the first round, 29th in the second and 22nd in the third. And he started the final round nine shots behind Purdy. Cink was one of the last anyone would have given a chance. But he caught fire in the fourth round, made six birdies and an eagle, and shot 64. It had to be slow torture for Purdy. He had to look at Cink's 64 for the entire second nine. Who knows whether it rattled him, but he did shoot 73 — missing a winning birdie from inside 10 feet at the 18th in regulation — and they were tied.

It was the Heritage's third playoff in four years, and Cink went out and beat Purdy, knocking in a six-footer on the fifth playoff hole. But the drama would not have been complete without the controversial episode at the "waste bunker." This is a sand-filled area that's not played like a regular bunker, meaning a golfer can remove stones and the like, and ground his club.

Cink drove into a waste bunker at the fifth playoff hole, No. 16. He checked with a rules official and was informed that he could do a little housekeeping in there. Then he flew a brilliant 75-yard wedge shot to within six feet of the pin. He made the putt for the win. Or was it?

The ever-present television viewers called in to report that Cink had violated the rules, improving his lie by lifting impediments and running his finger through the sand behind the ball. Cink was distressed. He took off the champion's jacket he had just put on. "I didn't feel right wearing it if there was some question about whether I'd earned it," Cink said. Rules officials reviewed the videotape over and over and confirmed that Cink had not violated any rules. "What I was afraid of is somehow I win this tournament and there may be question marks about it, or an asterisk," he said. "And if that's the case, I'm really sorry."

So Cink had his third career victory and his first since he won the Heritage in 2000 when he trailed Ernie Els by five shots before closing with a 65 to win. And if he wasn't nearly as happy with this one, Ted Purdy had no reservations.

"I didn't see anything I didn't like," Purdy said, "except he whipped me, and I wanted to win."

Shell Houston Open—$5,000,000
Winner: Vijay Singh

Poor Rod Pampling. Let him take a first-round lead, and the old story pops back up — of how he took the first-round lead in the 1999 Open Championship in Britain and then missed the cut, going 71-86. The story got trotted out again at the Shell Houston Open when Pampling, a third-year player from Australia, took the first-round lead with a 66. Then he shot 79. He didn't miss the cut this time. He made it right on the money, at 145.

Meanwhile, whipped by the mid-April wind and rain, the tournament was forced to a Monday finish. And there stood Vijay Singh, with his second victory of the year and the 17th of his career. He started far back in the pack with a 74 and then he put together 66, 69 and 68, for an 11-under-par 277 total at Redstone Golf Club to beat Scott Hoch by two strokes.

"Vijay was just too tough," said Hoch, who started the final round three strokes behind co-leaders Singh and John Huston. "He didn't leave any openings." Hoch closed with a 67, and Huston shot 71 and finished third.

"Today was the best I've played in a long, long time," said Singh, leaving people wondering what he could be talking about. This was not only his second victory of the season, but his sixth top-10 finish in 11 starts.

With the opening 74, Singh started "under the radar," as the current vernacular terms the unnoticed. Pampling birdied his first three holes before the weather kicked up in the first round. He ended his bogey-free 71 with a two-putt birdie at the 18th. It gave him a one-shot lead when Chris Riley, shrugging off heavy winds, birdied his last two holes for a 67. In the second round, Singh got noticed. He vaulted all the way from 94th to fourth, one stroke behind the three-way lead of Zach Johnson, Steve Stricker and Steve Lowery.

When the third round Saturday was suspended, Singh was four under par and still on the course. When the third round was completed the next morning, Singh was atop the leaderboard tied with Huston at seven-under 209. His third-round 69 included a chip-in eagle from 88 feet at No. 12. And when play was suspended again on Sunday, Singh only shrugged. "My mind is all set to play," he said. "I'm just waiting."

Singh came out firing when the waiting was finally over. He birdied two of his first three holes in the final round, dropping a 20-foot putt at the par-five No. 1 and tapping in a three-footer at the 209-yard, par-three No. 3. He was nine under par and leading. Hoch had started even hotter, with birdies on his first three holes. He didn't birdie again until the 12th, and at the par-five 15th, he lofted his 79-yard approach to six feet and made the birdie. Singh had run off seven pars, birdied the 11th, and at the 15th, when Hoch got a tad too close for comfort, he dropped a birdie from 10 feet.

There were two subplots in the tournament. In one, Jay Haas, age 50 but not yet ready to head for the Champions Tour, wanted to become the third player to win on the PGA Tour in four different decades, joining Sam Snead and Raymond Floyd. But more than that, he wanted to make the Ryder Cup team, even if as a captain's pick. He tied for 43rd. Said U.S. captain Hal Sutton, "The way he's swinging, the way he's putting, I don't think he's going to have to worry about being picked."

Singh was the star of the other subplot. He wanted to knock Tiger Woods off the top perch and take over the No. 1 spot in the Official World Golf Ranking. He may have found just the ticket at the Shell Houston Open. Said Singh, "I'd like to play this way all the time."

HP Classic of New Orleans—$5,100,000
Winner: Vijay Singh

When last seen, Vijay Singh was holding the MCI Heritage trophy. When next seen, Vijay Singh was holding the HP Classic of New Orleans trophy. Just a week later, in fact. And Singh, ranked No. 2 in the world, continued to roll on a collision course with No. 1 Tiger Woods. A multiple winner every year, Woods had won only once so far this year. Singh, on the other hand, had just gone back-to-back for his second and third victories of 2004.

And Singh won on Monday again. Heavy spring rains hit the New Orleans area and, what with delays and wash-outs, the tournament ran over into Monday again. This was his third Monday victory on the PGA Tour and the fourth of his career. And of his 18 career wins, it was his eighth come-from-behind victory.

Joe Ogilvie, seeking his first PGA Tour victory, started the final round with a two-stroke lead, and he closed strong enough to win most events, playing English Turn in four-under-par 68. In the process, he found himself just one hole from winning. That lone hole was the last hole in Singh's round. Singh trailed Ogilvie by four starting the final round, and worse, was six behind with eight holes to play. And then he dropped a 25-foot putt for a birdie on his final hole, and that ended Ogilvie's dreams.

"I shot 32 on the front side and I felt I was in control pretty much the whole way around," said Ogilvie. "What can you say? I mean, that's why he's probably the best player in the world right now. He shot 29 on the back nine."

After going 70-65-68, Singh closed with a 63 for a 22-under-par 266 total. There was nothing flimsy about the victory. He had to catch Ogilvie. This he did by playing the final eight holes in seven under par.

Poor Ogilvie. Consider that over his last 46 holes, he made 14 birdies and no bogeys, he got up and down for pars 20 times out of the 22 that he missed the green, and he closed with a 68 — his fourth straight round in the 60s — for a 21-under 267 total. And for that he would lose by a stroke and tie for second with Phil Mickelson. Playing for the first time since winning the Masters, Mickelson birdied three of the last four holes for a 66.

Danny Ellis, a veteran of three back surgeries, had an unceremonious end. Ellis, who regained his PGA Tour card in the 2003 qualifying, led through the first two rounds with an encouraging 63-66–129. The prospects for his first victory were a little brighter. Then he shot 82 in the third round.

Singh, who had five birdies and an eagle on the second nine, at first didn't give himself much of a chance. "I looked up after nine holes and I said, 'Well, it's over,'" Singh said. "But then I made a birdie on 11, 12 and 13, and all of a sudden I said I've got a chance."

He caught Ogilvie with an eagle on the island 15th, dangerously bunkered on both sides. "If I had made a birdie there, I may still not have won," he said. "I think that kind of tightened up the guys behind me as well."

It all came down to Singh's ultimate secret. It sounds simple enough.

"I had patience out there," Singh said. "Like the front nine, when nothing was happening. I was just two under and everybody was way ahead. So I said, 'Just keep going, there is another nine to go. Just play a solid nine and see what happens.' And the putts started going in, and throwing in an eagle here and there, and all of a sudden everything changed."

Wachovia Championship—$5,600,000
Winner: Joey Sindelar

The Wachovia Championship in Charlotte, North Carolina, had something for everyone. You had a troubled Tiger Woods posting his first bogey-free round of the year. There was Vijay Singh gunning for a third victory in three weeks. And there was Phil Mickelson pushing hard, Davis Love catching a hot hand and Kirk Triplett shooting a course record. What you didn't have was anyone noticing that pleasing and self-effacing veteran Joey Sindelar, age 46, who, if not out of place in this traffic, was at least something of a stranger. He hadn't won in 13 years, eight months and 370 starts — since 1990, that is — and for the past five years he had labored just to keep his PGA Tour playing card.

So when it came down to decision time, golf fans could be forgiven if they looked at the final two contenders and said, "Who?" These were Sindelar and Arron Oberholser, 29, best known as the Nationwide Tour graduate who threatened at the AT&T Pebble Beach National Pro-Am early in the year. The rest of the cast had fallen away, and Sindelar ran off three birdies and a par down the stretch, tied Oberholser, then beat him on the second hole of a playoff. This was not only a great relief, it would please his two sons, who never saw him win. Son No. 1 was still in diapers when he last won, at the 1990 Hardee's Golf Classic, and Son No. 2 was still three years away.

"They think those trophies in my case ... I picked them up at a local sporting goods store, to fool them," Sindelar cracked. "Now we've got a real one to show them."

The odds on Sindelar's getting this trophy, though, were on the prohibitive side. Woods, Singh and others made moves. But Oberholser turned them away and looked like a winner when he eagled the par-five 15th, after firing a five-wood second shot to eight feet to get to 13 under par. Then came trouble. He bogeyed the 16th from under a bush and birdied the par-three 17th with a wide tee shot and long chip. And he managed to save par at the 18th to force a playoff with Sindelar.

Sindelar trailed Oberholser by three going into the final round, and after a birdie at the 15th, he still trailed by three with three holes to play, a tough closing stretch at the Quail Hollow Club. Sindelar, nervous, refused to look at the leaderboard. But he turned to his caddie, John Buchna, and asked what it would take to win.

"A couple of birdies," Buchna said bluntly, "and a possible accident."

Sindelar, playing two groups ahead of Oberholser, did his part. He got the two birdies — a 15-foot putt at the 16th and a tee shot to three feet at the par-three 17th. Oberholser closed with a par 72, Sindelar a 69. They tied at 11-under 277. Oberholser bogeyed once more — fatally. They had tied at the first playoff hole, No. 18, and at the second, the 16th, Oberholser bogeyed out of a bunker and Sindelar two-putted from 30 feet for the victory.

Overall, the Wachovia Championship was a series of tight little dramas. Kirk Triplett experienced "Tigermania" first-hand in the first round. Thousands tramped after Woods, watching him do nothing more than break 70 for the second time this year with a 69. Meanwhile, two groups behind, there was Triplett, with practically no gallery, shooting a course-record 64 for a two-stroke lead. Woods rewarded the faithful in the second round with a 66 and 135 total for a two-stroke lead. He had just 22 putts, including seven consecutive one-putts. Said Woods, "It's just a matter of time before it starts coming together." Then he shot 75 in the third round, on his way to finish tied for third.

Davis Love opened his bid in the second round, birdieing four of his last five holes for a 66. Then he was flirting with the lead in the third round until he double-bogeyed the 11th. He would slip to a tie for 21st.

Singh got to within a stroke of the lead in the final round with a chip-in eagle at the 15th. He could smell that third straight victory. But he double-bogeyed the 18th for a 72 and dropped to a tie for 10th. The final drama was Joey Sindelar's to write, and he did, with a two-putt par at the second playoff hole.

"It will take me awhile to understand this is real," Sindelar said. He could always go check the Wachovia Championship trophy his kids were admiring.

EDS Byron Nelson Championship—$5,800,000
Winner: Sergio Garcia

With the arrival of the EDS Byron Nelson Championship in mid-May, the PGA Tour had just about reached the halfway point of the season. Tiger

Woods, the No. 1 player in the world, had won once, the WGC Accenture Match Play in February. That's a good year by most standards, but the world was accustomed to much more from him, and so it was generally agreed that it was high time Tiger Woods started playing like Tiger Woods again.

Accordingly, the real Tiger Woods surfaced in the second round, shooting a 67 and taking a one-stroke lead over who else but his best friend, Mark O'Meara.

"I've always felt comfortable when I've been in the lead," Woods said, which had to be disturbing news to the rest of the field. Alas for him, the spirit didn't last. Woods would fade — not by much, but just enough — and the title went instead to a young man in line behind him in the youth parade.

Sergio Garcia, the 24-year-old Spanish whiz with the retooled swing, had the kind of control Woods was searching for and won on the PGA Tour for the first time in two years. He did it with a tap-in for par on the first playoff hole against Robert Damron and Dudley Hart. Woods tied for fourth, Ernie Els tied for seventh, and Vijay Singh, a contender going into the final round, closed with a 78 and plunged to a tie for 59th. One member of the game's hierarchy wasn't in the picture at all. Phil Mickelson, who won the Masters a month earlier, shot 69-72 and missed the cut.

"Winning is always great," Garcia said. "I pulled it through and I'm happy."

In the third round, Garcia missed only one fairway and hit every green in regulation, posting a five-under-par 65 for a two-stroke lead over Jerry Kelly going into the finale. Woods, for the second consecutive week, held the 36-hole lead and let it get away. He was erratic, to say the least. He lost the lead with a three-putt bogey at No. 2, and he went the last seven holes without hitting a fairway or making a birdie. Singh also had his troubles. He was one of eight players who had a share of the lead at one point, but he went the final 10 holes in two over par and shot 68. And so Garcia entered the final round three shots ahead of Woods, four ahead of Vijay Singh. Who was the bigger threat?

"Myself," the cagey Garcia said. "If I don't beat myself out there, I should be okay."

Damron and Hart both closed strongly to take the clubhouse lead. Damron eagled the 15th with a seven iron from the fairway and shot 66. Hart birdied three of the last five holes for a 67. They shared the lead at 10-under 270. Garcia, bogeying from sand and trees, shot a one-over 71, the first Byron Nelson winner in 11 years not to break par in the final round. In the playoff, Damron three-putted from 50 feet for a bogey, and Hart missed the fairway, missed the green, and flubbed a chip shot and double-bogeyed. Garcia tapped in for the victory.

Bank of America Colonial—$5,300,000
Winner: Steve Flesch

The Bank of America Colonial was a time for everyone to get well, what with near-career rounds, tying the course record, resurrections and the like.

The problem for Steve Flesch is that he had to get well in a hurry. In the last two holes, in fact.

"I knew I was two ahead going into 17," Flesch said. "I don't think that affected anything, other than I probably just lost my focus for a second."

He lost it long enough to miss the green from the fairway, then — horrors — leave a chip in the rough. Finally, he had to sink a five-foot putt to hold the damage to a bogey. Then Flesch parred the 18th and — giving himself a heck of a present on his 37th birthday — won by one stroke over Chad Campbell.

"I wouldn't change the way any of it worked out," said Flesch, posting his second career victory. He hung in tight at the par-70 Colonial Country Club in Fort Worth, Texas. Shooting 66-69-67-67–269, Flesch was two strokes behind the resurrected Craig Perks in the first round, one behind Justin Leonard and J.L. Lewis in the second, and tied for a two-stroke lead with Campbell and Brian Gay going into the final round.

The Colonial was a joy for Perks, the unknown Australian who came from nowhere to win the 2002 Players Championship. Then he decided to retool his swing and disappeared. Early in 2004 Perks had missed 10 of 12 cuts, so his first-round 64 was a deliverance. "I could play okay," he said. "But when it was crunch time, I messed up." And this 64? "It shows me I can still play," he said. He went on to finish fourth.

Flesch birdied four of his first five holes, but found a stubborn course from there. "I just kept hitting it about 20, 25 feet," he said, "but I had putts that were breaking two or three feet."

Leonard had opened with a par 70, back in the pack, and seemed to be on his way to a record in the second round. He was seven under through the 11th. Then two bogeys — a three-putt and a missed green — gave him a 64 for a 134 total. "That was a little bit deflating," Leonard said. Lewis, who missed five cuts in 12 starts since the Bob Hope Chrysler Classic, was bogey-free in his 66. Flesch stayed close with his 69.

Then Campbell came barreling along in the third round with a 61, the third player in two years to tie the course record. He started with an eagle and three straight birdies, and had a run of five birdies from the 11th. "Shooting 61 here, with all the history, it doesn't get much better than that," Campbell said. Gay was eight under par through the 12th but bogeyed three of the last four holes for 65, and Flesch's modest-looking 67 tied him for the lead at 202.

In the final round, a new challenger was heard from. Jesper Parnevik eagled No. 1 and by the turn was only a shot off the lead. Then he crashed to a 41 on the last nine.

Flesch took the lead with a six-foot birdie at the par-four seventh. He missed three birdie tries from five feet or less, but a curling 16-footer at the par-three 16th gave him a two-shot lead on Campbell, who missed a birdie from 13 feet. Flesch's bogey at the 17th didn't ruin him, because Campbell caught a bunker and also bogeyed it. Campbell closed with a last-gasp birdie from five feet at the 18th, but Flesch wrapped it up with a par.

"I hit it so well," Flesch said. "It would have been a shame not to win."

FedEx St. Jude Classic—$4,700,000
Winner: David Toms

It could be said that David Toms hardly had the qualifications for winning anything, much less winning by six strokes. Consider that he had surgery on his left wrist for bone chips after the 2003 season, that he spent three months with the wrist in a cast and that he had made only two cuts in his previous seven outings before the FedEx St. Jude Classic late in May. Never mind the odds. Toms, the defending champion — he hadn't won since the 2003 event — won again by six strokes. And just how did he turn the tournament into a battle for second place?

"I just had to grind it out all the way," Toms said. He was referring to dealing with the winds that whipped the TPC at Southwind in Memphis, Tennessee. "I knew it would be tough for anybody to shoot a low score," he said. "I knew as long as I could hang in there and make a lot of pars, I'd be okay." He started the final round leading by seven and won by six. Toms shot 67-63-65-73 for a 16-under-par 268 total. There were only eight cards in the 60s the last day and Bob Estes had one of them, a 69 that locked up second place by a stroke over Tim Herron (70) and Steve Lowery (67).

The only time Toms trailed was in the first round, and then by only a stroke. Vaughn Taylor needed only 24 putts in a 66 for a one-stroke lead in the first round. "There's three more days left and a lot of golf to play," said Taylor, who had made only five cuts in 11 starts. "I'm just going to enjoy it and hopefully keep it up." He did, fairly well. He tied for fifth.

On a course dried out and buffeted by winds, only eight players broke 70 in the first round. Said Toms, tied for second with Paul Stankowski with 67s, "When you were aggressive, you had to make sure you knew what the wind was doing and get the right club." Toms had a chance to take the lead but bogeyed two of his last five holes, including his final, No. 9, where his wedge approach from 137 yards was a foot short of safety and drew back into the water.

Come the second round and Toms was on his way. "It seems the more I've played this tournament, the better I've played," he said after an eight-under 63 for a one-stroke lead on Taylor (65) at the halfway point. Toms caught Taylor with a birdie at the second, then took the lead with an eagle from two feet at the par-five third. He birdied the fifth and sixth, then got three more birdies on his last seven holes, including a seven iron to five feet at the 18th.

It was something of a cakewalk the rest of the way. In the third round, he birdied five of his first seven holes on his way to the 65, his 11th straight round in the 60s on Southwind. "What Dave is doing today is phenomenal," said John Daly, a victim of the winds. A 72 dropped him from a tie for fourth to 19th with a round to play.

Toms was right. In those winds, no one could go low enough in the final round. He hit only nine greens and his putting wasn't as sharp as usual in a five-bogey, three-birdie 73. But it was far more than enough.

"This does a lot for me," Toms said. "Makes me feel a lot better about my game, about myself."

Memorial Tournament—$5,250,000
Winner: Ernie Els

It was Jack Nicklaus' tournament on his golf course, and all at Muirfield Village were there to see — well, at age 64, to see whether he would make the 36-hole cut. Nicklaus rewarded the faithful by doing just that. Even better, he treated them to an almost-ace.

At the par-three 12th hole in the second round, his tee shot smashed into the hole on the fly — but rocketed back out and ended up on the fringe. "I end up missing the green after holing it," Nicklaus said. He two-putted for a par, shot 74, and made the cut at 147. He finished 77-71 and tied for 63rd place at 295, seven over par.

Meanwhile, the tournament was a mad scramble until Ernie Els finally took control in the fourth round to win by four strokes over Fred Couples, a former Memorial champion but an unlikely challenger this time, a 44-year-old with a bad back and creaky game.

First, no one was going anywhere who couldn't handle Muirfield's 18th hole, an uphill, dogleg-right par-four. In the first round alone, five players came to the 18th with at least a share of the lead and all got hurt. The worst hurt were J.L. Lewis, who made a seven, and South Africa's Darren Fichardt, a six, after their delicate chip shots rolled down into the fairway.

Els and Ben Curtis, a local favorite from just 20 minutes away, escaped the monster with pars — Els from a bunker and Curtis with a delicate chip — to tie for the first-round lead at 68. Eight other players were in a crunch at 69. Curtis was bogey-free, but Els had a wild time, including a 50-foot putt for an eagle at No. 7, three-putting from 20 feet for a bogey, and holing out a bunker shot for a birdie at the 17th. "It was quite a ride there at the end," Els said.

Curtis was still bogey-free through the second round for a 69 that tied him with England's Justin Rose (67) for the halfway lead at 137. Neither Tiger Woods nor Vijay Singh had made a move to this point. Woods, still erratic, opened with a 72. His 68 in the second round, including a double bogey, lifted him to within three strokes of the lead. Singh, vexed by his putting, shot 73 and 72.

Els asserted himself in the third round and took the 54-hole lead. "He attacked the course today," Couples said. "He had a couple breaks, but it was an easy 66." At 204, Els held a two-stroke lead on Couples (68), South Korea's K.J. Choi (68) and Rose (69). Els bolted home with two late birdies. He got up-and-down at the par-five 15th and holed a six-footer at the par-three 16th. Earlier, he birdied the fifth and sixth holes, and then turned disaster into a birdie at the par-five 11th. He had to chop his tee shot back to the fairway, then hit a daring five iron from 203 yards into a breeze to 18 feet and holed it.

Els' display in the final round moved Nicklaus to grin and ask, "What was the key putt — 12, 13, 14, 15, 16, 17?"

Well, there was the five-footer at the seventh that cooled Tiger Woods. Then a 10-footer to save par at the 12th, a 30-footer for birdie at the 13th, a 15-footer to keep his two-shot lead at the 17th. And so forth, until he beat a game Couples (68) by four. "It's tough to call one a key putt," Els said. "As Jack says, I made almost every putt I had to make."

Buick Classic—$5,250,000
Winner: Sergio Garcia

"I've been fortunate enough to do well pretty well in playoffs — not only here but also around the world," Sergio Garcia was saying. "I feel pretty comfortable in them."

This time it was the Buick Classic at Westchester Country Club in Rye, New York, in mid-June, and it was not only his second win of the season but his second in a playoff. A month earlier he won the EDS Byron Nelson Championship on the first extra hole. Here, Garcia, now age 24 and still pretty much the bouncy Spanish kid and emerging from a protracted swing change, beat South Africa's Rory Sabbatini and Ireland's Padraig Harrington.

All three were comparatively late coming into view, the early fireworks having been provided by Vijay Singh and his hot putter, Fred Couples sporting acupuncture rings, and even ageless Loren Roberts, outrunning the kids.

Garcia, who trailed by as much as seven strokes from the start, worked his way up the leaderboard, shooting 70-67-68-67. All three birdied the 18th in regulation to tie at 12-under-par 272. Garcia holed about a five-footer, Harrington holed a 16-foot chip shot for a 68, and Sabbatini, in the final threesome, holed a seven-foot putt for a 70.

Harrington, whom Garcia beat in a playoff in the 1999 German Masters, missed a chance to win on the first extra hole when a seven-foot birdie putt slid by. He bogeyed the second extra hole and was gone. At the third extra hole, the par-five 18th, Garcia floated a 90-yard wedge shot to within seven feet of the cup. Sabbatini's third shot, from 70 yards, didn't reach the upper level of the green, leaving him a 21-footer. Sabbatini missed, but Garcia didn't.

Garcia did not start the final round with promise. He bogeyed the second and third holes. Then he surged with four straight birdies from the seventh. He three-putted the 12th for a bogey, but birdied the 13th and got to 11 under par with another birdie at the par-three 16th. The closing birdie clinched a spot for him. "I felt like if I was patient and I just kept playing my game, I could make some birdies, because I've done well on this course and feel comfortable on it," Garcia said.

Vijay Singh, taking the first-round lead with an eight-under 63, solved his putting problems by hitting the ball closer to the hole. "From three, four feet," Singh offered, "you can't pick out too many bad lines." With a second-round 70, he slipped a stroke behind Fred Couples (65–132), who played wearing acupuncture rings in his ears. "I don't get it," said Couples, after visiting an acupuncturist for his aching back, "but I'm going to keep trying it."

Loren Roberts, age 48, upstaged the youth with a 64 for a 12-under 201 total and the third-round lead by one stroke over Sabbatini (65) and Cameron Beckman (66), who birdied the last five holes — three of them on chip-ins. Beckman would fade to a 75 in the final round and Roberts to a 78.

U.S. Open Championship—$5,650,000
Winner: Retief Goosen

See Chapter 3.

Booz Allan Classic—$4,800,000
Winner: Adam Scott

Adam Scott, a 23-year-old Australian and part of golf's youth movement, and also winner of The Players Championship in March, got a lot closer to his hero than he really wanted to in the Booz Allan Classic. That would be Greg Norman, and there is much about Norman a young golfer would want to emulate. But he wouldn't want to follow him off the end of the pier.

"I was getting a little nervy on the back nine," said Scott, "nervy" sounding like the Aussie equivalent of "antsy." He was on his way to a four-stroke victory over Charles Howell, another member of the youth movement, that wasn't nearly as easy at it seemed. For a while he seemed headed for a Normanesque collapse in the final round. Scott remembers much about Norman, including his crash at the 1996 Masters. Norman led by six going into that final round; Scott led by six going into this final round.

The drama of this story started with the venue, the par-71 TPC at Avenel, near Washington, D.C. Was the course vulnerable? Anyone not in the 60s needn't apply. In fact, anyone not under par, 142, missed the halfway cut.

Howell set the pace in the first round with a course-record 10-under-par 61. "It was one of those funny days where everything tends to work your way," Howell said. "The best you can do is get out of the way and let it continue to happen." Howell had a birdie and two eagles on the par-fives and made six putts of 15 or more feet, but at one point in front of only 32 spectators. The tournament came the week after the U.S. Open and many of the top players took the week off.

Scott took the lead for good with a 62 in the second round for a 36-hole Avenel record of 128 and a two-stroke lead on Howell and Olin Browne. Scott hit all 18 greens in regulation and needed only 28 putts. By the third round, Scott had turned the tournament into a shambles, shooting a 67 in strong winds for a six-stroke lead. Could he be beaten?

"We could slip him something in his food tonight," said Browne, in second place those six huge strokes behind.

"It was playing tough at the end, and I just managed to hang on," said Scott, after a 67 for a 195 total. Managing to hang on included, for example, slugging a drive 300 yards into the wind at the 18th to wrap up a round that had seven birdies, three bogeys and an assortment of shots from rough, sand and the like. Fighting the same conditions, Browne (71) bogeyed two of his last three holes, and Rich Beem, who tied Scott briefly, bogeyed four straight holes coming in for a 72.

It got tight in the final round. Scott had got up by seven through the sixth hole, and then Howell got cooking and closed to within two strokes. Starting at the 11th, he ran off five consecutive birdies and got another boost when Scott put his tee shot on a cart path at the 13th. Scott scrambled to a par, birdied the next two holes, then had to save par again at the 16th, this time with an 11-foot putt. Finally, Scott got home with a 68 and a 21-under 263 total that tied the tournament and course records and that won by four.

Said Howell, who closed with a 65, "Starting as far back as I did today, it's nice to play golf with nothing to lose."

Said Scott, who had the most to lose, "It's nice to be able to respond to a bit of pressure."

Cialis Western Open—$4,800,000
Winner: Stephen Ames

Words to live by: Never make a promise you can't keep. Especially to the kids.

Early in the week of the Cialis Western Open, Stephen Ames had sat down with his two boys and said, "Guys, I'm going to win this week for you." And so he did, not only keeping his word but, at age 40, notching his first victory on the PGA Tour in his 166th start. His biggest problem down the final stretch was his emotions, realizing he was about to keep faith with his boys.

"The last three holes, I was watching the leaderboard and it was tough," Ames said. "I kept asking where my wife was because I wanted to make sure my boys were there to enjoy this with me." And they were. First, Ames hugged his brother and caddie, Robert, and then his sons ran to him.

That first win was in doubt when Ames followed an opening 67 with a 73 that shoved him deep in the pack. He bounced back into a tie for the lead with a third-round 64, then held off Steve Lowery with a 70 for a two-stroke victory on a 10-under-par 274 total at Cog Hill Country Club in Lemont, Illinois, near Chicago. And the PGA Tour had its first champion from Trinidad and Tobago, a nation of islands in the Caribbean.

The tournament was notable for another reason. It was early July and Tiger Woods was still trying to find his second victory of the year. He started 70-73 and was as deep as 50th place, and he finished 65-71 and tied for seventh. "I was putting well," Woods said, "but when you've got 20-, 30-footers, it's hard to make a run at the leaders."

Loren Roberts, age 49, known as the "Boss of the Moss" for his putting touch, posted a bogey-free 64 for a one-stroke edge over Robert Allenby in the first round. "I drove the ball in the fairway just about every hole," Roberts said. "If you're going to make some putts, it equates to a low score." A second-round 75 ended his bid. A three-way tie popped up in the second round at six-under 136 — Lowery (68), Matt Gogel (64) and Charles Howell (67) — leaving Ames four shots astern. In the third round, Australian Mark Hensby, who used to sleep in his car because he couldn't afford better, shot a bogey-free 67 to tie with Ames, who climbed with a 64. In the fourth round, Hensby struggled to a 73, leaving the battle between Ames and Lowery.

It seemed one of those golf oddities would thwart Ames in the final round. At No. 3, he was in his backswing when a marshal yelled at fans to stand. Ames yanked the shot behind a tree, then caught a bunker, and then two-putted for a bogey. "The day is long," Ames told himself. "There's a lot of holes to play."

He caught Lowery at the par-three 12th, dropping a five-footer for birdie, and Lowery fell out at the 13th with a double bogey, going from rough to more rough. Ames was alone in the lead. All he had to do was get safely to the 18th to see the kids. "I just had to wait for it to happen," Ames said. "This week, it happened."

Other notables of the week: The second-most important shot of the tournament, after Ames' winning putt, was the eight-footer Lowery dropped for a par at the final hole. It gave him a second place and thus a spot in The Open Championship as the lowest finisher not otherwise exempt ... Casey Wittenberg, age 19, low amateur at the Masters and sophomore-to-be at Oklahoma State, made his professional debut here and missed the cut with 77-75 ... Defending U.S. Open champion Jim Furyk tied for seventh place in his second start after wrist surgery in March.

John Deere Classic—$3,800,000
Winner: Mark Hensby

A funny thing happened to Mark Hensby on his way to victory. The slight, 33-year-old Australian, who came up the hard way, made the John Deere Classic his first career PGA Tour win. Then to the disbelief of all, he turned down the berth in The Open Championship in Britain that was waiting for the highest finisher not otherwise qualified. Hensby said that he had no experience on links courses and wouldn't have enough time to prepare to play at Royal Troon the following week.

"It was really a no-brainer," Hensby said. "I've never played a course like that." That was merely the first surprise. In turning down the berth, Hensby said he was giving it to England's John Morgan, whom he had just beaten in a playoff. When Morgan contacted the Royal and Ancient Golf Club of St. Andrews to claim his prize, the R&A informed him that the berth was not Hensby's to give. It would go to whomever was next in the R&A procedure.

The victory was nonetheless sweet for the little-known Hensby. He had been laboring on the Nationwide Tour on and off for six years, and he came to the PGA Tour after finishing seventh on the Nationwide money list in 2003. Things had been looking up on the big tour in 2004: He had finished second in the BellSouth Classic and tied for third in both the Western Open and the Chrysler Classic.

All in all, at the par-71 TPC at Deere Run at Silvis, Illinois, this was the tournament of improbables. First, it belonged to Argentina's Jose Coceres. Shooting 62-68-68, Coceres led through the first three rounds and then parred the first seven holes in the final round. Then he double-bogeyed No. 8. Hensby started the final round four strokes behind Coceres, Morgan five behind, and they were already breathing down his neck before he crashed at the eighth.

Hensby birdied five of the first eight holes, including a tap-in after just missing an eagle from seven feet at the par-five second hole and a 16-foot putt at the sixth. Morgan pulled within a stroke of Hensby with three straight birdies. Hensby got not one but two great breaks at the 17th. His drive went into the trees and bounced back into the fairway, then his second shot also went into the trees and bounced back into the fairway. He finally reached the green and saved par. "You need some luck," Hensby explained, wrapping up a card of 68-65-69-66. Morgan, after posting 66-69-68, birdied four of his last five holes — including a 30-footer at the 18th — for a 65 to tie Hensby at 16-under-par 268.

At the second hole of the playoff, Morgan hit his tee shot far to the left and just waved goodbye to it. Hampered by an awkward stance, he chipped across the green and into a bunker. He nearly holed the bunker shot for a par, but that was his last chance. Hensby, who had hit the green, two-putted for a par.

The Open Championship—€6,001,690
Winner: Todd Hamilton

See Chapter 4.

B.C. Open—$3,000,000
Winner: Jonathan Byrd

As the contestants in the B.C. Open were grinding down the final stretch, they didn't need scorekeepers. They needed traffic cops. Jonathan Byrd, leader through the middle rounds, had slipped into an eight-way tie for the lead. As he came to the 15th tee, he had an odd reaction. "It almost made the last four holes easier," Byrd said, "because I knew I had to make birdies to win."

Everyone was making birdies at En-Joie Golf Club, in Endicott, New York, soggy from storms and being played under the lift-clean-place provision. Kelly Gibson, 40 and winless since turning professional in 1986, took the first-round lead with an eight-under-par 64 and hoped for heavier weather. Said Gibson, "I hope a hurricane comes tomorrow and there's a one-round winner." Alas, the affable Gibson was not long for the leaderboard.

Another unfamiliar name popped up in the first round — Camilo Villegas, age 22, from Colombia and a former University of Florida star, in only his fourth tournament. He was one stroke off the lead in the first round with a 65 that included a 29 on his second nine. "It's not hard," he said, "when you're in the middle of the fairway and the greens are that soft."

"It's a horse race," said Notah Begay, who shot a 62 in the second round. "The guys in front aren't guaranteed anything."

Byrd could vouch for that. He rang up nine birdies in the second round for a 65 and a one-stroke lead at 132, but the pack was still tight. Daniel Chopra (65) and John Morgan (68), the playoff loser in the John Deere Classic the week before, were tied at 133. Four others were one stroke further behind, and the cast kept changing as the birdies flew. Robert Gamez, for example, had 11 birdies and tied the course record with a 61 and was four strokes off the lead.

Byrd's performance was all the more encouraging to him because of the hip surgery he underwent in February. "I felt good the last three months," Byrd said. "I haven't got it done, but I've seen a lot of good signs." The next good sign was his 68 in the third round. He still led by one, and he had never led after three rounds. He birdied the first three holes, and Morgan, his playing partner, birdied two. "I thought we were going to run away with it," Byrd said. Not quite. Morgan took the lead briefly at the par-five No. 5, two-putting from 65 feet for a fourth straight birdie against Byrd's three-putt bogey from a mere 17 feet.

Begay's horse race came down to the 72nd hole, but he wasn't in it. First, Byrd bogeyed the 12th hole and was in that eight-way tie for the lead. As he thought to himself at the 15th tee, he needed a couple of birdies, and he got them, retaking the lead. Then it was almost snatched away from him.

Ted Purdy, playing with Byrd, cut his lead to one with a birdie at the 17th. Then at the 18th, Byrd put his approach 20 feet from the cup, but Purdy put his eight-iron second shot to three feet, and darkness was falling. "I thought we'd have a playoff tomorrow," Byrd said. A birdie would have won for Byrd, but he missed the try from 20 feet, and then Purdy addressed his three-footer for a tying birdie. He missed it. "I pulled it," Purdy said. "I'm heartbroken right now. Now I won't be able to sleep for a couple of weeks."

Byrd had his second career victory and also a new look at himself. "I could easily have put my head down," he said, contemplating his errors, "but I was still in the driver's seat. I'm proud of the way I finished."

U.S. Bank Championship in Milwaukee—$3,500,000
Winner: Carlos Franco

Carlos Franco is from Paraguay and Vijay Singh is from Fiji, and thus they are about half a world apart, give or take. And Franco is also about that far away from Singh when it comes to practicing his golf. Singh is the demon of the practice tee. Franco regards practice with an exceedingly jaundiced eye.

Singh has mentioned this a time or two. Franco said, "He tells me, 'Practice more, practice more,' and I say, 'I don't like it. Maybe I need it, but I don't like it.' I'd rather go fishing."

Fishing is pretty much what Franco did during the week of the U.S. Bank Championship, while he was in the process of winning it. It was his second victory in the tournament, which was the Greater Milwaukee Open when he first won it in 1999. It was also his first victory in about four years.

Franco had to work his way up. Brown Deer Park, a par-70 course of 6,759 yards, one of the shortest on the PGA Tour, was under heavy assault. A total of 62 players broke par in the first round and eight tied for the lead at five-under-par 65, tying the PGA Tour record for a single-round tie. Of them, Brett Quigley fared the best at the end. He finished tied for second behind Franco.

Franco shot a 68 in the first round. From there, he led or shared the lead, shooting 63-69-67 for a 13-under-par 267 total and a two-stroke victory over Quigley (69) and Fred Funk (66).

"I'm double-happy," Franco said. First for the win, and second that his wife Celsa, who had only watched him on television when he began playing the tour five years earlier, was with him this time. And what did she say when he hefted a check for $630,000, his biggest ever? "She doesn't speak to me," Franco said. "Only crying."

In the second round, without so much as hitting a ball on the practice range, Franco took the lead with a 63 for a 131 total and a one-stroke lead on Rich Beem (66). "When I came here in 1999 — 100 percent no practice," Franco said. "When I practice, I come to the golf course a little tired. A lot of guys hit 200 balls. If I do, I have no chance to play 18 holes."

Practice or not, Franco found himself in a dogfight in the third round. Quigley shot the day's best, 64; Patrick Sheehan, who was part of the first-round traffic jam, shot 67, and Franco a 69, and they were tied going into the final round.

"I'm sure I'll be nervous tomorrow," Sheehan said. "But there's 25 guys that can win this." He led Franco by a stroke going into the final nine and blew four shots through three holes — at bogey at the 11th, a double bogey off a tree at the 12th and a bogey at the 13th. He shot 70 and tied for fourth. Quigley shot 69 and was co-runner-up with Fred Funk (66). "I thought I'd be more nervous than I was today," Quigley said. "I played good golf, just didn't make the putts."

And Franco, who spent his free time fishing at a friend's pond, shot the 67 and won by two.

Buick Open—$4,500,000
Winner: Vijay Singh

Vijay Singh, the Fijian who wears holes in practice tees, won the Buick Open by changing two fundamental things — his putter and his focus.

The combination was as impressive as it was successful in what clearly was already Singh's year, although it had only reached August. Except for a tie at 36 holes, and also for an uneasy nine holes in the final round, Singh was in command all the way en route to his fourth victory of the year and the 19th of his career. Singh shot 63-70-65-67–265, 23 under par at Warwick Hills at Grand Blanc, Michigan, beating a surging John Daly by one stroke.

For the most obvious reason for all this success, you didn't have to look any further than the putter in his hands. It was now the conventional-sized putter, not the long "belly putter" he had used for over two years. "I'm a great chipper and a good bunker player," Singh said, "but if you keep missing short putts, that kind of eats into your game. And you put so much pressure into going for the flags, that whenever you make a mistake, it's a bogey."

The other reason was that Singh had decided to quit thinking about Tiger Woods and the No. 1 ranking and stick to playing golf. "I put too much pressure on myself trying to get that spot in the beginning of the year," Singh admitted. "I have not been playing that well, and maybe [I was] focusing on the wrong things. I'm really not worried about who is No. 1 now."

Warwick Hills, a relatively short, open course with greens holding after soaking rains, was a sitting duck for Singh in the first round. He warmed up with a nine-under-par 63 in which he ran off eight straight threes, starting at No. 8. Five were birdies, one was an eagle, the other two pars.

"I've never made so many threes in my life — except on a par-three course," Singh cracked.

The 63 gave him a one-stroke lead on Olin Browne, but he cooled to a 70 in the second round and was caught at 133 by Jim Furyk (67). Tiger Woods couldn't quite get it all together, but added a 68 to his opening 67 and was two behind. "There are some good names, but no matter who is on board, you're going to have to make a bunch of birdies," Woods said. "You can't go out there and make a bunch of pars." John Daly was one of the names. He shot a 64 that drew him within one. "I needed a round like this to get some confidence," Daly said. And that confidence served him well in the final round.

Singh added a 65 for 198 in the third round and pulled two ahead of Daly (66) and three ahead of Woods (66) and Carlos Franco (67). History was on Singh's side. He won the last six tournaments that he led after 54 holes. This ended up as the seventh, but not without some suspense. Woods and Franco both kept the heat on with 66s, but gained only a stroke, tying two strokes back. Daly was a different matter. This turned into a game of tag.

Daly eagled the second hole from 142 yards to tie Singh, then pulled ahead with a birdie at the third. Then Singh birdied the 12th to tie, then made the decisive birdie at the 14th that put him ahead to stay. Daly just missed one last chance to tie. At the 18th, Singh caught the rough and bogeyed for a 67. And Daly faced a makeable putt for the par that would tie him. But he also bogeyed, two-putting for a 66 to fall one stroke short.

The International—$5,000,000
Winner: Rod Pampling

Anyone venturing into The International in Castle Rock, Colorado, has to know first that scoring is done by something called a modified Stableford System. Forget the usual over-par and under-par numbers. This was by points. Birdies were worth two points, pars zero, bogeys worth minus one point, and double bogeys and worse, minus three points.

Oh, and eagles were worth five points, which is what Australian Rod Pampling rang up at the 17th hole of the final round to beat Germany's Alex Cejka. Pampling went into the scorebook with 31 points, two better than Cejka and the lowest winning total since the event returned to cumulative four-round scoring in 1993.

Pampling, age 34, a former greenskeeper, to his chagrin was still remembered as the person who led the 1999 Open Championship in Britain in the first round, then shot 86 and missed the cut. "I just keep myself in the present," Pampling insisted, defensively. "I knew I could celebrate after I had finished my job."

The International field was not one of the strongest. Some players were elsewhere, warming up for the PGA Championship the following week, among them Phil Mickelson, Tiger Woods, Vijay Singh and Sergio Garcia.

Of the top players, Ernie Els and defending champion Davis Love were in the field. Love ran away with the 2003 tournament with 46 points.

Chris DiMarco seemed bent on running away with this one. After the rain-interrupted first round was completed the next day, he found conditions in the second round benign and much to his liking, and so ripped off nine birdies and took only one bogey for 17 points. That gave him a robust 12-point lead over Pampling, who hadn't finished his round because of bad weather. "You're seeing a lot of good scores out there," DiMarco said. "I'm rolling the ball really well on the greens. To make 17 birdies the last two days is pretty impressive."

What looked like a runaway turned out to be anything but when DiMarco shot the equivalent of a stroke-play 77 in the third round, allowing 17 players to move within 10 points of him.

"I was plus-seven and I didn't think that would be good enough, but obviously Chris didn't play as well as he could have," Pampling said. "He let us back in." DiMarco had eight bogeys and three birdies in the third round Saturday to drop into a tie for the lead with Pampling. Cejka was two points back after a six-birdie round, and Tom Pernice and Bob Tway were tied for fourth with 26.

"I guess I made it a good tournament, eh?" DiMarco said.

Cejka started the final round one point behind, but dropped six points with double bogeys at the eighth and sixteenth. Then Pampling jumped on his chance at the 492-yard, par-five 17th. His tee shot left him 183 yards to the green, and he smacked a seven iron to the right fringe, pin-high, 21 feet from the flag. He rolled in the breaking putt for a five-point eagle that held up for a two-point win over Cejka. Said Pampling: "It was just a matter of hanging in there."

PGA Championship—$6,500,000
Winner: Vijay Singh

See Chapter 5.

WGC - NEC Invitational—$7,000,000
Winner: Stewart Cink

It was one of those curious questions that comes back on itself. Stewart Cink was cruising along in the WGC - NEC Invitational, and after another outstanding day in the third round, someone asked what went right. Cink, sitting comfortably atop the leaderboard, contemplated the matter for a moment, and then had to concede the point. "Well, nothing went wrong," Cink said. "I guess that's what went right."

Cink may have felt just a smidgen of heat from Rory Sabbatini on the final nine, but if so, he brushed it away and completed a wire-to-wire run — making 60 of 64 putts inside 10 feet — to win by a luxurious four strokes. "It's just indescribable how it feels," Cink said, still irked by the memory of the 2001 U.S. Open, which he lost when he missed a short putt on the final hole and double-bogeyed.

If anything, the pressure should have been off for Cink that week late in August in Akron, Ohio. He had just been made a captain's pick for the U.S. Ryder Cup team. But if anything, Cink himself cranked up the pressure, grinding through the select field at long and testing Firestone Country Club. But before that, there was a sequence of events Cink would never forget.

The Monday of this week — which was the day after the end of the PGA Championship — Ryder Cup captain Hal Sutton made Cink and Jay Haas his two choices for the United States team. Cink finally could admit that he was concerned all along about making the team. "I said it a bunch of times — I'm not playing for the Ryder Cup," Cink said. "I'm just trying to play The International, trying to play the Buick Open. But the truth is I was trying to make the Ryder Cup, too. Now I don't have to do that."

Tomorrow meant the final round. Cink opened with a 63-68, and now in the third round he chipped in at the 18th for a 68, an 11-under-par 204 total and a five-stroke lead. This fourth round was a crucial time for Cink. He was 0-for-6 in tournaments he had led after 54 holes. "I wanted to get that monkey off my back," he said.

There was that one brief moment Sunday. Sabbatini made three straight birdies on the first nine and birdied the 14th to close within two strokes of Cink. But a pair of bogeys stalled him, and this was a different Cink under the pressure. He bogeyed the 10th, but then ran off seven solid pars, and at the 18th, he stuck his seven-iron approach 15 feet from the flag and birdied. It was a 70, an 11-under-par 269 total and a four-stroke victory over Sabbatini (68) and Tiger Woods (69). It was the second win of the season for Cink, the fourth of his career, the first when he was leading after 54 holes.

"It's probably more nerve-wracking than sleeping with a one-shot lead or being tied, because everybody expects you to win, and the only other thing you can do is mess up," Cink said. "I can be a frontrunner like anybody else, and I can polish it off."

Reno-Tahoe Open—$3,000,000
Winner: Vaughn Taylor

The Reno-Tahoe Open was Steve Allan's tournament to lose, as he was leading by two strokes coming to the final hole that wind-whipped Sunday in Nevada. Alas, Allan, an Australian in his fourth year on the PGA Tour and looking for his first victory, did lose it. He double-bogeyed the 18th to fall into a four-way playoff, which Vaughn Taylor converted into his first victory in his first full year on the circuit.

Taylor was as much a survivor as a winner, what with just about all the weather anyone could want hitting the tournament that August week, opposite the WGC - NEC Invitational. Rain and lightning delayed play for hours in the first two rounds, and heavy winds struck in the fourth round, so severe that officials considered suspending play. Only 11 players broke par in the final round, and the scoring average for the round at the par-72 Montreux Golf and Country Club was 74.352, second only to the 78.727 at the U.S. Open.

Under the circumstances, the final four players looked pretty good. Taylor closed with a 75, Scott McCarron a 71, rookie Hunter Mahan a 74 and Allan a 74 to tie at 10-under-par 278. Taylor made two clutch putts in the process — a 14-footer on the last hole of regulation to join the tie and then an 11-footer to win on the first extra hole.

"I can't believe it," said Taylor, age 28, a Nationwide Tour alumnus and a rookie on the PGA Tour. "I stayed relaxed out there. I hung in there. I just can't believe it." Taylor came through the weather impressively, shooting 67-67-69, and trailing in the first round by one stroke, leading the second round by two, and trailing by one going into the fourth. In the final round he suffered two double bogeys and two bogeys in winds that gusted to 45 miles an hour and forced officials to take away the scoring standards that accompany each group.

Taylor started the final round at 13 under, trailing Roland Thatcher by one stroke. At the second hole, he had to hit a six iron to get home from only 150 yards, but he got it to 17 feet and holed the putt for a birdie to tie Thatcher. Taylor double-bogeyed the par-four third and the par-four 14th, then bogeyed the par-four 15th. He had slipped back to nine under par, but made it 10 under with the birdie at the 18th.

McCarron, a hometown favorite, made three birdies, saved par after bouncing off a cart path at the 15th, and bogeyed the 16th, but got up and down for a par at the 18th for his 71. Mahan made four birdies, four bogeys and a double bogey, but saved par with a 14-footer at the 18th for his 74. And Allan was 12 under and had a two-stroke lead over McCarron and Mahan coming to the 18th. Then he caught a greenside bunker with his approach, flew the green with his blast out, chipped back, and had a four-footer for a winning bogey. But he missed, shot 74, and joined the tie.

In the playoff at the 18th, a par-four of 429 yards, Allan was short of the green with his approach, Mahan missed a birdie from 16 feet, McCarron missed one from 14, and Taylor dropped his 11-footer for the victory. "I didn't play my best today, but I just tried to hang in there," Taylor said. "I never gave up one ounce. I've battled that in the past. I'll get down on myself and put my head down. Today, I gave it my all, and I'm proud of myself for doing that."

Buick Championship—$4,200,000
Winner: Woody Austin

The gods of golf seem never to tire of taunting Woody Austin, leaving him to work as a bank teller at times to make ends meet. And then there was the Buick Championship: They allowed Austin to get incredibly hot on the final nine and come from nowhere, and then with the victory at his fingertips on the last hole, his tee shot ended up not just in the fairway, but in a divot hole. No one can predict what that kind of shot will do. Austin fired this one over the green, about 80 feet past the pin, and he bogeyed and finished in a tie with Tim Herron. So the gods dragged it out to a playoff, and Austin birdied the first extra hole and at last had the second victory of his nine-year career. Relieved wasn't the word to describe him.

"I feel that deep down, I never really showed the true talent that I have," said Austin. "I feel like I'm one of the best players out here, and I've never shown it."

Whether that was realistic or not, Austin — the 1995 Rookie of the Year and now 40, the eighth player of that age level to win this season — did show a lot in the Buick Championship. And he wasn't even noticed for the first three rounds.

The tournament, formerly known as the Greater Hartford Open, was being played at the par-70 TPC at River Highlands in Cromwell, Connecticut. Gutsy Corey Pavin, slumping since winning the 1995 U.S. Open, burned the course with an eight-under-par 62 for a three-stroke lead in the first round. "Any time you get to a golf course you feel comfortable on, you just feel good that you might shoot a good score or things are going to come together," Pavin said.

Not so in the second round. Pavin slipped to a 72, and Zach Johnson and the durable Fred Funk took over. Johnson, a rookie and winner of the BellSouth Classic in April, shot 65, and Funk, age 48 and a career five-time winner, shot 66 to tie at 132 for a one-stroke lead. Funk praised Johnson and the rest of the new generation. "They're not scared of anything," Funk said. Then Johnson drifted astern with a 73, and Funk, with a 69, took a one-stroke lead over Tom Byrum (67) and Pavin (68) into the final round.

Austin, on 68-70-66, rising from the depths, was tied for sixth with Tim Herron and a whopping seven others going into the final round. They were three behind.

Some say a tournament begins on the final nine, and this one surely did. Austin made the turn, then exploded with five birdies over the next six holes to charge in among the leaders. But his chance to win in regulation died when his tee shot at the 18th ended up in a divot hole and cost him a bogey. Herron, playing with him, shook off a double bogey at the 17th and dropped a 24-footer for a birdie at the 18th to force the playoff. They closed with 66s and tied at 10-under 270.

Then the gods made Herron their target in the playoff. Herron caught the left rough with his tee shot, reached the green anyway, but was 55 feet from the cup. His birdie try left him a six-footer. Austin had bombed his drive 345 yards into the fairway and stuck his approach about six feet from the pin. Herron, putting first, made the clutch save. So Austin faced a six-footer for a birdie. And the nervous man with the balky putter rolled it right in for the victory and a new lease on life.

"I'm a little bit pessimistic, I guess, when it comes to my golf game," Austin said. "I certainly wanted to feel vindicated after my victory my rookie year."

Deutsche Bank Championship—$5,000,000
Winner: Vijay Singh

This is the entry for the history books: The Deutsche Bank Championship, at the TPC of Boston, September 6, 2004 — Tiger Woods' five-year reign as No. 1 in the world comes to an end.

And who to end it but the irrepressible Vijay Singh, who had been grinding his way through the season, and then just a few weeks after winning the PGA Championship he beat Woods head-to-head to take both the tournament and the No. 1 ranking from him. Woods had been No. 1 for 264 weeks, since August 8, 1999.

"I'm not disappointed about the ranking," Woods said. "I'm disappointed in not winning."

Said Singh, age 41: "I never thought I would be sitting here — the best player in the world right now." About a month earlier, Singh had said he would swear off concentrating on the No. 1 position and said instead he would focus on playing golf. This was his third victory in seven weeks and his sixth of the season, and this was only the first week of September. And then there was this curious wrinkle: This was Singh's fourth Monday victory in 12 months. But this one wasn't due to weather delays. It was scheduled as part of the Labor Day holiday.

Woods had won only once this season, taking the WGC - Accenture World Match Play in February. For most golfers, winning once would be an accomplishment. But not for the dominant Woods. This had turned into a down year. Still, he opened on an encouraging note, with a six-under-par 65 to share the lead with rookie Ryan Palmer. It was the last time Woods would lead. Woods and Palmer were a good story — Woods was trying to keep his No. 1 ranking, and Palmer, nearing age 28, was trying to get into the top 125 money leaders so that he could be exempt from qualifying in 2005. "It's a struggle getting up here," Palmer said, meaning the PGA Tour. He had two eagles, one on a 15-foot putt at No. 2 and the other a bunker hole-out at No. 7. He would cool off, but a tie for 17th at four-under 280 was pretty strong.

Singh, who opened with a 68, three behind Woods and Palmer, took over in the second round with an eight-under 63 triggered by a hole-out eagle two from a bunker at the first hole followed by eight birdies. With a 68 in the third round, Singh led by three going into the fourth, ran into trouble, but survived. Singh closed with a 69 and a 16-under 268, beating Woods (69) and Adam Scott (65) by three strokes.

Comments by Singh and Woods throughout the tournament told the story, or else shielded it. It was almost as though no one would admit to the drama that was taking place. For example, when Singh shot 63 in the second round and took over the lead, he noted, "It's not going to affect me one way or another if I overtake him." Said Woods, "The No. 1 ranking takes care of itself. If you win consistently, you don't have to worry abut that." And in the third round, when Singh shot 68 to widen his lead over Woods by three strokes, he offered, "It's better to be three up than two up. Every shot in front of Tiger is important." And said Woods of going up against Singh, "I think it will just be a blast."

Quite apart from his winning margin, Singh proved his right to the No. 1 spot by the way he faced down disaster in the final round. He had birdied the first hole to increase his lead to four. But it melted away, and when Woods chipped in for a birdie at the 12th and Singh missed the 13th green and bogeyed, they were tied at 13 under. Scott, coming fast, was one stroke behind. At the 14th, Singh and Woods were both about nine feet from the flag. Singh saved par and Woods bogeyed. Singh then rebuilt his lead. At the par-five 15th, Singh put his approach to within four feet and birdied, while Woods two-putted for par from 17 feet and was two behind. At the 17th, another birdie put Singh three up, and he could finally smile.

"I made the putts that counted," said Singh, who also birdied the 18th. "The big putt was on 17. When I made that one, I said, 'That's it.'"

Bell Canadian Open—$4,500,000
Winner: Vijay Singh

In a year that was bordering somewhere between unreal and unbelievable for him, Vijay Singh, the world's new No. 1 player, made the Bell Canadian Open his second victory in a row, his fourth in his last five starts and his seventh of the season. But he almost didn't want this one.

"I feel for Mike," Singh said. "That was the one person I didn't want to beat."

This was going to be the Mike Weir Show. He would be the first Canadian since Pat Fletcher in 1954 to win the Canadian Open. Weir had already thrilled his countrymen by winning the Masters in 2003. Now he had fans standing eight deep and on the verge of hysteria as he made his way around Glen Abbey, at Oakville, Ontario, inching ever closer to the championship. And then it didn't happen. Weir had led through the second and third rounds and was up by three convincing strokes with eight holes to play. Then the left-hander unraveled, got caught by Singh, and lost to him on the third hole of a playoff. And so Singh joined exclusive company. Only three players had won seven times in a year since 1950 — Tiger Woods (twice), Jack Nicklaus (twice) and Johnny Miller.

"For whatever reasons, I couldn't gather my emotions like I normally do," said Weir, buffeted by the roars of thousands of homefolks.

Weir had center stage, but he had to share at least a bit of it with Singh, who was world No. 1 for less than a week. But was this any way for the No. 1 to act? Singh, a late starter in the first round, took a triple-bogey seven on his second hole (No. 11) and was three over through five holes when a five-hour rain delay forced the first round over into the next day. The veteran Joey Sindelar captured the early attention with a five-under 66 and a two-stroke lead over Pat Perez. David Duval, still going through an agonizing struggle to reclaim his game, shot a par 71. He wasn't happy with it, but conceded, "That's a lot of progress from where I was a couple of months ago." (He would make a rare cut, but a third-round 76 would knock him down to a tie for 52nd finish.)

After tying Singh with a 68 in the first round, Weir took the lead in the second with a 65 triggered by one break and two stunning shots. He got the break at No. 10, his first hole, when his tee shot bounced off a tree and into an adjacent fairway. He rifled a six iron to 10 feet and made the birdie. At the 16th, he put an eight iron to 12 feet for another birdie, and at his final hole he ran a three iron to within three feet and eagled. Singh's opening 68 consisted of a 40 on his first nine, then a tournament-record 28 on the second nine. "I just started hitting it close, and all of a sudden I noticed it was 28," Singh said. He shot 66 in the second round, but then couldn't quite get a grip on his game. In the third round, he bogeyed three of his first four holes, put another ball into the creek at the 11th — which he played in seven over par for the tournament — and made another triple bogey, and then ran off three straight birdies. He shot a one-over 72 and trailed Weir by three. Weir, meantime, hit the ball well but couldn't talk to his putter. With 13 chances for birdies, he made only one, at the 18th, for a one-under 70 and a 10-under 203 total, three ahead of Singh, Jesper Parnevik and Cliff Kresge.

Weir's collapse down the final nine was worse than the numbers indicate. After some skirmishing, he birdied the 10th from 12 feet and was back to three up on Singh. Then he bogeyed the 11th out of a fairway bunker, and then the par-five 13th, where he got a 30-foot putt maybe only halfway there. Weir was still leading Singh by two with three holes to play, but at the 16th he had an eight-footer for birdie, knocked it four feet past, and missed that coming back and bogeyed. Singh caught Weir at the par-five 18th. He boomed a drive 371 yards and was long with his approach, chipped back eight feet past the hole, but made the putt for a birdie for 69 and a nine-under 275 total. Weir could have won it at the 18th, but missed his 10-foot birdie putt, shot 72, and they went into the playoff. On the third extra hole, No. 18, Weir pulled his tee shot, laid up, and then hit his approach into the water. He was done.

"I think maybe in the end," a saddened Weir said, "I was trying too hard."

Ryder Cup
Winner: Europe

See Chapter 7.

Valero Texas Open—$3,500,000
Winner: Bart Bryant

Before the 2004 Valero Texas Open, Bart Bryant, age 41, was best known for taking five cracks at the PGA Tour qualifying tournament, for partnering brother Brad in their victory in the 1995 Walt Disney World/Oldsmobile Classic, and individually, for going 0-for-186 tournaments without winning on the PGA Tour. Ah, but No. 187 was a charm.

"One tournament does not make a career," Bryant said. "This is just the beginning — that's what I'd like to think."

It was a comfortable three-stroke win over Patrick Sheehan, thanks to a sparkling second half of the tournament.

Bryant's best was seventh in the 1991 Honda Classic. So it looked like just another fruitless week at the office for Bryant, the office being LaCantera Golf Club near San Antonio. But who would notice in this third week of September? Practically everyone was occupied with the Ryder Cup going on at Oakland Hills near Detroit at the same time.

Bryant had no reason to expect anything different in this one, not after a first-round 67 tied him for 29th place behind Ted Purdy, who blistered LaCantera with a career-low, nine-under-par 61, tying the course record.

Purdy started on the back nine and finished the day eagle-birdie for a three-stroke lead. "I hit the ball better today than I have maybe ever in my life," said Purdy, who missed the cuts in five of his last seven events.

Dean Wilson took the halfway lead with a 65, knocking Purdy back to second place by one stroke. Wilson, at 11-under 129, was leading a tournament for the first time. Bryant, still no threat, shot another 67 and climbed to a tie for 13th with his big brother Brad, age 49, among others. Purdy and Wilson were both doomed. Bryant's time had come.

Bryant burst into the lead in the third round. He torched LaCantera with a career-low, 10-under 60, the tournament record. It left him at 16-under 194, leading Hunter Mahan (62) by three strokes. Bryant, starting the round five strokes off the lead, birdied six of his first eight holes for a 29. He birdied Nos. 7 and 8 from five feet each. He birdied three of the first five holes on the back, and got his 10th birdie of the round with a 30-footer at the 18th for the 60. "The whole way around, I was really trying to shoot 59," Bryant said. "My goal was to be 10 under going into that last hole."

What does a guy do the night before he's going to face his biggest challenge? Well, Bart Bryant went out to dinner and a movie with big brother Brad. "We didn't talk about golf," Brad said. "He's a big boy. He knew what to do."

Bryant turned protective on Sunday. He had only one birdie in his first 10 holes, knowing his lead was not entirely safe. "I tried to play aggressive, but didn't want to play stupid," he said. He made a great birdie at the par-four 11th. He drove into the left rough, then put his approach 30 feet from the hole and dropped the putt to go to 18 under par. That eased the tension. At the par-five 14th, he just missed an eagle from 40 feet and got the birdie. He finished with a 67 for a 19-under 261 total and a three-stroke win over Sheehan (66), who sealed his own fate when he three-putted the 16th for a bogey.

"This," Bryant said, "is unbelievable."

84 Lumber Classic of Pennsylvania—$4,200,000
Winner: Vijay Singh

The 84 Lumber Classic, played at Nemacolin Woodlands, a resort in the forested Laurel Highlands southeast of Pittsburgh, was the tournament for the golfer who already had everything. Those who went found themselves with butlers, sumptuous on-site accommodations, a small pride of lions (on course), and, among other things, a free round-trip flight to and from the WGC - American Express Championship in Ireland the following week. The only thing that would make the week sweeter would be a victory.

That was Vijay Singh's territory.

Singh continued to turn the 2004 season into a lark. He started out fast and battled at the end to win, led wire-to-wire and won by a stroke. It was his third victory in a row, his fifth in six tournaments, seventh in his last 16 starts and his eighth of the year. And the $756,000 first prize lifted him to a single-season record $9,455,566, breaking Tiger Woods' record from his nine wins in 2000.

"I want to win, I want to play well, and it's a good habit," Singh said.

Chris DiMarco, who chased Singh and fell short, tying for third, put it another way. Said DiMarco, "It's ridiculous the way he's playing right now."

The tournament has a historical significance beyond Singh's accomplishments. It underlined the difficulties of professional golf in the autumn, when interest in the game begins to wane and big name golfers have headed for home. And worse, golf is difficult at that time in metropolitan areas that have major sports. It debuted in 2000, to alternate between the Philadelphia and Pittsburgh areas, but not to rave reviews.

Joe Hardy, a Pittsburgh-based lumber baron, decide to provide a permanent home at Nemacolin Woodlands in 2003. His principal challenge still was drawing a field, but more so in 2004 because the tournament fell between the Ryder Cup and the WGC event. Hardy tried to offset all difficulties with numerous perks for players, including the free round trip to Ireland for the golfer and four guests. Which, by the way, went sour when one of the two chartered jets going over had to be delayed for repairs. One large jet then brought everyone back.

Meanwhile, at the tournament itself:

The course, Mystic Rock, a Pete Dye creation, had been renovated to provide a sterner test than J.L. Lewis faced when he won the inaugural at 22 under par in 2003. Singh staked his claim immediately with an eight-under 64 and a three-stroke lead over former British Open champion Ben Curtis, among others. Singh had three birdies and an eagle on his front nine, then birdied the 13th and 16th from eight feet and the 18th from 12 feet. "I don't know if I can hit it any better," Singh said. It looked like a runaway in the second round when he birdied the first two holes, but he cooled a bit and settled for a 68–132 and a two-stroke lead over Curtis. Curtis, who had missed five straight cuts and seven out of 11, made this one with another 67. "It's going to be a long weekend," Curtis said. "I haven't played 72 holes in a long time." (An 81 in the third round finished him.)

The third round was one of Singh's toughest in weeks. "My rhythm wasn't there," Singh said after a good-shot, bad-shot par 72. His lead shrank to one when he bogeyed the 11th, but DiMarco then bogeyed the 14th. In a scrambling finish, Singh saved par at the 15th and saved again from the water with a 25-foot chip-in at the par-five 16th. Singh bogeyed the 18th, but DiMarco bogeyed the last two holes and three of the last five for a 71 and a 206, two behind Singh's 12-under 204 total.

Singh dropped out of the solo lead only once, this when a bogey at the third hole tied him with DiMarco and Jonathan Byrd. But Singh birdied the par-four fourth to regain the lead for good. His last real threat came out of nowhere. Stewart Cink, who started the final round five strokes off the lead, turned up the heat with five birdies in a row from the seventh. Singh got to four up with birdies at the 11th and 13th, but Cink closed in again with birdies at the 16th and 17th, and he got to within the final stroke when Singh bogeyed the 18th.

For the statistically inclined, Singh had compiled some revealing numbers. Once again, exceptional fairway play allowed him to conquer a long course. He had won on four of the eight longest courses on the PGA Tour this year. He was 11th in driving distance, but only 145th in driving accuracy, but he was No. 1 in hitting greens in regulation.

Singh had another way of putting it: "I had my driver working, my irons working, and I made the putts I needed to make."

WGC - American Express Championship—€5,639,287
Winner: Ernie Els

See European Tours chapter.

Southern Farm Bureau Classic—$3,000,000
Winner: Fred Funk

Here is the wisdom according to Fred Funk: "There are just so many great things that go along with winning. And there just aren't that many good things, except the money, that go along with finishing second."

And here is also the wisdom of Fred Funk (on seeing the scores after the second round): "I've got to shoot at least two seven-unders just to have a chance."

That was after he had opened the Southern Farm Bureau Classic in Madison, Mississippi, with 69-67, and at eight-under-par 136 found himself in a big traffic jam, tied for 13th place and four strokes off the lead. The popular Funk did not shoot two seven-unders, but he did shoot a 64 and a 66, which amounted to the same thing, and thus by a single stroke he had his first victory since winning the same tournament six years earlier (when it was the Deposit Guaranty Classic).

"It's been a long, long road since 1998," said Funk, age 48 and heading for the Champions Tour. And he didn't really see the end until he birdied the final hole. Funk was in the final pairing and said he was able to keep his eyes off the scoreboard until he accidentally caught a glimpse of it on the final nine.

"I wondered, 'Where did all those 20s [under] come from?' " he said. "I figured somebody would get to 21 under for sure." Which meant he was dead-on with another prediction. He figured he would need 22 under to win. That's what he needed and that's what he got, tying the course record of 22-under 266 at Annandale Golf Club. The course was pummeled for 56 eagles, the most on tour this season. Funk had a crack at No. 57 at the par-five 18th. He was lying two, 75 feet from the hole. He gave the ball a good rap, but left it four feet short. Then he rolled that in, wrapping up a seven-birdie, one-bogey 66, picking up his sixth career victory.

The drop of that putt left PGA Tour rookie Ryan Palmer in second place. Palmer almost eagled the 18th. He was lying two, 49 feet from the hole. He rapped the putt, and it headed home. "I thought it was in, 10 feet from the hole," Palmer said. But the ball pulled up five inches short. He tapped in for a birdie, a 64 and the first top-10 finish of his career.

The tournament was notable for two other players who could figure heavily in the future. There was the emergence of Korean Kevin Na, age 21, the youngest member of the PGA Tour. Shooting 71-65-66-66–268, Na tied for third, his best finish of the year. At the other extreme was the struggling and puzzling David Duval, who shot 71-72 and missed the cut by three.

It was his fifth miss in seven starts. "I don't have a lot to say about it," Duval said. "I'm real disappointed."

Funk, practically fresh from an 0-3 appearance in the U.S. Ryder Cup loss to Europe, was well back in the first two rounds. In the third, he exploded for seven birdies and an eagle (and one bogey) for the 64 and a one-stroke lead. It changed the whole face of the tournament. John Senden, Harrison Frazar and Glen Day had tied for the first-round lead with 65s. Steve Pate joined the chase in the second round, closing with two birdies for a 65 and a share of the 36-hole lead with Frazar at 12-under 132.

Enter Funk, with a bounce in his step and a smile on his face. "There are a lot of birdies out there," Funk said. "Making a birdie is like making a deposit in the bank." In the third round, Funk eagled No. 5, hitting a 216-yard approach to nine feet. Then he birdied the next three, then the 10th, then the 17th and 18th. And in the final round, he held off the fast-closing Palmer for the 66 he needed for the win. And how did he know he would need a pair of seven-unders — or the equivalent thereof?

Funk summoned the crackpot clairvoyant character on the old Johnny Carson television show. "Carnac," Funk said.

Michelin Championship at Las Vegas—$4,000,000
Winner: Andre Stolz

What are the odds against a rookie who's barely hanging on and who has missed 10 of 11 cuts in one stretch, winning at Las Vegas?

That was Andre Stolz, a 34-year-old Australian, who had come to the Michelin Championship at Las Vegas in mid-October with less than $90,000 in winnings. He wasn't even in the picture until the third round, and even after that hardly anybody took him seriously until that final putt dropped, when he himself — much to his own surprise — was informed that he had won.

Stolz just calmly dropped his three-footer at the final hole. He thought it had got him into a playoff. "That's why I wasn't so excited," he said. "I thought I had more work to do." He had already done enough: 67-67-65-67—266, for a one-stroke victory over Harrison Frazar (67), Tag Ridings (61) and Tom Lehman (69).

So a tournament that ended with the longest of long shots winning was a different kind of tournament from the beginning. First, it was reduced from the regular 90 to 72 holes so that players who were at the WGC - American Express Championship in Ireland could get back to play. Next, the scoring was more like advanced accounting. The field took turns at three different courses — the TPC at the Canyons, a par-71, and two par-72s, the TPC at Summerlin and Bear's Best. So scoring was in relation to par. The tournament went this way:

First Round — Seven tied for the lead, two with 63s and the others with 64s, all eight under par. Among them was the puzzling Harrison Frazar, with a bogey-free 64, who had taken a month off trying to figure out how it was that he won most of his $1.1 million by the end of February and then went sour. "I'm happy to be here, and I don't feel like I'm going through the motions," he said. Danny Ellis, one of the eight-unders, had the most intriguing line of the day. "I've been playing good," he said, "but I've just been making a lot of bogeys."

Second Round — Three players were at 130, but one was J.L. Lewis at 14 under par, leading by one over Chez Reavie, Alex Cejka and Olin Browne. Lewis was puzzled. He had his best year in 2003, and now his statistics were up but he had dropped from 28th to 97th on the money list. "It's kind of a hard game to explain," he said. Explain this: He needed only 25 putts this round, and at the par-five 12th, he hit a seven iron over the green then chipped in for an eagle, and birdied the 13th and 18th as well. Reavie (64), a former Arizona State University star, was making his professional debut, but he enjoyed a career finish. He almost aced the par-three 17th, leaving the ball on the lip. Then he holed out a nine iron from 151 yards for eagle at the 18th. "It was," he conceded, "a great way to finish."

Third Round — Stolz surfaced. He shot 65 and made a precious cut (the cut being made after the third round here). He and Dicky Pride (66) were one stroke behind Tom Lehman (66–198), who hit 17 greens, made eight birdies, and held his first 54-hole lead in five years. Lehman had gone back to the long putter, with which he was 37 under in his last 10 rounds. Stolz, who rarely gets to speak from the leader's chair, explained himself. "I'm kind of weird," he said. "When I play well, I play really, really well. But when I play bad, I'm horrible. I need to fix that."

Fourth Round — Stolz was nothing but grace under pressure. At the 16th, after Lehman eagled to join the tie at 20 under par, Stolz holed an eight-footer for birdie to re-take the lead. Except he thought he was tied. At the 18th, Stolz two-putted from 45 feet, the last putt the three-footer for par. The marshal ordered Stolz's caddie, Tony Lingard, to put the flag back in the hole. "For what?" Lingard asked. "For the playoff," the marshal says.

Stolz had the last word. "I told my wife last night I had a feeling I was going to win," he said. With a feeling like that, what about the Las Vegas tables? "Golf's enough of a gamble," Stolz said.

Chrysler Classic of Greensboro—$4,600,000
Winner: Brent Geiberger

For anyone handicapping the Chrysler Classic of Greensboro, there were these things to consider about Brent Geiberger: He had a nerve problem that caused numbness in his arm, a sore hip, a bone spur in his right heel, an occasional problem with vertigo, and as to performance, he had nothing more to recommend him than 144th place on the PGA Tour money list and his only victory had come five years earlier. In short, his chances of winning were the classical slim and none. Talk about beating the odds.

Geiberger took the lead in the second round, shared it with Tom Lehman in the third, and rallied to get to the finish line two strokes ahead of anyone else. In the process, he made himself and his dad, Al, the 1976 Greensboro winner, the only father-son duo to win the same tournament other than, of course, the two Willie Parks and two Tom Morrises from the dawn of Open Championship golf in Scotland. Apart from that tidbit of history,

Geiberger jumped to No. 52 on the money list, made himself exempt for two years on the tour, and saved the $3,500 entry fee it would have cost him for the tour's qualifying tournament.

"It's pretty neat to be able to put my name on a trophy with my dad," Geiberger said. "I always — and still do — look up to my dad." And said the proud dad, from the Champions Tour's SBC Championship, "It's just wonderful to see him win in the same place that I did."

Brent Geiberger, who played the Forest Oaks Country Club course in Greensboro, North Carolina, in 66-67-71-66–270, 18 under par, looked every bit the winner from the start. He was one off the lead in the first round and led the rest of the way, winning by two over Michael Allen, age 45, whose career-best second place was worth $496,800, enough to get exempt status and spare him a 12th trip to the qualifying tournament. "What a good time," said Allen, who closed with a 67. A rejuvenated Lehman, now age 40, closed with a 70 that included a one-stroke penalty incurred when his ball moved as he was tapping it in. He tied for fourth, his third top-four finish in his last four starts.

Geiberger suffered from the first of his ailments in the second round when his ailing hip acted up and he needed a heat wrap. He saved par from 12 feet at No. 2, birdied No. 5 from three feet, and birdied his last from 20 feet for a 67 and his second bogey-free round. In the third round, suffering from a cold, he bogeyed the 17th out of a bunker. "I was on fumes," he said. "I just wanted to keep my head on straight. I did a pretty good job of it."

So did Lehman, shooting a 69 to tie him at 12-under 204. "I'm sick and tired of finishing second," said Lehman, heaping more pressure on Geiberger. Said Geiberger, "I'm looking forward to it, looking forward to the challenge."

He opened the fourth round with back-to-back birdies and took the lead for good with a 31 on the first nine. He scrambled to a par at the par-five 13th after topping a fairway wood 70 yards short of the green. And at the 14th, he left a 60-foot birdie putt eight feet short, but dropped that for par, then birdied the 16th and was on his way.

Chris Smith was another relieved golfer. He bogeyed the 11th and 12th, then eagled the 13th and birdied the next three for a 67 to finish third to win $312,800, which allowed him to keep his playing card. "I can breathe again," Smith said.

As a postscript to the tournament, U.S. Amateur champion Ryan Moore, having one of the greatest amateur seasons in history, played in his first regular PGA Tour event. Moore, playing on a sponsor's exemption, shot 281 and tied for 24th.

Funai Classic at the Walt Disney World Resort—$4,200,000
Winner: Ryan Palmer

Someone finally figured a way to beat the mighty Vijay Singh: Let him get a head start, then shoot 62 in the final round.

And that's how Ryan Palmer, age 28, from Amarillo, Texas, became the fifth rookie winner and 10th first-time winner on the PGA Tour this season in the Funai Classic at the Walt Disney World Resort. And maybe the most nervous. Palmer was not on anybody's list of probables. He was six strokes off the lead in the first round and five off in the next two rounds, and who makes up five shots on Singh, seeking his ninth win of the year, and Mark Calcavecchia, Tom Lehman, et al.? But Palmer not only did so, he beat Singh and Briny Baird by three strokes. And not that they folded. Singh played Disney's Magnolia Course in five-under-par 67, Baird in 70.

Palmer was uncertain almost to the end. He was already in with his 22-under 266 total and there were eight twosomes still on the course. "I thought there were too many holes left, especially for Vijay," Palmer said. "I figured a playoff, maybe."

So did a lot of people. An official announced that the first hole for the playoff would be No. 18. Palmer, starting the final round five strokes out of the lead, was high on his iron game. He holed a 25-footer for birdie at No. 1, then began sticking his irons close. He wedged to three feet at the par-five 14th and birdied for the solo lead. He chipped in from 40 feet at the 15th. At the 16th, he put his approach to two feet, and then at the 17th, where Ernie Els once putted off the green, he canned a 45-footer for birdie. He put his hands on his head. Could this be his time? He had to wait to see. His challengers were still out on the course.

Singh was trying to win his fourth straight tournament. With a string of three birdies, he closed to within two of the lead with four holes to play. Then he bogeyed the 16th with three putts from 50 feet after catching a fairway bunker off the tee, and that was that. "I played well," Singh said. "My game is coming back. I'm in that mood again. Ryan played well, and you can't take a good round away."

Baird got within two with a birdie from 15 feet at the par-five 14th and was the last man with a chance to catch Palmer. But like Singh, he also stumbled at the 16th. He missed the fairway and ended up three-putting.

Palmer, shooting 68-68-68, just moseyed along in obscurity through the first three rounds. J.L. Lewis, putting for birdie on 11 holes and making most of them, shot a 62 for the first-round lead by two. Briny Baird took over the second with a 66–131, one stroke ahead of the resurgent Tom Lehman (66). Some tournaments are like marathons, Lehman said. You have to pace yourself. But this one, he said, is like a sprint. "You've got to put the pedal to the metal and go as hard as you can for four days," he said. And so it was that he shot 67 in the third round and caught Baird at 17-under 199, with Scott Verplank a stroke back, Singh three back, and an unnoticed Ryan Palmer five back.

And late the next day, when Palmer realized no one could catch him, he covered his face with his hands, and then hugged his wife, Jennifer, and thought of domestic things. They had bought a house in the spring. "Needs some decorating," he said.

Chrysler Championship—$5,000,000
Winner: Vijay Singh

It's not really instructive to compare winnings in different periods of golf because that measures the increase in purses as much as anything. But there was an interesting way to look at Vijay Singh when he made the Chrysler Championship, the final full-field tournament of the season, his ninth victory of the year. And it is this: It took Singh eight years and 173 tournaments to win $10 million on the PGA Tour. With this win late in October, he became the first in history to win $10 million in one year — $10,725,166 to be precise. And the nine victories matches Tiger Woods of 2000 for most in a season since Sam Snead logged 11 in 1950. Also for the history book: Singh shot 65-69-67-65 for a tournament-record 266, 18 under par at the Copperhead Course at Westin Innisbrook at Palm Harbor, Florida, for a five-stroke victory over Tommy Armour and Jesper Parnevik.

It had got so that anytime Singh teed it up, he was expected to win. So lost in the flash of the Vijay Singh Light Show was the fact that Jeff Sluman had opened the tournament with a sizzling nine-under 62. That was good only for a two-stroke lead, given the beating being administered to the tough Copperhead Course. Even so, a 62 shocked the field. Said Peter Jacobsen to Sluman, "Tell me you stopped after 16." And said Singh, "One hell of a score." Said Sluman, "You kind of wonder to yourself why in the world you can't do that more often, because it seems so easy."

Sluman answered his own question in the second round, missing a half dozen good chances at birdies and settling for a 70. "Some days it's easy," Sluman said, "and some days it's a little more difficult." Still, he had a share of the lead, this with B.C. Open champion Jonathan Byrd, who shot a second 66 to tie him at 10-under 132. (Neither would last. Sluman would close with 74-73 and tie for 20th, and Byrd would blow to 75-76 and tie for 44th.) The two other notable developments in the second round: Masters champion Phil Mickelson shot 76–147 and missed the cut by five strokes. "I don't know what to say," he said. And Singh, with a 69, moved up to a tie for third. "You certainly shouldn't be surprised to see Vijay up there," Sluman said. And no one was.

Singh's victory wasn't a foregone conclusion, especially not after he made two bogeys early in the third round. He birdied twice to get even, then got down to business. He birdied the seventh from 12 feet, two-putted for a birdie at the par-five 11th, and at the par-five 14th he lifted a flop shot from deep rough to about four feet, setting up a birdie. But Singh wasn't the solo leader until he dropped a 30-footer for a birdie at the 17th for the 67 and a 12-under 201 total and a one-stroke lead on Armour, who made a miracle par at the 18th. His approach hit the bleachers, bounced off a tree and dropped into the rough near the green, and he got up-and-down to salvage a 68–202 total.

It was more or less over in a hurry in the final round. Singh birdied the first two holes, getting up-and-down at No. 1 and holing an eight-footer at No. 2. And he finished like a champ, coming out of a fairway bunker to 15 feet and holing that for a birdie and the five-stroke win. Golf's new No. 1 was ruling the game.

"The wins keep coming," Singh said. "It's good to see my name up there and see people worry about me instead of me worrying about others. It's a great feeling. I'm enjoying it. I love it. Come and get me."

Tour Championship—$6,000,000
Winner: Retief Goosen

The first round of the Tour Championship was notable for a number of reasons, none of them having anything to do with Retief Goosen. For one thing, Darren Clarke, Jerry Kelly and Jay Haas, all seeking their first victory of the season in the last official tournament, tied for the lead at three-under-par 67. All-conquering Vijay Singh, seeking his 10th win of the year, shot 69, and Tiger Woods, playing for the first time since his wedding, shot 72. And Ernie Els, having to putt with his sand wedge after accidentally breaking his putter in frustration, also shot 72. That was the first round. By the end of the tournament, golf had an identity problem. Now, if someone should ask, "How's the South African doing?" the correct answer should be "Which one?"

Retief Goosen, the "other" South African, emerged about the same time as Ernie Els on the Southern Africa Tour, but didn't have the early success elsewhere. Even after winning the U.S. Open in 2001, and then the U.S. Open again earlier in 2004, he was probably known more for the oddity of his name than the quality of his game. But this week Goosen came from behind, overran Tiger Woods, and took the Tour Championship. This kind of thing will start attracting attention. Of course, when it comes to attention, it doesn't help that Goosen is even quieter than a church mouse.

Goosen was so quiet in the tournament that hardly anyone knew he was on the grounds at East Lake Golf Club in Atlanta until his charge in the final round. He shot 70-66-69 in the first three rounds, and trailed by three strokes in the first round, three in the second, and going into the final round, he was four behind Woods and Haas. Then Goosen hit the shot of the tournament at the 481-yard, par-four 16th hole, a five iron out of the rough from 195 yards that ended up three feet from the pin. He got the birdie and closed with a 64 for an 11-under-par 269 total. Woods ended a year gone sour almost from the start with a 72 and was second, four strokes behind. No one was more surprised at the victory over Woods than Goosen himself.

"We all thought he was going to be the guy to beat," Goosen said after his bogey-free finale. This was the fifth career victory for Goosen, who joined the PGA Tour in 2001.

"He did absolutely everything he needed to do," Woods said. "Posted a number, and hopefully it would be good enough. And it was." Woods had won 14 consecutive times when he led or shared the lead after three rounds. Goosen was only the third player to overtake Woods in the final round of a PGA Tour event. The last time he lost was in the 2000 Tour Championship, to Phil Mickelson, and the time before that was in his third professional start in the 1996 Quad City Classic, to Ed Fiori.

Goosen couldn't have done it without help from Woods and Haas, co-leaders by four strokes going into the final round. Woods did the unthinkable. He bogeyed three of his first seven holes on his way to a 72. Haas, at age 50 the oldest competitor ever in the Tour Championship, was inspirational from the start. He tied for the first-round lead with 67, then took the lead by two with a 66 in the second round, then shot 68 to share the lead with

Woods (65) in the third round. But in the end, Haas struggled down the stretch, shot 75, and tied for seventh in the 29-man field.

For Goosen, the quiet one, it was the second time this year he had swept in and plucked the title from a big name. He one-putted his way merrily along in the last round of the U.S. Open and won by two when Phil Mickelson double-bogeyed the 17th. This time, he heard some pro-Tiger comments from the gallery coming in. Said Goosen, "It makes me a little bit more determined."

Special Events

Tavistock Cup—US$1,500,000
Winner: Isleworth

In the past couple of decades Orlando, Florida, has become the home of numerous professional golfers, and many have taken residences beside the golf courses at Isleworth and Lake Nona, or become members of one of the two clubs owned by British billionaire Joe Lewis. This led to the creation of the Tavistock Cup, with nine players representing each club in a two-day event at Lake Nona, with $1.5 million in prize money and television coverage on The Golf Channel.

Isleworth was the winner of the inaugural event by a margin of 14½ points to 9½ points, even though Isleworth's best player, Tiger Woods, did not participate.

With Mark O'Meara as the captain, Isleworth's team consisted of such players as Charles Howell and Australian stars Stuart Appleby and Robert Allenby. The captain of the Lake Nona team was Ernie Els, and his squad included Retief Goosen, Sergio Garcia and Annika Sorenstam.

The teams split the four better-ball matches with two points each on the first day for a 4-4 deadlock. On the second day, there were singles matches versus both players on the opposing teams in the draw, and Isleworth took 10½ of the 16 points. Appleby received the most money — $100,000 as a member of the winning team and $100,000 for having one of the three lowest scores on the second day.

CVS Charity Classic—$1,300,000
Winners: Jay and Bill Haas

The Haas Boys — okay, so they're father and son, Jay, age 50, and Bill, 22 — made big news as the charming story in an uncharming week at the U.S. Open at Shinnecock Hills. Just over a week later, they made news again, this time as winners of the CVS Charity Classic, a two-round better-ball team special event at Rhode Island Country Club in Barrington.

Bill played in the U.S. Open as an amateur, then made his professional debut the following week in the Booz Allen Classic, where he tied for 33rd and won $23,280.

In the CVS Charity Classic, Bill may have been a raw rookie, but he held up his end. He picked up three quick strokes in the second round. At the 311-yard No. 6, he drove the green and dropped a 25-foot putt for an eagle. Then he birdied the par-four No. 7. Then it was Dad to the rescue. It came down to the 18th. David Toms and Chad Campbell, tied with the Haases, both missed long birdie putts. Jay then put his approach 12 feet from the pin, but Bill put his to 10 feet and figured to be the key.

"I was almost resigned to the fact it was going to be him making the putt," Jay said. But Bill never got the chance. Jay, putting first, rolled in his 12-footer for a birdie and a team nine-under-par 62 and a 20-under 122 total. It was a one-stroke victory over Toms and Campbell, and it turned Jay into a proud father.

"Being paired with him, and having him play ... with these other great players is victory enough for me," Haas said. "To win the tournament was icing on the cake."

Ryder Cup
Winner: Europe

See Chapter 7.

Franklin Templeton Shootout—$2,500,000
Winners: Hank Kuehne and Jeff Sluman

In a rousing post-season, unofficial three-round event with something to delight every weekend golfer, Hank Kuehne and Jeff Sluman raced home with birdies on four of the last five holes to beat Justin Leonard and Steve Flesch by two strokes in the Franklin Templeton Shootout.

"We came in, I think, the same way we came in last year — just kind of loose and carefree," said Sluman, who was paired again with Kuehne in the field of 12 two-man teams. They combined for an 11-under-par 61 in the final-round scramble, racking up a 29-under 187 total at Tiburon Golf Club in Naples, Florida. That was six strokes better than when they won in a three-way playoff in 2003.

The tournament started with a modified alternate-shot format, and the second round was better ball. Then came scramble, everyone's favorite.

In the first round, Leonard and Flesch started off flaming, with six birdies in their first 10 holes, then birdied the 12th, 14th and 17th, combining for a nine-under 63 and a one-stroke lead over Kuehne and Sluman. Flesch made five birdie putts, including a 30-footer at the 12th, and Leonard made four. The heroics brought back a name from the recent past — tournament host Greg Norman, combining with Scott McCarron for a 65 and a share of third place. Norman was playing for the first time since injuring his back in August and was encouraged. "It's just working a little bit, a little bit at a time every day," he said.

In Saturday's better-ball format, Kuehne and Sluman shot a 62 to tie Leonard and Flesch (63). Kuehne holed a 15-footer for birdie at the 17th and an eight-footer for another birdie at the 18th to get the team to 18 under par. Flesch noted that the final round would belong to the team putting best. "That's all a scramble really is," he said. "No matter if you're playing on your club level or if you're out here, you've got to make the putts."

How right Flesch was. He and Leonard each missed an eight-foot birdie putt at the 15th, and missed a chance to tie. Said Sluman, "I said to Hank, 'Christmas came a little early.' They didn't look like they were going to miss it." Flesch hit the pin with a birdie chip at the 16th, and Sluman dropped a nine-foot putt for birdie. Kuehne just missed on a long eagle putt at the par-five 17th, and Sluman tapped in the birdie putt for a two-stroke lead. It was just as Sluman said — loose and carefree.

Callaway Golf Pebble Beach Invitational—$300,000
Winner: Jeff Brehaut

"It was a tough day to get a birdie and an easy day to get bogeys," Jeff Brehaut was saying. "The final putt was a perfect, easy putt, and I knew I had to do something with it." And what he did with that final putt was win the Callaway Golf Pebble Beach Invitational.

Brehaut was winless in five seasons on the PGA Tour, had a tie for eighth as his best finish of 2004, and he finished 149th on the money list, 24 spots from the magic all-exempt 125 level. But he got himself a measure of consolation when he won the Callaway event in November winds on California's Monterey Peninsula. He earned the $60,000 first prize and the confidence-building pleasure of knowing he could prevail against a quality field under tough circumstances.

That final putt was a five-footer. Brehaut dropped it for a three-under-par 69 and a one-stroke victory over Kevin Sutherland. In the rotating event, Brehaut shot 69 at Del Monte, 67 at Spyglass Hill and 74-69 at Pebble Beach for a nine-under 279 total. Todd Fischer (76) and Tom Lehman (73) tied for third place, five strokes behind. Pebble Beach's celebrated winds were also tough for the third round, when Triplett took a one-stroke lead with 72. That day, just five professionals shot in the 60s, and 10 players shot 80 and higher. It was more of the same for the final round.

"All of us were in trouble out there," Brehaut said, "but I hung in there and did what I had to do." What he had to do, first, was keep his head in strong winds and handle greens that were drying out hard. With his 69, he was just one of three golfers — with Sutherland (68) and Kent Jones (71) — to break par in the final round. Triplett shot 78 and fell to a tie for fifth place.

The 72-hole event brought together players from the PGA, Nationwide, Champions and LPGA Tours. The first three rounds were played over the three courses, and the low 40 pros and ties played the final round at Pebble.

WGC - World Cup—$4,000,000
Winners: Luke Donald and Paul Casey

See European Tours Chapter.

UBS Cup—$3,000,000
Winner: United States

Whatever it is Arnold Palmer does with his American team in the UBS Cup, the folks at the Ryder Cup, Solheim Cup and Walker Cup could use a dose of it. Even Colin Montgomerie couldn't penetrate Palmer's force. The United States took this one, 14-10, to post a record of three victories and one tie against the Rest of the World in the event's four years. "Our guys just played really good golf," said Palmer, who was now 3-0-1 as the U.S. captain in the UBS Cup and 6-0-1 overall as a team captain. "Today was probably the best example of how well they played."

The UBS Cup is a match play event for two 12-man teams, each with six players ages 40-49 and six 50 and over. This one, played in November at Kiawah Island, South Carolina, hung in the balance for a while. The Americans, trailing by one point entering the second day, moved into a 6½-5½ lead after Saturday's better-ball play. It was a question of strategy.

"I had great strategy coming in today," said Raymond Floyd. "I said, 'Just stay back out of the way and try not to interfere,' and Freddie handled the case." Fred Couples, his partner, made nine birdies as they took a 4-and-2 win over Sandy Lyle and Ian Woosnam. Tom Watson, partnering Hal Sutton, made seven birdies in their 3-and-2 win over Rodger Davis and Peter Senior.

The Americans led by a point going into the singles the final day, and it was there they dominated again. Floyd was the early sparkplug. He was 3 down with three holes to play against Mark McNulty, but McNulty three-putted the 16th and hit his approach shot into the water at the 17th and lost both, and Floyd holed a 10-footer for birdie at the 18th to halve their match. "I just kept hanging in there, hanging in there," Floyd said. "It's incredible how match play can swing."

Craig Stadler started with an eagle at No. 1, holing his approach shot, and kept on going for a 5-and-4 win over Ian Woosnam. "I was 7 under through 11 holes with a bogey — kind of overkill," Stadler said. "Kept aiming at the hole and it kept going in."

Scott Hoch beat Carl Mason, 2 and 1, guaranteeing the tie that meant the U.S. would retain the cup. Then Couples did what no American ever did in Ryder Cup singles — beat Colin Montgomerie. Monty, who is 5-0-2 in Ryder Cup singles, played beautifully. He made three birdies and no bogeys over 15 holes. Couples, on the other hand, made six birdies and an eagle in a 5-and-3 win that gave the United States the outright victory. "I've done that myself in these competitions," Montgomerie said. "Being at the receiving end — it's unbelievable."

It left Gary Player, captain of the Rest of the World team, to figure a way to break the American domination. "Congratulations to the U.S., but we're creeping closer," Player said. "Maybe next year we can entice Vijay

Singh and some others to compete — if we can just get them to give up their millions for a week."

PGA Grand Slam of Golf—$1,000,000
Winner: Phil Mickelson

The dates are important here. The Ryder Cup was played in mid-September, and the PGA Grand Slam of Golf just past mid-November. About two months. There was a Phil Mickelson in each one, but a different one. The first Phil Mickelson was not able to successfully renegotiate his endorsement contract with Titleist. So about two weeks before the Ryder Cup, he switched to Callaway and would start with their driver and fairway woods — in the Ryder Cup.

The switch may or may not have had anything to do with it, but Mickelson had a wretched time of it in the Ryder Cup, hitting the ball everywhere and finishing with a 1-3-0 record as the Americans were routed by the Europeans.

Then, not having touched a club for two weeks, Mickelson went to the PGA Grand Slam of Golf, an event for the winners of the year's four major championships, at Poipu Bay in Hawaii, and proceeded to shoot a 13-under-par 59. For the complete record, he shot 68-59–127 in the two-round event, beating Vijay Singh, the PGA Championship winner, by five strokes; Retief Goosen (U.S. Open), by six, and Todd Hamilton (Open Championship) by 18.

"It was certainly unexpected," said Mickelson. "I didn't hit it great today and somehow I shot 59. So go figure. It just all kind of came together."

They say golf is a funny game. Consider this: In the Ryder Cup, Mickelson could barely hit a fairway and was one of the goats of the event. In this 59, the lowest round he ever shot, he was just as bad or worse. He hit only five fairways. Yet he broke the previous record of 61, set by Tiger Woods in 2003. "Phil outplayed everybody — or outscored everybody," said Singh. "It was incredible. After about the 12th hole, we were just watching him."

Mickelson had 24 putts, 14 greens hit in regulation (to go with the five fairways), 11 birdies, one eagle, six pars. "So go figure," he said.

Shinhan Korea Golf Championship—$3,550,000
Winner: Arron Oberholser

Arron Oberholser — best-remembered from the AT&T Pebble Beach National Pro-Am and the Wachovia Championship earlier in the year — officially remained winless for his two full seasons on the PGA Tour. But the $1 million he earned at the Shinhan Korea Golf Championship would go far toward easing the disappointment.

Oberholser, who did not lead in any of the first three rounds, closed with a three-under-par 69 and a 284 total (72-73-70-69). It gave him a two-stroke victory over Spain's Miguel Angel Jimenez (72) and South Korea's Kevin Na (70). South Africa's Trevor Immelman leaped to fourth place with a 65, the best round of the final day. K.J. Choi, the only South Korean to have won on the PGA Tour, closed with a 68 and finished 28th.

The tournament, though not official, was historic in that it was the first PGA Tour-sanctioned event on Korean soil. With a field of 38 players from nine countries, it was played late in November on South Korea's southernmost island of Jeju, on the par-72 Jungmun Golf Club course.

American Ted Purdy solved the high winds of the first day for seven birdies for a 65 and a one-stroke lead over Ireland's Padraig Harrington, who had two eagles, three birdies and a bogey. All bets were off in the rainy second round, when winds gusting to 40 miles an hour left 12 of the 38 players unable to break 80. This forlorn group included Purdy, who soared to an 84, and Nick Faldo, who shot 80. South Korea's Y.E. Yang took the lead with a hard-fought 75. The wind fell to a mere 25 miles an hour in the third round, and Jimenez, already a four-victory man for the year on the European Tour, managed six birdies against three bogeys for a 69 and a two-under 214 total. And here was where Oberholser surfaced, shooting 70 to climb to within a stroke.

Oberholser, a two-time winner on the Nationwide Tour in 2002, kept threatening to break through on the big tour. He challenged for a while at Pebble Beach early in the year and was a playoff runner-up to Joey Sindelar in the Wachovia Championship in May. Overall, he made the cut in 17 of his 23 starts on the PGA Tour. Finally, he pulled it all together in the final round in South Korea, coming from behind and shaking off two bogeys with five birdies for the two-stroke victory.

Office Depot Father-Son Challenge—$1,000,000
Winners: Larry and Drew Nelson

"We wanted to make sure we would be back next year," Larry Nelson was saying at the Office Depot Father-Son Challenge. It was easy. Larry and son Drew simply went on a birdie rampage for two days to streak to a three-stroke victory over Bob and David Charles. The Nelsons finished the two-day scramble at 25-under-par 119 at the par-72 Champions Gate Resort in Orlando, Florida.

The two-day event is reserved for fathers who have won major championships and their sons. There were two exceptions this time. Arnold Palmer, who has no sons, was playing with his grandson, Sam Saunders, and Lee Janzen was partnering Aaron Stewart, the son of the late Payne Stewart.

The Nelsons combined for a 12-under 60 and a one-stroke lead on Saturday and a 13-under 59 on Sunday. As for their easy-looking victory, well, nothing's ever quite that simple, of course. Hot as they were, they had a real fight on their hands in the second round. They started with three straight birdies, but the Charleses, who started the day two strokes behind, ran off nine birdies in succession, starting from No. 2. "We had a two-shot lead at one point," said Bob Charles. "We had some momentum with nine birdies in a row."

Momentum? It was more like a steamroller. But the Nelsons responded with some steamroller of their own. First, they started with three straight birdies, but it wasn't enough to keep the lead. They birdied the fifth and eighth, then went on a spree of their own. Larry Nelson dropped a 20-footer for birdie at the 11th, then birdied three more in succession. The one at the 14th, on a six-foot putt by Drew, gave the Nelsons the lead for good. After birdies at the 15th and 16th, Drew hit a wedge to 10 feet, setting up another birdie at the 17th, and he closed it out with a 15-footer at the 18th for a run of eight birdies and a second-nine 27 that tied the tournament record.

Target World Challenge—$5,250,000
Winner: Tiger Woods

It was only a 16-man field, and it was one of those unofficial late-year events — although there's nothing silly about a $5,250,000 purse — so no one was making any extravagant claims. But it was a hugely encouraging sign for Tiger Woods.

Woods had won the WGC - Accenture Match Play Championship way back in February, then spent the year in limbo, coming close but always faltering with a game he was trying to reshape. This time, he looked pretty much like the real Tiger Woods. He had already outdistanced Colin Montgomerie in the final round, and with a burst at the start of the final nine and a solid finish, he held off Padraig Harrington to win by two strokes. It was his first stroke-play win in the United States in 2004 and his second in a few weeks. He had broken his long drought with an eight-stroke victory at the Dunlop Phoenix tournament in Japan in November.

"This is the way I played in Japan," said Woods. He played the Sherwood Country Club course in Thousand Oaks, California, in 67-66-69-66 for a 16-under-par 268 total against Harrington's 66–270. Harrington surged into contention with a 31 on the first nine, but a couple errant shots over the last three holes cooled him down.

Montgomerie opened with an encouraging 67 to tie Woods for the first-round lead and stayed with him with a 66 in the second round. Someone mentioned the tournament was in his hands, and Monty, age 41, still seeking his first stroke-play victory ever in the U.S., smiled and said, "It's in Tiger's hands."

And it was. Montgomerie pulled ahead of Woods and the field with a 67 in the third round and led by two strokes going into the fourth. He then bogeyed the first hole, and Woods was on his way, with a birdie from 10 feet at No. 1, a bunker blast to six feet for another at No. 2, and a two-putt birdie from 30 feet at the par-five No. 5. Harrington, meanwhile, was chasing him. Woods took the lead at the 10th with a 335-yard drive and a sand wedge to six inches. Harrington tied him with a birdie at the 13th, and Woods, in the group behind him, edged back in front with a two-putt birdie there. Five closing pars plus Harrington's errors sealed it.

All that remained was Woods' assessment of it all, which was: "I felt very comfortable with my swing. I had to take baby steps all year. I was working in the right direction. Sometimes it might have been just three or four holes in one round that I played great, and then the rest of it wasn't so good. Eventually it became nine holes, then 18, then 36 and 54. Now it's a whole tournament. It's exciting."

And a new season lay just over the horizon.

Nationwide Tour

Maybe the next time they'll find a way to get Daniel Chopra into their tournament. Otherwise, he'll go somewhere else and break their records.

That was Chopra in 2004, a graduate of the Nationwide Tour and now a member of the PGA Tour who stopped by at his old digs to see the guys. Jimmy Walker won the Player of the Year Award, but Chopra should have won the Mr. Efficiency Award, if there was one. Maybe never has anyone done so much with so little. Chopra played in only three Nationwide events in 2004, but he won two and set a record. That's a .667 batting average in any league.

The other two-time winners were Walker, who had seven top-10 finishes and topped the money list with $371,346; D.A. Points, second in money with $332,815; and Charles Warren and Kevin Stadler (son of Craig Stadler). They were among the 20 Nationwide Tour players advancing to the PGA Tour for 2005. There were no "battlefield promotions" — no three-time winners with automatic entries.

In April, Chopra wasn't eligible for the MCI Heritage on the PGA Tour and so he entered the First Tee Arkansas Classic. Chopra had to birdie the final hole for a first-round 75. Then he shot 66 in the second round, and started the final round three strokes off the lead. He went on a four-birdie tear in five holes starting at No. 6, and birdied the last hole on an up-and-down for a 66 to win by one stroke.

"I felt at home this week," Chopra said. "I almost felt like a farm boy who had gone to the big city." It was a quaint notion coming from a person with one of the most traveled backgrounds in the game. Chopra was born in Sweden of an Indian father and Swedish mother, moved to India at age seven and was raised by grandparents, and was living in Australia. He also played in Asia and Japan, and won the 2002 Mercuries Masters on the Asian Tour. A note for history: He says he was the first person to hit a golf ball off the Great Wall of China.

The First Tee Arkansas Classic was just a warm-up. Late in May, the PGA Tour was at the Bank of America Colonial and Chopra again wasn't eligible, so he headed to the Henrico County Open in Virginia. There he ran off scores of 65, 63, 65 and 65 for a 258 total — 30 under par, a Nationwide Tour record. He won by four strokes. He became only the second person, after Ernie Els, to reach 30 under par in a 72-hole U.S. event. Els set the record at 31 in the 2003 Mercedes Championships. The previous Nationwide low was 26 under par, set by Chris Smith in the 1997 Omaha Classic.

"That's something to put on my resume," Chopra said. He also finished 108th on the PGA Tour money list with $763,253 in 33 events.

Others also worked up some nice resume entries in 2004.

Walker announced himself in the season-opening BellSouth Panama Championship by running off with a five-stroke victory — his own first victory. "Yo Amo a Panama," said Walker, a Texan and a former All-American at Baylor University, who knew how to say "I love you" in the native tongue.

He was one of just three to finish under par for the tournament. The win had a double blessing. Not only did he pick up the $90,000 first prize, he also became exempt on the Nationwide Tour for all of 2004 and 2005. The win also added to a bright record. It was his 17th top-25 finish in 32 Nationwide tournaments.

This was, by the way, the Nationwide Tour's first visit to Central America, and it left its mark as one of the toughest tournaments. Panama Golf Club, a par-70, played to an average of 72.812 for the week, and Sunday's final-round average was 73.238.

Walker then became the fastest player in Nationwide Tour history to score multiple victories in a season when he took the fourth event on the schedule, the Chitimacha Louisiana Open late in March. Walker, who had come from eight strokes behind, birdied four of the last five holes for a seven-under-par 65 to win by one stroke. He did it with a flair, dropping a 30-foot birdie putt on the last hole. "It was probably the best feeling in golf I've ever had," he said. How did he do it? Native cooking. "I ate crawfish every night this week except Friday," Walker said.

It's the kind of thing that turns a guy into the Player of the Year.

There seemed to be an interesting matter of timing for the two-time winners. All struck while the irons were still hot. Walker won his two in four weeks, although on back-to-back starts, and likewise for Chopra, but five weeks apart. Points won the Northeast Pennsylvania Classic in mid-June and the Pete Dye West Virginia Classic a month later. Warren won the Samsung Canadian PGA Championship and the Cox Classic three weeks apart, and Stadler won the Lake Erie Charity Classic and the Scholarship America Showdown three weeks apart.

Points played the Northeast Pennsylvania Classic sort of by ear. "I didn't look at the leaderboard one time today," he said. "I could tell by the crowd around me that I was either in the lead or close to it." Eight players were within two shots of the lead in the final round. A playoff seemed certain and a playoff is what it took. Points beat James Driscoll on the first extra hole for his first win since 2001.

As for Kevin Stadler, he put it best when he said, "The whole thing is unreal." Minutes after Craig Stadler won the Bank of America Championship on the Champions Tour, son Kevin, age 24, won the Nationwide's Lake Erie Charity Classic, and in a three-way playoff. Then Stadler made history two weeks later when he won the Scholarship America Showdown, his second victory in just his fourth career start. The previous record was six starts. Stadler took this one in a playoff, too. "To win one was beyond my expectations, but to win two is beyond words," Stadler said. "It is just insane. I've been happy with my play since I turned pro, but I just haven't finished well."

And Warren, after taking the Samsung Canadian PGA in a walk, by seven strokes, did it the hard way in the Cox Classic. He fired a final-round 66 and had to par the last hole to win by a stroke. "I've never had to come up the last hole needing a par or birdie to win," said Warren, referring to his two previous Nationwide wins.

Elsewhere on the Nationwide Tour:

Frank Langham, a six-year PGA Tour veteran, regained his card by finishing fourth on the Nationwide Tour money list ($312,896). He had one win, a third and eight top-10 finishes overall.

On the down side, the sad story of Ty Tryon dragged on. Tryon, who turned professional as a teenager and spent two fruitless years on the PGA Tour, continued to have trouble on the Nationwide Tour. He made just six cuts in 22 starts, had a best finish of a tie for 48th, and won only $9,058. He was 199th on the money list. And Dave Stockton Jr., a PGA Tour member for eight years, made just seven cuts in 23 tournaments and finished 145th on the money list with $21,547.

Seven of the 2004 top-20 money winners were not U.S. players, and they won eight tournaments ... Bubba Watson hit the longest recorded drive in tour history, a 422-yarder at the Gila River Golf Classic ... Paul Gow went winless but came as close as he could — he lost in three playoffs ... Darron Stiles had nine top-10 finishes, the most on the tour, and shot the most rounds in the 60s, 43.

Canadian Tour

It's part of a golfer's makeup to wonder what might have been. In other words, a case of the "coulda's-woulda's." Accordingly, maybe Erik Compton had to come away wondering what might have been if he hadn't signed that incorrect scorecard and got disqualified that one time. Even so, 2004 was a good year for him — two victories and enough good finishes to ring up $85,000 in eight starts and top the Canadian Tour's Order of Merit. No complaints, but playing the way he was, who knows what might have happened in the Michelin Guadalajara Classic.

Compton, Chris Wisler and Stephen Woodard each won twice in the 13-event season. Compton also had two seconds and a third, and he logged a Canadian Tour-best 69.36 scoring average. Only Canadian David Hearn prevented an American sweep of the 13 events. Hearn, the 2002 Rookie of Year, also had three consecutive top-four finishes. Seven players scored their first Canadian Tour victories — Hearn, Woodard, Brad Sutterfield, Ben Pettitt, Jason Higton, Stephen Gangluff and Ryan Miller.

Erik Compton, a former University of Georgia player, who had a heart transplant at the age of 12, completed a wire-to-wire run to take the E-Loan Central Valley Classic at Brookside Golf Club in Stockton, California. With a final-round 68 and total of 15-under-par 273, he won comfortably by three strokes over Australian Ben Gallie. Compton shared the first-round lead, and in the final round shot 34 on the first nine and cruised home. Compton needed some heroics for more comfort, and so at the 522-yard, par-five 18th, he fired a two iron from 240 yards to within 10 feet. An easy two-putt from there, and that was it. Any problems? "It's tough trying to sleep on a lead and come out the next day and keep momentum," Compton said. "I wouldn't say I was relaxed this morning, but I was ready to go."

In the MTS Classic in Winnipeg, Compton seemed easily on his way to his second victory when he birdied his first two holes and increased his lead to four shots. Then he double-bogeyed the par-five fourth and had to duel Hearn down the stretch. Compton won with an eight-foot par putt at the 18th.

The Barton Creek Challenge at the Barton Creek Crenshaw Cliffside Course in Austin, Texas, was shortened to three rounds because of Thursday rains. Chris Wisler, after a stunning first-round 62 and 66 in the second round, took a three-stroke lead into the final round and stretched it to six after four holes. Then strong and gusty winds came up and all bets were off. Wisler won with a six-foot birdie at the 17th hole that put his lead at two. His closing birdie didn't hurt. He won by one stroke over Canadian Adam Short, who solved the winds for a closing 65. Said Wisler, "I tell you, his 65 in that wind today is more impressive than my 62 was."

Wisler followed that victory with his second late in August in the season-ending Bay Mills Open Players Championship at Wild Bluff, Brimley, Michigan. He led by four strokes going into the final round and shot 70 for a 12-under-par 276 total, the best winning score in the three years for a five-stroke victory, biggest on the Canadian Tour this season.

Stephen Woodard of Charlotte, North Carolina, winless since he joined the Canadian Tour in 1996, ended the drought with a playoff victory over Steve Scott in the Telus Edmonton Open in mid-July. Woodard's final-round 68 at the Derrick Golf and Winter Club tied Scott at 12-under-par 272. Woodward won with a two-putt par at the second playoff hole, the par-three 17th, when Scott was short of the green with his tee shot and his chip. "The way I've been playing the past few weeks, I felt I could put myself in position to win," Woodard said.

Woodard's second victory came the following week at the Montreal Open at Ile de Montreal Golf Club, a event reduced to three rounds by heavy rains. Woodard began the final round with a two-stroke edge and shot an even-par 70 on a windy day. He had a 54-hole total of four-under-par 206 and won by three strokes over Craig Taylor, the only other player under par in the gusting winds and sloppy conditions.

Hearn, of Brantford, Ontario, rallied at the Times Colonist Open to take his first Canadian Tour victory and head off an impending American sweep. He started the final round one stroke off the lead, posted 68 for a 15-under-par 273 total and a three-stroke win over Canadian amateur standout James Lepp. Hearn took the lead at the fourth hole, but seemed to be in trouble when he double-bogeyed the 10th. He rebounded for two straight birdies. "Wow, it is great to finally get it done," he said. "Coming close so many times, it sure feels special to win."

The Greater Vancouver Classic was a chance for redemption for Ryan Miller of West Alexandria, Ohio. He was still smarting from his rookie season of 2003 when he made just two cuts in 11 appearances and lost his playing card. Starting the final day a stroke behind the leaders, he closed strong at Mayfair Lakes, making a clutch save for par at the 14th and birdieing his last two holes for 66 for a 14-under-par 270 total, and waited to see if they could catch him. Erik Compton was one behind and nearly eagled the 18th out of a bunker. Canadians David Hearn and Derek Gillespie tied for third, three behind, and both shot 66s. Said a relieved Miller, "Winning a tournament of this caliber makes it all worthwhile."

For sheer drama, maybe nothing topped the season-opener, the Barton Creek Classic at the Fazio Foothills Course at Austin, Texas. Brad Sutterfield of St. George, Utah, looking for his first Canadian Tour victory, seemed to be in command, leading by one stroke coming down the home stretch. Then he bogeyed the 15th hole, and up ahead Mario Tiziani birdied the 16th and took the lead. Later, Tiziani birdied the 18th while Sutterfield was back at the 17th, making a birdie to stay within one stroke. Sutterfield needed a birdie at the 18th to tie, and he got it with a 15-foot downhill putt for 69. In the playoff, at the 18th, Tiziani hit his second shot over the green and watched helplessly as his gentle chip back rolled across the green and down into the creek. It was a formality for Sutterfield to wrap up the victory at that point.

Tiziani shrugged. "It's tough to take, but what can you do?" he said. "There will be other days."

"After what happened today," Sutterfield said, "I will never give up in any situation. I will give it my all."

Tour de las Americas (South America)

Argentina's Rafael Gomez was looking for a television cameraman to thank properly. "If you see him," a beaming Gomez said, "tell him to send me a bill." Without the cameraman's accidental help, Gomez might not have won the Mexico Open, and without the Mexico Open, Gomez would not have won the Tour de las Americas' Order of Merit for the second time.

Some call it great luck, which it is, and golf calls it the rub of the green. Gomez's approach shot to the final hole at Club de Golf La Hacienda in Mexico City, a 603-yard par-five, rolled over the back of the green and was heading for trouble and maybe even out of bounds. But it hit the cameraman or his equipment and left Gomez with an easier chip shot than he might have had. He chipped down to 18 inches, tapped that in for a birdie, the championship and $48,000, which lifted him to the top of the Order of Merit in only four appearances.

Gomez trailed all the way in the tournament and entered the final round one stroke behind Eduardo Herrera. "I chatted with my caddie, and we both agreed I needed to shoot 65," Gomez said. And that's what he shot for a 14-under 270 total and a two-stroke victory over Herrera, a colleague from the Nationwide Tour. Gomez was sixth in the Panasonic Panama Open, tied for 14th in the TIM Peru Open and tied for 23rd in the Abierto del Sur, piling up $59,222 to win the Order of Merit handily over Paraguay's Marco Ruiz, who was second with $43,688. Ruiz had no victories but had two seconds, a tie for fifth and a tie for 10th in six starts. Argentina's Rodolfo Gonzalez, winner of the American Express Puerto Rico Open, finished third.

Gomez could look forward to 2005. His Mexico win also gave him exempt status on the 2005 European Challenge Tour, and he retained his Nationwide Tour status by finishing 76th.

Gonzalez led the merit race most of the season, thanks mostly to his victory in the Puerto Rico Open. He locked up the win with a sand-save birdie at the last hole for a one-stroke victory over Argentina's Eduardo Argiro and Canada's David Morland. Gonzalez handled blustery conditions for a two-under 70 and a six-under 282 total. There would have been a tie except for an unusual penalty. American Mike San Filippo, the third-round leader, was assessed two strokes for practicing before the final round in an area designated as golf course. He finished fourth with 75–284 — two strokes behind Gonzalez.

"I played the last five holes with all my heart," Gonzalez said. "I knew it would be very hard to get out of the clutch, but I forced my way out. My bread-and-butter game is around the greens, and I felt pretty confident about that long bunker shot on the 18th. I thought I could lay the ball anywhere within two meters and fortunately I got it a bit loser, and a one-meter putt to win is a lot nearer than two."

Argiro was a bridesmaid again, thanks to his three-putt bogey at the 17th. "Two three-putts today, otherwise a very good round," he said. "I completely misjudged the first putt on 17, and for that I paid the price. You just can't afford to make any mistakes when you're in position."

Two others also had costly putting problems. At the 16th, San Filippo missed from less than three feet and lost the chance for the solo lead, and at the 18th he chipped well past the hole and bogeyed. "In all," San Filippo said, "that was not my best of days." He finished a solo fourth. Said Argentina's Miguel Guzman, after tying for sixth, "I could have kicked the ball better than I putted today."

In the Summit Panama Masters, at the Summit Resort in Panama City, Argentina's Miguel Fernandez got a break something like Gonzalez's. He also hit something, only much bigger than a cameraman. Fernandez was playing the par-five 18th when his ball hit a water tower that was off the course — and caromed back into the middle of the fairway.

"That said something good was happening to me," he said. Indeed. He eagled the hole to tie Welshman Mark Pilkington, who chipped in to birdie it. Fernandez (66) and Pilkington (67) tied at 14-under 274, tying the tournament record. Fernandez's eagle was his second, along with two birdies, for 30 on the second nine.

England's Ian Garbutt raced home in 66 for 13 under, only to watch Fernandez's ball bounce back into play to set up the eagle and then to see Pilkington's final pitch-in birdie. "I'm not really disappointed because I played well," Garbutt said, "but what I've just seen is really truly amazing!"

The playoff went to the friendly 18th. Fernandez made a long, delicate chip to within a foot for a winning birdie, while Pilkington missed the green and couldn't get close. For his trouble, Fernandez not only won the $18,000 first prize, he gained playing rights for a year on the European Tour and he got thrown into the swimming pool by his Argentine colleagues.

It also took a playoff to settle the Costa Rica Open. Italy's Alessandro Tadini birdied the third extra hole to edge Spain's Carlos Quevedo. Tadini finished with 70 and Quevedo 69 to tie at six-under 278 at Valle del Sol Golf Club in San Jose.

Tadini and Quevedo birdied the first playoff hole with delicate approaches and parred the 18th the next time around. Then Tadini played a superb approach to the 521-yard 10th and sank a six-foot putt for the winning birdie.

It very nearly was a four-way playoff. Argentina's Mauricio Molina (66) and Ariel Canete (69) both blew good chances at the 18th and finished a stroke behind, tied for third. Molina had rung up six birdies and a chip-in eagle, then missed a two-footer at the 18th. Canete lay two just short of the 18th green, but muffed a wedge shot.

"This has been the most thrilling event of my life," Tadini said. " I am very happy. I thought my three-putt on 17 had cost me the tournament, but I hung in when it got tough and survived."

Said Quevedo, "I'm content. Only one person can win a golf tournament. I came very close and I enjoyed it."

Finally, the TLA Players Championship was called the Acapulco Fest, but it ended up as Rafael Ponce's personal fest. The Fairmont Acapulco Princess has a par of 70 and measures only 6,355 yards, but Ponce, a 15-year veteran of the Asian Tour from Ecuador, reduced it to a miniature golf course, shooting 65-65-62-68 for a sizzling 20-under 260 and a nine-stroke victory over Rodolfo Gonzalez.

If the closing 68 seemed out of place, Ponce explained. "I was just trying to play safe, steady golf on the front nine," he said, "and I was doing that, more or less, but not making any putts when Rodolfo started to make his move and closed to within six. I was never really concerned, however, but the turnaround at the 11th and 12th made the last few holes much easier to play."

A curling 15-footer at the 11th gave Ponce a birdie, and Gonzalez double-bogeyed the 12th from a downhill lie in a bunker. Gonzalez fired back with a birdie on a long putt at the 13th, but Ponce was again eight ahead and out of reach. And when Ponce answered by sticking a seven iron from 148 yards to inches from the flag, Gonzalez did the only thing left to do. He waved a white towel.

10. European Tours

For the fifth successive year no European golfer won a major championship in 2004. For a brief period early in the year, there was no European in the top 10 of the Official World Golf Ranking for the first time since it was created in 1986. For the fourth season running the European Order of Merit was won by a South African, Ernie Els clinching his second title ahead of his predecessor, Retief Goosen, who had topped the money list for the previous two years.

But was European golf downhearted? It was not. By the time the year ended there was optimism in the air. The prime reason, although not the only one, was, of course, the overwhelming Ryder Cup victory at Oakland Hills. The rout was masterminded by Bernhard Langer, but the German was frank enough to suggest Europe could have picked from a pool of perhaps 18 players and still come back with the cup.

European golf has been undergoing a transition for a few years since it relied on major champions such as Langer, Seve Ballesteros, Nick Faldo and others. But the evidence appeared to be mounting that the transformation was nearing completion in 2004. More PGA European Tour players than ever before were set to finish the year in the top 50 on the World Ranking — there were 20 when the season finished after the Volvo Masters — and when talking about strictly European golfers, the figures were similarly encouraging.

When America achieved a nine-point victory in the Ryder Cup of 1981 at Walton Heath, they possessed what most judges rate as their strongest-ever team. No less than 11 of the 12 players either were, or went on to be, major champions. When Langer's team at Oakland Hills also won by nine points, not a single one of them had won a major — yet. The German captain promised that would change and, as everything else he forecast that week eventually proved correct, it would be foolish to dispute the issue.

"They always forget to say, 'the best player yet to win a major who is 24 years old,'" said Sergio Garcia, who joined Padraig Harrington back in the world's top 10 during the season. "I'm not worried. If I'm lucky and injuries behave, I'm going to have so many chances to win majors. I'm sure it will happen."

As for the Order of Merit, that has changed to the extent that majors and world championship events are now included. Players like Greg Norman, Nick Price and Vijay Singh came to Europe and then went on to the United States. Els and Goosen now live in London, remain members of the European Tour and still play all the big events.

Els came agonizingly close to winning not just one major championship, but all four. He put the disappointments behind him to win his first World Golf Championship event at the American Express Championship and then claimed the HSBC World Match Play title for a record sixth time. Goosen won the U.S. Open at Shinnecock Hills, but later suffered a hip injury in a jet ski accident which halted his summer campaign.

Harrington, ever consistent, finished third on the Order of Merit, just beating Miguel Angel Jimenez, who enjoyed the season of his life having just turned age 40. There was a relaxed air about the Spaniard. He smoked his cigars and drank his Rioja and his espressos and never got too worried by anything as trivial as a poor shot, and it seemed to bring out the best in his game. He won five times and returned to the Ryder Cup team.

Thomas Levet, who finished fifth on the money list, played for Europe for the first time at Oakland Hills and highlighted what was a golden year for French golf. They had four winners on tour, including Levet in the Barclays Scottish Open at Loch Lomond and Jean-Francois Remesy at the Open de France. There was no more joyous occasion on the circuit all year as when Remesy became the first Frenchman to win his national title since 1969.

Raphael Jacquelin was not among the French winners, but was highly consistent to prove himself as one of the many Europeans awaiting their turn for the big breakthrough. Graeme McDowell, a 24-year-old from Northern Ireland, did win the Italian Open to finish sixth on the Order of Merit. He stated his determination to gain a place on the Ryder Cup team at the K Club in Ireland in 2006.

English golf, however, is perhaps the most promising of all, with five players finishing in the top 20 of the money list. Lee Westwood did not win but continued his renaissance of the previous autumn by matching Garcia in earning four and a half points out of five at the Ryder Cup. He was joined at Oakland Hills by Ian Poulter, David Howell, Paul Casey and Luke Donald.

Poulter found himself the center of attention for wearing Union Jack flag trousers at the Open Championship; but when it comes to his game, he won the Volvo Masters to extend his steak of winning every year he has played on the European Tour. Howell produced one of the shots of the year, a six iron at the par-three 17th at Oakland Hills, to help himself and Casey win a crucial Saturday morning fourball after being 1 down with two to play.

Casey went on to another team triumph with Donald in claiming the WGC - World Cup for England. Donald enjoyed a fairy tale summer on the European Tour after spending the earlier part of his professional career in the United States. There were no more significant conversations all year than those Donald had with Langer and Ken Schofield, the executive director of the European Tour, persuading him to return to Europe. He won twice and received a Ryder Cup wild card from Langer.

"European golf is in good shape," said Colin Montgomerie. "There has been a good mood since September. We should build on the Ryder Cup and we are doing so. When there was no European in the top 10 of the world, that was just a blip. That's not going to happen again. It's like when there was only one Englishman in the top 100. Now there's loads" — seven, in fact — "but these things do change. It's been a fabulous year for European golf, of course it has."

For Montgomerie, it had been a turbulent year with the break-up of his marriage, but he found sanctuary on the golf course and ended up holing the winning putt at Oakland Hills. "My fellow competitors have been super," he said. "They have given me great support, as everyone has, including the lads and ladies in the press.

"The key to European golf is the camaraderie. It is a competitive place, as it should be, but it is also like a very big family. The man who has to take the credit for that is Ken Schofield. He has lived and breathed his job, and the players should be thankful that he has put in so much."

At the end of the year Schofield stepped down as executive director of the European Tour after 30 years in charge. George O'Grady, his deputy for most of that time, took over. During Schofield's reign the prize money went from under £500,000 to over £80 million, astounding figures. In that time there were six Ryder Cup victories and one tie, plus enormous change with the tour expanding outside its geographical boundaries. In 2004 there was a tournament in China for the first time; in 2005 there will be four.

O'Grady was confident of an ever prosperous future, partly thanks to the success of the teamwork at the Ryder Cup. "We will not lose sight of the sportsmanship and the spirit of the game, but it will be driven in a hard, business manner," O'Grady said, laying out his blueprint. "If you look at our schedule, you will see people who have used golf with all the values it stands for as part of their marketing platform.

"But the team spirit that came out of the Ryder Cup has traveled to our sponsors. It has brought an enormously positive response from people who want to ally their commercial brand to the sport.

"We are poised to bring something very unusual. We've amalgamated so many different countries, so many different cultures, and we've made it one big team. That's a very positive force for anybody prepared to invest their sponsorship dollars and we're going to drive that message forward."

PGA European Tour

South African Airways Open—£500,000
Winner: Trevor Immelman

See African Tours chapter.

Dunhill Championship—£500,000
Winner: Marcel Siem

See African Tours chapter.

Johnnie Walker Classic—US$1,800,000
Winner: Miguel Angel Jimenez

See Asia/Japan Tours chapter.

Heineken Classic—A$2,000,000
Winner: Ernie Els

See Australasian Tour chapter.

ANZ Championship—A$1,750,000
Winner: Brian Davis

See Australasian Tour chapter.

Carlsberg Malaysian Open—US$1,210,000
Winner: Thongchai Jaidee

See Asia/Japan Tours chapter.

Dubai Desert Classic—€1,607,591
Winner: Mark O'Meara

A few days after Tiger Woods and Mark O'Meara paid a surprise visit to American troops in the Arabian Gulf, it was O'Meara and not the world No. 1 who was victorious in the Dubai Desert Classic. O'Meara had not won for six years, since his glorious year of Masters and Open Championship success in 1998, but Woods was standing behind the 18th green at the Emirates Golf Club to congratulate his 47-year-old friend.

"It makes it even more special for Tiger to be there with a big bear hug at the finish," said O'Meara. "Tiger is the ultimate competitor, but he is also the ultimate champion and he knew what this means to me."

O'Meara started the final round tied with Paul McGinley, but a closing 69 gave the American a one-stroke victory at 271, 17 under par. After the Irishman found the water at the ninth, he could not get on terms again. O'Meara was relentless in finding every green on the back nine, holing from six feet for a birdie at the 11th, but not needing to match McGinley's four at the par-five 18th.

"He didn't give me an inch," said McGinley. "You have to hand it to him, being that tough when he hasn't been in that situation for so long. It looked like he was used to winning all the time. It was fun but I feel like I've been in a boxing match."

Ernie Els, with a closing round of 65, and David Howell finished tied for third place, three behind McGinley, while Woods was a shot further back.

"Chalk one up for the old boys," said O'Meara. "It's a big day for me and a huge boost of confidence. It's been a long time since I've won and you do wonder when you are battling away and low on confidence whether you will get the chance again."

O'Meara, who started the week in 201st place on the World Ranking, credited a new putting grip for his success. Although he won the Skins Game in 2002, the following year in the same event he won not a dollar, while Annika Sorenstam challenged Fred Couples for the title.

It was then that his coach, Hank Haney, suggested O'Meara adopt a variant on Chris DiMarco's "claw" putting grip. With the fingers of the right hand on top of the shaft and the thumb under it, the opposite of the natural grip, O'Meara was able to lock the right wrist as when using a saw.

On the perfect greens of the Middle East, O'Meara's confidence soared. "I'm calling it the 'saw' and we're going to have to get some copyrights sorted out," said O'Meara. "Trust me, it works. It has certainly rejuvenated my career. I was definitely a little nervous on the 18th green, but I hit a lot of great putts under pressure on the closing holes.

"By the end of last year I was getting frustrated. I was putting as badly as is humanly possible. It felt like it was time to turn things around. I needed to get a passion for the game of golf again and I feel a lot more relaxed on the course now."

On the eve of the tournament, Woods and O'Meara flew on a private jet to Bahrain, then by military plane to the aircraft carrier *USS George Washington* where they gave a clinic for 2,000 troops and handed out golf equipment. "It was one of the most awe-inspiring afternoons in my life," said Woods. "They are out there protecting us and putting their lives on the line, so it's the least we can do to put a smile on their faces."

Qatar Masters—€1,231,150
Winner: Joakim Haeggman

Joakim Haeggman's wait for a victory was even longer than Mark O'Meara's. The 34-year-old Swede had not won for seven years when he claimed the Qatar Masters, his third title on the European Tour. But Haeggman was only playing at Doha thanks to a medical exemption. He missed the first seven months of the 2003 season after breaking his ankle playing hockey the previous December.

It was the second time Haeggman's career had been interrupted by an injury caused by heading onto the ice. He was not intending to make it third time unlucky. "I'm not even thinking about playing again," he admitted. "I'm not going to put my skates back on."

A victory in Doha looked unlikely after an opening 75 left him trailing at the end of the field, but he played the last 54 holes in 19 under par, spurred on by a 64 in the second round. With one round to play, Haeggman trailed the leaders Nobuhito Sato and Raphael Jacquelin by two strokes.

Haeggman went to the turn in 31 to tie Sato and then birdied the 10th and 13th holes. He dropped a shot at the 14th, but holed from 15 feet on the final green for a closing 65 and to set the target with a 272 total, 16 under par. Both Sato and Jacquelin needed an eagle at the last to tie.

Sato's pitch for his third at the par-five 18th finished close and the birdie gave the Japanese player second place, his highest finish on the European Tour after coming through the qualifying tournament the previous autumn. Jacquelin could not get his bunker shot close at all and his par left the Frenchman tied for third place with Brian Davis and Jose Manuel Lara.

"Obviously, relief is the first word that comes to mind," said Haeggman, who was the first Swede to play for the European Ryder Cup team in 1993.

In 2002 at the Belfry, Haeggman had been an assistant to Sam Torrance, the European captain, but this victory gave Haeggman hope of qualifying to play in the match at Oakland Hills later in the year.

"I feel I'm back," he said. "I think I can cope with the pressure again and play at the highest level. Walking down the fairways with Sam at the Belfry, I was enjoying it, but I couldn't see why I shouldn't be playing instead."

Caltex Masters—US$900,000
Winner: Colin Montgomerie

See Asia/Japan Tours chapter.

Madeira Island Open—€600,000
Winner: Christopher Hanell

By emphasizing quality rather than quantity, Christopher Hanell quickly earned his first victory on the European Tour at the Madeira Island Open. Hanell was playing in his first event of the year, and the exemption status that the win brought the 30-year-old Swede ensured he would play in all the big events in the season, making it easier for him to stick to his plan of only playing 20 events.

"Not having a win after five years on tour was getting to me," Hanell admitted. "I felt I needed to make changes, but I'm so happy now. This gets me into the events I want to play in, like the Deutsche Bank, the Volvo PGA and the German Masters."

As well as skipping the early part of the season when the tour goes globetrotting, Hanell made several changes. He moved from Monaco to Scottsdale, Arizona, where he had attended college, employed a new coach and took up yoga.

High up at the Santo da Serra course it was wet and windy all week and Hanell had to play 27 holes on the final day, first completing a 73 in the third round to lie four strokes off the lead and then adding a 71 to reach 284 total, four under par, and win by one stroke over Brad Kennedy, Steven Jeppesen and Rob Rashell.

Both Jeppesen and Knud Storgaard fell away in the final round after starting three ahead of the field. After Hanell set the clubhouse target, Rashell, an American who shares Tiger Woods' birthday, missed a birdie putt at the last to tie, while Kennedy bogeyed the 18th.

Kennedy was left ruing a scorecard error from the third round which also involved the 18th hole. The Australian's drive finished in the left-hand rough but in a position where he could take a free drop. But then a gust of wind blew the ball 30 yards away up against the curb of a path. He was again entitled to a free drop, but the nearest point of relief was in heavy rough so Kennedy declared the ball unplayable and went back to the tee. He eventually three-putted for a triple-bogey seven, but was convinced he had taken an eight, the score he signed for on the card, and so condemned himself to start the final round a stroke further back than he needed to be.

Algarve Open de Portugal—€1,250,000
Winner: Miguel Angel Jimenez

A few weeks earlier, Miguel Angel Jimenez was disqualified from the Qatar Masters, which had prevented him from having any chance of earning a last-minute call-up from the top 50 of the World Ranking for the first major championship of the season at the Masters. Jimenez was penalized for an incident where his ball appeared to have moved, but although he disagreed with the referee at the time, he took his punishment in a sporting manner. The ball had oscillated while Jimenez took a practice chip, but he thought it had returned to the same position; the referee felt the balance of probability was that it had not.

So instead of heading to Augusta, Jimenez found himself on the Algarve, and a victory in the Portuguese Open confirmed the 40-year-old Spaniard was playing some of the best golf of his career. It was his second title of the season and his third since the previous October, which meant he was almost assured of earning a place on the European team for the Ryder Cup at Oakland Hills.

Jimenez, who won the Johnnie Walker Classic in Bangkok in January, was sharing the lead with Ignacio Garrido and David Lynn after three rounds. His 67 on the final day gave him a 272 total and a two-stroke victory over Terry Price, with Klas Eriksson and Graeme McDowell sharing third place.

Jimenez played a superb bunker shot at the last hole to finish off with a birdie after earlier going to the turn in 31. Price equaled the Penina course record of 64 set earlier in the day by Robert Karlsson.

"It is history," Jimenez said of the Qatar incident. "You have to forget and move on. You have to live for the moment and put it all behind you. I lost my chance to play in the Masters with what happened, but now I go home and spend time with my family. You can't compare this with the Masters. You have to take what comes. I am very happy to win the Portuguese Open as it is a victory and for your career that is important."

As for the Ryder Cup, the possibility of adding to his 1999 appearance was something he was not prepared to rely on with so much of the season still to play.

Open de Sevilla—€1,000,000
Winner: Ricardo Gonzalez

Statistics, who needs them? From the barrage of information collected every week, there came the conclusion that it was far better to be in the rough than the sand at Real Golf de Sevilla. Being in the sand was no good. Jose Manuel Lara tried it 31 times, almost eight times a day, but could only get up and down 14 times. He did not figure on the leaderboard at the inaugural Open de Sevilla.

When it came to hitting fairways, or missing them, in fact, it did not matter to Ricardo Gonzalez. The 34-year-old Argentinean went around in 69 strokes in the third round after hitting only one of the 14 fairways, and that on the one occasion he went with a two iron rather than a driver. He still had a one-stroke lead.

The following day Gonzalez hit only three more fairways, but also went around in 69 strokes for a 274 total to win by two shots over Jonathan Lomas and Stephen Gallacher. Overall for the week, Gonzalez hit less than a third of the fairways, but finished at 14 under par. He was helped by the rough not having grown much early in the spring, by hitting the ball over 300 yards and by a dazzling putting display. To prove the old adage that you drive for show and putt for dough, Gonzalez had the best putting average of anyone in the event.

It was Gonzalez's third win on the European Tour, but he achieved it only after birdieing three of the last five holes and by sinking a 40-foot putt on the final green. Earlier in the round it looked as if Lomas might claim only his second title when he holed in one at the third and eagled the fifth to take a five-stroke lead. But he finished with a bogey at the 18th. Gallacher's challenge also evaporated when he dropped a shot at the 15th and then parred in. Jean-Francois Remesy and Louis Oosthuizen tied for fourth place with Robert-Jan Derksen.

"I'm embarrassed at my driving, but I'm obstinate," Gonzalez said. "I kept on trying to hit the driver because I knew I was hitting the ball to the right and there isn't much trouble on the right."

Canarias Open de Espana—€1,650,000
Winner: Christian Cevaer

In order to counteract the five bogeys that Christian Cevaer suffered during the final round of the Canarias Open de Espana, the Frenchman needed a boost. The extra bit of magic that took the 34-year-old to his first title came in the form of two eagles, neither of which involved any putting.

Two behind overnight leader David Park and Ricardo Gonzalez, Cevaer made the perfect start when he holed a wedge shot from 137 yards for an eagle at the first hole. For good measure he also holed a chip-and-run shot from 53 yards for another eagle at the 16th hole.

It was all too much for Gonzalez, who was attempting to win for a second week running and had birdied three holes out of four from the third earlier in the day. Three strokes ahead with four to play, Gonzalez dropped back with the aid of a double bogey at the 16th, where he drove out of bounds and also took three putts.

Cevaer's up-and-down closing round of 69, one under par, put him at 271, nine under par, and gave him a one-stroke victory over Gonzalez, Peter Hedblom and Park. Bradley Dredge and Jarmo Sandelin shared fifth place another shot back.

Cevaer, who was born on the island of New Caledonia and has a degree in psychology from Stanford University, had twice finished second on the European Tour. "I've had a lot of podium finishes, but it is very encouraging to actually win," he said.

His career was interrupted early in 2002 when he fractured his right elbow while snowboarding. Like Joakim Haeggman before him, Cevaer almost faced the end of his playing days and took part in only six events that year. "I am a good skier so I thought I would try snowboarding, but found out it was totally different," he said.

"I struggled for about an hour, but then I was beginning to get the hang of it. Had I not had the accident I might have become very good. But at the end of a four-hour session, I misjudged a jump on a ramp and broke my elbow. When a thing like that happens it gives you a big jump of maturity. You realize that the boy in you likes the challenge, but the most important thing for me now is golf. I have been lucky to be able to continue playing and swinging so smoothly. There will be no more snowboarding."

Telecom Italia Open—€1,200,000
Winner: Graeme McDowell

When the Italian Police marching band is booked for an appearance, they will turn up exactly on time at the specified venue unless informed otherwise. Sadly, there was no otherwise at 7 p.m. on the Sunday evening of the Telecom Italia Open. The band arrived exactly on time for the prize giving ceremony on the 18th hole of Castello di Tolcinasco course in Milan.

Unfortunately, that was exactly the moment that play in the third and, as it turned out, final round was resuming after an earlier delay due to a flooded course. The band marched straight back to the car park without missing a note and was never seen again.

There was certainly no such fanfare when Graeme McDowell brought the rain-ruined tournament to a conclusion early on Monday morning. McDowell, after rounds of 66 and 66, completed a final round of 65 to join Thomas Levet in a playoff at 197, 19 under par. Levet had also scored a 65 in the last round, as did Gregory Havret, who finished in third place one stroke behind and one ahead of Angel Cabrera, who led by one over Joakim Haeggman and two over McDowell and Levet after two rounds.

Levet holed from eight feet at the 18th to get into the playoff. The same hole was then halved twice in pars, before both Levet and McDowell birdied the 17th. They went back to the 18th and this time Levet put his second shot into the water on the left of the green and McDowell was able to two-putt for victory.

It was the 24-year-old Northern Irishman's second European Tour title. The first came in the Scandinavian Masters in 2002 in only his fourth tournament since leaving the amateur ranks. "When I won in Sweden I still felt I was an amateur," said McDowell, who comes from Portrush and had borrowed a putter from Darren Clarke for the week.

"I feel this is my first professional victory and I am very happy with it. Looking back and knowing what I know now, and that my game is so much better, I realize I was playing as an amateur in Sweden. I have had two years of working and grinding out on tour and it is a different world. I feel I really worked for this one."

A trainer, a psychologist and a coach, Claude Harmon, son of Butch, all contributed to the victory which came with his weight in cheese, even if it was not serenaded by the Italian Police marching band.

Daily Telegraph Damovo British Masters—€2,370,800
Winner: Barry Lane

Since he had last won, Barry Lane had traveled a particularly long and winding road, but you would not have known from the way he won the Damovo Daily Telegraph British Masters at the Forest of Arden.

Though the eventual winning margin was three strokes, the moment of truth came at the 16th hole. Lane had dropped his only shot of the day at the previous hole, cutting his advantage to two strokes, but found his drive in the thickest of rough to the right of the fairway. Two days before, Lane had only been able to chip sideways to the fairway from a similar position. With Argentineans Eduardo Romero and Angel Cabrera breathing down his neck, the braver option had to be taken. Lane's recovery cleared the pond in front of the green and left the Englishman with a birdie chance from 25 feet that he holed.

"That's the worst lie I've ever seen," he said. "I'm glad I've got strong forearms. I was aiming for the right corner of the green but it came out a little left, but to get onto the green was unbelievable."

Lane, a month short of his 40th birthday, had chipped in for an eagle at the seventh to put him clear of the field and he finished with a 66 for a 272 total, 16 under par. Romero and Cabrera tied for second place, with Paul Broadhurst, the overnight leader, dropping back to a tie for fifth place.

This was Lane's 499th tournament on the European Tour, but he almost did not play. He was unable to walk the previous Monday and had his left knee strapped all week. The last of his previous four official titles came 10 years and 57 days ago, or 252 events, in Spain. An unofficial victory, and $1 million, followed in the forerunner to the Accenture World Match Play in 1995, but then nothing.

"This is a wonderful feeling," Lane said. "This is what we strive to do, win tournaments. I lost a bit of motivation and got fed up with all the traveling for a while, but this year my attitude has been good. I never stopped believing in myself."

Colin Montgomerie, lifted by the warmth of the crowd's reaction, was glad to get his first tournament since announcing the break-up of his marriage out of the way. "It has been a very difficult week, but now I can move on with confidence," said the Scot. "I've got a lot of time on my hands now, so you may see me practicing an awful lot more. You never know, it may help."

Deutsche Bank - SAP Open—€3,000,000
Winner: Trevor Immelman

There was much talk about belly putters at the Deutsche Bank - SAP Open. Ernie Els called for them to be banned, only to have his countryman, Trevor Immelman, wield his own implement to such good effect he took the title at St. Leon-Rot.

"I think it is an easier way to putt," Els said of belly and broom-handled putters. "It's braced against your body and you just have to move your bottom hand. It's just doesn't feel right to me. I think nerves and the skill of putting is part of the game. Take a tablet if you can't handle it."

It was watching Vijay Singh win back-to-back titles on the U.S. PGA Tour that inspired the 24-year-old Immelman to turn to the belly putter and he had used it at only one tournament previously. "I didn't have the yips," he said. "I just felt it was a technical thing for me. I felt I needed to release it better, and with the belly putter anchored in your stomach, the thing has to swing like a pendulum. It is as if I have learned how to putt all over again. Right from the start I could see this is something I could work with."

Immelman had only 24 putts on the final day when he beat Padraig Harrington by one stroke. It was a brilliant shootout between the pair and was only settled on the final green. Immelman rolled in a seven-footer for his seventh birdie of the day just moments after Harrington had missed from 10 feet for his eighth birdie.

Immelman closed with a 65 for a total of 271, 17 under par, while Harrington had to settle for a 66. Joakim Haeggman and Darren Clarke finished in third place, four strokes behind Harrington, while Els tied for fifth.

Immelman felt it was unfair that the issue of belly putters had come up just that week when plenty of others have won tournaments using non-conventional methods. "It is not just about one club," he said. "You have to hit the ball well to win tournaments as well. You don't just hole putts. I feel we've got a lot of our top players on the tour using the belly putter and I've never read much about them using it."

Volvo PGA Championship—€3,750,000
Winner: Scott Drummond

On Saturday night, Scott Drummond and his wife Claire went out to dinner to celebrate his 30th birthday. It was the first time they had had a couple of hours away from their four-week-old baby girl, Kiera, who was in the capable hands of grandparents. Otherwise, Drummond spent the week of his debut in the Volvo PGA Championship sharing a small hotel room with wife and baby, having takeaways in the evening, and sleeping on the floor for an hour in the morning.

But by the end of the week everything had changed. While Ernie Els opened up on the West course with an ominous 64 in pursuit of a title he has not yet won, it was a 64 for a 269 total on the final day by Drummond which secured victory by two strokes over Angel Cabrera.

It was a win to rank with that of Ben Curtis at the Open Championship the previous summer. Drummond was in his rookie season on the European Tour, had missed seven of his previous eight cuts, and earned only £35,000 in his career. He was ranked 186th on the Order of Merit and 435th in the world. But that didn't stop Drummond from playing with a maturity far beyond his years and producing a staggering result, one that was all the better for the impressive leaderboard that he topped.

Joakim Haeggman was third, with Darren Clarke, Nick Faldo and Anders Hansen tied for fourth and Ernie Els seventh. The in-form Vijay Singh finished even further adrift. Drummond joined Arnold Palmer, at Royal St. George's in 1975, as the only other player to win the title at his first attempt. He was also only the second player after Denmark's Hansen to make the PGA his first title, in the process matching Hansen's record score of 19 under par.

Born of Scottish parents in Shropshire, the Drummonds now live in Devon. Although he played amateur golf for England, like Sandy Lyle before him, Drummond became another Shropshire lad to elect to play for the land of his father, Scotland, on becoming a professional. That was back in 1996, but it was only after a successful season on the Challenge Tour in 2003 that he made it onto the main circuit full time.

He was the fourth reserve for the PGA when entries closed, but found out he was playing a week before the tournament. He had not played the West course at Wentworth prior to the week, but his sports psychologist thought odds of 500-to-1 were too tempting to miss out on and placed £10 on his man. When Drummond heard about the bet, for the first time ever he also placed a similar wager on himself.

After rolling in a 10-foot putt at the final green, Drummond appeared as stunned as everyone else. "I really can't comprehend it," he said. "It was surreal out there. I had to remind myself that it was the Sunday of the PGA."

Drummond received €625,000 for the victory. "It's a little bit more than I've won in the past," he said. "I wasn't thinking about winning, or the big paychecks," he said. "But, obviously, things are going to change now. It's always expensive to play on the tour as a rookie and at times you wonder what you are going to do next year. With Kiera coming along, obviously I wanted to be financially secure. You couldn't ask for me. It's a dream."

One behind Cabrera after 54 holes, Drummond was playing alongside the big-hitting Argentinean, who duly made the first two par-fives, the fourth and 12th, look puny with a pair of eagles.

Drummond, not to be outdone, would birdie all four of the par-fives and make four other birdies without dropping a shot. Cabrera made few errors, but his bogeys at the short holes, the fifth and 14th, proved costly. After Drummond had holed a 45-footer on the 13th green to tie, Cabrera left the 14th green now one behind. Drummond's amazing putting continued at the 17th, where he rolled in a 40-footer when it looked as if the Argentinean would draw even.

Again at the par-five 18th, Cabrera was pin-high in two, Drummond down the fairway after his drive finished in the rough. But with a superb wedge shot to six feet, Drummond put the pressure back on Cabrera, whose chip ran on 15 feet past the pin. His birdie effort finished on the lip and then Drummond had two for the win. Not that he knew. "I promised my caddie, Kevin Smith, that I wouldn't look at the leaderboard all day, not even on the last green. I could sense from the gallery that I was near the lead or tied, but obviously when the putt went in I knew from the roar and Kevin's reaction that I had won."

Celtic Manor Wales Open—€2,250,560
Winner: Simon Khan

While Scott Drummond was winning the PGA Championship, Simon Khan was sitting at home watching on television. He had been playing at Wentworth but was back early on the Sunday afternoon, having finished well down the field, not helped by a one-stroke penalty for slow play in the third round. Khan and Drummond were friends from their days playing the less celebrated byways of professional golf.

"As we were watching Scott, I said to my wife that I had played well at Wentworth but not really holed a putt. Lesley is pretty direct and said 'It's not going to get any better just sitting there and talking about it.' So I got my putting track out and hit 300 putts right there and then. Scott's win did get me thinking, but my wife again said, 'You used to play to win, even if it was a local PGA event or a pro-am.'

"You can fall into a trap on tour of trying to have a good finish, a top 10 to secure your card. It was almost like someone turning on a light. I had a different mindset this week. Watching Scott win definitely hit home."

Khan, a 31-year-old from Essex who spent time driving a taxi in London to support his early career, won his first title in the Wales Open at Celtic Manor. There were signs something was different on Friday morning when Khan played the first nine in nine under par, with seven birdies and an eagle. He scored a 61 to take the lead, but Paul Casey, with a 65, went three ahead after 54 holes.

Casey extended that lead to four with seven holes to play, but Khan birdied three holes out of four while Casey had a double bogey at the 15th and had to birdie the 18th to join Khan in a playoff at 267, 21 under par. Jean-Francois Remesy finished in third place, four shots adrift, with Nick O'Hern fourth.

Khan had missed a seven-footer for victory at the last, but after the 18th was halved at the first extra hole, playing the same hole again, Casey carved his approach and fluffed a chip to take a six and give Khan the victory. "I still think of all the hard times earlier in my career and it makes this all the sweeter," Khan said.

Diageo Championship at Gleneagles—€2,116,550
Winner: Miles Tunnicliff

Miles Tunnicliff claimed his second European Tour title with a convincing victory in the Diageo Championship at Gleneagles. He was never headed. A 67 on the opening day left him sharing the lead with Nick O'Hern. A 68 in the second round gave the 35-year-old a five-stroke lead. Even after a 72 on Saturday the field could only close within three strokes, and a 68 to finish left him at 275, 13 under par, and five in front of Graeme McDowell.

Tunnicliff, after repeated trips to the qualifying tournament earlier in his career, won for the first time in 2002. A second title meant even more, but for the second week running the victor thanked his immediate predecessor, namely Simon Khan. "I saw something Simon said that I concentrated on," Tunnicliff said. "He said he tried to think only of winning. After I opened up so well, that's what I tried and it worked well.

"I was a little bit nervous at the start of the final round, but I was so focused all day long. The only time I looked at the leaderboard was at the last." By then any danger had passed.

Tunnicliff looked to have sealed things up with birdies at the first two holes and another at the ninth to be out in 33. McDowell, a 24-year-old Ulsterman, suddenly produced five birdies in a row around the turn and another at the 15th to cut the deficit to two strokes, but he immediately took a double bogey at the 16th. Steven O'Hara and O'Hern were tied for third place, with David Lynn and Andrew Oldcorn tied for fifth.

Aa St. Omer Open—€400,000
Winner: Philippe Lima

One look at the prize money for the Aa St. Omer Open suggests that it is not a usual PGA European Tour event. Philippe Lima won "only" €66,660, but that did not stop it being a life-changing victory for the 22-year-old Frenchman. Lima was little more than a journeyman professional on the Challenge Tour until his first title came along at the Segura Viudas Challenge de Espana.

The very next week he was playing in the next stop on the Challenge Tour, the Aa St. Omer Open, which also has co-sanctioned status on the main European Tour. Victory meant he was exempted to play in all the elite events, starting with the following week's French Open.

"This has changed my life," said the player from Versailles. "It is hard to take in at the moment, but I know for sure that my life is changing. It has been an unbelievable two weeks for me, first with my victory in Spain last week and then to win here is a dream come true. I don't know what my schedule will be like now, but I will definitely go to the Open de France and play on the European Tour."

Lima opened with three successive rounds of 71 which left him three strokes behind the lead going into the final round. It was not the differential in strokes that was the problem, but the number of players in contention. No less than six players shared the lead after 54 holes: David Geall, whose 67 in the third round had jumped him furthest up the leaderboard, Carl Suneson, the halfway leader, Massimo Florioli, Simon Dyson, Finland's Pasi Purhonen and Jean-Francois Lucquin, another Frenchman who the home crowd were cheering on.

But their attention was soon taken by Lima, whose six birdies and only one bogey gave him a 66 and a 279 total, five under par. Alessandro Tadini, who had started one shot behind the leading sextet, was Lima's biggest threat and came to the 18th tied for the lead. He had a 40-foot birdie chance for the title and did not leave it short. Unfortunately, it ran on just enough to leave a trembler back from four feet to make the playoff, but he missed. Geall finished in third place, with Suneson and Dyson among those sharing fourth place.

Open de France—€3,000,000
Winner: Jean-Francois Remesy

The celebrations that greeted Philippe Lima's victory on home soil were nothing in comparison with the joy that erupted when another Frenchman won in front of his own supporters at the Open de France. What made Jean-Francois Remesy's victory at the National Club in Paris so special was that it was the first time since 1969 that a native player had won their national championship.

Remesy celebrated by throwing himself into the lake by the 18th green, but had dried off by the time he received the trophy from none other than Jean Garaialde, the last French winner of the title. The victory came 19 years after Remesy was the French Amateur champion and five years after his only other win on the European Tour. The 40-year-old's early career was not a huge success and he went 11 years before recording his first top-10 finish.

But that was all forgotten on a brilliant summer's day in Paris with a victory that grabbed the attention of the French media in a way the game has rarely enjoyed before. Remesy was the halfway co-leader with former Masters champion Ian Woosnam and then produced his lowest-ever round on the European Tour, a 65 that put him three ahead of Richard Green and seven ahead of Woosnam.

This was on a course that had rough so severe it was likened to U.S. Open conditions. But at the first hole on the final round Remesy was in worse trouble. He pulled his opening drive into a pond and took a double bogey. Though he birdied the second, a bogey followed at the third. It was hardly the start to calm the nerves.

But from then on Remesy never made a mistake and he finished with a 72 for a total of 272, 12 under par. Green's challenge floundered with bogeys at the 10th, 13th, 14th and 18th. Remesy's winning margin of seven strokes, improbable earlier in the afternoon, was the largest of the year on the European Tour to date. Green tied for second with fellow Australian Nick O'Hern. Jonathan Lomas and Graeme McDowell tied for fourth place, with Woosnam, despite the help of a trusty one iron that he reckoned he had used for 21 years, tied for sixth.

"I started really badly and perhaps that was the best thing to happen," Remesy said. "I was a little bit cramped and the double bogey just released me. After that I just played my game and it was really, really good. The reaction from the crowd was just unbelievable. It's what I've worked for and it's a great moment.

"If I look back a few years, I could not imagine that I win this tournament. After a major championship, I cannot win bigger. The pressure was unbelievable and it's fantastic for me and for the people who support me."

Smurfit European Open—€3,334,680
Winner: Retief Goosen

It was perfectly understandable for Retief Goosen to arrive in Ireland suffering from exhaustion. If the mental strain of winning the U.S. Open Championship at Shinnecock Hills was not enough, there followed the usual post-major maelstrom of interviews and appearances. There were also some more enjoyable moments for the quiet-spoken South African. There was a day at Wimbledon watching tennis and a barbeque at Ernie's Els' house at Wentworth.

All of which did not leave a lot of time for golf. "The first time I unpacked my clubs was when I arrived here," Goosen said on the eve of the tournament. "I should have taken another week off." His 155 opponents in the Smurfit European Open all wish that he had done exactly that.

Apparently showing few ill-effects on the golf course, Goosen cruised to a second victory in successive tournaments with a mighty transatlantic double. He eased away to a five-stroke victory on a course he, and everyone else, were seeing for the first time.

While the Ryder Cup in 2006 will be played on the Arnold Palmer-designed course that has hosted all the previous European Opens staged at the K Club — and will do so again except for when it is rested in 2006 prior to the Europe-America contest — this year's tournament was moved to the new Smurfit layout. With heavy rough and winds of up to 25 miles an hour, Nick Faldo described it as a "brutish" test.

But having been the last man standing at Shinnecock Hills, Goosen is a proven grinder in difficult conditions. His 66 in the second round took the 35-year-old to the top of the leaderboard, and even though he described his third round of 72 as "rubbish," he still led by one over Jose Manuel Lara, with Lee Westwood a further stroke back.

Goosen did not drop a shot in the final round. He pulled away with birdies at the third and fifth, added another at the 10th, and finished off a fourth at the 18th for a 68 and a 275 total, 13 under par. Westwood, with a 71, posted only his second top-10 finish of the season; but with his form the previous autumn, his second place here practically guaranteed his Ryder Cup position.

Westwood shared second place at eight under with Richard Green and Peter O'Malley, who earned a spot in the Open Championship by being the highest finisher not otherwise exempt. The event also saw the end of the mini-order of merit qualifying table for the Open which saw Green and Jean-Francois Remesy earn places at Royal Troon. Justin Rose, who failed to qualify at the new International Qualifier at Sunningdale earlier in the week, was still left looking for a place in the Open despite a last round of 65, the lowest of the week and, as such, the new course record.

Rose had one last chance in the Barclays Scottish Open, an event that Goosen withdrew from immediately after winning at the K Club. "I was tired at the beginning of the week and now I'm really tired," he said. "You are always under pressure. It's part of the game. I am just learning to trust my abilities under pressure and that's what it is all about. We all hit the ball well, but it's the guys who putt well and hit the right shots under pressure that come out winning." It was Goosen's 20th career victory.

Barclays Scottish Open—€3,305,600
Winner: Thomas Levet

It can take some ingenuity on occasions, but the Scots will stop at nothing to find a home link with the winners of their tournaments. There was not a local in sight when the Barclays Scottish Open reached its conclusion, but in order to put the bonnie into the Bonnie, Bonnie Banks, Edinburgh's Sir Logan Campbell, the great-great-great-grandfather of Michael Campbell, was resurrected, and when that did not look like doing the trick, the old alliance, Mary, Queen of Scots, and all that, was invoked on behalf of France's Thomas Levet.

With a brilliant stretch of golf on the back nine which would have taken even Sir Logan's breath away, Levet came home in 29 strokes to claim the title. He became the third French winner in the last month, after Philippe Lima and Jean-Francois Remesy, an unprecedented achievement for Gallic golf.

What could be better than joining a roll of honor at Loch Lomond that included Ernie Els, Tom Lehman, Colin Montgomerie and Lee Westwood and collecting €545,200? A place in the Open Championship at Royal Troon the following week was a mighty bonus for Levet, who took the one spot available for the player finishing highest who was not exempt.

"This is probably the best thing," Levet said. "A win is a win, but playing in the Open is something else." The runner-up in a playoff to Els at Muirfield in 2002 left it late, but the 35-year-old Parisian, who now lives in Berkshire in England, rallied from seven behind the overnight leaders. Marcus Fraser and Gregory Havret were also both chasing the last spot in the Open, but neither was able to break par in the final round.

"Life is strange, but golf is worse," Levet said. "I was playing so awful before this week I had spiders and ghosts in my mind. It's unbelievable." Levet withdrew from the Open qualifier at Sunningdale after one round because he was shaking with fatigue after a hectic schedule that had included the U.S. and French Opens. The win caused a few more headaches, but ones he was happy to have. "I have to go home," he said. "This is my last shirt. We were going to go on holiday. I need to find a hotel for Troon. I don't know what I am doing."

It was the run of three birdies and an eagle from the 11th which put Levet right in contention. At the par-five 13th he hit a three wood to 10 feet and at the next he played a superb chip. He would single-putt the last eight greens as he saved par on each of the 15th, 16th and 17th holes. Though playing ahead of the other contenders, Levet knew exactly what he needed to do at the last. "I was not afraid to go for broke," he said. "I knew I didn't need a par, I didn't need a bogey, I needed a birdie or nothing."

Hitting a driver off the tee instead of the safe play with a three wood, he had 151 yards left for his second shot and hit an eight iron to two and a half feet. "The drive was my best of the week, and on the second shot I said to myself to go straight for it, forget everything, wind, distance, doesn't matter, just hit the shot."

Levet holed the putt, despite backing off it due to the reversing alarm of a cart, for a closing birdie and a round of 63. Now 15 under par, 269, was the target, but Els, the defending champion, could get no closer than 13 under, where he tied with England's David Howell for third place.

Campbell birdied the 12th and the par-five 13th to go in front briefly, but then bogeyed the next two. A three at the 16th got the Kiwi to within one of the Frenchman, and Campbell gave himself a 15-footer to tie at the 18th but missed it on the left. Fraser could have tied by holing his second at the 18th, but finished with a bogey.

The Open Championship—€6,001,690
Winner: Todd Hamilton

See Chapter 4.

Nissan Irish Open—€1,900,000
Winner: Brett Rumford

It took Brett Rumford 57 holes to get into the lead in the Nissan Irish Open, but once the Australian was there he never lost his dominant position. So two days before his 27th birthday, Rumford claimed a four-stroke victory at the County Louth course in Baltray.

This was a second successive week of links golf following the Open Championship, and the course, which was staging Ireland's national championship for the first time, was revealed as something of a gem. No one was ever safe, as Peter Lonard found out in the third round when he took a triple bogey at the short seventh but still managed to maintain his lead.

Rumford was one behind his fellow Australian starting out in the final round, but a hat trick of birdies from the second hole swept him into the lead. He also birdied the 10th and 12th and recovered from a bogey at the 13th by chipping in for a birdie at the 15th. He could afford a bogey at the 18th and still finished with a 67 for a 274 total, 14 under par, with a handsome winning margin.

Rumford was a star amateur in his homeland, but lost his European Tour card after the 2002 season. He was playing on the Challenge Tour when he won the Aa St. Omer Open, a "double-badge" tournament, which earned him an exemption back on the main circuit. At Baltray he proved he could triumph against a full field of European Tour regulars.

Lonard dropped to fourth place, with Padraig Harrington and Raphael Jacquelin sharing the runner-up honors at 10 under par. Harrington had been 11 strokes behind with 27 holes to play, but in the final round, six groups ahead of the final pairing, the Irishman birdied the first three holes, then the sixth, 12th and 14th before his challenge stalled with a bogey at the 16th.

It was Harrington's 24th career second place and his fourth of the season, but then, as he says, often it is achieved by a good finish when too far back to contend. "I should have a post to notch up all these seconds," he joked.

Scandinavian Masters—€1,600,000
Winner: Luke Donald

After being at Northwestern University in Chicago for three years, it seemed the natural thing for Luke Donald to attend the U.S. qualifying tournament when he turned professional. His experience on the college circuit helped him secure a card on the U.S. PGA Tour and at the end of the 2002 season he won the Southern Farm Bureau Classic. The following season was not quite as successful as he slipped to 89th on the money list, and his priority in 2004 was to secure his status in the United States and work his way up the World Ranking.

All of which explains why the 26-year-old from High Wycombe was playing only his ninth event as a professional on the European Tour at the Scandinavian Masters. It was also why his parents, Colin and Ann, were present at Barseback, which was just as well because Donald won by five strokes.

It was a command performance by the former Walker Cup star for Great Britain and Ireland. He took the lead at the halfway stage and stamped his authority on the event by holing his second shot from 198 yards with a six iron for an eagle. His iron play is rated up there with the very best in the game and he is rarely less than pin-point accurate.

He led by three strokes over Peter Hanson after 54 holes and was never less than two ahead in the final round. He lost his earlier course record of 65 from the second day to Peter Lawrie's 64, but holed a putt from 50 feet at the sixth and saved par at the 11th before birdieing the next two holes. He ended up with a 69 and a total of 272, 16 under par. Henrik Stenson tied for second with Hanson, while Ian Poulter and Colin Montgomerie, both contenders for Ryder Cup places, Poulter from the qualifying list, Monty as a potential wild card, tied for fourth.

The victory also lifted Donald into contention for a Ryder Cup spot, even though a few weeks previously he had not been a member of the European Tour. Membership is a prerequisite to be eligible for the European team, but it necessitates playing 11 times on the European Tour. As he started the year not exempt for the majors and the World Championship events, which count on both the U.S. and European tours, Donald did not think he would complete his 11 in Europe.

At the end of May he withdrew from membership on the European Tour, meaning that he was no longer eligible to collect Ryder Cup qualifying points. But after discussions with both Bernhard Langer, the European captain, and Ken Schofield, the executive director of the European Tour, Donald agreed to rejoin in June.

Suddenly, the possibility of playing at Oakland Hills in September had increased. "This opens up a lot for me," Donald said. "It gives my chances of making the Ryder Cup team a great boost. In an ideal world I'd like to play myself onto the team, but I was hoping I was in Bernhard Langer's mind as a wild card even before this week. This is a special win and very important for my career."

KLM Open—€1,200,000
Winner: David Lynn

David Lynn opened the KLM Open with a seven-under-par 63, but if he was hoping to sweep majestically on to victory from there, then it did not quite work out like that. It rarely does in golf. But the important thing was Lynn's closing round of 66 which gave him a 264 total and a three-stroke victory and his first title on the European Tour at his 168th attempt.

"It means a lot, as it does for everyone who wins for the first time," said the 30-year-old Lynn. "It probably is more so for me. I feel absolutely awesome. I was getting a bit carried away going down the 17th and there was a tear in my eye. I had to pull myself together."

Lynn had turned to a sports psychologist, John Allsop, to help him find the missing key. "There are key moments where you have to start talking to yourself and make sure you put the foot down. This is something I have always thought I was capable of doing. Hopefully, having got the first win out of the way, this can be a stepping stone for me."

What happened in the middle rounds was that Richard Green scored 63 and 67 on Friday and Saturday to move three strokes ahead of Lynn. Green's advantage increased to four early in the final round, but by the turn they were even, Lynn's contribution being birdies at the second, seventh and ninth holes.

Lynn dropped his only shot at the 11th, but a birdie at the 14th, where Green could only make a par five, put the Englishman into the lead. Green bogeyed the 16th, while Lynn escaped from the trees for a par, and that was the tournament settled. While Lynn finished at 16 under par, Green shared second place with Paul McGinley, whose final round of 65 was a strong finish by an Irishman determined to retain his Ryder Cup place.

BMW Russian Open—€407,433
Winner: Gary Emerson

Yet another Englishman claimed his first European Tour victory with Gary Emerson winning the BMW Russian Open in Moscow. It took Emerson 10 years to achieve the feat, but came after losing his European Tour card the previous year. The 40-year-old from Wiltshire regained his status by winning an event that was co-sanctioned by both the Challenge Tour, where he played most of the season, and the main circuit.

He had to do it the hard way with most of Saturday's play having been lost to a rainstorm that saturated the fairways. Emerson had played only one hole of his third round and so had 35 left on the final day. But a pair of 68s, the first giving him a share of the lead alongside Kariem Baraka, and the second a two-stroke victory over Austria's Markus Brier with a 272 total.

"I feel as though I've got my job back," said Emerson. "I've been playing on tour for 10 years and I always thought I had underachieved. This is massive for me. Hopefully, I can go on from here."

Baraka, the nephew of Bernhard Langer, had led since a first-day 63, but collapsed to a 76 in the last round. Emerson birdied the first two holes, and despite a bogey at the 11th, he picked up another three shots in four holes from the 14th to finish at 16 under par. Brier closed with a 69 for second place, while Kyron Sullivan celebrated his best-ever finish in third place.

BMW International Open—€1,800,000
Winner: Miguel Angel Jimenez

Bernhard Langer, the European Ryder Cup captain, could not have been happier that Miguel Angel Jimenez won the BMW International over Thomas

Levet, proving two members of his team were in fine form. But Langer had far more on his mind as the last qualifying places were decided and the German selected his two wild cards.

It turned into a frantic afternoon at Eichenreid. Six players already knew they had qualified to play the Americans at Oakland Hills: Padraig Harrington, Sergio Garcia, Darren Clarke, Jimenez and Lee Westwood were the five players to come off the table based on World Ranking points after the NEC World Invitational. Levet was already assured of making it from the table based on money from the European Tour, while Paul Casey was almost safe and so it proved.

But David Howell, Ian Poulter and Paul McGinley had to defend their positions, although their task was made easier by Brian Davis and Jean-Francois Remesy missing the cut. Fredrik Jacobson was trying to play his way onto the team and opened up with birdies at four of the first seven holes.

Poulter, however, was going in the opposite direction. The 28-year-old from Milton Keynes went out of bounds for a double-bogey seven at the sixth hole and then was in the water and a ditch, taking two penalty shots, for a quadruple-bogey eight at the 10th. From there, Poulter responded magnificently by playing the last eight holes in six under. "I hadn't felt under pressure all week until then. I was up, well, you know, without a paddle," he said. "Darren Clarke and his caddie, Billy Foster, told me to try and make as many birdies as I could and to get myself back on the team."

He eagled the next, the 11th, then birdied the 15th and 16th holes, before adding another eagle at the 18th. "The only time I felt nervous was on the second shot at the last," he said. "I wanted to make a three so badly." A three wood from 277 yards finished 10 feet away and he holed the putt for a brilliant finale. "That's the biggest three of my life," he said of the second eagle.

Poulter was utterly stunned when he finished, but had risen from 56th place after 10 holes — and possibly out of the team with Jacobson contending for the title — to finish at 10 under par in 25th place. "What a day. I'm going home to be with my little boy and my little girl, and whatever happens, I'll have a glass of champagne. I could have let the wheels fall off and finished 70th, but that's not me and that's why I want to be part of the Ryder Cup side."

Howell played 15 strong holes before a blip with a double at the 16th and a bogey at the 17th, but birdied the last to finish at 11 under. "It was stressful, but I wasn't shaking over any shot as I have sometimes in the past," said the Swindon man. "I was a lot calmer than I thought I would be. I played my heart out. This is the biggest thing I've achieved."

McGinley was playing alongside Jacobson, but a 68 was good enough to finish tied with the Swede at 15 under in sixth place. McGinley kept the drama going by hitting his second shot at the 18th into a ditch. "It was a Van de Velde thing," he said. "If it hadn't hit the stand it would have been a simple chip." He took a penalty drop, but got up and down for a par. Even if he had taken a six and Jacobson had made his 14-foot birdie putt to finish tied for third, it would not have been enough for the Swede to dislodge any of those ahead of him.

McGinley, the hero of the Belfry two years previously, was looking for a week off after playing 10 tournaments in a row. "My whole life has been on hold for 10 weeks," the Irishman said. "It was a rollercoaster, but I didn't want to let it go. It was so important to finish in the top 10 because there were so many people deserving to be picked that I didn't want to add to Bernhard's problems."

While previous European Ryder Cup captains might have had to select an obvious player, such as a major winner, Langer now had a difficult choice between Jacobson, who missed out by one place on both the qualifying lists, more newcomers in Alex Cejka, who closed with a 65 to be tied for third, and Luke Donald, and the experience of Colin Montgomerie.

In the end Montgomerie, for all his personal trauma earlier in the year, was a clear-cut choice, and Langer also went with Donald, a former Walker Cup star. Montgomerie finished tied for third, his best result since the break-up of his marriage, but it was not until after the round he was told by Langer he would be making his seventh appearance in the match. "He knew he still needed to impress me here," Langer said. "But I know he will rise to the occasion."

"Bernhard knows what I can do and he felt I could help," Monty said. "It's been a tough year for me, but this is great news." Jimenez won for the fourth time in the season after a 66 which contained nine birdies and left the 40-year-old Spaniard at 267, 21 under par and two strokes ahead of Levet.

Omega European Masters—€1,600,000
Winner: Luke Donald

Luke Donald immediately repaid the faith of Bernhard Langer by matching Stewart Cink in winning a tournament the week after being selected as a wild card for the Ryder Cup. Donald's victory at the Omega European Masters was his second in little more than a month after deciding to play some tournaments in Europe rather than concentrate solely on the PGA Tour in the United States.

What was clear was the way members of Langer's team were playing. There were only three present at Crans-sur-Sierre, but they all teed off in the final group on Sunday. The indefatigable Miguel Angel Jimenez was leading by one stroke over Donald and Sergio Garcia, but it was the 26-year-old Englishman who took the best start by eagling the first hole to jump into the lead.

Donald never lost the lead again, even though he bogeyed the 11th and 13th, but there were plenty of birdies to counter those mistakes and a closing 66 put him at 265, 19 under par. He stretched his advantage to five strokes over Jimenez, who closed with a 72, as did Garcia to tie for third place with Eduardo Romero. Garcia went out of bounds for a double bogey on the 14th to end his challenge. The defending champion, Ernie Els, finished back in seventh place.

"I am over the moon right now," said Donald. "This win means even more than Sweden. That win got me into the Ryder Cup, but personally this means a lot going up against a stronger field. I was up against Sergio and Miguel and Ernie was just behind. To play well and beat these guys means a lot."

Donald also thanked Langer for his wild card selection. Donald had found out the news in a text message as he flew from Munich to Crans in a private plane with Garcia the previous Sunday evening. "Thanks to Bernhard for choosing me and I hope this week validates that selection. I just hope I can take this form to Detroit, but there are a lot of Ryder Cup players playing well right now."

Linde German Masters—€3,000,000
Winner: Padraig Harrington

Bernhard Langer led a contented team of players on the airplane to Detroit with yet another member of the European Ryder Cup side celebrating a victory on the eve of the match against the Americans. Following Miguel Angel Jimenez and Luke Donald in the previous two weeks, Padraig Harrington completed the hat trick by winning the Linde German Masters by three shots over Australian Nick O'Hern.

Harrington, the only player in the team in the top 10 of the World Ranking, had not won so far in the year despite finishing second another four times. More than that, the Dubliner had come to Gut Larchenhof looking to rekindle his form. Frustrated by not playing as well on the course as he thought he was on the range, Harrington had missed the cut in Munich a fortnight earlier.

Having consulted his coach, Bob Torrance, and his sports psychologist, Bob Rotella, Harrington arrived with a new attitude and he hauled in Northern Ireland's Graeme McDowell despite slipping six strokes behind after only two holes. Harrington opened with a couple of bogeys in the windy conditions while McDowell birdied the first. But the 25-year-old former American college player, so composed in maintaining his lead on Saturday, could not repeat the previous day's form.

Still three ahead at the ninth, McDowell found an awkward lie in a greenside bunker. Water awaited on the other side of the green and every golfer's worst nightmare in that situation visited McDowell. He thinned his recovery over the green and had to take a penalty drop before getting up and down for a double bogey.

Harrington, meanwhile, had driven into the rough on the right but played his approach to 15 feet and holed for a birdie to draw even. McDowell also found a bunker at the short 11th and could not get up and down before taking three from the edge of the 14th green to fall two behind.

Harrington all but sealed his ninth European Tour title by holing from nine feet for a birdie at the 15th, while McDowell's challenge sunk further when he found the water at the par-three 16th. Harrington's 70 gave him a total of 275, 13 under par, three ahead of O'Hern, with McDowell, after a 77, tying for third place with Raphael Jacquelin.

"There have been a few inquests and a lot of gnashing of teeth at home, but in the end I realized I shouldn't be so hard on myself," said Harrington, who five days before the event had undergone laser surgery on his dominant left eye. Langer had mentioned to one of his assistants, Thomas Bjorn, on the eve of the tournament that Harrington was his only concern, but the Dane had replied, "Don't worry, he'll be fine. The only thing you have to worry about is beating him this week." No one did.

Ryder Cup
Winner: Europe

See Chapter 7.

The Heritage—€2,000,000
Winner: Henrik Stenson

The Ryder Cup put in an appearance at Woburn Abbey on Wednesday evening prior to The Heritage tournament for Ken Schofield's retirement party. Schofield was stepping down as executive director of the European Tour after 30 years, during which time Europe had beaten the Americans six times and tied once.

The evening was the players' chance to say farewell to Schofield, whose first office was at the Oval cricket ground in London. Their gift was a painting of the ground by Jack Russell, the former England cricketer, and it was presented to Schofield by two other famous cricketers of an earlier era, twins Sir Alec and Eric Bedser, on behalf of the players.

There were more members of the victorious European team from Oakland Hills at the Abbey than remained at The Heritage into the weekend. Five did not enter, three withdrew with exhaustion, two missed the cut — the heroic Colin Montgomerie and Ian Poulter, none too pleased since he is the Woburn touring professional — leaving only Padraig Harrington and David Howell.

Neither had quite the reserves of energy to contend for the title, but there was plenty of evidence on the Duke's course at Woburn that Europe is overflowing with promising players. Former Walker Cup players Graeme McDowell, determined to play in the Ryder Cup in Ireland in 2006, and Nick Dougherty were on the leaderboard, but the Walker Cup is restricted only to players from Great Britain and Ireland.

When Continental Europe is added on, the picture only gets rosier. Having won the Benson and Hedges International at the Belfry in his rookie season three years ago, Henrik Stenson then lost his game and confidence. But he claimed The Heritage title in handsome fashion by birdieing four of the last five holes.

The 28-year-old Malmo resident won by four strokes over Carlos Rodiles, who was also runner-up at the Volvo Masters last year, a performance that put the young Spaniard in the running for a Ryder Cup place until a rib injury earlier in the season.

In each of his three victories on the Challenge Tour and now two on the main circuit, Stenson has led from the front, and he was never caught here as he closed with a 66 to finish at 269, 19 under par. "There was a time when I totally lost confidence and you wonder what you are doing, but I've fought my way back," he said.

"Some stay and fight the battle and others give up. I fought the battle. After a while you are scared of hitting a wild shot and it gets to you mentally. I lost it so bad that I had to start all over again. But I don't regret it. I've done a lot of hard work and my swing is better than when I won at the Belfry.

"Obviously, I watched the Ryder Cup and there was a function on Wednesday night where they showed some clips and interviewed some of the players, and that was inspiring going into a tournament," he added. "I will be trying my best to be on the next team."

WGC - American Express Championship—€5,639,287
Winner: Ernie Els

Having missed out at all four of the majors during the season, Ernie Els rewarded himself with the next best thing by winning the WGC - American Express Championship. A man known for his celebrations, this was the first time Els had enjoyed one in Ireland, a country where he certainly appreciates the local brews.

It was also Els' first World Golf Championship title as an individual and in the process he relegated Tiger Woods to third place in the World Ranking. "It's nice, but I'm still number two," Els joked. "I've been chasing Tiger for five years and now I'm chasing Vijay (Singh). The game is on well and truly."

In horrid weather, wet and windy but not quite the tournament-delaying storm that had been predicted, Els beat Thomas Bjorn by a stroke. Avoiding mistakes appeared impossible in the conditions, but had the South African holed his par putt at the 18th he would have been the only player not to have dropped a shot.

"I think I showed that I didn't want to lose today," Els said. "It was a tough day with the weather and Thomas keeping me on my toes all the way to the end. There was a lot of pressure, but I wanted to draw a line under the disappointments of the summer."

Els arrived at Mount Juliet after two weeks off in which he decided to put behind him the near-misses in the majors. "I needed to get that out of my system and start going forward again in my career. You can't keep looking back. I was despondent for a while and there was a negative spin on the whole thing, but from a positive point of view I came close to winning all four majors. In three of them I was right in there at the death and I've got to feel encouraged by that. Obviously, as an athlete and a competitor you play to win, but now I can move on."

By comparison Bjorn had an even tougher summer, walking off the course "fighting demons" on his last visit to Ireland in July at the European Open and then taking a five-week break after the Open. Being part of the back room at the Ryder Cup gave the Dane his first positive memories on a golf course for months, but the turnaround in his game was still astonishing.

"This is a massive improvement," said Bjorn, who recorded his best result since January. "It's been a long trip, but this is a sign that I can play with the big boys again and that's where I want to be." There had been hard work with his coach, Pete Cowen, and he was back with his old caddie,

Ken Comboy. He almost holed his approach at the first for an eagle, but Els also birdied and the pair matched each other again with twos at the third.

Bjorn added another birdie at the fifth but never drew even, with Els' birdies at the 10th and 17th keeping him in front. A closing 69 left Els at 270, 18 under par. It was another fine week for European players with David Howell four behind Bjorn, Sergio Garcia and two locals, Padraig Harrington and Darren Clarke, all on the leaderboard.

Woods, who started the week with his back in spasm but remarkably managed a 68 on the first day, finished in ninth place, but no longer held a stroke play title for the first time since his first professional win. He left for a week in Barbados where he would wed his fiancée, Elin Nordegren. "I'm ready to go diving. I'm ready to hop in that water and shoot some fish," he said, refusing to confirm his wedding plans to the press.

Dunhill Links Championship—€3,888,387
Winner: Stephen Gallacher

Before this Sunday evening at the home of golf, Stephen Gallacher's best moment in golf came when he was part of the winning Great Britain and Ireland Walker Cup team at Royal Porthcawl in 1995. That September was a good month for the Gallacher family as uncle Bernard captained Europe to victory in the Ryder Cup at Oak Hill.

As well as being winner early and often in his professional career, Bernard Gallacher made a lasting contribution to the game as a three-time captain and the longtime professional at Wentworth. His nephew enjoyed a fine amateur career, but had to wait nine years for his first professional victory.

But beating Graeme McDowell at the first extra hole at the Old Course brought a check for €645,162 and the Dunhill Links title. "It's definitely one of the titles you want to win on the European Tour," Gallacher said. "It's been frustrating, but a lot of guys have to wait until their late 30s or 40s for a win. You can't let it get to you."

This victory was hard-earned all right. A 67 in the final round had put Gallacher at 269, 19 under par, a score McDowell tied with a closing 68. Luke Donald, who was poised to win for a third time in seven events, had to settle for third place alongside Ian Poulter. Lee Westwood and David Howell tied for fifth, and Ernie Els and Fred Couples for seventh. Vijay Singh was also in the strong field.

Gallacher put McDowell under pressure in the playoff by hitting a wedge to a couple of feet. "It was the best shot I hit all week," he said. McDowell then put his approach into the Swilken Burn. "This really is like a dream come true," Gallacher said. "I've worked hard to get here and it was tough out there today with the standard of players so good, but it gives me great pleasure to win."

Gallacher made a brilliant assault on the final round with birdies at the fourth, fifth and seventh on the way out, and then at the 10th, 12th and 13th as he made his way out of the loop at the far end of the course.

A long hold-up on the 17th led to all the leaders taking a bogey. Having pulled his drive left, Gallacher laid up and pitched on but could not hole from 25 feet for the par. Both McDowell and Donald three-putted from the front of the green. With Gallacher parring the last, McDowell saw his approach spin back off the green. But after leaving his chip 10 feet short, he holed to make the playoff. Donald then had an 18-footer for a birdie and a place in the playoff, but it came up 18 inches short.

Earlier in the week McDowell enjoyed a piece of history when he played the Old Course in 62 strokes, only the fourth time the score has been made at the home of golf. He had a 15-footer at the 18th to break the record, but it just lipped by. "I knew exactly where it was going from having seen that putt millions of times of television," he said. "It wasn't the greatest effort, but it's not exactly the putt you would want to leave yourself for a 61."

McDowell's 62 matched the record set by Curtis Strange in 1987 at the Dunhill Cup, and matched by Brian Davis in the 2003 Dunhill Links Championship and Kevin McAlpine, a 20-year-old in a qualifying round for the 2004 Amateur Championship.

HSBC World Match Play—£2,440,000
Winner: Ernie Els

See Chapter 8.

Mallorca Classic—€1,000,000
Winner: Sergio Garcia

Sergio Garcia passed up the chance to win £1 million at the HSBC World Match Play to play for his sponsors and supporters in Spain, and a second title on home soil duly followed for the 24-year-old at the Mallorca Classic at Pula. The world No. 11 was ranked 57 places above anyone else in the field and he collected a modest €166,660 compared to the riches on offer at Wentworth, but Garcia could not have been happier.

A four-stroke victory over Simon Khan, winner of the Wales Open, may have looked comfortable, but he was three behind after bogeying the first two holes. But with Khan also making the odd error, a birdie at the sixth brought Garcia back even and another at the ninth put him ahead for the first time.

There was a two-stroke swing at the 11th when Khan went over the green and Garcia holed from four feet for a birdie. He finished at 268, 12 under par, after a 67, following rounds of 66, 67 and 68. Another Spaniard, Carlos Rodiles, finished in third place, with Markus Brier, Francois Delamontagne and Santiago Luna sharing fourth place.

"I said from the beginning of the week this was a great decision to come here," Garcia said after adding to his two victories in the United States earlier in the season. "I feel the Spanish people deserve to see me play and, unfortunately, I haven't been able to play here until this late in the season.

"I was really committed to coming here and trying to win. I only have a few chances to win in Europe, so to be able to win it in Spain makes it even sweeter. The way I was playing maybe I would have had a chance at Wentworth, but I don't care. I'm happy here with my people, and it's a wonderful feeling to come through like I did and play the last 13 holes in five under par."

Open de Madrid—€1,000,000
Winner: Richard Sterne

The last full-field event of the season always produces plenty of drama as the Order of Merit is finalized. Not at the top of it — Ernie Els had already wrapped that up — but down where players are trying to keep their cards for the following season. Richard Sterne, a 23-year-old South African, booked two more years on the European Tour by winning the Open de Madrid by two strokes over Anders Hansen.

Sterne's previous best result had been a tie for 16th the previous week in Mallorca. But he came through on the final day with a brilliant 65 — tournament host Seve Ballesteros said as much — to finish at 266, 18 under par. He had started the week in 122nd place on the Order of Merit, with only the top 116 retaining their playing privileges.

Sterne was able to unbook his flights to the qualifying tournament in November. "A bad round today and I would have been back," he said. "I can't believe I am standing here with the trophy. I knew a top 12 or top 15 could be good enough, but I didn't look at a leaderboard until the ninth and then not again until the 16th."

An eagle at the fourth had set him on the way to an outward 31, and his birdie at the 14th followed by four pars as the wind picked up was more than good enough. Hansen just pipped Terry Price for second place, with Raphael Jacquelin and Paul Broadhurst sharing fourth place.

Australian Wade Ormsby was another player celebrating not having to go to the qualifying tournament when he came back from being four over after 12 holes of the first round to finish with a birdie at the 72nd hole for 13 under and a tie for sixth place. But there was misery for plenty of others, including another Australian, Jarrod Moseley, who missed the cut and wound up just €13.57 behind Sweden's Robert Karlsson, who sneaked into last place on the Order of Merit.

Another bad luck story befell Johan Edfors, the Swede who led the Challenge Tour in 2003. He needed to win or finish second and was leading with a hole to play in the third round. But his drive hooked into the trees and it could not be found. It was suspected that a spectator had picked it up, but an appeal in Spanish and English brought no information so the referee ruled that Edfors had to go back to the tee. He took a double bogey, but then a woman spectator informed him that she had seen his original ball being picked up. Edfors worked his way back to second place during the final round, but then fell away to ninth.

Volvo Masters Andalucia—€3,750,000
Winner: Ian Poulter

Two days after Ian Poulter rated his season as "one out of 10 — and the one was the Ryder Cup victory," he was able to update that assessment by winning the season-ending Volvo Masters Andalucia after a playoff with his Oakland Hills teammate, Sergio Garcia. At the last gasp Poulter continued his run of winning every season on the European Tour since 2000. "Let's make it a five, possibly a six, but no higher than a seven," said Poulter, who has never been afraid to be hard on himself.

The 28-year-old from Milton Keynes, known for his flamboyant attire and fancy hairstyles, and the local hero, Garcia, tied at 277, seven under par, after both posted final rounds of 70. Garcia was attempting to win for the second tournament running in Spain, but missed his chance on the 18th in regulation by missing from four feet. In the playoff he was struggling from the moment he pushed his drive. Blocked out by the cork trees, his second shot went left and his third came up short.

A bogey five was the best he could do, but Poulter, who went left off the tee and just made the fringe with his second, chipped to two feet and holed for the victory. "I refused to lose," Poulter said. "I feel I have to win every year. It's a nice way to end what was a disappointing season, the Ryder Cup apart, but which turned out to be a great one. This is a great tournament to win. By winning every year, you keep moving up the World Ranking, and this really helps.

"I am very hard on myself. I'm a bad loser and I'm not ashamed to admit it. I don't like finishing second, third or fourth. I feel I'm capable of winning two, three, four or fives times a season. I've had a few chances this year, but not been able to finish it off until now. The Ryder Cup definitely helped. If you play well under that pressure, it helps to keep you cool. It was a massive boost, great to play in, great to win and great to get a point in the singles."

Poulter, with the biggest title of his career to date, earned €625,000 to finish ninth on the Order of Merit and moved up into the top 50 on the World Ranking. Alastair Forsyth led by three strokes entering the final round, but bogeyed the first two holes. The Scot remained in contention until his drive at the 16th finished in the right-hand trees and he took three shots to find the green, holing from five feet for a bogey.

Otherwise, Forsyth compiled 15 pars and so his 74 left him at six under and one outside the playoff. Poulter took the lead with three birdies in a row from the eighth as he holed from eight, 18 and then 30 feet. But by failing to get up and down at the 13th, he fell back into a three-way tie. Garcia's final nine was blemish free, but after the birdies at the 11th and 12th, he was unable to find the extra one he needed.

WGC - World Cup—US$4,000,000
Winners: Luke Donald/Paul Casey

After a week he might want to forget, it was appropriate that Paul Casey should hole the clinching putt as England won the WGC - World Cup for only the second time. Controversy raged around Casey ever since an interview appeared with the 27-year-old Englishman saying he had "hated" the Americans at the Ryder Cup. He later admitted it was the wrong word to use, but the damage was done when another newspaper took the remarks out of context and came up with the exaggerated headline: "Americans are stupid. I hate them."

These were the words subsequently reported around the globe and Casey received much negative reaction. "People are very angry and I fully understand that," Casey said. "I don't hate Americans. I have an American girlfriend, an American coach and I have a home there."

A second team victory went some way to compensating for failing to win individually during the season. Casey had finished fifth, third and second in the last three World Cups, but with a new partner in Luke Donald the progression reached a happy conclusion. England beat host Spain, in the form of Sergio Garcia and Miguel Angel Jimenez, by one stroke after a thrilling final round at Real Sevilla.

Only the pairing of Nick Faldo and David Carter in 1998 had previously claimed the World Cup for England since it began in 1953. To win, Casey and Donald had to produce the lowest final-round score since the event came into its present format in 2000.

A poor day on Saturday had allowed the Spaniards to take over at the top of the leaderboard when Garcia had contributed five birdies and two eagles to a better-ball of 61. But the format switched back to foursomes in the final round and, as on the Friday, the Englishmen produced a 64. Remarkably, in their total of 257, 31 under par, they were 16 under at foursomes and only 15 under at fourballs.

It is not as if they have similar styles, Donald being surgically precise, Casey inspired but occasionally erratic, but there is no bar to well-attuned opposites succeeding at this ticklish format. "I can't explain it," said Casey. "We just seem to click. We know each other's games and how we think and we never apologize. We trust each other. But I still can't believe we scored lower in foursomes than fourballs."

Donald said, "This course allowed us to play to our strengths, with my iron play and Paul's putting. It was a different pressure to the Ryder Cup, but our experience there helped us handle this."

Donald holed at the first to bring them even with the hosts, who dropped a shot at the short third to fall behind despite the encouragement of a large gallery of Sevillians. Due to the sequence of par-threes, fours and fives on this course, it falls to one player to face most of the birdie putts. Casey had holed all nine on Friday and seven of their nine on Sunday.

He rolled in putt after putt, including a 50-footer at the 10th hole, as England birded seven holes between the fourth and 12th to go four ahead. Ireland's Padraig Harrington and Paul McGinley eagled the 13th and birdied the 14th to draw within two, but finished third after a 65. Spain also eagled the 13th, after a wonderful long approach from Jimenez, and birdied the 15th to draw within one.

But at the par-five 16th, Garcia went for an aggressive shot from a poor lie and finished in the water. Jimenez's fourth shot gave them a chance of a par, but Garcia missed from eight feet as England's ninth birdie put them three ahead.

That was the margin teeing off at the 18th, but Casey drove into the rough on the bank of a bunker and Donald had to lay up. Casey's pitch came up on the lower tier and then Donald's long putt ran three feet past. Garcia had hit a brilliant second shot and Jimenez holed the four-footer for the birdie to put the pressure on Casey's bogey putt.

"At least we made them win it," Garcia said. "It was gutsy for Paul to hole that putt. You have to give them all the credit. They were unbelievable. I thought our 66 was a flipping good score, but it was not enough. It's disappointing, but you feel worse for the people. They were amazing, there was so much energy. It was a great atmosphere."

Looking back on an emotional week, Casey said, "I am proud of the way I handled myself this week. I was upset with what happened earlier in the week and it has been a distraction, but I put all my focus into the golf. I'll be more thick-skinned from now on. I'm going to worry about working on my golf game, but if I can repair any of the damage, I will."

Volvo China Open—US$1,000,000
Winner: Stephen Dodd

See Asia/Japan Tours chapter.

Omega Hong Kong Open—US$800,000
Winner: Miguel Angel Jimenez

See Asia/Japan Tours chapter.

Dunhill Championship—£500,000
Winner: Charl Schwartzel

See African Tours chapter.

Challenge Tour

A career put on halt by the debilitating effects of glandular fever appeared to be back on track stronger than ever as Lee Slattery won the 2004 Challenge Tour after topping the money list with €95,979. Two years earlier, Slattery, a 26-year-old Englishman, was working in a clothes shop, having given up his interest in golf and attempting to make it at the top level.

After six months of folding clothes, stacking shelves and smiling at customers, Slattery's appetite for the game returned and he began rebuilding his career. First he went to play in South Africa at the end of 2003. In 2004 he played on both the Europro Tour and the Challenge Tour, and on the latter he put together a mighty impressive run of form.

He finished second three times and third twice, but after the third of those runners-up finishes, Slattery made the breakthrough to win the Telia Grand Prix in Sweden in September. A fifth place in the Bouygues Telecom Grand Final in France was enough then to clinch the No. 1 spot on the money list over Italy's Alessandro Tadini, who had been high up the list ever since winning the Costa Rica Open in February.

"My goal for next year is to get into the top 50 on the Order of Merit on the European Tour," said Slattery, who is from the prime golfing terrain of Southport in Lancashire. "At the moment I know that my game is strong enough to take it up to the European Tour. I'm sure that I can go out there and get results. Once you realize how good your game has to be, you know whether or not you can get there, and I proved to myself this year that I have the game to do it."

Graeme Storm and Matthew King both won twice on the Challenge Tour as they also secured their cards for the European Tour in 2005. Scotland's David Drysdale left it late to get into the top 15 on the money list when he won the last tournament, the Grand Final at Medoc in Bordeaux, in a playoff over Mattias Eliasson, who had the consolation of also getting his card.

The other players to finish in the top 15 were Marc Cayeux, Johan Axgren, Leif Westerberg, Philip Archer, Henrik Nystrom, Garry Houston, Richard Bland, Fredrik Henge and Oliver Wilson.

Philippe Lima of France also won twice and did so in successive weeks. He triumphed at the Segura Viudas Challenge de Espana and then on home soil at the Aa St. Omer Open. As the latter event was also co-sanctioned by the European Tour, Lima was immediately promoted to the main circuit, as was Christopher Hanell for winning the Madeira Island Open and Gary Emerson for the BMW Russian Open.

11. Asia/Japan Tours

When Isao Aoki was inducted into the World Golf Hall of Fame in Florida in late 2004, it brought back memories of those exciting seasons in the latter 1990s when he and Masashi (Jumbo) Ozaki and Tsuneyuki (Tommy) Nakajima were jointly and at times separately dominating the Japan Tour. How times have changed. The 2004 season in Japan, in fact, was almost faceless with 23 different players winning the 29 tournaments on the schedule. Not even the singular performance of 14-year-old Ryota Ito making the cut in the Suntory Open added much to the rather drab season.

Somebody had to be the leading money winner and it happened to be Shingo Katayama, who took the No. 1 position for a second time, but in less than overly impressive fashion. The 31-year-old Katayama, the 2000 leader, took the title even though winning just two tournaments in the first half of the season — the Chunichi Crowns and the Woodone Open Hiroshima — and his official earnings total of ¥119,512,374 was the lowest to top the list since 1991.

Five other players won twice during the season, but, unusually, nobody did any better. Two of the dual titlists — Paul Sheehan (Fujisankei and Nippon Series) and Y.E. Yang (Sun Chlorella and Yomiuri Memorial) — won for the first time in Japan. They were among nine first-time winners on that tour, including Tiger Woods with his meaningful victory in the Dunlop Phoenix.

The gallery of winners had a distinctly international appearance. Fifteen of the 29 official events went to foreign players from seven countries, many of them competing on the Japan Tour on a fairly regular basis as exempt players. One of them — S.K. Ho of South Korea — seemed headed for a big season when he won the two early-season majors — the PGA and Tour Championships — but little was heard from him the rest of the year. He entered just 19 events and finished fourth on the money list (¥90,176,104) behind Toru Taniguchi, the top man in 2002, with ¥101,773,301 and Yang with ¥99,540,333. Taniguchi won the Japan and Bridgestone Opens in consecutive weeks.

History was made on the Asian Tour. The name was pretty much the same, but the Asian Tour teed off in January as the "new regional organization sanctioning professional tournament golf in Asia," said Chief Executive Louis Martin. The tour previously was operated by the Asian PGA. Now it was owned and operated by the players, Martin said.

Fittingly, the new year and the new organization debuted with Thailand's Boonchu Ruangkit hitting the first shot in the Areeya Thailand Open and going on to become — at the age of 47 years and 258 days — the tour's oldest winner. He also finished second twice and was seventh on the Asian Tour Order of Merit with a career-high $220,293.

The tour had 22 tournaments and $12.3 million in prize money, its highest ever. Thailand's Thongchai Jaidee won the Myanmar Open and the Carlsberg Malaysian Open back-to-back and had four other top-10 finishes to take the Order of Merit with a record $381,929. The Malaysian Open, co-sponsored with the European Tour, was especially pleasing to him. First, he came from behind with a back-nine 30 that included a hole-in-one, and second, as he put it, "Finally, I have won a big one — a joint-sanctioned tournament."

Spain's Miguel Angel Jimenez won three co-sponsored events, and Colin Montgomerie, the big Scot whose game was in disrepair, scored his one victory of the year in the Caltex Masters.

The season also saw the rise of new talents such as Angelo Que of the Philippines. Que had just submitted his entry for the qualifying school field, then won the Carlsberg Masters 2004 Vietnam, the first golf tournament ever held in that Communist country.

And speaking of golf in a Communist nation, China continued to be the fastest-growing golf country in the world. Four tournaments were played there, and rookie Rahil Gangjee, 25, of India, in only his fourth event, broke through with his first win.

The Asian Tour was growing in stature as more and more Asian players expanded onto the global stage. Korea's K.J. Choi, for example, who played on the U.S. PGA Tour and won twice there in 2002, tied for third in the 2004 Masters. Another Korean, Charlie Wi, won the Taiwan Open and later won his playing card for the U.S. PGA Tour. India's Arjun Atwal also won his U.S. card and earned nearly $500,000 in 2004. And Zhang Lian-wei, China's pioneering professional, became the first Chinese to be invited to the Masters. He missed the halfway cut by only one stroke.

Asian Tour

Areeya Thailand Open—US$300,000
Winner: Boonchu Ruangkit

It was like old times for Thailand's Boonchu Ruangkit. He rallied in the final round to win the Areeya Thailand Open, his second victory in this tournament, after winning it in 1992. The victory made him the oldest winner ever in the region, at 47 years and 258 days, succeeding American Mike Cunning, who won the 2003 Indian Open at 44 years and 243 days.

"This is by far the best win of my career," said Boonchu, who hit the opening drive when the Asian Tour was launched in 1995. This was the sixth win of his career, his fifth on the tour. He shot 68-66-69-67—270, 18 under par at the Royal Thai Air Force Club, and won by two over Thailand's Prayad Marksaeng and Korea's Kim Jong-duck.

Boonchu, never more than three off the lead, caught and passed third-round leader Kang Wook-soon of Korea in the fourth round. Boonchu birdied the first two holes, bogeyed No. 4, then birdied No. 5 with a tap-in and No. 7 on a 20-foot putt. "After those, I felt I had a good chance of winning," he said. His chances got even better at the closing hole. "I hit a nice approach at the 18th, and after that, I knew I would win," he said.

Prayad pulled within a stroke with a birdie at the 14th, but that was the end of his bid. Kang led on rounds of 63, 69 and 68, then came undone quickly in the final round with three bogeys and a double bogey on the first nine. He shot 77 and finished tied for eighth. "I didn't have any control with my irons today," Kang said.

Taiwan's Chen Chung-cheng couldn't upstage Boonchu, but he did grab the spotlight with two holes-in-one at the 187-yard No. 4, in the first and third rounds. Some luck. The car prize was at another hole. Cheng shrugged. "No car keys again," he said.

Johnnie Walker Classic—US$1,800,000
Winner: Miguel Angel Jimenez

The Final-Nine Devil, that fearsome monster, jumped up and grabbed Thomas Bjorn again. Last July, it cost him The Open Championship in Britain when it took him three shots to get out of a bunker just three holes from taking the old claret jug. This time, he lost the Johnnie Walker Classic in Bangkok, stumbling down the final stretch. Spain's Miguel Angel Jimenez, the pony-tailed 40-year-old, was only too happy to accept the gift.

"Thomas played well, but he opened the door," said Jimenez, taking his eighth PGA European Tour victory (the tournament was co-sponsored by the European, Asian and Australasian tours). Bjorn led from the start, and Jimenez, playing the Alpine Golf & Sports Club in 70, 66 and 67, closed the gap on him relentlessly. He trailed by six shots in the first round, then four, then one, and the final round turned into fierce match play.

The lead changed hands three times over the last 11 holes. Jimenez pulled ahead with four straight birdies from No. 6, but he bogeyed the 10th and 12th. Bjorn inched ahead with birdies at the 11th and 13th. Then he made two fatal errors, watering his tee shots at both back-nine par-fives, the 14th and 17th. He bogeyed both. "At worst, you're looking to be one under for those two holes — and that's the tournament for you," Bjorn said.

Jimenez leaped at his chance. He birdied both holes. The second was especially pleasing. "I didn't hole many putts," Jimenez said, "but I made that one on 17 (a 20-footer), which was important." It gave him a comfortable two-stroke lead going into the 18th, which he parred for a 68 and a 17-under-par 271. He won by two over Bjorn, who finished with a 71, and India's Jyoti Randhawa, who eagled the seventh and 16th en route to a 64. "I only started practicing two days before coming out here," Randhawa said. "Maybe I need to rest more to play good golf."

Myanmar Open—US$200,000
Winner: Thongchai Jaidee

In the Myanmar Open, it was a tale of more experience vs. less experience, and more experience will win just about every time. This was the case with Thongchai Jaidee, the star from Thailand, outlasting American Andrew Pitts over a final nine holes that were more like match play. Two statements pretty well summed things up.

"I didn't panic after falling behind," said Thongchai, seasoned by years on the Asian Tour and four earlier victories. "I knew that I could catch Andrew, as I like the back nine on this course." (Actually, the final eight. After a bogey at the 10th, he made five birdies the rest of the way.)

Said a disappointed Pitts, "I played flawlessly on the front nine, but then made some small mistakes, which are magnified on this course."

Thongchai played the Yangon Golf Club in 69, 72, 66 and 69, a 12-under-par 276 total, for a three-stroke victory. But the Thongchai-Pitts battle had to wait. The first-round spotlight was on little-known Korean Mo Joong-kyung, age 32. He opened with a six-birdie, one-bogey 67 for a one-stroke lead. "I'm quite surprised to be in the lead," said Mo. A 74 in the second round ended his dreams. He finished eighth. Australian rookie Alistair Presnell shot a 71 in tough weather for a one-stroke lead through the second round. A closing 73 dropped him to a tie for fourth.

The stage for that final battle was set in the third round when Thongchai exploded into the lead with a six-under-par 66 and Pitts got within a stroke with a 68. Then came a drama that Thongchai himself authored with a shaky 37 on the first nine while Pitts birdied the fifth and sixth holes and took a two-stroke lead heading into the final nine. Then Thongchai, staring at defeat, came to life.

Both bogeyed the 10th. But Pitts also bogeyed the next two holes, a stretch in which Thongchai caught and passed him. "I just kept telling myself to hit fairways and greens," Thongchai said. He birdied the 14th, then the 16th, 17th — where Pitts eagled on a three wood to three feet — and the 18th.

"It seems," said Thongchai, "that I always do well here."

Carlsberg Malaysian Open—US$1,210,000
Winner: Thongchai Jaidee

It's said that the Masters doesn't begin until the final nine on Sunday. Maybe it's always the Masters for Thailand's Thongchai Jaidee. He did it again.

A week earlier, Thongchai charged down the final nine to win the Myanmar Open. This time it was the Carlsberg Malaysian Open at Saujana Golf and Country Club in Kuala Lumpur, co-sponsored by the Asian and PGA European Tours. He punctuated his statement with a hole-in-one in a final-nine 30 for a two-stroke victory.

"I was able to change gears on the back nine," said Thongchai, meaning that after a struggling 38 on the first nine, he birdied the 10th, the 13th (on a chip-in), the 15th, aced the 188-yard par-three 16th, and birdied the 18th from four feet for a 30 and a four-under-par 68. His 14-under 274 was good for a two-stroke win over Australian Brad Kennedy.

The tournament had its unusual moments. England's Jamie Elson shared the first-round lead on a 66 after getting no practice, thanks to a case of food poisoning. Korea's Lee Sung-man, who has the distinction of being perhaps the only deaf golfer in tour golf, emerged in the second round. "Being deaf helps with my concentration," said Lee, who played for several years on the American Nationwide Tour. He led Thongchai by two going into the final round, then shot 77.

Thongchai, it will be noted, did not win against an empty field. Thomas Levet was the top European, finishing fifth, and Miguel Angel Jimenez tied for sixth. Among others, Paul McGinley finished 12th, Colin Montgomerie 16th, and Padraig Harrington 37th. It was Thongchai's sixth career victory, but not an ordinary one.

"Finally," Thongchai said, "I have won a big one — a joint-sanctioned tournament."

DHL Philippine Open—US$150,000
Winner: Edward Michaels

It was never like this on the American Hooters Tour. He had a bunch of birdies here, a handful of bogeys there, a really dumb penalty and an eagle. That was the adventure of Edward Michaels, age 27, an Atlanta-based American, former Hooters Tour player and now a rookie on the Asian Tour via the qualifying tournament. But that wild scramble was no mere adventure. It was Michaels' ticket to the championship in the DHL Philippine Open, only his second Asian Tour outing.

When that mad ride had ended, Michaels had himself a two-under-par 69, a two-under 282 total and a three-stroke victory over Filipino amateur Juvic Pagunsan. Michaels was, by the way, the only one in the field to finish under par at Manila's Riviera Golf and Country Club.

Until Michaels came smashing through, it seemed that the Asian Tour was going to have its third amateur winner. Pagunsan, age 25, had a hot third round, a seven-birdie 66, and was tied for the lead going into the final. Then he succumbed to amateur pressure and bogeyed his first two holes — just when Michaels was getting four birdies over the first six holes.

That easily put Michaels into the lead. Then he bogeyed three straight from No. 7. He eagled the par-five 10th, then blundered at the 15th. He plucked a loose impediment from the bunker, and that cost him a two-stroke penalty and a double bogey. No matter. No one was pressuring him anyway. So he birdied the 16th and went on to the three-stroke win.

The Philippine Open will be noted for another reason. Tournament officials, seeking to keep pace with golf elsewhere in the world, decided to invite a woman. The honor went to Ria Denise Quiazon of the Philippines. The result was about the same as with the others. She shot 86-84–170 and missed the cut by 20 strokes.

Caltex Masters—US$900,000
Winner: Colin Montgomerie

Everything else was a diversion at the Caltex Masters. There was, for example, Eddie Lee, age 20, a Korean-born New Zealander, one hole short of finishing the storm-battered first round. Could he bring in that eight-under-par 64 the next morning? (Yes.) Next there was Singapore's Mardan Mamat, taking the lead in the second round and thrilling the homefolks at Laguna National with thoughts of a home winner. (He didn't.) Then in the third round came American veteran Greg Hanrahan and England's Barry Lane, shooting 67s to tie for the lead. So there was plenty of the good golf and suspense that make for a fine tournament. But that's not what spectators had come to see.

They came to see Scotland's Colin Montgomerie, No. 1 in Europe for years but now just trying to crack the top 50 to get into The Players Championship in the United States the next week, to say nothing of regaining self-respect. This tournament was co-sponsored by the Asian and PGA European Tours, and a good showing was important.

Montgomerie just hung around for the first three rounds, then he came from four strokes off the lead and shot a dazzling 65 to race past the failing Hanrahan and Lane and sweep up his 37th career title. He had a total of 272, 16 under par, on his scores of 71, 69, 67 and the final 65 to win by three strokes over Hanrahan, who finished with a 72. Lane shot a final 75, falling to a tie for fifth place at 278.

"I haven't won in Europe for a year and a half, and it's a long time," said Montgomerie, who had won twice in Asia in the interim. "It's nice to get a victory to push me up the world rankings. I did have a bad year last year, and it's amazing how quickly you fall."

It's amazing how fast you can come back, too. Just bogey one hole for an entire tournament and make 17 birdies, and that ought to do it. Montgomerie tied Lane for the lead with a par at the ninth and took the lead with a birdie at the 13th. He locked up the victory at the par-three 17th, firing a six iron to two feet and dropping the birdie putt.

"This means an awful lot to me," Montgomerie said. "It means confidence to me. I lost my confidence. I have it back now."

Royal Challenge Indian Open—US$300,000
Winner: Mardan Mamat

When all else fails, try divine intervention. That seemed to be the case in the Royal Challenge Indian Open in mid-March.

Mexico's Pablo Del Olmo had it first, and he figured it worked, until he quit paying attention. Then came Singapore's Mardan Mamat, and he did pay attention. It paid off in his first important championship.

"...A little help from above," the 35-year-old Mamat admitted. If it included a 25-foot birdie putt on the final hole, so be it. Whatever it was, Mamat finished with an 18-under-par 270 total at the Delhi Golf Club and a five-stroke win over Del Olmo.

Poor Del Olmo. Things had been so promising. He broke out of a jam in the third round with a five-under 67, taking a three-stroke lead on Mamat and South Africa's Keith Horne. "A three-stroke lead is much better than two," Del Olmo said, "but it is nothing considering there are still 18 holes remaining."

Divine help? At the 17th, his bunker blast was too strong, but the ball hit the flagstick and dropped in tap-in range for a par. At the 18th, his errant three-iron shot hit a tree branch and dropped safely into a fairway bunker, setting up another par. "I think the Indian gods were looking out for me," he said. But not in the final round. He had three birdies, but two bogeys and a double bogey for a 73. "Unfortunately," he said, "I got ahead of myself and started thinking about winning."

Not Mamat. "I didn't think about winning," he said. "I just took things one at a time, and it worked for me." His "little help" in the final round bordered on the remarkable. He birdied the first two holes, birdied the sixth, eighth and 12th, and then the 17th and 18th for a seven-under 65. He offered thanks to his helpers, and also gave them a little scolding.

"I have waited 10 years for this," Mamat said, "and I think it was high time I got something."

Volkswagen Masters China—US$300,000
Winner: Rahil Gangjee

Rahil Gangjee, age 25, a third-year professional from India, wasn't merely a rookie on the Asian Tour, he was playing in only his fourth event in the inaugural Volkswagen Masters China at Pine Valley Golf Club in Beijing. He had a great golf story for a friend who lived down the street from him in Calcutta. It was all about how he won the tournament. Actually, he wanted to thank him. The friend was none other than Arjun Atwal, the great Indian golfer then playing on the U.S. PGA Tour.

"Arjun is my idol," Gangjee said. "Arjun showed belief in me even before I started believing in myself." Now Gangjee had good reason to believe in himself, not just for winning but for the way he won. He took the lead in the second round like a veteran, with two birdies in the last three holes for a six-under-par 66. In the third round, Gangjee battled such competition as Phillip Price, Nick Faldo, two-time Asian No. 1 Kang Wook-soon and Zhang Lian-wei, recently back from the Masters Tournament in the United States and the first Chinese ever to play in the storied tournament. Gangjee bogeyed the 18th, shot 70, and backed up into a five-way tie for the lead. Was the rookie beginning to crack?

Gangjee answered that question in the fourth round with a 68 that outran everybody but Korea's Mo Joong-kyung, who came out of the pack with a 66 to tie him at 15-under-par 273. Gangjee won on the first playoff hole, two-putting from 15 feet for a par after Mo hit into a greenside bunker.

"You practice for this all your life, and suddenly it happens," said Gangjee. "I can't describe what I'm feeling right now."

Zhang tied for seventh and was embarrassed that he couldn't win this first Chinese Masters on home soil. It didn't help that the world's most famous Chinese golfer twice was turned away from the locker room. The security guards didn't recognize him.

Macau Open—US$275,000
Winner: Jason Knutzon

Padraig Harrington, even with his Irish sense of humor, might not have been amused at the notion that he was something of a good luck charm.

Little-known American Jason Knutzon, playing with Harrington in the last round, came from behind with a strong final nine and won the Macau

Open. Knutzon noted that his good friend, Zach Johnson, had recently won the BellSouth Classic on the American PGA Tour while playing with Harrington in the final group. Conclusion? "I don't know if it was destiny that I should be playing with Padraig and winning today," Knutzon said.

Until then, the tournament was under the control of Amandeep Johl, who had opened with a nine-under-par 62, a course record at the Macau Golf and Country Club. Johl, seeking his first Asian Tour victory, led from there, and even by three shots over Knutzon going into the final round. He was still up by two going into the final turn. Then he double-bogeyed the 10th from the bushes and missed two-foot putts at the 12th and 13th. "That," said a deflated Johl, "was the turning point."

Maybe it was destiny. Of other contenders, Australian Scott Barr took the lead at the 12th but double-bogeyed the 13th. Harrington birdied three of his first six holes but triple-bogeyed the eighth. Earlier, Thailand's Thaworn Wiratchant closed with a 65 for the lead, but watched helplessly at the 18th as Knutzon edged him by a stroke.

Of course, Knutzon gave destiny a good nudge. With opportunities developing, Knutzon birdied the 13th and 14th, and then delivered in the clutch. He chipped in for a birdie at the 17th, and at the 18th, fired his approach from 117 yards to three feet and rolled that in for the winning birdie. He had a total of 268, 16 under par, on scores of 65, 68, 68 and the closing 67.

Knutzon spoke of times when he was in contention and didn't come through. "This," he said, "is nice."

BMW Asian Open—US$1,500,000
Winner: Miguel Angel Jimenez

Poor Simon Dyson. Now he knows exactly how Greg Norman felt. But he found out the hard way. It will be remembered that Norman led the 1996 Masters by six strokes going into the final round, shot 78 and lost. Dyson led the BMW Asian Open at the Tomson Golf Club in Shanghai by six strokes going into the final round, then shot 76, opening the door to Miguel Angel Jimenez. It was a stunning finish to the first event in China co-sponsored by the Asian and PGA European Tours.

"I didn't drive the ball well. I didn't putt that well," said Dyson, a 26-year-old Englishman, who was No. 1 on the Asian Tour when he won three times in 2000. Dyson was sparkling after a seven-week injury absence, dominating the first three rounds on scores of 66, 69 and 66. He led Jimenez by six strokes going into the fourth round. A bogey at No. 1 set the tone, and he was on his way to a 76. Jimenez, meantime, caught fire. He notched three birdies on the first nine, birdied the 10th and eagled the 13th, and was home free with a 67 for a 274 total, 14 under par, and a three-stroke victory, his third of the year.

"If I play like this," the exuberant Jimenez said, "I can do anything."

Norman was in the BMW Asian Open until the third round. He took an illegal drop from a water hazard, playing it as a lateral instead of a regular hazard, and was disqualified, as he had been in the Honda Classic on the U.S. PGA Tour earlier in the season. The pity was, Norman was playing well. He was eight under par when he hit his tee shot into the water at the 17th. The hazard line was yellow, signifying a regular hazard. Norman said he thought it was red, signifying a lateral hazard. He said he misread the line. "I was oblivious," Norman said. "I can't blame anybody but myself."

SK Telecom Open—US$400,000
Winner: Simon Yates

It was a case of two putts for Scotland's Simon Yates — two misses, three years apart. In the 2001 SK Telecom Open, Yates was six feet from winning on the final hole, but his birdie putt curled away at the last instant. A short while later, he bowed out of a playoff on the fifth hole. Now, in 2004, Yates again found himself at the final hole facing a makeable putt for the victory, a five-footer. Again he missed, and Canadian Rick Gibson had a four-footer to tie him.

"And Rick misses a short one for me to win today," said Yates, who shot a nine-under-par 279 total on rounds of 70, 69, 70 and 70. "That's golf, and I was a bit lucky on the 18th hole." There was a further irony. Yates also beat Korea's Charlie Wi, who tied for second with Gibson. It was Wi who beat Yates back in 2001.

Gibson finished at 280 with a closing 72, and Wi shot 71 to match him.

Defending champion K.J. Choi, the Korean star now playing on the American PGA Tour, and American star Fred Couples both came to play at Baekahmvista Country Club in Seoul. Neither really threatened. Couples tied for fifth, Choi for 14th.

Wi, a two-time winner of the SK Telecom Open, led through the middle rounds, and Yates (70) and Gibson (67) closed to within one of him through the third round. Wi faded just enough in the final round (72) to leave the battle to Yates and Gibson. Yates took a one-stroke lead with a first-nine 33, then led by two at the 15th when he saved par from eight feet against Gibson's bogey. Gibson cut it back to one with a birdie at the 16th, setting the stage for the drama at the 18th. It had been six years since Yates won. "It's nice," he said. "It's been a long time."

Tianjin TEDA Open—US$200,000
Winner: Thammanoon Srirot

It was instant replay five years later for Thailand's Thammanoon Srirot in the Tianjin TEDA Open presented by Rolls Royce. He won when it was last played in 1999. He won by a single stroke this time, too, playing the Tianjin Warner International Golf Club in Tianjin, China, in 19-under-par 265 to edge fellow Thai Boonchu Ruangkit. This was Thammanoon's first win since then, in a tournament otherwise marked by a sizzling final-round 61 by the unheralded Lu Wei-chih of Taiwan.

"When I came back here this week and had my practice round, I picked up a lot of confidence and felt I could win here again," said Thammanoon.

He was under pressure all the way and didn't flinch. Shooting rounds of 64, 67, 69 and 65, he was the tour's first wire-to-wire winner this year. He started strong and missed only two fairways in the first round. Keep this up, he said, "I'll have a chance of winning here again."

The driving didn't last, but Srirot had only one really awkward moment, topping his ball at his seventh hole after an emergency stop in the second round. But he survived the embarrassment to hold off Korea's Chung Joon, whose rollercoaster 68 included a double bogey at No. 1, a 30-foot birdie, two others of 25 feet and a 90-yard fairway hole-out for an eagle.

Thammanoon's driving turned sour in the third round. He opened with three straight birdies, then hooked his way to four bogeys over the next six holes. "I reminded myself to take deep breaths and relax," he said. It worked. He birdied the 12th and 14th, and salvaged a 69 to set up a showdown with Boonchu. In the fourth round, Thammanoon birdied the second, third, seventh and eighth holes, but credited a pedestrian eight-foot par putt at No. 1 for settling him down. "Boonchu put on some pressure on the back nine ... and I had to control my game," Thammanoon said.

Boonchu started two stokes behind, shot 31 on the first nine, and birdied the 10th, 12th and 13th to tie Thammanoon. But Boonchu torpedoed himself at the 14th, ignoring his caddie and hitting driver off the tee. He caught the rough and bogeyed. "That," he said, "cost me the tournament." But Thammanoon had to share the final curtain with Lu Wei-chih, age 26, a four-year professional on the Asian Tour, who shot 61 and leaped to a third-place finish. "This is the first 61 of my career," Lu said, in neat understatement. "I'm very happy, especially when I've won only $500 from my previous starts this year."

Kolon Korean Open—US$400,000
Winner: Edward Loar

The Kolon Korean Open began with Ernie Els, No. 3 in the world and favored to win, being upstaged by Hendrik Buhrmann, a countryman known best to fans of the Asian Tour. It ended with Els still being upstaged, this time by Edward Loar, a little-known American left-hander whose first win was in the 2003 Thailand Open. Loar shot a final-round 71 and was the only player to finish in red numbers, at two-under-par 286 at Woo Jeong Hills Country Club in Cheonan, South Korea, a tough par-72 course made tougher by blustery weather.

"The second one is always better, they say, especially with Ernie Els in the field and playing with him for two rounds at the weekend," said Loar. He beat Scotsman Simon Yates, who closed with a 69, by three, and Els was a stroke further back in third place after his second straight 75.

Said Els, "I haven't played well all weekend. I thought I hit it better today but the putter went kind of cold. I think I lost all the momentum when I missed those little putts on 10 and 11 in the third round. Three-putting No. 9 today was big. It just horseshoed out. Every time I got something going, I gave it back."

Buhrmann shot 68 for the first-round lead, three ahead of Els, and Australian Terry Pilkadaris matched Els' 69 in the second round to stay one stroke ahead. Els and Loar were tied a stroke behind going into the final round, and then Loar took over in the final round. He shook off three mid-round bogeys with four birdies, and then birdied the 11th, 15th and 18th — the last from 15 feet — to stay comfortably ahead of Yates, who started the round six strokes behind.

"I think it helped playing with Ernie yesterday," Loar said. "It gave me the comfort level of playing with him. I think I did a pretty good job of it."

Mercuries Taiwan Masters—US$390,000
Winner: Thaworn Wiratchant

Thailand's Thaworn Wiratchant, a man torn between the two drivers he was carrying, hadn't won in so long he had almost forgotten what it felt like. Three years, in fact. And the way Anthony Summers had started off the Mercuries Taiwan Masters, it didn't seem things would change.

Summers, a 34-year-old Australian in his first year on the tour, ended with a 67, five under par at the Taiwan Golf and Country Club's Tamsui Course. He led by two over Thaworn, Uttam Singh Mundy and Lin Wen-ko, the defending champion and one of three brothers in the field. Then the fates kicked in for Thaworn — once he got his driving sorted out.

Summers blew to a 77 in the second round, and Thaworn rejected his favorite driver and used the other. It worked. He missed only two fairways, made only one bogey, and shot another 67 for a one-stroke lead after 36 holes. "If I can keep driving it straight, I'll have a chance of winning this week," he said. His short game helped, of course. He birdied his first from 18 feet, the fourth from eight, and birdied the par-fives, Nos. 6 and 7.

The third round was an unsettled thing — four birdies, three bogeys and four par saves for a 71 in hot weather that wearied him. "I kept hooking my drives," he said. He bogeyed two of his first four holes, but steadied himself coming home. He birdied the 14th and 16th for the 71 and a luxury few golfers ever know — the rosy glow of no pressure in the final round.

"I thought the field would catch up on the back nine, as I wasn't playing solidly," Thaworn said. "I just played it safe coming in. I had a good lead."

Thaworn started the final round with a two-stroke lead on South Africa's Chris Williams and upped that to four by the turn with nothing more than a 35 that included a birdie at the fourth hole on an eight-foot putt and another at the par-five seventh on a six-footer.

"My putting was steady this week," Thaworn said. "At the turn, I was leading by four, and although I dropped bogeys at 10 and 16, I still had a good lead. I just avoided the big numbers."

Well, bigger numbers, that is. Thaworn closed with a two-over-par 74 for a five-under 283 total. He won by two strokes over Williams, who shot 74 without a birdie, and Chen Yuan-chi, who rolled in a 30-footer at the 18th for a 72. "It was hard to catch Thaworn," Chen said, "so joint second was pretty good."

Taiwan Open—US$300,000
Winner: Charlie Wi

A golfer who opens a tournament 76-76 probably won't be voted "Most Likely to Succeed." But Charlie Wi, a California-based South Korean, had plenty of bounce-back plus an accommodating field, and unlikely as it seemed, he did succeed with the Taiwan Open, his sixth career victory and his first since 2000. Never mind that wobbly start. Wi won by a comfortable three strokes.

Actually, 76-76–152 would ordinarily be far over the cut. But the scores were generally soaring, with strong September winds and rain from Typhoon Meari approaching Taipei, and the cut came in at 154.

The weather calmed for the first time in the week in the third round, and Wi rocketed out of the pack with a bogey-free, eight-under-par 64, tying the North Bay Golf and Country Club course record. The putter did it. "I just holed so many long ones today," said Wi, who had three top-five finishes on the Asian Tour this season. He rolled in a number from inside 20 feet, logging six birdies, and he eagled No. 5 on a three iron to three feet. The 64 hurled him up the leaderboard to even-par 216 and a tie for fourth with Thailand's Thammanoon Srirot (73) and Taiwan's Lin Wen-tang (65).

The third-round lead belonged to India's Gaurav Ghei (69) and Taiwan's Lin Chie-hsiang (71), tied at two-under 214. It was a high moment for Ghei, 36, who suffered a variety of injuries since winning in 1995. His round included a hole-out eagle at the par-four 16th on a wedge from 105 yards. "I'm really happy to be in the joint lead," Ghei said. "I feel lucky, and hopefully it'll go my way on Sunday."

Charlie Wi rendered Ghei's hopes academic with 68 in the final round for a three-stroke victory over Pilkadaris (72), who enjoyed second place alone and his best finish ever on the Asian Tour. Ghei tied for third, four strokes behind. When all was said and done, Charlie Wi was a puzzled winner.

Crowne Plaza Open—US$200,000
Winner: Terry Pilkadaris

Not that confidence plays a great part in golf, but Terry Pilkadaris had this to say about the inaugural Crowne Plaza Open: "I told my wife two months ago that I was going to win in Shanghai."

And Pilkadaris made good, scoring his first victory on the Asian Tour. But he strained the crystal ball. He entered the final round with a two-stroke lead. Then he promptly bogeyed the first two holes. He missed a seven-foot putt on the first hole and bunkered his approach at the second. But he steadied things soon enough, getting birdies at the fifth and ninth holes, then parred the second nine. He wrapped up the victory with a two-foot putt on the last hole for an eight-under-par 280 total to win by a stroke over Thailand's Boonchu Ruangkit at the Tomson Shanghai Pudong Golf Club.

"That," Pilkadaris said, with a relieved grin, "was the longest two-foot putt you'll ever make."

Pilkadaris took the lead in the third round with a par 72, inching two strokes ahead of Marcus Both, not only a fellow Australian but a roommate for the week. Both caught him with consecutive birdies at the 13th and 14th holes, but Pilkadaris moved back in front with a birdie of his own at the 14th. He then got his two-stroke lead when Both bogeyed the 17th from a bunker. Japan's Eiji Mizoguchi, the overnight leader, soared to a 76 and slumped to third place.

In the final round, Pilkadaris knew the threat from Boonchu, a very accomplished veteran, who finally got his putter working for a 68. "I hit the ball really well all week," Boonchu said. "I said yesterday that I would not be able to win unless I putted better, and that's what happened."

Pilkadaris needed that final two-footer, and he got it. "It's a big relief," Pilkadaris said, clutching his first win. "It's fun. I look forward to more."

Sanya Open—US$250,000
Winner: Terry Pilkadaris

Sometimes a caddie can make a world of difference. That seemed to be the case for Australian Terry Pilkadaris. After scoring his first victory the week before in the inaugural Crowne Plaza Open in Shanghai with a strange caddie, Pilkadaris had his favorite caddie in Beijing for the Sanya Open. Thus comfortably teamed, Pilkadaris scored his second victory — and second straight — this time in a playoff. He beat American Clay Devers on the second extra hole.

The caddie was his wife, Monique. "She wasn't with me when I won in Shanghai, so I was more determined to get over the line today with her," Pilkadaris said. "She's like my rock, and I'm glad we did it."

Pilkadaris, who turned age 31 on the day of the third round, took the lead in the second round and stayed there. He played the par-72 Yalong Bay Golf Club in 68-66-66-70, having an 18-under-par 270 total. Devers caught him with a final-round 65. In the playoff, Pilkadaris just missed winning on the first extra hole when his 20-footer burned the edge of the cup. At the second hole, he nearly holed out his approach shot from 170 yards. Devers caught a bunker with his approach shot.

"Terry just gets it on the fairway and gets it on the green," Devers said. He was pleased with his play, except, he said, "I left myself yardages that I'm not used to."

China's Liang Wen-chong nearly made it a three-way playoff, but his birdie try from 15 feet at the 18th just missed, and he had to settle for a 67 and a tie for third place with Thailand veteran Boonchu Ruangkit at 271, one stroke out of the playoff.

Pilkadaris started four shots behind the career-best 64 by first-round leader Zheng Wen-gen of China. Then he took over with a 66 of his own for a two-stroke lead through the second round. "My confidence is pretty good now, and I've got good control of the ball," Pilkadaris said. "I'll just go out there and have some fun."

In fact, he had a blast.

Carlsberg Masters 2004 Vietnam—US$200,000
Winner: Angelo Que

The first surprise was that a golf tournament, the epitome of capitalism, was being played in Vietnam — the Carlsberg Masters 2004 Vietnam, in Hanoi, the first professional golf tournament ever in that Communist country. The next surprise was the winner — an obscure Filipino named Angelo Que, age 26, a lowly 122nd on the Asian Tour Order of Merit. He won for the first time and in the process upstaged such challengers as Thongchai Jaidee, the celebrated Thai veteran and No. 1 on the Asian Tour, and Corey Pavin, a former U.S. Open champion.

Que shot 70-66-70-70 for a 12-under-par 276 total at the newly opened Chi Linh Star Golf and Country Club. He held a three-stroke lead in the second round and was in second place, just two behind Thongchai, through the third round.

"My confidence was low coming into this week, but I told myself to start believing in myself," Que said. "I knew I could play the game."

Que, a former two-time Philippine Amateur champion, started birdie-bogey in the second round, then got four more birdies for a first-nine 32 on his way to the 66 and a three-stroke lead. Thongchai dislodged him with a 64 in the third round and led him by two going into the final round. Que, showing nothing but great confidence, caught up with a birdie on No. 1 against Thongchai's bogey at No. 3. Then came the big strike. Que drove the shortish par-four No. 5 and dropped the 15-foot putt for an eagle two, to lead by a stroke through the turn. Thongchai's putter went sour and he bogeyed the 11th, 12th and 15th, shot 74, and finished second by two. Pavin birdied the third, fifth and seventh, but got chilled by a bogey at the 13th, shot 70, and finished third.

"It was very scary at the start," Que said. "I was playing the top player in Asia." He earned an exemption to play on the Asian Tour. His timing was impeccable. It never dawned on him that he might win, so he had sent in his application for the tour's qualifying tournament the day before the event started. Scratch one entry.

Volvo China Open—US$1,000,000
Winner: Stephen Dodd

It turned out that Shanghai is not all that good this time of year. Accordingly, the Volvo China Open — jointly sanctioned by the Asian and European Tours — was a matter of survival for a while. And in the midst of late November temperatures and cutting winds in the second round, it was Stephen Dodd, a 38-year-old Welshman, who survived the best. He grabbed the lead and kept it the rest of the way for his first professional victory. And he beat Danish Ryder Cupper Thomas Bjorn by three strokes in the process.

"My emotions at the moment?" said Dodd. "I can't really put it into words. Maybe you can ask me tomorrow."

Said Bjorn, who seemed well on his way back from a tough stretch, "There wasn't much I could do. He played really well."

Dodd, not nearly as tournament-tested as Bjorn, was therefore an odds-on favorite to fold when the going got tight down the final stretch. Dodd had never led going into the final round, but he was up by three going into this one. And this was with a 70 that included a watery triple bogey at No. 7. Not a cinch, but not bad, either. In the fourth round, Dodd held steady on the first nine and still led by three after both made the final turn in 35. Then he went four up with birdies at the 10th, 11th and 13th while Bjorn chased him with birdies at the 10th, 12th and 15th. Then the tension increased. Dodd bogeyed the 17th, and his lead was down to two.

Now Dodd — he played Shanghai Silport in 68-70-70-68 for a 12-under-par 276 total — needed the resolve that got him through the bitter weather of the second round, when he posted that four-birdie 70 with the temperature near freezing. And he found it. At the par-five 18th, he hit the fairway, and when he hit the green with his second shot, he broke into a smile. He knew it was his. He two-putted for the birdie.

And Bjorn tipped his cap. "You just have to take your hat off to him," Bjorn said. "Here's a win for the good guy, and Stephen is definitely one of the good guys."

Omega Hong Kong Open—US$800,000
Winner: Miguel Angel Jimenez

This was the 46th playing of the Omega Hong Kong Open, the longest-running sports event in Hong Kong, and the first round belonged to Adam Groom, another in the unending supply of talented golfers coming out of Australia. Groom, having a strong rookie year on the Asian Tour, took the lead with a bogey-free, six-under-par 64. After that, the tournament, co-sanctioned by the Asian and European Tours, belonged to the veterans.

At the very end, it belonged to Miguel Angel Jimenez, the smiling Spaniard who sports a cigar in the front and a ponytail at the back. Jimenez outran South Africa's James Kingston and Ireland's Padraig Harrington, defending champion and ranked No. 6 in the world, and picked off his fifth title of the year and third in Asia. The three started the final round tied for the lead. It came down to the final hole, with Jimenez shooting a four-under 66 and Kingston and Harrington 67s at the Hong Kong Golf Club.

Harrington, who birdied the last two holes to win by a shot last year, this time ran into trouble at the 16th. "Obviously it cost me the round," he said. "I probably missed six very makeable putts, and that's what cost me." Harrington could have forced a playoff with a birdie at the 18th, but his putt from 25 feet died just short. Kingston took the lead, dropping a 30-footer at the 17th, but Jimenez matched him from 25 feet.

They were tied coming to the 18th tee, and that's where it ended for Kingston when he hit his tee shot into the trees. "I went with the three wood, and a good swing would have given me a nice aggressive shot into the green and a chance for the win," he said. "Obviously I made a bad swing there, and that was it." He had to take a penalty drop, and finished by making a 15-footer for bogey. The door was wide open for Jimenez, who was comfortably just eight feet from the pin. He two-putted for his par for a 14-under 266 total and the victory.

"Five victories this year — nobody can think you can win so many times at the start of the year," Jimenez said. "Every win is different. I like to live the moment. This means exactly like any other one. It shows me that I'm still in form."

A jacket of rich red also went to the winner. This pleased Jimenez. "I've got my Ferraris in red," he said. "This jacket is going to match my cars."

Volvo Masters of Asia—US$550,000
Winner: Jyoti Randhawa

For India's Jyoti Randhawa, it turned out the most important lesson he would learn from his golf coach was to be patient. For Australia's Terry Pilkadaris, it was the ability to accept reality when, truth be known, there was nothing else left to do.

And that pretty well summed up the Volvo Masters of Asia at the Kota Permai Golf and Country Club in Kuala Lumpur early in December. India's Randhawa led through the first two rounds, rebounded in the final round, and beat Pilkadaris in a playoff, scoring his only victory of the year.

"It was a great finish," Randhawa said. "It was nerve-wracking, but I handled myself well."

Indeed he did. But the key to his victory probably was the way he bounced back from a shaky third round. He was in a fairly commanding position through the first two rounds, shooting 63-70, and led by two. But then he broke out in a rash of errors in the third round and shot a two-over-par 74. The field didn't wait. Thailand's Prayad Marksaeng came out "99 percent" confident he could win after tying Taiwan's Wang Ter-chang for the third-round lead. Prayad shot a five-under 67 and Wang posted a 69 to share the lead at 12-under-par 204. Randhawa's 74 put him at 207. It was a five-shot swing.

In the final round, Randhawa needed some of the magic he enjoyed in that first-round 63, which he called "the best round of my career." And he found it. He labored all the way back for a 67 to tie Pilkadaris at 14-under 274. Pilkadaris, seeking his third win in four months, had come from the pack with a seven-under 65. But Randhawa denied him, dropping an eight-foot birdie putt at the 18th to tie him. In the playoff, they birdied the first hole of the playoff. At the second, Pilkadaris was seven feet from a birdie while Randhawa sat 15 feet away after a poor chip shot. Then Randhawa rolled his home for the birdie, and Pilkadaris missed.

Reality? "It was a bitter pill to swallow," Pilkadaris said. "But you can't complain if you lose to a birdie."

Said Randhawa, "I started to doubt myself after making a few swing changes. I've not won for nearly two years. But my coach, Kel Llewellyn, told me to be patient."

Asia/Japan Okinawa Open—¥100,000,000
Winner: Kiyoshi Miyazato

See Japan Tour section.

Japan Tour

Token Homemate Cup—¥100,000,000
Winner: Hiroyuki Fujita

Hiroyuki Fujita turned a slow start into the third victory of his seven-season career as the Japan Tour season began its 2004 run with the Token Home-mate Cup tournament at Tado, Mie Prefecture. The actual opener was the Asia/Japan Okinawa Open the previous December, a tournament that Fujita won in December 2002. At the Token, he shot a final-round, two-under-par 69 at Token Tado Country Club to post a two-stroke victory with his three-under-par 281 total.

Although he registered a one-under-par 70 in the opening round, Fujita found himself in a massive tie for 35th place in the standings at the end of the day. He was six strokes off the lead as Shigemasa Higaki and Toshimitsu Izawa, the tour's leading money winner in 2001 and 2003, fired 64s and led by one stroke over Ryoken Kawagishi and two over Kaname Yokoo. On a very windy Friday, though, Fujita shot 68, the round's best score and one of only two sub-par cards, and took the lead by two strokes with 138 over the other under-par shooter — Tsukasa Watanabe (70-70) — and three others — ageless Masashi Ozaki (69-71), Steve Conran of Australia (69-71) and Higaki (64-76).

Charlie Wi, who started the third round at 141, shot 70 Saturday for 211 and a one-shot lead over Fujita (74). Izawa bounced back from his second-round 77 with 72 and kept his hopes alive at 213 with Shingo Katayama (71) and Ryuichi Oda (70). Fujita picked up the win Sunday when he shot the 69 for the two-stroke victory over Wi (72) and Katayama (70).

Tsuruya Open—¥100,000,000
Winner: Brendan Jones

Brendan Jones has a modest goal as he plays on the Japan Tour. "I want to win at least one tournament a year," the Australian said. Thus far, he has accomplished that aim, doing it quickly in the 2004 season, capturing the Tsuruya Open, the second event on the year's calendar in late April when the circuit resumed its regular schedule a month after the Token opener. Jones won the Sun Chlorella in 2003 and the Philip Morris in 2002.

Jones' victory was a bitter disappointment for Tatsuya Mitsuhashi, who led the tournament for three days in quest of his first Japan Tour victory in six years on the circuit. Jones dogged Mitsuhashi all the way. Mitsuhashi opened with a splendid, eight-under-par 63 and found himself on top of the leaderboard for the first time in his career, but Jones nearly matched him with a 64, and six players, including Shingo Katayama, the perennial contender for the money title, were at 65. Joining Katayama there were Tsuyoshi Yoneyama, Tomohiro Kondo, Tadahisa Inoue, Katsumasa Miyamoto and Scott Laycock.

Scoring was higher Friday. Jun Kikuchi had the only low round among the contenders, carding a 65 to join Mitsuhashi at the top. Mitsuhashi shot 70 for 133. Jones slipped four strokes behind with 73–137, but remained confident because "I was putting well." That confidence was rewarded Saturday when he produced a 69 that moved him within a stroke of Mitsuhashi, who settled for a one-over-par 72.

The final round was a real dogfight. Jones climbed in front early with a bogey-free, two-birdie first nine, but opened the door coming in when he incurred a bogey and a double bogey. Still, he mustered three birdies and held off Shinichi Yokota and Taichi Teshima, who shot 67s, Keiichiro Fukabori (68), Laycock (70) and crestfallen Mitsuhashi, who again shot 72. They all wound up at 277, two behind the winner, whose closing 69 gave him a 275 total.

Chunichi Crowns—¥120,000,000
Winner: Shingo Katayama

After laying in wait in the first two tournaments of the season, Shingo Katayama struck in the third one — the Chunichi Crowns, the early season's richest event. Katayama, seeking to regain the money-winning crown he wore in 2000, etched three consecutive rounds in the low 60s and coasted to a two-stroke victory with his 16-under-par 264. It was the 15th victory for Katayama in his 10 years on the Japan Tour.

Katayama began the week at the par-70 Nagoya Golf Club course with a 65 that left him in a three-way tie with Nozomi Kawahara and Keiichiro Fukabori one stroke behind Dinesh Chand, Fiji's other international professional player and winner. (Need I mention Vijay Singh?) Chand, a two-time winner in Japan, was seeking his first victory since the 2001 Munsingwear KSB Cup, but he couldn't cope with Katayama the rest of the week.

Katayama took the lead Friday. His 64, the product of eight birdies, three on the last four holes, and two bogeys, vaulted him three strokes in front of Naomichi (Joe) Ozaki, who also shot 64, and Kawahara (65-67). The beat went on Saturday. Katayama again racked up eight birdies and took a single bogey for 63–192. That padded his margin to seven strokes over Brendan Jones (65), the previous week's Tsuruya Open winner, and Hisayuki Sasaki, who shot 64.

Katayama's torrid streak cooled off Sunday. He slipped to a two-over-par 72, but his huge margin still enabled him to post a two-stroke victory with the 264 despite a major rally by Paul Sheehan, who jumped from a ninth-place tie into second place with a 63. Sasaki shot 68 and finished third.

Fujisankei Classic—¥110,000,000
Winner: Paul Sheehan

Paul Sheehan hinted at things to come in the Fujisankei Classic with his hot finish and runner-up position in the Chunichi Crowns. Those things materialized when he stepped out to a four-stroke victory at the par-71

Kawana Hotel golf course, the second victory by an Australian in the first four events of the Japan Tour season and his first on the circuit.

The momentum of his closing 63 in the Crowns didn't kick in at the start. Course-record-breaking rounds of 63 by veteran Nobuo Serizawa, age 44 and a five-time winner over his 21 seasons on the tour, and lesser-known Takashi Iwamoto put Sheehan five strokes in arrears with his 68. He fell even farther behind in Friday's second round. While he was shooting a one-under-par 70, Serizawa followed his blazing start with a 68 for 131 and a two-stroke advantage over Kiyoshi Maita (68-65). Iwamoto fell from contention with 73.

Then the Australian did some record-breaking of his own. After taking a bogey on the first hole Saturday, Sheehan reeled off an eagle and eight birdies over the next 17 for a 62 to break the two-day-old record on the Kawana course. That vaulted him from a 17th-place tie into a two-stroke lead over Serizawa (71) and Daisuke Maruyama (67), three ahead of six other players who were at 213.

Sheehan closed out his initial Japanese victory decisively on Sunday. He put together an impeccable, four-birdie 67 for 267 and finished with a four-stroke margin over Mitsuhiro Tateyama and Kaname Yokoo, who closed with 68s. Another 71 dropped Serizawa into a tie for fifth as his bid for his first win in four seasons failed.

Japan PGA Championship—¥110,000,000
Winner: S.K. Ho

S.K. Ho of South Korea became the third overseas winner of the early season when he landed the important Japan PGA Championship, a nearly 80-year-old fixture on the Japan Tour. Following in the footsteps of Australians Brendan Jones and Paul Sheehan, Ho picked up his second title in Japan in a final-round duel with Keiichiro Fukabori in the rain-shortened championship.

Those two men played lead roles from the start. Heavy rains and strong winds forced cancellation of Thursday's first round at Kochi Kuroshio Country Club at Geisel, Kochi Prefecture, converting it to a 54-hole event. When Friday's opening round played out, Ho and Fukabori had shares of the lead with 49-year-old David Ishii, the Hawaiian-born American who landed the money crown in 1987 when he won six of his 13 titles on the circuit. They shot six-under-par 66s.

From then on, though, it was virtually all Ho and Fukabori. As Ishii, whose last victory was in the 1994 Maruman Open, tumbled from contention, Ho shot 68 for 134 and Fukabori 69 for 135. Yasuharu Imano intervened with a 65 that tied him for the lead with the South Korean, but he, like Ishii, faded the next day, leaving the decision in the hands of Ho and Fukabori. And that came down to the final hole, where Ho birdied for 68 and edged Fukabori by one stroke with his 14-under-par 202. Fukabori also had a 68 for his 203. Next in line were Kaname Yokoo and Hideto Tanihara at a distant 209.

Munsingwear Open KSB Cup—¥100,000,000
Winner: Tatsuya Mitsuhashi

Six virtually fruitless years on the Japan Tour ended for Tatsuya Mitsuhashi in the Munsingwear Open KSB Cup tournament. Mitsuhashi, never before a serious contender on the circuit, was in the hunt all week at Tojigaoka Marine Hills Golf Club as he registered a two-stroke victory with an 18-under-par 270 in a tournament that has a penguin as a mascot and "Get fun! Get together!" as a theme for its players and galleries.

He started things in the opening round when he shot 66 for a share of the lead with Thailand's Thammanoon Srirot, one stroke in front of another Thai, Chawalit Plaphol, Taichiro Kiyota and veteran Toru Suzuki. A three-putt bogey at No. 12 was the only blemish on Mitsuhashi's six-under-par card. He slipped three shots behind Friday when he took a 71. India's Jeev Milkha Singh, with 65, the day's low round, and Shinichi Yokota (66) moved in front with 134. They led Suzuki (69) by two, Mitsuhashi and three others by three at the midpoint of the tournament.

Mitsuhashi blitzed the field Saturday, putting his maiden victory well within reach when he shattered the Tajigaoka course record with a nine-under-par 63 and raced to a four-stroke lead. "I had no idea that I had set a record even after I'd finished," said Mitsuhashi, who started the round with an eagle at the second hole and tapped in for his seventh birdie on the 18th green in the bogey-free round that broke the four-year-old record by a stroke.

Singh, also winless in Japan, where he has been an occasional player since 1996, shot 70 and held second place at 204 by a shot over Koki Idoki and Toru Taniguchi.

Mitsuhashi was a bit shaky Sunday, taking a double bogey at the fourth hole and two bogeys, but rebounded with six birdies for 70 and the two-stroke win. Shingo Katayama, the money list leader, completed a big resurgence to join Singh and Nobuhiro Masuda in second place with his second straight 66. Singh closed with 68, Masuda with 66.

Mitsubishi Diamond Cup—¥110,000,000
Winner: Tetsuji Hiratsuka

Tetsuji Hiratsuka, the No. 2 money winner of 2003, even though he didn't acquire his first-ever victory on the Japan Tour until the Nippon Series, the final event of the season, validated his reputation with his 2004 victory in the Mitsubishi Diamond Cup at Oarai Golf Club in Ibaraki Prefecture in late May. The 33-year-old Hiratsuka, a professional since 1994, broke from a four-way tie at the halfway mark and rolled to a five-stroke victory.

Hiratsuka was deadlocked with Hiroshi Goda, Makoto Inoue and Hideto Tanihara at 138 after the first 36 holes. He started with a 68, trailing first-round leader Masayuki Kawamura by two, and followed with a 70 to join Goda, Inoue and Tanihara, all of whom also had 68-70 starts. Actually, Hiratsuka could easily have had first place to himself. He ran off six birdies Friday, but gave back four strokes with bogeys.

Hiratsuka eliminated the bogeys Saturday and stepped out to a two-shot lead. His four-birdie 68 put him at 206, two in front of Tanihara, who shot 70. Three strokes further back were Shinichi Yokota, Ryuichi Oda and Kawamura. Hiratsuka completed his sweep to victory Sunday, again avoiding the bogeys. He posted a comfortable 69 for 275, 13 under par for the distance. Hidemasa Hoshino jumped into second place at 280 with a final-round 66, one stroke better than S.K. Ho's final posting.

JCB Classic Sendai—¥100,000,000
Winner: Takashi Kamiyama

It took him more than seven years to do it, but Takashi Kamiyama finally nailed down a victory on the Japan Tour. The 31-year-old Kamiyama emerged from the season's first playoff in the JCB Classic Sendai tournament as the third first-time winner of 2004, joining Paul Sheehan (Fujisankei) and Tatsuya Mitsuhashi (Munsingwear) in that category.

Kamiyama was little noticed until the final day. The focus Thursday and Friday was on another unheralded player, Ryuichi Oda, who, in a year of low scores and records challenges, matched the all-time low at the par-71 Omotezao Kokusai Golf Club at Shibata, Miyagi Prefecture, with a 62. It gave the 27-year-old Oda, another non-winner, a two-stroke lead over Shinichi Yokota after 18 holes. South Korea's Kim Jong-duck trailed by three. Although he slipped to a one-over-par 72 Friday, Oda retained the lead, but only by one over the experienced Kazuhiko Hosokawa and two over Kim.

Little had been heard to that point of the season from Toru Taniguchi, the 2002 money winner and regular contender for that title in recent years. He made his presence felt Saturday when he shot a one-bogey 65, his last of seven birdies a nine-foot putt on the 18th green to take the lead at 202. He was one stroke in front of Hisayuki Sasaki and two ahead of veteran star Tsuneyuki Nakajima, who turned 50 in 2004; Kim (68) and Kamiyama (67). Nakajima bolted into the picture with 63, his best round in many seasons.

Surprisingly, Taniguchi stumbled with a 74 in Sunday's final round, opening the door to Kamiyama (67 again), Nakajima (67) and Kondo (64) to knot the final score at 271 and bring about the playoff. It ended quickly when Kamiyama birdied the first extra hole.

Mandom Lucido Yomiuri Open—¥100,000,000
Winner: Dinesh Chand

Dinesh Chand, the Fiji regular on the Japan Tour, couldn't have picked a better time to equal a somewhat unlikely circuit record. Nursing a one-stroke lead as he teed off in the final round of the Mandom Lucido Yomiuri Open, Chand eagled the seventh, 11th and 18th holes at Hyogo's par-72 Yomiuri Country Club en route to a four-stroke victory, his third in Japan and first since the 2001 Munsingwear KSB Cup.

The record-tying three-eagle round created quite a stir, as did the Thursday performance of the tour's all-time tournament winner (94) — 57-year-old

Masashi Ozaki. Just a tournament after Tsuneyuki Nakajima, another of Japan's aging superstars, lost in the JCB Classic Sendai at age 50, Ozaki opened the Yomiuri Open with a six-under-par 66 and found himself in a four-way tie for the lead. Ozaki, who had gained confidence from his 67-65 close at that JCB Classic Sendai and sixth-place finish, shared the Yomiuri lead with Kazuhiro Fukunaga, Mitsuhiro Tateyama and Chand.

Katsunori Kuwabara, who had opened with 67, climbed into the lead Friday with a sparkling 64, but Ozaki stayed in the race with 67–133, two back in second place with Toru Suzuki (67-66). Kuwabara had an eagle, seven birdies and a bogey for the 64, matching the day's best score. Chand was another shot back after rounds of 66-68, and when he repeated the 68 Saturday with seven birdies and three bogeys, the Fijian claimed his one-stroke margin over Kuwabara (72) and S.K. Ho (69).

Then came the flurry of eagles, accompanied by three birdies and three bogeys for the winning 66–268. Ho shot 69 and shared second place with Tetsuji Hiratsuka, the Diamond Cup winner. Ozaki, unable to maintain the fast pace, finished with rounds of 72-74 over the weekend and tied for 24th place.

Mizuno Open—¥100,000,000
Winner: Brendan Jones

Brendan Jones returned to action with a bang on the Japan Tour. Idle for a month, the Australian wasted no time becoming the circuit's first multiple winner of the 2004 season when he grabbed the Mizuno Open title at the end of June in overtime.

Jones, who won his third Japanese tournament in the Tsuruya Open in late April, was never out of the lead at Setonaikai Golf Club at Kasaoka, Okayama Prefecture. In the first round, he was one of five players who opened with 67, the largest leadership bunching of the season to date. Nobuhito Sato, Kaname Yokoo, Yusaku Miyazato and Hiroyuki Fujita, the Token Homemate Cup winner, also had 67s.

The Aussie stepped ahead Friday, shooting his second straight bogey-free round, 68 for 135. That put him one stroke in front of Fujita (69) and New Zealand's David Smail (68-68) and two ahead of Miyazato, Hiroaki Iijima, Kim Jong-duck of South Korea and Lin Keng-chi of Taiwan. The top of the standings snarled again Saturday, but Jones remained one of the leaders with his 70–205. Miyazato joined him with a 68 and two others — Naruhito Ueda and Hidemasa Hoshino — made it a foursome when they shot the day's best rounds of 65.

Fujita and Iijima trailed by a stroke at 206, and it was the unlikely Iijima who wound up in the playoff with Jones after blowing the victory when he bogeyed the final hole for 68–274. Jones forced the playoff when he finished moments later with 69 for his 274 total and took the title with a par to another Iijima bogey on the second extra hole. With the victory, Jones inched ahead of Shingo Katayama on the money list and earned a spot in the Open Championship at Royal Troon.

Japan Golf Tour Championship—¥120,000,000
Winner: S.K. Ho

S.K. Ho rang up two firsts and a second when he won the Japan Golf Tour Championship, the circuit's newest prestige tournament the first week of July.

The firsts: The South Korean was the first non-Japanese winner in the five-year history of the lucrative tournament and the first to pair up that victory with the earlier Japan PGA Championship. The second: Ho became the second multiple winner of the season, following in the footsteps of Brendan Jones, who won his second of the season the week before in the Mizuno Open.

For the first three days at Shishido Hills Country Club at Tomobe, Ibaraki Prefecture, Tomohiro Kondo, a winless 27-year-old, was the man to beat, and Ho didn't appear to be the man who would do it. Kondo, who tied for 10th in the previous week's Mizuno Open, his best finish ever, began his title bid Thursday with a five-under-par 66 — seven birdies and two bogeys — and a two-stroke lead over New Zealand's David Smail and Kiyoshi Miyazato. He followed with a 70 for 136 Friday, but led by just a stroke over two other non-winners — Satoru Hirota (69-68) and Yoshiaki Mano, who shot the day's best round of 66 for his 137. Meanwhile, Ho had fallen eight strokes behind the leader with rounds of 70-74, sitting in a 19th-place tie.

Things looked bright for Kondo after three rounds. Despite a closing bogey, he shot another 70 Saturday and widened the gap to three strokes over Hidemasa Hoshino, who fired a 65 with the aid of a hole-in-one, and Australia's Scott Laycock, who followed a pair of 69s with a 71. Ho gained ground with a 67, but still trailed the leader by five strokes going to the final round.

An ace at the par-three third hole ignited the South Korean's charge Sunday. He went on to a 68 and that was good enough for a tie when Kondo came home with a 73 for his five-under-par 279. Ho then won the third playoff on the tour in four weeks with a par on the second extra hole and supplanted Jones as the money list leader. The victory brought two valuable bonuses — a five-year exemption on the tour and a spot in the WGC - NEC Invitational at America's Firestone Country Club — not to mention a ¥1 million reward for the hole-in-one.

Woodone Open Hiroshima—¥100,000,000
Winner: Shingo Katayama

The list of two-time winners on the 2004 Japan Tour continued to grow at the Woodone Open Hiroshima and the addition there was no surprise. Shingo Katayama, the circuit's most successful player in the new century, parlayed two brilliant rounds on the Hachihonmatsu course of Hiroshima Country Club and walked off with a five-stroke victory to go with his early-season triumph in the Chunichi Crowns.

For most of the tournament, it didn't appear that it would be that easy. Especially the first day, when Katayama shot a two-under-par 70 and rested in a 19th-place tie, four strokes behind leader Tadahiro Takayama. Katayama bolted all the way into the lead Friday when he shot a course-record-tying 63 — an eagle and seven birdies — for 133, 11 under par. For the second time in four weeks, Masashi Ozaki came to the fore. The 57-year-old Japanese golf hero, who won the variously titled version of the tournament at Hiroshima nine times over the years, shot 65 and trailed Katayama by just a stroke. Y.E. Yang was next at 135.

Katayama failed to provide himself with a cushion Saturday. He scored a two-under-par 70 for 203 and still led by a stroke, but he had the likes of Tateo Ozaki at 204 and brother Masashi, Toru Taniguchi and first-round-leader Takayama at 205. As it turned out, Katayama needed no margin Sunday. He repeated his course-record-tying performance, the 63 this time the product of two eagles and five birdies. Ryuichi Oda shot 65 to take the runner-up slot. Takayama, the third-place finisher, was eight shots behind Katayama, who regained the money list lead with the first-place prize of ¥20 million for his 10th career victory.

Sato Foods NST Niigata Open—¥50,000,000
Winner: Kim Jong-duck

Kim Jong-duck joined South Korean countryman S.K. Ho in the 2004 winner's circle on the Japan Tour when he rolled to a five-stroke victory in the Sato Foods NST Niigata Open. Like Ho, Kim had established his credentials as a winner in earlier years. In fact, when he won his most recent second and third titles during the 1999 season, he was the first South Korean to have scored three victories in Japan.

With most of the leading players skipping the tournament because of its half-sized purse — at ¥50 million by far the smallest of the season — the 43-year-old Kim could easily have enjoyed a wire-to-wire triumph at Niigata Prefecture's Forest Golf Club. He began the week with a seven-under-par 64, which normally would put its shooter in the lead. Instead, Hirokazu Kuniyoshi, an eight-year veteran without a win on his record, came up with a 63 and a brief flirt with glory.

The next day, Kuniyoshi managed just a 74 on his way to a 50th-place finish and Kim took charge. His four-birdie 67 for 131 put him on top by a stroke over Kazuhiro Kinjo, another unlikely challenger. Kinjo was also winless in his 12th season. Gregory Meyer of Australia and Tetsuji Hiratsuka were at 133.

Touched off by an eagle on the par-five first hole, Kim fashioned a six-under-par 65 with four subsequent birdies and two bogeys Saturday and stretched his lead to four strokes with his 196. Although he lost ground, Kinjo held onto second place with 68–200. Meyer remained in third place, sharing the 201 slot with Tomohiro Kondo, Hisao Ahara and Makoto Inoue. Kim remained solid Sunday, shooting 67, his fourth straight round of 67 or better, to build the five-stroke victory margin with his 263, the lowest 72-hole score of the season. Any hopes the surprising Kinjo had of catching Kim went out the window when he double-bogeyed the third hole, but he rallied to a 68 and finished second at 268.

Aiful Cup—¥120,000,000
Winner: Takuya Taniguchi

The location of the 2004 Aiful Cup tournament wasn't the only thing that was new that late July week. The 20-year-old tournament was moved to Daisen Ark Country Club at Mikokuchi, becoming the first Japan Tour event ever played in Tottori Prefecture. At week's end, the circuit had its fourth new winner of the season — 24-year-old Takuya Taniguchi, a Tohoku Fukushi University graduate in just his second year on tour.

Taniguchi set up the victory in the third round when he shot a five-under-par 66 for 201 that gave him a two-stroke lead, and he carried that margin to the bank. The lead had changed hands twice before that. Takenori Hiraishi, without a victory since the 2001 KBC Augusta tournament, fired the week's best round Thursday, a 64 that staked him to a two-stroke lead over Keiichiro Fukabori and Hideki Kase.

Makoto Inoue, making another run at his first career victory after seven years of trying, took over first place Friday when he rang up a 65 for 134. Taniguchi made his first move that day with a 67 that moved him into a second-place tie at 135 with Fukabori (69). Taniguchi then shot the 66–201 that put him two shots in front of two-time 2004 winner S.K. Ho of South Korea (66) and Fukabori (68).

Those two players appeared to be the only ones in position to challenge Takuya, with the rest of the field at least three shots farther back. But veteran Katsumasa Miyamoto jumped into second place at the finish Sunday, shooting a 66 to their 70s. Still, it was not enough to overtake Taniguchi, who put together a six-birdie, four-bogey 69 for the winning 270.

Sun Chlorella Classic—¥150,000,000
Winner: Y.E. Yang

Y.E. Yang took the first important step toward his dream of international fame and fortune when he landed his initial victory on the Japan Tour, a decisive three-stroke triumph in the rich Sun Chlorella Classic the first week of August. "It is unbelievable that I won such a big title," said the South Korean. "I believe that to become a top player in Asia it is necessary to become a top player in Japan. Then my aim is to become a successful player in the United States like (countryman) K.J. Choi (South Korea's most prominent world competitor)."

Yang, competing in his first full season in Japan after leading the qualifier for the 2004 circuit, joined S.K. Ho (two) and Kim Jong-duck as South Korean winners during the season's first 15 events and was the fifth first-time victor of the year.

Yang was in contention all the way at Otaru Country Club, a 7,327-yard challenge in Hokkaido. He started the week with a 67 and was just two strokes off the pace of Hideto Tanihara, who won the 2003 Asia/Japan Okinawa Open, the opening event of the 2004 season. Tanihara nearly set a new nine-hole tour record that day, shooting a 28 and just missing a seven-foot eagle putt on the ninth hole that would have established a new standard.

Third-year professional Ryuichi Oda, whose big game suited the long course, took the lead Friday with his second straight 68, but Yang moved within a stroke with his 70–137, tied for second place with David Smail (69-68) and Tsuyoshi Yoneyama (66-71). Oda had six of his seven birdies on the first nine. Yang made it to the top Saturday, piecing five birdies and two bogeys into a 69 for 206, joined there by Thailand's Prayad Marksaeng, a 38-year-old without a victory in Japan, who bogeyed his final hole for 67 and his 206.

Yang played on edge but steady in Sunday's final round en route to his closing 69 and 13-under-par 275 total. He had two birdies on the first nine, two more and a bogey on the second. "I was nervous," admitted the South Korean, "until I finished the 17th hole with a three-stroke lead." Smail (71) and Taiwan's Yeh Wei-tze (66) shared second place, a shot in front of Marksaeng (73) and Hideki Kase (71).

Hisamitsu KBC Augusta—¥100,000,000
Winner: Steve Conran

The run of first-time winners reached three in a row when the Japan Tour resumed action after a two-week layoff with the Hisamitsu KBC Augusta tournament at the end of August. In a not overly surprising development, Australian Steve Conran followed in the maiden-victory footsteps of Takuya Taniguchi (Aiful Cup) and Y.E. Yang (Sun Chlorella), the third player from Down Under to grab a title in Japan in 2004.

Conran, an occasional contender in the past on the circuit, never led until the very end at Keya Golf Club at Kyushu, Fukuoka Prefecture. Another Australian — Craig Jones — occupied the top spot Thursday with his six-under-par 65, manufactured from an eagle, five birdies and a bogey. He had a one-stroke lead over Riki Ikeda. Conran was three back at 68. The week's low round of 64 propelled Thailand's Thammanoon Srirot into the lead Friday with 136, one better than the 137s of Kazuhiko Hosokawa and Masaya Tomida. Conran (70) was then two back with four others, including Jones, who slipped back with a 73.

A proven winner took his turn in front Saturday. Frankie Minoza, the 44-year-old Philippine veteran who has seven Japan Tour titles on his record, squeezed ahead by a stroke with his 67–207, one shot better than the 208s of Conran (70), Toru Taniguchi (69), Liang Wen-chong (70) and Hosokawa (71). The victory was up for grabs all day Sunday until Conran birdied the final two holes for 69, 277 total and a one-stroke victory over Taniguchi (70) and Takashi Kamiyama (67). Minoza dropped into a six-way tie for fourth place when he slipped to a one-over-par 72.

Suntory Open—¥100,000,000
Winner: Hideki Kase

The Suntory Open, one of the formal Japan Tour's original events in the 1973 consolidation, provided the setting for a veteran's week in the sun. Hideki Kase, who had three victories spread over the previous 14 seasons, added his fourth at the par-70 Sobu Country Club course at Inzai, Chiba Prefecture. The 44-year-old broke from a three-way tie after 54 holes and posted a three-stroke victory.

Kase received minimal attention all week as international star Retief Goosen of South Africa drew much of the media splash but came up empty in his eighth career appearance in Japan. The U.S. Open champion, who had an otherwise outstanding season, put himself hopelessly behind with a 70-71 start, then rallied to finish in a five-way tie for seventh.

South Korean Y.E. Yang took a run at his second victory in the last three events, opening with 65 and tying for the lead with Scott Laycock of Australia, who won his only Japanese tournament in the 2002 Bridgestone Open. Both had unflawed five-birdie cards. Laycock pushed in front by a stroke Friday when he birdied the last three holes for 69 and 134. Yang shot 70 and was joined in the runner-up spot by Toru Taniguchi, Katsuya Nakagawa and Hideto Tanihara. Of interest that day, too, was 14-year-old, junior high school student Ryota Ito, who became the youngest player to ever make the cut on the circuit. He made it with three strokes to spare with 70-69 and eventually tied for 44th place.

Enter a man from the other end of the spectrum — 44-year-old Kase. He began the third round two strokes off the pace, shot 66, and climbed into a first-place tie at 202 with Yang and Tanihara, who both had 67s. Kase, the 1990 PGA champion, then wrapped up his first win since the 1996 Nikkei Cup with a solid 65 finish. The 267 total gave him the three-stroke margin over Taniguchi and Tomohiro Kondo, both of whom also shot 65s, and Nakagawa (66). Yang and Tanihara both had 70s and tied for fifth.

ANA Open—¥100,000,000
Winner: Chawalit Plaphol

Chawalit Plaphol's mid-September victory in the ANA Open had dual significance. Not only was it his first victory in seven years of campaigning on the Japan Tour, but it was also the first win ever on the circuit by a Thailand player. Chawalit played impressively in becoming the seventh first-time winner of 2004, starting the ANA Open one stroke off the pace and taking the lead for keeps the next day. He wound up with a one-stroke victory with a 17-under-par 271 total.

The 30-year-old Thai opened with a 66 on Sapporo Golf Club's Wattsu course in Kitahiroshima, Hokkaido Prefecture, joining Taichi Teshima, Toshimitsu Izawa and Katsumune Imai, one stroke behind the 65s of Mamoru Osanai, Takashi Kanemoto and India's Jyoti Randhawa, a first-time winner in the 2003 Suntory Open.

On Friday, Chawalit birdied five of the last eight holes for 65–131 and took a two-stroke lead over hot-running Y.E. Yang of South Korea. Imai (68) was at 134. Yang inched a stroke closer to the top Saturday. He shot 69 while Chawalit was keeping things together despite three bogeys and a double bogey and managing a 70 for 201. Izawa, the defending circuit champion who was far down the current money list while playing in just eight events, shot 67 and took over third place, three shots behind Chawalit.

Things turned into a final-pairing duel Sunday and nothing changed. Both Chawalit and Yang mustered 70s to finish one-two, the Thai hanging on despite three bogeys for the winning 271. Imai (69) and Hideto Tanihara (67), fourth on the money list even though winless during the season, finished at 204.

Acom International—¥120,000,000
Winner: Toru Suzuki

Timing was everything for Toru Suzuki at the Acom International, the tournament that carried the Japan Tour season into October and its run of bigger-money events. The 38-year-old Suzuki, who had scattered six victories over 11 previous seasons, walloped the field with a stunning, eight-under-par 63 in Saturday's third round to whip into a three-stroke lead at 13-under-par 200.

Suzuki never had to find out if it would hold up. Typhoon-induced heavy rains inundated the Ishioka Golf Club at Ogawa, Ibaraki Prefecture, Sunday and washed out the final round. The Acom became a 54-hole tournament and Suzuki a winner for a seventh time.

Obviously, the weather was a disappointment to the closest contenders. Paul Sheehan of Australia, seeking his second win of the season, had been the leader before Suzuki's charge and finished second at 203. The others with dashed hopes were at 205 — Steve Conran, Gregory Meyer, Yeh Wei-tze and Masashi Ozaki.

Sheehan and Meyer, among nine 68-shooters, were the only ones among the ultimate leading finishers who appeared high on the leaderboard after the first 18 holes. Chawalit Plaphol retained his momentum from his ANA Open victory, shot 67, and trailed only little-known Richard Lee of New Zealand. Suzuki was far down the standings with 72 and still trailed Sheehan by four strokes when he shot 65 Friday. Sheehan, the Fujisankei winner in May, had rounds of 68-65 for his second-round lead. Lee, with 69, slipped to second place at 135 with Yeh (66). Then came Suzuki's winning 63, the result of an eagle, seven birdies and a bogey.

Coca-Cola Tokai Classic—¥120,000,000
Winner: Katsumune Imai

Typhoons continued to play havoc with the Japan Tour as the players moved to Miyoshi in Aichi Prefecture for the Coca-Cola Tokai Classic, bringing about a 54-hole tournament for the second week in a row. The victory this time went to Katsumune Imai, who had broken through with his first win by an overwhelming seven-stroke margin in the top-level Casio World Open at the end of the 2003 season. The 32-year-old Imai had a much harder time of it in the Tokai Classic, though, having to defeat veteran Kazuhiko Hosokawa in the season's last playoff to claim the title.

The tournament started routinely at Miyoshi Country Club with Australian Craig Jones taking the first-round lead with 65, just as he did in August in the KSB Augusta then fell from contention. This time, it was a plunge as he came back Friday with 84 after the 65 at Miyoshi had given him a two-stroke lead over Paul Sheehan and Yusaku Miyazato.

The second round didn't have a true leader until early Saturday morning when Imai, one of 38 men who were still on the course when play was suspended Friday after two rain delays, posted his 68 for 138. He led by three over Hosokawa (71-70), whose most recent of seven victories was in the 2001 Acom International, and Toru Suzuki (74-67), the previous week's Acom winner. After squeezing in the completion of that round, officials cancelled the scheduled third round because of the pouring rains from an approaching typhoon.

Imai struggled a bit with his game in improved weather Sunday, giving up two strokes of his lead on the first eight holes. Ultimately, he birdied the 18th hole for 72 to match Hosokawa's 69–210 and parred the 18th on the first hole of the playoff to land the title.

Japan Open—¥120,000,000
Winner: Toru Taniguchi

Pickings had been rather slim for the better part of the last two seasons for Toru Taniguchi as he prepared to play in the Japan Open on the testing Katayamazu Golf Club's Hakusan course at Kaga, Ishikawa Prefecture. Taniguchi, age 36, was winless and had managed only a handful of high finishes since his pinnacle 2004 season when he rode four victories to the year's money title.

Then things changed for the better. His game jelled and he sailed to a four-stroke victory with the season's first wire-to-wire performance. Unshaken by another week affected by bad weather that skied the scoring in the final two rounds, Taniguchi posted the only sub-par total — a three-under 285 — and won the circuit's most important title by four strokes. It was his eighth career victory in Japan.

Taniguchi began his march to the title with a four-under-par 68 Thursday, taking a one-stroke lead over Dinesh Chand of Fiji and two over four others, including four-time Open champion Tsuneyuki Nakajima. Storm delays and darkness prevented completion of the second round Friday, but when Taniguchi finished Saturday morning with another 68, he had opened a four-shot lead over Chand, the Yomiuri Open winner in June, and Nobuhiro Masuda.

The windy conditions were so fierce Saturday, though, that David Smail's 69, the only score in the 60s in the round, enabled him to cut Taniguchi's margin in half. Taniguchi struggled to a 75, bogeying four of the last six holes, but remained two in front of Smail with his 211. Masuda shot 74 and went into the last round three behind and tied there with Toshimitsu Izawa (73), the 2003 season champion.

Matters got even worse Sunday. Not a single player broke par on the demanding course, so Taniguchi's 74 turned the trick. He eased home with the four-stroke margin over Smail, who shot 76; Yeh Wei-tze of Taiwan, whose par 72 was the best score of the day, and Izawa (75). They were one over par at 289.

Bridgestone Open—¥110,000,000
Winner: Toru Taniguchi

Toru Taniguchi remained on a high from his Japan Open victory when the tour moved on to Sodegaura Country Club in Chiba for the Bridgestone Open, and he became the season's first and only winner of back-to-back tournaments. This time, though, Taniguchi had his hands full as he had to overcome a three-stroke deficit in the final round and fend off challenges by Shigeki Maruyama, Japan's best known international star, back from America and playing in his first tournament in his home country in three years, and Shinichi Yokota.

Still riding the victory momentum, Taniguchi registered a six-birdie 66 in the opening round and tied Tomohiro Kondo and Dinesh Chand for the lead. Four others, including KBC Augusta winner Steve Conran and China's Liang Wen-chong, had 67s. Takahiro Takayama, a newcomer to contending positions, surged in front Friday. Takayama birdied six of his first nine holes, added two more birdies and a bogey on his second nine for 65–134 and a one-stroke lead over Katsumune Imai (69-66), the Tokai Classic winner. Taniguchi fell three off the pace when he finished bogey, double bogey for 71–137, tied there with, among others, David Smail, the Japan Open runner-up. Maruyama seemed out of contention eight back after rounds of 74-68.

Takayama held onto first place Saturday with his second 69 for 203, but was joined at the top by Smail (66) and Imai (68). Taniguchi shot 69 for his 206 and Maruyama edged closer with 67–209. Yokota also was at 209 and both came out firing Sunday. Both shot 64s, Maruyama with an eagle, seven birdies and a bogey and Yokota with two eagles and four birdies. "It looked like things might be heading for a playoff," Taniguchi noted later, but he was nearly as hot as those pursuers. He reeled off six birdies for 66, and his 16-under-par 272 total slid him into victory by the single stroke. His ninth career triumph made Taniguchi the fourth two-time winner of the season.

ABC Championship—¥120,000,000
Winner: Makoto Inoue

On Monday morning of ABC Championship week in Tojo, Makoto Inoue was on the outside looking in. He was merely one of a large group of players trying to win one of the few spots allotted to the tournament qualifier that week. Six days later, Inoue was standing on the 18th green acknowledging the gallery applauding him as the new ABC Championship winner. He had just accomplished what only two other players had done in the history of the Japan Tour — won a tournament as a Monday qualifier — and the last time it happened was in 1985.

Inoue, without a victory since beginning his tour career late in the 1998 season, became the eighth first-time winner when he nipped Toru Suzuki, the Acom champion, and Ryoken Kawagishi by a stroke at the ABC Golf Club at the end of October. The 29-year-old finished with a 15-under-par 273 total.

First-round laurels went to veteran Hisayuki Sasaki, a successful player in the 1990s but winless since 1997. Sasaki opened with a six-birdie 66 and took a one-stroke edge over Toshimitsu Izawa, a successful player in the 2000s. The lead changed hands Friday as Takashi Kamiyama, the JCB Sendai winner in June, shot 66 for 134 and moved one shot in front of Sasaki (69) and two ahead of Toru Suzuki (71-65), Taichi Teshima (68-68) and Inoue (69-67).

Inoue rolled in an 18-foot eagle putt on the 18th green Saturday to cap a 66 and went two strokes up on the field with his 202. He also had five birdies and a bogey in the round. The 37-year-old Kawagishi, who has never matched his "rookie of the year" season of 1990 when he scored three of his six career victories, bolted into the picture Saturday with 64, the week's lowest round, to join Kamiyama (70) and Suzuki (68) at 203.

The outcome was in doubt until the final hole Sunday. Inoue lost the lead to Kawagishi with bogeys at the 11th and 12th holes, drew even again, and finally wrapped up the victory with a birdie at the 18th hole for 71 and the 273. Suzuki and Kawagishi had 70s for 274, and Kamiyama 71 for 275 and solo fourth place.

Asahi-Ryokuken Yomiuri Aso-Iizuka Memorial Open—¥100,000,000
Winner: Y.E. Yang

The new kid on the block — the Asahi-Ryokuken Yomiuri Aso-Iizuka Memorial Open — was established in northern Kyushu as a three-fold recognition of successful history and at the same time as somewhat of a reclamation project. For three days it appeared that Toshimitsu Izawa was going to use it as a reclamation project for his frustrating season only to watch Y.E. Yang snatch the victory when his game crumbled in the final round.

Hoping to attract new activity to an old coal-mining area that had been devastated by heavy rains the previous summer, organizers filled the late-season gap in the schedule with the tournament which celebrated two anniversaries of Yomiuri newspapers, national and local, and the 30th year of the tournament site at the Aso-Iizuka Golf Club.

They got a plus right away when Izawa, the No. 1 player on the tour in 2003 and winner of 14 tournaments in his fine career, and Ryoken Kawagishi, another popular player hungry for a victory, opened with exciting, seven-under-par 65s for the lead. Izawa's round was topped by the second albatross (double eagle) of his career on the par-five 17th hole, where he holed his five-wood second shot from 252 yards. Kawagishi birdied his last four holes for his 65. Kaname Yokoo was just a stroke back.

Izawa maintained his hot pace Friday, shooting 67 for 132 and a three-stroke lead over Katsumasa Miyamoto (68-67), four over Kawagishi (65-71), Tatsuya Mitsuhashi and Taichiro Kiyota, both with 71-65 cards. Izawa had six birdies and a bogey in the round. Miyamoto narrowed Izawa's lead to two Saturday, shooting another 67–202 to Izawa's 68–200. Shingo Katayama and Shinichi Yokota were three shots further back, and South Korea's Yang was at 206 after rounds of 69-68-69.

Izawa's hopes vanished Sunday. He suffered through a 75 that dropped him to a four-way tie for third in the final standings. Yang, on the other hand, caught fire. He seized the lead with five birdies on the first 10 holes, added two more coming in for 65 and the winning 17-under-par 271. That victory, coupled with his earlier win in the Sun Chlorella Classic, made him the season's fifth double winner. Katayama padded his money list lead by picking off second place with 68–273.

Mitsui Sumitomo Visa Taiheiyo Masters—¥150,000,000
Winner: Darren Clarke

Talk about living up to expectations! The committee of the Mitsui Sumitomo Visa Taiheiyo Masters issued three special invitations to the 2004 tournament to PGA European Tour stars Darren Clarke, Lee Westwood and Graeme McDowell and were rewarded when Clarke led from start to finish, Westwood tied for second and McDowell shot four rounds in the 60s to finish in a three-way tie for sixth.

Actually, Clarke's was not an outright wire-to-wire victory. The burly shot-maker from Northern Ireland shared the first-round lead with Ryoken Kawagishi, who was in the same position the week before at Aso-Iizuka. They shot 66s. Clarke birdied his first three holes en route to a 31 on his first nine, while Kawagishi's round was highlighted by a third-hole eagle. Toru Taniguchi, making a late-season surge, was one back with Hideki Kase, Nozomi Kawahara and Taiwan's Yeh Wei-tze.

Clarke advanced to a two-stroke lead Friday on the Gotemba course of the Taiheiyo Club in Shizuoka Prefecture. He had two eagles to go with three birdies as he posted a bogey-free 65 for 131 and went two strokes up on Shingo Katayama. The money list leader also shot 65 and, in turn, was two ahead of Yeh and three in front of Kawagishi (70) and Kawahara (69).

Clarke birdied two of his last three holes Saturday for 67, as he widened his margin to four strokes at 198. Kawahara produced a 66 and climbed into second place at 202. Westwood, who won the Taiheiyo Masters three years in a row in the late 1990s, shot 67 for 204, tied with Yeh (69). Clarke put on the finishing touches Sunday, noting, "I didn't think I'd have too much trouble winning, but you never know what can happen." He ran off five birdies and took a lone bogey for 68 and finished six strokes in front of Westwood (67) and Kawahara (66). It was his second victory in Japan, where he won the Chunichi Crowns in 2001.

Dunlop Phoenix—¥200,000,000
Winner: Tiger Woods

Only time would tell, of course, but the significance of Tiger Woods' blow-away victory in the Dunlop Phoenix tournament in late November may turn out to be far greater than the respect it may have gotten in world circles at the time. By the high standards expected of him, Woods had gone through a mediocre year, with only a victory in the WGC - Accenture Match Play to add to his impressive win column when he arrived at the par-70 Phoenix Country Club course.

Andrew Redington/Getty Images

Phil Mickelson shot 31 on the final nine and held off Ernie Els for his first major victory.

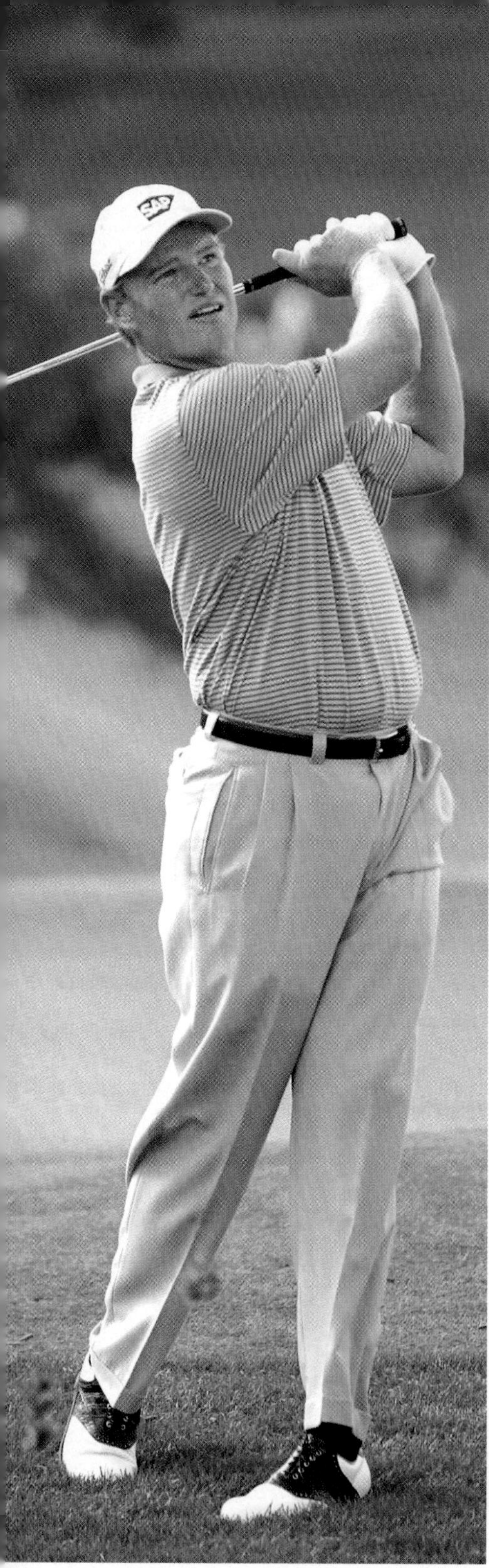

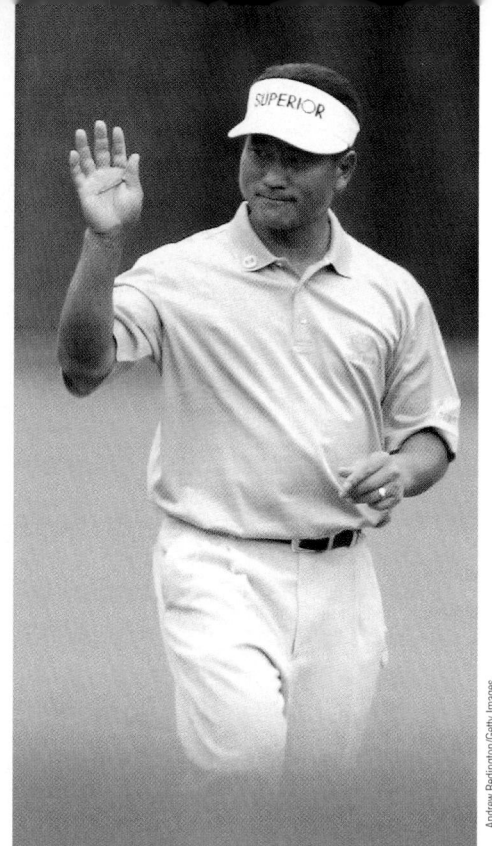

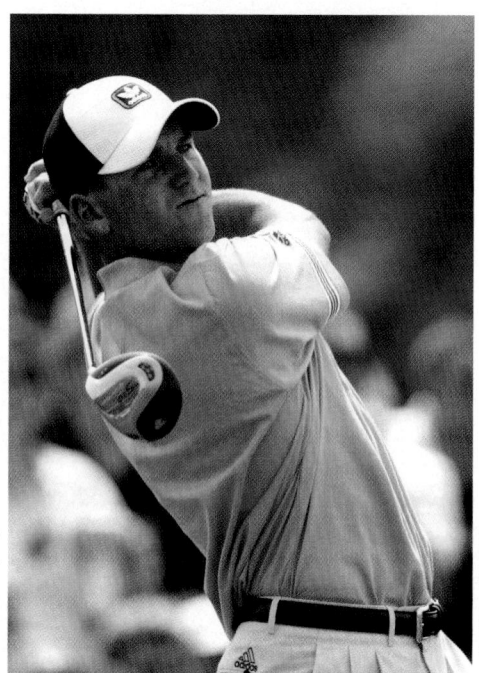

Ernie Els closed with 67, one stroke short.

David Cannon/Getty Images

K.J. Choi's 69 brought him to third place.

Andrew Redington/Getty Images

Sergio Garcia shot 66 to tie for fourth.

David Cannon/Getty Images

Andrew Redington/Getty Images

Bernhard Langer's strong play was surprising.

Andrew Redington/Getty Images

Justin Rose led through 36 holes.

Harry How/Getty Images

Chris DiMarco struggled in the final group.

Harry How/Getty Images

Arnold Palmer played his 50th and final Masters.

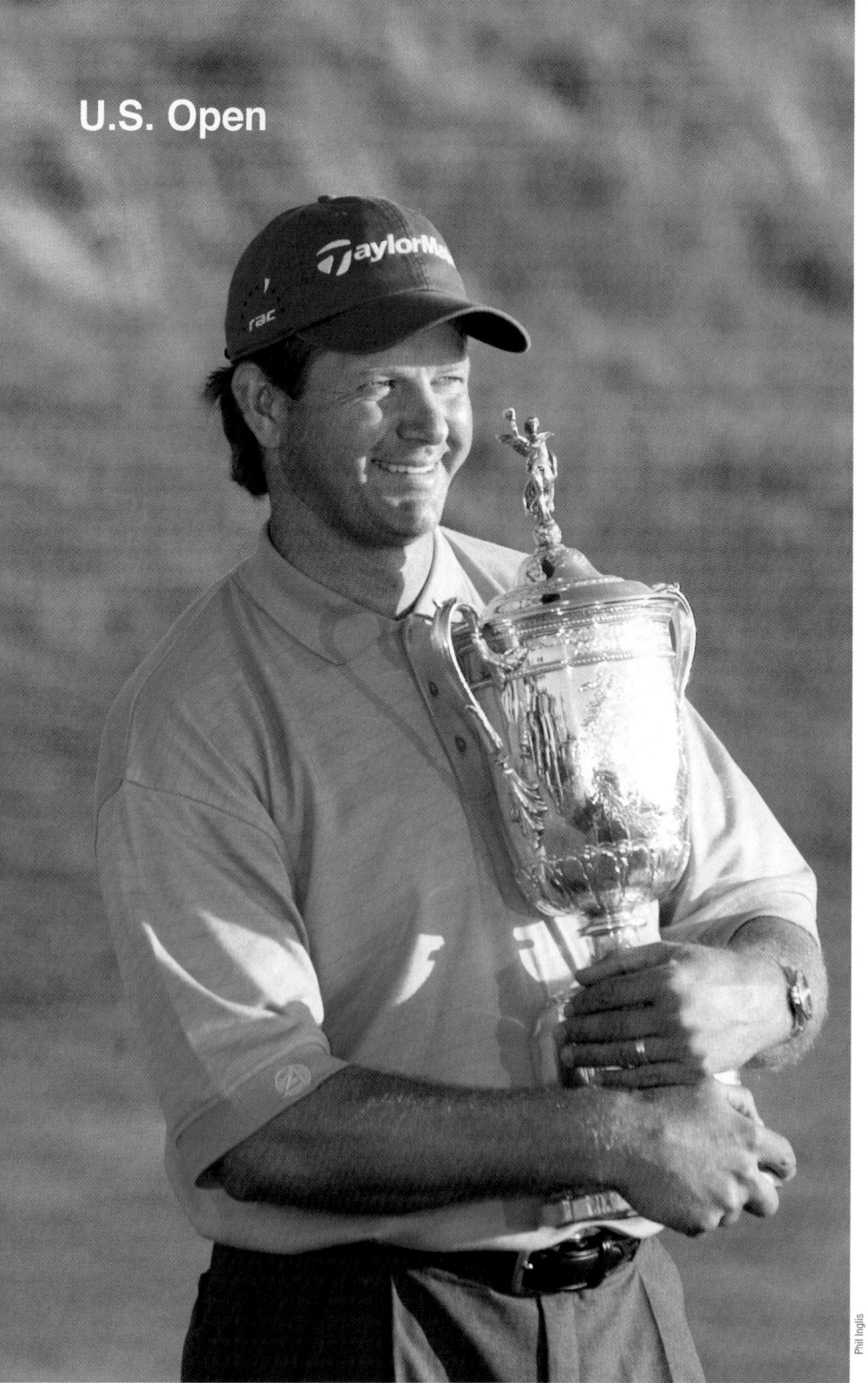

Retief Goosen won his second U.S. Open title with his miraculous short game.

Phil Mickelson double-bogeyed the 71st hole.

Jeff Maggert placed third, five shots back.

Jay Haas had a 66 to start.

Ernie Els shot 80 in the final group.

Shigeki Maruyama tied for the opening lead.

The unflappable Todd Hamilton sank a two-foot putt to win after a pitch-and-run from 30 yards.

Ernie Els had a putt to win in regulation.

Phil Mickelson was one stroke behind.

A final 67 lifted Lee Westwood to fourth place.

Colin Montgomerie carried the Scottish hopes.

All Tiger Woods could do was tie for ninth.

PGA Championship

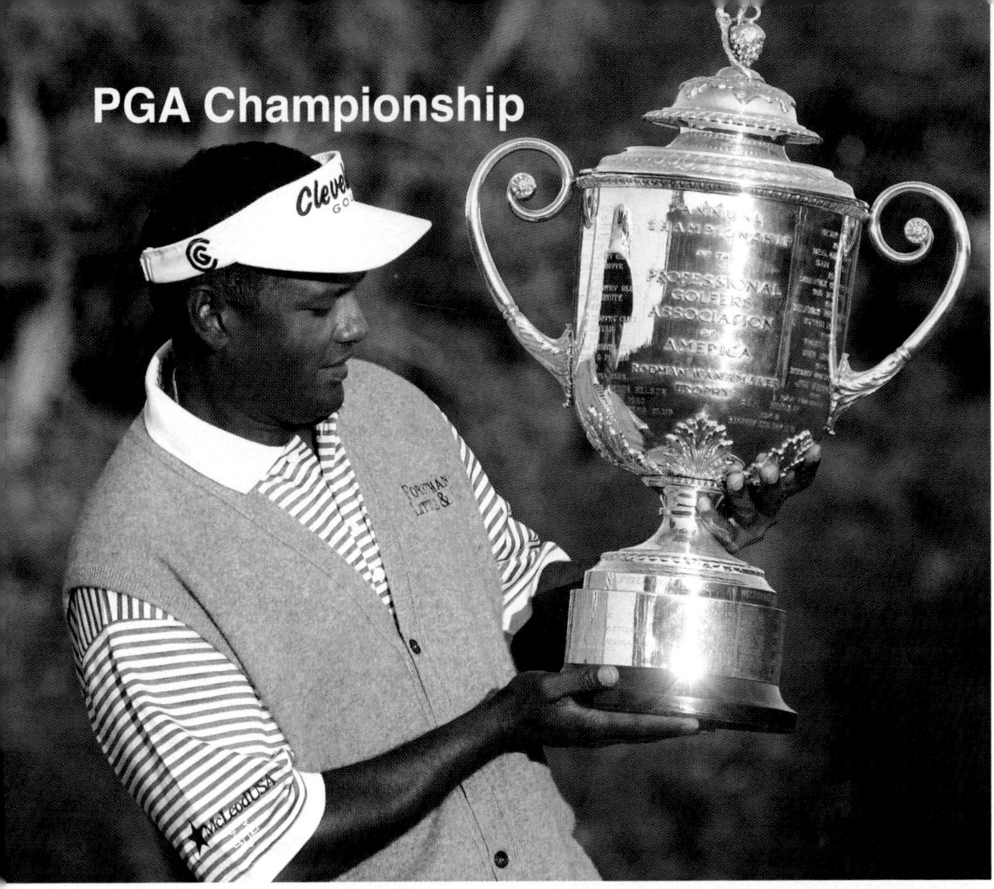

Ross Kinnaird/Getty Images

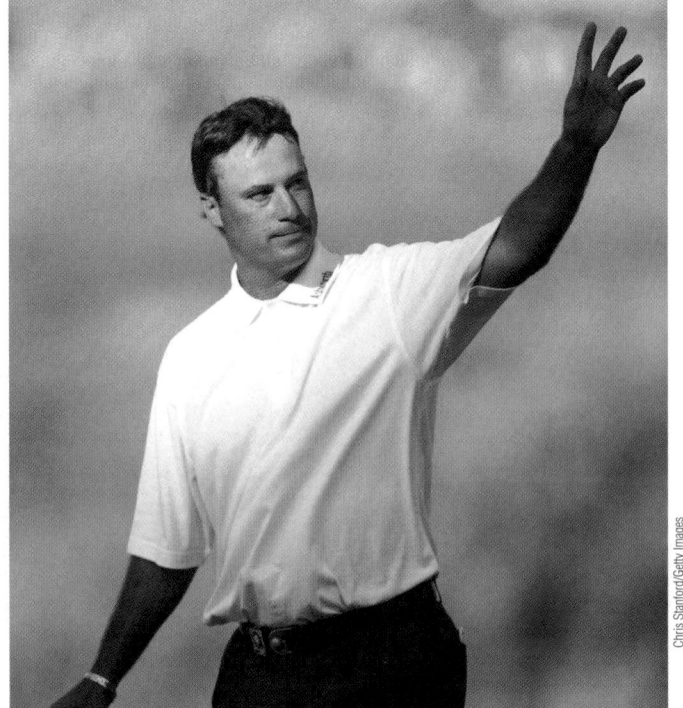

After 76 in the final round, Vijay Singh won his second title in the PGA Championship in a playoff.

Chris Stanford/Getty Images

Chris DiMarco got in the playoff with 71 in the fourth round.

A 75 put Justin Leonard in the playoff.

Ernie Els tied for fourth, one behind.

Chris Riley shot 73 to share fourth place.

Darren Clarke opened with 65.

U.S. PGA Tour

Victory in the Deutsche Bank Championship made Vijay Singh No. 1 in the world.

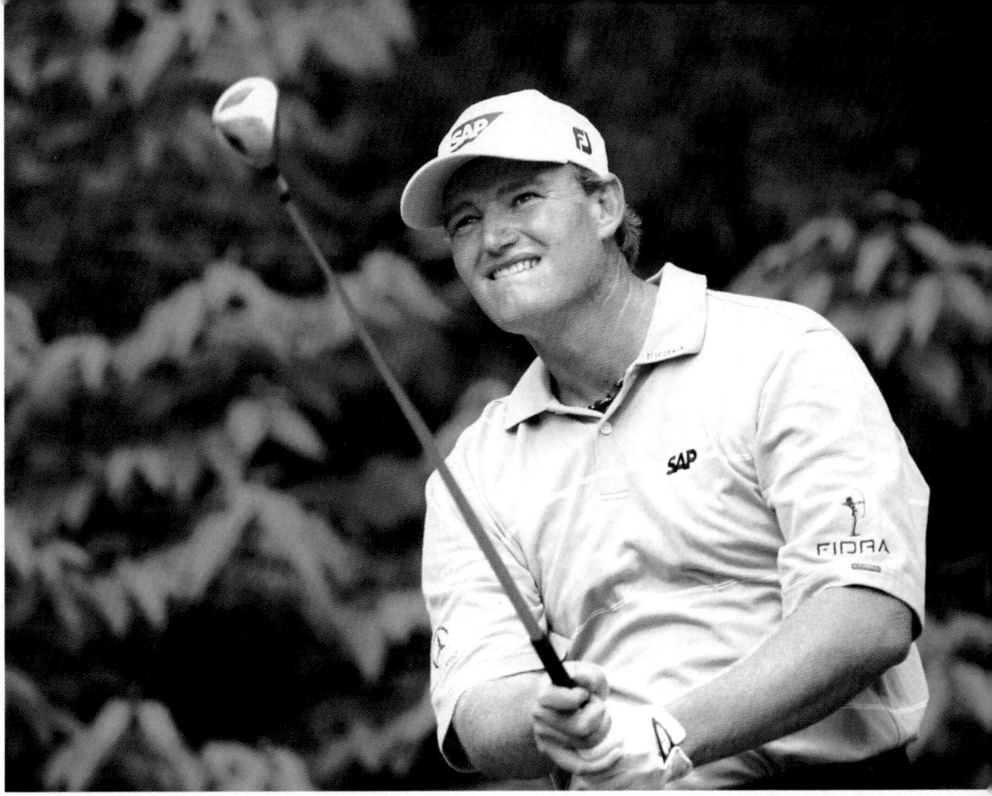

Scott Halleran/Getty Images

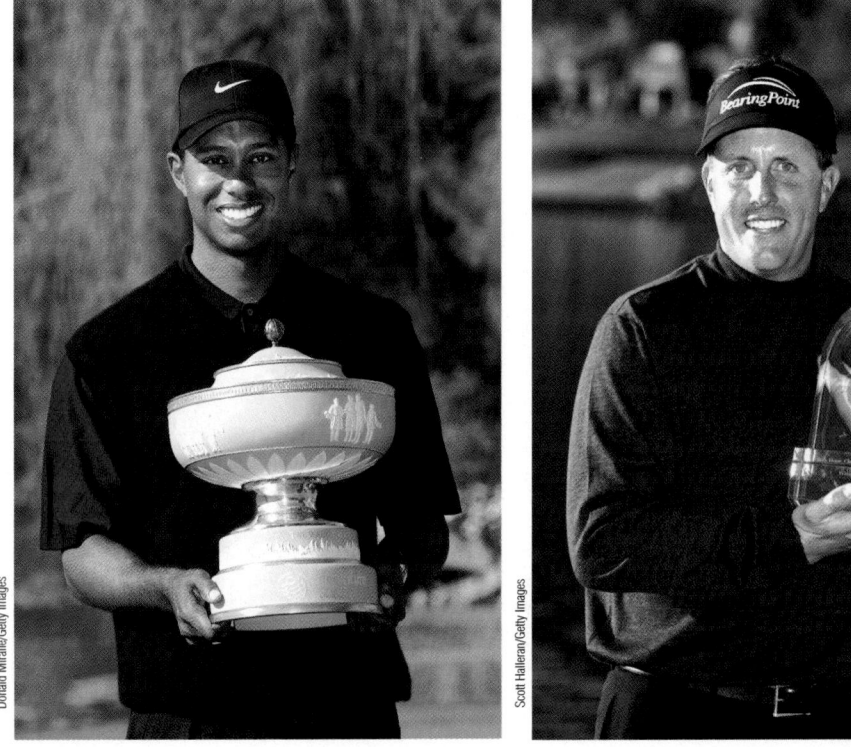

Arguably Ernie Els had a better year than all but Singh, winning five times worldwide.

Donald Miralle/Getty Images

Tiger Woods' Accenture win avoided a shutout.

Scott Halleran/Getty Images

Phil Mickelson won early in the year too.

Retief Goosen had two big U.S. wins.

Stuart Appleby opened the year with a win.

Todd Hamilton also won at Honda.

Australian Adam Scott posted two victories.

Ronald Martinez/Getty Images

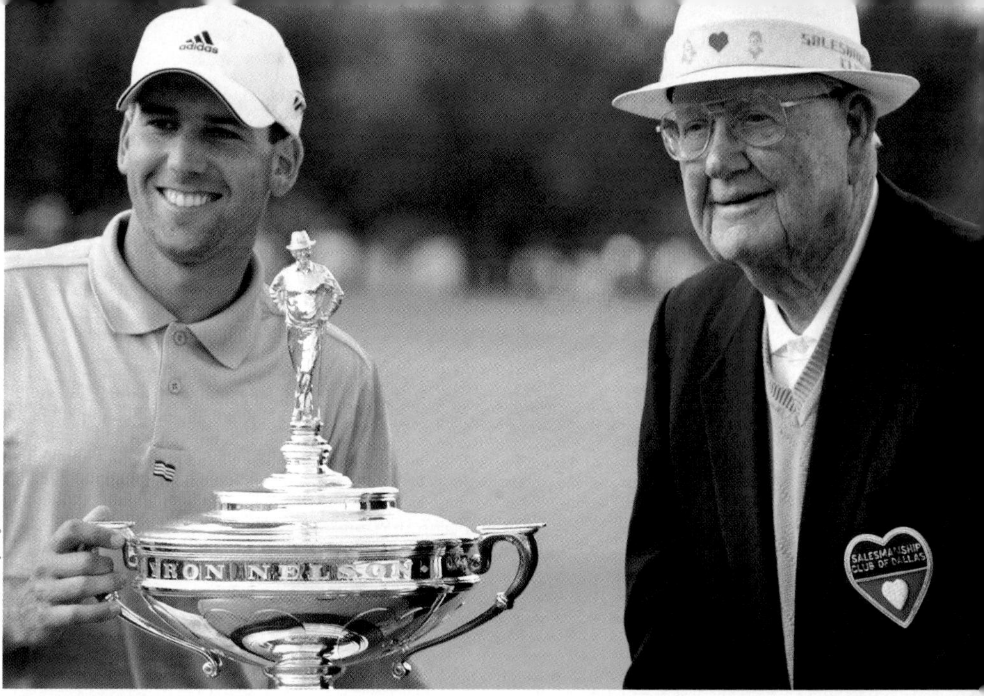

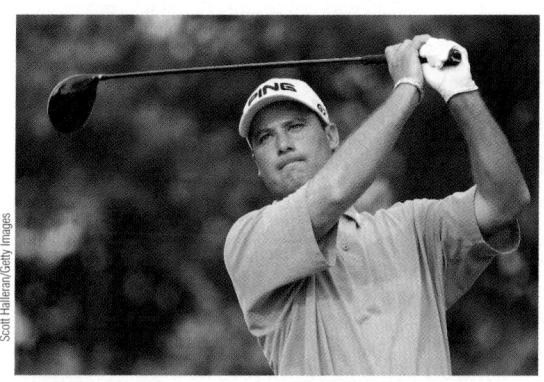

Sergio Garcia received the prize from host Byron Nelson for one of his three worldwide wins.

Scott Halleran/Getty Images

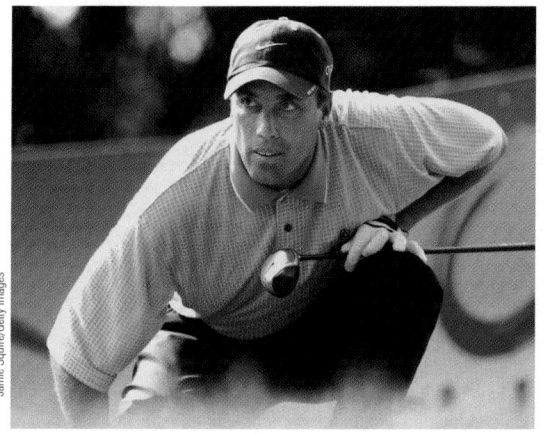

Chris DiMarco was second in the PGA and FBR Open.

Jamie Squire/Getty Images

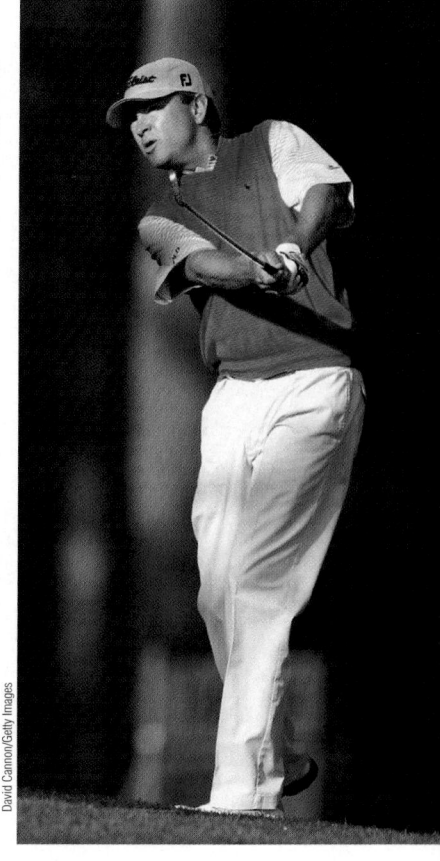

Stephen Ames took the Western Open trophy.

David Cannon/Getty Images

Davis Love was runner-up at Accenture.

Mike Weir won, but not in Canada.

Stewart Cink was the Heritage and NEC champion.

Chad Campbell had to play like Arnold Palmer.

Mark Hensby won, but skipped the Open.

Zack Johnson got his first at BellSouth.

David Toms fell 11 places to world No. 20.

Wrist surgery held back Jim Furyk.

Jay Haas didn't play like a senior.

Kenny Perry tied for third in The Players.

Ever-popular John Daly made a comeback.

David Duval rejoined the tour in June.

The Players Championship

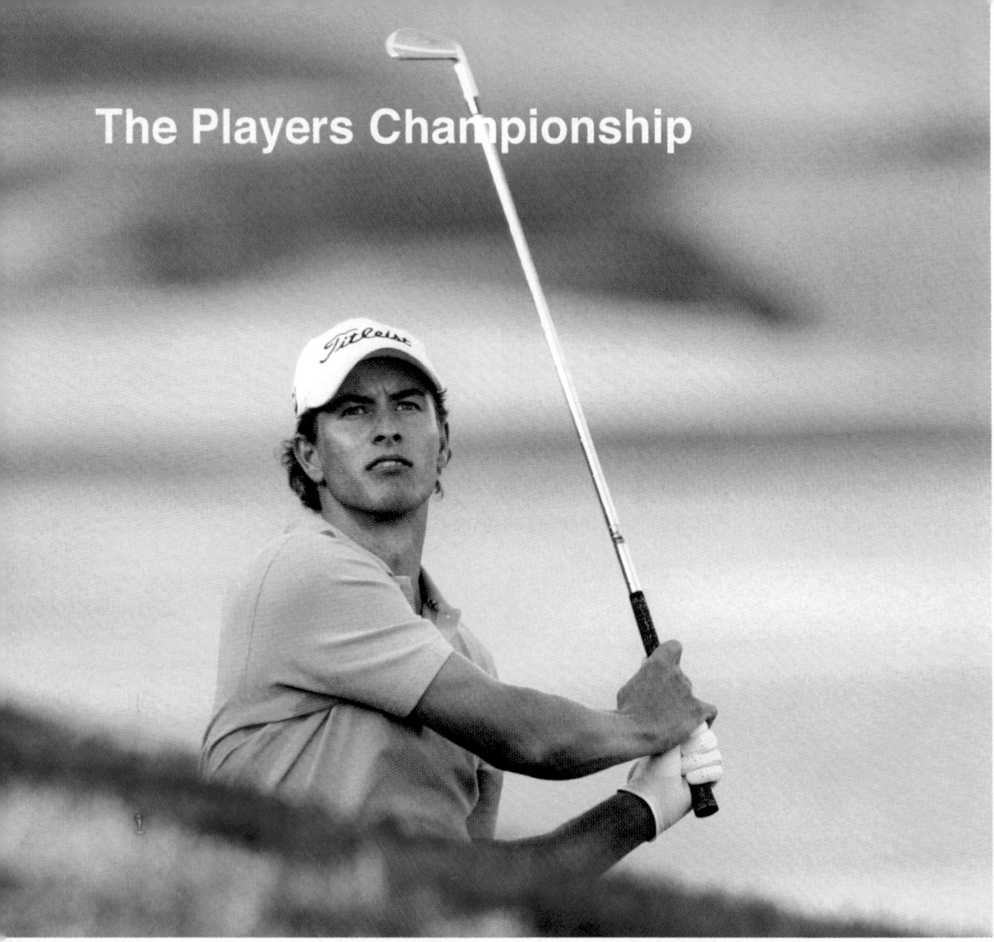

Andy Lyons/Getty Images

At age 23, and with a tip from Greg Norman, Adam Scott became the youngest winner.

Andy Lyons/Getty Images

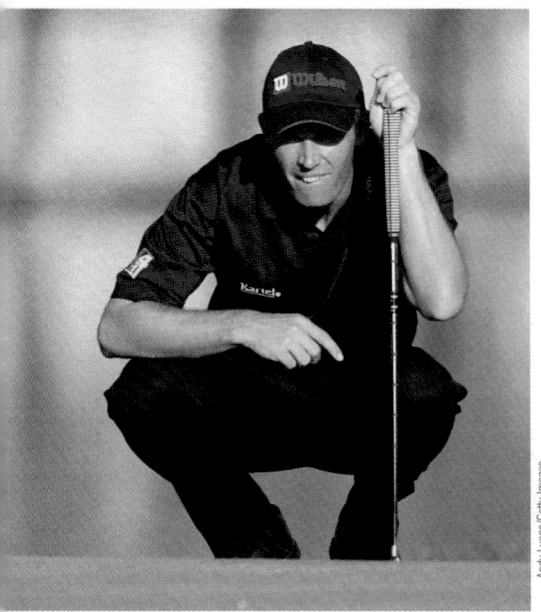

A final 66 lifted Padraig Harrington to second.

Donald Miralle/Getty Images

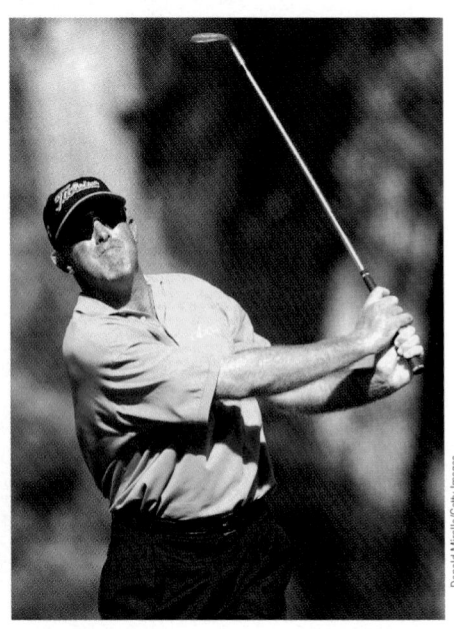

Frank Lickliter was in a tie for third.

"It's huge," he said of his eight-stroke triumph, his first ever in Japan. "Just look at the past champions of this tournament. It's one of the biggest tournaments in Japan." (Actually, by far the richest, with its ¥200 million purse.)

"I'm sure it's not going to be important everywhere. But just the way I played here with four solid rounds is enough for me. I'm very excited about the prospects for next year because of the way I played here."

The way he played there was vintage Woods. He birdied his first hole, made four other birdies, and jumped off to a three-stroke lead with a 65 in a steady rain in Thursday's first round. It was the first time all season that Tiger led after 18 holes and he never looked back. In his immediate wake that day were Kaname Yokoo at 68, Hideto Tanihara, Kim Jong-duck and Craig Parry at 69.

Woods retained his three-stroke lead Friday when both he and Yokoo put up 67s, Tiger for 132, Kaname for 135. American Christian Pena, a regular in Japan, fired the day's best round of 63 and took over third place. Woods had four birdies and took his first bogey of the tournament when he trapped his approach at the 16th hole.

If there had been any doubt about the outcome, Woods ended that uncertainty Saturday. With a solid 65, he ballooned his lead to 10 strokes, matching the 54-hole position he had in the 2000 U.S. Open Championship at Pebble Beach. He had six birdies and a bogey as he left the rest of the field in the dust. Behind him at 207 in what obviously had become a fight for second place were Naomichi Ozaki, Sweden's Daniel Chopra and Ryoken Kawagishi, making his presence known in a third straight tournament.

Kawagishi won that secondary battle with a closing 65 for 272, putting him two shots ahead of K.J. Choi, South Korea's international star. Kawagishi's 65 also reduced Woods' final margin to eight strokes as he breezed to a 67 with five birdies and a pair of bogeys for a final 264. "Going through all the changes I've made in my swing, it was just a matter of time," he summarized. As for his record, the Dunlop Phoenix victory was the 56th of his career — 40 on the U.S. PGA Tour, eight on other world tours and eight others in unofficial events.

Casio World Open—¥140,000,000
Winner: David Smail

The Casio World Open — the third and last in the November series of rich events on the Japan Tour — didn't bring in quite the international star power of the two previous events, but it certainly had a foreign flavor all week, ending with New Zealand's David Smail, the 2002 Casio winner, scoring a one-stroke victory with his 12-under-par 276 total. It was his third victory in eight seasons on the circuit, the highlight of which was his triumph in the 2002 Japan Open.

The tournament also unveiled the potential of young American Hunter Mahan. The 22-year-old from Oklahoma State, the 2002 U.S. Amateur runner-up, made his first challenging bid for a professional victory in the Casio, contending all the way and finishing second with 277.

While Smail made his moves over the weekend, Mahan was at the top from the start. Mahan opened with 66 and tied veteran Katsunori Kuwabara for the lead, one stroke in front of Hideki Kase, the Suntory winner in September, and moment-of-glory Tadahisa Inoue. Another of the visitors entered the picture Friday. Charl Schwartzel of South Africa shot 67–135 and edged in front by a stroke over Mahan (70), Smail (70-66), Takahiro Takayama (70-66) and Hisayuki Sasaki (68-68).

Smail took over Saturday. He shot a three-under-par 69 for 205 and went two ahead of Mahan (71) and three in front of Takashi Kamiyama (68) and Schwartzel, who slipped to 73. Smail was not rock solid Sunday, but his three-birdie, two-bogey 71 was enough to hold off Mahan, who closed with 70–277 to match his highest finish in a tour tournament.

Golf Nippon Series JT Cup—¥100,000,000
Winner: Paul Sheehan

Australian Brendan Jones made an effort to become the Japan Tour season's only player with more than two victories in the bag. But at the end, another Australian — Paul Sheehan — joined the sizeable group of double winners when he stepped out to a four-stroke victory in the season-ending Golf Nippon Series JT Cup, the tournament with a 26-player field of the year's victors and major money winners.

Jones, who scored early-season victories in the Tsuruya and Mizuno Opens, went after No. 3 early when he began the tournament at Tokyo's Yomiuri Country Club with five birdies and a five-under-par 65. That was one stroke better than Hideki Kase, the 44-year-old Suntory winner who enjoyed the most lucrative season of his career. Kase repeated his 66 Friday and moved into a first-place deadlock with Jones, who shot 67. Sheehan remained close with his 69-65–134, joined there by Keiichiro Fukabori (also 69-65) and David Smail (67-67), coming off his Casio World Open victory the previous Sunday.

Fukabori inched a shot in front of Sheehan (66) and Kase (68) Saturday with his 65 for 199 as Jones faltered with 70–202. In between at 201 were Katsumasa Miyamoto and Smail, who shot his third straight 67. Nobody had an answer for Sheehan Sunday. The Aussie fired another 66 for his 14-under-par 266 total and the four-shot win, winding up his best season in Japan with his first two victories and fifth place on the final money list. Y.E. Yang placed third when he finished with 68 and took one of the second-place checks for ¥10.55 million. The other went to Miyamoto, who had 69 for his 270.

Although he didn't finish higher than sixth place in the final month of the season, Shingo Katayama held onto the No. 1 position on the money list, finishing with ¥119,512,374, nearly ¥18 million better than runner-up Toru Taniguchi. Katayama also won the money title in 2000.

Asia/Japan Okinawa Open—¥100,000,000
Winner: Kiyoshi Miyazato

Proud as he was of his little sister and her tremendous achievements during the 2004 Japan LPGA Tour season, Kiyoshi Miyazato just couldn't let Ai have the family stage completely to herself. He gave the fans in his native Okinawa one final chance to unleash partisan cheers with a remarkable victory in the mid-December Asia/Japan Okinawa Open, the event that, for the last three years, has launched the Japan Tour's new season and ended the 2004 Asian Tour campaign.

While 19-year-old Ai was dazzling the world of women's golf with her brilliant five-victory rookie season on the Japan LPGA Tour, Kiyoshi and brother Yusaku were laboring on the Japan Tour with middling success, finishing 75th and 50th on the money list respectively. Then came the Okinawa Open on the familiar Naha Golf Club course at Kochinda.

Early rounds indicated that India's Jeev Milkha Singh was heading for his first victory in Japan. After Charlie Wi of South Korea surrendered his first-round lead (65) to Singh on Friday, the international player took control of the tournament. Singh, who had started the tournament two back at 67, generated an overwhelming nine-under-par 62 and roared four strokes in front with 129. It was Singh's lowest score ever on a par-71 course. Lin Chie-hsiang, who had shared the runner-up slot the first day at 66 with Dinesh Chand of Fiji, remained second after shooting 67–133 Friday. Wi had 69 for 134. Although both Miyazatos made the 36-hole cut, Kiyoshi rested in 21st place with 138 and Yusaku in 57th with 141.

Singh returned to earth Saturday, but his 69–198 enabled him to preserve his four-stroke lead going into the final round. Hideki Kase was at 202, Scott Barr, Soshi Tajima and Wi at 203. After a 68, Kiyoshi Miyazato seemed too far back in an 18th-place tie with an eight-stroke deficit. But Sunday afternoon at Naha turned into one of most exciting and competitive battles imaginable. Nearly a dozen players could have won the title when Singh let his big lead slip away.

Miyazato birdied the first two holes, and by the time he had worked out five more, he found himself in the lead. He dropped back into a deadlock when he bogeyed the 16th with a trapped approach, but gained his final narrow margin when his charmed round got one more boost as a 30-foot putt dropped for the winning birdie, a round of 64 and a winning score of 270, his first career victory. Six players finished at 271 — Masahiro Kuramoto and Mamoru Osanai with 67s, Wi and Barr with 68s, Kase with 69 and the disappointed Singh with 73.

12. Australasian Tour

Peter Lonard overcame Ross River Fever, a debilitating mosquito-carried disease, to become one of Australia's most consistent performers both at home and abroad. During the first half of 2004 Lonard also had to put up with a rib injury. He struggled in America and Europe. Although he retained his card comfortably on the European Tour, it was a different matter in the United States after slipping to 118th on the money list, just enough but disappointing after two solid top-50 seasons in the previous two years.

But when Lonard returned to Australia at the end of the year it all came right as he won three tournaments in a row. The first was at the New South Wales Open, a fine reward for supporting his state championship despite the event being on the second-tier circuit, the Von Nida Tour.

The following week it was a different story entirely as Lonard won his second successive Australian Open. There are some pretty strong names who have successfully defended the championship in the last 50 years, and Lonard is now ranked along with Arnold Palmer, Jack Nicklaus, Greg Norman and Aaron Baddeley. But what made Lonard's victory at the Australian Club all the more special was that it was the centenary edition of the Australian Open. "Hopefully, I'll always be known as the Centenary champion," said Lonard.

Lonard held his nerve again a week later to win the Cadbury Schweppes Australian PGA Championship. "Last week was fantastic, this is unbelievable," Lonard said. Reflecting on his season, the 37-year-old said, "It has been tough. Over the last three months I have felt it coming back together. I've been working on the same things week after week, and when I do the video stuff it all looks the same."

Lonard did not qualify for the Order of Merit, so Richard Green's victory in the MasterCard Masters, the last event of the year, clinched the No. 1 position on the money list. It was the left-handed Green's first victory on home soil and came in his hometown. Ironic, then, that it should give him exemptions to some of the biggest events all around the world. It would give Green the chance to play more in America, but with a three-year-old daughter, he said he would still base himself in Europe.

With Ernie Els retaining the Heineken Classic and England's Brian Davis winning the ANZ Championship, there was only one Australian to win on the European Tour in 2004, Brett Rumford claiming the Nissan Irish Open. Nick O'Hern, yet another of the Australian left-handers, finished 12th on the Order of Merit and was a relentless lurker on the leaderboard, finishing with an impressive 11 top-10 finishes.

Stuart Appleby got the season in America off to a fine start with victory at the Mercedes Championships, and there followed victories for Mark Hensby, Rod Pampling and Andre Stolz. But the highlight of the year was Adam Scott's win at The Players Championship at Sawgrass, despite a harrowing final hole when he found the water with his approach shot. Scott added a victory in the Booz Allen Classic, and the young Australian finished the year seventh on the money list and challenging for a top-10 place on the Official World Golf Ranking.

Holden New Zealand Open—NZ$700,000
Winner: Terry Price

The season very nearly opened with a fairy tale. Indeed, it is rare that the winner of a tournament admits to wishing he had lost, but that was the case with Terry Price at the Holden New Zealand Open. Price won by a single shot over the New Zealand amateur Brad Heaven at the Grange Club in Auckland.

Heaven appeared to be having a week that was entirely in keeping with his name. He shared the lead after the first round with a six-under-par score of 64. After two days he led by two strokes after adding a 66. He slipped back with a third round of 72, but going into the final day found himself only a shot behind Price, who had opened with rounds of 69, 65 and 67.

It was a fine dual in the last round, with both men scoring 70s, although it was only at the 16th that Price birdied to go ahead for good. Heaven had the chance to get into a playoff at the last, but his birdie putt came up six inches short. Peter Senior and David Smail shared third place, three strokes behind Price's nine-under-par 271 total.

It was the 43-year-old Price's second victory in the New Zealand Open, but he was fully aware of the impact that a win for Heaven would have made. "What a great story it would have been for New Zealand golf," Price said. "I got a bit hypocritical out there today, because as much as I wanted to win it myself, it would have been a great event for Brad to win."

Heaven was intending to remain an amateur at least until the Eisenhower Trophy later in the year. Price, ironically, was helped to victory by a tip from a player who did win his national title as an amateur, Aaron Baddeley. "I had been putting atrociously, but with Aaron's help I no longer feel I am taking a knife to a gun fight."

Johnnie Walker Classic—US$1,800,000
Winner: Miguel Angel Jimenez

See Asia/Japan Tours chapter.

Heineken Classic—A$2,000,000
Winner: Ernie Els

Ernie Els produced two supreme efforts during the Heineken Classic. One was an opening round of 60, the other, his earlier brilliance notwithstanding, was to win the tournament for the third successive year from the depths of despair on the final day.

First, the South African's astonishing first round when he lowered the record for the composite course at Royal Melbourne by two strokes and so nearly broke 60. He had 11 birdies, an eagle and one bogey. He birdied the three par-threes and was four under for the three par-fives. He birdied five of the first eight holes and then eagled the ninth with a three iron from 262 yards to seven feet to be out in 29.

He birdied the first five holes on the second nine to be 12 under after 14 holes, and eight under for his last seven holes. But there the glorious deeds ended. At the 15th he missed the green and failed to get up and down, and although he birdied the 16th, he could not add another at either of the last two holes. It was the lowest round of his career and he led the field by four strokes.

After adding rounds of 66 and 68, Els was eight clear of the field going into the final round. But there was to be no coasting to victory. He started the last day with a bogey and a birdie, then a bogey and a triple bogey. He went to the turn in 42, and suddenly his advantage had been all eaten up and now he shared the lead with Adam Scott at 16 under par.

Most might have crumbled at this point, but Els rallied with birdies at the 10th, 12th, 13th and 14th. He had a spurt of genius that Scott, having worked himself into contention after starting the day playing for second place, could not quite match. However, the young Australian did birdie the 17th to be only one stroke behind before missing the 12-footer at the last that would have meant a playoff.

Scott closed with a 67 compared to the 74 of Els, but the South African sneaked home by one stroke at 268, 20 under par. "When things go bad, what do you do?" asked the shell-shocked Els after his afternoon fright. "You've got to keep playing, put shots together, make putts, hang in there. It's not the easiest game in the world.

"A tournament is not lost in two or three days. That is something everybody can learn. I learned a lot from that. I think I crossed a little hurdle. I don't think anybody gets too old to learn. If I have another big lead, I now know you've got to go out and play as hard as you can."

ANZ Championship—A$1,750,000
Winner: Brian Davis

Australians like nothing better than to mock the sporting calamities of their auld enemy, the English, but at the Horizons resort they came to praise. They had to as Brian Davis walked off with the ANZ Championship by one point over Paul Casey, who made a thoroughly decent effort at defending his title.

The tournament was played under a modified-Stableford scoring format, and another Englishman, Steve Webster, led the way after the second and third rounds. But the format rewards players who charge out of the pack, and that is just what Davis did on the final day with 17 points, his 10 birdies and three bogeys being the equivalent of a round of 65.

Davis, buoyed by a putting lesson from friend Gary Evans the previous night, finished at 44 points, with Casey finishing at 43 after 14 points in the final round. Webster needed an eagle at the 18th to win, but his aggressive play led to him driving out of bounds and he picked up when he could do no better than a double bogey.

For the 29-year-old Davis it was a second title on the PGA European Tour, which was co-sanctioning the event, but his first since the 2000 Spanish Open. Not only did it bolster his attempt to earn a place on the European Ryder Cup team, but the victory took Davis into the top 64 on the World

Ranking just in time to play in the WGC - Accenture World Match Play later in the month.

"A few years ago they were saying what a poor state English golf was in, but now all of a sudden here we are with lots of us challenging for the Ryder Cup team," Davis said. "I'm sure Paul will be there in September. He is a great player."

Laura Davies became the first woman to compete in a men's European Tour event after receiving an invitation from the sponsors, but missed the cut and finished next to last.

Jacob's Creek Open—A$1,050,000
Winner: Euan Walters

In the first of two events co-sanctioned with the U.S. Nationwide Tour, Euan Walters cruised to a five-stroke victory in the Jacob's Creek Open at the Kooyonga Club in Adelaide.

Walters never wavered on the way to victory. He did not drop a shot on the second nine during a final round of three-under-par 68 which gave the Victorian a nine-under-par 275 total. Former U.S. PGA champion Wayne Grady, Anthony Painter and Brendan Jones shared second place with scores of 280.

New Zealand PGA Championship—A$1,000,000
Winner: Gavin Coles

A three-stroke victory for Australian Gavin Coles does not convey the drama of the closing holes at the New Zealand PGA Championship. Coles came to the final hole at the Clearwater Resort in Christchurch just hoping to get into a playoff. With the hole location on the final green perilously close to the water on the left, Coles came up short and right over 50 feet away.

But with unerring accuracy, Coles' putt went right into the heart of the cup. American Bill Lunde then bogeyed both the 17th and 18th holes, and the result was clear cut. Coles closed with a 68 for a six-under-par total of 282 in what were tricky conditions all week. Brendan Jones, Bradley Hughes and Lunde shared second place, with Euan Walters, the previous week's winner, joining those in fifth place.

Hillross Centenary Australian Open—A$1,500,000
Winner: Peter Lonard

Peter Lonard chose a good moment to defend a title successfully for the first time. Lonard won the Hillross Australian Open in 2003 and returned to triumph again at the centenary edition in 2004. He followed Arnold Palmer, Jack Nicklaus, Greg Norman and Aaron Baddeley in winning back-to-back titles in the last 50 years.

"This win was a lot bigger than last year, because it's the 100th anniversary, and I hope I am always known as the Centenary champion," Lonard said. "It's fantastic because I've never defended a title. As a kid growing up anywhere in the world, you want to win your national open, and now that I've done it twice, it really is something special. I guess it proves last year wasn't a fluke."

Lonard made a memorable charge for victory at the Australian Club in Sydney. The 37-year-old Australian parred the first 10 holes of the final round, at which point he had made just six birdies in 64 holes. He then birdied five of the next seven holes before bogeying the last.

His second shot on the 18th went well left of the fairway at the par-five hole, but after finding the green for his third, he then three-putted. "I thought they were going to lead me to the hall of shame after that," said Lonard, who was left preparing for a possible playoff as Stuart Appleby closed to within a stroke with a birdie at the 16th.

Appleby came to the 18th needing a birdie to tie and had a 15-foot putt to do so, but it just missed. Lonard closed with a 68 for a three-under-par total of 281 to win by one over Appleby, with Steven Bowditch and Rod Pampling sharing third place one stroke further back.

Cadbury Schweppes Australian PGA Championship—A$1,000,000
Winner: Peter Lonard

Proving himself to be the master of the Sunday charge, Peter Lonard again powered to victory with an impressive closing display. It was a formidable double for Lonard after his win in the Australian Open, but in fact this represented the 37-year-old's third win in successive weeks. The run had started with victory in the New South Wales Open on the Von Nida Tour, Australia's second-string circuit.

At the Hyatt Regency Coolum Resort on Queensland's Sunshine Coast, Lonard won the Cadbury Schweppes Australian PGA Championship with a closing round of 65, his second seven-under-par round of the tournament. At one point there were 14 players within five strokes of the lead, but Lonard soon blew them away. At the par-five eighth hole, Lonard was 60 yards short of the green by a tree in two strokes but conjured up a recovery to six feet for the first of five birdies in six holes.

Another birdie at the 16th and Lonard was two clear and feeling comfortable. He finished at 270 total, 18 under par, and maintained that two-stroke advantage over James Nitties, a rookie playing only his fourth event as a professional. American Bob Estes, the first-round leader after a 63, bogeyed the 72nd hole to fall back to third place, one ahead of countryman Corey Pavin and Australian left-hander Nick O'Hern.

Lonard had tied for the Australian PGA title in 2002 when his playoff with Jarrod Moseley could not be completed due to darkness. This time the New South Welshman was able to lift the Kirkwood Cup on his own. "Last week was fantastic and this week just measures into the unbelievable category," Lonard said. "I don't think I have had to shoot seven under with tougher pin placements to win a tournament. After the birdie on 16 to get two ahead, I felt pretty good."

MasterCard Masters — A$1,250,000
Winner: Richard Green

It had been a long wait for Richard Green in his quest to win on home soil, so having to go to an extra hole at Huntingdale to claim the MasterCard Masters was not a problem. Green won the Dubai Classic on the European Tour in 1997 when he defeated Ian Woosnam and his boyhood idol, Greg Norman, also in a playoff.

But the man from Melbourne had not won in Australia until his victory in his hometown. "Out of all the tournaments I play, this is the one I wanted," Green said. "I did not want to became a player who played internationally and won events, but did not win here in Australia."

Green, age 33, became the first left-hander to win the prestigious title. "That's a nice one as well," he said. The victory also clinched the top spot on the 2004 Australasian Tour Order of Merit.

Not that it was straightforward. There was a moment when there were 25 players within five strokes of the lead, and many players made a run up the leaderboard. Peter Lonard, going for a fourth consecutive win, was one of them, but he dropped three strokes over the last two holes to finish four back. Former U.S. Open champion Corey Pavin was another, but he finished two strokes behind the playoff.

Greg Chalmers, another Australian left-hander, closed with a 65 with five birdies on the back nine to set the clubhouse target at 271, 17 under par. Green was the next to post that score. Four birdies in a row at the start of the final nine had given him the lead briefly, but a bogey at the 17th left him nervously awaiting the efforts of those behind him.

Those included overnight leader David McKenzie, who endured a roller-coaster final round which started with a double bogey. He managed to keep in contention, but then bogeyed the 15th and 16th before brilliantly holing from six feet at the 18th to get into the playoff.

But Bradley Hughes, hoping for a third gold jacket, was not so fortunate. Hughes arrived at the 18th with a one-stroke lead but pushed his drive so badly that he had to take an unplayable lie. He could not reach the green in three and had a 12-foot putt to get into the playoff, but it did not drop. The double bogey dropped him into a share of fourth place with Brad Kennedy and Steven Bowditch.

In the playoff it was back to the 18th hole, and Chalmers was in the trees on the right but found the green with his recovery. McKenzie came up just short. But whatever the two men did, it was outshone by Green, who fired his approach brilliantly to four feet and holed the putt for a winning birdie.

13. African Tours

Apart from having his season interrupted by a jet ski accident in Barbados which resulted in a pelvis injury, Retief Goosen had just about the perfect year in 2004.

Under intense pressure in extraordinary conditions at Shinnecock Hills, Goosen won the U.S. Open for the second time. He held off the challenge of Masters champion Phil Mickelson, suddenly the man to beat in the major championships. A measure of how difficult scoring was on the final day, Goosen's playing partner, his compatriot Ernie Els, slumped to an 80.

A few weeks later Goosen added the Smurfit European Open title to his collection, but then had to miss the PGA Championship with his injury. It took time to regain his best form, but once he had, he held off a resurgent, and newly married Tiger Woods to win the Tour Championship.

As if his mastery of golf in America and Europe, where he was second on the Order of Merit, was not enough, Goosen returned home to South Africa to win the Nedbank Golf Challenge for the first time at Sun City. Off the course, life was good, too, as baby daughter Ella joined elder brother Leo in the Goosen household.

What to make of Els' year? It was perhaps close to being one of the best seasons ever seen in golf ... but it was not. There was a second successive Order of Merit victory on the European Tour, although that is not something high on his priority list. His record of 14 top-10 finishes in 15 events was truly sensational, however. Along the way, Els won the Heineken Classic in Melbourne for the third successive year after an opening round of 60, although there was still a desperate rearguard action on the last day.

It was in the majors that Els came so close but could not award himself a cigar. At Augusta National, in one of the most exciting finishes the Masters has seen, Els made two eagles on the final day but lost out to Mickelson's birdie at the 18th. The uncharacteristic collapse at the U.S. Open was followed by his playoff defeat to Todd Hamilton at the Open Championship and he finished one stroke out of the playoff at the PGA Championship.

Els brooded on his disappointments for a couple of weeks and then put them behind him with his first WGC title at the American Express Championship and then won the HSBC World Match Play title for a record sixth time at Wentworth. He promised there would be more to come.

The same could be said of South African golf in general if the number of promising young players on the tour was anything to go by. Some have already ventured overseas, and there could be no more important victory than by Charl Schwartzel at the Dunhill Championship at the end of the year, a first PGA European Tour win for the 20-year-old former English Amateur Stroke Play champion. On the other hand, the likes of Thomas Aiken was aiming to gain experience by staying at home and celebrated his 21st birthday with three victories in the Vodacom Origins of Golf series.

In the important early tournaments, Trevor Immelman got the New Year underway with a repeat victory in the South African Airways Open, followed by the victories of Marcel Siem in the Dunhill Championship and Darren Fichardt in the Dimension Data Pro-Am. As the year went on, Andrew McLardy and Bradford Vaughan each won twice.

South African Airways Open—£500,000
Winner: Trevor Immelman

Retaining the South African Airways Open not only proved how well Trevor Immelman plays on his home course of Erinvale, but that his new motto was working well. Annoyed at playing some of his best golf in the pro-am prior to tournaments, Immelman's New Year resolution was to "Peak on Sundays."

He did that so well that there was not only another celebration of winning his national title at Erinvale, but the knowledge that the 24-year-old was the first to win successive South African Opens since Gary Player in 1976-77. It was Immelman's second victory on the European Tour and his fourth in South Africa.

"I have always played my best leading up to tournaments, and when the tournaments came round, ended up getting in my own way because I was thinking too much," Immelman admitted. "The thing you have to work out is that you have to go out and play as if you were playing with your mates. Also, if you are not hitting it well in the warm-up, it doesn't mean you are not going to play well in the tournament."

Immelman crept quietly into contention during the week, lying two strokes behind third-round leaders Craig Lile and Anders Hansen. Hansen and Alastair Forsyth led at the turn, but when the wind picked up, Immelman felt right at home. Hansen played the last three holes in five over par, but by then Immelman was away, with birdies at the 10th, the 13th, where he played an exquisite chip from a bank beside the green, and the 16th.

Immelman missed a three-footer at the 18th for a bogey, but his closing round of 67 gave him a 12-under-par 276 total and a three-stroke victory over Forsyth and Steve Webster, while Darren Fichardt finished fourth.

Immelman had been disappointed to miss out on the Presidents Cup when it was played in South Africa a couple of months earlier, but he finished the 2003 season by winning the World Cup with Rory Sabbatini and that was the perfect start to the new season. "I definitely feel I am a better player this year," Immelman said. "I am stronger, have more control, and my timing has improved dramatically." Particularly on a Sunday.

Dunhill Championship—£500,000
Winner: Marcel Siem

Marcel Siem's father, Heinz, was a German international handball player, but his son soon got into golf at the age of six. From the age of 13, Siem was intent on a career as a professional. Father and son both thought it would take until around the age of 25 to gain his first win. "But I am 23, so it is two years too early," joked Siem after winning the Dunhill Championship.

In a low-scoring week at Houghton Golf Club in Johannesburg, Siem had to win a playoff for the title after tying at 22-under-par 266 with two Frenchmen, Raphael Jacquelin and Gregory Havret. Siem closed with a 66, while his opponents both had 67s after birdieing the last hole to set up the three-way playoff.

Playing the 18th hole repeatedly, Siem had a chance to win with an eight-foot birdie putt at the first extra hole but it just slipped by. He had a similar chance the second time around, but it was third time lucky as a birdie finally saw off the dual French challenge.

Siem had altered his grip — it was too open he felt — prior to the start of the season and also tried chewing gum and other relaxation tips which obviously seemed to work. But the young German has one more thing he wanted to change. "I smoke and I want to put a stop to that," he said.

"That doesn't look good on the course and I want to look good, especially to young people in Germany and Europe. I would like to be an idol for them and when I smoke I can't be that. Smoking is a bad thing."

Dimension Data Pro-Am—R2,000,000
Winner: Darren Fichardt

Darren Fichardt had never forgotten a lesson in winning he received from Mark McNulty and put it to good effect while weathering a final-round charge from Ulrich van den Berg to win the Dimension Data Pro-Am by two strokes at the Gary Player Country Club at Sun City.

Fichardt and van den Berg challenged for the title in a final round which both led at various stages. They were tied for the lead after both dropped shots at the par-four 14th, Fichardt taking a bogey but van den Berg suffering a double bogey. Van den Berg, whose three birdies in a row around the turn had put him in the lead, went on to bogey the 17th as well, while Fichardt birdied the 18th for victory with 10-under-par 278 total after a 68. Van den Berg and Nick Price shared second place at eight under with respective final rounds of 69 and 68.

It was at the 2002 Vodacom Players Championship that Fichardt had gotten a bit over-excited and handed the title to the calm veteran McNulty. "Mark told me afterwards just to be more patient in situations like that and not force things," Fichardt, the Pretoria professional, said. "I was a bit upset when he first told me that, because he'd just whipped me.

"But I never stopped thinking about it. I used his advice when I won the Qatar Masters in March last year, and again today. It's just a case of keeping the ball in play and waiting for your opponent to make the mistakes."

Nashua Masters—R1,000,000
Winner: Andrew McLardy

Wild Coast, the venue for the Nashua Masters, is a world away from Johannesburg, and Andrew McLardy insisted on treating the week like a holiday. It was a vacation with a bonus as he held up the trophy at the end of the tournament for his first victory on the main summer leg of the Southern Africa Tour.

McLardy, age 30, won by three strokes over Desvonde Botes, but it was a close duel for much of the day. McLardy handed a boost to his rival with a double bogey at the fifth hole when his approach flew the green into the bush. But the 11th proved the turning point.

McLardy hit a five iron to 18 feet at the testing par-three, but Botes, who had led by one, took a bogey to fall one behind. Botes then drove into a bunker at the 12th and, too aggressive with his second shot, ended up taking a double bogey. Both men closed with rounds of 67 on the par-70 course, but McLardy finished at 264, 16 under par, with Titch Moore and Keith Horne sharing third place four strokes behind.

"After the fifth, I just hit my shots and tried not to think ahead," said McLardy. "I can't believe I won, because I just came down here to get away from Johannesburg for a week. I did nothing. I just watched cricket, played golf and braaied (barbequed). All I had to do was get up and play golf."

Telkom PGA Championship—R1,500,000
Winner: Warrick Druian

Warrick Druian broke a seven-year victory drought in emphatic fashion, storming to a five-stroke victory in the Telkom PGA Championship at Woodhill. A composed final round of 66 earned him victory at 267, 21 under par. Michiel Bothma, the defending champion, Mark Murless, the man Bothma beat for the title in 2003, and Desvonde Botes shared second place at 16 under.

Druian's victory, witnessed by his mother but not his father who was too nervous to attend, was his first since winning the 1997 Royal Swazi Sun Open and was the epitome of the 34-year-old's quest to manage his anger on the course. Druian admitted that after finishing tied for 24th in the Dimension Data Pro-Am at Sun City three weeks earlier, he snapped his irons in the parking lot. At Wild Coast a week later, he was in contention for the Nashua Masters before a 10 on the 14th hole on the final day saw him crash off the leaderboard.

"My anger was getting the better of me. I actually wanted to ask Hennie Otto for the name of his sports psychologist," he said in reference to Otto's famous act of throwing his clubs into the Wild Coast river after a particularly bad round during the Nashua Masters one year. Druian settled on working with sports psychologist Ken Jennings, who advised Druian to assess his anger level after every hole during a round and write it down on a scale of one to 10 in his yardage book.

At Woodhill, there was not a single high number written in that yardage book. "I couldn't have asked for anything better. I was so calm," Druian said.

Southern Africa Tour Championship—R2,000,000
Winner: Andrew McLardy

Andrew McLardy finished the 2003-04 season strongly with his second victory in three weeks at the Southern Africa Tour Championship at Leopard Creek. McLardy, age 30, went into the final round with a seven-stroke lead and had to weather a strong charge from Louis Oosthuizen before signing off a successful season with a final round of 72 to win at 15-under-par 273. Oosthuizen finished second at 12 under par with a closing 66.

McLardy earned a check for R317,000 which enabled him to finish second on the final Order of Merit behind Darren Fichardt. "Now I can afford to build my house at Pecanwood," said McLardy.

With such a commanding lead on Saturday night, McLardy read motivational books by Deepak Chopra and about Zen and the martial arts in order to stay focused and calm. He played conservative golf on the final day, preferring instead to let the rest of the field try to catch him.

Oosthuizen birdied four of his first six holes for an outward nine of 31 and then reeled off three birdies from the 12th to close to within three of McLardy. But he could get no closer. McLardy hoped the experience had helped him overcome the loss of playing privileges on both the European and American circuits earlier in his career.

"I achieved that early in my career and then lost them both, so my confidence took a big whack. I thought I couldn't compete at that level. But hopefully with a bit more experience and being a bit older, we can get there again and stay there," he said.

Ashleigh Simon, a 14-year-old amateur, became the first woman to play in a Southern Africa Tour event, but closed with a 79 for last place at 28 over par.

Stanbic Zambia Open—€100,000
Winner: Michael Kirk

Michael Kirk denied Leonard Loxton, a player without privileges on the Southern Africa Tour, as he claimed a three-stroke victory in the Stanbic Zambia Open in Lusaka.

Kirk and Loxton were tied for the lead playing the crucial par-four 17th in the joint-sanctioned European Challenge Tour event. Kirk holed a 15-footer for birdie while Loxton missed a two-footer for par for a two-shot swing that Kirk carried with him down the last. Loxton bogeyed the 18th as well for three bogeys in his final four holes, costing him the title. Kirk's five-under 68 gave him a total of 274, 18 under, and his first victory as a professional. Loxton, the leader by three strokes with a round to play, closed with a 74.

"I knew that if I could get to a total of 18 or 19 under par, then I would stand a chance," said Kirk, who had finished second in the event the previous year. "I didn't make a bogey in my round, which was key to the victory. The greens are very tricky on this course. They're quite grainy and you've got to be patient. I think that why I've always done well here is because I've made the putts over the years. But, of course, that two-shot swing on 17 was huge in the outcome of the tournament."

Kenya Open—€110,000
Winner: Marc Cayeux

Marc Cayeux, a big-hitting 26-year-old from Zimbabwe, overcame Sweden's Leif Westerberg in a playoff to claim the Kenya Open in his first outing of the season on the joint-sanctioned European Challenge Tour. The pair finished at 10-under-par 270 after 72 holes, with Cayeux shooting a three-under 67 and Westerberg a six-under 66 at the Karen Golf Club before heading to the par-four 12th for the shoot-out.

Westerberg was the one to falter, and he three-putted to allow Cayeux to claim his second title on the Challenge Tour. "I do feel a sense of pride," Cayeux said. "I said the other day about how tough it had become for me two years ago, and it is a really nice feeling to be back on the Challenge Tour.

"I'll have my category one membership for the Challenge Tour after this victory, and that gives me a great opportunity to finish in the top 15 on the rankings. This could be a career changing win I suppose. When I think back to just a few days ago, I had no thoughts about playing in the Madeira Island Open, but now I'll be entered in a full European Tour event, so it has already changed things."

FNB Botswana Open—R250,000
Winner: Barry Painting

Zimbabwean Barry Painting claimed his first victory on the Southern Africa Tour with a three-stroke wire-to-wire triumph in the FNB Botswana Open at Gaborone. Painting closed with a 68 to win at 195, 18 under par, with Omar Sandys his nearest challenger at 15 under, also after a 68. Mark Murless was third at 14-under-par 199 following a final-round 70.

"It's all a bit of a blur at the moment, but jeez I'm really happy," said Painting, who had won on the Diner's Club mini-tour and on his home tour in Zimbabwe, but never on the Southern Africa Tour. "This is the big one for me. I'm going to phone my folks in Bulawayo and let them know, and then I'm certainly going to go and have a couple of beers."

Painting did not hit the ball at all well on the final day, but his saving grace was once again a putter that had been hot all week. "I really didn't hit many good shots. I hit a couple of mediocre shots and made putts," he said. "I made birdie on the first and I think that really relaxed my nerves. I think I dropped at the last, but it's such a blur I couldn't tell you."

Parmalat Classic—R200,000
Winner: Justin Walters

Justin Walters, an Englishman born in South Africa but best known on the American college circuit, produced a brilliant closing round to win the Parmalat Classic at the De Zalze Golf Club in Stellenbosch. The 23-year-old Walters carded a superb seven-under 65 to move to 11-under 205, holding off South Africa's Nicholas Lawrence by two strokes after he shot a 69.

It was Walters' first victory as a professional in less than a year in the paid ranks. Walters was born and raised in South Africa, but owes his English passport to his English-born mother. He attended North Carolina State on a golf scholarship, where he won four titles and became a four-time All American.

After going to the turn in 33, Walters holed from 30 feet for a par at the 12th to get in the hunt before making four consecutive birdies from the next, holing another 30-footer at the 16th to get to 11 under. "I was trying not to look at the scoreboards down the stretch, but on 17 there was a huge scoreboard right in my line and I couldn't miss it," Walters said.

"Even after I made par there, I didn't think I had it wrapped up. I really played solidly on the front nine. I didn't really do anything wrong, and then I just got going on the back nine. It's great to win as a professional and I suppose this will always be a special moment in my life."

Capital Alliance Royal Swazi Sun Open—R400,000
Winner: Nic Henning

Nic Henning benefited from both his own inspired play and some errors from others to claim his third victory on the Southern Africa Tour at the Capital Alliance Royal Swazi Sun Open. It was a result that few expected when Walter Coetsee stepped onto the par-three 18th hole with a one-point lead over Henning and overnight leader Titch Moore in the Stableford-style event.

But when Coetsee left his tee shot in the front bunker and then fluffed his second short of the green, a playoff seemed the likely outcome. And when he missed a six-footer for bogey moments later, the astonishing climax ended with a bemused Henning looking on. Coetsee's double bogey on the closing hole dropped him into third place, while Moore's bogey four saw him claim outright second.

Henning had almost gone home when he finished his round, a nine-under 63, the lowest of the week, that included seven birdies and an eagle at the 12th as well as earning him 19 points. "I was never expecting to win it," said Henning. "But I played really well today and it could have been even better.

"I thought I had to birdie 17 to have a chance, but as it happened none of us birdied it. That was surprising. It's a great feeling to win. It's always nice to know you were the best player out there that week."

Vodacom Origins of Golf Tour at Pezula—R300,000
Winner: Patrick O'Brien

Patrick O'Brien held his nerve to claim his first Southern Africa Tour victory at the weather-delayed Vodacom Origins of Golf Tour at Pezula. O'Brien had two holes to play early in the morning after the final round of the 54-hole event had been extended to an extra day.

The 29-year-old kept his composure to make par on both the 17th and 18th holes, which added the finishing touches to a magnificent closing six-under 66, the lowest round of the week. O'Brien then endured an agonizing wait as Ulrich van der Berg, one stroke behind with six holes to play at the beginning of the day, kept him guessing right until the final moment. But after dropping a shot early on, van der Berg arrived at the last two holes needing two birdies, but could only claim one at the 18th to finish one behind O'Brien's 210 total.

"I couldn't hope for a better venue for my first win, it's an unbelievable golf course in unbelievable shape," said an ecstatic O'Brien after surviving gale force winds and heavy rain during the week. "I had no bogeys and hit 18 greens, and I must say, I putted really well."

Vodacom Origins of Golf Tour at Schoeman Park—R300,000
Winner: Steve van Vuuren

Steve van Vuuren turned back the clock to win on the Southern Africa Tour for the first time in almost a decade at the Vodacom Origins of Golf Tour at Schoeman Park in Bloemfontein. In the end, van Vuuren's victory margin was four shots as he eagled the par-five 18th hole to finish at 16-under-par 200.

But it was a lot closer than that with Ulrich van den Berg hot on his heels all afternoon and only one stroke behind going down the 54th hole. For the 44-year-old van Vuuren, it was an emotional return to the winner's circle after eight years without victory. "It's been a long time," said van Vuuren. "Eight years since my last win. I've been pretty blessed this week. I kept my cool and kept the ball in play today. It's just fantastic."

The turning point was on the 17th hole when van Vuuren rolled in a six-foot putt for birdie that heaped the pressure on van den Berg, who then missed a birdie effort of similar length. And after van Vuuren's approach to the 18th came to rest just 15 feet from the flag, van den Berg was forced to go for broke.

"I knew I had to go for it, but made a terrible swing and hooked it well left," said van den Berg. From an atrocious lie in the trees to the left of the green, van den Berg hacked out into the front bunker and went on to make a bogey six to finish alone in second place for the second successive tournament.

Royal Swazi Sun Classic—R250,000
Winner: Bradford Vaughan

Bradford Vaughan clearly feels at home at the Royal Swazi Sun course and this was the third of his four victories on the Southern Africa Tour to be achieved here. He won the Royal Swazi Sun Classic with a dazzling eight-under-par 64 which featured nine birdies.

Vaughan swept past the overnight leaders with an opening half of four-under 32, and his only bogey came at the 18th. Nevertheless, he secured a four-stroke victory with 199 total over Ashley Roestoff, who scored a 68 playing alongside Vaughan. Ulrich van den Berg briefly tied for the lead with Vaughan, but after a triple bogey at the 10th had to settle for a share of third place, his third top-three finish in successive tournaments.

The victory meant reclaimed exempt status on both the winter and summer legs of the Southern Africa Tour. "It's such a relief," said Vaughan. "I was determined all day, made a fast start, and kept my focus. Winning means I won't have to qualify for events and that's the best part about this.

"I was sick for the main part of the Sunshine Tour in January and February and lost my card. It's been my goal just to keep making cuts."

Vodacom Origins of Golf Tour at Zimbali—R292,650
Winner: Thomas Aiken

Thomas Aiken claimed his first victory on the Southern Africa Tour with a dramatic playoff win over Keith Horne at the Vodacom Origins of Golf Tour at Zimbali. A par on the first extra hole, the tricky par-four 18th, was enough to see the 20-year-old Aiken through as Horne failed to get up and down from short of the green.

Moments earlier, Horne had bogeyed the very same hole from a greenside bunker to keep Aiken's hopes alive after arriving at the 54th hole with a one-stroke lead. Horne's dropped shot meant a closing 69 that would have seemed enough at the beginning of the day but for the 66 from Aiken, which started with five successive birdies. Both players finished with 204 totals.

"I needed to get off to a good start being three shots back, and after three in a row I was thinking, 'This is unbelievable,'" said Aiken. "Before I knew it, I had made the turn with a three-shot lead. There were nerves there, but I just stuck to my game plan, which all week has been to keep it in play. I'm delighted with this win and hopefully it will give me confidence in the future."

James Kamte, a 21-year-old black professional from Glendower who held a share of the lead with Aiken after the first round, closed with a steady one-under-par 71 to make third place his own at nine under.

For Aiken, victory on home soil came as a resounding affirmation of his decision to turn professional at the tender age of 18. "People put me down when I turned pro so young, but I'm glad I did it," said Aiken. "My dad and I agreed that whenever you take the step you have to start from the bottom, so then was as good a time as any."

Vodacom Origins of Golf Tour at Sun City—R294,330
Winner: Thomas Aiken

Having won once at home, Thomas Aiken immediately added another title with the Vodacom Origins of Golf Tour at Sun City. Having started the final day with a five-stroke cushion, Aiken held off a charging Des Terblanche with a nerveless one-under-par 71 to win by three strokes with a 204 total, 12 under par.

Terblanche outscored Aiken by two strokes on the final day, but squandered any chance he had of stealing the trophy when he found the water off the 18th tee. Grant Muller, the final member of the last group, holed a slippery 10-foot putt on the final green to complete a closing 70 and claim third spot for himself at seven under.

Terblanche made three early birdies and then saw Aiken birdie the eighth and ninth, but the youngster responded by birdieing the 10th and 11th and then parred his way home. It was an exciting month for Aiken, which also included a top-10 finish on the European Challenge Tour and his 21st birthday.

"My heart was pumping and the adrenaline was flowing just like at Zimbali, so I was glad to get it over with in the end," said a relieved Aiken. "Five shots is a lot, but it's not a hell of a lot, it can disappear in three holes. When I saw Des making his run I just kept thinking, 'He can't keep doing this.'

"It feels great to win again and I look forward to a break now. I'm having my 21st birthday party next Saturday, and it's going to be great to see all my friends again."

Vodacom Origins of Golf Tour at Arabella—R300,000
Winner: Louis Oosthuizen

Louis Oosthuizen became yet another first-time winner on the Southern Africa Tour at the Vodacom Origins of Golf Tour at Arabella. Oosthuizen came from behind to edge overnight leader Keith Horne by one stroke, his closing 71 including seven birdies and completing a 54-hole score of 215, one under par.

After a double bogey at the 15th, Horne birdied two of the last three holes, but missed out when Oosthuizen birdied the par-five 18th. The 21-year-old was taking a break from the European Tour, where he had secured his card for 2005.

"Those are such tough holes coming in and I needed to play some good shots to get through them. When Keith birdied the 16th and I dropped on the 17th, it was not over," said Oosthuizen. "I hit a perfect two iron from 240 yards on the 18th that finished on the green, and fortunately I two-putted from there. It feels great to win here. And it's very special with my parents watching as well."

Bearingman Highveld Classic—R220,000
Winner: Divan van den Heever

Divan van den Heever kept up the trend of the season with his first victory by a comfortable five strokes at the Bearingman Highveld Classic. The 21-year-old made amends for his near-miss at Witbank 12 months earlier, when he bogeyed the 18th hole to finish second by one shot to Dion Fourie.

This time he never looked back after an outward half of 33 and completed an eight-under-par 64 for a 54-hole score of 198, 18 under. "That was fun," said van den Heever. "I felt good this morning and just went out to have a good time and it came off. Over the last few holes I just wanted to keep the ball in play. I really didn't want to finish like last year with a bogey."

A birdie at the 15th and an eagle at the 17th meant van den Heever had a nice cushion at the last, where his chip hit the pin to ensure a par. Leonard Loxton also parred the 18th to finish alone in second place.

Limpopo Eskom Classic—R500,000
Winner: Bradford Vaughan

Bradford Vaughan came from behind to win his second title within two months in a tense final round at the Limpopo Eskom Classic. Vaughan bogeyed the 18th hole for a closing five-under-par 67 and a 54-hole winning score of 18-under 198.

"I'm glad I made that putt on 17," said Vaughan. "I wouldn't have enjoyed a slider on the last green to win. It was a pretty soft bogey on the last, but you know what they say, 'If you need five to win, make five.' I didn't want to get too clever.

"It's such a good feeling to win," Vaughan added. "Having lost my exemption last year I needed to come out and prove myself this season, so I'm very pleased. In hindsight, losing my card was probably the best thing that's ever happened to me. It made me more motivated than ever."

Vodacom Origins of Golf Championship—R300,000
Winner: Thomas Aiken

Thomas Aiken became the first player to win three times in the season with his victory in the Vodacom Origins of Golf Championship by seven shots at The Links at Fancourt. Aiken rolled in a birdie on the par-five 18th hole to ensure an even-par closing 73 for a score of 214, five under par, making him the only player to finish the tournament in red figures.

Jean Hugo and Hennie Otto, his partners in the final threesome, both fell apart in a stiff breeze over the closing holes to hand Aiken an easy victory. Hugo signed for a 79 to finish alone in second place at two over par, while Andre Cruse ground out a 75 to claim outright third two strokes further back. Otto, who made a quadruple-bogey eight on the 15th hole en route to a closing 82, was one of four players tied for fourth at five over par.

Aiken had to work hard for his victory despite the winning margin after following an eagle at the fifth by dropping six shots in five holes from the sixth. "We turned into the wind on seven, eight and nine, and it was really tough. My putter went cold and I needed to keep my composure over the last few holes," said Aiken, who stayed in South Africa after struggling in his rookie season on the European Challenge Tour in 2003.

"I'm really chuffed with how it turned out. This is one of the toughest golf courses I've ever played on, and to play three rounds without going over par here is pretty good. This win is really good for my confidence. I've been a bit shaky over the last few weeks, so I really needed a boost."

Platinum Classic—R550,000
Winner: Titch Moore

Titch Moore came from behind to win his second Platinum Classic title in three years at Mooi Nooi. Moore closed with the final day's lowest round of six-under-par 66 to finish the tournament at 200, 16 under par, three strokes clear of Hennie Otto.

Otto's second successive 67 saw him claim outright second place, with Nic Henning, Thomas Aiken and Charl Schwartzel all tied for third at 12 under. Moore, winning for the fifth time, kept his composure as others lost theirs in a tense finish in breezy conditions.

Starting the day two shots behind Ulrich van den Berg, Moore erased the deficit with an eagle on the first hole and never looked back. "I told my caddie, James, we needed a fast start, and that was just right," said Moore. "It's awesome coming back here and winning again. The course was in brilliant condition all week and it suits my game.

"This is absolutely perfect for me ahead of the European Qualifying School next week," he added. "I drove the ball so well all week, my wedge play was good and my putting was very solid too, so I'm confident going overseas."

MTC Namibian PGA Championship—R500,000
Winner: Mark Murless

Mark Murless closed with a six-under 65 to win his first title in eight years at the inaugural MTC Namibian PGA Championship by two strokes with 202 total. The 28-year-old came from two shots behind at the beginning of the day to end a title drought on home soil that dated back to his breakthrough win at the 1996 Platinum Classic.

Qualifier Bradley Davison, who played with Murless in the third-to-last group, closed with a 67 to finish second with Zimbabwe's Sean Farrell. Murless' main concern was shaking off his tenacious playing partner Davison, who eagled the par-five seventh for the third successive round and matched Murless with birdies on the 10th and 11th.

"Brad was one shot behind me for most of the day," said Murless. "I just couldn't shake him." That was until Murless rolled in a 30-foot birdie putt on the 16th hole to stretch his lead to two shots with just two holes to play.

"That was the key putt of the tournament for me. I'm absolutely thrilled to be back in the winner's circle again," Murless added. "It's been a long time and I've had so many close calls. It just feels fantastic."

Seekers Travel Pro-Am—R230,000
Winner: Ulrich van den Berg

Ulrich van den Berg claimed the victory that had been eluding him all season when he won the Seekers Travel Pro-Am in a playoff over Patrick O'Brien and Mark Murless. After pars all around at the 18th for the first extra hole, the next time the 29-year-old van den Berg birdied to win his third Southern Africa Tour title.

After playing second fiddle all season with two second-place finishes and five other top-10s, it was a fitting finale to the winter season. Van den Berg had to work hard to join his opponents in the winner's circle. Coming down the stretch it seemed likely that he would add another near-miss to his collection when he faded his drive into the trees off the tee on the last hole of regulation play.

But after hitting a masterful long iron under the branches and onto the back of the 18th green, van den Berg holed a 30-foot putt that roused the galleries and saw him post a closing five-under-par 67 to join Murless, who closed with a 66, in the clubhouse lead at 203, 13 under par. O'Brien then very nearly followed suit with his 25-foot effort to win the tournament, but watched in agony as his ball shaved the right lip of the hole, and he had to settle for a 66 of his own.

"That 30-foot putt I holed was definitely the one that won me the tournament," said van den Berg. "I only had half a shot from under the tree, and I was just hoping to get it on the green and do something special."

He had been inspired by the form of U.S. Open champion Retief Goosen. "I'm very chuffed," said van den Berg. "I've been in position so often this season, but I knew I had the heart to win. I was inspired by Retief's win at the U.S. Tour Championship recently. I tend to get a bit emotional, being half Italian, but this week I was a lot calmer and realized the benefit of staying composed like the Goose."

Nelson Mandela Invitational—R125,000
Winners: Ernie Els and Vincent Tshabalala

South Africans Ernie Els and Vincent Tshabalala claimed the fifth annual Nelson Mandela Invitational better-ball title at the Arabella Country Club. The pair completed the 36-hole tournament, hosted by Gary Player, at 14-under-par 130 to claim a one-stroke victory over England's Lee Westwood and South Africa's Simon Hobday.

Tshabalala outplayed Els coming down the stretch with birdies at the par-four 16th and par-five 18th to ensure victory. Els started slowly but came in with five birdies overall, although he admitted that Tshabalala had carried the team with his steady game.

"Vincent is the whole story, he made five birdies and a lot of good pars which gave us victory," Els said. "It was an honor to play with him." Tshabalala was equally impressed with Els. "This tournament is all about giving, and I can honestly say that playing with the world's No. 3 gave me great inspiration this week," Tshabalala said.

Nedbank Golf Challenge—US$4,060,000
Winner: Retief Goosen

If Retief Goosen was feeling under the weather it was hard to tell, as his superb consistency helped the U.S. Open champion claim a six-stroke victory in the Nedbank Golf Challenge at the Gary Player Country Club at Sun City. Goosen, who earned $1.2 million, won the tournament for the first time at 281, seven under par.

But he had almost not played due to the illness of his new baby daughter, Ella, and having picked up the flu at the PGA Grand Slam of Golf in Hawaii. But in blustery conditions on the final day, his outward nine of 31 was crucial, as his closing 69 proved the only sub-70 of the day. In second place were Australia's Stuart Appleby and compatriot Ernie Els, who stood by the 18th green and watched in surprise as his finishing 71 improved his position with almost every shot played by the men still out on the course.

Lee Westwood, the third-day leader, crashed to an 80 in the final round, with a final nine of 43. Nick Price came home in 42, and Sergio Garcia, who beat Goosen in a playoff in 2003 after finishing at 14 under par, was trailing at 15 over.

Goosen's first nine started with a birdie at the second hole. He added another at the sixth, almost holed in one at the seventh, and then hit a drive and an eight iron onto the island green at the ninth and holed from only three feet for an eagle that handed him a five-stroke lead. He bogeyed the 18th, but that was irrelevant, and Goosen headed home to rest after a superb season.

Dunhill Championship—£500,000
Winner: Charl Schwartzel

With the Dunhill Championship moving to a pre-Christmas slot on the European Tour schedule at a new venue of Leopard Creek, the tournament was being played for the second time in 2004, but the trend of providing first-time winners was continued as Charl Schwartzel lived up to his billing as one of South Africa's most exciting youngsters.

Schwartzel recovered from a poor finish in regulation to win at the first playoff hole against England's Neil Cheetham, who was also hoping for his first title. Schwartzel closed with a one-under-par 71, while Cheetham, the third-round leader, scored a 73, leaving both players at 281, seven under.

Schwartzel had a chance to win in regulation, but he three-putted the 17th for a bogey and also three-putted the 18th for par. Cheetham appeared to be slipping from contention when he three-putted the 15th and 16th holes for bogeys.

On the playoff hole, the par-five 18th, Schwartzel chipped to five feet and birdied the hole, while Cheetham made par. Schwartzel admitted he was nervous making the chip. "But shots like that and positions like that are what you practice for," said Schwartzel. "So I am very, very happy."

The 20-year-old former English Amateur Open Stroke Play champion added, "It's an unbelievable feeling, indescribable. This is something I've always worked for, and to finally break through is an amazing feeling. I could have made it easier for myself, two-putting on 17 and 18. But there is a lot of pressure out there, and it is difficult."

The leading pair finished one stroke ahead of Warren Abery, Ernie Els and Oliver Whiteley. Defending champion Marcel Siem and David Frost were another shot back.

14. Senior Tours

Though never as spectacular and acclaimed as some of his peers despite a successful career spanning more than two decades on the PGA Tour, Craig Stadler followed a pattern that has marked the Champions Tour over much of its quarter century when he arrived in the middle of the 2003 season and moved through the 2004 campaign. Other than the consistently high level of play of Hale Irwin for nearly all of the last decade, the dominant professionals year in and year out on the senior circuit have been those who are just getting their wind back after blowing out the 50 candles on their birthday cakes.

The delightfully grumpy Stadler, who hadn't won since 1996, played his first Champions Tour golf right after turning 50 in June of 2003 and picked off three victories, including the Ford Senior Players Championship, before the end of the season. Not to mention his regular tour win in the B.C. Open in July. Things got even better in 2004 as Stadler barreled to five more victories and led all money winners with earnings of $2,306,066 during the 30-tournament season. The venerable Walrus did most of his damage in the latter half of the campaign, especially when he ran off three wins in a row starting with the major JELD-WEN Tradition in late August.

Irwin finished second on the money list. One of four men with two victories in 2004, Irwin won the rain-plagued Senior PGA Championship at Valhalla as well as the Legends of Golf. Since his first full season in 1996, Irwin has won the money title three times, finished second three other times, third twice and had his worst showing — fifth — in 2003. Bruce Fleisher (Royal Caribbean, Bruno's), Jim Thorpe (Farmer's, Long Island) and Larry Nelson (Kinko's, Administaff) were the other double winners.

Mark McNulty carried on the "young seniors" pattern. The native Zimbabwean, one of just two non-Americans with victories on the tour in 2004, won in his first Champion Tour start at the Outback Steakhouse Pro-Am in Tampa in February, then closed the year in high style by scoring back-to-back triumphs in the SBC Championship and the grand finale Charles Schwab Cup Championship. The other winner from overseas — Mark James, the former Ryder Cup captain from England — took the Ford Senior Players Championship.

The victors in the two Senior Opens were surprising, particularly in the case of the Senior British Open won at Royal Portrush by little-known American club professional Pete Oakley, who promptly faded from sight the rest of the year. Peter Jacobsen, though still not fully recovered after hip surgery, survived a 36-hole final day and nailed the U.S. Senior Open Championship at Bellerive in just his third start on the Champions Tour.

Besides Jacobsen, James, Oakley and McNulty, only one other player — Ed Fiori at the MasterCard Classic in Mexico — registered a first victory during the 2004 season.

The European Seniors Tour season had a remarkable similarity to that of the Champions Tour. Although not nearly as successful a player in his younger days as was Craig Stadler, Carl Mason virtually duplicated Stadler's first year and a half in senior golf. Just three weeks younger than Stadler,

Mason got off to the same kind of start in Europe as Stadler did in the United States. He won four times, including his last three starts of the 2003 season, to reign as the Order of Merit leader. He continued the onslaught by making it an interrupted four-in-a-row at Tobago in the 2004 opening tournament and acquiring four more titles, most importantly the De Vere PGA Seniors, to repeat as Order of Merit king.

That achievement gave Mason one of the two plums that the UBS Cup team matches allot annually to the European Seniors Tour. The other went to John Chillas at the final tournament of the season. At the end of a season in which he did everything else but win and finished second four times, the Scot hooked the Estoril Seniors Tour Championship, jumped into third place in the Order of Merit, and was awarded the other trip to Kiawah in America with the Rest of the World team because No. 2 was Pete Oakley, the American who won the Senior British Open and wasn't eligible.

Other than Mason, only three players were multiple winners in the 21-tournament 2004 season — Bill Longmuir (Mobile Cup, Scottish Open), Luis Carbonetti (Jamaica, European Masters) and Bob Cameron (French, San Remo). Besides Carbonetti, Cameron and Oakley, retiring Ryder Cup captain Sam Torrance and Gavan Levenson won for the first time on the circuit in 2004, Levenson in his second start in Barbados.

Katsunari Takahashi remained the dean of the Japan Senior Tour in 2004. He was the only double winner in the skimpy but drawn out season, taking the first event — Castle Hill in May — and the sixth and last — the Japan Senior Open at the end of October. It was his third Open victory and, with 10 senior titles, Takahashi is tied with Seiichi Kanai and just one behind Fujio Kobayashi on the career victory list.

Champions Tour

MasterCard Championship—$1,600,000
Winner: Fuzzy Zoeller

His victory in the season-opening MasterCard Championship was just Fuzzy Zoeller's second after two full seasons on the Champions Tour, but the irrepressible one looks at it a little differently. "I win every day I'm out here," he insists. "I've had three back surgeries and I'm still walking and I'm still playing the game. I might not come home with the hardware, but I'm winning."

Zoeller did leave Hawaii with the full winner's spoils, taking along the hardware and the $268,000 first-place check after besting Dana Quigley by one stroke in an exciting finish to the elite 39-player event that had special invitee Hall-of-Famers Jack Nicklaus, Arnold Palmer, Gary Player and Lee Trevino in the field. The other 35 either won a senior major during the previous five seasons or were tournament winners in 2002 or 2003.

For two days at Hualalai Golf Club on the Big Island of Hawaii, Doug Tewell held sway. Tewell opened with an eight-under-par 64 that gave him a one-stroke lead over James Mason and two over four others. Zoeller and Quigley began with 67s in the weather-interrupted round, followed with 65s, but still trailed by three when Tewell put up a 65 of his own for 129. Dave Eichelberger was at 131. Nicklaus, who celebrated his 64th birthday, shot himself into contention with 68-66–134.

Tewell, who suffered an overnight kidney stone attack Saturday, lost his sharpness Sunday, enabling Zoeller, Quigley and Craig Stadler to forge into contention. Stadler wound up shooting 63 and tied for third with Tewell as Zoeller and Quigley, playing in the 233rd consecutive tournament for which he was eligible, edged a stroke in front when they both birdied the 17th hole. Zoeller, who had a five-birdie run on the first nine and had birdied the 16th to tie for the lead, topped it off when he ran in an 18-foot birdie putt on the last green for 64–196 and the one-stroke victory to go with his 2002 triumph in the Senior PGA Championship. Nicklaus shot 67 and placed sixth at 201, his highest finish on the Champions Tour since the 2001 U.S. Senior Open.

Royal Caribbean Golf Classic—$1,450,000
Winner: Bruce Fleisher

The Royal Caribbean Golf Classic is where it all began for Bruce Fleisher — and the beat goes on. Fleisher, who lives in Miami, launched his Champions Tour career in 1999 with a victory in the Royal Caribbean Classic in his hometown, won again there the next winter, and socked away a third title in the first full-field event of 2004. It took a birdie on the final green to do it, his one-under-par 71 giving him a one-stroke victory over Dana Quigley on a windy Sunday on a Crandon Park Golf Club layout that Quigley described as "as hard a golf course as we play all year." Only six players broke par that day.

The gusty conditions prevailed through the entire tournament. Tom Kite held a one-shot lead at day's end Friday with his four-under-par 68, the highest starting score to lead the Royal Caribbean Classic since 1992, and he had five players, including Fleisher, right on his tail at 69. Don Pooley, who missed much of the 2003 season with a shoulder injury and also was in that quintet, matched the score Saturday and shared the lead with Wayne Levi (70-68). South African John Bland climbed into contention with a 67, joining Fleisher, J.C. Snead and Bruce Summerhays (with 70s) at 139.

Only two players broke 70 in the tough conditions Sunday. One was Quigley, who was seven strokes off the lead when he made the turn but racked up four birdies coming in to put a target score on the board. Fleisher ran off eight pars on the back nine through No. 17, where Bland fell back with a bogey. Needing a birdie at the par-five 18th to beat Quigley, Fleisher lofted a splendid pitch from the grassy upslope of a greenside bunker and holed the five-foot putt for 71–210 and his 17th victory on the Champions Tour.

"It was a struggle out there," he remarked afterward. "I certainly didn't want to go down 18 again with him (Quigley)." Fleisher's total was the highest winning score in tournament history. Bland, who bogeyed the last two holes, tied for third with Gil Morgan at 212.

ACE Group Classic—$1,600,000
Winner: Craig Stadler

Craig Stadler surprised himself when he wound up with the title in the ACE Group Classic in Naples, Florida. "There's no rhyme or reason I should've won the golf tournament," said Stadler, who pieced together a final-round par 72 that included a double bogey and slipped into a three-way deadlock at 210 with Gary Koch and Tom Watson. Then, on the subsequent playoff hole, he holed a 27-foot birdie putt to score his fourth Champions Tour victory in less than a year of action. Another reason for his incredulity about winning was the fact that the West Coaster was 0-forever in Florida during his long and lucrative 21-victory career.

Stadler took a one-stroke lead into the final round and, as he had twice before on the Champions Tour, carried the lead to victory. Stadler shot an impressive 67 Saturday as 30-mile-an-hour winds made the TwinEagles Golf Club course play four shots tougher than it had the day before when Koch, winless after his first full season on the tour, blistered the course with a tournament-record 62 that included a holed 50-foot bunker shot for an eagle. Yet he only led Lonnie Nielsen by one stroke as more than half the field broke par.

Koch struggled in the wind Saturday, made only one birdie, and shot 73, dropping a stroke behind Stadler and his 134. Only nine players broke par that day, among them Watson, whose 69 left him five strokes off the lead. As Koch put it, "It was the kind of day that every time I made a par, it was kinda like. 'Whew, one less hole to play.'"

When he drove out of bounds and double-bogeyed the 13th hole Sunday, Stadler fell three shots behind his friend Koch and admitted later that he then hoped that Gary would notch his first Champions Tour victory. But Stadler kept plugging along and birdied the 15th as Koch faltered with bogeys at the 14th and 17th. Meanwhile, Watson birdied two of the last three holes for 67 and his 210, and Larry Nelson missed the playoff when he bogeyed the 18th and finished with 211.

Like Stadler, Watson had never won in Florida, and he had the best chance on the extra hole, but, after Koch missed from 31 feet and Stadler made his 27-footer, Watson failed to convert from 10 feet and was forced to settle for second place at Naples for the fourth time in five years.

Outback Steakhouse Pro-Am—$1,600,000
Winner: Mark McNulty

Mark McNulty joined some high-class company when he won in his first start on the Champions Tour in the annual event at Tampa, Florida, renamed by its new sponsor as the Outback Steakhouse Pro-Am. Among the 10 other players who accomplished the same thing their first times out in senior competition were Arnold Palmer, Jack Nicklaus and Gary Player. Just as satisfying to the native Zimbabwean, though, was the fact that, although he had compiled a tremendous record around the world with 55 victories, he had never won in the United States. "Even though it's the Champions Tour, it's still a big deal," McNulty said. "It's my first win in America and I will enjoy it."

McNulty had planned to launch his Champions Tour career at the start of the season, but an attack of shingles in January had delayed the debut. At that, his victory was no surprise, considering his career record and his medalist performance in the qualifying tournament for the 2004 circuit.

He won by just one stroke, but that was deceiving, since he reached the 72nd hole with a three-shot lead, then took a bogey while runner-up Larry Nelson was notching a birdie. Both players shot 68s, McNulty for a 13-under-par 200 and Nelson for 201. But, for most of the afternoon, much of the attention was on Fuzzy Zoeller and his run at the Champion Tour's first-ever 59. Zoeller rang up 11 birdies over the first 14 holes, including seven in a row, one shy of the tour record, and he still had a shot at 59 until he bogeyed the last hole. His 61 tied the course record at the TPC at Tampa Bay and jumped him from nowhere into a third-place tie at 202 with Tom Purtzer.

McNulty began the tournament solidly with 67, sitting four strokes off the lead as Tom Kite took advantage of benign conditions, ran off eight birdies, and posted a 63, good for a one-stroke lead over Nelson and Mike McCullough. The wind picked up Saturday, to Kite's detriment (74), but to McNulty's advantage. He shot 65 and jumped into a one-stroke lead over Nelson (69) and D.A. Weibring, who matched McNulty's effort to reach his 133.

Although McNulty surrendered the lead to the streaking Zoeller at one point Sunday, he built a comfortable lead on the back nine, the cushion he needed at the end to hold off Nelson, a winner 17 times in his six-plus years.

MasterCard Classic—$2,000,000
Winner: Ed Fiori

The odds were stacked against Ed Fiori when he teed off in the final round of the MasterCard Classic in the Champion Tour's only foray into Mexico. It wasn't enough that he was seven strokes behind leader Graham Marsh at that time. Only once in tour history had a winner made up more shots the last day — Jay Sigel won from 10 strokes back in the GTE West Classic in 1994. Nor was it that he hadn't won a tournament of any kind in nearly eight years, before which he was on the verge of a career change to charter boat captain.

There he was in thin air at 8,100 feet on the Bosque Real Golf Club course, having spent part of the previous night being treated for high blood pressure just two months after suffering a heart attack. The chunky Texas resident overcame all of those obstacles, winning the early March tournament — and he even had to go three extra holes to do it.

While Fiori was muddling along unnoticed with a 72-71 start, others were showing their mettle. Andy Bean, a strong player on the regular tour in the 1980s from whom little had been heard since, popped up in the lead Friday with 67, one stroke ahead of Jim Colbert and Stewart Ginn of Australia. Marsh made his move Saturday, shooting 66 for 136 and a one-stroke lead over Hugh Baiocchi of South Africa.

On Sunday, though, Marsh, trying to be the first 60-or-over to win on the Champions Tour in three seasons, struggled with a cold putter. After three-putting the 16th and 17th holes, he missed a winning birdie putt on the 54th hole to fall into the playoff with Fiori, who made his massive move with "just" a 67. Both players bogeyed the first playoff hole, Marsh hitting a wedge approach into the water at the 18th. They parred the second extra hole, the 16th, before Fiori's par at the 17th accounted for the victory.

Although Fiori won four times during his career on the regular PGA Tour, he called his victory in Tampa "the thrill of my life." Marsh, on the other hand, singled out the putting for his failure. "I didn't lose in the playoff," said the Australian, who had six wins on his Champions Tour record since 1994. "I lost with the two three-putts and that pathetic wedge into the water hazard" at the 18th hole in the playoff.

SBC Classic—$1,500,000
Winner: Gil Morgan

Gil Morgan continued his climb up the ladder of all-time career winners on the Champions Tour when he won the SBC Classic at Valencia Country Club in Southern California in mid-March. It was his 23rd victory on the senior circuit, elevating him into a tie for fourth place with Bob Charles behind Hale Irwin, Lee Trevino and Miller Barber.

Interestingly, his victory run began in 1996, his first season, in the same tournament when it was known as the Ralphs Senior Classic and was played at Wilshire Country Club. He repeated the following year, yet he admitted that he was nervous this time coming down the stretch, still haunted by memories of the remarkable turn of events that cost him a third SBC title in 2003. Leading by two strokes playing the 36th and final hole, he bogeyed, and Tom Purtzer snatched the victory with a 58-foot eagle putt.

This time, Morgan saw a five-stroke lead through 11 holes dwindle to two, but he made a good par putt at the 15th and carried that margin to victory. He shot 69 Sunday for a 14-under-par 202. Like Purtzer the previous year, Larry Nelson eagled the 18th Sunday, jumping into second place, one stroke ahead of Peter Jacobsen, who was making his Champions Tour debut. Two-time SBC Classic winner Joe Inman shot 64 Sunday and tied Graham Marsh for fourth place.

Jacobsen, just a week beyond his 50th birthday, launched his Champions Tour career adroitly with a five-under-par 67, making an eight-foot birdie putt on the final hole to join Craig Stadler, Don Pooley and Mike McCullough atop the field after the first round. Morgan took possession of the lead Saturday with a little help from Nelson. Morgan fired a solid 66 with a lone bogey at the 17th hole, but Nelson, who started the day a stroke off the lead, blazed around the first nine in 30 strokes, eagled the ninth hole, and overtook Morgan at 10 under par. But Nelson drove into the water at the 10th, took two later bogeys, and came in with 68 for 136, holding the runner-up slot but three behind Morgan's 133.

Stadler and Jacobsen pulled within two strokes after eight holes Sunday before Morgan hit the afterburners and birdied the next three holes to establish a comfortable five-shot cushion. That enabled him to ease to the eventual two-stroke victory, his fifth all-time in the Los Angeles area.

Toshiba Senior Classic—$1,600,000
Winner: Tom Purtzer

Only once before in the 25-year history of the Champions Tour did a player shoot an opening-round 60 as Tom Purtzer did. Like Bruce Fleisher before him in the 2002 RJR Championship, Purtzer carried the record-tying start to victory in the Toshiba Senior Classic at Newport Beach, California, but not with the same ease as Fleisher enjoyed two years earlier in North Carolina. Purtzer, picking up his second Champions Tour title, had to battle to the final hole to notch a one-stroke victory over Morris Hatalsky. Purtzer, a five-time winner on the PGA Tour in his younger days, followed the 60 with 71 and 67 to finish at 15-under-par 198.

Things were a bit anticlimactic at Newport Beach Country Club after Purtzer's 60, when he took a four-stroke lead over Joe Inman, who had posted all three of his Champions Tour triumphs up the road in the Los Angeles area in successive years in the SBC and its predecessor Pacific Bell tournaments. Purtzer had a valid shot at tour golf's record low of 59 that day. He eagled the par-five 15th and birdied the 16th to get to 10 under par, but he failed to birdie the 17th before reaching a greenside bunker at the par-five 18th and getting down in two for the birdie and 60.

"Nothing felt as good as yesterday," said Purtzer after his par 71 for 131 dropped him into a first-place tie with Hatalsky. "It was kind of like a comedy of errors most of the day." In fact, Purtzer was fortunate not to turn the lead over to Hatalsky. Hatalsky birdied the first two holes Saturday, but lost his ball in a tree at the fifth and took a double bogey. Unrattled, he birdied three of the next five holes and picked up two more strokes on the back nine for his 66–131. John Jacobs (68) and Keith Fergus (69) were right there at 132.

Only Hatalsky challenged Purtzer seriously Sunday. Purtzer opened a three-stroke lead over Hatalsky with birdies at the 15th and 16th, but gave Hatalsky a chance when he bogeyed the 17th. Hatalsky responded with a birdie at the par-five finishing hole, but Purtzer's routine par wrapped up the one-stroke victory as the circuit headed into a three-week break.

Blue Angels Classic—$1,500,000
Winner: Tom Jenkins

With the rest of the field in the Blue Angels Classic just along for the ride, Tom Jenkins qualified for a very fast one of his own when he ran away with the title at Pensacola, Florida, in mid-April. When Jenkins notched his fifth Champions Tour victory by a five-stroke margin at the Moors Golf Club, he not only acquired the $225,000 first-place check and a handsome trophy depicting the Navy's famous precision flight team, but the offer of a ride in one of the Blue Angels' Hornet jets as an added bonus.

The victory by the 56-year-old Jenkins was a virtual copy of Bob Gilder's 2003 win. Jenkins matched Gilder's final-round 63 as pulled away from Gil Morgan, the second-round leader, to win by the largest margin in the event's 10-year history. The 63 gave him a 54-hole total of 196, three strokes higher than Gilder's victory total the previous season. Jenkins was the eighth different winner of the 2004 circuit.

Fuzzy Zoeller, who won the season-opening MasterCard Championship but was coming off a surprisingly poor showing the previous week in the Masters, rebounded with a five-under-par 65 in the opening round, staking himself to a one-stroke lead over Gilder and Morgan. Jenkins was one of 15 players who shot 68 in the renamed Emerald Coast Classic.

Morgan, who made just one bogey over the first 36 holes, took over the lead Saturday when he shot his second straight 66 on the treeless, wind-blown course as Zoeller fell back with a 71–136. Morgan, also a winner earlier in the season at the SBC Classic, led Jenkins by one stroke as he eyed his 24th victory on the Champions Tour. Jenkins shot 65 for his 133 and had two strokes on third-place Wayne Levi and Gary Koch.

Things changed quickly on Sunday. Jenkins birdied the first hole and seized the lead for good on the second when Morgan bogeyed. Jenkins, who won the Bruno's Memorial almost a year earlier, then birdied four of the next seven holes. Despite a bogey at the sixth, Jenkins led Morgan by four at the turn. He never slowed down, getting back-to-back birdies at the 12th and 13th, and observed afterward, "I felt like get me on the green and I might birdie every hole coming in."

Morgan wound up shooting 70, making just one birdie Sunday, and dropped to third place with Levi and Jim Ahern, as Rodger Davis, the Toshiba Classic winner, completed a major rebound with a 65 for 201. The Australian had been three-over-par after the first six holes of the tournament.

Liberty Mutual Legends of Golf—$2,300,000
Winner: Hale Irwin

It was not one of Hale Irwin's classier victories, he would be the first to agree. Still, the all-time king of the Champions Tour embellished his brilliant record with his 39th triumph on the circuit and 59th of his career by a shaky one-stroke margin in the Liberty Mutual Legends of Golf at The Club at Savannah Harbor in the Georgia coastal city. Irwin, who has now won at least one title in each of his 10 seasons on the Champions Tour, frittered away a three-stroke lead on the final nine Sunday before capturing the title with a par on the final hole for 11-under-par 205. He edged Gil Morgan, who bogeyed the last hole for 73, his first over-par round in his previous 24, and Gary Koch, who was already in with 206 after parring the final four holes.

Morgan, who had won three weeks earlier in the SBC Classic, had the lead the first two days. "I felt like I had a chance to birdie every hole,"

Morgan said after running off eight birdies and shooting 65 in the opening round of the hybrid event which, in its original better-ball format, led to the formation of the senior circuit in 1980. He was one stroke up on Canadian Dave Barr and Irwin, making his first start in four weeks on the Champions Tour.

Morgan shot 68 Saturday, but the top of the leaderboard remained the same as Irwin and Barr matched that score, Irwin despite a double bogey at the sixth hole. Craig Stadler started strongly and had a two-stroke lead over Morgan at the turn, but faltered on the second nine and also wound up with a 68 for 135, two strokes behind the leader, who regained the top spot with a 17-foot birdie putt at the 16th hole. Koch shot 67 to join Stadler in a fourth-place tie.

Irwin built a three-stroke lead over Barr, four over Morgan, when he birdied the ninth hole for an outgoing 33 Sunday. However, he bogeyed the 12th and 16th, the latter miscue dropping him into a deadlock with Morgan. But Morgan drove into a fairway bunker at the last hole and eventually two-putted from 20 feet for the costly bogey as Irwin parred out.

Bruno's Memorial Classic—$1,500,000
Winner: Bruce Fleisher

"He just obliterated the rest of us." That was the appraisal of Hale Irwin after Bruce Fleisher's runaway victory in the Bruno's Memorial Classic in Birmingham, Alabama, in early May. It was no exaggeration. Fleisher's seven-stroke margin was the widest in tournament history and the biggest on the Champions Tour in nearly three years as he became the first multiple winner in the season's 10th event. On the other hand, he was the 13th consecutive different winner in the event's history.

The rout began Friday. Sharpened by a remedial session on the range after a poor effort in the pro-am, Fleisher nailed an eight-under-par 64 at Greystone Golf and Country Club and jumped off with a two-stroke lead over Lonnie Nielsen. That set the stage for his wire-to-wire victory, the first for an outright leader each day in the Bruno Memorial's history.

Fleisher widened his margin to four strokes Saturday. He birdied the last hole for 68 and 132 with only one bogey after 36 holes. D.A. Weibring, seeking his second Champions Tour victory, moved into second place, shooting 68 despite a bogey at the 18th. Defending champion Tom Jenkins fired a 66 and was five behind Fleisher with Hale Irwin and Jay Siegel, who had 67s. "That's a nice lead," conceded Fleisher, "but we'll see."

The field saw an invincible leader Sunday, undisturbed by a late start following a two-hour delay forced by heavy overnight rains. Fleisher maintained his margin through the first nine, then made three birdies coming in for another 68 and his 16-under-par 200. Only Weibring made any sort of challenge Sunday. He got within two strokes briefly early on the first nine, but Fleisher responded promptly with a birdie and any threat ended.

"Bruce played a terrific, real solid round and made a couple of putts to put it away on the back nine," observed Weibring, who shot 71 and tied for second at 207 with Bruce Lietzke, who closed with a 67.

"I was very focused," said the 55-year-old Fleisher about the wrap-up of his 18th victory on the senior circuit. "No matter how good you're striking it, it can come up and bite you." The only bite he suffered, though, was from the victory bug.

FedEx Kinko's Classic—$1,600,000
Winner: Larry Nelson

Larry Nelson thought and tinkered his way to his first victory of 2004 in the FedEx Kinko's Classic in Austin, Texas. The 56-year-old Nelson, an often short-changed three-time major championship winner during his solid PGA Tour career, racked up his 18th title on the senior circuit without benefit of his "A" game, if you accept his post-victory analysis.

"I really didn't hit the ball that well, but I really did think well," said the soft-spoken Georgian, who emerged from a pack of contenders with a final-round 67 for a seven-under-par 209 total that gave him a one-stroke triumph over Bruce Lietzke at The Hills Country Club in early May.

Like Arnold Palmer, born on the same September 10th date 18 years earlier, Nelson constantly fiddles with his clubs. Although one of the circuit's best on the greens, Nelson decided to saw two inches off his putter before the start of the tournament. It may have been the secret, but not at the start. He opened with 73 and was six strokes behind leaders Raymond Floyd and Scot Sam Torrance, the 2002 European Ryder Cup captain making his initial full-time foray on the Champions Tour. Floyd had endured back problems and prostate cancer surgery since his 14th and last win on the circuit, the 2000 Senior Players Championship. Torrance called his 67 his best round to date in America.

Bob Charles, professional golf's original left-handed star whose sparkling record of 29 titles is topped by the 1963 British Open, popped into a three-way tie for the second-round lead with Wayne Levi and Mark McNulty at 139. Had he gone on to a 24th victory on the Champions Tour, Charles, at age 68, would have been the circuit's oldest winner ever by five years.

However, Charles couldn't maintain the pace Sunday, faltering with a 76. Nor could Levi (72) or McNulty (75) hold on as Nelson came on strong with his 67, sparked by an eagle at the eighth hole. When he birdied the 10th and 13th holes, Nelson had a share of the lead with Lietzke, and when he rolled in a 39-footer with his shortened putter for a final birdie at the 16th, Nelson had the lead for keeps. He gave Lietzke one last chance at the par-five 18th when he missed a fairly short birdie putt after nearly holing his wedge shot to the green. But Lietzke overshot the green with his four-iron second shot, chipped long and, with Nelson watching, missed the tying putt.

Allianz Championship—$1,500,000
Winner: D.A. Weibring

In its own way, "youth" always seems to be served in the Allianz Championship. In the first three seasons of its existence, youngsters by Champions Tour standards — Jim Thorpe (52), Bob Gilder (51) and Don Pooley (51)

— walked off the Glen Oaks Country Club course in West Des Moines, Iowa, with the title, and nothing changed in 2004. D.A. Weibring was two days short of his 51st birthday when he spurted to a three-stroke victory in the tournament's renewal in late May.

Weibring, whose greatest success has come in the Midwest, scored his second victory on the senior circuit with a closing 71 and a nine-under-par total of 204, finishing three in front of Tom Jenkins, who was gunning for his second 2004 triumph. Of Weibring's five victories on the regular PGA Tour, four came in his native state of Illinois — three in the Quad Cities in Coal Valley and the 1987 Western Open in Chicago. His other Champions Tour win occurred in the SAS Championship in Raleigh, North Carolina, in his rookie 2003 season.

His putter contributed heavily to Weibring's fast start on a Glen Oaks course that, in its late spring position on the schedule, played much tougher than in previous years when the event was staged in drier summer conditions. Weibring, one of just 11 players in the 60s Friday, compared to 31 in 2003's opening round, made six birdies on the first 12 holes — three with putts of 30 feet or longer — and parred in for the 65 that staked him to a two-stroke lead over Tom Wargo, off to his best start in a mediocre season.

Weibring never trailed after that. He holed a 60-footer early in his second-round 68 and held off a challenge from Bobby Walzel, an illness-and-injury-plagued man who hadn't played on the circuit since the previous October. Tom Jenkins (67), Tom Watson (68) and Tom Kite (69) were tied for third, four off the lead. Wargo fell back with back-to-back double bogeys and 72.

Sunday turned blustery and overcast, virtually precluding any sizzling rounds. That enabled Weibring to win easily with an even-par final round. He held himself together early when he put his tee shot in the water at the second hole and double-bogeyed. He went birdie-bogey-birdie on the next three holes, ran off nine straight pars, stiffed his approach for a birdie at the 15th, and coasted home with a nine-under-par 204. He won by three strokes over Jenkins (70), four over Watson (71) and five over Kite (72), Raymond Floyd (66), Jim Thorpe and Jay Sigel (68s). Walzel's bubble burst and he finished with an 80.

Senior PGA Championship—$2,000,000
Winner: Hale Irwin

The Senior PGA Championship wound up resoundingly weather-beaten, but with as proper a winner as anybody could have expected. What seemed like constant rain drove the Champion Tour's first major of the year to a further-delayed Monday finish, and when things sloshed to a climax, Hale Irwin had his fourth Senior PGA Championship. Only Sam Snead won the Senior PGA more often — six times — and those came in the years when only a handful of players in the fields had tour experience.

Irwin, just short of his 59th birthday, shot a final-round, even-par 71 that Monday after sitting around at water-logged Valhalla Golf Club in rain-drenched Louisville, Kentucky, half the day as the final-round start had to be delayed five hours while a flooded creek subsided. It gave him his seventh major title and a tour-record 40th victory by one stroke over Jay Haas, who was making his Champions Tour debut while still playing most of his golf on the regular PGA Tour.

In the course of the first four days, Valhalla absorbed seven inches of rain, according to the weatherman, and it began right out of the box. Play was delayed two hours Thursday because of heavy overnight rain, and only half the field finished the first round Thursday. Irwin and Tom Watson posted 67s that day, and Haas and Gil Morgan matched that score when they finished their first rounds on Friday afternoon.

Play didn't start Friday until 4:30, and Irwin and Watson were among 78 players who did not even begin their second rounds that day. Kentucky got some much-needed sun Saturday. Everyone completed their second rounds, Irwin claiming possession of the lead with a four-birdie run and 69 for 136 total, placing him a stroke in front of John Harris (70-67) and Wayne Levi (69-68). Morgan and Haas (both 67-71) were next.

Hopes of completing the tournament Sunday were dashed when weather reared its disruptive head again. Before a line of heavy weather, including tornadoes in nearby Indiana, forced the tournament's fourth suspension of play, Irwin finished the last nine holes of his third round with a 69 and bogeyed the first hole of his final round. At that point, he led Haas and Dave Barr by a stroke.

When play finally began Monday afternoon after the five-hour delay, Irwin put together a 71 and needed a birdie on the 72nd hole to edge Haas by one stroke with his eight-under-par 276. He two-putted the par-five 18th for the birdie after Haas, playing in the preceding group, overshot the green with his fairway wood and missed a 10-footer on his birdie try. He shot 70 for his 277. Craig Stadler was third, shooting 69 for 279. Irwin's comment as he left the 18th green said it for the field, "I'm pooped."

Farmers Charity Classic—$1,600,000
Winner: Jim Thorpe

Just when it appeared that Andy Bean, the deep-voiced Floridian, was on the verge of winning a tour event for the first time in 18 years, fate struck him a cruel blow. Less than an hour before he would be taking a share of the lead in the Farmers Charity Classic into the final round, Bean became ill on the practice tee and passed out in the caddie tent at Egypt Valley Golf Club at Grand Rapids, Michigan, the victim of an allergic reaction to his sausage-and-muffin breakfast. Although he came around quickly, doctors insisted that he go by ambulance to the hospital. So he missed his starting time and his chance at the long-sought victory.

What was a bitter disappointment for Bean worked eventually to the benefit of Jim Thorpe, who ended a parade of near-misses at Egypt Valley. Barely. He nearly squandered a three-stroke lead with a double bogey at the 72nd hole, edging Fred Gibson by a stroke with his six-under-par 66 and 203 total. Gibson, a non-winner, also shot 66 and conceded that, although "it was nip and tuck for a while, it was real difficult for me."

Thorpe, who has won at least once in his last five years on the Champions Tour, had finished second, third and fourth in previous Farmers Charity Classics. It was his eighth victory in his sixth season on the circuit.

"Golf is a funny game," observed the 55-year-old Thorpe. "We take turns every week beating one another. One thing that shocked me is how good the level of play still is out here." He was the 11th different winner in the first 13 events of the season.

The powerful man with an unorthodox swing trailed Bean and Bob Gilder by three strokes after 36 holes, sitting in a five-way tie for third place. He had rounds of 67 and 70, joining Tom Purtzer, Vicente Fernandez, Stewart Ginn and first-round-leader Sammy Rachels at 137. Rachels, who was out most of the 2003 season with injuries suffered in a motorcycle accident, shot 64 Friday, the week's lowest round, but wound up far down the standings when he followed with 73 and 76.

Gilder, who also was shooting for an eighth Champions Tour title, managed only a 71 Sunday and tied for third with Gil Morgan, whose check made him the year's first $1 million winner, the eighth straight season he has posted seven-digit earnings.

Bayer Advantage Celebrity Pro-Am—$1,650,000
Winner: Allen Doyle

Little did Allen Doyle know how important was the eight-foot birdie putt he holed on the 18th green to conclude the second round of the Bayer Advantage Celebrity Pro-Am with a 66 and inch back into a one-stroke lead in the tournament. He found out the next day after overnight thunderstorms raked the Kansas City area with heavy rains and winds up to 75 miles an hour. The violent weather left the National Golf Club course littered with debris, fallen television towers and downed tents Sunday. When it was clear that the course could not be made playable again, tournament officials cancelled the round and declared Doyle the winner.

It was the first time in two years that a Champions Tour event was shortened to 36 holes. Ironically, that also happened in Kansas City in the predecessor TD Waterhouse Championship.

Doyle, 57, obviously had no complaint about the decision that gave him his ninth victory on the circuit and first of the 2004 season. "I know it's not the way Bayer and the tournament people wanted it to end, but I'm thrilled to be the champion," he remarked. "In a couple of years, nobody will remember that it was shortened by rain."

Jerry Pate, who was making his strongest bid for his initial triumph on the Champions Tour, had good reason to be unhappy with the outcome. He trailed Doyle by a single stroke after rounds of 67 and 65 and was three shots ahead of the rest of the field, but masked any negative feelings.

"I'm not disappointed at all because I'm excited for Allen," said the personable Pate, who is hoping to regain the winning form he had before serious shoulder trouble and a series of operations cut short his bright career on the PGA Tour in the early 1980s. "I'm feeling great about my game, and I know I've got more opportunities ahead of me."

Doyle shared the first-round lead at seven-under-par 65 with John Harris, a long-time amateur, and Andy Bean, bouncing back from the shock of his forced withdrawal from the Farmers Charity Classic the previous Sunday when he collapsed from an allergy attack shortly before he was to tee off in the final round with a share of the lead. Mark James and Morris Hatalsky shot 66s, and Pate was one of six players at 67.

The bad weather was forecast to hit the area earlier than it did, enabling the field to complete the second round and set what turned out to be the final order of finish. Doyle ran off six birdies over the first 16 holes before taking his first bogey of the tournament when he three-putted No. 17 and making the winning birdie at No. 18. Meanwhile, Pate, who finished his round on the first nine, birded the fifth, seventh and ninth holes for 65 and his 132 total. James, Bean, Bob Gilder and David Eger tied for third at 135.

Bank of America Championship—$1,550,000
Winner: Craig Stadler

"This is probably the best golfing day I will ever have," pronounced Craig Stadler after winning the Bank of America Championship in late June. The victory certainly was meaningful, but was just one of five he had accumulated in his first 12 months on the Champions Tour. He had also won 13 titles during his fine career on the regular PGA Tour, one of which was the coveted Masters.

So why would Stadler make such a strong statement? Very simple. On the same day that Stadler won the Bank of America Championship in Massachusetts, his son Kevin scored the biggest victory of his young career when he won the Lake Erie Charity Classic, the Nationwide Tour tournament in upstate New York. "I don't think another win will ever come close to this. I am so happy for him and so proud of him. I never even dreamed of us both winning on the same day," explained the veteran Californian. Those dual victories perhaps are only paralleled by the same-day victories in 1999 of David Duval in The Players Championship and his father, Bob, in the Emerald Coast Classic on the Champions Tour.

Craig Stadler rested four strokes off the lead after two rounds at Nashawtuc Country Club in suburban Boston. Then, on Sunday, although aware of his son's prospects of victory, Stadler focused on the business at hand and fired a blazing eight-under-par 64 to establish his tournament-leading score of 15-under-par 201. When he finished, Stadler was less concerned whether that score would hold up than what Kevin was doing. He went into the scoring trailer and watched as his son won the Nationwide Tour event on the fourth playoff hole.

Meanwhile, Tom Purtzer, who led the tournament for the first two rounds, came to the 17th hole two strokes off Stadler's final score. But, as with Stadler earlier, Purtzer had trouble with the par-three hole, only worse. He double-bogeyed from a bunker and dropped into a three-way tie for second place at 205 with Tom Kite and D.A. Weibring.

Purtzer opened the tournament with a seven-under-par 65, hoping that a cranky back would hold up as it sometimes hadn't earlier in the season, even though he had won the Toshiba Senior Classic in March and had six top-10 finishes, helping him to an eighth-place position on the money list.

The 65 gave him a one-stroke lead over John Harris. Stadler opened with 68 and he slipped four back Saturday with 68-69–137 as Purtzer widened his margin with 68–133. At that point, Purtzer led John Jacobs and Walter Hall by two strokes and, among others, Stadler by four.

The tables turned drastically Sunday. As Purtzer faltered with an even-par 72, Stadler was roaring obliviously along. "I was just a wreck out there, watching Kevin all day. I wasn't paying attention to my own game. That's probably why I played well." By the time he reached No. 17, Stadler had built a three-stroke lead. He skulled a sand shot over the green at the par-three and was fortunate to save bogey there. He finished with 64 despite that mishap and won handily with his 201 total.

Commerce Bank Long Island Classic—$1,500,000
Winner: Jim Thorpe

It was the middle of July and the 2004 Champions Tour had been distinguished by the way the titles had been spread around. Only three players — Bruce Fleisher, Hale Irwin and Craig Stadler — were multiple winners, each with just a pair of victories. But the unlikely happened at the Commerce Bank Long Island Classic when Jim Thorpe became the fourth player with more than a single victory and the first of the year to successfully defend a championship — by the skin of an 18-foot par putt on the final hole.

Thorpe, who had won the Farmers Charity Classic three Sundays earlier, edged Bobby Wadkins, Andy Bean and Wayne Levi by one stroke with that clutch putt and a 67 for 201 total, nine under par. He followed an unusual pattern in the long-standing Long Island event with the repeat. Its other three two-time winners — George Archer, Lee Trevino and Bruce Fleisher — all did it back to back.

The exciting finish developed when Jerry Pate, who had taken command of the tournament Saturday, saw victory hopes go by the boards for the second time in three weeks when he stumbled to a 73 in the final round. Pate, the one-time star on the PGA Tour seeking his first Champions Tour win, had shared the first-round lead at six-under-par 64 with Wadkins and Peter Jacobsen, who was making his first start in three months after undergoing arthroscopic hip surgery. Thorpe was right there with a 65 at the tournament's new venue — the Red course at Eisenhower Park, a public facility at East Meadow.

Pate, who didn't have a bogey Friday, followed with a one-bogey 66 Saturday and took a two-stroke lead at 130, thanks to a misplay by Wadkins at the final hole. An errant drive and a weak chip resulted in a double bogey that cost Wadkins a share of the lead. Instead, Pate was atop the standings going into the final round for the first time in 23 years, when he led the 1981 Pensacola Open and went on to victory. Tom Jenkins (66) and Mike Hill (67) were three off the lead at 133, and Thorpe added a 69 for 134, tied there with Levi. Jacobsen fell from contention with a 74–138.

Thorpe made up ground early Sunday with three birdies on the first nine. His surge faltered when he bogeyed the 16th hole, but he birdied the par-five 17th and shared the lead with Wadkins after Bobby birdied the 17th as well. Playing ahead of him, Thorpe missed his five-iron approach short right of the green. "That was a bad place to miss the green," Thorpe said later. "I told myself, 'Don't get stupid. Just put it on the green and make the putt.'" He did.

Bean, in the previous threesome, missed a birdie putt at the 18th for 201 total, and so did Levi, who was playing with Thorpe. Levi's birdie bid from the fringe just missed. That left it up to Wadkins, who put his approach on the last hole in virtually the same place as Thorpe, pitched 15 feet long and failed to drop the tying putt. Bean shot 67, Levi 68, and Wadkins 70. Thorpe was 15 under par at 195 when he won at Eisenhower in 2003 and declared that he was able to win with a nine-under score in 2004 because "it was a different course, longer and with higher rough."

Ford Senior Players Championship—$2,500,000
Winner: Mark James

Were it not for the 1999 Ryder Cup Matches, Mark James likely would have been tagged a little-known Englishman in stories describing how he hung on for a one-stroke victory in the Ford Senior Players Championship, the Champions Tour's second major of the season. Although James had 22 amateur and professional titles on his record and had played on seven Ryder Cup teams before joining the senior circuit in 2004, he had never won an important event in Europe and rarely played in America during his earlier career. But he was the captain of the European team in the hotly contested Ryder Cup at Boston's The Country Club in 1999 and got a great deal of attention before, during and after that controversial event.

When he turned 50, James elected to play on the more lucrative Champions Tour rather than on the European Seniors Tour, and it proved to be a wise choice. With strong showings at the Senior PGA Championship (fourth) and the Bayer Advantage Celebrity Pro-Am (third), James came to Dearborn's TPC of Michigan comfortable with his game. He began with a competitive 68, three strokes behind Gil Morgan, the first-round leader, but in a tie for second place with Dana Quigley, Allen Doyle, Bruce Fleisher, Isao Aoki and Jose Maria Canizares, who, as it turned out, was his strongest challenger over the weekend.

Gary McCord, the zany CBS commentator, took over a share of first place Friday with Canizares. McCord, who also fulfilled a television role that week, shot 64 with nine birdies and a bogey, one short of the tournament record, to go 10 under par. Canizares caught him when he birdied the last six holes of his round for 66 and his 134. Morgan slipped to 70, and James and Quigley shot 67s to stand just a stroke off the pace at 135.

From there in, James was in the forefront. He fired a solid 67 Saturday to post a 14-under-par 202 and jump three strokes in front of the field. McCord and Canizares shot 71s and shared second place at 205. A promising day turned into a huge disappointment for Quigley, who was tied for the lead with James before putting two balls in the water at the challenging par-five 17th and taking a quadruple-bogey nine. He finished with 72 for a 207 total. Morgan faded with a 75 for 210.

Canizares mounted the strongest challenge Sunday. James remained at least two strokes in front until he bogeyed the ninth hole. When the

Spaniard birdied the 10th, he moved into a first-place tie, and Canizares was in and out of the lead until he went in front with a birdie at the 16th before James bogeyed the hole. But, trying to play safe at the risky 17th, Canizares scuttled his hopes, as Quigley had the day before, with a ball into the lake and took a fatal double bogey that dropped him a stroke off the pace. James parred in behind him for 73–275 and clinched the one-stroke victory, the first ever in a Champions Tour major championship by a European. Scores of 71 carried Fleisher into third place at 277 and Bruce Lietzke into fourth at 278.

Interestingly, James was the third straight player and sixth in history to score an initial Champions Tour victory in the Senior Players Championship. "It's been a dream really," said James, whose playing career had been in doubt through two surgeries for testicular cancer at the turn of the century.

Senior British Open—€1,504,220
Winner: Pete Oakley

See European Seniors Tour section.

U.S. Senior Open—$2,600,000
Winner: Peter Jacobsen

It defied logic. Common sense dictated that Peter Jacobsen could not possibly win the U.S. Senior Open, given the circumstances that he faced after 36 holes. The personable Jacobsen "almost didn't come" to St. Louis and Bellerive Country Club for perhaps the most important tournament of the year. He had had hip surgery in late April and had pulled out of two earlier tournaments because he felt it would be too painful to walk 18 holes each day. So, when another siege of bad weather hit at the end of July in St. Louis, forcing a 36-hole Sunday finish of the Senior Open, it didn't seem likely that Jacobsen, sharing the lead after the drawn-out first two rounds, could get around the course twice that Sunday and win the title. But he did. Upholding the adage warning the field to "beware the injured player," Jacobsen ground out rounds of 69 and 68 and made the Senior Open his first Champions Tour victory in just his third start since turning 50 in March.

Jacobsen staked out his bid from the start. His six-under-par 65, his third consecutive opening round in the 60s, gave him a one-stroke lead over Craig Stadler and two over Jay Haas, who was making just his second start on the circuit while focusing on his efforts to qualify for the U.S. Ryder Cup team on the regular tour. The day before the rains came was marked by an off-beat record occurrence as three players — Mike McCullough and club professionals John Aubrey and Pat Tallent — made holes-in-one. Aubrey's was the first shot of the tournament at the third hole.

The first of the rains came through the night and into Friday morning, forcing a cancellation of the round and mandating the 36-hole finish Sunday, which some questioned as too arduous for the senior players.

Jacobsen's hip withstood another test Saturday. He shot 70, chipping in from 40 feet for a birdie on the last hole, and finished in a tie for the lead with Stadler, who birdied three holes coming in for 69 and his 135. Jose Maria Canizares birdied the last three holes for 68–136, and a host of strong players remained in striking distance — Tom Kite, Fuzzy Zoeller, Bob Gilder and D.A. Weibring at 137 and Gil Morgan and Hale Irwin at 138.

Jacobsen's victory on Sunday came at the painful expense of Kite, whose run for a Senior Open title to go with his 1992 U.S. Open victory deflated in the stretch Sunday. Kite, going after his first Champions Tour victory in 21 months, fashioned a 65 in the morning round and jumped into a two-stroke lead over Jacobsen (69) and Gilder (67). He remained in command in the early stages of the afternoon round until he threw a shoe on the last four holes, finishing bogey-bogey-par-double bogey for 72, which left him in a tie for third with Haas (68) at 274. The week before, Kite lost the Senior British Open to club professional Pete Oakley by a stroke. Irwin slipped into second place with 68–273, parring the 18th after giving himself a shot at the title with a birdie at the 17th.

Jacobsen birdied the first two holes in the afternoon, fell three back after six, then battled back and challenged Kite for the lead the rest of the day until Kite took the fatal double bogey ahead of him at the 18th. Kite drove into a fairway bunker and caught the lip heavily coming out, the ball going only a few feet and into heavy rough. Jacobsen parred the last three holes for 68 and the winning 272 total. He was the seventh man to make the Senior Open his first victory on the Champions Tour and was the third straight first-time winner on the circuit.

3M Championship—$1,750,000
Winner: Tom Kite

Tom Kite was a frustrated man when he arrived in Minnesota to play in the 3M Championship at the TPC of the Twin Cities the first week of August. Two major titles on the Champions Tour had just slipped through his grasp the previous two weeks when he finished second in the Senior British Open at Royal Portrush and in a third-place tie in the U.S. Senior Open when he double-bogeyed the 72nd hole. Those were his latest bids to end a non-winning streak that extended through 47 starts dating back to the fall of 2002, an unexpected run for one of the game's most successful players through the years.

End it Kite did in suburban Minneapolis with a solid finish for a 69, a 13-under-par 203 total and a one-stroke victory over Craig Stadler. Kite birdied three of the last seven holes to hold off Stadler, already a two-time winner in 2004. It was the new Hall-of-Famer's seventh Champions Tour victory, and he became the 17th different winner in the first 21 events of the season.

Three players — Kite, Stadler and Tom Purtzer — dominated the tournament from the start. Birdie runs highlighted the 64s shot by Stadler and Purtzer to take the opening-day lead. Stadler birdied his last four holes, including a 61-footer at the 16th after "the only bad iron shot I had all day." Purtzer, the Toshiba Classic winner in March, ran off five birdies in a row after the turn. Shaking off the bitter loss on Sunday, Kite shot 65 and was just one back, tied with Sammy Rachels.

Purtzer, who had a good shot at the 3M title in his first appearance in 2003 until he put two shots in the water at the 53rd hole, established a two-stroke lead Saturday, when gusty winds and cooler temperatures elevated the scoring considerably. Purtzer shot 68, with two others the low score of the day, for 132 and the two-stroke margin over Kite, with whom he had been tied until that troublesome 17th of 2003. Stadler shot 71 and settled into third place at 135.

For the second year in a row, Purtzer failed to convert a victory in the 3M Championship. A double bogey at the seventh and a bogey at the ninth headed him toward a 75 that dropped him into a three-way tie for third place with Larry Nelson (66) and Vicente Fernandez (68). Kite took the lead after consecutive birdies at the 12th and 13th, saved par with a five-footer at the 16th, and rolled a 60-foot eagle putt to tap-in range on the final green to secure the victory over Stadler, who missed an eagle putt from 15 feet at the 18th that would have forced a playoff.

Greater Hickory Classic at Rock Barn—$1,600,000
Winner: Doug Tewell

When a player goes an entire tournament without making a bogey, he should wind up in first place, which is what Doug Tewell did when he won the Greater Hickory Classic at Rock Barn in mid-August. But Tewell had to hole a 12-foot birdie putt with a borrowed putter on the 18th green Sunday to finish off a 64 and pull out a one-stroke victory over Bruce Fleisher, an 18-time winner on the Champions Tour who had seemed on the way to becoming the first three-time winner of the season. Philosophized Fleisher, "When you shoot 64, you're supposed to win."

Fleisher had taken a three-stroke lead Saturday on the Jones course at Rock Barn Golf and Spa at Conover, in the North Carolina mountains, with a low round of his own. His eight-birdie, seven-under-par 65–135 had created that margin over Tewell (69-69) and Mark Lye (66-72), the surprise first-round leader who got into the field on a sponsor's exemption and was playing in just his second tournament since undergoing gall bladder surgery in May.

Another 72 Sunday took Lye, the long-time Golf Channel analyst, out of the picture, leaving Tewell as the only challenger in the way of Fleisher's 19th Champions Tour victory. Tewell came out of the box sizzling with three straight birdies, including a holed bunker shot at the second, to pull within a stroke. The tight battle followed as Fleisher twice gave up the lead on the second nine, for the last time when "I got careless" at the 15th. He buried a sand wedge approach and fell a shot behind when he bogeyed and Tewell parred.

Both men birdied the 16th, and Tewell saved par from the front bunker at the par-three 17th. Fleisher's hopes grew when he reached the green with his second shot at the par-five finishing hole and Tewell's shot trickled into the sand. But Fleisher missed his eagle putt from 18 feet before Tewell holed his 22nd putt of the round with the putter on loan from Walter Hall for a birdie and the victory, his eighth on the circuit. He finished with 202, 14 under par. Morris Hatalsky took third place with 206, and Jerry Pate had another top-10 finish with his 68–207.

The 18th different winner of the season, Tewell left town with a $240,000 check and Hall's Ping Anser, assuring one and all that "Walter is not going to get that putter back."

JELD-WEN Tradition—$2,300,000
Winner: Craig Stadler

Craig Stadler rained on Peter Jacobsen's parade — and the rain was a shower of stretch-run birdies on the final day of the relocated JELD-WEN Tradition, the Champions Tour season's last major championship at the end of August.

Jacobsen, a rookie on the senior circuit who won the U.S. Senior Open in July, had played a big part in the move of the Tradition to his hometown area of Portland, Oregon, in 2003 after 14 years in Arizona. Furthermore, his company runs the tournament, so he elected to stay home instead of going to Hartford, Connecticut, where he would have been defending the title he won on the regular PGA Tour in 2003.

The decision looked like a sage one when he played solidly for the first three days and shared the lead after 54 holes with Vicente Fernandez. But Stadler became a spoilsport Sunday at Reserve Vineyards and Golf Club when he birdied the last four holes for 67 to eke out a one-stroke victory, his third of the season and sixth in just 30 starts in 14 months on the Champions Tour. He finished with a 13-under-par 275, one shot ahead of Jerry Pate and Allen Doyle.

Stadler barely made his presence known the first three days. In Thursday's opening round, which was plagued with rain that had soaked the course earlier in the week, Fernandez shared the first-round lead with Bruce Summerhays and Jose Maria Canizares at 67. Jacobsen was in a huge group at 69, and Stadler had 70. When Stadler shot another 70 Friday, he slipped five strokes off the pace of Jacobsen, who jumped into the lead with 66 for 135 total, one stroke better than Bruce Lietzke. Fernandez shot 71 for 138 after nearly withdrawing with neck and back pains. "I don't think I could have played but for the trainers here," he said afterward.

The 58-year-old Argentinean poured in a 66 Saturday and took a piece of first place when Jacobsen bogeyed the 17th and left a 12-foot birdie putt at the 18th three inches short for 69 and his 204. Doyle vaulted into third place when he eagled the 15th hole and birdied in for 64–205. Again Stadler was quiet, shooting 68 for 208, four strokes behind the leaders.

Sunday's finale turned into a wild scramble. Stadler "didn't think I was in it" until he made the third of his four-birdie spurt at the 17th hole. He then played a skillful shot from the rough to four feet at the 18th, made the putt for the 67, and looked on as five players failed to catch him. Both Jacobsen and Fernandez closed with 73s, Jacobsen missing a four-foot birdie putt for the lead at the 16th then taking a double bogey at the 17th when he put his second shot in the water. They and five others wound up tied for fourth at 277.

The First Tee Open at Pebble Beach—$2,000,000
Winner: Craig Stadler

A new tournament had an old winner at famed Pebble Beach, California, the first week of September. Craig Stadler, already a three-time winner on the 2004 Champions Tour, strengthened his grip on the circuit's money lead when he finished decisively on the storied Monterey Peninsula links to win the inaugural First Tee Open on the heels of his victory the previous week in the JELD-WEN Tradition.

In fact, it was a double-edged victory for the second-season senior. The new event was created to support and focus attention on The First Tee program that is bringing golf primarily to young, underprivileged golfers around America, and its unique feature is the pairing of leading juniors with the Champions Tour professionals. Stadler and his junior partner, Aaron Woodard, a 16-year-old from Denver, finished four strokes atop the field with a 22-under-par 194. Stadler's individual total was 201, three better than that of Jay Haas, the 50-year-old who was still playing primarily on the regular PGA Tour and headed for the Ryder Cup Matches.

Benign summer weather led to low scoring, not usually the case when the PGA Tour's tournament is played in winter conditions. David Eger, the former rules official who won the MasterCard Classic in Mexico in 2003, jumped in front in Friday's opening round with a five-under-par 67 at Pebble Beach, one ahead of D.A. Weibring, the Allianz Championship winner in May, who also played on that course. Half the field played at the Bayonet Golf Course Friday, then switched for Saturday's second round.

Stadler, who had a nondescript 72 at Bayonet Friday, blistered Pebble Beach with a 63 Saturday to seize a lead he never relinquished. His torrid round, which included two eagles and six birdies, pushed him into a one-stroke lead over Haas, who shot 66 on top of his 70 at Bayonet. Those two outdistanced the rest of the field. Tom Kite, Hale Irwin (66s), Gary McCord (68) and Weibring (71) sat four off the lead at 139.

Stadler maintained his sizzling pace Sunday as he became the first player since Bob Gilder in 2002 to score back-to-back victories on the Champions Tour. He shot 66, widening his final margin to three over Haas, who closed with a 68 for 204, five better than Irwin and Kite, who tied for third place. The second-place posting gave Haas his second runner-up finish in his only three starts on the circuit. He tied for third in the Senior Open. Stadler had the two eagles and 13 birdies as he matched the season's best final two rounds with his 129 total. He had just one bogey in the final 27 holes. Eger closed with 70 for 210 and tied for fifth with Weibring (71).

Kroger Classic—$1,500,000
Winner: Bruce Summerhays

Sixty-year-old players sitting six strokes off the lead going into the final round do not figure to contend for a tournament title, particularly if they haven't won on the Champions Tour in more than six years. Bruce Summerhays defied those compelling negatives in the Kroger Classic by posting an eight-under-par 64 on the closing September Sunday in Cincinnati,

Ohio, and snaring his third career seniors victory by a single stroke at the Tournament Players Club at River's Bend.

Summerhays, the first former club professional to win on the 2004 tour, staged the greatest come-from-behind victory in tournament history as he added the Kroger Classic to his triumphs in 1997 and 1998. Ironically, before the tournament, he predicted 201 to be the winning score and that's what his nine-birdie 64 gave him as he became the 20th different winner in the season's first 26 events.

Needless to say, Summerhays attracted no attention during the first two rounds at River's Bend. Instead, Irishman Des Smyth and colorful television announcer Gary McCord got the headlines Friday on a day when officials squeezed in a full round despite a five-hour fog delay in the morning. Their seven-under-par 65s were the best among 50 sub-pars scores posted after the fog lifted. McCord won twice in 1999, while Smyth, a winner on the European Tour in his younger days, had done little in America and was struggling to climb the money list high enough to be an exempt player in 2005.

Doug Tewell, the Greater Hickory Classic winner in August and runner-up in the Kroger Classic in 2003, slipped into the lead Saturday with a 65 for 131 and a one-stroke advantage over Smyth (67) and three over McCord (69). "Maybe it's my turn to win it this year," Tewell observed. "I'd feel better if I had a six- or seven-shot lead." His seven-foot birdie putt at the 18th lipped out and that turned out to be the margin of victory for Summerhays, who had opening rounds of 67 and 70.

"I didn't go out to shoot 64. It just happened," said Summerhays of his sizzling finish. "When I got to 14 under, I said, 'Now you can get to 15 under.' It took me to the last hole to get to 15." Tewell, who still led by one after the 15th hole and was 15 under, bogeyed from the sand at the par-three 16th and failed to birdie the 18th. That left him in a three-way tie for second at 202 with Jim Thorpe and Morgan, who both closed with 66s.

SAS Championship—$1,800,000
Winner: Craig Stadler

He said it in jest, but Tom Jenkins probably expressed what many players on the Champions Tour were feeling at the end of that September week in Raleigh, North Carolina. Jenkins, the runner-up in the SAS Championship, quipped, "I told him (Craig Stadler) ... that he's too good. He needs to go back to the PGA Tour."

Stadler had just wrapped up his third victory in a row in record fashion — with a six-stroke margin and a tournament-record score of 17-under-par 199. In just 15 months on the senior circuit, the erstwhile Walrus had rung up eight victories along with a second place, two thirds and 10 top-10 finishes in his 18 starts this season. When he returned to the tour after skipping the Kroger Classic and tacked the SAS title onto his back-to-back wins in the JELD-WEN Tradition and The First Tee Open at Pebble Beach, he became the first player to win in three straight starts since Gil Morgan prevailed in his last two starts of 1997 and first start in 1998.

"I guess you get to the point where you expect things, you expect to hit good shots," said Stadler of his performance at Prestonwood Country Club in suburban Cary. "You get in a zone where you just go out and play."

Stadler was in that zone from the start, opening with a 65 and a two-stroke lead over D.A. Weibring, the defending champion, and Wayne Levi. He shook off a one-over-par status after six holes, eagled the par-five seventh with a 40-foot putt, and ran off six birdies on the back nine to take a lead he never relinquished.

He followed with a four-under-par 68 Saturday, doubling his lead to four strokes with the 133 total. Jenkins took over second place at 137 with a 65 in the second round. Weibring, Stewart Ginn and John Harris were two strokes further back. In a similar start to his opening round, Stadler missed three greens and was one over par after six holes. Again, the par-five seventh ignited his game. He birdied it, followed with another at the ninth, and picked off three more on his incoming nine for the 68.

His mastery of the second nine continued Sunday as he breezed to his easiest of five 2004 victories. He shot 66 for the 199 and was five under par on the last nine, turning the finish into a laugher with birdies on the final three holes. For the week, he was 14 under on the second nine, and in the three straight wins he was 35 under par.

Constellation Energy Classic—$1,600,000
Winner: Wayne Levi

Craig Stadler gave the other guys a chance when he bypassed the Constellation Energy Classic in Baltimore the first weekend of October, and Wayne Levi not only took advantage of his absence but also duplicated his effort in the SAS Championship by rolling to a wire-to-wire victory at Hayfields Country Club in Hunt Valley, Maryland. It was the 52-year-old Levi's second victory on the Champions Tour, coming more than a year after the initial one in the 3M Championship. He became the 21st different winner on the 2004 tour.

Although it only gave him a one-stroke lead over Rodger Davis, Levi's opening 64 clearly sparked him to the victory. "It felt like the old days when I was out on the regular tour shooting low," enthused the upstate New Yorker, whose excellent record bearing 12 victories on that circuit is often overlooked by tour followers. "I used to shoot a lot of these rounds." He fashioned the Constellation Energy round with eight birdies, tying the course record held jointly by Jose Maria Canizares (2000) and J.C. Snead (2002).

A 68 Saturday widened Levi's margin to two strokes, then over Canizares and Graham Marsh, who both shot 66s for 134. Gil Morgan and Bob Gilder, with 67s, were at 135, and another stroke back were Jerry Pate (66) and Tom Watson (68), playing in his final tournament before undergoing arthroscopic surgery on his left hip that was expected to sideline him for six months. Levi scored three birdies on the first five holes, eagled the 16th and bogeyed the 17th in shooting the 68.

Levi clung to his two-stroke edge through most of the final round, fending off challenges from Hale Irwin, Jim Thorpe and Davis. Irwin and Thorpe matched Levi's 64 of Friday, Irwin's jumping him into a second-place finish. Levi's birdie at the 16th was key to his 68 for 200 total and the victory. Irwin was at 202, Davis at 203, and Thorpe and Marsh at 204.

"This feels great," said the elated Levi. "It's not like I'm winning one of these every month."

Administaff Small Business Classic—$1,600,000
Winner: Larry Nelson

Larry Nelson turned another final-round rally into a victory on the Champions Tour. Just as he did in an earlier win in the FedEx Kinko's Classic in Austin in May, Nelson came from well off the pace over the last 18 holes to climb into a first-place tie in the new Administaff Small Business Classic in Houston when the circuit returned to Texas for a late-season pair of events. His strong finish enabled him to overtake Hale Irwin at 202, and he birdied the first playoff hole to put his 19th Champions Tour victory in the bank.

In both victorious events, the soft-spoken Georgian finished with 67s. In the Kinko's Classic, he made up a three-stroke deficit to win by a shot. In the Administaff event, he came from seven shots off the lead to gain the tie and wind up in the playoff, just the third of the season and the first since March, when Ed Fiori also made up seven strokes in the MasterCard Classic in Mexico.

For two days, Wayne Levi seemed headed for consecutive victories. Coming off his win in the Constellation Energy Classic in Maryland, Levi fired an eight-birdie 64 at Augusta Pines Golf Club and shared the first-round lead with Walter Hall. They had two strokes on Jim Dent and three over four others, including Irwin.

Levi followed with a 67 Saturday to move two strokes in front at 131. D.A. Weibring, gunning for his second 2004 victory, advanced to the runner-up position with 65 for 133, and Irwin remained in contention with 68–135. Hall dropped into a five-way tie at 136 and Nelson stood at 138 after rounds of 68 and 70.

As the leaders fell back Sunday, the 57-year-old Nelson began his climb up the standings. Out in 33 with four birdies and a bogey, Nelson birdied three of the first four holes on the second nine to overtake Peter Jacobsen, who had seized the lead earlier in the round. Nelson bogeyed again at the 17th, but he posted the leading score when he birdied the par-five 18th after Jacobsen drove into the water and finished a stroke behind at 203. Irwin also birdied the 18th to match Nelson's 202 and set up the playoff on the same hole.

Nelson birdied again and won when Irwin, on the back fringe, approached poorly with his putter and missed a 19-footer he needed to keep the match alive. Irwin got some solace as his second-place finish rewarded him with enough points to regain first place in the lucrative Schwab Cup competition over Craig Stadler, who finished at 211 in his failed quest for a fourth consecutive victory.

SBC Championship—$1,500,000
Winner: Mark McNulty

Mark McNulty stated his case for post-season honors on the Champions Tour with a resounding victory in the SBC Championship in San Antonio, Texas, in mid-October. His eight-stroke runaway at Oak Hills Country Club, coupled with his win in his first start on the Champions Tour at Tampa in the Outback Steakhouse Pro-Am in February, made him the only 2004 rookie with more than a single victory and just the sixth multiple winner of the season. It was only the third win by a foreign player all year, ex-Ryder Cup Captain Mark James bagging the other with his triumph in the Ford Senior Players Championship.

The Zimbabwean's victory margin, the largest in more than three years since Doug Tewell won by nine in the 2001 Countrywide Tradition, swelled over the weekend after he started the tournament one stroke off the 66 pace of four co-leaders — Tom Kite, Dave Stockton, Tom Jenkins and James Mason.

McNulty exploded in the middle of the second round with an eagle and five birdies in a seven-hole stretch, went on to a 63, and raced four strokes ahead of the field with his 130 total. Gary McCord, Morris Hatalsky and 2002 winner Dana Quigley were at 134. Only one under par for the day after eight holes, McNulty nearly holed his tee shot at the par-three ninth, followed with a 18-foot eagle putt at the 10th, and birdied the 11th, 13th, 14th and 15th, all with short putts. "I hit a lot of very good quality iron shots and followed them up with good putts," said McNulty, evaluating his dominating round.

The outcome was never in doubt Sunday. En route to a 65 and his 18-under-par total of 195, McNulty banged out four birdies on the first nine to quash any hopes his pursuers may have had. He kept it going with a three-birdie run starting at the 14th to widen the gap to an immense 10 strokes, which would have been an all-time Champions Tour record if he could have maintained it. But runner-up McCord birdied the 17th and McNulty took his only bogey on the final hole to prevent that achievement. Still, McNulty's eight-stroke victory margin was the widest of the season. McCord shot 69–203 and edged Bobby Wadkins (67) for second place by a stroke.

"If your putting stats are the best and your greens stats are the best, you are going to win by eight strokes," said McNulty, noting also that he only three-putted once over the 54 holes. "That doesn't happen often."

Charles Schwab Cup Championship—$2,500,000
Winner: Mark McNulty

The finale of the 2004 Champions Tour season turned into an emotional mixture of impressive triumph and unexpected disappointment in the Charles Schwab Cup Championship in the wine country of northern California in late October. Even though he was coming off a victory the previous Sunday in the SBC Championship, Mark McNulty seemed an unlikely winner at Sonoma Golf Club until he turned on the afterburners on the final nine-hole stretch and snatched a one-stroke victory, his third of the season.

It was a triumphant day, too, for Hale Irwin. The Champion Tour's all-time records-holder, struggling after a sleepless night with a stiff neck that nearly forced him to withdraw, finished high enough in the standings — joint seventh — to win the season-long Charles Schwab Cup competition and its million dollar annuity. "I'm in a mild state of shock," said Irwin as he accepted his second Schwab Cup. "I really did not think for one moment that I was going to get through the day."

The disappointed figure was Tom Kite, whose shaky game, particularly off the tee, betrayed him in the early stages of the final round after he carried a two-stroke lead into Sunday's wind-up. His closing 72 not only left him a single stroke behind McNulty, but cost him the Schwab Cup as well. It was the last of several missed opportunities during the season. A first-place finish would have jumped him past Irwin in the final points tally. "I'm disappointed that I didn't close the door in more tournaments," Kite said remorsefully.

The win was a real surprise to McNulty, who became the first international player since David Graham in 1997 to win three times in a Champions Tour season. "After Friday's round, I wasn't thinking about winning," said the 50-year-old Zimbabwe native. For good reason. He was then nine strokes behind Kite, who had opened the championship with an eight-under-par 64 and, with 70–134 at the halfway mark, led Irwin (66-69) and Morris Hatalsky (68-67) by a stroke.

The third round was played on an already saturated golf course in a steady, moderate rain, and Kite, not burdened by the glasses he wore through most of his career before undergoing laser surgery in 1998, managed a par 72 for 206 on what he called "a brutal day." He stood two shots in front of Jose Maria Canizares, three ahead of Irwin. McNulty was tied for fourth after a 68, but was five strokes back at 211.

Kite was in trouble from the start Sunday, bogeying three of the first four holes. When he bogeyed again at the seventh hole, he fell a stroke behind Allen Doyle. Even an eagle at the 13th hole didn't help, as McNulty and Doyle dueled for the lead ahead of him. McNulty ran off four birdies in a row starting at the 11th and made what proved to be the winning birdie when he holed a 15-foot putt at the 17th. Par at the 18th gave him a 66 and 277 total. Kite had one last shot at the title at the 18th, which he had birdied each of the first three days, but he missed the green with his long approach and had to settle for par, another 72 and 278 total. Doyle shot 69 and finished third at 280.

European Seniors Tour

Tobago Plantations Seniors Classic—€183,980
Winner: Carl Mason

Carl Mason continued to follow in the footsteps of Tommy Horton with his season-opening victory in the Tobago Plantations Seniors Classic. Mason, who had not yet put in a full season on the European Seniors Tour, has a long way to go to equal Horton's 23 victories, but tacked onto the spillover of three year-ending victories in 2003, the Tobago win enabled Mason to match Horton's tour record of four wins in a row. In 2003 Mason had already joined Horton as the second man in circuit history to have a four-victory season.

Mason won easily at the Tobago Plantations Beach and Golf Resort, where, somewhat incongruously, the European Seniors Tour again began its season in the Caribbean. He shot a shaky final-round 72 for 207 total, nine under par, and a three-stroke victory over Australian David Good. "That was a most uncomfortable day," remarked Mason after he frittered away a five-stroke lead, then rallied bravely with three closing birdies to establish the winning margin. "You try not to do anything silly, and because of that you end up doing something silly."

Mason bolted into the five-stroke lead Saturday when he fired a course-record, eight-under-par 64, taking first place away from first-round leader John Grace. Grace, a 55-year-old Texan who was winless since posting three victories in his first full season in 2000, had opened with 69 in strong winds. One over par after a bogey at No. 3, Mason birdied nine of the remaining 15 holes for a 135 total. John Chillas, runner-up at Tobago the previous two years, was second again at 140.

But it was Good who gave Mason a scare Sunday as he shot 67 for 210 and the runner-up slot. Mason was one over at the turn, then double-bogeyed the 11th and bogeyed the 15th. That reduced his margin over the Australian to a stroke, but he finished brilliantly with the three birdies, holing a 45-foot putt for a deuce on the par-three 17th. Defending champion Terry Gale and newcomer Jeff Hawkes placed third at 212.

DGM Barbados Open—€187,393
Winner: Gavan Levenson

Gavan Levenson wasted no time making his mark on the European Seniors Tour. The 50-year-old South African, a winner in his younger years in both Europe and South Africa, put his first senior title on his record in just his second start. He eked out a one-stroke victory in the DGM Barbados Open the last week of March in the second of the European Tour's two stops in the Caribbean launching the season.

In the process, Levenson denied Carl Mason's strong bid for a fifth consecutive victory, which would have been a tour record. Mason made a final-day run at the top. He shot 68 to Levenson's 71 Sunday, but a bogey at the 15th hole proved fatal to the title bid. Mason finished in a tie for second place with fellow Englishman Denis Durnian at 206, one stroke behind the winner.

Levenson entered the final round at Royal Westmoreland Golf Club with a three-stroke lead over Durnian after tying the course record on Saturday with an eight-under-par 64 for 133. He relished the challenge, observing, "I have not been in the lead in a tournament for years because I have not played in one." Noting that he had stopped playing on the regular European Tour in 1997 to concentrate on running a golf academy in Johannesburg, "I am really looking forward to being under the gun, which is what it is all about."

The victory didn't come easily. Durnian, seeking his first victory in 18 months, not only made up the three-stroke deficit, but went a shot ahead with a three-birdie spurt starting at the 13th hole. However, things swung dramatically back in Levenson's favor at the par-three 16th: Levenson scored a deuce and Durnian took a double-bogey five. The South African then widened the gap to four with a birdie to a Durnian bogey at the 17th, but almost needed that big margin when Durnian birdied and he closed with a bogey for 71–204. Durnian's 70 tied him with Mason at 206. John Morgan, age 60, the first-round leader with 66, finished far off the pace when he closed with a 76.

Open de France Seniors—€200,000
Winner: Bob Cameron

The promise Bob Cameron showed during his first season on the European Seniors Tour in 2003 came to fruition early in the 2004 campaign when the circuit resumed action six weeks after its two-tournament start in March in the Caribbean. The Englishman stormed the Omaha Beach Golf Club with a final-round 67 and pulled away to a three-stroke victory in the new Open de France Seniors that was part of the 60th anniversary of the D-Day invasion that led to the Allied victory in World War II.

Cameron, a club professional who occasionally played on the European Tour in his younger days, finished 15th on the 2003 money list with two seconds and a third in his rookie season. He started the new season slowly with middle-of-the-field finishes before finding his game in France. His opening 70 put him in a four-way tie for third behind Alan Mew (68), the surprise leader better known in Britain as a builder than as a golfer, and David J. Russell (69), who was making his Senior Tour debut. Mew, a native of Trinidad & Tobago, has lived in England since 1984, played amateur golf until 2002 when he tired of the construction business — he remodeled the clubhouse at famed Wentworth — and qualified for the 2003 tour as a professional.

Cameron's reign as a contender was short-lived with 78-77 the next two days, but he moved into position Saturday despite a 73. It was a cold, windy day and only two players broke par. One of them — John Chillas — joined Cameron and Brian Jones (71-72) in first place with his 71–143.

Cameron's 73 was hard-attained. He bounced back from an outgoing nine of 39 with a two-under performance coming in. On the other hand, Jones had sole leadership in his hands until he lost his ball on his five-iron second shot and double-bogeyed the 17th. A birdie at the 18th put him in the first-place deadlock.

Cameron's 67 finish for his winning 210 total matched the lowest score of the week. It was tight Sunday until he ran off three consecutive birdies starting at the 12th. Russell, whose victory hopes had been severely damaged with two double bogeys Saturday, edged into second place with a 68–213. Chillas (71) tied for third with Manuel Pinero (68).

"I have been working very hard to get to this position," said Cameron. "I was quite relaxed, which was pleasing. It was my goal to win and thankfully it came a bit sooner than I thought."

Bosch Italian Seniors Open—€160,152
Winner: Terry Gale

Terry Gale, a strong force on the 2003 European Seniors Tour, made his first emphatic move of the 2004 season with his triumph in the inaugural Bosch Italian Seniors Open. Gale, age 57, birdied the final two holes at Venezia Golf Club to take victory away from David J. Russell, who had to settle for runner-up status for the second week in a row at the start of his European Seniors career. The win, the Australian's sixth in his eight seasons on the circuit, came on the heels of his three-victory campaign in 2003 when he placed third on the money list.

Gale had fallen two strokes off the pace in Saturday's second round at the course on Lido Island just outside the historic city of Venice after sharing the opening-day lead with Gavan Levenson, the rookie winner of the DGM Barbados Open in March. Both had posted three-under-par 69s on a course Levenson called "tighter than tight" to jump off a stroke in front of Argentina's Horacio Carbonetti and American Hank Woodrome.

Gale faltered Saturday with a 74 as Russell stirred up a memory of years gone by when he shot 67 and moved into a three-way tie for the lead with Levenson (72) and Woodrome (71), winner of the Wallonia Open in Belgium in 2003. Upon learning that his 67 matched the course record set by Arnold Palmer in an exhibition event there in 1979, Russell reacted: "Arnold Palmer and me, hey! That's great." Gale, who bogeyed the last two holes, was tied for fourth with frequent contender John Chillas of Scotland.

Russell led for most of the round Sunday and remarked afterward, "I should have really nailed it. I kept getting under and then throwing it away again." Russell had a one-stroke lead after 14 holes, but was overwhelmed by Gale's storming finish. Gale birdied the 15th, made a great par save at the 16th, where he almost holed a chip shot, then sank putts of five and eight feet for the birdies on the last two holes for 68–211 and a one-stroke victory over Russell and two over Levenson and Chillas.

"It's a funny game, isn't it," observed the Australian veteran. "I finished bogey, bogey yesterday and birdie, birdie today. The pleasing thing about today was that I was able to hit the shots when it mattered."

Digicel Jamaica Classic—€233,030
Winner: Luis Carbonetti

It was younger brother's turn. Argentinean Horacio Carbonetti scored his first European Seniors Tour at Bad Ragaz in Switzerland during the 2003 season. Luis Carbonetti, six years his junior, joined his brother in the winners' ranks in 2004 when the circuit made a one-stop return to the Caribbean for the Digicel Jamaica Classic in late May. The first-year player did it the hard way, coming from behind in the final-round stretch to force a playoff and winning with a birdie on the first extra hole. In the process, Carbonetti deprived Terry Gale, the playoff loser, of a second consecutive win to go with his victory the previous Sunday in Italy.

Carbonetti's fortunes fluctuated wildly the first two days at Half Moon Bay. He came within one stroke of the tour's all-time record round on Friday when he shot a nine-under-par 63 and staked himself to a huge, five-stroke lead over Gale and American Jerry Bruner. Carbonetti launched the round with a 15-foot eagle putt on the par-five first hole and subsequently rang up nine birdies and took a pair of bogeys as he came within a stroke of Tommy Horton's all-time low, shot in the 1997 Scottish Seniors Open.

"It was one of those days when golf felt so easy," reflected Carbonetti, who played his first senior golf without success on the Champions Tour in the United States and lost his playing privileges.

Things went the other way for the Argentinean Saturday. He made only one birdie, absorbed four bogeys, and shot 75, dropping two strokes behind surprise leader Philippe Dugeny, also a rookie on the circuit. Frenchman Dugeny, playing in just his third event, had seven birdies and a bogey as he shot 66 for 136 and finished the day a stroke in front of Gale. Carbonetti was tied for third at 138 with native son Delroy Cambridge, the winner of four tour titles during his previous three seasons. Dugeny's goal Sunday was "to make it a special day for France." Only Jean Garaialde, the country's first international star, had a win in the tour's record book.

But it was not to be. Gale moved in front with a birdie on the first hole and never trailed. Carbonetti stayed close but "I thought I was out of it. I did not think I could catch Terry." A crucial birdie at the 17th led Carbonetti to a 70–208, and he watched as Gale, playing in the final group behind him and needing just a par at the 18th, bogeyed the hole off a poor drive, shot 71 and slipped into a tie at 208. Cambridge missed the playoff by a stroke, placing third with his 209.

In the season's first playoff, Carbonetti ran in a 12-foot birdie putt on the first extra hole to claim the title.

AIB Irish Seniors Open—€330,930
Winner: Carl Mason

Carl Mason continued his highly impressive run on the European Seniors Tour when he picked up his sixth victory in less than a year in the AIB Irish Seniors Open. In a hard-to-beat sequence, the Englishman won his last three starts in 2003 and the 2004 season-opening Tobago Plantations Seniors, tied for second in Barbados, skipped the next two tournaments while nursing a back ailment, and tied for fourth in Italy two weeks before nailing No. 6 in Ireland and regaining first place on the money list.

Actually, Mason was on the rebound at the Irish Open from his only glitch of the season. He had missed the cut in the U.S. Senior PGA Championship the week before, as did Australia's David Good. So what happens? Good shot 67 and Mason 68 in the opening round at Adare Manor and Golf Resort to finish 1-2 in the standings. Good scored his sixth birdie on the par-five 18th to inch ahead of Mason, who holed a 12-foot par putt there to complete a bogey-free round. "It felt familiar and I'm where I like to be," Mason remarked.

Good slipped back with a 73 Saturday, but Mason moved into a three-way tie for the lead with Nick Job and Noel Ratcliffe when he shot 69 for 137. Australian Ratcliffe, whose most recent of seven tour victories was in the 2003 Irish Seniors, shot 67, and Englishman Job had 68 to join the leadership deadlock. They were three strokes ahead of Good in fourth place. Mason had the lead to himself before three-putting for a bogey at the 17th hole. Job had five birdies after bogeying the first hole.

Ratcliffe fell out of the mix early in Sunday's final round with an outgoing 41, leaving the two Englishmen to compete for the title. The two were still tied for the lead at the turn, but Mason birded the 12th, 13th and 14th to take a two-stroke lead. Job pulled within a stroke when he birdied the 17th, and nearly forced a playoff at the par-five 18th when he dropped his third shot nine feet from the cup. But he missed the putt and Mason two-putted for another 69, the winning 10-under-par 206 and a one-stroke victory. Ratcliffe and Gery Watine finished four behind Job in a tie for third place.

Interestingly, Carl Mason won the tournament that he worked as a referee in 2003 before he had turned 50 and joined the circuit.

Irvine Whitlock Jersey Seniors Classic—€179,804
Winner: Jim Rhodes

Jim Rhodes ended a long dry spell on the European Seniors Tour on the Isle of Jersey. The 58-year-old Englishman, who joined the circuit in 1996 and scored his only win in 2001 in its match play championship, went wire to wire in the Irvine Whitlock Jersey Seniors Classic in mid-June and fashioned a three-stroke victory with his 11-under-par 205.

Although he was a bit unhappy with his less-than-dashing finish — "I played so well but finished so badly" — he proclaimed himself "very pleased with my overall performance. It's my first stroke-play win, so I feel as if I have arrived. It's especially nice to have won it from the front."

Rhodes got in front right away at La Moye Golf Club, the event's long-time venue. Switching to an old putter he acquired in 1966, Rhodes came in late in the first round with a 66 to take the lead away from old friend David Creamer, who shot 67. The Ping putter that he used when he won the match play championship worked beautifully for Rhodes as he ran off five birdies on his incoming nine and didn't have a bogey on his card. The ever-present but luckless John Chillas shot 68 and tied for third with Bill Longmuir and Eddie Polland.

Rhodes' margin grew to two strokes Saturday when he put together six birdies and a bogey for 67. His short approach game was strong, but he opined that "I can't remember putting so well and holing so many putts." Chillas also shot 67 and moved into the runner-up spot at 135. Longmuir was next with 68-69–137.

Sunday did not begin well for Rhodes. Chillas caught him at the sixth hole, only to bogey the next three holes, starting with a three-putt at the seventh and ending when he drove into a bush at the ninth. Rhodes took advantage with his best stretch of the day, registering birdies at the 12th and 13th to open a four-stroke lead. But bogeys at the 15th and 17th tarnished the finish. He had to settle for a par 72 and the 205 total. Finishing second at 208, Chillas posted his highest of four top-five finishes in six 2004 starts.

The Mobile Cup—€189,150
Winner: Bill Longmuir

The 2004 season had not been as productive as might have been expected from Bill Longmuir, the No. 2 man on the 2003 European Seniors Tour money list. Although he had three top-10 finishes and tied for fourth in Barbados, Longmuir had not seriously challenged for a title. "I've had a frustrating start to the year ... I've played well but I keep doing crazy things," he observed.

Deep into the final round of The Mobile Cup at the Oxfordshire Golf Club, it didn't appear things were going to change at the circuit's first stop of the season in England. With four holes to play, Longmuir was three strokes off the lead and just two under par for the round. However, he caught fire at that point, birdied three of the last four holes, and picked up his first win of the season when leader Seiji Ebihara bogeyed the 72nd hole. The 50-year-old Scotsman, who won twice in his rookie 2003 season, finished with a 67 and nine-under-par 207.

Early on, Carl Mason appeared headed for yet another victory at the site where his run of success had begun the year before. The defending champion, who lives 30 minutes from Oxfordshire and had played it frequently, had skipped the Jersey Seniors to prepare for his Mobile Cup defense. It paid off as he opened Friday with a seven-under-par 65 and jumped off to a three-stroke lead over American Steve Stull, Frenchman Gerry Watine, Argentinean Luis Carbonetti and fellow Englishman Bob Cameron.

But for the second time this season, Mason incurred a back ailment that ultimately forced him to withdraw. A muscle spasm during his morning shower contributed heavily to his 74 in Saturday's second round. It worsened overnight and he decided not to play Sunday. Mike Miller took the biggest advantage of Mason's misfortune, whipping up a 64 to vault two strokes in front of Canadian Bill Hardwick, Spaniard Manuel Pinero and Carbonetti. Miller, a 53-year-old Scot who won the Nigel Mansell Classic in 2003, solved nagging putting woes in the middle of the opening round "by going back to the basics and letting the putter do the job." The 64 proved the difference.

At that point Longmuir sat in a tie for eighth place five strokes off the lead after rounds of 72 and 68. On Sunday, Longmuir's hopes soared, then sagged over the first 14 holes. He raced to nine under par on the first nine with a blistering 31, only to make a wild drive and a bogey at the 12th and a double bogey at the par-three 13th, where he overshot the green and wound up in a water hazard. "I felt off the pace then," he said, "but then I holed from 10 feet at the 15th, hit a great bunker shot at 17 to five feet for another birdie, and sank it from 18 feet for three at the last hole."

Ebihara, a five-time winner on the European Seniors Tour, started the day one stroke behind Longmuir, also shot 31, and seemed certain of at least a tie until he drove into a fairway bunker on the 18th. But he couldn't reach the green in two and missed his par putt for 67–208 and the runner-up slot. Miller managed only a 74 and finished third at 209.

De Vere Northumberland Seniors Classic—€227,363
Winner: Malcolm Gregson

"I gave everyone an eight-tournament head start." Malcolm Gregson was speaking about his victory in the De Vere Northumberland Seniors Classic, the European Seniors Tour's ninth event, and alluding to a failed experiment with his golf clubs. Gregson, a one-time Ryder Cup player, had tried three different sets of clubs as he sought unsuccessfully to get out of the doldrums earlier in the season. In despair, he went back to the set he used in winning four times during his previous 10 years on the circuit and look what happened. Gregson, approaching his 61st birthday, posted rounds of 69, 68 and 73 for a six-under-par total of 210 and a two-stroke victory over Seiji Ebihara, runner-up for the second straight week.

Gregson trailed leader John Chillas by three after the opening round at the De Vere Slaley Hall Golf Club. Despite a second and two thirds earlier in the season and his second-place finish at Slaley Hall in 2003, Chillas was not overly optimistic about the weekend. "It wasn't a comfortable day. I didn't know where the ball was going next," he said. "I had luck all over the place … holed one from about 17 yards at the last hole."

Chillas' pessimism proved well-founded Saturday. He slumped to 76, going five over par on a five-hole stretch on the second nine, and eventually tied for 10th. Gregson came to the fore that day. The Englishman gathered an eagle, three birdies and a bogey into the 68 that gave him a 137 and a two-stroke lead over David J. Russell (72) and three over Australian Brian Jones (73).

Gregson frittered away a fast start Sunday. He went four strokes ahead with birdies at the second and fourth holes, but nine holes later his lead was down to one after he double-bogeyed the fifth and bogeyed the 10th and 13th. After the 15th, he remained just a stroke in front of Ebihara and Russell, but his birdie at the 16th established his victory margin.

"It was quite windy and I don't feel comfortable putting in the wind, but I managed to hold it together. It was so much better using my old irons," Gregson remarked.

Ryder Cup Wales Seniors Open—€753,732
Winner: Ray Carrasco

The American presence on the European Seniors Tour, which had been noticeably absent during the first six months of the 2004 season, loomed dominantly in the Ryder Cup Wales Seniors Open. Ray Carrasco led the Yankee charge, picking up a victory for the third year in a row in sensational fashion with two birdies on the final three holes to edge fellow American David Oakley by one stroke. Las Vegas resident Bob Lendzion tied for third, with New Zealander Simon Owen two shots further back.

"It feels absolutely miraculous," beamed Carrasco as he reflected on the 45-foot birdie putt he dropped on the final green to claim the victory. "I was just trying to get it close, and to have it curl in was just an incredible surprise." The monster putt gave him the triumph, but, as Oakley pointed out, the bunker shot he holed for a deuce at the 16th was "the one that won it for him."

The 57-year-old Carrasco, in his sixth season on the tour, was heading in the other direction until he made that shot. After taking a one-stroke lead into the final round at Royal St. David's Golf Club, a par-69 layout in Wales, and remaining in front in the early going Sunday, Carrasco stumbled and fell behind Oakley when he bogeyed the 11th, 13th and 15th holes before righting the ship and shooting 67 for the victorious, four-under-par 203 total.

The self-taught professional, one of 15 children in a California family, who played most of his earlier golf and won more than 100 times on mini-tours in the United States, picked the right time to win. His first-place check — €112,503 — was the second largest of the year on the circuit.

Cold, windy conditions made the going rough the first two days as Carrasco forged his one-stroke lead with a pair of 68s. The first one put him in a tie with David Good of Australia, two behind leaders Noel Ratcliffe, a seven-time winner on the tour, and Owen, who hadn't won since his initial victory in Tunisia in 2001. A 25-foot birdie putt on the opening hole Saturday "kind of got things going" for Carrasco, and he matched four subsequent birdies with four bogeys for the 68 and his one-stroke lead over Oakley and Owen.

The winner even thought he might have gotten some spiritual help at Royal St. David's, explaining that his late father-in-law had Welsh ancestry.

Nigel Mansell Sunseeker International Classic—€223,255
Winner: Seiji Ebihara

A year in America was enough for Seiji Ebihara, who celebrated his return to the European Seniors Tour in 2004 with an exciting victory in the Nigel Mansell Sunseeker International Classic in July. "I have really enjoyed my golf since coming back to the European Seniors Tour and I am so happy to have won again," said the 55-year-old Japanese player after registering a two-stroke victory at Woodbury Park. Ebihara, who led the 2002 money list on the strength of three wins, decided to give the more rewarding Champions Tour in America a try in 2003. He earned his card at the qualifying tournament, but did not fare well in tour events and returned to Europe in 2004.

Runner-up finishes on successive weeks in two of the three events preceding the Mansell tournament signaled the victory, but Ebihara needed some heavy duty scrambling during the final round to produce a six-under-par 66, his 203 total and his sixth victory on the tour. That was twice the number he won on the regular Japan Tour in his younger days.

David Oakley was Ebihara's primary adversary in the final round, but he also had to contend with Carl Mason, the current No. 1 player who had shaken off an injury that had slowed him down in preceding weeks, and Tommy Horton, the circuit's all-time leading performer. Oakley, coming off a second-place finish at the Wales Open the previous Sunday, started fast with a five-under-par 67 at Woodbury Park and shared the first-round lead with Australian Bob Shearer, a four-time winner on the circuit but winless since 2001. They led five others by one stroke while Mason opened with a 69 and Ebihara a 70.

When the dust settled Saturday, Oakley had retained his share of the lead, shooting 70–137, and was joined at the top by Ebihara (67) and Mason (68). Mason withdrew prior to the final round in The Mobile Cup three weeks earlier after suffering back spasms, skipped a week, and didn't contend the week before in Wales. "It's a great feeling to play like that again after a difficult few weeks," he said of his finish Saturday which included a birdie at the 14th, eagle at the 16th and birdie at the 17th. Horton, with 23 titles on his gaudy senior record but none since 2000, had his second 69 and shared the 138 slot with Dragon Taki.

Ebihara never trailed Sunday, but had to deal with some wild shots on the closing nine holes. He caught trees off the tee at the par-five 16th, but put his long-iron third shot six feet from the hole to set up a birdie. He drove into an unplayable lie on the 17th and saved par with another brilliant iron shot to three feet. That prompted tournament namesake Nigel Mansell, the Formula One driving great and crack golf amateur who owns Woodbury Park, to call him Houdini after watching the finish. Oakley shot 68 and finished second again, two strokes ahead of Mason (70) and Horton (69).

Senior British Open—€1,504,220
Winner: Pete Oakley

The Senior British Open has had a few unlikely winners among the established stars who have claimed the title in the 18-year-old event — Bob Verwey, John Fourie, Tom Wargo and Noburo Sugai, to name names. But none came out of the blue quite as Pete Oakley did at Royal Portrush Golf Club in Northern Ireland in late July.

Although fairly successful in club professional competition in America, Oakley had just picked up his playing credentials on the European Seniors Tour for the 2004 season and had finished no higher than eighth (twice) in his first 10 starts. He got into the elite field through the qualifying route and went on to become the first qualifier to win the circuit's richest and most prestigious event. Ironically, the most likely Oakley to claim that title would seem to have been older brother David, a four-time winner since 1999 who had finished second in the two previous tournaments.

But 55-year-old Pete Oakley upstaged his 59-year-old brother all week, traveling in high-class company the final three rounds after opening modestly with 73. He was four strokes off the first-round pace of Englishman Jim Rhodes, the Jersey winner in June, constant contender John Chillas of Scotland, fellow American Don Pooley, the 2002 U.S. Senior Open champion, and Argentinean Eduardo Romero, making his first start as a senior. Pooley had back-to-back eagles in his 69.

Oakley made his move Friday, shooting 68, the day's best round, despite three bogeys. That thrust him into a four-way tie for the lead at 141 with three established winners — Pooley (72), Mark McNulty (69) and Carl Mason (71), the current leader on the money list and the defending champion.

When only two players broke par and nobody shot in the 60s in windy conditions at Royal Portrush Saturday, Oakley found himself atop the classy field with his 73 and two-under-par 214, one stroke ahead of Pooley and McNulty, who both shot 74s, and two in front of Mark James and Tom Kite, two former Ryder Cup captains who have U.S. senior major championships on their records. Though seven strokes off the pace, 60-year-old Graham Marsh grabbed headlines when he aced the 182-yard, par-three 11th for the second time in three days, an unheard of feat in professional tour competition.

"Not in my wildest dreams," said Oakley of his exalted position. "I was a little bit antsy getting ready to tee it up with Tom Kite and Mark James, but I was more nervous trying to qualify — 132 players for 20 spots."

Oakley, whose biggest victory ever was in the 1999 Senior Club Professional Championship in Florida, held his nerve and his lead Sunday on another cold and windy day. He led by three strokes after 15 holes, but bogeyed the 16th, giving Kite and Romero an opening. Kite, who had made a costly, three-putt bogey at the 14th, birdied the 17th to narrow the margin to one, and Romero made his third straight birdie there to join him. The drama heightened when Oakley, needing a par to win, trapped his approach at the 18th. His bunker shot stopped 12 feet past the cup and he sank the €237,000 putt for 70–284 and a host of other rewards, including a year's exemption on the Champions Tour in America.

"I'm still trying to rationalize at the moment," he said. "My world is changing at this very moment."

Bad Ragaz PGA Seniors Open—€190,000
Winner: Horacio Carbonetti

Horacio Carbonetti achieved a first for the 2004 European Seniors Tour season when he successfully defended his Bad Ragaz PGA Seniors Open in Switzerland, but he had to do it the hard way. Carbonetti, who rolled to a three-stroke victory at Bad Ragaz in his rookie 2003 season, came from four strokes off the lead on the final three holes in 2004 to overtake Denis Durnian, then defeated the shocked Englishman with a par on the first extra hole.

"It is always difficult to defend a title, but I guess I just feel so comfortable on this course," said the victorious, 56-year-old Argentinean, who joined his younger brother, Luis, as a 2004 winner. Luis, age 51, won the Digicel Jamaica Open in May.

Once again, the par-70 Bad Ragaz course was a patsy for the birdie shooters. Durnian, a three-time winner on the circuit who said he had been "playing dreadful lately," shot the lowest round of his career — an eight-under-par 62. That gave him a three-stroke lead over fellow Englishman Bob Cameron, the French Senior Open winner, in an opening round that saw 29 players break 70. Carbonetti, John Chillas, Nick Job and South African John Mashego had 66s.

A fast finish after a four-bogey stretch in the middle of the second round enabled Durnian to cling to a one-stroke lead Saturday. Durnian eagled the 16th and birdied the 18th for 68–130 and the narrow advantage over Carbonetti, who produced a 65–131. Cameron shot 68 for 133 and third place in the standings.

Durnian clung to the lead through the first 15 holes Sunday before Carbonetti eagled the par-five 16th to catch him. Playing together, the two matched birdies on the final two holes, Durnian sinking a monster 40-foot putt on the 18th green, for the tying score of 195. Carbonetti shot 64, Durnian 65. Par on the first playoff hole was good enough for Carbonetti's victory as Durnian bunkered his approach and missed the par putt. Bill Longmuir and Guiseppe Cali of Italy tied for third place, six strokes behind.

De Vere PGA Seniors Championship—€305,852
Winner: Carl Mason

Carl Mason resumed his domination of the European Seniors Tour when he rallied in the final round to win the circuit's second major — the De Vere PGA Seniors Championship at De Vere Carden Park — in the season's third and last playoff. He added that major title to his surprise 2003 victory in the Senior British Open and five other wins in just a year on the circuit after being slowed down a bit by back trouble during the previous month or so.

Mason did all his damage at Carden Park on the final day after treading water for three rounds when the lead bounced around among three other players. Noel Ratcliffe opened on fire Thursday with a 10-under-par 62, the lowest score of his 30-year career, a match for the tour's all-time record low and a course record by two strokes. The Australian, the No. 2 all-time money winner on the tour with seven victories to his credit, grabbed a three-stroke lead with his two-eagle, six-birdie round before bad weather ended play in mid-afternoon.

Ratcliffe managed only a par round Friday and slipped back into a tie for the lead with Seiji Ebihara, the 2002 Senior PGA champion, who put a 68 with his opening 66 for his 134 total. Bunched one stroke behind them were Delroy Cambridge, Giuseppe Cali and Denis Durnian, the playoff loser the previous Sunday in Switzerland.

The top of the standings was scrambled Saturday. Frenchman Gery Watine, in his first full season on the circuit, jumped in front with 66 for 202. Cali remained a shot off the lead with 68–203, but frequent contender David

Good took over third place at 204 with 66. At that point, Carl Mason was five back with rounds of 67-71-69.

Mason produced a 68 Sunday and got the negative help he needed from the frontrunners to get into contention. Watine shot 74, Cali 73 and Good 77. That put Mason in early with 275 total and ultimately a spot in a three-man playoff with Ebihara, who shot 70, and Jim Rhodes, who missed a three-foot birdie putt at the 18th to join the group with 68. Rhodes' disappointment magnified when he was eliminated on the first extra hole with a shot into the water from a bad lie. Mason lipped out a putt for the victory there, but won when they replayed the 18th and he birdied from 12 feet after Ebihara missed the green and failed to save par.

Travis Perkins Senior Masters—€338,436
Winner: Sam Torrance

For the second week in a row, the European Seniors Tour record for lowest round (62) was equaled and the feat rewarded Sam Torrance, the former Ryder Cup player and captain, with his first victory in seniors competition in the Travis Perkins Senior Masters at the Wentworth Club. The 10-under-par round brought the tournament to a spectacular finish as the popular Scot came from three strokes back to score a two-stroke triumph with his 203 total, vindicating his decision to drop off the Champions Tour and stay in Britain following the Senior British Open. It was just his third start in Europe in 2004 and sixth since turning 50 the preceding August.

"I got off to a wonderful start today," said Torrance. "It was as good as I have ever played from tee to green. I played great the first two days and I knew if I kept playing that way, things would happen."

Despite the solid play, Torrance, who lives within walking distance of Wentworth's Edinburgh course, didn't score all that well in Friday's opening round, shot 72, and trailed co-leaders Jeff Hawkes and Seiji Ebihara by three strokes. Hawkes, a South African who delayed his debut on the European Seniors Tour for a year because of his work as a golf commentator on the SKY network, had done little after his third-place finish in the season opener in Tobago, but Ebihara had a win and three seconds so far in the season. Carl Mason, who had scored his third victory of the season the previous Sunday in the Senior PGA Championship, was just one stroke back with Bob Cameron and Canadian Bruce Heuchan.

Although Torrance shot 69 Saturday, he remained three off the pace, then set by Ebihara, who repeated his Friday 69 for 138 and a one-stroke advantage over David Good and American Alan Tapie. Hawkes fell out of contention with 74–143.

Torrance turned it on early in Sunday's final round. He birdied the first four holes plus two others to turn in 30, then eagled the 10th hole to take the lead for good. Ebihara remained in contention with an eagle at the 16th, trailing by just a stroke as Torrance birdied both the 15th and 16th to get to the 10-under score. Six under for the day and needing a birdie at the 18th to tie, Ebihara bunkered his approach and bogeyed for 67–205 and his fourth second-place finish of the season. Tapie shot 69 and finished in third place, four strokes behind Ebihara.

While Torrance was the eighth player in tour history to shoot 62, he was just the third to do it on a par-72 course. Tommy Horton did it in 1997 and Noel Ratcliffe matched it in the first round of the De Vere PGA Championship the preceding Thursday, but finished in a 10th-place tie.

Charles Church Scottish Seniors Open—€221,677
Winner: Bill Longmuir

Bill Longmuir will always remember his fifth victory on the European Seniors Tour. Not that the three he won in his 2003 rookie season or his earlier 2004 triumph in The Mobile Cup weren't meaningful and gratifying, but No. 5, his come-from-behind victory in the Charles Church Scottish Seniors Open, was special because his caddie was his 13-year-old son Callum. Plus he was raised as a Scot and won at The Roxburghe in Kelso, Scotland. "All my wins are sweet," Longmuir said, "but this one is special because I have Callum on my bag for the first time. I just wish my father had been here to witness it."

Longmuir took victory away from another Scot — the luckless John Chillas — when he came from three strokes behind in the final round with a four-under-par 68 for the winning six-under-par 210 total. Chillas, who had let slip several opportunities earlier in the season, led or shared the lead the first two days only to come up one stroke short Sunday in a runner-up tie with Carl Mason.

Chillas pieced together an eagle, four birdies and two bogeys for his leading 68 the first day, finishing a stroke in front of Longmuir, Englishman Tony Allen and Seiji Ebihara, the second-place finisher in the previous two tournaments. Those were the only scores below 71 on the windy day. Chillas, who gave up his head professional and coaching duties in Stirling to concentrate on the tour, "was very awkward with the breeze" and was "delighted with that start."

Chillas added a 71 Saturday for 139 and stayed on top, sharing the lead with Australian David Good, who came from far back with a stunning 64, the best round of the week by four strokes. Good, brandishing a putter he bought in the Roxburghe pro shop, made an eagle and seven birdies and was headed for 63 until the putter finally betrayed him and he three-putted the 18th hole. Giuseppe Cali was at 140 and, following a 73, Longmuir was in a four-way tie at 142 with Guillermo Encina, Nick Job and David J. Russell.

The occasional bad holes that cost Chillas in other events crippled his hopes for victory Sunday. He had the lead at seven under par until he over-clubbed at the 15th and plugged his approach in a greenside bunker at the 16th for the bogeys that eventually killed his chances. Ahead of him, Longmuir had birdied the 17th to get to six under and parred the 18th for the decisive 68. Mason went from horrid to hot with his putter, making four birdies on the final nine to shoot 68, but he missed from 15 feet on the 18th to finish one short. Chillas also missed his chance to tie on the last green when his 15-footer lipped out.

Bovis Lend Lease European Senior Masters—€335,638
Winner: Luis Carbonetti

Luis Carbonetti exceeded his own expectations when he won the Bovis Lend Lease European Senior Masters in early September. "This is unexpected," proclaimed the Argentinean. "My goal was to win once this year. To win again is just great." Carbonetti, playing his first full season on the European Seniors Tour after an unsuccessful shot at America's Champions Tour, had won in late May in the Digicel Jamaica Classic. He became just the third multiple victor of the season, joining Carl Mason, a three-time winner, and Bill Longmuir, who had scored his second victory the previous week in Scotland.

The Bovis Lend Lease triumph came more easily than he experienced in Jamaica, where he came from two strokes off the pace the last day and won in a playoff. At England's Woburn Golf and Country Club, Carbonetti entered the final round in a first-place tie with Sam Torrance, shot 71 for 209 total, and won by two strokes over John Chillas (69–211), runner-up for the second week in a row and third time in the season. Carl Mason, the tour's leading player, finished another stroke back in third place with 68–212.

Eamonn Darcy, the former Ryder Cupper who played just a handful of events in his first two years as a senior, opened a bid for his first win on the circuit Friday with a five-under-par 67. He was two strokes in front of American Jerry Bruner and three ahead of five others, including Sam Torrance, who was coming off a two-week vacation following his initial seniors victory in the Travis Perkins Masters. Torrance would have been right on Darcy's heels if he hadn't three-putted two of the last four holes.

Carbonetti vaulted into contention Saturday with a seven-birdie 65 for 138, a total matched by Torrance (70-68), as Darcy shot himself out of contention with 73–143. Torrance compiled an eagle, three birdies and a bogey for the 68. Delroy Cambridge, the Jamaican who won the Bovis Lend Lease in 2002, was just one stroke behind after a 69.

Torrance went south Sunday, shooting 76 with a double bogey and two bogeys on the first nine. That left Carbonetti setting the pace as he birdied the first two holes. He added another birdie and absorbed two bogeys the rest of the way for 71 and his seven-under 209 total.

"I was playing well when I arrived here, but you never know how you will perform," assessed Carbonetti. "I just kept my concentration very well and held things together."

Daily Telegraph Turismo Andaluz Seniors Match Play—€147,353
Winner: Carl Mason

Carl Mason must have a particularly fond spot in his heart for the Daily Telegraph Turismo Andaluz Seniors Match Play. Not only is he two for two in the change-of-pace event at Flamingos Golf Club in Marbella, Spain, but it was there he launched the three-victory spree at the end of 2003 that brought him the money list title in his "rookie" season.

In 2004 Mason defeated John Chillas, 3 and 2, in a superbly played match by both men, but he had to travel a much more difficult road to the finals. In the previous four matches, Mason won twice at the 18th hole and at the 19th in the last two. Chillas, swallowing his third straight runner-up finish, had a much easier time, never reaching the final hole in any of his four matches.

In the opening round of 16 matches, Chillas thumped Gavan Levenson, 4 and 3, and Mason edged Delroy Cambridge, 1 up, with a decisive birdie at the 17th hole. In the second round Mason overcame a two-stroke deficit on the second nine to nip Noel Ratcliffe, 2 up, as Chillas again won handily, 4 and 2, after racing to a 5-up lead at the turn.

Guiseppe Cali could have sidetracked Mason in the quarter-finals. His caddie cost him a hole when he rode in a cart on the 16th hole — a rules violation — and the two subsequently wound up tied after the 18th before Mason holed a 10-foot birdie putt on the first extra hole. A string of four birdies at mid-round spurred Chillas to his quarter-final triumph over Seiji Ebihara, 3 and 1. Chillas remained hot in the morning semi-finals, birdied four of the last six holes to nip Bob Cameron, 2 and 1, while Mason was going an extra hole again to survive. He and Guillermo Encina both shot 66s over the 18 holes before Encina bogeyed the 19th.

Mason was virtually unbeatable in the afternoon finals, winning 3 and 2, and prompting the disappointed Chillas to quip: "I don't know what he had for lunch." The Scot had five birdies, didn't have a bogey, but couldn't cope with the eight-birdie barrage that Mason fired at him to score his fourth win of the season. That matched his 2003 output and moved him ahead of Pete Oakley into the top position on the money list.

"I played solid as a rock all day," Mason observed. "I played some great golf this morning, and the start this afternoon (four birdies on the first four holes) was unbelievable."

ADT English Seniors Open—€221,029
Winner: Carl Mason

Carl Mason clinched his hold on the money list's No. 1 position when he put together back-to-back victories and scored his fifth and final win of the 2004 European Seniors Tour season in the ADT English Seniors Open at Formby Hall in Merseyside. It was the first time consecutive victories were posted during the season and pushed Mason's 18-month win total to nine for his senior career, this by a man who won only twice in more than 20 years on the regular European Tour. With more than €354,000 for the year, Mason had nearly double the money earned by his nearest pursuer, John Chillas, and was uncatchable.

Coming off five grueling matches en route to his Seniors Match Play victory the previous week in Spain, Mason and Chillas, his victim in the title match, started slowly at Formby Hall, Mason shooting 71 and Chillas 73. They were back in the pack behind Scotland's Martin Gray, who grabbed the lead with a four-under-par 68, one stroke in front of fellow Scot Bill Longmuir and American Steve Stull.

Mason made a quantum leap in Saturday's second round. After starting with a three-putt double bogey on the first hole, he ran off seven birdies over the remaining holes, shot 67, and roared into a five-stroke lead at 138. No other player broke 70. Bob Cameron, with 71, climbed into a second-place tie with Grace (75) and Longmuir (74) at 143.

Blustery weather Sunday took its toll on the field. Nobody shot better than 70, and Mason struggled home with the victory despite a shaky 75 and a final nine that he called "horrendous." Even with the 75, he won by three strokes over Cameron (73) and Chillas (71) at even-par 216, Chillas finishing second for the fourth week in a row.

Mason was one under par on the first nine. Then, after two birdies after the turn, he went four over par on the 13th, 14th and 15th and finished with a three-under 213. "The conditions were tough," said Mason. "I never felt as good as I did in the second round, but at least I got the job done."

Sanremo Masters—€200,000
Winner: Bob Cameron

All it took for Bob Cameron to win the Sanremo Masters was the lowest score in the history of the European Seniors Tour. His confidence buoyed by his second-place finish the previous week in the ADT English Seniors Open, the 51-year-old Cameron scored his second victory at the tail-end of his second season on the circuit by shooting a 61 in the final round and racking up a two-stroke victory. Sanremo is a par-69 course, so his winning total of 193, the fewest strokes ever for 54 holes, was "just" 14 under par.

When matched against par, neither the 61 nor the 193 were new records, but Cameron could have cared less. "It's wonderful to win, with such a low finishing round as well. It was close all the way through," he said.

His first obstacle was Carl Mason, shooting for three straight wins coming off his fifth victory of the season. Mason opened his play at the Sanremo Country Club in Italy with a 63 and shared the first-round lead with Bill Longmuir, another multiple winner in 2004. Two other winners — Seiji Ebihara and Luis Carbonetti — were just one stroke back, and Cameron was in a logjam of seven at 66.

The score of 63 was the number again in Saturday's second round. This time Chilean Guillermo Encina and Australian David Good shot 63s to take over first place with nine-under-par 129 totals as Longmuir and Mason fell back with 69 and 70, respectively. Encina, who had an eagle, five birdies and a bogey, had several fruitless chances for his first victory in 2002 and 2003, and it was not to be again at Sanremo.

Birdies continued to fly Sunday, and Cameron, playing bogey-less golf, forged two strokes in front. Then Frenchman Gery Watine and national favorite Giuseppe Cali overtook him, forging a three-way tie through 15 holes. Cameron put the victory away when he birdied the last two holes for the two-stroke triumph. Cali finished with 64–195 and Watine took third place with 66–196. A triple bogey ruined Encina, who shot 68–197, and Good suffered three late bogeys, took 69 and dropped into a fifth-place tie at 198 with Mason (65) and Longmuir (66).

Estoril Seniors Tour Championship—€240,000
Winner: John Chillas

The situation was all too familiar to John Chillas. Time and again during the European Seniors Tour season, Chillas had entered the final round either as co-leader or close contender only to come up short. Five times he finished second, four of them in consecutive tournaments late in the season, adding to his frustration. The money he had made was fine, but victory was all-important to him as the circuit reached its final stop in Portugal for the Estoril Seniors Tour Championship.

When it finally happened at Quinta da Marinha Oitavos Golfe, it not only gave him the satisfaction of the victory but also vaulted him ahead of Seiji Ebihara, who tied for 32nd, and Bill Longmuir, who tied for 38th, in the final money list. That earned him the second and last berth on the Rest of the World Team for the international UBS Cup Matches in November at Kiawah Island in America.

Chillas knew what he had to do when he went into the final 18 holes of a third 2004 tournament in which he shared first place. He was sitting at three-under-par 139 with Italian Guiseppe Cali and Frenchman Gery Watine, like Chillas winless all season. Chillas had opened the tournament with 69, one stroke behind leaders Watine and fellow Scot Martin Gray.

The third time was the charm. Despite the pressure — "I knew mathematically that I could still make the UBS Cup but only by winning" — Chillas moved in front with a one-under-par first nine. He went birdie-bogey-birdie starting the back nine and he established his two-stroke victory with a final birdie at the 15th hole. With 68, he finished with a six-under-par 207 total, two ahead of Australia's David Good, who had a season similar to Chillas but wound up winless. It was Chillas' second Estoril Seniors Tour Championship victory, added to his 2003 triumph in the Travis Perkins Masters. "To win in the last event is something I'm over the moon about," chimed the "absolutely delighted" Scotsman.

Carl Mason wrapped up his sensational season with a third-place-tie finish at 210 with Gray and American John Benda. Mason was the other UBS qualifier as he led the money list for the second year.

Japan Senior Tour

Castle Hill Open—¥30,000,000
Winner: Katsunari Takahashi

Katsunari Takahashi picked up where he left off in May in the Castle Hill Open, the usual first event of the Japan Senior Tour. Takahashi, who won the final two tournaments of the 2003 season, jumped in front in the first round at Castle Hill Country Club, Aichi Prefecture, and never trailed en route to victory by six strokes, the biggest margin of the year.

Takahashi, who has won at least once in the last five years on the circuit, started his run toward his ninth senior victory with a four-under-par 68. Only two other players broke par Friday — Takeru Shibata with 70 and Hikeru Emoto with 71. Seven players were at 72. Takahashi, a 13-tournament winner in his regular tour days, widened his margin to four Saturday with 70 for 138. Hiroshi Ishii, a four-time winner on the Japan Senior Tour, took over second place with 73-69–142, one stroke in front of Yurio Akitomi (75-68), Koji Nakajima (72-71), Yoshitaka Yamamoto (73-70) and Emoto (71-72).

With the four-stroke cushion, Takahashi cruised to victory with another 70 Sunday for 208 total. Six shots back in second place were Ishii, who closed with 72, and Akitomi, who finished with 71 for his 214.

Aderans Wellness Open—¥60,000,000
Winner: Toyotake Nakao

Toyotake Nakao raced from four strokes off the pace with a final-round 64 to capture the Aderans Wellness Open in June at the Nakajo Golf Club, Niigata Prefecture, his first victory on the Japan Senior Tour. With his 11-under-par 205, Nakao finished with a three-stroke margin over Yuichi Yokoshima, the second-round co-leader.

Tateo (Jet) Ozaki, the eldest of Japan's most famous golfing brothers and winner of 15 titles on the regular Japan Tour, signaled his arrival on the senior circuit when he shot 68 and shared the first-round lead with Takaaki Fukuzawa. They led Koichi Uehara, Masaru Amano and Yokoshima by a stroke.

Ozaki remained on top Saturday, but again had company in first place. He shot 69 for 137 and Yokoshima joined him at that score with a 68. They led Fukuzawa (70) and Amano (68) by one stroke, Uehara (70) by two going into the final round. Nakao was at 141 after rounds of 72 and 69. His Sunday round blew everybody away. In fact, only Takashi Miyoshi (68) and Takeru Shibata (69) also broke 70 and they tied for third at 209 with Ozaki (72) and Fukuzawa (71).

PGA Philanthropy Rebornest Senior Open—¥30,000,000
Winner: Shuichi Sano

Shuichi Sano emerged a winner from a peculiar final round in the PGA Philanthropy Rebornest Senior Open. Even though he began the day one stroke off the lead and shot a one-over-par 73, Sano wound up with his first title on the Japan Senior Tour in the July tournament at Biglayzac Country Club, Miyagi Prefecture. Sano posted a six-under-par 282 and won by a stroke over Takashi Miyoshi.

Four players tied for the lead in the opening round of the four-day tournament. Hisao Inoue, Dragon Taki, Noboru Fujiike and Tadao Furuichi shot 67s. Sano trailed by just a stroke, tied for fifth with Katsumi Nanjo. When he matched the 68 Friday, Sano took over the top spot in the standings, one ahead of Miyoshi (70-67).

Sano scored his first of two 73s Saturday and it dropped him a stroke behind Norihiko Matsumoto, who posted a 208 total after his third-round 69. Miyoshi shot himself off the leaderboard with a 77, a score just one stroke too many to overcome with his closing 69 Sunday. His 283 total left him a shot behind Sano on a day when six of the top seven finishers, excepting Miyoshi, had rounds of par or higher.

Fancl Senior Classic—¥60,000,000
Winner: Yuichi Yokoshima

The Japan Senior Tour had a first-time winner in its third consecutive tournament — the Fancl Senior Classic — as Yuichi Yokoshima registered a one-stroke victory at Susono Country Club, Shizuoka Prefecture, in August. Yokoshima, runner-up in the Aderans Wellness Open earlier in the season, finished with a nine-under-par 207.

Yokoshima took command of the tournament the second day when he shot 65, the week's lowest score, and jumped from a four-stroke deficit into a two-shot lead with his 136.

Veteran Teruo Nakamura, age 54, a 20-tournament winner on the Japan Tour in his younger days, grabbed the first-round lead with a 67, two strokes ahead of runners-up Noboru Fujiike and Katsuji Hasegawa. Yokoshima was in a four-way tie for fifth place with 71. Nakamura followed with 72 Saturday and slipped three strokes behind Yokoshima and one back of Hikaru Emoto, who climbed into second place with 66 for his 138.

Only Motomasa Aoki challenged Yokoshima Sunday. He shot 68 as Yokoshima was putting together a 71 to claim the one-stroke victory. The third-place finishers — Takaaki Fukuzawa, Takeru Shibata, Fujiike and Nakamura — were three behind Aoki at 211.

Japan PGA Senior Championship—¥40,000,000
Winner: Takaaki Fukuzawa

Tired of just coming close, Takaaki Fukuzawa took charge early and never let up as he rolled to a three-stroke victory in the Japan PGA Senior Championship at Yamada Golf Club, Chiba Prefecture, at the end of September. He had tied for third place in the previous three tournaments on the Japan Senior Tour.

Fukuzawa, who won the Japan Senior Open in 2002, fired an exceptional 63 in the opening round and staked himself to a four-stroke lead over Kenjiro Iwama and at least five over the rest of the field. Chen Tze-ming, the talented Taiwanese player who played most of his career in Japan, made a powerful attack at the leader Friday. He shot 64 for 132 and moved within two of Takaaki, who had 67 for 130. Teruo Nakamura was a distant third in the standings at 137.

Fukuzawa shot his highest score of the week, a 69 on Saturday, yet opened a five-stroke lead as Chen faltered with 72 for 204 to Takaaki's 199. Nakamura scored 71 and still held onto third place, but nine behind the leader, who had his highest round of the week Sunday (71) and settled for the three-stroke final margin with his 270 total. Chen shot 69 for 273 and Katsunari Takahashi, the most successful player on the circuit the last few years, soared into third place at 275 with a closing 65.

Japan Senior Open Championship—¥50,000,000
Winner: Katsunari Takahashi

Katsunari Takahashi finished the Japan Senior Tour season as he had started it — with a victory. Surviving the year's only playoff, Takahashi recorded his 10th win in five seasons on the circuit as he won the coveted Japan Senior Open Championship, the season's late October finale, for the third time in five years. The 2004 repeat triumph tied him with Seiichi Kanai on the tour's career victory list and left him only one win behind leader Fujio Kobayashi, who has 11 titles.

The 54-year-old Takahashi frittered away a four-stroke lead in the final round at Ibaraki Golf Club's East Course, Saitama Prefecture, forcing him into a playoff against visiting Scot Bill Longmuir, a leading player on the European Seniors Tour, and Katsuyoshi Tomori as the three players finished with seven-under-par 281 totals. Tomori went out on the second extra hole and Takahashi ousted Longmuir with a birdie on the next hole.

Although overshadowed by Takahashi's fine performance, Tateo (Jet) Ozaki made another strong showing in the tour's most prestigious event. Ozaki, who tied for third in the Aderans Wellness Open, launched another bid with an opening 66, taking a one-stroke lead over Takahashi and Akira Yabe. Ozaki doubled his margin over Takahashi Friday, shooting 68–134 to Takahashi's 69–136. Longmuir was then at 138 (68-70) and Tomori at 140 (71-69).

Nobody shot in the 60s Saturday, and Takahashi established his four-stroke lead with a two-under-par 70 as Ozaki stumbled with a 76 and dropped into a second-place tie with Longmuir (72) at 210. Tomori was next at 211 after a 71. Takahashi opened the door to the playoff for Longmuir and Tomori when he muddled to a 75 Sunday while the Scotsman was shooting 70 and Tomori 71.

15. Women's Tours

It was becoming next to automatic for Annika Sorenstam. The victories kept piling up, the honors, the money. To borrow from a ragged sports cliché, it was almost as if she could put her ball on the tee and the tournament was hers. But wait. It wasn't automatic. Perhaps the best way to look at her year in 2004 is to look where things weren't so rosy. Keeping in mind, of course, that she won eight times on the LPGA Tour in 2004, that she won another major title (McDonald's LPGA Championship), notched two additional international victories, and was runner-up four times. And she won $2,544,707 for her seventh LPGA money title and $2,746,824 to lead the Women's World Money List for the fourth consecutive year. Keeping in mind also that Sorenstam finished in the top 10 in 16 of her 18 LPGA Tour starts. And there's the rub. What went wrong in those other two?

Sorenstam had announced that she was aiming at the LPGA Grand Slam for 2004. It was just about the only thing she hadn't accomplished. The bid would start with the Kraft Nabisco Championship in March, and that's where it would end. Grace Park won. Sorenstam, who won the Safeway International the week before, opened with 71 and trailed by five strokes, then shot 76, and that was that. She tied for 13th place. "It's disappointing," Sorenstam conceded. "But on the other hand, it gets me fired up for the other three. That's why I set high goals for myself."

Her next disappointment came in the Weetabix Women's British Open. She had won in 2003 and now was trying to match Mickey Wright, of some 40 years earlier, in winning back-to-back titles in all four major championships. This was the only one left. Sorenstam was also going for her eighth career major title and also her second major of the season, after the McDonald's LPGA Championship, and her fifth victory of the season. While Karen Stupples was winning the championship heroically, Sorenstam was having a restless time of it. She couldn't keep up and tied for 13th place again. "I gave it all I got," Sorenstam said. "I missed a few shots here and there, and I really couldn't get it going. Life goes on."

The way she won the McDonald's LPGA Championship showed yet another side of her. Meaning she can win from in front, she can come from behind, and she can start to collapse then pull herself together. Which was the case here. She had a seven-stroke lead and, in un-Sorenstam fashion, blew most of it coming down the stretch. At the 16th hole, she was so wild off the tee that she played from an adjoining fairway, then hit a blind approach shot to three feet and made the birdie. She said something about golf being a funny game.

There really was life on the LPGA Tour beyond Sorenstam. Lorena Ochoa, for example, took Rookie of the Year honors hands down with victories in the Franklin American Mortgage Championship in May and the Wachovia LPGA Classic in August.

The Franklin American event was sort of a sister-brother act. Her brother Alejandro was climbing Mt. Everest at the time, and she had made a deal with him — if he could climb Everest, she would win the tournament. "I just knew I was going to," Ochoa said. Her brother kept his end of the bargain. In the Wachovia tournament, Ochoa came from behind in the final round to win. This was a rookie sounding like an instant veteran.

If anyone could have upstaged Sorenstam, it was Meg Mallon, at age 41, who got her share of the spotlight with back-to-back national championships — the U.S. Women's Open and the Canadian Women's Open. In the U.S. Women's, she came from nowhere with a final-round 65 to beat Sorenstam by two. "I'm 41 years old," Mallon said, "and you've got to enjoy your days, enjoy when things like this happen." She enjoyed them the next week all over again, the first to win both the U.S. Women's Open and the BMO Financial Group Canadian Women's Open in the same year.

The big news off the course came from LPGA Tour Commissioner Ty Votaw, who announced that he would step down after the 2005 season. It came as a shock inasmuch as the LPGA Tour was in the best shape of his history. The 2005 schedule already had 32 tournaments listed and all but two of them had purses of at least $1 million and four were over $4 million.

"I feel very much at peace with this decision," Votaw said. "I feel very good about having given the LPGA everything I've got, and I feel good about the results. It was a difficult decision simply because of the love I have for the organization. But it was made easier by the fact that I think the LPGA foundation is so strong and the future is bright."

Golf is no respecter of age or geography. Michelle Wie, a 15-year-old high school girl from Hawaii, was clearly the most famous female amateur in the world. She played on both the LPGA Tour and PGA Tour on sponsor's exemptions. Right behind her came Paula Creamer, 18, who won the LPGA's qualifying tournament in earning her playing card for 2005.

Youth led the way on the Nedbank Women's Tour of South Africa. Finland's Minea Blomqvist, 19, won two of the four tournaments — the Pam Golding Ladies International and the Telkom Women's Classic — led the Order of Merit, and posted the lowest scoring average, 69.92. At that, she may have been overshadowed by Ashleigh Simon of South Africa, who was only 14 years old. Simon won the Acer Women's South African Open — including a record final-round 63 — becoming the first amateur and youngest player ever to win it. And she was second by one shot to Blomqvist in the Pam Golding Ladies International. Sweden's Helena Alterby won the Nedbank Women's Masters, the fourth South African event.

In Japan, Ai Miyazato, 19, turned professional and took the Japan LPGA Tour by storm, and in the process nearly dethroned the veteran Yuri Fudoh, age 27, the No. 1 player. Fudoh won seven tournaments, including two of the three majors — the Japan Women's Open and Japan LPGA Tour Championship. Miyazato won five times and became the only teenager on either the women's or men's tours to win over ¥100 million in one season. While she was the youngest of the new crop, she wasn't the only talented one. Yukari Baba, age 21, won the Yonex Ladies wire-to-wire; Miho Koga, age 22, won the Hisako Higuchi event; amateur Mika Miyazato (no relation to Ai), was just 14 years old when she finished 17th in the Stanley Ladies, and Kumiko Kaneda, also age 14, finished third in the Golf 5 Ladies and played in the final round with Fudoh, who won it.

The old gag goes that you can't tell who's who without a scorecard. In women's golf these days, an age card might be more to the point.

U.S. LPGA Tour

Welch's/Fry's Championship—$800,000
Winner: Karen Stupples

When you open up with a career-low 63 and you're still nowhere near the lead, you get the idea you're in for a long week. So pity Karen Stupples, former British Curtis Cup player, in the Welch's/Fry's Championship that kicked off the 2004 LPGA Tour in mid-March. She did open with a 63, only to find herself trailing by three strokes. Where did she go wrong? "I didn't take advantage of the par-fives on the first nine like I should have done," she said, "because I can get to both of those very easily."

But don't pity her for too long. Stupples — age 30, a patient and resolved Englishwoman looking for her first victory in six years on the LPGA Tour — took the lead in the second round, outran a strong field down the closing holes, and stormed to a five-stroke victory. Perhaps she'd had a sign that she was about to break through. Just two weeks earlier, in the ANZ Ladies Masters, she had her best finish — runner-up to Annika Sorenstam, the No. 1 player in the world.

"It's unbelievable," said Stupples. "I had no idea all of that was going to happen."

She led by one shot with six holes to play, then stretched that into a stunning five-shot victory over Grace Park and Jung Yeon Lee, on a card of 63-66-66-63 for the best 72-hole total in LPGA history, a 22-under-par 258 at the Dell Urich Course in Tucson, Arizona.

An opening 63 should be enough to lead anywhere, but Jung Yeon Lee, a London-born South Korean, shot a 10-under-par 60. Lee came within a whisker of Sorenstam's LPGA Tour record 59, missing birdies from 20 feet at the 17th and 10 feet at the 18th. Still, a 60 was nothing to sneeze at. Stupples, after bogeying No. 6, the easiest par-five on the course, went on to notch six of her eight birdies for the 63.

The second round was a test of between-clubs golf. Lee didn't pass it, Stupples did. Said Stupples, "It was a day for being patient and biding my time. The yardages for me always seemed to be in-between, and sometimes committing to the shot was a little tougher today." Said Lee, "It was a struggle. The club selection — the between-clubs. I chose the wrong club." So Stupples, shooting the 66, ran her bogey-free streak to 30 holes and found herself at 11-under-par 129 and one stroke ahead of Lee (70) and Davies (65), the former tour dominator who was seeking her first victory since 2001. Now, could Stupples withstand the mounting pressure?

In the third round, at least, the answer was yes. The turning point was the narrow, 427-yard 14th hole. Stupples birdied to get to 16 under par while Davies bogeyed and slipped three behind her, and Lee bogeyed and fell four behind. Stupples tripped just once, a bogey at the 18th that ended her string of bogey-free holes at 47. It left her with a 66 and a one-stroke lead over Davies (66) and Grace Park, the former Arizona State star who made five birdies on the tough back nine for a career-low 61.

Stupples faced greater heat in the final round. She not only survived it, she seemed to thrive on it.

Stupples made only three bogeys in the entire tournament, but two came back-to-back on two days — No. 18 in the third round, and now No. 1 in the fourth. Was she starting to crack? No. She bounced back with birdies at Nos. 2 and 3 for a one-stroke lead on Park, and the duel was on. Park tied her with a birdie at the fifth hole, and both birdied the sixth and parred the seventh. At the eighth, Stupples' approach ended up 10 inches behind the flag. She tapped in for another birdie. Then Stupples all but locked up the win when she coolly holed a 30-foot putt for an eagle at the 13th.

"But even after that I still felt like I had some chance as long as I made a couple of birdies to push her," Park said. "But I couldn't, and she kept making pars and made a great birdie on 16, and the game was over." And the formidable Laura Davies, on a run of 12 straight pars, became a nonfactor.

Eventually, Stupples' scariest opponent was herself. "I really struggled emotionally," she said. "My caddie was telling me, 'Keep it under control.' But every time I gave myself a second to think about what was happening, it just overwhelmed me." But she was composed enough to drop her final putt, an eight-footer to save par. Then she hugged her caddie and cried.

Safeway International—$1,200,000
Winner: Annika Sorenstam

The 2004 Safeway International went down in history for two reasons. First, Annika Sorenstam, in her LPGA season debut, scored the 49th victory of her career, and second, teenage whiz Michelle Wie replaced her father as caddie.

Wie, age 14, and the future of women's golf by many accounts, came out for the Safeway International, near Phoenix, Arizona, without her father on the bag for the first time in an LPGA event. "It's actually kind of nice," said Wie, a ninth grader. "There's a lot less arguing."

Wie threatened to upstage Sorenstam, the world's No. 1 female player, making the cut and staying on the fringe of the hunt until she closed with a 77 and tied for 19th place at two-under-par 286.

Sorenstam headed into the final round with no lack of confidence. "I think Phoenix has been good to me," she said. Well, yes and almost. The previous three Safeway events were played at Moon Valley. She won in 2001, when she shot her historic 59. The next two years, she led heading into the final round but couldn't hold on. Now here she was again, two strokes ahead with one round to go.

Sorenstam simply outlasted the field in the final round on a late March day of withering 97-degree heat and 25 mile-an-hour winds that baked the Superstition Mountain Golf Club and all the souls on it. Only four players could break par, led by Becky Morgan's three-under 69. Against a wilting field, Sorenstam ground out a 70 and won by four strokes over Cristie Kerr, who rallied for a 71. "I hit just eight greens and shot one under," Kerr marveled. "It was a very, very tough day." The other challengers couldn't come close. Se Ri Pak shot 74, Laura Davies 76, and Kim Saiki, who led the first round with a 64, closed with a 79. Perhaps the most noticeable fold was by 19-year-old South Korean rookie Shi Hyun Ahn. She started the final round in second place, just two behind Sorenstam, and shot 77.

Sorenstam, winner of the ANZ Masters in Australia three weeks earlier, took the lead in the second round. "I'm playing smart and giving myself good opportunities," she said, after a bogey-free 65 put her one up on Kerr. "If I hit a good drive, I'm playing aggressive. If I hit it poorly off the tee, I play it conservatively."

She was smart and steady in the third round. She eagled No. 2, made a bogey and a birdie along the way, then birdied the 17th and 18th for a solid 68 and a 16-under 200 total, two ahead of Ahn. "I'm proud to play with Annika," said Ahn, who closed the gap from four to two strokes with a seven-birdie 66. "I want to learn from Annika."

Maybe the best lesson Ahn learned was how to keep your head in punishing weather. The heat in the final round sapped the players' strength, and the wind called for as much as three more clubs. Said Sorenstam, "It tests your ability to hit the shots, your ability to putt, but most of all — your patience. It's all about being patient and not getting too ahead of yourself."

While Ahn was laboring to a 77, Sorenstam dueled the course and the elements on better than even terms. She had four birdies and two bogeys in that final round. Her final birdie was like a gesture of triumph. At the 18th, a 508-yard par-five, she rolled in a 25-footer. Then she could finally relax.

"Now," Sorenstam said, "I'm tired."

Kraft Nabisco Championship—$1,600,000
Winner: Grace Park

The Kraft Nabisco Championship in Rancho Mirage, California, first of the LPGA Tour's four majors, arrived late in March with all eyes focused on three golfers, none of them Grace Park. There was Annika Sorenstam, the world's No. 1 female golfer, who had boldly announced she was taking aim at the Grand Slam, all four major championships in the same year.

Then there were the two kids. Aree Song, a native of Thailand and now a Florida resident, who first played in this tournament in 2000 as a 13-year-old amateur named Aree Wongluekiet, was 17 now and a rookie on the tour. This was her first major since turning professional the previous summer. And then there was Michelle Wie, 14, from Hawaii, the tall, slender amateur sensation who experts said would make fans forget everyone else.

Four days later all eyes were on Park, age 25, a fifth-year professional from Korea and Phoenix, Arizona, at the final green, facing the longest, scariest six-foot putt of her life. "My knees, my arms, my whole body was shaking," said Park. "I didn't know if I could start the club back."

It was enough to unnerve a saint, because moments earlier, Song had poured in a 30-foot putt for an eagle to force Park's hand. Park's six-footer was for a birdie — and the first major of her career. And so Park was a quivering, nervous wreck. "If you want it really, really badly, you can do it," Park was to say later. "I guess I was the one who wanted it most."

She holed that six-footer for a birdie, a three-under-par 69 and an 11-under 277 total to strike a blow for the "old folks" of the LPGA Tour. Song finished second, one stroke back, and the amazing Wie finished fourth, playing the Mission Hills Country Club course in a seven-under total of 281, four strokes behind Park.

As for Sorenstam, who won the Safeway International the week before, the Kraft Nabisco Championship wasn't in the cards. An opening 71 left her five strokes behind and a second-round 76 buried her. She tied for 13th at three-under 285, eight behind Park. "It's disappointing," Sorenstam said. "But on the other hand, it gets me fired up for the other three. That's why I set high goals for myself."

But Park wasn't without other challengers. There was feisty Dottie Pepper, the 1999 winner, tying for the halfway lead with Korea's Jung Yeon Lee. A 74-78 close knocked Pepper out. Jung bowed out with a closing 75. Karrie Webb seemed to be recovering her form. Needing only 111 putts, she shot 69-71-71-69 and finished third, two strokes back.

Wie had the time of her young life. She hung around stubbornly, shooting 69, 72, 69 and 71. "I promised myself, whatever happened, I would fight to the end," Wie said, "and I did. I was proud of myself."

It came down to a duel between Song and Park.

"You know, I like my chances here," said Song after taking a one-shot lead in the first round with a bogey-free 66. Park was six strokes back at 72. In the second round, Song shot a 73 and was a stroke behind the co-leaders, Pepper and Jung. Park, at 69–141, climbed to within three strokes.

Then the third round took shape abruptly. Park erupted with four straight birdies, from a punch nine iron into No. 7 to a four-foot putt at No. 10 en route to a bogey-free 67. Song notched five birdies, including a 60-footer at the 17th for a 69, setting the stage for a shootout. Going into the final round, Song and Park were tied for the lead at eight-under 208, one stroke ahead of the soon-departing Jung.

Park was on her way out, too, early in the final round. By the eighth, a sour putter left her two shots behind Song. Then Park exploded again — four straight birdies, starting with a wedge to three feet at No. 9. She was leading for the first time, and for good. She was two up on Song, who bogeyed the 16th. Now came the 18th, a 485-yard par-five with an island green — a perfect stage for a closing drama.

Song had nothing to lose. She went for the island green in two, hitting a seven wood from 210 yards to 30 feet. Park laid up from 199 yards, then lofted a pitching wedge to six feet. Song holed the 30-footer for the eagle, leaving Park quivering over the six-footer for the championship.

Said Song, "I wasn't disappointed when it went in, because I felt like I couldn't have done any more."

Said Park, "I don't remember what it was like out there, but I know I won. I did it. I'm shaking like a baby."

Office Depot Championship—$1,750,000
Winner: Annika Sorenstam

What's Swedish for "front runner?"

"Annika Sorenstam" will do quite nicely.

Not that Sorenstam, the Swedish golfing machine, can't come from behind. She just doesn't have to very often, and that was the case again in the Office Depot Championship at El Caballero Country Club near Los Angeles. Sorenstam led all the way — though not without incident — shooting 68, 70 and 69 for a nine-under-par 207 total and a three-stroke victory over Ashli Bunch and Meg Mallon.

This was Sorenstam's 50th win on the LPGA Tour. It was her second in three starts this year — it was early April — and with the ANZ Masters in Australia earlier, it was her third victory in four starts. (This was also her third Office Depot victory.) As to front-running — of her 50 LPGA victories, 34 came when she was leading going into the final round. She is expected to win every time, but she missed at the Kraft Nabisco Championship a week earlier.

"I just lost the touch," said Sorenstam, who tied for 13th there. She was referring to her short game, which generally is considerable, as it was in the Office Depot Championship.

In the first round, Sorenstam hit just 11 greens in regulation, yet shot a 68 to lead Jill McGill and Meg Mallon by a stroke. Her approach shots set up four birdies on putts of eight feet or less. Then there was the 12-footer for a birdie on her sixth hole and the snaky 31-footer on her 17th. "I do think I love this place," Sorenstam said. "I putted very well today. I saw the lines. The greens are so undulating and tricky."

Otherwise, the big news of the first round was that Karrie Webb, who dominated the LPGA Tour through the late 1990s and early 2000s, shot an 81, and Laura Diaz shot 82. Both would miss the cut.

Sorenstam did not have a trouble-free week. Getting out of trouble is her specialty. Take El Caballero's par-five 17th hole in the second round. She pulled her tee shot into the woods on the left. This left her in an awkward stance against a tree. She punched the ball 150 yards up the fairway and was still 102 yards from the green. She lofted a wedge that hit beyond the cup and spun back, rimming the hole. She tapped in for a birdie. "You've got to keep on grinding," she said.

"She is a very, very strong player on Sunday," said Rosie Jones, who would go from a tie for second to a closing 79. "She usually makes fewer mistakes than the rest of us."

Sorenstam couldn't rest in the final round. Meg Mallon kept the pressure on and Ashli Bunch leaped up the leaderboard with a 65. "I felt the heat and thought that I've got to do something," Sorenstam said. The "something" was to birdie three of the last five holes to beat them both by three strokes. Sorenstam became the sixth LPGA player to win 50 or more tournaments and the first since Kathy Whitworth in 1969.

"Fifty is kind of a magical number," Sorenstam said. "I've thought about this for a while. I really wanted to do it this week."

LPGA Takefuji Classic—$1,100,000
Winner: Cristie Kerr

Cristie Kerr has been an LPGA Tour golfer since 1997. Before that, she was an outstanding junior and amateur, and was a Curtis Cup player. She's a left-hander but plays golf right-handed. Her favorite hobbies are fishing and baking. Whoever sketched her biography left out the part where she likes working the high wire without a net. How else to explain how she notched her second career victory in the LPGA Takefuji Classic in Las Vegas — leading from start to finish, blowing a big lead, then winning in a playoff.

The climax actually was anti-climax. Kerr dueled with the surprised and grateful Korean rookie Seol-An Jeon for six tense extra holes and finally won with a three-foot putt for par on the seventh. Maybe it was more than just a test of golf. April winds, cold and rain had hit Las Vegas Country Club. "It was getting a lot colder and it was getting windier," Kerr said. "I think it was just a matter of survival."

It was a playoff that shouldn't have been. Kerr had a four-stroke lead with six holes to play and squandered it all. She bogeyed four of the last six, including missing a three-foot par putt at the 18th that would have won for her in regulation. Her closing one-over-par 73 dropped her into a tie with Jeon at seven-under 209 in the three-round tournament. Jeon had come in earlier with a 69 and was delighted. She thought she had finished second. Then her caddie came to her. "Now a playoff," he said.

The playoff was a grind. They halved the first six holes in pars, and tough pars at that. Jeon piled on the pressure with a 15-footer for par at the par-three 17th, their fourth playoff hole. But Kerr responded with a six-footer to stay alive. Jeon just missed a birdie from 18 feet at the sixth extra hole. Then it was Kerr's turn. She could have won with her 14-footer, but it pulled up a tad short.

Then came the decisive seventh playoff hole, the 16th. Jeon hit her second shot over the green, then nicked a tree limb coming back and dropped short of the green. Then she chipped 35 feet below the hole. Kerr had put her second shot on the fringe and two-putted for the title.

Putting had fuelled Kerr early on. In the windy first round she sank a 30-footer at No. 7 and a 15-footer at No. 8 on her way to a 69 and a share of the lead with Jackie Gallagher-Smith, Stacy Prammanasudh and rookie Nadina Taylor. Kerr took a four-stroke lead through the second round with a bogey-free 67, thanks to sharp putting on the second nine — birdies from seven, 15 and eight feet, and a tap-in after a 45-foot eagle try just missed. Then came the crumbling finish in the final round and the playoff battle with the surprised rookie who won her admiration.

"With the exception of the last playoff hole," Kerr said, "I think she played better than I did."

Chick-Fil-A Charity Championship—$1,600,000
Winner: Jennifer Rosales

This was a basic all-star cast at the Chick-Fil-A Charity Championship. There was Aree Song, trying to give herself a present for her 18th birthday

— her first professional victory in Stockbridge, Georgia. Annika Sorenstam was going for her third victory in the first six weeks of the season. Grace Park was challenging for her second victory in four weeks, and Se Re Pak was warming up. Jennifer Rosales, a 25-year-old Filipino, was just another player hoping for that first win.

For the curious, Rosales was the one pacing nervously behind the scoring tent after the fourth round. She had posted a 65 for a 274 total, 14 under par, for the clubhouse lead. Would it hold up? She was twitching as fans asked for autographs. "I couldn't even sign my name," Rosales said. "My hands were shaking. I never felt like that before in my life."

Little-known Christina Kim took the first-round lead with a seven-under-par 65 at Eagles Landing Country Club, but Sorenstam stole the scene with her fight to get under par for the 11th time in 12 rounds. She did it, birdieing the last two holes for a one-under-par 71. She stayed under par the rest of the way but never seriously challenged, tying for 10th. Kim was out of the chase on a second-round 74, and Song took a two-stroke halfway lead with a 66. She would turn 18 years old the next day, May 1, and if she could hold on, she would be the youngest LPGA champion ever. But she didn't. She shot 78.

Rosales had come close once, losing in a playoff to Rachel Teske in the 2003 Giant Eagle Classic. Her prospects weren't good this time. She started the final round four strokes off the lead, and with 12 women ahead of her, including such campaigners as Sorenstam, Pak, Park and Song. But Rosales, playing four threesomes ahead of the last group, was ready. She birdied No. 1 with a 12-foot putt, then No. 3 from 20 feet. Then she birdied the 14th, and looked up and was stunned to see her name atop the leaderboard.

"I started taking deep breaths," Rosales said. "That helped me a lot."

But Rosales was still too charged up at the par-five 18th. She knocked her second shot into the club seats left of the green. "Too much adrenaline," she said. "Thank God the grandstand was there." Her free drop ended up in thick rough. She blasted out, missed a long birdie putt, and tapped in for a par and a bogey-free 65. Then she went out behind the scoring tent for the wait to see whether her 274 would hold up. It did, but just. Four golfers fell a stroke short — Jung Yeon Lee (65), Rosie Jones (67), Becky Morgan (68) and Park (68).

Rosales, having won $240,000, uttered that all-liberating phrase, "I'm going to shop 'til I drop."

Michelob Ultra Open at Kingsmill—$2,200,000
Winner: Se Ri Pak

When Korea's Se Ri Pak joined the LPGA Tour in 1998, experts agreed it was only a question of time before she would be in the LPGA's Hall of Fame. And after one fine week in May 2004, that's exactly what it was — a question of time. Three more years, to be precise. Her victory in the Michelob Ultra Open at Kingsmill gave her the 27th point she needed to enter the hall. But there was another qualification — 10 years on the Tour, and her 10th year was now three years away.

No one would have given her half a chance this time. She trailed through three rounds and by 10 strokes after the second round. She entered the final round four strokes behind Cristie Kerr and Lorena Ochoa, then sprinted to a 65 and won by two over Ochoa and Juli Inkster at the Kingsmill Resort in Williamsburg, Virginia.

"One of my dreams came true," said Pak. "My biggest goal was trying to join the Hall of Fame, and I worked so hard for the past seven years. This is the best day of my life."

"She's a fast finisher," said Inkster, herself a Hall of Famer. "She usually starts off kind of plodding, kind of gets herself in the hunt; then Sunday she let's it all go." Inkster made a run at Pak, birdieing three of the first seven holes. But two bogeys before the turn cooled her off.

Pak followers might have seen this one coming. She's been great with come-from-behind wins. Of her previous 21 victories, she won nine when she trailed entering the final round. Now she was 10-for-22.

She got started this time with birdies at Nos. 2, 3 and 5 on putts of 35, 18 and 25 feet. She bogeyed No. 6, and then she was off again from No. 8, with five one-putt birdies over eight holes, ranging from a tap-in to a 22-footer. A two-putt bogey at the 16th served to prove that she was human. She had come from behind again to win. "I have done that so many times," Pak said. "I don't know why. Tell you the truth, I am not really trying to do that. It just happens."

So Pak's "just happens" ruined some dreams. Korean star Soo-Yun Kang took a big step toward her first LPGA Tour victory with the first-round lead on a 65, thanks to some pinpoint work with her 60-degree wedge. She tied for 16th. Kim Williams took the second-round lead with a tournament-record 63 and refused to let it excite her. "All it gets you is making the cut," she said. She tied for 12th. Kerr and Ochoa shared the third-round lead. Then Ochoa (71) tied for second and Kerr (75) tied for sixth as Pak went sweeping by.

All that was left, then, was for Pak to celebrate May 9, 2004, as the best day of her life. But only until one day in 2007.

Franklin American Mortgage Championship—$900,000
Winner: Lorena Ochoa

Lorena Ochoa had this pact with her big brother Alejandro (he's age 27, she's 22). If he would scale his mountain, she would scale hers. Her mountain would be her first victory. His was Everest. They both made it.

Ochoa spent a nearly sleepless night before the final round of the inaugural Franklin American Mortgage Championship at the Legends Club in Franklin, Tennessee. She was nervous enough with a one-stroke lead, and she was also waiting for word on Alejandro, who was on top of the world halfway around the globe.

"Climbing Mt. Everest has been his dream," Ochoa said. "Before he left, we made a promise that I will win my first tournament, and he will get to the summit." Finally, about 4:30 a.m., the call came — Alejandro had reached Everest's summit and was safely back in camp. Ochoa could sleep a little. Then she went out and finished climbing her own mountain. She was the first Mexican to win on the LPGA Tour.

Ochoa, the LPGA Tour's 2003 Rookie of the Year, was having a remarkable early career. She'd had 13 top-10 finishes, including three seconds and three thirds. But that first win kept eluding her. It was in her sights just a week earlier, in the Michelob Ultra Open, until Se Ri Pak exploded in the final round and left her tied for second. But this was a new week.

In this tournament, Ochoa would get the test of her young career, with veterans coming at her from all directions. She opened with a two-under-par 70, four strokes behind an elated Nancy Scranton, whose career had tailed off since the last of her three wins in 2000. In a rain-interrupted second round, Ochoa was steady under heat from three-time winner Pat Hurst. Ochoa hit 12 of the 14 driving fairways and 16 greens in shooting a 67 that tied at her at 137 with Hurst, who shook off two wind-blown bogeys for a 69. "I need to try and go for it, go straight for the pin and make a lot of birdies," Ochoa said. Hurst felt pretty much the same way. "This is a birdie course," she said. "It's going to take a lot of birdies."

And birdies it was for Ochoa in a third-round 67 — but only after two early bogeys and a quick chat with her caddie on the subject of reading greens. She bounced back with birdies on six of the next nine holes to take the lead by one stroke. "That was the key of my day," Ochoa said. "I didn't have time to get frustrated or angry." She dropped Hurst (68) to a tie for second place with Mi Hyun Kim, who tied the course record with a 64.

Then came the nearly sleepless night. If Ochoa needed to prove herself, three-time winner Wendy Ward gave her the chance. Ward tied Ochoa for the lead three times with birdies on four of her first eight holes. And for one last blast, Ward (67) eagled the par-five 18th. Ochoa took the challenge. Instead of laying up at the 18th, she went for the green, nearly watered her approach, chipped to 15 feet and two-putted for the birdie and a 68 and a 16-under-par 272 total. It was the stroke she needed for the win.

"I just knew I was going to," Ochoa said.

Sybase Classic—$1,250,000
Winner: Sherri Steinhauer

The Sybase Classic opened with high hopes for three women — Silvia Cavalleri, Nadina Taylor and Young-A Yang. But it opened with practically no hope for Sherri Steinhauer. Then fate played a trick on all four.

Cavalleri, age 31, a fifth-year professional from Italy; Taylor, 25, an Australian rookie, and Korea's Yang, 26, a second-year player, were looking for that first victory or at least for a top-20 finish for the first time this year. Good sign: They tied for the first-round lead with five-under-par 66s at Wykagyl Country Club in New Rochelle, New York.

Steinhauer, age 41, a 19-year veteran from Madison, Wisconsin, wasn't feeling bubbly. She had won five times, including a major championship, the 1992 du Maurier Classic, but she was coming off her worst year. In 2003, she made only eight cuts in 21 starts and won $40,174. A year like that can wear on a person.

But at the end of this week late in May, Steinhauer was asking, "Are we dreaming? Did this happen? It's amazing." The answers: No, yes, and only if you say so.

Steinhauer would turn things around and win by two strokes, her sixth career victory and her first since winning both the Sybase Classic and the Weetabix Women's British Open in 1999. But first she would have to fester awhile longer.

The hopeful trio of the first round did get one prayer answered. They cracked the top 20.

Steinhauer, just a stroke behind in the first round, got knocked six strokes back in the second round with a 70 when Becky Morgan, a winless fourth-year player from Wales, shot a tournament-low 64 for a 131 total. But it was Steinhauer's time, and it arrived in the third round.

"There's nothing," Steinhauer said, "like hitting a golf shot that you've pictured in your mind before." This picture was a masterpiece. At the 18th, she put a three wood from 245 yards to within five feet of the pin, and then made the putt for an eagle three for a 66 to tie Morgan for the third-round lead.

In the final round, Morgan had a bumpy front nine with four birdies, two bogeys and a double bogey. Steinhauer made nine pars. Morgan got to 13 under par and led by three strokes through the sixth, but couldn't make another birdie. "The three-putt on No. 5 dented the confidence a little," Morgan said, "and the bad tee shot on No. 9 killed it." They were still tied at 10 under making the turn, and Grace Park was a stoke behind. Morgan continued to slip.

Steinhauer birdied the 10th, 14th and 15th to lead Park by three. A bogey at the 16th cut her lead to two, but she saved par at the 17th and parred the 18th to win by two over Park and three over Morgan.

"After last year, playing so horribly," Steinhauer said, "it's an unbelievable feeling."

LPGA Corning Classic—$1,000,000
Winner: Annika Sorenstam

Annika Sorenstam was playing the LPGA Corning Classic for the first time in nine years. It was as though she had never been away.

She was in her second year on the LPGA Tour when she first played it in 1995 and tied for seventh place. When she returned in 2004, she was the No. 1 female golfer in the world. A year earlier, this week, she was making her historic appearance against men on the PGA Tour. She was now expected to win every time she entered a tournament, and so at Corning (New York) Country Club she obliged her fans with a dramatic performance. Michelle Estill, who won as a rookie in 1991, got within four holes of her second career victory. But once Sorenstam got within view of the title, she made a break for it and overran the unfortunate Estill with four birdies on the second nine for a two-stroke victory.

It was Sorenstam's third victory in six tournaments this season, her 51st overall and her 16th come-from-behind win. And she did it without benefit of a practice round. She didn't arrive in Corning until Wednesday. "Maybe I should always come the night before," Sorenstam said.

Sorenstam tied Liselotte Neumann for the first-round lead with a seven-under-par 65, one stroke ahead of a group that included Estill. She hit every green but one in regulation. After a couple of three-putt bogeys, she birdied No. 8, then ran off three more birdies from the 10th and shot 31 on the second nine with scarcely a glance at the formidable Laura Davies, who eagled both par-fives on the first nine before cooling down to a 70.

Sorenstam was looking solid with an early 67 in the second round, but then Estill came to life, shooting a 64 for a two-round total of 131 and a one-stroke lead on Sorenstam. "There's two days left," said Estill.

True enough. But the third round still belonged to Estill. She was paired with Sorenstam, but instead of being intimidated, she seemed inspired. She matched Sorenstam stroke for stroke, and coolly holed a four-footer for a birdie at the 18th to take a one-stroke lead.

"Wow!" Estill said. "It's exciting just to be here." Indeed. While Sorenstam was struggling, Estill built a four-stroke lead with a birdie at the eighth while Sorenstam bogeyed three of the last four holes on the first nine. Then Estill burned off three shots of that four-shot lead with a triple bogey at the par-four No. 9. She regained her balance and wrapped up the 70 that kept her one-stroke lead. "Today was a gift," Estill said. "If it's your turn, it's your turn. If it isn't, that's all right, too."

Alas, Estill would need that fatalistic view to sustain her at the end. She started the final round with birdies on two of her first four holes and still led by one through No. 7. Sorenstam, meanwhile, bogeyed twice. "I came to the point where I got totally frustrated with myself." But at No. 8, Estill overshot the green and bogeyed, and Sorenstam birdied No. 9 from nine feet. The duel was on. Estill birdied the 11th and 12th and led by one, but bogeyed the 13th from under a tree. Sorenstam took the lead for good at the 14th with a birdie from seven feet. Estill had to save par at the 16th, but Sorenstam birdied and closed with a 68 and an 18-under-par 270 total and a two-stroke victory. Estill shot one-under 71 and tied for second with Vicki Goetze-Ackerman (67).

Said the disappointed Estill, "Today was kind of a test. It was fun to battle with Annika. It was fun to be in the hunt." Said Sorenstam, "I'll be back. I should have been here sooner."

Kellogg-Keebler Classic—$1,200,000
Winner: Karrie Webb

Annika Sorenstam was teeing it up again in the Kellogg-Keebler Classic and again she was expected to win. She seemed to own Stonebridge Country Club in Aurora, Illinois. She won on the last two visits, by 11 strokes in 2002 and by three in 2003. She was the No. 1-ranked female in the world, and she was on a roll, with three victories in six starts by the first week of June. So no one noticed long-slumping Karrie Webb — until the second round.

Webb had won 29 times on the LPGA Tour and owned six major titles, and twice was the LPGA Player of the Year. But she had won just once in 2003 and she dropped out of the top 10 in the World Ranking for the first time since joining the LPGA Tour in 1996. She opened with a three-under-par 69 and trailed by three strokes. Then things changed abruptly.

In the second round, she birdied four of the last five holes for a tournament-low 64, vaulting into the lead. The burst included a 40-foot putt at the 14th and birdies at the last two holes. At 11-under-par 133, she led by two over Jill McGill and Seol-An Jeon.

"I know I'm on the right track," Webb said. "If I don't win tomorrow, still, these are the two most solid rounds I've put together this year."

Of course, there was always the menace of Sorenstam hovering over all contenders and pretenders. "I didn't get off to a hot start like in the past," she said, after opening with a 71 to trail by five, "but I feel really good about my game." She rang up seven birdies in the second round, but a three-putt bogey at the 17th left her with a 66. She had picked up a stroke, but four strokes were just too much to pick up on a vintage Karrie Webb in the final round.

Webb led McGill and Jeon by two heading into the final round, and ran that into a five-stroke victory with a bogey-free 67. What little trouble popped up, she brushed off. At the par-four sixth, she drove into thick rough and could only get her approach to 20 feet. She holed the putt for a birdie and a four-shot lead over Jeong Jang with nine holes to play. At the par-four 16th, she bunkered her approach, came out to 15 feet, and saved par. At the 18th, she holed a 10-footer for birdie and a 67 for a 16-under-par 200 total.

Crowds, meantime, watched in vain for fire from Sorenstam. "It was just one of those days where I started out with nine solid pars," she said. She shot 68 and tied for second with Jang (69) and Siew-Ai Lim (66).

Tina Barrett, hoping for a second career victory, shot a 66 for the first-round lead, thanks to an eagle at No. 2, where her 89-yard sand wedge shot hung on the lip before dropping, and thanks also to a bounce off a bank that set up her 10-foot birdie at the 18th. A second-round 74 killed her chances. But then, once Karrie Webb got rolling, no one had a chance.

McDonald's LPGA Championship—$1,600,000
Winner: Annika Sorenstam

Sweden is quite some distance to the north of Spain, and by most perceptions, it seems the cool Swedes are about the same distance from the passionate Spaniards in temperament. Even so, Annika Sorenstam has proved herself to be golfing kin to Seve Ballesteros.

Take Sorenstam, the defending champion, coming down the final stretch of the McDonald's LPGA Championship. She had blown most of a seven-shot lead, and what looked like a comfortable victory was fast unraveling. Then Sorenstam reversed the collapse. At the par-five 16th, she missed the fairway so far to the left that she had to play her second shot down the 11th fairway. Then, for her approach, she was faced with a blind shot over 60-foot-high trees from 94 yards. She put it three feet from the pin and made the birdie. If this wasn't the Ballesteros style of winning, what was it? And it came just in time.

"I had a nice little lead going to the last 10 holes," Sorenstam said. "But this game is so funny that way — you never know."

Indeed. On a 36-hole Sunday, forced by rains, Sorenstam dominated much of it, then had a brief but scary wreck on the final nine, and then regained her touch and wrapped up her second consecutive McDonald's LPGA Championship. She shot 68-67-64-72 for a 13-under-par 271 total at the DuPont Country Club in Wilmington, Delaware. She won by three strokes over Shi Hyun Ahn and by five over Grace Park.

The book on Sorenstam now reads: Seven career major victories (tied with Juli Inkster for sixth place on the all-time list), fourth win of the year (and it was only mid-June), and 52nd career victory. This was the third time she successfully defended a major championship, the others being the 1995 and 1996 U.S. Women's Open and the 2001 and 2002 Kraft Nabisco Championship.

Sorenstam was, of course, the prohibitive favorite. Considering that she led by as much as seven strokes, her three-stroke win wasn't quite as easy at it looked. Her first obstacle was Jennifer Rosales, who had scored her first win just six weeks earlier in the Chick-Fil-A Charity Championship. Rosales, 25, was the bright light the first day with a bogey-free, five-under-par 66. "I hit a lot of fairways — that was the key," Rosales said. "I kept putting and putting until I made some, and kept going." She led by one over Gloria Park, Karen Stupples and Chiharu Yamaguchi.

In her opening 68, Sorenstam birdied two of her first three holes, then could have used a Ballesteros at her 16th hole, the par-four No. 7. She was wide off the tee, hacked a seven iron just 40 yards out of trees and rough, and bogeyed. But she birdied the last two holes: a five iron to four feet at the par-three No. 8, then a four wood from 238 yards and two putts from 30 feet for a birdie at No. 9, her 18th.

Heavy rains forced the second round into Saturday, and from there on it was Sorenstam's championship to win or lose. She did give the faithful more of a thrill than they wanted in the final round, but before that she had them cheering.

Sorenstam took over in that second round. A burst of four straight birdies carried her to a seven-under 67 and a 135 total. Her only bogey was a three-putt from 40 feet at the final hole. It left her with a one-stroke lead over Inkster and Rosales. Inkster, who came from two behind to beat Sorenstam in the U.S. Women's Open two years earlier, trailed her by a stroke this time. "I like my position," she said. "I have a chance on Sunday, and that's pretty much what you want to do." A bold birdie at her final hole, the par-five ninth — a big drive, a seven wood and two putts from the front of the green — got her to 66–136. Rosales bogeyed two of her first three holes but rallied for a 70, joining Inkster at 136.

Come Sunday and the third round in the morning, Sorenstam was turning the tournament into a shambles. She blistered the field with a bogey-free, seven-under 64. That gave her a 14-under 199 total, the 54-hole record.

"It was one of those rounds you remember forever," Sorenstam said. She was leading Lorena Ochoa (67) by six shots, Inkster (70) by seven. When Sorenstam birdied the eighth in the final round that afternoon, she was leading by seven.

Then abruptly, she gave most of it away. She double-bogeyed the par-five ninth, wedging too far and chipping back too short. She bogeyed the 10th, missing the green and chipping weakly, and bogeyed the 11th, three-putting.

Then Sorenstam regained her game. She holed a 40-footer for birdie at the 12th. Ahn kept the pressure on with birdies at the 15th and 16th that got her within two. Sorenstam kept her at arm's length, holing a 25-foot putt for a birdie at the 14th.

Then came the birdie at the 16th, via the 11th fairway, and a 15-foot birdie at the 17th. All in all, another round you remember forever.

ShopRite LPGA Classic—$1,300,000
Winner: Cristie Kerr

The 2004 ShopRite Classic belonged to a 17-year-old amateur who did everything but win it. This was Paula Creamer, a high school senior from Pleasanton, California, who was so good that some were thinking perhaps Michelle Wie wasn't the only young phenom on the scene. In this instance, Creamer went all the way to the 54th and final hole on the verge of becoming the first amateur to win an LPGA event since 1969, only just failing.

"She's going to be a star," said Cristie Kerr, on picking up her second victory of the season. "She's absolutely fearless."

Kerr had some encouraging words for herself as well. "I don't want to get ahead of myself, but why not think about Player of the Year?" she said. "Why not dare to dream?"

Creamer came within an inch of her own dream, right to the final hole. She had a 10-foot birdie putt that would have forced a playoff. She missed. Then Kerr coolly dropped an eight-footer for her own birdie. It was, she said, a "perfect" putt. But Giulia Sergas still had a crack at her. Sergas needed a birdie at the 18th to win. She missed the green, then missed an eight-footer for the birdie, and Kerr had her second title of the season and career-third by a stroke over her and Creamer.

Kerr shot 66-68-68 for an 11-under-par 202 total at the Seaview Resort Bay Course in Galloway Township, New Jersey. She had the lead briefly with the 66 in the first round, until Sergas and Denise Killeen came in with 65s. "I didn't do anything yet," said Sergas. "This is just the start." Killeen, winless in her 12 years as a professional, was also realistic, but found the heavy June heat and a native insect called the green fly a tad much. "If I could just get through 18 holes without getting bitten by those bugs, I'd be happy," Killeen said. Kerr was much pleased with her results. "To not play your best golf and shoot five or six under is pretty encouraging." Creamer, with a 70, faced a tough task for any golfer — making up a five-stroke deficit in two rounds.

Creamer stopped the show in the second round. "I've been in a couple of LPGA tournaments and I really didn't do much," Creamer said. "And I thought, 'Paula, you need to kick it in gear here.'" Which she did, making nine birdies, including a 35-foot downhiller at No. 4, for a seven-under 64, tying her career low. Killeen's collapse boosted Creamer into contention. Killeen, age 42, after another 65 in the second round, was at 130 and two up on Sergas (67) and four up on Kerr (68) and the streaking Creamer (64). Then in the final round, while Killeen was blowing to a 79, Kerr, Sergas and Creamer made a run for it.

Creamer bogeyed the second hole, birdied the third and fifth, then made a brilliant birdie at the par-four seventh on a wedge over a tree to inside

10 feet. She tied Kerr, who was having an iffy time. Kerr missed an 18-inch putt and bogeyed the 12th, then bogeyed the 14th, missing her par from 10 feet. She left a five-foot birdie try a foot short at the 17th, and came to the 18th tied with Creamer, her playing partner, and Sergas, in the group behind.

Kerr hit the final fairway, put her approach eight feet from the pin, and she finished it off perfectly.

"It's the stuff you dream about," Kerr said.

Wegmans Rochester LPGA—$1,500,000
Winner: Kim Saiki

It was the third round of the Wegmans Rochester LPGA, and Kim Saiki, age 38, having just shot a 68, was saying, "I think of myself as a successful player." There were those who might point out that she hadn't won. Saiki corrected the record the next day by completing a wire-to-wire run and making the tournament her first victory. And after waiting 12 years and 277 events for that magical moment, Saiki was almost speechless.

"It was incredible!" Saiki said. "No words could describe it. Chills!"

She didn't break through against a weak field. Eight of the top 10 on the money list were on hand. She came from behind three times in the final round against Rosie Jones, who had won 13 times, twice on this very course, Locust Hill Country Club in Rochester, New York. Also in the field were No. 1 Annika Sorenstam, seeking her fifth victory (and it was only late June), Laura Davies and Juli Inkster. Saiki shot 66-69-68-71 for a 14-under-par 274 total and won by four strokes.

Saiki started hot, making four birdies to the turn on her first nine, and closed with a 15-footer for birdie for a six-under 66 and a one-stroke lead over Candie Kung, a three-time winner the year before. Inkster was at 68, and Jones, Se Ri Pak and amateur whiz Paula Creamer were at 69. Sorenstam shot 72 and noted, "A few breaks here and there, things could have been different." Saiki was aware that Sorenstam could be making her own breaks at any time. "I know I have the ability to win," Saiki said. "That's why I'm still out here."

In the second round, sure enough, here came Sorenstam, surging on a 66. "I've struggled with my swing," she said, "but now I think I've got it back." Kung dropped three bending 12-footers and shot 68 to tie Saiki for the lead at nine-under 135. Becky Morgan (67) was one stroke back, Inkster (69) and Jones (68) two, and Sorenstam three. Saiki took her first bogey of the tournament, three-putting the 16th, but answered with a birdie at the 17th on a nine-footer and shot 69 for the tie. Could she hold up? Said Saiki, "If I play well enough, I'll come out on top."

Kung, Sorenstam and Morgan all fell back in the third round, but Jones came on as a serious threat and even led briefly, shooting a 67. She birdied the 10th from seven feet, dropped a 30-footer at the 14th, chipped in at the 15th, and birdied the 17th from four feet. Saiki never flinched. She ran off three straight birdies — a wedge to inches at the 11th, a 10-foot putt at the 12th, and a chip-in at the 13th. Saiki shot 68 and led Jones by one. Now could she win? "It's what I'm out here for," she said.

In the final round, Jones led three different times, then did herself in with a three-putt, double-bogey six from 18 feet at the 14th. Saiki sank a curving five-footer for birdie and a three-stroke swing. Jones fought on. She birdied the 15th from 25 feet while Saiki faced a 22-footer just to save par. And she saved it. At the 16th, Jones was short of the green, then two-putted from three feet for another bogey, shot 74, and dropped into a tie for second with Mi Hyun Kim (69). And Saiki had her first win.

"Oh, yes," Saiki said. "I got the monkey off my back!"

U.S. Women's Open—$3,100,000
Winner: Meg Mallon

Meg Mallon, a freckle-faced 41-year-old born near Boston, put an awesome burden on the long-suffering Boston Red Sox baseball club.

Moments after she won the 2004 U.S. Women's Open, played at The Orchards Golf Club at South Hadley, Massachusetts, a fan yelled, "If the Red Sox can't do it, you can do it today."

"I figure if I can win the U.S. Open," said Mallon, "the Red Sox can win the World Series."

Boston hadn't won the World Series since 1918, and their fans despaired they ever would. This was early July and the Red Sox were in second place in the American League East behind the hated New York Yankees. Well, Mallon did her part — and several months later, so did the Red Sox. She came from deep in the pack in the first round to turn back Annika Sorenstam, the world's No. 1 woman golfer, and win the Open by two strokes.

Mallon won with the greatest final round by a winner in the 59-year history of the Women's Open. After moving up the leaderboard with rounds of 73-69-67, she closed with a six-under 65, not only making up a three-stroke deficit on Jennifer Rosales but turning away Sorenstam. Mallon totaled a 10-under 274. Sorenstam closed with a 67, and Rosales, who got her first victory in May, helped Mallon by shooting a 75 in the final round.

By anybody's reckoning, Mallon was not even a long shot for this Open. Mallon's best year was 1991, when she won four times, including the Women's Open and the LPGA Championship. Her latest win was the 2003 season-ending ADT Championship, beating Sorenstam by a stroke. Sorenstam had already won four times on the LPGA Tour this season, and Mallon didn't make a peep in the first round, not with a 73 that left her tied for 40th behind Brittany Lincicome, age 18, who tied the amateur record with a 66. Mallon got little or no notice when a second-round 69 tied her for 13th at the halfway point.

It was Mallon's 67 in the third-round fireworks that finally reminded people that she was there.

Rosales shot a 69 for a 206 total and a three-stroke lead on Sorenstam, Mallon and Kelly Robbins. "I was kind of nervous at the end a little bit," Rosales said. Sorenstam bogeyed two of the first four holes, then made two birdies to make the turn in even par. She eagled the par-five 13th with a 20-foot putt and birdied the 14th from 12 feet for a 70, tying for second with Mallon and Kelly Robbins (68), who spurted to four birdies on the front nine and briefly tied for the lead. The three ended up at 209, three shots behind Rosales.

"I didn't get off to the start I wanted, but I kept grinding," Sorenstam said. Mallon's 67, the best of the day, put her in the final pairing with Rosales.

In the last round, the spirited Rosales birdied the first hole with a five-foot putt that upped her lead to four. Then, starting at the seventh, she bogeyed five of her last 12 holes.

Meanwhile, Mallon was making her move. She birdied from short range at the third hole, then rolled in a 50-footer for another at the fourth. At this point, Mallon would have to fight off some bad memories of previous Opens. In 1995, she blew a three-stroke lead over Sorenstam and finished second to her. In 2000, she three-putted for bogeys four times on the final nine and was co-runner-up to Karrie Webb. But that was all behind her.

"The cup looked like a bucket," Mallon said with a big grin. "And it was a great day for that to happen."

What happened was she birdied the ninth, 11th (from 18 feet, for the lead for good), 12th and 14th and saved par from 25 feet at the 15th. She needed just 24 putts for the round.

Sorenstam birdied the last two holes for her 67. "I did what I could," Sorenstam said. "I got outplayed."

Said Rosales, "I was just grinding out there. I was trying too hard, and I couldn't make anything happen."

This U.S. Women's Open will also be noted as the Open of the teenage amateurs. Michelle Wie, the 14-year-old whiz kid, was the headliner. The U.S. Golf Association gave her a special exemption. Wie and Paula Creamer, 17, tied for 13th place at 285 and shared low-amateur honors. Lincicome, 18, the first-round leader, finished 55th. But the kids couldn't overshadow Meg Mallon.

"I'm 41 years old," Mallon said, "and you've got to enjoy your days, enjoy when things like this happen."

BMO Financial Group Canadian Women's Open—$1,300,000
Winner: Meg Mallon

"This has been my 18th year on tour and it's been such a rewarding career," Meg Mallon said, "but I've never had two weeks like this."

Indeed, who had?

In the U.S. Women's Open, Mallon had to come from behind to win, but this time she broke on top and stayed there, racing off with the BMO Financial Group Canadian Women's Open by four stokes. Her toughest time was a one-stroke lead after 36 holes.

Beth Daniel, four shots behind after the third round, had the answer. "I'm having dinner with Meg tonight," Daniel said. "Maybe I can poison her food."

Not really. Just steal her putter.

Daniel should have swiped it early. In the first round, through the sun, wind and rain at the par-72 Legends course at Niagara Falls, Ontario, Mallon birdied four of her first five holes, hit 14 of the 18 greens, needed only 25 putts, and shot a seven-under-par 65 for a two-stroke lead. This extended her bogey-free streak to 43 holes. She birdied the first hole from nine feet and was five under through the eighth. She dropped a 30-footer at the 14th. The idea was taking root that Mallon had tapped into some mysterious force.

"You have to carry your momentum and know how to handle that," Mallon said. "And when you're playing well, you have to go with it and don't fight it." And so she did, living up to her own word and shooting 65-70-65-70–270, 18 under par.

Mallon also showed she could handle a little friction. In the second round, at the par-four 12th, her third hole, she put her approach shot into a bunker and two-putted from 15 feet for the bogey that ended her bogey-free string at 45 holes. She bogeyed the 13th as well, hooking her tee shot into the rough and hitting a tree with her second. Then she regained her senses in the third round, shooting another 65. And in the fourth, things were relentlessly much the same, moving Lorena Ochoa, the bright young player, to lament, "I wish there were more holes."

In closing, Mallon saved par with a five-footer at the second hole and another with a sloping nine-footer at the par-three third. She saved par once again at the 16th with a four-footer. She did find time for two birdies, with a 15-foot putt at the fifth and an eight-footer at the eighth. Probably the best indication of the roll Mallon was on was this: Except for the two bogeys in the second round, she had made par or better in 95 of her last 97 holes, and she was 28 under for her last six rounds.

Giant Eagle LPGA Classic—$1,000,000
Winner: Moira Dunn

Not to indulge in stereotypes, but it was the case of a woman shopping. She said so herself. "... I couldn't leave without buying something," Moira Dunn confessed, and the something she bought at the pro shop was a new putter — and a new lease on life. Three days later, in her 245th tournament, she won her first LPGA title.

"It's been a long time," said Dunn, fighting back the tears. "I always believed it would come. That's what got me here."

The persistent and believing Dunn, nearing age 33 and in her 10th year on the LPGA Tour, closed with a seven-under-par 65 to take the Giant Eagle LPGA Classic by two strokes over Korea's Young-A Yang. There being no champagne handy, A.J. Eathorne and Amy Fruhwirth made do with beer and doused the new champion after she tapped in a short par putt that wrapped up rounds of 70, 69 and 65, for a 10-under 204 total at Squaw Creek Country Club in Vienna, Ohio.

Dunn, whose previous best was a couple of ties for second in 2001, was barely in the picture at first. Gloria Park, a two-time winner this season, had blistered Squaw Creek with a 10-birdie 66, and this was after nearly withdrawing with a stomach problem. She would feel worse the next day — a 76 would knock her out of the picture. "It was just a tough day," Park said. "I just had one or two bad holes."

Michelle Estill, seeking her first victory in 13 years, shot 67 in the second round and tied for the lead with Yang (71), a sophomore, at six-under 138. "After the last couple of years, a win would help my self-confidence," said Estill, age 41. She holed a seven iron from 143 yards for an eagle at No. 3 and had four birdies and a bogey, and was surprised. "I didn't realize I shot a 67," she said. "I kept adding it over and over."

Dunn solved all problems with her new putter. She needed 31 putts in her first round, then 27 putts, and finally 26.

Dunn started the final round a stroke behind Yang and Estill and caught them with a birdie on the first hole. She and Yang, in the same threesome, were tied for the lead on the last nine when a storm forced suspension of play. Yang then took the lead with a birdie at the 14th, and Dunn caught her at the par-three 15th. "I would make a birdie, and then she would make a birdie," Yang said. "After that, she just made two more birdies."

At the 16th, Dunn put her seven-iron approach from 150 yards to 18 feet above the hole and made the birdie to take the lead. Then she birdied the 17th, firing a six iron from 161 yards to five feet. A short while later Dunn had her first championship. Patience and perseverance were the key words for her.

"I was just trying to hang around and see what happened," Dunn said. She got a beer shower for her trouble.

Evian Masters—€1,977,826
Winner: Wendy Doolan

See Ladies European Tour section.

Weetabix Women's British Open—€1,050,000
Winner: Karen Stupples

See Ladies European Tour section.

Jamie Farr Owens Corning Classic—$1,100,000
Winner: Meg Mallon

Karen Stupples was picking up where she left off a week earlier in the Weetabix Women's British Open, but then Meg Mallon decided to pick up where she left off a little earlier. Mallon was standing over a 10-foot putt for a birdie on the final hole of the Jamie Farr Owens Corning Classic and called on a fresh memory to steady her nerves.

"I was set over that putt and I was thinking, 'I've won the U.S. Open. I don't get nervous,'" Mallon said. "But I'll tell you what — I was nervous."

Nerves and all, Mallon rolled in that 10-footer to beat Stupples and defending champion Se Ri Pak by one stroke, notching her third victory of the season following two national championships — the U.S. Women's Open and the BMO Financial Group Canadian Women's Open back-to-back just a month earlier. It was the 18th win of her career.

Mallon shot 66-69-74-68–277, a seven-under-par total at Highland Meadows, near Toledo, Ohio. Stupples closed with a 73 and Pak with a 68, both at 278, and both just missed birdie putts at the 18th that would have forced a playoff. Pak, a four-time winner here, was trying to match Mickey Wright as a five-time winner of the same event.

"I really have no complaints," Stupples said. "If somebody had told me I would tie for second at the start of the week, I would have jumped all over it. I gave it a good try, but it just wasn't in me. Give more credit to Meg. She played superb, brought it to me, and won the tournament."

Mallon, who had slipped behind after tying for the second-round lead, started the last round four shots behind Stupples' lead. She pulled within a stroke with a birdie at No. 3 shortly before Stupples bogeyed it off a hooked tee shot. Stupples then became erratic, setting off a tight skirmish down the final nine.

Stupples bogeyed again off a hooked shot into trees at the 12th and bogeyed the 13th on a three-putt from 35 feet. "That was ridiculous," she said. Pak caught up with a birdie from 15 feet at the 16th. Pak narrowly missed a 10-footer for the lead at the 17th. Mallon joined the fray with back-to-back birdies — a chip-in at the 15th (her second chip-in of the round), then a 20-foot putt at the 16th.

At the decisive par-five 18th, Pak's birdie try from 18 feet just missed. Mallon, in the next-to-last group, flipped a wedge from 100 yards to 10 feet. She swallowed hard and holed the putt. Stupples watched from down in the fairway, then hit her approach to 14 feet. Her try for the tying birdie slipped past, and Mallon had her third victory of the season.

"At this stage of my career," said Mallon, age 41, "I can't tell you how much I enjoy this. I know how fleeting it is."

Wendy's Championship for Children—$1,100,000
Winner: Catriona Matthew

Catriona Matthew, queen of the top-10 finish, hadn't led in so long she had practically forgotten what it felt like. She didn't lead in the rain-interrupted Wendy's Championship for Children, either — until the instant it counted.

Matthew, a native of Scotland, was probably best known for scoring the winning point for Europe in the 2003 Solheim Cup. She had won only once in her 10 years on the LPGA Tour. That was the 2001 Cup Noodles Hawaiian Ladies Open. Add to that 47 other top-10 finishes — four this year — and that should be a measure of her frustration.

But no frustration this time. Make that two victories.

Matthew was hardly a threat through the first three rounds at Tartan Fields Golf Club in Dublin, Ohio. Shooting 72-67-71, she trailed by six strokes in the first round, by four after 36 holes, and by three strokes with six holes to play. Her chances for another top-10 finish — but somewhere under first — were looking good if tiresome.

Then, abruptly, opportunity presented itself in the form of some shaky putting by her playing partner, defending champion Hee-Won Han, who led the tournament by two coming into the final round. Han birdied two of the first four holes, bogeyed the sixth, and birdied the 10th and 12th. Then came trouble.

Han came out of a bunker at the par-five 14th, but missed a four-footer for par. At the par-three 15th, Matthew fired a five iron to three feet and birdied. Then Matthew caught Han with a birdie from 12 feet at the 17th and shot a bogey-free 68. They tied at 10-under-par 278.

In the playoff, at the 18th, Matthew put her approach to 15 feet. She missed the birdie putt, got the par, and waited to go on to the second playoff hole. But she never got there. Han's first putt from 60 feet turned five feet to the right of the hole, and she missed the second — the tying par putt. Matthew, in her first playoff, was a winner.

"I'm just absolutely delighted," Matthew said. I played well the last few years, but haven't managed to win. To hold it together and come out with the win — it's fantastic."

But it was almost an anticlimax to the rest of the week. Fans were following the two teen sensations, Michelle Wie, age 14, and Paula Creamer, 17. Wie tied for sixth at 282, her second-best finish in an LPGA tournament, and Creamer was 18th at 286.

Wachovia LPGA Classic—$1,000,000
Winner: Lorena Ochoa

It was what's called a rousing start. The first round of the Wachovia LPGA Classic looked this way: Laura Diaz ran off five straight birdies to tie for the lead with Hillary Lunke and Jill McGill at six-under-par 66. Hee-Won Han, the playoff runner-up the week before, birdied five of her first seven holes, then cooled off and joined a crowd of nine at 67 that included Lorena Ochoa. Five others were at 68, including tournament host Betsy King. A throng of 12 at 69 included U.S. Women's Open champion Meg Mallon. There were 26 within three strokes of the lead. At Berkleigh Country Club in Kutztown, Pennsylvania, it looked more like a stampede than a golf tournament.

McGill, 32, a nine-year veteran seeking her first victory, called on her new-found attitude and raced to a three-stroke lead with a 64 for a 130 total through the second round. "I've worn myself down being so nervous and uptight," McGill said. "So I have taken a new approach to my game." Something worked. She birdied six of seven holes from No. 8, and ended up three ahead of Soo-Yun Kang (66) and Suzann Pettersen (63). The race would shake itself down. Karrie Webb, briefly hopeful, was sidetracked by a 75 in the third round, and all three co-leaders of the first round would fall out in the fourth — McGill with a 73, Diaz, 75, and Lunke, 76.

Grace Park, four strokes off the halfway lead, logged four birdies and an eagle on the second nine for a 65 to bolt to the top in the third round. Her 199 total was a record, 17 under par, good for a one-stroke lead over McGill. Then came the fall.

"I don't think I have ever played a final round this bad with the lead," said Park, who for the first time in her professional career lost a tournament after leading through the third round. "Seventeen under par for three days, then even par — that tells it all. I just played bad."

Ochoa was there to pick up the pieces. "I was five shots out of the lead, but Grace gave us a chance and I took advantage," said Ochoa, who got her first victory in May and had a top-10 finish in each of her last five tournaments.

Ochoa started this time with three birdies on the first nine. Park birdied twice before the turn, but bogeyed the 10th and 13th. That was the opening Ochoa needed. She birdied the 10th, then edged closer when Park missed a par putt from two feet. Ochoa tied Park with a birdie at the 15th, then had the lead alone when Park, in the group behind her, bogeyed it, two-putting from 40 feet. Ochoa then birdied the 18th for a 65 and a two-stroke victory over Park on a 19-under 269 total.

The only problem was with the folks back home in Guadalajara, Mexico. Ochoa called her mother to say she had won, only to discover that the family was watching the tournament on tape-delay television. "I'm not going to tell anyone," her mother said, "because they are watching you play on 14."

State Farm Classic—$1,200,000
Winner: Cristie Kerr

Not that there's a world of difference between ages 26 and 20, but there clearly was between eight years and two on the LPGA Tour, and it was that difference that got Cristie Kerr past Christina Kim in the State Farm Classic.

Kerr, age 26 and in her eighth season on tour, let a four-stroke lead get away in the final round, but reached down and found some reserve at the final hole and scrambled out of trouble and won. Then it was tears all around. Kim, age 20, led for the first two rounds, chased Kerr in the last two rounds, and regained the lead, but only briefly. So Kim missed a short birdie putt and broke down and cried. And Kerr, who missed the cut in her last two tournaments, had her third victory of the season and cried because Kim was crying.

It was just a two-player race at the Rail Golf Course in Springfield, Illinois. Kerr shot 69-63-63-69, a 24-under 264 total. Kim's results read 62-66-71-66–265. Mi Hyun Kim was third at 270. Christina's opening 62, good for a two-stroke lead on Swedish rookie Mikaela Parmlid, came on a bogey and 11 birdies of all sizes — from five feet, three from within 20 feet, a 15-footer and a few shorter ones coming in. She could have used a bit of that touch at the final hole. Kerr pulled to within four of Kim in the second round with a 63 that included an eagle and four birdies on the second nine. Kerr then took the lead with another 63 against Kim's 71 in the third round.

Kim, trailing by four strokes going into the final round, notched five birdies, then an eagle at the par-five 15th that returned her to the lead. A poor tee shot and two bad chips cost her a bogey at the par-three 16th. Kerr regained the lead at the 17th, dropping her wedge approach to five feet.

Next is where experience told. Kim played the 18th hole beautifully — a drive into the fairway and an eight iron to four feet. Kerr had driven into the right rough, under a tree, and punched her second into a greenside bunker. Then, coolly, she blasted out to three feet. It jarred Kim.

"I was terrified," Kim said. "I kept telling myself, just breathe. I've never had it come down to the wire like that." Kim missed her short putt. Kerr made hers and won.

Said Kim, "I am so damn proud of how I played."

Said Kerr, "I dug deep and I found a way to go within myself and be at peace."

John Q. Hammons Hotel Classic—$1,000,000
Winner: Annika Sorenstam

Christina Kim, so crushed at just missing her first victory a week before, regrouped and set out take on the John Q. Hammons Hotel Classic near Tulsa, Oklahoma. Alas, it was not to be. It was Annika Sorenstam's week. She hadn't played in about a month and hadn't won since mid-June. She ran away with the Hammons event by four strokes, making it her fifth victory of the season and the 53rd of her career.

Kim served notice that she had recovered from her disappointment at the State Farm Classic a week earlier by playing Cedar Ridge Country Club in six-under-par 65, notching seven birdies and only one bogey for the one-stroke lead over Sorenstam and rookie Shi Hyun Ahn. "I felt rusty," said Sorenstam, after her 66. "It doesn't seem like it with the score. I'm surprised myself."

For anyone else, the surprise ended the next day. Sorenstam hit 16 greens in regulation. So much for rest. The three-round tournament was all but over. Kim double-bogeyed the first hole out of the water and was on her way to a second-round 75 and eventually a tie for 12th place. Sorenstam, after a brief exchange with England's Joanne Morley, regained the lead with a birdie at the ninth, then pulled away with birdies at the 11th and par-five 14th. Only 13 players were under par for two rounds on the tight par-71 course, and Sorenstam was already eight under par and leading by three.

Sorenstam last played competitively in Sweden in early August; she hadn't played in the United States since the U.S. Women's Open early in July. She spent part of that break cleaning up hurricane damage at her Orlando home. So a month later, she was hitting the narrow fairways and sloping greens and making putts as though she had never been away.

In the third round, Morley moved to within a stroke of Sorenstam with birdies at the first two holes, but then bogeyed five of the next six holes. Sorenstam wrapped up the victory with a one-under 70, tossing her ball into the gallery with a smile after a bogey at the 18th cut her winning margin to four over Shi Hyun Ahn. Sorenstam was back from her break. She had hit 31 of 42 fairways in regulation and 44 of 54 greens, and she broke par in all three rounds.

"I'm just really surprised how well I hit it and putted," said Sorenstam, but probably no one else was surprised.

Safeway Classic—$1,200,000
Winner: Hee-Won Han

It seems there's nothing routine about any tournament Annika Sorenstam plays. Accordingly, she came to the Safeway Classic looking to make that the third tournament that she's won three years in succession, adding it to the Michelob Light Classic, 1997-1999, and the Mizuno Classic, 2001-2003. She was a two-time defending champion coming to Columbia Edgewater Country Club in Portland, Oregon, in mid-September. And that's where that string ended. Sorenstam kept threatening, but she just couldn't crack the top and finished tied for fourth place.

In the end, it was Hee-Won Han beating Lorie Kane on the first extra hole for her first victory of the year, the third of her LPGA career, and improving her record to 2-3 in playoffs. Just a month earlier, Han missed a five-foot putt and lost to Catriona Matthew in a playoff for the Wendy's Championship for Children.

This time, Han birdied the 18th twice within minutes, first on an eight-footer for a 67 to force the playoff and then on a four-footer for the win after Kane's 80-footer took her breath away, just missing. Kane made the eight-foot return for her par, but Han rendered it meaningless with her four-footer.

Kane shook off bad weather to grab a share of the second-round lead with a 69, tying Candie Kung (68) at seven-under-par 137. Han (71) was three back at 140, setting up the final-round duel. Kung was about to make it a three-way playoff. Standing on the final green she was tied for the lead with Kane at nine under, but she four-putted for a double bogey for 72 and a tie for fourth. Janice Moodie was also a victim of the 18th. She was just one off the lead, then hit into the trees twice, water once, and finally dropped an 18-foot putt for a double-bogey six, a 71, and finished seventh.

Kane made three birdies and a bogey for her closing 70. Han, playing comfortably, made up a three-stroke deficit with a 67, and they tied at nine-under-par 207 in regulation.

"Playing from behind is better than being the leader," Han said. "Not as much pressure."

Longs Drugs Challenge—$1,000,000
Winner: Christina Kim

It seems free-spirited Christina Kim grew up in an awful hurry. It was just three weeks earlier at the State Farm Classic that the 20-year-old LPGA Tour player was so scared she blew a four-foot putt on the final hole that would have forced a playoff. "I was terrified," she admitted, saying she had never been in that kind of pressure before. Now, just three tournaments later, here she was in the heat again. Then she was crying again, but this time for a different reason. She had stood up under the pressure and won the Longs Drugs Challenge for her first LPGA Tour victory.

This time, Kim, who contended for the title after taking the first-round lead with a 64, was under the pressure longer. She was coming down the stretch against Karrie Webb, owner of 29 career victories in her nine years. Kim made five birdies on the final nine — three on the last five holes, in fact — for a six-under-par 65 and a 266 total at the Ridge Golf Course near Sacramento, California. Webb herself was on a roll, on her way to a 64, and she was tied for the lead with Kim — until Kim birdied the 17th. Then, at the 18th, Webb had a seven-foot putt for birdie to tie Kim and force a playoff. Her putt just missed to the left, and Kim had her victory by a stroke.

Kim was also under pressure from another great veteran, Juli Inkster, herself a two-time Longs Drugs Challenge winner. With three birdies on the first nine, Inkster led by two strokes going through the turn. She played the last nine in even par for a 68 and got outrun by the surging Kim and finished third.

Kim became a quick success story on the tour. She opted to turn professional rather than go to college. She won $215,632 in 2003, her rookie year. Working up to this victory in 2004, she was second once and had four other top-10 finishes, two in majors — a tie for eighth in the Kraft Nabisco Championship and a tie for sixth in the McDonald's LPGA Championship. And now the victory.

"I hope it doesn't change me," Kim said. "I'm sure it will. I just have to make sure that, if it does, it changes me for the better."

Asahi Ryokuken International—$1,000,000
Winner: Liselotte Neumann

Liselotte Neumann, age 38, one of the first of the outstanding Swedes to come to the LPGA Tour and a rookie in 1988, forgot how long it had been since she was in the thick of things. She got a hint at the Asahi Ryokuken International, the last full-field event of the 2004 schedule, early in October at Mount Vintage Plantation Golf Club in North Augusta, South Carolina. The name on her caddie's back was "Newmann."

They got it right on the scoreboard, however. It was at the top from the second round on. It was her first victory since 1998 and the 13th of her LPGA career. "I'm so relieved, so happy, I don't even know what else to say," Neumann said. The combination of tears and laughter said it all for her.

Grace Park, Kim Saiki and Silvia Cavalleri shared the first-round lead with six-under-par 66s. Neumann, unnoticed, was at 68. It would come down to a shootout with Park before Neumann would win by three strokes. First, she had to exercise some old physical and psychological muscle before she could win.

Neumann shot another 68 in the second round and shared a two-stroke lead with Donna Andrews (68) and Becky Morgan (69) at eight-under 136. Neumann caught a hot hand with the putter. She had a stretch of birdie putts of 15, 17, 25 and 30 feet. A pair of bogeys dropped her back into the tie.

She had the lead to herself with a third-round 69 that put her one stroke ahead of Morgan (70). Neumann birdied two of the first three holes and took the lead outright when Andrews was foiled by a downhill chip at the fourth and bogeyed. Coming home, Neumann birdied the 10th and 12th holes and salvaged a bogey at the par-three 15th when she had to chip backwards from a tree. Then she saved pars at the 17th, holing a seven-foot putt, and at the 18th, on a three-footer for a 69, an 11-under 205 and a one-stroke lead.

Grace Park, co-leader in the first round and hurt by a 74 in the second, suddenly was a threat in the fourth round. Neumann stretched her lead to four with birdies at the eighth and ninth, but she quickly found herself in trouble. She bogeyed the 10th and 11th, and Park eagled the par-five 12th. Neumann birdied the 12th and was back to two ahead, and Park answered with a 30-footer from the edge at the 14th that got her back to within one. The head-to-head battle lasted for two more holes. Neumann birdied the 14th with a 10-footer to go back to two ahead. Park birdied the 16th to get within one again, and for the last time, when Neumann answered with a birdie on a six-footer. The battle was all but over when Park hit a tree with her approach at the 17th and bogeyed.

Neumann, with a 68 for a 15-under 273 total, had her first victory in six years.

Samsung World Championship—$825,000
Winner: Annika Sorenstam

Annika Sorenstam was contemplating life as the leader. "When you are in the lead," she was saying, "my experience has been, you look at the leaderboards a lot. You wonder if somebody is going to get hot. Are they going to catch me?"

Whether that was precisely the case in the Samsung World Championship must be left for the golfers themselves to answer, but the fact is, Sorenstam picked up two strokes on Grace Park in the third round, then stormed from three strokes behind over the final five holes in the fourth round to win. This, in mid-October, was her sixth win in 15 LPGA Tour starts in 2004 and her career 54th victory. Sorenstam shot 66-68-69-67, an 18-under par 270 total at Bighorn Golf Club in Palm Desert, California, to outrun Park by three strokes

"This is special — to come from behind," Sorenstam said. "You've got the 20 best players in the world and you've got to really play some good golf."

Park opened with a 10-under 62, the lowest start in the tournament's 24 years, and was leading all the way. She was three strokes up on Sorenstam and Cristie Kerr going into the final round. Then she helped Sorenstam by shooting 73. "I fell apart," Park said. "I didn't get the job done, and that's it. I'm playing good golf but just not getting it done." Park, No. 2 most of the year to Sorenstam's No. 1 in the world rankings, thus finished second for the sixth time. She had one victory, the Kraft Nabisco Championship in March.

Sorenstam caught up with Park with a chip-in eagle at the par-five 15th, then took the lead at the 17th, holing a six-foot birdie putt. Park, in the twosome behind Sorenstam, bogeyed the last two holes.

Two other golfers did notable work. Michelle Wie, the sensational teen amateur, now 15 and a 10th-grader, was there on a sponsor's exemption. She tied for 13th place with a five-under 283 total. "I had a lot of fun," Wie said, "and now it's back to school."

Se Ri Pak was notable for a different reason. The former sensation continued her mysterious slide. Even after taking an extended break from early September, she couldn't find her game. She had closing rounds of 80 and 78 and finished at 15-over 303, the only player over par.

CJ Nine Bridges Classic—$1,350,000
Winner: Grace Park

This was a new and rejuvenated Grace Park at the CJ Nine Bridges Classic late in October. Just two weeks earlier she was saying, "I fell apart" after losing the lead in the final round of the Samsung World Championship and getting overrun by Annika Sorenstam. And now Park was saying, "I can't describe my happiness with words." This was after sharing the lead through the first two rounds with 66-69, then sprinting home with a 65 to beat Sorenstam and Carin Koch by five strokes. It was enough to perk anybody up.

"Even though I had several mistakes in my putting from the beginning," Park said after the victory, "I didn't really have any danger of a bogey because my shots were really good today."

The tournament was played at the Nine Bridges Golf Club on Jeju Island, off the southern coast of Korea, and Koch greeted the event with birdies on her first four holes. Mexico's Lorena Ochoa stole some of her thunder with an ace at the par-three 13th and an eagle at the par-five 18th in her 68. Sorenstam, rarely out of the picture, had an erratic four-birdie, three-bogey 71. Park bogeyed the 13th, but recovered with birdies at the 16th and 18th to tie Koch at 66.

Park birdied the 18th again in the second round, this time tying at nine-under-par 135 with Kate Golden, a former University of Texas star and one-time winner on the LPGA Tour, who shot 64. "Today was a little bit of everything that did not work out," said Park. "My shots were not great and neither was my putting. There was not a big difference, but it was still good enough."

It was good enough to keep Sorenstam three off the lead with her 67–138. But three shots don't mean that much to Sorenstam, and Park understood this more than anyone when she bogeyed to start the third and final round. There came that sinking feeling. Was this going to be a repeat of the Samsung? No, Park wouldn't let it. She went on to rack up eight birdies for the day, outdistancing the field. For Sorenstam, it took an eagle at the final hole to get her within five.

The Mitchell Company Tournament of Champions—$800,000
Winner: Heather Daly-Donofrio

Heather Daly-Donofrio, a graduate of Yale and Oxford and former women's golf coach at Yale, was thinking about her first three rounds at The Mitchell Company Tournament of Champions. "I've put three days together that are by far the best golf I've ever played," she said. "Regardless of what happens, these are three of the best days I've ever had."

Daly-Donofrio had just shot a 64 in the third round, eight under par at Magnolia Grove's Crossings course near Mobile, Alabama. It was her career-low by a stroke, and with a 69-66 start, it was the first time in her seven-year career she had three rounds in the 70s. More to the point, she was 17 under par at 199, and leading by three strokes.

"When you get this close, though," she said, "you want to close it out."

So she did close it out, shooting 70 for a four-stroke victory over Laura Diaz. She was more than a surprise winner. The first surprise was that she was even in the field. She got in because officials had extended the eligibility to include winners from 2001, when she won the First Union Betsy King Classic, her only victory. The other surprise was that coming into this tournament, her average in three previous years at Magnolias Grove's Crossing was 75.6. This time she averaged 67.25, a whopping 8.35 strokes lower.

Daly-Donofrio was a little ways back in the field with her first-round 69. Grace Park birdied the last three holes to crash into a tie at 66 with Laura Diaz, Christina Kim and Juli Inkster. There must have been a spell on Magnolia's last three holes. Diaz birdied them in the second round for a 67, jumping out to a two-stroke lead at 133. Diaz had two goals. For the short-term, she wanted to finish no lower than fifth to get into the top 30 on the money list to qualify for the season-ending ADT Championship the following week. And for the long-term, "To make the Hall of Fame, and you do that by winning tournaments."

Diaz led by two over Daly-Donofrio, who was so relieved by her 66. "I had a horrible history here," she said. "It's been abysmal. I would get off the golf course and think I'm so frazzled that the course got the better of me, I don't ever want to come back. This is much better golf than I have ever played here before."

Daly-Donofrio then stunned the field in the third round, leapfrogging from two behind to three ahead with a career-low 64 she finished with a four-foot birdie putt on the 18th. That put her three up on Sophie Gustafson, who missed short birdie putts at the 16th and 18th for a 65. "That's just going to make me hungrier for tomorrow," Gustafson said.

No matter. The next day, Daly-Donofrio holed out a nine iron from 123 yards for an eagle two at No. 3. "I can still feel that swing," she said. "It hit about eight feet in front of the pin, and then everybody started cheering. That was the good start I needed." The eagle put her five ahead, and except for a bogey at the final hole, she had a fairly uneventful day. If one considers winning uneventful.

ADT Championship—$1,000,000
Winner: Annika Sorenstam

Annika Sorenstam started off like gangbusters in the ADT Championship, the end of the LPGA season, but there was a touch of T.S. Eliot in her finish:

not with a bang but a whimper. But it was a win — her 10th worldwide in a spectacular season for the No. 1 female golfer.

Sorenstam led with her customary authority through the first three rounds. Then came one of those great golf puzzles — the collapse. Ultimately, she found herself trailing in the final round. As though the entire season had been scripted for this critical moment, she beat Cristie Kerr in a playoff. The whimper? For all of her great game, Sorenstam won on the first extra hole — with a bogey.

"I was so nervous the last two holes," said Sorenstam. "I wanted to do it so badly."

It was not only her eighth LPGA Tour victory of the season, but the 56th of her career, moving her past Betsy Rawls into fifth place on the all-time victory list.

The ADT Championship brought together the top 30 players of the year to Trump International in West Palm Beach, Florida, and lest anyone forget that Sorenstam was the huge favorite, in the first round she blistered the last five holes for four birdies, for a six-under-par 66 and a one-stroke lead. Sorenstam had worked on her swing and had come in confident.

"Now I'm not afraid of being a little more aggressive because I have a better feel," she said. Two of the birdies came on elegant seven irons. At the par-four 16th, she ignored the two bunkers and fired her approach to nine feet on a sloping two-tiered green. At the 18th, she stopped her shot about eight feet to the right of a deep-cut pin, made the putt, and led by one over Kerr.

Sorenstam bumped through the turn in the second round. She lost the lead at the eighth, then turned disaster into a silk purse at the par-five ninth — and nearly disaster for her mom. Her seven-wood shot from 214 yards drifted to the right and almost hit her mother. "I saw my mom standing there, and she said, 'Are you trying to hit me?'" Sorenstam grinned and flipped a wedge to six feet and made the birdie. Then a burst of four birdies coming home put her at 68–134, three ahead of Kerr (70), Laura Diaz (68) and Karrie Webb (69), tied at 137. "You don't want to be too much more than three behind going into Sunday," said Kerr, who hurt herself with two weak bogeys. She three-putted the sixth and missed the green with a wedge at the 12th.

In the third round, Sorenstam blew her three-stroke lead over the first five holes, then had to make three birdies over the last six holes for a par 72. "I don't know if I'd call it a roller-coaster day, but it was tough," she said. But at 10-under 206, she was still leading, with Jennifer Rosales (69) and Kerr (70) her closest threats.

The tournament came down to the last two groups in the final round, with Kerr in the next-to-last group and Rosales and Sorenstam in the final one. Rosales birdied the second hole from three feet to get to 10 under par. Kerr dropped a short birdie putt at the second for 10 under, then birdied the third from eight feet. Sorenstam fell back, missing birdie chances at the first four holes. She bogeyed the fifth, three-putting from 60 feet. Then click: She birdied the sixth from 20 feet and the seventh from 45 feet.

At the par-five ninth, Rosales hit her tee shot into water, double-bogeyed, and was out of the running. Kerr and Sorenstam both birdied from short range. Then Kerr took the lead at the 15th with a tap-in birdie while Sorenstam parred on three putts from 40 feet. In an exchange at the 16th, Kerr two-putted from eight feet for par and Sorenstam birdied from eight feet, and they were tied. Kerr just missed a 20-footer for birdie at the 17th and another at the 18th. Sorenstam saved par with a six-footer at the 17th and also two-putted from 12 feet to par the 18th. Kerr shot 68, Sorenstam 69, and they tied with 13-under 275 totals.

The playoff, at the par-five 18th, was anything but artful. Kerr, who hadn't made a bogey in 44 holes, hit a so-so drive, then hit her seven-wood approach shot into the water, and double-bogeyed. All Sorenstam had to do for the easy victory was hit the green. Instead, she hit a spectator. From there, she bogeyed — and won. It was the exclamation point to 2004.

Ladies European Tour

ANZ Ladies Masters—A$800,000
Winner: Annika Sorenstam

See Australian Women's Tour section.

AAMI Women's Australian Open—A$550,000
Winner: Laura Davies

See Australian Women's Tour section.

Tenerife Ladies Open—€220,000
Winner: Diana Luna

With the help of one of only two other Italian players to win on the Ladies European Tour, Diana Luna secured her first title at the Tenerife Ladies Open. Federica Dassu, who retired at the end of 2003 with six victories to her name, also enjoyed success in her new role as coach and caddie to Luna. Stefania Croce, Italy's other winner, was ready to spray the pair with champagne after the final putt.

Luna, starting her third season as a professional, entered the final round with a two-stroke lead and closed with a 69 for a 279 total to win by two over Becky Brewerton, who was also the runner-up the previous year when still an amateur. Georgina Simpson finished a stroke further back, and the first-round leader, Minea Blomqvist, was fourth.

Luna charged ahead with three birdies and an eagle on the first nine, but her afternoon was eased by Simpson bogeying the 16th and 17th holes in windy conditions on the Seve Ballesteros-designed Buenavista course.

"Federica has been so good to me and she's coaching me full time now," said Luna, a 21-year-old from Rome. "She has really helped me with my confidence on the course, and that's why I feel so good when I am playing now. She has helped me get to the next level."

Ladies Open of Portugal—€300,000
Winner: Cecilia Ekelundh

Cecilia Ekelundh escaped from the trees and overcame the loss of her late mother's lucky necklace to win her first title and a €3,500 diamond ring at the Ladies Open of Portugal. The 26-year-old Swede also coped with the torrential, cold rain for a closing 67 and a 206 total at Aroeira to be 10 under par and win by three strokes over Linda Wessberg.

Three times around the turn Ekelundh went into the trees but emerged with birdies. At the 12th this was achieved by holing a wedge shot from 60 yards, but she immediately bogeyed the next after discovering the loss of her lucky charm. Birdies at the 15th and 17th sealed the victory as Wessberg finished with a 70 and Trish Johnson, who had shared the overnight lead with the two Swedes, shot a 72 to be third.

"You definitely need skill and lots of luck to win and it's an amazing feeling now," Ekelundh said. "I felt the pressure all day long out there and then I noticed I lost my mum's heart necklace. I've been thinking about her a lot this week and I think she was looking down on me, too. I did this for her."

Union Fenosa Open de Espana Feminino Xacobeo—€275,000
Winner: Stephanie Arricau

In what was becoming something of a trend, another player won for the first time when France's Stephanie Arricau took the Union Fenosa Open de Espana Feminino Xacobeo. She triumphed at the first extra hole of a playoff against Gina Scott at La Coruna.

Defending her overnight lead with a final round of 71, Arricau was caught at nine-under-par 279 by Scott's closing 69. But it was hardly that simple. Arricau led by two strokes approaching the final hole thanks to five birdies in six holes on the second nine. But the 30-year-old's approach at the 18th hit one of the tall conifers and rebounded almost to where she stood. Her next was punched under the branches of the tree onto the green, but her par putt from 30 feet finished three feet away and then she missed that. They returned to the 18th for the playoff and this time it was Scott's turn to miss a short putt as Arricau made a safe par.

"I was feeling really good after all those birdies, but at the final hole I just played my second shot too quickly," Arricau said. "It wasn't a good shot and I thought I could just get on with it, make bogey and still win. But I've done it now!"

BMW Ladies Italian Open—€275,000
Winner: Ana Belen Sanchez

Ana Belen Sanchez became the fourth first-time winner in a row as the 28-year-old from Malaga won the BMW Ladies Italian Open at Parco di Roma. Sanchez had posted 17 top-10 finishes prior to what was considered an overdue victory.

A three-hour thunderstorm during the final round did not help her nerves, but Sanchez birdied the seventh, ninth, 11th and 13th holes to lead by four strokes. She and Germany's Martina Eberl both birdied the 17th, but there was still drama at the last. While Eberl chipped in for an eagle, Sanchez had driven into a pond on the left of the fairway and was left with a 35-foot putt for her par and two putts for victory. Her first putt was a beauty and the Solheim Cup player needed only a tap-in for the title. She shot 69 for a 281 total, seven under par.

"That was definitely the hardest two-putt I have ever had in my life," admitted the Spaniard. "Right now, I just can't describe what I feel ... but I think I'm happy."

Arras Open de France Dames—€275,000
Winner: Stephanie Arricau

Stephanie Arricau ended the run of maiden titles on the Ladies European Tour by becoming the third French player to win her national championship. Victory in the Arras Open de France Dames at Golf d'Arras in northern France was Arricau's second victory in three weeks. The 30-year-old from Orthez won by two strokes over Austria's Natascha Fink.

Arricau finished with a seven-under-par 281 total after a 67 in the final round, the only player under par from the final three groups to tee off. Her charge began with four birdies in the first six holes, but she did not take the outright lead until a birdie at the 13th.

She bogeyed the 15th but picked the shot back up at the next and then parred the last two holes, avoiding the disaster at the last hole that dropped her into a playoff in Spain for her earlier win. "I did the same score last year in the final round, so I was thinking about that all day long," said Arricau, who joined Patricia Meunier-Lebouc and Marie-Laure de Lorenzi as the only French women to win the French Open.

"I think this win was more difficult than La Coruna, because when I began the day playing very well, I knew very quickly that I was in contention. It's an incredible feeling. When I got onto the flight to Spain, I could not imagine that I would be having three weeks like this. When I won there, I knew I could win again."

KLM Ladies Open—€165,000
Winner: Elisabeth Esterl

Elisabeth Esterl won her second title with a two-stroke victory in the KLM Ladies Open at Kennemer. The 27-year-old German came from three shots behind the overnight leader, Georgina Simpson, with a closing 68 to finish at two under par with a 214 total. She was the only player to complete the three rounds in red figures.

Spain's Marta Prieto finished second at even par, and Becky Brewerton was one stroke further back along with Simpson, who dropped shots at the last two holes to fall out of second place.

"I found my rhythm on the course today," Esterl said. "It was just a day when I had to hang in there, as this is a tough course and you must be patient, and that's what I needed to do to play well. Everything was solid in the swing and I like courses this tough, as it forces me to play better golf."

Esterl was involved in a curious rules incident when her playing partner in the final round, Trish Johnson, who was one stroke off the lead at the time, discovered from the German that she was not entitled to a drop from a path as she had done in the previous round. Johnson immediately disqualified herself for signing for a wrong score in the second round. "I really feel for her," said Esterl. "It goes to show that Trish is such a fantastic sportswoman to do that when you are in contention."

Ladies English Open—€179,063
Winner: Maria Hjorth

It took eight years for Maria Hjorth to win her first title on the Ladies European Tour, but when she did, at the Ladies English Open, the 30-year-old Swede did so in record-breaking fashion. Her final round of 64 equaled the course record at Chart Hills, while her 54-hole total of 197, 19 under par, was a new record for the tour.

Hjorth opened with rounds of 66 and 67, but still only led by two shots over a group of three players. But she skated away from the field with eight birdies on the final day, including at the last three holes, to win by six strokes over Joanne Mills. Karen Stupples, playing in her home county of Kent, finished tied for third place with Asa Gottmo.

Hjorth, known as "Mimmi," qualified for both the Evian Masters and the Weetabix Women's British Open to put behind her a poor season up to that point in the United States.

"It's been very frustrating over the last 18 months. It's been very hard, but you just never know when the game is going to come round again," Hjorth said. "It's been a tough year in America, but I've been playing a lot better the last month or so. It's pretty nice to know I broke the tour record."

OTP Bank Ladies Central European Open—€165,000
Winner: Minea Blomqvist

After "Mimmi," next came "Minni," the exciting new player from Finland, Minea Blomqvist. The 19-year-old became the first rookie to win on the Ladies European Tour in three years with her victory in the OTP Bank Ladies Central European Open at Old Lake in Tata, Hungary.

Blomqvist, who won twice in her first three starts as a professional in South Africa earlier in the year, opened with a 62 to equal the lowest score ever recorded on the European Tour, although this was a nine-under-par score, while Trish Johnson had been 11 under with her 62 in France in 1996.

Blomqvist, who was still playing junior golf the previous season and appeared for Europe in the Junior Solheim Cup in September 2003, then added rounds of 67 and 70 for a 14-under total of 199. She won by four strokes over Gina Scott, her second runner-up finish of the season, and Emma Zackrisson.

Four ahead with one round to play, Blomqvist was one over par on the first nine. Virginie Auffret, with a eagle at the 13th, closed to within one stroke, but then fell back to tie for fourth place with Karine Icher. Auffret and Zackrisson both double-bogeyed at the last hole to leave Blomqvist in the clear.

At 19 years and 128 days, she was the third youngest player to win on the Ladies European Tour. "Last night we went out to eat, and I just couldn't eat anything, as I was thinking that this was my dream if I should win," Blomqvist said. "I knew it was going to be a tough day out there after about six holes and I was so tense. I've dreamed of this moment all my life. This was my goal this year and I still can't believe I've won on the European Tour. I have always tested myself and try to make my goals and now it has come true."

Evian Masters—€1,977,826
Winner: Wendy Doolan

Annika Sorenstam, leading by three strokes with one round to play, was denied a third victory in the Evian Masters by a superb finish by Wendy Doolan. The 35-year-old Australian scored a 65 in the final round to Sorenstam's 71 to win by one stroke at 18 under par with a 270 total.

Doolan was five behind Sorenstam at the start of the day, but went to the turn in 30. From the sixth she went birdie, eagle, birdie, eagle, birdie to be seven under for those five holes and move into the lead.

Even Sorenstam could not respond to that sort of pressure, but the Swede did birdie the last three holes. Doolan, however, also birdied the 18th by two-putting from 45 feet. It was her third win on the LPGA circuit, but her first in Europe at the co-sanctioned event.

"I knew I had it in me to make a lot of birdies on this course," said Doolan. "There were a lot of birdies and eagles there in a few holes and I'll cherish that for a long time. Every win is a special win and that's why we are out here practicing hard each week, and when it came down to it, I made the putts that mattered."

Sorenstam finished behind, with Lorena Ochoa in third place and Karen Stupples was fourth. Sorenstam said, "I was a little surprised when I got to the ninth hole and saw Wendy at 17 under. I knew she must have made eagle or something, but there weren't many cheers out there. I figured someone would do something out there today and I was kind of hoping it was going to be me.

"I gave it my all, but today I made a few mistakes and didn't play as well as the first three days. This is a big tournament for me and I'm disappointed, and it goes to show there are a lot of good players out there. The golf is getting better and better, so I have to keep sharp."

Weetabix Women's British Open—€1,050,000
Winner: Karen Stupples

With a brilliance rarely seen on the final day of a major championship, Karen Stupples became the first home player to win the Weetabix Women's British Open in 13 years. It was a day of days at Sunningdale, in front of many family and friends, for Stupples, who virtually bankrupted herself when starting out as a professional.

Stupples, a 31-year-old Englishwoman whose first ever win in the United States had come at the start of the year, marched up the last hole with a five-stroke lead accompanied by a thundering standing ovation. The eventual margin of victory appeared emphatic, yet only became so after three birdies on the Old Course's devious final four holes.

But it was the start that will be long remembered by the player and everyone who witnessed it. Beginning the final round one stroke off the lead, Stupples' first five strokes were as near perfection as could be imagined. Can a player in a major championship ever have followed an eagle with an albatross (or double eagle)? It was only the second time the latter rare bird had been achieved in a women's major. After two holes, both par-fives, Stupples was five under par. At the first she hit a five iron for her second shot to 15 feet and holed the putt.

It was the sort of start she had hoped for to put pressure on the leaders, but after driving over the road at the second hole it became the stuff of fairy tales. This time another five iron from 205 yards rolled gently up to the hole, knocked against the flagstick, and fell in.

The gallery, including many who had made the journey from her home town of Deal on the Kent coast, burst into cheers. "I couldn't see the ball go into the hole, but the cheer from the crowd was unbelievable and I knew it must have gone in," she said. "I've never had an albatross before, so it was a good time to have one. I knew from then on I was going to enjoy the day regardless of what happened."

Rachel Teske, one of the overnight leaders, birdied the first two holes but was still two behind. The Australian twice drew level with Stupples, but her bogey at the 12th dropped her out of the lead. Stupples quickly drew away by holing from 30 feet at the 15th, hitting yet another superb five iron at the 16th to six feet, and then, to gild the lily, holing a 40-footer at the 17th. "The atmosphere was fantastic, I enjoyed it so much," she said. "My family weren't there when I won in the States, so it makes this even more special for them all to be here today."

Stupples was the first home player to win since Penny Grice-Whittaker in 1991 at Woburn and the first British winner of a major for six years. A closing 64 meant she tied the major championship record of 19 under par with a 269 total. Teske finished second, five behind, with Heather Bowie third and Lorena Ochoa in fourth place. "It's mind-blowing," Stupples said.

"It just goes to show, if you have a dream, you should never give up. You should always fight on, you never know what might happen."

Minea Blomqvist, who only just made the cut with a second round of 78, set a new record for a woman's major championship with a third round of 62, 10 under par. The 19-year-old Finn had six birdies and two eagles to add another 62 to her opening round at the Central European Open earlier in the month.

HP Open—€465,563
Winner: Annika Sorenstam

Tired after seeing her chances of winning the last two tournaments disappear and playing in stifling heat in Stockholm, Annika Sorenstam collected her fifth victory on home soil by winning the HP Open at Ullna. Sorenstam came from two behind in the final round with a brilliant 64, a new course record.

Sorenstam won for the sixth time in the season by two strokes over compatriot Carin Koch with a 275 for a 13-under-par total. Becky Morgan finished third, with Janice Moodie in fourth place and Stephanie Arricau in fifth.

Sorenstam got her round going by eagling the fourth hole on the way to an outward 33. Koch was still leading at that stage, but Sorenstam birdied the 11th, chalked up another eagle at the 12th, and then birdied the 13th and 15th.

"I'm very happy and I thought it was amazing to come out today and play the way I did," Sorenstam said. "I really don't know where I got the energy from, but I couldn't ask for a better day at home and in front of my home crowd, and it's very special. I was tired earlier in the week, and yesterday there were some signs of some good golf, and it all came right today."

Wales "Golf as it should be" Ladies Open—€501,375
Winner: Trish Johnson

Two of Europe's finest players, Laura Davies and Helen Alfredsson, went out tied for the lead in the final round of the Wales "Golf as it should be" Ladies Open. But it was another, Trish Johnson, who came from four strokes behind to win at Royal Porthcawl with a closing round of 65, eight under par, for a 277 total.

Johnson finished at 15 under to win by three strokes over Davies, who shot a 72, and Iben Tinning (68), while Alfredsson tied for fourth place with Marta Prieto and Asa Gottmo. It was Johnson's 17th career title, but the 38-year-old's first triumph for four years.

Johnson went to the turn in 32, but Davies was still three strokes ahead with nine to play. When Davies ran into trouble, Tinning made four birdies in six holes to take the lead, then she fell back to 12 under and was swept away by Johnson, who birdied the 12th and then each of the last three holes.

"I always thought I would win again, but I didn't realize it had been that long," said Johnson, who played much of her early golf in the West Country and just over the border in southern Wales. "I knew I could still win, otherwise there would have been no point me being out here.

"This event is a fabulous event and it's very important to me, as I know the area so well. I spent 10 years down here, and a lot of my friends and family came down to support me, and that stood me in good stead all day."

Catalonia Ladies Masters—€180,000
Winner: Karine Icher

After a season when so many records were set or equaled, it was entirely in keeping that Karine Icher should win the Catalan Ladies Masters by scoring the third and fourth 62s of the season. They came in the first and third rounds at Sant Cugat to give the 25-year-old Frenchwoman a nine-stroke victory over compatriot Stephanie Arricau and Spain's Paula Marti.

Icher, from Chateauroux, finished at 17 under par, having shot a mere 66 in the middle round. Her 190 total lowered the record for best score in a 54-hole event set earlier in the season, although this was a par-69 course.

From two ahead at the start of the final day, Icher turned it into a procession with four birdies in the first five holes. It was her fourth victory but her first since the 2002 Spanish Open. "I am very happy, as it has been a long time since my last win," Icher said. "I was really focused all day long and my putting was excellent all day. It is the sort of course you can make a lot of birdies, and I did that at the start of the round, which made me feel a bit more relaxed. From the second to the 13th hole, I was very concentrated, and when I looked up at the leaderboard at the 14th, I think I was five shots clear, so I began to relax. It was a great feeling to be able to walk down the last few holes with a big lead."

Arricau, who won twice during the season, had the consolation of winning the Players' Player of the Year award. Laura Davies led the money list for the sixth time, with Trish Johnson second and Arricau in third place. Minea Blomqvist, the 19-year-old Finn who also scored 62s twice in the season, including at the Weetabix Women's British Open, won the Rookie of the Year title.

Japan LPGA Tour

Daikin Orchid Ladies—¥60,000,000
Winner: Ai Miyazato

Ai Miyazato took little time proving her decision to turn professional right out of high school was a solid one. Less than six months after the 18-year-old left the amateur ranks to join the Japan LPGA Tour, she scored her first pro victory, a decisive, three-stroke triumph in the season-opening Daikin Orchid Ladies tournament at Ryukyu Golf Club on her home island of Okinawa.

Actually, it was Miyazato's second victory on the Japan circuit. While still an amateur and holder of the Japan Women's Amateur title, Miyazato won the Miyagi TV Cup in September. The youngest winner ever in Japan, she turned professional a month later.

A sparkling, six-under-par 66 in Saturday's second round spurred Miyazato to victory. The young lady trailed by three strokes after the first 18 holes, when Mikiyo Nishizaka, Yukari Baba and amateur Shinobu Moromizato opened with 67s. Four players were at 68 and Yuri Fudoh, who counted the Daikin Orchid among her 10 victories in 2003, was among four others at 69. With the day's only round in the 60s Saturday, Miyazato raced three strokes in front with her 136. Closest then were Kaori Higo, Toshimi Kimura and Moromizato at 139. Again Sunday, rounds in the 60s were hard to come by and Miyazato's 70 cemented her three-shot lead and led to the victorious 206 total. Higo also shot 70 to finish second. Fudoh had uncharacteristic rounds of 76 and 74 on the weekend and tied for 23rd.

Saishunkan Ladies Hinokuni Open—¥60,000,000
Winner: Yuri Fudoh

Yuri Fudoh had more than a month to wipe out memories of a bad weekend in Okinawa. When the Japan LPGA Tour resumed action in mid-April with the Saishunkan Ladies Hinokuni Open, she made amends, snagging her 26th victory in a three-way playoff at Kumamoto Airport Country Club.

She didn't rebound, though, until the second day. Fudoh struggled to a 76 Friday and at the end of the day was eight strokes behind Yuka Sakaguchi, the unlikely leader. Sakaguchi, winless in six seasons on the tour, had an eagle and five birdies as she shot 68 and led by one over Miho Koga, who had just returned to Japan after playing in some early tournaments on the LPGA Tour in America. Ji-Yeon Han of South Korea was also alone at 70.

Scoring continued high Saturday and Fudoh's 68 moved her into contention as Sakaguchi shot 73 for 141 and led by two strokes over Ji-Hee Lee of South Korea, a four-time winner in 2003. Fudoh was then just three off the pace, sharing third place with Michie Ohba, Maki Sasayama, Woo-Soon Ko and Nikki Campbell.

Nerves caught up to Sakaguchi Sunday. She stumbled to a 77, opening the door for Fudoh, Ko and amateur Sakura Yokomine, the other 18-year-old in the field. One round of 70 was the day's best, so Yokomine, with 71, and Fudoh and Ko, with 73s, wound up tied for first place at 215 after the regulation 54 holes. The South Korean bogeyed her way out of the playoff on the first extra hole and Fudoh wrapped up the victory with a seven-foot birdie putt on the next one.

Katokichi Queens — ¥60,000,000
Winner: Hsiao-Chuan Lu

Another Taiwanese player became a winner on the Japan LPGA Tour in the Katokichi Queens tournament. Hsiao-Chuan Lu, playing in her fourth season on the circuit, picked up the victory in the tour's second straight playoff, sinking a birdie putt on the first extra hole to defeat Michie Ohba at Yashima Country Club in Mure, Kagawa Prefecture.

The two players bided their time during the first two rounds. Toshima Kimura, seeking her first win in two years and ninth of her career, and Mihoko Takahashi, going after her fourth, began on top with five-under-par 67s. Ohba was one back at 68 with Kasumi Fujii, Ayako Uehara and Atomi Shiota and Lu opened with 69. Kimura faltered Saturday, but Takahashi shot 69 for 136 and she was joined in the lead by Fujii, who eagled her final hole for 68. Lu (68) and Ohba (69) trailed by just a shot.

On Sunday, Takahashi and Fujii blew to 77 and 78, respectively, and Lu and Ohba created the playoff situation when they both posted 71s, as did Yuri Fudoh, who missed the playoff by a single stroke.

Nichirei Cup World Ladies — ¥60,000,000
Winner: Rui Kitada

Rui Kitada joined a distinguished cast of Nichirei Cup World champions when she captured the fourth tournament of the season at Tokyo's Yomiuri Country Club in early May. Yuri Fudoh, holder of the circuit's money title the last four years, numbered the Nichirei Cup among her 10 victories in 2003, and winners of the previous three editions of that event were no less than Annika Sorenstam in 2002 and Karrie Webb in 2001 and 2000. (Neither was in the 2004 field.) Unlike those three ex-champions, though, Kitada began play that week without a victory to show for her three years on the Japan LPGA Tour.

Interestingly, she won her first title at the expense of Fudoh in a weekend that the two dominated from start to finish. Fudoh, who already had a 2004 victory (Saishunkan), got off to a terrific start at Yomiuri, firing rounds of 64 and 65 to take a three-stroke halfway lead over Kitada. Fudoh had no bogeys as she reeled off eight birdies Thursday and seven Friday.

Kitada matched the 64 Friday after an opening 68, then jumped in front to stay Saturday with 67–199 as Fudoh faltered with 74 for 203, one stroke back of runner-up Shinobu Moromizato, another promising young amateur. Kitada had her weakest round of the tournament Sunday, slipping to 73, but

Fudoh couldn't take advantage of the opening. She mustered only a 71, but that was enough to put her into second place at the finish as Moromizato slumped to 75. Kitada's 16-under-par 272 total gave her a two-stroke victory.

Vernal Ladies—¥100,000,000
Winner: Yuri Fudoh

Yuri Fudoh made the best of a bad weather day in the Vernal Ladies when she came from two strokes off the lead on the rain-swept Fukuoka Century Country Club course with a two-under-par 70 Sunday and nailed her second victory of the season by one stroke over Toshima Kimura. The win was the 27th in the last five years for the 10-season professional who has dominated the Japan LPGA Tour in the 2000s.

Midori Yoneyama, age 27, a four-time winner in her first three seasons but without a victory since 2001, got off to a good start with a 69 and a two-stroke lead over four players — Ai Miyazato, Englishwoman Samantha Head, Shiho Ohyama and Mika Adaniya. Fudoh shot her first of two 72s.

The second one Saturday left Fudoh two behind Kimura and Kasumi Fujii (69s), Miyazato (71) and Yoneyama (73), tied with the lead at 142. Fudoh's 70 Sunday was a solid one in miserable playing conditions on the wet day. She made a birdie on each nine (No. 4 and No. 14) and ran off 16 pars for the winning, two-under-par 214 total to edge Kimura, who shot 73. Miyazato had 74 and tied for third with Akiko Fukushima, who had the day's best round of 69.

Chukyo TV Bridgestone Ladies Open—¥50,000,000
Winner: Yuko Saitoh

The long wait ended for Yuko Saitoh. The 36-year-old had labored on the Japan LPGA Tour for 15 years without enjoying the fruits of victory until it happened pretty much out of the blue at the Chukyo TV Bridgestone Ladies Open in late May on the Ishino course of Chukyo Golf Club. Nowhere in sight after 18 holes, Saitoh put rounds of 65 and 67 back to back and picked off a three-stroke victory with her eight-under-par 208 total.

Saitoh opened the tournament with a nondescript 74 that put her five strokes off the leading pace of local favorite Midori Yoneyama on the windy Friday at Toyota, Aichi Prefecture. The 69 duplicated Yoneyama's leading start the preceding Friday in the Vernal Ladies, where she led or shared the lead for two rounds before finishing seventh with a closing 76. This time, the 69 gave her a one-stroke lead over six players and two over defending champion Yuri Fudoh.

Aki Takamura emerged from the six pack Saturday and took over first place with 68–138, but her lead was a shaky stroke over four others — Shiho Ohyama (73-66), Kaori Suzuki (72-67), Fudoh (71-68) and Saitoh (74-65). An eagle at the seventh hole Sunday sparked Saitoh to the victory. It gave her the lead and she maintained it with three birdies later in the round for the 67 that earned her the long-awaited title by one stroke over Kaori

Harada, who shot 68 for 209. Fudoh never challenged Sunday, managing just a 73 to tie for eighth.

Saitoh was the second first-time winner of the young season.

Kosaido Ladies Golf Cup—¥60,000,000
Winner: Yuri Fudoh

Yuri Fudoh bounced back from a poor finish at Chukyo with a solid start-to-finish performance in the Kosaido Ladies Golf Cup to ice her third victory of the season and consolidate her No. 1 position on the money list. In winning her 28th career title, Fudoh tied together three rounds in the 60s and finished first by two strokes over Hsiu-Feng Tseng.

Fudoh shot 69 the first day and rested just two shots off the lead of second-year professional Ikue Asama. Five players — Noriko Aso, Junko Yoshida, Fumiko Muraguchi, Shiho Ohyama and Rie Fujiwara — were at 68. Then Fudoh asserted herself and her fine game. She forged two strokes into the lead Saturday, running off four of her five birdies on the second nine en route to a 68 and 137. Tseng moved into second place with 71-68–139, joined there by Muraguchi, who shot 71.

Although she only won by two strokes, Fudoh never seemed to be in trouble Sunday. She mustered three birdies, avoided bogeys and shot 69–206 to post the two-stroke victory over Tseng, who also had a 69 Sunday. Rui Kitada jumped into third place at 209 with a 66.

Resort Trust Ladies—¥50,000,000
Winner: Hiromi Mogi

Hiromi Mogi won the first tournament of her young career on the Japan LPGA Tour the hard way. Mogi, playing in just her second season on the circuit, had to go four extra holes before capturing the title in the Resort Trust Ladies tournament at Grande Hamanako Golf Club.

Mogi had ground to make up after the first round. She shot 71 and trailed leaders Hsiao-Chuan Lu, Chihiro Nakajima and Yuka Sakaguchi by four strokes. A 67 of her own Saturday brought Mogi into the picture. At 138, she shared first place with Sakaguchi (71), and they, in turn, led Lu by a stroke.

Both Mogi and Sakaguchi shot 70s Sunday for eight-under-par 208 totals, forcing the season's third and longest playoff in a duel between two winless ladies. They matched pars for three holes before Sakaguchi faltered with a bogey at the fourth extra hole and Mogi seized the victory when she holed a par-saving putt.

We Love Kobe Suntory Ladies Open—¥60,000,000
Winner: Ai Miyazato

Ai Miyazato became the season's second multiple winner at the We Love Kobe Suntory Ladies Open, picking up the second victory of her rookie season. Joining leading money winner Yuri Fudoh, who already had three wins, Miyazato came from behind in the final round and rolled to a six-stroke victory, the biggest margin of the year that far. Miyazato had opened her first professional season with victory in the Daikin Orchid curtain-raiser.

The first round belonged to the veterans. Chieko Amanuma, a five-time winner, and South Korea's Young-Me Lee, with eight titles on her record but none since 1999, opened with 66s and led Mikiyo Nishizuka by a stroke.

Rain cut short Friday's second round. Miyazato, who followed her opening 69 with a 70 for 139, was in front when play was suspended and trailed by only one when Hiroko Yamaguchi finished the next morning with 68-70–138. Toshima Kimura (71-69) and Young-Me Lee (66-74) shared third place at 140. Midori Yoneyama, who had made two strong runs earlier in the season, matched the Japan Memorial Golf Club's course record Saturday with an eight-under-par 64 and jumped into a two-stroke lead over Miyazato (70) and Yamaguchi (71).

Miyazato overran the field Sunday. Shooting the only score in the 60s — 68 — she raced in front early and rolled to the six-stroke victory with her 11-under-par 277 total. Kimura's 71 and Yamaguchi's 74 put them in a runner-up tie at 283.

Apita Circle K Sankus Ladies—¥50,000,000
Winner: Ai Miyazato

It wasn't as easy for Ai Miyazato in the Apita Circle K Sankus Ladies, but the outcome was a second consecutive victory. The sensational teenager, who won by six strokes the previous Sunday in the Suntory Open, hung on to nip the mighty Yuri Fudoh by one stroke in the Apita Circle K at Nagatsugawa Golf Club. The victory, the third of the season for the rookie who celebrated her 19th birthday on the Saturday, matched Fudoh's victory total at that stage of the 2004 season.

Chihiro Nakajima, a tour veteran twice the age of the ultimate winner, had a limelight moment in the opening round, shooting a four-under-par 68 for a one-stroke lead over Miyazato, Mitsuko Kawasaki, Miyuki Shimabukuro, and Hiromi Mogi, the Resort Trust winner a month earlier. Miyazato duplicated her first-round 69 and slipped into a one-stroke lead on her birthday Saturday. She had a chance to open a wider gap after running off her first tour eagle and three birdies on the first nine, but gave two strokes back with bogeys on the second nine. Miyazato led Yun-Jye Wei, the defending champion, by a stroke, Aki Nakano by two, and Fudoh and three others by three.

Only Fudoh threatened Miyazato Sunday. She shot 70 and fell a stroke short as Miyazato managed just a par round for a six-under-par 210 and the one-shot triumph. She became the youngest winner of back-to-back tournaments since the tour system was established in 1988.

Promise Ladies—¥60,000,000
Winner: Kasumi Fujii

Ai Miyazato's bid for three victories in a row virtually ended before it started when she shot 75 in the first round of the Promise Ladies tournament. Rui Kitada, another young player on the circuit, made a run at her second win of the season with a sparkling 65 in the second round that vaulted her into the lead. But, when push came to shove Sunday, the issue was decided between two veterans — Kasumi Fujii, in her ninth season, and Toshimi Kimura, who has been around even longer at age 35. Fujii prevailed in a six-hole playoff, the season's longest.

Akiko Fukushima, just back from the American tour, where she has played most of her golf after collecting most of her 16 victories in Japan, made her presence felt immediately at Tojo's Water Hills Golf Club. She shot 68 and shared the first-round lead with Michie Ohba, a three-time winner whose last victory came in 2001.

Neither was around at the end, though, as Kitada jumped in front at 137 with the 65, leading Fujii and Yasuko Sato by a stroke. Kitada ran off eight birdies in the sparkling round. But she used them up the next day, managing only a 73 Sunday as Fujii shot 69 and Kimura 68 to create the deadlock at 207. The next five players in the standings were at 210. Fujii and Kimura matched scores for five holes in the ensuing playoff before Kimura bogeyed and Fujii took the title with a par. It was her sixth tour victory.

Belluna Ladies Cup—¥60,000,000
Winner: Mitsuko Kawasaki

The ranks of winners on the Japan LPGA Tour expanded rapidly in the 2004 season. In just the first week of July, Mitsuko Kawasaki became the fifth first-time winner when she won the Belluna Ladies Cup by one stroke over Junko Omote, an occasional contender who also is without a victory on her record.

Actually, it was a week for non-winners at Obatago Golf Club, Kanra in Gunma Prefecture. Misato Nishikawa, who is still looking for her first, shot the best round of her career in the opening round and joined Takayo Bandoh in the lead with 68s. On Saturday, Michiko Mitsui established her bid for a maiden victory when she fired a 67 for 137 and took a one-stroke lead over Omote (68) and Mika Adaniya (69).

At that point, Kawasaki lay three strokes off the pace after rounds of 69 and 71. On Sunday she fashioned a flawless 67 — five birdies, no bogeys — to snatch the title from Omote, who finished a shot behind at 208 when she took a bogey at the last hole for 70. Neither three-time 2004 winner — Yuri Fudoh or Ai Miyazato — played in the Belluna, Miyazato withdrawing before its start, suffering with a cold.

Chateaureze Queens Cup—¥50,000,000
Winner: Akiko Fukushima

Akiko Fukushima came up with one of the most impressive and certainly most decisive victories of her fine career when she ran away with the Chateaureze Queens Cup in mid-July. Fukushima, presently Japan's best-known international player, recorded her 17th career victory by overwhelming the field by 10 strokes, the biggest margin so far in the Japan LPGA Tour season.

Fukushima, who was playing in just her third tournament since deciding she had had enough of the LPGA Tour in America and returning to her native land, dominated the Chateaureze from the beginning. Scoring conditions were quite difficult at Sapporo's Chateaureze Country Club in Friday's first round and Fukushima acquired a three-stroke lead with her two-under-par 70. At that, only Kasumi Fujii, the Promise winner two weeks earlier, and Midori Yoneyama even had 73s.

Fukushima blew the gap wide open in a fog-ridden second round. After a three-hour delay of the start of play because of heavy fog, she headed for the day's only round in the 60s. When she completed play early Sunday, her 66–136 gave her a nine-stroke margin over Seiko Watanabe (75-70). Yoneyama shot another 73 and was at 146 with Kaori Higo (76-70) and Eriko Moriyama (74-72). Fukushima completed her wire-to-wire victory with a 71 Sunday for 207. Yoneyama took the runner-up spot with 71–217. Ai Miyazato with 68 had the only other round in the 60s and tied for third place with Woo-Soon Ko of South Korea despite an opening 78.

Stanley Ladies—¥60,000,000
Winner: Yuri Fudoh

The Stanley Ladies tournament didn't suffer from any lack of star power. Not only did the Japan LPGA Tour's dominating duo of Yuri Fudoh and Ai Miyazato both play for the first time in three weeks and wage a mighty battle for the title, but Japanese golf fans got a hint of things to come with a stunning performance by Mika Miyazato, the country's 14-year-old counterpart to the world-acclaimed Michelle Wei.

Mika attracted the early acclaim. Mika, who had been the youngest player ever to win the Japan Women's Amateur a month earlier, fired a dazzling 67 in the opening round and wound up in a tie for the lead with Fudoh, the defending champion, and Yukari Horikoshi. All three players had six birdies and one bogey on their cards. The better-known Miyazato, Ai, was just a stroke behind, tied at 68 with Aki Nakano, Mika Tajiri and Kumiko Hiyoshi. (By the way, the Miyazatos are not related.)

Mika was not able to maintain the pace, slipping back to a 17th-place finish with further rounds of 71-73, a remarkable performance for such a young, inexperienced player. The pace, instead, was set by Ai Miyazato, who was even par after 10 holes, then made an eagle and three birdies coming in for 67–135 to jump a stroke in front of Fudoh (69) and veteran Michiko Hattori, a 16-tournament winner.

Ai Miyazato and Fudoh went head to head in Sunday's final round in a thrilling battle in which Fudoh gained the upper hand early and went on to a one-stroke victory, the 29th of her sparkling career. It was her first of two successful defenses of her 10 victories in 2003. While Fudoh was shooting 68 and winning, Ai was gathering only a par 72, dropping to a tie for fifth place, opening the way for Hattori to garner the second spot with 69–205, one stroke behind the winner.

Golf 5 Ladies—¥50,000,000
Winner: Yuri Fudoh

It was another big week for Yuri Fudoh anyway, but she got something a little extra when she rolled to a three-stroke victory in the Golf 5 Ladies tournament at Bibai in Hokkaido. In the first place, the win was Fudoh's fifth of the season and second in a row, matching the feat of her closest rival, Ai Miyazato, earlier in the season. It widened her lead over Miyazato in the money race. The bonus was a security blanket. As if she will ever need it, by winning her 30th event on the Japan LPGA Tour, Fudoh gained lifetime exemption status.

Things were tough on the Alpen Golf Club's Miuta course. The best scores of the week on the par-73 layout were 72s, and virtual unknown Yui Kawahara had one of them to lead the tournament after the first round by a stroke over six par-shooters — Shiho Ohyama, Noriko Aso, Yun-Jye Wei, Aki Nakano, Kyoko Kadokawa and Harumi Sakagami.

Fudoh, who opened with 75, had one of only two 72s Saturday and moved into the lead, but for the second week in a row, one of Japan's budding young amateurs excited the crowd. Kumiko Kaneda, who is still in junior high school like Mika Miyazato, the previous tournament's teen sensation, shot a second straight 74, took over second place and faced a final-round pairing with Fudoh. Ji-Yeon Han and Yun-Jye Wei, both from Taiwan, were at 149.

Fudoh pulled away to a three-stroke victory Sunday, even though she shot a one-over-par 74 and finished two over par with 221 total. Wei posted a 75 and took second place with 224. The youngster, Kaneda, understandably succumbed to the final-group pressure, shot 77 and tied for third with Woo-Soon Ko (74) at 225.

NEC Karuizawa 72—¥60,000,000
Winner: Rui Kitada

Rui Kitada stepped up into exclusive company when she landed the NEC Karuizawa 72 tournament as the Japan LPGA Tour returned to action after a two-week mid-summer hiatus in early August. The two-stroke victory was Kitada's second of the year and she became just the third player with multiple 2004 victories on her record, joining Yuri Fudoh and Ai Miyazato.

The triumph was a hard-fought one for the 22-year-old against one of Japan's brighter and more experienced stars — Akiko Fukushima — who also was gunning for a second victory of the year and her third consecutive win in the NEC Karuizawa 72.

Another veteran — Woo-Soon Ko — set the early pace. The South Korean, who has eight victories in Japan on her record, shot 66 in the first round and was followed by lesser-known Noriko Aso at 67 and veteran winner Mayumi Murai and Namika Omata at 68.

But the race took a different shape Saturday. Fukushima fired a 65 and Kitada a 66, both for 135s, as they moved three shots in front of the rest of the field going into the final round. Kitada's closing 67 — six birdies and a bogey — for 14-under-par 202 established the two-stroke margin over Fukushima (69) and Ai Miyazato, who capped another strong performance with an incendiary 64. The 202 total tied the tournament record.

New Caterpillar Mitsubishi Ladies—¥60,000,000
Winner: Toshimi Kimura

Three times earlier in the season, Toshimi Kimura came up second best in efforts to win her first tournament in almost two years on the circuit. Most disappointing was her loss to Kasumi Fujii on the sixth hole of a playoff in the Suntory Open in June. She wasn't going to let it happen again in the New Caterpillar Mitsubishi Ladies tournament.

Kimura grabbed a one-stroke lead after 36 holes at Dai Hakone Country Club in Kanagawa Prefecture and parlayed it into a three-stroke victory with a solid performance in Sunday's final round. She shot 71 for 210 total on the par-73 course in scoring the ninth victory of her career.

The 35-year-old player, competing in her 18th season on tour, came just one stroke short of a wire-to-wire victory. She shot 70 in the opening round and trailed the leader, Kyoko Kadokawa, by a stroke. Kadokawa, an eight-year professional, got a big lift when two of her birdies came via chip-ins.

As this hinted, Kadokawa couldn't come close to matching that score in Saturday's second round. She shot 77 as Kimura moved atop the standings with her 69–139. Kimura made five birdies and took a lone bogey as she went a stroke in front of Kyoko Ono, whose 68 equaled the day's low round.

Even a double bogey could not sidetrack Kimura Sunday. She notched five birdies and took a lone bogey at the 14th hole that merely cut her lead to two strokes before she picked up a sixth birdie to establish the final margin. Yuri Fudoh, the tour's No. 1 player, duplicated Kimura's 71 and tied for second place with Fujii, who had the tables turned on her by Kimura this time.

Yonex Ladies—¥60,000,000
Winner: Yukari Baba

What sort of odds could a gambler have gotten on Yukari Baba just to score her first Japan LPGA Tour victory in the Yonex Ladies tournament, let alone go wire-to-wire in doing so? After three years on the circuit, the 21-year-old's best finish was a tie for sixth in this year's Golf 5 Ladies tournament a month earlier in the season.

Baba beat those odds convincingly and withstood the late pressure of a charge by No. 1 Yuri Fudoh to register a two-stroke triumph with her 10-under-par 206 at Yonex Country Club at the end of August.

The diminutive young lady played a solid opening round, her first of three without a bogey, and chalked up a 67. That gave her a one-stroke lead over Noriko Aso and Yuriko Ohtsuka and she never let the lead get away. Baba followed with a 69 Saturday for a 136 that preserved her one-stroke lead. The runner-up then was Miho Koga, who jumped into contention with a 66, the day's lowest round. Ohtsuka shot 71 and dropped into a tie for third at 139 with Kasumi Fujii and Mikiyo Nishizuka.

Baba, the sixth first-time winner of the season, wrapped up the victory Sunday with a two-bogey 70 for 206 total, 10 under par. She held steady for the two-stroke victory in the face of the onrushing Fudoh, who fell two short with her 68–208, but had second place to herself in the final standings.

Fujisankei Ladies Classic—¥60,000,000
Winner: Kasumi Fujii

The players in the Fujisankei Ladies Classic were in a fog ... literally. Earlier in the season, the Chateaureze Queens tournament was victimized by fog but got the 54 holes in by finishing the delayed round the following day. At the Fujisankei in Narusawa, heavy fog — and rain — waited until Sunday to put in an appearance. Unable to carry the tournament over to Monday, tournament officials had no choice but to declare it a 36-hole event and distribute three-quarters of the prize money.

The largest check — ¥8,100,000 — went to Kasumi Fujii, who had held a three-stroke lead overnight. It was the second win of the season for the unexpected beneficiary and the seventh of her career.

Fujii led from the start. She opened with a four-under-par 68, establishing a two-stroke margin with 18-foot putts for her third and fourth birdies on the second nine. Australian Nikki Campbell, Mikiyo Nishizuka and Junko Yoshida had 70s, and yet another promising young Japanese player — 18-year-old Sakura Yokomine — shot 71 in her first round as a professional.

Fujii padded her lead Saturday. Putting four birdies and three bogeys on her card for 71–139, she widened the gap to what proved to be the winning three strokes. Junko Omote posted a 70 for 142, and Ai Miyazato added another high finish to her impressive season with 74-69–143. Yokomine placed fourth with 71-73–144 and collected ¥2,700,000 as her initial prize money.

Japan LPGA Championship—¥70,000,000
Winner: Kaori Higo

The wins have occurred less frequently in recent years for Kaori Higo, but the veteran still has the ability to shine when the important events come up on the schedule. Higo displayed that talent brilliantly when the Japan

LPGA Championship rolled around in early September, breaking away from the pack in the final round to score a five-stroke victory, the 17th of her 16-year career that began when she was just 19.

Most noteworthy about the win at the Mashiko course of the Taiheiyo Club was the fact that it made Higo just the fifth player in Japan LPGA history to have won all three of the circuit's major titles. She had won the 2000 Japan Women's Open and the 2001 Japan LPGA Tour Championship.

Higo improved her scores and positions every day in the LPGA Championship. She started the week with 73, four strokes in arrears of leader Yun-Jye Wei. Higo moved up to a fifth-place tie Friday with her 73-72—145, but remained four strokes off the lead, still held by Wei, who added a 72 for 141. She led Junko Omote by two strokes at that juncture.

Higo revved up on the weekend. She fired a 69 Saturday for 214, joined at the top by Omote, who shot 71. Hiroko Fujishima vaulted into contention with 66 for 215. Tour standouts Akiko Fukushima (215) and Yuri Fudoh (217) moved close, too, as Wei slumped with a 76 for 217. Nobody had an answer to Higo's flashy finish Sunday. Her concluding 67 for 281 total built the five-stroke margin over Omote, who shot 72—286 to finish the runner-up for the second week in a row. Fukushima was third at 287, and Fudoh tied with Ai Miyazato for fourth at 290.

Munsingwear Ladies Tokai Classic—¥60,000,000
Winner: Hiromi Mogi

Obviously, it was a coincidence, but with the first two victories of her career, both in 2004, her second season, Hiromi Mogi won tournaments in which Yuri Fudoh, the Japan LPGA Tour's leading light, was the defending champion. It was the Resort Trust in June, then the Munsingwear Ladies Tokai Classic in mid-September. Fudoh put up a spirited defense in the Tokai Classic, losing to Mogi by a stroke in a flurry of final-round scoring.

It was virtually a two-player duel from the start. Fudoh, Mogi and Michie Ohba carved six-under-par 66s out of the short (6,477 yards) Ryosen Golf Club course and shared the first-round lead. Then Mogi edged a stroke in front Saturday with 68—132 as Ohba shot 69 and Fudoh took 70. Four others, including Ai Miyazato, were three back at 137.

It came down pretty much to Mogi and Fudoh Sunday. Mogi needed the second straight 68 she shot — five birdies and a bogey — to avoid a playoff with Fudoh, who closed strongly with 67, but came up one short with her 13-under-par 203 total. Midori Yoneyama shot 68 and finished third at 205. Miyazato was next with 70—207, while Ohba faded to 208 with a 73.

Miyagi TV Cup Dunlop Ladies Open—¥60,000,000
Winner: Yoko Yamagishi

Yoko Yamagishi wiped out a decade of disappointment at the Miyagi TV Cup Dunlop Ladies Open when she became the seventh first-time winner of the season. Even then, it didn't come easy. Yamagishi had to birdie the 54th hole to force a playoff, the first on the tour in three months, and birdie again on the first extra hole to land the title.

Another country was heard from in the opening round, when England's Samantha Head shot a course-record, seven-under-par 65 at Rifu Golf Club and led Woo-Soon Ko of South Korea, Miho Koga and Yamagishi by two strokes. As usually happens, Head could not maintain such a fast pace, shot 71 Saturday, and dropped into a three-way tie for the lead at 136 with Yamagishi (67-69) and Michie Ohba, who matched Head's day-old record after opening with 71.

Koga, beginning her final round two shots off the lead, produced a 69 and watched as Yamagishi birdied the final hole to join her at 207 and force the playoff, then as she holed the three-foot birdie putt in overtime for the win. Kaori Higo jumped into third place with 68–208, while Ohba and Head took 74s and fell into a three-way tie for fourth at 210 with Yuri Fudoh.

Ai Miyazato did not fare well in the first title defense of her burgeoning career. She was never in contention and tied for 23rd place in the tournament, which was the scene of her "coming-out party" in 2003, when, at age 18, she became the first amateur winner on the circuit in 30 years.

Japan Women's Open—¥70,000,000
Winner: Yuri Fudoh

Yuri Fudoh picked the perfect time to reassert herself as a winner on the Japan LPGA Tour. Fudoh, who had run up five 2004 victories through July, put No. 6 onto her record in the Japan Women's Open, the most cherished event on the circuit and the lone tour major that had escaped her remarkable accumulation of titles over the past five seasons. With that win, she became the sixth player to have won all three majors, a feat Kaori Higo achieved three weeks earlier when she won the LPGA Championship.

Fudoh took charge of the Women's Open at Hiroshima Country Club in Saturday's third round after a slow start. She shot 74 in the first round and found herself five strokes off the lead as Namika Omata, winless in six seasons, opened with 69. That was one stroke better than Yukari Horikoshi and Fuki Kido, a six-time winner during her long career. Fudoh moved up into a third-place tie with teenager Sakura Yokomine Friday when she shot 70–144. Rie Murata also shot 70–142, and that gave her a one-stroke lead over Kido (73).

Fudoh made the big move Saturday when she shot 69 and soared to a four-stroke lead at 213. She ran off seven birdies to more than offset four bogeys and was the only player under par. Taiwan's Hsiao-Chuan Lu was at 217, and Aki Nakano and Yokomine (74) were at 218.

Fudoh obliterated the opposition in Sunday's final round. With 67, the lowest round of the week, Fudoh raced to an 11-stroke victory with her eight-under-par 280 total. Kaori Higo shot 69 and bolted into a second-place tie at 293 with young Yokomine. It was Yokomine's best finish in her first three professional starts. On the other hand, Ai Miyazato, suffering from a muscle strain in her lower back, missed the cut.

Sankyo Ladies Open—¥60,000,000
Winner: Rui Kitada

The Japan LPGA Tour wound up with its second unintended 36-hole tournament of the 2004 season when the effects of a typhoon forced cancellation of the second round of the Sankyo Ladies Open at Niisato in Gunma Prefecture. The beneficiary, of sorts, was Rui Kitada.

After the first round, Toshimi Kimura was in front with her 70 at Akagi Country Club, but six players, including Kitada, were just one stroke behind. Also at 71 were Kasumi Fujii, a two-time 2004 winner; Ji-Hee Lee, the defending champion from South Korea; Yuka Irie, Mineko Nasu and Masaki Maeda. After the storm blew through, play resumed with the final round Sunday.

Kitada made the most of her opportunity. She shot 69 for 140 and won by two over Midori Yoneyama, Mikiyo Nishizuka, Fujii and Junko Omote, who finished second for the third time in six weeks. The victory, Kitada's third of the year after going winless in her first three years on the tour, made her the only player other than Yuri Fudoh and Ai Miyazato with more than two victories on their 2004 record.

Fujitsu Ladies—¥60,000,000
Winner: Michiko Hattori

Michiko Hattori, whose fame and success in Japanese golf spans two decades, put another feather in her cap by winning the Fujitsu Ladies tournament in mid-October. The victory in a two-hole playoff was Hattori's first of the season and 16th of her career. Among those on the record of the 35-year-old veteran, who first drew international attention when she won the 1985 U.S. Women's Amateur as a 15-year-old, were the 1994 Women's Open and the 1998 PGA Championship.

Another of her victories was the Fujitsu Ladies in 1999, and she and another former Fujitsu winner, Hiromi Kobayashi, took the first-round lead with 68s, two better than Miho Koga, Yasuko Sato, Ji-Yeon Han and Mikiyo Nishizuka. Hattori wasn't as solid Saturday. She made four birdies again, but had three bogeys to go with them. Still, she held onto a share of the lead with her 71–139. Nishizuka added a 69 to her opening 70 to match the 139. Ai Miyazato, back in action after missing a week with a muscle pull, was at 140 (73-67) with Kobayashi (68-72).

Hattori repeated her 71 Sunday for 210 total, missing a makeable birdie putt on the last hole to wind up tied with Keiko Sasaki, who had finished earlier with a 69 for her 210. Hattori had another birdie opportunity on the second extra hole and dropped that one to claim the title. Miyazato and Nishizuka tied for third place, three shots back at 213.

Masters Golf Club Ladies—¥100,000,000
Winner: Ai Miyazato

Ai Miyazato revived her battle with Yuri Fudoh for the money title and No. 1 ranking on the Japan LPGA Tour when she won the Masters Golf Club Ladies tournament, the second richest event of the season with a powerhouse field to match. The ¥18 million first-place check for her fourth victory of the season pulled her within range of Fudoh, who avoided losing more ground with her third-place finish at Miki in Hyogo Prefecture.

Miyazato's prime opposition at the Masters Golf Club was Miho Koga, age 22, a two-time winner in 2003, her third season on the Japan LPGA Tour. Koga shot 68 to edge a stroke in front of a headline seven-player battery of 69-shooters that included Miyazato, Fudoh, Australia's Karrie Webb, South Korea's Se Ri Pak and Akiko Fukushima, along with constant contender Junko Omote and Aki Nakano.

Miyazato roared past Koga in Saturday's second round when she shot 68–137 with five birdies and a bogey and took a three-stroke lead over Koga (72–140). Koga was right on Miyazato's heels until she triple-bogeyed the 17th hole. Four players — Fukushima, Midori Yoneyama, Naoko Takahashi and Ayako Uehara — were at 141.

Miyazato needed all of that margin Sunday as Koga made a strong run at her. Koga came up with a six-under-par 66, and Miyazato needed the birdie she made on the last hole for 68 and a one-stroke victory over Koga with her 11-under-par 205 total. Fudoh shot 67 to claim her third-place finish.

Hisako Higuchi Hall of Fame Commemoration—¥60,000,000
Winner: Miho Koga

Miho Koga capitalized on momentum to pick off her first victory of the season in the Hisako Higuchi Hall of Fame Commemoration tournament at the end of October. Coming off a near-miss at the previous week's Masters title when she shot 66 in the final round, Koga fashioned a 68, took the first-round lead and went on to a two-stroke win at the Musashigaoka Golf Course. It was the 22-year-old's third victory in her four seasons on tour.

Koga managed the 68 start despite a double bogey at the third hole, where she drove out of bounds, and led Rui Kitada, Yuriko Ohtsuka and Misato Nishikawa by a stroke after 18 holes. Koga kept the lead in the second round, but didn't post the 71–139 until Sunday morning. She was one of nine players still on the course Saturday when play was suspended because of darkness. At 139, she had a three-stroke margin over Australia's Nikki Campbell and South Korea's Young-Me Lee. Six others were at 143, including Ai Miyazato and Sakura Yokomine.

Koga shot 71 for 210 Sunday and won by two strokes, but it was far from a breeze. Both Yuri Fudoh and Yokomine made runs at her during the final round. Fudoh posted 66–212 early to challenge the leader still on the course, and Yokomine matched the 212 with a 69 before Koga completed the round.

Mizuno Classic—¥110,000,000
Winner: Annika Sorenstam

Annika Sorenstam's wonderful 2004 season included a victory stop in Japan, where she won the joint U.S./Japan LPGA Tours' Mizuno Classic for the fourth consecutive year, tying an all-time record on the American circuit set by Laura Davies from 1994 to 1997 in the Ping tournament in Arizona. The Swedish great has to have a soft spot in her heart for Japan. This year's Mizuno victory was her seventh in the Land of the Rising Sun, as well as her seventh of the season.

The scoring was astounding at the Seta Golf Club's North course. In the first round, for instance, Sorenstam eagled the first hole, added seven birdies, shot 63, and still didn't have the lead to herself. Chihiro Nakajima also posted a nine-under-par score, taking just 30 strokes on her second nine. They had a three-stroke advantage over Australia's Rachel Teske and Thailand's Aree Song, and a host of strong players, including Laura Davies, Grace Park, Karrie Webb and Lorena Ochoa, were just another stroke back at 67.

Sorenstam followed with a 66–129 Saturday and stepped out to a four-stroke lead over Nakajima, who shot 70–133. Seven players tied for third, seven distant strokes off the pace. Sorenstam polished things off Sunday with a 65, making an eagle and three birdies in one front-nine stretch. The 194 she posted was the lowest 54-hole score of the season by far in Japan, and the nine-stroke margin duplicated her performance in the Mizuno in 2003. Ai Miyazato and Michie Ohba, much too late with a pair of 63s, and Grace Park (67) shared the runner-up position as Nakajima plummeted down the standings with a 74.

Itoen Ladies—¥60,000,000
Winner: Yuriko Ohtsuka

Yuriko Ohtsuka became the eighth and final first-time winner of the 2004 Japan LPGA Tour season in the Itoen Ladies tournament, the third event of the year shortened to 36 holes because of bad weather. Thunderstorms raked the Great Island Club at Chonan, Chiba Prefecture, Friday, wiping out the round and forcing tournament officials to go with the abbreviated format.

Mitsuko Kawasaki, one of the earlier seven first-time winners (Belluna Cup), went after a second title when play began Saturday. She shot 69 and grabbed a share of the lead with Taiwanese players Yun-Jye Wei and Hsiao-Chuan Lu, one stroke ahead of Yuri Fudoh, Michie Ohba and Kasumi Fujii.

Two other players came from further back in the standings Sunday and wound up in a playoff. Michiko Hattori, winner of the Fujitsu in a playoff in mid-October, shot 71-69 for 140 to tie with Ohtsuka, who had rounds of 72 and 68. This time, the much more experienced Hattori failed in overtime, as Ohtsuka dropped a birdie putt on the fourth extra hole to nail the victory. Kaori Higo and Lu missed the playoff by a stroke.

Daioseishi Elleair Ladies Open—¥80,000,000
Winner: Ai Miyazato

Ai Miyazato did all she could in her futile attempt to overtake Yuri Fudoh in the race for the Japan LPGA Tour money title in the next-to-last tournament of the season. The 19-year-old won her fifth title of the year with a three-stroke victory in the Daioseishi Elleair Ladies Open at Elleair Golf Club in Saita, Kagawa Prefecture.

Miyazato took charge of the competition the second day after sitting just a stroke off the lead after Friday's opening round. Shiho Ohyama, age 27, who won her first tournament (Belluna Cup) in 2003, shot a seven-under-par 65 and led Miyazato, Rui Kitada and Hsiao-Chuan Lu by a stroke. Miyazato followed with a 67 Saturday and advanced two strokes into the lead with her 133. She had six birdies and a bogey. Little-known Yuko Saitoh had a 68 and moved into second place with 135.

Miyazato put the victory on ice with a closing 69 for a 202 total, 14 under par. Chieko Amanuma shot 66 and Kitada 69 to tie for second place at 205. Even though she could still lose the money race under an unlikely combination of circumstances, Fudoh did not play at Elleair.

Japan LPGA Tour Championship—¥60,000,000
Winner: Yuri Fudoh

Yuri Fudoh must have had a good feeling about what would happen in the Japan LPGA Tour season finale — the major LPGA Tour Championship. Although she knew there was a slim chance that the money title could slip from her grasp, she allowed that possibility to exist by skipping the penultimate Elleair event on the schedule. Perhaps it was because she had won the 2003 Tour Championship by five strokes on the Miyazaki Country Club where the 2004 edition was about to be played.

Nearly ¥20 million separated Fudoh and Ai Miyazato at week's end, but only because Fudoh performed like the talented champion that she is and made the Tour Championship her seventh victory of the season and 32nd of her relatively short career. And Miyazato did not go down without a fight.

At the end of the first round, Fudoh and Miyazato were first and second among the players who qualified for the select field of 23 who either won during the 2004 season or finished in the top 20 on the money list. Fudoh shot 68 with five birdies and a bogey, and Miyazato scored 69. Quite a turnabout occurred in Friday's second round. Fudoh struggled to a 76 and Miyazato was only one stroke better, opening the door to Toshimi Kimura and Michie Ohba, who slipped one stroke into the lead with 143s.

The tide turned again on a windy Saturday. Miyazato took her final shot with a 69–213 that moved her two strokes in front of Fudoh (71) and Ohba (72). But the champion prevailed in the final-day showdown. Fudoh worked out a 71 for a two-under-par 286 total, just good enough to edge Miyazato (74) and Ohba (73), making her the tour's No. 1 money winner for a remarkable fifth year in a row.

Australian Women's Tour

ABC Learning Centres Ladies Classic—A$100,000
Winner: Mardi Lunn

Mardi Lunn won for the first time since she triumphed on the LPGA circuit in America in 1999 at the ABC Learning Centres Ladies Classic at the Lakelands course on the Gold Coast. Lunn, with a final round of 67 following opening efforts of 71 and 65, finished with a 203 total, one stroke ahead of fellow Australian Shani Waugh.

Lunn and Waugh were tied entering the final round with Laura Davies, who all played in the final group. While Waugh's closing 68 kept her in touch with the winner's 13-under-par total, Davies's 72 left her five strokes behind, tied for third place with Australian rookie Kylie Pratt. England's Georgina Simpson was one stroke further back in fifth place.

Lunn's struggles in recent seasons had seen her drop to 125th on the LPGA Tour in 2003 and this was a welcome upturn in her fortunes. "I started to hit the ball well late last year, but I couldn't putt to save my life," she said. "But I didn't have one three-putt this week, and it's a great confidence boost."

ANZ Ladies Masters—A$800,000
Winner: Annika Sorenstam

Annika Sorenstam got her season off to the perfect start by winning her opening tournament at the ANZ Ladies Masters. The 33-year-old Swede repeated her victory from 2002 at Royal Pines, on Queensland's Gold Coast, for the 58th victory of her career.

Sorenstam was in scintillating form over the weekend as she scored matching rounds of 65, seven under par, each of the last two days to finish with a 269 total, 19 under par. Having led by one stroke entering the last round over England's Karen Stupples, Sorenstam pulled away to win by four strokes. Stupples clinched second place, four shots ahead of Kylie Pratt and Jennifer Rosales, with Anne-Marie Knight a further stroke back.

"It got to the stage where I was thinking 'what do I have to do?'" admitted Stupples. "Annika played supremely well." The Swede was six under for the first eight holes and finished with an eagle, five birdies and no bogeys.

"I'm glad to have got off to a hot start," Sorenstam said. "To finish this weekend 65-65 was perfect preparation for me, and I feel sharpened up for the next few weeks." Having won two major championships and shared the lead on the final nine in the other two in 2003, Sorenstam was setting out in 2004 to win the Grand Slam of all four.

AAMI Women's Australian Open—A$550,000
Winner: Laura Davies

Laura Davies extended her run of winning every season in her 19-year career as a professional and added to a lengthy list of national championships by winning the AAMI Women's Australian Open at Concord. Davies had already won the Opens of Britain, America, England, Scotland, Wales, Ireland, Italy, Spain, Switzerland, Belgium, Denmark and Thailand.

It was her 66th career title, but the 40-year-old Englishwoman had to wait until Monday morning to collect her check for A$82,500 because bad weather had earlier delayed play. Davies had to finish her last six holes, and with birdies at the 14th and the 17th, she claimed a six-stroke victory over Australian Rachel Teske.

Davies, with a 283 total, five under par, recovered from a third round of 77 with a closing 70 and was the only player to finish under par for the week. Trish Johnson was third, two strokes behind Teske, with Michelle Ellis and Martina Eberl tied for fourth.

"The AAMI is a tournament I rank very highly and it's great to get my first victory this year out of the way early," Davies said. "I played really well all week. It's nice to know, when I play my best, I can still win. Hopefully it will be the start of a fun year."

Mianne Bagger's appearance in the tournament created more headlines than scores of 84 and 74, to miss the cut by four strokes, would suggest. The 37-year-old transsexual, who had turned professional in 2003, was invited to play by Women's Golf Australia even though the women's professional tours around the world state that players must be female at birth to become members. Following the Danish-born Australian's appearance at Concord, the Ladies European Tour revoked the rule later in the year.

Nedbank Women's Tour of South Africa

Acer Women's South African Open—R250,000
Winner: Ashleigh Simon

Ashleigh Simon did far more than show she was a player for the future by winning the Acer Women's South African Open. She already has a place in the record books after a breathtaking performance on her home course of Royal Johannesburg and Kensington. At 14 years old, Simon became the youngest winner of the Acer Women's South African Open.

She also became the first amateur to win the title, or any women's professional tournament in South Africa. Coming from eight strokes behind Denmark's Carina Vagner, Simon's closing round of 63 equaled the lowest ever recorded on the Women's Tour of South Africa. She began the day at one over par, but nine birdies and nine pars left her with an eight-under 208 total and a shot ahead of Vagner and Sweden's Johanna Westerberg, with Cecilia Ekelundh three strokes further back.

Two months before her 15th birthday, it was the culmination of an incredible few weeks for Simon. She became the first woman to appear on the men's Sunshine Tour when she played at the Tour Championship, finishing last in the no-cut event, and then became the youngest winner of both the SA Women's Amateur Stroke Play and Match Play titles.

"It's been a roller-coaster ride the past few weeks," Simon said. "I don't know how I'm going to celebrate this because I'm too young to do anything. My goal this year was to win the double in the SA Women's Amateur and I achieved that. Then somebody said to me, 'The Women's SA Open is at your home course, why don't you go and win it,' and I was like, 'Yeah, sure thing.'"

Simon added, "I didn't think I could catch the leader. I just set myself the goals of finishing as the best amateur and under par for the tournament. I was aiming for a 68, but this is my best score ever. I've had a few 67s before, but never a 63. I felt like I could hole everything I looked at. I hit a lot of wedges close. Every time I had a wedge in my hand, I hit it stiff. It was strange because you start saying to yourself that you have to drop a shot sometime. I usually go low on the front nine and then lose concentration on the second nine, but I just kept going at it."

Pam Golding Ladies International—R250,000
Winner: Minea Blomqvist

Ashleigh Simon came so close to winning for the second week running but eventually lost out to another teenager, albeit five years older, as Minea Blomqvist won the Pam Golding Ladies International at Glendower. Blomqvist, a 19-year-old from Finland, was playing in only her second professional tournament, and the previous autumn, when still an amateur, had represented Europe in the Junior Solheim Cup.

Simon opened with a 68 to be one shot off the lead, but then added a 76. Blomqvist had rounds of 71 and 73, but then found herself tied with Simon after 15 holes of the final round. It was Blomqvist who sneaked ahead at the 16th with a birdie after she put her approach to four feet. Her closing 69 left her at six-under-par 213 and one stroke ahead of Simon, who had a 70. Denmark's Lisa Holm Sorensen was a stroke further behind in third place.

"I feel absolutely great," said Blomqvist. "I wanted to win one of these four tournaments on the tour while I was out here, because I felt it would give me the perfect start to my professional career. I was just trusting myself out there. My confidence was good and I hit the ball well, but I was really nervous over that putt on the 16th."

Telkom Women's Classic—R250,000
Winner: Minea Blomqvist

Another week, the same result, almost. Minea Blomqvist won for the second tournament in a row, giving her a record of two out of three as a professional, at the Telkom Women's Classic at Randpark. And amateur Ashleigh Simon was second for the second week running, but this time she was seven strokes behind, along with Laurette Maritz.

"This is becoming quite fun," was how the 19-year-old Blomqvist started her winner's speech. She set up the victory with a 63 in the second round which gave her a three-stroke lead. In the final round she did not drop a shot and four birdies gave her a 68 for a total of 204, 12 under par. Simon and Maritz both scored 70s to be five under, with Johanna Westerberg two shots further back.

"I had set myself the target of 68 today," said the Helsinki teenager. "I was just so relaxed, especially on the back nine. I was just trusting my game. A year ago, if I'd had a six- or seven-shot lead, I would have been thinking about how a double or triple bogey could cost me. But this time I just trusted my game.

"This Tour has given me so much experience. After every round I feel more clever. I was much more comfortable with my game this week than last week."

Nedbank Women's South African Masters—R250,000
Winner: Helena Alterby

Putting her computer science degree to one side, Helena Alterby won her first-ever title at the Nedbank Women's South African Masters at the Johannesburg Country Club. Alterby birdied five holes out of seven around the turn and briefly led by five before securing a two-stroke victory.

The 26-year-old Swede from Gothenburg closed with a 68 for a 12-under-par 204 total to win the R37,500 first prize. Compatriot Asa Gottmo finished second, with Denmark's Lisa Holm Sorensen and local Laurette Maritz tying for third place.

Alterby had played golf only part-time while working on her Master's degree in computing, but decided to try the sport full-time after earning her European Tour card for 2004 at the qualifying tournament. "This win means a lot to me," she said. "I thought if I made enough birdies early in the round then I could afford a few drops over the closing holes.

"This is my first year on the Ladies European Tour, so it's good to win now. Hopefully I get a lot of money with this win. But more importantly, I don't have a sponsor yet, so I hope this helps."

Finland's Minea Blomqvist tied for fifth to top of the Order of Merit with earnings of R91,708, while 14-year-old Ashleigh Simon, after her victory and two second places, tied for 19th here and got set to head to San Diego for the World Junior Championship.

APPENDIXES

Official World Golf Ranking
(As of December 31, 2004)

Ranking		Player	Country	Points Average	Total Points	No. of Events	02/03 Points Lost	2004 Points Gained
1	(2)	Vijay Singh	Fiji	12.79	767.61	60	-496.66	+707.57
2	(1)	Tiger Woods	USA	11.60	463.99	40	-521.61	+402.52
3	(3)	Ernie Els	SAf	10.98	581.97	53	-438.55	+574.68
4	(7)	Retief Goosen	SAf	7.47	396.15	53	-307.94	+354.65
5	(15)	Phil Mickelson	USA	7.00	336.10	48	-272.60	+413.46
6	(8)	Padraig Harrington	Ire	5.55	277.27	50	-249.89	+268.21
7	(36)	Sergio Garcia	Spn	5.40	259.24	48	-169.77	+285.37
8	(6)	Mike Weir	Can	5.40	237.50	44	-264.75	+201.62
9	(4)	Davis Love	USA	5.38	253.03	47	-318.33	+202.58
10	(53)	Stewart Cink	USA	4.65	269.90	58	-139.80	+285.04
11	(25)	Adam Scott	Aus	4.33	224.98	52	-197.81	+243.33
12	(94)	Miguel A. Jimenez	Spn	4.32	220.27	51	-86.78	+231.07
13	(14)	Stuart Appleby	Aus	4.16	236.97	57	-214.01	+220.41
14	(11)	Darren Clarke	NIr	4.14	240.20	58	-200.90	+202.45
15	(26)	Chris DiMarco	USA	3.86	208.39	54	-178.78	+217.18
16	(82)	Todd Hamilton	USA	3.72	189.64	51	-82.33	+204.94
17	(105)	Stephen Ames	T&T	3.59	194.04	54	-97.25	+219.84
18	(10)	Kenny Perry	USA	3.53	172.85	49	-218.46	+122.23
19	(13)	Chad Campbell	USA	3.51	196.29	56	-198.46	+156.48
20	(9)	David Toms	USA	3.44	171.86	50	-227.62	+129.85
21	(5)	Jim Furyk	USA	3.44	140.85	41	-255.08	+41.94
22	(24)	Scott Verplank	USA	3.38	168.86	50	-146.17	+155.20
23	(19)	Thomas Bjorn	Den	3.24	162.20	50	-131.33	+127.94
24	(65)	Lee Westwood	Eng	3.21	182.83	57	-87.04	+153.86
25	(21)	K.J. Choi	Kor	3.13	203.23	65	-186.30	+179.44
26	(130)	Luke Donald	Eng	3.05	170.65	56	-83.68	+188.92
27	(29)	Jay Haas	USA	3.02	144.98	48	-134.99	+138.67
28	(39)	Shigeki Maruyama	Jpn	2.99	164.28	55	-137.97	+168.74
29	(23)	Paul Casey	Eng	2.97	148.42	50	-135.43	+123.50
30	(66)	Angel Cabrera	Arg	2.96	124.52	42	-99.73	+132.62
31	(37)	Fred Couples	USA	2.92	116.67	40	-100.33	+108.75
32	(33)	Jerry Kelly	USA	2.77	163.43	59	-163.46	+159.11
33	(16)	Robert Allenby	Aus	2.77	160.64	58	-177.62	+125.24
34	(75)	Rory Sabbatini	SAf	2.73	144.53	53	-98.89	+151.41
35	(42)	Ian Poulter	Eng	2.66	159.62	60	-112.58	+136.48
36	(54)	Steve Flesch	USA	2.63	170.75	65	-140.89	+171.00
37	(28)	Peter Lonard	Aus	2.62	165.18	63	-152.23	+125.60
38	(373)	Mark Hensby	Aus	2.60	137.98	53	-34.11	+158.45
39	(20)	Justin Leonard	USA	2.59	124.41	48	-153.92	+114.13
40	(17)	Fredrik Jacobson	Swe	2.55	119.98	47	-130.19	+84.63
41	(281)	John Daly	USA	2.51	120.53	48	-64.28	+157.79
42	(124)	Thomas Levet	Frn	2.50	152.25	61	-78.35	+160.95
43	(111)	David Howell	Eng	2.49	137.21	55	-60.60	+134.97
44	(207)	Zach Johnson	USA	2.49	126.77	51	-46.47	+145.17
45	(103)	Nick O'Hern	Aus	2.36	122.49	52	-69.19	+121.01
46	(27)	Chris Riley	USA	2.32	123.20	53	-145.04	+100.91
47	(32)	Jonathan Kaye	USA	2.29	119.05	52	-142.37	+104.61
48	(327)	Joakim Haeggman	Swe	2.23	89.25	40	-43.14	+116.32
49	(55)	Trevor Immelman	SAf	2.19	129.25	59	-137.47	+129.71
50	(110)	Rod Pampling	Aus	2.19	126.88	58	-74.71	+122.27

( ) Ranking in brackets indicates position as of December 31, 2003.

Ranking		Player	Country	Points Average	Total Points	No. of Events	02/03 Points Lost	2004 Points Gained
51	(12)	Nick Price	Zim	2.15	85.92	40	-143.62	+67.22
52	(56)	Kirk Triplett	USA	2.13	104.37	49	-100.18	+98.15
53	(38)	Fred Funk	USA	2.12	131.14	62	-153.45	+111.12
54	(59)	Shingo Katayama	Jpn	2.11	114.01	54	-97.17	+94.18
55	(234T)	Graeme McDowell	NIr	2.10	124.16	59	-42.98	+140.21
56	(43)	Alex Cejka	Ger	2.10	130.30	62	-119.29	+114.15
57	(18)	Charles Howell	USA	2.08	127.07	61	-185.79	+92.53
58	(132)	Jeff Maggert	USA	2.03	91.38	45	-75.29	+109.70
59	(88)	Tom Lehman	USA	2.03	91.26	45	-69.09	+85.87
60	(31)	Stephen Leaney	Aus	2.02	95.07	47	-123.38	+78.35
61	(243)	Richard Green	Aus	2.01	112.76	56	-40.88	+121.97
62	(104)	Toru Taniguchi	Jpn	2.01	98.44	49	-61.06	+92.97
63	(22)	Brad Faxon	USA	1.98	108.88	55	-129.19	+66.43
64	(30)	Bob Tway	USA	1.92	99.94	52	-119.98	+64.94
65	(50)	Tim Herron	USA	1.91	105.29	55	-112.04	+84.35
66	(231)	Stephen Gallacher	Sco	1.90	102.35	54	-35.47	+103.64
67	(85)	Duffy Waldorf	USA	1.86	94.72	51	-82.83	+93.14
68	(157)	Paul McGinley	Ire	1.80	95.59	53	-57.79	+100.61
69	(68)	Briny Baird	USA	1.77	111.64	63	-99.53	+81.19
70	(76)	Geoff Ogilvy	Aus	1.77	99.05	56	-86.99	+80.15
71	(52)	Justin Rose	Eng	1.77	106.09	60	-124.68	+99.78
72	(195)	Carlos Franco	Par	1.76	103.76	59	-56.12	+112.34
73	(46)	Shaun Micheel	USA	1.74	99.35	57	-109.28	+69.39
74	(67)	Tim Clark	SAf	1.74	99.15	57	-100.50	+80.25
75	(181)	Jesper Parnevik	Swe	1.71	97.34	57	-57.04	+106.97
76	(40)	Bob Estes	USA	1.70	85.03	50	-104.81	+62.36
77	(688)	Y.E. Yang	Kor	1.67	66.66	40	-10.22	+73.38
78	(71)	Craig Parry	Aus	1.67	79.97	48	-107.56	+88.77
79	(51)	Loren Roberts	USA	1.63	74.85	46	-92.76	+57.93
80	(89)	Bernhard Langer	Ger	1.62	72.99	45	-82.24	+76.97
81	(41)	Colin Montgomerie	Sco	1.62	89.15	55	-129.73	+83.80
82	(48)	Phillip Price	Wal	1.57	76.75	49	-80.00	+43.72
83	(49)	Toshimitsu Izawa	Jpn	1.56	67.19	43	-71.45	+33.07
84	(60)	Brian Davis	Eng	1.53	90.29	59	-96.28	+68.26
85	(57)	John Huston	USA	1.53	65.72	43	-89.28	+51.91
86	(183)	Joey Sindelar	USA	1.52	91.21	60	-59.45	+101.40
87	(118)	Carl Pettersson	Swe	1.52	85.03	56	-67.69	+84.90
88	(148)	S.K. Ho	Kor	1.52	66.73	44	-48.71	+70.85
89	(44)	Michael Campbell	NZl	1.52	78.84	52	-103.25	+61.37
90	(62)	Scott Hoch	USA	1.50	60.08	40	-88.42	+66.21
91	(196)	Arron Oberholser	USA	1.50	72.01	48	-47.65	+84.67
92	(123)	Raphael Jacquelin	Frn	1.50	83.78	56	-59.03	+76.62
93	(306)	Ryan Palmer	USA	1.49	91.02	61	-17.76	+91.30
94	(34)	Ben Curtis	USA	1.49	74.55	50	-71.84	+36.90
95	(150)	Thongchai Jaidee	Tha	1.49	62.54	42	-45.59	+65.90
96	(173)	Brent Geiberger	USA	1.49	69.96	47	-34.44	+66.48
97	(45)	Eduardo Romero	Arg	1.48	59.13	40	-93.61	+47.72
98	(69)	Jonathan Byrd	USA	1.46	81.90	56	-100.11	+62.55
99	(100)	Alastair Forsyth	Sco	1.46	78.86	54	-61.23	+67.29
100	(126)	Anders Hansen	Den	1.46	71.45	49	-64.80	+75.28

( ) Ranking in brackets indicates position as of December 31, 2003.

Ranking		Player	Country	Points Average	Total Points	No. of Events	02/03 Points Lost	2004 Points Gained
101	(171)	Harrison Frazar	USA	1.43	74.35	52	-58.28	+85.67
102	(98)	David Smail	NZl	1.43	74.12	52	-69.46	+67.58
103	(198)	Mark O'Meara	USA	1.42	62.32	44	-57.23	+81.17
104	(86)	Tim Petrovic	USA	1.39	93.01	67	-88.65	+77.27
105	(136)	Skip Kendall	USA	1.38	81.48	59	-69.54	+85.37
106	(158)	Paul Sheehan	Aus	1.38	74.51	54	-39.69	+70.30
107	(122)	Tom Pernice, Jr.	USA	1.38	85.48	62	-65.44	+78.44
108	(79)	Steve Lowery	USA	1.38	78.52	57	-89.20	+68.17
109	(429)	Bo Van Pelt	USA	1.37	74.10	54	-33.20	+93.95
110	(342)	Scott Drummond	Sco	1.37	71.17	52	-29.17	+82.18
111	(137)	Tommy Armour	USA	1.36	70.78	52	-42.05	+54.99
112	(114)	Woody Austin	USA	1.33	79.90	60	-69.48	+65.39
113	(81)	Ricardo Gonzalez	Arg	1.32	55.48	42	-58.57	+43.29
114	(185)	David Lynn	Eng	1.31	73.19	56	-45.53	+72.14
115	(133)	Jyoti Randhawa	Ind	1.30	72.62	56	-44.31	+68.01
116	(102)	Brendan Jones	Aus	1.29	74.94	58	-69.33	+68.14
117	(61)	Jeff Sluman	USA	1.27	74.85	59	-117.27	+59.54
118	(92)	Ben Crane	USA	1.25	68.65	55	-77.71	+58.72
119	(192)	Steven Conran	Aus	1.23	66.46	54	-30.27	+54.26
120	(129)	Joe Durant	USA	1.23	66.39	54	-57.64	+61.29
121	(90)	Tetsuji Hiratsuka	Jpn	1.23	70.06	57	-63.03	+44.34
122	(308)	Joe Ogilvie	USA	1.23	73.71	60	-32.15	+82.77
123	(180)	Barry Lane	Eng	1.23	68.62	56	-52.17	+73.53
124	(63)	John Rollins	USA	1.22	69.70	57	-102.58	+44.90
125	(64)	Scott McCarron	USA	1.22	66.03	54	-87.49	+41.56
126	(93)	Jose M. Olazabal	Spn	1.22	70.52	58	-72.38	+56.33
127	(95)	Lee Janzen	USA	1.21	60.55	50	-70.84	+52.65
128	(230)	Jean-F. Remesy	Frn	1.20	62.14	52	-44.04	+73.77
129	(153)	Keiichiro Fukabori	Jpn	1.19	66.59	56	-38.03	+51.62
130	(127)	Frank Lickliter	USA	1.16	66.20	57	-71.96	+70.17
131	(109)	Matt Gogel	USA	1.16	57.99	50	-50.75	+44.49
132	(77)	J.L. Lewis	USA	1.14	72.10	63	-84.13	+46.93
133	(456)	Hunter Mahan	USA	1.14	47.98	42	-10.80	+50.10
134	(135)	Hideto Tanihara	Jpn	1.12	61.36	55	-34.20	+47.06
135	(91)	Mark Calcavecchia	USA	1.11	54.50	49	-65.74	+45.50
136	(263)	Simon Khan	Eng	1.11	54.26	49	-24.68	+56.86
137	(97)	Kevin Sutherland	USA	1.09	59.06	54	-74.09	+53.66
138	(164)	Dudley Hart	USA	1.09	49.20	45	-49.72	+55.71
139	(418)	Vaughn Taylor	USA	1.09	49.01	45	-13.92	+52.43
140	(399)	Bart Bryant	USA	1.08	43.38	40	-15.07	+46.96
141	(119)	Katsumasa Miyamoto	Jpn	1.08	58.47	54	-46.76	+39.88
142	(35)	Rocco Mediate	USA	1.07	46.17	43	-99.11	+17.67
143	(1141)	Takashi Kamiyama	Jpn	1.07	42.74	40	-6.73	+49.06
144	(434)	Ted Purdy	USA	1.07	73.68	69	-30.23	+87.77
145	(317)	Henrik Stenson	Swe	1.06	58.16	55	-20.58	+58.43
146	(96)	Carlos Rodiles	Spn	1.06	58.15	55	-52.33	+36.61
147	(204)	Jose Coceres	Arg	1.05	43.04	41	-26.88	+41.47
148	(304)	Marcel Siem	Ger	1.04	52.24	50	-29.14	+60.10
149	(101)	Andre Stolz	Aus	1.03	53.42	52	-47.08	+43.73
150	(333)	Ryoken Kawagishi	Jpn	1.02	53.24	52	-8.33	+46.36

( ) Ranking in brackets indicates position as of December 31, 2003.

Ranking		Player	Country	Points Average	Total Points	No. of Events	02/03 Points Lost	2004 Points Gained
151	(309)	Hideki Kase	Jpn	1.02	57.15	56	-19.20	+52.06
152	(285)	Brett Rumford	Aus	1.02	52.90	52	-29.08	+54.32
153	(255)	Corey Pavin	USA	1.02	54.82	54	-33.33	+60.33
154	(73)	Nick Faldo	Eng	1.01	40.56	40	-61.48	+31.13
155	(172)	Tom Byrum	USA	1.01	56.66	56	-46.04	+56.97
156	(58)	Niclas Fasth	Swe	1.01	55.43	55	-86.03	+32.30
157	(159)	Peter O'Malley	Aus	1.01	52.29	52	-50.75	+51.73
158	(116)	Hidemichi Tanaka	Jpn	0.99	57.26	58	-68.74	+46.33
159	(80)	Robert Gamez	USA	0.97	60.28	62	-75.69	+41.64
160	(296)	Miles Tunnicliff	Eng	0.97	43.71	45	-27.40	+52.47
161	(262)	Patrick Sheehan	USA	0.97	62.88	65	-33.70	+64.96
162	(203)	Brett Quigley	USA	0.94	54.51	58	-39.29	+51.65
163	(149)	Hank Kuehne	USA	0.93	51.86	56	-44.02	+47.61
164	(112)	Hiroyuki Fujita	Jpn	0.92	48.03	52	-61.18	+40.20
165	(72)	Mathias Gronberg	Swe	0.92	54.49	59	-60.22	+36.67
166	(512)	Tag Ridings	USA	0.91	36.51	40	-7.83	+37.45
167	(87)	Gary Evans	Eng	0.90	40.63	45	-64.43	+20.35
168	(115)	Greg Owen	Eng	0.90	35.97	40	-52.89	+24.07
169	(202)	Peter Senior	Aus	0.88	35.25	40	-22.16	+28.69
170	(295)	Stephen Dodd	Wal	0.86	49.21	57	-24.53	+46.66
171	(139)	Soren Kjeldsen	Den	0.86	43.04	50	-48.38	+34.85
172	(504)	Daniel Chopra	Swe	0.86	58.49	68	-18.67	+65.31
173	(121)	Taichi Teshima	Jpn	0.86	46.44	54	-46.07	+24.86
174	(201)	Darren Fichardt	SAf	0.86	45.52	53	-46.36	+49.02
175	(299)	Terry Price	Aus	0.86	46.26	54	-28.45	+55.12
176	(197)	Cameron Beckman	USA	0.86	47.89	56	-39.22	+46.95
177	(223)	James Kingston	SAf	0.85	44.86	53	-30.92	+44.37
178	(297)	Kevin Na	USA	0.85	43.11	51	-23.85	+48.54
179	(233)	Yeh Wei-tze	Twn	0.84	41.36	49	-17.88	+33.24
180	(186)	Prayad Marksaeng	Tha	0.84	47.71	57	-36.07	+38.85
181	(267)	Dennis Paulson	USA	0.83	34.21	41	-29.29	+37.33
182	(107)	Maarten Lafeber	Neth	0.83	46.29	56	-54.83	+24.94
183	(170)	Kim Jong-duck	Kor	0.83	39.61	48	-37.45	+36.29
184	(330)	Paul Broadhurst	Eng	0.82	43.65	53	-18.73	+43.65
185	(269)	Toru Suzuki	Jpn	0.82	47.74	58	-22.26	+41.89
186	(240)	Robert Damron	USA	0.82	49.22	60	-35.51	+49.28
187	(752)	Michael Allen	USA	0.82	42.43	52	-7.14	+45.94
188	(428)	Brian Bateman	USA	0.81	40.26	50	-25.57	+51.27
189	(190)	Marcus Fraser	Aus	0.80	44.24	55	-27.06	+39.55
190	(914)	Terry Pilkadaris	Aus	0.80	32.15	40	-2.04	+32.83
191	(276)	Simon Yates	Sco	0.80	31.93	40	-21.48	+32.50
192	(165)	Tsuyoshi Yoneyama	Jpn	0.79	38.01	48	-32.12	+21.24
193	(140)	Peter Fowler	Aus	0.79	46.60	59	-50.32	+34.14
194	(219)	Charl Schwartzel	SAf	0.79	48.91	62	-21.28	+44.11
195	(338)	Peter Hanson	Swe	0.78	39.95	51	-17.91	+41.03
196	(292)	Tomohiro Kondo	Jpn	0.78	43.78	56	-26.69	+44.10
197	(224)	John Senden	Aus	0.78	52.18	67	-40.31	+47.73
198	(83)	Bradley Dredge	Wal	0.77	41.78	54	-76.49	+32.90
199	(221)	Kent Jones	USA	0.77	43.76	57	-35.55	+42.05
200T	(273)	Jose M. Lara	Spn	0.76	38.13	50	-20.86	+38.40
200T	(305)	Dinesh Chand	Fiji	0.76	43.47	57	-22.74	+40.15

( ) Ranking in brackets indicates position as of December 31, 2003.

Age Groups of Current Top 100 World Ranked Players

Under 25	25-28	29-30	31-32	33-34	35-36	37-38	39-42	Over 43
					Els			
				Mickelson	Goosen			
	Donald			Harrington	Clarke			K. Perry
	Casey			Weir	DiMarco			Haas
	Sabbatini			Appleby	Maruyama		Singh	Couples
	Poulter			Furyk	Cabrera		Love	N. Price
	Z. Johnson			Bjorn	Levet		Jimenez	Funk
	Immelman	Woods		K.J. Choi	Haeggman	Toms	Hamilton	Lehman
	McDowell	C.Campbell	Cink	Allenby	Pampling	Kelly	Ames	Faxon
	C. Howell	Jacobson	Westwood	Hensby	Leaney	Flesch	Verplank	Tway
	Ogilvy	D. Howell	Leonard	O'Hern	Taniguchi	Lonard	Triplett	Roberts
	Pettersson	Gallacher	C. Riley	Kaye	Micheel	Daly	Maggert	Langer
	R. Palmer	T. Clark	Katayama	Cejka	Izawa	McGinley	Waldorf	Huston
Garcia	Curtis	B. Davis	Baird	R. Green	M.Campbell	Estes	Franco	Sindelar
Scott	Byrd	Oberholser	Y.E. Yang	Herron	Thongchai	Parry	Parnevik	Hoch
Rose	Forsyth	Jacquelin	S.K. Ho	A. Hansen	Geiberger	P. Price	Montgomerie	Romero

2004 World Ranking Review

Major Movements

Upward

Name	Net Points Gained	Position 2003	2004
Vijay Singh	211	2	1
Stewart Cink	145	53	10
Miguel A. Jimenez	144	94	12
Phil Mickelson	141	15	5
Ernie Els	136	3	3
Mark Hensby	124	373	38
Todd Hamilton	123	82	16
Stephen Ames	123	105	17
Sergio Garcia	116	36	7
Luke Donald	105	130	26
Zach Johnson	99	207	44
Graeme McDowell	97	234	55
John Daly	94	281	41
Thomas Levet	83	124	42
Richard Green	81	243	61
David Howell	74	111	43
Ryan Palmer	74	306	93
Joakim Haeggman	73	327	48
Stephen Gallacher	68	231	66
Lee Westwood	67	65	24
Y.E. Yang	63	688	77

Downward

Name	Net Points Lost	Position 2003	2004
Jim Furyk	213	5	21
Tiger Woods	119	1	2
Davis Love	116	4	9
Rich Beem	110	47	266
David Toms	98	9	20
Kenny Perry	96	10	18
Charles Howell	93	18	57
Rocco Mediate	81	35	142
Nick Price	76	12	51
Len Mattiace	74	70	233
Mike Weir	63	6	8
Brad Faxon	63	22	63
Jeff Sluman	58	61	117
John Rollins	58	63	124

Highest-Rated Events of 2004

	Event	No. of World Ranked Players Participating					World Rating Points
		Top 5	Top 15	Top 30	Top 50	Top 100	
1	PGA Championship	5	14	27	48	95	767
2	U.S. Open Championship	5	15	30	49	76	751
3	The Open Championship	5	15	29	44	71	710
4	Masters Tournament	5	14	29	47	71	711
5	The Players Championship	5	14	29	48	80	739
6	WGC NEC Invitational	4	14	29	47	69	700
7	WGC Accenture Match Play	4	13	28	47	64	681
8	WGC American Express	3	12	26	44	55	586
9	Memorial Tournament	4	9	21	36	66	574
10	Bay Hill Invitational	4	9	19	34	62	543
11	Buick Classic	4	12	23	34	57	529
12	Nissan Open	2	8	18	34	61	508
13	Wachovia Championship	4	8	19	32	55	487
14	The Tour Championship	5	15	23	29	31	476
15	EDS Byron Nelson Champ.	4	9	17	28	51	463
16	Volvo PGA Championship	2	5	6	12	26	222
17	Chrysler Championship	3	8	14	24	52	420
18	FBR Open	1	5	17	29	57	434
19	Bank of America Colonial	2	7	15	26	52	393
20	Mercedes Championships	5	11	13	19	26	370
21	Buick Invitational	2	6	16	24	42	377
22	Sony Open	4	9	13	20	35	355
23	Cialis Western Open	3	7	13	20	36	345
24	MCI Heritage	2	5	11	24	52	357
25	The International	2	4	13	20	45	321
26	Dunhill Links Championship	3	6	10	15	30	287
27	Funai Classic at Disney	1	4	7	16	48	305
28	Bob Hope Chrysler Classic	0	4	13	22	43	311
29	84 Lumber Classic	1	4	12	20	39	311
30	Ford Championship	0	4	13	20	41	297
31	Buick Open	2	4	11	14	30	263
32	Bell Canadian Open	3	7	11	14	26	251
33	Honda Classic	1	4	10	16	36	250
34	Deutsche Bank Championship	2	4	6	12	34	247
35	Deutsche Bank SAP Open	1	5	8	12	25	209
36	HP Classic of New Orleans	1	4	10	15	32	241
37	Barclays Scottish Open	2	3	5	11	28	205
38	AT&T Pebble Beach Pro-Am	2	4	7	13	30	234
39	HSBC World Match Play	3	5	9	13	15	230
40	Dubai Desert Classic	2	4	6	9	21	190

World Golf Rankings 1968-2004

Year	No. 1	No. 2	No. 3	No. 4	No. 5
1968	Nicklaus	Palmer	Casper	Player	Charles
1969	Nicklaus	Player	Casper	Palmer	Charles
1970	Nicklaus	Player	Casper	Trevino	Charles
1971	Nicklaus	Trevino	Player	Palmer	Casper
1972	Nicklaus	Player	Trevino	Crampton	Palmer
1973	Nicklaus	Weiskopf	Trevino	Player	Crampton
1974	Nicklaus	Miller	Player	Weiskopf	Trevino
1975	Nicklaus	Miller	Weiskopf	Irwin	Player
1976	Nicklaus	Irwin	Miller	Player	Green
1977	Nicklaus	Watson	Green	Irwin	Crenshaw
1978	Watson	Nicklaus	Irwin	Green	Player
1979	Watson	Nicklaus	Irwin	Trevino	Player
1980	Watson	Trevino	Aoki	Crenshaw	Nicklaus
1981	Watson	Rogers	Aoki	Pate	Trevino
1982	Watson	Floyd	Ballesteros	Kite	Stadler
1983	Ballesteros	Watson	Floyd	Norman	Kite
1984	Ballesteros	Watson	Norman	Wadkins	Langer
1985	Ballesteros	Langer	Norman	Watson	Nakajima
1986	Norman	Langer	Ballesteros	Nakajima	Bean
1987	Norman	Ballesteros	Langer	Lyle	Strange
1988	Ballesteros	Norman	Lyle	Faldo	Strange
1989	Norman	Faldo	Ballesteros	Strange	Stewart
1990	Norman	Faldo	Olazabal	Woosnam	Stewart
1991	Woosnam	Faldo	Olazabal	Ballesteros	Norman
1992	Faldo	Couples	Woosnam	Olazabal	Norman
1993	Faldo	Norman	Langer	Price	Couples
1994	Price	Norman	Faldo	Langer	Olazabal
1995	Norman	Price	Langer	Els	Montgomerie
1996	Norman	Lehman	Montgomerie	Els	Couples
1997	Norman	Woods	Price	Els	Love
1998	Woods	O'Meara	Duval	Love	Els
1999	Woods	Duval	Montgomerie	Love	Els
2000	Woods	Els	Duval	Mickelson	Westwood
2001	Woods	Mickelson	Duval	Els	Love
2002	Woods	Mickelson	Els	Garcia	Goosen
2003	Woods	Singh	Els	Love	Furyk
2004	Singh	Woods	Els	Goosen	Mickelson

(The World of Professional Golf 1968-1985; World Ranking 1986-2004)

Year	No. 6	No. 7	No. 8	No. 9	No. 10
1968	Boros	Coles	Thomson	Beard	Nagle
1969	Beard	Archer	Trevino	Barber	Sikes
1970	Devlin	Coles	Jacklin	Beard	Huggett
1971	Barber	Crampton	Charles	Devlin	Weiskopf
1972	Jacklin	Weiskopf	Oosterhuis	Heard	Devlin
1973	Miller	Oosterhuis	Wadkins	Heard	Brewer
1974	M. Ozaki	Crampton	Irwin	Green	Heard
1975	Green	Trevino	Casper	Crampton	Watson
1976	Watson	Weiskopf	Marsh	Crenshaw	Geiberger
1977	Marsh	Player	Weiskopf	Floyd	Ballesteros
1978	Crenshaw	Marsh	Ballesteros	Trevino	Aoki
1979	Aoki	Green	Crenshaw	Ballesteros	Wadkins
1980	Pate	Ballesteros	Bean	Irwin	Player
1981	Ballesteros	Graham	Crenshaw	Floyd	Lietzke
1982	Pate	Nicklaus	Rogers	Aoki	Strange
1983	Nicklaus	Nakajima	Stadler	Aoki	Wadkins
1984	Faldo	Nakajima	Stadler	Kite	Peete
1985	Wadkins	O'Meara	Strange	Pavin	Sutton
1986	Tway	Sutton	Strange	Stewart	O'Meara
1987	Woosnam	Stewart	Wadkins	McNulty	Crenshaw
1988	Crenshaw	Woosnam	Frost	Azinger	Calcavecchia
1989	Kite	Olazabal	Calcavecchia	Woosnam	Azinger
1990	Azinger	Ballesteros	Kite	McNulty	Calcavecchia
1991	Couples	Langer	Stewart	Azinger	Davis
1992	Langer	Cook	Price	Azinger	Love
1993	Azinger	Woosnam	Kite	Love	Pavin
1994	Els	Couples	Montgomerie	M. Ozaki	Pavin
1995	Pavin	Faldo	Couples	M. Ozaki	Elkington
1996	Faldo	Mickelson	M. Ozaki	Love	O'Meara
1997	Mickelson	Montgomerie	M. Ozaki	Lehman	O'Meara
1998	Price	Montgomerie	Westwood	Singh	Mickelson
1999	Westwood	Singh	Price	Mickelson	O'Meara
2000	Montgomerie	Love	Sutton	Singh	Lehman
2001	Garcia	Toms	Singh	Clarke	Goosen
2002	Toms	Harrington	Singh	Love	Montgomerie
2003	Weir	Goosen	Harrington	Toms	Perry
2004	Harrington	Garcia	Weir	Love	Cink

World's Winners of 2004

U.S. PGA TOUR

Mercedes Championships	Stuart Appleby
Sony Open in Hawaii	Ernie Els
Bob Hope Chrysler Classic	Phil Mickelson
FBR Open	Jonathan Kaye
AT&T Pebble Beach National Pro-Am	Vijay Singh
Buick Invitational	John Daly
Nissan Open	Mike Weir
WGC - Accenture Match Play	Tiger Woods
Chrysler Classic of Tucson	Heath Slocum
Ford Championship at Doral	Craig Parry
Honda Classic	Todd Hamilton
Bay Hill Invitational	Chad Campbell
The Players Championship	Adam Scott
BellSouth Classic	Zach Johnson
Masters Tournament	Phil Mickelson (2)
MCI Heritage	Stewart Cink
Shell Houston Open	Vijay Singh (2)
HP Classic of New Orleans	Vijay Singh (3)
Wachovia Championship	Joey Sindelar
EDS Byron Nelson Championship	Sergio Garcia
Bank of America Colonial	Steve Flesch
FedEx St. Jude Classic	David Toms
Memorial Tournament	Ernie Els (3)
Buick Classic	Sergio Garcia (2)
U.S. Open Championship	Retief Goosen
Booz Allen Classic	Adam Scott (2)
Cialis Western Open	Stephen Ames
John Deere Classic	Mark Hensby
B.C. Open	Jonathan Byrd
U.S. Bank Championship in Milwaukee	Carlos Franco
Buick Open	Vijay Singh (4)
The International	Rod Pampling
PGA Championship	Vijay Singh (5)
WGC - NEC Invitational	Stewart Cink (2)
Reno-Tahoe Open	Vaughn Taylor
Buick Championship	Woody Austin
Deutsche Bank Championship	Vijay Singh (6)
Bell Canadian Open	Vijay Singh (7)
Valero Texas Open	Bart Bryant
84 Lumber Classic	Vijay Singh (8)
Southern Farm Bureau Classic	Fred Funk
Michelin Championship at Las Vegas	Andre Stolz
Chrysler Classic of Greensboro	Brent Geiberger
Funai Classic at the Walt Disney World Resort	Ryan Palmer
Chrysler Championship	Vijay Singh (9)
Tour Championship	Retief Goosen (3)

SPECIAL EVENTS

Tavistock Cup	Isleworth
CVS Charity Classic	Jay Haas/Bill Haas
Ryder Cup	Europe
Franklin Templeton Shootout	Hank Kuehne/Jeff Sluman
Callaway Golf Pebble Beach Invitational	Jeff Brehaut
UBS Cup	United States
PGA Grand Slam of Golf	Phil Mickelson (3)

Shinhan Korea Golf Championship	Arron Oberholser
Office Depot Father-Son Challenge	Larry Nelson (3)/Drew Nelson
Target World Challenge	Tiger Woods (3)

NATIONWIDE TOUR

BellSouth Panama Championship	Jimmy Walker
Chitimacha Louisiana Open	Jimmy Walker (2)
First Tee Arkansas Classic	Daniel Chopra
Rheem Classic	Franklin Langham
BMW Charity Pro-Am at The Cliffs	Ryuji Imada
Chattanooga Classic	Justin Bolli
Henrico County Open	Daniel Chopra (2)
SAS Carolina Classic	Chris Anderson
Knoxville Open	Hunter Haas
LaSalle Bank Open	Brendan Jones (2)
Northeast Pennsylvania Classic	D.A. Points
Lake Erie Charity Classic	Kevin Stadler
Reese's Cup Classic	Ben Bates
Scholarship America Showdown	Kevin Stadler (2)
Pete Dye West Virginia Classic	D.A. Points (2)
Samsung Canadian PGA Championship	Charles Warren
Preferred Health Systems Wichita Open	Bradley Hughes
Cox Classic	Charles Warren (2)
Price Cutter Charity Championship	Brad Ott
Alberta Classic	David Hearn (2)
Envirocare Utah Classic	Brett Wetterich
Virginia Beach Open	James Driscoll
Oregon Classic	Jeff Quinney
Albertsons Boise Open	Scott Gump
Mark Christopher Charity Classic	Scott Dunlap
Gila River Classic at Wild Horse Pass Resort	Chris Nallen
Permian Basin Charity Golf Classic	Charley Hoffman
Miccosukee Championship	D.J. Trahan
Nationwide Tour Championship	Nick Watney

CANADIAN TOUR

Barton Creek Classic	Brad Sutterfield
Barton Creek Challenge	Chris Wisler
Greater Sacramento Open	Ben Pettitt
E-Loan Central Valley Classic	Erik Compton
Michelin Guadalajara Classic	Rob Johnson
Corona Ixtapa Classic	Jason Higton
Lewis Chitengwa Memorial	Stephen Gangluff
Times Colonist Open	David Hearn
Greater Vancouver Classic	Ryan Miller
MTS Classic	Erik Compton (2)
Telus Edmonton Open	Stephen Woodard
Montreal Open	Stephen Woodard (2)
Bay Mills Open Players Championship	Chris Wisler (2)
Casino de Charlevoix Cup	Dirk Ayers/Stephen Woodard (3)

TOUR DE LAS AMERICAS (SOUTH AMERICA)

Caribbean Open	Tim Conley
Albierto del Sur	Angel Cabrera
Summit Panama Masters	Miguel Fernandez
Costa Rica Open	Alessandro Tadini
Albierto Telefonica	Daniel Vancsik
American Express Puerto Rico Open	Rodolfo Gonzalez
American Express Dominican Open	Wilfredo Morales
Acapulco Fest	Rafael Ponce
Cantv Venezuela Open	Miguel Martinez

Mexico Open	Rafael Gomez
Panasonic Panama Open	Richard McEvoy
TIM Peru Open	Brad Sutterfield (2)

PGA EUROPEAN TOUR

Dubai Desert Classic	Mark O'Meara
Qatar Masters	Joakim Haeggman
Madeira Island Open	Christopher Hanell
Algarve Open de Portugal	Miguel Angel Jimenez (2)
Open de Sevilla	Ricardo Gonzalez
Canarias Open de Espana	Christian Cevaer
Telecom Italia Open	Graeme McDowell
Daily Telegraph Damovo British Masters	Barry Lane
Deutsche Bank - SAP Open	Trevor Immelman (2)
Volvo PGA Championship	Scott Drummond
Celtic Manor Wales Open	Simon Khan
Diageo Championship at Gleneagles	Miles Tunnicliff
Aa St. Omer Open	Philippe Lima (2)
Open de France	Jean-Francois Remesy
Smurfit European Open	Retief Goosen (2)
Barclays Scottish Open	Thomas Levet
The Open Championship	Todd Hamilton (2)
Nissan Irish Open	Brett Rumford
Scandinavian Masters	Luke Donald
KLM Open	David Lynn
BMW Russian Open	Gary Emerson
BMW International Open	Miguel Angel Jimenez (4)
Omega European Masters	Luke Donald (2)
Linde German Masters	Padraig Harrington
The Heritage	Henrik Stenson
WGC - American Express Championship	Ernie Els (4)
Dunhill Links Championship	Stephen Gallacher
HSBC World Match Play	Ernie Els (5)
Mallorca Classic	Sergio Garcia (3)
Open de Madrid	Richard Sterne
Volvo Masters Andalucia	Ian Poulter
WGC - World Cup	Luke Donald (3)/Paul Casey

CHALLENGE TOUR

Al Ahram-Jolie Ville Sharm El Sheikh Challenge	Gareth Davies
Peugeot Challenge de Leon	Edward Rush
Tessali-Metaponto Open di Puglia e Basilicata	Leif Westerberg
Nykredit Danish Open	Matthew Morris
Segura Viudas Challenge de Espana	Philippe Lima
Galeria Kaufhof Pokal Challenge	Garry Houston
Volvo Finnish Open	*Roope Kakko
Open des Volcans Challenge de France	Johan Axgren
Texbond Open	Sam Little
JJB Sports North West Challenge	Fredrik Henge
Ryder Cup Wales Challenge	Graeme Storm
Rolex Trophy	Philip Archer
Norwegian Challenge	Stephen Browne
Skandia PGA Open	Matthew King
BA-CA Golf Open	Marcus Brier
Telia Grand Prix	Lee Slattery
Open de Toulouse	Marc Cayeux (2)
Estoril Challenge Open Portugal Telecom	Tom Whitehouse
Attijari Wafa - Tikida Beach Moroccan Classic	Graeme Storm (2)
Donnington Grove Computacenter English Open	Matthew King (2)
Bouygues Telecom Grand Final	David Drysdale

ASIAN TOUR

Areeya Thailand Open	Boonchu Ruangkit
Johnnie Walker Classic	Miguel Angel Jimenez
Myanmar Open	Thongchia Jaidee
Carlsberg Malaysian Open	Thongchia Jaidee (2)
DHL Philippine Open	Edward Michaels
Caltex Masters	Colin Montgomerie
Royal Challenge Indian Open	Mardan Mamat
Volkswagen Masters China	Rahil Gangjee
Macau Open	Jason Knutzon
BMW Asian Open	Miguel Angel Jimenez (3)
SK Telecom Open	Simon Yates
Tianjin TEDA Open	Thammanoon Srirot
Kolon Korean Open	Edward Loar
Mercuries Taiwan Masters	Thaworn Wiratchant
Taiwan Open	Charlie Wi
Crowne Plaza Open	Terry Pilkadaris
Sanya Open	Terry Pilkadaris (2)
Carlsberg Masters 2004 Vietnam	Angelo Que
Volvo China Open	Stephen Dodd
Omega Hong Kong Open	Miguel Angel Jimenez (5)
Volvo Masters of Asia	Jyoti Randhawa

JAPAN TOUR

Token Homemate Cup	Hiroyuki Fujita
Tsuruya Open	Brendan Jones
Chunichi Crowns	Shingo Katayama
Fujisankei Classic	Paul Sheehan
Japan PGA Championship	S.K. Ho
Munsingwear Open KSB Cup	Tatsuya Mitsuhashi
Mitsubishi Diamond Cup	Tetsuji Hiratsuka
JCB Classic Sendai	Takashi Kamiyama
Mandom Lucido Yomiuri Open	Dinesh Chand
Mizuno Open	Brendan Jones (3)
Japan Golf Tour Championship	S.K. Ho (2)
Woodone Open Hiroshima	Shingo Katayama (2)
Sato Foods NST Niigata Open	Kim Jong-duck
Aiful Cup	Takuya Taniguchi
Sun Chlorella Classic	Y.E. Yang
Hisamitsu KBC Augusta	Steve Conran
Suntory Open	Hideki Kase
ANA Open	Chawalit Plaphol
Acom International	Toru Suzuki
Coca-Cola Tokai Classic	Katsumune Imai
Japan Open	Toru Taniguchi
Bridgestone Open	Toru Taniguchi (2)
ABC Championship	Makoto Inoue
Asahi-Ryokuken Yomiuri Memorial Open	Y.E. Yang (2)
Mitsui Sumitomo Visa Taiheiyo Masters	Darren Clarke
Dunlop Phoenix	Tiger Woods (2)
Casio World Open	David Smail
Golf Nippon Series JT Cup	Paul Sheehan (2)
Asia/Japan Okinawa Open	Kiyoshi Miyazato

AUSTRALASIAN TOUR

Holden New Zealand Open	Terry Price
Heineken Classic	Ernie Els (2)
ANZ Championship	Brian Davis
Jacob's Creek Open	Euan Walters
New Zealand PGA Championship	Gavin Coles
Hillross Centenary Australian Open	Peter Lonard

Cadbury Schweppes Australian PGA Champ.	Peter Lonard (2)
MasterCard Masters	Richard Green

AFRICAN TOURS

South African Airways Open	Trevor Immelman
Dunhill Championship	Marcel Siem
Dimension Data Pro-Am	Darren Fichardt
Nashua Masters	Andrew McLardy
Telkom PGA Championship	Warrick Druian
Southern Africa Tour Championship	Andrew McLardy (2)
Stanbic Zambia Open	Michael Kirk
Kenya Open	Marc Cayeux
FNB Botswana Open	Barry Painting
Parmalat Classic	Justin Walters
Capital Alliance Royal Swazi Sun Open	Nic Henning
Vodacom Origins of Golf Tour at Pezula	Patrick O'Brien
Vodacom Origins of Golf Tour at Schoeman Park	Steve van Vuuren
Royal Swazi Sun Classic	Bradford Vaughan
Vodacom Origins of Golf Tour at Zimbali	Thomas Aiken
Vodacom Origins of Golf Tour at Sun City	Thomas Aiken (2)
Vodacom Origins of Golf Tour at Arabella	Louis Oosthuizen
Bearingman Highveld Classic	Divan van den Heever
Limpopo Eskom Classic	Bradford Vaughan (2)
Vodacom Origins of Golf Championship	Thomas Aiken (3)
Platinum Classic	Titch Moore
MTC Namibian PGA Championship	Mark Murless
Seekers Travel Pro-Am	Ulrich van den Berg
Nelson Mandela Invitational	Ernie Els (6)/Vincent Tshabalala
Nedbank Golf Challenge	Retief Goosen (4)
Dunhill Championship	Charl Schwartzel

CHAMPIONS TOUR

MasterCard Championship	Fuzzy Zoeller
Royal Caribbean Golf Classic	Bruce Fleisher
ACE Group Classic	Craig Stadler
Outback Steakhouse Pro-Am	Mark McNulty
MasterCard Classic	Ed Fiori
SBC Classic	Gil Morgan
Toshiba Senior Classic	Tom Purtzer
Blue Angels Classic	Tom Jenkins
Liberty Mutual Legends of Golf	Hale Irwin
Bruno's Memorial Classic	Bruce Fleisher (2)
FedEx Kinko's Classic	Larry Nelson
Allianz Championship	D.A. Weibring
Senior PGA Championship	Hale Irwin (2)
Farmers Charity Classic	Jim Thorpe
Bayer Advantage Celebrity Pro-Am	Allen Doyle
Bank of America Championship	Craig Stadler (2)
Commerce Bank Long Island Classic	Jim Thorpe (2)
Ford Senior Players Championship	Mark James
U.S. Senior Open	Peter Jacobsen
3M Championship	Tom Kite
Greater Hickory Classic at Rock Barn	Doug Tewell
JELD-WEN Tradition	Craig Stadler (3)
The First Tee Open at Pebble Beach	Craig Stadler (4)
Kroger Classic	Bruce Summerhays
SAS Championship	Craig Stadler (5)
Constellation Energy Classic	Wayne Levi
Administaff Small Business Classic	Larry Nelson (2)
SBC Championship	Mark McNulty (2)
Charles Schwab Cup Championship	Mark McNulty (3)

EUROPEAN SENIORS TOUR

Tobago Plantations Seniors Classic	Carl Mason
DGM Barbados Open	Gavan Levenson
Open de France Seniors	Bob Cameron
Bosch Italian Seniors Open	Terry Gale
Digicel Jamaica Classic	Luis Carbonetti
AIB Irish Seniors Open	Carl Mason (2)
Irvine Whitlock Jersey Seniors Classic	Jim Rhodes
The Mobile Cup	Bill Longmuir
De Vere Northumberland Seniors Classic	Malcolm Gregson
Ryder Cup Wales Seniors Open	Ray Carrasco
Nigel Mansell Sunseeker International Classic	Seiji Ebihara
Senior British Open	Pete Oakley
Bad Ragaz PGA Seniors Open	Horacio Carbonetti
De Vere PGA Seniors Championship	Carl Mason (3)
Travis Perkins Senior Masters	Sam Torrance
Charles Church Scottish Seniors Open	Bill Longmuir (2)
Bovis Lend Lease European Senior Masters	Luis Carbonetti (2)
Daily Telegraph Turismo Andaluz Match Play	Carl Mason (4)
ADT English Seniors Open	Carl Mason (5)
Sanremo Masters	Bob Cameron (2)
Estoril Seniors Tour Championship	John Chillas

JAPAN SENIOR TOUR

Castle Hill Open	Katsunari Takahashi
Aderans Wellness Open	Toyoyake Nakao
PGA Philanthropy Rebornest Senior Open	Shuichi Sato
Fancl Senior Classic	Yuichi Yokoshima
Japan PGA Senior Championship	Takaaki Fukuzawa
Japan Senior Open Championship	Katsunari Takahashi (2)

U.S. LPGA TOUR

Welch's/Fry's Championship	Karen Stupples
Safeway International	Annika Sorenstam (2)
Kraft Nabisco Championship	Grace Park
Office Depot Championship	Annika Sorenstam (3)
LPGA Takefuji Classic	Cristie Kerr
Chick-Fil-A Charity Championship	Jennifer Rosales
Michelob Ultra Open at Kingsmill	Se Ri Pak
Franklin American Mortgage Championship	Lorena Ochoa
Sybase Classic	Sherri Steinhauer
LPGA Corning Classic	Annika Sorenstam (4)
Kellogg-Keebler Classic	Karrie Webb
McDonald's LPGA Championship	Annika Sorenstam (5)
ShopRite LPGA Classic	Cristie Kerr (2)
Wegmans Rochester LPGA	Kim Saiki
U.S. Women's Open	Meg Mallon
BMO Financial Group Canadian Women's Open	Meg Mallon (2)
Giant Eagle LPGA Classic	Moira Dunn
Jamie Farr Owens Corning Classic	Meg Mallon (3)
Wendy's Championship for Children	Catriona Matthew
Wachovia LPGA Classic	Lorena Ochoa (2)
State Farm Classic	Cristie Kerr (3)
John Q. Hammons Hotel Classic	Annika Sorenstam (7)
Safeway Classic	Hee-Won Han
Longs Drugs Challenge	Christina Kim
Asahi Ryokuken International	Liselotte Neumann
Samsung World Championship	Annika Sorenstam (8)
CJ Nine Bridges Classic	Grace Park (2)
The Mitchell Company Tournament of Champions	Heather Daly-Donofrio
ADT Championship	Annika Sorenstam (10)

LADIES EUROPEAN TOUR

Tenerife Ladies Open	Diana Luna
Ladies Open of Portugal	Cecilia Ekelundh
Union Fenosa Open de Espana Xacobeo	Stephanie Arricau
BMW Ladies Italian Open	Ana Belen Sanchez
Arras Open de France Dames	Stephanie Arricau (2)
KLM Ladies Open	Elisabeth Esterl
Ladies English Open	Maria Hjorth
OTP Bank Ladies Central European Open	Minea Blomqvist (3)
Evian Masters	Wendy Doolan
Weetabix Women's British Open	Karen Stupples (2)
HP Open	Annika Sorenstam (6)
Wales "Golf as it should be" Ladies Open	Trish Johnson
Catalonia Ladies Masters	Karine Icher

JAPAN LPGA TOUR

Daikin Orchid Ladies	Ai Miyazato
Saishunkan Ladies Hinokuni Open	Yuri Fudoh
Katokichi Queens	Hsiao-Chuan Lu
Nichirei Cup World Ladies	Rui Kitada
Vernal Ladies	Yuri Fudoh (2)
Chukyo TV Bridgestone Ladies Open	Yuko Saitoh
Kosaido Ladies Golf Cup	Yuri Fudoh (3)
Resort Trust Ladies	Hiromi Mogi
We Love Kobe Suntory Ladies Open	Ai Miyazato (2)
Apita Circle K Sankus Ladies	Ai Miyazato (3)
Promise Ladies	Kasumi Fujii
Belluna Ladies Cup	Mitsuko Kawasaki
Chateaureze Queens Cup	Akiko Fukushima
Stanley Ladies	Yuri Fudoh (4)
Golf 5 Ladies	Yuri Fudoh (5)
NEC Karuizawa 72	Rui Kitada (2)
New Caterpillar Mitsubishi Ladies	Toshimi Kimura
Yonex Ladies	Yukari Baba
Fujisankei Ladies Classic	Kasumi Fujii (2)
Japan LPGA Championship	Kaori Higo
Munsingwear Ladies Tokai Classic	Hiromi Mogi (2)
Miyagi TV Cup Dunlop Ladies Open	Yoko Yamagishi
Japan Women's Open	Yuri Fudoh (6)
Sankyo Ladies Open	Rui Kitada (3)
Fujitsu Ladies	Michiko Hattori
Masters Golf Club Ladies	Ai Miyazato (4)
Hisako Higuchi Hall of Fame Commemoration	Miho Koga
Mizuno Classic	Annika Sorenstam (9)
Itoen Ladies	Yuriko Ohtsuka
Daioseishi Elleair Ladies Open	Ai Miyazato (5)
Japan LPGA Tour Championship	Yuri Fudoh (7)

AUSTRALIAN WOMEN'S TOUR

ABC Learning Centres Ladies Classic	Mardi Lunn
ANZ Ladies Masters	Annika Sorenstam
AAMI Women's Australian Open	Laura Davies

NEDBANK WOMEN'S TOUR OF SOUTH AFRICA

Acer Women's South African Open	*Ashleigh Simon
Pam Golding Ladies International	Minea Blomqvist
Telkom Women's Classic	Minea Blomqvist (2)
Nedbank Women's South African Masters	Helena Alterby

Multiple Winners of 2004

PLAYER	WINS	PLAYER	WINS
Annika Sorenstam	10	Todd Hamilton	2
Vijay Singh	9	David Hearn	2
Yuri Fudoh	7	S.K. Ho	2
Ernie Els	6	Trevor Immelman	2
Miguel Angel Jimenez	5	Hale Irwin	2
Carl Mason	5	Shingo Katayama	2
Ai Miyazato	5	Matthew King	2
Craig Stadler	5	Philippe Lima	2
Retief Goosen	4	Peter Lonard	2
Thomas Aiken	3	Bill Longmuir	2
Minea Blomqvist	3	Andrew McLardy	2
Luke Donald	3	Hiromi Mogi	2
Sergio Garcia	3	Lorena Ochoa	2
Brendan Jones	3	Grace Park	2
Cristie Kerr	3	Terry Pilkadaris	2
Rui Kitada	3	D.A. Points	2
Meg Mallon	3	Adam Scott	2
Mark McNulty	3	Paul Sheehan	2
Phil Mickelson	3	Kevin Stadler	2
Larry Nelson	3	Graeme Storm	2
Stephen Woodard	3	Karen Stupples	2
Tiger Woods	3	Brad Sutterfield	2
Stephanie Arricau	2	Katsunari Takahashi	2
Bob Cameron	2	Toru Taniguchi	2
Luis Carbonetti	2	Thongchia Jaidee	2
Marc Cayeux	2	Jim Thorpe	2
Daniel Chopra	2	Bradford Vaughan	2
Stewart Cink	2	Jimmy Walker	2
Erik Compton	2	Charles Warren	2
Bruce Fleisher	2	Chris Wisler	2
Kasumi Fujii	2	Y.E. Yang	2

World Money List

This list of the 400 leading money winners in the world of professional golf in 2004 was compiled from the results of men's (excluding seniors) tournaments carried in the Appendixes of this edition. This list includes tournaments with a minimum of 36 holes and four contestants and does not include such competitions as skins games, pro-ams and shootouts.

In the 39 years during which World Money Lists have been compiled, the earnings of the player in the 200th position have risen from a total of $3,326 in 1966 to $524,905 in 2004. The top 200 players in 1966 earned a total of $4,680,287. In 2004, the comparable total was $308,780,682.

The world money list of the International Federation of PGA Tours was used for the official money list events of the U.S. PGA Tour, PGA European Tour, PGA Tour of Japan, Asian Tour, Southern Africa Tour and PGA Tour of Australasia. The conversion rates used for 2004 for other events and other tours were: Euro = US$1.22; British pound = US$1.81; Japanese yen = US$0.00909; South African rand = US$0.154; Australian dollar = US$0.77; Canadian dollar = US$0.75.

POS.	PLAYER, COUNTRY	TOTAL MONEY
1	Vijay Singh, Fiji	$11,638,699
2	Ernie Els, South Africa	9,368,386
3	Tiger Woods, USA	7,069,407
4	Retief Goosen, South Africa	6,589,631
5	Phil Mickelson, USA	6,184,823
6	Padraig Harrington, Ireland	5,008,167
7	Stewart Cink, USA	4,680,554
8	Sergio Garcia, Spain	4,656,917
9	Adam Scott, Australia	4,099,782
10	Stuart Appleby, Australia	3,802,507
11	Todd Hamilton, USA	3,679,986
12	Jay Haas, USA	3,641,046
13	Stephen Ames, Trinidad & Tobago	3,458,205
14	Chris DiMarco, USA	3,431,842
15	Miguel Angel Jimenez, Spain	3,410,906
16	Luke Donald, England	3,367,763
17	Davis Love, USA	3,312,592
18	Darren Clarke, N. Ireland	3,116,701
19	Mike Weir, Canada	2,934,788
20	Chad Campbell, USA	2,774,985
21	Steve Flesch, USA	2,757,540
22	Mark Hensby, Australia	2,752,176
23	Rory Sabbatini, South Africa	2,672,897
24	Lee Westwood, England	2,644,772
25	John Daly, USA	2,639,839
26	Jerry Kelly, USA	2,543,722
27	K.J. Choi, Korea	2,474,568
28	Paul Casey, England	2,459,721
29	Zach Johnson, USA	2,447,185
30	David Toms, USA	2,445,031
31	Shigeki Maruyama, Japan	2,419,105

POS.	PLAYER, COUNTRY	TOTAL MONEY
32	Scott Verplank, USA	2,413,092
33	Arron Oberholser, USA	2,355,433
34	Fred Funk, USA	2,317,481
35	Kenny Perry, USA	2,242,043
36	Thomas Levet, France	2,152,427
37	Graeme McDowell, N. Ireland	2,056,318
38	Carlos Franco, Paraguay	2,035,272
39	Ian Poulter, England	2,019,700
40	Angel Cabrera, Argentina	1,919,462
41	Fred Couples, USA	1,883,184
42	David Howell, England	1,872,387
43	Charles Howell, USA	1,865,860
44	Nick O'Hern, Australia	1,857,700
45	Rod Pampling, Australia	1,824,601
46	Trevor Immelman, South Africa	1,775,269
47	Robert Allenby, Australia	1,752,699
48	Tim Herron, USA	1,727,577
49	Justin Leonard, USA	1,718,523
50	Alex Cejka, Germany	1,706,278
51	Thomas Bjorn, Denmark	1,695,353
52	Jonathan Kaye, USA	1,695,332
53	Ted Purdy, USA	1,657,876
54	Jeff Maggert, USA	1,636,136
55	Jesper Parnevik, Sweden	1,633,730
56	Richard Green, Australia	1,598,423
57	Duffy Waldorf, USA	1,597,912
58	Ryan Palmer, USA	1,597,284
59	Bo Van Pelt, USA	1,584,558
60	Kirk Triplett, USA	1,575,076
61	Scott Hoch, USA	1,569,599
62	Fredrik Jacobson, Sweden	1,568,447
63	Colin Montgomerie, Scotland	1,538,155
64	Joey Sindelar, USA	1,536,881
65	Chris Riley, USA	1,525,984
66	Craig Parry, Australia	1,514,749
67	Tom Pernice, Jr., USA	1,502,274
68	Harrison Frazar, USA	1,496,764
69	Woody Austin, USA	1,495,980
70	Justin Rose, England	1,483,801
71	Joe Ogilvie, USA	1,483,363
72	Tom Lehman, USA	1,417,682
73	Stephen Gallacher, Scotland	1,409,568
74	Joakim Haeggman, Sweden	1,385,367
75	Paul McGinley, Ireland	1,384,583
76	Tim Petrovic, USA	1,383,691
77	Carl Pettersson, Sweden	1,367,962
78	Jeff Sluman, USA	1,360,135
79	Peter Lonard, Australia	1,358,815
80	Jean-Francois Remesy, France	1,315,839
81	Frank Lickliter, USA	1,299,234
82	Geoff Ogilvy, Australia	1,263,578
83	Brent Geiberger, USA	1,259,779
84	Tim Clark, South Africa	1,250,528
85	Bernhard Langer, Germany	1,235,605

POS.	PLAYER, COUNTRY	TOTAL MONEY
86	Patrick Sheehan, USA	1,234,344
87	Stephen Leaney, Australia	1,231,351
88	Kevin Na, Korea	1,229,947
89	Jim Furyk, USA	1,206,675
90	Skip Kendall, USA	1,206,438
91	Barry Lane, England	1,203,071
92	Steve Lowery, USA	1,191,245
93	Vaughn Taylor, USA	1,183,684
94	Daniel Chopra, Sweden	1,182,057
95	Scott Drummond, Scotland	1,169,205
96	Briny Baird, USA	1,156,517
97	Jonathan Byrd, USA	1,135,540
98	Hank Kuehne, USA	1,116,889
99	Bob Estes, USA	1,115,265
100	Loren Roberts, USA	1,111,177
101	Shingo Katayama, Japan	1,104,303
102	Shaun Micheel, USA	1,085,887
103	Brad Faxon, USA	1,071,898
104	Eduardo Romero, Argentina	1,070,381
105	Nick Price, Zimbabwe	1,068,841
106	Heath Slocum, USA	1,066,837
107	Y.E. Yang, Korea	1,044,204
108	Lee Janzen, USA	1,040,482
109	Ben Crane, USA	1,036,958
110	Brian Bateman, USA	1,029,255
111	Mark O'Meara, USA	1,025,455
112	Bob Tway, USA	1,014,053
113	Bart Bryant, USA	983,562
114	Corey Pavin, USA	963,767
115	Kevin Sutherland, USA	961,060
116	Hunter Mahan, USA	958,117
117	Toru Taniguchi, Japan	955,002
118	Joe Durant, USA	952,547
119	Robert Damron, USA	933,388
120	Raphael Jacquelin, France	932,066
121	Brett Quigley, USA	923,463
122	Simon Khan, England	921,716
123	Michael Campbell, New Zealand	920,165
124	J.J. Henry, USA	920,073
125	Anders Hansen, Denmark	919,507
126	David Lynn, England	918,231
127	Alastair Forsyth, Scotland	904,425
128	Michael Allen, Ireland	882,872
129	Scott McCarron, USA	881,220
130	Brian Davis, England	878,718
131	Paul Sheehan, New Zealand	877,078
132	Mark Calcavecchia, USA	876,444
133	John Huston, USA	874,280
134	Tom Byrum, USA	873,139
135	Henrik Stenson, Sweden	870,196
136	Todd Fischer, USA	861,496
137	Dudley Hart, USA	854,638
138	Tommy Armour, USA	853,284
139	Brendan Jones, Australia	850,787

POS.	PLAYER, COUNTRY	TOTAL MONEY
140	David Smail, New Zealand	839,403
141	Peter O'Malley, Australia	826,672
142	Hidemichi Tanaka, Japan	826,456
143	Matt Gogel, USA	823,617
144	Andre Stolz, Australia	821,780
145	Miles Tunnicliff, England	816,908
146	S.K. Ho, Korea	811,999
147	J.L. Lewis, USA	807,345
148	Cameron Beckman, USA	801,272
149	Jose Coceres, Argentina	779,196
150	Marcel Siem, Germany	773,476
151	Jose Maria Olazabal, Spain	773,038
152	John Rollins, USA	767,457
153	Brett Rumford, Australia	752,769
154	John Senden, Australia	748,487
155	Robert Gamez, USA	745,868
156	Thongchai Jaidee, Thailand	724,241
157	Pat Perez, USA	723,724
158	Neal Lancaster, USA	701,239
159	Phillip Price, Wales	695,782
160	Chris Smith, USA	692,785
161	Kent Jones, USA	683,559
162	Mathias Gronberg, Sweden	679,339
163	Billy Andrade, USA	678,643
164	Dennis Paulson, USA	677,035
165	Christian Cevaer, France	675,268
166	Brian Gay, USA	672,194
167	Paul Azinger, USA	671,438
168	Olin Browne, USA	671,334
169	Jay Williamson, USA	660,038
170	Aaron Baddeley, Australia	655,174
171	Peter Hanson, Sweden	652,589
172	Steve Allan, Australia	648,480
173	Stephen Dodd, Wales	639,306
174	Tag Ridings, USA	623,262
175	Terry Price, Australia	622,622
176	Matt Kuchar, USA	619,257
177	Jyoti Randhawa, India	617,685
178	Hideki Kase, Japan	605,339
179	Craig Barlow, USA	595,820
180	Paul Broadhurst, England	595,633
181	Notah Begay, USA	583,537
182	Bob Burns, USA	581,421
183	Takashi Kamiyama, Japan	575,029
184	Billy Mayfair, USA	574,501
185	Steven Conran, Australia	570,106
186	Jason Bohn, USA	569,821
187	Soren Kjeldsen, Denmark	568,329
188	Dean Wilson, USA	561,340
189	Keiichiro Fukabori, Japan	561,137
190	Carlos Rodiles, Spain	558,066
191	Lucas Glover, USA	557,454
192	Jose Manuel Lara, Spain	551,049
193	Marcus Fraser, South Africa	546,971

POS.	PLAYER, COUNTRY	TOTAL MONEY
194	Martin Maritz, South Africa	541,140
195	Scott Hend, Australia	536,989
196	James Kingston, South Africa	534,317
197	Ricardo Gonzalez, Argentina	533,917
198	Bill Haas, USA	532,854
199	Ben Curtis, USA	527,480
200	Brenden Pappas, South Africa	524,905
201	Hideto Tanihara, Japan	524,209
202	Glen Day, USA	519,935
203	Jonathan Lomas, England	516,939
204	Craig Bowden, USA	515,568
205	Tetsuji Hiratsuka, Japan	508,994
206	Jeff Brehaut, USA	508,914
207	Greg Chalmers, Australia	506,207
208	Ryoken Kawagishi, Japan	505,966
209	Tomohiro Kondo, Japan	504,222
210	David Park, Wales	500,289
211	John E. Morgan, England	499,010
212	Niclas Fasth, Sweden	498,373
213	Patrik Sjoland, Sweden	496,320
214	Bradley Dredge, Wales	494,586
215	Danny Ellis, USA	490,413
216	Toru Suzuki, Japan	488,685
217	Arjun Atwal, India	486,052
218	Robert-Jan Derksen, Netherlands	485,576
219	Nick Faldo, England	484,834
220	David Peoples, USA	479,464
221	Ian Woosnam, Wales	476,203
222	Hiroyuki Fujita, Japan	473,645
223	Charl Schwartzel, South Africa	471,691
224	Richard Johnson, Sweden	467,954
225	Prayad Marksaeng, Thailand	464,085
226	Paul Stankowski, USA	463,122
227	Dinesh Chand, Fiji	459,585
228	Maarten Lafeber, Netherlands	453,413
229	Craig Perks, New Zealand	447,998
230	Katsumasa Miyamoto, Japan	446,670
231	Darren Fichardt, South Africa	446,476
232	David Frost, South Africa	441,460
233	Steve Stricker, USA	440,906
234	Gregory Havret, France	438,135
235	Steve Webster, England	429,894
236	John Riegger, USA	423,263
237	Kaname Yokoo, Japan	412,233
238	Peter Senior, Australia	412,144
239	Louis Oosthuizen, South Africa	406,115
240	Danny Briggs, USA	400,206
241	Soren Hansen, Denmark	399,372
242	Markus Brier, Austria	396,516
243	Tom Carter, USA	395,780
244	Christopher Hanell, Sweden	394,041
245	Chawalit Plaphol, Thailand	391,616
246	Takuya Taniguchi, Japan	386,845
247	Richard Sterne, South Africa	384,608

POS.	PLAYER, COUNTRY	TOTAL MONEY
248	Peter Fowler, Australia	378,329
249	Spike McRoy, USA	377,687
250	Rocco Mediate, USA	373,942
251	Jimmy Walker, USA	371,346
252	Peter Hedblom, Sweden	369,948
253	Tatsuya Mitsuhashi, Japan	368,629
254	Yeh Wei-tze, Taiwan	364,744
255	Hidemasa Hoshino, Japan	360,026
256	D.J. Brigman, USA	356,943
257	Deane Pappas, South Africa	353,568
258	Bill Glasson, USA	347,693
259	Omar Uresti, USA	345,797
260	Kenneth Ferrie, England	344,478
261	Steven O'Hara, Scotland	341,615
262	Bradley Hughes, Australia	338,372
263	Nobuhiro Masuda, Japan	336,767
264	Mark Roe, England	335,973
265	Toshimitsu Izawa, Japan	335,813
266	D.A. Points, USA	335,565
267	Andrew Oldcorn, Scotland	335,484
268	Makoto Inoue, Japan	333,922
269	Kim Jong-duck, Korea	332,943
270	Jeev Milkha Singh, India	332,011
271	John Bickerton, England	331,526
272	Franklin Langham, USA	331,346
273	Gary Evans, England	330,902
274	Brad Kennedy, Australia	327,041
275	Gary Murphy, Ireland	327,011
276	Mark Wilson, USA	326,425
277	Kiyoshi Miyazato, Japan	325,311
278	Jason Dufner, USA	323,315
279	Anthony Wall, England	322,804
280	Katsumune Imai, Japan	321,209
281	Miguel Angel Martin, Spain	320,914
282	Simon Dyson, England	320,719
283	David McKenzie, Australia	316,223
284	Dan Forsman, USA	315,540
285	Hisayuki Sasaki, Japan	314,721
286	Ryuji Imada, Japan	313,185
287	Ken Duke, USA	312,074
288	Klas Eriksson, Sweden	307,881
289	Nick Watney, USA	307,038
290	Steve Elkington, Australia	306,988
291	Robert Coles, England	305,564
292	Peter Lawrie, Ireland	305,451
293	Sandy Lyle, England	301,431
294	Taichi Teshima, Japan	299,763
295	Pat Bates, USA	299,384
296	Paul Gow, Australia	295,993
297	David Branshaw, USA	295,005
298	Joel Kribel, USA	290,162
299	Raymond Russell, Scotland	287,420
300	Gene Sauers, USA	287,151
301	Stephen Scahill, New Zealand	286,828

POS.	PLAYER, COUNTRY	TOTAL MONEY
302	Andrew Marshall, England	286,697
303	Thammanoon Srirot, Thailand	284,384
304	Nobuhito Sato, Japan	284,137
305	Yasuharu Imano, Japan	283,620
306	James Driscoll, USA	281,161
307	Tsuyoshi Yoneyama, Japan	278,005
308	Kevin Stadler, USA	277,542
309	Damian McGrane, Ireland	275,399
310	Charles Warren, USA	275,138
311	Mark Foster, England	274,834
312	Justin Bolli, USA	273,387
313	Nick Dougherty, England	272,052
314	Rich Beem, USA	271,778
315	Kiyoshi Maita, Japan	271,557
316	Brandt Jobe, USA	270,953
317	Ryuichi Oda, Japan	268,882
318	Roland Thatcher, USA	267,252
319	Greg Owen, England	266,940
320	Mark Brooks, USA	266,451
321	Camilo Villegas, Colombia	264,729
322	Emanuele Canonica, Italy	264,065
323	Euan Walters, Australia	262,056
324	J.P. Hayes, USA	260,816
325	John Cook, USA	260,448
326	Zhang Lian-wei, China	259,937
327	Shinichi Yokota, Japan	259,690
328	Nozomi Kawahara, Japan	258,429
329	Cliff Kresge, USA	258,062
330	Tadahiro Takayama, Japan	257,531
331	Hal Sutton, USA	253,698
332	Brett Wetterich, USA	253,637
333	Gavin Coles, Australia	252,863
334	Aaron Barber, USA	251,320
335	Mikko Ilonen, Finland	249,013
336	Katsunori Kuwabara, Japan	247,781
337	Michael Long, New Zealand	242,042
338	Dicky Pride, USA	242,024
339	Liang Wen-chong, Taiwan	240,004
340	Grant Waite, New Zealand	239,318
341	Terry Pilkadaris, Australia	238,778
342	David Carter, England	235,041
343	Roger Tambellini, USA	234,164
344	Santiago Luna, Spain	233,741
345	Mamoru Osanai, Japan	232,395
346	Kazuhiko Hosokawa, Japan	232,174
347	Charlie Wi, Korea	230,742
348	Daisuke Maruyama, Japan	228,298
349	Christian Pena, USA	226,871
350	Jean-Francois Lucquin, France	226,824
351	Rich Barcelo, USA	225,577
352	Kiyoshi Murota, Japan	224,229
353	Wade Ormsby, Australia	223,453
354	Scott Laycock, Australia	219,415
355	David Sutherland, USA	218,123

POS.	PLAYER, COUNTRY	TOTAL MONEY
356	Len Mattiace, USA	217,207
357	Scott Gutschewski, USA	216,166
358	Thaworn Wiratchant, Thailand	215,865
359	Marten Olander, Sweden	213,152
360	Boonchu Ruangkit, Thailand	212,926
361	Darron Stiles, USA	212,894
362	Gary Emerson, England	212,243
363	Hunter Haas, USA	212,065
364	Mads Vibe-Hastrup, Denmark	210,225
365	Curtis Strange, USA	209,800
366	Kris Cox, USA	206,715
367	Jarmo Sandelin, Sweden	206,181
368	David Hearn, Canada	205,552
369	Chris Anderson, USA	203,794
370	Takashi Kanemoto, Japan	202,891
371	Fredrik Andersson, Sweden	201,276
372	Andrew McLardy, South Africa	200,787
373	Nathan Green, Australia	199,828
374	Naomichi Ozaki, Japan	199,653
375	Steve Pate, USA	199,569
376	Doug Barron, USA	198,882
377	Mathew Goggin, Australia	198,595
378	Chris Tidland, USA	196,251
379	Kyle Thompson, USA	195,935
380	Katsuyoshi Tomori, Japan	192,556
381	Scott Simpson, USA	190,986
382	Jay Delsing, USA	190,184
383	Rolf Muntz, Netherlands	189,837
384	Philippe Lima, France	189,086
385	Shane Bertsch, USA	189,046
386	Charley Hoffman, USA	185,379
387	Russ Cochran, USA	185,108
388	Ricky Barnes, USA	184,057
389	Jarrod Moseley, Australia	183,900
390	Brandt Snedeker, USA	183,573
391	Robert Karlsson, Sweden	183,438
392	Tsuneyuki Nakajima, Japan	183,414
393	D.J. Trahan, USA	183,030
394	Rob Rashell, USA	181,507
395	Simon Yates, Scotland	180,297
396	Alessandro Tadini, Italy	179,332
397	Yoshiaki Mano, Japan	178,844
398	Jason Caron, USA	177,629
399	Craig Jones, Australia	177,597
400	Simon Wakefield, England	175,619

World Money List Leaders

YEAR	PLAYER, COUNTRY	TOTAL MONEY
1966	Jack Nicklaus, USA	$168,088
1967	Jack Nicklaus, USA	276,166
1968	Billy Casper, USA	222,436
1969	Frank Beard, USA	186,993
1970	Jack Nicklaus, USA	222,583
1971	Jack Nicklaus, USA	285,897
1972	Jack Nicklaus, USA	341,792
1973	Tom Weiskopf, USA	349,645
1974	Johnny Miller, USA	400,255
1975	Jack Nicklaus, USA	332,610
1976	Jack Nicklaus, USA	316,086
1977	Tom Watson, USA	358,034
1978	Tom Watson, USA	384,388
1979	Tom Watson, USA	506,912
1980	Tom Watson, USA	651,921
1981	Johnny Miller, USA	704,204
1982	Raymond Floyd, USA	738,699
1983	Seve Ballesteros, Spain	686,088
1984	Seve Ballesteros, Spain	688,047
1985	Bernhard Langer, Germany	860,262
1986	Greg Norman, Australia	1,146,584
1987	Ian Woosnam, Wales	1,793,268
1988	Seve Ballesteros, Spain	1,261,275
1989	David Frost, South Africa	1,650,230
1990	Jose Maria Olazabal, Spain	1,633,640
1991	Bernhard Langer, Germany	2,186,700
1992	Nick Faldo, England	2,748,248
1993	Nick Faldo, England	2,825,280
1994	Ernie Els, South Africa	2,862,854
1995	Corey Pavin, USA	2,746,340
1996	Colin Montgomerie, Scotland	3,071,442
1997	Colin Montgomerie, Scotland	3,366,900
1998	Tiger Woods, USA	2,927,946
1999	Tiger Woods, USA	7,681,625
2000	Tiger Woods, USA	11,034,530
2001	Tiger Woods, USA	7,771,562
2002	Tiger Woods, USA	8,292,188
2003	Vijay Singh, Fiji	8,499,611
2004	Vijay Singh, Fiji	11,638,699

Career World Money List

Here is a list of the 50 leading money winners for their careers through the 2004 season. It includes players active on both the regular and senior tours of the world. The World Money List from this and the 38 previous editions of the annual and a table prepared for a companion book, *The Wonderful World of Professional Golf* (Atheneum, 1973) form the basis for this compilation. Additional figures were taken from official records of major golf associations, although shortcomings in records-keeping outside the United States in the 1950s and 1960s and a few exclusions from U.S. records during those years prevent these figures from being completely accurate, although the careers of virtually all of these top 50 players began after that time. Conversion of foreign currency figures to U.S. dollars is based on average values during the particular years involved.

POS.	PLAYER, COUNTRY	TOTAL MONEY
1	Tiger Woods, USA	$55,452,437
2	Ernie Els, South Africa	49,822,769
3	Vijay Singh, Fiji	46,554,712
4	Davis Love, USA	37,439,036
5	Phil Mickelson, USA	32,223,742
6	Hale Irwin, USA	30,739,017
7	Nick Price, Zimbabwe	29,865,440
8	Colin Montgomerie, Scotland	29,141,298
9	Bernhard Langer, Germany	25,928,285
10	Fred Couples, USA	25,775,335
11	Greg Norman, Australia	23,937,082
12	Retief Goosen, South Africa	23,572,634
13	Scott Hoch, USA	23,321,205
14	Jim Furyk, USA	22,596,568
15	Tom Kite, USA	22,419,143
16	Masashi Ozaki, Japan	21,703,563
17	Gil Morgan, USA	21,216,043
18	Mark Calcavecchia, USA	20,913,089
19	Tom Lehman, USA	20,840,193
20	David Toms, USA	20,663,616
21	Darren Clarke, N. Ireland	20,349,194
22	Sergio Garcia, Spain	20,296,772
23	Nick Faldo, England	20,030,383
24	Justin Leonard, USA	19,826,336
25	David Duval, USA	19,774,559
26	Raymond Floyd, USA	19,591,722
27	Mark O'Meara, USA	19,386,682
28	Tom Watson, USA	19,315,092
29	Padraig Harrington, Ireland	19,261,853
30	Jose Maria Olazabal, Spain	19,030,639
31	Larry Nelson, USA	18,639,199
32	Brad Faxon, USA	18,537,301
33	Jeff Sluman, USA	18,194,537
34	Ian Woosnam, Wales	17,756,099
35	Lee Westwood, England	17,536,095
36	Isao Aoki, Japan	17,471,436
37	Jay Haas, USA	17,200,611

POS.	PLAYER, COUNTRY	TOTAL MONEY
38	Kenny Perry, USA	17,197,283
39	Lee Trevino, USA	17,153,663
40	Craig Stadler, USA	17,124,248
41	Mike Weir, Canada	17,102,557
42	David Frost, South Africa	16,552,233
43	Fred Funk, USA	16,536,339
44	Hal Sutton, USA	16,277,916
45	Shigeki Maruyama, Japan	15,749,556
46	Stuart Appleby, Australia	15,616,512
47	Paul Azinger, USA	15,600,251
48	Stuart Cink, USA	15,597,008
49	Chris DiMarco, USA	15,432,693
50	Robert Allenby, Australia	15,405,596

These 50 players have won $1,117,669,572 in their careers.

Senior World Money List

This list includes official earnings from the world money list of the International Federation of PGA Tours, U.S. Senior PGA Tour, European Seniors Tour and Japan Senior Tour, along with other winnings in established unofficial events when reliable figures could be obtained.

POS.	PLAYER, COUNTRY	TOTAL MONEY
1	Craig Stadler, USA	$2,681,041
2	Hale Irwin, USA	2,228,397
3	Tom Kite, USA	2,058,315
4	Larry Nelson, USA	1,628,224
5	Gil Morgan, USA	1,606,453
6	Bruce Fleisher, USA	1,537,571
7	Mark McNulty, Zimbabwe	1,528,988
8	D.A. Weibring, USA	1,413,795
9	Jim Thorpe, USA	1,378,343
10	Peter Jacobsen, USA	1,331,041
11	Allen Doyle, USA	1,298,555
12	Wayne Levi, USA	1,272,227
13	Doug Tewell, USA	1,179,440
14	Dana Quigley, USA	1,155,649
15	Tom Purtzer, USA	1,149,447
16	Tom Jenkins, USA	1,138,843
17	Morris Hatalsky, USA	1,066,506
18	Jerry Pate, USA	1,006,740
19	Mark James, England	952,289
20	Graham Marsh, Australia	926,694
21	Jose Maria Canizares, Spain	905,989
22	Bruce Lietzke, USA	838,874
23	Bruce Summerhays, USA	832,442

POS.	PLAYER, COUNTRY	TOTAL MONEY
24	Jay Sigel, USA	813,107
25	Bob Gilder, USA	791,452
26	Fuzzy Zoeller, USA	787,838
27	Andy Bean, USA	777,361
28	David Eger, USA	773,443
29	Ed Fiori, USA	689,420
30	Bobby Wadkins, USA	676,461
31	Vicente Fernandez, Argentina	657,367
32	Tom Watson, USA	635,553
33	Dave Stockton, USA	605,673
34	Walter Hall, USA	576,425
35	Rodger Davis, Australia	567,843
36	John Harris, USA	557,479
37	Des Smyth, Ireland	536,904
38	Carl Mason, England	532,829
39	Lonnie Nelson, USA	529,262
40	Don Pooley, USA	524,974
41	Raymond Floyd, USA	521,312
42	John Bland, South Africa	516,605
43	John Jacobs, USA	508,682
44	Gary McCord, USA	497,325
45	Gary Koch, USA	485,129
46	Jim Ahern, USA	463,243
47	Dave Barr, Canada	436,531
48	Sam Torrance, Scotland	425,159
49	Dave Eichelberger, USA	422,755
50	Joe Inman, USA	420,051
51	Pete Oakley, USA	403,268
52	J.C. Snead, USA	378,261
53	Mike McCullough, USA	370,263
54	John Chillas, Scotland	366,304
55	Isao Aoki, Japan	351,183
56	Mike Hill, USA	339,355
57	Hugh Baiocchi, South Africa	327,791
58	Bob Charles, New Zealand	323,937
59	Keith Fergus, USA	321,717
60	Jim Dent, USA	295,750
61	Stewart Ginn, Australia	294,425
62	Bill Longmuir, Scotland	292,635
63	Sammy Rachels, USA	290,030
64	Fred Gibson, USA	285,924
65	Tom Wargo, USA	272,876
66	Seiji Ebihara, Japan	260,896
67	James Mason, USA	256,929
68	Bobby Lincoln, South Africa	249,952
69	David Good, Australia	234,275
70	Jim Colbert, USA	232,522
71	Bob Cameron, England	230,936
72	Leonard Thompson, USA	228,672
73	Bob Murphy, USA	224,572
74	Bobby Walziel, USA	219,682
75	Luis Carbonetti, Argentina	215,367
76	Katsunari Takahashi, Japan	206,955
77	Yuichi Yokoshima, Japan	206,734

POS.	PLAYER, COUNTRY	TOTAL MONEY
78	Eamonn Darcy, Ireland	202,255
79	Mark McCumber, USA	200,020
80	Mike Reid, USA	190,824
81	Bob Eastwood, USA	189,578
82	Terry Gale, Australia	188,602
83	Ray Carrasco, USA	183,421
84	Jim Rhodes, England	182,429
85	David Oakley, USA	181,424
86	Mike Smith, USA	180,999
87	Giuseppe Cali, Italy	177,913
88	Hajime Meshiai, Japan	177,728
89	Gary Player, South Africa	171,287
90	Jack Spradlin, USA	163,875
91	Bill Rogers, USA	161,702
92	Nick Job, England	161,508
93	Lee Trevino, USA	159,435
94	Jim Albus, USA	155,145
95	Takaaki Fukuzawa, Japan	153,899
96	Simon Owen, New Zealand	135,299
97	Mark Johnson, USA	134,261
98	Mark Lye, USA	132,463
99	Denis Durnian, England	132,005
100	Jay Overton, USA	131,465
101	Toyotake Nakao, Japan	129,173
102	Lanny Wadkins, USA	125,604
103	Ed Dougherty, USA	125,074
104	Rocky Thompson, USA	124,834
105	Dale Douglass, USA	123,781
106	Martin Gray, Scotland	122,073
107	Darrell Kestner, USA	121,873
108	Tateo Ozaki, Japan	119,788
109	Noel Ratcliffe, Australia	118,781
110	Delroy Cambridge, Jamaica	118,184
111	Horacio Carbonetti, Argentina	117,225
112	Jack Nicklaus, USA	116,594
113	Gavan Levenson, South Africa	115,581
114	R.W. Eaks, USA	114,135
115	Charles Coody, USA	113,416
116	Ben Crenshaw, USA	113,343
117	John Grace, USA	109,434
118	David J. Russell, England	108,636
119	Arnold Palmer, USA	105,312
120	Terry Dill, USA	104,320
121	Gery Watine, France	103,363
122	Gibby Gilbert, USA	103,005
123	Howard Twitty, USA	97,037
124	Guillermo Encina, Chile	93,176
125	Mike Miller, Scotland	92,916

Women's World Money List

This list includes official earnings on the U.S. LPGA Tour, Ladies European Tour and Japan LPGA Tour, along with other winnings in established unofficial events when reliable figures could be obtained.

POS.	PLAYER, COUNTRY	TOTAL MONEY
1	Annika Sorenstam, Sweden	$2,746,824
2	Grace Park, Korea	1,525,471
3	Lorena Ochoa, Mexico	1,450,824
4	Meg Mallon, USA	1,358,623
5	Yuri Fudoh, Japan	1,297,816
6	Cristie Kerr, USA	1,189,990
7	Ai Miyazato, Japan	1,117,819
8	Karen Stupples, England	1,043,064
9	Mi-Hyun Kim, Korea	931,693
10	Hee-Won Han, Korea	840,605
11	Karrie Webb, Australia	779,439
12	Jennifer Rosales, Philippines	730,393
13	Se Ri Pak, Korea	697,213
14	Jeong Jang, Korea	680,080
15	Juli Inkster, USA	654,967
16	Catriona Matthew, Scotland	650,444
17	Christina Kim, USA	636,490
18	Shi Hyun Ahn, Korea	628,804
19	Rui Kitada, Japan	627,373
20	Rachel Teske, Australia	626,753
21	Carin Koch, Sweden	626,055
22	Candie Kung, Taiwan	600,713
23	Wendy Doolan, Australia	597,481
24	Toshimi Kimura, Japan	587,241
25	Kaori Higo, Japan	563,332
26	Michie Ohba, Japan	563,241
27	Lorie Kane, Canada	530,078
28	Laura Davies, England	519,584
29	Pat Hurst, USA	491,227
30	Kim Saiki, USA	490,747
31	Michele Redman, USA	473,886
32	Rosie Jones, USA	473,616
33	Becky Morgan, Wales	468,235
34	Laura Diaz, USA	465,700
35	Gloria Park, Korea	464,543
36	Kasumi Fujii, Japan	439,516
37	Junko Omote, Japan	438,499
38	Miho Koga, Japan	436,805
39	Akiko Fukushima, Japan	436,616
40	Aree Song, Thailand	426,327
41	Beth Daniel, USA	419,610
42	Michiko Hattori, Japan	387,985
43	Stacy Prammanasudh, USA	381,333
44	Wendy Ward, USA	378,915
45	Sherri Steinhauer, USA	376,795

POS.	PLAYER, COUNTRY	TOTAL MONEY
46	Woo-Soon Ko, Korea	376,355
47	Shiho Ohyama, Japan	368,797
48	Jung Yeon Lee, Korea	360,672
49	Hiromi Mogi, Japan	357,402
50	Moira Dunn, USA	355,024
51	Midori Yoneyama, Japan	350,532
52	Kelly Robbins, USA	324,868
53	Hsiao-Chuan Lu, Taiwan	321,303
54	Patricia Meunier-Lebouc, France	319,070
55	Liselotte Neumann, Sweden	311,543
56	Mikiyo Nishizuka, Japan	303,086
57	Angela Stanford, USA	297,790
58	Heather Bowie, USA	280,572
59	Seol-An Jeon, Korea	280,166
60	Natalie Gulbis, USA	277,093
61	Hiroko Yamaguchi, Japan	273,462
62	Young Kim, Korea	264,072
63	Mitsuko Kawasaki, Japan	262,228
64	Soo-Yun Kang, Korea	260,608
65	Brandie Burton, USA	256,189
66	Giulia Sergas, Italy	244,420
67	Janice Moodie, Scotland	243,910
68	Heather Daly-Donofrio, USA	243,734
69	Dorothy Delasin, USA	241,826
70	Yuriko Ohtsuka, Japan	241,364
71	Jill McGill, USA	240,331
72	Yuko Saitoh, Japan	232,487
73	Yukari Baba, Japan	225,239
74	Tina Barrett, USA	220,728
75	Michelle Estill, USA	217,933
76	Kate Golden, USA	215,463
77	Jamie Hullett, USA	212,667
78	Ashli Bunch, USA	212,659
79	Stephanie Arricau, France	208,795
80	Chieko Amanuma, Japan	208,739
81	Helen Alfredsson, Sweden	207,317
82	Suzann Pettersen, Norway	202,214
83	Michelle Ellis, Australia	201,662
84	Yun-Jye Wei, Taiwan	197,191
85	Trish Johnson, England	196,836
86	Dawn Coe-Jones, Canada	195,151
87	Young-A Yang, Korea	191,124
88	Kelli Kuehne, USA	188,312
89	Keiko Sasaki, Japan	181,519
90	Sophie Gustafson, Sweden	180,429
91	Vicki Goetze-Ackerman, USA	179,199
92	Siew-Ai Lim, Malaysia	177,377
93	Nadina Taylor, Australia	175,753
94	Paula Marti, Spain	165,636
95	Candy Hannemann, Brazil	164,527
96	Reilley Rankin, USA	162,987
97	Silvia Cavalleri, Italy	162,141
98	Yasuko Satoh, Japan	161,721
99	Tammie Green, USA	161,298

POS.	PLAYER, COUNTRY	TOTAL MONEY
100	Johanna Head, England	160,193
101	Sakura Yokomine, Japan	157,690
102	Katherine Hull, Australia	156,760
103	Donna Andrews, USA	152,321
104	Jean Bartholomew, USA	146,555
105	Kristi Albers, USA	144,429
106	Noriko Aso, Japan	144,425
107	Yuka Sakaguchi, Japan	144,086
108	Karine Icher, France	143,377
109	Michiko Mitsui, Japan	142,899
110	Minea Blomqvist, Finland	142,248
111	Jackie Gallagher-Smith, USA	140,698
112	Yuka Shiroto, Japan	140,553
113	Emilee Klein, USA	140,320
114	Nancy Scranton, USA	140,299
115	Riko Higashio, Japan	139,944
116	Asa Gottmo, Sweden	137,970
117	Kaori Suzuki, Japan	137,600
118	Leta Lindley, USA	136,144
119	Nikki Campbell, Canada	135,956
120	Yoko Yamagishi, Japan	131,344
121	Betsy King, USA	126,966
122	Hsiu-Feng Tseng, Taiwan	125,638
123	Chihiro Nakajima, Japan	125,457
124	Kaori Harada, Japan	124,408
125	Samantha Head, England	122,822
126	Isabelle Beisiegel, Canada	120,586
127	Fuki Kido, Japan	120,192
128	Catherine Cartwright, USA	120,171
129	Marcy Hart, USA	119,814
130	Deb Richard, USA	119,239
131	Fumiko Muraguchi, Japan	118,297
132	Mhairi McKay, Scotland	116,371
133	Ana Belen Sanchez, Spain	115,605
134	Cecilia Ekelundh, Sweden	114,929
135	Shani Waugh, Australia	113,199
136	Yu Ping Lin, Taiwan	111,844
137	A.J. Eathorne, Canada	111,698
138	Yuka Irie, Japan	109,142
139	Soo Young Moon, Korea	105,545
140	Becky Brewerton, Wales	105,260
141	Seiko Watanabe, Japan	105,176
142	Martina Eberl, Germany	103,524
143	Joanne Mills, Australia	102,951
144	Stephanie Louden, USA	102,457
145	Kuniko Maeda, Japan	100,921
146	Ji-Hee Lee, Korea	100,514
147	Linda Wessberg, Sweden	100,288
148	Iben Tinning, Denmark	100,140
149	Ji-Yeon Han, Korea	99,522
150	Lynnette Brooky, New Zealand	98,913

American Tours

Mercedes Championships

Plantation Course at Kapalua, Maui, Hawaii
Par 36-37–73; 7,263 yards

January 8-11
purse, $5,300,000

	SCORES				TOTAL	MONEY
Stuart Appleby	66	67	66	71	270	$1,060,000
Vijay Singh	68	64	69	70	271	600,000
Darren Clarke	67	69	69	70	275	400,000
Tiger Woods	71	70	65	71	277	275,000
Retief Goosen	70	70	64	73	277	275,000
Kirk Triplett	68	69	71	70	278	204,000
Adam Scott	69	74	68	68	279	180,000
Scott Hoch	68	71	69	72	280	170,000
Davis Love	69	71	69	72	281	155,000
Ben Crane	71	74	66	70	281	155,000
Jim Furyk	70	71	68	74	283	140,000
Jonathan Kaye	74	70	66	74	284	130,000
Shaun Micheel	70	71	69	75	285	115,000
Justin Leonard	68	73	71	73	285	115,000
Tommy Armour	73	71	73	70	287	89,166.67
Peter Jacobsen	70	71	73	73	287	89,166.67
Kenny Perry	73	71	68	75	287	89,166.66
Steve Flesch	73	72	72	70	287	89,166.67
Chad Campbell	71	76	65	75	287	89,166.66
Shigeki Maruyama	69	72	72	74	287	89,166.67
Fred Couples	69	72	72	75	288	79,000
J.L. Lewis	70	71	69	78	288	79,000
Ernie Els	73	70	73	72	288	79,000
Mike Weir	71	70	73	75	289	75,000
Rory Sabbatini	73	74	74	70	291	73,000
John Huston	69	72	71	81	293	70,000
Frank Lickliter	73	76	70	74	293	70,000
Craig Stadler	73	78	68	75	294	67,500
Bob Tway	76	74	72	72	294	67,500
Ben Curtis	73	80	70	74	297	66,000

Sony Open in Hawaii

Waialae Country Club, Honolulu, Hawaii
Par 35-35–70; 7,060 yards

January 15-18
purse, $4,800,000

	SCORES				TOTAL	MONEY
Ernie Els	67	64	66	65	262	$864,000
Harrison Frazar	67	63	66	66	262	518,400
(Els defeated Frazar on third playoff hole.)						
Davis Love	70	65	63	67	265	326,400
Frank Lickliter	71	62	65	68	266	230,400
Jerry Kelly	68	65	69	65	267	182,400
Briny Baird	68	66	66	67	267	182,400
John Riegger	68	66	67	67	268	160,800

	SCORES				TOTAL	MONEY
Stephen Ames	66	70	65	68	269	144,000
Craig Barlow	66	69	66	68	269	144,000
Paul Azinger	67	66	66	71	270	110,400
John Huston	67	67	69	67	270	110,400
Vijay Singh	69	68	67	66	270	110,400
Omar Uresti	72	66	67	65	270	110,400
Retief Goosen	67	69	65	69	270	110,400
Craig Bowden	70	64	69	68	271	76,800
Jesper Parnevik	65	68	70	68	271	76,800
Brenden Pappas	67	69	69	66	271	76,800
Aaron Baddeley	66	72	67	66	271	76,800
Bo Van Pelt	71	65	67	68	271	76,800
Corey Pavin	68	67	66	71	272	50,057.14
Michael Allen	68	69	65	70	272	50,057.14
Shaun Micheel	72	64	68	68	272	50,057.14
Joe Durant	70	66	69	67	272	50,057.15
Carlos Franco	63	72	68	69	272	50,057.14
Chris Riley	69	69	67	67	272	50,057.15
Luke Donald	66	66	71	69	272	50,057.14
Robert Gamez	67	66	72	68	273	34,800
Cameron Beckman	70	69	66	68	273	34,800
Steve Allan	67	62	70	74	273	34,800
Charles Howell	68	68	69	68	273	34,800
Tim Herron	67	69	69	69	274	28,464
Mark Hensby	68	69	68	69	274	28,464
Ben Crane	68	70	68	68	274	28,464
Pat Perez	70	69	65	70	274	28,464
Jonathan Byrd	67	69	66	72	274	28,464
Bart Bryant	68	70	70	67	275	22,608
Fred Funk	69	64	74	68	275	22,608
Duffy Waldorf	70	67	68	70	275	22,608
Brian Gay	69	67	73	66	275	22,608
D.J. Brigman	69	65	72	69	275	22,608
Tommy Armour	72	67	70	67	276	16,800
Pat Bates	68	65	72	71	276	16,800
John Maginnes	68	68	69	71	276	16,800
Brent Geiberger	70	67	68	71	276	16,800
Shigeki Maruyama	71	67	69	69	276	16,800
Kevin Na	68	67	70	71	276	16,800
Jason Dufner	69	70	65	72	276	16,800
Olin Browne	70	68	73	66	277	12,064
Russ Cochran	69	69	71	68	277	12,064
Peter Jacobsen	69	70	69	69	277	12,064
Tjaart van der Walt	69	68	69	71	277	12,064
Hideto Tanihara	67	66	72	72	277	12,064
Ted Purdy	66	71	71	69	277	12,064
Danny Briggs	71	67	69	71	278	10,944
Jonathan Kaye	67	68	68	75	278	10,944
Rod Pampling	72	67	72	67	278	10,944
Andre Stolz	68	70	70	70	278	10,944
Kenichi Kuboya	73	66	70	69	278	10,944
David Ishii	66	71	74	68	279	10,464
Tom Lehman	72	67	71	69	279	10,464
Scott Simpson	70	66	73	70	279	10,464
Bob Burns	71	67	70	71	279	10,464
Ken Duke	70	69	68	72	279	10,464
Brad Lardon	69	69	69	73	280	9,648
Woody Austin	69	70	71	70	280	9,648
Todd Fischer	69	70	70	71	280	9,648
Hidemichi Tanaka	67	70	71	72	280	9,648

	SCORES				TOTAL	MONEY
John Senden	71	67	69	73	280	9,648
Arjun Atwal	71	68	68	73	280	9,648
Bobby Kalinowski	70	68	71	71	280	9,648
Joe Ogilvie	71	68	73	68	280	9,648
Ryan Palmer	70	66	70	74	280	9,648
Jason Bohn	69	66	72	73	280	9,648
Lucas Glover	71	68	74	67	280	9,648
Richard S. Johnson	68	67	71	74	280	9,648
Jeff Brehaut	69	69	71	72	281	9,024
Heath Slocum	67	71	72	73	283	8,928
Loren Roberts	71	68	75	70	284	8,832
Tom Carter	70	69	75	72	286	8,736

Bob Hope Chrysler Classic

PGA West, Palmer Course: Par 36-36–72; 6,930 yards
Indian Wells CC: Par 36-36–72; 6,478 yards
Bermuda Dunes CC: Par 36-36–72; 6,927 yards
La Quinta CC: Par 36-36–72; 7,060 yards
La Quinta, California

January 21-25
purse, $4,500,000

	SCORES					TOTAL	MONEY
Phil Mickelson	68	63	64	67	68	330	$810,000
Skip Kendall	63	68	68	66	65	330	486,000
(Mickelson defeated Kendall on first playoff hole.)							
Jay Haas	65	68	64	67	67	331	306,000
Jonathan Kaye	67	70	66	65	64	332	216,000
Kenny Perry	64	66	69	64	71	334	164,250
Jesper Parnevik	67	68	66	65	68	334	164,250
Ben Crane	68	64	65	69	68	334	164,250
Bernhard Langer	67	67	69	68	64	335	139,500
Paul Azinger	67	65	66	69	69	336	104,142.85
J.L. Lewis	68	68	69	64	67	336	104,142.86
Kirk Triplett	66	65	68	63	74	336	104,142.85
Kent Jones	69	65	68	68	66	336	104,142.86
Chris Riley	68	64	69	70	65	336	104,142.86
Rod Pampling	70	67	67	66	66	336	104,142.86
Harrison Frazar	73	67	66	63	67	336	104,142.86
Rocco Mediate	70	67	65	69	66	337	69,750
Mark O'Meara	72	69	67	65	64	337	69,750
Jeff Sluman	68	67	66	70	66	337	69,750
Steve Flesch	72	66	63	68	68	337	69,750
Loren Roberts	67	67	66	66	72	338	48,750
Scott Verplank	70	64	71	68	65	338	48,750
Duffy Waldorf	71	67	65	69	66	338	48,750
Stephen Ames	68	72	64	69	65	338	48,750
Geoff Ogilvy	69	67	63	71	68	338	48,750
Zach Johnson	66	67	70	66	69	338	48,750
Joe Durant	74	67	68	65	65	339	33,975
Dean Wilson	67	65	69	68	70	339	33,975
Danny Ellis	71	63	67	64	74	339	33,975
Retief Goosen	71	64	70	67	67	339	33,975
John Daly	68	68	65	72	67	340	27,337.50
John Riegger	69	63	71	70	67	340	27,337.50
Jerry Kelly	65	71	70	67	67	340	27,337.50
Justin Leonard	65	71	69	68	67	340	27,337.50
Joe Ogilvie	66	67	68	68	71	340	27,337.50

		SCORES				TOTAL	MONEY
Richard S. Johnson	66	70	64	68	72	340	27,337.50
Bob Estes	69	68	71	66	67	341	21,195
Lee Janzen	66	73	67	68	67	341	21,195
Tom Pernice, Jr.	70	65	68	69	69	341	21,195
Robert Damron	72	67	64	70	68	341	21,195
Stephen Leaney	69	71	67	68	66	341	21,195
Billy Andrade	69	68	71	63	71	342	16,200
Steve Pate	67	67	67	72	69	342	16,200
Bob Burns	68	69	63	71	71	342	16,200
Mike Weir	70	67	68	70	67	342	16,200
Notah Begay	68	66	67	71	70	342	16,200
John Senden	66	72	62	73	69	342	16,200
Marco Dawson	69	73	66	66	69	343	12,360
Paul Stankowski	68	69	69	69	68	343	12,360
Kevin Na	68	68	68	71	68	343	12,360
Robert Gamez	71	69	60	69	75	344	10,770
Peter Jacobsen	67	70	69	71	67	344	10,770
Michael Allen	70	67	68	71	68	344	10,770
Stewart Cink	71	68	68	70	67	344	10,770
Fredrik Jacobson	67	69	66	71	71	344	10,770
Carl Pettersson	74	69	69	64	68	344	10,770
Steve Elkington	68	70	68	71	68	345	10,035
Donnie Hammond	68	72	68	67	70	345	10,035
Neal Lancaster	70	69	68	70	68	345	10,035
Scott McCarron	76	64	69	65	71	345	10,035
Chad Campbell	70	68	70	67	70	345	10,035
Todd Fischer	68	67	63	70	77	345	10,035
Mark Calcavecchia	72	65	68	67	74	346	9,450
John Huston	70	70	66	68	72	346	9,450
Grant Waite	68	67	68	73	70	346	9,450
Kevin Sutherland	74	67	66	68	71	346	9,450
Spike McRoy	74	67	67	69	69	346	9,450
Chris Couch	66	67	70	70	73	346	9,450
Mathias Gronberg	67	66	71	73	69	346	9,450
Corey Pavin	70	71	68	68	70	347	8,955
Tim Petrovic	69	68	73	66	71	347	8,955
Per-Ulrik Johansson	67	74	64	68	74	347	8,955
J.J. Henry	72	70	70	65	70	347	8,955
Patrick Sheehan	69	69	72	66	72	348	8,730
Steve Lowery	73	70	69	65	72	349	8,595
Glen Hnatiuk	67	74	65	71	72	349	8,595
Cameron Beckman	72	68	69	68	73	350	8,415
Brenden Pappas	67	69	71	70	73	350	8,415
Ian Leggatt	73	70	68	65	75	351	8,280
Patrick Moore	72	71	68	66	76	353	8,190

FBR Open

TPC of Scottsdale, Scottsdale, Arizona
Par 35-36–71; 7,216 yards

January 29-February 1
purse, $5,200,000

		SCORES			TOTAL	MONEY
Jonathan Kaye	65	68	66	67	266	$936,000
Chris DiMarco	68	67	64	69	268	561,600
Vijay Singh	71	69	63	66	269	301,600
Steve Flesch	66	69	68	66	269	301,600
Duffy Waldorf	70	68	68	65	271	197,600

	SCORES				TOTAL	MONEY
Mike Weir	65	69	68	69	271	197,600
Phil Mickelson	64	68	68	72	272	167,700
Scott Verplank	63	70	70	69	272	167,700
Kevin Sutherland	72	65	68	68	273	130,000
Justin Leonard	69	67	66	71	273	130,000
Retief Goosen	70	68	68	67	273	130,000
Sergio Garcia	71	67	65	70	273	130,000
Fredrik Jacobson	68	68	67	70	273	130,000
Stephen Ames	72	64	69	69	274	78,115.55
Robert Allenby	71	68	68	67	274	78,115.56
Stewart Cink	69	70	67	68	274	78,115.55
Alex Cejka	70	67	68	69	274	78,115.55
Rod Pampling	66	71	69	68	274	78,115.56
Brenden Pappas	66	70	70	68	274	78,115.56
Heath Slocum	71	69	67	67	274	78,115.56
Bo Van Pelt	66	69	70	69	274	78,115.56
Ricky Barnes	67	67	68	72	274	78,115.55
Tom Lehman	71	69	66	69	275	54,080
Bob Tway	69	71	67	69	276	45,760
Tim Herron	72	70	68	66	276	45,760
Charles Howell	68	71	68	69	276	45,760
Bob Estes	68	72	66	71	277	36,140
Bernhard Langer	69	67	66	75	277	36,140
Jeff Sluman	66	67	71	73	277	36,140
Marco Dawson	71	69	68	69	277	36,140
Brandt Jobe	70	65	71	71	277	36,140
Glen Hnatiuk	68	71	69	69	277	36,140
Paul Azinger	71	66	70	71	278	27,473.34
Mark Calcavecchia	71	66	70	71	278	27,473.34
Jay Haas	68	72	67	71	278	27,473.33
Glen Day	72	68	67	71	278	27,473.33
Kent Jones	67	70	68	73	278	27,473.33
Chris Riley	66	69	75	68	278	27,473.33
Lee Janzen	68	67	70	74	279	22,360
Chad Campbell	70	70	70	69	279	22,360
Brent Geiberger	71	66	70	72	279	22,360
Tom Byrum	71	69	67	73	280	18,720
Jim Carter	72	69	69	70	280	18,720
Mark O'Meara	68	68	71	73	280	18,720
Joey Sindelar	70	70	69	71	280	18,720
J.P. Hayes	72	70	66	73	281	15,149.34
Arron Oberholser	75	66	70	70	281	15,149.33
Carl Pettersson	73	69	70	69	281	15,149.33
Steve Elkington	69	68	72	73	282	12,833.60
Tim Petrovic	68	73	70	71	282	12,833.60
Paul Stankowski	70	70	69	73	282	12,833.60
Jesper Parnevik	70	72	70	70	282	12,833.60
Carlos Franco	68	70	70	74	282	12,833.60
John Daly	71	70	71	71	283	11,908
Steve Lowery	70	70	70	73	283	11,908
Notah Begay	68	70	73	72	283	11,908
John Senden	69	71	73	70	283	11,908
Briny Baird	70	69	70	75	284	11,648
Tom Pernice, Jr.	69	72	70	74	285	11,388
John Riegger	71	69	71	74	285	11,388
Jeff Brehaut	70	70	73	72	285	11,388
Scott McCarron	66	72	68	79	285	11,388
Esteban Toledo	69	72	77	68	286	10,972
Steve Stricker	69	73	71	73	286	10,972
Shigeki Maruyama	73	66	77	70	286	10,972

	SCORES			TOTAL	MONEY
John Rollins	72	68	72	74	286	10,972
Tommy Armour	70	70	72	75	287	10,712
Fred Funk	69	73	76	72	290	10,556
Chris Smith	69	72	70	79	290	10,556
David Gossett	70	72	74	75	291	10,400

AT&T Pebble Beach National Pro-Am

Pebble Beach GL: Par 36-36–72; 6,816 yards
Poppy Hills GC: Par 36-36–72; 6,833 yards
Spyglass Hill GC: Par 36-36–72; 6,862 yards
Pebble Beach, California

February 5-8
purse, $5,300,000

	SCORES				TOTAL	MONEY
Vijay Singh	67	68	68	69	272	$954,000
Jeff Maggert	71	68	67	69	275	572,400
Phil Mickelson	68	68	71	69	276	360,400
Mike Weir	73	70	66	70	279	219,066.67
Arron Oberholser	69	67	67	76	279	219,066.66
K.J. Choi	67	70	71	71	279	219,066.67
Tom Pernice, Jr.	67	68	73	72	280	165,183.33
Jesper Parnevik	70	67	73	70	280	165,183.34
Mark Hensby	70	67	73	70	280	165,183.33
Bill Glasson	73	69	66	73	281	127,200
Corey Pavin	69	68	73	71	281	127,200
Scott McCarron	69	68	71	73	281	127,200
Kent Jones	67	71	74	69	281	127,200
Peter Jacobsen	70	71	70	71	282	95,400
Kirk Triplett	69	70	70	73	282	95,400
Todd Fischer	72	70	72	68	282	95,400
Mark Brooks	71	72	68	72	283	76,850
Phillip Price	67	70	69	77	283	76,850
Ted Purdy	68	73	70	72	283	76,850
Luke Donald	69	65	72	77	283	76,850
Tim Petrovic	71	71	70	72	284	57,240
Paul Stankowski	69	71	72	72	284	57,240
Arjun Atwal	72	70	72	70	284	57,240
Rich Barcelo	72	69	73	70	284	57,240
Fred Couples	70	71	73	71	285	37,126.50
Todd Hamilton	71	69	73	72	285	37,126.50
Tom Lehman	70	69	72	74	285	37,126.50
Brian Bateman	69	71	69	76	285	37,126.50
Woody Austin	69	71	72	73	285	37,126.50
Boyd Summerhays	69	74	70	72	285	37,126.50
Niclas Fasth	69	71	72	73	285	37,126.50
Daniel Chopra	71	71	68	75	285	37,126.50
Bo Van Pelt	72	68	73	72	285	37,126.50
Carl Pettersson	69	74	72	70	285	37,126.50
Craig Stadler	68	71	71	76	286	25,572.50
Willie Wood	72	70	71	73	286	25,572.50
Jerry Kelly	71	72	70	73	286	25,572.50
Craig Barlow	67	75	71	73	286	25,572.50
Charles Howell	69	73	72	72	286	25,572.50
Ryan Palmer	74	72	68	72	286	25,572.50
Jay Don Blake	71	74	70	72	287	18,550
Jay Delsing	73	66	73	75	287	18,550
David Edwards	74	68	72	73	287	18,550

	SCORES				TOTAL	MONEY
Loren Roberts	72	68	72	75	287	18,550
Greg Chalmers	71	70	72	74	287	18,550
J.J. Henry	65	70	75	77	287	18,550
Steve Friesen	69	70	73	75	287	18,550
Danny Briggs	70	70	74	74	288	13,320.66
Tom Byrum	74	68	72	74	288	13,320.67
John Senden	71	68	73	76	288	13,320.67
Mark Wilson	70	74	71	73	288	13,320.66
Joel Kribel	68	73	72	75	288	13,320.67
Matt Kuchar	65	74	74	75	288	13,320.67
David Sutherland	74	70	69	76	289	12,084
Kevin Sutherland	70	69	73	77	289	12,084
J.P. Hayes	72	70	73	74	289	12,084
Ken Duke	67	68	76	78	289	12,084
Joe Ogilvie	71	67	77	74	289	12,084
Neal Lancaster	72	72	71	75	290	11,713
Zach Johnson	71	71	72	76	290	11,713
Robert Gamez	67	69	76	79	291	11,501
Kevin Stadler	69	73	72	77	291	11,501
Dennis Paulson	69	68	78	77	292	11,236
David Branshaw	71	71	73	77	292	11,236
Patrick Sheehan	71	67	75	79	292	11,236
Trevor Dodds	74	72	69	78	293	11,024
Deane Pappas	68	73	74	80	295	10,918
Per-Ulrik Johansson	73	71	71	81	296	10,812

Buick Invitational

Torrey Pines Golf Course, La Jolla, California
South Course: Par 36-36–72; 7,568 yards
North Course: Par 36-36–72; 6,874 yards

February 12-15
purse, $4,800,000

	SCORES				TOTAL	MONEY
John Daly	69	66	68	75	278	$864,000
Chris Riley	67	71	71	69	278	422,400
Luke Donald	69	69	71	69	278	422,400
(Daly defeated Riley and Donald on first playoff hole.)						
Phil Mickelson	74	69	69	67	279	174,000
Duffy Waldorf	68	70	71	70	279	174,000
Thomas Bjorn	70	69	72	68	279	174,000
Jesper Parnevik	65	73	70	71	279	174,000
Shigeki Maruyama	72	67	71	69	279	174,000
Bo Van Pelt	68	68	73	70	279	174,000
Jay Haas	70	69	70	71	280	106,400
Billy Mayfair	72	65	72	71	280	106,400
Tom Pernice, Jr.	71	68	69	72	280	106,400
Brandt Jobe	69	69	70	72	280	106,400
Tiger Woods	71	68	72	69	280	106,400
Stewart Cink	70	63	71	76	280	106,400
Tom Lehman	66	73	70	72	281	72,000
Steve Flesch	67	68	72	74	281	72,000
Brett Quigley	70	68	72	71	281	72,000
Craig Barlow	66	73	71	71	281	72,000
Niclas Fasth	70	68	74	69	281	72,000
Bob Tway	66	73	71	72	282	51,840
Stephen Leaney	72	65	71	74	282	51,840
Hank Kuehne	73	67	71	71	282	51,840

	SCORES				TOTAL	MONEY
Rory Sabbatini	69	73	71	69	282	51,840
Dennis Paulson	69	69	67	79	284	37,440
Woody Austin	70	71	70	73	284	37,440
Roger Tambellini	68	71	70	75	284	37,440
Vaughn Taylor	74	65	72	73	284	37,440
K.J. Choi	68	73	74	69	284	37,440
David Peoples	73	70	72	70	285	28,525.71
Joey Sindelar	67	73	72	73	285	28,525.72
Tommy Tolles	68	73	71	73	285	28,525.72
Danny Ellis	71	71	71	72	285	28,525.72
Jonathan Kaye	71	68	73	73	285	28,525.71
Sergio Garcia	67	71	73	74	285	28,525.71
Arjun Atwal	73	70	75	67	285	28,525.71
Tripp Isenhour	74	67	73	72	286	22,560
Briny Baird	72	69	73	72	286	22,560
Heath Slocum	67	73	75	71	286	22,560
Grant Waite	73	69	74	71	287	18,720
Robert Allenby	74	67	70	76	287	18,720
Stuart Appleby	73	70	70	74	287	18,720
Aaron Baddeley	68	74	72	73	287	18,720
Zach Johnson	73	70	75	69	287	18,720
Tim Petrovic	67	74	77	70	288	13,212
Stephen Ames	73	69	77	69	288	13,212
Michael Allen	72	69	75	72	288	13,212
Kevin Sutherland	66	74	75	73	288	13,212
Kent Jones	70	73	72	73	288	13,212
Tom Carter	76	66	73	73	288	13,212
Mathias Gronberg	66	73	74	75	288	13,212
Brenden Pappas	69	70	72	77	288	13,212
Bernhard Langer	71	70	72	76	289	11,008
Neal Lancaster	71	70	76	72	289	11,008
Jay Williamson	70	69	78	72	289	11,008
Chad Campbell	69	73	74	73	289	11,008
Todd Fischer	68	71	76	74	289	11,008
Hidemichi Tanaka	69	72	74	74	289	11,008
Corey Pavin	70	73	75	72	290	10,368
Hal Sutton	67	70	76	77	290	10,368
Jose Maria Olazabal	76	67	73	74	290	10,368
Bob Burns	71	70	72	77	290	10,368
Craig Bowden	70	70	74	76	290	10,368
Ken Duke	70	70	76	74	290	10,368
Kevin Stadler	64	74	75	77	290	10,368
Brian Bateman	70	73	74	74	291	9,744
Rod Pampling	70	70	75	76	291	9,744
Fredrik Jacobson	67	74	79	71	291	9,744
Charles Howell	69	74	75	73	291	9,744
Jason Bohn	74	67	74	76	291	9,744
Jason Dufner	70	71	72	78	291	9,744
Billy Andrade	72	68	77	75	292	9,216
Jay Delsing	71	72	76	73	292	9,216
Arron Oberholser	71	70	70	81	292	9,216
Ted Purdy	65	75	71	81	292	9,216
Kevin Na	72	69	78	73	292	9,216
Chris Smith	71	72	77	73	293	8,880
Dean Wilson	70	68	77	78	293	8,880
Robert Damron	68	71	77	78	294	8,736
Keiichiro Fukabori	70	67	83	75	295	8,592
Patrick Sheehan	72	65	77	81	295	8,592
Spike McRoy	72	71	77	80	300	8,448

Nissan Open

Riviera Country Club, Pacific Palisades, California
Par 35-36–71; 7,222 yards

February 19-22
purse, $4,800,000

	SCORES				TOTAL	MONEY
Mike Weir	66	64	66	71	267	$864,000
Shigeki Maruyama	64	66	71	67	268	518,400
Stuart Appleby	70	64	70	66	270	326,400
John Daly	68	64	72	67	271	230,400
Hank Kuehne	65	72	68	67	272	192,000
Kirk Triplett	66	67	72	68	273	172,800
Jay Williamson	69	69	72	64	274	149,600
Tiger Woods	72	66	72	64	274	149,600
J.J. Henry	71	69	65	69	274	149,600
Bob Tway	68	67	71	69	275	110,400
Tim Clark	72	69	64	70	275	110,400
Briny Baird	69	62	73	71	275	110,400
Loren Roberts	70	65	69	71	275	110,400
Jeff Maggert	67	66	69	73	275	110,400
Corey Pavin	68	69	72	67	276	76,800
Rory Sabbatini	70	67	71	68	276	76,800
Robert Allenby	66	69	72	69	276	76,800
Brandt Jobe	72	69	66	69	276	76,800
Brent Geiberger	70	67	69	70	276	76,800
Neal Lancaster	69	68	72	68	277	55,920
Sergio Garcia	71	65	72	69	277	55,920
Tim Petrovic	68	68	74	67	277	55,920
Scott McCarron	66	65	72	74	277	55,920
Stephen Ames	70	67	72	69	278	37,140
Vijay Singh	71	70	68	69	278	37,140
Joe Durant	71	65	72	70	278	37,140
Shaun Micheel	64	70	73	71	278	37,140
Mathias Gronberg	68	69	71	70	278	37,140
Hidemichi Tanaka	72	68	71	67	278	37,140
Russ Cochran	67	66	73	72	278	37,140
Carl Pettersson	68	69	68	73	278	37,140
Steve Elkington	73	68	68	70	279	25,988.58
Jose Maria Olazabal	71	65	74	69	279	25,988.57
Fred Funk	71	66	71	71	279	25,988.57
Tim Herron	69	64	73	73	279	25,988.57
Paul Stankowski	69	68	70	72	279	25,988.57
Stewart Cink	69	67	70	73	279	25,988.57
Aaron Baddeley	70	66	69	74	279	25,988.57
Kevin Sutherland	69	69	71	71	280	19,680
Chad Campbell	70	71	69	70	280	19,680
Jay Haas	71	66	70	73	280	19,680
Michael Allen	71	66	70	73	280	19,680
Fredrik Jacobson	72	69	73	66	280	19,680
Chris DiMarco	70	67	72	72	281	14,166.86
Joe Ogilvie	67	73	69	72	281	14,166.86
Bo Van Pelt	68	73	69	71	281	14,166.86
Paul Azinger	74	64	73	70	281	14,166.86
Lee Westwood	73	67	67	74	281	14,166.86
Hal Sutton	72	68	71	70	281	14,166.85
Carlos Franco	69	72	70	70	281	14,166.85
Tom Carter	70	71	68	73	282	11,366.40
Per-Ulrik Johansson	71	68	71	72	282	11,366.40
Billy Andrade	69	68	73	72	282	11,366.40
Bernhard Langer	73	68	69	72	282	11,366.40

	SCORES				TOTAL	MONEY
Tom Byrum	69	72	70	71	282	11,366.40
Rich Beem	73	67	71	72	283	10,848
Tom Lehman	70	70	72	71	283	10,848
Zach Johnson	71	68	77	67	283	10,848
Frank Lickliter	74	65	70	75	284	10,416
Woody Austin	67	69	71	77	284	10,416
Justin Rose	75	65	67	77	284	10,416
Spike McRoy	71	69	71	73	284	10,416
Ben Crane	73	67	73	71	284	10,416
Fred Couples	66	70	77	71	284	10,416
K.J. Choi	69	72	71	73	285	10,032
Phillip Price	68	73	74	70	285	10,032
Steve Flesch	70	69	72	75	286	9,792
Lee Janzen	70	66	76	74	286	9,792
Luke Donald	69	71	74	72	286	9,792
Jeff Brehaut	69	72	70	76	287	9,504
Thomas Bjorn	69	71	73	74	287	9,504
Brenden Pappas	68	73	73	73	287	9,504
Charles Howell	70	71	75	72	288	9,312
Matt Gogel	70	70	72	77	289	9,120
Pat Perez	71	68	75	75	289	9,120
Jerry Kelly	71	69	76	73	289	9,120
John Riegger	68	71	73	78	290	8,928
Jesper Parnevik	69	69	83	74	295	8,832

WGC - Accenture Match Play

La Costa Resort and Spa, Carlsbad, California   February 25-29
Par 36-36–72; 7,029 yards   purse, $7,000,000

FIRST ROUND

Padraig Harrington defeated Toshimitsu Izawa, 2 and 1.
Bob Estes defeated Scott Verplank, 19 holes.
David Toms defeated Niclas Fasth, 19 holes.
Shaun Micheel defeated Paul Casey, 21 holes.
Thomas Bjorn defeated Scott Hoch, 4 and 3.
Fredrik Jacobson defeated Phillip Price, 5 and 4.
Tiger Woods defeated John Rollins, 1 up.
Trevor Immelman defeated Shigeki Maruyama, 2 and 1.
Duffy Waldorf defeated Jonathan Kaye, 5 and 4.
Ian Poulter defeated Chris Riley, 1 up.
John Huston defeated Retief Goosen, 2 and 1.
Peter Lonard defeated Rocco Mediate, 1 up.
Colin Montgomerie defeated Nick Price, 20 holes.
Stewart Cink defeated K.J. Choi, 4 and 2.
Mike Weir defeated Rich Beem, 3 and 2.
Stephen Leaney defeated Fred Funk, 1 up.
Darren Clarke defeated Eduardo Romero, 25 holes.
Alex Cejka defeated Justin Leonard, 4 and 3.
Kenny Perry defeated Jeff Sluman, 6 and 4.
Steve Flesch defeated Brad Faxon, 19 holes.
Chad Campbell defeated Tim Herron, 3 and 2.
Loren Roberts defeated Jay Haas, 1 up.
Vijay Singh defeated Shingo Katayama, 5 and 3.
Jerry Kelly defeated Sergio Garcia, 1 up.
Stuart Appleby defeated Justin Rose, 5 and 4.
Chris DiMarco defeated Michael Campbell, 2 up.
Phil Mickelson defeated Lee Westwood, 3 and 1.

Ben Curtis defeated Charles Howell, 2 up.
Robert Allenby defeated Brian Davis, 3 and 2.
Adam Scott defeated Miguel Angel Jimenez, 2 and 1.
Davis Love defeated Briny Baird, 2 up.
Fred Couples defeated Bob Tway, 3 and 2.

(Each losing player received $35,000.)

SECOND ROUND

Woods defeated Immelman, 5 and 4.
Jacobson defeated Bjorn, 5 and 4.
Toms defeated Micheel, 4 and 3.
Harrington defeated Estes, 3 and 2.
Leaney defeated Weir, 3 and 2.
Montgomerie defeated Cink, 5 and 4.
Huston defeated Lonard, 1 up.
Poulter defeated Waldorf, 7 and 5.
Kelly defeated Singh, 4 and 2.
Campbell defeated Roberts, 3 and 1.
Perry defeated Flesch, 1 up.
Clarke defeated Cejka, 6 and 5.
Love defeated Couples, 3 and 2.
Scott defeated Allenby, 23 holes.
Mickelson defeated Curtis, 7 and 6.
DiMarco defeated Appleby, 19 holes.

(Each losing player received $75,000.)

THIRD ROUND

Woods defeated Jacobson, 5 and 4.
Harrington defeated Toms, 1 up.
Leaney defeated Montgomerie, 1 up.
Poulter defeated Huston, 2 and 1.
Kelly defeated Campbell, 1 up.
Clarke defeated Perry, 3 and 2.
Love defeated Scott, 4 and 3.
Mickelson defeated DiMarco, 3 and 2.

(Each losing player received $115,000.)

QUARTER-FINALS

Woods defeated Harrington, 2 and 1.
Leaney defeated Poulter, 1 up.
Clarke defeated Kelly, 5 and 3.
Love defeated Mickelson, 1 up.

(Each losing player received $225,000.)

SEMI-FINALS

Woods defeated Leaney, 2 and 1.
Love defeated Clarke, 21 holes.

PLAYOFF FOR THIRD-FOURTH PLACE

Clarke defeated Leaney, 2 up.

(Clarke earned $530,000; Leaney earned $430,000.)

FINAL

Woods defeated Love, 3 and 2.

(Woods earned $1,200,000; Love earned $700,000.)

Chrysler Classic of Tucson

Omni Tucson National Resort, Tucson, Arizona

Par 36-36–72; 7,109 yards

February 26-29

purse, $3,000,000

	SCORES				TOTAL	MONEY
Heath Slocum	67	64	70	65	266	$540,000
Aaron Baddeley	68	69	64	66	267	324,000
Mark Hensby	65	68	69	68	270	156,000
Harrison Frazar	66	67	71	66	270	156,000
Rory Sabbatini	69	68	69	64	270	156,000
Bill Glasson	66	66	71	68	271	104,250
Per-Ulrik Johansson	65	69	69	68	271	104,250
Mike Heinen	66	71	65	70	272	84,000
Carlos Franco	65	69	68	70	272	84,000
Todd Fischer	68	68	69	67	272	84,000
Tim Clark	66	68	72	66	272	84,000
Dan Olsen	69	69	66	69	273	63,000
Garrett Willis	71	69	67	66	273	63,000
Angel Cabrera	66	71	68	68	273	63,000
Michael Clark	68	65	72	69	274	52,500
Notah Begay	68	70	69	67	274	52,500
Mark Calcavecchia	67	69	69	70	275	45,000
Geoff Ogilvy	67	66	72	70	275	45,000
Hunter Mahan	69	68	69	69	275	45,000
Danny Briggs	67	72	70	67	276	31,285.71
Blaine McCallister	71	67	69	69	276	31,285.71
Dennis Paulson	67	72	69	68	276	31,285.72
Brian Bateman	73	66	69	68	276	31,285.72
Brian Gay	69	70	70	67	276	31,285.71
Hidemichi Tanaka	69	70	69	68	276	31,285.72
Ted Purdy	69	66	72	69	276	31,285.71
Billy Mayfair	71	68	70	68	277	20,400
Larry Mize	68	72	70	67	277	20,400
Chris Smith	68	70	70	69	277	20,400
Frank Lickliter	63	73	72	69	277	20,400
Cameron Beckman	70	68	70	69	277	20,400
David Branshaw	70	67	71	69	277	20,400
Patrick Sheehan	68	69	72	68	277	20,400
Olin Browne	66	72	70	70	278	15,150
David Edwards	69	68	71	70	278	15,150
Steve Elkington	69	66	70	73	278	15,150
J.L. Lewis	71	67	69	71	278	15,150
Steve Pate	71	69	68	70	278	15,150
Vaughn Taylor	66	68	69	75	278	15,150
Todd Hamilton	70	68	70	71	279	12,300
Dean Wilson	69	71	69	70	279	12,300
Brent Geiberger	67	70	72	70	279	12,300
Russ Cochran	67	70	72	71	280	9,620
Omar Uresti	68	70	71	71	280	9,620
John Maginnes	70	69	68	73	280	9,620
Tripp Isenhour	71	69	70	70	280	9,620
Cliff Kresge	70	67	71	72	280	9,620

	SCORES				TOTAL	MONEY
Brenden Pappas	70	69	75	66	280	9,620
David Frost	68	71	70	72	281	7,404
Steve Lowery	71	67	73	70	281	7,404
Deane Pappas	70	70	75	66	281	7,404
Tag Ridings	67	68	72	74	281	7,404
Ricky Barnes	68	72	75	66	281	7,404
Brian Watts	67	72	72	71	282	6,780
Guy Boros	68	71	71	72	282	6,780
Pat Bates	71	69	72	70	282	6,780
Kris Cox	69	69	75	69	282	6,780
Dicky Pride	71	68	72	71	282	6,780
Keiichiro Fukabori	72	67	73	70	282	6,780
D.J. Brigman	70	67	71	74	282	6,780
Andre Stolz	69	70	72	72	283	6,480
Don Yrene	68	72	71	72	283	6,480
Jason Bohn	71	68	69	75	283	6,480
Tom Lehman	67	70	72	75	284	6,360
Brian Henninger	66	71	72	76	285	6,240
Greg Chalmers	70	70	70	75	285	6,240
Steve Allan	65	72	76	72	285	6,240
Roger Tambellini	69	69	75	73	286	6,120
John Daly	67	73	76	74	290	6,000
Casey Martin	69	70	77	74	290	6,000
Joel Kribel	69	70	75	76	290	6,000

Ford Championship at Doral

Doral Golf Resort & Spa, Blue Course, Miami, Florida   March 4-7
Par 36-36–72; 7,219 yards   purse, $5,000,000

	SCORES				TOTAL	MONEY
Craig Parry	71	65	67	68	271	$900,000
Scott Verplank	67	72	65	67	271	540,000
(Parry defeated Verplank on first playoff hole.)						
Retief Goosen	67	68	71	66	272	340,000
Joe Durant	66	72	67	68	273	240,000
Bernhard Langer	75	68	66	65	274	175,625
Gene Sauers	70	70	64	70	274	175,625
David Toms	72	68	65	69	274	175,625
K.J. Choi	70	69	66	69	274	175,625
Mark Calcavecchia	68	69	70	68	275	140,000
Danny Ellis	69	69	67	70	275	140,000
Nick Price	72	70	65	69	276	110,000
Chris DiMarco	68	70	67	71	276	110,000
Neal Lancaster	71	68	72	65	276	110,000
Shigeki Maruyama	70	69	69	68	276	110,000
Todd Hamilton	68	68	71	70	277	87,500
Alex Cejka	69	68	69	71	277	87,500
Fred Funk	71	69	70	68	278	65,428.57
Robert Gamez	73	71	66	68	278	65,428.57
John Riegger	68	73	66	71	278	65,428.57
Woody Austin	73	69	70	66	278	65,428.58
Stewart Cink	70	69	69	70	278	65,428.57
Angel Cabrera	70	69	69	70	278	65,428.57
Heath Slocum	70	74	68	66	278	65,428.57
Russ Cochran	74	71	66	68	279	44,000
Phil Mickelson	67	69	69	74	279	44,000

	SCORES				TOTAL	MONEY
Dennis Paulson	68	70	71	70	279	44,000
Chris Smith	65	76	71	68	280	36,250
Stephen Ames	71	69	70	70	280	36,250
Craig Perks	68	69	73	70	280	36,250
Jesper Parnevik	71	70	67	72	280	36,250
Kenny Perry	72	70	68	71	281	31,000
Ryan Palmer	72	70	73	66	281	31,000
Bo Van Pelt	70	74	70	67	281	31,000
Jay Haas	73	67	71	71	282	23,150
Jeff Sluman	70	72	69	71	282	23,150
Shaun Micheel	72	71	70	69	282	23,150
Brian Bateman	70	75	71	66	282	23,150
Brett Quigley	73	70	67	72	282	23,150
Cliff Kresge	74	71	70	67	282	23,150
Briny Baird	68	75	70	69	282	23,150
Rod Pampling	74	71	66	71	282	23,150
Peter Lonard	74	69	66	73	282	23,150
Patrick Sheehan	71	74	70	67	282	23,150
Tommy Armour	71	72	68	72	283	14,450
Skip Kendall	69	70	76	68	283	14,450
Billy Mayfair	70	74	69	70	283	14,450
Joey Sindelar	74	71	70	68	283	14,450
Dan Olsen	72	71	71	69	283	14,450
Jerry Kelly	70	74	70	69	283	14,450
Justin Leonard	70	69	74	70	283	14,450
Jose Coceres	71	72	67	73	283	14,450
Paul Azinger	71	70	71	72	284	11,725
Olin Browne	70	74	71	69	284	11,725
David Peoples	71	71	72	70	284	11,725
Craig Barlow	70	74	68	72	284	11,725
Scott Hoch	70	74	71	70	285	11,050
Marco Dawson	72	72	68	73	285	11,050
Michael Allen	72	71	69	73	285	11,050
Dean Wilson	72	71	73	69	285	11,050
Sven Struver	73	70	74	68	285	11,050
Hank Kuehne	72	71	69	73	285	11,050
Erik Compton	73	70	70	72	285	11,050
Hunter Mahan	74	69	73	69	285	11,050
Lee Janzen	72	70	69	75	286	10,350
Omar Uresti	73	72	71	70	286	10,350
Notah Begay	76	69	72	69	286	10,350
John Senden	71	73	70	72	286	10,350
Arjun Atwal	77	68	75	66	286	10,350
Joe Ogilvie	72	73	71	70	286	10,350
Bill Glasson	73	72	73	69	287	9,900
J.L. Lewis	73	72	71	71	287	9,900
Ted Purdy	71	73	70	73	287	9,900
Niclas Fasth	73	72	71	72	288	9,700
Tom Carter	74	71	72	72	289	9,450
Carlos Franco	71	74	70	74	289	9,450
Brenden Pappas	71	72	69	77	289	9,450
J.J. Henry	73	70	71	75	289	9,450
Tim Clark	68	76	75	71	290	9,200
Tripp Isenhour	70	75	73	74	292	9,100

Honda Classic

The Country Club of Mirasol, Sunrise Course,
Palm Beach Gardens, Florida
Par 36-36–72; 7,468 yards

March 11-14
purse, $5,000,000

	SCORES				TOTAL	MONEY
Todd Hamilton	68	66	68	74	276	$900,000
Davis Love	69	69	70	69	277	540,000
Brian Bateman	71	69	70	68	278	340,000
Woody Austin	71	69	69	70	279	196,875
Robert Allenby	68	74	67	70	279	196,875
Fredrik Jacobson	67	69	70	73	279	196,875
Kevin Na	67	72	71	69	279	196,875
Brad Faxon	68	66	76	70	280	155,000
Tommy Armour	69	69	73	70	281	130,000
Lee Janzen	74	66	70	71	281	130,000
Chad Campbell	71	70	71	69	281	130,000
Rory Sabbatini	66	72	71	72	281	130,000
Tom Pernice, Jr.	70	68	70	74	282	83,125
Craig Bowden	69	69	72	72	282	83,125
Chris Riley	72	67	68	75	282	83,125
Mark Hensby	65	73	71	73	282	83,125
Rod Pampling	75	67	67	73	282	83,125
Geoff Ogilvy	73	70	70	69	282	83,125
Zach Johnson	69	75	66	72	282	83,125
Carl Pettersson	63	68	76	75	282	83,125
Larry Mize	68	71	70	74	283	54,000
Briny Baird	68	71	73	71	283	54,000
Aaron Baddeley	72	69	67	75	283	54,000
Luke Donald	70	69	75	69	283	54,000
Fred Couples	68	70	73	73	284	39,000
David Toms	72	72	69	71	284	39,000
Brett Quigley	69	74	71	70	284	39,000
Justin Leonard	71	73	69	71	284	39,000
Brenden Pappas	69	72	70	73	284	39,000
Chris DiMarco	74	68	74	69	285	30,375
Steve Flesch	66	76	71	72	285	30,375
Jesper Parnevik	66	72	74	73	285	30,375
John Senden	72	66	75	72	285	30,375
Ted Purdy	69	73	70	73	285	30,375
Ryan Palmer	72	68	74	71	285	30,375
Craig Parry	73	68	72	73	286	24,583.33
Cliff Kresge	73	70	72	71	286	24,583.34
Justin Rose	71	70	71	74	286	24,583.33
Notah Begay	72	72	72	71	287	22,000
Roger Tambellini	70	70	74	73	287	22,000
Billy Mayfair	70	69	73	76	288	18,500
Craig Perks	72	70	74	72	288	18,500
Hidemichi Tanaka	71	68	72	77	288	18,500
Patrick Sheehan	71	71	76	70	288	18,500
D.J. Brigman	72	69	73	74	288	18,500
Mark O'Meara	71	73	74	71	289	13,371.43
John Riegger	67	75	71	76	289	13,371.42
Chris Smith	70	73	73	73	289	13,371.43
Brandt Jobe	69	73	74	73	289	13,371.43
Glen Hnatiuk	69	72	72	76	289	13,371.43
Carlos Franco	67	75	73	74	289	13,371.43
Ken Duke	68	74	71	76	289	13,371.43
Joe Durant	73	71	70	76	290	11,700
Charles Howell	72	71	75	72	290	11,700

	SCORES				TOTAL	MONEY
Per-Ulrik Johansson	74	70	70	77	291	11,350
Dean Wilson	70	73	72	76	291	11,350
Craig Barlow	73	70	72	76	291	11,350
J.J. Henry	74	68	79	70	291	11,350
Skip Kendall	71	73	76	72	292	10,850
Jeff Sluman	72	68	80	72	292	10,850
Pat Bates	72	72	69	79	292	10,850
Glen Day	69	70	74	79	292	10,850
Robert Damron	69	72	74	77	292	10,850
David Gossett	69	74	73	76	292	10,850
Bernhard Langer	71	71	75	76	293	10,350
Scott McCarron	69	74	73	77	293	10,350
Danny Ellis	71	69	75	78	293	10,350
Mathias Gronberg	71	72	75	75	293	10,350
Jason Dufner	72	72	79	71	294	10,100
Jay Delsing	72	72	73	78	295	9,900
Gene Sauers	68	73	76	78	295	9,900
Joe Ogilvie	71	70	77	77	295	9,900
Michael Allen	69	73	76	80	298	9,700

Bay Hill Invitational

Bay Hill Club & Lodge, Orlando, Florida
Par 36-36–72; 7,239 yards

March 18-21
purse, $5,000,000

	SCORES				TOTAL	MONEY
Chad Campbell	66	68	70	66	270	$900,000
Stuart Appleby	67	67	66	76	276	540,000
Scott Verplank	68	68	73	68	277	290,000
Adam Scott	68	70	68	71	277	290,000
Jerry Kelly	67	69	73	69	278	200,000
Stephen Ames	72	65	73	70	280	161,875
Shigeki Maruyama	66	66	75	73	280	161,875
Darren Clarke	66	68	74	72	280	161,875
Zach Johnson	67	68	75	70	280	161,875
John Daly	68	70	70	73	281	130,000
Dennis Paulson	72	67	72	70	281	130,000
Tom Lehman	70	74	70	68	282	115,000
Mathias Gronberg	69	72	72	70	283	100,000
Bo Van Pelt	72	72	70	69	283	100,000
Fred Couples	76	67	68	73	284	70,333.33
J.L. Lewis	71	70	71	72	284	70,333.33
Steve Lowery	70	67	71	76	284	70,333.33
Kenny Perry	69	72	72	71	284	70,333.34
John Riegger	72	67	72	73	284	70,333.33
Lee Westwood	73	69	74	68	284	70,333.34
Mark Hensby	72	70	70	72	284	70,333.33
Fredrik Jacobson	70	69	70	75	284	70,333.33
Charles Howell	71	71	71	71	284	70,333.34
Brad Faxon	68	73	77	67	285	39,571.43
Jeff Sluman	72	68	73	72	285	39,571.43
Tim Herron	70	73	71	71	285	39,571.43
Craig Barlow	72	68	72	73	285	39,571.43
Rod Pampling	69	70	69	77	285	39,571.42
Justin Rose	71	70	69	75	285	39,571.43
Ryan Palmer	71	72	72	70	285	39,571.43
Lee Janzen	70	66	78	72	286	27,166.67

	SCORES				TOTAL	MONEY
Davis Love	69	74	71	72	286	27,166.67
Kirk Triplett	72	68	73	73	286	27,166.67
Vijay Singh	68	72	70	76	286	27,166.66
Brett Quigley	71	70	72	73	286	27,166.67
Thomas Bjorn	71	70	73	72	286	27,166.67
Frank Lickliter	74	67	73	72	286	27,166.67
Niclas Fasth	71	71	70	74	286	27,166.66
Sergio Garcia	73	66	70	77	286	27,166.66
Bernhard Langer	72	70	71	74	287	19,000
Jose Maria Olazabal	73	71	71	72	287	19,000
Joe Durant	72	70	73	72	287	19,000
Steve Flesch	73	68	72	74	287	19,000
Patrick Sheehan	70	71	74	72	287	19,000
Ben Curtis	69	69	77	72	287	19,000
Loren Roberts	70	71	72	75	288	12,850
Gene Sauers	75	69	72	72	288	12,850
Neal Lancaster	76	67	75	70	288	12,850
Tiger Woods	67	74	74	73	288	12,850
Kent Jones	72	70	75	71	288	12,850
Brian Gay	68	71	71	78	288	12,850
Stewart Cink	73	71	74	70	288	12,850
Alex Cejka	72	70	71	75	288	12,850
Arron Oberholser	71	73	70	74	288	12,850
Trevor Immelman	73	69	76	70	288	12,850
Mark O'Meara	69	73	73	74	289	11,250
Omar Uresti	71	71	73	74	289	11,250
Danny Ellis	70	67	77	75	289	11,250
Aaron Baddeley	68	74	71	76	289	11,250
Harrison Frazar	76	68	71	75	290	10,950
Ben Crane	72	71	73	74	290	10,950
Tim Petrovic	72	72	69	78	291	10,650
Woody Austin	73	70	77	71	291	10,650
Phillip Price	73	71	72	75	291	10,650
Hunter Mahan	69	69	79	74	291	10,650
Billy Andrade	72	72	73	75	292	10,350
Tom Watson	70	74	75	73	292	10,350
Nick Faldo	70	72	77	74	293	10,200
Todd Hamilton	71	70	77	76	294	10,050
Mike Heinen	71	71	75	77	294	10,050
Scott McCarron	69	71	82	74	296	9,900
Stephen Leaney	72	71	78	76	297	9,800
Dicky Pride	72	71	80	75	298	9,700

The Players Championship

TPC at Sawgrass, Stadium Course,
Ponte Vedra Beach, Florida
Par 36-36–72; 7,093 yards

March 25-28
purse, $8,000,000

	SCORES				TOTAL	MONEY
Adam Scott	65	72	69	70	276	$1,440,000
Padraig Harrington	68	70	73	66	277	864,000
Phil Mickelson	70	69	70	71	280	416,000
Kenny Perry	69	71	69	71	280	416,000
Frank Lickliter	69	71	68	72	280	416,000
Jay Haas	72	73	70	66	281	268,000
Kevin Sutherland	66	69	73	73	281	268,000

	SCORES				TOTAL	MONEY
Jerry Kelly	69	66	74	72	281	268,000
Shaun Micheel	70	76	69	67	282	232,000
Fred Funk	73	71	68	71	283	200,000
Bob Burns	67	72	72	72	283	200,000
Paul Casey	72	70	69	72	283	200,000
Craig Parry	74	72	64	74	284	154,666.66
Stephen Ames	75	69	72	68	284	154,666.67
Vijay Singh	70	68	72	74	284	154,666.67
Tom Byrum	74	71	71	69	285	116,000
Woody Austin	76	69	66	74	285	116,000
Paul Stankowski	73	70	66	76	285	116,000
Tiger Woods	75	69	68	73	285	116,000
Geoff Ogilvy	73	70	72	70	285	116,000
Matt Kuchar	74	67	71	73	285	116,000
J.P. Hayes	72	73	72	69	286	80,000
Glen Day	71	75	67	73	286	80,000
Thomas Bjorn	67	76	73	70	286	80,000
Stewart Cink	70	73	74	69	286	80,000
Steve Elkington	69	76	70	72	287	56,800
John Huston	72	71	71	73	287	56,800
Jeff Sluman	69	70	73	75	287	56,800
Scott Verplank	68	75	73	71	287	56,800
Ernie Els	68	69	72	78	287	56,800
Cameron Beckman	70	71	72	74	287	56,800
Darren Clarke	71	74	73	69	287	56,800
Davis Love	77	68	70	73	288	39,644.44
Jeff Maggert	73	73	70	72	288	39,644.45
Len Mattiace	74	69	74	71	288	39,644.45
Corey Pavin	74	67	74	73	288	39,644.45
Robert Allenby	71	73	70	74	288	39,644.44
Jesper Parnevik	72	71	73	72	288	39,644.45
Alex Cejka	69	71	73	75	288	39,644.44
Briny Baird	71	74	70	73	288	39,644.44
Ian Poulter	70	73	71	74	288	39,644.44
Brad Faxon	70	75	73	71	289	24,087.27
Scott Hoch	70	71	77	71	289	24,087.28
David Peoples	72	72	73	72	289	24,087.27
Nick Price	75	69	73	72	289	24,087.27
Pat Bates	73	73	73	70	289	24,087.28
Brett Quigley	73	73	69	74	289	24,087.27
Colin Montgomerie	73	73	73	70	289	24,087.28
Justin Leonard	75	69	72	73	289	24,087.27
Chad Campbell	75	69	71	74	289	24,087.27
Rory Sabbatini	73	68	75	73	289	24,087.27
K.J. Choi	67	79	69	74	289	24,087.27
Tim Petrovic	71	72	74	73	290	18,432
Matt Gogel	72	71	70	77	290	18,432
Scott McCarron	76	70	69	75	290	18,432
Shigeki Maruyama	70	73	74	73	290	18,432
Sergio Garcia	68	73	72	77	290	18,432
Todd Hamilton	71	72	76	72	291	17,360
Billy Mayfair	76	70	70	75	291	17,360
Joe Durant	74	71	72	74	291	17,360
Carlos Franco	74	70	74	73	291	17,360
Rod Pampling	73	71	72	75	291	17,360
John Senden	73	72	70	76	291	17,360
Heath Slocum	73	73	72	73	291	17,360
Justin Rose	73	73	70	75	291	17,360
Mark Calcavecchia	71	72	72	77	292	16,240
Loren Roberts	73	70	79	70	292	16,240

	SCORES				TOTAL	MONEY
Craig Stadler	70	76	74	72	292	16,240
Spike McRoy	74	71	75	72	292	16,240
Arron Oberholser	73	73	75	71	292	16,240
Ben Crane	71	72	71	78	292	16,240
Nick Faldo	71	75	71	76	293	15,600
Tom Pernice, Jr.	72	71	70	80	293	15,600
Joey Sindelar	73	70	73	78	294	15,200
Duffy Waldorf	66	73	71	84	294	15,200
Brandt Jobe	68	75	76	75	294	15,200
Bernhard Langer	71	74	73	77	295	14,800
Bob Tway	69	71	78	77	295	14,800
John Daly	69	73	76	80	298	14,560
Peter Jacobsen	72	73	71	83	299	14,400
Greg Norman	72	73	77	79	301	14,160
Hidemichi Tanaka	72	71	74	84	301	14,160
Neal Lancaster	72	71	80	79	302	13,920

BellSouth Classic

TPC at Sugarloaf, Duluth, Georgia
Par 36-36–72; 7,293 yards

April 1-4
purse, $4,500,000

	SCORES				TOTAL	MONEY
Zach Johnson	69	66	68	72	275	$810,000
Mark Hensby	73	70	66	67	276	486,000
Scott Hend	72	66	68	71	277	306,000
Padraig Harrington	70	69	67	72	278	216,000
Peter Lonard	73	67	69	71	280	180,000
Lee Janzen	75	67	68	71	281	156,375
Ben Crane	68	69	71	73	281	156,375
Stewart Cink	75	67	69	71	282	135,000
Luke Donald	72	70	71	69	282	135,000
Phil Mickelson	69	72	71	71	283	121,500
David Peoples	73	72	66	73	284	103,500
Tim Petrovic	67	70	75	72	284	103,500
Grant Waite	73	72	70	69	284	103,500
Neal Lancaster	70	75	66	74	285	74,250
Craig Bowden	66	71	72	76	285	74,250
Brian Gay	68	70	69	78	285	74,250
Steve Allan	71	72	71	71	285	74,250
Roger Tambellini	65	78	72	70	285	74,250
Tag Ridings	73	69	71	72	285	74,250
Blaine McCallister	71	69	71	75	286	45,393.75
Chris Smith	70	70	74	72	286	45,393.75
Duffy Waldorf	73	70	71	72	286	45,393.75
Chris DiMarco	75	70	72	69	286	45,393.75
Jeff Brehaut	71	74	69	72	286	45,393.75
Glen Hnatiuk	70	72	68	76	286	45,393.75
Briny Baird	74	69	70	73	286	45,393.75
Arron Oberholser	72	68	71	75	286	45,393.75
Larry Mize	76	69	70	72	287	32,625
Kevin Na	73	71	69	74	287	32,625
Steve Lowery	71	73	67	77	288	27,945
Shaun Micheel	67	72	75	74	288	27,945
Steve Stricker	69	76	73	70	288	27,945
Kris Cox	71	70	70	77	288	27,945
David Morland	72	70	72	74	288	27,945

	SCORES				TOTAL	MONEY
Steve Elkington	70	75	71	73	289	23,175
Harrison Frazar	71	74	69	75	289	23,175
Rich Beem	69	75	73	72	289	23,175
Robert Gamez	71	70	76	73	290	18,450
John Huston	70	73	72	75	290	18,450
Steve Flesch	71	73	71	75	290	18,450
Franklin Langham	74	70	72	74	290	18,450
Brent Geiberger	73	70	72	75	290	18,450
Joe Ogilvie	70	75	69	76	290	18,450
Pat Perez	73	71	74	72	290	18,450
Jose Maria Olazabal	65	77	73	76	291	12,612.85
Bob Burns	76	69	73	73	291	12,612.86
Brian Bateman	73	70	75	73	291	12,612.86
Brett Quigley	73	71	74	73	291	12,612.86
Spike McRoy	70	73	74	74	291	12,612.86
Deane Pappas	72	72	71	76	291	12,612.85
Mike Weir	73	70	73	75	291	12,612.86
Guy Boros	72	73	71	76	292	10,552.50
Chris Couch	72	69	75	76	292	10,552.50
Carl Pettersson	76	68	73	75	292	10,552.50
Richard S. Johnson	72	73	73	74	292	10,552.50
Billy Mayfair	68	76	73	76	293	9,945
Dennis Paulson	72	73	71	77	293	9,945
Scott Simpson	68	76	70	79	293	9,945
Scott McCarron	74	71	72	76	293	9,945
Jonathan Kaye	73	72	71	77	293	9,945
Rory Sabbatini	68	75	75	75	293	9,945
Kevin Durkin	71	73	72	77	293	9,945
Lucas Glover	75	70	72	76	293	9,945
Danny Briggs	70	74	75	75	294	9,495
David Branshaw	72	73	72	77	294	9,495
Brian Kortan	69	73	73	80	295	9,315
Bo Van Pelt	75	70	74	76	295	9,315
Roland Thatcher	72	71	72	81	296	9,180
Daniel Chopra	71	73	76	77	297	9,090
Hirofumi Miyase	70	73	75	80	298	9,000
Brian Watts	71	73	77	79	300	8,910

Masters Tournament

Augusta National Golf Club, Augusta, Georgia
Par 36-36–72; 7,290 yards

April 8-11
purse, $6,000,000

	SCORES				TOTAL	MONEY
Phil Mickelson	72	69	69	69	279	$1,170,000
Ernie Els	70	72	71	67	280	702,000
K.J. Choi	71	70	72	69	282	442,000
Bernhard Langer	71	73	69	72	285	286,000
Sergio Garcia	72	72	75	66	285	286,000
Fred Couples	73	69	74	70	286	189,893
Davis Love	75	67	74	70	286	189,893
Nick Price	72	73	71	70	286	189,893
Kirk Triplett	71	74	69	72	286	189,893
Chris DiMarco	69	73	68	76	286	189,893
Vijay Singh	75	73	69	69	286	189,893
Paul Casey	75	69	68	74	286	189,893
Retief Goosen	75	73	70	70	288	125,667

	SCORES				TOTAL	MONEY
Padraig Harrington	74	74	68	72	288	125,667
Charles Howell	71	71	76	70	288	125,667
*Casey Wittenberg	76	72	71	69	288	
Jay Haas	69	75	72	73	289	97,500
Steve Flesch	76	67	77	69	289	97,500
Stewart Cink	74	73	69	73	289	97,500
Stephen Leaney	76	71	73	69	289	97,500
Fredrik Jacobson	74	74	67	74	289	97,500
Shaun Micheel	72	76	72	70	290	70,200
Tiger Woods	75	69	75	71	290	70,200
Stuart Appleby	73	74	73	70	290	70,200
Justin Rose	67	71	81	71	290	70,200
Alex Cejka	70	70	78	73	291	57,200
Mark O'Meara	73	70	75	74	292	51,025
Bob Tway	75	71	74	72	292	51,025
Scott Verplank	74	71	76	72	293	48,100
Jose Maria Olazabal	71	69	79	75	294	46,150
Bob Estes	76	72	73	74	295	41,275
Brad Faxon	72	76	76	71	295	41,275
Jerry Kelly	74	72	73	76	295	41,275
Ian Poulter	75	73	74	73	295	41,275
Justin Leonard	76	72	72	76	296	35,913
Phillip Price	71	76	73	76	296	35,913
Sandy Lyle	72	74	75	76	297	32,663
Paul Lawrie	77	70	73	77	297	32,663
Eduardo Romero	74	73	74	77	298	30,550
Todd Hamilton	77	71	76	75	299	29,250
Tim Petrovic	72	75	75	78	300	27,950
*Brandt Snedeker	73	75	75	77	300	
Jeff Sluman	73	70	82	77	302	26,650
Chris Riley	70	78	78	78	304	25,350

Out of Final 36 Holes

Ben Crenshaw	74	75		149
John Daly	78	71		149
Raymond Floyd	73	76		149
J.L. Lewis	77	72		149
Craig Stadler	74	75		149
Mike Weir	79	70		149
Robert Allenby	73	76		149
Craig Perks	76	73		149
Darren Clarke	70	79		149
Michael Campbell	76	73		149
Peter Lonard	74	75		149
John Rollins	74	75		149
Zhang Lian-wei	77	72		149
Fred Funk	80	70		150
Jeff Maggert	78	72		150
Larry Mize	76	74		150
Jack Nicklaus	75	75		150
Craig Parry	74	76		150
Briny Baird	77	73		150
Ben Curtis	73	77		150
Rich Beem	77	73		150
*Nathan Smith	78	72		150
Nick Faldo	76	75		151
Len Mattiace	76	75		151
Rocco Mediate	75	76		151
David Toms	78	73		151

	SCORES	TOTAL
Ian Woosnam	76 75	151
Colin Montgomerie	71 80	151
Jonathan Kaye	79 72	151
Angel Cabrera	74 77	151
Kenny Perry	74 78	152
Tom Watson	76 76	152
Toshimitsu Izawa	76 76	152
*Nick Flanagan	78 74	152
*Gary Wolstenholme	77 76	153
Chad Campbell	76 77	153
Shigeki Maruyama	82 71	153
Trevor Immelman	77 76	153
Adam Scott	80 73	153
Jonathan Byrd	79 74	153
Tim Herron	80 74	154
Tim Clark	73 81	154
Brian Davis	82 73	155
Thomas Bjorn	80 77	157
Fuzzy Zoeller	79 81	160
Gary Player	82 80	162
Charles Coody	88 79	167
Arnold Palmer	84 84	168
Tommy Aaron	87 83	170

(Professionals who did not complete 72 holes received $5,000.)

MCI Heritage

Harbour Town Golf Links, Hilton Head Island, South Carolina   April 15-18
Par 36-35–71; 6,973 yards   purse, $4,800,000

	SCORES	TOTAL	MONEY
Stewart Cink	72 69 69 64	274	$864,000
Ted Purdy	69 67 65 73	274	518,400
(Cink defeated Purdy on fifth playoff hole.)			
Ernie Els	69 70 68 69	276	249,600
Patrick Sheehan	71 66 69 70	276	249,600
Carl Pettersson	72 71 66 67	276	249,600
Fred Funk	69 69 69 70	277	172,800
Jay Haas	68 69 70 71	278	144,600
Scott Hoch	70 68 71 69	278	144,600
Stephen Ames	70 68 68 72	278	144,600
Justin Rose	73 69 66 70	278	144,600
Darren Clarke	71 66 71 72	280	101,760
Jose Coceres	71 68 72 69	280	101,760
Jonathan Kaye	70 70 68 72	280	101,760
Geoff Ogilvy	71 73 70 66	280	101,760
Kevin Na	69 68 70 73	280	101,760
Tim Petrovic	69 72 71 69	281	63,040
Bob Burns	73 70 67 71	281	63,040
Jay Williamson	71 72 69 69	281	63,040
Kent Jones	72 72 68 69	281	63,040
Cliff Kresge	71 70 74 66	281	63,040
Rod Pampling	68 72 69 72	281	63,040
Fredrik Jacobson	73 69 68 71	281	63,040
Jonathan Byrd	68 71 70 72	281	63,040
Lucas Glover	73 70 66 72	281	63,040

	SCORES				TOTAL	MONEY
John Huston	69	68	74	71	282	35,862.86
Skip Kendall	72	71	69	70	282	35,862.86
Mark O'Meara	71	67	73	71	282	35,862.86
Dennis Paulson	73	70	70	69	282	35,862.86
Nick Price	69	71	74	68	282	35,862.86
Alex Cejka	70	71	68	73	282	35,862.85
Ben Curtis	68	66	75	73	282	35,862.85
Tom Byrum	74	68	69	72	283	25,988.57
Davis Love	72	70	69	72	283	25,988.57
Scott Verplank	73	69	72	69	283	25,988.58
Woody Austin	71	71	69	72	283	25,988.57
Chad Campbell	69	69	70	75	283	25,988.57
Heath Slocum	68	67	70	78	283	25,988.57
Matt Kuchar	72	70	70	71	283	25,988.57
David Frost	71	68	75	70	284	19,200
Lee Janzen	71	72	70	71	284	19,200
Bernhard Langer	71	71	70	72	284	19,200
Craig Bowden	70	72	74	68	284	19,200
Spike McRoy	69	71	71	73	284	19,200
Justin Leonard	71	72	73	68	284	19,200
Robert Gamez	69	70	73	73	285	13,212
Jeff Maggert	73	66	70	76	285	13,212
Dudley Hart	74	68	70	73	285	13,212
Jeff Brehaut	74	66	73	72	285	13,212
Cameron Beckman	67	72	74	72	285	13,212
John Rollins	71	70	71	73	285	13,212
Tim Clark	70	71	72	72	285	13,212
Ben Crane	74	67	74	70	285	13,212
Billy Andrade	77	64	71	74	286	10,908
J.L. Lewis	69	75	72	70	286	10,908
Scott Simpson	73	69	72	72	286	10,908
Brian Bateman	69	71	75	71	286	10,908
Glen Day	72	68	72	74	286	10,908
Frank Lickliter	71	71	71	73	286	10,908
Dean Wilson	72	71	67	76	286	10,908
Zach Johnson	69	72	75	70	286	10,908
Loren Roberts	69	73	72	73	287	10,320
Craig Barlow	71	71	76	69	287	10,320
Scott Hend	73	70	66	78	287	10,320
Ian Poulter	70	70	73	74	287	10,320
Bob Estes	71	72	71	74	288	10,080
Robert Damron	74	69	72	74	289	9,984
Dan Olsen	71	72	73	74	290	9,840
Matt Gogel	71	71	76	72	290	9,840
Brad Faxon	71	71	81	68	291	9,648
Billy Mayfair	76	68	73	74	291	9,648
Tommy Armour	76	68	77	71	292	9,456
Todd Fischer	72	72	75	73	292	9,456

Shell Houston Open

Redstone Golf Club, Fall Creek Course, Humble, Texas
Par 35-37–72; 7,508 yards
(Tournament extended to Monday—rain.)

April 22-26
purse, $5,000,000

	SCORES				TOTAL	MONEY
Vijay Singh	74	66	69	68	277	$900,000
Scott Hoch	73	68	71	67	279	540,000
John Huston	71	71	67	71	280	340,000
Stephen Ames	68	76	69	69	282	220,000
Dudley Hart	69	72	71	70	282	220,000
Paul Azinger	73	67	72	71	283	161,875
John Daly	76	69	67	71	283	161,875
Jose Coceres	73	69	68	73	283	161,875
Rory Sabbatini	74	70	69	70	283	161,875
Geoff Ogilvy	71	70	71	72	284	135,000
David Peoples	70	71	73	71	285	96,250
Paul Stankowski	72	70	71	72	285	96,250
Tim Herron	73	71	70	71	285	96,250
Ted Purdy	72	73	71	69	285	96,250
Patrick Sheehan	69	71	74	71	285	96,250
Zach Johnson	71	68	74	72	285	96,250
D.J. Brigman	71	72	70	72	285	96,250
K.J. Choi	74	70	72	69	285	96,250
Mark Calcavecchia	72	69	72	73	286	52,611.11
Steve Lowery	70	69	76	71	286	52,611.11
Tim Petrovic	69	73	72	72	286	52,611.11
Steve Stricker	69	70	77	70	286	52,611.11
Carlos Franco	73	72	69	72	286	52,611.11
Joe Ogilvie	72	70	68	76	286	52,611.11
Bo Van Pelt	74	71	69	72	286	52,611.11
Jason Bohn	71	72	73	70	286	52,611.12
Kevin Na	72	70	72	72	286	52,611.11
Brian Bateman	77	68	71	71	287	37,000
Len Mattiace	75	70	71	72	288	30,437.50
Billy Mayfair	74	71	72	71	288	30,437.50
Tom Pernice, Jr.	70	73	73	72	288	30,437.50
John Riegger	69	71	74	74	288	30,437.50
Neal Lancaster	70	71	76	71	288	30,437.50
Justin Leonard	71	70	72	75	288	30,437.50
Tom Carter	71	73	71	73	288	30,437.50
Lucas Glover	68	77	75	68	288	30,437.50
Russ Cochran	70	74	70	75	289	22,000
Blaine McCallister	74	70	74	71	289	22,000
Hal Sutton	69	73	74	73	289	22,000
Chris Riley	67	74	76	72	289	22,000
Ben Crane	72	72	72	73	289	22,000
Hank Kuehne	74	70	72	73	289	22,000
Danny Briggs	73	72	71	74	290	16,033.33
Jay Haas	72	73	70	75	290	16,033.33
Jeff Brehaut	71	74	73	72	290	16,033.33
Mathias Gronberg	73	72	72	73	290	16,033.34
Rod Pampling	66	79	73	72	290	16,033.33
Arron Oberholser	73	71	70	76	290	16,033.34
Fred Couples	71	74	74	72	291	12,340
Robert Allenby	72	71	76	72	291	12,340
Frank Lickliter	68	77	73	73	291	12,340
Lee Westwood	76	69	73	73	291	12,340
Alex Cejka	72	71	72	76	291	12,340

	SCORES				TOTAL	MONEY
David Frost	71	73	72	76	292	11,400
Dennis Paulson	71	74	73	74	292	11,400
Brian Kortan	71	74	74	73	292	11,400
Heath Slocum	73	70	74	75	292	11,400
Edward Loar	74	71	72	75	292	11,400
Robert Gamez	74	71	75	73	293	10,850
Mike Heinen	73	72	71	77	293	10,850
Joel Kribel	71	72	77	73	293	10,850
Scott Hend	73	71	72	77	293	10,850
Roger Tambellini	71	74	78	70	293	10,850
J.J. Henry	71	74	76	72	293	10,850
Daniel Chopra	72	73	74	75	294	10,450
Aaron Baddeley	71	72	77	74	294	10,450
Brian Gay	72	73	74	76	295	10,250
Tjaart van der Walt	71	74	75	75	295	10,250
Phil Blackmar	76	67	76	78	297	10,100
Deane Pappas	68	77	78	75	298	9,950
Dicky Pride	71	73	76	78	298	9,950

HP Classic of New Orleans

English Turn Golf & Country Club, New Orleans, Louisiana   April 29-May 3
Par 36-36–72; 7,078 yards   purse, $5,100,000
(Tournament extended to Monday — rain.)

	SCORES				TOTAL	MONEY
Vijay Singh	70	65	68	63	266	$918,000
Phil Mickelson	67	65	69	66	267	448,800
Joe Ogilvie	66	67	66	68	267	448,800
Hidemichi Tanaka	69	64	69	67	269	244,800
Charles Howell	66	64	71	70	271	193,800
Justin Rose	67	70	65	69	271	193,800
Stephen Ames	67	69	71	65	272	158,950
Brian Bateman	67	67	69	69	272	158,950
K.J. Choi	67	68	68	69	272	158,950
Joe Durant	67	70	67	69	273	132,600
Matt Kuchar	69	63	71	70	273	132,600
David Frost	69	69	70	66	274	107,100
Ken Duke	64	68	72	70	274	107,100
Ryan Palmer	68	64	72	70	274	107,100
Paul Azinger	66	66	71	72	275	81,600
Steve Pate	75	65	68	67	275	81,600
David Sutherland	66	67	72	70	275	81,600
Bob Burns	69	64	75	67	275	81,600
Carl Pettersson	68	68	73	66	275	81,600
Dan Forsman	71	68	69	68	276	57,324
Steve Stricker	71	69	67	69	276	57,324
John Senden	70	67	72	67	276	57,324
Pat Perez	70	70	70	66	276	57,324
James McLean	70	67	71	68	276	57,324
Bob Estes	69	65	75	68	277	36,493.34
J.L. Lewis	69	67	71	70	277	36,493.33
Hal Sutton	69	66	76	66	277	36,493.33
Robert Damron	66	70	70	71	277	36,493.33
Mathias Gronberg	67	70	72	68	277	36,493.34
Briny Baird	73	67	71	66	277	36,493.33
Ted Purdy	68	68	68	73	277	36,493.33

	SCORES				TOTAL	MONEY
Geoff Ogilvy	68	69	72	68	277	36,493.34
Jonathan Byrd	70	70	71	66	277	36,493.33
Russ Cochran	70	69	70	69	278	23,089.09
Skip Kendall	71	64	73	70	278	23,089.09
Steve Lowery	70	65	72	71	278	23,089.09
Dennis Paulson	66	72	72	68	278	23,089.09
Joey Sindelar	71	69	72	66	278	23,089.09
David Toms	69	66	72	71	278	23,089.09
Jerry Kelly	69	67	71	71	278	23,089.09
Deane Pappas	68	69	68	73	278	23,089.09
Andre Stolz	70	69	71	68	278	23,089.09
Daniel Chopra	73	65	67	73	278	23,089.09
Steve Allan	72	68	68	70	278	23,089.10
Scott Hoch	70	69	71	69	279	14,932.80
Bob Tway	67	70	70	72	279	14,932.80
Steve Flesch	68	67	74	70	279	14,932.80
Kent Jones	68	71	69	71	279	14,932.80
Chris Riley	68	68	73	70	279	14,932.80
Kelly Gibson	68	67	76	69	280	12,418.50
Craig Bowden	66	66	73	75	280	12,418.50
Hirofumi Miyase	69	68	73	70	280	12,418.50
Harrison Frazar	74	66	68	72	280	12,418.50
Olin Browne	70	68	73	70	281	11,526
Ken Green	70	66	76	69	281	11,526
Scott Verplank	68	70	71	72	281	11,526
Dean Wilson	70	68	71	72	281	11,526
Greg Chalmers	67	72	70	72	281	11,526
Andrew McLardy	70	69	73	69	281	11,526
Joel Kribel	72	64	72	73	281	11,526
Chris Smith	72	68	68	74	282	11,016
Kirk Triplett	66	69	75	72	282	11,016
Guy Boros	70	70	63	79	282	11,016
Pat Bates	71	69	70	73	283	10,761
Omar Uresti	69	69	70	75	283	10,761
Blaine McCallister	68	71	68	77	284	10,557
Esteban Toledo	69	69	72	74	284	10,557
Dan Olsen	68	69	75	73	285	10,302
Vaughn Taylor	69	70	72	74	285	10,302
John E. Morgan	69	71	74	71	285	10,302
Danny Ellis	63	66	82	75	286	10,098
John Riegger	68	69	75	75	287	9,945
D.J. Brigman	70	68	73	76	287	9,945
Fulton Allem	69	67	78	74	288	9,792
Jeff Brehaut	69	70	73	77	289	9,690
Chris DiMarco	69	69	72	80	290	9,537
Mike Heinen	74	65	79	72	290	9,537
Tommy Tolles	69	71	73	79	292	9,384

Wachovia Championship

Quail Hollow Club, Charlotte, North Carolina
Par 36-36–72; 7,396 yards

May 6-9
purse, $5,600,000

	SCORES				TOTAL	MONEY
Joey Sindelar	69	69	70	69	277	$1,008,000
Arron Oberholser	69	68	68	72	277	604,800

(Sindelar defeated Oberholser on second playoff hole.)

	SCORES				TOTAL	MONEY
Tiger Woods	69	66	75	68	278	324,800
Carlos Franco	68	71	69	70	278	324,800
Jeff Maggert	71	69	67	72	279	196,700
Phil Mickelson	70	70	72	67	279	196,700
Steve Flesch	72	72	66	69	279	196,700
Notah Begay	67	70	69	73	279	196,700
Mathias Gronberg	69	71	71	69	280	162,400
Vijay Singh	68	70	71	72	281	128,800
Kevin Sutherland	71	68	71	71	281	128,800
Geoff Ogilvy	69	71	66	75	281	128,800
Heath Slocum	67	75	67	72	281	128,800
Lucas Glover	74	70	68	69	281	128,800
Tom Byrum	74	69	71	68	282	86,800
Kirk Triplett	64	73	71	74	282	86,800
Matt Gogel	69	72	70	71	282	86,800
Jonathan Kaye	68	74	69	71	282	86,800
Stuart Appleby	66	72	70	74	282	86,800
Luke Donald	67	73	73	69	282	86,800
Todd Hamilton	71	71	70	71	283	54,160
Davis Love	73	66	72	72	283	54,160
Nick Price	74	69	70	70	283	54,160
Mike Weir	67	72	75	69	283	54,160
Chad Campbell	70	74	66	73	283	54,160
J.J. Henry	72	70	70	71	283	54,160
Pat Perez	73	70	70	70	283	54,160
Jay Haas	71	73	71	69	284	38,920
Spike McRoy	69	74	71	70	284	38,920
Cameron Beckman	67	72	71	74	284	38,920
Joe Ogilvie	68	71	76	69	284	38,920
Gene Sauers	70	72	71	72	285	33,133.34
John Senden	69	73	71	72	285	33,133.33
Jason Bohn	71	70	72	72	285	33,133.33
John Cook	74	70	67	75	286	25,293.33
Donnie Hammond	72	70	73	71	286	25,293.34
John Riegger	74	70	73	69	286	25,293.34
Pat Bates	75	68	72	71	286	25,293.33
Stephen Leaney	71	72	71	72	286	25,293.33
Daniel Chopra	73	68	71	74	286	25,293.33
Ben Curtis	71	71	74	70	286	25,293.34
Rich Beem	70	73	68	75	286	25,293.33
K.J. Choi	71	73	69	73	286	25,293.33
Jeff Sluman	70	73	70	74	287	16,930.66
Shaun Micheel	70	72	74	71	287	16,930.67
Brett Quigley	66	72	74	75	287	16,930.66
Dean Wilson	73	71	74	69	287	16,930.67
Peter Lonard	73	68	72	74	287	16,930.67
Scott Hend	73	71	71	72	287	16,930.67
Chris DiMarco	69	70	76	73	288	13,402.67
Tripp Isenhour	71	71	75	71	288	13,402.67
Robert Allenby	72	68	74	74	288	13,402.67
Rich Barcelo	74	68	72	74	288	13,402.66
Rory Sabbatini	66	74	74	74	288	13,402.66
Richard S. Johnson	72	69	76	71	288	13,402.67
Brad Faxon	73	71	72	73	289	12,544
David Peoples	70	71	75	73	289	12,544
Shigeki Maruyama	69	75	72	73	289	12,544
Kelly Mitchum	72	69	77	71	289	12,544
Steve Allan	69	74	72	74	289	12,544
Billy Mayfair	70	74	76	70	290	12,096
Brent Geiberger	70	74	74	72	290	12,096

	SCORES				TOTAL	MONEY
Sergio Garcia	73	71	76	70	290	12,096
Tom Carter	73	70	73	75	291	11,816
Tim Clark	73	69	71	78	291	11,816
Michael Allen	74	69	70	79	292	11,536
Jerry Kelly	69	74	75	74	292	11,536
Robert Damron	72	71	73	76	292	11,536
Grant Waite	72	71	76	74	293	11,312
Blaine McCallister	70	74	78	73	295	11,144
Matt Kuchar	76	68	73	78	295	11,144
Hidemichi Tanaka	72	71	77	80	300	10,976

EDS Byron Nelson Championship

TPC Four Seasons Resort at Las Colinas: May 13-16
Par 35-35–70; 7,022 yards purse, $5,800,000
Cottonwood Valley Course: Par 34-36–70; 6,846 yards
Irving, Texas

	SCORES				TOTAL	MONEY
Sergio Garcia	66	68	65	71	270	$1,044,000
Dudley Hart	65	71	67	67	270	510,400
Robert Damron	67	69	68	66	270	510,400
(Garcia defeated Hart and Damron on first playoff hole.)						
Duffy Waldorf	67	70	66	68	271	239,733.33
Tiger Woods	65	67	70	69	271	239,733.33
Tim Herron	69	70	68	64	271	239,733.34
Nick Price	66	71	69	66	272	174,725
Ernie Els	69	70	66	67	272	174,725
Shigeki Maruyama	70	70	66	66	272	174,725
Stephen Leaney	66	69	69	68	272	174,725
Mark O'Meara	67	66	70	70	273	133,400
Jerry Kelly	66	68	67	72	273	133,400
Deane Pappas	67	69	66	71	273	133,400
Scott Verplank	71	66	67	70	274	92,800
Chris DiMarco	69	70	65	70	274	92,800
Brian Bateman	69	69	69	67	274	92,800
Matt Gogel	69	69	68	68	274	92,800
Carlos Franco	70	70	67	67	274	92,800
David Branshaw	70	69	67	68	274	92,800
Luke Donald	68	71	64	71	274	92,800
Tom Carter	68	69	69	69	275	58,000
Briny Baird	69	69	65	72	275	58,000
Rod Pampling	66	72	66	71	275	58,000
Tjaart van der Walt	69	68	68	70	275	58,000
Rory Sabbatini	69	69	70	67	275	58,000
Bo Van Pelt	70	69	66	70	275	58,000
John Daly	68	71	71	66	276	39,440
Chris Smith	66	72	70	68	276	39,440
Shaun Micheel	67	68	71	70	276	39,440
Harrison Frazar	68	69	70	69	276	39,440
Ted Purdy	68	69	67	72	276	39,440
Jonathan Byrd	67	67	70	72	276	39,440
Brandt Snedeker	70	66	71	69	276	39,440
Russ Cochran	70	68	68	71	277	28,668.57
Kent Jones	68	72	67	70	277	28,668.57
Justin Leonard	69	70	68	70	277	28,668.57
Jesper Parnevik	67	73	69	68	277	28,668.58

	SCORES				TOTAL	MONEY
Hank Kuehne	70	69	65	73	277	28,668.57
Carl Pettersson	67	71	69	70	277	28,668.57
Kevin Na	71	66	69	71	277	28,668.57
Tommy Armour	73	65	68	72	278	20,300
Bob Tway	68	69	69	72	278	20,300
Kevin Sutherland	68	71	68	71	278	20,300
Robert Allenby	69	67	68	74	278	20,300
John Senden	72	68	71	67	278	20,300
J.J. Henry	68	71	66	73	278	20,300
Zach Johnson	68	69	68	73	278	20,300
Bart Bryant	70	70	70	69	279	14,577.34
J.L. Lewis	64	74	68	73	279	14,577.33
Chad Campbell	73	67	69	70	279	14,577.34
Cameron Beckman	70	67	71	71	279	14,577.33
Peter Lonard	64	70	71	74	279	14,577.33
Jason Bohn	69	69	67	74	279	14,577.33
Tom Byrum	71	69	68	72	280	13,224
Jay Williamson	66	71	73	70	280	13,224
Craig Perks	70	69	71	70	280	13,224
Daniel Chopra	66	68	72	74	280	13,224
Rich Barcelo	68	71	69	72	280	13,224
Jay Delsing	69	68	69	75	281	12,470
Todd Hamilton	74	65	70	72	281	12,470
Kenny Perry	67	70	71	73	281	12,470
Neal Lancaster	70	67	71	73	281	12,470
Vijay Singh	68	67	68	78	281	12,470
Mike Weir	69	69	69	74	281	12,470
Notah Begay	68	72	70	71	281	12,470
Todd Fischer	70	67	70	74	281	12,470
John Cook	67	73	75	67	282	11,716
Lee Janzen	70	68	71	73	282	11,716
Mark Hensby	68	71	67	76	282	11,716
Greg Chalmers	68	68	73	73	282	11,716
Pat Perez	71	68	71	72	282	11,716
Billy Andrade	70	70	71	72	283	11,252
Steve Lowery	68	69	70	76	283	11,252
Kevin Durkin	66	70	73	74	283	11,252
Scott Simpson	71	69	74	71	285	11,020
Tommy Tolles	69	69	68	80	286	10,904
Ken Duke	70	70	73	74	287	10,788
Gene Sauers	71	69	75	73	288	10,672
Vaughn Taylor	71	69	73	77	290	10,556
Aaron Baddeley	70	69	79	77	295	10,440

Bank of America Colonial

Colonial Country Club, Fort Worth, Texas
Par 35-35–70; 7,080 yards

May 20-23
purse, $5,300,000

	SCORES				TOTAL	MONEY
Steve Flesch	66	69	67	67	269	$954,000
Chad Campbell	70	71	61	68	270	572,400
Stephen Ames	70	69	68	64	271	360,400
Craig Perks	64	71	70	68	273	254,400
Robert Gamez	71	64	71	68	274	186,162.50
Skip Kendall	68	71	68	67	274	186,162.50
Tim Petrovic	66	71	69	68	274	186,162.50

	SCORES				TOTAL	MONEY
Bo Van Pelt	68	69	72	65	274	186,162.50
Mark Brooks	71	68	67	69	275	143,100
Jeff Maggert	66	69	73	67	275	143,100
John Senden	66	74	70	65	275	143,100
Kenny Perry	67	71	70	68	276	116,600
Loren Roberts	68	70	71	67	276	116,600
Tom Byrum	68	69	71	69	277	72,433.34
Lee Janzen	70	66	71	70	277	72,433.34
Kirk Triplett	69	69	71	68	277	72,433.34
Brian Bateman	69	69	68	71	277	72,433.33
Justin Leonard	70	64	72	71	277	72,433.33
Jesper Parnevik	65	72	68	72	277	72,433.33
Brian Gay	70	67	65	75	277	72,433.33
Chris Riley	67	71	69	70	277	72,433.33
Stewart Cink	66	70	71	70	277	72,433.33
Joe Ogilvie	71	70	68	68	277	72,433.34
Tim Clark	68	70	69	70	277	72,433.33
Zach Johnson	71	65	68	73	277	72,433.33
Fred Funk	70	72	65	71	278	42,400
J.L. Lewis	68	66	75	70	279	38,425
Bob Tway	70	69	68	72	279	38,425
Stephen Leaney	70	68	71	70	279	38,425
Peter Lonard	71	71	67	70	279	38,425
Dennis Paulson	67	70	71	72	280	32,131.25
Corey Pavin	70	70	72	68	280	32,131.25
Glen Day	72	71	67	70	280	32,131.25
Rory Sabbatini	72	69	67	72	280	32,131.25
Davis Love	74	67	72	68	281	25,572.50
Phil Mickelson	71	66	70	74	281	25,572.50
Scott Verplank	72	68	67	74	281	25,572.50
Joe Durant	70	73	69	69	281	25,572.50
Brett Quigley	70	68	68	75	281	25,572.50
Sergio Garcia	72	67	73	69	281	25,572.50
Joey Sindelar	71	69	72	70	282	20,670
Hal Sutton	71	67	73	71	282	20,670
Dudley Hart	73	70	66	73	282	20,670
Tommy Armour	69	74	71	69	283	16,023.67
Todd Hamilton	72	71	70	70	283	16,023.67
David Toms	72	70	68	73	283	16,023.66
Chris DiMarco	69	71	72	71	283	16,023.67
Frank Lickliter	68	70	68	77	283	16,023.66
Rod Pampling	72	71	69	71	283	16,023.67
Brad Faxon	70	68	75	71	284	12,905.50
Kent Jones	70	69	73	72	284	12,905.50
Briny Baird	71	69	71	73	284	12,905.50
Aaron Baddeley	68	71	74	71	284	12,905.50
Steve Elkington	71	71	73	70	285	11,978
Rocco Mediate	72	71	71	71	285	11,978
Neal Lancaster	73	70	70	72	285	11,978
Matt Gogel	70	73	76	66	285	11,978
Robert Allenby	67	76	73	69	285	11,978
Mathias Gronberg	70	70	71	74	285	11,978
Carl Pettersson	67	74	73	71	285	11,978
Mike Weir	68	73	71	74	286	11,501
Scott Hend	69	74	72	71	286	11,501
Tim Herron	69	72	72	74	287	11,130
Geoff Ogilvy	74	69	69	75	287	11,130
Patrick Sheehan	71	70	69	77	287	11,130
Luke Donald	69	74	73	71	287	11,130
Hunter Mahan	70	71	71	75	287	11,130

	SCORES				TOTAL	MONEY
Steve Lowery	69	74	75	70	288	10,706
Dan Pohl	71	72	72	73	288	10,706
Jeff Sluman	72	70	74	72	288	10,706
Len Mattiace	71	71	74	73	289	10,441
Brenden Pappas	73	70	72	74	289	10,441
Mark Calcavecchia	72	68	75	75	290	10,282
Bob Estes	68	74	72	77	291	10,176

FedEx St. Jude Classic

TPC at Southwind, Memphis, Tennessee
Par 35-36–71; 7,030 yards

May 27-30
purse, $4,700,000

	SCORES				TOTAL	MONEY
David Toms	67	63	65	73	268	$846,000
Bob Estes	74	64	67	69	274	507,600
Steve Lowery	74	64	70	67	275	272,600
Tim Herron	72	64	69	70	275	272,600
Brian Gay	71	66	66	73	276	165,087.50
Stewart Cink	68	70	69	69	276	165,087.50
Fredrik Jacobson	75	68	64	69	276	165,087.50
Vaughn Taylor	66	65	71	74	276	165,087.50
Craig Bowden	72	68	66	71	277	122,200
Paul Stankowski	67	69	71	70	277	122,200
Hirofumi Miyase	68	69	67	73	277	122,200
Charles Howell	70	70	68	69	277	122,200
Michael Bradley	70	70	67	71	278	85,540
Dennis Paulson	72	68	67	71	278	85,540
Michael Allen	71	68	70	69	278	85,540
Brian Kortan	75	67	66	70	278	85,540
Joel Kribel	73	65	70	70	278	85,540
Tom Pernice, Jr.	75	68	63	73	279	61,288
Loren Roberts	71	71	67	70	279	61,288
Kris Cox	72	67	68	72	279	61,288
John Senden	74	69	65	71	279	61,288
Steve Allan	70	67	69	73	279	61,288
Joe Ogilvie	74	69	66	71	280	45,120
Ted Purdy	72	64	71	73	280	45,120
Hank Kuehne	73	66	70	71	280	45,120
Billy Andrade	75	67	67	72	281	33,370
Danny Briggs	74	68	67	72	281	33,370
Fred Funk	73	68	66	74	281	33,370
David Peoples	71	69	68	73	281	33,370
Patrick Sheehan	69	70	70	72	281	33,370
Matt Kuchar	73	66	70	72	281	33,370
Hunter Mahan	73	67	70	71	281	33,370
Joel Edwards	73	68	67	74	282	23,291.11
Mike Grob	75	67	66	74	282	23,291.11
J.P. Hayes	70	71	70	71	282	23,291.11
Michael Clark	81	62	70	69	282	23,291.11
Brent Geiberger	69	72	74	67	282	23,291.11
Notah Begay	75	65	69	73	282	23,291.12
Doug Barron	76	67	67	72	282	23,291.11
Ben Crane	70	65	73	74	282	23,291.11
Rich Beem	73	64	68	77	282	23,291.11
John Daly	71	65	72	75	283	16,450
Robert Gamez	72	71	68	72	283	16,450

	SCORES				TOTAL	MONEY
Matt Gogel	72	69	69	73	283	16,450
Cameron Beckman	73	68	70	72	283	16,450
Robert Damron	71	69	69	74	283	16,450
Bart Bryant	72	68	69	75	284	12,072.29
Gene Sauers	74	66	69	75	284	12,072.29
Jim McGovern	75	66	71	72	284	12,072.28
Brett Quigley	75	68	68	73	284	12,072.28
Ken Duke	74	66	70	74	284	12,072.29
Tjaart van der Walt	72	69	70	73	284	12,072.28
Zhang Lian-wei	68	72	70	74	284	12,072.29
Jay Delsing	72	70	67	76	285	10,716
Kirk Triplett	73	69	70	73	285	10,716
Brian Bateman	73	65	73	74	285	10,716
J.J. Henry	70	70	71	74	285	10,716
Bryce Molder	74	69	69	73	285	10,716
Tom Lehman	70	70	71	75	286	10,434
David Edwards	73	70	69	75	287	10,246
Stan Utley	72	70	69	76	287	10,246
Brenden Pappas	71	69	71	76	287	10,246
Tripp Isenhour	70	67	73	78	288	9,964
Jose Coceres	74	64	74	76	288	9,964
Scott Hend	73	70	72	73	288	9,964
Vance Veazey	71	70	73	75	289	9,776
Greg Chalmers	70	70	72	78	290	9,635
Pat Perez	72	70	70	78	290	9,635
Tom Carter	72	66	74	79	291	9,494
Chris Smith	74	69	77	72	292	9,353
Rich Barcelo	70	71	73	78	292	9,353
Mike Springer	75	67	72	80	294	9,165
Brandt Snedeker	74	69	76	75	294	9,165
Deane Pappas	72	69	74	83	298	9,024

Memorial Tournament

Muirfield Village Golf Club, Dublin, Ohio — June 3-6
Par 36-36–72; 7,265 yards — purse, $5,250,000

	SCORES				TOTAL	MONEY
Ernie Els	68	70	66	66	270	$945,000
Fred Couples	69	69	68	68	274	567,000
Tiger Woods	72	68	67	69	276	357,000
Justin Rose	70	67	69	71	277	252,000
K.J. Choi	71	67	68	72	278	210,000
Kenny Perry	72	72	66	69	279	182,437.50
Stephen Ames	69	68	70	72	279	182,437.50
Jay Haas	70	72	69	71	282	152,250
Retief Goosen	70	72	69	71	282	152,250
Ben Curtis	68	69	73	72	282	152,250
John Daly	72	69	73	69	283	111,300
J.L. Lewis	70	72	70	71	283	111,300
Stephen Leaney	71	71	71	70	283	111,300
Peter Lonard	71	73	70	69	283	111,300
Rory Sabbatini	71	71	71	70	283	111,300
Davis Love	70	73	72	69	284	84,000
Tom Pernice, Jr.	73	71	71	69	284	84,000
Jerry Kelly	74	70	70	70	284	84,000
John Cook	71	74	71	69	285	65,887.50

	SCORES				TOTAL	MONEY
Brad Faxon	72	74	71	68	285	65,887.50
Scott McCarron	72	69	75	69	285	65,887.50
Tim Herron	76	71	66	72	285	65,887.50
Harrison Frazar	73	72	69	72	286	54,600
Dan Forsman	73	73	67	74	287	39,725
Tom Lehman	74	69	73	71	287	39,725
Chris DiMarco	71	74	72	70	287	39,725
Vijay Singh	73	72	71	71	287	39,725
Chad Campbell	72	73	74	68	287	39,725
Sergio Garcia	73	69	72	73	287	39,725
Ted Purdy	74	70	72	71	287	39,725
Geoff Ogilvy	74	68	71	74	287	39,725
Zach Johnson	69	73	70	75	287	39,725
Todd Hamilton	69	70	73	76	288	27,150
Lee Janzen	69	73	72	74	288	27,150
Jeff Sluman	70	73	73	72	288	27,150
Kevin Sutherland	71	70	72	75	288	27,150
Steve Flesch	72	73	72	71	288	27,150
Robert Allenby	74	74	74	66	288	27,150
Hidemichi Tanaka	73	75	72	68	288	27,150
Tim Petrovic	75	69	71	74	289	19,950
Stewart Cink	70	74	75	70	289	19,950
Padraig Harrington	71	74	74	70	289	19,950
John Rollins	69	74	74	72	289	19,950
Tim Clark	73	75	69	72	289	19,950
Rich Beem	71	71	72	75	289	19,950
Len Mattiace	70	73	73	74	290	14,553
Jesper Parnevik	75	71	74	70	290	14,553
Shigeki Maruyama	71	71	76	72	290	14,553
Mark Hensby	74	74	73	69	290	14,553
Trevor Immelman	73	73	69	75	290	14,553
Jeff Maggert	73	69	76	73	291	12,521.25
Nick Price	74	73	72	72	291	12,521.25
Briny Baird	76	69	71	75	291	12,521.25
Niclas Fasth	75	70	73	73	291	12,521.25
Tommy Armour	72	72	72	76	292	11,812.50
Skip Kendall	77	71	69	75	292	11,812.50
Rocco Mediate	71	73	73	75	292	11,812.50
Arron Oberholser	69	74	72	77	292	11,812.50
Brenden Pappas	73	74	72	73	292	11,812.50
Keiichiro Fukabori	72	74	74	72	292	11,812.50
Hunter Mahan	74	70	75	74	293	11,445
Mark Calcavecchia	74	72	73	75	294	11,340
Billy Andrade	71	73	75	76	295	11,130
Jack Nicklaus	74	73	77	71	295	11,130
Stuart Appleby	73	74	70	78	295	11,130
Paul Azinger	69	74	78	76	297	10,815
Craig Parry	71	72	79	75	297	10,815
Woody Austin	73	74	78	72	297	10,815
Shaun Micheel	73	73	80	72	298	10,552.50
Aaron Baddeley	74	74	78	72	298	10,552.50
Corey Pavin	71	75	76	77	299	10,342.50
Frank Lickliter	71	75	73	80	299	10,342.50
Thomas Bjorn	71	76	78	75	300	10,132.50
Darren Fichardt	70	78	74	78	300	10,132.50
Hirofumi Miyase	73	75	77	78	303	9,975

Buick Classic

Westchester Country Club, West Course,
Harrison, New York
Par 36-35–71; 6,751 yards

June 10-13
purse, $5,250,000

	SCORES				TOTAL	MONEY
Sergio Garcia	70	67	68	67	272	$945,000
Padraig Harrington	68	68	68	68	272	462,000
Rory Sabbatini	69	68	65	70	272	462,000
(Garcia defeated Harrington on second and Sabbatini on third playoff hole.)						
Tom Byrum	71	64	68	71	274	217,000
Fred Couples	67	65	74	68	274	217,000
Vijay Singh	63	70	71	70	274	217,000
Luke Donald	67	66	70	72	275	175,875
Fredrik Jacobson	64	69	74	69	276	162,750
Kenny Perry	69	71	71	66	277	131,250
Chris DiMarco	69	69	69	70	277	131,250
Cameron Beckman	68	68	66	75	277	131,250
Tim Clark	68	72	68	69	277	131,250
Bo Van Pelt	68	71	68	70	277	131,250
Robert Allenby	69	71	69	69	278	97,125
Scott Hend	68	68	72	70	278	97,125
Phil Mickelson	69	68	69	73	279	73,650
Craig Parry	73	66	69	71	279	73,650
Loren Roberts	67	70	64	78	279	73,650
Ernie Els	68	69	72	70	279	73,650
Brett Quigley	69	68	72	70	279	73,650
Joe Ogilvie	72	66	70	71	279	73,650
J.J. Henry	68	73	69	69	279	73,650
Brad Faxon	68	73	67	72	280	46,725
Dennis Paulson	70	68	68	74	280	46,725
Kris Cox	67	71	68	74	280	46,725
Stuart Appleby	69	70	69	72	280	46,725
Zach Johnson	74	66	70	70	280	46,725
Davis Love	68	71	70	72	281	36,487.50
Tim Petrovic	69	69	71	72	281	36,487.50
Scott Verplank	69	70	69	73	281	36,487.50
Brian Gay	70	68	68	75	281	36,487.50
Bart Bryant	72	68	72	70	282	26,670
Dan Forsman	70	71	69	72	282	26,670
Steve Lowery	69	70	72	71	282	26,670
Joey Sindelar	68	72	70	72	282	26,670
Neal Lancaster	70	71	70	71	282	26,670
Dudley Hart	67	71	73	71	282	26,670
Kevin Sutherland	68	70	73	71	282	26,670
Jerry Kelly	71	69	72	70	282	26,670
Ted Purdy	69	70	69	74	282	26,670
Adam Scott	71	70	72	69	282	26,670
Skip Kendall	68	71	68	76	283	15,807.27
Rocco Mediate	71	67	71	74	283	15,807.27
Tom Pernice, Jr.	71	70	72	70	283	15,807.28
Pat Bates	72	69	67	75	283	15,807.27
Glen Day	71	70	73	69	283	15,807.28
David Morland	69	70	70	74	283	15,807.27
Peter Lonard	67	74	72	70	283	15,807.28
John Senden	70	68	71	74	283	15,807.27
Daniel Chopra	69	70	71	73	283	15,807.27
D.J. Brigman	71	69	71	72	283	15,807.27
Pat Perez	73	66	70	74	283	15,807.27

	SCORES				TOTAL	MONEY
Omar Uresti	70	71	74	69	284	12,285
Stephen Leaney	73	67	73	71	284	12,285
David Frost	66	72	70	77	285	11,865
Bob Tway	71	69	71	74	285	11,865
Craig Bowden	71	69	72	73	285	11,865
Todd Fischer	69	71	70	75	285	11,865
John Rollins	72	66	74	73	285	11,865
Danny Ellis	75	66	75	70	286	11,287.50
Carlos Franco	68	69	74	75	286	11,287.50
Robert Damron	67	70	73	76	286	11,287.50
Jose Coceres	69	68	70	79	286	11,287.50
Tjaart van der Walt	71	65	75	75	286	11,287.50
Arjun Atwal	73	67	76	70	286	11,287.50
Esteban Toledo	71	69	72	75	287	10,815
Niclas Fasth	69	71	75	72	287	10,815
Richard S. Johnson	69	72	73	73	287	10,815
Alex Cejka	70	69	73	76	288	10,552.50
Jonathan Byrd	67	70	71	80	288	10,552.50
Billy Andrade	70	70	75	74	289	10,237.50
Chris Smith	71	70	70	78	289	10,237.50
Notah Begay	69	72	73	75	289	10,237.50
Jason Bohn	72	68	76	73	289	10,237.50
Billy Mayfair	68	68	76	78	290	9,975
Joel Edwards	69	72	71	79	291	9,712.50
Tom Carter	70	69	77	75	291	9,712.50
Miguel Angel Jimenez	70	67	76	78	291	9,712.50
Brad Adamonis	69	72	73	77	291	9,712.50
Grant Waite	72	69	75	76	292	9,397.50
Jonathan Kaye	73	66	73	80	292	9,397.50
Patrick Sheehan	71	69	76	78	294	9,240

U.S. Open Championship

Shinnecock Hills Golf Club, Southampton, New York
Par 35-35–70; 6,996 yards

June 17-20
purse, $6,250,000

	SCORES				TOTAL	MONEY
Retief Goosen	70	66	69	71	276	$1,125,000
Phil Mickelson	68	66	73	71	278	675,000
Jeff Maggert	68	67	74	72	281	424,604
Mike Weir	69	70	71	74	284	267,756
Shigeki Maruyama	66	68	74	76	284	267,756
Fred Funk	70	66	72	77	285	212,444
Robert Allenby	70	72	74	70	286	183,828
Steve Flesch	68	74	70	74	286	183,828
Jay Haas	66	74	76	71	287	145,282
Stephen Ames	74	66	73	74	287	145,282
Chris DiMarco	71	71	70	75	287	145,282
Ernie Els	70	67	70	80	287	145,282
Tim Herron	75	66	73	74	288	119,770
*Spencer Levin	69	73	71	75	288	
Tim Clark	73	70	66	79	288	119,770
Angel Cabrera	66	71	77	75	289	109,410
Skip Kendall	68	75	74	73	290	98,477
Tiger Woods	72	69	73	76	290	98,477
Corey Pavin	67	71	73	79	290	98,477
Mark Calcavecchia	71	71	74	75	291	80,644

	SCORES				TOTAL	MONEY
David Toms	73	72	70	76	291	80,644
Kirk Triplett	71	70	73	77	291	80,644
Sergio Garcia	72	68	71	80	291	80,644
Daniel Chopra	73	68	76	75	292	63,328
Tim Petrovic	69	75	72	76	292	63,328
Nick Price	73	70	72	77	292	63,328
Lee Janzen	72	70	71	79	292	63,328
Vijay Singh	68	70	77	78	293	51,774
Shaun Micheel	71	72	70	80	293	51,774
Ben Curtis	68	75	72	79	294	46,089
Peter Lonard	71	73	77	74	295	41,759
K.J. Choi	76	68	76	75	295	41,759
Padraig Harrington	73	71	76	75	295	41,759
David Roesch	68	73	74	80	295	41,759
Bo Van Pelt	69	73	73	80	295	41,759
*Casey Wittenberg	71	71	75	79	296	
Lee Westwood	73	71	73	79	296	36,813
Hidemichi Tanaka	70	74	73	79	296	36,813
Charles Howell	75	70	68	83	296	36,813
Joe Ogilvie	70	75	74	78	297	30,672
Pat Perez	73	67	76	81	297	30,672
Spike McRoy	72	72	72	81	297	30,672
Jerry Kelly	76	69	71	81	297	30,672
*Bill Haas	72	73	71	81	297	
Geoffrey Sisk	72	72	71	82	297	30,672
Scott Verplank	71	71	72	83	297	30,672
Stephen Leaney	72	70	71	84	297	30,672
John Rollins	76	68	76	78	298	23,325
Kris Cox	68	74	77	79	298	23,325
Jim Furyk	72	72	75	79	298	23,325
Zach Johnson	70	73	75	80	298	23,325
Chris Riley	72	71	72	83	298	23,325
Scott Hoch	75	70	73	81	299	19,390
Dudley Hart	71	73	70	85	299	19,390
Trevor Immelman	69	70	79	82	300	18,405
Tom Carter	74	71	70	85	300	18,405
Joakim Haeggman	74	69	76	83	302	17,304
Phillip Price	70	73	75	84	302	17,304
Tom Kite	72	71	75	84	302	17,304
Craig Parry	70	73	75	85	303	16,353
Alex Cejka	75	70	73	85	303	16,353
Cliff Kresge	72	73	77	82	304	15,888
*Chez Reavie	73	72	71	88	304	
J.J. Henry	75	69	86	76	306	15,630
Kevin Stadler	68	72	82	85	307	15,372
Billy Mayfair	70	70	81	89	310	15,089

Out of Final 36 Holes

Duffy Waldorf	72	74		146
Rory Sabbatini	72	74		146
Chad Campbell	72	74		146
Jonathan Kaye	77	69		146
J.P. Hayes	72	74		146
Bob Tway	73	73		146
Miguel Angel Jimenez	77	69		146
Justin Leonard	71	75		146
Omar Uresti	75	71		146
Justin Hicks	75	71		146
Brian Davis	73	73		146

	SCORES		TOTAL
John Senden	76	70	146
Eduardo Romero	72	74	146
Rich Beem	74	72	146
Tom Byrum	76	70	146
Michael Campbell	78	68	146
Dan Forsman	74	72	146
Brad Faxon	74	72	146
Ian Poulter	74	72	146
Bob Estes	74	72	146
Bubba Watson	73	74	147
Dan Olsen	73	74	147
Tripp Isenhour	74	73	147
Darren Clarke	73	74	147
Briny Baird	73	74	147
Kevin Sutherland	76	71	147
Paul Casey	74	73	147
Craig Bowden	76	71	147
Dennis Paulson	72	76	148
Joey Sindelar	79	69	148
Toshimitsu Izawa	72	76	148
Steve Stricker	75	73	148
Chris Smith	77	71	148
J.L. Lewis	73	75	148
Robert Garrigus	74	74	148
John Douma	76	72	148
Brad Lardon	73	75	148
Brian Gay	69	79	148
Thomas Bjorn	77	71	148
Tom Pernice, Jr.	73	75	148
Stuart Appleby	79	70	149
Stewart Cink	74	75	149
Brendan Jones	71	78	149
Parker McLachlin	75	74	149
*Brock Mackenzie	73	76	149
*Nathan Smith	73	76	149
John Elliott	76	73	149
Camilo Villegas	73	76	149
Steve Allan	74	75	149
Andrew Tschudin	73	76	149
Eric Axley	72	77	149
Thomas Levet	75	75	150
Adam Scott	75	75	150
Scott Weatherly	76	74	150
Charleton Dechert	73	77	150
Raymond Floyd	75	75	150
David Morland	75	75	150
Aaron Baddeley	79	72	151
Todd Hamilton	77	74	151
Pete Jordan	79	72	151
Davis Love	76	75	151
Nick Faldo	81	70	151
Kenny Perry	74	77	151
Matt Gogel	76	75	151
David Faught	75	76	151
Fredrik Jacobson	75	77	152
Fred Couples	75	77	152
Roger Tambellini	79	73	152
Jonathan Byrd	74	78	152
Gabriel Hjertstedt	75	77	152
Mark Brooks	74	78	152

	SCORES	TOTAL
Jimmy Green	78 74	152
Jeff Gove	75 77	152
John Connelly	73 79	152
Payton Osborn	76 77	153
Paul Lawrie	76 77	153
Scott Hend	75 78	153
Carl Paulson	72 81	153
Leif Olson	76 77	153
Steve Sokol	75 79	154
Johnson Wagner	77 77	154
*Nick Flanagan	80 74	154
Steve Gotsche	76 78	154
Justin Rose	77 78	155
Casey Bourque	78 79	157
*Oscar Alvarez	78 80	158
Joey Maxon	78 82	160
David Duval	83 82	165
David Carr	83 83	166
Carlos Franco		WD

(Professionals who did not complete 72 holes received $5,000.)

Booz Allen Classic

TPC at Avenel, Potomac, Maryland
Par 36-35–71; 6,987 yards

June 24-27
purse, $4,800,000

	SCORES				TOTAL	MONEY
Adam Scott	66	62	67	68	263	$864,000
Charles Howell	61	69	72	65	267	518,400
Rory Sabbatini	67	67	69	66	269	326,400
Tim Herron	69	68	68	67	272	198,400
Arron Oberholser	69	65	68	70	272	198,400
Bo Van Pelt	69	68	68	67	272	198,400
Olin Browne	64	66	71	72	273	154,800
Alex Cejka	74	63	67	69	273	154,800
Frank Lickliter	67	69	72	66	274	134,400
Aaron Barber	70	68	68	68	274	134,400
Tom Lehman	66	67	71	71	275	101,760
Jeff Sluman	65	71	69	70	275	101,760
Duffy Waldorf	67	71	66	71	275	101,760
Harrison Frazar	67	69	70	69	275	101,760
Ryan Palmer	70	69	68	68	275	101,760
Tom Pernice, Jr.	68	71	69	68	276	79,200
Rich Barcelo	71	69	69	67	276	79,200
Guy Boros	68	69	71	69	277	67,200
J.J. Henry	68	69	70	70	277	67,200
Kevin Na	68	71	64	74	277	67,200
Billy Andrade	68	71	72	67	278	45,060
Bart Bryant	71	67	67	73	278	45,060
Joe Durant	69	71	68	70	278	45,060
David Morland	69	71	72	66	278	45,060
Danny Ellis	67	69	71	71	278	45,060
Scott Hend	66	72	69	71	278	45,060
Vaughn Taylor	68	71	68	71	278	45,060
Ben Crane	70	70	66	72	278	45,060
Michael Allen	70	71	69	69	279	31,920

	SCORES				TOTAL	MONEY
Matt Gogel	69	70	71	69	279	31,920
Craig Barlow	69	68	69	73	279	31,920
Hidemichi Tanaka	70	65	73	71	279	31,920
Bill Glasson	72	69	67	72	280	23,280
Esteban Toledo	69	71	68	72	280	23,280
Pete Jordan	72	67	72	69	280	23,280
Shaun Micheel	67	72	66	75	280	23,280
Steve Stricker	67	68	71	74	280	23,280
Brent Geiberger	71	68	72	69	280	23,280
Notah Begay	72	65	71	72	280	23,280
Chris Riley	72	66	69	73	280	23,280
Mark Wilson	69	72	69	70	280	23,280
Bill Haas	69	65	73	73	280	23,280
Michael Bradley	70	65	70	76	281	14,616
Danny Briggs	70	69	69	73	281	14,616
John Cook	71	69	69	72	281	14,616
Corey Pavin	70	68	70	73	281	14,616
Glen Day	69	62	79	71	281	14,616
Mark Hensby	68	72	70	71	281	14,616
David Branshaw	69	70	71	71	281	14,616
Luke Donald	72	68	70	71	281	14,616
Brad Faxon	74	66	71	71	282	11,296
Jeff Brehaut	70	69	71	72	282	11,296
Charley Hoffman	69	70	71	72	282	11,296
Rich Beem	64	67	72	79	282	11,296
Carl Pettersson	67	71	70	74	282	11,296
Richard S. Johnson	72	67	72	71	282	11,296
David Edwards	68	73	71	71	283	10,512
Len Mattiace	71	69	71	72	283	10,512
Tommy Tolles	69	72	71	71	283	10,512
Pat Bates	70	71	72	70	283	10,512
Cameron Beckman	70	68	79	66	283	10,512
Garrett Willis	71	68	70	74	283	10,512
Daniel Chopra	72	69	70	72	283	10,512
Steve Allan	69	67	75	72	283	10,512
Billy Mayfair	66	70	75	73	284	10,080
Cliff Kresge	71	68	74	72	285	9,888
Kelly Mitchum	72	69	76	68	285	9,888
Heath Slocum	70	69	74	72	285	9,888
Tom Byrum	72	69	76	69	286	9,648
Jonathan Kaye	70	70	71	75	286	9,648
Kelly Gibson	71	70	72	74	287	9,312
Geoff Ogilvy	70	68	74	75	287	9,312
Aaron Baddeley	67	74	74	72	287	9,312
Patrick Sheehan	68	71	77	71	287	9,312
Hunter Mahan	69	70	73	75	287	9,312
Mike Grob	72	68	72	77	289	9,024
Steve Pate	68	73	76	73	290	8,880
Dicky Pride	68	71	76	75	290	8,880
John Daly	70	70	76	77	293	8,736
Jay Don Blake	69	70	77	85	301	8,640

Cialis Western Open

Cog Hill Golf & Country Club, Lemont, Illinois
Par 36-36–72; 7,073 yards

July 1-4
purse, $4,800,000

	SCORES				TOTAL	MONEY
Stephen Ames	67	73	64	70	274	$864,000
Steve Lowery	68	68	70	70	276	518,400
Mark Hensby	67	70	67	73	277	278,400
Luke Donald	72	68	70	67	277	278,400
Stuart Appleby	71	68	67	72	278	182,400
Geoff Ogilvy	68	69	68	73	278	182,400
Davis Love	70	74	67	68	279	144,600
Tiger Woods	70	73	65	71	279	144,600
Jim Furyk	69	71	68	71	279	144,600
Carl Pettersson	71	70	69	69	279	144,600
Scott Hoch	69	69	73	69	280	98,400
Loren Roberts	64	75	73	68	280	98,400
Scott Verplank	72	71	67	70	280	98,400
Robert Allenby	65	73	71	71	280	98,400
Shigeki Maruyama	70	72	67	71	280	98,400
Pat Perez	69	73	71	67	280	98,400
Robert Gamez	67	71	72	71	281	64,960
Vijay Singh	72	71	68	70	281	64,960
Matt Gogel	72	64	74	71	281	64,960
Carlos Franco	74	69	70	68	281	64,960
Charles Howell	69	67	74	71	281	64,960
John Rollins	71	69	69	72	281	64,960
J.J. Henry	69	73	68	72	282	49,920
Billy Mayfair	69	74	69	71	283	42,240
Peter Lonard	72	70	70	71	283	42,240
D.J. Brigman	68	70	75	70	283	42,240
Bart Bryant	71	71	71	71	284	33,360
Michael Allen	68	72	72	72	284	33,360
Bob Burns	74	68	72	70	284	33,360
Mike Small	69	70	69	76	284	33,360
David Branshaw	68	74	72	70	284	33,360
Jonathan Byrd	67	72	71	74	284	33,360
Steve Stricker	69	75	71	70	285	24,822.86
Jerry Kelly	72	72	72	69	285	24,822.85
Tom Carter	71	72	71	71	285	24,822.86
Jose Coceres	72	69	74	70	285	24,822.86
Jason Bohn	71	73	71	70	285	24,822.85
Kevin Na	70	69	75	71	285	24,822.86
Richard S. Johnson	70	71	73	71	285	24,822.86
David Frost	75	68	71	72	286	17,760
Steve Pate	73	70	67	76	286	17,760
Brett Quigley	73	71	71	71	286	17,760
Briny Baird	70	73	70	73	286	17,760
Mark Wilson	72	71	71	72	286	17,760
Rich Beem	69	73	71	73	286	17,760
K.J. Choi	68	71	74	73	286	17,760
Skip Kendall	68	75	71	73	287	12,912
Jeff Sluman	72	70	71	74	287	12,912
Scott McCarron	71	72	74	70	287	12,912
Stephen Leaney	76	66	70	75	287	12,912
Steve Elkington	72	72	72	72	288	11,232
Scott Simpson	68	71	73	76	288	11,232
Chris Smith	68	72	70	78	288	11,232
Jay Williamson	69	73	74	72	288	11,232

	SCORES				TOTAL	MONEY
Chad Campbell	67	76	73	72	288	11,232
Patrick Sheehan	73	70	69	76	288	11,232
Jason Dufner	71	72	75	70	288	11,232
Brad Lardon	76	68	71	74	289	10,560
Pat Bates	72	70	77	70	289	10,560
Todd Fischer	70	74	72	73	289	10,560
Steve Allan	72	69	72	76	289	10,560
Aaron Baddeley	75	69	73	72	289	10,560
Dan Forsman	68	72	72	78	290	9,936
Len Mattiace	74	70	72	74	290	9,936
Gene Sauers	73	68	75	74	290	9,936
Joey Sindelar	72	70	77	71	290	9,936
Brian Bateman	74	67	74	75	290	9,936
Robert Damron	70	74	73	73	290	9,936
Vaughn Taylor	71	69	72	78	290	9,936
Hank Kuehne	70	73	76	71	290	9,936
Tommy Armour	72	72	73	74	291	9,264
Kevin Sutherland	68	73	71	79	291	9,264
Craig Bowden	69	72	73	77	291	9,264
Glen Day	74	69	73	75	291	9,264
Brent Geiberger	72	70	74	75	291	9,264
Lucas Glover	75	68	79	69	291	9,264
Heath Slocum	71	68	75	78	292	8,928
J.P. Hayes	74	68	74	77	293	8,832
Joel Edwards	74	70	76	74	294	8,688
J.L. Lewis	67	74	78	75	294	8,688
Trevor Dodds	73	71	75	76	295	8,496
Ryan Palmer	74	69	76	76	295	8,496

John Deere Classic

TPC at Deere Run, Silvis, Illinois
Par 35-36–71; 7,183 yards

July 8-11
purse, $3,800,000

	SCORES				TOTAL	MONEY
Mark Hensby	68	65	69	66	268	$684,000
John E. Morgan	66	69	68	65	268	410,400
(Hensby defeated Morgan on second playoff hole.)						
Jose Coceres	62	68	68	71	269	258,400
Steve Stricker	71	67	64	68	270	149,625
Vijay Singh	69	67	67	67	270	149,625
Greg Chalmers	64	67	69	70	270	149,625
Joel Kribel	70	65	70	65	270	149,625
Jeff Sluman	69	68	66	68	271	110,200
Stewart Cink	70	65	67	69	271	110,200
John Rollins	66	69	69	67	271	110,200
Jay Haas	67	68	67	70	272	87,400
Scott Hoch	68	68	68	68	272	87,400
Jeff Brehaut	65	70	68	69	272	87,400
Robert Gamez	67	68	67	71	273	62,700
Scott McCarron	70	69	65	69	273	62,700
Carl Paulson	68	72	67	66	273	62,700
Patrick Sheehan	69	66	69	69	273	62,700
Vaughn Taylor	63	69	70	71	273	62,700
Jason Bohn	67	71	68	67	273	62,700
Len Mattiace	68	68	69	69	274	44,270
Jim McGovern	67	69	68	70	274	44,270

	SCORES				TOTAL	MONEY
Zach Johnson	70	69	65	70	274	44,270
Casey Wittenberg	68	71	66	69	274	44,270
Olin Browne	68	71	68	68	275	33,440
Joe Durant	66	69	67	73	275	33,440
Glen Day	70	68	70	67	275	33,440
J.L. Lewis	67	73	68	68	276	26,980
Tom Pernice, Jr.	68	68	67	73	276	26,980
Shigeki Maruyama	70	70	69	67	276	26,980
David Morland	71	69	66	70	276	26,980
Hank Kuehne	69	68	68	71	276	26,980
Joel Edwards	71	68	70	68	277	20,574.29
Stan Utley	70	69	67	71	277	20,574.29
Chris DiMarco	72	66	72	67	277	20,574.28
Kevin Sutherland	67	69	73	68	277	20,574.29
Aaron Barber	66	70	76	65	277	20,574.28
Ben Crane	69	71	70	67	277	20,574.28
Lucas Glover	68	67	72	70	277	20,574.29
Bart Bryant	70	68	69	71	278	14,820
Neal Lancaster	70	70	69	69	278	14,820
Wes Short, Jr.	68	71	71	68	278	14,820
John Senden	70	69	72	67	278	14,820
Daniel Chopra	64	72	73	69	278	14,820
Harrison Frazar	69	71	70	68	278	14,820
Mark Wilson	68	68	70	72	278	14,820
Nick Price	68	70	69	72	279	9,880
Woody Austin	69	70	68	72	279	9,880
Mike Heinen	70	66	71	72	279	9,880
Kris Cox	69	71	68	71	279	9,880
Todd Fischer	69	70	69	71	279	9,880
Briny Baird	69	68	68	74	279	9,880
Hidemichi Tanaka	72	67	70	70	279	9,880
Ted Purdy	65	71	73	70	279	9,880
Jason Dufner	68	72	71	68	279	9,880
Donnie Hammond	71	67	72	70	280	8,626
Mike Springer	70	70	71	69	280	8,626
J.P. Hayes	69	68	68	75	280	8,626
Carlos Franco	70	67	73	70	280	8,626
Todd Hamilton	67	70	71	73	281	8,284
Chris Smith	67	73	73	68	281	8,284
Kirk Triplett	68	72	68	73	281	8,284
Willie Wood	70	68	74	69	281	8,284
Camilo Villegas	71	68	68	74	281	8,284
Jonathan Byrd	67	72	70	73	282	8,018
Richard S. Johnson	68	68	72	74	282	8,018
Pat Perez	70	69	75	69	283	7,904
David Edwards	69	70	73	72	284	7,752
Kevin Na	70	70	71	73	284	7,752
Roland Thatcher	70	68	73	73	284	7,752
Tripp Isenhour	70	70	71	74	285	7,486
Roger Tambellini	68	70	74	73	285	7,486
J.J. Henry	68	72	74	71	285	7,486
D.J. Brigman	69	71	74	71	285	7,486
Patrick Moore	72	68	68	78	286	7,258
Matt Kuchar	69	70	72	75	286	7,258

The Open Championship

See European Tours chapter.

B.C. Open

En-Joie Golf Club, Endicott, New York
Par 37-35–72; 6,974 yards

July 15-18
purse, $3,000,000

	SCORES				TOTAL	MONEY
Jonathan Byrd	67	65	68	68	268	$540,000
Ted Purdy	69	67	65	68	269	324,000
Notah Begay	73	62	66	69	270	144,000
Todd Fischer	65	69	71	65	270	144,000
Robin Freeman	70	67	67	66	270	144,000
Hidemichi Tanaka	68	68	68	66	270	144,000
Neal Lancaster	67	67	69	68	271	93,500
Vaughn Taylor	71	66	68	66	271	93,500
Camilo Villegas	65	70	67	69	271	93,500
Jim Gallagher, Jr.	70	68	66	68	272	75,000
Robert Gamez	75	61	65	71	272	75,000
John Senden	71	66	67	68	272	75,000
Hank Kuehne	70	68	67	68	273	56,250
John Morgan	65	68	68	72	273	56,250
Chris Smith	69	65	69	70	273	56,250
Tommy Tolles	67	69	65	72	273	56,250
Steve Allan	72	68	64	70	274	43,500
Bill Haas	74	66	66	68	274	43,500
Joey Sindelar	68	69	68	69	274	43,500
Jay Williamson	68	67	70	69	274	43,500
Pat Bates	70	68	67	70	275	28,162.50
Jason Bohn	67	68	69	71	275	28,162.50
Wayne Levi	72	67	69	67	275	28,162.50
Brenden Pappas	66	73	67	69	275	28,162.50
John Rollins	71	65	72	67	275	28,162.50
Craig Stadler	67	69	71	68	275	28,162.50
Esteban Toledo	71	66	70	68	275	28,162.50
Omar Uresti	71	67	67	70	275	28,162.50
Jim Carter	70	68	68	70	276	19,075
Greg Chalmers	68	71	70	67	276	19,075
Daniel Chopra	68	65	72	71	276	19,075
John Cook	69	68	68	71	276	19,075
Jason Dufner	69	71	69	67	276	19,075
Mark Wiebe	69	70	69	68	276	19,075
David Edwards	71	71	66	69	277	14,790
Gabriel Hjertstedt	67	68	70	72	277	14,790
Richard Johnson	69	68	70	70	277	14,790
David Peoples	70	66	69	72	277	14,790
Stan Utley	68	69	71	69	277	14,790
Fred Funk	74	68	68	68	278	12,300
Lucas Glover	67	74	70	67	278	12,300
Kevin Stadler	65	70	71	72	278	12,300
Michael Clark	70	69	71	69	279	9,900
Mike Grob	71	71	67	70	279	9,900
Brian Kortan	69	68	73	69	279	9,900
Wes Short, Jr.	72	69	68	70	279	9,900
Roland Thatcher	66	68	76	69	279	9,900
Craig Bowden	68	71	71	70	280	7,387.50
Olin Browne	67	71	70	72	280	7,387.50
Tom Carter	67	72	70	71	280	7,387.50
Hiroyuki Fujita	72	70	68	70	280	7,387.50
Brock Mackenzie	69	71	69	71	280	7,387.50
Carl Paulson	69	70	74	67	280	7,387.50
Brett Quigley	66	69	71	74	280	7,387.50

	SCORES				TOTAL	MONEY
Garrett Willis	66	71	70	73	280	7,387.50
Kelly Gibson	64	74	71	72	281	6,750
Matt Hendrix	72	70	68	71	281	6,750
Kevin Muncrief	70	71	69	71	281	6,750
Roger Tambellini	69	69	70	73	281	6,750
Billy Andrade	72	68	73	69	282	6,420
Tim Conley	72	70	72	68	282	6,420
Trevor Dodds	74	68	70	70	282	6,420
Ken Duke	73	68	74	67	282	6,420
John Morse	71	70	69	72	282	6,420
David Ogrin	73	68	70	71	282	6,420
Mark Wilson	70	69	71	72	282	6,420
Danny Briggs	72	69	73	69	283	6,150
Kevin Na	70	70	70	73	283	6,150
Mike Heinen	67	75	70	72	284	6,000
Mike Springer	71	71	73	69	284	6,000
Mike Standly	72	68	71	73	284	6,000
Jim Benepe	67	68	76	74	285	5,820
Ken Green	69	71	71	74	285	5,820
Grant Waite	71	69	74	71	285	5,820
David Sutherland	73	69	68	76	286	5,700
Brad Bryant	72	70	71	74	287	5,610
Brandt Snedeker	69	73	71	74	287	5,610
Mike Sullivan	71	71	73	74	289	5,520

U.S. Bank Championship in Milwaukee

Brown Deer Park Golf Course, Milwaukee, Wisconsin
Par 34-36–70; 6,759 yards

July 22-25
purse, $3,500,000

	SCORES				TOTAL	MONEY
Carlos Franco	68	63	69	67	267	$630,000
Fred Funk	68	68	67	66	269	308,000
Brett Quigley	65	71	64	69	269	308,000
Billy Andrade	72	64	67	67	270	144,666.67
Olin Browne	65	70	68	67	270	144,666.67
Patrick Sheehan	65	68	67	70	270	144,666.66
Danny Briggs	65	70	68	68	271	109,083.33
Kenny Perry	69	67	65	70	271	109,083.33
Bo Van Pelt	65	68	71	67	271	109,083.34
Scott Hoch	68	65	70	69	272	94,500
Scott Verplank	66	69	67	71	273	84,000
Jason Dufner	67	67	68	71	273	84,000
Tom Byrum	69	70	65	70	274	63,700
Corey Pavin	70	68	66	70	274	63,700
Jerry Kelly	66	72	67	69	274	63,700
Scott McCarron	70	68	69	67	274	63,700
Frank Lickliter	70	69	68	67	274	63,700
Bart Bryant	70	68	71	66	275	47,250
Kirk Triplett	68	67	70	70	275	47,250
Craig Bowden	66	70	69	70	275	47,250
Todd Fischer	65	70	72	68	275	47,250
Jeff Sluman	66	72	71	67	276	33,600
Jay Williamson	67	68	68	73	276	33,600
Dean Wilson	67	71	68	70	276	33,600
Aaron Barber	73	68	69	66	276	33,600
Lucas Glover	69	72	64	71	276	33,600

	SCORES				TOTAL	MONEY
Brad Faxon	71	68	67	71	277	25,375
Dan Forsman	66	68	71	72	277	25,375
Brian Gay	70	66	67	74	277	25,375
Richard S. Johnson	70	70	66	71	277	25,375
Cameron Beckman	66	72	68	72	278	20,755
Hideto Tanihara	69	70	69	70	278	20,755
Roger Tambellini	73	65	70	70	278	20,755
Ryan Palmer	67	73	68	70	278	20,755
J.J. Henry	69	71	70	68	278	20,755
Robert Gamez	65	71	73	70	279	14,365.91
Steve Stricker	75	66	68	70	279	14,365.91
Tommy Tolles	70	70	68	71	279	14,365.91
Wes Short, Jr.	66	71	74	68	279	14,365.91
Kent Jones	69	71	70	69	279	14,365.91
Brent Geiberger	68	72	69	70	279	14,365.91
Brenden Pappas	69	71	70	69	279	14,365.91
Daniel Chopra	68	69	68	74	279	14,365.90
Mark Wilson	71	70	66	72	279	14,365.91
Matt Kuchar	68	70	70	71	279	14,365.91
Rich Barcelo	68	70	74	67	279	14,365.91
John Cook	72	66	70	72	280	8,708
Jay Delsing	70	70	66	74	280	8,708
Steve Elkington	68	72	70	70	280	8,708
Bob Estes	72	69	70	69	280	8,708
Len Mattiace	69	72	72	67	280	8,708
Joey Sindelar	69	70	69	72	280	8,708
Mike Grob	70	71	70	69	280	8,708
Spike McRoy	71	69	70	70	280	8,708
Tripp Isenhour	68	71	71	70	280	8,708
Greg Chalmers	67	69	73	71	280	8,708
Paul Azinger	66	72	70	73	281	7,770
Steve Allan	69	70	71	71	281	7,770
Harrison Frazar	70	70	70	71	281	7,770
Rich Beem	66	66	76	73	281	7,770
Kevin Muncrief	66	73	73	69	281	7,770
Jim Carter	69	68	72	73	282	7,385
Jim Gallagher, Jr.	71	65	73	73	282	7,385
Loren Roberts	71	70	71	70	282	7,385
Scott Simpson	71	70	67	74	282	7,385
Ted Purdy	74	65	68	75	282	7,385
Jonathan Byrd	68	72	72	70	282	7,385
Tom Carter	70	70	71	72	283	7,140
J.L. Lewis	69	72	73	70	284	7,000
Steve Lowery	70	71	76	67	284	7,000
Camilo Villegas	72	68	75	69	284	7,000
Mark Calcavecchia	69	70	71	75	285	6,790
Skip Kendall	71	68	72	74	285	6,790
Joe Durant	71	70	73	71	285	6,790
Ken Green	70	66	72	78	286	6,510
Dan Olsen	69	70	73	74	286	6,510
Kris Cox	68	73	71	74	286	6,510
Jason Bohn	70	70	74	72	286	6,510
Nick Gilliam	70	69	75	72	286	6,510
Steve Pate	69	72	74	72	287	6,265
David Roesch	74	67	69	77	287	6,265
Cliff Kresge	72	67	75	76	290	6,125
Kevin Na	71	70	78	71	290	6,125
Brad Lardon	70	71	73	77	291	6,020
David Edwards	70	70	72	82	294	5,950

Buick Open

Warwick Hills Golf & Country Club,
Grand Blanc, Michigan
Par 36-36–72; 7,127 yards

July 29-August 1
purse, $4,500,000

	SCORES				TOTAL	MONEY
Vijay Singh	63	70	65	67	265	$810,000
John Daly	70	64	66	66	266	486,000
Carlos Franco	67	67	67	66	267	261,000
Tiger Woods	67	68	66	66	267	261,000
Stewart Cink	69	65	70	66	270	180,000
Jim Furyk	66	67	70	68	271	156,375
Jeff Sluman	70	67	68	66	271	156,375
Daniel Chopra	68	68	66	70	272	135,000
Jerry Kelly	71	66	69	66	272	135,000
Mark O'Meara	67	70	70	66	273	117,000
Scott Verplank	70	67	70	66	273	117,000
Craig Barlow	66	69	72	68	275	94,500
Jose Maria Olazabal	70	67	69	69	275	94,500
Brenden Pappas	66	73	69	67	275	94,500
Billy Andrade	68	65	73	70	276	76,500
Chris DiMarco	69	68	73	66	276	76,500
Kenny Perry	69	68	72	67	276	76,500
Jim Carter	69	69	70	69	277	56,700
Paul Casey	72	66	69	70	277	56,700
J.P. Hayes	72	68	69	68	277	56,700
Hank Kuehne	69	69	68	71	277	56,700
Geoff Ogilvy	69	70	69	69	277	56,700
Bob Tway	68	67	73	69	277	56,700
Woody Austin	72	68	69	69	278	36,450
Olin Browne	64	70	69	75	278	36,450
Glen Day	68	71	71	68	278	36,450
Brian Gay	68	70	69	71	278	36,450
Justin Rose	68	70	71	69	278	36,450
Wes Short, Jr.	70	68	71	69	278	36,450
Steve Allan	67	72	68	72	279	25,600
Paul Azinger	72	68	70	69	279	25,600
Rich Barcelo	70	69	70	70	279	25,600
Danny Briggs	68	72	72	67	279	25,600
Bob Burns	70	70	71	68	279	25,600
Neal Lancaster	71	68	70	70	279	25,600
Hunter Mahan	70	68	77	64	279	25,600
Scott McCarron	68	69	70	72	279	25,600
Brett Quigley	72	68	69	70	279	25,600
Tom Byrum	71	69	72	68	280	19,350
Matt Gogel	68	68	68	76	280	19,350
Patrick Sheehan	71	69	70	70	280	19,350
Bill Glasson	75	63	71	72	281	17,550
Jeff Brehaut	70	69	72	71	282	13,410
Robert Damron	67	71	73	71	282	13,410
Jason Dufner	71	69	71	71	282	13,410
Steve Flesch	69	71	69	73	282	13,410
Billy Mayfair	71	69	73	69	282	13,410
Larry Mize	70	70	71	71	282	13,410
David Peoples	66	71	71	74	282	13,410
Tom Pernice, Jr.	70	70	69	73	282	13,410
Jay Williamson	70	69	72	71	282	13,410
Pat Bates	70	65	74	74	283	10,552.50
Greg Chalmers	69	71	73	70	283	10,552.50

	SCORES				TOTAL	MONEY
Dan Forsman	68	71	76	68	283	10,552.50
Mathias Gronberg	69	71	73	70	283	10,552.50
John Morgan	70	70	73	71	284	10,080
Dan Olsen	72	68	70	74	284	10,080
Pat Perez	73	67	70	74	284	10,080
Carl Pettersson	69	71	73	71	284	10,080
Roland Thatcher	69	71	72	72	284	10,080
Lucas Glover	70	69	76	70	285	9,765
Steve Stricker	69	71	71	74	285	9,765
Bill Haas	72	65	76	73	286	9,585
Joe Ogilvie	73	67	72	74	286	9,585
Robert Gamez	68	68	78	73	287	9,405
J.L. Lewis	72	67	75	73	287	9,405
Ken Duke	69	71	71	77	288	9,180
Mike Grob	65	73	74	76	288	9,180
David Morland	70	70	78	70	288	9,180
Len Mattiace	66	73	73	77	289	9,000
Hideto Tanihara	73	67	77	74	291	8,910

The International

Castle Pines Golf Club, Castle Rock, Colorado
Par 36-36–72; 7,594 yards

August 5-8
purse, $5,000,000

	POINTS				TOTAL	MONEY
Rod Pampling	15	7	7	2	31	$900,000
Alex Cejka	8	9	11	1	29	540,000
Tom Pernice, Jr.	5	10	11	1	27	340,000
Duffy Waldorf	8	3	7	8	26	240,000
Jay Haas	10	3	8	4	25	200,000
Tim Petrovic	9	5	8	2	24	167,500
Stewart Cink	6	5	11	2	24	167,500
Chris DiMarco	14	17	(-2)	(-5)	24	167,500
Mathias Gronberg	2	6	9	6	23	135,000
Bernhard Langer	7	7	5	4	23	135,000
Bob Tway	9	9	8	(-3)	23	135,000
Kevin Sutherland	5	10	4	3	22	105,000
Todd Hamilton	6	8	7	1	22	105,000
Jose Maria Olazabal	11	3	9	(-1)	22	105,000
Justin Leonard	6	7	1	7	21	82,500
Corey Pavin	4	6	8	3	21	82,500
Davis Love	8	8	5	0	21	82,500
Rocco Mediate	7	7	7	0	21	82,500
Notah Begay	1	13	0	6	20	60,600
Stuart Appleby	2	6	6	6	20	60,600
Chad Campbell	6	3	7	4	20	60,600
Kevin Na	5	4	8	3	20	60,600
Justin Rose	9	2	10	(-1)	20	60,600
John Cook	3	5	6	5	19	41,500
Harrison Frazar	2	9	3	5	19	41,500
Mark Hensby	2	8	4	5	19	41,500
Olin Browne	(-1)	18	(-1)	3	19	41,500
John Rollins	8	6	4	1	19	41,500
Ernie Els	4	8	4	2	18	35,500
Bart Bryant	8	1	6	2	17	34,000
Bill Haas	10	0	4	2	16	31,000
Brad Faxon	9	(-1)	9	(-1)	16	31,000

	POINTS			TOTAL	MONEY
Danny Ellis	1	15	5 (-5)	16	31,000
Lucas Glover	4	2	8 1	15	27,000
Brian Bateman	(-2)	12	6 (-1)	15	27,000
Arron Oberholser	6	7	9 (-7)	15	27,000
J.P. Hayes	6	10	4 (-6)	14	24,500
Billy Mayfair	4	6	4 (-1)	13	23,500
Danny Briggs	8	10	0 (-6)	12	22,500
Kirk Triplett	3	4	7 (-4)	10	20,500
Brett Quigley	6	4	4 (-4)	10	20,500
Tom Lehman	11	(-5)	9 (-5)	10	20,500
Jose Coceres	14	(-1)	1 (-5)	9	18,500
Geoff Ogilvy	14	3	(-1) (-8)	8	17,500

Out of Final 18 Holes

Brent Geiberger	3	4	6	13	16,000
John Senden	(-3)	9	7	13	16,000
Brenden Pappas	0	11	1	12	13,220
Rory Sabbatini	5	6	1	12	13,220
Dicky Pride	0	9	3	12	13,220
Craig Perks	5	4	3	12	13,220
Robert Allenby	8	(-1)	5	12	13,220
Steve Elkington	4	6	1	11	11,600
Tag Ridings	7	4	0	11	11,600
David Toms	6	2	3	11	11,600
Bo Van Pelt	4	3	4	11	11,600
Jason Bohn	4	3	4	11	11,600
Ryan Palmer	5	1	5	11	11,600
Cameron Beckman	1	7	2	10	11,150
Carl Pettersson	3	4	3	10	11,150
D.J. Brigman	5	4	0	9	10,900
Brian Kortan	8	5	(-4)	9	10,900
Roger Tambellini	7	(-1)	3	9	10,900

PGA Championship

Whistling Straits, Sheboygan, Wisconsin
Par 36-36–72; 7,590 yards

August 12-15
purse, $6,250,000

	SCORES				TOTAL	MONEY
Vijay Singh	67	68	69	76	280	$1,125,000
Chris DiMarco	68	70	71	71	280	550,000
Justin Leonard	66	69	70	75	280	550,000
(Singh defeated DiMarco and Leonard in three-hole playoff.)						
Ernie Els	66	70	72	73	281	267,500
Chris Riley	69	70	69	73	281	267,500
Paul McGinley	69	74	70	69	282	196,000
K.J. Choi	68	71	73	70	282	196,000
Phil Mickelson	69	72	67	74	282	196,000
Robert Allenby	71	70	72	70	283	152,000
Ben Crane	70	74	69	70	283	152,000
Adam Scott	71	71	69	72	283	152,000
Stephen Ames	68	71	69	75	283	152,000
Arron Oberholser	73	71	70	70	284	110,250
Brad Faxon	71	71	70	72	284	110,250
Brian Davis	70	71	69	74	284	110,250
Darren Clarke	65	71	72	76	284	110,250

	SCORES				TOTAL	MONEY
Stuart Appleby	68	75	72	70	285	76,857.15
Jean Francois Remesy	72	71	70	72	285	76,857.15
Stewart Cink	73	70	70	72	285	76,857.14
David Toms	72	72	69	72	285	76,857.14
Fredrik Jacobson	72	70	70	73	285	76,857.14
Matt Gogel	71	71	69	74	285	76,857.14
Loren Roberts	68	72	70	75	285	76,857.14
Tom Byrum	72	73	71	70	286	46,714.29
Shaun Micheel	77	68	70	71	286	46,714.29
Chad Campbell	73	70	71	72	286	46,714.29
J.L. Lewis	73	69	72	72	286	46,714.29
Tiger Woods	75	69	69	73	286	46,714.28
Geoff Ogilvy	68	73	71	74	286	46,714.28
Luke Donald	67	73	71	75	286	46,714.28
Miguel Angel Jimenez	76	65	75	71	287	34,250
Chip Sullivan	72	71	73	71	287	34,250
Carlos Franco	69	75	72	71	287	34,250
Bo Van Pelt	74	71	70	72	287	34,250
Charles Howell	70	71	72	74	287	34,250
Nick O'Hern	73	71	68	75	287	34,250
Todd Hamilton	72	73	75	68	288	24,687.50
Brett Quigley	74	69	73	72	288	24,687.50
Trevor Immelman	75	69	72	72	288	24,687.50
Ian Poulter	73	72	70	73	288	24,687.50
Zach Johnson	75	70	69	74	288	24,687.50
Briny Baird	67	69	75	77	288	24,687.50
Steve Flesch	73	72	67	76	288	24,687.50
Jay Haas	68	72	71	77	288	24,687.50
Tommy Armour	72	71	74	72	289	18,500
Niclas Fasth	74	70	73	72	289	18,500
David Howell	72	72	70	75	289	18,500
Padraig Harrington	68	71	72	78	289	18,500
Patrick Sheehan	70	71	75	74	290	14,660
Nick Faldo	72	70	74	74	290	14,660
Joe Ogilvie	75	68	70	77	290	14,660
Michael Campbell	71	73	69	77	290	14,660
Duffy Waldorf	69	72	70	79	290	14,660
Carl Pettersson	71	71	76	73	291	13,600
Paul Azinger	74	71	74	73	292	13,200
S.K. Ho	72	73	73	74	292	13,200
Craig Parry	70	75	71	76	292	13,200
Bob Tway	71	70	74	77	292	13,200
Eduardo Romero	72	73	70	77	292	13,200
Hidemichi Tanaka	72	71	71	78	292	13,200
Rod Pampling	73	69	70	80	292	13,200
Jeff Sluman	72	72	79	70	293	12,650
Scott Verplank	67	76	77	73	293	12,650
Shingo Katayama	74	70	76	73	293	12,650
Woody Austin	74	71	74	74	293	12,650
Scott Drummond	71	72	76	75	294	12,350
Bernhard Langer	74	70	75	75	294	12,350
Robert Gamez	72	73	76	75	296	12,150
Mark Hensby	74	69	77	76	296	12,150
Colin Montgomerie	73	72	78	74	297	12,000
Roy Biancalana	73	72	75	79	299	11,900
Jeff Coston	77	68	79	77	301	11,800
Skip Kendall	72	73	79	80	304	11,700

Out of Final 36 Holes

Brian Bateman	73	73	146
Jonathan Byrd	73	73	146
Paul Casey	74	72	146
Alex Cejka	75	71	146
Joe Durant	71	75	146
Fred Funk	74	72	146
Sergio Garcia	73	73	146
Hale Irwin	73	73	146
Raphael Jacquelin	74	72	146
Thomas Levet	74	72	146
Peter Lonard	74	72	146
Rocco Mediate	74	72	146
Jose Maria Olazabal	70	76	146
Tim Petrovic	68	78	146
Heath Slocum	74	72	146
Kevin Sutherland	74	72	146
Mike Weir	73	73	146
Lee Westwood	75	71	146
Bill Britton	77	70	147
Ben Curtis	73	74	147
Quinn Griffing	76	71	147
Stephen Leaney	74	73	147
Jesper Parnevik	76	71	147
Tom Pernice, Jr.	75	72	147
Phillip Price	72	75	147
Ted Purdy	73	74	147
Justin Rose	73	74	147
Hal Sutton	73	74	147
Mark Brooks	73	75	148
Timothy Clark	75	73	148
Bob Estes	75	73	148
Ricardo Gonzalez	75	73	148
Davis Love	79	69	148
Scott McCarron	70	78	148
Brenden Pappas	74	74	148
Joey Sindelar	71	77	148
Craig Thomas	73	75	148
Kirk Triplett	77	71	148
Zane Zwemke	72	76	148
Tim Fleming	76	73	149
Harrison Frazar	72	77	149
Mark O'Meara	73	76	149
Kenny Perry	76	73	149
Angel Cabrera	74	76	150
John Huston	71	79	150
Shigeki Maruyama	72	78	150
Rich Beem	78	73	151
Brendan Jones	72	79	151
Alan Schulte	75	76	151
Mike Small	75	76	151
Frank Bensel	76	76	152
Graeme McDowell	77	75	152
Billy Andrade	74	79	153
Jim Furyk	75	78	153
Joakim Haeggman	78	75	153
Cary Hungate	77	76	153
Jerry Kelly	76	77	153
Steve Schneiter	75	78	153
Ian Woosnam	79	74	153

	SCORES				TOTAL	
Tetsuji Hiratsuka	80	74			154	
Steve Lowery	80	74			154	
Rory Sabbatini	81	73			154	
Bruce Smith	77	77			154	
Jonathan Kaye	74	81			155	
Mike Northern	77	78			155	
Ron Philo, Jr.	76	79			155	
Bob Sowards	78	77			155	
Tim Herron	77	79			156	
J.R. Roth	79	77			156	
Dave Tentis	76	80			156	
Robert Thompson	77	79			156	
Mike Baker, Jr.	80	77			157	
John Daly	81	76			157	
David Duval	77	81			158	
Thongchai Jaidee	80	78			158	
Mike Schuchart	79	79			158	
Sean English	75	84			159	
Jeffrey Lankford	77	83			160	
Mark Evenson	80	82			162	
Dudley Hart					WD	
Scott Hoch					WD	
Frank Lickliter					WD	
Mark Calcavecchia					DQ	

(Professionals who did not complete 72 holes received $2,000.)

WGC - NEC Invitational

Firestone Country Club, South Course, Akron, Ohio
Par 35-35–70; 7,230 yards

August 19-22
purse, $7,000,000

	SCORES				TOTAL	MONEY
Stewart Cink	63	68	68	70	269	$1,200,000
Rory Sabbatini	68	66	71	68	273	552,500
Tiger Woods	68	66	70	69	273	552,500
Davis Love	68	68	72	66	274	282,500
Angel Cabrera	69	70	67	68	274	282,500
Bob Tway	67	73	67	68	275	178,333.33
David Toms	69	66	69	71	275	178,333.34
Chris DiMarco	68	69	67	71	275	178,333.33
Alex Cejka	72	67	71	66	276	116,000
Stuart Appleby	69	70	69	68	276	116,000
Lee Westwood	69	69	69	69	276	116,000
Robert Allenby	71	67	69	69	276	116,000
Charles Howell	71	67	68	70	276	116,000
Darren Clarke	71	70	68	68	277	87,500
Rod Pampling	68	67	70	72	277	87,500
Paul Casey	72	70	68	68	278	79,333.33
Sergio Garcia	68	70	70	70	278	79,333.33
Luke Donald	71	70	65	72	278	79,333.34
Jerry Kelly	69	73	64	73	279	74,000
Scott Verplank	69	69	67	74	279	74,000
Todd Hamilton	69	67	71	73	280	71,000
Zach Johnson	65	73	73	70	281	65,000
Jim Furyk	68	72	71	70	281	65,000
Jesper Parnevik	69	72	70	70	281	65,000

	SCORES				TOTAL	MONEY
Stephen Ames	69	70	69	73	281	65,000
Stephen Leaney	73	67	68	73	281	65,000
Kenny Perry	72	75	69	66	282	58,000
Brett Rumford	71	73	69	69	282	58,000
Miguel Angel Jimenez	71	70	72	69	282	58,000
S.K. Ho	70	67	73	72	282	58,000
Shigeki Maruyama	69	68	72	73	282	58,000
Thongchai Jaidee	71	71	76	65	283	51,000
Peter Lonard	71	69	76	67	283	51,000
Trevor Immelman	73	69	72	69	283	51,000
Vijay Singh	73	73	67	70	283	51,000
Brad Faxon	72	72	69	70	283	51,000
Joey Sindelar	70	70	71	72	283	51,000
Thomas Levet	68	73	70	72	283	51,000
Fred Couples	72	68	69	74	283	51,000
Fredrik Jacobson	69	72	68	74	283	51,000
Mike Weir	70	67	73	74	284	45,500
Jay Haas	70	69	71	74	284	45,500
John Daly	71	69	74	71	285	43,000
Phil Mickelson	70	75	68	72	285	43,000
Chris Riley	72	69	71	73	285	43,000
Paul McGinley	73	72	69	72	286	40,750
Nick Price	69	73	72	72	286	40,750
Steve Flesch	75	70	71	71	287	39,750
Tim Clark	71	70	72	74	287	39,750
Tommy Armour	76	72	70	70	288	38,000
Ricardo Gonzalez	73	75	70	70	288	38,000
Justin Leonard	73	71	72	72	288	38,000
Phillip Price	72	70	74	72	288	38,000
Shaun Micheel	71	72	73	72	288	38,000
J.L. Lewis	73	71	73	72	289	36,000
Barry Lane	67	77	73	72	289	36,000
Adam Scott	71	67	75	76	289	36,000
Carlos Franco	69	73	75	73	290	34,500
Colin Montgomerie	69	71	75	75	290	34,500
K.J. Choi	71	73	69	77	290	34,500
Bernhard Langer	74	69	75	74	292	32,750
Scott Drummond	69	75	73	75	292	32,750
Fred Funk	69	75	71	77	292	32,750
Niclas Fasth	75	68	70	79	292	32,750
Ernie Els	72	77	72	72	293	30,750
Craig Parry	79	69	71	74	293	30,750
Mark Hensby	71	70	78	74	293	30,750
Jonathan Kaye	71	75	72	75	293	30,750
Kirk Triplett	73	67	79	75	294	29,250
Chad Campbell	74	74	71	75	294	29,250
Andrew McLardy	73	83	69	70	295	28,500
Peter Senior	69	77	74	76	296	27,750
Mark O'Meara	71	72	77	76	296	27,750
Padraig Harrington	77	74	70	76	297	27,000
Pierre Fulke	73	77	78	76	304	26,500

Reno-Tahoe Open

Montreux Golf & Country Club, Reno, Nevada
Par 36-36–72; 7,577 yards

August 19-22
purse, $3,000,000

	SCORES				TOTAL	MONEY
Vaughn Taylor	67	67	69	75	278	$540,000
Steve Allan	68	68	68	74	278	224,000
Hunter Mahan	69	67	68	74	278	224,000
Scott McCarron	69	67	71	71	278	224,000
(Taylor won on first playoff hole.)						
Carl Pettersson	69	67	74	69	279	109,500
Roland Thatcher	66	68	68	77	279	109,500
Mark Wilson	67	71	69	72	279	109,500
Woody Austin	71	67	70	72	280	93,000
Michael Allen	71	66	75	71	283	75,000
Daniel Chopra	67	70	73	73	283	75,000
Ken Duke	71	67	73	72	283	75,000
Joe Ogilvie	72	64	72	75	283	75,000
Dennis Paulson	68	75	69	71	283	75,000
Corey Pavin	68	65	76	75	284	52,500
John Rollins	69	70	74	71	284	52,500
Grant Waite	70	69	72	73	284	52,500
Dean Wilson	74	69	67	74	284	52,500
Craig Barlow	72	69	69	75	285	37,800
Steve Elkington	71	69	70	75	285	37,800
Spike McRoy	73	69	72	71	285	37,800
Scott Simpson	67	71	71	76	285	37,800
Garrett Willis	72	66	74	73	285	37,800
Willie Wood	72	70	70	73	285	37,800
Jason Bohn	70	71	73	72	286	24,900
Jay Delsing	76	68	69	73	286	24,900
John Senden	73	65	73	75	286	24,900
Hidemichi Tanaka	68	68	75	75	286	24,900
Jay Williamson	73	68	71	74	286	24,900
Cameron Beckman	72	69	77	69	287	19,075
Ben Crane	73	68	71	75	287	19,075
Trevor Dodds	71	71	71	74	287	19,075
David Edwards	73	70	73	71	287	19,075
Matt Gogel	71	73	73	70	287	19,075
J.J. Henry	69	75	69	74	287	19,075
Rich Beem	68	71	75	74	288	14,790
John Cook	75	69	68	76	288	14,790
Danny Ellis	71	69	75	73	288	14,790
Brent Geiberger	71	67	75	75	288	14,790
Duffy Waldorf	71	68	75	74	288	14,790
David Branshaw	72	72	71	74	289	11,700
Jeff Brehaut	70	74	70	75	289	11,700
Lucas Glover	70	71	75	73	289	11,700
J.P. Hayes	71	72	71	75	289	11,700
Richard Johnson	72	71	82	64	289	11,700
Todd Fischer	71	72	72	75	290	9,030
Brian Gay	73	70	73	74	290	9,030
Bill Haas	71	68	67	84	290	9,030
Jose Maria Olazabal	69	72	72	77	290	9,030
Guy Boros	73	71	74	73	291	7,800
Jay Don Blake	70	69	74	79	292	7,305
Olin Browne	70	67	74	81	292	7,305
Chris Smith	74	69	70	79	292	7,305
Roger Tambellini	73	69	73	77	292	7,305

	SCORES				TOTAL	MONEY
Arjun Atwal	74	70	76	73	293	6,930
Glen Day	70	69	79	75	293	6,930
Mark Calcavecchia	67	77	74	76	294	6,750
Mike Heinen	70	73	80	71	294	6,750
Len Mattiace	71	69	76	78	294	6,750
Gene Sauers	72	71	77	74	294	6,750
Michael Clark	74	70	78	73	295	6,540
David Morland	76	68	77	74	295	6,540
Phil Tataurangi	73	71	71	80	295	6,540
Dicky Pride	72	71	76	77	296	6,360
Jyoti Randhawa	74	69	77	76	296	6,360
Mark Wiebe	67	73	79	77	296	6,360
Michael Bradley	73	70	79	75	297	6,180
Nick Flanagan	72	72	80	73	297	6,180
Matt Kuchar	72	72	72	81	297	6,180
Ryan Palmer	71	73	80	75	299	6,060
Jim McGovern	69	72	84	75	300	6,000
Scott Hend	70	74	85	80	309	5,940

Buick Championship

TPC at River Highlands, Cromwell, Connecticut
Par 35-35–70; 6,820 yards

August 26-29
purse, $4,200,000

	SCORES				TOTAL	MONEY
Woody Austin	68	70	66	66	270	$756,000
Tim Herron	70	69	65	66	270	453,600
(Austin defeated Herron on first playoff hole.)						
Fred Funk	66	66	69	70	271	218,400
Zach Johnson	67	65	73	66	271	218,400
Tom Pernice, Jr.	70	66	68	67	271	218,400
Jason Bohn	71	67	69	65	272	140,700
Matt Gogel	67	69	69	67	272	140,700
Corey Pavin	62	72	68	70	272	140,700
Tom Byrum	69	66	67	71	273	109,200
Todd Fischer	71	69	67	66	273	109,200
Jeff Sluman	72	69	70	62	273	109,200
Kevin Sutherland	70	70	67	66	273	109,200
Arjun Atwal	68	72	70	64	274	69,825
Robert Damron	71	68	68	67	274	69,825
Brad Faxon	69	68	70	67	274	69,825
Jerry Kelly	66	71	70	67	274	69,825
Hank Kuehne	68	65	71	70	274	69,825
Hidemichi Tanaka	68	69	67	70	274	69,825
Kirk Triplett	68	67	69	70	274	69,825
Omar Uresti	68	70	67	69	274	69,825
Craig Barlow	73	66	69	67	275	42,000
Jose Coceres	68	66	70	71	275	42,000
Frank Lickliter	73	68	67	67	275	42,000
Hunter Mahan	71	67	65	72	275	42,000
Loren Roberts	67	72	69	67	275	42,000
Bo Van Pelt	69	68	68	70	275	42,000
Olin Browne	69	68	71	68	276	29,820
Brent Geiberger	71	67	68	70	276	29,820
David Peoples	66	70	73	67	276	29,820
Tim Wilkinson	67	71	74	64	276	29,820
Garrett Willis	72	66	71	67	276	29,820

	SCORES				TOTAL	MONEY
Cameron Beckman	71	69	67	70	277	20,440
Craig Bowden	66	73	71	67	277	20,440
Daniel Chopra	71	68	65	73	277	20,440
Joe Durant	69	69	68	71	277	20,440
J.L. Lewis	71	70	67	69	277	20,440
Kevin Na	72	67	69	69	277	20,440
Tim Petrovic	68	70	74	65	277	20,440
Ted Purdy	73	66	68	70	277	20,440
John Senden	69	70	70	68	277	20,440
Joey Sindelar	68	67	68	74	277	20,440
Heath Slocum	70	71	69	67	277	20,440
Jay Williamson	68	71	67	71	277	20,440
Billy Andrade	72	67	71	68	278	13,053.60
Jonathan Byrd	72	67	70	69	278	13,053.60
Jason Dufner	66	70	70	72	278	13,053.60
Brian Kortan	70	71	69	68	278	13,053.60
Billy Mayfair	68	71	69	70	278	13,053.60
Aaron Barber	70	69	70	70	279	10,365.60
Pat Bates	70	70	71	68	279	10,365.60
Ken Duke	68	69	70	72	279	10,365.60
Skip Kendall	69	69	66	75	279	10,365.60
Chris Nallen	69	70	74	66	279	10,365.60
Bart Bryant	70	69	69	72	280	9,618
Mike Heinen	70	69	72	69	280	9,618
J.J. Henry	69	72	71	68	280	9,618
Vaughn Taylor	71	69	70	70	280	9,618
Bob Burns	65	70	70	76	281	9,324
Bill Haas	70	69	69	73	281	9,324
Matt Weibring	65	72	74	70	281	9,324
Michael Allen	69	72	68	73	282	8,946
Aaron Baddeley	68	70	71	73	282	8,946
Ryan Palmer	68	73	71	70	282	8,946
Pat Perez	69	69	70	74	282	8,946
Craig Perks	69	71	75	67	282	8,946
Esteban Toledo	69	66	74	73	282	8,946
Russ Cochran	68	73	71	71	283	8,526
Robert Gamez	69	66	70	78	283	8,526
Hirofumi Miyase	72	68	73	70	283	8,526
Steve Pate	71	70	69	73	283	8,526
Justin Rose	71	70	71	72	284	8,232
Scott Simpson	67	69	76	72	284	8,232
Roland Thatcher	70	69	75	70	284	8,232
*Brian Harman	73	67	71	73	284	
Tag Ridings	67	71	77	70	285	8,022
Patrick Sheehan	70	71	73	71	285	8,022
Deane Pappas	68	73	73	72	286	7,854
Dicky Pride	71	70	78	67	286	7,854
Scott Hend	71	70	71	80	292	7,728

Deutsche Bank Championship

TPC of Boston, Norton, Massachusetts
Par 36-35–71; 7,415 yards

September 3-6
purse, $5,000,000

	SCORES				TOTAL	MONEY
Vijay Singh	68	63	68	69	268	$900,000
Adam Scott	69	67	70	65	271	440,000

	SCORES				TOTAL	MONEY
Tiger Woods	65	68	69	69	271	440,000
Daniel Chopra	68	69	70	67	274	220,000
John Rollins	67	66	75	66	274	220,000
Hank Kuehne	68	68	71	68	275	173,750
Shigeki Maruyama	68	66	71	70	275	173,750
Jay Williamson	68	68	70	70	276	155,000
Brad Faxon	72	69	68	68	277	135,000
Bill Haas	69	64	71	73	277	135,000
Charles Howell	67	68	76	66	277	135,000
Camilo Villegas	69	68	72	69	278	115,000
David Duval	72	70	70	67	279	93,750
Zach Johnson	68	72	71	68	279	93,750
Dennis Paulson	69	70	71	69	279	93,750
David Toms	69	71	73	66	279	93,750
Dan Forsman	68	72	69	71	280	70,000
Richard Johnson	70	69	73	68	280	70,000
Matt Kuchar	69	73	70	68	280	70,000
Ryan Palmer	65	69	74	72	280	70,000
Deane Pappas	67	70	72	71	280	70,000
Skip Kendall	69	69	71	72	281	52,000
Neal Lancaster	72	69	70	70	281	52,000
Tim Petrovic	70	68	71	72	281	52,000
Todd Fischer	72	67	73	70	282	39,875
Frank Lickliter	68	67	76	71	282	39,875
Hunter Mahan	72	69	71	70	282	39,875
David Peoples	73	66	73	70	282	39,875
Aaron Baddeley	68	70	74	71	283	31,791.67
Brent Geiberger	72	70	70	71	283	31,791.67
Jesper Parnevik	70	71	73	69	283	31,791.67
Justin Rose	72	70	74	67	283	31,791.67
Jonathan Byrd	66	71	72	74	283	31,791.66
Dean Wilson	71	71	68	73	283	31,791.66
Jeff Brehaut	71	68	78	67	284	26,375
Jim Furyk	69	70	77	68	284	26,375
John Daly	71	70	73	71	285	19,500
Jason Dufner	71	69	75	70	285	19,500
Ken Green	72	68	74	71	285	19,500
Mike Heinen	72	70	74	69	285	19,500
J.J. Henry	70	71	75	69	285	19,500
Mark Hensby	69	70	73	73	285	19,500
Lee Janzen	70	69	74	72	285	19,500
Kent Jones	71	68	74	72	285	19,500
Arron Oberholser	70	69	71	75	285	19,500
Jeff Sluman	70	68	77	70	285	19,500
Hidemichi Tanaka	70	72	72	71	285	19,500
John Senden	71	69	79	68	287	12,428.58
Cameron Beckman	66	71	76	74	287	12,428.57
Jason Bohn	72	70	73	72	287	12,428.57
Tim Clark	70	67	75	75	287	12,428.57
Robert Gamez	71	71	74	71	287	12,428.57
Steve Pate	71	71	72	73	287	12,428.57
Craig Perks	67	71	74	75	287	12,428.57
Danny Briggs	68	73	73	74	288	11,350
Trevor Immelman	71	70	74	73	288	11,350
Billy Mayfair	67	72	77	72	288	11,350
Joey Sindelar	72	69	74	73	288	11,350
Michael Allen	72	69	77	71	289	11,000
Robert Damron	69	72	71	77	289	11,000
Mark Wilson	73	68	73	75	289	11,000
Briny Baird	72	69	76	73	290	10,700

	SCORES			TOTAL	MONEY
Ben Crane	69	72	75	74	290	10,700
Danny Ellis	72	68	74	76	290	10,700
Bob Burns	71	66	77	77	291	10,450
Harrison Frazar	70	71	74	76	291	10,450
Pat Bates	70	72	78	73	293	10,300
Brian Kortan	72	70	74	78	294	10,200
Guy Boros	72	70	74	79	295	10,100
Mark O'Meara	66	74	82	76	298	10,000

Bell Canadian Open

Glen Abbey Golf Club, Oakville, Ontario, Canada
Par 35-36–71; 7,222 yards

September 9-12
purse, $4,500,000

	SCORES				TOTAL	MONEY
Vijay Singh	68	66	72	69	275	$810,000
Mike Weir	68	65	70	72	275	486,000
(Singh defeated Weir on third playoff hole.)						
Joe Ogilvie	70	69	69	69	277	306,000
Stewart Cink	72	68	69	69	278	177,187.50
Tom Lehman	74	70	70	64	278	177,187.50
Hunter Mahan	72	69	69	68	278	177,187.50
Justin Rose	70	70	75	63	278	177,187.50
Robert Damron	72	71	70	66	279	139,500
Mark Hensby	70	69	70	71	280	126,000
Jesper Parnevik	69	66	71	74	280	126,000
Billy Andrade	67	75	71	68	281	103,500
D.J. Brigman	67	74	67	73	281	103,500
David Sutherland	69	72	68	72	281	103,500
David Branshaw	71	65	75	71	282	76,500
Cliff Kresge	69	70	67	76	282	76,500
Steve Lowery	70	69	70	73	282	76,500
Pat Perez	68	68	78	68	282	76,500
Dean Wilson	71	70	69	72	282	76,500
Arjun Atwal	71	67	75	70	283	54,540
Jose Coceres	72	70	74	67	283	54,540
Glen Day	70	69	70	74	283	54,540
Bill Haas	71	71	67	74	283	54,540
Kenny Perry	71	67	74	71	283	54,540
Chris DiMarco	69	71	73	71	284	41,400
Casey Wittenberg	73	72	71	68	284	41,400
Craig Barlow	67	69	75	74	285	29,992.50
Chad Campbell	73	68	72	72	285	29,992.50
Bill Glasson	72	70	73	70	285	29,992.50
Corey Pavin	73	70	72	70	285	29,992.50
David Peoples	69	70	73	73	285	29,992.50
Craig Perks	70	72	75	68	285	29,992.50
Brett Quigley	69	71	73	72	285	29,992.50
Joey Sindelar	66	73	74	72	285	29,992.50
Roland Thatcher	72	72	71	70	285	29,992.50
Bob Tway	74	71	70	70	285	29,992.50
David Edwards	72	69	74	71	286	21,656.25
Dudley Hart	72	73	73	68	286	21,656.25
Richard Johnson	73	70	71	72	286	21,656.25
Roger Tambellini	71	71	69	75	286	21,656.25
Jason Bohn	73	70	72	72	287	18,000
Greg Chalmers	71	72	70	74	287	18,000

	SCORES				TOTAL	MONEY
David Frost	73	71	71	72	287	18,000
Davis Love	72	73	68	74	287	18,000
Jonathan Byrd	72	70	69	77	288	14,850
Esteban Toledo	76	68	72	72	288	14,850
Tommy Tolles	72	70	78	68	288	14,850
Mark Brooks	69	73	76	71	289	11,898
Fred Funk	74	70	72	73	289	11,898
Tim Petrovic	72	70	73	74	289	11,898
Jim Rutledge	74	71	75	69	289	11,898
Mark Wilson	74	70	71	74	289	11,898
David Duval	71	72	76	71	290	10,494
Todd Fischer	71	71	75	73	290	10,494
Steve Flesch	73	71	75	71	290	10,494
Tag Ridings	68	76	72	74	290	10,494
Omar Uresti	74	70	74	72	290	10,494
Neal Lancaster	71	70	75	75	291	10,035
Billy Mayfair	70	74	72	75	291	10,035
Jim McGovern	71	72	76	72	291	10,035
Phil Mickelson	75	69	79	68	291	10,035
Paul Azinger	72	68	74	78	292	9,630
Tom Carter	72	71	76	73	292	9,630
Brian Kortan	71	74	70	77	292	9,630
Dennis Paulson	69	72	75	76	292	9,630
Garrett Willis	71	74	75	72	292	9,630
Aaron Barber	72	73	75	73	293	9,225
Danny Briggs	69	73	77	74	293	9,225
Jim Carter	72	69	78	74	293	9,225
Justin Leonard	76	66	77	74	293	9,225
Larry Mize	76	68	74	76	294	8,865
David Morland	70	73	73	78	294	8,865
Dicky Pride	72	72	77	73	294	8,865
Grant Waite	75	70	73	76	294	8,865
Dirk Ayers	72	71	79	73	295	8,550
John Rollins	74	71	74	76	295	8,550
Kevin Sutherland	74	71	75	75	295	8,550
Andre Stolz	71	74	77	74	296	8,370
Chris Couch	71	71	79	83	304	8,280

Ryder Cup

See Special Events section.

Valero Texas Open

LaCantera Golf Club, Resort Course, San Antonio, Texas
Par 35-35–70; 7,001 yards

September 16-19
purse, $3,500,000

	SCORES				TOTAL	MONEY
Bart Bryant	67	67	60	67	261	$630,000
Patrick Sheehan	65	68	65	66	264	378,000
Todd Fischer	68	67	63	67	265	203,000
Dean Wilson	64	65	70	66	265	203,000
Tim Clark	64	70	64	68	266	118,650
J.J. Henry	64	67	67	68	266	118,650
Jerry Kelly	66	67	68	65	266	118,650
Hunter Mahan	68	67	62	69	266	118,650

	SCORES				TOTAL	MONEY
Ted Purdy	61	69	71	65	266	118,650
Justin Leonard	65	68	68	66	267	84,000
J.L. Lewis	69	67	68	63	267	84,000
Scott Simpson	65	67	66	69	267	84,000
Heath Slocum	66	69	64	68	267	84,000
Brent Geiberger	66	68	67	67	268	63,000
Joe Ogilvie	67	70	61	70	268	63,000
Duffy Waldorf	66	67	67	68	268	63,000
Olin Browne	69	67	66	67	269	50,750
Bob Estes	68	66	70	65	269	50,750
Tom Lehman	66	70	68	65	269	50,750
Justin Rose	68	68	65	68	269	50,750
John Senden	66	65	69	70	270	42,000
Scott McCarron	65	69	68	69	271	31,550
Brenden Pappas	68	69	65	69	271	31,550
Jesper Parnevik	69	65	67	70	271	31,550
Pat Perez	66	69	63	73	271	31,550
Loren Roberts	66	68	69	68	271	31,550
Vaughn Taylor	70	68	67	66	271	31,550
Jay Williamson	71	66	64	70	271	31,550
Jay Delsing	65	72	64	71	272	21,306.25
Joel Edwards	70	67	69	66	272	21,306.25
Brian Gay	66	70	65	71	272	21,306.25
Jason Hartwick	70	66	69	67	272	21,306.25
Fredrik Jacobson	68	68	64	72	272	21,306.25
Ryan Palmer	66	65	67	74	272	21,306.25
Tim Thelen	68	70	66	68	272	21,306.25
Bo Van Pelt	66	69	69	68	272	21,306.25
Brad Bryant	66	68	68	71	273	16,100
Daniel Chopra	68	69	70	66	273	16,100
Kent Jones	69	67	68	69	273	16,100
David Peoples	67	64	70	72	273	16,100
Tommy Armour	67	70	68	69	274	11,917.50
D.J. Brigman	66	72	66	70	274	11,917.50
Tom Byrum	68	68	67	71	274	11,917.50
Tom Carter	69	68	67	70	274	11,917.50
Ben Crane	66	72	68	68	274	11,917.50
Matt Kuchar	68	68	67	71	274	11,917.50
Corey Pavin	67	69	71	67	274	11,917.50
Bob Tway	70	68	64	72	274	11,917.50
Mark Wilson	65	72	70	68	275	8,843.34
Arjun Atwal	67	67	66	75	275	8,843.33
Deane Pappas	67	70	68	70	275	8,843.33
Jim Benepe	70	67	68	71	276	8,080
Steve Elkington	68	69	70	69	276	8,080
Lucas Glover	71	66	69	70	276	8,080
Gabriel Hjertstedt	69	69	72	66	276	8,080
Dan Olsen	68	69	67	72	276	8,080
Rod Pampling	70	68	68	70	276	8,080
Brian Watts	69	69	68	70	276	8,080
Shaun Micheel	67	69	72	69	277	7,735
Tim Petrovic	67	67	70	73	277	7,735
Brian Bateman	70	68	70	70	278	7,490
Pat Bates	68	70	69	71	278	7,490
Guy Boros	68	69	73	68	278	7,490
Adam Meyer	70	68	68	72	278	7,490
Andre Stolz	71	66	69	72	278	7,490
Willie Wood	69	69	67	74	279	7,280
Briny Baird	70	66	69	75	280	7,140
David Branshaw	69	68	74	69	280	7,140

	SCORES				TOTAL	MONEY
Kevin Muncrief	66	68	73	73	280	7,140
Brad Lardon	68	68	74	71	281	6,965
David Sutherland	68	69	70	74	281	6,965
Aaron Baddeley	67	69	70	76	282	6,860
Jose Coceres	68	67	70	78	283	6,755
Hank Kuehne	68	67	72	76	283	6,755
Jeff Brehaut	71	66	73	74	284	6,650
Brandel Chamblee	68	69	74	74	285	6,580
Omar Uresti	68	69	72	77	286	6,510
Jeff Maggert	67	68	70	82	287	6,440

84 Lumber Classic

Nemacolin Woodlands Resort & Spa, Mystic Rock Course,
Farmington, Pennsylvania
Par 36-36–72; 7,276 yards

September 23-26
purse, $4,200,000

	SCORES				TOTAL	MONEY
Vijay Singh	64	68	72	69	273	$756,000
Stewart Cink	71	71	67	65	274	453,600
Jonathan Byrd	68	72	67	69	276	201,600
Chris DiMarco	70	65	71	70	276	201,600
Zach Johnson	69	69	70	68	276	201,600
Pat Perez	67	73	69	67	276	201,600
K.J. Choi	71	68	73	65	277	135,450
Duffy Waldorf	70	69	70	68	277	135,450
Frank Lickliter	71	72	67	68	278	117,600
Jose Maria Olazabal	73	70	70	65	278	117,600
Bob Burns	73	68	68	70	279	100,800
Matt Gogel	71	68	68	72	279	100,800
Cameron Beckman	67	73	73	67	280	72,000
John Daly	68	72	70	70	280	72,000
Robert Gamez	69	70	70	71	280	72,000
Kent Jones	69	68	71	72	280	72,000
Billy Mayfair	71	69	71	69	280	72,000
Tim Petrovic	75	67	70	68	280	72,000
Tag Ridings	71	71	68	70	280	72,000
Robert Allenby	67	74	72	68	281	47,208
Jonathan Kaye	73	69	71	68	281	47,208
Shigeki Maruyama	72	71	68	70	281	47,208
John Rollins	72	70	69	70	281	47,208
Chris Smith	69	72	71	69	281	47,208
Jeff Brehaut	69	71	72	70	282	31,380
Charles Howell	70	70	70	72	282	31,380
Richard Johnson	67	71	72	72	282	31,380
Ted Purdy	73	70	70	69	282	31,380
Patrick Sheehan	72	69	69	72	282	31,380
Roland Thatcher	72	70	70	70	282	31,380
David Toms	70	71	72	69	282	31,380
Mark Brooks	70	73	68	72	283	24,307.50
Ben Curtis	67	67	81	68	283	24,307.50
Lee Janzen	68	73	71	71	283	24,307.50
Jerry Kelly	76	67	70	70	283	24,307.50
Tim Clark	71	71	69	73	284	19,355
Len Mattiace	70	68	71	75	284	19,355
Brenden Pappas	72	68	72	72	284	19,355
David Peoples	71	69	73	71	284	19,355

	SCORES				TOTAL	MONEY
Justin Rose	69	72	71	72	284	19,355
Steve Stricker	71	71	70	72	284	19,355
Jason Bohn	72	68	70	75	285	13,513.50
Glen Day	72	71	70	72	285	13,513.50
Brian Gay	75	67	71	72	285	13,513.50
Brent Geiberger	69	69	73	74	285	13,513.50
J.P. Hayes	68	69	73	75	285	13,513.50
Joey Sindelar	68	69	72	76	285	13,513.50
Vaughn Taylor	74	69	73	69	285	13,513.50
Grant Waite	72	70	73	70	285	13,513.50
Carlos Franco	71	71	71	73	286	10,332
Skip Kendall	72	71	71	72	286	10,332
Rod Pampling	70	73	70	73	286	10,332
Steve Allan	71	69	71	76	287	9,544.50
Mark Calcavecchia	72	71	71	73	287	9,544.50
Robert Damron	70	73	70	74	287	9,544.50
Steve Flesch	71	72	68	76	287	9,544.50
Todd Hamilton	72	68	72	75	287	9,544.50
Fredrik Jacobson	72	70	74	71	287	9,544.50
Kevin Na	68	73	69	77	287	9,544.50
Omar Uresti	72	70	73	72	287	9,544.50
Billy Andrade	69	73	71	75	288	9,072
Gene Sauers	74	67	75	72	288	9,072
Mike Weir	69	72	74	73	288	9,072
Tom Carter	72	69	76	72	289	8,862
David Frost	72	71	76	70	289	8,862
Greg Chalmers	71	71	71	77	290	8,652
Tom Pernice, Jr.	69	74	71	76	290	8,652
Roger Tambellini	68	75	73	74	290	8,652
Dan Forsman	68	73	73	77	291	8,442
Cliff Kresge	72	71	73	75	291	8,442
Neal Lancaster	71	71	75	75	292	8,316
Tommy Armour	68	74	73	78	293	8,232
Kris Cox	68	72	75	80	295	8,148
Tim Herron	72	71	73	80	296	8,064

WGC - American Express Championship

See European Tours chapter.

Southern Farm Bureau Classic

Annandale Golf Club, Madison, Mississippi
Par 36-36–72; 7,199 yards

September 30-October 3
purse, $3,000,000

	SCORES				TOTAL	MONEY
Fred Funk	69	67	64	66	266	$540,000
Ryan Palmer	69	68	66	64	267	324,000
Glen Day	65	70	70	63	268	144,000
J.J. Henry	70	67	66	65	268	144,000
Kevin Na	71	65	66	66	268	144,000
Loren Roberts	66	69	68	65	268	144,000
Kirk Triplett	69	69	65	66	269	100,500
Jonathan Byrd	70	69	66	65	270	90,000
Tim Clark	68	69	67	66	270	90,000
Pat Bates	69	66	68	68	271	72,000

	SCORES				TOTAL	MONEY
Greg Chalmers	68	67	67	69	271	72,000
Chris Couch	70	63	68	70	271	72,000
Carl Pettersson	67	69	67	68	271	72,000
Steve Allan	69	69	67	67	272	52,500
Danny Briggs	72	65	69	66	272	52,500
Rod Pampling	69	71	68	64	272	52,500
John Senden	65	68	69	70	272	52,500
Heath Slocum	70	67	70	66	273	45,000
Robert Damron	70	65	71	68	274	33,857.15
Brent Geiberger	71	66	72	65	274	33,857.15
Craig Barlow	67	71	68	68	274	33,857.14
Tom Carter	69	69	67	69	274	33,857.14
Bill Glasson	66	70	68	70	274	33,857.14
Ted Purdy	69	69	66	70	274	33,857.14
Patrick Sheehan	66	67	72	69	274	33,857.14
Woody Austin	72	64	70	69	275	21,750
Aaron Barber	69	68	71	67	275	21,750
Daniel Chopra	70	70	66	69	275	21,750
Lucas Glover	73	67	64	71	275	21,750
Richard Johnson	73	66	68	68	275	21,750
Steve Pate	67	65	69	74	275	21,750
Joe Durant	68	69	70	69	276	18,150
Chris Smith	67	71	69	69	276	18,150
Billy Andrade	67	70	71	69	277	14,200
Jason Bohn	69	71	68	69	277	14,200
Harrison Frazar	65	67	73	72	277	14,200
Shaun Micheel	70	68	69	70	277	14,200
David Morland	68	67	70	72	277	14,200
Deane Pappas	66	70	70	71	277	14,200
Omar Uresti	70	70	70	67	277	14,200
Camilo Villegas	72	64	68	73	277	14,200
Jay Williamson	68	71	68	70	277	14,200
Cameron Beckman	72	68	66	72	278	10,500
Brad Bryant	69	70	69	70	278	10,500
Dan Forsman	69	69	70	70	278	10,500
Olin Browne	69	68	71	71	279	8,316
Jay Delsing	73	67	72	67	279	8,316
David Frost	71	69	66	73	279	8,316
Brenden Pappas	66	72	72	69	279	8,316
Joey Sindelar	70	69	69	71	279	8,316
Jay Don Blake	68	67	71	74	280	7,060
Matt Gogel	71	66	70	73	280	7,060
Kent Jones	68	71	69	72	280	7,060
Brad Lardon	70	70	66	74	280	7,060
Tommy Tolles	71	67	72	70	280	7,060
Garrett Willis	69	70	71	70	280	7,060
Rich Beem	70	67	72	72	281	6,720
Larry Mize	68	71	72	70	281	6,720
Dicky Pride	72	67	72	70	281	6,720
Kris Cox	70	69	73	70	282	6,570
David Sutherland	66	73	69	74	282	6,570
Jeff Brehaut	68	69	74	72	283	6,420
J.P. Hayes	71	69	73	70	283	6,420
Craig Perks	72	68	71	72	283	6,420
Paul Azinger	71	68	74	71	284	6,240
Brian Bateman	71	66	73	74	284	6,240
Grant Waite	72	68	72	72	284	6,240
David Peoples	71	69	71	74	285	6,120
Ken Duke	70	69	73	74	286	6,030
Kelly Gibson	71	69	70	76	286	6,030

Michelin Championship at Las Vegas

TPC at Summerlin: Par 36-36–72; 7,243 yards
TPC at The Canyons: Par 36-35–71; 7,193 yards
Bear's Best GC: Par 36-36–72; 7,381 yards
Las Vegas, Nevada

October 7-10
purse, $4,000,000

	SCORES				TOTAL	MONEY
Andre Stolz	67	67	65	67	266	$720,000
Harrison Frazar	64	68	68	67	267	298,666.67
Tag Ridings	67	66	73	61	267	298,666.67
Tom Lehman	64	68	66	69	267	298,666.66
Carl Pettersson	68	68	65	67	268	152,000
Dicky Pride	66	67	66	69	268	152,000
Danny Ellis	63	70	73	63	269	120,500
David Frost	69	71	67	62	269	120,500
Lee Janzen	68	66	70	65	269	120,500
Tim Petrovic	66	66	68	69	269	120,500
Bob Estes	67	65	68	70	270	88,000
Jim Furyk	67	67	70	66	270	88,000
Brian Gay	68	70	65	67	270	88,000
Duffy Waldorf	65	66	69	70	270	88,000
Greg Chalmers	69	67	64	71	271	58,100
Jose Coceres	66	68	69	68	271	58,100
Ben Crane	68	65	69	69	271	58,100
Lucas Glover	68	68	67	68	271	58,100
Kent Jones	64	68	70	69	271	58,100
Scott Verplank	64	72	66	69	271	58,100
Jay Williamson	69	62	74	66	271	58,100
Mark Wilson	68	73	63	67	271	58,100
Stuart Appleby	69	67	69	67	272	32,133.34
Danny Briggs	65	71	68	68	272	32,133.34
Omar Uresti	67	65	72	68	272	32,133.34
Briny Baird	72	63	70	67	272	32,133.33
Jason Bohn	63	70	70	69	272	32,133.33
Olin Browne	67	64	69	72	272	32,133.33
Justin Leonard	65	70	67	70	272	32,133.33
J.L. Lewis	67	63	70	72	272	32,133.33
Pat Perez	70	68	66	68	272	32,133.33
Tom Byrum	66	70	65	72	273	22,640
Alex Cejka	65	65	72	71	273	22,640
Dudley Hart	69	70	65	69	273	22,640
Billy Mayfair	64	69	71	69	273	22,640
Scott McCarron	66	71	67	69	273	22,640
Billy Andrade	68	68	68	70	274	16,800
Woody Austin	74	66	66	68	274	16,800
Paul Azinger	69	65	71	69	274	16,800
David Duval	67	68	68	71	274	16,800
Robert Gamez	67	66	70	71	274	16,800
Geoff Ogilvy	66	67	70	71	274	16,800
Chris Smith	70	66	67	71	274	16,800
Bo Van Pelt	72	68	65	69	274	16,800
Steve Allan	67	70	68	70	275	11,211.43
Robert Allenby	69	68	68	70	275	11,211.43
Craig Barlow	66	71	69	69	275	11,211.43
Donnie Hammond	68	65	71	71	275	11,211.43
Corey Pavin	68	70	68	69	275	11,211.43
Tom Pernice, Jr.	66	72	69	68	275	11,211.43
Rich Barcelo	69	66	72	68	275	11,211.42
Cameron Beckman	67	66	69	74	276	9,104

	SCORES				TOTAL	MONEY
David Branshaw	67	66	71	72	276	9,104
Glen Day	68	64	72	72	276	9,104
Paul Goydos	66	68	70	72	276	9,104
Richard Johnson	66	69	71	70	276	9,104
Jonathan Kaye	65	71	69	71	276	9,104
Ryan Palmer	71	71	65	69	276	9,104
Deane Pappas	74	70	63	69	276	9,104
Craig Perks	69	70	66	71	276	9,104
Dean Wilson	68	64	72	72	276	9,104
Daniel Chopra	72	64	70	72	278	8,520
Ted Purdy	71	67	69	71	278	8,520
Jeff Sluman	70	67	68	73	278	8,520
Steve Stricker	68	72	67	71	278	8,520
John Rollins	72	65	69	74	280	8,320
Skip Kendall	66	72	66	77	281	8,160
Frank Lickliter	69	69	69	74	281	8,160
Spike McRoy	66	70	70	75	281	8,160
Kris Cox	68	71	67	76	282	8,000
Mark Brooks	70	73	64	76	283	7,920
Chez Reavie	66	64	75	85	290	7,840

Chrysler Classic of Greensboro

Forest Oaks Country Club, Greensboro, North Carolina
Par 36-36–72; 7,311 yards

October 14-17
purse, $4,600,000

	SCORES				TOTAL	MONEY
Brent Geiberger	66	67	71	66	270	$828,000
Michael Allen	70	67	68	67	272	496,800
Chris Smith	70	69	67	67	273	312,800
Tom Lehman	69	66	69	70	274	202,400
David Toms	69	65	71	69	274	202,400
Arjun Atwal	71	70	68	66	275	165,600
Tom Pernice, Jr.	66	68	73	69	276	154,100
Jerry Kelly	70	65	72	70	277	110,975
Jeff Brehaut	68	66	73	70	277	110,975
Matt Gogel	70	69	66	72	277	110,975
Joe Ogilvie	68	67	70	72	277	110,975
Ted Purdy	71	68	74	64	277	110,975
Ben Crane	68	69	70	70	277	110,975
Jason Dufner	65	70	73	69	277	110,975
Richard S. Johnson	67	71	69	70	277	110,975
Cameron Beckman	71	67	71	69	278	73,600
Rod Pampling	69	71	70	68	278	73,600
Bo Van Pelt	66	69	74	69	278	73,600
Jay Delsing	67	72	73	68	280	55,752
Brett Quigley	66	71	72	71	280	55,752
Shigeki Maruyama	68	70	68	74	280	55,752
Carlos Franco	70	70	69	71	280	55,752
Hank Kuehne	67	69	73	71	280	55,752
David Frost	70	66	71	74	281	42,320
Blaine McCallister	67	70	70	74	281	42,320
*Ryan Moore	68	69	73	71	281	
Brad Faxon	68	70	71	73	282	31,970
Fred Funk	69	71	69	73	282	31,970
Jeff Sluman	68	71	72	71	282	31,970
Steve Stricker	70	71	71	70	282	31,970

		SCORES			TOTAL	MONEY
Jesper Parnevik	72	68	69	73	282	31,970
John Rollins	68	73	72	69	282	31,970
Jason Bohn	70	70	71	71	282	31,970
Roland Thatcher	70	69	73	70	282	31,970
Billy Andrade	67	71	72	73	283	20,825.45
Mark Calcavecchia	69	69	71	74	283	20,825.45
Corey Pavin	70	69	72	72	283	20,825.45
Mike Springer	70	68	74	71	283	20,825.46
Kevin Sutherland	70	71	72	70	283	20,825.46
Deane Pappas	70	70	70	73	283	20,825.45
Cliff Kresge	69	72	70	72	283	20,825.45
Todd Fischer	67	74	71	71	283	20,825.46
Arron Oberholser	71	70	71	71	283	20,825.46
Tag Ridings	69	71	72	71	283	20,825.46
Carl Pettersson	67	72	72	72	283	20,825.45
Skip Kendall	70	71	71	72	284	13,468.80
Dan Olsen	67	73	74	70	284	13,468.80
Robert Allenby	71	69	73	71	284	13,468.80
Danny Ellis	69	72	73	70	284	13,468.80
Brenden Pappas	66	71	76	71	284	13,468.80
Steve Pate	69	70	75	71	285	11,009.33
Tim Petrovic	69	69	79	68	285	11,009.34
Ken Duke	72	69	72	72	285	11,009.33
Fredrik Jacobson	70	69	73	73	285	11,009.33
Mark Wilson	68	72	72	73	285	11,009.33
D.J. Brigman	67	74	77	67	285	11,009.34
Geoff Ogilvy	69	72	78	67	286	10,350
Hunter Mahan	70	69	75	72	286	10,350
Lucas Glover	70	68	73	75	286	10,350
Chris Stroud	69	71	73	73	286	10,350
Zach Johnson	68	73	72	74	287	10,120
Rocco Mediate	70	71	73	74	288	9,844
Guy Boros	70	70	75	73	288	9,844
Frank Lickliter	70	70	74	74	288	9,844
Niclas Fasth	70	71	73	74	288	9,844
Scott Hend	71	69	77	71	288	9,844
Craig Parry	69	69	75	76	289	9,568
Jose Coceres	69	72	71	79	291	9,476
Robert Damron	71	70	79	73	293	9,384
Billy Mayfair	73	68	81	73	295	9,292

Funai Classic at the Walt Disney World Resort

Walt Disney World Resort, Lake Buena Vista, Florida
Magnolia Course: Par 36-36–72; 7,200 yards
Palm Course: Par 36-36–72; 6,957 yards

October 21-24
purse, $4,200,000

		SCORES			TOTAL	MONEY
Ryan Palmer	68	68	68	62	266	$756,000
Briny Baird	65	66	68	70	269	369,600
Vijay Singh	66	71	65	67	269	369,600
Cameron Beckman	68	65	68	69	270	184,800
Joey Sindelar	66	70	67	67	270	184,800
Mark Calcavecchia	71	66	65	69	271	135,975
Tim Clark	69	69	64	69	271	135,975
Mark Hensby	64	71	68	68	271	135,975
Tom Lehman	66	66	67	72	271	135,975

	SCORES				TOTAL	MONEY
Lucas Glover	68	68	68	68	272	93,100
John Huston	64	71	69	68	272	93,100
Neal Lancaster	69	69	67	67	272	93,100
Geoff Ogilvy	68	67	67	70	272	93,100
Carl Pettersson	70	70	68	64	272	93,100
Vaughn Taylor	68	66	72	66	272	93,100
Billy Andrade	69	69	69	66	273	57,015
Bart Bryant	66	71	67	69	273	57,015
Ben Curtis	66	71	66	70	273	57,015
Chris DiMarco	69	65	70	69	273	57,015
Dan Forsman	68	70	66	69	273	57,015
Jerry Kelly	67	68	71	67	273	57,015
Skip Kendall	66	67	72	68	273	57,015
Scott Verplank	70	65	65	73	273	57,015
J.L. Lewis	62	73	72	67	274	35,805
Loren Roberts	71	67	66	70	274	35,805
Justin Rose	71	68	69	66	274	35,805
Kirk Triplett	66	67	72	69	274	35,805
Stephen Ames	65	71	67	72	275	28,560
Richard Johnson	68	67	71	69	275	28,560
Zach Johnson	68	72	68	67	275	28,560
Scott McCarron	69	67	68	71	275	28,560
Spike McRoy	68	72	71	64	275	28,560
Steve Allan	67	72	71	66	276	21,262.50
Arjun Atwal	68	71	73	64	276	21,262.50
Brian Bateman	68	70	67	71	276	21,262.50
Joe Durant	69	70	71	66	276	21,262.50
Stephen Leaney	70	69	68	69	276	21,262.50
Steve Lowery	72	67	67	70	276	21,262.50
Pat Perez	69	71	66	70	276	21,262.50
Craig Perks	73	65	70	68	276	21,262.50
Michael Allen	73	67	69	68	277	14,301
Bob Estes	69	70	69	69	277	14,301
Steve Flesch	67	71	71	68	277	14,301
Fred Funk	69	69	71	68	277	14,301
Brian Gay	67	72	68	70	277	14,301
Fredrik Jacobson	69	70	68	70	277	14,301
Jose Maria Olazabal	65	72	69	71	277	14,301
Brenden Pappas	67	67	74	69	277	14,301
Daniel Chopra	67	71	68	72	278	10,262
Carlos Franco	69	71	69	69	278	10,262
Paul Goydos	70	70	66	72	278	10,262
Hank Kuehne	69	64	71	74	278	10,262
John Rollins	68	71	70	69	278	10,262
Omar Uresti	67	71	70	70	278	10,262
Chad Campbell	69	67	70	73	279	9,408
Michael Clark	67	71	72	69	279	9,408
Danny Ellis	69	71	70	69	279	9,408
Harrison Frazar	67	67	70	75	279	9,408
Robert Gamez	68	71	70	70	279	9,408
J.J. Henry	69	68	70	72	279	9,408
Deane Pappas	70	70	69	70	279	9,408
John Cook	68	70	71	71	280	8,862
David Frost	71	68	68	73	280	8,862
Charles Howell	67	71	72	70	280	8,862
Matt Kuchar	69	70	71	70	280	8,862
Jeff Maggert	68	71	70	71	280	8,862
Dean Wilson	69	71	68	72	280	8,862
Stuart Appleby	69	66	73	73	281	8,358
Ben Crane	71	69	72	69	281	8,358

	SCORES				TOTAL	MONEY
Lee Janzen	71	69	70	71	281	8,358
Kent Jones	69	70	71	71	281	8,358
Hunter Mahan	69	70	71	71	281	8,358
Rod Pampling	69	69	71	72	281	8,358
Rich Beem	70	70	70	72	282	7,896
Shaun Micheel	69	71	72	70	282	7,896
Arron Oberholser	69	71	72	70	282	7,896
Tom Pernice, Jr.	67	69	74	72	282	7,896
Bob Tway	69	71	72	70	282	7,896
Bob Burns	69	70	75	70	284	7,602
Esteban Toledo	73	67	71	73	284	7,602
Tom Carter	69	70	72	74	285	7,434
Jay Williamson	68	68	76	73	285	7,434
David Branshaw	67	73	73	73	286	7,266
Jose Coceres	70	70	70	76	286	7,266
Gene Sauers	69	71	73	75	288	7,140
Ken Duke	72	64	75	80	291	7,056

Chrysler Championship

Westin Innisbrook Resort, Copperhead Course,
Palm Harbor, Florida
Par 36-35–71; 7,315 yards

October 28-31
purse, $5,000,000

	SCORES				TOTAL	MONEY
Vijay Singh	65	69	67	65	266	$900,000
Tommy Armour	70	64	68	69	271	440,000
Jesper Parnevik	68	67	68	68	271	440,000
Joe Durant	68	71	70	63	272	240,000
Kirk Triplett	64	71	68	70	273	200,000
Robert Allenby	70	67	69	68	274	173,750
David Toms	70	69	67	68	274	173,750
Spike McRoy	69	72	66	68	275	145,000
Kenny Perry	70	68	70	67	275	145,000
Carl Pettersson	68	68	70	69	275	145,000
Tim Clark	69	69	70	68	276	120,000
Tag Ridings	72	69	71	64	276	120,000
Tom Carter	73	67	65	72	277	93,750
Jay Haas	67	70	70	70	277	93,750
Lee Janzen	67	72	70	68	277	93,750
Kevin Na	70	70	68	69	277	93,750
Bob Estes	70	70	70	68	278	75,000
Kent Jones	64	71	75	68	278	75,000
Craig Parry	68	72	69	69	278	75,000
Retief Goosen	69	73	66	71	279	58,250
Matt Kuchar	69	72	66	72	279	58,250
Geoff Ogilvy	72	67	70	70	279	58,250
Jeff Sluman	62	70	74	73	279	58,250
Briny Baird	70	68	72	70	280	40,500
Tim Herron	70	69	67	74	280	40,500
Bernhard Langer	70	69	71	70	280	40,500
Shaun Micheel	73	69	70	68	280	40,500
Jose Maria Olazabal	67	71	67	75	280	40,500
Hidemichi Tanaka	70	70	70	70	280	40,500
Woody Austin	68	71	70	72	281	29,062.50
Pat Bates	72	68	73	68	281	29,062.50
Jeff Brehaut	72	69	69	71	281	29,062.50

	SCORES				TOTAL	MONEY
Harrison Frazar	68	74	70	69	281	29,062.50
Chris Riley	68	72	67	74	281	29,062.50
Justin Rose	65	71	71	74	281	29,062.50
Vaughn Taylor	70	65	73	73	281	29,062.50
Dean Wilson	72	68	68	73	281	29,062.50
David Frost	73	69	73	67	282	21,000
Stephen Leaney	67	70	72	73	282	21,000
Justin Leonard	71	71	68	72	282	21,000
Rocco Mediate	76	66	69	71	282	21,000
Arron Oberholser	71	68	73	70	282	21,000
Tom Pernice, Jr.	71	71	70	70	282	21,000
Bart Bryant	70	71	71	71	283	15,116.67
Tom Byrum	68	70	72	73	283	15,116.67
Mark Calcavecchia	68	71	73	71	283	15,116.67
Fred Funk	70	70	76	67	283	15,116.67
Jonathan Byrd	66	66	75	76	283	15,116.66
John Huston	70	68	71	74	283	15,116.66
Brian Gay	69	73	73	69	284	11,966.67
Charles Howell	68	71	72	73	284	11,966.67
Neal Lancaster	70	72	70	72	284	11,966.67
Duffy Waldorf	69	73	72	70	284	11,966.67
Stephen Ames	70	71	69	74	284	11,966.66
Patrick Sheehan	71	71	68	74	284	11,966.66
Skip Kendall	70	70	69	76	285	11,350
Billy Mayfair	69	71	73	72	285	11,350
Glen Day	71	70	70	75	286	11,050
Peter Jacobsen	71	70	73	72	286	11,050
Ryan Palmer	70	69	75	72	286	11,050
Brenden Pappas	70	72	70	74	286	11,050
Brian Bateman	69	70	78	70	287	10,600
Chad Campbell	70	72	72	73	287	10,600
Rod Pampling	69	65	76	77	287	10,600
Brett Quigley	69	73	73	72	287	10,600
Bo Van Pelt	75	67	73	72	287	10,600
Aaron Baddeley	70	70	74	74	288	10,300
Loren Roberts	71	68	81	70	290	10,200
Len Mattiace	71	71	74	77	293	10,100
Carlos Franco	73	67	73	82	295	9,950
J.L. Lewis	68	72	77	78	295	9,950
Jay Williamson	72	69	77	82	300	9,800

Tour Championship

East Lake Golf Club, Atlanta, Georgia
Par 35-35–70; 7,141 yards

November 4-7
purse, $6,000,000

	SCORES				TOTAL	MONEY
Retief Goosen	70	66	69	64	269	$1,080,000
Tiger Woods	72	64	65	72	273	648,000
Jerry Kelly	67	71	71	65	274	414,000
Stephen Ames	69	66	70	70	275	248,000
Mark Hensby	69	70	69	67	275	248,000
Mike Weir	69	69	67	70	275	248,000
Jay Haas	67	66	68	75	276	198,000
Scott Verplank	74	67	68	67	276	198,000
Vijay Singh	69	73	70	65	277	180,000
Ernie Els	72	71	68	67	278	158,200

	SCORES				TOTAL	MONEY
Rory Sabbatini	71	68	71	68	278	158,200
David Toms	68	73	70	67	278	158,200
Zach Johnson	68	71	71	69	279	141,600
Padraig Harrington	69	75	68	68	280	134,400
Stuart Appleby	69	72	71	69	281	123,800
Darren Clarke	67	73	70	71	281	123,800
Sergio Garcia	71	70	69	71	281	123,800
John Daly	69	72	71	70	282	117,000
Shigeki Maruyama	73	76	67	68	284	112,500
Phil Mickelson	71	72	67	74	284	112,500
Stewart Cink	70	73	71	71	285	105,600
Steve Flesch	69	78	67	71	285	105,600
Adam Scott	75	71	69	70	285	105,600
Chris DiMarco	72	71	70	73	286	98,400
Carlos Franco	72	68	78	68	286	98,400
Fred Funk	73	70	75	68	286	98,400
K.J. Choi	73	73	72	70	288	94,800
Todd Hamilton	72	72	76	70	290	93,600
Kenny Perry	76	72	70	73	291	92,400
Chad Campbell	73	73			WD	
Davis Love					WD	

Special Events

Tavistock Cup

Lake Nona Golf and Country Club, Orlando, Florida
Par 36-36–72; 7,016 yards

March 29-30
purse, $1,500,000

FIRST DAY
(Team better ball; 2 points for win, 1 point for tie)

Ernie Els and Sven Struver (Lake Nona) 65, Mark O'Meara and Darren Clarke (Isleworth) 68
Charles Howell and John Cook (Isle.) 66, Nick Faldo and Trevor Immelman (LN) 67
Stuart Appleby and Robert Allenby (Isle.) 67, Ian Poulter and Justin Rose (LN) 69
Retief Goosen and Sergio Garcia (LN) 62, Scott Hoch and Lee Janzen (Isle.) 67

POINTS: Isleworth 4, Lake Nona 4

SECOND DAY
(Singles versus both players on other team; 1 point for win, ½ point for tie)

Goosen 67 and Garcia 73 (LN) versus Clarke 72 and Appleby 66 (Isle.)
Poulter 76 and Faldo 78 (LN) versus O'Meara 69 and Craig Parry 69 (Isle.)
Immelman 72 and Rose 70 (LN) versus Howell 71 and Hoch 72 (Isle.)
Els 72 and Annika Sorenstam 77 (LN) versus Allenby 75 and Janzen 73 (Isle.)

POINTS: Isleworth 10½ (Clarke 1, Appleby 2, O'Meara 2, Parry 2, Howell 1, Hoch ½, Allenby 1, Janzen 1); Lake Nona 5½ (Goosen 1, Immelman ½, Rose 2, Els 2)

TWO-DAY TOTAL: Isleworth 14½, Lake Nona 9½

(Each member of the winning team received $100,000; each member of the losing team received $50,000. Cook/Parry and Struver/Sorenstam split shares. Appleby and Goosen received $100,000 each and O'Meara and Parry received $50,000 each for the three lowest scores on the second day.)

CVS Charity Classic

Rhode Island Country Club, Barrington, Rhode Island   July 28-29
Par 36-35–71; 6,694 yards   purse $1,300,000

	SCORES		TOTAL	MONEY (Team)
Jay Haas/Bill Haas	60	62	122	$250,000
David Toms/Chad Campbell	60	63	123	175,000
Mike Weir/Davis Love	63	61	124	130,000
Dana Quigley/Brett Quigley	63	61	124	130,000
Peter Jacobsen/Chris Riley	64	61	125	115,000
Brad Faxon/Greg Norman	66	60	126	110,000
Jeff Sluman/Rocco Mediate	62	66	128	105,000
Billy Andrade/Arnold Palmer	64	65	129	95,000
Kenny Perry/Shaun Micheel	67	62	129	95,000
Craig Stadler/Jerry Kelly	68	61	129	95,000

Ryder Cup

Oakland Hills Country Club, South Course,   September 17-19
Bloomfield Hills, Michigan
Par 453 444 443–35, 445 344 434–35–70; 7,077 yards

FIRST DAY
Morning Fourballs

Colin Montgomerie and Padraig Harrington (Europe) defeated Phil Mickelson and Tiger Woods (USA), 2 and 1.

Montgomerie	3			3	3	4		4								4	3
Harrington		4	2		5			3	4		4	4	3	3	4		
Mickelson						4	3	4		4	4		3	4	4	3	3
Woods	4	4	3	3	3			3			5						

Darren Clarke and Miguel Angel Jimenez (Europe) defeated Davis Love and Chad Campbell (USA), 5 and 4.

Clarke	4			3	3	4		4		4		3	4
Jimenez		4	3				4		3		3	4	
Love	4	5							4		4		4
Campbell			3	4	4	4	4	4		4		3	

Paul McGinley and Luke Donald (Europe) halved with Chris Riley and Stewart Cink (USA).

McGinley	4		3			3	3	4	3		5	3	4		
Donald		5		4	4					4	4			4	4	3	4
Riley		5			4			3		4			4		4		4
Cink	4		3	4		4	3		3		4	5	4		3		3

Sergio Garcia and Lee Westwood (Europe) defeated David Toms and Jim Furyk (USA), 5 and 3.

	1	2	3	4	5	6	7	8	9	10	11	12	13	14	15
Garcia	3		3			3	4	4	3	4	5			4	4
Westwood		4		3	4							4	2		
Toms				4						4	4	5			
Furyk	4	5	3		4	3	4	4	4				3	3	5

TOTAL: Europe 3½, United States ½

Afternoon Foursomes

Chris DiMarco and Jay Haas (USA) defeated Miguel Angel Jimenez and Thomas Levet (Europe), 3 and 2.

	1	2	3	4	5	6	7	8	9	10	11	12	13	14	15	16
Jimenez/Levet	4	4	3	5	5	4	4	4	3	5	5	5	3	4	4	4
DiMarco/Haas	4	5	3	4	4	3	4	4	4	4	4	5	4	4	4	3

Colin Montgomerie and Padraig Harrington (Europe) defeated Davis Love and Fred Funk (USA), 4 and 2.

	1	2	3	4	5	6	7	8	9	10	11	12	13	14	15	16
Montgomerie/Harrington	3	4	4	4	3	3	5	4	2	4	4	5	3	5	4	4
Love/Funk	4	4	3	4	3	4	5	4	3	5	5	5	3	4	4	6

Darren Clarke and Lee Westwood (Europe) defeated Phil Mickelson and Tiger Woods (USA), 1 up.

	1	2	3	4	5	6	7	8	9	10	11	12	13	14	15	16	17	18
Clarke/Westwood	4	5	4	5	4	4	3	5	3	3	4	5	3	4	4	4	4	5
Mickelson/Woods	4	4	3	4	4	5	4	5	3	4	5	5	3	4	4	4	3	6

Sergio Garcia and Luke Donald (Europe) defeated Kenny Perry and Stewart Cink (USA), 2 and 1.

	1	2	3	4	5	6	7	8	9	10	11	12	13	14	15	16	17
Garcia/Donald	5	4	3	4	4	4	4	4	3	4	5	4	3	5	4	5	3
Perry/Cink	5	5	3	4	4	4	4	4	4	5	4	5	2	4	5	5	3

TOTAL: Europe 6½, United States 1½

SECOND DAY
Morning Fourballs

Sergio Garcia and Lee Westwood (Europe) halved with Jay Haas and Chris DiMarco (USA).

	1	2	3	4	5	6	7	8	9	10	11	12	13	14	15	16	17	18
Garcia	4		2	4		4	3	4			3	4			4	4	3	
Westwood		5			4				2	4			3	3				5
Haas	3		3	4	3			4	2			4	3	3			3	5
DiMarco		5				3	4			4	4				4	4		

Tiger Woods and Chris Riley (USA) defeated Darren Clarke and Ian Poulter (Europe), 4 and 3.

	1	2	3	4	5	6	7	8	9	10	11	12	13	14	15
Clarke	5	5	3	4	4		4		3	4	4				3
Poulter						3		4				5	3	4	
Woods	4		4	4	3	3	4	4	3	4	4			4	
Riley		4										4	2		3

Paul Casey and David Howell (Europe) defeated Jim Furyk and Chad Campbell (USA), 1 up.

	1	2	3	4	5	6	7	8	9	10	11	12	13	14	15	16	17	18
Casey	4		3				4	3	3	3		5	3	4				4
Howell		4		4	4	3					4				3	4	2	
Furyk		4		4	4	4		3		4	3	4	2	4	3			5
Campbell	4		3				4		3							4	3	

Stewart Cink and Davis Love (USA) defeated Colin Montgomerie and Padraig
Harrington (Europe), 3 and 2.

Montgomerie	5				4		3		3				3	4	4	
Harrington		4	2	5		4		4		4	4	5				3
Cink	4							4		3				4	4	3
Love		4	2	3	4	3		4		4	4	4	3			

TOTAL: Europe 8, United States 4

Afternoon Foursomes

Darren Clarke and Lee Westwood (Europe) defeated Jay Haas and Chris DiMarco
(USA), 5 and 4.

| Clarke/Westwood | 4 | 5 | 4 | 4 | 3 | 4 | 4 | 3 | 4 | 4 | 3 | 4 | 3 | 5 |
| Haas/DiMarco | 6 | 5 | 4 | 4 | 4 | 4 | 4 | 4 | 2 | 6 | 4 | 5 | 3 | 5 |

Phil Mickelson and David Toms (USA) defeated Miguel Angel Jimenez and Thomas
Levet (Europe), 4 and 3.

| Jimenez/Levet | 4 | 4 | 4 | 3 | 4 | 4 | 4 | 5 | 4 | 4 | 4 | 5 | 3 | 4 | 5 |
| Mickelson/Toms | 4 | 5 | 3 | 4 | 3 | 3 | 4 | 5 | 4 | 4 | 4 | 4 | 2 | 4 | 4 |

Sergio Garcia and Luke Donald (Europe) defeated Jim Furyk and Fred Funk (USA),
1 up.

| Garcia/Donald | 3 | 5 | 3 | 4 | 4 | 3 | 4 | 3 | 3 | 4 | 4 | 6 | 3 | 3 | 4 | 4 | 4 | 4 |
| Furyk/Funk | 5 | 5 | 4 | 3 | 4 | 3 | 4 | 5 | 3 | 5 | 4 | 5 | 3 | 4 | 3 | 4 | 2 | 4 |

Padraig Harrington and Paul McGinley (Europe) defeated Davis Love and Tiger Woods
(USA), 4 and 3.

| Harrington/McGinley | 5 | 5 | 3 | 3 | 4 | 4 | 4 | 3 | 4 | 4 | 5 | 3 | 4 | 3 |
| Love/Woods | 4 | 3 | 3 | 4 | 4 | 4 | 4 | 5 | 4 | 4 | 5 | 5 | 4 | 4 |

TOTAL: Europe 11, United States 5

THIRD DAY
Singles

Tiger Woods (USA) defeated Paul Casey (Europe), 3 and 2.

| Casey | 5 | 5 | 4 | 4 | 5 | 3 | 4 | 5 | 3 | 4 | 4 | 4 | 3 | 4 | 4 | 4 |
| Woods | 4 | 5 | 4 | 4 | 4 | 3 | 4 | 5 | 3 | 4 | 4 | 3 | 3 | 4 | 4 | 4 |

Sergio Garcia (Europe) defeated Phil Mickelson (USA), 3 and 2.

| Garcia | 5 | 4 | 4 | 4 | 4 | 4 | 4 | 5 | 2 | 3 | 3 | 5 | 3 | 4 | 4 | 4 |
| Mickelson | 5 | 4 | 3 | 4 | 4 | 4 | 4 | 3 | 3 | 4 | 4 | 5 | 4 | 4 | 4 | 5 |

Darren Clarke (Europe) halved with Davis Love (USA).

| Clarke | 4 | 5 | 2 | 4 | 5 | 4 | 4 | 4 | 3 | 4 | 3 | 4 | 3 | 5 | 4 | 3 | 2 | 5 |
| Love | 4 | 4 | 3 | 4 | 4 | 3 | 4 | 5 | 3 | 4 | 3 | 4 | 3 | 4 | 4 | 4 | 3 | 5 |

Jim Furyk (USA) defeated David Howell (Europe), 6 and 4.

| Howell | 5 | 6 | 3 | 4 | 3 | 4 | 4 | 5 | 3 | 5 | 4 | 5 | 5 | 4 |
| Furyk | 4 | 4 | 3 | 3 | 3 | 4 | 3 | 4 | 3 | 5 | 5 | 5 | 3 | 3 |

Lee Westwood (Europe) defeated Kenny Perry (USA), 1 up.

| Westwood | 4 | 4 | 3 | 4 | 5 | 5 | 4 | 4 | 4 | 4 | 4 | 4 | 3 | 5 | 4 | 4 | 3 | 4 |
| Perry | 4 | 5 | 2 | 4 | 3 | 4 | 4 | 5 | 4 | 4 | 4 | 5 | 4 | 4 | 5 | 4 | 3 | 4 |

Colin Montgomerie (Europe) defeated David Toms (USA), 1 up.

| Montgomerie | 3 | 4 | 3 | 4 | 5 | 3 | 4 | 4 | 3 | 5 | 4 | 5 | 2 | 4 | 6 | 3 | 3 | 4 |
| Toms | 4 | 4 | 2 | 5 | 5 | 4 | 4 | 4 | 3 | 5 | 3 | 4 | 3 | 4 | 5 | 4 | 3 | 4 |

Chad Campbell (USA) defeated Luke Donald (Europe), 5 and 3.

Donald	4	5	4	5	3	4	4	4	4	5	4	5	3	5	5	
Campbell	4	5	3	3	3	4	4	3	4	4	4	4	4	5	4	

Chris DiMarco (USA) defeated Miguel Angel Jimenez (Europe), 1 up.

Jimenez	4	4	4	4	4	3	3	4	3	4	4	5	3	5	4	5	3	4
DiMarco	4	6	3	4	4	4	3	4	4	4	4	3	4	5	4	3	4

Thomas Levet (Europe) defeated Fred Funk (USA), 1 up.

Levet	4	4	3	3	4	4	3	4	4	4	5	6	2	4	5	4	3	5
Funk	4	4	3	4	5	4	4	4	4	4	4	5	2	5	4	4	3	5

Ian Poulter (Europe) defeated Chris Riley (USA), 3 and 2.

Poulter	4	5	3	4	5	3	4	4	3	5	3	5	3	4	3	4
Riley	5	4	3	4	5	3	5	4	3	5	4	4	3	5	4	4

Padraig Harrington (Europe) defeated Jay Haas (USA), 1 up.

Harrington	6	3	3	4	4	3	3	4	4	4	3	5	3	3	3	6	4	4
Haas	3	4	3	5	4	4	4	5	3	4	4	4	2	5	3	5	4	4

Paul McGinley (Europe) defeated Stewart Cink (USA), 3 and 2.

McGinley	4	4	3	4	5	3	4	4	3	4	3	4	4	4	3	4
Cink	6	4	4	5	4	4	4	5	2	4	3	5	3	4	3	4

TOTAL: Europe 18½, United States 9½

Franklin Templeton Shootout

Tiburon Golf Course, Naples, Florida
Par 36-36–72; 7,193 yards

November 12-14
purse, $2,500,000

	SCORES			TOTAL	MONEY (Each)
Hank Kuehne/Jeff Sluman	64	62	61	187	$300,000
Steve Flesch/Justin Leonard	63	63	63	189	187,500
Mark Calcavecchia/Loren Roberts	66	63	61	190	112,500
Bill Haas/Jay Haas	69	61	61	191	87,500
Scott McCarron/Greg Norman	65	64	62	191	87,500
Scott Hoch/Kenny Perry	67	65	60	192	77,500
John Daly/Rory Sabbatini	65	68	60	193	72,500
Paul Azinger/Olin Browne	68	65	62	195	70,000
Chad Campbell/Chris Riley	71	66	59	196	67,500
Steve Elkington/Rocco Mediate	70	65	64	199	63,750
Nick Faldo/Fred Funk	70	66	63	199	63,750
Charles Howell/Lee Janzen	71	65	64	200	60,000

Callaway Golf Pebble Beach Invitational

Pebble Beach GL: Par 36-36–72; 6,737 yards
Spyglass Hills GC: Par 36-36–72; 6,862 yards
Del Monte GC: Par 36-36–72; 6,357 yards
Pebble Beach, California

November 18-21
purse, $300,000

	SCORES				TOTAL	MONEY
Jeff Brehaut	69	67	74	69	279	$60,000
Kevin Sutherland	70	69	73	68	280	32,200
Todd Fischer	70	71	67	76	284	13,500
Tom Lehman	68	71	72	73	284	13,500
Kirk Triplett	69	66	72	78	285	8,650
Tommy Armour	68	69	73	75	285	8,650
Bo Van Pelt	76	69	68	72	285	8,650
Kent Jones	73	67	74	71	285	8,650
Matt Gogel	70	70	70	76	286	6,500
Curt Byrum	72	72	68	75	287	5,750
Matt Hansen	74	74	66	73	287	5,750
Nick Watney	68	67	76	77	288	5,050
Rich Beem	69	69	74	76	288	5,050
Olin Browne	66	72	73	78	289	4,300
J.J. Jakovac	66	75	70	78	289	4,300
Janice Moodie	75	69	73	72	289	4,300
Ryan Palmer	69	66	74	81	290	3,500
Spike McRoy	70	71	75	74	290	3,500
Len Mattiace	69	71	77	73	290	3,500
Steve Scott	68	73	71	79	291	3,000
Scott McCarron	71	74	74	72	291	3,000
D.A. Points	69	72	76	75	292	2,750
Rob Oppenheim	70	75	75	72	292	2,750
Charles Howell	71	74	73	75	293	2,375
Jonathan Byrd	72	75	72	74	293	2,375
Per-Ulrik Johansson	71	73	75	74	293	2,375
David Frost	74	73	72	74	293	2,375
Mark Brooks	69	77	74	73	293	2,375
Shawn McEntee	75	72	73	73	293	2,375
Jill McGill	69	73	74	78	294	2,150
Kyle Thompson	70	76	70	79	295	2,100
Tom Purtzer	68	78	73	77	296	2,080
Brian Miller	72	74	71	80	297	2,050
Brian Mogg	72	76	71	78	297	2,050
Roger Maltbie	73	74	74	78	299	2,020
Tommy Masters	74	71	74	81	300	1,990
Scott Miller	70	75	74	81	300	1,990
Rick Hartmann	74	70	77	80	301	1,960
Ron Skayhan	68	75	78	81	302	1,940
Mark Hensby	72	68	76		WD	1,910
Andrew Magee	74	76	71		WD	1,910

WGC - World Cup

See European Tours chapter.

UBS Cup

Kiawah Island Club, Cassique Course,　　　　　　　November 19-21
Kiawah Island, South Carolina　　　　　　　　　　purse, $3,000,000
Par 35-35–70; 6,945 yards

FIRST DAY
Alternate Shot

Arnold Palmer and Jay Haas (US) halved with Gary Player and Mark McNulty.
Colin Montgomerie and Bernhard Langer (World) defeated Tom Kite and Raymond Floyd, 1 up.
Hale Irwin and Fred Funk (US) defeated Sam Torrance and Barry Lane, 5 and 3.
Ian Woosnam and Sandy Lyle (World) defeated Tom Watson and Scott Hoch, 4 and 3.
John Chillas and Carl Mason (World) defeated Curtis Strange and Craig Stadler, 4 and 3.
Hal Sutton and Fred Couples (US) defeated Peter Senior and Rodger Davis, 3 and 2.

POINTS: United States 2½, Rest of the World 3½

SECOND DAY
Best-Ball

Player and McNulty (World) halved with Palmer and Haas.
Torrance and Lane (World) halved with Stadler and Kite.
Sutton and Watson (US) defeated Davis and Senior, 4 and 2.
Hoch and Strange (US) defeated Mason and Chillas, 2 and 1.
Floyd and Couples (US) defeated Woosnam and Lyle, 4 and 2.
Montgomerie and Langer (World) defeated Irwin and Funk, 2 and 1.

POINTS: United States 4, Rest of the World 2
TWO-DAY TOTAL: United States 6½, Rest of the World 5½

THIRD DAY
Singles

Player (World) defeated Palmer, 6 and 5.
Haas (US) defeated Lane, 5 and 3.
Stadler (US) defeated Woosnam, 5 and 4.
Kite (US) defeated Davis, 1 up.
Torrance (World) defeated Strange, 5 and 3.
Senior (World) defeated Funk, 1 up.
Floyd (US) halved with McNulty.
Watson (US) defeated Lyle, 1 up.
Hoch (US) defeated Mason, 2 and 1.
Irwin (US) halved with Chillas.
Couples (US) defeated Montgomerie, 5 and 3.
Sutton (US) halved with Bernhard Langer.

POINTS: United States 7½, Rest of the World 4½
TOTAL POINTS: United States 14, Rest of the World 10

(Each member of the United States team received $150,000; each member of the Rest of the World team received $100,000.)

PGA Grand Slam of Golf

Poipu Golf Club, Kauai, Hawaii
Par 36-36–72; 7,081 yards

November 23-24
purse, $1,000,000

	SCORES		TOTAL	MONEY
Phil Mickelson	68	59	127	$400,000
Vijay Singh	66	66	132	250,000
Retief Goosen	65	68	133	200,000
Todd Hamilton	70	75	145	150,000

Shinhan Korea Golf Championship

Jungmun Golf Club, Jeju Island, South Korea
Par 36-36–72; 7,431 yards

November 25-28
purse, $3,550,000

	SCORES				TOTAL	MONEY
Arron Oberholser	72	73	70	69	284	$1,000,000
Kevin Na	70	74	72	70	286	325,000
Miguel Angel Jimenez	70	75	69	72	286	325,000
Trevor Immelman	70	74	78	65	287	200,000
Tim Petrovic	70	77	72	70	289	147,500
Daniel Chopra	71	76	71	71	289	147,500
Duffy Waldorf	73	78	71	68	290	110,000
Matt Kuchar	72	74	74	70	290	110,000
Mathias Gronberg	74	75	71	70	290	110,000
Brian Bateman	68	75	73	74	290	110,000
Billy Mayfair	72	77	74	68	291	71,250
Y.E. Yang	66	75	80	70	291	71,250
Padraig Harrington	66	77	76	72	291	71,250
J.J. Henry	73	73	72	73	291	71,250
Carlos Franco	71	73	76	72	292	55,000
Harrison Frazar	70	80	76	67	293	50,000
Frank Lickliter	83	80	73	68	294	40,000
Mark Calcavecchia	70	76	76	72	294	40,000
Joe Ogilvie	71	76	72	75	294	40,000
Mark Hensby	73	77	76	69	295	31,500
Zach Johnson	70	80	74	72	296	29,500
John Rollins	71	80	71	74	296	29,500
Tom Pernice, Jr.	68	80	87	71	297	27,000
Brian Gay	77	78	70	72	297	27,000
Shaun Micheel	71	78	76	72	297	27,000
Nick Faldo	74	80	73	71	298	24,500
Jang Ik-jae	77	76	73	72	298	24,500
K.J. Choi	76	77	78	68	299	23,000
Brett Quigley	74	83	72	72	301	22,083
Cameron Beckman	73	73	80	75	301	22,083
Bo Van Pelt	73	77	74	77	301	22,083
Rich Beem	69	81	78	75	303	21,500
Craig Bowden	73	83	76	72	304	21,000
Park No-seok	74	80	77	73	304	21,000
Ted Purdy	65	84	80	74	304	21,000
Robert Gamez	74	78	76	75	305	20,500
Paul Stankowski	79	78	74	75	306	20,250
Alex Cejka	72	80	81	75	308	20,000

Office Depot Father-Son Challenge

Champions Gate Golf Resort, Orlando, Florida
Par 37-35–72; 7,111 yards

December 4-5
purse, $1,000,000

	SCORES		TOTAL	MONEY
				(Won by professional)
Larry/Drew Nelson	60	59	119	$200,000
Bob/David Charles	62	60	122	105,000
Jerry/Wesley Pate	61	64	125	59,800
Tom/David Kite	63	62	125	59,800
Raymond/Raymond Jr. Floyd	63	62	125	59,800
Bill/Ben Rogers	64	61	125	59,800
Curtis/Thomas Strange	66	59	125	59,800
Dave/Ronnie Stockton	65	61	126	48,000
Vijay/Qass Singh	66	62	128	46,500
Bernhard/Stefan Langer	63	65	128	46,500
Lee/Rick Trevino	66	63	129	45,000
Arnold Palmer/Sam Saunders	65	65	130	43,000
Hale/Steve Irwin	65	65	130	43,000
Lee Janzen/Aaron Stewart	64	66	130	43,000
Lanny/Travis Wadkins	67	65	132	41,000
Craig/Chris Stadler	67	67	134	40,000

Target World Challenge

Sherwood Country Club, Thousand Oaks, California
Par 36-35–71; 7,206 yards

December 9-12
purse, $5,250,000

	SCORES				TOTAL	MONEY
Tiger Woods	67	66	69	66	268	$1,250,000
Padraig Harrington	68	69	67	66	270	750,000
Jay Haas	69	66	67	69	271	447,500
Colin Montgomerie	67	66	67	71	271	447,500
Miguel Angel Jimenez	68	69	66	70	273	290,000
Jim Furyk	67	68	67	74	276	240,000
Stewart Cink	70	69	69	70	278	220,000
Fred Couples	68	70	71	70	279	205,000
Vijay Singh	74	69	68	68	279	205,000
Chad Campbell	70	68	69	73	280	190,000
Chris DiMarco	69	67	70	75	281	185,000
John Daly	73	69	75	65	282	172,500
Davis Love	70	66	74	72	282	172,500
Kenny Perry	73	73	69	69	284	165,000
Stephen Ames	74	69	74	72	289	155,000
Todd Hamilton	73	69	74	73	289	155,000

Advancing from No. 94 to No. 12 in the world, Miguel Angel Jímenez won five times.

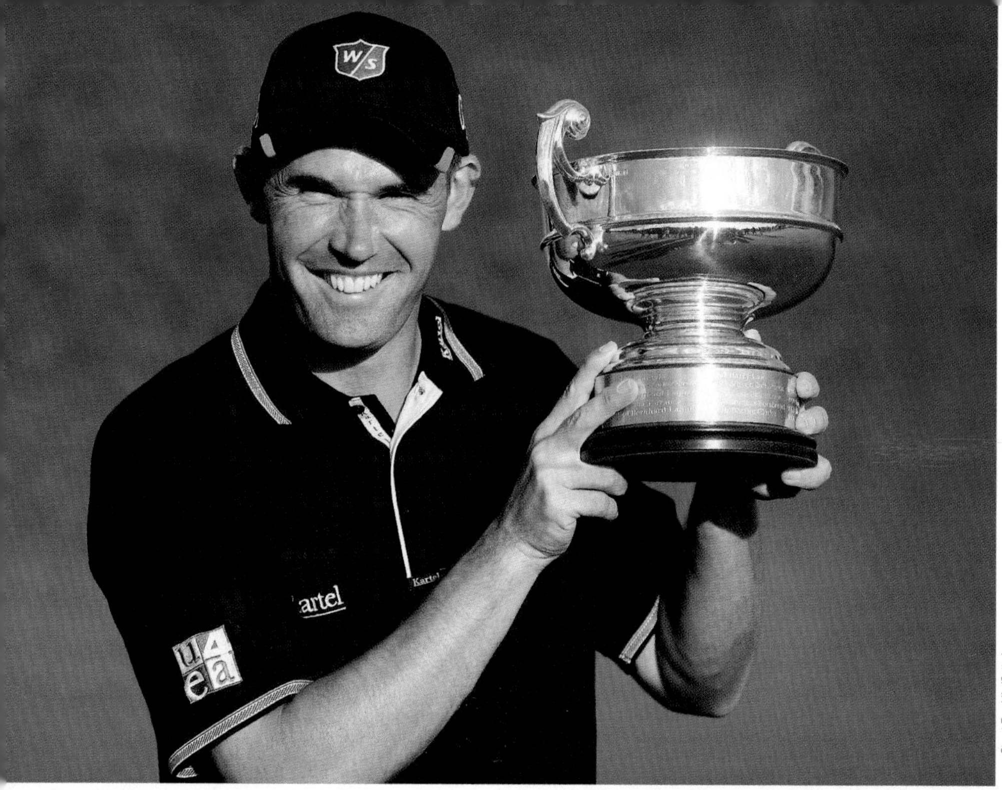

Stuart Franklin/Getty Images

With a victory in the Linde German Masters, Padraig Harrington was third on the Order of Merit.

Warren Little/Getty Images

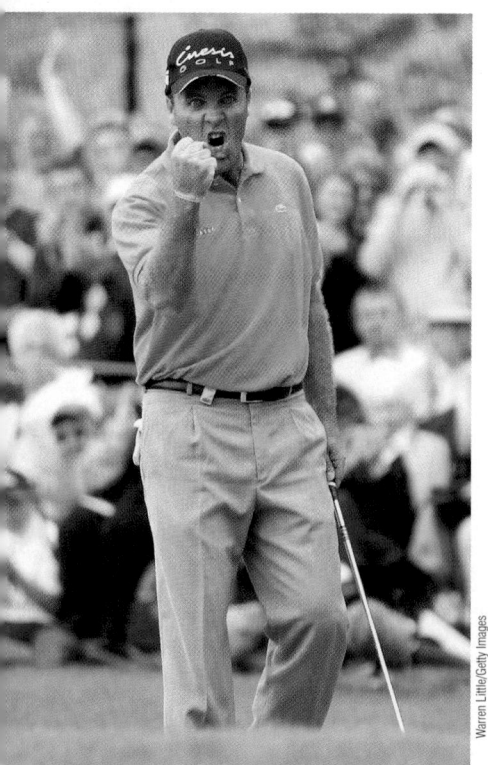

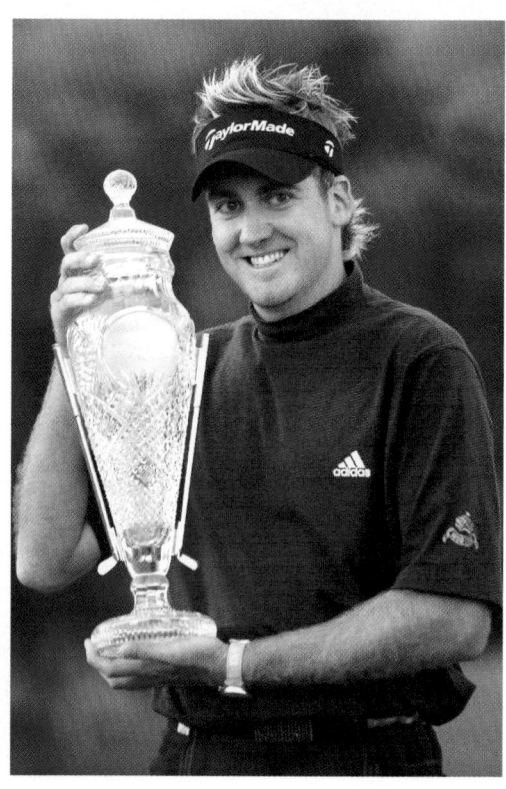

Thomas Levet won in Scotland.

Phil Inglis

Ian Poulter took the Volvo Masters first prize.

Michael C. Cohen

Stuart Franklin/Getty Images

Ernie Els was Europe's money leader with over €4 million.

Graeme McDowell won in Italy.

Andrew Redington/Getty Images

Retief Goosen was second behind Els and had a victory in the Smurfit European Open.

Andrew Redington/Getty Images

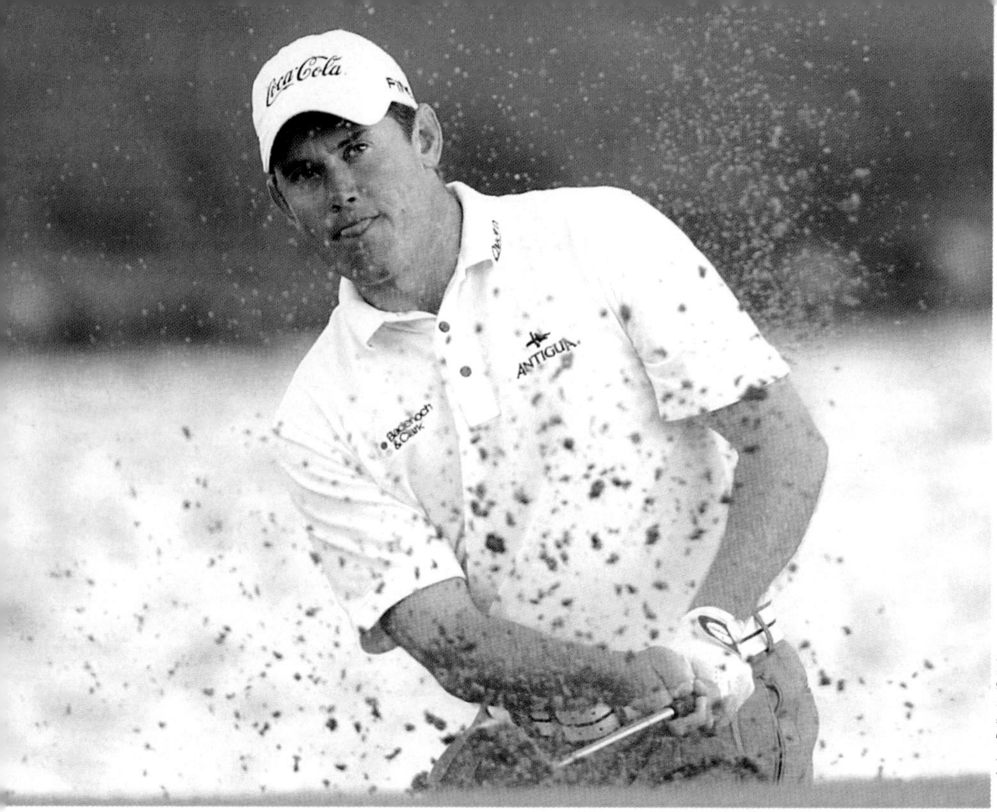

Although Lee Westwood did not win, he placed seventh on the European Tour.

Andrew Redington/Getty Images

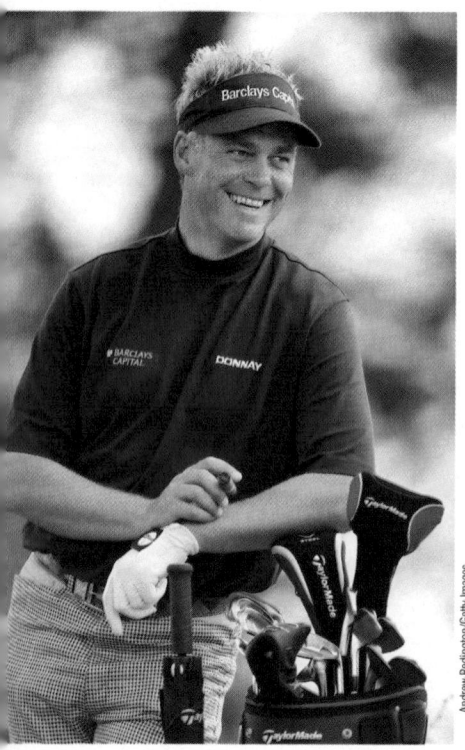

Darren Clarke was third at Accenture.

Phil Inglis

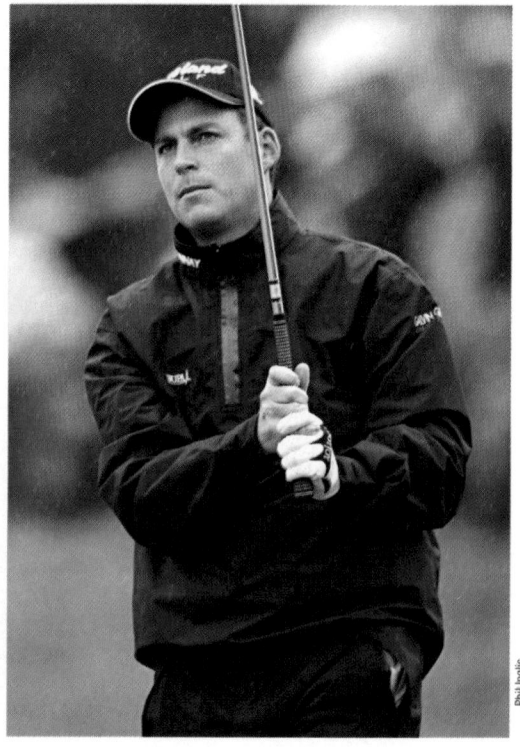

David Howell had two third-place finishes.

Luke Donald and Paul Casey won the WGC - World Cup.

Trevor Immelman won in Germany.

Angel Cabrera posted two seconds.

Stephen Gallacher held the trophy at St. Andrews.

Jean F. Remesy was the French champion.

Nick O'Hern had three top-three finishes.

Thomas Bjorn was a runner-up twice.

Scott Drummond took the Volvo PGA title.

Shigeki Maruyama was No. 28, Japan's best.

Shingo Katayama won ¥105 million in Japan.

Korea's S.K. Ho was third in Japan.

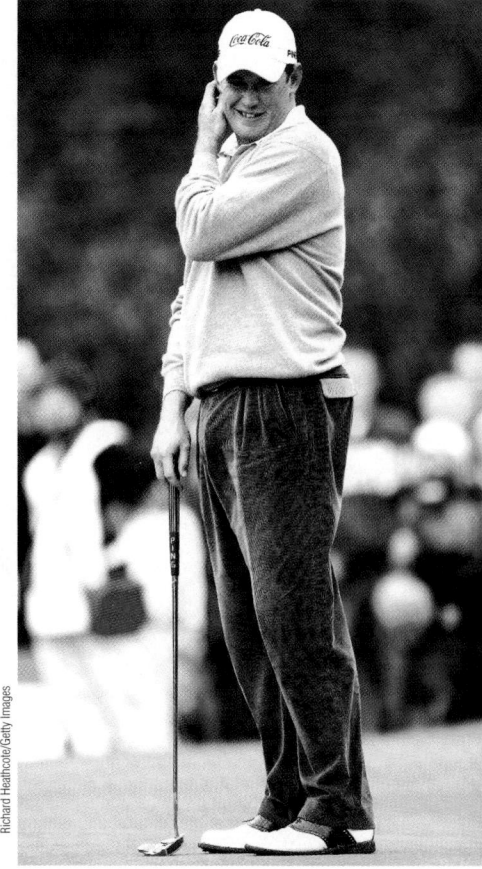

HSBC World Match Play

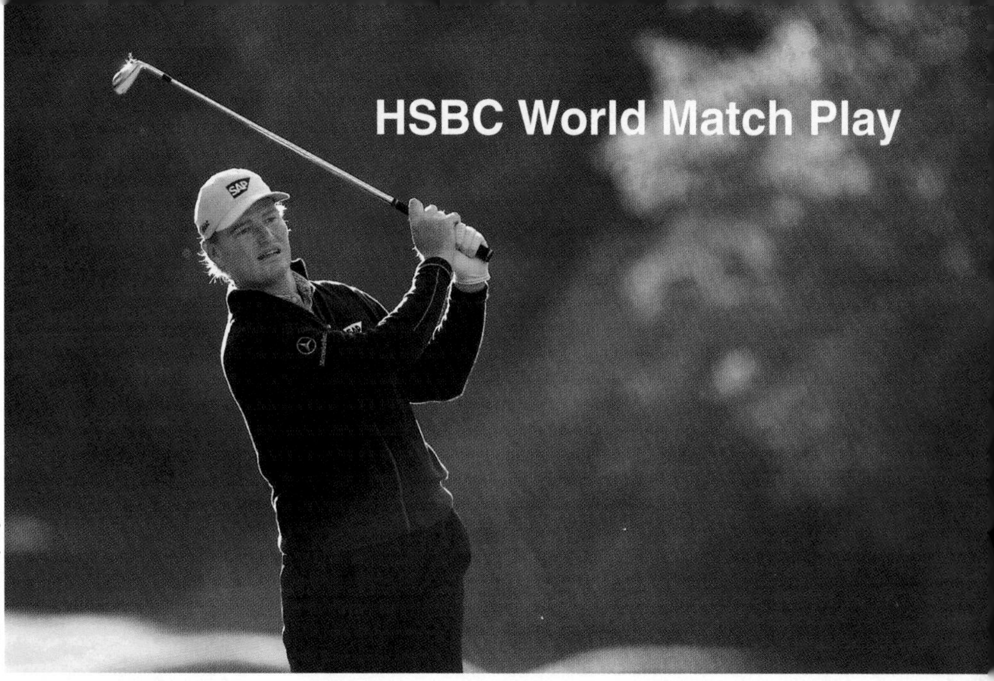

Julian Herbert/Getty Images

Ernie Els won the title for a record sixth time, passing Gary Player and Seve Ballesteros.

Richard Heathcote/Getty Images

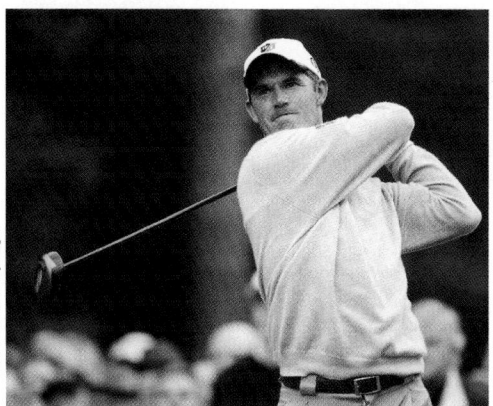

Padraig Harrington lost to Els in the semi-finals.

Richard Heathcote/Getty Images

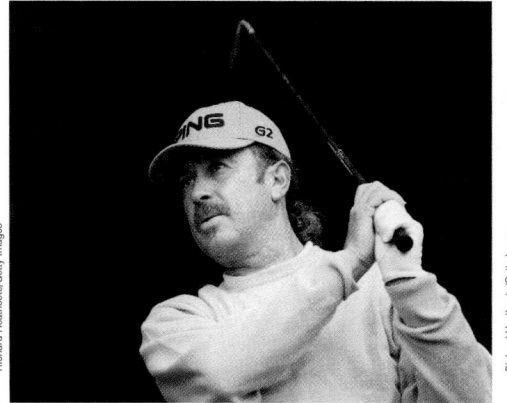

Miguel Angel Jimenez fell on the 36th hole.

Richard Heathcote/Getty Images

Lee Westwood lost 2 & 1 in the final.

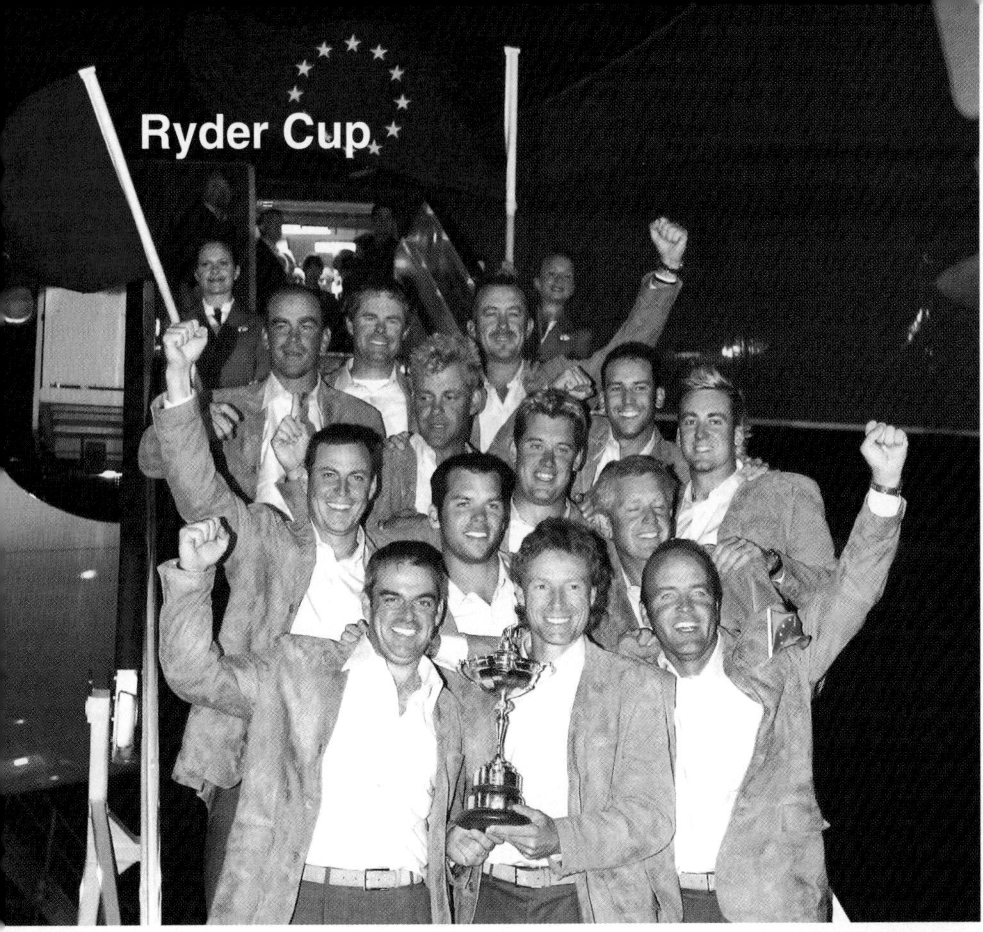

Ryder Cup

Captain Bernhard Langer held the Ryder Cup upon the victorious European team's return home.

Colin Montgomerie made the winning point.

Sergio Garcia posted a 4-0-1 record.

Lee Westwood had four wins and a halve.

Padraig Harrington won four of five.

Tiger Woods left with a 2-3 record.

Phil Mickelson stirred a controversy.

Women's Tours

The ADT Championship was Annika Sorenstam's 10th victory and eighth on the LPGA Tour.

Warren Little/Getty Images

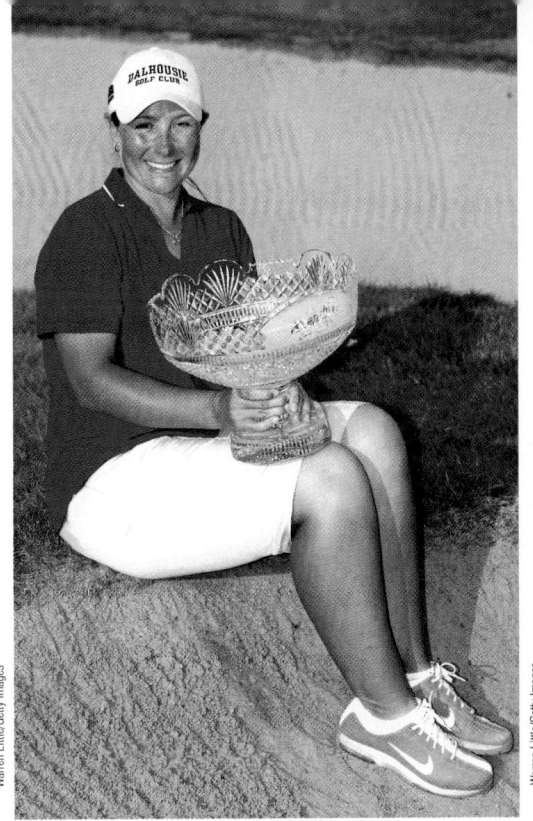

Karen Stupples won the Weetabix British title.

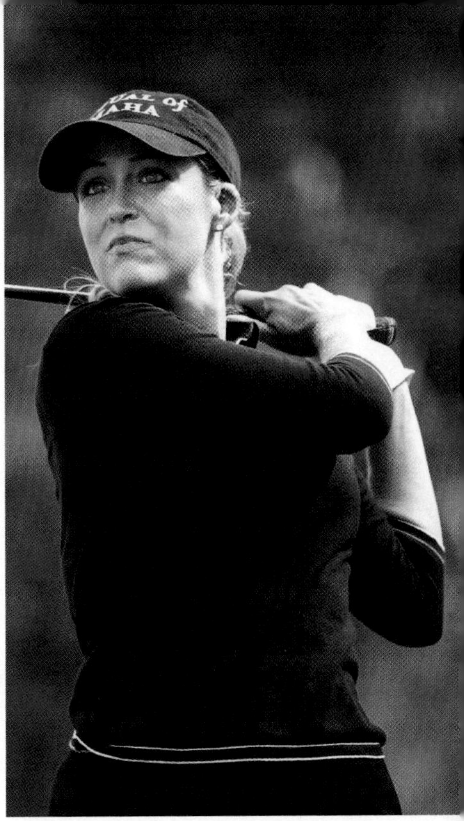

Warren Little/Getty Images

Cristie Kerr posted three LPGA triumphs.

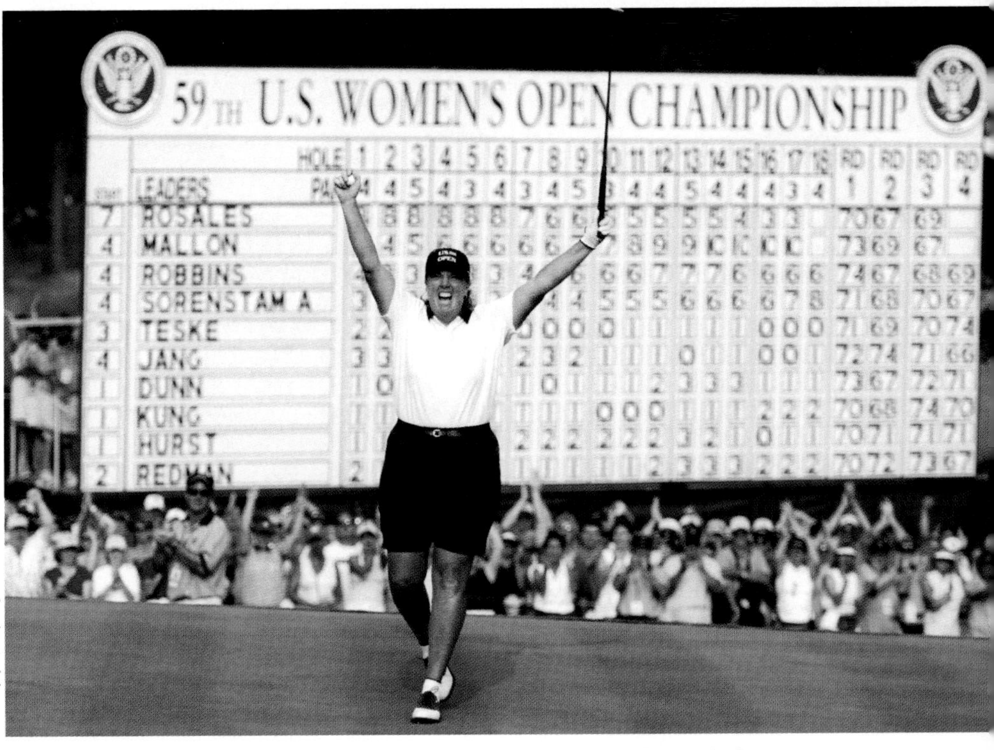

Andy Lyons/Getty Images

Meg Mallon closed with 65, the lowest final round ever in the U.S. Women's Open.

Grace Park was second on the LPGA Tour.   Hee-Won Han was a winner.

Mi Hyun Kim was No. 7 in money won.   At age 14, Michelle Wei was a strong competitor.

Yuri Fudoh won seven times in Japan.

Stephanie Arricau won twice in Europe.

Young Ai Miyazato won five times.

Lorena Ochoa had two LPGA victories.

Senior Tours

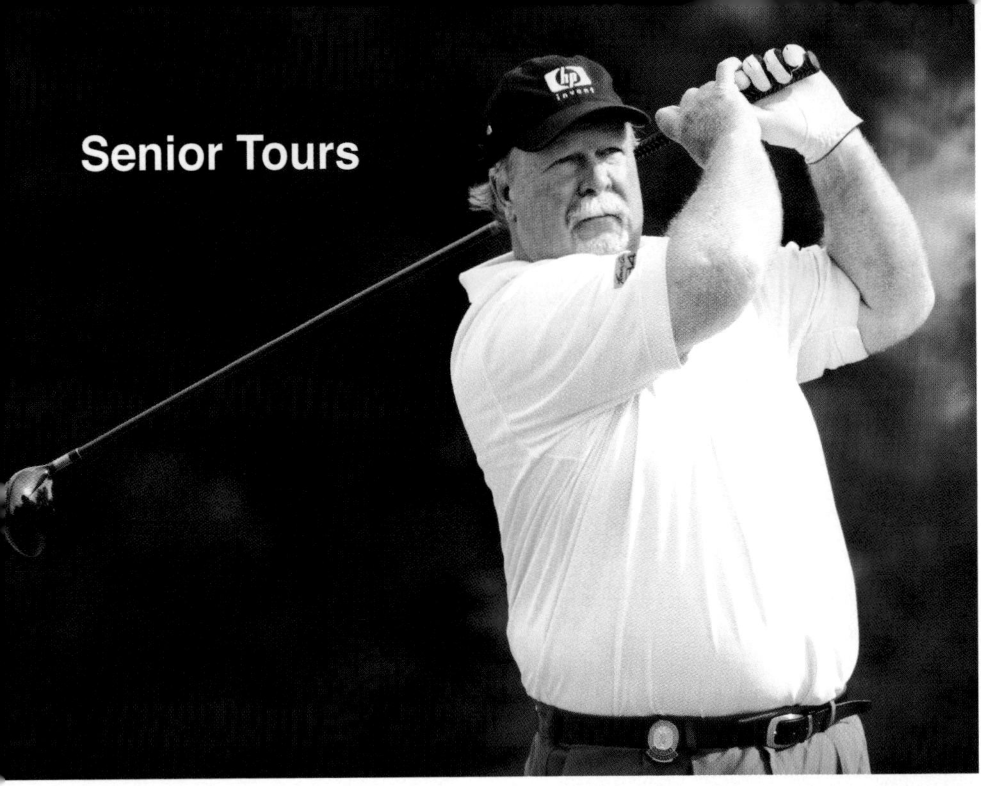

Andy Lyons/Getty Images

The Champions Tour leader was Craig Stadler with five victories and $2.3 million.

Scott Halleran/Getty Images

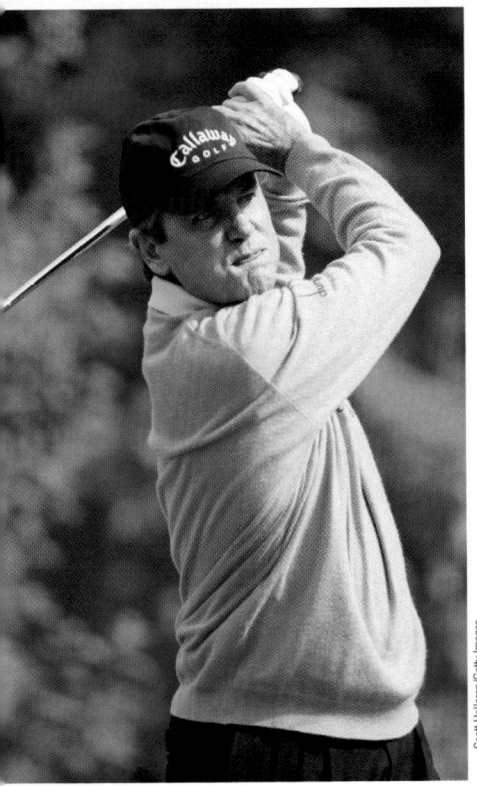

Mark McNulty won the last two events.

Andy Lyons/Getty Images

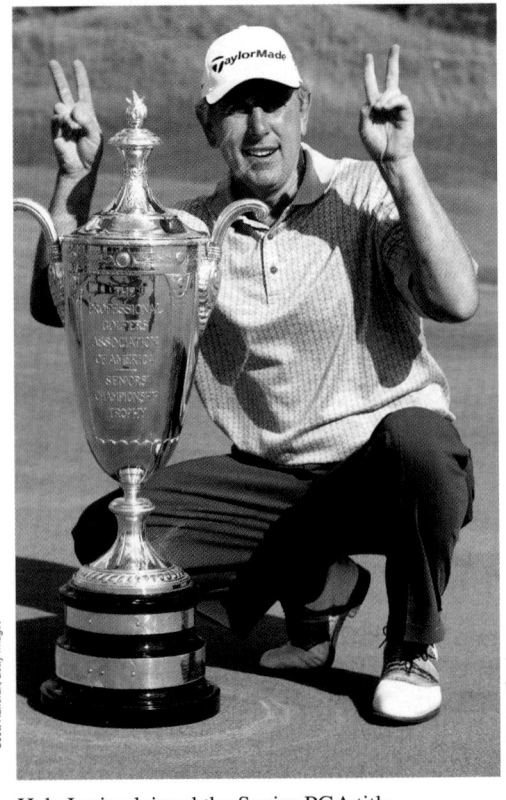

Hale Irwin claimed the Senior PGA title.

Scott Halleran/Getty Images

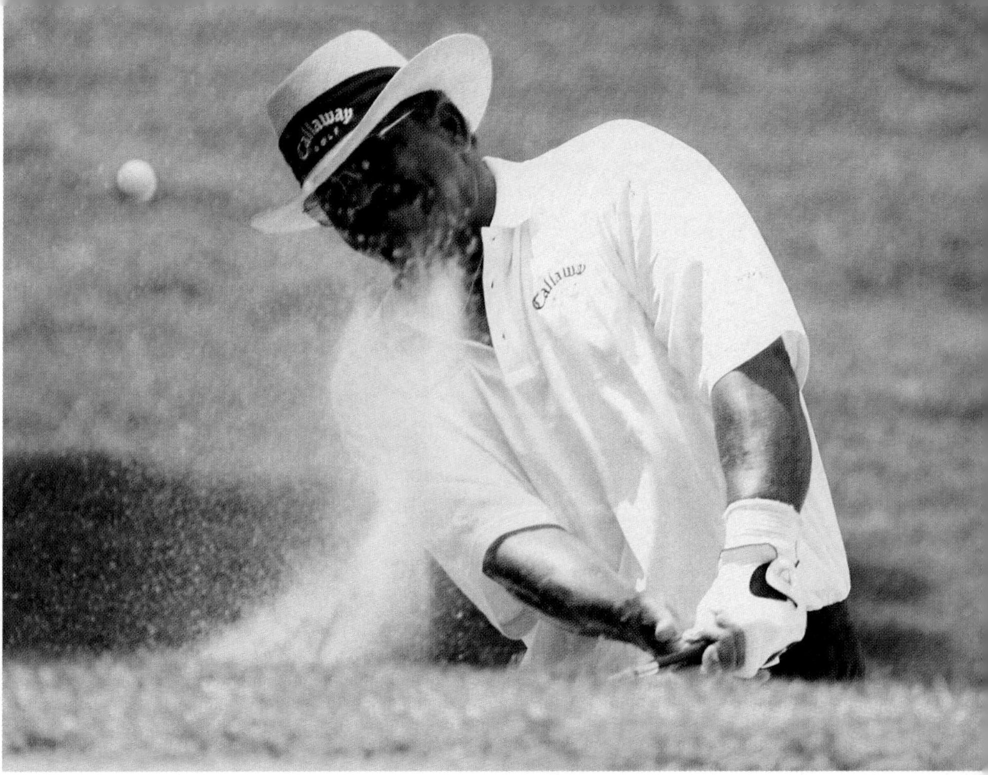

With a two-victory year, Jim Thorpe was among the top 10 money winners.

Scott Halleran/Getty Images

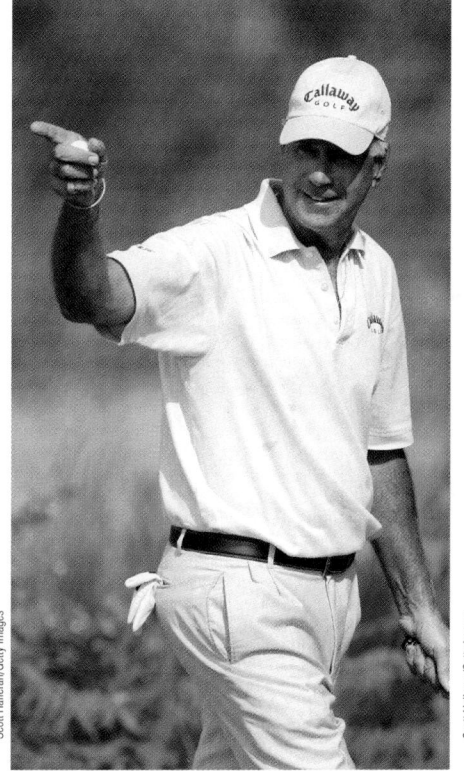

Bruce Fleisher had two early wins.

Scott Halleran/Getty Images

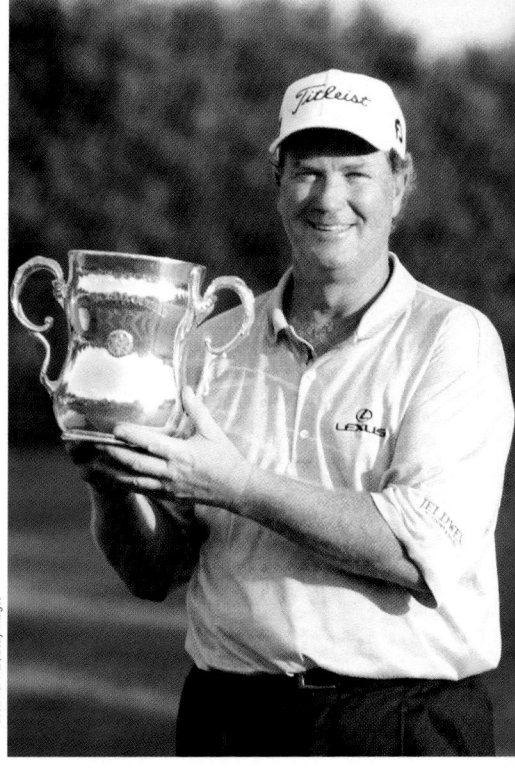

Peter Jacobsen won the U.S. Senior Open.

Mark James took the Ford Senior Players.

Pete Oakley won the Senior British Open.

Carl Mason led in Europe with five wins.

Tom Kite placed third on the money list.

At age 50, Jay Haas stayed on the PGA Tour.

Nationwide Tour

BellSouth Panama Championship

Panama Golf Club, Panama City, Panama
Par 35-35–70; 6,818 yards

February 5-8
purse, $500,000

	SCORES				TOTAL	MONEY
Jimmy Walker	65	69	70	69	273	$90,000
Tom Scherrer	66	69	71	72	278	54,000
Ryan Armour	69	72	68	70	279	34,000
Steve Ford	71	73	67	70	281	19,687.50
Paul Gow	71	68	69	73	281	19,687.50
Jason Caron	67	71	70	73	281	19,687.50
Chris Sessler	69	73	69	70	281	19,687.50
Greg Bruckner	65	71	71	75	282	15,500
Curt Byrum	72	72	67	72	283	13,500
Chris Zambri	70	70	70	73	283	13,500
Jeff Klauk	68	71	73	71	283	13,500
Jim Rutledge	68	74	72	70	284	9,800
Jeff Freeman	67	72	74	71	284	9,800
Matt Bettencourt	72	70	71	71	284	9,800
Rafael Gomez	72	68	73	71	284	9,800
Jon Mills	66	71	75	72	284	9,800
Jess Daley	73	69	68	75	285	7,750
Bryant Odom	68	70	71	76	285	7,750
Barry Cheesman	72	72	69	73	286	5,462.50
Kenneth Staton	71	71	71	73	286	5,462.50
Jason Buha	72	72	69	73	286	5,462.50
Hunter Haas	69	73	70	74	286	5,462.50
Nick Cassini	70	69	73	74	286	5,462.50
Brian McCann	68	69	74	75	286	5,462.50
Troy Matteson	69	75	72	70	286	5,462.50
Steve LeBrun	70	72	70	74	286	5,462.50
Sonny Skinner	71	71	71	74	287	3,485.71
Richard Massey	72	71	69	75	287	3,485.71
Doug Barron	71	69	73	74	287	3,485.71
Richie Coughlan	66	75	76	70	287	3,485.72
Jason Schultz	72	69	70	76	287	3,485.71
Miguel Fernandez	69	72	73	73	287	3,485.72
Brett Wetterich	73	70	73	71	287	3,485.72

Jacob's Creek Open
See Australasian Tour chapter.

New Zealand PGA Championship
See Australasian Tour chapter.

Chitimacha Louisiana Open

Le Triomphe Country Club, Broussard, Louisiana
Par 36-36–72; 7,004 yards

March 25-28
purse, $475,000

	SCORES				TOTAL	MONEY
Jimmy Walker	69	64	74	65	272	$85,500
Rick Price	69	67	69	68	273	51,300
Charley Hoffman	68	70	70	66	274	32,300
Jon Mills	69	67	73	67	276	22,800
Justin Bolli	71	68	69	69	277	18,050
Robert Garrigus	66	65	68	78	277	18,050
Mike Springer	71	63	74	70	278	13,339.58
Craig Lile	76	66	69	67	278	13,339.59
Darron Stiles	70	66	70	72	278	13,339.58
D.J. Trahan	69	69	71	69	278	13,339.58
Scott Gutschewski	71	66	70	71	278	13,339.58
Steve LeBrun	70	69	71	68	278	13,339.59
Jim Rutledge	70	71	71	67	279	9,183.34
Charles Warren	71	67	70	71	279	9,183.33
Boo Weekley	72	69	70	68	279	9,183.33
Franklin Langham	70	70	71	69	280	7,600
Todd Demsey	69	69	70	72	280	7,600
Brad Ott	71	67	70	72	280	7,600
Ben Bates	72	69	70	70	281	5,757
Bart Bryant	71	69	72	69	281	5,757
Dan Pohl	71	69	70	71	281	5,757
Dave Stockton, Jr.	72	66	69	74	281	5,757
Rafael Gomez	66	74	70	71	281	5,757
Charles Raulerson	71	70	70	71	282	4,243.33
Chris Tidland	73	66	72	71	282	4,243.33
Brian Kortan	71	70	73	68	282	4,243.34
Scott Petersen	71	70	73	69	283	3,515
Ken Duke	73	67	73	70	283	3,515
Hunter Haas	72	68	71	72	283	3,515
Roland Thatcher	73	68	72	70	283	3,515

First Tee Arkansas Classic

Diamante Country Club, Hot Springs Village, Arkansas
Par 36-36–72; 7,519 yards

April 15-18
purse, $500,000

	SCORES				TOTAL	MONEY
Daniel Chopra	75	66	68	66	275	$90,000
John Elliott	73	66	71	66	276	54,000
Ryuji Imada	72	70	66	70	278	26,000
James Driscoll	69	70	67	72	278	26,000
Justin Bolli	73	70	65	70	278	26,000
Chris Tidland	73	68	68	70	279	18,000
Robert Garrigus	76	69	68	67	280	16,750
Ben Bates	70	68	73	71	282	14,500
Tjaart van der Walt	72	69	70	71	282	14,500
Bill Lunde	68	71	70	73	282	14,500
Robin Freeman	73	72	68	70	283	12,000
Kelly Gibson	71	66	72	74	283	12,000
Bob Heintz	72	71	66	75	284	9,666.66
Charley Hoffman	70	76	69	69	284	9,666.67

	SCORES				TOTAL	MONEY
Aaron Barber	74	69	69	72	284	9,666.67
Gary Hallberg	70	69	77	69	285	7,250
Vance Veazey	72	69	76	68	285	7,250
Ken Duke	72	74	69	70	285	7,250
Keoke Cotner	73	69	71	72	285	7,250
Vaughn Taylor	69	71	74	71	285	7,250
Jimmy Walker	75	70	70	70	285	7,250
Dicky Pride	71	73	70	72	286	4,700
Mike Sposa	71	74	69	72	286	4,700
Paul Claxton	72	71	72	71	286	4,700
Darron Stiles	73	71	71	71	286	4,700
Scott Gutschewski	72	69	73	72	286	4,700
Patrick Damron	73	71	73	69	286	4,700
Brad Fabel	75	71	71	70	287	3,400
Andy Morse	72	73	71	71	287	3,400
Ryan Armour	69	72	73	73	287	3,400
Sean O'Hair	73	69	69	76	287	3,400
Nick Watney	67	70	72	78	287	3,400
Scott Weatherly	72	69	71	75	287	3,400

Rheem Classic

Hardscrabble Country Club, Fort Smith, Arkansas
Par 35-35–70; 6,619 yards

April 22-25
purse, $475,000

	SCORES				TOTAL	MONEY
Franklin Langham	67	61	71	66	265	$85,500
Keoke Cotner	65	65	70	67	267	51,300
Shane Bertsch	68	69	65	67	269	32,300
Mike Sullivan	69	66	68	67	270	22,800
Jeff Hart	67	68	68	69	272	18,050
Ahmad Bateman	68	70	66	68	272	18,050
Andy Morse	67	72	67	67	273	15,912.50
Paul Gow	73	66	66	69	274	13,775
James Driscoll	69	68	66	71	274	13,775
Justin Bolli	67	67	69	71	274	13,775
Vance Veazey	66	71	68	70	275	10,450
Paul Claxton	67	71	70	67	275	10,450
Ryuji Imada	68	67	73	67	275	10,450
Bryce Molder	66	69	70	70	275	10,450
Jim Rutledge	68	69	71	68	276	7,837.50
Michael Long	72	68	68	68	276	7,837.50
Jeff Klauk	72	67	68	69	276	7,837.50
Rafael Gomez	68	65	69	74	276	7,837.50
Donnie Hammond	68	70	70	69	277	5,035
David Ogrin	69	70	69	69	277	5,035
Scott Petersen	67	73	68	69	277	5,035
Todd Demsey	69	70	70	68	277	5,035
Michael Clark	70	69	67	71	277	5,035
Darron Stiles	71	69	68	69	277	5,035
Chris Anderson	67	68	72	70	277	5,035
Ryan Hietala	74	66	67	70	277	5,035
Jason Caron	69	66	69	73	277	5,035
Fran Quinn	67	69	71	71	278	3,230
Rick Price	69	70	72	67	278	3,230
Charley Hoffman	67	68	70	73	278	3,230
Ryan Gioffre	69	70	69	70	278	3,230

	SCORES				TOTAL	MONEY
Hunter Haas	69	67	71	71	278	3,230
D.A. Points	73	66	70	69	278	3,230

BMW Charity Pro-Am at The Cliffs

The Cliffs Golf & Country Club, Travelers Rest, South Carolina   April 29-May 2
Cliffs Valley Course: Par 36-36–72; 7,023 yards   purse, $600,000
Cliffs at Keowee Vineyards: Par 36-35–71; 7,006 yards

	SCORES				TOTAL	MONEY
Ryuji Imada	70	66	65	69	270	$108,000
Paul Gow	68	67	69	66	270	64,800
(Imada defeated Gow on fifth playoff hole.)						
Rick Price	69	65	68	69	271	27,060
Shane Bertsch	65	68	70	68	271	27,060
Richie Coughlan	67	69	67	68	271	27,060
Jason Gore	69	68	67	67	271	27,060
Bryant Odom	69	70	65	67	271	27,060
Kyle Thompson	67	67	67	71	272	18,000
Jeff Klauk	70	65	71	66	272	18,000
Brad Bryant	66	68	69	70	273	12,857.14
Sonny Skinner	70	66	69	68	273	12,857.15
Vance Veazey	68	69	68	68	273	12,857.14
Anthony Painter	67	71	64	71	273	12,857.14
Steven Alker	67	71	66	69	273	12,857.14
Tony Carolan	65	67	70	71	273	12,857.14
Darron Stiles	68	69	70	66	273	12,857.15
Jody Bellflower	69	67	69	69	274	9,300
Tyler Williamson	72	67	66	69	274	9,300
Ben Duncan	68	70	68	69	275	6,771.43
Jeff Freeman	67	70	71	67	275	6,771.43
Franklin Langham	67	69	69	70	275	6,771.43
Ahmad Bateman	66	70	69	70	275	6,771.43
Ryan Armour	71	66	69	69	275	6,771.43
Euan Walters	66	70	68	71	275	6,771.42
Richard Johnson	69	66	73	67	275	6,771.43
Steve Haskins	70	68	69	69	276	4,140
Mark Wurtz	68	69	72	67	276	4,140
Bradley Hughes	65	73	70	68	276	4,140
Craig Lile	69	70	69	68	276	4,140
Brett Wetterich	68	64	72	72	276	4,140
Bill Lunde	67	70	67	72	276	4,140
Justin Bolli	68	69	69	70	276	4,140
Jimmy Walker	67	68	70	71	276	4,140
Jon Mills	70	65	71	70	276	4,140
Johnson Wagner	72	65	72	67	276	4,140

Chattanooga Classic

Black Creek Club, Chattanooga, Tennessee   May 6-9
Par 36-36–72; 7,044 yards   purse, $450,000

	SCORES				TOTAL	MONEY
Justin Bolli	72	67	63	65	267	$81,000
Chris Anderson	63	70	66	69	268	39,600

	SCORES				TOTAL	MONEY
Johnson Wagner	68	66	68	66	268	39,600
Doug Barron	67	68	73	62	270	19,800
Matthew Jones	66	66	72	66	270	19,800
Bart Bryant	70	65	66	70	271	15,637.50
Tyler Williamson	67	67	67	70	271	15,637.50
Todd Demsey	70	67	63	72	272	13,050
Chris Tidland	67	69	68	68	272	13,050
Roland Thatcher	70	68	66	68	272	13,050
Shane Bertsch	67	67	71	68	273	8,935.72
Paul Claxton	67	70	68	68	273	8,935.72
Brad Ott	68	68	68	69	273	8,935.71
Gavin Coles	67	69	69	68	273	8,935.71
Darron Stiles	69	70	66	68	273	8,935.71
Elliot Gealy	65	68	71	69	273	8,935.71
D.A. Points	70	68	68	67	273	8,935.72
Robin Freeman	71	66	65	72	274	6,075
Mathew Goggin	69	70	64	71	274	6,075
Kelly Sellers	68	69	68	69	274	6,075
Scott Weatherly	68	67	69	70	274	6,075
Jeff Hart	70	68	70	67	275	4,114.29
Charles Raulerson	72	66	72	65	275	4,114.29
John Connelly	66	67	69	73	275	4,114.28
Randy Leen	69	69	67	70	275	4,114.28
Hunter Haas	70	68	68	69	275	4,114.29
Doug Garwood	72	66	69	68	275	4,114.29
Nick Watney	67	71	65	72	275	4,114.28
Jim Rutledge	70	67	70	69	276	3,150
Andy Morse	67	72	69	68	276	3,150

Henrico County Open

The Dominion Club, Glen Allen, Virginia
Par 36-36–72; 7,089 yards

May 20-23
purse, $450,000

	SCORES				TOTAL	MONEY
Daniel Chopra	65	63	65	65	258	$81,000
Franklin Langham	64	64	67	67	262	39,600
Nathan Green	62	69	67	64	262	39,600
Ryuji Imada	67	64	67	65	263	19,800
James Driscoll	69	66	65	63	263	19,800
Jimmy Walker	66	67	66	65	264	16,200
Bryant MacKellar	66	67	64	69	266	14,512.50
Johnson Wagner	67	66	65	68	266	14,512.50
Jason Buha	66	67	67	67	267	13,050
Mark Wilson	67	68	67	66	268	11,700
David Faught	67	66	67	68	268	11,700
Scott Sterling	65	63	71	70	269	9,450
Shane Bertsch	69	66	65	69	269	9,450
Kyle Thompson	67	68	68	66	269	9,450
Jeff Street	65	66	70	69	270	7,200
Han Lee	68	69	67	66	270	7,200
Matthew Jones	69	66	69	66	270	7,200
John E. Morgan	69	63	69	69	270	7,200
Patrick Damron	64	69	70	67	270	7,200
Mathew Goggin	68	67	66	70	271	5,625
Justin Bolli	68	65	67	71	271	5,625
Ben Bates	67	68	66	71	272	4,500

	SCORES				TOTAL	MONEY
Mike Grob	70	66	67	69	272	4,500
Mike Henderson	68	69	71	64	272	4,500
Bubba Dickerson	66	68	69	69	272	4,500
Chip Sullivan	64	69	69	71	273	3,510
Guy Boros	69	65	71	68	273	3,510
Scott Petersen	66	69	74	64	273	3,510
Scott Weatherly	71	66	67	69	273	3,510
Tim Simpson	69	66	71	68	274	2,700
Michael Long	67	67	70	70	274	2,700
Gavin Coles	65	70	69	70	274	2,700
Charles Warren	69	68	64	73	274	2,700
Jason Caron	68	65	69	72	274	2,700
Kelly Sellers	70	66	70	68	274	2,700
Scott Gutschewski	68	67	70	69	274	2,700
Nick Cassini	71	64	69	70	274	2,700
Troy Matteson	66	68	69	71	274	2,700

SAS Carolina Classic

TPC at Wakefield Plantation, Raleigh, North Carolina   May 27-30
Par 35-36–71; 7,257 yards   purse, $525,000

	SCORES				TOTAL	MONEY
Chris Anderson	67	70	66	68	271	$94,500
Paul Gow	67	70	64	70	271	39,200
Brendan Jones	68	65	65	73	271	39,200
Jason Buha	66	72	68	65	271	39,200
(Anderson defeated Gow and Buha on first, Jones on eighth playoff hole.)						
Brett Wetterich	68	67	68	70	273	21,000
Franklin Langham	68	67	70	69	274	18,900
Kyle Thompson	67	68	70	70	275	16,931.25
Scott Gutschewski	70	71	67	67	275	16,931.25
Eduardo Herrera	72	69	64	71	276	14,700
Hunter Haas	68	67	71	70	276	14,700
Shane Bertsch	73	68	66	70	277	12,075
Todd Demsey	68	69	69	71	277	12,075
Doug LaBelle	67	72	67	71	277	12,075
Tim Simpson	65	67	75	71	278	8,137.50
Sonny Skinner	69	71	67	71	278	8,137.50
Kevin Johnson	70	71	70	67	278	8,137.50
Dave Cunningham	68	71	68	71	278	8,137.50
Bradley Hughes	70	71	67	70	278	8,137.50
Darron Stiles	68	70	73	67	278	8,137.50
Jeff Klauk	69	71	67	71	278	8,137.50
Jeremy Wilkinson	66	69	69	74	278	8,137.50
P.H. Horgan	66	71	69	73	279	5,082
Wes Short, Jr.	70	70	70	69	279	5,082
Brad Ott	70	70	65	74	279	5,082
Jason Schultz	71	70	71	67	279	5,082
Craig Lile	68	73	69	69	279	5,082
Jeff Gove	69	69	73	69	280	3,990
Jason Enloe	68	70	70	72	280	3,990
Bryant Odom	73	67	71	69	280	3,990
Ben Bates	71	68	72	70	281	3,045
Jeff Hart	68	73	72	68	281	3,045
Zoran Zorkic	68	73	68	72	281	3,045
Dave Stockton, Jr.	67	72	69	73	281	3,045

	SCORES				TOTAL	MONEY
Ahmad Bateman	69	70	73	69	281	3,045
Bob Sowards	71	69	71	70	281	3,045
Michael Long	67	70	72	72	281	3,045
Mathew Goggin	70	71	72	68	281	3,045
Brendon de Jonge	68	73	67	73	281	3,045
Han Lee	66	73	71	71	281	3,045
Patrick Damron	70	71	69	71	281	3,045

Knoxville Open

Fox Den Country Club, Knoxville, Tennessee
Par 36-36–72; 7,142 yards

June 3-6
purse, $475,000

	SCORES				TOTAL	MONEY
Hunter Haas	71	68	67	69	275	$85,500
Shane Bertsch	67	70	67	71	275	41,800
Justin Bolli	72	67	65	71	275	41,800
(Haas defeated Bertsch and Bolli on first playoff hole.)						
Zoran Zorkic	70	67	74	66	277	19,633.34
Brendan Jones	70	70	68	69	277	19,633.33
Jimmy Walker	69	69	64	75	277	19,633.33
Jeff Freeman	70	71	69	68	278	15,318.75
Tim Wilkinson	71	69	67	71	278	15,318.75
John Elliott	72	69	69	69	279	10,992.86
Vance Veazey	69	65	72	73	279	10,992.85
Kang Wook-soon	67	71	71	70	279	10,992.86
Darron Stiles	71	69	67	72	279	10,992.85
Bryce Molder	70	69	71	69	279	10,992.86
Jeff Quinney	69	70	73	67	279	10,992.86
Nick Watney	70	68	70	71	279	10,992.86
Curt Byrum	69	72	69	70	280	5,846.82
Guy Boros	66	72	70	72	280	5,846.81
Kevin Johnson	68	70	71	71	280	5,846.82
Dan Olsen	66	71	72	71	280	5,846.82
Matt Bettencourt	71	70	71	68	280	5,846.82
Michael Long	71	69	70	70	280	5,846.82
Gavin Coles	72	65	71	72	280	5,846.82
Kyle Thompson	68	68	70	74	280	5,846.81
Jess Daley	70	70	69	71	280	5,846.82
Dave Christensen	69	71	73	67	280	5,846.82
D.A. Points	70	71	72	67	280	5,846.82
Tom Scherrer	70	70	68	73	281	3,439
Bob Sowards	69	73	67	72	281	3,439
Chris Tidland	70	70	71	70	281	3,439
Brett Wetterich	71	69	68	73	281	3,439
Patrick Damron	75	66	69	71	281	3,439

LaSalle Bank Open

The Glen Club, Glenview, Illinois
Par 36-36–72; 7,217 yards

June 10-13
purse, $650,000

	SCORES				TOTAL	MONEY
Brendan Jones	67	70	64	67	268	$117,000
D.A. Points	70	62	68	69	269	70,200

	SCORES				TOTAL	MONEY
Mike Springer	67	65	69	72	273	44,200
Fran Quinn	67	67	68	72	274	28,600
Doug LaBelle	67	67	70	70	274	28,600
Brett Wetterich	65	69	69	72	275	22,587.50
Bryce Molder	69	66	69	71	275	22,587.50
Ryan Armour	69	70	68	69	276	19,500
Mathew Goggin	66	68	68	74	276	19,500
Scott Petersen	67	70	66	74	277	14,408.33
Mark Wilson	66	67	67	77	277	14,408.33
Craig Lile	67	70	70	70	277	14,408.34
Jeff Klauk	67	66	72	72	277	14,408.33
Ricky Barnes	66	68	69	74	277	14,408.33
Nick Watney	69	72	65	71	277	14,408.34
Ryan Howison	69	72	69	68	278	10,400
Ryuji Imada	67	69	71	71	278	10,400
Aaron Barber	69	69	71	69	278	10,400
Jim Rutledge	69	70	71	69	279	8,157.50
Vance Veazey	70	70	69	70	279	8,157.50
Kyle Thompson	70	71	66	72	279	8,157.50
Andrew Barnes	67	71	70	71	279	8,157.50
Scott Gump	67	71	65	77	280	5,427.50
Tom Scherrer	68	69	71	72	280	5,427.50
Brian Kortan	69	67	74	70	280	5,427.50
Victor Schwamkrug	65	69	73	73	280	5,427.50
Charles Warren	70	70	69	71	280	5,427.50
James Driscoll	66	69	72	73	280	5,427.50
Jason Caron	71	66	74	69	280	5,427.50
Boo Weekley	69	72	67	72	280	5,427.50

Northeast Pennsylvania Classic

Glenmaura National Golf Club, Moosic, Pennsylvania
Par 35-36–71; 6,933 yards

June 17-20
purse, $450,000

	SCORES				TOTAL	MONEY
D.A. Points	67	66	71	66	270	$81,000
James Driscoll	67	69	67	67	270	48,600
(Points defeated Driscoll on first playoff hole.)						
Ryuji Imada	70	69	67	66	272	30,600
Darron Stiles	65	72	65	71	273	21,600
Bryce Molder	70	67	66	71	274	17,100
Justin Bolli	71	67	67	69	274	17,100
Nick Cassini	68	66	69	72	275	14,512.50
Boo Weekley	67	68	68	72	275	14,512.50
Charles Warren	69	70	68	69	276	12,600
Nathan Green	66	67	72	71	276	12,600
Brad Fabel	66	71	71	70	278	9,900
Jim McGovern	68	71	70	69	278	9,900
Dave Cunningham	70	69	72	67	278	9,900
Troy Matteson	69	69	71	69	278	9,900
Willie Wood	67	70	72	70	279	6,750
Scott Sterling	68	71	70	70	279	6,750
Shane Bertsch	66	70	74	69	279	6,750
Bradley Hughes	66	70	69	74	279	6,750
Rob McKelvey	70	69	68	72	279	6,750
Euan Walters	72	67	71	69	279	6,750
Jason Enloe	70	69	68	72	279	6,750

	SCORES				TOTAL	MONEY
Dicky Pride	67	71	69	73	280	4,356
Ahmad Bateman	74	65	69	72	280	4,356
Chris Tidland	71	70	70	69	280	4,356
Brad Elder	66	72	72	70	280	4,356
Jeff Klauk	71	68	68	73	280	4,356
Ben Bates	70	65	77	69	281	3,195
Sonny Skinner	66	71	71	73	281	3,195
Rick Price	71	69	69	72	281	3,195
Vance Veazey	69	70	67	75	281	3,195
Chris Zambri	71	68	74	68	281	3,195
Mathew Goggin	71	69	69	72	281	3,195

Lake Erie Charity Classic

Peek'n Peak Resort, Upper Course,
Findley Lake, New York
Par 35-36–71; 6,888 yards

June 24-27
purse, $450,000

	SCORES				TOTAL	MONEY
Kevin Stadler	66	70	69	74	279	$81,000
Michael Long	74	70	68	67	279	39,600
Bubba Watson	77	65	69	68	279	39,600
(Stadler defeated Long on first and Watson on fourth playoff hole.)						
Kevin Johnson	71	72	69	69	281	18,600
Gavin Coles	72	64	73	72	281	18,600
Jeff Quinney	71	64	75	71	281	18,600
Bob Heintz	72	70	70	70	282	14,512.50
Bryce Molder	72	68	72	70	282	14,512.50
Sonny Skinner	68	69	72	74	283	10,414.28
Robin Byrd	73	70	70	70	283	10,414.29
John Morse	73	69	72	69	283	10,414.29
Doug Barron	73	70	69	71	283	10,414.29
Victor Schwamkrug	67	71	72	73	283	10,414.28
Craig Lile	69	72	69	73	283	10,414.28
Chris Anderson	73	69	71	70	283	10,414.29
Ben Bates	70	74	71	69	284	6,525
Matt Peterson	69	68	72	75	284	6,525
Jeff Freeman	72	70	74	68	284	6,525
Lee Porter	68	72	75	69	284	6,525
Jason Buha	70	73	67	74	284	6,525
Troy Matteson	71	71	73	69	284	6,525
Keith Clearwater	72	72	70	71	285	4,500
Andy Morse	71	71	73	70	285	4,500
Ryan Armour	72	70	71	72	285	4,500
Jason Caron	70	68	74	73	285	4,500
Franklin Langham	70	70	74	72	286	3,510
Phil Tataurangi	75	67	69	75	286	3,510
David McKenzie	67	70	79	70	286	3,510
Scott Gutschewski	73	70	70	73	286	3,510
Jaxon Brigman	69	67	74	77	287	2,790
Warren Schutte	71	72	72	72	287	2,790
Ahmad Bateman	69	68	75	75	287	2,790
Paul Claxton	70	71	72	74	287	2,790
Anthony Painter	69	66	82	70	287	2,790
Hunter Haas	68	73	73	73	287	2,790
Kevin Durkin	74	70	71	72	287	2,790

Reese's Cup Classic

Hershey Country Club, East Course, Hershey, Pennsylvania
Par 36-35–71; 7,154 yards

July 1-4
purse, $450,000

	SCORES				TOTAL	MONEY
Ben Bates	70	69	66	73	278	$81,000
Paul Gow	68	68	70	72	278	48,600
(Bates defeated Gow on eighth playoff hole.)						
Doug Barron	71	72	65	72	280	26,100
Jason Caron	66	73	71	70	280	26,100
Michael Long	68	72	67	74	281	16,425
Kenneth Staton	73	71	64	73	281	16,425
Nick Watney	73	64	72	72	281	16,425
Mike Springer	68	71	70	73	282	12,150
Paul Claxton	72	69	72	69	282	12,150
Ryuji Imada	70	73	69	70	282	12,150
Charles Warren	69	71	71	71	282	12,150
Dave Christensen	72	68	73	69	282	12,150
Barry Cheesman	71	73	70	69	283	7,950
Dave Cunningham	72	71	70	70	283	7,950
Scott Sterling	69	69	72	73	283	7,950
Charley Hoffman	71	73	70	69	283	7,950
Brent Schwarzrock	73	69	72	69	283	7,950
Kevin Durkin	70	73	65	75	283	7,950
John Morse	72	64	77	71	284	5,647.50
Mike Grob	71	70	72	71	284	5,647.50
Jeff Gove	71	73	70	70	284	5,647.50
James Driscoll	72	71	70	71	284	5,647.50
John Elliott	75	68	71	71	285	3,857.14
Jeff Freeman	74	69	74	68	285	3,857.15
Bob Heintz	72	70	77	66	285	3,857.15
D.J. Trahan	74	70	72	69	285	3,857.14
Robert Garrigus	74	70	68	73	285	3,857.14
Rafael Gomez	68	72	73	72	285	3,857.14
Patrick Damron	72	71	72	70	285	3,857.14
Eduardo Herrera	70	73	69	74	286	2,745
Jim Rutledge	73	70	73	70	286	2,745
Bradley Hughes	72	71	70	73	286	2,745
Ryan Howison	71	68	72	75	286	2,745
Brian Guetz	71	70	74	71	286	2,745
Brad Adamonis	71	70	71	74	286	2,745
Justin Bolli	75	66	71	74	286	2,745
Kyle Gallo	71	69	70	76	286	2,745

Scholarship America Showdown

Troy Burne Golf Club, Hudson, Wisconsin
Par 36-35–71; 7,003 yards

July 8-11
purse, $475,000

	SCORES				TOTAL	MONEY
Kevin Stadler	69	65	67	68	269	$85,500
Chris Tidland	69	65	67	68	269	35,466.66
Mathew Goggin	67	70	68	64	269	35,466.67
Kyle Thompson	68	62	71	68	269	35,466.67
(Stadler won on third playoff hole.)						
Jason Caron	66	69	67	68	270	19,000

	SCORES				TOTAL	MONEY
Ryuji Imada	70	67	67	68	272	16,506.25
Darron Stiles	67	72	68	65	272	16,506.25
Rick Fehr	67	71	68	67	273	14,250
Johnson Wagner	68	68	69	68	273	14,250
Mario Tiziani	71	66	66	71	274	11,875
Conrad Ray	69	71	66	68	274	11,875
Dave Christensen	69	66	68	71	274	11,875
Scott Petersen	69	66	71	69	275	8,906.25
Doug LaBelle	68	69	68	70	275	8,906.25
Keith Huber	69	71	64	71	275	8,906.25
Jimmy Walker	68	65	72	70	275	8,906.25
Todd Demsey	69	68	70	69	276	6,887.50
Nathan Green	69	69	69	69	276	6,887.50
John Douma	69	67	70	70	276	6,887.50
Matthew Jones	69	69	68	70	276	6,887.50
Ahmad Bateman	68	70	69	70	277	4,781.67
Charley Hoffman	70	70	70	67	277	4,781.66
Joe Daley	69	68	71	69	277	4,781.67
Steven Alker	68	70	72	67	277	4,781.66
Richie Coughlan	70	70	68	69	277	4,781.67
J.J. Wall	70	68	70	69	277	4,781.67
John Morse	71	68	72	67	278	3,439
Jason Schultz	69	69	69	71	278	3,439
Chris Anderson	72	67	70	69	278	3,439
Charles Warren	67	70	68	73	278	3,439
Nick Watney	67	71	67	73	278	3,439

Pete Dye West Virginia Classic

Pete Dye Golf Club, Bridgeport, West Virginia
Par 36-36—72; 7,248 yards

July 15-18
purse, $600,000

	SCORES				TOTAL	MONEY
D.A. Points	65	62	68	70	265	$108,000
Nick Cassini	66	69	67	68	270	64,800
Darron Stiles	66	67	69	69	271	40,800
Jess Daley	71	65	70	67	273	26,400
Vance Veazey	69	67	65	72	273	26,400
Jason Schultz	70	71	66	67	274	20,850
D.J. Trahan	66	70	68	70	274	20,850
Jeff Gove	70	69	66	70	275	18,000
Bob Heintz	69	69	67	70	275	18,000
Greg Bruckner	68	70	71	67	276	15,600
Jon Mills	74	68	65	69	276	15,600
Jason Caron	71	69	66	71	277	12,600
Craig Lile	68	70	69	70	277	12,600
Chris Tidland	70	69	67	71	277	12,600
Stephen Gangluff	72	68	70	68	278	9,300
Bradley Hughes	71	69	68	70	278	9,300
Bryce Molder	66	67	71	74	278	9,300
Fran Quinn	71	71	70	66	278	9,300
Charles Warren	69	73	69	67	278	9,300
Nick Watney	63	71	69	75	278	9,300
Ryan Armour	75	67	67	70	279	6,240
Greg Boyette	72	68	68	71	279	6,240
Andrew McLardy	73	69	65	72	279	6,240
Bryant Odom	70	65	71	73	279	6,240

	SCORES				TOTAL	MONEY
Scott Sterling	70	71	70	68	279	6,240
Jason Buha	71	69	71	69	280	4,560
Nathan Green	70	68	69	73	280	4,560
Troy Matteson	69	71	72	68	280	4,560
Keith Nolan	70	71	71	68	280	4,560
Tom Scherrer	68	71	71	70	280	4,560

Samsung Canadian PGA Championship

Whistle Bear Golf Club, Cambridge, Ontario, Canada — July 22-25
Par 36-36–72; 7,305 yards — purse, $450,000

	SCORES				TOTAL	MONEY
Charles Warren	71	65	66	67	269	$81,000
Doug Barron	68	68	71	69	276	39,600
Dave Christensen	69	70	68	69	276	39,600
David McKenzie	70	66	69	72	277	21,600
Dave Cunningham	70	67	67	74	278	18,000
Scott Dunlap	69	71	68	71	279	15,075
Kenneth Staton	68	68	72	71	279	15,075
Bill Lunde	68	68	73	70	279	15,075
John Morse	70	68	70	72	280	11,700
Rob Bradley	69	70	71	70	280	11,700
Jason Gore	75	66	71	68	280	11,700
Johnson Wagner	71	66	71	72	280	11,700
Ryan Howison	70	73	66	72	281	8,437.50
Michael Long	70	72	69	70	281	8,437.50
Carl Desjardins	70	71	72	68	281	8,437.50
Bubba Watson	74	69	67	71	281	8,437.50
Kevin Johnson	72	71	68	71	282	6,090
Franklin Langham	72	70	71	69	282	6,090
Tim Conley	72	70	68	72	282	6,090
Shane Bertsch	70	73	71	68	282	6,090
Paul Gow	69	72	69	72	282	6,090
Erik Compton	70	72	70	70	282	6,090
Ben Bates	71	67	71	74	283	3,857.14
Sonny Skinner	71	70	71	71	283	3,857.14
Scott Petersen	69	71	69	74	283	3,857.14
Jason Buha	73	70	73	67	283	3,857.15
Jeff Klauk	71	69	68	75	283	3,857.14
David Hearn	70	73	71	69	283	3,857.15
Patrick Damron	74	67	71	71	283	3,857.14
Scott Gump	70	71	74	69	284	2,790
Rick Price	72	69	72	71	284	2,790
Richard Massey	73	69	70	72	284	2,790
John Connelly	72	71	74	67	284	2,790
Brad Elder	71	69	72	72	284	2,790
Stephen Gangluff	70	70	73	71	284	2,790
Dan Buchner	71	69	75	69	284	2,790

Preferred Health Systems Wichita Open

Crestview Country Club, Wichita, Kansas
Par 35-36–71; 6,913 yards

July 29-August 1
purse, $475,000

	SCORES				TOTAL	MONEY
Bradley Hughes	71	65	69	65	270	$85,500
Hunter Haas	67	66	72	65	270	35,466.67
Scott Harrington	66	71	68	65	270	35,466.67
Erik Compton	68	68	66	68	270	35,466.66
(Hughes won on first playoff hole.)						
Dave Christensen	68	68	69	66	271	18,050
Brad Elder	69	63	67	72	271	18,050
David Hearn	70	66	67	69	272	13,822.50
Richard Massey	66	70	70	66	272	13,822.50
Darron Stiles	66	67	69	70	272	13,822.50
D.J. Trahan	67	69	71	65	272	13,822.50
Johnson Wagner	65	70	69	68	272	13,822.50
Nathan Green	69	67	69	68	273	10,450
Anthony Painter	66	72	64	71	273	10,450
Jason Buha	66	69	69	70	274	7,837.50
Gavin Coles	65	69	70	70	274	7,837.50
Keoke Cotner	64	67	72	71	274	7,837.50
Joe Daley	70	67	71	66	274	7,837.50
Stephen Gangluff	68	65	70	71	274	7,837.50
Craig Lile	67	72	66	69	274	7,837.50
Ben Bates	65	68	72	70	275	5,731.67
Jim Rutledge	67	68	73	67	275	5,731.67
Jimmy Walker	67	67	70	71	275	5,731.66
Justin Bolli	66	72	65	73	276	3,966.25
Paul Claxton	68	71	68	69	276	3,966.25
Tim Conley	70	69	69	68	276	3,966.25
John Kidwell	69	66	70	71	276	3,966.25
Bryant Odom	71	68	69	68	276	3,966.25
Jason Schultz	67	69	73	67	276	3,966.25
Kenneth Staton	69	70	69	68	276	3,966.25
Brett Wetterich	67	68	72	69	276	3,966.25

Cox Classic

Champions Run, Omaha, Nebraska
Par 36-36–72; 7,099 yards

August 5-8
purse, $600,000

	SCORES				TOTAL	MONEY
Charles Warren	65	71	65	66	267	$108,000
John Elliott	66	65	67	70	268	64,800
Doug LaBelle	69	69	68	63	269	40,800
Jeff Hart	69	70	64	68	271	26,400
Brett Wetterich	69	70	65	67	271	26,400
Patrick Damron	68	72	66	66	272	19,425
Rafael Gomez	72	67	66	67	272	19,425
Jon Mills	66	71	69	66	272	19,425
Bryant Odom	72	67	65	68	272	19,425
Chad Collins	65	71	69	68	273	13,800
Dave Cunningham	65	74	65	69	273	13,800
Mathew Goggin	68	67	69	69	273	13,800
Jeff Klauk	66	71	66	70	273	13,800

	SCORES				TOTAL	MONEY
Michael Long	71	69	65	68	273	13,800
Chris Anderson	69	65	67	73	274	9,300
Robin Freeman	68	66	69	71	274	9,300
Jeff Gove	67	71	70	66	274	9,300
Ryuji Imada	72	64	70	68	274	9,300
Fran Quinn	72	65	69	68	274	9,300
Jimmy Walker	69	67	71	67	274	9,300
Jason Caron	65	73	71	66	275	6,240
Scott Gutschewski	67	68	68	72	275	6,240
Hunter Haas	68	70	65	72	275	6,240
Lee Porter	66	71	65	73	275	6,240
Chris Tidland	67	69	66	73	275	6,240
Ahmad Bateman	70	69	68	69	276	4,290
Nick Cassini	73	67	69	67	276	4,290
Jess Daley	70	69	72	65	276	4,290
Joe Daley	69	65	75	67	276	4,290
Todd Demsey	69	70	68	69	276	4,290
Steve Ford	68	72	70	66	276	4,290
Steve Runge	67	68	70	71	276	4,290
Bubba Watson	73	66	71	66	276	4,290

Price Cutter Charity Championship

Highland Springs Country Club, Springfield, Missouri
Par 36-36–72; 7,060 yards

August 12-15
purse, $525,000

	SCORES				TOTAL	MONEY
Brad Ott	65	66	68	64	263	$94,500
Brandt Snedeker	68	66	67	63	264	56,700
David McKenzie	67	67	68	64	266	30,450
Tyler Williamson	66	70	70	60	266	30,450
Michael Letzig	68	69	68	62	267	21,000
Tom Scherrer	66	72	65	66	269	18,900
Ryan Armour	72	66	69	64	271	15,815.63
Jeff Freeman	72	68	66	65	271	15,815.63
Nathan Green	73	63	66	69	271	15,815.62
Andrew McLardy	68	65	69	69	271	15,815.62
Daniel Chopra	70	70	68	64	272	11,130
Chad Collins	64	69	68	71	272	11,130
Jess Daley	71	66	64	71	272	11,130
Fran Quinn	69	67	67	69	272	11,130
Kyle Thompson	69	70	66	67	272	11,130
Steven Alker	68	67	72	66	273	7,875
Ben Bates	71	69	67	66	273	7,875
Greg Bruckner	68	68	68	69	273	7,875
Robert Garrigus	70	65	68	70	273	7,875
Jeff Gove	71	66	67	69	273	7,875
Jeff Klauk	70	70	66	68	274	6,090
Dave Stockton, Jr.	73	65	66	70	274	6,090
Chris Anderson	75	62	69	69	275	5,250
Jason Caron	70	67	69	69	275	5,250
Dave Christensen	71	66	71	68	276	3,850
Paul Claxton	68	66	73	69	276	3,850
Kevin Durkin	71	67	70	68	276	3,850
Scott Gump	70	69	68	69	276	3,850
Franklin Langham	68	69	70	69	276	3,850
Kevin Stadler	68	68	72	68	276	3,850

	SCORES				TOTAL	MONEY
Johnson Wagner	69	68	68	71	276	3,850
Jimmy Walker	69	68	65	74	276	3,850
Nick Watney	69	71	67	69	276	3,850

Alberta Classic

Redwood Meadows Golf & Country Club, Calgary, Alberta, Canada
Par 36-36–72; 7,058 yards

August 19-22
purse, $450,000

	SCORES				TOTAL	MONEY
David Hearn	70	65	67	71	273	$81,000
David McKenzie	65	70	70	69	274	48,600
Mathew Goggin	68	71	68	68	275	30,600
Nick Watney	66	73	66	72	277	21,600
Kevin Johnson	68	70	70	71	279	16,425
Jim Rutledge	75	68	70	66	279	16,425
Charles Warren	71	69	69	70	279	16,425
Jason Buha	68	71	70	71	280	12,150
Paul Gow	68	70	71	71	280	12,150
Jon Mills	71	69	71	69	280	12,150
John Morse	68	70	71	71	280	12,150
Jason Schultz	70	67	72	71	280	12,150
Steven Alker	71	68	74	68	281	8,700
Matthew Jones	67	69	73	72	281	8,700
Lee Porter	67	74	70	70	281	8,700
Erik Compton	65	72	73	72	282	7,200
Wes Martin	75	68	67	72	282	7,200
Kelly Sellers	69	69	73	71	282	7,200
Bradley Hughes	72	70	71	70	283	6,075
Warren Schutte	70	73	71	69	283	6,075
Ricky Barnes	70	70	71	73	284	4,680
John Elliott	72	70	70	72	284	4,680
Keith Nolan	70	68	73	73	284	4,680
Bubba Watson	69	70	73	72	284	4,680
Brett Wetterich	72	71	68	73	284	4,680
Nick Cassini	72	69	75	69	285	3,160
Chad Collins	76	67	71	71	285	3,160
John Connelly	69	74	71	71	285	3,160
Jeff Freeman	73	70	70	72	285	3,160
Tom Gillis	72	71	72	70	285	3,160
Jeff Klauk	71	67	74	73	285	3,160
D.A. Points	70	69	73	73	285	3,160
Jeff Quinney	69	72	71	73	285	3,160
Johnson Wagner	70	72	74	69	285	3,160

Envirocare Utah Classic

Willow Creek Country Club, Sandy, Utah
Par 35-37–72; 7,104 yards

August 26-29
purse, $450,000

	SCORES				TOTAL	MONEY
Brett Wetterich	67	69	65	71	272	$81,000
Ryuji Imada	72	69	65	67	273	39,600
Franklin Langham	71	67	69	66	273	39,600
Doug Barron	70	67	69	68	274	18,600

	SCORES				TOTAL	MONEY
David McKenzie	67	70	68	69	274	18,600
Bubba Watson	69	67	70	68	274	18,600
Scott Gutschewski	70	70	67	68	275	14,025
Scott Petersen	70	70	64	71	275	14,025
D.A. Points	69	70	68	68	275	14,025
Jason Caron	68	68	73	67	276	11,700
Tyler Williamson	70	66	69	71	276	11,700
Jeff Freeman	67	72	69	69	277	8,550
Nathan Green	67	73	69	68	277	8,550
Hunter Haas	69	67	72	69	277	8,550
John Merrick	71	65	75	66	277	8,550
Warren Schutte	68	72	69	68	277	8,550
Nick Watney	69	71	68	69	277	8,550
Jaxon Brigman	70	71	68	69	278	5,868
John Douma	71	68	71	68	278	5,868
James Driscoll	69	70	70	69	278	5,868
John Elliott	68	72	69	69	278	5,868
Steve Schneiter	65	70	74	69	278	5,868
Dave Cunningham	70	69	70	70	279	3,857.15
Keith Nolan	72	68	70	69	279	3,857.15
Tim Conley	72	67	69	71	279	3,857.14
Ryan Hietala	67	74	68	70	279	3,857.14
Darron Stiles	70	67	71	71	279	3,857.14
Chris Tidland	72	69	68	70	279	3,857.14
Zoran Zorkic	72	68	69	70	279	3,857.14
Joe Daley	69	71	74	66	280	2,835
Ryan Howison	68	71	73	68	280	2,835
Todd Rose	67	66	73	74	280	2,835
Chris Sessler	69	67	67	77	280	2,835
Jeff Street	72	68	70	70	280	2,835
Johnson Wagner	69	70	71	70	280	2,835

Virginia Beach Open

TPC of Virginia Beach, Virginia Beach, Virginia
Par 36-36–72; 7,432 yards

September 9-12
purse, $450,000

	SCORES				TOTAL	MONEY
James Driscoll	70	69	66	68	273	$81,000
Jason Buha	71	67	71	68	277	33,600
Kyle Thompson	68	68	67	74	277	33,600
Jimmy Walker	72	67	70	68	277	33,600
Richie Coughlan	69	71	68	70	278	16,425
Ryan Hietala	72	67	70	69	278	16,425
Tom Scherrer	69	68	69	72	278	16,425
Brandt Snedeker	71	67	67	74	279	13,950
Dave Cunningham	68	75	65	72	280	11,250
John Douma	72	65	75	68	280	11,250
Jeff Gove	71	68	70	71	280	11,250
Hunter Haas	71	67	70	72	280	11,250
Brian McCann	69	68	71	72	280	11,250
Chris Anderson	71	71	70	69	281	7,650
Doug Barron	73	70	68	70	281	7,650
Jody Bellflower	73	70	70	68	281	7,650
Todd Demsey	74	66	71	70	281	7,650
Michael Long	67	70	72	72	281	7,650
Fran Quinn	71	69	70	72	282	6,075

	SCORES				TOTAL	MONEY
Jason Schultz	73	68	68	73	282	6,075
*Ryan Blaum	71	69	72	70	282	
John Klauk	73	68	72	70	283	4,397.15
Bill Lunde	73	69	74	67	283	4,397.15
Barry Cheesman	70	73	70	70	283	4,397.14
Charley Hoffman	68	72	72	71	283	4,397.14
Han Lee	72	70	71	70	283	4,397.14
Tim Simpson	69	70	73	71	283	4,397.14
Johnson Wagner	67	70	71	75	283	4,397.14
Chad Collins	69	70	70	75	284	3,060
Andy Doeden	67	74	70	73	284	3,060
Scott Gump	73	70	70	71	284	3,060
Andrew McLardy	68	74	67	75	284	3,060
Bryce Molder	70	72	72	70	284	3,060
Nick Watney	70	72	71	71	284	3,060

Oregon Classic

Shadow Hills Country Club, Junction City, Oregon
Par 36-36–72; 7,007 yards

September 16-19
purse, $450,000

	SCORES				TOTAL	MONEY
Jeff Quinney	71	71	70	63	275	$81,000
Barry Cheesman	71	70	69	68	278	39,600
David McKenzie	68	70	71	69	278	39,600
Jason Gore	69	73	68	69	279	19,800
Jason Schultz	65	70	72	72	279	19,800
David Hearn	69	68	72	71	280	15,637.50
Michael Long	70	66	74	70	280	15,637.50
Doug Barron	70	73	72	66	281	12,600
Paul Gow	66	71	72	72	281	12,600
Scott Petersen	68	70	73	70	281	12,600
Brandt Snedeker	73	71	71	66	281	12,600
Scott Gutschewski	71	68	70	73	282	9,112.50
Doug LaBelle	69	71	73	69	282	9,112.50
Casey Martin	71	68	71	72	282	9,112.50
Vance Veazey	71	70	74	67	282	9,112.50
Stephen Gangluff	72	71	74	66	283	6,975
Scott Gump	70	67	74	72	283	6,975
Charley Hoffman	70	71	71	71	283	6,975
Franklin Langham	67	75	70	71	283	6,975
Robin Byrd	70	70	73	71	284	4,875
Brendon de Jonge	69	73	71	71	284	4,875
Rick Fehr	75	67	72	70	284	4,875
Ryan Howison	72	70	72	70	284	4,875
Tim Simpson	66	73	75	70	284	4,875
Bubba Watson	73	71	70	70	284	4,875
Steven Alker	71	71	72	71	285	3,420
Jason Caron	74	69	71	71	285	3,420
Tim Conley	69	70	74	72	285	3,420
Brent Schwarzrock	70	71	69	75	285	3,420
Mike Sposa	70	67	74	74	285	3,420

Albertsons Boise Open

Hillcrest Country Club, Boise, Idaho
Par 36-35–71; 6,698 yards

September 23-26
purse, $600,000

	SCORES				TOTAL	MONEY
Scott Gump	66	68	68	68	270	$108,000
Michael Long	71	67	64	70	272	52,800
Jimmy Walker	67	72	63	70	272	52,800
Scott Gutschewski	68	71	64	70	273	24,800
Bradley Hughes	69	69	68	67	273	24,800
Kyle Thompson	66	68	69	70	273	24,800
Justin Bolli	63	69	69	73	274	18,700
David Hearn	70	67	65	72	274	18,700
Chris Tidland	68	67	69	70	274	18,700
Nick Cassini	70	66	68	71	275	13,300
Kelly Gibson	68	69	70	68	275	13,300
Joel Kribel	69	69	66	71	275	13,300
Franklin Langham	70	70	67	68	275	13,300
Tom Scherrer	67	71	67	70	275	13,300
Nick Watney	69	71	67	68	275	13,300
Chris Anderson	68	71	69	68	276	9,000
James Driscoll	70	71	65	70	276	9,000
Jeff Gove	70	66	70	70	276	9,000
Brad Ott	71	63	70	72	276	9,000
Tyler Williamson	65	70	69	72	276	9,000
Bobby Gage	73	65	69	70	277	6,480
Ryan Hietala	73	67	71	66	277	6,480
David McKenzie	70	68	69	70	277	6,480
Kevin Stadler	65	69	74	69	277	6,480
Shane Bertsch	68	68	69	73	278	4,800
Ryuji Imada	68	68	70	72	278	4,800
Scott Petersen	70	70	71	67	278	4,800
Johnson Wagner	71	69	70	68	278	4,800
Bubba Watson	70	69	72	67	278	4,800
Steven Alker	70	68	68	73	279	3,540
Gavin Coles	69	72	68	70	279	3,540
Rick Fehr	67	74	72	66	279	3,540
Robert Garrigus	67	70	70	72	279	3,540
Steve Haskins	67	69	72	71	279	3,540
Casey Martin	71	67	68	73	279	3,540
John Merrick	67	69	71	72	279	3,540
Andy Morse	67	73	73	66	279	3,540
Victor Schwamkrug	68	65	73	73	279	3,540
Brent Schwarzrock	70	71	68	70	279	3,540

Mark Christopher Charity Classic

Empire Lakes Golf Club, Rancho Cucamonga, California
Par 36-35–71; 7,017 yards

September 30-October 3
purse, $450,000

	SCORES				TOTAL	MONEY
Scott Dunlap	65	69	72	66	272	$81,000
Scott Gutschewski	65	69	69	72	275	39,600
Bubba Watson	66	64	75	70	275	39,600
Brad Adamonis	67	71	70	69	277	15,717.86
Ryan Armour	72	64	72	69	277	15,717.86

	SCORES				TOTAL	MONEY
Ricky Barnes	65	73	72	67	277	15,717.86
Brandt Snedeker	69	72	68	68	277	15,717.86
Nick Watney	68	71	70	68	277	15,717.86
Kevin Durkin	66	72	68	71	277	15,717.85
Chris Tidland	69	71	66	71	277	15,717.85
Matt Bettencourt	71	66	74	67	278	9,540
Jeff Gove	67	70	70	71	278	9,540
Bradley Hughes	72	69	67	70	278	9,540
Jon Mills	69	70	71	68	278	9,540
Darron Stiles	68	69	68	73	278	9,540
Robin Byrd	68	64	73	74	279	6,750
Brendon de Jonge	69	70	70	70	279	6,750
Bob Heintz	70	69	69	71	279	6,750
Charley Hoffman	68	69	72	70	279	6,750
Troy Matteson	71	69	66	73	279	6,750
Shane Bertsch	66	69	76	69	280	4,397.15
Johnson Wagner	71	68	71	70	280	4,397.15
Jason Enloe	66	73	69	72	280	4,397.14
Jason Gore	68	73	65	74	280	4,397.14
Kyle Kovacs	68	66	72	74	280	4,397.14
Anthony Painter	70	70	69	71	280	4,397.14
Zoran Zorkic	68	72	65	75	280	4,397.14
Steven Alker	67	72	72	70	281	2,674.29
Chris Anderson	71	69	70	71	281	2,674.29
Dave Cunningham	70	68	72	71	281	2,674.29
Patrick Damron	70	71	70	70	281	2,674.29
Scott Gump	70	71	71	69	281	2,674.29
Ryuji Imada	70	70	70	71	281	2,674.29
Sean Murphy	71	69	70	71	281	2,674.29
D.A. Points	68	70	72	71	281	2,674.29
John Connelly	71	70	66	74	281	2,674.28
Nathan Green	66	73	70	72	281	2,674.28
Gabriel Hjertstedt	67	69	73	72	281	2,674.28
Matthew Jones	68	69	68	76	281	2,674.28
Scott Petersen	70	71	68	72	281	2,674.28
Jeff Quinney	64	67	77	73	281	2,674.28

Gila River Classic at Wild Horse Pass Resort

Whirlwind Golf Club, Cattail Course, Chandler, Arizona
Par 36-36–72; 7,240 yards

October 7-10
purse, $475,000

	SCORES				TOTAL	MONEY
Chris Nallen	60	66	67	71	264	$85,500
Troy Matteson	66	69	67	70	272	51,300
Jason Schultz	65	73	65	70	273	32,300
Matthew Jones	66	68	69	72	275	20,900
Kevin Stadler	68	64	67	76	275	20,900
Steven Alker	69	70	70	67	276	14,368.75
Jason Buha	73	65	69	69	276	14,368.75
Scott Petersen	66	65	70	75	276	14,368.75
Brent Schwarzrock	62	72	69	73	276	14,368.75
Darron Stiles	69	68	72	67	276	14,368.75
Tyler Williamson	70	68	68	70	276	14,368.75
Barry Cheesman	68	66	74	69	277	9,025
Paul Claxton	70	69	69	69	277	9,025
Jeff Freeman	67	65	70	75	277	9,025

	SCORES				TOTAL	MONEY
Scott Gutschewski	65	67	71	74	277	9,025
Eduardo Herrera	69	68	73	67	277	9,025
Michael Letzig	69	67	70	71	277	9,025
Shane Bertsch	70	68	74	66	278	5,095.46
Brad Elder	67	70	73	68	278	5,095.46
Charley Hoffman	68	69	71	70	278	5,095.46
Rick Price	68	68	73	69	278	5,095.46
Boo Weekley	69	67	72	70	278	5,095.46
Ben Bates	65	69	70	74	278	5,095.45
Robin Byrd	69	69	69	71	278	5,095.45
Bill Haas	68	68	69	73	278	5,095.45
Ryan Howison	66	71	70	71	278	5,095.45
Bryant Odom	70	67	68	73	278	5,095.45
Brad Ott	65	69	69	75	278	5,095.45
Ahmad Bateman	69	70	70	70	279	2,858.64
Justin Bolli	67	68	74	70	279	2,858.64
Steve Ford	67	72	70	70	279	2,858.64
Jeff Gove	65	69	75	70	279	2,858.64
Hunter Haas	71	66	72	70	279	2,858.64
Richard Massey	67	71	71	70	279	2,858.64
Don Yrene	67	69	74	69	279	2,858.64
Steve Holmes	64	70	72	73	279	2,858.63
Ryuji Imada	67	69	71	72	279	2,858.63
Kenneth Staton	67	66	70	76	279	2,858.63
Brett Wetterich	62	70	75	72	279	2,858.63

Permian Basin Charity Golf Classic

Midland Country Club, Midland, Texas
Par 36-36–72; 7,354 yards

October 14-17
purse, $450,000

	SCORES				TOTAL	MONEY
Charley Hoffman	72	67	71	72	282	$81,000
Jeff Gove	68	75	70	69	282	39,600
Craig Lile	72	71	67	72	282	39,600
(Hoffman defeated Gove and Lile on third playoff hole.)						
Scott Gump	77	69	70	67	283	19,800
Steven Alker	72	69	72	70	283	19,800
Chris Tidland	72	72	70	70	284	14,568.75
Matt Bettencourt	72	72	70	70	284	14,568.75
Euan Walters	73	72	67	72	284	14,568.75
David Hearn	69	70	73	72	284	14,568.75
Shane Bertsch	73	71	74	67	285	10,800
Paul Claxton	75	71	67	72	285	10,800
James Driscoll	72	69	70	74	285	10,800
D.J. Trahan	74	71	69	71	285	10,800
Eduardo Herrera	68	75	71	72	286	8,325
Matthew Jones	74	68	72	72	286	8,325
Ryan Howison	72	73	71	71	287	7,425
Gabriel Hjertstedt	73	72	72	70	287	7,425
Mike Grob	74	71	73	70	288	6,300
Rafael Gomez	75	71	67	75	288	6,300
Bubba Watson	71	76	66	75	288	6,300
Brad Fabel	71	71	75	72	289	5,220
Mathew Goggin	73	70	75	71	289	5,220
Steve Haskins	74	71	74	71	290	3,960
Robin Byrd	74	73	73	70	290	3,960

	SCORES			TOTAL	MONEY
Keoke Cotner	73	74	72	71	290	3,960
Justin Bolli	72	73	70	75	290	3,960
Kelly Sellers	74	70	75	71	290	3,960
Matt Hendrix	73	72	70	75	290	3,960
Brad Ott	76	72	73	70	291	3,037.50
Bryce Molder	70	78	74	69	291	3,037.50
Kevin Stadler	72	71	72	76	291	3,037.50
Troy Matteson	73	75	72	71	291	3,037.50

Miccosukee Championship

Miccosukee Golf & Country Club, Miami, Florida
Par 36-35–71; 7,200 yards

October 21-24
purse, $500,000

	SCORES			TOTAL	MONEY
D.J. Trahan	68	67	68	65	268	$90,000
Nick Watney	72	63	64	71	270	54,000
James Driscoll	68	66	70	68	272	34,000
Chris Tidland	65	72	64	72	273	24,000
Ryan Armour	67	67	69	71	274	17,562.50
Scott Gutschewski	71	69	66	68	274	17,562.50
Bryce Molder	64	70	69	71	274	17,562.50
Tim Wilkinson	64	68	71	71	274	17,562.50
Franklin Langham	69	72	68	66	275	14,500
Rafael Gomez	71	65	71	69	276	11,083.34
Hunter Haas	72	69	67	68	276	11,083.34
Brendon de Jonge	70	70	67	69	276	11,083.33
Mathew Goggin	70	69	66	71	276	11,083.33
Kelly Sellers	66	70	68	72	276	11,083.33
Chris Sessler	66	70	70	70	276	11,083.33
Greg Kraft	69	68	70	70	277	8,250
D.A. Points	70	66	68	73	277	8,250
Jeff Gove	67	73	68	70	278	6,520
Dan Olsen	68	70	69	71	278	6,520
Tom Scherrer	68	70	69	71	278	6,520
Jason Schultz	69	71	68	70	278	6,520
Mike Sposa	70	67	71	70	278	6,520
Steven Alker	69	69	74	67	279	4,285.72
Matthew Jones	69	72	72	66	279	4,285.72
Brad Ott	72	69	70	68	279	4,285.72
Scott Gump	67	73	69	70	279	4,285.71
Eduardo Herrera	70	68	69	72	279	4,285.71
Ryan Howison	67	67	73	72	279	4,285.71
Brandt Snedeker	68	69	69	73	279	4,285.71
Tony Carolan	70	68	67	75	280	3,250
Brad Fabel	67	68	71	74	280	3,250
Stephen Gangluff	68	72	69	71	280	3,250
Troy Matteson	67	73	72	68	280	3,250

Nationwide Tour Championship

Robert Trent Jones Golf Trail at Capitol Hill,
Senator Course, Prattville, Alabama
Par 36-36–72; 7,661 yards

October 28-31
purse, $625,000

	SCORES				TOTAL	MONEY
Nick Watney	69	64	71	69	273	$112,500
Brett Wetterich	66	69	71	70	276	67,500
Jason Caron	66	68	77	66	277	36,250
Franklin Langham	67	65	77	68	277	36,250
Justin Bolli	67	64	73	74	278	21,187.50
Mathew Goggin	73	67	68	70	278	21,187.50
Nathan Green	68	69	69	72	278	21,187.50
Brandt Snedeker	73	70	68	67	278	21,187.50
Kevin Stadler	68	67	70	73	278	21,187.50
Jason Schultz	68	71	72	68	279	15,625
Darron Stiles	65	72	72	70	279	15,625
Kyle Thompson	69	66	72	72	279	15,625
David Hearn	75	64	71	70	280	12,500
Ryuji Imada	69	67	70	74	280	12,500
Jeff Gove	72	67	71	71	281	10,625
Bill Lunde	72	67	73	69	281	10,625
D.J. Trahan	70	66	70	75	281	10,625
Doug LaBelle	73	70	70	69	282	8,750
D.A. Points	70	69	71	72	282	8,750
Chris Tidland	68	69	74	71	282	8,750
Ryan Armour	70	70	71	72	283	6,312.50
John Elliott	73	72	68	70	283	6,312.50
Scott Gump	71	71	70	71	283	6,312.50
Charley Hoffman	70	68	73	72	283	6,312.50
Jon Mills	68	71	71	73	283	6,312.50
Charles Warren	72	69	72	70	283	6,312.50
Jason Buha	69	70	70	75	284	5,062.50
Scott Gutschewski	67	69	74	76	286	4,572.92
Bradley Hughes	72	72	70	72	286	4,572.92
Brad Ott	73	68	71	74	286	4,572.91

Canadian Tour

Barton Creek Classic

Barton Creek, Fazio Foothills Course, Austin, Texas
Par 36-36–72; 6,956 yards

February 26-29
purse, C$150,000

	SCORES				TOTAL	MONEY
Brad Sutterfield	70	69	72	69	280	C$24,000
Mario Tiziani	67	73	75	65	280	14,400
Craig Taylor	73	70	71	70	284	9,000
Erik Compton	72	71	74	68	285	6,600
Dan Swanson	73	75	68	69	285	6,600
Steve Scott	73	75	68	70	286	5,400
Jason Allred	72	73	75	68	288	4,500
Philip Jonas	71	71	71	75	288	4,500
Rob McMillan	67	74	77	70	288	4,500
Kris Mikkelsen	70	72	73	73	288	4,500
Derek Gillespie	77	70	69	73	289	3,450
Craig Kanada	78	68	73	70	289	3,450
Bryce Molder	75	69	74	71	289	3,450
Ben Bunny	73	72	70	75	290	2,550
Nick Davey	72	74	71	73	290	2,550
Keith Fergus	70	72	76	72	290	2,550
Ryan Miller	73	68	76	73	290	2,550
Stephen Woodard	72	74	76	68	290	2,550
Dirk Ayers	72	75	74	70	291	1,931
Paul Danielson	70	74	76	71	291	1,931
Wes Heffernan	70	74	76	71	291	1,931
Rob Oppenheim	72	70	78	71	291	1,931
Andy Matthews	74	69	78	71	292	1,650
Jason Schultz	70	72	74	76	292	1,650
Chris Wollmann	72	73	77	70	292	1,650
Rob Labritz	74	74	77	68	293	1,440
Tele Wightman	73	72	78	70	293	1,440
Lee Williamson	71	73	78	71	293	1,440
Chris Greenwood	70	74	77	73	294	1,226
Matt Hansen	73	73	72	76	294	1,226
Andy Johnson	75	70	74	75	294	1,226
Alex Quiroz	72	76	78	68	294	1,226
Chris Wall	72	71	80	71	294	1,226
Dong Yi	73	71	77	73	294	1,226

Barton Creek Challenge

Barton Creek, Crenshaw Cliffside Course, Austin, Texas
Par 35-35–70; 6,523 yards
(Event shortened to 54 holes—rain.)

March 4-7
purse, C$150,000

	SCORES			TOTAL	MONEY
Chris Wisler	62	66	71	199	C$24,000
Adam Short	69	66	65	200	14,400

	SCORES			TOTAL	MONEY
Craig Kanada	65	66	70	201	6,900
Darren Griff	70	65	66	201	6,900
Andy Johnson	66	67	68	201	6,900
Jason Schultz	68	68	65	201	6,900
Matt Hansen	67	69	66	202	4,800
Chris Wollmann	67	71	64	202	4,800
Jason Allred	69	66	68	203	3,471
Scott Ford	70	69	64	203	3,471
Rafael Gemoets	69	66	68	203	3,471
Derek Gillespie	72	67	64	203	3,471
Danny Mijovic	69	65	69	203	3,471
Rob Oppenheim	70	64	69	203	3,471
Dan Swanson	68	64	71	203	3,471
Paul Devenport	68	67	69	204	2,475
Danny Paniccia	65	69	70	204	2,475
Lee Curry	69	66	70	205	1,995
Paul Danielson	66	71	68	205	1,995
Clint Jensen	69	63	73	205	1,995
Rob McMillan	70	66	69	205	1,995
Peter Wilson	68	66	71	205	1,995
Casey Bourque	67	68	71	206	1,409
Josh Habig	71	67	68	206	1,409
David Howser	69	68	69	206	1,409
Cory Jones	70	68	68	206	1,409
Chris Locker	65	71	70	206	1,409
Chris Parra	70	69	67	206	1,409
Alex Rocha	69	66	71	206	1,409
Michael Sabo	71	67	68	206	1,409
Craig Taylor	67	68	71	206	1,409
Chris Wall	71	67	68	206	1,409
Stephen Woodard	70	66	70	206	1,409

Greater Sacramento Open

Whitney Oaks Golf Club, Rocklin, California
Par 71; 6,919 yards

April 15-18
purse, C$150,000

	SCORES				TOTAL	MONEY
Ben Pettitt	68	69	68	70	275	C$24,000
Rob McMillan	72	68	68	71	279	14,400
Kyle Kovacs	69	73	70	68	280	9,000
Craig Kanada	71	73	69	69	282	7,200
Steve Scott	72	68	69	74	283	6,000
Matt Hansen	74	67	71	72	284	5,175
Kris Mikkelsen	72	68	75	69	284	5,175
Joe Acosta, Jr.	72	69	76	68	285	3,900
David Hearn	71	72	69	73	285	3,900
Casey Martin	72	69	72	72	285	3,900
Rob Oppenheim	73	71	70	71	285	3,900
Craig Taylor	67	75	73	70	285	3,900
Mario Tiziani	73	71	69	72	285	3,900
Brett Carman	74	73	69	70	286	2,775
Brad Sutterfield	71	67	74	74	286	2,775
Ben Ferguson	75	67	80	65	287	2,188
Wes Heffernan	73	69	70	75	287	2,188
Doug McGuigan	69	72	73	73	287	2,188
David McKenzie	76	70	71	70	287	2,188

	SCORES				TOTAL	MONEY
Ray Stewart	72	70	72	73	287	2,188
Chris Wisler	69	73	74	71	287	2,188
Steve Schneiter	75	71	70	72	288	1,725
Dan Swanson	70	76	73	69	288	1,725
Chris Wall	73	72	70	73	288	1,725
Dirk Ayers	72	74	70	73	289	1,395
Andrew Barnes	76	70	66	77	289	1,395
Robert Hamilton	75	68	74	72	289	1,395
Billy Noon	73	72	74	70	289	1,395
Alex Rocha	70	71	74	74	289	1,395
Stephen Woodard	71	72	72	74	289	1,395
Rick Woodson	69	73	73	74	289	1,395

E-Loan Central Valley Classic

Brookside Country Club, Stockton, California
Par 36-36–72; 6,720 yards

April 22-25
purse, C$150,000

	SCORES				TOTAL	MONEY
Erik Compton	69	65	71	68	273	C$24,000
Ben Gallie	72	68	68	68	276	14,400
Chris Wall	71	72	71	63	277	9,000
Brian Unk	71	69	71	67	278	6,600
Dirk Ayers	74	68	68	68	278	6,600
Iain Steel	77	69	64	69	279	4,837
Rob Oppenheim	69	70	70	70	279	4,837
Jeff Wood	75	67	68	69	279	4,837
Wes Martin	72	64	72	71	279	4,837
Brad Sutterfield	76	68	68	68	280	3,750
Andrew Smeeth	73	72	72	63	280	3,750
Rob Johnson	70	69	71	70	280	3,750
Stephen Woodard	72	71	70	68	281	3,150
Adam Short	77	69	69	67	282	2,775
Chris Greenwood	74	72	67	69	282	2,775
Eugene Smith	76	69	69	69	283	2,132
David McKenzie	74	71	68	70	283	2,132
Adam Speirs	76	69	67	71	283	2,132
Jon Turcott	73	73	65	72	283	2,132
Jason Higton	73	68	70	72	283	2,132
Marcus Jones	74	71	66	72	283	2,132
Casey Martin	74	69	68	72	283	2,132
David Hearn	76	67	71	70	284	1,688
Matt McQuillan	73	71	72	68	284	1,688
Dan Swanson	75	70	70	70	285	1,505
Joe Acosta, Jr.	74	67	72	72	285	1,505
Doug McGuigan	71	68	73	73	285	1,505
Rob Labritz	76	70	69	71	286	1,248
Ben Pettitt	73	71	70	72	286	1,248
Dean North	75	70	71	70	286	1,248
Rod Spittle	75	70	71	70	286	1,248
Conrad Ray	76	70	70	70	286	1,248
Ben Ferguson	71	74	66	75	286	1,248
Andrew Barnes	73	71	76	66	286	1,248

Michelin Guadalajara Classic

Atlas Golf & Country Club, Guadalajara, Mexico   May 6-9
Par 36-36–72; 7,204 yards   purse, C$175,000

	SCORES				TOTAL	MONEY
Rob Johnson	71	68	68	69	276	C$28,000
Alex Quiroz	69	70	67	71	277	16,800
Rob McMillan	68	69	70	72	279	9,450
Jon Turcott	70	72	71	66	279	9,450
Paul Danielson	70	70	69	71	280	7,000
Jason Higton	69	75	69	68	281	5,833
Kris Mikkelsen	71	69	69	72	281	5,833
Matt Weibring	69	70	70	72	281	5,833
Anders Hultman	71	68	73	70	282	4,375
Jeff McCammon	68	74	68	72	282	4,375
Rob Oppenheim	70	69	68	75	282	4,375
Antonio Serna	70	73	69	70	282	4,375
Stephen Woodard	71	68	71	72	282	4,375
Matt Hansen	72	72	68	71	283	2,975
Rob Labritz	72	68	71	72	283	2,975
Doug McGuigan	72	70	67	74	283	2,975
Steve Schneiter	68	75	73	67	283	2,975
Brad Sutterfield	73	71	71	68	283	2,975
Rafael Alarcon	70	70	73	71	284	2,205
George Bradford	70	74	68	72	284	2,205
Robert Hamilton	75	70	70	69	284	2,205
Clint Jensen	70	71	71	72	284	2,205
Andy Matthews	67	71	73	73	284	2,205
Lee Curry	72	69	71	73	285	1,727
Craig Kanada	67	76	71	71	285	1,727
Ryan Miller	71	72	71	71	285	1,727
Conrad Ray	70	70	74	71	285	1,727
Dan Swanson	73	68	73	71	285	1,727
Tele Wightman	72	66	76	71	285	1,727
Dave Levesque	72	73	75	66	286	1,452
Antonio Maldonado	71	70	77	68	286	1,452
Ben Pettitt	72	74	73	67	286	1,452

Corona Ixtapa Classic

Palma Real Golf Club, Ixtapa, Mexico   May 12-15
Par 36-36–72; 6,875 yards   purse, C$175,000

	SCORES				TOTAL	MONEY
Jason Higton	66	68	67	70	271	C$28,000
Will Moore	68	70	67	67	272	16,800
Erik Compton	71	66	70	68	275	7,595
Derek Gillespie	68	70	67	70	275	7,595
Clint Jensen	67	67	70	71	275	7,595
Brad Sutterfield	68	67	69	71	275	7,595
Chris Wall	71	67	67	70	275	7,595
Rafael Alarcon	70	70	65	71	276	5,075
Clodomiro Carranza	67	75	69	65	276	5,075
Ben Pettitt	66	71	66	73	276	5,075
Miguel Guzman	72	67	68	70	277	4,025
Brennan Webb	69	69	70	69	277	4,025

	SCORES				TOTAL	MONEY
Stephen Woodard	71	70	68	68	277	4,025
Scott Ford	72	69	66	71	278	3,062
Bryce Molder	72	71	70	65	278	3,062
Steve Scott	72	71	67	68	278	3,062
Lee Williamson	71	70	70	67	278	3,062
Dirk Ayers	73	70	69	67	279	2,384
Rob Oppenheim	70	69	69	71	279	2,384
Michael Sims	69	71	69	70	279	2,384
Eugene Smith	70	72	70	67	279	2,384
Rob McMillan	71	73	67	69	280	1,925
Mauricio Molina	67	71	72	70	280	1,925
Conrad Ray	71	67	69	73	280	1,925
Andres Romero	72	72	70	66	280	1,925
Jose Trauwitz	70	73	70	67	280	1,925
Dave Levesque	71	70	70	70	281	1,616
Danny Mijovic	67	72	69	73	281	1,616
Kris Mikkelsen	73	70	68	70	281	1,616
Bryan Novoa	73	71	68	70	282	1,479
Matt Weibring	69	69	71	73	282	1,479

Lewis Chitengwa Memorial

Stoney Creek at Wintergreen, Wintergreen, Virginia
Par 36-36–72; 7,004 yards

June 10-13
purse, C$150,000

	SCORES				TOTAL	MONEY
Stephen Gangluff	72	66	68	69	275	C$24,000
Dirk Ayers	69	69	68	73	279	8,400
Erik Compton	69	69	69	72	279	8,400
Wes Heffernan	70	73	68	68	279	8,400
Rob Labritz	70	70	71	68	279	8,400
Chris Wollmann	71	67	69	72	279	8,400
Paul Danielson	70	69	70	71	280	4,650
Brian Nosler	69	74	66	71	280	4,650
Steve Schneiter	71	72	70	67	280	4,650
Anders Hultman	72	69	68	72	281	4,050
Alex Rocha	70	68	71	73	282	3,600
Lee Williamson	70	71	70	71	282	3,600
Steve Scott	69	72	73	69	283	3,000
Chris Wall	73	70	70	70	283	3,000
Jason Allred	73	71	72	68	284	2,475
Chris Carnahan	71	68	72	73	284	2,475
Matt Seppanen	71	71	71	71	284	2,475
Stephen Woodard	70	73	67	74	284	2,475
Chris Baryla	71	73	71	70	285	1,772
George Bradford	72	71	71	71	285	1,772
Robert Hamilton	69	67	74	75	285	1,772
Dean North	71	71	73	70	285	1,772
Todd Tanner	71	72	76	66	285	1,772
Mario Tiziani	70	72	70	73	285	1,772
Chris Wood	71	67	72	75	285	1,772
Jeff Wood	70	72	68	75	285	1,772
Nathan Fritz	70	72	71	73	286	1,385
Chris Locker	69	70	72	75	286	1,385
*Andrew Parr	74	71	69	72	286	
Brad Sutterfield	71	72	68	75	286	1,385

Times Colonist Open

Gorge Vale Golf Club, Victoria, British Columbia   June 24-27
Par 37-35–72; 6,820 yards   purse, C$150,000

	SCORES				TOTAL	MONEY
David Hearn	70	71	64	68	273	C$24,000
*James Lepp	70	71	68	67	276	
Jason Allred	70	67	72	68	277	10,200
Clint Jensen	67	69	72	69	277	10,200
Brad Sutterfield	68	66	71	72	277	10,200
Brad Fritsch	68	69	68	73	278	5,700
Adam Short	69	70	71	68	278	5,700
Alex Rocha	71	69	64	75	279	4,800
Steve Scott	72	68	68	71	279	4,800
Craig Kanada	70	70	69	71	280	4,050
Eddie Maunder	70	71	66	73	280	4,050
Chris Wall	69	71	71	69	280	4,050
Dirk Ayers	72	70	69	70	281	2,850
Robert Hamilton	69	71	72	69	281	2,850
Chris Parra	72	65	73	71	281	2,850
Craig Taylor	66	71	72	72	281	2,850
Mario Tiziani	70	68	70	73	281	2,850
Bjorn Widerstedt	70	71	71	69	281	2,850
Chris Baryla	73	66	71	72	282	1,825
Ben Bunny	72	71	69	70	282	1,825
Ryan Ellis	70	68	73	71	282	1,825
Chris Greenwood	72	67	73	70	282	1,825
Kyle Kovacs	72	67	75	68	282	1,825
Rob McMillan	72	70	70	70	282	1,825
Brian Nosler	71	71	70	70	282	1,825
Craig Scott	72	70	68	72	282	1,825
Lee Williamson	73	69	74	66	282	1,825
Ben Ferguson	70	69	72	72	283	1,385
Will Moore	71	68	74	70	283	1,385
Matt Weibring	70	71	70	72	283	1,385

Greater Vancouver Classic

Mayfair Lakes Golf Club, Richmond, British Columbia   July 1-4
Par 35-36–71; 6,641 yards   purse, C$150,000

	SCORES				TOTAL	MONEY
Ryan Miller	69	69	66	66	270	C$24,000
Erik Compton	67	65	71	68	271	14,400
Derek Gillespie	69	69	69	66	273	8,100
David Hearn	68	72	67	66	273	8,100
Jason Allred	68	70	68	68	274	6,000
Ben Ferguson	76	67	64	68	275	4,837
Robert Hamilton	69	67	69	70	275	4,837
Matt McQuillan	71	67	68	69	275	4,837
Mario Tiziani	70	69	65	71	275	4,837
Rob Labritz	69	73	64	70	276	3,750
Wes Martin	71	70	70	65	276	3,750
Brian Nosler	68	72	64	72	276	3,750
Brett Carman	66	70	74	67	277	2,812
Chris Carnahan	70	71	69	67	277	2,812

	SCORES				TOTAL	MONEY
Wes Heffernan	69	65	69	74	277	2,812
Andrew Smeeth	70	71	69	67	277	2,812
Anders Hultman	68	68	75	67	278	2,250
David Mathis	68	69	70	71	278	2,250
Alex Rocha	72	69	70	67	278	2,250
Rob McMillan	67	70	74	68	279	1,875
Matt Weibring	74	69	68	68	279	1,875
Stephen Woodard	70	67	70	72	279	1,875
Stuart Anderson	69	66	73	72	280	1,460
Scott Ford	74	69	70	67	280	1,460
Chris Greenwood	71	72	70	67	280	1,460
Will Moore	68	72	71	69	280	1,460
Bryan Novoa	67	68	70	75	280	1,460
Justin Peters	73	69	68	70	280	1,460
Steve Schneiter	75	68	69	68	280	1,460
Dan Swanson	70	71	70	69	280	1,460
Peter Wilson	73	69	65	73	280	1,460

MTS Classic

Pine Ridge Golf Club, Winnipeg, Manitoba
Par 36-35–71; 6,522 yards

July 8-11
purse, C$150,000

	SCORES				TOTAL	MONEY
Erik Compton	66	68	64	69	267	C$24,000
David Hearn	70	63	67	68	268	14,400
Stephen Woodard	70	66	68	67	271	9,000
Steve Scott	68	67	70	67	272	7,200
Stuart Anderson	71	67	67	70	275	5,250
Ryan Ellis	71	69	66	69	275	5,250
Matt McQuillan	67	71	68	69	275	5,250
Russell Surber	69	68	70	68	275	5,250
Kyle Kovacs	72	66	71	68	277	4,350
Bryan Wright	68	72	72	66	278	4,050
Lee Curry	67	72	71	69	279	2,979
David Faught	70	72	72	65	279	2,979
David Mathis	67	74	68	70	279	2,979
Alex Quiroz	72	70	68	69	279	2,979
Brad Sutterfield	72	71	72	64	279	2,979
Todd Tanner	68	68	72	71	279	2,979
Chris Wall	75	66	69	69	279	2,979
Brett Carman	69	71	72	68	280	1,995
Paul Danielson	69	72	67	72	280	1,995
Darren Griff	68	72	69	71	280	1,995
Wes Martin	67	71	71	71	280	1,995
Michael Sabo	69	69	73	69	280	1,995
Jason Allred	66	77	66	72	281	1,487
Brian Flugstad	77	66	70	68	281	1,487
Derek Gillespie	68	74	69	70	281	1,487
Rob Labritz	68	70	73	70	281	1,487
Rob Oppenheim	68	67	72	74	281	1,487
Ben Pettitt	71	72	70	68	281	1,487
Dustin Risdon	70	67	70	74	281	1,487
Dan Swanson	68	68	71	74	281	1,487

Telus Edmonton Open

Derrick Golf & Winter Club, Edmonton, Alberta
Par 35-36–71; 6,691 yards

July 15-18
purse, C$150,000

	SCORES				TOTAL	MONEY
Stephen Woodard	68	67	69	68	272	C$24,000
Steve Scott	66	66	69	71	272	14,400
(Woodard defeated Scott on second playoff hole.)						
Matt McQuillan	65	70	70	68	273	8,100
Craig Scott	68	68	68	69	273	8,100
Jason Allred	72	68	68	66	274	5,070
George Bradford	69	72	64	69	274	5,070
Brad Fritsch	70	71	66	67	274	5,070
David Hearn	67	67	68	72	274	5,070
Cory Jones	68	69	67	70	274	5,070
Jason Higton	67	66	73	69	275	3,900
Marcus Jones	72	70	66	67	275	3,900
Ben Ferguson	67	71	69	69	276	2,850
Rob Johnson	71	68	69	68	276	2,850
Jim Lemon	71	68	69	68	276	2,850
David Mathis	68	72	69	67	276	2,850
Todd Tanner	65	76	65	70	276	2,850
Chris Wall	71	69	70	66	276	2,850
*Mike Mezei	70	72	68	67	277	
Michael Sabo	72	69	69	67	277	2,175
Zoltan Veress	72	69	69	67	277	2,175
Chris Baryla	67	70	72	69	278	1,800
Tyler Erickson	68	68	74	68	278	1,800
Josh Habig	66	72	71	69	278	1,800
Chris Locker	70	67	70	71	278	1,800
Peter Wilson	73	69	68	68	278	1,800
Dustin Risdon	68	71	70	70	279	1,575
Lee Curry	75	65	69	71	280	1,298
Brian Flugstad	70	68	71	71	280	1,298
Robert Hamilton	69	73	69	69	280	1,298
Masaharu Kawaguchi	69	73	70	68	280	1,298
Bryan Novoa	71	70	69	70	280	1,298
Rob Oppenheim	69	67	75	69	280	1,298
Chris Parra	72	69	71	68	280	1,298
Brian Payne	72	67	73	68	280	1,298
Brad Sutterfield	69	71	69	71	280	1,298

Montreal Open

Ile de Montreal Golf, South Course, Montreal, Quebec
Par 35-35–70; 7,219 yards
(Event shortened to 54 holes—rain.)

July 29-August 1
purse, C$150,000

	SCORES			TOTAL	MONEY
Stephen Woodard	67	69	70	206	C$24,000
Craig Taylor	72	67	70	209	14,400
Chez Reavie	70	69	71	210	9,000
Dave Levesque	71	72	68	211	7,200
Stuart Anderson	70	69	73	212	5,250
Clint Jensen	71	67	74	212	5,250
Brad Sutterfield	68	72	72	212	5,250

	SCORES			TOTAL	MONEY
Bryan Wright	69	71	72	212	5,250
Jason Allred	69	71	73	213	3,900
George Bradford	69	69	75	213	3,900
Brad Fritsch	70	71	72	213	3,900
Darren Griff	69	70	74	213	3,900
Dirk Ayers	74	66	74	214	2,812.50
Paul Danielson	70	74	70	214	2,812.50
Kent Fukushima	70	69	75	214	2,812.50
Dustin Risdon	70	71	73	214	2,812.50
Ryan Ellis	72	69	74	215	2,062.50
David Mathis	74	69	72	215	2,062.50
Mac McLeod	68	76	71	215	2,062.50
John O'Leary	71	72	72	215	2,062.50
Rob Oppenheim	70	73	72	215	2,062.50
Ben Pettitt	69	73	73	215	2,062.50
Marc Girouard	70	74	72	216	1,545
Andy Johnson	74	70	72	216	1,545
Rob Labritz	76	67	73	216	1,545
Craig Matthew	69	75	72	216	1,545
Matt McQuillan	71	71	74	216	1,545
Chris Wall	72	71	73	216	1,545
Lee Curry	72	73	72	217	1,090.96
Tyler Erickson	74	70	73	217	1,090.96
Scott Ford	71	71	75	217	1,090.96
Cory Jones	70	73	74	217	1,090.96
Rob McMillan	75	70	72	217	1,090.96
Kris Mikkelsen	70	74	73	217	1,090.96
Bryan Novoa	72	72	73	217	1,090.96
Craig Scott	68	73	76	217	1,090.96
Brian Unk	70	74	73	217	1,090.96
Matt Weibring	72	73	72	217	1,090.96
Peter Wilson	74	70	73	217	1,090.96
Chris Wisler	69	71	77	217	1,090.96
Ron Won	68	73	76	217	1,090.96

Bay Mills Open Players Championship

Wild Bluff Golf Club, Brimley, Michigan
Par 36-36–72; 6,988 yards

August 26-29
purse, C$225,000

	SCORES				TOTAL	MONEY
Chris Wisler	72	66	68	70	276	C$36,000
Dirk Ayers	66	75	72	68	281	13,725
Brad Fritsch	73	69	72	67	281	13,725
Scott Hawley	70	75	70	66	281	13,725
Clint Jensen	71	67	75	68	281	13,725
*Jeff Cuzzort	66	73	71	72	282	
David Faught	73	71	66	72	282	8,100
Rob Oppenheim	70	67	73	73	283	7,425
Scott Ford	76	71	65	72	284	6,750
Sal Spallone	72	72	71	69	284	6,750
Ben Ferguson	73	69	73	70	285	5,625
Craig Matthew	74	70	71	70	285	5,625
Will Moore	71	73	68	73	285	5,625
Gary Pike	71	73	66	76	286	3,857
Matt Seppanen	72	71	72	71	286	3,857
Adam Short	73	70	70	73	286	3,857

	SCORES				TOTAL	MONEY
Mario Tiziani	71	71	73	71	286	3,857
Brian Unk	71	72	71	72	286	3,857
Chris Wall	74	71	69	72	286	3,857
Stephen Woodard	75	71	70	70	286	3,857
Alex Rocha	78	68	70	71	287	2,869
Lee Williamson	73	72	71	71	287	2,869
Josh Habig	71	73	71	73	288	2,644
Jason Higton	78	68	76	66	288	2,644
Bryan Conway	73	67	75	74	289	2,312
Dave Levesque	71	75	72	71	289	2,312
Steve Scott	69	76	76	68	289	2,312
Drew Symons	74	72	74	69	289	2,312
Paul Danielson	74	71	71	74	290	1,903
Brian Flugstad	76	70	71	73	290	1,903
Anders Hultman	71	75	73	71	290	1,903
Rob Labritz	75	71	71	73	290	1,903
Kris Mikkelsen	73	71	73	73	290	1,903
Bryan Novoa	71	73	74	72	290	1,903

Casino de Charlevoix Cup

Le Manoir Richelieu Golf Club, Pointe-au-Pic, Quebec   August 31-September 4
Par 71; 6,225 yards   purse, C$100,000

FIRST DAY
Canadian Tour
Dirk Ayers and Stephen Woodard defeated Craig Scott and Ben Bunny, 1 up
Matt McQuillan and Anthony Warren defeated Rob Labritz and Jon Turcott, 5 and 4
Danny Paniccia and Matt Hansen defeated Chris Greenwood and Chris Wall, 3 and 1
Jason Allred and Jason Higton defeated Philip Dawson Jr. and Robert Hamilton, 20th
hole
Nick Goetze and Alex Rocha defeated Steve Scott and Brad Sutterfield, 2 and 1
Scott Ford and Rob Johnson defeated Lee Curry and Dan Swanson, 2 and 1
Paul Danielson and Rory Scrymgeour defeated Ben Pettitt and Bryan Wright, 3 and 2
Brennan Webb and Chris Wisler defeated Darren Griff and Paul Devenport, 3 and 2

Quebec Tour
Pete Bousquet and Jean Louis Lamarre defeated Jean Laforce and Eric Mercier, 4 and 3
Serge Thivierge and Claude Tremblay defeated Jerome Blais and Jason Morin, 5 and 4
P. Luc Bergeron and Dave Levesque defeated Remi Bouchard and Kevin Senecal, 1 up
Carl Desjardins and Marc Girouard defeated Jean-Claude Leblanc and Patrick Loiselle,
7 and 6
Gregg Cuthill and Dave Kelly defeated Louis Bourgeois and Eric Laporte, 2 and 1
Chris Learmonth and Dwight Reinhart defeated Blais Guillaume and Jean-Francois
Perron, 1 up
Olivier Edmond and Pascal Edmond defeated Robert Flaro and Michel Latulipe, 2 and 1
Guillaume Doucet and Nicolas Huot defeated Pierre Bernatchez and Earl Lasalle, 4 and 3

(Each losing team received C$1,000.)

SECOND DAY
Canadian Tour
Ayers and Woodard defeated McQuillan and Warren, 5 and 4
Allred and Higton defeated Paniccia and Hansen, 3 and 2
Ford and Johnson defeated Goetze and Rocha, 2 and 1
Webb and Wisler defeated Danielson and Scrymgeour, 4 and 3

Quebec Tour
Thivierge and Tremblay defeated Bousquet and Lamarre, 1 up

Bergeron and Levesque defeated Desjardins and Girouard, 1 up
Learmonth and Reinhart defeated Cuthill and Kelly, 1 up
Olivier Edmond and Pascal Edmond defeated Doucet and Huot, 1 up

(Each losing team received C$2,000.)

QUARTER-FINALS

Ford and Johnson defeated Webb and Wisler, 6 and 5
Ayers and Woodard defeated Allred and Higton, 22nd hole
Thivierge and Tremblay defeated Bergeron and Levesque, 4 and 3
Olivier Edmond and Pascal Edmond defeated Learmonth and Reinhart, 4 and 3

(Each losing team received C$4,000.)

SEMI-FINALS

Ayers and Woodard defeated Ford and Johnson, 6 and 5
Thivierge and Tremblay defeated Olivier Edmond and Pascal Edmond, 4 and 2

(Each losing team received C$8,000.)

FINAL

Ayers and Woodard defeated Thivierge and Tremblay, 5 and 3

(Ayers and Woodard received C$20,000; Thivierge and Claude Tremblay received C$16,000.)

Tour de las Americas (South America)

Caribbean Open

Our Lucaya Golf Resort, Freeport, Bahamas
Par 36-36–72; 6,824 yards

January 7-10
purse, US$40,000

	SCORES				TOTAL	MONEY
Tim Conley	71	69	72	72	284	US$9,000
Peter Horrobin	72	74	69	73	288	6,000
Juan Salazar	74	69	75	71	289	4,000
Jeff Yeckes	70	78	69	72	289	4,000
Michael Sims	72	77	74	68	291	2,500
Chris Taylor	73	73	74	72	292	1,550
John Gerber	71	75	74	72	292	1,550
Emalcus Hield	77	70	73	72	292	1,550
Jimmy Delancey	76	71	71	74	292	1,550
Eduardo Herrera	81	76	66	70	293	1,050
Adam Spring	74	74	73	72	293	1,050
Itamar Cohen	76	72	72	74	294	900
Louis Luke	77	73	75	74	299	800
Jeff Olson	79	78	73	70	300	709.50

	SCORES				TOTAL	MONEY
Miguel Martinez	77	72	78	73	300	709.50
John Bloomfield	78	73	76	73	300	709.50
Michael Brown	76	74	75	75	300	709.50
Victor Leoni	76	72	76	77	301	612
*Dion Gonsalves	79	79	71	75	304	
Santiago Larrea	78	71	75	80	304	550
Austin Chase	78	75	74	78	305	375
Magnus A. Carlsson	77	80	70	78	305	375
Matthew Pittsley	86	75	74	71	306	250
Jim Fuller	78	82	74	74	308	250
Huel Riley	74	77	80	77	308	250
Keno Turnquest	79	77	72	81	309	250
Alex Dominguez	78	73	82	77	310	200
Paul Johnson	78	78	79	76	311	200
*Ralph Knapp	76	79	74	82	311	
Jeronimo Esteve	83	73	82	73	311	200

Abierto del Sur

Mar del Plata Golf Club, Mar del Plata, Argentina   January 29-February 1
Par 35-35–70; 6,082 yards   purse, US$50,000

	SCORES				TOTAL	MONEY
Angel Cabrera	65	69	69	67	270	US$9,000
Miguel Guzman	72	65	66	68	271	5,700
Raul Perez	67	69	73	63	272	4,000
Andres Romero	70	66	73	65	274	2,900
Daniel Vancsik	66	65	75	68	274	2,900
Rafael Echenique	65	67	76	67	275	1,900
Alfonso Barrera	65	72	71	67	275	1,900
Raul Fretes	66	71	71	68	276	1,250
Gustavo Acosta	67	69	71	69	276	1,250
Clodomiro Carranza	66	72	68	70	276	1,250
Cesar Monasterio	67	71	68	70	276	1,250
Eduardo Romero	67	70	73	67	277	950
Daniel Barbetti	68	71	70	68	277	950
Cesar Costilla	65	73	69	70	277	950
Ricardo Ferrin	69	66	75	68	278	825
Eduardo Argiro	67	68	74	69	278	825
Miguel Fernandez	67	71	75	66	279	750
Rodolfo Gonzalez	66	70	72	72	280	700
Luis Carbonetti	66	72	74	69	281	625
Miguel Rodriguez	68	71	70	72	281	625
Omar Solis	66	67	79	70	282	530
Ariel Canete	69	69	73	71	282	530
Rafael Gomez	70	70	76	67	283	450
Marco Ruiz	72	66	77	68	283	450
Pedro Martinez	71	70	74	68	283	450
Ruben Alvarez	67	70	74	72	283	450
Mauricio Molina	67	75	74	68	284	400
*Victor Argonz	64	74	79	68	285	
Diego Ortiz	70	72	73	70	285	380
*Emilio Dominguez	72	67	75	71	285	

Summit Panama Masters

Summit Golf & Resort, Panama City, Panama
Par 36-36–72; 6,676 yards

February 12-15
purse, US$100,000

	SCORES				TOTAL	MONEY
Miguel Fernandez	72	68	68	66	274	US$18,000
Mark Pilkington	69	68	70	67	274	11,400
(Fernandez defeated Pilkington on first playoff hole.)						
Ian Garbutt	70	72	67	66	275	8,000
Richard Bland	66	70	70	70	276	6,400
Gary Clark	76	65	68	68	277	4,700
Greig Hutcheon	70	65	69	73	277	4,700
Lee S. James	72	69	71	66	278	3,100
Eduardo Argiro	70	72	68	68	278	3,100
Cesar Monasterio	73	67	73	66	279	2,500
John Mellor	67	69	74	69	279	2,500
Kevin Haefner	70	70	71	69	280	1,920
Alexandre Rocha	68	70	72	70	280	1,920
Miguel Rodriguez	72	69	68	71	280	1,920
Manuel Inman	71	66	70	73	280	1,920
Bubba Dickerson	69	69	69	73	280	1,920
Jamie Little	71	72	71	67	281	1,500
Rodolfo Gonzalez	71	69	68	73	281	1,500
Oliver Wilson	66	68	73	74	281	1,500
Andrew Raitt	73	70	73	66	282	1,200
Alex Balicki	72	71	67	72	282	1,200
Andres Romero	70	70	69	73	282	1,200
Ariel Canete	70	70	75	68	283	806.66
Paul Dwyer	69	72	72	70	283	806.66
Steven Bowditch	73	69	71	70	283	806.66
Sion Bebb	67	70	75	71	283	806.66
Edward Rush	72	71	69	71	283	806.66
Mauricio Molina	74	66	71	72	283	806.66
Graeme Storm	68	70	72	73	283	806.66
Philip Archer	69	70	71	73	283	806.66
Carlos Larrain	70	73	67	73	283	806.66
Magnus A. Carlsson	67	68	73	75	283	806.66
Carlos Quevedo	69	66	73	75	283	806.66
Marco Ruiz	65	72	70	76	283	806.66

Costa Rica Open

Valle del Sol Golf Club, San Jose, Costa Rica
Par 36-35–71; 6,961 yards

February 19-22
purse, US$110,000

	SCORES				TOTAL	MONEY
Alessandro Tadini	72	68	68	70	278	US$20,000
Carlos Quevedo	67	72	70	69	278	12,540
(Tadini defeated Quevedo on third playoff hole.)						
Mauricio Molina	76	68	69	66	279	7,920
Ariel Canete	74	68	68	69	279	7,920
Kyron Sullivan	71	70	71	68	280	5,170
Pasi Purhonen	75	65	71	69	280	5,170
Van Phillips	73	70	70	68	281	3,410
Michael Sims	72	69	68	72	281	3,410
Gary Clark	72	71	67	72	282	2,860

	SCORES				TOTAL	MONEY
Cesar Monasterio	75	69	71	68	283	2,200
Steve Sokol	70	75	70	68	283	2,200
Marco Ruiz	75	66	72	70	283	2,200
Darren Leng	68	72	72	71	283	2,200
Sam Little	71	73	68	71	283	2,200
Sion Bebb	77	67	67	72	283	2,200
Carl Suneson	71	72	69	72	284	1,705
Gregory Bourdy	78	67	66	73	284	1,705
Sergio Acevedo	70	72	75	68	285	1,207.25
Gustavo Rojas	73	70	73	69	285	1,207.25
Oliver Wilson	71	73	71	70	285	1,207.25
Ian Garbutt	73	71	70	71	285	1,207.25
Kariem Baraka	72	73	69	71	285	1,207.25
Michael Henderson	72	70	71	72	285	1,207.25
Daniel Escalera	74	71	68	72	285	1,207.25
Rafael Echenique	73	65	73	74	285	1,207.25
Henrik Nystrom	69	72	77	68	286	849.20
Shannon Sykora	72	71	73	70	286	849.20
Fabian Gomez	73	67	75	71	286	849.20
Eduardo Argiro	71	71	73	71	286	849.20
Magnus A. Carlsson	74	71	70	71	286	849.20

Abierto Telefonica

Hacienda Neuva Country Club, Guatemala City, Guatemala
Par 36-36–72; 7,043 yards

February 26-29
purse, US$100,000

	SCORES				TOTAL	MONEY
Daniel Vancsik	65	73	65	69	272	US$18,000
Marco Ruiz	68	70	70	66	274	11,400
Diego Vanegas	70	69	67	70	276	8,000
Ariel Canete	68	74	71	64	277	4,100
Neil Cheetham	67	73	70	67	277	4,100
Mikael Lundberg	71	70	69	67	277	4,100
Hernan Rey	69	73	68	67	277	4,100
Marco Soffietti	68	72	68	69	277	4,100
Kyron Sullivan	70	66	71	70	277	4,100
Bubba Dickerson	70	73	69	66	278	2,060
Graeme Storm	74	67	70	67	278	2,060
Henrik Nystrom	70	71	68	69	278	2,060
Jeff Burns	72	68	68	70	278	2,060
Garry Houston	69	65	69	75	278	2,060
Andrew Raitt	70	72	70	67	279	1,352.50
Johan Skold	72	68	71	68	279	1,352.50
Tim Conley	70	69	71	69	279	1,352.50
Oliver Wilson	67	72	70	70	279	1,352.50
Richard Bland	72	69	68	70	279	1,352.50
Philip Archer	68	72	68	71	279	1,352.50
Andres Romero	75	66	67	71	279	1,352.50
Miguel Rodriguez	68	74	65	72	279	1,352.50
Rodolfo Gonzalez	68	73	74	65	280	880
Sion Bebb	67	73	70	70	280	880
Philippe Lima	71	70	69	70	280	880
Alex Balicki	68	69	72	71	280	880
Jamie Little	68	71	67	74	280	880
Carl Suneson	69	73	71	68	281	730
John Pitt	73	70	70	68	281	730

	SCORES				TOTAL	MONEY
David Geall	71	71	70	69	281	730
Jim Fuller	66	71	74	70	281	730

American Express Puerto Rico Open

Costa Caribe Resort, Ponce, Puerto Rico
Par 36-36–72; 7,266 yards

March 18-21
purse, US$110,000

	SCORES				TOTAL	MONEY
Rodolfo Gonzalez	71	72	69	70	282	US$19,890
Eduardo Argiro	74	68	72	69	283	10,718.50
David Morland	74	68	68	73	283	10,718.50
Mike San Filippo	67	72	70	75	284	7,072
Mauricio Molina	70	71	75	69	285	5,746
Miguel Rodriguez	72	70	73	71	286	3,830.66
Miguel Guzman	75	68	71	72	286	3,830.66
Wilfredo Morales	72	71	71	72	286	3,830.66
Andres Romero	76	67	73	71	287	2,873
Miguel Fernandez	74	73	71	70	288	2,652
Alex Quiroz	69	70	80	70	289	2,431
Michael Sims	75	74	71	70	290	2,210
Richard Terga	69	74	75	73	291	2,044.25
Geoffry Schacher	73	74	71	73	291	2,044.25
Martin Velazquez	74	74	74	70	292	1,712.75
John Gerber	76	70	75	71	292	1,712.75
Tim Conley	72	74	75	71	292	1,712.75
Manuel Inman	70	76	74	72	292	1,712.75
Adam Spring	73	72	75	73	293	1,381.25
Peter Horrobin	72	75	73	73	293	1,381.25
Yoyo Rosario	73	73	79	69	294	965.77
James Muir	70	76	79	69	294	965.77
Mario Hurtado	70	73	81	70	294	965.77
Manuel Bermudez	71	71	79	73	294	965.77
Fabrizio Zanotti	76	73	72	73	294	965.77
Daniel Barbetti	74	75	72	73	294	965.77
Gustavo Mendoza	68	78	73	75	294	965.77
Diego Vanegas	70	73	74	77	294	965.77
Daniel Escalera	73	71	73	77	294	965.77
Ryan Grant	73	72	71	78	294	965.77

American Express Dominican Open

Casa de Campo Resort, Dye Fore Course,
Altos de Chavon, Dominican Republic
Par 36-36–72; 7,102 yards

March 24-27
purse, US$70,000

	SCORES				TOTAL	MONEY
Wilfredo Morales	72	70	72	72	286	US$12,600
Tim Conley	73	72	75	67	287	6,790
Shannon Sykora	72	72	69	74	287	6,790
Martin Velazquez	73	70	76	70	289	4,060
Rodolfo Gonzalez	72	71	71	75	289	4,060
Mauricio Molina	74	74	73	69	290	2,426.66
Miguel Guzman	72	73	73	72	290	2,426.66
Geoffry Schacher	75	71	70	74	290	2,426.66

	SCORES				TOTAL	MONEY
Jeronimo Esteve	68	75	75	73	291	1,750
Jim Fuller	67	75	75	74	291	1,750
Clodomiro Carranza	75	76	71	70	292	1,540
Andres Romero	71	77	72	74	294	1,330
Daniel Escalera	77	73	69	75	294	1,330
Eduardo Argiro	71	73	72	78	294	1,330
Julio Zapata	75	75	71	75	296	1,171
Fabrizio Zanotti	73	76	71	76	296	1,171
Miguel Rodriguez	77	74	71	75	297	1,080
Christian Reimbold	70	75	75	77	297	1,080
Patricio Vilaclara	76	74	74	74	298	1,000
Michael Sims	73	77	75	74	299	900
Pedro Martinez	77	71	74	77	299	900
Amadeo Calzada	71	74	76	79	300	844
Craig Marseilles	77	77	74	73	301	802
Manuel Bermudez	78	80	73	71	302	746
Ramiro Goti	78	75	74	75	302	746
John Bloomfield	72	82	69	79	302	746
Antonio Olivo	71	85	71	77	304	690
Adam Stierman	75	80	76	75	306	648
Armando Saavedra	77	82	72	75	306	648
Marcelo Soria	78	78	73	77	306	648

Acapulco Fest

Fairmont Acapulco Princess, Acapulco, Mexico
Par 35-35–70; 6,355 yards

May 26-29
purse, US$50,000

	SCORES				TOTAL	MONEY
Rafael Ponce	65	65	62	68	260	US$9,000
Rodolfo Gonzalez	68	68	66	67	269	5,700
Julio Zapata	68	69	66	68	271	4,000
Miguel Rodriguez	70	61	72	70	273	3,200
Miguel Carballo	69	71	68	66	274	2,600
Eduardo Argiro	66	68	70	71	275	2,100
Jose Trauwitz	69	71	69	67	276	1,490
Alex Quiroz	68	68	70	70	276	1,490
Miguel Guzman	70	71	65	70	276	1,490
Michael Sims	69	65	70	72	276	1,490
Octavio Gonzalez	69	72	67	70	278	1,220
Nicolas Sedler	69	65	77	68	279	1,070
John Gerber	67	70	73	69	279	1,070
Jeff Yeckes	72	67	71	69	279	1,070
Sergio Acevedo	72	70	69	69	280	920
Martin Velazquez	72	70	67	71	280	920
Antonio Serna	73	63	71	73	280	920
Mauricio Molina	73	73	66	69	281	795
Daniel Barbetti	68	65	71	77	281	795
Clay Devers	74	72	66	70	282	673.33
Julian Nicolosi	69	74	67	72	282	673.33
Victor Leoni	74	70	66	72	282	673.33
Tim Conley	67	79	71	66	283	600
Andres Romero	78	74	68	64	284	590
Horacio Morales	72	75	71	68	286	560
Ramiro Goti	72	73	70	71	286	560
Juan Ibarreche	72	72	72	72	288	520
Alejandro Mastreta	74	70	70	74	288	520

	SCORES				TOTAL	MONEY
Manuel Bermudez	73	69	75	72	289	500
Ricardo Samar	76	72	71	71	290	490

Cantv Venezuela Open

Valle Arriba Golf Club, Venezuela
Par 35-35–70; 6,372 yards

June 3-6
purse, US$50,000

	SCORES				TOTAL	MONEY
Miguel Martinez	65	66	64	70	265	US$9,000
Wilfredo Morales	65	70	67	64	266	5,700
Angel Romero	69	66	67	67	269	3,600
Nicolas Sedler	64	66	66	73	269	3,600
Rodolfo Gonzalez	68	70	63	69	270	2,600
Mauricio Molina	67	70	69	65	271	2,100
Andres Romero	72	67	64	70	273	1,700
Miguel Guzman	67	72	71	64	274	1,420
Eduardo Argiro	68	69	70	67	274	1,420
Julio Zapata	68	69	68	69	274	1,420
Gustavo Mendoza	68	71	67	69	275	1,170
Miguel Carballo	68	67	69	71	275	1,170
*Daniel Laughlin	69	72	66	70	277	
Miguel Rodriguez	70	70	68	70	278	1,070
Ramiro Goti	65	77	70	67	279	995
Jesus Amaya	73	65	70	71	279	995
Mario Hurtado	62	77	69	73	281	920
Christoph Guenther	70	72	70	70	282	795
*Julio Nutt	67	74	74	67	282	
Sergio Acevedo	72	67	72	71	282	795
Fernando Posada	71	70	70	71	282	795
Daniel Barbetti	71	71	68	72	282	795
Rodrigo Castaneda	73	69	75	66	283	670
Jesus Osmar	75	68	72	69	284	615
Ramon Munoz	71	72	70	71	284	615
Carlos Larrain	72	70	70	73	285	590
Diego Vanegas	74	69	69	74	286	570
Tim Conley	73	67	76	71	287	530
Ali Ibarra	67	73	73	74	287	530
Julian Nicolosi	71	70	72	74	287	530

Mexico Open

Club de Golf La Hacienda, Mexico City, Mexico
Par 35-36–71; 7,306 yards

November 25-28
purse, US$300,000

	SCORES				TOTAL	MONEY
Rafael Gomez	67	70	68	65	270	US$48,000
Eduardo Herrera	70	65	69	68	272	33,000
David Higgins	72	67	67	68	274	21,000
James Heath	69	69	68	69	275	18,000
Rafael Echenique	68	71	70	69	278	12,200
Miguel Carballo	68	71	69	70	278	12,200
Van Phillips	70	68	69	71	278	12,200
Sebastian Fernandez	66	69	73	71	279	7,800
Antonio Maldonado	70	68	70	71	279	7,800

	SCORES				TOTAL	MONEY
Gustavo Rojas	71	69	68	72	280	6,600
Chris Gane	71	71	71	68	281	5,700
Octavio Gonzalez	72	72	66	71	281	5,700
Rodolfo Gonzalez	68	71	70	72	281	5,700
Miguel Rodriguez	72	73	69	68	282	4,800
Richard McEvoy	69	71	71	71	282	4,800
Antonio Serna	67	73	68	74	282	4,800
Michael Hoey	72	70	72	69	283	3,787.50
Manuel Inman	71	74	69	69	283	3,787.50
Kalle Brink	70	73	70	70	283	3,787.50
Julien Van Hauwe	70	73	69	71	283	3,787.50
Michael Kirk	74	70	72	68	284	2,940
Jan-Are Larsen	71	72	69	72	284	2,940
Kevin Haefner	73	66	69	76	284	2,940
Jorge Berendt	69	74	73	69	285	2,670
Horacio Morales	72	73	70	70	285	2,670
Alex Quiroz	74	71	69	71	285	2,670
Kariem Baraka	72	71	70	72	285	2,670
Kyle Dobbs	73	72	68	72	285	2,670
Ross Fisher	69	70	71	75	285	2,670
Rafael Alarcon	73	72	71	70	286	2,400
Andrew Butterfield	70	71	73	72	286	2,400
Sam Osborne	72	73	69	72	286	2,400

Panasonic Panama Open

Coronado Golf Resort, Coronado, Panama
Par 36-36–72; 7,048 yards

December 2-5
purse, US$200,000

	SCORES				TOTAL	MONEY
Richard McEvoy	67	72	71	67	277	US$32,000
Marco Ruiz	69	69	69	71	278	22,000
Michael Hoey	74	67	66	72	279	14,000
Benn Barham	72	71	68	69	280	11,000
Andres Romero	69	70	70	71	280	11,000
Rafael Gomez	68	71	70	72	281	8,000
Cesar Monasterio	72	70	67	73	282	6,400
Miguel Fernandez	73	72	68	71	284	5,600
Christian Reimbold	74	70	72	69	285	4,600
Rafael Echenique	69	76	71	69	285	4,600
Stephen Gangluff	71	71	70	74	286	4,000
Michele Reale	67	72	76	72	287	3,700
David Kirkpatrick	74	72	69	72	287	3,700
John Bloomfield	72	74	70	72	288	3,300
Stuart Davis	71	69	75	73	288	3,300
Miguel Rodriguez	69	75	77	68	289	2,900
Ken Duke	75	68	75	71	289	2,900
Daniel Barbetti	76	72	73	69	290	2,325
Magnus Persson Atlevi	74	74	71	71	290	2,325
Gustavo Acosta	72	75	71	72	290	2,325
Ross Fisher	71	66	76	77	290	2,325
Marcus Higley	75	74	71	71	291	1,900
Marc Warren	71	74	74	72	291	1,900
Eduardo Argiro	73	72	74	72	291	1,900
Martin Wiegele	74	72	72	73	291	1,900
Oskar Bergman	74	73	77	68	292	1,680
Brad Sutterfield	73	72	77	70	292	1,680

	SCORES				TOTAL	MONEY
Martin Velazquez	73	73	75	71	292	1,680
Chris Gane	72	76	73	71	292	1,680
Kevin Haefner	73	73	74	72	292	1,680
Brad Fritsch	74	72	73	73	292	1,680
Michael Sims	70	74	72	76	292	1,680

TIM Peru Open

Los Incas Golf Club, Lima, Peru
Par 36-36—72; 6,924 yards

December 9-12
purse, US$168,000

	SCORES				TOTAL	MONEY
Brad Sutterfield	70	66	71	69	276	US$26,880
Michael Hoey	69	69	70	69	277	15,120
Stuart Davis	71	70	67	69	277	15,120
Sebastian Fernandez	66	70	75	67	278	10,080
Marco Ruiz	72	73	67	67	279	6,832
Carlos Franco	67	73	71	68	279	6,832
Gustavo Rojas	71	68	70	70	279	6,832
Paul Dwyer	69	74	68	69	280	4,704
Eduardo Argiro	71	74	68	68	281	3,864
Kariem Baraka	72	69	69	71	281	3,864
Andrew Butterfield	73	70	70	69	282	3,192
Mauricio Molina	72	73	68	69	282	3,192
Gustavo Mendoza	69	71	71	71	282	3,192
Rafael Gomez	69	70	72	72	283	2,772
Roberto Coceres	73	72	66	72	283	2,772
Stephen Gangluff	70	70	72	72	284	2,436
Ariel Canete	71	73	67	73	284	2,436
Christian Reimbold	73	72	70	70	285	2,044
Clodomiro Carranza	73	74	68	70	285	2,044
Julio Zapata	67	69	73	76	285	2,044
Matthew Abbott	72	70	74	70	286	1,680
Ben Portie	70	74	73	70	287	1,579.20
Miguel Carballo	72	71	73	71	287	1,579.20
Shannon Sykora	71	72	73	71	287	1,579.20
Tim Rice	73	71	71	72	287	1,579.20
Sergio Acevedo	72	70	71	74	287	1,579.20
Fabrizio Zanotti	75	73	69	71	288	1,411.20
Francisco Ojeda	69	69	78	72	288	1,411.20
Ross Fisher	74	70	72	72	288	1,411.20
Alvaro Pinedo	72	73	71	72	288	1,411.20
Julian Nicolosi	72	72	71	73	288	1,411.20

European Tours

South African Airways Open
See African Tours chapter.

Dunhill Championship
See African Tours chapter.

Johnnie Walker Classic
See Asia/Japan Tours chapter.

Heineken Classic
See Australasian Tour chapter.

ANZ Championship
See Australasian Tour chapter.

Carlsberg Malaysian Open
See Asia/Japan Tours chapter.

Dubai Desert Classic

Emirates Golf Club, Dubai, United Arab Emirates
Par 35-37–72; 7,264 yards

March 4-7
purse, €1,607,591

	SCORES				TOTAL	MONEY
Mark O'Meara	70	64	68	69	271	€267,929.13
Paul McGinley	68	65	69	70	272	178,619.42
David Howell	67	71	70	67	275	90,507.37
Ernie Els	70	68	72	65	275	90,507.37
Tiger Woods	70	69	69	68	276	53,211.26
Brian Davis	70	66	69	71	276	53,211.26
Marcel Siem	70	70	70	66	276	53,211.26
Thongchai Jaidee	69	67	73	67	276	53,211.26
Peter Lawrie	69	69	71	68	277	32,580.51
Joakim Haeggman	70	70	68	69	277	32,580.51
Greg Owen	71	65	72	69	277	32,580.51
Colin Montgomerie	70	69	71	68	278	24,885.51
Andrew Marshall	72	71	67	68	278	24,885.51
Bradley Dredge	64	71	72	71	278	24,885.51
Lee Westwood	70	71	68	69	278	24,885.51
Paul Casey	69	68	70	71	278	24,885.51
Damien McGrane	72	70	68	69	279	20,791.51
Gary Orr	69	75	68	67	279	20,791.51
Michael Campbell	74	69	70	66	279	20,791.51
Raphael Jacquelin	68	72	73	67	280	18,447.11
Jean Van de Velde	73	68	68	71	280	18,447.11
Simon Dyson	68	69	70	73	280	18,447.11
Wade Ormsby	70	73	70	67	280	18,447.11
Padraig Harrington	69	72	70	70	281	16,718.94
Steve Webster	70	73	68	70	281	16,718.94
Marcus Fraser	69	70	71	71	281	16,718.94
Richard Green	68	71	72	71	282	15,272.11

	SCORES				TOTAL	MONEY
Brett Rumford	74	69	70	69	282	15,272.11
Louis Oosthuizen	74	69	72	67	282	15,272.11
Nick Faldo	73	69	73	68	283	13,584.14
Paul Broadhurst	70	74	73	66	283	13,584.14
Phillip Price	71	72	71	69	283	13,584.14
Charl Schwartzel	69	71	70	73	283	13,584.14
Zhang Lian-wei	71	70	72	71	284	11,413.90
Maarten Lafeber	72	72	71	69	284	11,413.90
Ian Poulter	73	70	70	71	284	11,413.90
Simon Khan	69	71	74	70	284	11,413.90
Jarmo Sandelin	70	74	70	70	284	11,413.90
Stephen Gallacher	72	71	73	68	284	11,413.90
Martin Maritz	70	72	71	71	284	11,413.90
Mark Foster	74	70	70	71	285	9,645.55
Anders Hansen	72	70	70	73	285	9,645.55
Raymond Russell	70	73	71	71	285	9,645.55
Michael Jonzon	74	70	73	68	285	9,645.55
Gary Murphy	71	67	76	72	286	7,877.20
Kenneth Ferrie	70	70	74	72	286	7,877.20
Henrik Stenson	72	71	71	72	286	7,877.20
Gregory Havret	70	71	70	75	286	7,877.20
James Kingston	73	70	72	71	286	7,877.20
Mikko Ilonen	70	71	73	72	286	7,877.20
Martin LeMesurier	70	73	70	73	286	7,877.20
Peter Hanson	71	73	72	71	287	6,108.85
Emanuele Canonica	72	70	74	71	287	6,108.85
Stephen Scahill	69	73	74	71	287	6,108.85
John Bickerton	71	71	71	74	287	6,108.85
Stuart Little	74	69	72	73	288	4,943.34
Soren Hansen	69	75	70	74	288	4,943.34
Robert Karlsson	71	70	75	72	288	4,943.34
Christian Cevaer	70	73	72	73	288	4,943.34
Mark Roe	71	72	75	71	289	4,260.12
Peter Baker	69	73	76	71	289	4,260.12
Miles Tunnicliff	71	73	76	69	289	4,260.12
Gary Evans	71	73	73	72	289	4,260.12
Darren Fichardt	72	71	70	77	290	3,697.46
Thaworn Wiratchant	74	70	74	72	290	3,697.46
Richard Sterne	73	70	73	74	290	3,697.46
Alastair Forsyth	70	73	76	72	291	3,375.94
Andrew Coltart	72	72	73	75	292	3,134.80
Mads Vibe-Hastrup	71	72	72	77	292	3,134.80
Ben Banks	73	70	79	73	295	2,933.85
Carlos Rodiles	72	72	69		WD	

Qatar Masters

Doha Golf Club, Doha, Qatar
Par 36-36–72; 7,167 yards

March 11-14
purse, €1,231,150

	SCORES				TOTAL	MONEY
Joakim Haeggman	75	64	68	65	272	€201,596.75
Nobuhito Sato	68	70	67	68	273	134,392.46
Jose Manuel Lara	72	67	68	67	274	62,494.99
Brian Davis	69	70	68	67	274	62,494.99
Raphael Jacquelin	73	67	65	69	274	62,494.99
Martin Maritz	73	67	68	67	275	42,335.32

	SCORES				TOTAL	MONEY
Greg Owen	70	71	70	65	276	36,287.41
Roger Chapman	70	71	66	70	277	25,945.50
David Howell	71	69	67	70	277	25,945.50
Robert-Jan Derksen	74	67	71	65	277	25,945.50
Stephen Gallacher	70	72	68	67	277	25,945.50
Soren Hansen	72	70	72	64	278	20,139.51
Thongchai Jaidee	72	70	68	68	278	20,139.51
Mark Roe	73	67	70	69	279	17,417.96
Anders Hansen	72	68	67	72	279	17,417.96
Phillip Price	74	66	69	70	279	17,417.96
Bradley Dredge	71	72	71	65	279	17,417.96
Andrew Oldcorn	68	70	73	69	280	14,152.09
Ian Woosnam	69	69	72	70	280	14,152.09
Jean-Francois Remesy	71	69	69	71	280	14,152.09
Jonathan Lomas	76	64	66	74	280	14,152.09
Ricardo Gonzalez	75	67	69	69	280	14,152.09
Alastair Forsyth	70	73	70	67	280	14,152.09
Charl Schwartzel	72	71	66	71	280	14,152.09
Kenneth Ferrie	72	67	71	71	281	11,853.89
Henrik Bjornstad	72	70	70	69	281	11,853.89
Robert Karlsson	73	70	71	67	281	11,853.89
Stephen Dodd	72	69	69	71	281	11,853.89
Brett Rumford	72	69	73	67	281	11,853.89
Mark Foster	69	73	71	69	282	9,878.24
Barry Lane	72	71	71	68	282	9,878.24
Rolf Muntz	69	73	71	69	282	9,878.24
James Kingston	72	70	70	70	282	9,878.24
Marcus Fraser	73	67	72	70	282	9,878.24
Wade Ormsby	70	71	68	73	282	9,878.24
Santiago Luna	75	67	71	70	283	7,257.48
Warren Bennett	71	71	71	70	283	7,257.48
Cesar Monasterio	72	71	72	68	283	7,257.48
Darren Fichardt	70	69	71	73	283	7,257.48
Peter Lawrie	71	72	67	73	283	7,257.48
Jean Van de Velde	73	68	70	72	283	7,257.48
Marcel Siem	75	68	64	76	283	7,257.48
Pierre Fulke	68	71	71	73	283	7,257.48
Christian Cevaer	72	70	69	72	283	7,257.48
Paul Lawrie	71	72	69	71	283	7,257.48
Simon Khan	71	72	70	70	283	7,257.48
Jarmo Sandelin	69	72	71	71	283	7,257.48
Terry Price	69	72	71	71	283	7,257.48
Richard McEvoy	72	67	74	70	283	7,257.48
Peter Hanson	69	73	69	73	284	4,596.41
Paul Broadhurst	68	73	72	71	284	4,596.41
Gregory Havret	70	68	71	75	284	4,596.41
Stuart Little	72	71	72	69	284	4,596.41
Peter Hedblom	70	69	72	73	284	4,596.41
Per Nyman	72	71	72	69	284	4,596.41
David Park	70	71	76	67	284	4,596.41
Steven O'Hara	69	70	70	75	284	4,596.41
Thomas Levet	70	71	75	69	285	3,447.30
Ignacio Garrido	71	72	71	71	285	3,447.30
Stephen Scahill	75	68	75	67	285	3,447.30
James Hepworth	71	71	69	74	285	3,447.30
Gary Murphy	71	67	74	74	286	2,664.66
Jose Manuel Carriles	74	69	70	73	286	2,664.66
Jarrod Moseley	73	67	72	74	286	2,664.66
Diego Borrego	71	70	73	72	286	2,664.66
Andrew Raitt	73	69	69	75	286	2,664.66
Fredrik Andersson Hed	72	71	71	72	286	2,664.66

	SCORES				TOTAL	MONEY
Raymond Russell	72	70	72	72	286	2,664.66
Michael Jonzon	70	69	72	75	286	2,664.66
David Carter	73	70	71	72	286	2,664.66
Ian Garbutt	74	68	72	73	287	1,819.50
Matthew Blackey	68	73	71	75	287	1,819.50
Nick Dougherty	74	68	74	71	287	1,819.50
Paul Marantz	72	67	76	72	287	1,819.50
Emanuele Canonica	72	67	76	73	288	1,800.50
Martin Wiegele	68	71	75	74	288	1,800.50
Robert Rock	72	70	72	75	289	1,796
Richard Green	73	70	76	71	290	1,793
Sandy Lyle	72	68	76	76	292	1,787
Johan Edfors	73	70	75	74	292	1,787
Iain Pyman	70	72	78	72	292	1,787
Patrik Sjoland	73	70	77	73	293	1,781
Maarten Lafeber	72	69			WD	
Miguel Angel Jimenez	71	68			DQ	

Caltex Masters

See Asia/Japan Tours chapter.

Madeira Island Open

Santo da Serra Golf Club, Madeira, Portugal
Par 36-36–72; 6,826 yards

March 25-28
purse, €600,000

	SCORES				TOTAL	MONEY
Christopher Hanell	73	67	73	71	284	€100,000
Brad Kennedy	62	72	80	71	285	44,740
Steven Jeppesen	69	70	70	76	285	44,740
Rob Rashell	69	67	76	73	285	44,740
Garry Houston	71	69	72	74	286	23,220
Sam Walker	69	72	75	70	286	23,220
Knud Storgaard	69	67	73	78	287	13,896
Jamie Spence	66	67	80	74	287	13,896
Markus Brier	70	70	76	71	287	13,896
John Mellor	71	73	72	71	287	13,896
Graeme McDowell	73	69	72	73	287	13,896
Miguel Angel Martin	71	72	70	75	288	9,990
Warren Bennett	72	69	71	76	288	9,990
Santiago Luna	69	76	71	73	289	7,987.50
Robert-Jan Derksen	75	68	73	73	289	7,987.50
Paul Broadhurst	68	70	76	75	289	7,987.50
Mattias Nilsson	70	74	73	72	289	7,987.50
Fernando Roca	73	72	68	76	289	7,987.50
Bradley Dredge	69	73	74	73	289	7,987.50
Peter Gustafsson	72	69	76	72	289	7,987.50
Craig Williams	70	73	72	74	289	7,987.50
Euan Little	68	72	72	78	290	6,600
Sam Little	75	71	69	75	290	6,600
Jesus Maria Arruti	73	70	75	72	290	6,600
Fredrik Andersson Hed	72	71	73	75	291	5,970
Mark Sanders	74	69	71	77	291	5,970
David Dixon	68	73	74	76	291	5,970
Jamie Elson	73	70	72	76	291	5,970

	SCORES				TOTAL	MONEY
Maarten Lafeber	70	73	75	74	292	5,250
Shaun Webster	71	73	70	78	292	5,250
Paul Eales	70	71	75	76	292	5,250
Philippe Lima	70	73	74	75	292	5,250
Klas Eriksson	73	73	74	73	293	4,450
Anthony Wall	69	71	76	77	293	4,450
Simon Wakefield	69	72	78	74	293	4,450
Henrik Nystrom	70	75	74	74	293	4,450
Robert Rock	72	71	74	76	293	4,450
Richard Sterne	71	73	69	80	293	4,450
Magnus Persson Atlevi	67	76	74	77	294	3,720
Fredrik Henge	74	71	74	75	294	3,720
David Lynn	70	71	75	78	294	3,720
James Hepworth	71	70	75	78	294	3,720
David Drysdale	71	74	77	72	294	3,720
Matthew Morris	71	68	76	79	294	3,720
Marc Cayeux	70	72	76	77	295	3,060
Massimo Florioli	68	73	73	81	295	3,060
Matthew Cort	70	68	78	79	295	3,060
Mikko Ilonen	71	69	79	76	295	3,060
Michael Kirk	69	75	75	76	295	3,060
Greig Hutcheon	72	73	75	76	296	2,460
Jean-Francois Lucquin	74	72	74	76	296	2,460
Van Phillips	76	70	72	78	296	2,460
Andrew Raitt	73	73	77	73	296	2,460
Andreas Ljunggren	71	72	71	82	296	2,460
Chris Gane	71	70	78	78	297	1,980
Rolf Muntz	72	69	74	82	297	1,980
Raphael Pellicioli	72	69	76	80	297	1,980
Mattias Eliasson	69	73	78	78	298	1,710
Raul Ballesteros	69	77	78	74	298	1,710
Alan McLean	73	70	76	79	298	1,710
Daniel Gaunt	71	73	74	80	298	1,710
Iain Pyman	70	72	79	78	299	1,530
Jeppe Huldahl	69	76	78	76	299	1,530
Martin Erlandsson	70	72	77	81	300	1,380
Paul Streeter	67	77	82	74	300	1,380
Antonio Sobrinho	73	71	76	80	300	1,380
Wayne Westner	70	76	76	79	301	1,200
Cesar Monasterio	71	71	80	79	301	1,200
Mikael Lundberg	73	71	74	83	301	1,200
Marc Farry	71	75	79	80	305	1,000
Jarmo Sandelin	77	69	82	77	305	1,000
Gustavo Rojas	70	76	81	79	306	897
Titch Moore	74	71	83	79	307	894
Fredrik Widmark	73	73	82	80	308	891
Johan Kok	70	71	79	89	309	888

Algarve Open de Portugal

Le Meridien Penina Golf & Resort, Portimao, Portugal
Par 35-37–72; 6,799 yards

April 1-4
purse, €1,250,000

	SCORES				TOTAL	MONEY
Miguel Angel Jimenez	69	66	70	67	272	€208,330
Terry Price	68	68	74	64	274	138,880
Klas Eriksson	71	72	65	67	275	70,375

	SCORES				TOTAL	MONEY
Graeme McDowell	69	70	69	67	275	70,375
Jean-Francois Remesy	70	68	70	68	276	41,375
Ignacio Garrido	69	67	69	71	276	41,375
David Lynn	71	68	66	71	276	41,375
David Park	70	71	66	69	276	41,375
Jose Manuel Lara	68	74	66	69	277	22,160.71
Damien McGrane	70	66	72	69	277	22,160.71
Desvonde Botes	70	70	69	68	277	22,160.71
Gregory Havret	67	72	68	70	277	22,160.71
Paul Eales	71	69	69	68	277	22,160.71
Emanuele Canonica	71	67	70	69	277	22,160.71
Fredrik Andersson Hed	71	70	67	69	277	22,160.71
Robert-Jan Derksen	71	71	71	65	278	15,678.57
Peter Lawrie	66	71	70	71	278	15,678.57
Robert Karlsson	69	70	75	64	278	15,678.57
Mads Vibe-Hastrup	74	69	66	69	278	15,678.57
Francois Delamontagne	74	68	70	66	278	15,678.57
Sam Walker	68	71	71	68	278	15,678.57
Jamie Spence	71	72	70	66	279	12,625
Soren Hansen	73	69	69	68	279	12,625
Jarmo Sandelin	67	71	76	65	279	12,625
Patrik Sjoland	70	69	71	69	279	12,625
Nick Dougherty	72	68	73	66	279	12,625
Sebastian Fernandez	72	71	69	67	279	12,625
Gabriel Canizares	67	75	70	67	279	12,625
Andrew Oldcorn	71	71	69	69	280	10,208.33
Barry Lane	68	71	71	70	280	10,208.33
Gary Emerson	69	71	70	70	280	10,208.33
Nicolas Colsaerts	67	71	70	72	280	10,208.33
Matthew Cort	69	69	70	72	280	10,208.33
Jamie Elson	73	70	69	68	280	10,208.33
Ian Woosnam	71	66	71	73	281	8,250
Jesus Maria Arruti	68	71	70	72	281	8,250
Stephen Dodd	67	73	68	73	281	8,250
Bradley Dredge	72	70	68	71	281	8,250
John Mellor	71	70	70	70	281	8,250
Richard Sterne	74	67	70	70	281	8,250
Martin LeMesurier	69	71	70	71	281	8,250
Richard McEvoy	71	69	75	66	281	8,250
Miguel Angel Martin	68	74	72	68	282	6,375
Jose Manuel Carriles	71	70	73	68	282	6,375
Kenneth Ferrie	69	72	70	71	282	6,375
Julien Clement	70	69	72	71	282	6,375
Gary Orr	70	73	70	69	282	6,375
Michael Jonzon	75	68	69	70	282	6,375
Louis Oosthuizen	72	66	75	69	282	6,375
Steve Webster	72	66	72	73	283	4,515.63
Chris Gane	70	72	74	67	283	4,515.63
Joakim Haeggman	71	72	71	69	283	4,515.63
Diego Borrego	74	68	70	71	283	4,515.63
Simon Khan	73	68	72	70	283	4,515.63
David Carter	74	68	69	72	283	4,515.63
Christopher Hanell	67	73	70	73	283	4,515.63
David Dixon	71	72	68	72	283	4,515.63
Philip Walton	68	74	71	71	284	3,312.50
Gary Murphy	69	72	72	71	284	3,312.50
Paul Broadhurst	75	68	73	68	284	3,312.50
Peter Baker	71	70	76	67	284	3,312.50
Raymond Russell	71	71	65	77	284	3,312.50
Steven Jeppesen	72	71	72	69	284	3,312.50

	SCORES				TOTAL	MONEY
Fernando Roca	73	68	74	70	285	2,812.50
Mikko Ilonen	71	70	72	72	285	2,812.50
Alan McLean	72	68	78	68	286	2,625
David Gilford	72	70	68	77	287	2,388.33
Maarten Lafeber	68	74	71	74	287	2,388.33
Andrew Raitt	67	73	67	80	287	2,388.33
Nathan Fritz	70	73	72	74	289	1,875
Raul Ballesteros	70	69	76	78	293	1,872
*Sam Osborne	72	70	73	78	293	
Robert Rock	71	72	76	80	299	1,869

Open de Sevilla

Real Club de Golf, Sevilla, Spain

Par 36-36–72; 7,140 yards

April 15-18

purse, €1,000,000

	SCORES				TOTAL	MONEY
Ricardo Gonzalez	70	66	69	69	274	€166,660
Jonathan Lomas	73	68	69	66	276	86,855
Stephen Gallacher	70	68	70	68	276	86,855
Robert-Jan Derksen	70	70	68	70	278	42,466.67
Jean-Francois Remesy	67	74	69	68	278	42,466.67
Louis Oosthuizen	74	71	67	66	278	42,466.67
Soren Hansen	69	72	68	70	279	25,800
Peter Hedblom	72	69	70	68	279	25,800
Alan McLean	69	69	68	73	279	25,800
David Park	75	69	71	65	280	19,200
Steven O'Hara	68	76	65	71	280	19,200
Mattias Nilsson	70	69	69	73	281	15,825
Bradley Dredge	70	74	67	70	281	15,825
Matthew Blackey	69	68	74	70	281	15,825
Nick Dougherty	68	71	71	71	281	15,825
Klas Eriksson	76	68	66	72	282	12,350
Jose Manuel Carriles	71	69	69	73	282	12,350
Cesar Monasterio	68	67	76	71	282	12,350
Garry Houston	67	75	71	69	282	12,350
Simon Khan	69	69	70	74	282	12,350
David Lynn	68	73	70	71	282	12,350
Francois Delamontagne	69	72	68	73	282	12,350
Richard McEvoy	75	70	67	70	282	12,350
Kenneth Ferrie	70	68	74	71	283	10,250
Martin Erlandsson	69	70	71	73	283	10,250
Stephen Dodd	74	71	66	72	283	10,250
Benoit Teilleria	75	68	69	71	283	10,250
Marc Farry	72	70	71	71	284	8,900
Soren Kjeldsen	71	67	72	74	284	8,900
Miguel Angel Jimenez	68	73	72	71	284	8,900
Nicolas Colsaerts	65	75	70	74	284	8,900
Ivo Giner	67	72	71	74	284	8,900
Miguel Angel Martin	72	71	70	72	285	7,111.11
Mark Roe	73	70	68	74	285	7,111.11
Gary Murphy	70	71	71	73	285	7,111.11
Mark Foster	71	70	72	72	285	7,111.11
Raul Ballesteros	68	68	74	75	285	7,111.11
Julien Clement	70	70	74	71	285	7,111.11
Emanuele Canonica	67	69	70	79	285	7,111.11
Sebastian Fernandez	70	72	76	67	285	7,111.11

	SCORES				TOTAL	MONEY
Bruno-Teva Lecuona	71	70	67	77	285	7,111.11
Jose Manuel Lara	71	72	70	73	286	5,600
Alex Balicki	70	73	72	71	286	5,600
Scott Drummond	71	73	73	69	286	5,600
Fernando Roca	71	73	77	65	286	5,600
Tom Whitehouse	71	69	74	72	286	5,600
Charl Schwartzel	69	72	75	70	286	5,600
Jamie Spence	69	70	72	76	287	4,500
Christian Cevaer	70	71	70	76	287	4,500
Sion Bebb	73	68	75	71	287	4,500
David Carter	75	70	75	67	287	4,500
Stuart Davis	72	72	69	74	287	4,500
Paul Streeter	72	70	74	72	288	3,416.67
Raymond Russell	70	73	72	73	288	3,416.67
Robert Rock	75	69	69	75	288	3,416.67
Graeme McDowell	72	73	70	73	288	3,416.67
Martin Maritz	72	72	73	71	288	3,416.67
Wade Ormsby	71	73	69	75	288	3,416.67
Santiago Luna	71	72	71	75	289	2,500
Andrew Oldcorn	75	66	73	75	289	2,500
Peter Lawrie	71	74	72	72	289	2,500
Sam Little	69	76	71	73	289	2,500
Jean-Francois Lucquin	72	73	69	75	289	2,500
Miles Tunnicliff	72	71	72	74	289	2,500
Gustavo Rojas	71	73	72	73	289	2,500
Benn Barham	70	73	70	76	289	2,500
Jamie Donaldson	75	70	72	72	289	2,500
Desvonde Botes	70	75	69	76	290	1,703.50
Gary Emerson	70	75	72	73	290	1,703.50
Gregory Havret	66	77	70	77	290	1,703.50
Domingo Hospital	70	73	72	75	290	1,703.50
Jesus Maria Arruti	69	75	74	72	290	1,703.50
Gabriel Canizares	68	76	75	71	290	1,703.50
Wayne Westner	68	76	76	72	292	1,489.50
Federico Bisazza	72	73	73	74	292	1,489.50
Roger Chapman	69	70	74	80	293	1,482
Jorge Berendt	71	74	72	76	293	1,482
Rob Rashell	74	71	74	74	293	1,482
Henrik Nystrom	74	71	73	76	294	1,476
Chris Gane	73	71	76	76	296	1,473
Gary Evans	68	76	80	76	300	1,470

Canarias Open de Espana

Fuerteventura Golf Club, Fuerteventura, Canary Islands
Par 35-35–70; 6,638 yards

April 22-25
purse, €1,650,000

	SCORES				TOTAL	MONEY
Christian Cevaer	66	67	69	69	271	€275,000
Peter Hedblom	68	66	68	70	272	123,040
Ricardo Gonzalez	67	70	64	71	272	123,040
David Park	64	65	71	72	272	123,040
Bradley Dredge	70	69	64	70	273	63,855
Jarmo Sandelin	67	71	69	66	273	63,855
Jose Manuel Lara	69	68	69	68	274	42,570
Miles Tunnicliff	70	66	71	67	274	42,570
Charl Schwartzel	69	70	67	68	274	42,570

	SCORES				TOTAL	MONEY
Marcus Fraser	68	68	69	70	275	33,000
Jean-Francois Remesy	67	68	71	70	276	29,370
Louis Oosthuizen	72	70	66	68	276	29,370
Santiago Luna	69	67	69	72	277	25,355
Nicolas Colsaerts	72	67	67	71	277	25,355
Rob Rashell	72	67	67	71	277	25,355
Alvaro Salto	69	70	72	67	278	21,037.50
Klas Eriksson	70	67	67	74	278	21,037.50
Emanuele Canonica	71	69	70	68	278	21,037.50
David Lynn	67	68	72	71	278	21,037.50
Fredrik Andersson Hed	72	68	67	71	278	21,037.50
Stephen Gallacher	72	69	66	71	278	21,037.50
Miguel Angel Martin	67	70	72	70	279	17,655
Jesus Maria Arruti	74	65	71	69	279	17,655
Diego Borrego	67	73	66	73	279	17,655
Pedro Linhart	73	66	70	70	279	17,655
Steven Jeppesen	68	73	68	70	279	17,655
Mark Roe	73	70	69	68	280	14,208.33
Jose Manuel Carriles	68	69	72	71	280	14,208.33
Soren Kjeldsen	73	69	70	68	280	14,208.33
Gregory Havret	73	63	69	75	280	14,208.33
Jean-Francois Lucquin	68	72	68	72	280	14,208.33
Stephen Dodd	71	70	68	71	280	14,208.33
David Carter	73	67	69	71	280	14,208.33
Martin Maritz	72	69	68	71	280	14,208.33
Richard McEvoy	71	69	71	69	280	14,208.33
Euan Little	68	70	73	70	281	11,550
Jorge Berendt	72	67	71	71	281	11,550
Sion Bebb	70	69	71	71	281	11,550
Sebastian Fernandez	71	70	71	69	281	11,550
Roger Chapman	66	71	74	71	282	10,230
Joakim Haeggman	69	72	71	70	282	10,230
Henrik Nystrom	70	65	72	75	282	10,230
*Rafael Cabrera	70	68	70	74	282	
Jeppe Huldahl	74	69	71	68	282	10,230
Gary Murphy	70	72	70	71	283	8,910
Peter Hanson	74	69	72	68	283	8,910
Matthew Cort	67	74	71	71	283	8,910
Martin LeMesurier	70	70	73	70	283	8,910
Cesar Monasterio	73	70	71	70	284	6,930
Philip Golding	69	73	69	73	284	6,930
Paul Eales	70	70	70	74	284	6,930
Robert Coles	71	69	70	74	284	6,930
Simon Wakefield	71	70	71	72	284	6,930
Michael Jonzon	71	68	71	74	284	6,930
Francois Delamontagne	73	70	71	70	284	6,930
Alastair Forsyth	72	71	73	68	284	6,930
Marc Pendaries	72	66	73	74	285	5,280
Rolf Muntz	73	70	72	70	285	5,280
Jamie Spence	71	71	75	69	286	4,620
Carlos Rodiles	70	73	74	69	286	4,620
Marcel Siem	67	68	75	76	286	4,620
Julien Clement	73	63	71	79	286	4,620
Graeme McDowell	71	72	72	71	286	4,620
Maarten Lafeber	71	72	74	70	287	3,960
Greig Hutcheon	70	72	76	69	287	3,960
Tom Whitehouse	70	70	71	76	287	3,960
Kenneth Ferrie	72	70	71	75	288	3,630
Carl Suneson	70	73	77	69	289	3,382.50
Terry Price	73	70	72	74	289	3,382.50

	SCORES			TOTAL	MONEY
Simon Khan	71	72	72	75	290	3,135
Nobuhito Sato	70	72	74	75	291	2,742.50
Matthew Blackey	70	73	74	74	291	2,742.50
Stephen Scahill	74	69	67	82	292	2,472
Thomas Levet	72	67	76	79	294	2,469
Damien McGrane	75	68	79	73	295	2,463
Desvonde Botes	71	72	77	75	295	2,463
Luis Claverie	69	72	77	77	295	2,463
*Miguel Cabrera	71	72	74	78	295	
Ricardo Jimenez	71	71	74	80	296	2,457

Telecom Italia Open

Castello di Tolcinasco Golf & Country Club, Milan, Italy
Par 36-36–72; 7,224 yards
(Reduced to 54 holes, Monday finish—rain.)

April 29-May 3
purse, €1,200,000

	SCORES			TOTAL	MONEY
Graeme McDowell	66	66	65	197	€200,000
Thomas Levet	67	65	65	197	133,330
(McDowell defeated Levet on fourth playoff hole.)					
Gregory Havret	64	69	65	198	75,120
Angel Cabrera	67	63	69	199	60,000
Alastair Forsyth	69	65	67	201	50,880
Ian Poulter	68	66	68	202	36,000
Marcel Siem	67	66	69	202	36,000
Joakim Haeggman	67	64	71	202	36,000
Anders Hansen	68	69	66	203	24,320
Martin Maritz	67	66	70	203	24,320
Charl Schwartzel	72	64	67	203	24,320
Robert Coles	68	67	69	204	20,640
Eduardo Romero	69	67	69	205	17,688
Mark Roe	64	69	72	205	17,688
Jose Manuel Lara	68	70	67	205	17,688
Martin Erlandsson	67	66	72	205	17,688
*Francesco Molinari	73	63	69	205	
Simon Khan	70	68	67	205	17,688
Mark Foster	66	69	71	206	14,448
Peter Hanson	74	68	64	206	14,448
Gary Evans	67	69	70	206	14,448
David Lynn	66	70	70	206	14,448
Markus Brier	72	69	65	206	14,448
Barry Lane	73	65	69	207	12,660
Richard Green	72	69	66	207	12,660
Paul Broadhurst	69	69	69	207	12,660
Philip Golding	71	68	68	207	12,660
Damien McGrane	68	72	68	208	9,880
Cesar Monasterio	66	70	72	208	9,880
Anthony Wall	67	70	71	208	9,880
Henrik Stenson	70	67	71	208	9,880
Jean Van de Velde	71	66	71	208	9,880
Fredrik Andersson Hed	73	69	66	208	9,880
Ivo Giner	71	70	67	208	9,880
Michael Campbell	65	72	71	208	9,880
Paul Marantz	69	69	70	208	9,880
Thongchai Jaidee	70	67	71	208	9,880
Steven O'Hara	69	70	69	208	9,880

	SCORES			TOTAL	MONEY
Marcus Fraser	70	69	69	208	9,880
Santiago Luna	70	70	69	209	7,680
David Park	69	72	68	209	7,680
Raymond Russell	71	71	67	209	7,680
Terry Price	69	69	71	209	7,680
Marc Farry	70	72	68	210	6,720
Andrew Marshall	70	71	69	210	6,720
Emanuele Canonica	72	68	70	210	6,720
Christopher Hanell	65	74	71	210	6,720
David Howell	69	72	70	211	5,160
Jose Manuel Carriles	70	71	70	211	5,160
Soren Kjeldsen	70	71	70	211	5,160
Fernando Roca	69	70	72	211	5,160
Stephen Gallacher	68	72	71	211	5,160
Robert Rock	71	70	70	211	5,160
Brett Rumford	68	69	74	211	5,160
Sebastian Fernandez	70	68	73	211	5,160
Wade Ormsby	71	70	70	211	5,160
Darren Fichardt	69	69	74	212	3,690
Jesus Maria Arruti	71	68	73	212	3,690
Jonathan Lomas	72	69	71	212	3,690
James Hepworth	69	70	73	212	3,690
Jamie Spence	67	69	77	213	3,180
Henrik Bjornstad	71	70	72	213	3,180
Gianluca Baruffaldi	70	71	72	213	3,180
Gary Orr	73	69	71	213	3,180
Maarten Lafeber	75	67	72	214	2,700
Alessandro Tadini	69	73	72	214	2,700
Gary Emerson	73	68	73	214	2,700
Alan McLean	68	73	73	214	2,700
Paul Eales	72	70	73	215	2,093.40
Paul Lawrie	69	72	74	215	2,093.40
Andrew Coltart	69	72	74	215	2,093.40
Matthew Blackey	69	73	73	215	2,093.40
Steven Jeppesen	72	68	75	215	2,093.40
Peter Baker	70	70	77	217	1,792.50
Per Nyman	69	73	75	217	1,792.50
Martin LeMesurier	72	69	81	222	1,788

Daily Telegraph Damovo British Masters

Marriott Forest of Arden Hotel, Warwickshire, England
Par 36-36–72; 7,213 yards

May 6-9
purse, €2,370,800

	SCORES				TOTAL	MONEY
Barry Lane	70	69	67	66	272	€395,123.46
Eduardo Romero	67	68	71	69	275	205,911.39
Angel Cabrera	70	68	70	67	275	205,911.39
Patrik Sjoland	69	65	73	69	276	118,540
Anders Hansen	69	71	72	65	277	78,473.48
Nick O'Hern	69	68	72	68	277	78,473.48
Paul Broadhurst	69	70	66	72	277	78,473.48
Darren Clarke	70	73	69	65	277	78,473.48
Alastair Forsyth	70	70	69	69	278	53,105.92
Kenneth Ferrie	67	73	70	69	279	45,519.36
Stephen Gallacher	69	68	74	68	279	45,519.36
Trevor Immelman	67	72	71	70	280	39,473.82

	SCORES				TOTAL	MONEY
Paul Casey	72	70	69	69	280	39,473.82
Robert-Jan Derksen	69	71	71	70	281	35,562
Paul McGinley	70	72	70	69	281	35,562
Miguel Angel Martin	69	73	73	67	282	31,353.83
Ian Woosnam	70	70	70	72	282	31,353.83
Colin Montgomerie	72	69	70	71	282	31,353.83
Michael Campbell	67	71	73	71	282	31,353.83
David Howell	66	73	71	73	283	27,204.93
Raphael Jacquelin	68	75	71	69	283	27,204.93
Ian Poulter	73	71	68	71	283	27,204.93
Carlos Rodiles	69	72	74	68	283	27,204.93
Jean-Francois Lucquin	70	68	77	69	284	23,945.08
Jarrod Moseley	68	72	72	72	284	23,945.08
Gary Evans	73	68	75	68	284	23,945.08
Graeme McDowell	73	68	73	70	284	23,945.08
Martin Maritz	69	72	68	75	284	23,945.08
Martin Erlandsson	71	72	74	68	285	20,388.88
Henrik Stenson	75	67	74	69	285	20,388.88
Thomas Levet	70	70	73	72	285	20,388.88
Gary Orr	71	72	72	70	285	20,388.88
Terry Price	70	72	68	75	285	20,388.88
Sandy Lyle	70	71	78	67	286	16,595.60
Santiago Luna	70	68	75	73	286	16,595.60
Brian Davis	68	67	79	72	286	16,595.60
Sven Struver	72	70	75	69	286	16,595.60
Maarten Lafeber	68	72	72	74	286	16,595.60
Richard Green	72	70	73	71	286	16,595.60
Emanuele Canonica	75	67	74	70	286	16,595.60
Thongchai Jaidee	73	71	74	68	286	16,595.60
Klas Eriksson	71	70	75	71	287	12,802.32
Jean-Francois Remesy	70	73	73	71	287	12,802.32
Soren Kjeldsen	73	71	74	69	287	12,802.32
Anthony Wall	70	69	74	74	287	12,802.32
David Lynn	72	71	74	70	287	12,802.32
Simon Wakefield	70	72	71	74	287	12,802.32
Lee Westwood	71	65	75	76	287	12,802.32
Rob Rashell	72	71	73	71	287	12,802.32
Cesar Monasterio	69	73	75	71	288	10,431.52
Louis Oosthuizen	72	72	75	69	288	10,431.52
David Gilford	72	71	76	70	289	8,534.88
Soren Hansen	69	75	75	70	289	8,534.88
Stephen Dodd	71	72	74	72	289	8,534.88
Bradley Dredge	73	70	77	69	289	8,534.88
Retief Goosen	72	71	75	71	289	8,534.88
Christopher Hanell	71	72	75	71	289	8,534.88
Mark Roe	71	71	76	72	290	6,756.78
Henrik Bjornstad	76	66	73	75	290	6,756.78
Greg Owen	72	72	79	67	290	6,756.78
Steven O'Hara	73	71	78	68	290	6,756.78
David Carter	71	72	74	74	291	5,927
Mads Vibe-Hastrup	74	70	74	73	291	5,927
Paul Marantz	69	75	75	72	291	5,927
Peter Baker	72	72	75	73	292	5,452.84
Ivo Giner	71	71	78	73	293	5,215.76
Jonathan Lomas	70	72	78	74	294	4,741.60
Raymond Russell	71	73	81	69	294	4,741.60
Daniel Gaunt	72	71	75	76	294	4,741.60
Philip Golding	73	71	78	73	295	3,948.76
Miguel Angel Jimenez	72	71	75	77	295	3,948.76
*Gary Wolstenholme	72	72	76	75	295	

	SCORES				TOTAL	MONEY
Damien McGrane	71	71	80	74	296	3,551.50
Mattias Nilsson	72	72	78	74	296	3,551.50
Andrew Coltart	67	77	81	76	301	3,547

Deutsche Bank - SAP Open

St. Leon-Rot Golf Club, Heidelberg, Germany   May 20-23
Par 36-36–72; 7,255 yards   purse, €3,000,000

	SCORES				TOTAL	MONEY
Trevor Immelman	65	72	69	65	271	€500,000
Padraig Harrington	70	68	68	66	272	333,330
Joakim Haeggman	69	72	66	69	276	168,900
Darren Clarke	70	67	70	69	276	168,900
David Howell	65	71	75	66	277	107,400
Soren Kjeldsen	70	70	71	66	277	107,400
Ernie Els	67	72	72	66	277	107,400
Louis Oosthuizen	69	68	71	72	280	75,000
Alex Cejka	69	64	76	72	281	63,600
Retief Goosen	70	72	69	70	281	63,600
Anders Hansen	68	70	73	71	282	55,200
Nick Price	74	66	70	73	283	51,600
Jean-Francois Remesy	71	68	73	72	284	44,220
Richard Green	70	73	73	68	284	44,220
Soren Hansen	70	71	70	73	284	44,220
Emanuele Canonica	68	76	72	68	284	44,220
David Carter	71	71	71	71	284	44,220
Klas Eriksson	69	69	74	73	285	36,120
Thomas Bjorn	71	68	72	74	285	36,120
Stephen Scahill	68	69	74	74	285	36,120
David Lynn	72	72	75	66	285	36,120
Michael Campbell	73	68	78	66	285	36,120
Barry Lane	67	77	73	69	286	31,200
Andrew Marshall	73	70	73	70	286	31,200
Gregory Havret	65	71	68	82	286	31,200
Phillip Price	68	77	70	71	286	31,200
Jarmo Sandelin	69	70	76	71	286	31,200
Jose Maria Olazabal	66	79	72	70	287	26,250
Brian Davis	73	72	74	68	287	26,250
Paul Broadhurst	70	73	72	72	287	26,250
Carlos Rodiles	71	71	74	71	287	26,250
Nobuhito Sato	72	70	75	70	287	26,250
Robert Karlsson	71	72	71	73	287	26,250
Santiago Luna	74	67	76	71	288	21,900
Miguel Angel Jimenez	67	77	73	71	288	21,900
Marcel Siem	66	72	73	77	288	21,900
Alan McLean	66	72	74	76	288	21,900
Christopher Hanell	70	76	72	70	288	21,900
Eduardo Romero	69	69	74	77	289	19,500
Johan Edfors	73	71	75	70	289	19,500
John Bickerton	71	70	76	72	289	19,500
Henrik Stenson	73	73	72	72	290	17,100
Fredrik Andersson Hed	74	70	74	72	290	17,100
Stephen Gallacher	70	74	74	72	290	17,100
Paul Casey	70	76	75	69	290	17,100
Ben Curtis	68	73	75	74	290	17,100
Thongchai Jaidee	71	73	77	70	291	15,300

	SCORES				TOTAL	MONEY
Robert-Jan Derksen	66	79	73	74	292	14,100
Patrik Sjoland	71	71	77	73	292	14,100
Robert Rock	70	72	73	77	292	14,100
Marten Olander	69	77	74	73	293	11,700
Martin Erlandsson	74	71	75	73	293	11,700
Stuart Little	68	75	77	73	293	11,700
Nick Dougherty	77	67	78	71	293	11,700
Jamie Elson	68	76	76	73	293	11,700
Gary Murphy	71	73	75	75	294	9,225
Andre Cruse	70	71	76	77	294	9,225
Kariem Baraka	67	77	76	74	294	9,225
Rob Rashell	72	70	80	72	294	9,225
Ian Woosnam	72	72	75	76	295	7,800
Peter Fowler	70	73	77	75	295	7,800
Darren Fichardt	71	74	76	74	295	7,800
Simon Khan	73	69	80	73	295	7,800
Sebastian Fernandez	72	72	76	75	295	7,800
Costantino Rocca	73	73	75	75	296	6,750
Miles Tunnicliff	70	76	79	71	296	6,750
Lee Westwood	71	75	75	76	297	6,300
Ignacio Garrido	71	72	81	74	298	6,000
Martin Wiegele	76	70	77	76	299	5,585
Tobias Dier	72	72	80	75	299	5,585
Thomas Levet	70	74	77	80	301	4,498.50
Diego Borrego	77	67	78	79	301	4,498.50

Volvo PGA Championship

Wentworth Club, Surrey, England
Par 35-37–72; 7,072 yards

May 27-30
purse, €3,750,000

	SCORES				TOTAL	MONEY
Scott Drummond	66	71	68	64	269	€625,000
Angel Cabrera	67	69	68	67	271	416,660
Joakim Haeggman	68	67	70	67	272	234,750
Nick Faldo	70	69	68	66	273	159,250
Anders Hansen	67	69	73	64	273	159,250
Darren Clarke	68	67	71	67	273	159,250
Ernie Els	64	71	72	68	275	112,500
Darren Fichardt	68	69	68	71	276	84,250
Thomas Levet	72	66	70	68	276	84,250
Miguel Angel Jimenez	65	74	70	67	276	84,250
Justin Rose	67	66	72	72	277	62,812.50
Retief Goosen	68	74	67	68	277	62,812.50
Christopher Hanell	65	73	72	67	277	62,812.50
Adam Scott	69	74	67	67	277	62,812.50
Vijay Singh	66	73	71	68	278	54,000
Mikko Ilonen	69	72	67	70	278	54,000
Pierre Fulke	72	69	68	70	279	50,625
Peter O'Malley	69	74	69	68	280	47,437.50
Thomas Bjorn	72	66	69	73	280	47,437.50
Richard Green	67	75	69	70	281	43,031.25
Peter Hanson	70	73	68	70	281	43,031.25
Stephen Gallacher	74	70	69	68	281	43,031.25
Mads Vibe-Hastrup	70	72	69	70	281	43,031.25
Anthony Wall	68	72	70	72	282	39,000
Peter Hedblom	69	68	74	71	282	39,000

	SCORES				TOTAL	MONEY
Simon Khan	68	72	72	70	282	39,000
Sandy Lyle	71	70	74	68	283	31,800
Eduardo Romero	69	71	73	70	283	31,800
Barry Lane	72	72	69	70	283	31,800
Jean-Francois Remesy	71	69	72	71	283	31,800
David Gilford	67	72	75	69	283	31,800
Soren Kjeldsen	71	71	67	74	283	31,800
Nick O'Hern	71	73	70	69	283	31,800
Phillip Price	70	65	73	75	283	31,800
Graeme McDowell	71	73	70	69	283	31,800
Marcus Fraser	71	73	69	70	283	31,800
Steve Webster	71	69	73	71	284	25,125
Marcel Siem	69	67	75	73	284	25,125
Peter Lonard	69	72	72	71	284	25,125
David Park	72	70	71	71	284	25,125
Paul Casey	68	73	70	73	284	25,125
Jose Maria Olazabal	72	72	68	73	285	21,375
Peter Lawrie	69	73	73	70	285	21,375
Stephen Dodd	65	71	77	72	285	21,375
John Bickerton	68	73	71	73	285	21,375
Richard Sterne	69	73	71	72	285	21,375
David Howell	72	69	74	71	286	17,625
Maarten Lafeber	68	71	75	72	286	17,625
Colin Montgomerie	70	70	73	73	286	17,625
Robert Rock	72	72	69	73	286	17,625
Chris Kelly	69	71	70	76	286	17,625
Mark Roe	70	73	72	72	287	14,625
Ian Poulter	68	68	77	74	287	14,625
Ignacio Garrido	67	76	69	75	287	14,625
Thongchai Jaidee	69	71	75	73	288	13,125
Brian Davis	75	68	68	78	289	12,000
Kenneth Ferrie	73	70	70	76	289	12,000
Marten Olander	70	74	70	76	290	10,687.50
Nicolas Colsaerts	67	72	73	78	290	10,687.50
Miles Tunnicliff	69	74	72	75	290	10,687.50
James Kingston	69	73	75	73	290	10,687.50
Raymond Russell	71	73	75	72	291	9,562.50
David Higgins	73	71	71	76	291	9,562.50
Raphael Jacquelin	71	71	77	73	292	8,625
Ricardo Gonzalez	72	71	68	81	292	8,625
Barry Austin	71	72	75	74	292	8,625
Jamie Spence	70	72	76	75	293	7,335
Paul Wesselingh	71	71	78	73	293	7,335
Gary Orr	70	74	74	75	293	7,335
Paul Lawrie	72	71	76	74	293	7,335
Ross Drummond	74	69	76	75	294	5,623.50
Fredrik Andersson Hed	69	74	73	78	294	5,623.50
Jarmo Sandelin	71	72	77	79	299	5,619

Celtic Manor Wales Open

Celtic Manor Resort, Wentwood Hills Course,
Newport, Wales
Par 36-36–72; 7,379 yards

June 3-6
purse, €2,250,560

	SCORES				TOTAL	MONEY
Simon Khan	69	61	70	67	267	€375,092.50
Paul Casey	69	63	65	70	267	250,051.70
(Khan defeated Casey on second playoff hole.)						
Jean-Francois Remesy	71	69	66	65	271	140,884.80
Nick O'Hern	70	67	68	68	273	112,527.80
David Howell	65	74	67	68	274	74,493.38
John Bickerton	70	71	63	70	274	74,493.38
Alastair Forsyth	74	66	65	69	274	74,493.38
Martin Maritz	69	71	67	67	274	74,493.38
Ian Poulter	71	69	66	70	276	45,611.25
Stephen Dodd	70	69	67	70	276	45,611.25
James Kingston	70	66	66	74	276	45,611.25
Marten Olander	72	66	69	70	277	36,458.99
Thomas Levet	69	71	67	70	277	36,458.99
Peter O'Malley	70	71	68	68	277	36,458.99
Santiago Luna	70	69	73	66	278	27,538.61
Miguel Angel Martin	69	69	70	70	278	27,538.61
Colin Montgomerie	67	68	69	74	278	27,538.61
Marcel Siem	66	72	70	70	278	27,538.61
Jarrod Moseley	68	72	66	72	278	27,538.61
Joakim Haeggman	73	69	68	68	278	27,538.61
Robert Karlsson	68	72	69	69	278	27,538.61
Robert Coles	70	70	68	70	278	27,538.61
Fredrik Andersson Hed	69	71	70	68	278	27,538.61
Mads Vibe-Hastrup	70	69	72	67	278	27,538.61
Marcus Fraser	72	66	70	70	278	27,538.61
Ian Woosnam	71	69	69	70	279	21,380.27
Damien McGrane	76	67	67	69	279	21,380.27
David Carter	68	69	70	72	279	21,380.27
Terry Price	71	69	70	69	279	21,380.27
Steven O'Hara	67	73	70	69	279	21,380.27
Martin Erlandsson	71	69	68	72	280	18,679.61
Philip Golding	71	66	67	76	280	18,679.61
Stuart Little	68	72	71	69	280	18,679.61
Mark Foster	71	69	68	73	281	15,978.94
Barry Lane	69	74	68	70	281	15,978.94
Miles Tunnicliff	69	71	69	72	281	15,978.94
Andrew Coltart	70	72	70	69	281	15,978.94
Michael Campbell	72	70	71	68	281	15,978.94
Stephen Gallacher	71	66	70	74	281	15,978.94
Mikko Ilonen	68	70	68	75	281	15,978.94
Peter Hanson	69	70	72	71	282	12,603.11
Peter Lawrie	71	64	70	77	282	12,603.11
Andrew Marshall	75	68	69	70	282	12,603.11
Nicolas Colsaerts	73	67	70	72	282	12,603.11
Jonathan Lomas	70	72	71	69	282	12,603.11
Paul McGinley	70	71	69	72	282	12,603.11
Christian Cevaer	67	70	74	71	282	12,603.11
Stephen Scahill	73	68	71	70	282	12,603.11
Robert-Jan Derksen	71	71	68	73	283	9,227.27
Anthony Wall	72	70	75	66	283	9,227.27
Jean-Francois Lucquin	73	70	65	75	283	9,227.27
Phillip Price	72	70	68	73	283	9,227.27

	SCORES				TOTAL	MONEY
Christopher Hanell	73	69	70	71	283	9,227.27
Francois Delamontagne	72	69	70	72	283	9,227.27
Steven Jeppesen	71	65	70	77	283	9,227.27
Gary Murphy	68	71	73	72	284	6,796.68
Gary Evans	71	69	73	71	284	6,796.68
Gary Orr	70	70	74	70	284	6,796.68
David Lynn	69	70	71	74	284	6,796.68
Michael Jonzon	71	70	70	73	284	6,796.68
Per Nyman	70	68	72	75	285	5,738.92
Simon Wakefield	71	71	70	73	285	5,738.92
Graeme McDowell	73	70	71	71	285	5,738.92
David Dixon	70	70	71	74	285	5,738.92
Peter Baker	70	68	80	68	286	5,063.75
Jarmo Sandelin	72	71	74	69	286	5,063.75
Gordon Brand, Jr.	73	69	70	75	287	4,501.11
Patrik Sjoland	71	71	69	76	287	4,501.11
Barry Austin	71	68	72	76	287	4,501.11
Richard Green	71	71	75	72	289	3,743.51
Emanuele Canonica	66	75	72	76	289	3,743.51
Soren Kjeldsen	69	70	73	78	290	3,373
Roger Chapman	72	71	70	78	291	3,370
Richard Sterne	71	69	72	80	292	3,365.50
Louis Oosthuizen	71	71	78	72	292	3,365.50
Sven Struver	69	74	72	78	293	3,361
Warren Bennett	70	73	76	78	297	3,358

Diageo Championship at Gleneagles

Gleneagles Hotel, PGA Centenary Course,
Perthshire, Scotland
Par 36-36–72; 7,060 yards

June 10-13
purse, €2,116,550

	SCORES				TOTAL	MONEY
Miles Tunnicliff	67	68	72	68	275	€349,614.70
Graeme McDowell	69	71	73	67	280	233,071.50
Nick O'Hern	67	73	70	71	281	118,101.50
Steven O'Hara	73	72	69	67	281	118,101.50
Andrew Oldcorn	74	73	68	67	282	81,181.69
David Lynn	71	73	70	68	282	81,181.69
Russell Claydon	70	72	69	72	283	54,121.13
Paul McGinley	68	73	73	69	283	54,121.13
Raymond Russell	75	67	70	71	283	54,121.13
Gary Murphy	70	74	70	70	284	36,500.29
Richard Green	69	74	72	69	284	36,500.29
Anthony Wall	74	72	69	69	284	36,500.29
Peter O'Malley	71	75	70	68	284	36,500.29
Stephen Gallacher	72	73	69	70	284	36,500.29
Ross Drummond	73	75	69	68	285	30,207.14
Anders Hansen	72	74	64	75	285	30,207.14
Mark Roe	70	73	69	74	286	26,179.52
Soren Kjeldsen	74	70	67	75	286	26,179.52
Greig Hutcheon	74	70	72	70	286	26,179.52
Gary Evans	73	69	69	75	286	26,179.52
Henrik Nystrom	72	73	67	74	286	26,179.52
Santiago Luna	68	75	67	77	287	22,130.93
David Howell	73	68	72	74	287	22,130.93
Gary Emerson	73	70	71	73	287	22,130.93

	SCORES				TOTAL	MONEY
Colin Montgomerie	71	73	71	72	287	22,130.93
Peter Baker	70	72	73	72	287	22,130.93
Richard Sterne	73	72	68	74	287	22,130.93
David Gilford	74	72	70	72	288	18,669.69
Raphael Jacquelin	72	76	69	71	288	18,669.69
Henrik Stenson	71	70	71	76	288	18,669.69
Peter Hedblom	73	74	69	72	288	18,669.69
Ben Mason	72	72	69	75	288	18,669.69
Paul Broadhurst	75	72	71	71	289	15,995.10
Andrew Marshall	74	74	69	72	289	15,995.10
Scott Henderson	77	71	72	69	289	15,995.10
David Drysdale	72	76	70	71	289	15,995.10
Jonathan Lomas	74	72	70	74	290	14,054.71
Robert Coles	75	72	76	67	290	14,054.71
Patrik Sjoland	69	75	71	75	290	14,054.71
Terry Price	73	69	73	75	290	14,054.71
Alastair Forsyth	76	71	71	72	290	14,054.71
Steve Webster	74	72	74	71	291	11,956.99
Carlos Rodiles	70	75	68	78	291	11,956.99
Paul Eales	73	70	73	75	291	11,956.99
Stephen Scahill	76	72	71	72	291	11,956.99
Marcus Fraser	74	73	72	72	291	11,956.99
Matthew Blackey	70	74	71	77	292	10,069.05
Francois Delamontagne	71	75	72	74	292	10,069.05
Jamie Elson	72	73	75	72	292	10,069.05
Craig Williams	70	76	72	74	292	10,069.05
Sandy Lyle	72	75	74	72	293	7,971.33
Euan Little	71	76	72	74	293	7,971.33
Pierre Fulke	72	76	69	76	293	7,971.33
Ivo Giner	72	75	70	76	293	7,971.33
Sam Walker	72	73	72	76	293	7,971.33
Marc Warren	74	74	74	71	293	7,971.33
Philip Walton	71	76	71	76	294	6,293.15
Jorge Berendt	74	73	76	71	294	6,293.15
Rolf Muntz	74	73	72	75	294	6,293.15
Richard McEvoy	74	74	75	72	295	5,873.61
Mark King	71	76	74	75	296	5,558.95
Brett Rumford	70	75	73	78	296	5,558.95
Warren Bennett	72	75	74	76	297	4,719.87
Sven Struver	70	77	73	77	297	4,719.87
Scott Drummond	73	75	70	79	297	4,719.87
Ian Garbutt	71	77	76	73	297	4,719.87
Chris Kelly	70	76	73	78	297	4,719.87
Daniel Gaunt	72	73	75	77	297	4,719.87
Gordon Law	70	77	79	72	298	3,656.16
Emanuele Canonica	74	73	75	76	298	3,656.16
Matthew Cort	72	74	72	80	298	3,656.16
Mattias Eliasson	73	75	75	76	299	3,142.50
Hennie Otto	73	75	75	76	299	3,142.50
Alex Balicki	77	69	72	82	300	3,138
Mattias Nilsson	71	77	78	76	302	3,135
Jeppe Huldahl	73	74	74	82	303	3,132

Aa St. Omer Open

Aa St. Omer Golf Club, Lumbres, France
Par 36-35–71; 6,852 yards

June 17-20
purse, €400,000

	SCORES				TOTAL	MONEY
Philippe Lima	71	71	71	66	279	€66,660
Alessandro Tadini	70	74	67	69	280	44,440
David Geall	70	73	67	71	281	25,040
Carl Suneson	70	67	73	72	282	15,740
James Hepworth	75	67	72	68	282	15,740
Iain Pyman	71	72	72	67	282	15,740
Simon Dyson	70	70	70	72	282	15,740
Jean-Francois Lucquin	68	73	69	74	284	8,986.67
Massimo Florioli	69	72	69	74	284	8,986.67
Johan Skold	72	72	69	71	284	8,986.67
Jamie Little	70	76	69	70	285	6,536
Pasi Purhonen	71	71	68	75	285	6,536
Didier de Vooght	74	73	66	72	285	6,536
Murray Urquhart	70	68	75	72	285	6,536
Sebastien Delagrange	72	72	73	68	285	6,536
Miguel Angel Martin	73	72	73	68	286	4,593.85
Sven Struver	76	71	71	68	286	4,593.85
Titch Moore	75	67	71	73	286	4,593.85
Michael Hoey	72	70	74	70	286	4,593.85
Jorge Berendt	71	74	73	68	286	4,593.85
Benn Barham	67	75	71	73	286	4,593.85
Simon Wakefield	75	69	71	71	286	4,593.85
John Mellor	72	70	72	72	286	4,593.85
Leif Westerberg	71	76	73	66	286	4,593.85
Kariem Baraka	74	72	70	70	286	4,593.85
Tom Whitehouse	71	71	71	73	286	4,593.85
Brad Kennedy	72	72	74	68	286	4,593.85
Johan Kok	71	72	74	69	286	4,593.85
Knud Storgaard	74	72	72	69	287	3,560
Stephen Browne	69	69	75	74	287	3,560
Gareth Paddison	76	71	69	71	287	3,560
Magnus Persson Atlevi	74	71	73	70	288	3,150
Paul Dwyer	76	68	75	69	288	3,150
Gustavo Rojas	70	74	73	71	288	3,150
Paul Marantz	71	71	75	71	288	3,150
Garry Houston	72	71	71	75	289	2,720
Olivier David	73	71	75	70	289	2,720
Ian Garbutt	76	71	72	70	289	2,720
Paul Streeter	71	74	72	72	289	2,720
Graeme Storm	76	71	74	68	289	2,720
Kyron Sullivan	66	72	75	76	289	2,720
Greig Hutcheon	70	72	75	73	290	2,200
Fernando Roca	74	70	77	69	290	2,200
Tim Milford	71	71	73	75	290	2,200
Simon Hurd	72	73	73	72	290	2,200
David Drysdale	73	71	72	74	290	2,200
Francois Delamontagne	73	73	71	73	290	2,200
Juan Abbate	69	71	78	72	290	2,200
Gianluca Baruffaldi	73	72	77	69	291	1,760
Mark Pilkington	72	74	73	72	291	1,760
Peter Gustafsson	73	74	73	71	291	1,760
Gregory Bourdy	70	73	75	73	291	1,760
Marc Farry	69	72	73	78	292	1,337.14
Alex Balicki	74	73	74	71	292	1,337.14

	SCORES				TOTAL	MONEY
Jean Marc de Polo	74	73	71	74	292	1,337.14
Marc Cayeux	69	77	74	72	292	1,337.14
Carlos Quevedo	74	68	76	74	292	1,337.14
Darren Leng	72	71	74	75	292	1,337.14
Brian Akstrup	75	67	82	68	292	1,337.14
Alvaro Salto	70	73	75	75	293	1,080
Marco Soffietti	72	75	71	75	293	1,080
Jean Hugo	72	74	75	72	293	1,080
Jan-Are Larsen	71	76	77	70	294	900
Sion Bebb	75	71	71	77	294	900
Henrik Nystrom	74	72	73	75	294	900
Mikael Lundberg	69	73	81	71	294	900
Daniel Vancsik	74	73	75	72	294	900
Alexandre Chopard	74	70	74	76	294	900
Warren Bennett	73	74	76	72	295	658.20
Roger Winchester	71	73	77	74	295	658.20
Pehr Magnebrant	73	73	77	72	295	658.20
Oyvind Rojahn	72	68	77	78	295	658.20
David Patrick	72	75	76	72	295	658.20
Jochen Lupprian	76	71	75	74	296	589.50
Benoit Teilleria	71	74	75	76	296	589.50
Joakim Rask	74	73	77	73	297	583.50
Steven Jeppesen	76	71	77	73	297	583.50
Sebastien Branger	77	70	80	71	298	574.50
Julien Van Hauwe	75	72	75	76	298	574.50
Andreas Ljunggren	73	74	74	77	298	574.50
Matthew Morris	73	71	78	76	298	574.50
Mark Sanders	73	73	77	76	299	567

Open de France

Le Golf National, Paris, France
Par 36-35–71; 7,202 yards

June 24-27
purse, €3,000,000

	SCORES				TOTAL	MONEY
Jean-Francois Remesy	69	67	65	71	272	€500,000
Richard Green	68	70	66	75	279	260,565
Nick O'Hern	73	68	70	68	279	260,565
Jonathan Lomas	73	70	69	69	281	138,600
Graeme McDowell	70	73	74	64	281	138,600
Ian Woosnam	67	69	72	74	282	97,500
Peter O'Malley	73	67	70	72	282	97,500
Miguel Angel Jimenez	75	72	68	69	284	71,100
Marcel Siem	71	73	69	71	284	71,100
Darren Fichardt	66	73	70	76	285	53,775
Soren Hansen	76	72	68	69	285	53,775
David Lynn	72	71	68	74	285	53,775
Paul Casey	77	70	65	73	285	53,775
David Howell	71	69	74	72	286	43,200
Jose Maria Olazabal	74	72	69	71	286	43,200
Ian Poulter	70	71	69	76	286	43,200
Robert Allenby	76	68	70	72	286	43,200
Gary Murphy	75	72	70	70	287	35,600
Damien McGrane	76	70	70	71	287	35,600
Steve Webster	74	71	73	69	287	35,600
Paul McGinley	75	72	68	72	287	35,600
James Kingston	77	72	68	70	287	35,600

	SCORES				TOTAL	MONEY
David Park	76	68	67	76	287	35,600
Mark Roe	70	71	74	73	288	30,300
Robert-Jan Derksen	75	70	72	71	288	30,300
Marten Olander	72	73	73	70	288	30,300
Gary Evans	72	70	68	78	288	30,300
John Bickerton	73	67	72	76	288	30,300
Andrew Oldcorn	77	70	73	69	289	25,800
Peter Fowler	71	75	70	73	289	25,800
Trevor Immelman	74	68	73	74	289	25,800
Andrew Marshall	73	73	74	69	289	25,800
Jarrod Moseley	73	76	70	70	289	25,800
Thomas Levet	76	66	75	73	290	22,800
James Hepworth	71	74	69	76	290	22,800
Roger Chapman	74	75	70	72	291	21,000
David Gilford	74	72	72	73	291	21,000
Raymond Russell	76	69	75	71	291	21,000
Christopher Hanell	78	70	73	70	291	21,000
Miguel Angel Martin	73	74	68	77	292	18,000
Anders Hansen	76	71	71	74	292	18,000
Peter Hanson	74	72	70	76	292	18,000
Jean-Francois Lucquin	73	73	71	75	292	18,000
Simon Khan	73	75	75	69	292	18,000
Robert Coles	75	73	73	71	292	18,000
Gordon Brand, Jr.	72	73	71	77	293	15,600
Matthew Blackey	72	76	74	71	293	15,600
Cesar Monasterio	70	73	78	73	294	13,500
Colin Montgomerie	74	75	73	72	294	13,500
Jorge Berendt	74	75	70	75	294	13,500
Bradley Dredge	73	74	77	70	294	13,500
Richard McEvoy	72	70	79	73	294	13,500
Paul Eales	72	70	79	74	295	10,500
Nicolas Colsaerts	69	77	75	74	295	10,500
Mikko Ilonen	78	71	67	79	295	10,500
Alastair Forsyth	75	68	77	75	295	10,500
Steven O'Hara	72	74	73	76	295	10,500
Scott Drummond	77	70	75	74	296	8,250
Jamie Spence	73	73	74	76	296	8,250
Gregory Havret	72	70	77	77	296	8,250
Ricardo Gonzalez	71	78	71	76	296	8,250
Markus Brier	72	77	70	77	296	8,250
David Dixon	71	72	77	76	296	8,250
Jose Manuel Carriles	76	72	77	72	297	6,750
Benjamin Nicolay	73	73	79	72	297	6,750
Francois Delamontagne	75	68	80	74	297	6,750
Bruno-Teva Lecuona	77	69	77	74	297	6,750
Jean Van de Velde	74	68	78	78	298	5,417.50
Stephen Gallacher	73	74	74	77	298	5,417.50
Mads Vibe-Hastrup	75	71	77	75	298	5,417.50
Philippe Lima	74	73	74	77	298	5,417.50
Justin Rose	75	71	77	76	299	4,495.50
Mattias Nilsson	74	75	78	72	299	4,495.50
David Carter	77	71	82	73	303	4,491

Smurfit European Open

The K Club, Dublin, Ireland
Par 36-36–72; 7,313 yards

July 1-4
purse, €3,334,680

	SCORES				TOTAL	MONEY
Retief Goosen	69	66	72	68	275	€550,004.69
Richard Green	70	78	66	66	280	246,086.57
Peter O'Malley	72	70	68	70	280	246,086.57
Lee Westwood	69	69	71	71	280	246,086.57
Jose Manuel Lara	73	68	67	73	281	127,713.41
Maarten Lafeber	67	70	75	69	281	127,713.41
David Howell	69	72	75	67	283	99,002.64
Soren Kjeldsen	71	75	69	69	284	78,212.09
Angel Cabrera	72	73	72	67	284	78,212.09
Nick O'Hern	67	72	72	74	285	59,154.08
Paul Broadhurst	67	74	69	75	285	59,154.08
Paul McGinley	70	71	71	73	285	59,154.08
Thongchai Jaidee	72	72	69	72	285	59,154.08
Gordon Brand, Jr.	74	68	75	69	286	45,596.22
Justin Rose	73	76	72	65	286	45,596.22
Joakim Haeggman	72	74	70	70	286	45,596.22
Gary Evans	70	74	68	74	286	45,596.22
Terry Price	73	72	70	71	286	45,596.22
Paul Casey	72	74	71	69	286	45,596.22
Gary Murphy	74	73	69	71	287	37,868.51
Jesper Parnevik	72	73	75	67	287	37,868.51
Phillip Price	75	72	70	70	287	37,868.51
Bradley Dredge	70	75	75	67	287	37,868.51
Andrew Oldcorn	74	73	71	70	288	33,825.90
Henrik Stenson	71	72	69	76	288	33,825.90
Markus Brier	73	73	75	67	288	33,825.90
Christopher Hanell	74	73	74	67	288	33,825.90
Jean-Francois Remesy	73	74	71	71	289	30,855.82
Kenneth Ferrie	77	66	71	75	289	30,855.82
Brian Davis	72	77	70	71	290	26,153.20
Steve Webster	76	73	68	73	290	26,153.20
Marcel Siem	74	74	70	72	290	26,153.20
Peter Hedblom	71	72	77	70	290	26,153.20
David Carter	75	72	71	72	290	26,153.20
Brett Rumford	72	73	77	68	290	26,153.20
Louis Oosthuizen	74	73	73	70	290	26,153.20
Marcus Fraser	72	73	74	71	290	26,153.20
Peter Lawrie	72	72	71	76	291	21,120.56
James Kingston	72	68	75	76	291	21,120.56
David Lynn	73	76	76	66	291	21,120.56
Mads Vibe-Hastrup	74	71	73	73	291	21,120.56
Charl Schwartzel	72	76	71	72	291	21,120.56
Rob Rashell	73	75	76	67	291	21,120.56
Anthony Wall	75	74	70	73	292	16,500.44
Christian Cevaer	73	69	76	74	292	16,500.44
Andrew Coltart	70	74	75	73	292	16,500.44
Niclas Fasth	70	71	73	78	292	16,500.44
Matthew Blackey	69	73	77	73	292	16,500.44
Stephen Gallacher	71	74	74	73	292	16,500.44
John Dwyer	73	75	71	73	292	16,500.44
Robert Rock	72	72	78	70	292	16,500.44
Nick Faldo	74	72	74	73	293	11,597.45
Padraig Harrington	70	76	76	71	293	11,597.45
Jose Manuel Carriles	71	77	72	73	293	11,597.45

	SCORES				TOTAL	MONEY
Philip Golding	75	73	73	72	293	11,597.45
Miles Tunnicliff	72	77	73	71	293	11,597.45
Emanuele Canonica	73	75	73	72	293	11,597.45
Stephen Dodd	74	75	75	69	293	11,597.45
Klas Eriksson	75	73	75	71	294	8,910.24
Darren Clarke	76	72	74	72	294	8,910.24
Robert Coles	74	73	75	72	294	8,910.24
Francois Delamontagne	71	76	78	69	294	8,910.24
Martin Maritz	76	73	77	68	294	8,910.24
Andrew Marshall	74	74	74	73	295	7,755.21
Jesus Maria Arruti	69	79	72	75	295	7,755.21
Sandy Lyle	75	74	78	69	296	7,095.19
Simon Dyson	73	76	79	68	296	7,095.19
Paul Eales	78	71	75	74	298	6,435.17
Simon Khan	74	74	77	73	298	6,435.17
Ivo Giner	76	73	78	72	299	6,030.16
Neil Manchip	73	76	73	78	300	4,948.50
Alastair Forsyth	72	73	77	78	300	4,948.50
Mark Foster	76	72	76	77	301	4,942.50
Iain Pyman	73	72	79	77	301	4,942.50
Ian Woosnam	75	74	78	75	302	4,938
Martin Erlandsson	71	76	81	78	306	4,933.50
Rolf Muntz	78	70	76	82	306	4,933.50

Barclays Scottish Open

Loch Lomond Golf Club, Glasgow, Scotland
Par 36-35–71; 7,088 yards

July 8-11
purse, €3,305,600

	SCORES				TOTAL	MONEY
Thomas Levet	70	67	69	63	269	€545,208.75
Michael Campbell	70	67	63	70	270	363,472.52
David Howell	70	64	67	70	271	184,174.87
Ernie Els	70	68	65	68	271	184,174.87
Peter Lonard	69	67	66	70	272	101,279.82
Niclas Fasth	70	69	66	67	272	101,279.82
Tim Clark	68	71	68	65	272	101,279.82
Martin Maritz	75	63	69	65	272	101,279.82
Marcus Fraser	67	68	64	73	272	101,279.82
Ian Poulter	67	67	69	70	273	58,638.27
Gregory Havret	69	64	66	74	273	58,638.27
Miguel Angel Jimenez	71	70	67	65	273	58,638.27
Lee Westwood	71	67	70	65	273	58,638.27
Eduardo Romero	65	72	69	68	274	49,069.68
Tom Lehman	67	68	68	71	274	49,069.68
Roger Chapman	69	66	68	72	275	44,162.71
Kenneth Ferrie	67	68	72	68	275	44,162.71
Thomas Bjorn	68	67	68	72	275	44,162.71
Barry Lane	72	69	69	66	276	39,910.01
Phillip Price	65	69	71	71	276	39,910.01
Henrik Stenson	68	71	69	69	277	37,456.52
Wade Ormsby	71	66	73	67	277	37,456.52
Stephen Scahill	70	70	67	71	278	34,512.34
Stephen Gallacher	68	69	72	69	278	34,512.34
Steven O'Hara	73	69	66	70	278	34,512.34
Tim Petrovic	71	66	72	69	278	34,512.34
Mark Roe	67	70	75	67	279	29,114.68

	SCORES				TOTAL	MONEY
Jose Maria Olazabal	71	70	69	69	279	29,114.68
Brian Davis	71	68	71	69	279	29,114.68
Anthony Wall	69	71	68	71	279	29,114.68
Christian Cevaer	67	68	71	73	279	29,114.68
David Lynn	72	69	68	70	279	29,114.68
Graeme McDowell	72	65	70	72	279	29,114.68
Colin Montgomerie	69	68	76	67	280	23,880.58
Nicolas Colsaerts	68	68	75	69	280	23,880.58
Angel Cabrera	74	64	67	75	280	23,880.58
Fredrik Jacobson	74	68	67	71	280	23,880.58
Tetsuji Hiratsuka	70	65	73	72	280	23,880.58
Maarten Lafeber	69	69	72	71	281	19,627.87
Joakim Haeggman	74	66	68	73	281	19,627.87
James Kingston	69	70	69	73	281	19,627.87
Robert Coles	69	73	68	71	281	19,627.87
Andrew Coltart	70	68	70	73	281	19,627.87
Terry Price	68	74	71	68	281	19,627.87
Ben Mason	71	71	69	70	281	19,627.87
Rob Rashell	70	72	69	70	281	19,627.87
Sandy Lyle	71	69	70	72	282	14,066.64
Miguel Ángel Martin	70	68	71	73	282	14,066.64
Ian Woosnam	73	69	68	72	282	14,066.64
Robert-Jan Derksen	69	72	71	70	282	14,066.64
Jose Manuel Lara	65	75	70	72	282	14,066.64
Soren Kjeldsen	71	70	72	69	282	14,066.64
Marcel Siem	69	71	73	69	282	14,066.64
Paul Lawrie	74	68	70	70	282	14,066.64
Raymond Russell	72	68	69	73	282	14,066.64
Peter Lawrie	71	71	70	71	283	10,059.29
Peter Hedblom	67	68	73	75	283	10,059.29
Emanuele Canonica	66	76	69	72	283	10,059.29
Gary Evans	70	70	71	72	283	10,059.29
Philip Golding	67	71	75	71	284	8,832.54
Gary Orr	69	71	73	71	284	8,832.54
Nick Dougherty	69	70	75	70	284	8,832.54
Stephen Dodd	74	67	70	74	285	8,014.72
Matthew Blackey	73	68	74	70	285	8,014.72
Chris Gane	72	68	72	74	286	7,033.32
Julien Clement	73	69	73	71	286	7,033.32
Patrik Sjoland	68	71	75	72	286	7,033.32
Martin Wiegele	73	68	73	72	286	7,033.32
Gordon Brand, Jr.	70	71	73	73	287	6,096.54
Bradley Dredge	70	70	71	76	287	6,096.54
Trevor Immelman	71	71	74	72	288	4,905.50
Peter O'Malley	71	71	72	74	288	4,905.50
Ricky Barnes	72	69	72	76	289	4,901
Damien McGrane	69	71	70	80	290	4,896.50
Ricardo Gonzalez	68	73	75	74	290	4,896.50
Marten Olander	73	68	75	76	292	4,892
Mark Calcavecchia	72	70	74	77	293	4,889

The Open Championship

Royal Troon Golf Club, Ayrshire, Scotland
Par 36-35–71; 7,175 yards

July 15-18
purse, €6,001,690

	SCORES				TOTAL	MONEY
Todd Hamilton	71	67	67	69	274	€1,078,430.41
Ernie Els	69	69	68	68	274	644,062.61
(Hamilton defeated Els, 15 to 16, in four-hole playoff.)						
Phil Mickelson	73	66	68	68	275	411,900.51
Lee Westwood	72	71	68	67	278	314,532.20
Davis Love	72	69	71	67	279	238,902.30
Thomas Levet	66	70	71	72	279	238,902.30
Scott Verplank	69	70	70	71	280	175,993.90
Retief Goosen	69	70	68	73	280	175,993.90
Mike Weir	71	68	71	71	281	134,054.90
Tiger Woods	70	71	68	72	281	134,054.90
Darren Clarke	69	72	73	68	282	103,848.90
Mark Calcavecchia	72	73	69	68	282	103,848.90
Skip Kendall	69	66	75	72	282	103,848.90
Stewart Cink	72	71	71	69	283	84,626.83
Barry Lane	69	68	71	75	283	84,626.83
Joakim Haeggman	69	73	72	70	284	70,397.54
Justin Leonard	70	72	71	71	284	70,397.54
Kenny Perry	69	70	73	72	284	70,397.54
K.J. Choi	68	69	74	73	284	70,397.54
Vijay Singh	68	70	76	71	285	57,066.94
Gary Evans	68	73	73	71	285	57,066.94
Bob Estes	73	72	69	71	285	57,066.94
Paul Casey	66	77	70	72	285	57,066.94
Michael Campbell	67	71	74	73	285	57,066.94
Ian Poulter	71	72	71	72	286	48,304.70
Colin Montgomerie	69	69	72	76	286	48,304.70
Jyoti Randhawa	73	72	70	72	287	43,436.78
Rod Pampling	72	68	74	73	287	43,436.78
Takashi Kamiyama	70	73	71	73	287	43,436.78
Shigeki Maruyama	71	72	74	71	288	36,696.59
David Toms	71	71	74	72	288	36,696.59
Bo Van Pelt	72	71	71	74	288	36,696.59
Keiichiro Fukabori	73	71	70	74	288	36,696.59
Mark O'Meara	71	74	68	75	288	36,696.59
Nick Price	71	71	69	77	288	36,696.59
Steve Lowery	69	73	75	72	289	28,084.13
Tjaart van der Walt	70	73	72	74	289	28,084.13
Tetsuji Hiratsuka	70	74	70	75	289	28,084.13
Stuart Appleby	71	70	73	75	289	28,084.13
Hunter Mahan	74	69	71	75	289	28,084.13
Kim Felton	73	67	72	77	289	28,084.13
Charles Howell	75	70	72	73	290	22,167.74
Adam Scott	73	68	74	75	290	22,167.74
Kenneth Ferrie	68	74	73	75	290	22,167.74
Trevor Immelman	69	74	71	76	290	22,167.74
Andrew Oldcorn	73	70	71	76	290	22,167.74
Alastair Forsyth	68	74	79	70	291	17,920.35
Jerry Kelly	75	70	73	73	291	17,920.35
Mathias Gronberg	70	74	73	74	291	17,920.35
Sean Whiffin	73	72	71	75	291	17,920.35
Miguel Angel Jimenez	74	71	71	75	291	17,920.35
Paul Bradshaw	75	67	72	77	291	17,920.35
Shaun Micheel	70	72	70	79	291	17,920.35

	SCORES				TOTAL	MONEY
Raphael Jacquelin	72	72	73	75	292	15,802
Ignacio Garrido	71	74	72	75	292	15,802
Steve Flesch	75	70	70	77	292	15,802
Paul McGinley	69	76	75	73	293	15,277.76
Carl Pettersson	68	77	74	74	293	15,277.76
James Kingston	73	72	74	74	293	15,277.76
Gary Emerson	70	71	76	77	294	14,828.42
Paul Broadhurst	71	74	72	77	294	14,828.42
Brad Faxon	74	68	73	79	294	14,828.42
Chris DiMarco	71	71	78	76	296	14,453.96
*Stuart Wilson	68	75	77	76	296	
Mark Foster	71	72	76	77	296	14,453.96
Marten Olander	68	74	78	77	297	14,154.40
Rory Sabbatini	71	72	73	81	297	14,154.40
Paul Wesselingh	73	72	76	77	298	13,854.83
Martin Erlandsson	73	70	77	78	298	13,854.83
Bob Tway	76	68	73	82	299	13,630.16
Rich Beem	69	73	77	81	300	13,405.49
Christian Cevaer	70	74	74	82	300	13,405.49
Sandy Lyle	70	73	81	79	303	13,180.82

Out of Final 36 Holes

	SCORES		TOTAL	MONEY
S.K. Ho	72	74	146	4,493.46
Chad Campbell	72	74	146	4,493.46
Jay Haas	70	76	146	4,493.46
Tim Clark	73	73	146	4,493.46
Scott Barr	70	76	146	4,493.46
Jim Furyk	73	73	146	4,493.46
Fredrik Jacobson	75	71	146	4,493.46
Luke Donald	75	71	146	4,493.46
Mathew Goggin	68	78	146	4,493.46
Euan Little	74	72	146	4,493.46
Klas Eriksson	73	73	146	4,493.46
Peter Lonard	76	71	147	3,744.55
Stephen Leaney	73	74	147	3,744.55
Robert Allenby	70	77	147	3,744.55
Jonathan Cheetham	72	75	147	3,744.55
Jean-Francois Remesy	74	73	147	3,744.55
Sven Struver	74	73	147	3,744.55
*Lloyd Campbell	73	74	147	
Grant Muller	73	74	147	3,744.55
Peter O'Malley	77	70	147	3,744.55
Craig Parry	76	71	147	3,744.55
Brendan Jones	71	76	147	3,744.55
Chris Riley	72	75	147	3,744.55
Paul Sheehan	75	72	147	3,744.55
Padraig Harrington	76	71	147	3,744.55
*Steven Tiley	71	76	147	
Glen Day	74	73	147	3,744.55
Barry Hume	72	75	147	3,744.55
John Huston	75	73	148	3,744.55
John Daly	70	78	148	3,744.55
Phillip Price	75	73	148	3,744.55
Arjun Atwal	74	74	148	3,744.55
Tim Herron	72	76	148	3,744.55
Daniel Sugrue	74	74	148	3,744.55
Ben Willman	72	76	148	3,744.55
Maarten Lafeber	74	74	148	3,744.55
*Nick Flanagan	72	76	148	

	SCORES			TOTAL	MONEY
Sergio Garcia	75	73		148	3,744.55
Aaron Baddeley	74	75		149	3,370.10
Miles Tunnicliff	74	75		149	3,370.10
Brian Davis	72	77		149	3,370.10
Greg Norman	73	76		149	3,370.10
Spike McRoy	71	78		149	3,370.10
Ben Curtis	75	74		149	3,370.10
Cameron Beckman	75	74		149	3,370.10
Zach Johnson	73	76		149	3,370.10
Stephen Ames	74	75		149	3,370.10
Matthew Hazelden	79	71		150	3,370.10
Anders Hansen	76	74		150	3,370.10
Simon Wakefield	73	77		150	3,370.10
Richard Green	74	76		150	3,370.10
Jonathan Kaye	74	76		150	3,370.10
Hidemasa Hoshino	76	74		150	3,370.10
Simon Dyson	75	76		151	3,370.10
Peter Hedblom	78	73		151	3,370.10
Tom Lehman	73	78		151	3,370.10
Craig Perks	74	77		151	3,370.10
Hennie Otto	74	77		151	3,370.10
Darren Fichardt	71	80		151	3,370.10
Eduardo Romero	77	75		152	2,995.64
*Brian McElhinney	76	76		152	
Scott Drummond	73	79		152	2,995.64
Graeme McDowell	79	73		152	2,995.64
Nick Faldo	76	77		153	2,995.64
David Griffiths	75	78		153	2,995.64
Thomas Bjorn	74	79		153	2,995.64
Jimmy Green	78	75		153	2,995.64
David Howell	78	76		154	2,995.64
Nicolas Colsaerts	77	77		154	2,995.64
Frank Lickliter	77	77		154	2,995.64
Dinesh Chand	80	74		154	2,995.64
Paul Lawrie	78	77		155	2,995.64
Louis Oosthuizen	74	82		156	2,995.64
Andrew Willey	80	76		156	2,995.64
Ian Spencer	79	78		157	2,995.64
Adam Le Vesconte	77	80		157	2,995.64
Andrew Buckle	76	82		158	2,995.64
Yoshinobu Tsukada	79	80		159	2,995.64
Tom Weiskopf	80	80		160	2,995.64
Brett Taylor	86	75		161	2,995.64
Neil Evans	85	78		163	2,995.64
Lewis Atkinson	79	85		164	2,995.64
Anthony Millar	78	86		164	2,995.64

Nissan Irish Open

County Louth Golf Club, Baltray, Ireland
Par 37-35–72; 7,031 yards

July 22-25
purse, €1,900,000

	SCORES				TOTAL	MONEY
Brett Rumford	66	71	70	67	274	€316,660
Padraig Harrington	70	70	71	67	278	165,025
Raphael Jacquelin	69	68	74	67	278	165,025
Peter Lonard	64	70	72	73	279	95,000

	SCORES			TOTAL	MONEY
Andrew Oldcorn	71	69	71	69	280	68,020
Paul Broadhurst	73	67	70	70	280	68,020
Paul McGinley	73	71	66	70	280	68,020
Peter Fowler	70	72	69	70	281	42,686.67
Nick O'Hern	64	74	72	71	281	42,686.67
Peter Baker	70	72	69	70	281	42,686.67
Sandy Lyle	67	74	71	70	282	30,336.67
Peter O'Malley	69	69	74	70	282	30,336.67
Gary Evans	77	66	72	67	282	30,336.67
James Kingston	68	68	72	74	282	30,336.67
Stephen Gallacher	66	70	75	71	282	30,336.67
Graeme McDowell	73	69	70	70	282	30,336.67
Miguel Angel Martin	70	68	74	71	283	23,712
Cesar Monasterio	70	73	73	67	283	23,712
Henrik Stenson	69	70	73	71	283	23,712
David Carter	70	70	70	73	283	23,712
Louis Oosthuizen	68	73	74	68	283	23,712
Niclas Fasth	70	71	72	71	284	20,615
Michael Campbell	70	72	73	69	284	20,615
Luke Donald	71	71	71	71	284	20,615
Robert Rock	72	70	72	70	284	20,615
Gary Murphy	71	73	71	70	285	18,050
Steve Webster	67	70	74	74	285	18,050
Anthony Wall	70	72	72	71	285	18,050
Soren Hansen	69	73	74	69	285	18,050
Julien Clement	70	71	69	75	285	18,050
Roger Chapman	69	68	74	75	286	14,582.50
Mark Roe	67	75	72	72	286	14,582.50
Robert-Jan Derksen	67	70	77	72	286	14,582.50
Peter Lawrie	67	73	75	71	286	14,582.50
Trevor Immelman	72	68	72	74	286	14,582.50
Miguel Angel Jimenez	73	69	69	75	286	14,582.50
Christian Cevaer	68	70	78	70	286	14,582.50
John Bickerton	71	73	69	73	286	14,582.50
Ian Woosnam	76	67	73	71	287	11,020
Jose Manuel Lara	70	70	74	73	287	11,020
Damien McGrane	71	71	73	72	287	11,020
Jean-Francois Lucquin	69	72	72	74	287	11,020
Stephen Dodd	69	69	76	73	287	11,020
Jorge Berendt	72	69	73	73	287	11,020
David Park	71	70	72	74	287	11,020
David Higgins	68	73	72	74	287	11,020
Terry Price	72	67	71	77	287	11,020
Wade Ormsby	68	75	71	73	287	11,020
Bradley Dredge	71	71	75	71	288	8,360
John Dwyer	72	71	71	74	288	8,360
Mikko Ilonen	71	71	73	73	288	8,360
Simon Dyson	72	71	73	72	288	8,360
Johan Edfors	73	71	74	71	289	6,840
Fredrik Andersson Hed	67	72	79	71	289	6,840
Nick Dougherty	71	72	72	74	289	6,840
Richard Sterne	70	73	74	72	289	6,840
Raymond Russell	70	73	74	73	290	5,890
Jamie Spence	73	71	75	72	291	5,225
Carlos Rodiles	71	72	71	77	291	5,225
Robert Karlsson	68	74	75	74	291	5,225
Iain Pyman	72	71	77	71	291	5,225
Michael Jonzon	74	70	73	74	291	5,225
Alastair Forsyth	73	71	73	74	291	5,225
Soren Kjeldsen	71	71	74	76	292	4,180

	SCORES				TOTAL	MONEY
Stuart Little	71	72	76	73	292	4,180
Darren Clarke	70	71	78	73	292	4,180
Christopher Hanell	70	71	78	73	292	4,180
Ben Mason	69	71	78	74	292	4,180
Gordon Brand, Jr.	70	73	76	74	293	3,540
Mark Foster	72	70	78	73	293	3,540
Ivo Giner	72	72	78	73	295	2,850
Martin Maritz	71	71	81	74	297	2,847
Nick Flanagan	70	70	79	79	298	2,844
Jean-Francois Remesy	72	70	79	82	303	2,841

Scandinavian Masters

Barseback Golf & Country Club, Malmo, Sweden
Par 36-36–72; 7,365 yards

July 29-August 1
purse, €1,600,000

	SCORES				TOTAL	MONEY
Luke Donald	69	65	69	69	272	€266,660
Peter Hanson	72	66	68	71	277	138,965
Henrik Stenson	68	70	70	69	277	138,965
Ian Poulter	72	68	74	65	279	73,920
Colin Montgomerie	72	68	72	67	279	73,920
David Lynn	72	68	69	71	280	56,000
Simon Khan	70	69	72	70	281	48,000
David Howell	67	71	74	70	282	30,720
Jesper Parnevik	69	70	71	72	282	30,720
Steve Webster	68	74	68	72	282	30,720
Peter Lawrie	72	74	72	64	282	30,720
Marcel Siem	71	74	69	68	282	30,720
Niclas Fasth	71	71	70	70	282	30,720
Adam Scott	72	71	70	69	282	30,720
Stephen Scahill	72	73	67	71	283	21,632
Markus Brier	70	71	71	71	283	21,632
Raymond Russell	72	72	68	71	283	21,632
Charl Schwartzel	73	69	69	72	283	21,632
Ross Fisher	71	71	70	71	283	21,632
Nick Faldo	71	72	69	72	284	18,360
Carlos Rodiles	71	69	71	73	284	18,360
Soren Hansen	69	71	73	71	284	18,360
Paul McGinley	69	68	74	73	284	18,360
Peter Fowler	73	69	70	73	285	15,680
Thomas Levet	69	71	72	73	285	15,680
Jorge Berendt	75	68	70	72	285	15,680
Greg Owen	71	75	68	71	285	15,680
Simon Wakefield	72	70	71	72	285	15,680
Christopher Hanell	68	69	74	74	285	15,680
Wilhelm Schauman	68	67	75	75	285	15,680
Damien McGrane	72	72	70	72	286	12,832
Soren Kjeldsen	73	67	74	72	286	12,832
Jean-Francois Lucquin	70	73	69	74	286	12,832
Peter Hedblom	71	70	73	72	286	12,832
Steven O'Hara	72	71	67	76	286	12,832
Sven Struver	73	73	69	72	287	10,880
Jesus Maria Arruti	70	72	72	73	287	10,880
Stephen Dodd	71	72	73	71	287	10,880
Pierre Fulke	71	70	73	73	287	10,880
Robert Coles	71	71	69	76	287	10,880

	SCORES				TOTAL	MONEY
Graeme McDowell	70	74	70	73	287	10,880
Jose Manuel Lara	76	70	71	71	288	9,120
Raphael Jacquelin	72	70	72	74	288	9,120
Nick O'Hern	73	69	80	66	288	9,120
Jamie Spence	74	72	70	72	288	9,120
Chris Gane	68	73	77	70	288	9,120
Ian Woosnam	72	73	70	74	289	7,360
Mark Foster	74	71	73	71	289	7,360
Paul Broadhurst	72	73	77	67	289	7,360
Robert Karlsson	75	70	69	75	289	7,360
Fernando Roca	71	75	73	70	289	7,360
Peter Gustafsson	72	73	74	70	289	7,360
Miguel Angel Martin	70	74	74	72	290	5,040
Costantino Rocca	71	72	76	71	290	5,040
Mark Roe	74	70	72	74	290	5,040
Johan Axgren	72	72	75	71	290	5,040
Peter Baker	74	71	76	69	290	5,040
Johan Skold	77	69	71	73	290	5,040
Andrew Coltart	70	72	74	74	290	5,040
Iain Pyman	75	70	68	77	290	5,040
Sebastian Fernandez	69	74	73	74	290	5,040
Philippe Lima	76	69	76	69	290	5,040
Richard Green	74	71	74	72	291	3,840
Scott Drummond	74	71	72	74	291	3,840
Wade Ormsby	76	70	75	70	291	3,840
Martin Erlandsson	73	72	78	69	292	3,520
Johan Edfors	67	71	75	80	293	3,360
Matthew Blackey	72	72	75	75	294	3,200
Tony Johnstone	73	72	76	75	296	2,790
Andrew Oldcorn	72	74	78	72	296	2,790
Gregory Havret	70	74	77	75	296	2,790
Henrik Nystrom	73	73	73	78	297	2,397
Rolf Muntz	72	74	76	77	299	2,394

KLM Open

Hilversumsche Golf Club, Hilversum, Netherlands
Par 35-35–70; 6,660 yards

August 5-8
purse, €1,200,000

	SCORES				TOTAL	MONEY
David Lynn	63	70	65	66	264	€200,000
Richard Green	65	63	67	72	267	104,225
Paul McGinley	65	69	68	65	267	104,225
Miles Tunnicliff	67	66	71	67	271	55,440
Andrew Raitt	64	67	71	69	271	55,440
Andrew Marshall	69	68	65	70	272	39,000
Paul Marantz	69	72	65	66	272	39,000
Per Nyman	66	67	70	70	273	30,000
Graeme McDowell	69	67	71	67	274	26,880
Ian Poulter	67	67	71	70	275	22,240
Stephen Scahill	65	71	67	72	275	22,240
Christopher Hanell	70	67	70	68	275	22,240
Steven O'Hara	69	67	72	68	276	19,320
Miguel Angel Martin	68	66	73	70	277	17,280
Jose Manuel Lara	70	69	68	70	277	17,280
Jamie Spence	70	71	69	67	277	17,280
Andrew Coltart	68	68	70	71	277	17,280

	SCORES				TOTAL	MONEY
David Howell	70	70	71	67	278	13,464
Kalle Brink	69	68	70	71	278	13,464
Marten Olander	68	71	68	71	278	13,464
Cesar Monasterio	69	71	66	72	278	13,464
David Park	67	72	70	69	278	13,464
Markus Brier	71	68	68	71	278	13,464
Patrik Sjoland	66	73	74	65	278	13,464
Mads Vibe-Hastrup	69	69	72	68	278	13,464
Fredrik Widmark	74	67	68	69	278	13,464
Craig Williams	69	68	70	71	278	13,464
Mark Roe	69	67	73	70	279	10,320
Robert-Jan Derksen	70	72	68	69	279	10,320
Peter Hanson	72	68	70	69	279	10,320
Peter Lawrie	73	66	71	69	279	10,320
Greg Owen	70	70	69	70	279	10,320
Michael Jonzon	70	70	69	70	279	10,320
David Dixon	67	70	72	70	279	10,320
Andrew Oldcorn	71	66	67	76	280	8,160
Costantino Rocca	70	67	70	73	280	8,160
Diego Borrego	68	71	70	71	280	8,160
James Hepworth	70	70	70	70	280	8,160
Jarmo Sandelin	68	69	71	72	280	8,160
Nick Dougherty	72	67	71	70	280	8,160
Tom Whitehouse	68	70	71	71	280	8,160
Rob Rashell	75	67	68	70	280	8,160
Marc Farry	73	66	71	71	281	6,120
Damien McGrane	70	69	67	75	281	6,120
Anders Hansen	77	65	73	66	281	6,120
Nicolas Colsaerts	68	72	69	72	281	6,120
Simon Khan	71	69	71	70	281	6,120
Simon Wakefield	68	73	69	71	281	6,120
Raymond Russell	66	71	69	75	281	6,120
Richard Sterne	69	71	68	73	281	6,120
Philippe Lima	72	69	70	70	281	6,120
Gordon Brand, Jr.	68	67	76	71	282	4,125
Gary Emerson	71	71	65	75	282	4,125
Rolf Muntz	69	73	72	68	282	4,125
Fredrik Andersson Hed	69	71	69	73	282	4,125
Matthew Blackey	73	68	70	71	282	4,125
Martin Wiegele	65	71	72	74	282	4,125
Guido Van Der Valk	74	68	73	67	282	4,125
Ross Fisher	69	68	70	75	282	4,125
Anthony Wall	70	70	68	75	283	3,060
Carlos Rodiles	69	72	65	77	283	3,060
Paul Eales	71	71	69	72	283	3,060
Bradley Dredge	73	67	71	72	283	3,060
Robert Rock	72	67	69	75	283	3,060
Simon Dyson	69	73	71	70	283	3,060
Stuart Little	74	67	71	72	284	2,305
Jean-Francois Lucquin	72	69	75	68	284	2,305
Russell Claydon	70	72	72	70	284	2,305
Ignacio Garrido	69	68	70	77	284	2,305
Sebastian Fernandez	70	69	69	76	284	2,305
Mark Reynolds	71	68	70	75	284	2,305
Euan Little	71	71	70	74	286	1,797
Pasi Purhonen	71	71	72	73	287	1,792.50
Daniel Gaunt	69	71	72	75	287	1,792.50
Steven Jeppesen	69	72	73	74	288	1,788
*James Heath	72	70	72	74	288	
David Carter	70	72	70	77	289	1,785

	SCORES				TOTAL	MONEY
*Edward De Jong	74	68	74	73	289	
Alan McLean	74	68	72	76	290	1,782
Gary Orr	69	69	80	74	292	1,779

BMW Russian Open

Le Meridien Moscow Country Club, Moscow, Russia

Par 36-36–72; 7,074 yards

August 12-15

purse, €407,433

	SCORES				TOTAL	MONEY
Gary Emerson	71	65	68	68	272	€67,902.73
Markus Brier	69	66	70	69	274	45,265.77
Kyron Sullivan	68	72	67	68	275	25,505.29
Mattias Eliasson	69	67	73	67	276	20,371.63
Henrik Nystrom	68	66	73	70	277	17,275.15
Philip Archer	68	70	75	65	278	13,241.56
Gregory Bourdy	71	69	68	70	278	13,241.56
Nick Dougherty	71	70	70	68	279	9,153.65
Chris Gane	73	67	70	69	279	9,153.65
Alessandro Tadini	72	70	70	67	279	9,153.65
Kariem Baraka	63	71	70	76	280	7,021.42
Oskar Bergman	70	68	73	69	280	7,021.42
Mikael Lundberg	67	71	70	72	280	7,021.42
David Griffiths	68	68	71	74	281	6,111.49
Johan Skold	69	73	69	70	281	6,111.49
Alex Balicki	69	67	74	72	282	5,031.79
Jorge Berendt	70	72	71	69	282	5,031.79
Matthew King	67	70	73	72	282	5,031.79
Gareth Paddison	69	73	73	67	282	5,031.79
Gustavo Rojas	71	70	73	68	282	5,031.79
Jamie Spence	69	72	71	70	282	5,031.79
Benoit Teilleria	69	70	73	70	282	5,031.79
Craig Williams	71	68	74	69	282	5,031.79
John Mellor	75	67	73	68	283	4,115.07
Alvaro Salto	68	68	75	72	283	4,115.07
Lee Slattery	71	67	74	71	283	4,115.07
Tom Whitehouse	72	68	72	71	283	4,115.07
Oliver Wilson	69	69	75	70	283	4,115.07
Magnus Persson Atlevi	69	71	72	72	284	3,286.62
Peter Baker	69	69	73	73	284	3,286.62
Stuart Davis	68	71	73	72	284	3,286.62
Steven Jeppesen	69	73	71	71	284	3,286.62
Roope Kakko	70	66	71	77	284	3,286.62
Wade Ormsby	71	69	72	72	284	3,286.62
David Ryles	70	70	73	71	284	3,286.62
Jarmo Sandelin	69	70	70	75	284	3,286.62
Leif Westerberg	69	72	70	73	284	3,286.62
Johan Axgren	71	68	75	71	285	2,607.57
Richard Bland	73	66	73	73	285	2,607.57
Paul Eales	71	70	72	72	285	2,607.57
Marc Pendaries	68	70	73	74	285	2,607.57
Graeme Storm	68	71	75	71	285	2,607.57
Carl Suneson	70	72	72	71	285	2,607.57
David Dixon	72	68	76	70	286	2,240.88
Jamie Elson	68	73	74	71	286	2,240.88
Sven Struver	68	73	73	72	286	2,240.88
Lee S. James	73	69	72	73	287	1,996.42

	SCORES				TOTAL	MONEY
Jean-Francois Lucquin	72	68	74	73	287	1,996.42
Iain Pyman	69	72	74	72	287	1,996.42
Sion Bebb	70	70	75	73	288	1,711.22
Andrew Coltart	69	71	75	73	288	1,711.22
Cesar Monasterio	69	73	74	72	288	1,711.22
Martin Wiegele	65	75	74	74	288	1,711.22
Neil Cheetham	73	69	73	74	289	1,385.27
Matthew Cort	67	73	75	74	289	1,385.27
Mattias Nilsson	72	70	73	74	289	1,385.27
Erol Simsek	71	69	73	76	289	1,385.27
Stephen Browne	74	67	72	77	290	1,201.93
Fernando Roca	72	67	78	73	290	1,201.93
Graham Gordon	69	73	75	74	291	1,100.07
Allan Hogh	71	70	74	76	291	1,100.07
Euan Little	67	68	77	79	291	1,100.07
Ivo Giner	72	69	77	74	292	957.47
Ben Mason	70	71	76	75	292	957.47
Tim Milford	70	71	76	75	292	957.47
Van Phillips	71	70	76	75	292	957.47
Jan-Are Larsen	69	71	81	72	293	835.24
Mark Mouland	71	71	73	78	293	835.24
Alan Mclean	70	71	78	75	294	774.12
Tony Edlund	71	71	79	74	295	749.68

BMW International Open

Golfclub Munchen Nord-Eichenreid, Munich, Germany
Par 36-36–72; 6,957 yards

August 26-29
purse, €1,800,000

	SCORES				TOTAL	MONEY
Miguel Angel Jimenez	68	66	67	66	267	€300,000
Thomas Levet	73	65	63	68	269	200,000
Colin Montgomerie	67	70	67	68	272	93,000
Alex Cejka	68	70	69	65	272	93,000
Paul Casey	69	69	69	65	272	93,000
Paul McGinley	70	68	67	68	273	47,664
Darren Clarke	72	68	68	65	273	47,664
Fredrik Jacobson	71	65	68	69	273	47,664
David Lynn	67	68	69	69	273	47,664
Retief Goosen	66	69	68	70	273	47,664
Soren Kjeldsen	70	67	69	68	274	29,412
Joakim Haeggman	69	70	70	65	274	29,412
Andrew Raitt	73	69	65	67	274	29,412
John Daly	67	70	72	65	274	29,412
Tino Schuster	70	68	68	68	274	29,412
Markus Brier	71	65	67	72	275	23,805
Lee Westwood	72	68	66	69	275	23,805
Graeme McDowell	72	72	69	62	275	23,805
Sebastian Fernandez	71	68	67	69	275	23,805
Peter Fowler	73	67	64	72	276	21,240
Luke Donald	68	71	68	69	276	21,240
David Howell	73	68	67	69	277	19,800
Raphael Jacquelin	68	72	71	66	277	19,800
Nick O'Hern	71	73	67	66	277	19,800
Sergio Garcia	71	69	70	68	278	18,180
Damien McGrane	73	70	67	68	278	18,180
Ian Poulter	73	66	69	70	278	18,180

	SCORES				TOTAL	MONEY
Miguel Angel Martin	72	69	68	70	279	16,020
Gary Murphy	71	72	70	66	279	16,020
Anders Hansen	72	65	73	69	279	16,020
Jean-Francois Lucquin	69	72	68	70	279	16,020
Emanuele Canonica	69	73	68	69	279	16,020
Robert-Jan Derksen	73	69	68	70	280	12,982.50
Mark Foster	69	72	71	68	280	12,982.50
Marten Olander	74	69	69	68	280	12,982.50
Henrik Stenson	69	69	76	66	280	12,982.50
Paul Broadhurst	70	72	71	67	280	12,982.50
Jonathan Lomas	73	71	66	70	280	12,982.50
Greg Owen	73	71	68	68	280	12,982.50
Ivo Giner	69	69	72	70	280	12,982.50
Klas Eriksson	72	71	67	71	281	10,800
Bradley Dredge	71	66	72	72	281	10,800
David Park	70	71	69	71	281	10,800
Alastair Forsyth	74	68	71	68	281	10,800
Mark Roe	71	67	71	73	282	9,180
Martin Erlandsson	72	69	69	72	282	9,180
Nobuhito Sato	72	69	69	72	282	9,180
Robert Coles	72	72	67	71	282	9,180
David Carter	73	71	67	71	282	9,180
Sven Struver	70	71	70	72	283	6,840
Anthony Wall	73	69	74	67	283	6,840
Jamie Spence	69	71	69	74	283	6,840
Miles Tunnicliff	75	65	74	69	283	6,840
Peter O'Malley	67	72	72	72	283	6,840
Pierre Fulke	74	67	69	73	283	6,840
Nick Dougherty	76	67	73	67	283	6,840
Charl Schwartzel	73	69	70	71	283	6,840
Hennie Otto	74	70	74	66	284	4,770
Thomas Gogele	73	69	70	72	284	4,770
Stephen Scahill	72	72	73	67	284	4,770
Simon Khan	72	72	72	68	284	4,770
Raymond Russell	73	70	70	71	284	4,770
Matthew Blackey	72	71	68	73	284	4,770
Stephen Gallacher	72	68	73	71	284	4,770
Steven O'Hara	73	70	72	69	284	4,770
Gary Emerson	71	73	71	70	285	3,870
Patrik Sjoland	69	73	73	70	285	3,870
Robert Karlsson	71	73	71	71	286	3,433.33
Ben Mason	73	71	73	69	286	3,433.33
Marcus Fraser	71	72	72	71	286	3,433.33
Andrew Oldcorn	74	67	74	72	287	2,695.50
Johan Edfors	69	69	75	74	287	2,695.50
Jarmo Sandelin	71	69	74	73	287	2,695.50
Rob Rashell	73	70	72	72	287	2,695.50
Andrew Marshall	71	73	73	71	288	2,685
Marcel Siem	74	70	70	74	288	2,685
Peter Hedblom	72	72	69	75	288	2,685
Michael Jonzon	68	76	70	75	289	2,679
Simon Dyson	70	74	74	72	290	2,676
Darren Fichardt	73	69	75	74	291	2,671.50
Carlos Rodiles	70	68	78	75	291	2,671.50
Marcel Haremza	74	68	78	74	294	2,665.50
Nicolas Colsaerts	72	72	72	78	294	2,665.50

Omega European Masters

Crans-sur-Sierre Golf Club, Crans Montana, Switzerland
Par 36-35–71; 6,808 yards

September 2-5
purse, €1,600,000

	SCORES				TOTAL	MONEY
Luke Donald	67	67	65	66	265	€266,660
Miguel Angel Jimenez	65	67	66	72	270	177,770
Eduardo Romero	68	67	67	69	271	82,666.66
Sergio Garcia	66	65	68	72	271	82,666.66
Robert Coles	70	68	69	64	271	82,666.66
Graeme McDowell	69	67	66	70	272	56,000
Ernie Els	69	67	66	71	273	48,000
K.J. Choi	76	65	66	67	274	37,920
Carlos Rodiles	67	69	72	66	274	37,920
Darren Fichardt	69	67	69	71	276	29,653.33
Peter O'Malley	72	65	71	68	276	29,653.33
Stephen Scahill	70	68	72	66	276	29,653.33
Craig Spence	69	67	66	75	277	24,586.67
Angel Cabrera	67	73	68	69	277	24,586.67
James Kingston	68	69	71	69	277	24,586.67
Mark Roe	72	69	68	69	278	21,160
Peter Fowler	67	68	71	72	278	21,160
Simon Dyson	68	68	74	68	278	21,160
Charl Schwartzel	68	66	71	73	278	21,160
Anthony Wall	70	72	67	70	279	18,360
Andrew Marshall	72	65	73	69	279	18,360
Bradley Dredge	69	68	72	70	279	18,360
Robert Rock	71	70	70	68	279	18,360
Miguel Angel Martin	69	70	72	69	280	16,880
Wade Ormsby	68	70	71	71	280	16,880
Robert-Jan Derksen	71	70	71	69	281	14,240
Marc Farry	66	70	71	74	281	14,240
Paul Broadhurst	68	71	71	71	281	14,240
Stuart Little	71	69	68	73	281	14,240
Soren Hansen	74	67	71	69	281	14,240
Johan Edfors	74	69	69	69	281	14,240
Per Nyman	70	71	71	69	281	14,240
Miles Tunnicliff	73	68	74	66	281	14,240
Thomas Bjorn	72	69	70	70	281	14,240
Maarten Lafeber	68	69	72	73	282	11,840
Matthew Blackey	70	69	72	71	282	11,840
Sven Struver	70	68	70	75	283	10,560
Peter Baker	66	73	74	70	283	10,560
Ricardo Gonzalez	76	67	71	69	283	10,560
Patrik Sjoland	74	69	70	70	283	10,560
Ivo Giner	71	70	72	70	283	10,560
Sebastian Fernandez	72	69	72	70	283	10,560
David Gilford	72	68	71	73	284	9,120
Philip Golding	70	70	71	73	284	9,120
Steven O'Hara	67	73	74	70	284	9,120
Mark Foster	70	73	72	70	285	7,040
Brian Davis	70	71	71	73	285	7,040
Jamie Spence	68	71	72	74	285	7,040
Marc Chatelain	73	69	70	73	285	7,040
Jesus Maria Arruti	68	74	69	74	285	7,040
Christian Cevaer	68	71	75	71	285	7,040
Paul Lawrie	70	71	71	73	285	7,040
Jarmo Sandelin	70	72	70	73	285	7,040
Iain Pyman	74	69	75	67	285	7,040

	SCORES				TOTAL	MONEY
John Bickerton	72	70	72	71	285	7,040
Simon Wakefield	67	73	70	76	286	4,920
Michael Campbell	70	69	75	72	286	4,920
Nick Dougherty	75	68	71	72	286	4,920
Brett Rumford	71	72	73	70	286	4,920
Gordon Brand, Jr.	72	70	73	72	287	4,080
Roger Chapman	71	65	72	79	287	4,080
Jose Manuel Lara	73	69	71	74	287	4,080
Hennie Otto	71	72	71	73	287	4,080
Diego Borrego	70	73	73	71	287	4,080
Fredrik Andersson Hed	70	68	72	77	287	4,080
Sandy Lyle	70	72	73	73	288	3,440
Peter Lawrie	71	71	73	73	288	3,440
Richard McEvoy	72	66	73	78	289	3,200
Cesar Monasterio	68	74	73	75	290	2,985
*Nicolas Sulzer	71	72	73	74	290	
Peter Hedblom	66	76	76	72	290	2,985
Jeev Milkha Singh	71	72	76	72	291	2,398.50
Tom Whitehouse	72	69	75	75	291	2,398.50
Thongchai Jaidee	73	70	73	76	292	2,392.50
David Dixon	73	69	73	77	292	2,392.50
Dean Robertson	70	73	76	74	293	2,388
Gary Orr	69	73	75	77	294	2,385
Daniel Gaunt	72	69	74	80	295	2,382
Francois Delamontagne	71	72	80	74	297	2,379

Linde German Masters

Gut Larchenhof, Cologne, Germany
Par 36-36—72; 7,289 yards

September 9-12
purse, €3,000,000

	SCORES				TOTAL	MONEY
Padraig Harrington	66	75	64	70	275	€500,000
Nick O'Hern	68	68	72	70	278	333,330
Raphael Jacquelin	68	68	70	73	279	168,900
Graeme McDowell	69	64	69	77	279	168,900
Alex Cejka	67	70	71	72	280	127,200
Richard Green	68	68	73	74	283	90,000
Nick Dougherty	72	71	71	69	283	90,000
Paul Casey	68	72	67	76	283	90,000
Kenneth Ferrie	73	71	72	68	284	67,200
Trevor Immelman	70	73	71	71	285	57,600
Alastair Forsyth	70	71	73	71	285	57,600
Jose Maria Olazabal	69	74	69	74	286	46,440
Thomas Levet	70	68	74	74	286	46,440
Joakim Haeggman	72	71	71	72	286	46,440
Stephen Dodd	72	71	70	73	286	46,440
Rolf Muntz	69	73	72	72	286	46,440
Klas Eriksson	71	74	71	71	287	36,850
Robert-Jan Derksen	70	69	73	75	287	36,850
Ricardo Gonzalez	77	70	71	69	287	36,850
Darren Clarke	71	70	71	75	287	36,850
Greg Owen	68	71	74	74	287	36,850
Markus Brier	73	72	70	72	287	36,850
Brian Davis	73	69	70	76	288	31,650
Thomas Gogele	71	76	72	69	288	31,650
Simon Khan	74	71	66	77	288	31,650

	SCORES				TOTAL	MONEY
Philippe Lima	75	69	73	71	288	31,650
Mark Roe	75	70	70	74	289	25,063.64
Jean-Francois Remesy	74	71	69	75	289	25,063.64
Steve Webster	73	70	70	76	289	25,063.64
Jamie Spence	73	73	74	69	289	25,063.64
Gregory Havret	72	73	70	74	289	25,063.64
Miles Tunnicliff	76	71	72	70	289	25,063.64
Peter O'Malley	71	69	75	74	289	25,063.64
Phillip Price	73	72	70	74	289	25,063.64
Angel Cabrera	70	75	71	73	289	25,063.64
Bradley Dredge	75	68	71	75	289	25,063.64
Brett Rumford	71	73	72	73	289	25,063.64
Miguel Angel Jimenez	75	69	73	73	290	20,400
Niclas Fasth	73	71	71	75	290	20,400
Anders Hansen	72	72	73	74	291	17,700
Soren Hansen	71	74	71	75	291	17,700
Jarrod Moseley	72	73	72	74	291	17,700
Thomas Bjorn	74	70	75	72	291	17,700
Gary Orr	71	73	73	74	291	17,700
Louis Oosthuizen	68	76	74	73	291	17,700
Marcus Fraser	73	72	73	73	291	17,700
Marten Olander	75	72	69	76	292	14,100
Alessandro Tadini	76	71	72	73	292	14,100
Peter Baker	73	73	72	74	292	14,100
Christian Cevaer	72	72	73	75	292	14,100
Michael Campbell	72	72	74	74	292	14,100
Eduardo Romero	75	72	76	70	293	11,700
Barry Lane	69	78	70	76	293	11,700
Anthony Wall	69	76	77	71	293	11,700
K.J. Choi	71	75	69	79	294	10,500
Sandy Lyle	78	69	74	74	295	9,060
Peter Hedblom	72	75	73	75	295	9,060
Diego Borrego	73	70	75	77	295	9,060
Robert Rock	72	70	74	79	295	9,060
Martin Maritz	74	72	73	76	295	9,060
Gary Murphy	69	78	71	78	296	7,800
Gary Emerson	73	72	70	81	296	7,800
Ignacio Garrido	73	74	73	76	296	7,800
Carlos Rodiles	74	72	75	76	297	7,050
James Kingston	75	72	71	79	297	7,050
Pierre Fulke	74	73	73	78	298	6,300
Raymond Russell	71	70	74	83	298	6,300
Erol Simsek	71	73	76	78	298	6,300
Marcel Siem	72	75	81	72	300	5,700
Marc Farry	70	76	72	83	301	5,470
David Geall	70	73	77	84	304	4,500
Andrew Oldcorn	73	72	80	80	305	4,497

Ryder Cup

See American Tours chapter.

The Heritage

Woburn Golf & Country Club, Duke's Course,
Buckinghamshire, England
Par 34-38–72; 6,979 yards

September 23-26
purse, €2,000,000

	SCORES				TOTAL	MONEY
Henrik Stenson	69	67	67	66	269	€333,330
Carlos Rodiles	70	71	67	65	273	222,220
Patrik Sjoland	68	68	68	71	275	125,200
Anders Hansen	72	68	71	65	276	100,000
Barry Lane	71	67	72	67	277	66,200
Stephen Dodd	76	68	67	66	277	66,200
Phillip Price	68	67	72	70	277	66,200
Simon Wakefield	70	68	67	72	277	66,200
Ian Woosnam	71	69	68	70	278	37,640
Gary Murphy	71	73	70	64	278	37,640
Nick O'Hern	67	72	71	68	278	37,640
Mikko Ilonen	70	71	65	72	278	37,640
Alastair Forsyth	73	68	66	71	278	37,640
Graeme McDowell	67	68	72	72	279	30,600
David Lynn	73	70	70	67	280	28,800
Retief Goosen	70	72	67	71	280	28,800
David Howell	71	70	73	67	281	24,566.67
Mark Foster	69	69	69	74	281	24,566.67
Jean-Francois Remesy	71	70	72	68	281	24,566.67
Nicolas Colsaerts	74	71	70	66	281	24,566.67
Bradley Dredge	70	74	66	71	281	24,566.67
Nick Dougherty	68	73	69	71	281	24,566.67
Gordon Brand, Jr.	70	70	71	71	282	20,500
Jose Manuel Lara	67	73	73	69	282	20,500
Sven Struver	75	69	67	71	282	20,500
Jean-Francois Lucquin	69	75	71	67	282	20,500
Jamie Elson	69	71	75	67	282	20,500
Marcus Fraser	70	69	70	73	282	20,500
Peter Senior	71	73	71	68	283	16,628.57
Raphael Jacquelin	68	73	72	70	283	16,628.57
Richard Green	73	70	70	70	283	16,628.57
Martin Erlandsson	70	70	70	73	283	16,628.57
Soren Hansen	70	71	72	70	283	16,628.57
Jarrod Moseley	68	75	71	69	283	16,628.57
David Park	71	70	69	73	283	16,628.57
*James Heath	73	70	70	70	283	
Miguel Angel Martin	73	69	75	67	284	14,400
Padraig Harrington	72	71	71	70	284	14,400
Klas Eriksson	69	71	75	70	285	12,800
David Gilford	73	68	74	70	285	12,800
Soren Kjeldsen	72	73	70	70	285	12,800
Jorge Berendt	74	69	71	71	285	12,800
Fredrik Andersson Hed	76	67	73	69	285	12,800
Martin Maritz	71	71	73	70	285	12,800
Sam Torrance	74	69	69	74	286	10,400
Peter Lawrie	72	72	74	68	286	10,400
Philip Golding	73	71	73	69	286	10,400
Raymond Russell	68	74	76	68	286	10,400
Sebastian Fernandez	73	68	75	70	286	10,400
Casey Wittenberg	73	70	71	72	286	10,400
Gary Emerson	73	69	72	73	287	7,800
Mattias Nilsson	70	70	73	74	287	7,800
Miles Tunnicliff	74	69	77	67	287	7,800

	SCORES				TOTAL	MONEY
Jonathan Lomas	72	73	74	68	287	7,800
Rolf Muntz	75	69	72	71	287	7,800
Stephen Gallacher	75	69	73	70	287	7,800
Robert Rock	73	70	77	67	287	7,800
Robert Karlsson	72	72	73	71	288	6,100
Jarmo Sandelin	74	70	71	73	288	6,100
Andrew Marshall	71	72	73	73	289	5,600
Gary Orr	75	70	72	72	289	5,600
Paul Lawrie	72	73	75	69	289	5,600
Jesus Maria Arruti	75	70	73	72	290	5,100
Ignacio Garrido	71	70	73	76	290	5,100
Roger Chapman	69	73	75	74	291	4,400
Robert-Jan Derksen	76	69	75	71	291	4,400
Kenneth Ferrie	72	73	72	74	291	4,400
Trevor Immelman	73	70	74	74	291	4,400
Ross Fisher	74	71	71	75	291	4,400
Michael Campbell	72	73	75	86	306	3,800

WGC - American Express Championship

Mount Juliet Conrad, Thomastown,
Co. Kilkenny, Ireland
Par 36-36–72; 7,256 yards

September 30-October 3
purse, €5,639,287

	SCORES				TOTAL	MONEY
Ernie Els	69	64	68	69	270	€979,113.80
Thomas Bjorn	68	69	66	68	271	550,751.50
David Howell	69	69	66	71	275	367,167.70
Sergio Garcia	67	72	67	70	276	251,305.90
Darren Clarke	71	72	65	68	276	251,305.90
Padraig Harrington	69	69	66	73	277	163,185.60
Todd Hamilton	66	69	69	73	277	163,185.60
Retief Goosen	68	69	68	72	277	163,185.60
Tiger Woods	68	70	70	70	278	126,468.90
Zach Johnson	68	71	69	71	279	110,150.30
Luke Donald	67	71	71	71	280	91,791.91
Mark Hensby	73	73	69	65	280	91,791.91
Brad Faxon	70	68	72	71	281	73,433.53
Lee Westwood	68	69	71	73	281	73,433.53
David Toms	70	74	68	69	281	73,433.53
Shigeki Maruyama	70	70	73	70	283	64,458.32
Stuart Appleby	67	74	70	72	283	64,458.32
Jerry Kelly	69	73	69	72	283	64,458.32
Miguel Angel Jimenez	67	68	75	73	283	64,458.32
Angel Cabrera	69	69	74	71	283	64,458.32
Paul Casey	72	70	71	71	284	58,746.82
Rory Sabbatini	71	70	70	73	284	58,746.82
Steve Flesch	67	70	74	74	285	53,035.33
Barry Lane	69	72	72	72	285	53,035.33
Stewart Cink	71	73	67	74	285	53,035.33
Trevor Immelman	71	71	72	71	285	53,035.33
Peter Lonard	69	70	70	76	285	53,035.33
Justin Leonard	68	68	77	73	286	44,570.07
Richard Green	72	70	72	72	286	44,570.07
Nick O'Hern	68	73	75	70	286	44,570.07
Thomas Levet	73	71	73	69	286	44,570.07
Bob Tway	71	70	72	73	286	44,570.07

	SCORES				TOTAL	MONEY
Alex Cejka	70	74	69	73	286	44,570.07
Carlos Franco	69	72	75	70	286	44,570.07
Paul McGinley	70	75	71	70	286	44,570.07
Jim Furyk	70	70	71	76	287	39,164.55
Fred Couples	73	67	70	77	287	39,164.55
Stephen Ames	73	72	70	72	287	39,164.55
Chris DiMarco	69	75	70	73	287	39,164.55
Adam Scott	67	74	73	73	287	39,164.55
Davis Love	74	69	69	76	288	36,308.80
Thongchai Jaidee	71	75	71	71	288	36,308.80
Peter Senior	69	74	74	72	289	34,268.98
Scott Drummond	69	71	73	76	289	34,268.98
Arjun Atwal	71	78	70	70	289	34,268.98
Jay Haas	72	71	70	76	289	34,268.98
Graeme McDowell	73	70	75	71	289	34,268.98
Desvonde Botes	70	72	75	74	291	32,841.11
Joakim Haeggman	71	71	73	76	291	32,841.11
Andrew McLardy	73	73	70	76	292	31,821.20
Chris Riley	70	75	73	74	292	31,821.20
Chad Campbell	70	79	71	72	292	31,821.20
S.K. Ho	71	76	72	74	293	31,005.27
Tim Herron	73	75	72	74	294	30,189.34
Scott Verplank	71	82	72	69	294	30,189.34
Robert Allenby	68	74	75	77	294	30,189.34
Jean-Francois Remesy	72	71	75	77	295	29,169.43
K.J. Choi	71	76	75	73	295	29,169.43
Darren Fichardt	76	71	74	75	296	27,945.54
Fredrik Jacobson	74	76	72	74	296	27,945.54
Jonathan Kaye	70	73	73	80	296	27,945.54
Charles Howell	74	73	71	78	296	27,945.54
Stephen Leaney	73	75	71	78	297	26,925.63
Y.E. Yang	75	76	71	77	299	26,517.66
Andre Stolz	70	76	75	79	300	26,109.70
Michael Campbell	74	77	73	80	304	25,701.74
Shingo Katayama	79	76	76	75	306	25,293.77
Zhang Lian-wei	75	77	76	79	307	24,885.81

Dunhill Links Championship

St. Andrews Old Course: Par 36-36–72; 7,115 yards   October 7-10
Carnoustie Championship Course: Par 36-36–72; 7,112 yards   purse, €3,888,387
Kingsbarns Golf Links: Par 36-36–72; 7,059 yards
St. Andrews, Scotland

	SCORES				TOTAL	MONEY
Stephen Gallacher	70	66	66	67	269	€645,162.40
Graeme McDowell	62	72	67	68	269	430,105.60
(Gallacher defeated McDowell on first playoff hole.)						
Ian Poulter	69	67	65	69	270	217,935.90
Luke Donald	66	65	68	71	270	217,935.90
David Howell	65	65	71	71	272	149,806.70
Lee Westwood	71	65	69	67	272	149,806.70
Fred Couples	70	66	69	69	274	106,451.80
Ernie Els	68	68	68	70	274	106,451.80
Richard Green	70	66	73	66	275	78,451.75
Nick O'Hern	71	69	67	68	275	78,451.75
Marcel Siem	73	66	67	69	275	78,451.75

	SCORES				TOTAL	MONEY
Mark Foster	72	66	67	71	276	58,645.27
Brian Davis	72	67	70	67	276	58,645.27
Rolf Muntz	73	63	69	71	276	58,645.27
Angel Cabrera	69	66	69	72	276	58,645.27
John Bickerton	71	67	66	72	276	58,645.27
Adam Scott	68	67	74	67	276	58,645.27
Peter Senior	70	68	67	72	277	46,606.54
Ian Woosnam	73	66	66	72	277	46,606.54
Vijay Singh	68	70	69	70	277	46,606.54
Miles Tunnicliff	73	68	69	67	277	46,606.54
Phillip Price	70	73	68	66	277	46,606.54
Eduardo Romero	70	71	71	66	278	39,677.49
Maarten Lafeber	72	70	70	66	278	39,677.49
Colin Montgomerie	68	67	72	71	278	39,677.49
James Kingston	65	72	69	72	278	39,677.49
Retief Goosen	65	72	69	72	278	39,677.49
Richard Sterne	66	68	75	69	278	39,677.49
Dean Robertson	70	70	70	69	279	33,290.38
Mikko Ilonen	71	69	71	68	279	33,290.38
Simon Dyson	69	68	73	69	279	33,290.38
Brett Rumford	71	67	68	73	279	33,290.38
Nathan Green	70	65	73	71	279	33,290.38
Jose Maria Olazabal	68	74	68	70	280	26,322.63
Soren Kjeldsen	74	69	69	68	280	26,322.63
Anthony Wall	72	70	68	70	280	26,322.63
Trevor Immelman	69	68	71	72	280	26,322.63
Emanuele Canonica	70	72	66	72	280	26,322.63
Darren Clarke	72	69	66	73	280	26,322.63
Peter Lonard	65	71	71	73	280	26,322.63
Bradley Dredge	70	70	71	69	280	26,322.63
David Lynn	73	69	68	70	280	26,322.63
Greg Owen	69	68	72	71	280	26,322.63
Gordon Brand, Jr.	67	72	71	71	281	18,580.68
Robert-Jan Derksen	69	70	69	73	281	18,580.68
Jyoti Randhawa	70	73	69	69	281	18,580.68
Stephen Dodd	69	69	74	69	281	18,580.68
Simon Khan	71	70	68	72	281	18,580.68
Paul Casey	70	70	69	72	281	18,580.68
Jamie Donaldson	69	65	73	74	281	18,580.68
Martin Maritz	69	69	71	72	281	18,580.68
Louis Oosthuizen	67	65	79	70	281	18,580.68
Marcus Fraser	70	67	67	77	281	18,580.68
Miguel Angel Martin	71	71	70	70	282	11,870.99
Zhang Lian-wei	74	68	70	70	282	11,870.99
Scott Drummond	73	68	69	72	282	11,870.99
Titch Moore	72	69	71	70	282	11,870.99
Gregory Havret	67	71	74	70	282	11,870.99
David Park	73	67	71	71	282	11,870.99
Raymond Russell	72	72	67	71	282	11,870.99
Rich Beem	71	65	70	76	282	11,870.99
Alastair Forsyth	70	69	73	70	282	11,870.99
Thomas Levet	68	72	71	72	283	8,903.24
Peter Hedblom	68	72	72	71	283	8,903.24
Paul McGinley	72	67	73	71	283	8,903.24
Stephen Scahill	69	68	72	74	283	8,903.24
Jason Dawes	71	66	70	76	283	8,903.24
Gary Orr	71	68	73	72	284	7,741.95
Arjun Singh	71	71	70	73	285	7,205.66
Simon Yates	70	70	71	74	285	7,205.66
Peter O'Malley	69	72	71	75	287	5,807

	SCORES				TOTAL	MONEY
Brad Kennedy	69	74	69	76	288	5,804
Sven Struver	70	71	71	78	290	5,801

HSBC World Match Play

Wentworth Club, West Course, Surrey, England
Par 434 534 444–35; 345 434 455–37–72; 7,072 yards

October 14-17
purse, £2,440,000

FIRST ROUND

Ernie Els defeated Scott Drummond, 2 and 1

Els	5	3	3	5	3	4	5	4	5	3	4	4	3	3	5	3	5	4
Drummond	4	3	3	5	3	4	4	6	4	3	4	4	5	3	3	4	4	5

Drummond leads, 1 up

Els	4	2	3	3	3	4	4	3	4		3	4	5	4	3	5	4	5
Drummond	4	3	5	3	3	4	4	4	5		3	3	5	5	3	4	4	5

Angel Cabrera defeated K.J. Choi, 1 up

Choi	5	2	4	4	3	4	5	3	5	3	4	4	5	3	3	4	4	3
Cabrera	4	3	4	3	3	4	4	5	4	3	4	4	4	3	4	4	4	C

Cabrera leads, 1 up

Choi	5	3	4	4	3	5	4	3	4	3	3	3	4	4	4	4	5	5
Cabrera	4	2	5	5	2	4	4	4	3	3	3	5	5	3	4	4	5	5

Padraig Harrington defeated Chris Riley, 2 and 1

Harrington	4	3	4	3	3	4	4	5	4	3	4	4	3	4	4	3	4	
Riley	5	3	4	4	3	4	4	4	4	3	3	5	3	3	4	4	5	4

Harrington leads, 1 up

Harrington	5	2	5	4	3	5	4	3	4	2	4	5	4	3	4	4	5	
Riley	4	3	5	4	2	4	4	4	4	4	4	5	3	3	5	5	5	

Thomas Levet defeated Mike Weir, 2 and 1

Weir	6	3	4	4	4	4	4	3	4	3	4	4	3	3	4	5	4	3
Levet	4	3	5	5	4	3	4	4	5	3	3	4	4	3	3	4	4	5

Weir leads, 1 up

Weir	4	3	4	4	3	3	5	5	4	2	3	4	4	3	4	5	6	
Levet	4	3	4	4	3	4	4	4	4	3	3	3	4	3	4	4	4	

Retief Goosen defeated Jeff Maggert, 12 and 11

Goosen	4	2	5	4	3	4	4	3	4	2	4	4	3	3	4	4	4	
Maggert	4	4	5	5	4	5	5	3	5	3	4	4	4	3	4	4	5	5

Goosen leads, 10 up

Goosen	4	2	5	4	2	4	3
Maggert	4	3	5	4	2	4	4

Lee Westwood defeated Todd Hamilton, 4 and 3

Hamilton	4	3	4	4	4	4	3	5	4	3	4	4	4	3	4	4	4	4
Westwood	4	3	4	5	3	4	4	4	4	3	4	4	4	3	5	3	3	4

Westwood leads, 1 up

Hamilton	4	4	4	5	3	3	3	3	5	3	4	5	4	3				
Westwood	5	2	4	4	3	4	4	3	4	2	3	4	5	3	3			

Miguel Angel Jimenez defeated Steve Flesch, 3 and 2

Jimenez	4	3	4	3	2	4	5	4	4	3	4	3	4	3	3	3	4	5
Flesch	5	3	4	4	3	4	4	4	4	3	4	6	3	2	4	4	4	4

Jimenez leads, 2 up

Jimenez	5	2	5	4	3	4	5	4	4	4	4	4	4	2	4	3		
Flesch	4	3	4	4	2	4	4	5	4	3	5	5	4	3	4	4		

Bernhard Langer defeated Vijay Singh, 1 up, 37th hole

Singh	4	4	4	4	2	4	4	4	4	3	4	4	4	3	4	4	4	5
Langer	4	3	4	4	3	3	4	4	4	3	4	5	4	2	4	4	5	5

Match all-square

Singh	4	3	5	4	3	5	4	4	4	2	5	4	4	3	3	3	4	5
Langer	5	2	5	4	2	4	3	5	4	3	4	4	4	2	4	4	5	5

Match all-square

Singh	5
Langer	4

QUARTER-FINALS

Ernie Els defeated Angel Cabrera, 1 up

Els	4	2	5	4	3	3	4	4	4	3	4	4	4	3	4	4	C	4
Cabrera	5	3	4	5	3	4	4	3	4	3	4	4	3	2	4	4	3	4

Cabrera leads, 1 up

Els	4	2	5	4	3	5	4	4	3	3	3	4	4	3	4	5	4	4
Cabrera	5	3	6	3	3	4	4	4	4	2	4	4	5	2	4	4	5	4

Padraig Harrington defeated Thomas Levet, 1 up

Harrington	3	3	4	4	2	3	5	3	4	3	4	5	3	2	4	3	4	4
Levet	4	2	3	5	3	4	4	4	4	3	3	4	4	3	5	5	5	4

Harrington leads, 5 up

Harrington	4	3	4	4	3	4	5	3	5	3	4	C	4	2	4	6	5	4
Levet	5	3	4	3	2	3	4	4	4	3	4	4	5	2	4	3	5	4

Lee Westwood defeated Retief Goosen, 2 and 1

Goosen	4	3	4	4	3	4	4	4	4	3	4	4	4	3	4	4	4	5
Westwood	4	2	4	5	3	4	4	4	4	2	3	4	4	3	4	4	4	4

Westwood leads, 3 up

Goosen	4	3	4	5	3	4	4	3	4	2	4	4	4	3	3	4	4
Westwood	4	3	4	3	2	4	4	C	3	3	4	4	4	3	4	5	4

Miguel Angel Jimenez defeated Bernhard Langer, 2 and 1

Jimenez	5	2	3	4	2	4	2	4	4	2	3	3	4	4	4	5	4	4
Langer	4	3	3	4	2	4	3	4	4	3	4	5	4	3	4	3	5	4

Jimenez leads, 3 up

Jimenez	5	3	5	4	2	4	5	4	4	3	4	5	3	3	6	4	4
Langer	5	3	3	4	3	4	5	4	4	3	4	4	4	2	4	4	5

SEMI-FINALS

Ernie Els defeated Padraig Harrington, 5 and 4

Els	4	3	4	4	3	4	3	4	4	2	4	4	4	3	5	5	4	4
Harrington	4	3	4	4	3	4	4	4	4	4	4	4	5	4	4	4	5	4

Els leads, 3 up

Els	4	3	4	4	3	4	3	4	4	3	3	4	4	3
Harrington	4	3	5	4	2	4	4	3	4	3	4	4	4	4

Lee Westwood defeated Miguel Angel Jimenez, 1 up

Jimenez	3	3	4	5	3	4	3	4	4	3	4	4	4	3	4	4	5	4
Westwood	4	3	4	5	3	3	4	3	5	2	4	3	4	3	3	3	4	5

Westwood leads, 3 up

Jimenez	5	3	4	5	3	3	3	4	4	2	4	3	3	3	4	3	5	4
Westwood	4	3	4	4	3	3	4	3	4	2	5	4	4	3	4	4	5	4

FINAL

Ernie Els defeated Lee Westwood, 2 and 1

Els	4	3	5	3	4	5	3	4	3	4	4	3	4	4	4	4	5	4
Westwood	5	3	4	3	2	4	4	4	4	3	4	4	4	4	4	3	6	4

Match all-square

Els	5	3	3	3	3	4	4	4	4	3	4	5	4	3	5	4	4
Westwood	5	3	4	4	2	4	4	4	4	4	4	5	4	3	3	5	4

PRIZE MONEY: Els £1,000,000; Westwood £400,000; Harrington, Jimenez £120,000 each; Cabrera, Goosen, Langer, Levet £80,000 each; Choi, Drummond, Flesch, Hamilton, Maggert, Riley, Singh, Weir £60,000 each.

LEGEND: C—conceded hole to opponent.

Mallorca Classic

Pula Golf Club, Majorca, Spain
Par 35-35–70; 6,568 yards

October 14-17
purse, €1,000,000

	SCORES				TOTAL	MONEY
Sergio Garcia	66	67	68	67	268	€166,660
Simon Khan	66	64	71	71	272	111,110
Carlos Rodiles	66	67	71	69	273	62,600
Santiago Luna	67	69	69	70	275	42,466.67
Markus Brier	68	68	67	72	275	42,466.67
Francois Delamontagne	65	71	71	68	275	42,466.67
Paul Broadhurst	68	72	69	67	276	25,800
Alastair Forsyth	67	68	73	68	276	25,800
Gonzalo Fernandez-Castan	72	64	69	71	276	25,800
Jose Maria Olazabal	73	68	70	66	277	20,000
Peter Fowler	66	70	73	69	278	16,340
Jose Manuel Lara	67	69	75	67	278	16,340
Paul Lawrie	68	70	70	70	278	16,340
David Park	75	65	70	68	278	16,340
Stephen Gallacher	70	67	71	70	278	16,340
Emanuele Canonica	67	67	76	69	279	13,500
Richard Sterne	69	69	71	70	279	13,500
Brad Kennedy	70	67	72	70	279	13,500
Jose Rivero	70	69	73	68	280	11,187.50
Anthony Wall	69	70	74	67	280	11,187.50
Darren Fichardt	65	71	72	72	280	11,187.50
Peter Lawrie	71	67	72	70	280	11,187.50
Paul Eales	74	66	70	70	280	11,187.50
Robert Coles	71	69	71	69	280	11,187.50
Michael Jonzon	70	71	69	70	280	11,187.50
Martin Maritz	73	68	70	69	280	11,187.50
Damien McGrane	71	71	68	71	281	9,200
Jean-Francois Lucquin	70	68	71	72	281	9,200
Fernando Roca	68	71	75	67	281	9,200
Ricardo Gonzalez	69	67	74	71	281	9,200
Steven O'Hara	69	69	74	69	281	9,200
Gordon Brand, Jr.	70	71	71	70	282	7,875
Mark Roe	68	68	72	74	282	7,875
Marten Olander	69	70	76	67	282	7,875
Philip Golding	71	69	71	71	282	7,875
Brian Davis	71	70	74	68	283	6,600
Sven Struver	71	67	77	68	283	6,600
Johan Edfors	71	71	69	72	283	6,600

	SCORES				TOTAL	MONEY
Tomas Jesus Munoz	67	69	73	74	283	6,600
Rolf Muntz	71	71	71	70	283	6,600
Van Phillips	69	73	72	69	283	6,600
Raymond Russell	72	71	69	71	283	6,600
Christopher Hanell	72	69	73	69	283	6,600
Miguel Angel Martin	71	72	72	69	284	5,400
Martin Erlandsson	69	72	73	70	284	5,400
Robert Karlsson	67	70	75	72	284	5,400
Wade Ormsby	70	73	70	71	284	5,400
Gary Murphy	76	67	70	72	285	4,700
Steve Webster	69	68	73	75	285	4,700
Fredrik Andersson Hed	70	63	78	74	285	4,700
Soren Hansen	69	69	76	72	286	4,100
Jesus Maria Arruti	73	70	73	70	286	4,100
Marcus Fraser	69	69	74	74	286	4,100
David Matthew	69	69	75	74	287	3,320
Stuart Little	75	68	71	73	287	3,320
Marcel Siem	69	73	74	71	287	3,320
Carlos Balmaseda	71	72	73	71	287	3,320
Oyvind Rojahn	69	69	75	74	287	3,320
Stephen Scahill	71	68	76	72	287	3,320
*Sebastian Garcia Grout	72	69	73	73	287	
Roger Chapman	72	69	71	76	288	2,850
Eduardo De La Riva	72	69	77	70	288	2,850
Paul Streeter	70	73	73	73	289	2,700
Iain Pyman	70	68	74	78	290	2,500
Dean Robertson	73	70	76	71	290	2,500
Rob Rashell	69	74	74	73	290	2,500
Jose Manuel Carriles	72	70	79	70	291	2,300
Gary Emerson	71	71	73	78	293	2,100
Jonathan Lomas	71	72	81	69	293	2,100
Robert Rock	72	71	75	75	293	2,100
Philip Walton	71	68	80	75	294	1,865
Peter Baker	73	70	79	72	294	1,865
Nick Dougherty	74	68	75	78	295	1,500
Daniel Gaunt	73	68	84	72	297	1,497
David Dixon	66	73	82	78	299	1,494
Carlos Garcia	70	73	84	74	301	1,491

Open de Madrid

Club de Campo, Madrid, Spain
Par 36-35–71; 6,967 yards

October 21-24
purse, €1,000,000

	SCORES				TOTAL	MONEY
Richard Sterne	70	65	66	65	266	€166,660
Anders Hansen	68	66	68	66	268	111,110
Terry Price	66	71	65	67	269	62,600
Raphael Jacquelin	74	64	64	68	270	46,200
Paul Broadhurst	67	65	68	70	270	46,200
Darren Fichardt	67	66	67	71	271	30,000
Ivo Giner	68	69	64	70	271	30,000
Wade Ormsby	72	66	67	66	271	30,000
Trevor Immelman	67	68	69	68	272	18,820
Henrik Stenson	69	71	64	68	272	18,820
Johan Edfors	66	67	69	70	272	18,820
Raymond Russell	71	69	68	64	272	18,820

	SCORES				TOTAL	MONEY
Brett Rumford	70	65	66	71	272	18,820
Philip Golding	69	67	68	69	273	14,100
Jesus Maria Arruti	67	70	68	68	273	14,100
Jonathan Lomas	70	71	67	65	273	14,100
David Park	71	67	67	68	273	14,100
Jamie Donaldson	68	67	68	70	273	14,100
Jose Manuel Lara	70	65	72	67	274	11,825
Joakim Haeggman	73	66	67	68	274	11,825
Graeme McDowell	70	64	67	73	274	11,825
Marcus Fraser	70	69	69	66	274	11,825
Gary Murphy	68	66	70	71	275	10,100
Robert-Jan Derksen	68	69	69	69	275	10,100
Jose Manuel Carriles	70	69	68	68	275	10,100
Miguel Angel Jimenez	70	63	69	73	275	10,100
Peter Hedblom	70	70	68	67	275	10,100
Bradley Dredge	67	71	67	70	275	10,100
Sebastian Fernandez	70	70	68	67	275	10,100
Peter Fowler	67	73	66	70	276	7,925
Steve Webster	70	71	67	68	276	7,925
Jamie Spence	71	66	69	70	276	7,925
Colin Montgomerie	68	71	67	70	276	7,925
Stuart Little	70	66	72	68	276	7,925
Peter O'Malley	70	69	70	67	276	7,925
Stephen Scahill	71	70	69	66	276	7,925
Martin Maritz	68	72	65	71	276	7,925
Santiago Luna	69	70	68	70	277	6,100
Ian Woosnam	72	67	72	66	277	6,100
Maarten Lafeber	70	71	69	67	277	6,100
Peter Lawrie	71	67	68	71	277	6,100
Miles Tunnicliff	70	69	69	69	277	6,100
Michael Jonzon	70	70	66	71	277	6,100
Matthew Blackey	68	73	66	70	277	6,100
Francois Delamontagne	70	69	69	69	277	6,100
Alastair Forsyth	68	72	68	69	277	6,100
Brian Davis	67	71	71	69	278	4,700
Nick O'Hern	67	69	70	72	278	4,700
Jean-Francois Lucquin	68	69	73	68	278	4,700
Ricardo Gonzalez	73	68	67	70	278	4,700
Mikko Ilonen	73	68	68	69	278	4,700
Miguel Angel Martin	70	69	74	66	279	3,437.50
Carlos Rodiles	72	69	70	68	279	3,437.50
Nicolas Colsaerts	70	71	71	67	279	3,437.50
David Lynn	71	70	68	70	279	3,437.50
Robert Rock	71	68	68	72	279	3,437.50
Gonzalo Fernandez-Castan	73	68	66	72	279	3,437.50
Jamie Elson	72	69	68	70	279	3,437.50
Charl Schwartzel	70	70	70	69	279	3,437.50
Gordon Brand, Jr.	72	67	70	71	280	2,600
Sam Torrance	71	69	72	68	280	2,600
Mark Foster	71	67	70	72	280	2,600
Andrew Marshall	69	71	68	72	280	2,600
Jarmo Sandelin	71	70	69	70	280	2,600
Julien Clement	64	72	72	73	281	2,150
Stephen Dodd	69	70	72	70	281	2,150
James Kingston	71	68	74	68	281	2,150
Francisco Cea	68	68	70	75	281	2,150
Rob Rashell	70	70	67	75	282	1,900
Gary Orr	69	69	74	71	283	1,665
Patrik Sjoland	72	69	65	77	283	1,665
Marten Olander	69	72	71	72	284	1,491

	SCORES				TOTAL	MONEY
Gregory Havret	68	72	71	73	284	1,491
Carlos Balmaseda	70	71	71	72	284	1,491
Martin Wiegele	70	71	69	74	284	1,491
Steven O'Hara	68	71	72	73	284	1,491
Robert Karlsson	70	71	70	74	285	1,480.50
Fernando Roca	69	70	73	73	285	1,480.50
Jose Rivero	71	69	73	74	287	1,476

Volvo Masters Andalucia

Club de Golf Valderrama, Sotegrande, Spain   October 28-31
Par 35-36–71; 6,961 yards   purse, €3,750,000

	SCORES				TOTAL	MONEY
Ian Poulter	71	67	69	70	277	€625,000
Sergio Garcia	67	69	71	70	277	416,660
(Poulter defeated Garcia on first playoff hole.)						
Alastair Forsyth	68	69	67	74	278	234,750
Peter Hanson	70	70	70	70	280	187,500
David Howell	73	69	73	66	281	145,125
Christian Cevaer	69	70	70	72	281	145,125
Scott Drummond	74	71	68	70	283	103,125
Lee Westwood	72	71	72	68	283	103,125
Trevor Immelman	70	73	68	73	284	79,500
Paul Casey	72	70	74	68	284	79,500
Paul Broadhurst	73	74	69	69	285	63,347.50
Jonathan Lomas	69	72	74	70	285	63,347.50
Darren Clarke	73	72	68	72	285	63,347.50
Thomas Bjorn	75	70	71	69	285	63,347.50
Richard Green	73	73	73	67	286	53,000
Stephen Dodd	71	72	69	74	286	53,000
Patrik Sjoland	73	70	73	70	286	53,000
Graeme McDowell	73	72	71	70	286	53,000
Padraig Harrington	72	70	71	74	287	45,600
Colin Montgomerie	75	74	69	69	287	45,600
Angel Cabrera	73	66	75	73	287	45,600
Terry Price	71	71	72	73	287	45,600
Luke Donald	69	76	74	68	287	45,600
Marcus Fraser	70	75	71	72	288	42,000
Soren Kjeldsen	73	71	71	74	289	38,400
Nick O'Hern	74	77	70	68	289	38,400
Marcel Siem	76	74	68	71	289	38,400
Joakim Haeggman	71	73	77	68	289	38,400
Phillip Price	76	71	72	70	289	38,400
Brian Davis	68	73	75	74	290	33,733.33
Miguel Angel Jimenez	73	76	69	72	290	33,733.33
Peter O'Malley	69	72	75	74	290	33,733.33
Thongchai Jaidee	72	71	73	75	291	32,000
Eduardo Romero	75	79	69	69	292	30,000
Jose Manuel Lara	67	79	72	74	292	30,000
Barry Lane	73	73	74	72	292	30,000
Bradley Dredge	70	73	77	72	292	30,000
Anders Hansen	78	69	73	73	293	27,200
David Lynn	74	71	74	74	293	27,200
Martin Maritz	76	71	73	73	293	27,200
Paul McGinley	76	72	71	75	294	25,600
David Park	73	71	74	77	295	24,400

	SCORES				TOTAL	MONEY
Brett Rumford	74	75	76	70	295	24,400
Raphael Jacquelin	76	73	71	76	296	22,000
Ricardo Gonzalez	71	72	74	79	296	22,000
James Kingston	71	72	75	78	296	22,000
Stephen Gallacher	77	74	71	74	296	22,000
Carlos Rodiles	78	77	74	70	299	19,600
Thomas Levet	75	77	78	69	299	19,600
Simon Khan	76	75	75	74	300	18,400
Jean-Francois Remesy	74	73	73	83	303	17,200
Miles Tunnicliff	75	76	81	71	303	17,200
Henrik Stenson	75	75	76	78	304	16,000
Michael Campbell	74	76	74	82	306	15,500

WGC - World Cup

Real Club de Golf de Sevilla, Sevilla, Spain   November 18-21
Par 36-36–72; 7,134 yards   purse, US$4,000,000

	INDIVIDUAL SCORES				TOTAL
ENGLAND—$1,400,000					
Luke Donald/Paul Casey	61	64	68	64	257
SPAIN—$700,000					
Miguel Angel Jimenez/Sergio Garcia	63	68	61	66	258
IRELAND—$400,000					
Padraig Harrington/Paul McGinley	60	71	64	65	260
SOUTH AFRICA—$200,000					
Rory Sabbatini/Trevor Immelman	66	65	64	68	263
NETHERLANDS—$135,000					
Robert-Jan Derksen/Maarten Lafeber	65	69	63	68	265
AUSTRIA—$135,000					
Martin Wiegele/Markus Brier	60	70	68	67	265
SWEDEN—$95,000					
Joakim Haeggman/Fredrik Jacobson	64	67	64	72	267
GERMANY—$95,000					
Kariem Baraka/Marcel Siem	64	69	66	68	267
UNITED STATES—$95,000					
Scott Verplank/Bob Tway	64	67	64	72	267
JAPAN—$62,500					
Shigeki Maruyama/Hidemichi Tanaka	62	69	65	73	269
AUSTRALIA—$62,500					
Stephen Leaney/Nick O'Hern	64	68	65	72	269
SOUTH KOREA—$62,500					
Kim Dae-sub/Shin Yong-jin	65	70	64	70	269
WALES—$62,500					
Phillip Price/Bradley Dredge	65	69	64	71	269

	INDIVIDUAL SCORES	TOTAL

DENMARK—$50,000
Anders Hansen/Soren Kjeldsen   64   73   67   66   270

NEW ZEALAND—$48,500
David Smail/Craig Perks   69   73   62   68   272

FRANCE—$48,500
Thomas Levet/Raphael Jacquelin   68   68   66   70   272

ITALY—$47,000
Alessandro Tadini/Andrea Maestroni   70   71   64   68   273

SCOTLAND—$46,000
Alastair Forsyth/Scott Drummond   64   72   66   72   274

ARGENTINA—$45,000
Eduardo Romero/Angel Cabrera   70   71   65   70   276

CANADA—$44,000
Darren Griff/Stuart Anderson   68   71   64   73   277

COLOMBIA—$43,000
Jose Garrido/Manuel Merizalde   67   73   65   75   280

MYANMAR—$42,000
Kyi Hla Han/Soe Kyaw Naing   69   73   67   73   282

TAIWAN—$41,000
Wang Ter-chang/Lu Wei-chih   70   70   68   75   283

MEXICO—$40,000
Pablo del Olmo/Alex Quiroz   74   72   68   74   288

Volvo China Open
See Asia/Japan Tours chapter.

Omega Hong Kong Open
See Asia/Japan Tours chapter.

Dunhill Championship
See African Tours chapter.

Challenge Tour

Summit Panama Masters
See American Tours chapter.

Costa Rica Open
See American Tours chapter.

Albierto Telefonica
See American Tours chapter.

Stanbic Zambia Open
See African Tours chapter.

Kenya Open
See African Tours chapter.

Madeira Island Open
See PGA European Tour section.

Al Ahram-Jolie Ville Sharm El Sheikh Challenge

Jolie Ville Golf Resort, Sharm El Skeikh, Egypt
Par 35-35–70; 6,546 yards

April 22-25
purse, €104,261

	SCORES				TOTAL	MONEY
Gareth Davies	69	67	63	66	265	€16,631.97
Neil Cheetham	67	64	70	66	267	11,434.48
Joachim Larsen	66	69	67	66	268	6,756.74
Jose Trauwitz	67	66	68	67	268	6,756.74
Andre Bossert	66	68	65	70	269	5,197.49
Johan Axgren	68	68	66	68	270	3,742.19
Oliver Whiteley	67	64	70	69	270	3,742.19
Lee S. James	66	71	65	69	271	2,442.82
Marco Bernardini	67	68	66	70	271	2,442.82
Richard Finch	70	65	69	67	271	2,442.82
Gregory Bourdy	70	64	68	69	271	2,442.82
Kalle Brink	66	70	68	68	272	1,819.12
Ilya Goroneskoul	68	68	69	67	272	1,819.12
Edward Rush	68	69	64	71	272	1,819.12
Justin Kehoe	67	66	70	69	272	1,819.12
Marcel Haremza	69	67	64	73	273	1,403.32
Julien Van Hauwe	67	69	69	68	273	1,403.32
Daniel Vancsik	69	65	72	67	273	1,403.32
Marc Warren	66	70	66	71	273	1,403.32
Massimo Florioli	71	62	69	72	274	1,084.54
Mark Pullan	70	67	69	68	274	1,084.54
Simon Hurd	69	69	68	68	274	1,084.54
Fredrik Orest	67	69	69	70	275	925.15
David Geall	70	63	71	71	275	925.15

	SCORES				TOTAL	MONEY
Mark Smith	66	70	67	72	275	925.15
Benoit Teilleria	69	68	69	69	275	925.15
Leif Westerberg	72	64	72	67	275	925.15
Gerard Bent	68	69	69	69	275	925.15
Stephen Browne	68	70	67	70	275	925.15
Hernan Rey	73	64	67	71	275	925.15

Peugeot Challenge de Leon

Club de Golf de Leon, Leon, Spain · April 29-May 2
Par 36-35–71; 6,916 yards · purse, €110,000

	SCORES				TOTAL	MONEY
Edward Rush	68	68	76	64	276	€17,600
Alvaro Salto	66	74	72	64	276	12,100
(Rush defeated Salto on first playoff hole.)						
Richard Finch	68	74	68	67	277	7,700
Sion Bebb	70	70	71	67	278	6,050
Mikael Lundberg	73	71	67	67	278	6,050
Julien Van Hauwe	74	68	70	68	280	4,400
Henrik Nystrom	71	67	73	70	281	3,080
Gregory Bourdy	75	67	70	69	281	3,080
Johan Kok	68	69	77	67	281	3,080
Simon Dyson	73	72	69	68	282	2,236.67
Marc Warren	70	72	66	74	282	2,236.67
Ariel Canete	69	74	68	71	282	2,236.67
Jamie Little	71	74	68	70	283	1,760
Michael Hoey	75	69	68	71	283	1,760
Carl Suneson	71	72	66	74	283	1,760
Gary Clark	67	72	71	73	283	1,760
Benn Barham	70	69	70	74	283	1,760
Peter Kaensche	71	72	73	68	284	1,338.33
Michael Kirk	74	73	70	67	284	1,338.33
Gabriel Canizares	68	78	68	70	284	1,338.33
Garry Houston	68	73	68	76	285	1,089
Jose Romero	75	71	69	70	285	1,089
Johan Axgren	72	76	67	71	286	1,001
Didier de Vooght	74	74	71	67	286	1,001
Peter Gustafsson	70	72	72	72	286	1,001
Peter Whiteford	75	72	71	68	286	1,001
Oliver Whiteley	73	75	70	68	286	1,001
Justin Kehoe	72	75	70	69	286	1,001
Juan Quiros	74	70	73	70	287	913
Pasi Purhonen	78	70	70	69	287	913
*Alvaro Quiros	71	71	75	70	287	

Tessali-Metaponto Open di Puglia e Basilicata

Riva dei Tessali: Par 35-36–71; 6,502 yards · May 6-9
Metaponto GC: Par 36-36–72; 6,873 yards · purse, €120,000
Castellaneta, Italy

	SCORES				TOTAL	MONEY
Leif Westerberg	68	68	71	67	274	€19,200
Oliver Wilson	69	71	65	70	275	13,200

	SCORES				TOTAL	MONEY
Craig Williams	71	69	65	71	276	8,400
Peter Gustafsson	72	70	69	67	278	7,200
Sam Little	68	73	70	69	280	4,500
Francesco Guermani	65	73	71	71	280	4,500
Andrew Butterfield	75	69	69	67	280	4,500
Daniel Vancsik	75	69	70	66	280	4,500
Alessandro Tadini	67	72	72	70	281	2,760
Kariem Baraka	70	70	69	72	281	2,760
Michael Ettl	70	71	70	71	282	2,160
Garry Houston	73	68	72	69	282	2,160
Christian Nilsson	71	71	64	76	282	2,160
Ariel Canete	70	68	71	73	282	2,160
Carlos del Corral	69	73	68	72	282	2,160
Paolo Terreni	73	72	69	69	283	1,740
Jean Marc de Polo	72	72	70	69	283	1,740
Johan Axgren	69	72	72	71	284	1,318
Marc Cayeux	73	70	69	72	284	1,318
Tim Milford	73	67	72	72	284	1,318
Brian Akstrup	66	71	76	71	284	1,318
Stephen Sokol	71	72	69	72	284	1,318
Oliver Whiteley	69	71	72	72	284	1,318
Marco Soffietti	67	74	71	73	285	1,080
Paul Dwyer	71	69	75	70	285	1,080
Gary Clark	71	73	70	71	285	1,080
Philippe Lima	68	77	68	72	285	1,080
Jean-Baptiste Gonnet	70	72	71	72	285	1,080
Neil Cheetham	69	73	73	71	286	972
Graeme Storm	72	65	78	71	286	972
David Patrick	69	72	69	76	286	972
Daniel Quiros	72	69	74	71	286	972

Nykredit Danish Open

Esbjerg Golfklub, Esbjerg, Denmark
Par 35-36–71; 6,944 yards

June 3-6
purse, €137,500

	SCORES				TOTAL	MONEY
Matthew Morris	67	68	68	72	275	€22,000
Simon Dyson	72	65	69	72	278	15,120
Paul Nilbrink	72	67	69	73	281	8,940
Marc Cayeux	69	73	70	69	281	8,940
Shaun Webster	72	68	70	72	282	6,187.50
Leif Westerberg	71	71	70	70	282	6,187.50
Joakim Rask	70	73	71	69	283	4,125
Lee S. James	74	68	70	71	283	4,125
Magnus Persson Atlevi	69	69	71	75	284	2,832.50
Alvaro Salto	72	71	69	72	284	2,832.50
Philip Archer	67	72	73	72	284	2,832.50
Massimo Florioli	70	73	71	70	284	2,832.50
Mark Pilkington	71	71	69	73	284	2,832.50
Jochen Lupprian	71	72	69	73	285	1,993.75
Julien Van Hauwe	73	71	70	71	285	1,993.75
Gary Clark	70	67	72	76	285	1,993.75
Mikael Lundberg	71	68	70	76	285	1,993.75
Jean-Baptiste Gonnet	72	70	72	71	285	1,993.75
David Patrick	69	70	78	68	285	1,993.75
Carlos Quevedo	70	70	73	73	286	1,478.13

	SCORES				TOTAL	MONEY
Henrik Nystrom	73	67	72	74	286	1,478.13
Alessandro Tadini	68	77	70	72	287	1,251.25
Pasi Purhonen	73	67	73	74	287	1,251.25
Carl Suneson	72	73	71	71	287	1,251.25
Gustavo Rojas	72	72	70	73	287	1,251.25
Andrew Butterfield	72	73	71	71	287	1,251.25
David Drysdale	69	76	69	73	287	1,251.25
Benoit Teilleria	71	73	67	76	287	1,251.25
Thomas Norret	68	74	75	70	287	1,251.25
Alex Balicki	73	72	71	72	288	1,003.75
Greig Hutcheon	74	70	74	70	288	1,003.75
Fredrik Henge	68	69	70	81	288	1,003.75
Richard Bland	75	70	70	73	288	1,003.75
Tim Milford	71	70	73	74	288	1,003.75
Andreas Ljunggren	72	71	70	75	288	1,003.75
Peter Gustafsson	69	73	71	75	288	1,003.75
Marco Ruiz	68	73	77	70	288	1,003.75
Philippe Lima	71	73	66	78	288	1,003.75
Gareth Paddison	72	72	71	73	288	1,003.75

Segura Viudas Challenge de Espana

Torremirona Golf Club, Girona, Spain
Par 36-36–72; 6,794 yards

June 10-13
purse, €135,000

	SCORES				TOTAL	MONEY
Philippe Lima	73	67	67	67	274	€21,600
Alessandro Napoleoni	70	65	66	73	274	14,850
(Lima defeated Napoleoni on first playoff hole.)						
Kariem Baraka	66	69	68	72	275	9,450
Alessandro Tadini	67	70	69	70	276	4,657.50
Garry Houston	70	66	68	72	276	4,657.50
Richard Bland	67	69	71	69	276	4,657.50
Jan-Are Larsen	69	68	66	73	276	4,657.50
Johan Skold	65	66	71	74	276	4,657.50
Mark Pilkington	69	71	64	72	276	4,657.50
Leif Westerberg	66	73	65	72	276	4,657.50
David Orr	66	69	71	70	276	4,657.50
Johan Axgren	70	66	68	73	277	2,160
Carl Suneson	70	67	69	71	277	2,160
Erol Simsek	70	68	67	72	277	2,160
Peter Gustafsson	64	74	69	70	277	2,160
Stephen Browne	69	68	69	71	277	2,160
Gregory Bourdy	69	63	70	75	277	2,160
Oliver Wilson	70	66	70	71	277	2,160
Alvaro Salto	69	69	67	73	278	1,461.38
Ignacio Feliu	70	67	74	67	278	1,461.38
Lee S. James	70	69	69	70	278	1,461.38
Kyron Sullivan	68	71	68	71	278	1,461.38
Simon Hurd	69	71	66	73	279	1,269
Benn Barham	67	73	67	72	279	1,269
Tuomas Tuovinen	69	65	73	72	279	1,269
Gabriel Canizares	67	72	66	74	279	1,269
Magnus Persson Atlevi	69	66	70	75	280	1,134
Fredrik Henge	71	66	70	73	280	1,134
Olivier David	68	69	67	76	280	1,134
Paul Dwyer	69	70	69	72	280	1,134

	SCORES				TOTAL	MONEY
Graeme Storm	67	68	73	72	280	1,134
Johan Kok	70	67	68	75	280	1,134
Julien Quesne	66	71	71	72	280	1,134

Aa St. Omer Open

See PGA European Tour section.

Galeria Kaufhof Pokal Challenge

Rittergut Birkhof Golf Club, Dusseldorf, Germany
Par 36-36–72; 6,807 yards

June 24-27
purse, €110,000

	SCORES				TOTAL	MONEY
Garry Houston	72	68	66	65	271	€17,600
Gary Emerson	67	69	66	69	271	12,100
(Houston defeated Emerson on fourth playoff hole.)						
Jean-Baptiste Gonnet	71	69	70	63	273	7,700
Massimo Florioli	71	71	67	66	275	6,050
Anders Hansen	73	69	64	69	275	6,050
John Mellor	69	67	64	76	276	3,960
Erol Simsek	75	70	64	67	276	3,960
Stefano Reale	73	67	69	68	277	2,713.33
Stuart Manley	72	69	69	67	277	2,713.33
Oliver Wilson	70	68	69	70	277	2,713.33
Fredrik Henge	73	70	66	69	278	2,090
Richard Finch	70	70	69	69	278	2,090
Johan Kok	70	68	68	72	278	2,090
*Nicolas Meitinger	71	71	69	67	278	
Denny Lucas	69	72	70	68	279	1,650
Gustavo Rojas	73	69	67	70	279	1,650
Marco Bernardini	68	70	72	69	279	1,650
Tino Schuster	71	67	69	72	279	1,650
Daniel Vancsik	73	69	70	67	279	1,650
Alessandro Tadini	69	70	70	71	280	1,190.75
Mark Pilkington	74	70	70	66	280	1,190.75
David Orr	73	66	71	70	280	1,190.75
Matthew King	72	68	70	70	280	1,190.75
Shaun Webster	71	68	67	75	281	1,034
Titch Moore	72	72	67	70	281	1,034
Michael Kirk	75	70	71	65	281	1,034
Euan Little	73	68	70	71	282	957
Michael Hoey	73	71	69	69	282	957
Kariem Baraka	72	67	69	74	282	957
Brad Heaven	73	68	71	70	282	957

Volvo Finnish Open

Espoon Golfseura, Espoo, Finland
Par 36-35–71; 6,768 yards
(Event shortened to 54 holes—rain.)

July 1-4
purse, €110,000

	SCORES			TOTAL	MONEY
*Roope Kakko	68	67	67	202	
Johan Axgren	65	69	68	202	€14,850
Philip Archer	67	68	67	202	14,850
(Kakko defeated Axgren and Archer on first playoff hole.)					
Alessandro Tadini	69	68	67	204	7,700
Andrew Butterfield	69	67	69	205	6,600
Henrik Nystrom	69	67	70	206	4,950
Graeme Storm	71	66	69	206	4,950
Jan-Are Larsen	67	72	68	207	3,300
John Mellor	70	69	68	207	3,300
Greig Hutcheon	72	69	67	208	2,266
Morten Hagen	71	67	70	208	2,266
Mark Pilkington	74	65	69	208	2,266
Joakim Rask	72	67	69	208	2,266
Daniel Vancsik	69	69	70	208	2,266
Mattias Eliasson	68	72	69	209	1,815
Christian Nilsson	75	68	66	209	1,815
Knud Storgaard	70	68	72	210	1,274.78
Shaun Webster	71	71	68	210	1,274.78
Richard Bland	71	67	72	210	1,274.78
Massimo Florioli	72	67	71	210	1,274.78
Pehr Magnebrant	72	68	70	210	1,274.78
Erol Simsek	69	71	70	210	1,274.78
Janne Mommo	69	71	70	210	1,274.78
Mark Sanders	71	69	70	210	1,274.78
Ariel Canete	70	69	71	210	1,274.78
Magnus Persson Atlevi	74	69	68	211	968
Oskar Bergman	74	69	68	211	968
Kyron Sullivan	72	70	69	211	968
*Érik Stenman	73	68	70	211	
David Patrick	71	70	70	211	968
Andrew Buckle	67	69	75	211	968

Open des Volcans Challenge de France

Golf des Volcans, Clermont Ferrand, France
Par 36-35–71; 7,054 yards

July 8-11
purse, €125,000

	SCORES				TOTAL	MONEY
Johan Axgren	75	67	67	71	280	€20,000
Richard Bland	69	73	71	68	281	13,750
Peter Gustafsson	75	68	71	69	283	8,750
Olivier David	79	68	65	72	284	6,875
Fredrik Widmark	74	72	67	71	284	6,875
Neil Cheetham	74	68	72	71	285	5,000
Ian Garbutt	78	71	70	67	286	3,150
Paul Dwyer	76	68	72	70	286	3,150
Lee S. James	72	74	66	74	286	3,150
Edward Rush	73	70	68	75	286	3,150
Gregory Bourdy	74	68	72	72	286	3,150

	SCORES				TOTAL	MONEY
Magnus Persson Atlevi	77	71	69	70	287	2,187.50
Fredrik Henge	75	68	71	73	287	2,187.50
Jean Marc de Polo	75	72	66	74	287	2,187.50
Stuart Manley	73	71	72	71	287	2,187.50
Marc Farry	72	75	70	71	288	1,637.50
Andrew Butterfield	77	67	69	75	288	1,637.50
Gary Clark	77	68	75	68	288	1,637.50
John Mellor	73	69	75	71	288	1,637.50
Ariel Canete	72	71	75	70	288	1,637.50
Marc Pendaries	71	75	72	71	289	1,200
Roger Sabarros	75	69	74	71	289	1,200
Marcus Higley	76	71	72	70	289	1,200
Titch Moore	74	74	70	71	289	1,200
Jamie Little	77	72	69	71	289	1,200
Mark Mouland	74	72	72	72	290	1,100
Thomas Besancenez	77	72	70	71	290	1,100
Gareth Davies	73	75	69	73	290	1,100
*Francois Calmels	78	69	70	73	290	
Michael Hoey	76	74	68	73	291	1,012.50
Marc Cayeux	76	70	74	71	291	1,012.50
Andrew Raitt	76	71	71	73	291	1,012.50
Nicolas Wrona	75	71	71	74	291	1,012.50

Texbond Open

Gardagolf Country Club, Brescia, Italy
Par 36-36–72; 7,112 yards

July 14-17
purse, €110,000

	SCORES				TOTAL	MONEY
Sam Little	71	65	67	66	269	€17,600
Massimo Scarpa	66	70	69	67	272	9,900
Henrik Nystrom	67	67	68	70	272	9,900
Shaun Webster	67	66	73	67	273	6,050
Mikael Lundberg	68	71	68	66	273	6,050
Ariel Canete	68	70	69	67	274	3,960
Thomas Aiken	73	68	67	66	274	3,960
Tim Milford	75	63	69	68	275	2,860
Johan Kok	72	70	68	65	275	2,860
Mark Mouland	72	68	71	65	276	2,172.50
Andrea Maestroni	70	67	73	66	276	2,172.50
Michael Hoey	70	67	71	68	276	2,172.50
Stuart Davis	69	70	69	68	276	2,172.50
Philip Archer	71	66	71	69	277	1,815
Massimo Florioli	67	69	70	71	277	1,815
Sion Bebb	70	68	70	70	278	1,595
Benn Barham	72	68	68	70	278	1,595
Pasi Purhonen	72	71	70	66	279	1,238.60
Van Phillips	69	72	69	69	279	1,238.60
Mauricio Molina	74	68	71	66	279	1,238.60
David Patrick	73	70	72	64	279	1,238.60
Stephen Browne	72	71	74	62	279	1,238.60
Stefano Reale	69	68	72	71	280	968
Julien Van Hauwe	70	70	68	72	280	968
Ian Garbutt	69	71	70	70	280	968
Federico Bisazza	72	70	70	68	280	968
Fredrik Widmark	71	68	71	70	280	968
Matthew King	70	68	72	70	280	968

	SCORES				TOTAL	MONEY
Edward Rush	69	68	73	70	280	968
Tuomas Tuovinen	70	73	67	70	280	968
Gregory Bourdy	72	66	74	68	280	968

JJB Sports North West Challenge

Marriott Worsley Park Hotel & Country Club,
Manchester, England
Par 35-35–70; 6,797 yards

July 22-25
purse, €152,904

	SCORES				TOTAL	MONEY
Fredrik Henge	67	69	69	67	272	€24,067.52
Lee Slattery	67	65	71	70	273	16,546.42
Marcus Higley	70	67	66	71	274	8,273.21
Jan-Are Larsen	66	65	73	70	274	8,273.21
Gary Clark	72	68	64	70	274	8,273.21
Oliver Wilson	67	68	69	70	274	8,273.21
Philip Archer	65	72	67	71	275	4,211.82
Simon Hurd	65	67	69	74	275	4,211.82
John Mellor	65	68	70	72	275	4,211.82
Marcel Haremza	67	66	74	69	276	3,058.58
David Fisher	66	68	70	72	276	3,058.58
Stephen Browne	69	67	68	72	276	3,058.58
Jamie Little	66	71	68	72	277	2,481.96
Ian Garbutt	69	69	71	68	277	2,481.96
David Orr	67	67	70	73	277	2,481.96
David Patrick	72	67	66	72	277	2,481.96
Johan Axgren	69	69	66	74	278	2,030.70
Matthew King	67	70	71	70	278	2,030.70
Garry Houston	69	71	68	71	279	1,679.71
Olivier David	65	68	71	75	279	1,679.71
Peter Gustafsson	66	68	75	70	279	1,679.71
Alex Balicki	69	70	71	70	280	1,398.92
Marc Cayeux	65	72	69	74	280	1,398.92
Paul Streeter	67	70	73	70	280	1,398.92
Benoit Teilleria	73	64	70	73	280	1,398.92
Fredrik Widmark	69	68	73	70	280	1,398.92
Michiel Bothma	68	70	71	71	280	1,398.92
Benn Barham	66	72	70	73	281	1,263.55
Chris Kelly	66	73	68	74	281	1,263.55
Johan Kok	75	64	69	73	281	1,263.55

Ryder Cup Wales Challenge

Northop Golf & Country Club, Chester, Wales
Par 35-36–71; 6,735 yards

August 5-8
purse, €125,000

	SCORES				TOTAL	MONEY
Graeme Storm	68	63	64	67	262	€20,000
Matthew King	64	65	66	70	265	13,750
Lee Slattery	70	65	66	67	268	8,125
Marc Warren	70	66	65	67	268	8,125
Leif Westerberg	65	69	68	67	269	6,250
David Griffiths	71	65	62	72	270	5,000
Henrik Nystrom	68	67	65	71	271	4,000

	SCORES				TOTAL	MONEY
Magnus Persson Atlevi	68	65	69	70	272	3,083.33
Mikael Lundberg	66	65	65	76	272	3,083.33
Gareth Paddison	69	69	65	69	272	3,083.33
Kariem Baraka	68	67	69	69	273	2,375
Matthew Griffiths	65	69	67	72	273	2,375
David Patrick	63	71	68	71	273	2,375
Garry Houston	67	70	69	68	274	1,875
Jan-Åre Larsen	69	69	65	71	274	1,875
Carl Suneson	68	70	67	69	274	1,875
Carlos Quevedo	70	65	67	72	274	1,875
Oskar Bergman	66	69	65	74	274	1,875
Olivier David	66	72	70	67	275	1,353.13
Lee S. James	67	68	71	69	275	1,353.13
Roope Kakko	71	68	67	69	275	1,353.13
Simon Dunn	66	68	71	70	275	1,353.13
Knud Storgaard	67	65	71	73	276	1,075
Pelle Edberg	67	72	68	69	276	1,075
Titch Moore	65	68	74	69	276	1,075
Denny Lucas	71	66	68	71	276	1,075
Jean Hugo	71	68	71	66	276	1,075
Marc Cayeux	65	68	70	73	276	1,075
Neil Cheetham	71	68	69	68	276	1,075
Carlos Balmaseda	69	70	67	70	276	1,075
Sean Whiffin	71	66	71	68	276	1,075
David Smith	66	66	73	71	276	1,075
Sebastien Delagrange	67	71	67	71	276	1,075

BMW Russian Open

See PGA European Tour section.

Rolex Trophy

Geneva Golf Club, Geneva, Switzerland
Par 36-36–72; 6,727 yards
(Event shortened to 54 holes—rain.)

August 19-22
purse, €163,500

	SCORES			TOTAL	MONEY
Philip Archer	65	67	66	198	€17,000
Lee Slattery	71	67	65	203	11,000
Marc Cayeux	68	69	67	204	8,500
Richard Bland	66	70	68	204	8,500
Graeme Storm	66	68	70	204	8,500
Ian Garbutt	73	67	65	205	6,500
Matthew King	69	67	69	205	6,500
Alvaro Salto	65	64	76	205	6,500
Steven Jeppesen	71	69	66	206	5,700
Henrik Nystrom	68	68	70	206	5,700
Ariel Canete	68	71	68	207	5,400
Garry Houston	68	67	73	208	5,200
Johan Axgren	71	69	70	210	4,720
Peter Gustafsson	68	71	71	210	4,720
Mikael Lundberg	70	68	72	210	4,720
Matthew Morris	69	69	72	210	4,720
Fredrik Henge	68	69	73	210	4,720
Michael Kirk	68	72	72	212	4,400

Norwegian Challenge

Vestfold Golf Club, Tonsberg, Norway
Par 36-36–72; 7,016 yards
(Event shortened to 54 holes—rain.)

August 19-22
purse, €105,000

	SCORES			TOTAL	MONEY
Stephen Browne	68	70	67	205	€16,800
Denny Lucas	68	69	71	208	8,400
Oskar Bergman	69	68	71	208	8,400
Mark Sanders	72	66	70	208	8,400
Andrew Butterfield	68	69	72	209	5,250
Paul Blaikie	71	68	71	210	4,200
Cesar Monasterio	70	72	69	211	2,646
Paul Nilbrink	71	74	66	211	2,646
Titch Moore	72	71	68	211	2,646
Morten Hagen	72	69	70	211	2,646
Sebastien Delagrange	70	71	70	211	2,646
Shaun Webster	70	71	71	212	1,837.50
Gustavo Rojas	68	72	72	212	1,837.50
David Drysdale	72	68	72	212	1,837.50
Magnus A. Carlsson	70	72	70	212	1,837.50
Julien Van Hauwe	71	72	71	214	1,522.50
Stuart Manley	72	71	71	214	1,522.50
Oyvind Rojahn	69	72	74	215	1,182.30
David Higgins	70	72	73	215	1,182.30
Brian Akstrup	69	70	76	215	1,182.30
Craig Williams	70	70	75	215	1,182.30
Jason Dransfield	68	77	70	215	1,182.30
Mark Mouland	71	72	73	216	976.50
Sean Whiffin	72	70	74	216	976.50
Sarel Son-Houi	67	75	74	216	976.50
Graham Gordon	68	75	73	216	976.50
Pelle Edberg	74	72	71	217	882
Linus Pettersson	73	71	73	217	882
Richard Finch	70	75	72	217	882
Peter Whiteford	72	72	73	217	882
Bruno-Teva Lecuona	71	72	74	217	882

Skandia PGA Open

Arlandastad Golf Club, Stockholm, Sweden
Par 34-36–70; 6,780 yards

August 26-29
purse, €109,038

	SCORES				TOTAL	MONEY
Matthew King	64	71	66	69	270	€17,393.89
Johan Axgren	70	67	67	68	272	8,696.94
Magnus A. Carlsson	67	70	69	66	272	8,696.94
Gareth Paddison	68	68	70	66	272	8,696.94
Kalle Brink	73	63	69	68	273	4,420.95
Per G. Nyman	69	67	70	67	273	4,420.95
Jan-Are Larsen	68	71	65	69	273	4,420.95
Hampus Von Post	67	69	69	69	274	2,826.51
Oliver Wilson	70	68	65	71	274	2,826.51
Fredrik Henge	71	69	66	69	275	2,286.51
Stuart Davis	70	69	67	69	275	2,286.51
Pelle Edberg	74	64	68	70	276	2,011.17

	SCORES				TOTAL	MONEY
Henrik Nystrom	64	69	71	72	276	2,011.17
Lee Slattery	72	65	70	70	277	1,848.10
Marc Cayeux	70	68	71	69	278	1,521.96
Adam Mednick	70	69	68	71	278	1,521.96
Oskar Bergman	71	67	70	70	278	1,521.96
Graeme Storm	70	68	67	73	278	1,521.96
Tuomas Tuovinen	69	68	70	71	278	1,521.96
Jean Hugo	69	71	68	71	279	1,134.23
Andrew Butterfield	71	68	70	70	279	1,134.23
Leif Westerberg	68	66	72	73	279	1,134.23
Mattias Eliasson	70	68	72	70	280	1,021.89
Titch Moore	67	70	72	71	280	1,021.89
Tom Whitehouse	68	67	71	74	280	1,021.89
Philip Archer	68	68	74	71	281	945.79
Peter Kaensche	69	68	72	72	281	945.79
Sion Bebb	69	71	72	69	281	945.79
Ari Savolainen	72	70	69	70	281	945.79
*Oskar Henningsson	73	69	67	72	281	

BA-CA Golf Open

Fontana Golf Club, Vienna, Austria
Par 35-36–71; 6,976 yards

September 2-5
purse, €150,000

	SCORES				TOTAL	MONEY
Markus Brier	65	63	66	67	261	€24,000
Lee Slattery	67	65	72	65	269	13,500
Roope Kakko	66	67	65	71	269	13,500
Sam Walker	64	68	65	73	270	9,000
*Bernd Wiesberger	71	65	67	67	270	
Van Phillips	67	71	66	67	271	6,100
Graeme Storm	70	69	65	67	271	6,100
Oliver Wilson	67	66	72	66	271	6,100
Johan Skold	67	70	66	69	272	3,900
Daniel Vancsik	72	67	64	69	272	3,900
Pasi Purhonen	71	66	66	70	273	2,962.50
Ian Garbutt	70	68	70	65	273	2,962.50
Ariel Canete	71	67	69	66	273	2,962.50
Gareth Paddison	71	65	69	68	273	2,962.50
Jan-Are Larsen	70	68	65	71	274	2,475
John Mellor	65	67	71	71	274	2,475
Alvaro Salto	71	68	65	71	275	1,965
Richard Bland	69	71	67	68	275	1,965
Sam Little	67	69	69	70	275	1,965
Claude Grenier	69	70	64	72	275	1,965
Mark Sanders	64	69	70	72	275	1,965
Fredrik Henge	72	66	69	69	276	1,440
Massimo Florioli	69	68	68	71	276	1,440
Benoit Teilleria	70	66	67	73	276	1,440
David Higgins	68	69	70	69	276	1,440
Craig Williams	72	68	72	64	276	1,440
Johan Axgren	66	72	72	67	277	1,290
Marcel Haremza	66	67	72	72	277	1,290
David Drysdale	69	71	69	68	277	1,290
Oskar Bergman	70	68	70	69	277	1,290
Kariem Baraka	69	69	68	71	277	1,290

Telia Grand Prix

Ljunghusens Golf Club, Stockholm, Sweden   September 9-12
Par 35-37–72; 6,790 yards   purse, €131,460

	SCORES				TOTAL	MONEY
Lee Slattery	66	75	66	74	281	€21,033.68
Hampus Von Post	67	71	71	73	282	14,460.66
Mattias Eliasson	66	72	70	75	283	8,544.93
Tom Whitehouse	67	68	68	80	283	8,544.93
Matthew Cort	71	70	72	71	284	4,056.50
Oliver Wilson	69	72	71	72	284	4,056.50
Richard Bland	69	73	69	73	284	4,056.50
Fredrik Henge	71	72	66	75	284	4,056.50
Mattias Nilsson	73	68	65	78	284	4,056.50
Johan Axgren	69	68	67	80	284	4,056.50
Graeme Storm	66	68	66	84	284	4,056.50
Jamie Little	70	71	72	72	285	2,366.29
Oliver Whiteley	74	70	69	72	285	2,366.29
Fredrik Widmark	72	70	66	77	285	2,366.29
Bruno Lecuona	67	71	71	77	286	1,971.91
Joakim Rask	72	70	65	79	286	1,971.91
John Mellor	74	65	68	79	286	1,971.91
Oskar Bergman	71	73	71	72	287	1,325.36
Stuart Davis	71	73	71	72	287	1,325.36
Per G. Nyman	70	73	70	74	287	1,325.36
Paul Dwyer	72	66	74	75	287	1,325.36
Alvaro Salto	68	72	71	76	287	1,325.36
Adam Mednick	69	69	73	76	287	1,325.36
Christian Nilsson	67	70	72	78	287	1,325.36
Thomas Nielsen	69	74	64	80	287	1,325.36
Peter Gustafsson	66	70	70	81	287	1,325.36
Sam Little	64	74	68	81	287	1,325.36
David Drysdale	67	69	67	84	287	1,325.36
David Patrick	69	73	71	75	288	1,025.39
Andre Bossert	69	74	70	75	288	1,025.39
Carlos Quevedo	68	75	68	77	288	1,025.39
Craig Spence	68	72	71	77	288	1,025.39
Ryan Reid	68	69	73	78	288	1,025.39
Gareth Paddison	73	69	67	79	288	1,025.39
Gregory Bourdy	69	69	71	79	288	1,025.39

Open de Toulouse

Golf de Toulouse-Palmola, Buzet-sur-Tarn, France   September 23-26
Par 36-36–72; 6,801 yards   purse, €110,000

	SCORES				TOTAL	MONEY
Marc Cayeux	65	71	72	68	276	€17,600
David Drysdale	70	69	69	68	276	12,100
(Cayeux defeated Drysdale on first playoff hole.)						
Lee Slattery	69	69	72	67	277	7,150
Jeppe Huldahl	71	69	68	69	277	7,150
Gregory Bourdy	66	75	67	71	279	5,500
Cedric Menut	68	70	72	71	281	4,400
Alex Balicki	70	74	69	69	282	2,772
Fredrik Henge	68	68	72	74	282	2,772

	SCORES				TOTAL	MONEY
Daniel Vancsik	74	67	73	68	282	2,772
Michael Kirk	71	69	67	75	282	2,772
Brian Akstrup	73	68	70	71	282	2,772
Marco Soffietti	71	68	71	73	283	1,925
Benn Barham	73	73	67	70	283	1,925
David Griffiths	72	70	73	68	283	1,925
Gabriel Canizares	72	66	71	74	283	1,925
Tom Whitehouse	74	68	71	71	284	1,595
Craig Williams	73	70	71	70	284	1,595
Alvaro Salto	71	71	69	74	285	1,338.33
Stefano Reale	67	73	74	71	285	1,338.33
Edward Rush	68	74	73	70	285	1,338.33
Sam Little	72	73	71	70	286	1,067
Didier de Vooght	71	74	73	68	286	1,067
Ariel Canete	70	76	72	68	286	1,067
Carlos de Corral	66	66	76	78	286	1,067
Johan Axgren	66	76	73	72	287	979
Andrew Butterfield	73	73	71	70	287	979
Sebastien Delagrange	70	75	68	74	287	979
Graeme Storm	66	71	76	74	287	979
Kalle Brink	71	72	76	69	288	847
Knud Storgaard	71	73	69	75	288	847
Renaud Guillard	74	69	74	71	288	847
Raimo Sjoberg	70	72	75	71	288	847
Erol Simsek	70	76	71	71	288	847
Fredrik Widmark	70	73	77	68	288	847
Raphael Pellicioli	70	73	72	73	288	847
Steven Jeppesen	71	72	71	74	288	847

Estoril Challenge Open Portugal Telecom

Oitavos Golf, Quinta da Marinha, Portugal
Par 36-35–71; 6,893 yards

September 30-October 3
purse, €113,000

	SCORES				TOTAL	MONEY
Tom Whitehouse	69	67	68	70	274	€18,080
Kalle Brink	74	69	70	65	278	12,430
Fredrik Henge	71	67	70	71	279	7,345
Sam Little	72	72	67	68	279	7,345
Olivier David	73	70	71	66	280	4,595.33
David Higgins	74	69	66	71	280	4,595.33
David Griffiths	71	73	69	67	280	4,595.33
Marcus Higley	70	70	70	71	281	2,938
Gregory Bourdy	72	71	70	68	281	2,938
Philip Archer	72	71	70	69	282	2,169.60
Sion Bebb	71	72	70	69	282	2,169.60
Henrik Nystrom	71	70	73	68	282	2,169.60
Erol Simsek	72	69	71	70	282	2,169.60
Mikael Lundberg	74	71	66	71	282	2,169.60
Magnus Persson Atlevi	74	70	69	70	283	1,638.50
Greig Hutcheon	71	68	70	74	283	1,638.50
Andre Bossert	72	69	71	71	283	1,638.50
Matthew King	70	72	71	70	283	1,638.50
Richard Bland	73	73	65	73	284	1,173.32
Paul Dwyer	68	72	70	74	284	1,173.32
Gary Clark	73	72	70	69	284	1,173.32
Johan Skold	71	71	72	70	284	1,173.32

	SCORES				TOTAL	MONEY
Magnus A. Carlsson	71	71	73	69	284	1,173.32
Oliver Wilson	72	74	68	70	284	1,173.32
Marc Pendaries	71	71	71	72	285	994.40
Marco Soffietti	77	67	69	72	285	994.40
Andrew Butterfield	73	72	69	71	285	994.40
Lee Slattery	71	70	71	73	285	994.40
Daniel Vancsik	73	73	67	72	285	994.40
Oyvind Rojahn	73	72	72	69	286	915.30
John Mellor	73	73	73	67	286	915.30

Attijari Wafa - Tikida Beach Moroccan Classic

Golf du Soleil, Agadir, Morocco
Par 35-35–70; 6,477 yards

October 7-10
purse, €130,000

	SCORES				TOTAL	MONEY
Graeme Storm	64	67	68	65	264	€20,800
Juan Abbate	67	69	66	66	268	14,300
Mark Mouland	72	62	70	65	269	8,450
Sion Bebb	64	69	70	66	269	8,450
Mattias Nilsson	67	66	69	68	270	4,875
David Higgins	69	69	65	67	270	4,875
Stephen Browne	68	67	70	65	270	4,875
Ariel Canete	64	68	71	67	270	4,875
Matthew King	75	66	67	63	271	2,990
Michael Kirk	72	65	70	64	271	2,990
Alessandro Napoleoni	69	67	71	65	272	2,275
Francesco Guermani	65	67	69	71	272	2,275
Peter Gustafsson	67	69	67	69	272	2,275
Daniel Vancsik	66	67	75	64	272	2,275
Gabriel Canizares	75	66	66	65	272	2,275
Gareth Paddison	70	70	68	64	272	2,275
Andre Bossert	70	70	68	65	273	1,690
David Drysdale	68	70	66	69	273	1,690
David Griffiths	68	72	64	69	273	1,690
Greig Hutcheon	68	69	65	72	274	1,240.78
Paul Dwyer	70	66	70	68	274	1,240.78
Simon Hurd	72	67	67	68	274	1,240.78
Benoit Teilleria	69	69	69	67	274	1,240.78
Mikael Lundberg	66	71	71	66	274	1,240.78
Francois Delamontagne	68	71	67	68	274	1,240.78
Kariem Baraka	69	70	70	65	274	1,240.78
Kyron Sullivan	74	64	69	67	274	1,240.78
David Dixon	72	67	63	72	274	1,240.78
Magnus Persson Atlevi	70	68	67	70	275	1,040
Niki Zitny	70	71	70	64	275	1,040
Richard Bland	67	68	69	71	275	1,040
Henrik Nystrom	67	68	75	65	275	1,040
Jeppe Huldahl	72	68	66	69	275	1,040

Donnington Grove Computacenter English Open

Donnington Grove Country Club, Donnington, England
Par 36-36–72; 7,108 yards

October 14-17
purse, €110,000

	SCORES				TOTAL	MONEY
Matthew King	67	70	66	69	272	€17,600
David Higgins	71	68	71	65	275	12,100
Oskar Bergman	68	69	69	71	277	7,700
Richard Bland	69	67	70	72	278	6,600
David Griffiths	66	73	70	70	279	5,500
Johan Kok	72	70	68	70	280	4,400
Mattias Eliasson	69	74	67	71	281	3,300
David Fisher	70	69	71	71	281	3,300
Erol Simsek	72	66	74	70	282	2,530
Tom Whitehouse	71	72	69	70	282	2,530
Marcus Higley	71	68	74	70	283	2,090
Russell Claydon	73	72	66	72	283	2,090
Kariem Baraka	72	70	70	71	283	2,090
Garry Houston	68	74	74	68	284	1,815
Ian Garbutt	70	71	71	72	284	1,815
Jan-Are Larsen	73	71	68	73	285	1,441
Benn Barham	72	71	70	72	285	1,441
Chris Rodgers	73	68	73	71	285	1,441
Peter Gustafsson	72	69	73	71	285	1,441
Phil Worthington	73	72	69	71	285	1,441
Magnus Persson Atlevi	73	71	67	75	286	1,023
Kalle Brink	72	73	70	71	286	1,023
Johan Axgren	73	68	70	75	286	1,023
Christian Nilsson	71	73	71	71	286	1,023
Andre Bossert	73	69	73	71	286	1,023
Johan Skold	72	74	71	69	286	1,023
Fredrik Widmark	71	69	72	74	286	1,023
Ariel Canete	72	70	72	72	286	1,023
Mark Mouland	73	71	70	73	287	869
Olivier David	70	72	71	74	287	869
Michael Hoey	75	67	74	71	287	869
Carl Suneson	68	71	72	76	287	869
Michele Reale	75	69	70	73	287	869
Mark Pullan	72	73	74	68	287	869

Bouygues Telecom Grand Final

Golf du Medoc, Bordeaux, France
Par 35-36–71; 6,917 yards

October 21-24
purse, €200,000

	SCORES				TOTAL	MONEY
David Drysdale	67	65	69	70	271	€34,250
Mattias Eliasson	67	65	71	68	271	22,800
(Drysdale defeated Eliasson on first playoff hole.)						
Oskar Bergman	71	65	67	70	273	12,890
Sam Walker	70	67	64	73	274	10,280
Lee Slattery	67	71	69	68	275	8,730
Neil Cheetham	65	75	70	66	276	7,685
Peter Gustafsson	67	71	72	66	276	7,685
Marc Cayeux	67	69	70	71	277	6,268.67
Matthew Morris	66	71	69	71	277	6,268.67

	SCORES				TOTAL	MONEY
Oliver Wilson	68	67	75	67	277	6,268.67
Daniel Vancsik	73	72	65	68	278	5,306
David Higgins	68	68	72	71	279	4,637.50
Edward Rush	68	68	74	69	279	4,637.50
Alessandro Tadini	68	68	72	72	280	3,598.93
Jan-Are Larsen	67	72	68	73	280	3,598.93
Gareth Paddison	68	69	75	68	280	3,598.93
Richard Bland	69	75	66	71	281	2,786.60
Henrik Nystrom	74	67	69	71	281	2,786.60
Philip Archer	71	71	71	69	282	2,550.20
Garry Houston	69	71	71	72	283	2,245.80
Ian Garbutt	70	69	71	73	283	2,245.80
Gary Clark	74	72	70	67	283	2,245.80
Johan Skold	67	69	72	75	283	2,245.80
Steven Jeppesen	71	71	72	69	283	2,245.80
John Mellor	73	70	69	72	284	1,892.04
Leif Westerberg	70	72	70	72	284	1,892.04
Kyron Sullivan	68	74	70	72	284	1,892.04
Michael Kirk	70	68	72	74	284	1,892.04
Ariel Canete	68	69	77	70	284	1,892.04
Kariem Baraka	71	72	67	75	285	1,686.40
Gregory Bourdy	67	74	70	74	285	1,686.40

Asian Tour

Areeya Thailand Open

Royal Thai Air Force Club, Bangkok, Thailand
Par 36-36–72; 7,240 yards

January 22-25
purse, US$300,000

	SCORES				TOTAL	MONEY
Boonchu Ruangkit	68	66	69	67	270	US$48,450
Prayad Marksaeng	70	66	67	69	272	25,995
Kim Jong-duck	69	67	65	71	272	25,995
Mardan Mamat	71	67	69	67	274	13,500
Craig Kamps	70	68	67	69	274	13,500
Richard Moir	66	71	73	66	276	9,750
Paul Spargo	67	70	68	71	276	9,750
Thongchai Jaidee	71	69	69	68	277	7,095
Kang Wook-soon	63	69	68	77	277	7,095
Thaworn Wiratchant	66	68	75	69	278	5,752.50
Jim Johnson	70	67	70	71	278	5,752.50
Edward Loar	71	69	71	68	279	4,641
Bryan Saltus	69	68	72	70	279	4,641
Adam Groom	65	72	70	72	279	4,641
Harmeet Kahlon	68	69	71	71	279	4,641
Thammanoon Srirot	69	69	65	76	279	4,641
Eiji Mizoguchi	70	72	71	67	280	3,810
Scott Taylor	71	71	69	69	280	3,810
Gary Rusnak	69	69	72	70	280	3,810
Mike Cunning	69	70	71	70	280	3,810
Yeh Chang-ting	72	71	71	67	281	3,420
Vivek Bhandari	71	71	71	68	281	3,420
Amandeep Johl	70	71	69	71	281	3,420
Gaurav Ghei	71	71	71	69	282	3,105
Somkiat Srisanga	70	71	70	71	282	3,105
Chawalit Plaphol	70	68	71	73	282	3,105
Uttam Singh Mundy	67	69	70	76	282	3,105
Gerald Rosales	71	70	70	72	283	2,880
Unho Park	70	72	74	68	284	2,655
Anthony Kang	74	69	71	70	284	2,655
Anthony Gilligan	70	71	72	71	284	2,655
Chen Chung-cheng	71	70	68	75	284	2,655

Johnnie Walker Classic

Alpine Golf & Sports Club, Bangkok, Thailand
Par 36-36–72; 7,072 yards

January 29-February 1
purse, US$1,800,000

	SCORES				TOTAL	MONEY
Miguel Angel Jimenez	70	66	67	68	271	US$301,787.93
Jyoti Randhawa	69	70	70	64	273	157,277.03
Thomas Bjorn	64	68	70	71	273	157,277.03
Boonchu Ruangkit	71	68	70	65	274	61,808.63
Shaun Micheel	70	70	67	67	274	61,808.63
Thongchai Jaidee	67	72	67	68	274	61,808.63
Raphael Jacquelin	71	68	67	68	274	61,808.63

	SCORES				TOTAL	MONEY
David Smail	67	69	69	69	274	61,808.63
Simon Yates	68	68	68	70	274	61,808.63
Ernie Els	70	67	69	69	275	33,560.15
Scott Gardiner	66	71	69	69	275	33,560.15
Ian Poulter	66	72	67	70	275	33,560.15
Anders Hansen	67	70	72	67	276	26,691.19
Nick Faldo	65	70	72	69	276	26,691.19
Colin Montgomerie	73	67	67	69	276	26,691.19
Miles Tunnicliff	69	70	68	69	276	26,691.19
Richard Green	73	64	67	72	276	26,691.19
Euan Walters	72	68	68	69	277	22,137.03
David Park	69	72	67	69	277	22,137.03
Barry Lane	70	70	67	70	277	22,137.03
Marcus Fraser	67	73	66	71	277	22,137.03
Scott Laycock	70	68	70	70	278	19,918.80
Unho Park	69	71	68	70	278	19,918.80
Y.E. Yang	70	70	66	72	278	19,918.80
Anthony Kang	71	69	71	68	279	17,202.60
David Howell	70	71	70	68	279	17,202.60
Jean-Francois Remesy	70	69	71	69	279	17,202.60
Zhang Lian-wei	68	71	70	70	279	17,202.60
Brad Kennedy	70	70	70	69	279	17,202.60
Brian Davis	71	71	66	71	279	17,202.60
David Lynn	68	66	71	74	279	17,202.60
Philip Golding	71	69	73	67	280	14,486.40
John Bickerton	70	70	73	67	280	14,486.40
Gary Rusnak	71	67	73	69	280	14,486.40
Stephen Dodd	69	70	71	71	281	12,856.68
Trevor Immelman	69	69	72	71	281	12,856.68
Soren Kjeldsen	68	69	72	72	281	12,856.68
Nick O'Hern	69	68	71	73	281	12,856.68
Adam Scott	70	69	67	75	281	12,856.68
Henrik Stenson	70	70	72	70	282	11,045.88
Justin Rose	72	68	71	71	282	11,045.88
Craig Carmichael	76	64	71	71	282	11,045.88
Michael Long	70	68	71	73	282	11,045.88
Mardan Mamat	70	70	70	72	282	11,045.88
Andrew Coltart	72	70	72	69	283	8,691.84
Lee Westwood	72	70	72	69	283	8,691.84
Charl Schwartzel	73	68	71	71	283	8,691.84
Christian Cevaer	70	67	75	71	283	8,691.84
Mike Cunning	68	70	73	72	283	8,691.84
Jarrod Moseley	66	71	74	72	283	8,691.84
Lin Wen-tang	70	70	71	72	283	8,691.84
Graeme McDowell	71	68	71	73	283	8,691.84
Ben Curtis	68	73	73	70	284	6,186.91
Chris Downes	74	67	73	70	284	6,186.91
Robert-Jan Derksen	70	72	74	68	284	6,186.91
Harmeet Kahlon	71	71	71	71	284	6,186.91
James Kingston	71	69	72	72	284	6,186.91
Gary Murphy	73	67	70	74	284	6,186.91
David Bransdon	69	71	74	71	285	5,160.78
Peter Lawrie	73	65	74	73	285	5,160.78
Prom Meesawat	68	72	74	72	286	4,617.54
Jason Knutzon	70	72	74	70	286	4,617.54
Thaworn Wiratchant	68	74	74	70	286	4,617.54
Kenneth Ferrie	70	71	72	73	286	4,617.54
Jean Van de Velde	71	71	70	75	287	3,983.76
Edward Loar	66	76	70	75	287	3,983.76
Jarmo Sandelin	71	71	71	74	287	3,983.76

	SCORES				TOTAL	MONEY
Andrew Pitts	72	67	74	75	288	3,458.63
Simon Dyson	71	66	75	76	288	3,458.63
Peter Fowler	74	68	71	75	288	3,458.63
Terry Price	70	71	74	74	289	2,713.94
Ted Oh	70	70	77	72	289	2,713.94
Andrew Bonhomme	71	71	72	76	290	2,708.29
Amandeep Johl	75	67	73	76	291	2,700.75
Jamie Donaldson	72	69	74	76	291	2,700.75
Frederik Andersson	69	70	76	76	291	2,700.75
Matthew Ecob	72	69	77	78	296	2,693.24

Myanmar Open

Yangon Golf Club, Yangon, Myanmar
Par 36-36–72; 7,011 yards

February 12-15
purse, US$200,000

	SCORES				TOTAL	MONEY
Thongchai Jaidee	69	72	66	69	276	US$32,300
Andrew Pitts	69	71	68	71	279	22,260
Unho Park	70	71	73	67	281	12,400
Mardan Mamat	73	71	70	68	282	9,000
Alistair Presnell	68	71	70	73	282	9,000
Akinori Tani	69	73	72	69	283	6,500
Anthony Kang	72	70	70	71	283	6,500
Mo Joong-kyung	67	74	70	73	284	5,000
Prayad Marksaeng	69	74	72	70	285	4,230
Aung Win	71	69	71	74	285	4,230
Thammanoon Srirot	75	71	73	67	286	3,264
Greg Hanrahan	72	72	71	71	286	3,264
Lin Wen-tang	73	69	71	73	286	3,264
Lee Sung-man	71	75	67	73	286	3,264
Chen Tsang-te	75	69	69	73	286	3,264
Rick Gibson	68	77	74	68	287	2,700
Craig Kamps	68	78	72	69	287	2,700
Frankie Minoza	72	73	72	70	287	2,700
Kenichi Ryu	71	74	74	69	288	2,282.86
David Gleeson	72	69	76	71	288	2,282.86
Rahil Gangjee	70	75	72	71	288	2,282.86
Danny Zarate	76	69	71	72	288	2,282.86
Ashok Kumar	70	74	72	72	288	2,282.86
Glenn Joyner	72	70	73	73	288	2,282.86
Mike Cunning	72	71	71	74	288	2,282.86
Pat Giles	73	74	72	70	289	1,980
Kyi Hla Han	76	71	72	70	289	1,980
Lin Wen-ko	69	75	72	73	289	1,980
Simon Yates	73	75	73	69	290	1,675
Gerry Norquist	73	75	73	69	290	1,675
Arjun Singh	73	76	71	70	290	1,675
Chris Williams	72	76	71	71	290	1,675
Prom Meesawat	77	71	71	71	290	1,675
Terry Pilkadaris	75	71	71	73	290	1,675
James Stewart	72	72	72	74	290	1,675
Yoshinobu Tsukada	71	70	73	76	290	1,675

Carlsberg Malaysian Open

Saujana Golf & Country Club, Kuala Lumpur, Malaysia
Par 36-36–72; 6,971 yards

February 19-22
purse, US$1,210,000

	SCORES				TOTAL	MONEY
Thongchai Jaidee	71	71	64	68	274	US$201,660
Brad Kennedy	69	70	70	67	276	134,440
Chawalit Plaphol	68	72	65	73	278	62,516.67
Thomas Levet	69	70	69	70	278	62,516.67
Prayad Marksaeng	70	69	69	70	278	62,516.67
Andrew Marshall	71	69	68	72	280	39,325
Miguel Angel Jimenez	70	72	67	71	280	39,325
Klas Eriksson	68	74	70	69	281	25,954.50
Thaworn Wiratchant	70	67	72	72	281	25,954.50
David Dixon	70	73	69	69	281	25,954.50
Lee Sung-man	69	68	67	77	281	25,954.50
Paul McGinley	68	70	74	70	282	19,148.25
Mikko Ilonen	68	68	75	71	282	19,148.25
Lin Wen-tang	70	75	67	70	282	19,148.25
Jason Knutzon	71	69	68	74	282	19,148.25
Jose Manuel Carriles	72	70	71	70	283	14,507.90
Colin Montgomerie	73	66	72	72	283	14,507.90
Robert Karlsson	68	71	73	71	283	14,507.90
Stephen Dodd	68	73	75	67	283	14,507.90
John Bickerton	70	75	71	67	283	14,507.90
Gregory Hanrahan	68	70	74	71	283	14,507.90
Y.E. Yang	71	70	75	67	283	14,507.90
Martin Maritz	66	74	72	71	283	14,507.90
Richard McEvoy	70	73	69	71	283	14,507.90
Marcus Fraser	69	72	67	75	283	14,507.90
Martin Erlandsson	68	74	71	71	284	11,495
Johan Edfors	74	69	69	72	284	11,495
Jyoti Randhawa	72	71	70	71	284	11,495
Wade Ormsby	73	70	69	72	284	11,495
Marcus Both	74	69	70	71	284	11,495
David Howell	69	71	78	67	285	9,559
Thammanoon Srirot	71	73	72	69	285	9,559
Joakim Haeggman	73	71	73	68	285	9,559
James Hepworth	69	70	73	73	285	9,559
Stephen A. Lindskog	72	73	71	69	285	9,559
Mads Vibe-Hastrup	72	69	69	75	285	9,559
Kyi Hla Han	73	70	72	71	286	8,228
Padraig Harrington	69	74	71	72	286	8,228
Martin LeMesurier	70	75	71	70	286	8,228
Chen Yuan-chi	73	70	73	70	286	8,228
Costantino Rocca	69	72	73	73	287	6,897
Andrew Pitts	71	69	71	76	287	6,897
Jose Manuel Lara	68	74	71	74	287	6,897
Chris Gane	74	69	72	72	287	6,897
Anthony Kang	68	74	73	72	287	6,897
Terry Price	66	73	77	71	287	6,897
Harmeet Kahlon	73	72	71	71	287	6,897
Charlie Wi	75	67	79	67	288	5,687
Fredrik Andersson Hed	75	64	74	75	288	5,687
Sushi Ishigaki	72	72	73	71	288	5,687
Jeev Milkha Singh	74	71	71	73	289	4,840
Damien McGrane	70	75	72	72	289	4,840
Stuart Little	73	72	69	75	289	4,840
Satoshi Tomiyama	71	71	71	76	289	4,840

	SCORES				TOTAL	MONEY
Mattias Eliasson	75	68	70	77	290	4,114
Amandeep Johl	73	72	72	73	290	4,114
Stephen Scahill	72	72	71	76	291	3,751
Warren Bennett	71	71	74	76	292	3,448.50
Mike Cunning	71	69	73	79	292	3,448.50
Sam Walker	70	72	73	77	292	3,448.50
Lin Wen-ko	72	73	76	71	292	3,448.50
Francois Delamontagne	71	74	73	75	293	3,085.50
Eddie Lee	70	75	69	79	293	3,085.50
Robert-Jan Derksen	69	74	77	74	294	2,843.50
Jeppe Huldahl	75	68	73	78	294	2,843.50
Robert Rock	74	70	75	76	295	2,601.50
Jamie Elson	66	74	78	77	295	2,601.50
Chris Williams	70	75	74	78	297	2,420
Sven Struver	72	73	76	77	298	2,299
Scott Taylor	71	72	80	77	300	2,216
Andrew Coltart	72	73	77		WD	

DHL Philippine Open

Riviera Golf & Country Club, Manila, Philippines
Par 71

February 26-29
purse, US$150,000

	SCORES				TOTAL	MONEY
Edward Michaels	70	74	69	69	282	US$24,225
*Juvic Pagunsan	75	70	66	74	285	
Jonathan Cheetham	70	71	74	73	288	12,998
Adam Groom	65	75	71	77	288	12,998
Chen Yuan-chi	71	74	73	71	289	6,750
Richard Moir	69	73	73	74	289	6,750
Mo Joong-kyung	73	72	76	69	290	5,250
Scott Taylor	72	73	75	71	291	3,865
Adam Fraser	71	73	74	73	291	3,865
Amandeep Johl	67	74	75	75	291	3,865
Rick Gibson	72	75	73	72	292	2,877
Antonio Lascuna	69	74	73	76	292	2,877
Greg Hanrahan	71	77	74	71	293	2,427
Alistair Presnell	71	74	74	74	293	2,427
Jeev Milkha Singh	68	71	75	79	293	2,427
*Jay Bayron	70	76	74	74	294	
Danny Zarate	72	73	74	75	294	2,160
Glenn Joyner	72	74	73	75	294	2,160
Jyoti Randhawa	72	73	77	73	295	1,980
Bryan Saltus	75	73	75	72	295	1,980
Clay Devers	73	75	78	70	296	1,781
Sushi Ishigaki	72	75	76	73	296	1,781
Angelo Que	72	71	77	76	296	1,781
David Gleeson	69	74	77	76	296	1,781
Gary Rusnak	71	74	79	73	297	1,575
Danilo Delos Santos	73	74	78	72	297	1,575
Ross Bain	72	76	76	73	297	1,575
*S. Sivachandran	71	76	76	74	297	
Lin Chie-hsiang	72	75	74	76	297	1,575
Attaphon Prathummanee	74	75	71	77	297	1,575

Caltex Masters

Laguna National Golf & Country Club, Singapore
Par 36-36–72; 7,145 yards

March 18-21
purse, US$900,000

	SCORES				TOTAL	MONEY
Colin Montgomerie	71	69	67	65	272	US$150,000
Gregory Hanrahan	68	68	67	72	275	100,000
Nick O'Hern	71	68	70	67	276	50,670
Jyoti Randhawa	72	64	74	66	276	50,670
Barry Lane	71	65	67	75	278	32,220
Patrik Sjoland	70	71	70	67	278	32,220
Wang Ter-chang	75	68	66	69	278	32,220
Mardan Mamat	67	68	70	74	279	21,330
Brett Rumford	71	69	70	69	279	21,330
Joakim Haeggman	73	70	69	68	280	18,000
Jean-Francois Remesy	72	69	72	68	281	14,370
Marten Olander	73	68	69	71	281	14,370
Thomas Levet	67	75	65	74	281	14,370
James Kingston	68	69	70	74	281	14,370
Matthew Blackey	70	73	67	71	281	14,370
David Gleeson	70	71	69	71	281	14,370
Kyi Hla Han	68	69	74	71	282	11,055
Damien McGrane	68	68	75	71	282	11,055
Kang Wook-soon	70	70	69	73	282	11,055
Anthony Kang	69	73	71	69	282	11,055
Terry Price	70	70	69	73	282	11,055
Y.E. Yang	74	69	66	73	282	11,055
Anders Hansen	74	70	70	69	283	8,685
Peter Hanson	68	73	69	73	283	8,685
Soren Hansen	73	68	71	71	283	8,685
Danny Chia	74	70	72	67	283	8,685
Jonathan Lomas	71	71	65	76	283	8,685
Boonchu Ruangkit	72	70	71	70	283	8,685
Mads Vibe-Hastrup	72	70	70	71	283	8,685
Kim Felton	73	69	71	70	283	8,685
Eddie Lee	64	72	75	72	283	8,685
Hideto Tanihara	71	70	74	68	283	8,685
Simon Yates	70	73	71	70	284	7,065
Thongchai Jaidee	71	68	70	75	284	7,065
Peter Lawrie	68	70	71	76	285	6,210
Emanuele Canonica	69	73	72	71	285	6,210
Michael Campbell	69	70	72	74	285	6,210
Chen Yuan-chi	68	71	76	70	285	6,210
Terry Pilkadaris	71	71	72	71	285	6,210
Adam Groom	72	68	74	71	285	6,210
Scott Barr	70	72	71	72	285	6,210
Richard Green	70	72	75	69	286	5,310
Michael Jonzon	71	73	72	70	286	5,310
Lin Wen-tang	68	73	75	70	286	5,310
Stephen Scahill	74	69	70	74	287	4,770
Brad Kennedy	73	70	70	74	287	4,770
Jason Knutzon	70	74	72	71	287	4,770
Stuart Little	70	73	69	76	288	4,140
Peter O'Malley	72	71	74	71	288	4,140
Unho Park	72	72	72	72	288	4,140
Lee Sung-man	72	69	74	73	288	4,140
Jose Manuel Lara	71	72	66	80	289	3,162.86
Soren Kjeldsen	73	69	74	73	289	3,162.86
Henrik Bjornstad	73	66	69	81	289	3,162.86

	SCORES				TOTAL	MONEY
Peter Hedblom	70	73	76	70	289	3,162.86
Lam Chih-bing	74	70	75	70	289	3,162.86
Jamie Elson	71	73	69	76	289	3,162.86
Hiroyuki Fujita	75	68	75	71	289	3,162.86
Simon Khan	70	69	78	73	290	2,475
Andrew Coltart	69	74	73	74	290	2,475
Daisuke Maruyama	73	70	75	72	290	2,475
Marcus Both	73	70	75	72	290	2,475
Clay Devers	71	70	72	78	291	2,160
Prayad Marksaeng	69	73	70	79	291	2,160
Charl Schwartzel	73	69	71	78	291	2,160
Costantino Rocca	72	70	76	74	292	1,728.26
Zhang Lian-wei	72	72	77	71	292	1,728.26
Thammanoon Srirot	69	70	73	80	292	1,728.26
Charlie Wi	72	72	72	76	292	1,728.26
Gerry Norquist	74	69	75	74	292	1,728.26
Lin Wen-ko	71	73	76	72	292	1,728.26
Roger Chapman	70	68	75	80	293	1,345.89
Arjun Singh	68	75	74	77	294	1,342.23
Chen Tze-chung	74	69	77	75	295	1,336.75
Kim Jong-duck	68	76	71	80	295	1,336.75
Edward Loar	70	73	72	81	296	1,331.26
Ivo Giner	73	68	75	81	297	1,327.60
Peter Fowler	67	77	80	75	299	1,323.95

Royal Challenge Indian Open

Delhi Golf Club, New Delhi, India
Par 36-36—72; 6,831 yards

March 25-28
purse, US$300,000

	SCORES				TOTAL	MONEY
Mardan Mamat	68	67	70	65	270	US$50,000
Pablo Del Olmo	69	66	67	73	275	33,090
Mo Joong-kyung	68	70	70	70	278	16,538
Keith Horne	63	72	70	73	278	16,538
Mukesh Kumar	67	71	71	70	279	11,038
Thaworn Wiratchant	66	69	71	73	279	11,038
Firoz Ali	72	70	69	69	280	8,825
Rick Gibson	70	71	73	67	281	7,375
Lee Sung-man	72	73	70	67	282	6,345
Gary Rusnak	68	69	71	74	282	6,345
Clay Devers	67	69	73	74	283	5,505
Adam Fraser	74	65	74	71	284	5,151
Vijay Kumar	71	68	75	71	285	5,151
Amritinder Singh	68	72	74	71	285	5,151
Kim Felton	71	73	69	73	286	4,230
Digvijay Singh	73	72	67	74	286	4,230
Rafiq Ali	69	71	72	74	286	4,230
Craig Kamps	69	74	72	72	287	3,730
Gerry Norquist	73	66	73	75	287	3,730
Lam Chih-bing	71	69	69	78	287	3,730
Harmeet Kahlon	72	69	77	70	288	3,285
Adam Le Vesconte	74	69	71	74	288	3,285
Edward Michaels	73	72	69	74	288	3,285
Bryan Saltus	68	72	72	76	288	3,285
Stephen Lindskog	69	69	71	79	288	3,285
Ross Bain	69	70	70	79	288	3,285

	SCORES				TOTAL	MONEY
Chris Williams	70	71	78	70	289	2,790
Gaurav Ghei	70	75	74	70	289	2,790
Yeh Chang-ting	68	75	72	74	289	2,790
Anthony Gilligan	72	70	72	75	289	2,790
Greg Hanrahan	70	68	75	76	289	2,790

Volkswagon Masters China

Pine Valley Golf Course, Beijing, China
Par 36-36–72; 7,050 yards

April 29-May 2
purse, US$300,000

	SCORES				TOTAL	MONEY
Rahil Gangjee	69	66	70	68	273	US$48,450
Mo Joong-kyung	70	70	67	66	273	33,390
(Ganjee defeated Mo on first playoff hole.)						
Richard Moir	67	70	69	68	274	14,025
Phillip Price	68	70	67	69	274	14,025
Kang Wook-soon	70	67	68	69	274	14,025
Adam Groom	67	69	69	69	274	14,025
Zhang Lian-wei	68	70	69	69	276	8,250
Kim Felton	70	67	68	71	276	8,250
Gerald Rosales	72	65	71	69	277	5,634
Mardan Mamat	70	68	70	69	277	5,634
Kyi Hla Han	70	68	70	69	277	5,634
Jason Knutzon	69	70	68	70	277	5,634
Alistair Presnell	71	68	68	70	277	5,634
Greg Hanrahan	70	70	70	68	278	4,590
David Hearn	70	69	69	71	279	4,410
Unho Park	71	67	72	70	280	4,140
Keith Horne	68	70	70	72	280	4,140
Chawalit Plaphol	69	71	71	70	281	3,675
Ross Bain	66	73	70	72	281	3,675
Sushi Ishigaki	70	71	69	71	281	3,675
Lee Sung-man	71	71	66	73	281	3,675
Amandeep Johl	71	69	72	70	282	3,285
Koji Katoh	73	69	70	70	282	3,285
Jason Dawes	73	72	66	71	282	3,285
Chris Williams	69	71	70	72	282	3,285
Rick Gibson	69	73	70	71	283	3,015
Ian Woosnam	75	71	66	71	283	3,015
Lin Chie-hsiang	73	73	72	66	284	2,588
Yoshinobu Tsukada	73	71	71	69	284	2,588
Adam Le Vesconte	74	69	71	70	284	2,588
Eddie Lee	71	71	71	71	284	2,588
Lin Wen-tang	71	70	71	72	284	2,588
Edward Michaels	72	69	71	72	284	2,588
Gary Rusnak	69	71	71	73	284	2,588
Anthony Kang	70	72	69	73	284	2,588

Macau Open

Macau Golf & Country Club, Macau
Par 35-36–71; 6,027 yards

May 6-9
purse, US$275,000

	SCORES				TOTAL	MONEY
Jason Knutzon	65	68	68	67	268	US$44,412.50
Thaworn Wiratchant	64	71	69	65	269	30,607.50
Lu Wen-teh	68	71	67	64	270	15,400
Amandeep Johl	62	69	67	72	270	15,400
Padraig Harrington	69	67	66	69	271	10,312.50
Scott Barr	66	70	66	69	271	10,312.50
Harmeet Kahlon	66	66	72	68	272	8,250
Edward Loar	71	67	66	69	273	6,875
Simon Yates	67	76	65	66	274	5,350.13
David Kang	66	69	72	67	274	5,350.13
Lin Wen-tang	65	73	69	67	274	5,350.13
Chen Tze-chung	69	71	62	72	274	5,350.13
Lu Wei-lan	68	71	69	67	275	4,137.38
Andrew Pitts	70	71	67	67	275	4,137.38
Prom Meesawat	68	75	62	70	275	4,137.38
Nico van Rensburg	63	70	71	71	275	4,137.38
Anthony Summers	71	70	70	65	276	3,556.67
Sushi Ishigaki	66	72	71	67	276	3,556.67
Zhang Lian-wei	70	69	69	68	276	3,556.67
Anthony Kang	68	71	70	68	277	2,970
Vivek Bhandari	66	69	73	69	277	2,970
Sung Mao-chang	69	74	65	69	277	2,970
Chen Tsang-te	70	69	69	69	277	2,970
Arjun Singh	69	72	67	69	277	2,970
Lee Sung-man	71	67	69	70	277	2,970
Wang Ter-chang	65	70	72	70	277	2,970
Ewan Porter	68	70	68	71	277	2,970
Des Terblanche	69	70	67	71	277	2,970
Richard Moir	72	70	66	70	278	2,516.25
Koji Katoh	69	68	70	71	278	2,516.25

BMW Asian Open

Tomson Golf Club, Shanghai, China
Par 36-36–72; 7,300 yards

May 13-16
purse, US$1,500,000

	SCORES				TOTAL	MONEY
Miguel Angel Jimenez	71	66	70	67	274	$250,000
Simon Dyson	66	69	66	76	277	166,660
Prayad Marksaeng	67	73	67	71	278	93,900
K.J. Choi	67	73	71	68	279	75,000
Paul McGinley	68	69	72	71	280	53,700
Zhang Lian-wei	70	69	70	71	280	53,700
Adam Groom	69	69	71	71	280	53,700
Unho Park	71	71	72	67	281	35,550
Jean-Francois Lucquin	72	66	70	73	281	35,550
Greg Hanrahan	67	71	75	69	282	26,887.50
Jeev Milkha Singh	71	71	70	70	282	26,887.50
Marcus Both	68	71	73	70	282	26,887.50
Jyoti Randhawa	70	74	68	70	282	26,887.50
Mo Joong-kyung	72	71	73	67	283	22,500

	SCORES				TOTAL	MONEY
Alex Cejka	68	70	72	73	283	22,500
Paul Eales	73	71	69	71	284	21,150
Terry Pilkadaris	75	71	70	69	285	19,400
Rafael Ponce	69	74	72	70	285	19,400
Sam Walker	72	73	68	72	285	19,400
Benn Barham	74	70	73	69	286	16,066.67
Andrew Raitt	71	72	73	70	286	16,066.67
Chris Gane	70	70	75	71	286	16,066.67
Adam Fraser	74	68	73	71	286	16,066.67
Gary Emerson	70	71	74	71	286	16,066.67
Thaworn Wiratchant	72	68	75	71	286	16,066.67
Eddie Lee	72	73	70	71	286	16,066.67
Tom Whitehouse	75	69	70	72	286	16,066.67
Des Terblanche	71	72	67	76	286	16,066.67
Mardan Mamat	74	71	73	69	287	13,125
Pasi Purhonen	74	71	73	69	287	13,125
Johan Axgren	76	70	72	69	287	13,125
Sushi Ishigaki	74	72	71	70	287	13,125
Lin Wen-tang	76	70	74	68	288	11,437.50
James Kingston	69	74	75	70	288	11,437.50
Craig Kamps	70	72	74	72	288	11,437.50
Eiji Mizoguchi	70	72	72	74	288	11,437.50
David Dixon	72	72	76	69	289	9,300
Gregory Bourdy	71	73	75	70	289	9,300
Kim Felton	75	69	74	71	289	9,300
Shaun Webster	72	69	76	72	289	9,300
Boonchu Ruangkit	70	72	75	72	289	9,300
Jonathan Cheetham	70	73	74	72	289	9,300
Matthew Cort	71	70	75	73	289	9,300
Pat Giles	76	69	71	73	289	9,300
Choi Gwang-soo	74	70	71	74	289	9,300
Chen Yuan-chi	74	71	67	77	289	9,300
Edward Loar	70	74	78	68	290	5,884.62
Charlie Wi	73	73	74	70	290	5,884.62
Prom Meesawat	70	74	75	71	290	5,884.62
Jason Dawes	73	70	76	71	290	5,884.62
Sven Struver	71	75	73	71	290	5,884.62
Brian Akstrup	71	72	75	72	290	5,884.62
Brad Kennedy	74	71	73	72	290	5,884.62
Olle Nordberg	77	69	72	72	290	5,884.62
Ted Oh	73	70	74	73	290	5,884.62
Fredrik Henge	72	73	72	73	290	5,884.62
Euan Little	71	69	75	75	290	5,884.62
Ian Garbutt	73	72	70	75	290	5,884.62
Hendrik Buhrmann	72	71	71	76	290	5,884.62
Kalle Brink	71	74	75	71	291	3,750
Benoit Teilleria	71	74	74	72	291	3,750
Craig Williams	71	72	75	73	291	3,750
Craig Spence	68	72	78	73	291	3,750
Jorge Berendt	76	70	72	73	291	3,750
Padraig Harrington	72	72	73	74	291	3,750
Gary Rusnak	69	74	72	76	291	3,750
David Drysdale	68	78	75	71	292	3,075
Andrew Pitts	73	70	71	78	292	3,075
Arjun Singh	72	73	74	74	293	2,850
Gustavo Rojas	75	71	75	73	294	2,369.70
Tim Milford	73	72	75	74	294	2,369.70
Harmeet Kahlon	72	71	76	75	294	2,369.70
Bryan Saltus	71	72	74	77	294	2,369.70
Mattias Eliasson	68	72	76	79	295	2,239.13

	SCORES				TOTAL	MONEY
Christian Reimbold	71	74	77	74	296	2,233.79
Shang Lei	71	74	72	79	296	2,233.79
Chawalit Plaphol	70	76	79	72	297	2,224.87
Andreas Ljunggren	76	70	77	74	297	2,224.87
Gareth Paddison	70	75	78	74	297	2,224.87
Scott Barr	73	73	81	73	300	2,217.74

SK Telecom Open

Baekahmvista Country Club, Seoul, Korea
Par 36-36–72; 7,079 yards

May 20-23
purse, US$400,000

	SCORES				TOTAL	MONEY
Simon Yates	70	69	70	70	279	US$85,470.09
Charlie Wi	70	66	72	72	280	34,188.03
Rick Gibson	70	72	67	71	280	34,188.03
Chung Joon	71	72	68	72	283	20,512.82
Anthony Kang	71	72	68	73	284	15,982.91
Fred Couples	70	74	69	71	284	15,982.91
Shin Yong-jin	72	73	70	70	285	12,991.45
Lee Sung-man	69	73	74	70	286	10,940.17
Kim Jong-duck	77	67	69	73	286	10,940.17
Jason Dawes	70	74	73	70	287	9,230.77
Edward Michaels	72	70	74	71	287	9,230.77
Jung Jae-hoon	76	67	75	70	288	7,863.25
S.K. Ho	72	72	70	74	288	7,863.25
Choi Gwang-soo	75	72	72	70	289	6,153.85
Jang Ik-jae	73	73	70	73	289	6,153.85
Kim Dae-sub	72	70	73	74	289	6,153.85
Thaworn Wiratchant	68	70	76	75	289	6,153.85
K.J. Choi	69	74	72	74	289	6,153.85
Ted Oh	70	71	75	74	290	4,957.26
Choi Ho-sung	71	72	73	74	290	4,957.26
Kang Ji-man	73	73	73	72	291	4,273.50
Paul Spargo	75	71	73	72	291	4,273.50
Chen Tze-chung	74	73	75	69	291	4,273.50
Park Jae-kyung	73	75	70	73	291	4,273.50
Bae Sung-chul	72	73	72	74	291	4,273.50
Eddie Lee	75	70	74	73	292	3,504.27
Harmeet Kahlon	75	72	73	72	292	3,504.27
*Kim Kyung-tae	78	69	71	74	292	
Adam Fraser	75	71	70	76	292	3,504.27
Edward Loar	69	74	72	77	292	3,504.27

Tianjin TEDA Open

Tianjin Warner International Golf Club, Tianjin, China
Par 71; 6,755 yards

August 19-22
purse, US$200,000

	SCORES				TOTAL	MONEY
Thammanoon Srirot	64	67	69	65	265	US$32,300
Boonchu Ruangkit	69	69	64	64	266	22,260
Lu Wei-chih	69	71	68	61	269	12,400
Chen Yuan-chi	67	68	71	65	271	10,000
Simon Yates	65	73	66	68	272	7,500

	SCORES				TOTAL	MONEY
Charlie Wi	67	66	68	71	272	7,500
Alistair Presnell	69	67	71	66	273	5,500
Chung Joon	64	68	71	70	273	5,500
Anura Rohana	66	70	68	70	274	4,460
Park No-seok	69	68	72	66	275	3,580
Chawalit Plaphol	69	68	69	69	275	3,580
Wang Ter-chang	70	67	69	69	275	3,580
Richard Moir	70	69	67	69	275	3,580
Amandeep Johl	68	70	71	67	276	2,940
Anthony Kang	67	70	71	68	276	2,940
Lu Wen-teh	69	70	69	68	276	2,940
Scott Barr	71	69	71	66	277	2,640
Chan Yih-shin	65	74	71	67	277	2,640
Jason Dawes	67	70	72	69	278	2,440
Andrew Pitts	68	66	71	73	278	2,440
Gerald Rosales	65	68	69	77	279	2,340
Gerry Norquist	69	66	75	70	280	2,100
Hao Yuan	70	68	72	70	280	2,100
Robert Jacobson	70	71	68	71	280	2,100
Terry Pilkadaris	68	74	67	71	280	2,100
Ewan Porter	70	68	70	72	280	2,100
Taimur Hussain	69	68	71	72	280	2,100
Lee Sung-man	70	68	69	73	280	2,100
M. Sasidaran	69	72	71	69	281	1,720
Kang Wook-soon	73	70	68	70	281	1,720
Lin Wen-tang	75	64	70	72	281	1,720
Arjun Singh	64	73	71	73	281	1,720
Li Chao	70	69	69	73	281	1,720
Prom Meesawat	69	68	68	76	281	1,720

Kolon Korean Open

Woo Jeong Hills Country Club, Cheonan, Korea
Par 36-36–72; 7,047 yards

September 9-12
purse, US$400,000

	SCORES				TOTAL	MONEY
Edward Loar	73	69	73	71	286	US$85,543
Simon Yates	72	75	73	69	289	42,771
Ernie Els	71	69	75	75	290	29,084
Hendrik Buhrmann	68	74	77	73	292	18,391
Terry Pilkadaris	70	69	75	78	292	18,391
Kang Wook-soon	76	73	72	72	293	14,798
Jang Ik-jae	77	75	70	72	294	12,403
Mo Joong-kyung	71	73	78	72	294	12,403
Ted Oh	74	71	75	74	294	12,403
Choi Sang-ho	71	72	79	73	295	8,839
Amandeep Johl	74	76	72	73	295	8,839
Park No-seok	73	71	77	74	295	8,839
Pat Giles	76	70	77	73	296	6,458
Kim Felton	74	74	74	74	296	6,458
Richard Moir	70	73	78	76	297	5,517
*Kim Bum-sik	79	72	77	70	298	
Choi Gwang-soo	74	73	76	75	298	5,175
Charlie Wi	77	72	73	76	298	5,175
Nam Young-woo	73	74	75	76	298	5,175
*Kang Sung-hoon	72	71	76	79	298	
Jo Hyo-jun	73	72	80	74	299	4,662

	SCORES				TOTAL	MONEY
Ahn Ju-hwan	77	72	74	76	299	4,662
Harmeet Kahlon	75	73	75	76	299	4,662
David Oh	76	69	77	79	301	4,319
Sushi Ishigaki	77	73	75	77	302	4,148
Park Do-kyu	73	75	80	75	303	3,789
Eiji Mizoguchi	78	74	75	76	303	3,789
Kevin Na	73	73	81	76	303	3,789
Edward Michaels	73	74	78	78	303	3,789
*Kim Kyung-tae	74	72	77	80	303	
Des Terblanche	75	71	75	82	303	3,789

Mercuries Taiwan Masters

Taiwan Golf & Country Club, Taiwan, Chinese Taipei
Par 36-36–72; 6,950 yards

September 16-19
purse, US$390,000

	SCORES				TOTAL	MONEY
Thaworn Wiratchant	69	69	71	74	283	US$77,968.10
Chris Williams	70	70	71	74	285	37,034.85
Chen Yuan-chi	74	71	68	72	285	37,034.85
Simon Yates	72	74	69	71	286	19,492.02
Richard Moir	70	74	71	73	288	14,619.02
Yeh Chang-ting	74	75	69	70	288	14,619.02
Chen Tsang-te	73	73	69	74	289	10,720.61
Chang Tse-peng	77	70	67	75	289	10,720.61
Lin Chie-hsiang	72	67	80	71	290	6,705.26
Kim Felton	74	69	75	72	290	6,705.26
Jason Knutzon	72	72	73	73	290	6,705.26
Boonchu Ruangkit	71	76	71	72	290	6,705.26
Gaurav Ghei	74	73	71	72	290	6,705.26
Chen Chung-cheng	70	75	75	71	291	5,132.90
Hsu Mong-nan	77	68	74	72	291	5,132.90
Kao Bo-song	72	73	74	72	291	5,132.90
Danny Chia	75	73	74	70	292	4,385.71
Mike Cunning	73	75	73	71	292	4,385.71
Alistair Presnell	73	75	72	72	292	4,385.71
Huang Tung-liang	76	71	72	73	292	4,385.71
Harmeet Kahlon	73	76	72	72	293	3,924.39
Su Chin-jung	74	75	71	73	293	3,924.39
Hsieh Min-nan	75	73	71	74	293	3,924.39
Gerald Rosales	73	74	75	72	294	3,625.52
Rick Gibson	72	76	72	74	294	3,625.52
Firoz Ali	72	73	74	75	294	3,625.52
Hsieh Chin-sheng	73	73	72	76	294	3,625.52
Olle Nordberg	71	75	75	74	295	3,313.64
Mardan Mamat	75	75	73	72	295	3,313.64
Yoshinobu Tsukada	73	75	72	75	295	3,313.64
Lin Wen-tang	74	74	73	74	295	3,313.64

Taiwan Open

North Bay Golf & Country Club, Chinese Taipei
Par 36-36–72

September 23-26
purse, US$300,000

	SCORES				TOTAL	MONEY
Charlie Wi	76	76	64	68	284	US$50,000
Terry Pilkadaris	72	73	70	72	287	33,090
Chang Tse-peng	75	74	71	68	288	16,537.50
Gaurav Ghei	73	72	69	74	288	16,537.50
Lin Wen-tang	78	73	65	73	289	11,037.50
Lin Chie-hsiang	72	71	71	75	289	11,037.50
Rick Gibson	79	69	72	70	290	` 8,100
Thammanoon Srirot	70	73	73	74	290	8,100
Hsieh Min-nan	72	73	74	73	292	5,836.50
Simon Yates	76	72	70	74	292	5,836.50
Chen Chung-cheng	76	71	71	74	292	5,836.50
Kim Felton	76	71	71	74	292	5,836.50
Wang Ter-chang	78	73	73	69	293	4,707
Lu Wen-teh	74	72	74	73	293	4,707
Chen Chih-hong	78	73	73	70	294	4,140
Clay Devers	78	76	68	72	294	4,140
Lu Wei-chih	77	76	68	73	294	4,140
Harmeet Kahlon	73	74	73	74	294	4,140
Su Chin-jung	79	72	73	71	295	3,610
*Kim Kyung-tae	79	75	69	72	295	
Sushi Ishigaki	75	75	73	72	295	3,610
Lin Keng-chi	73	76	71	75	295	3,610
Hsieh Yu-shu	77	77	71	71	296	3,240
Kao Bo-song	74	74	75	73	296	3,240
Chen Tze-chung	73	74	74	75	296	3,240
Brad Kennedy	74	75	72	75	296	3,240
Amandeep Johl	77	73	69	77	296	3,240
Chung Chun-hsing	79	70	76	72	297	2,925
Gerald Rosales	77	75	68	77	297	2,925
Jeev Milkha Singh	80	74	70	74	298	2,580
Prom Meesawat	78	74	74	72	298	2,580
Boonchu Ruangkit	75	78	70	75	298	2,580
Andrew Pitts	78	73	76	71	298	2,580
Rahil Gangjee	79	73	75	71	298	2,580
Hong Chia-yuh	78	67	75	78	298	2,580

Crowne Plaza Open

Tomson Golf Club, Shanghai, China
Par 36-36–72; 7,300 yards

October 21-24
purse, US$200,000

	SCORES				TOTAL	MONEY
Terry Pilkadaris	67	69	72	72	280	US$32,300
Boonchu Ruangkit	68	72	73	68	281	22,260
Gary Rusnak	70	74	69	70	283	11,200
Marcus Both	69	72	69	73	283	11,200
Craig Kamps	67	73	76	68	284	7,500
Anthony Summers	66	72	75	71	284	7,500
Greg Hanrahan	70	74	71	71	286	4,865
Satoshi Tomiyama	72	71	72	71	286	4,865
Somkiat Srisanga	64	74	75	73	286	4,865

	SCORES				TOTAL	MONEY
Eiji Mizoguchi	66	69	76	75	286	4,865
Hendrik Buhrmann	71	73	72	71	287	3,670
Amandeep Johl	74	72	72	70	288	3,094
Lu Wen-teh	70	74	73	71	288	3,094
David Gleeson	72	72	71	73	288	3,094
Nico van Rensburg	73	73	68	74	288	3,094
David Kang	68	72	73	75	288	3,094
Lai Hung-lin	72	74	72	71	289	2,586.67
Adam Fraser	72	71	73	73	289	2,586.67
Wang Ter-chang	71	72	70	76	289	2,586.67
Anura Rohana	71	75	73	71	290	2,340
Digvijay Singh	69	76	72	73	290	2,340
Gerald Rosales	67	72	75	76	290	2,340
Yoshinobu Tsukada	72	72	76	71	291	2,130
Zheng Wen-gen	71	76	73	71	291	2,130
Anthony Kang	68	75	75	73	291	2,130
Pat Giles	71	71	75	74	291	2,130
Stephen Lindskog	73	74	73	72	292	1,860
Adam Groom	69	74	75	74	292	1,860
Rafael Ponce	73	71	73	75	292	1,860
Prom Meesawat	71	75	70	76	292	1,860
Eddie Lee	72	73	70	77	292	1,860

Sanya Open

Yalong Bay Golf Club, Sanya, China   October 28-31
Par 36-36–72; 7,180 yards   purse, US$250,000

	SCORES				TOTAL	MONEY
Terry Pilkadaris	68	66	66	70	270	US$40,375
Clay Devers	69	70	66	65	270	27,825
(Pilkadaris defeated Devers on second playoff hole.)						
Boonchu Ruangkit	66	74	64	67	271	14,000
Liang Wen-chong	69	69	66	67	271	14,000
Anura Rohana	73	69	63	68	273	9,375
Chang Tse-peng	70	67	66	70	273	9,375
Gerald Rosales	66	70	69	69	274	6,875
Charlie Wi	73	67	65	69	274	6,875
Li Chao	72	69	67	67	275	5,575
Bryan Saltus	73	69	67	67	276	5,000
Shiv Kapur	68	70	72	67	277	4,181
Anthony Summers	71	69	68	69	277	4,181
*Hu Mu	74	65	68	70	277	
Yoshinobu Tsukada	69	67	70	71	277	4,181
Lin Wen-ko	70	70	66	71	277	4,181
Lu Wen-teh	70	68	73	67	278	3,525
Mo Joong-kyung	70	66	72	70	278	3,525
Gerry Norquist	66	73	66	73	278	3,525
Gary Rusnak	70	70	70	69	279	3,020
Prom Meesawat	69	71	70	69	279	3,020
Satoshi Tomiyama	71	69	69	70	279	3,020
Mardan Mamat	72	64	72	71	279	3,020
Alistair Presnell	68	71	69	71	279	3,020
Anthony Gilligan	69	69	70	72	280	2,737.50
Keith Horne	71	71	65	73	280	2,737.50
Eiji Mizoguchi	70	73	69	69	281	2,437.50
Adam Groom	71	71	69	70	281	2,437.50

	SCORES				TOTAL	MONEY
Ashok Kumar	72	69	70	70	281	2,437.50
Akinori Tani	66	70	73	72	281	2,437.50
Lu Wei-lan	70	74	64	73	281	2,437.50
David Kang	71	67	68	75	281	2,437.50

Carlsberg Masters 2004 Vietnam

Chi Linh Star Golf & Country Club, Hanoi, Vietnam   November 4-7
Par 36-36–72   purse, US$200,000

	SCORES				TOTAL	MONEY
Angelo Que	70	66	70	70	276	US$32,300
Thongchai Jaidee	70	70	64	74	278	22,260
Corey Pavin	71	68	71	70	280	12,400
Boonchu Ruangkit	70	69	70	72	281	9,000
Thaworn Wiratchant	68	71	68	74	281	9,000
Ashok Kumar	71	70	68	73	282	7,000
Rick Gibson	70	74	69	70	283	6,000
Chang Tse-peng	69	71	74	70	284	4,730
Lin Wen-ko	69	74	70	71	284	4,730
Li Chao	70	72	71	72	285	4,000
Bryan Saltus	73	70	73	70	286	3,552
Lin Chie-hsiang	75	68	72	71	286	3,552
Sushi Ishigaki	73	73	71	70	287	3,216
Scott Barr	67	73	76	72	288	3,060
Ewan Porter	72	73	74	70	289	2,760
Chris Williams	72	75	72	70	289	2,760
Kyi Hla Han	72	72	72	73	289	2,760
Anthony Kang	72	72	72	73	289	2,760
Prom Meesawat	75	72	72	71	290	2,375
Keith Horne	74	75	69	72	290	2,375
Alistair Presnell	70	71	73	76	290	2,375
Adam Fraser	73	70	71	76	290	2,375
R. Nachimuthu	74	73	73	71	291	2,100
Huang Tung-liang	70	74	73	74	291	2,100
Jerome Delariarte	69	70	76	76	291	2,100
Arjun Singh	72	74	70	75	291	2,100
Kasper Jorgensen	71	73	70	77	291	2,100
Richard Moir	74	73	76	69	292	1,800
Harmeet Kahlon	75	74	70	73	292	1,800
Amandeep Johl	77	68	73	74	292	1,800
Nam Young-woo	73	73	69	77	292	1,800
Anthony Summers	66	76	70	80	292	1,800

Volvo China Open

Shanghai Silport Golf Club, Shanghai, China   November 25-28
Par 36-36–72; 7,073 yards   purse, US$1,000,000

	SCORES				TOTAL	MONEY
Stephen Dodd	68	70	70	68	276	US$166,660
Thomas Bjorn	71	72	68	68	279	111,110
Chawalit Plaphol	75	69	72	66	282	51,666.67
Jason Dawes	68	74	74	66	282	51,666.67
Thaworn Wiratchant	71	74	69	68	282	51,666.67

	SCORES				TOTAL	MONEY
Steve Webster	70	75	70	68	283	32,500
Amandeep Johl	68	76	70	69	283	32,500
Jonathan Lomas	72	71	72	69	284	22,466.67
Barry Lane	68	75	70	71	284	22,466.67
Soren Hansen	70	71	70	73	284	22,466.67
Mark Foster	70	72	71	72	285	16,750
Chung Joon	69	72	72	72	285	16,750
Gregory Havret	71	75	67	72	285	16,750
Simon Yates	70	73	70	72	285	16,750
Liang Wen-chong	72	74	73	67	286	14,100
Anthony Wall	73	72	71	70	286	14,100
Bradley Dredge	67	75	70	74	286	14,100
David Park	73	77	70	67	287	12,225
Peter Lawrie	72	78	70	67	287	12,225
Damien McGrane	71	74	73	69	287	12,225
Mads Vibe-Hastrup	69	77	68	73	287	12,225
Chris Williams	72	72	73	71	288	11,150
Paul Broadhurst	73	73	71	71	288	11,150
Andrew Pitts	69	77	74	69	289	10,550
James Kingston	69	78	70	72	289	10,550
Edward Michaels	72	72	74	72	290	9,950
Philip Golding	71	75	70	74	290	9,950
Mikko Ilonen	72	78	73	68	291	8,600
Wang Ter-chang	72	74	73	72	291	8,600
Zhang Lian-wei	69	76	74	72	291	8,600
Prayad Marksaeng	70	76	73	72	291	8,600
Matthew King	68	73	77	73	291	8,600
Maarten Lafeber	74	75	70	72	291	8,600
Rick Gibson	70	79	68	74	291	8,600
Anthony Kang	72	76	73	71	292	7,400
Terry Pilkadaris	75	72	72	73	292	7,400
Graeme Storm	78	72	76	67	293	7,000
Pablo Del Olmo	72	76	73	72	293	7,000
Hendrik Buhrmann	71	79	73	71	294	5,900
Stephen Scahill	72	75	74	73	294	5,900
Simon Dyson	72	78	72	72	294	5,900
Louis Oosthuizen	72	75	74	73	294	5,900
Marc Cayeux	68	75	77	74	294	5,900
Fredrik Andersson-Hed	71	75	74	74	294	5,900
Unho Park	67	80	70	77	294	5,900
Gary Rusnak	73	75	69	77	294	5,900
Choi Gwang-soo	75	72	70	77	294	5,900
Scott Barr	73	78	74	70	295	4,400
Miguel Angel Martin	75	74	74	72	295	4,400
Robert Karlsson	74	75	73	73	295	4,400
Paul Lawrie	71	78	73	73	295	4,400
Nick Dougherty	72	79	69	75	295	4,400
Jyoti Randhawa	71	76	72	76	295	4,400
Pat Giles	75	74	74	73	296	3,500
Greg Hanrahan	73	71	77	75	296	3,500
Andrew Marshall	73	75	72	76	296	3,500
Robert-Jan Derksen	72	78	78	69	297	2,900
Des Terblanche	72	77	77	71	297	2,900
Mardan Mamat	71	80	74	72	297	2,900
Raymond Russell	70	80	71	76	297	2,900
Robert Coles	71	76	73	77	297	2,900
Thammanoon Srirot	72	77	77	72	298	2,600
*Henry Liaw	73	77	74	74	298	
Arjun Singh	73	77	78	72	300	2,400
Shang Lei	71	79	74	76	300	2,400

	SCORES				TOTAL	MONEY
Emanuele Canonica	76	70	74	80	300	2,400
Jamie Donaldson	73	78	75	75	301	2,150
Johan Axgren	76	75	73	77	301	2,150
Harmeet Kahlon	74	77	76	75	302	1,950
Danny Chia	72	79	75	76	302	1,950
Nobuhito Sato	75	76	78	74	303	1,665.24
Huang Ming-jie	73	77	76	77	303	1,665.24

Omega Hong Kong Open

Hong Kong Golf Club, Hong Kong   December 2-5
Par 34-36–70; 6,749 yards   purse, US$800,000

	SCORES				TOTAL	MONEY
Miguel Angel Jimenez	65	64	71	66	266	US$133,330
James Kingston	71	67	62	67	267	69,480
Padraig Harrington	65	68	67	67	267	69,480
Thomas Bjorn	69	67	65	69	270	36,960
Thammanoon Srirot	67	68	66	69	270	36,960
David Howell	65	66	70	71	272	26,000
Nick Faldo	69	67	65	71	272	26,000
Zhang Lian-wei	70	64	73	66	273	17,160
Jose Maria Olazabal	67	68	71	67	273	17,160
Alessandro Tadini	66	67	72	68	273	17,160
Charl Schwartzel	65	70	70	68	273	17,160
Robert-Jan Derksen	68	70	69	67	274	12,120
Miguel Angel Martin	68	69	69	68	274	12,120
Louis Oosthuizen	69	64	71	70	274	12,120
Bryan Saltus	66	68	71	69	274	12,120
Adam Groom	64	70	68	72	274	12,120
Gregory Havret	66	68	68	72	274	12,120
Andrew Pitts	72	66	69	68	275	10,320
Maarten Lafeber	72	67	70	67	276	9,328
Steve Webster	69	68	71	68	276	9,328
Soren Hansen	68	71	69	68	276	9,328
Jamie Donaldson	71	65	71	69	276	9,328
Liang Wen-chong	67	68	71	70	276	9,328
Christopher Hanell	72	68	69	68	277	8,080
Ted Oh	68	69	71	69	277	8,080
Amandeep Johl	71	69	68	69	277	8,080
Markus Brier	70	72	66	69	277	8,080
Philippe Lima	67	70	70	70	277	8,080
Clay Devers	67	72	73	66	278	6,760
Damien McGrane	72	67	71	68	278	6,760
Thaworn Wiratchant	69	70	70	69	278	6,760
Boonchu Ruangkit	71	71	67	69	278	6,760
Barry Lane	68	71	69	70	278	6,760
Terry Pilkadaris	68	73	67	70	278	6,760
Richard Bland	71	66	72	70	279	5,760
Nick Dougherty	69	67	72	71	279	5,760
Harmeet Kahlon	66	71	70	72	279	5,760
Mardan Mamat	68	72	67	72	279	5,760
Simon Wakefield	71	71	72	66	280	5,040
Robert Jacobson	70	70	73	67	280	5,040
Paul Lawrie	69	71	68	72	280	5,040
Thongchai Jaidee	67	68	72	73	280	5,040
Choi Gwang-soo	69	67	70	74	280	5,040

	SCORES				TOTAL	MONEY
Simon Yates	70	72	68	71	281	4,480
Leif Westerberg	70	70	70	71	281	4,480
Jonathan Lomas	72	68	76	66	282	3,920
Nico van Rensburg	70	69	74	69	282	3,920
Wang Ter-chang	71	71	70	70	282	3,920
Gaurav Ghei	68	70	72	72	282	3,920
Jason Knutzon	69	69	70	74	282	3,920
Adam Fraser	68	72	73	70	283	3,040
Raymond Russell	68	74	71	70	283	3,040
David Gleeson	69	72	71	71	283	3,040
Gerry Norquist	70	70	71	72	283	3,040
Prayad Marksaeng	69	68	74	72	283	3,040
Rick Gibson	70	66	72	75	283	3,040
Des Terblanche	71	69	73	71	284	2,400
Stephen Scahill	70	71	71	72	284	2,400
Jonathan Cheetham	68	73	71	72	284	2,400
Stephen Dodd	68	72	75	70	285	2,000
Philip Golding	73	69	73	70	285	2,000
Paul Broadhurst	69	71	74	71	285	2,000
Lam Chih Bing	68	69	75	73	285	2,000
Derek Fung	66	75	72	72	285	2,000
Pablo Del Olmo	67	72	71	75	285	2,000
Li Chao	69	69	69	78	285	2,000
Jeev Milkha Singh	69	73	72	72	286	1,600
Scott Barr	66	72	75	73	286	1,600
Gary Rusnak	69	71	71	75	286	1,600
Lee Sung-man	69	72	74	72	287	1,470
David Park	70	70	76	72	288	1,197.91
Jason Dawes	71	67	76	74	288	1,197.91
Lee Slattery	68	73	74	74	289	1,189.94
Nobuhito Sato	70	72	68	79	289	1,189.94
Andrew Marshall	70	72	78	70	290	1,179.97
Gary Emerson	71	71	74	74	290	1,179.97
Eiji Mizoguchi	71	71	73	75	290	1,179.97
Danny Chia	69	71	72	79	291	1,172
Edward Loar	70	70	74	78	292	1,168.01
Anthony Summers	71	71	72	79	293	1,164.03
Mike Cunning	74	67	75	81	297	1,160.04

Volvo Masters of Asia

Kota Permai Golf & Country Club, Kuala Lumpur, Malaysia
Par 36-36–72; 6,929 yards

December 9-12
purse, US$550,000

	SCORES				TOTAL	MONEY
Jyoti Randhawa	63	70	74	67	274	US$99,000
Terry Pilkadaris	70	70	69	65	274	62,254
(Randhawa defeated Pilkadaris on second playoff hole.)						
Prayad Marksaeng	68	69	67	72	276	31,254
Wang Ter-chang	69	66	69	72	276	31,254
Thongchai Jaidee	70	72	68	68	278	22,254
Edward Loar	70	68	71	70	279	19,754
Marcus Both	70	68	72	71	281	15,479.50
Ted Oh	70	71	67	73	281	15,479.50
Thaworn Wiratchant	71	70	72	69	282	10,956.25
Rahil Gangjee	69	73	69	71	282	10,956.25
Jeev Milkha Singh	67	73	68	74	282	10,956.25

	SCORES				TOTAL	MONEY
Chawalit Plaphol	69	69	68	76	282	10,956.25
Pablo Del Olmo	71	71	73	68	283	9,105
Gary Rusnak	69	75	72	68	284	7,584.38
Thammanoon Srirot	72	73	71	68	284	7,584.38
Rick Gibson	72	75	68	69	284	7,584.38
Chung Joon	70	73	71	70	284	7,584.38
Craig Kamps	68	70	72	74	284	7,584.38
Sushi Ishigaki	70	69	71	74	284	7,584.38
Lee Sung-man	68	71	71	74	284	7,584.38
Liang Wen-chong	68	67	73	76	284	7,584.38
Kyi Hla Han	72	71	72	70	285	6,360
Hendrik Buhrmann	74	73	68	70	285	6,360
Prom Meesawat	73	69	69	74	285	6,360
Chris Williams	69	74	76	67	286	5,700
Charlie Wi	72	72	72	70	286	5,700
Scott Barr	71	72	71	72	286	5,700
Jason Knutzon	70	73	70	73	286	5,700
Simon Dyson	68	76	68	74	286	5,700
Harmeet Kahlon	69	76	72	70	287	5,122.50
Lu Wen-teh	71	71	73	72	287	5,122.50

Asia/Japan Okinawa Open

See Japan Tour section.

Japan Tour

Token Homemate Cup

Token Tado Country Club, Mie
Par 35-36–71; 7,083 yards

March 25-28
purse, ¥100,000,000

	SCORES				TOTAL	MONEY
Hiroyuki Fujita	70	68	74	69	281	¥20,000,000
Shingo Katayama	69	73	71	70	283	8,400,000
Charlie Wi	69	72	70	72	283	8,400,000
Nobuhiro Masuda	67	78	72	67	284	4,400,000
Ryuichi Oda	68	75	70	71	284	4,400,000
S.K. Ho	67	76	71	71	285	3,600,000
Tsuyoshi Yoneyama	71	72	74	69	286	3,175,000
Hideto Tanihara	71	74	72	69	286	3,175,000
Kim Jong-duck	72	73	75	67	286	3,175,000
Kazuhiro Shimizu	68	74	76	69	287	2,520,000
Soshi Tajima	69	74	73	71	287	2,520,000
Toshimitsu Izawa	64	77	72	74	287	2,520,000
Azuma Yano	68	78	75	67	288	1,686,666
Takuya Taniguchi	73	72	74	69	288	1,686,666

	SCORES				TOTAL	MONEY
Yoshiaki Mano	67	76	75	70	288	1,686,666
Hidemasa Hoshino	68	76	73	71	288	1,686,666
Keiichiro Fukabori	73	72	71	72	288	1,686,666
Ryoken Kawagishi	65	78	71	74	288	1,686,666
Naoya Sugiyama	67	76	76	70	289	1,220,000
Shigemasa Higaki	64	76	78	71	289	1,220,000
Daisuke Maruyama	70	71	77	71	289	1,220,000
Katsunori Kuwabara	70	77	71	71	289	1,220,000
Takuya Ogawa	73	71	73	73	290	953,333
Tsukasa Watanabe	70	70	77	73	290	953,333
Steve Conran	69	71	75	75	290	953,333
Toru Taniguchi	69	77	74	71	291	820,000
Tadahiro Takayama	68	73	76	74	291	820,000
Craig Jones	73	71	72	75	291	820,000
Satoru Hirota	73	73	75	71	292	700,000
Frankie Minoza	70	71	76	75	292	700,000
Masashi Ozaki	69	71	75	77	292	700,000

Tsuruya Open

Sports Shinko Country Club, Kawanishi, Hyogo
Par 35-36–71; 6,759 yards

April 22-25
purse, ¥100,000,000

	SCORES				TOTAL	MONEY
Brendan Jones	64	73	69	69	275	¥20,000,000
Scott Laycock	65	70	72	70	277	5,840,000
Keiichiro Fukabori	66	73	70	68	277	5,840,000
Taichi Teshima	66	73	71	67	277	5,840,000
Shinichi Yokota	67	72	71	67	277	5,840,000
Tatsuya Mitsuhashi	63	70	72	72	277	5,840,000
Jun Kikuchi	68	65	73	72	278	3,056,666
Shingo Katayama	65	71	73	69	278	3,056,666
Toru Taniguchi	68	72	68	70	278	3,056,666
Steve Conran	68	72	69	70	279	2,520,000
Katsumasa Miyamoto	65	69	74	71	279	2,520,000
Lin Keng-chi	71	67	74	68	280	2,120,000
Hideto Tanihara	70	71	72	67	280	2,120,000
Kiyoshi Miyazato	67	70	73	71	281	1,670,000
Kazuhiko Hosokawa	67	70	73	71	281	1,670,000
Katsunori Kuwabara	70	71	69	71	281	1,670,000
Tadahisa Inoue	65	70	71	75	281	1,670,000
Unho Park	71	68	70	73	282	1,180,000
Y.E. Yang	66	72	74	70	282	1,180,000
Yusaku Miyazato	74	68	69	71	282	1,180,000
Prayad Marksaeng	72	65	76	69	282	1,180,000
Tsuyoshi Yoneyama	65	69	80	68	282	1,180,000
Kiyoshi Maita	69	67	74	72	282	1,180,000
Kiyoshi Murota	68	68	75	71	282	1,180,000
David Ishii	69	72	72	70	283	820,000
Paul Sheehan	71	70	72	70	283	820,000
Richard Backwell	70	69	74	70	283	820,000
Tsukasa Watanabe	70	71	70	72	283	820,000
Masayuki Kawamura	68	69	70	76	283	820,000
Toru Suzuki	71	69	70	74	284	647,500
Yoshitaka Yamamoto	68	74	72	70	284	647,500
Hideki Haraguchi	68	69	76	71	284	647,500
Shinichi Akiba	71	68	72	73	284	647,500

Chunichi Crowns

Nagoya Golf Club, Wago Course, Togo, Aichi
Par 35-35–70; 6,547 yards

April 29-May 2
purse, ¥120,000,000

	SCORES				TOTAL	MONEY
Shingo Katayama	65	64	63	72	264	¥24,000,000
Paul Sheehan	66	70	67	63	266	12,000,000
Hisayuki Sasaki	66	69	64	68	267	8,160,000
Brendan Jones	68	66	65	69	268	5,760,000
S.K. Ho	69	68	68	64	269	4,800,000
Toru Suzuki	69	67	67	67	270	4,320,000
Takenori Hiraishi	70	66	68	67	271	3,810,000
Y.E. Yang	66	68	69	68	271	3,810,000
Naomichi Ozaki	68	64	70	70	272	2,784,000
Taichi Teshima	68	70	64	70	272	2,784,000
Keiichiro Fukabori	65	72	69	66	272	2,784,000
Daisuke Maruyama	68	66	71	67	272	2,784,000
Kaname Yokoo	70	66	67	69	272	2,784,000
Nozomi Kawahara	65	67	68	72	272	2,784,000
Koki Idoki	71	66	65	71	273	1,944,000
Jun Kikuchi	71	68	68	66	273	1,944,000
Azuma Yano	71	67	70	65	273	1,944,000
Hiroyuki Fujita	69	68	70	67	274	1,656,000
Dinesh Chand	64	69	72	69	274	1,656,000
Masashi Ozaki	67	72	66	70	275	1,368,000
Tsukasa Watanabe	67	70	69	69	275	1,368,000
Yasuharu Imano	71	68	66	70	275	1,368,000
Scott Laycock	67	69	69	70	275	1,368,000
Katsunori Kuwabara	69	64	68	75	276	1,056,000
Yoshiaki Mano	67	66	73	70	276	1,056,000
Steve Conran	68	69	71	68	276	1,056,000
David Smail	66	67	72	71	276	1,056,000
Hideki Kase	69	71	67	70	277	842,400
Ryoken Kawagishi	72	65	68	72	277	842,400
Kim Jong-duck	67	70	69	71	277	842,400
Masao Nakajima	67	66	72	72	277	842,400
Christian Pena	67	71	74	65	277	842,400

Fujisankei Classic

Kawana Hotel Golf Club, Fuji Course, Ito, Shizuoka
Par 35-36–71; 6,694 yards

May 6-9
purse, ¥110,000,000

	SCORES				TOTAL	MONEY
Paul Sheehan	68	70	62	67	267	¥22,000,000
Mitsuhiro Tateyama	65	71	67	68	271	9,240,000
Kaname Yokoo	68	68	67	68	271	9,240,000
Kiyoshi Maita	68	65	71	68	272	5,280,000
Nobuo Serizawa	63	68	71	71	273	4,180,000
Yusaku Miyazato	69	66	68	70	273	4,180,000
Masayuki Kawamura	71	67	70	66	274	3,630,000
Takashi Kanemoto	70	67	66	72	275	3,113,000
Scott Laycock	69	67	67	72	275	3,113,000
Katsumune Imai	70	68	70	67	275	3,113,000
Kazuhiko Hosokawa	68	67	68	73	276	2,552,000
Lin Keng-chi	67	69	69	71	276	2,552,000

	SCORES				TOTAL	MONEY
Steve Conran	73	67	69	68	277	1,914,000
Dinesh Chand	68	71	70	68	277	1,914,000
Katsumasa Miyamoto	68	70	69	70	277	1,914,000
Takashi Iwamoto	63	73	73	68	277	1,914,000
Yeh Wei-tze	72	66	71	68	277	1,914,000
Katsunori Kuwabara	66	71	70	71	278	1,518,000
Jeev Milkha Singh	72	66	68	72	278	1,518,000
Koki Idoki	69	68	69	73	279	1,210,000
Keiichiro Fukabori	70	68	73	68	279	1,210,000
Mamoru Osanai	71	69	69	70	279	1,210,000
Tatsuya Mitsuhashi	70	69	71	69	279	1,210,000
Nobuhiro Masuda	70	67	72	70	279	1,210,000
Nobumitsu Yuhara	71	67	70	72	280	799,700
Hiroyuki Fujita	72	68	72	68	280	799,700
Yasuharu Imano	72	70	71	67	280	799,700
Daisuke Maruyama	68	67	67	78	280	799,700
David Smail	68	71	70	71	280	799,700
Hiroaki Iijima	70	68	70	72	280	799,700
Kodai Ichihara	69	72	68	71	280	799,700
Jyoti Randhawa	74	68	70	68	280	799,700
Tadahiro Takayama	70	71	68	71	280	799,700
Tadahisa Inoue	71	68	72	69	280	799,700

Japan PGA Championship

Kochi Kuroshio Country Club, Kochi
Par 36-36–72; 7,270 yards
(First round cancelled—rain.)

May 13-16
purse, ¥110,000,000

	SCORES			TOTAL	MONEY
S.K. Ho	66	68	68	202	¥16,500,000
Keiichiro Fukabori	66	69	68	203	8,250,000
Kaname Yokoo	67	71	71	209	4,785,000
Hideto Tanihara	71	72	66	209	4,785,000
Taichi Teshima	70	72	68	210	2,997,500
Hiroyuki Fujita	69	67	74	210	2,997,500
Katsumasa Miyamoto	74	70	66	210	2,997,500
Tsukasa Watanabe	70	70	71	211	2,083,125
Satoru Hirota	72	68	71	211	2,083,125
Yasuharu Imano	69	65	77	211	2,083,125
Hidemasa Hoshino	69	70	72	211	2,083,125
Paul Sheehan	71	71	69	211	2,083,125
Thammanoon Srirot	70	71	70	211	2,083,125
Tadahiro Takayama	72	69	71	212	1,298,000
Kazuhiko Hosokawa	71	70	71	212	1,298,000
Jun Kikuchi	69	74	69	212	1,298,000
Yasuaki Takashima	71	70	71	212	1,298,000
Kim Jong-duck	71	68	73	212	1,298,000
Brendan Jones	70	72	70	212	1,298,000
Tomohiro Kondo	71	70	72	213	940,500
Takuya Taniguchi	73	69	71	213	940,500
Fumihiro Ebine	73	71	69	213	940,500
Yeh Wei-tze	70	67	76	213	940,500
Hideki Kase	71	71	72	214	660,000
Hiroshi Tominaga	70	72	72	214	660,000
Takuya Ogawa	76	68	70	214	660,000
Nozomi Kawahara	72	70	72	214	660,000

	SCORES			TOTAL	MONEY
Shingo Katayama	72	71	71	214	660,000
Yui Ueda	69	72	73	214	660,000
Kazuhiro Shimizu	76	68	70	214	660,000
Tatsuya Mitsuhashi	72	72	70	214	660,000

Munsingwear Open KSB Cup

Tojigaoka Marine Hills Golf Club, Okayama
Par 36-36–72; 7,017 yards

May 20-23
purse, ¥100,000,000

	SCORES				TOTAL	MONEY
Tatsuya Mitsuhashi	66	71	63	70	270	¥20,000,000
Shingo Katayama	72	68	66	66	272	7,200,000
Nobuhiro Masuda	69	68	69	66	272	7,200,000
Jeev Milkha Singh	69	65	70	68	272	7,200,000
Hiroyuki Fujita	68	71	67	67	273	4,000,000
Lin Keng-chi	71	71	66	66	274	3,600,000
Takashi Kanemoto	68	70	68	69	275	3,175,000
Steve Conran	73	69	68	65	275	3,175,000
Hisayuki Sasaki	74	67	71	64	276	2,720,000
Prayad Marksaeng	68	70	73	65	276	2,720,000
Hideki Kase	71	67	72	67	277	1,970,000
Katsuyoshi Tomori	73	71	71	62	277	1,970,000
Toru Taniguchi	68	71	66	72	277	1,970,000
Kaname Yokoo	68	69	69	71	277	1,970,000
Tadahiro Takayama	75	67	67	68	277	1,970,000
Fumihiro Ebine	73	69	67	68	277	1,970,000
Taichi Teshima	72	67	68	71	278	1,344,000
Daisuke Maruyama	71	68	68	71	278	1,344,000
Tetsuji Hiratsuka	70	73	67	68	278	1,344,000
Chawalit Plaphol	67	70	73	68	278	1,344,000
Thammanoon Srirot	66	78	69	65	278	1,344,000
Koki Idoki	68	72	65	74	279	964,000
Toshimitsu Izawa	69	70	70	70	279	964,000
Toru Suzuki	67	69	74	69	279	964,000
Takuya Taniguchi	70	69	71	69	279	964,000
Christian Pena	68	75	68	68	279	964,000
Hiroya Kamide	73	69	68	70	280	688,750
Hideki Haraguchi	72	72	67	69	280	688,750
Kazuhiko Hosokawa	72	70	69	69	280	688,750
Katsuya Nakagawa	70	71	67	72	280	688,750
Tomohiro Kondo	71	72	67	70	280	688,750
Hideto Tanihara	69	74	69	68	280	688,750
Taichiro Kiyota	67	71	74	68	280	688,750
Y.E. Yang	72	71	69	68	280	688,750

Mitsubishi Diamond Cup

Oarai Golf Club, Ibaragi
Par 36-36–72; 7,200 yards

May 27-30
purse, ¥110,000,000

	SCORES				TOTAL	MONEY
Tetsuji Hiratsuka	68	70	68	69	275	¥22,000,000
Hidemasa Hoshino	68	71	75	66	280	11,000,000
S.K. Ho	71	68	73	69	281	7,480,000

	SCORES				TOTAL	MONEY
Toru Taniguchi	70	72	72	68	282	4,840,000
Hideto Tanihara	68	70	70	74	282	4,840,000
Shigemasa Higaki	75	68	70	70	283	3,511,750
Nobuhiro Masuda	67	77	70	69	283	3,511,750
Craig Jones	71	70	72	70	283	3,511,750
Y.E. Yang	69	74	70	70	283	3,511,750
Koki Idoki	73	72	71	68	284	2,772,000
David Smail	73	70	72	69	284	2,772,000
Katsuyoshi Tomori	70	71	73	71	285	1,672,000
Masayuki Kawamura	66	75	70	74	285	1,672,000
Taichi Teshima	71	68	75	71	285	1,672,000
Daisuke Maruyama	68	74	70	73	285	1,672,000
Shinichi Yokota	72	70	69	74	285	1,672,000
Jun Kikuchi	74	70	71	70	285	1,672,000
Yasuharu Imano	73	71	73	68	285	1,672,000
Kiyoshi Miyazato	73	72	70	70	285	1,672,000
Ryuichi Oda	68	73	70	74	285	1,672,000
Takuya Taniguchi	74	67	71	73	285	1,672,000
Christian Pena	70	73	71	71	285	1,672,000
Liang Wen-chong	73	73	68	71	285	1,672,000
Kiyoshi Murota	72	72	71	71	286	990,000
Kazuhiko Hosokawa	71	73	70	72	286	990,000
Chawalit Plaphol	72	71	73	70	286	990,000
Lin Keng-chi	72	74	73	68	287	741,888
Kaname Yokoo	71	70	72	74	287	741,888
Takashi Kamiyama	70	73	76	68	287	741,888
Makoto Inoue	68	70	77	72	287	741,888
Tomohiro Kondo	71	74	69	73	287	741,888
Masaya Tomida	69	75	69	74	287	741,888
Yoshikazu Haku	71	72	72	72	287	741,888
Kim Jong-duck	71	75	74	67	287	741,888
Jeev Milkha Singh	70	74	72	71	287	741,888

JCB Classic Sendai

Omotezao Kokusai Golf Club, Shibata, Miyagi
Par 36-35–71; 6,625 yards

June 3-6
purse, ¥100,000,000

	SCORES				TOTAL	MONEY
Takashi Kamiyama	68	69	67	67	271	¥20,000,000
Tsuneyuki Nakajima	74	67	63	67	271	8,400,000
Tomohiro Kondo	71	68	68	64	271	8,400,000
(Kamiyama defeated Nakajima and Kondo on first playoff hole.)						
Tetsuji Hiratsuka	66	72	67	68	273	4,400,000
Hidemasa Hoshino	68	70	69	66	273	4,400,000
Masashi Ozaki	71	71	67	65	274	3,192,500
Shinichi Yokota	64	73	68	69	274	3,192,500
Katsumasa Miyamoto	71	69	67	67	274	3,192,500
Thammanoon Srirot	69	69	68	68	274	3,192,500
Kiyoshi Murota	73	67	69	66	275	2,620,000
Toru Taniguchi	70	67	65	74	276	2,040,000
Yoshiaki Mano	68	69	70	69	276	2,040,000
Tadahiro Takayama	69	68	68	71	276	2,040,000
Ryuichi Oda	62	72	73	69	276	2,040,000
Kim Jong-duck	65	71	68	72	276	2,040,000
Hideki Kase	69	71	70	67	277	1,266,666
Shinichi Akiba	66	71	72	68	277	1,266,666

	SCORES				TOTAL	MONEY
Kazuhiko Hosokawa	70	65	72	70	277	1,266,666
Lin Keng-chi	71	69	67	70	277	1,266,666
Dinesh Chand	71	66	70	70	277	1,266,666
Nobuyuki Okuwa	73	70	67	67	277	1,266,666
Toshimasa Nakajima	72	71	67	67	277	1,266,666
Chawalit Plaphol	71	67	73	66	277	1,266,666
S.K. Ho	72	70	67	68	277	1,266,666
Hisayuki Sasaki	69	68	66	75	278	880,000
Shintaro Kai	68	73	67	70	278	880,000
Kaname Yokoo	72	67	70	70	279	721,666
Liang Wen-chong	69	69	71	70	279	721,666
Tatsuya Mitsuhashi	71	68	68	72	279	721,666
Nobuhiro Masuda	70	68	72	69	279	721,666
Christian Pena	68	71	70	70	279	721,666
Y.E. Yang	72	66	69	72	279	721,666

Mandom Lucido Yomiuri Open

Yomiuri Country Club, Nishinomiya, Hyogo
Par 36-36–72; 7,073 yards

June 17-20
purse, ¥100,000,000

	SCORES				TOTAL	MONEY
Dinesh Chand	66	68	68	66	268	¥20,000,000
Tetsuji Hiratsuka	72	66	68	66	272	8,400,000
S.K. Ho	67	67	69	69	272	8,400,000
Tsuyoshi Yoneyama	68	68	72	65	273	4,800,000
Katsunori Kuwabara	67	64	72	71	274	3,800,000
Keiichiro Fukabori	68	67	72	67	274	3,800,000
Kiyoshi Murota	70	66	71	68	275	3,175,000
Shingo Katayama	72	70	68	65	275	3,175,000
Masayuki Kawamura	71	68	68	69	276	2,620,000
Kazuhiro Fukunaga	66	70	70	70	276	2,620,000
Jun Kikuchi	71	71	69	65	276	2,620,000
Takashi Kanemoto	68	72	66	71	277	2,220,000
Toru Suzuki	67	66	73	72	278	1,456,363
Koki Idoki	68	71	69	70	278	1,456,363
Kim Jong-duck	70	71	70	67	278	1,456,363
Shigeru Nonaka	70	66	70	72	278	1,456,363
Shigemasa Higaki	68	72	69	69	278	1,456,363
Mitsuhiro Tateyama	66	71	70	71	278	1,456,363
Yoshiaki Mano	70	69	72	67	278	1,456,363
Takashi Kamiyama	70	68	69	71	278	1,456,363
Satoru Hirota	70	71	67	70	278	1,456,363
Takuya Taniguchi	70	69	72	67	278	1,456,363
Tatsuhiko Takahashi	69	67	73	69	278	1,456,363
Masashi Ozaki	66	67	72	74	279	880,000
Taichi Teshima	69	69	66	75	279	880,000
Shintaro Kai	68	68	73	70	279	880,000
Nobuhiro Masuda	72	70	71	66	279	880,000
Nobuo Serizawa	70	70	65	75	280	685,000
Lin Keng-chi	73	64	71	72	280	685,000
Zhang Lian-wei	71	70	72	67	280	685,000
Jeev Milkha Singh	71	69	68	72	280	685,000
Yusaku Miyazato	69	68	71	72	280	685,000
Masaya Tomida	70	67	71	72	280	685,000

Mizuno Open

Setonaikai Golf Club, Kasaoka, Okayama
Par 36-36–72; 7,256 yards

June 24-27
purse, ¥100,000,000

	SCORES				TOTAL	MONEY
Brendan Jones	67	68	70	69	274	¥20,000,000
Hiroaki Iijima	70	68	68	68	274	10,000,000
(Jones defeated Iijima on second playoff hole.)						
Takashi Kanemoto	69	70	69	67	275	5,800,000
Hiroyuki Fujita	67	69	70	69	275	5,800,000
Nobuhito Sato	67	74	69	66	276	3,633,333
Hidemasa Hoshino	68	72	65	71	276	3,633,333
Yusaku Miyazato	67	71	67	71	276	3,633,333
David Smail	68	68	71	70	277	2,935,000
Naruhito Ueda	72	68	65	72	277	2,935,000
Tomohiro Kondo	71	70	69	68	278	2,620,000
Y.E. Yang	71	72	69	67	279	2,120,000
Yasuharu Imano	70	72	70	67	279	2,120,000
Takenori Hiraishi	73	69	68	69	279	2,120,000
Kim Jong-duck	72	66	70	71	279	2,120,000
Tadahiro Takayama	74	70	65	71	280	1,620,000
Toru Taniguchi	69	74	65	72	280	1,620,000
Scott Laycock	73	66	68	73	280	1,620,000
Ryuichi Oda	70	72	71	68	281	1,260,000
Masayuki Kawamura	71	72	69	69	281	1,260,000
Chikara Ikeda	73	67	72	69	281	1,260,000
Kaname Yokoo	67	76	68	70	281	1,260,000
Lin Keng-chi	73	65	73	70	281	1,260,000
Peter Teravainen	74	69	71	68	282	1,020,000
Dinesh Chand	72	72	71	68	283	763,000
Jeev Milkha Singh	69	73	73	68	283	763,000
Tadahisa Inoue	70	72	72	69	283	763,000
Kazuhiro Kinjo	70	71	73	69	283	763,000
Masanari Kato	72	72	69	70	283	763,000
Craig Jones	70	71	72	70	283	763,000
Kiyoshi Maita	73	68	72	70	283	763,000
Nozomi Kawahara	69	72	72	70	283	763,000
Unho Park	72	69	70	72	283	763,000
Hirokazu Shimizu	75	65	67	76	283	763,000

Japan Golf Tour Championship

Shishido Hills Country Club, Tomobe, Ibaragi
Par 36-35–71; 7,170 yards

July 1-4
purse, ¥120,000,000

	SCORES				TOTAL	MONEY
S.K. Ho	70	74	67	68	279	¥24,000,000
Tomohiro Kondo	66	70	70	73	279	12,000,000
(Ho defeated Kondo on second playoff hole.)						
Tsuyoshi Yoneyama	72	70	72	68	282	8,160,000
Yoshiaki Mano	71	66	75	71	283	5,760,000
Scott Laycock	69	69	71	75	284	4,800,000
Prayad Marksaeng	72	68	72	73	285	3,693,600
Masayuki Kawamura	72	73	70	70	285	3,693,600
Liang Wen-chong	71	72	71	71	285	3,693,600
Shingo Katayama	73	71	69	72	285	3,693,600

	SCORES				TOTAL	MONEY
Takenori Hiraishi	71	71	70	73	285	3,693,600
Hiroyuki Fujita	74	73	69	70	286	2,544,000
Nobuo Serizawa	73	74	71	68	286	2,544,000
Nobuhito Sato	71	71	72	72	286	2,544,000
Satoru Hirota	69	68	73	76	286	2,544,000
Brendan Jones	71	74	72	70	287	2,004,000
Hidemasa Hoshino	72	72	65	78	287	2,004,000
Kiyoshi Miyazato	68	73	76	72	289	1,712,000
Shigemasa Higaki	77	71	70	71	289	1,712,000
Yoshikazu Haku	69	77	69	74	289	1,712,000
Yoshinori Mizumaki	75	73	72	70	290	1,280,000
Unho Park	74	73	72	71	290	1,280,000
Hiroshi Goda	73	68	78	71	290	1,280,000
Takashi Kanemoto	77	68	74	71	290	1,280,000
Keiichiro Fukabori	69	74	73	74	290	1,280,000
Kiyoshi Murota	70	72	74	74	290	1,280,000
Shigeru Nonaka	70	76	70	75	291	960,000
Hideto Tanihara	74	71	72	74	291	960,000
Mamoru Osanai	75	71	78	67	291	960,000
Makoto Inoue	70	73	77	71	291	960,000
Koki Idoki	74	71	74	73	292	777,000
Lin Keng-chi	72	73	75	72	292	777,000
David Smail	68	70	78	76	292	777,000
Takuya Taniguchi	72	73	71	76	292	777,000

Woodone Open Hiroshima

Hiroshima Country Club, Higashi, Hiroshima
Par 36-36–72; 7,010 yards

July 8-11
purse, ¥100,000,000

	SCORES				TOTAL	MONEY
Shingo Katayama	70	63	70	63	266	¥20,000,000
Ryuichi Oda	67	69	70	65	271	10,000,000
Tateo Ozaki	70	66	68	70	274	5,800,000
Tadahiro Takayama	66	75	64	69	274	5,800,000
Jun Kikuchi	72	71	66	67	276	3,800,000
Yasuharu Imano	68	69	69	70	276	3,800,000
Masashi Ozaki	69	65	71	72	277	3,175,000
Takuya Taniguchi	70	74	70	63	277	3,175,000
Nobuo Serizawa	69	73	71	65	278	2,320,000
Toru Taniguchi	72	66	67	73	278	2,320,000
Shigeru Nonaka	71	70	69	68	278	2,320,000
Katsumasa Miyamoto	73	71	69	65	278	2,320,000
Mamoru Osanai	71	70	69	68	278	2,320,000
Prayad Marksaeng	69	71	69	69	278	2,320,000
Kaname Yokoo	70	69	72	68	279	1,620,000
Tadahisa Inoue	70	73	69	67	279	1,620,000
Thammanoon Srirot	74	71	65	69	279	1,620,000
Kazuhiro Takami	71	72	68	69	280	1,300,000
Hiroaki Iijima	69	71	70	70	280	1,300,000
Christian Pena	73	71	68	68	280	1,300,000
Craig Jones	70	73	69	68	280	1,300,000
Masayuki Kawamura	72	69	70	70	281	917,142
Tsuyoshi Yoneyama	73	72	69	67	281	917,142
Taichi Teshima	69	72	72	68	281	917,142
Yudai Maeda	70	67	74	70	281	917,142
Tomohiro Kondo	71	70	69	71	281	917,142

	SCORES			TOTAL	MONEY
Kiyoshi Miyazato	68	73	71	69	281	917,142
Y.E. Yang	68	67	71	75	281	917,142
David Smail	70	73	67	72	282	720,000
Masanori Kijima	68	71	70	73	282	720,000

Sato Foods NST Niigata Open

Forest Golf Club, Toyoura, Niigata
Par 35-36–71; 7,000 yards

July 22-25
purse, ¥50,000,000

	SCORES				TOTAL	MONEY
Kim Jong-duck	64	67	65	67	263	¥10,000,000
Kazuhiro Kinjo	68	64	68	68	268	5,000,000
Hisao Ahara	71	65	65	68	269	2,900,000
Tomohiro Kondo	69	68	64	68	269	2,900,000
Tetsuji Hiratsuka	67	66	70	67	270	1,900,000
Masanori Kijima	70	65	69	66	270	1,900,000
Hideki Kase	68	67	68	69	272	1,473,750
Gregory Meyer	65	68	68	71	272	1,473,750
Yui Ueda	67	70	65	70	272	1,473,750
Ryuichi Oda	73	64	68	67	272	1,473,750
Masayuki Kawamura	73	66	67	67	273	1,110,000
Toshikazu Sugihara	71	70	65	67	273	1,110,000
Masao Nakajima	68	71	65	69	273	1,110,000
Makoto Inoue	65	69	67	73	274	885,000
Takuya Taniguchi	66	69	69	70	274	885,000
Koichi Hagiwara	71	70	69	65	275	716,000
Yutaka Horinouchi	67	68	70	70	275	716,000
Azuma Yano	74	65	67	69	275	716,000
Kiyoshi Miyazato	70	71	64	70	275	716,000
Y.E. Yang	68	68	66	73	275	716,000
Hiroya Kamide	67	70	68	71	276	500,000
Kazuhiro Fukunaga	72	65	69	70	276	500,000
Jun Kikuchi	66	72	70	68	276	500,000
Tadahisa Inoue	70	69	68	69	276	500,000
Toshinori Muto	69	66	67	74	276	500,000
Michael Wright	69	66	73	68	276	500,000
Yuji Takagi	69	69	67	72	277	337,222
Koki Idoki	72	69	67	69	277	337,222
Tatsuo Takasaki	72	69	69	67	277	337,222
Yasuharu Imano	72	66	68	71	277	337,222
Tatsuya Mitsuhashi	68	71	70	68	277	337,222
Tadahiro Takayama	69	71	69	68	277	337,222
Masaya Tomida	67	71	69	70	277	337,222
Ishimaru Masashi	71	67	70	69	277	337,222
Kaneyuki Aramoto	67	70	71	69	277	337,222

Aiful Cup

Daisen Ark Country Club, Tottori
Par 36-35–71; 7,014 yards

July 29-August 1
purse, ¥120,000,000

	SCORES				TOTAL	MONEY
Takuya Taniguchi	68	67	66	69	270	¥24,000,000
Katsumasa Miyamoto	71	67	68	66	272	12,000,000

	SCORES				TOTAL	MONEY
Keiichiro Fukabori	66	69	68	70	273	6,960,000
S.K. Ho	67	70	66	70	273	6,960,000
Yudai Maeda	69	71	66	68	274	4,800,000
Hideki Kase	66	71	69	69	275	3,980,000
Jyoti Randhawa	67	69	71	68	275	3,980,000
Liang Wen-chong	71	70	68	66	275	3,980,000
Yasuharu Imano	69	70	69	68	276	3,384,000
Kosaku Makisaka	69	71	68	69	277	3,024,000
Kaname Yokoo	70	68	69	70	277	3,024,000
Kiyoshi Murota	69	74	68	67	278	2,184,000
Gregory Meyer	68	70	70	70	278	2,184,000
Taichi Teshima	69	70	72	67	278	2,184,000
Makoto Inoue	69	65	72	72	278	2,184,000
Nobuhiro Masuda	71	69	68	70	278	2,184,000
Kiyoshi Miyazato	70	69	68	71	278	2,184,000
Hiroyuki Fujita	69	70	70	70	279	1,656,000
Prayad Marksaeng	72	68	67	72	279	1,656,000
Naomichi Ozaki	69	73	68	70	280	1,280,000
Kazuhiro Takami	71	69	69	71	280	1,280,000
Nozomi Kawahara	71	68	68	73	280	1,280,000
Satoru Hirota	72	71	68	69	280	1,280,000
Yui Ueda	73	68	68	71	280	1,280,000
Tadahiro Takayama	69	71	71	69	280	1,280,000
Dinesh Chand	70	73	71	67	281	1,008,000
Jeev Milkha Singh	70	72	68	71	281	1,008,000
Takenori Hiraishi	64	73	73	72	282	864,000
Katsunori Kuwabara	71	70	70	71	282	864,000
Yoichi Shimizu	70	72	69	71	282	864,000
Thammanoon Srirot	70	70	70	72	282	864,000

Sun Chlorella Classic

Otaru Country Club, Hokkaido
Par 36-36–72; 7,327 yards

August 5-8
purse, ¥150,000,000

	SCORES				TOTAL	MONEY
Y.E. Yang	67	70	69	69	275	¥30,000,000
David Smail	69	68	70	71	278	12,600,000
Yeh Wei-tze	73	70	69	66	278	12,600,000
Hideki Kase	70	68	70	71	279	6,600,000
Prayad Marksaeng	70	69	67	73	279	6,600,000
Tsuyoshi Yoneyama	66	71	72	71	280	4,617,000
Shingo Katayama	68	74	66	72	280	4,617,000
Kazuhiro Takami	66	74	70	70	280	4,617,000
Ryuichi Oda	68	68	74	70	280	4,617,000
Jyoti Randhawa	68	75	67	70	280	4,617,000
Naomichi Ozaki	72	71	68	70	281	3,180,000
Mitsuhiro Tateyama	69	71	74	67	281	3,180,000
Hideto Tanihara	65	74	72	70	281	3,180,000
Kim Jong-duck	73	70	67	71	281	3,180,000
Toru Taniguchi	67	74	72	69	282	2,505,000
Takashi Kamiyama	74	69	71	68	282	2,505,000
Mamoru Osanai	68	71	72	72	283	2,280,000
Kiyoshi Maita	73	68	71	72	284	1,890,000
Kiyoshi Murota	71	69	72	72	284	1,890,000
Hisayuki Sasaki	72	68	70	74	284	1,890,000
Tomohiro Kondo	71	73	71	69	284	1,890,000

	SCORES				TOTAL	MONEY
Naruhito Ueda	73	68	72	71	284	1,890,000
Tadahisa Inoue	70	74	69	72	285	1,470,000
Tadahiro Takayama	71	68	72	74	285	1,470,000
Katsuyoshi Tomori	73	70	71	72	286	1,260,000
Ryoken Kawagishi	68	75	73	70	286	1,260,000
Satoru Hirota	74	71	68	73	286	1,260,000
Yoichi Shimizu	71	70	73	72	286	1,260,000
Toshikazu Sugihara	71	72	71	73	287	1,080,000
Nobuhiro Hirai	72	70	73	72	287	1,080,000

Hisamitsu KBC Augusta

Keya Golf Club, Shima, Fukuoka
Par 35-36–71; 7,134 yards

August 26-29
purse, ¥100,000,000

	SCORES				TOTAL	MONEY
Steve Conran	68	70	70	69	277	¥20,000,000
Toru Taniguchi	68	71	69	70	278	8,400,000
Takashi Kamiyama	71	71	69	67	278	8,400,000
Hiroyuki Fujita	72	68	71	68	279	3,595,000
Kazuhiko Hosokawa	69	68	71	71	279	3,595,000
Mamoru Osanai	67	73	70	69	279	3,595,000
Masaya Tomida	68	69	72	70	279	3,595,000
Frankie Minoza	69	71	67	72	279	3,595,000
Thammanoon Srirot	72	64	73	70	279	3,595,000
Tsukasa Watanabe	67	72	74	67	280	2,220,000
Shigeru Nonaka	71	73	69	67	280	2,220,000
Daisuke Maruyama	71	67	72	70	280	2,220,000
Jeev Milkha Singh	73	68	71	68	280	2,220,000
Liang Wen-chong	67	71	70	72	280	2,220,000
Satoshi Higashi	67	73	69	72	281	1,620,000
Yasuharu Imano	70	72	73	66	281	1,620,000
Craig Jones	65	73	72	71	281	1,620,000
Hideki Kase	70	73	66	73	282	1,300,000
Yuji Takagi	70	71	70	71	282	1,300,000
Yoshiaki Mano	70	72	69	71	282	1,300,000
Tadahisa Inoue	71	69	73	69	282	1,300,000
Taichi Teshima	72	71	69	71	283	990,000
Tatsuhiko Takahashi	70	69	72	72	283	990,000
Hiroo Okamo	68	74	68	73	283	990,000
Yoshikazu Haku	70	69	70	74	283	990,000
Kazuhiro Takami	70	70	73	71	284	707,777
Kiyoshi Maita	71	69	73	71	284	707,777
Masayuki Kawamura	69	69	76	70	284	707,777
Ryoken Kawagishi	71	72	72	69	284	707,777
Atsushi Takamatsu	71	71	72	70	284	707,777
Shigemasa Higaki	69	73	73	69	284	707,777
Masanari Kato	70	71	72	71	284	707,777
Yasumasa Suzuki	67	72	71	74	284	707,777
Yusaku Miyazato	72	71	70	71	284	707,777

Suntory Open

Sobu Country Club, Inzai, Chiba
Par 35-35–70; 7,123 yards

September 9-12
purse, ¥100,000,000

	SCORES				TOTAL	MONEY
Hideki Kase	69	67	66	65	267	¥20,000,000
Tomohiro Kondo	71	66	68	65	270	7,200,000
Toru Taniguchi	68	67	70	65	270	7,200,000
Katsuya Nakagawa	68	67	69	66	270	7,200,000
Y.E. Yang	65	70	67	70	272	3,800,000
Hideto Tanihara	66	69	67	70	272	3,800,000
Shingo Katayama	68	69	67	70	274	2,842,000
Steve Conran	66	70	67	71	274	2,842,000
Thammanoon Srirot	69	68	68	69	274	2,842,000
Liang Wen-chong	69	67	71	67	274	2,842,000
Retief Goosen	70	71	66	67	274	2,842,000
Mamoru Osanai	68	72	67	68	275	2,120,000
Komei Oda	69	70	68	68	275	2,120,000
Katsunori Kuwabara	71	69	69	67	726	1,670,000
Nozomi Kawahara	71	67	71	67	726	1,670,000
Naomichi Ozaki	69	71	66	70	726	1,670,000
Kazuhiro Takami	70	72	67	67	726	1,670,000
Jeev Milkha Singh	72	70	70	65	277	1,300,000
Hisayuki Sasaki	69	70	71	67	277	1,300,000
Shigeru Nonaka	70	70	69	68	277	1,300,000
Craig Jones	70	69	70	68	277	1,300,000
Katsumasa Miyamoto	72	67	74	65	278	990,000
Scott Laycock	65	69	71	73	278	990,000
Koki Idoki	71	70	71	66	278	990,000
Toshimitsu Izawa	72	68	69	69	278	990,000
Paul Sheehan	67	72	72	68	279	860,000
David Smail	72	70	72	66	279	860,000
Prayad Marksaeng	70	69	75	66	279	860,000
Yusaku Miyazato	70	67	74	69	279	860,000
Hiroshi Goda	72	68	70	70	279	860,000
Yudai Maeda	68	72	69	71	279	860,000
Chawalit Plaphol	69	70	72	69	279	860,000
Soshi Tajima	71	68	72	69	279	860,000
David Ishii	71	69	69	71	279	860,000

ANA Open

Sapporo Golf Club, Wattsu Course,
Kitahiroshima, Hokkaido
Par 36-36–72; 7,063 yards

September 16-19
purse, ¥100,000,000

	SCORES				TOTAL	MONEY
Chawalit Plaphol	66	65	70	70	271	¥20,000,000
Y.E. Yang	69	64	69	70	272	10,000,000
Hideto Tanihara	68	67	72	67	274	5,800,000
Katsumune Imai	66	68	71	69	274	5,800,000
Masahiro Kuramoto	69	70	66	70	275	4,000,000
Keiichiro Fukabori	70	69	71	66	276	3,192,500
Mamoru Osanai	65	72	70	69	276	3,192,500
Toshimitsu Izawa	66	71	67	72	276	3,192,500
Zhang Lian-wei	71	68	67	70	276	3,192,500

	SCORES				TOTAL	MONEY
Tomohiro Kondo	69	70	66	72	277	2,320,000
Hisayuki Sasaki	70	69	68	70	277	2,320,000
Daisuke Maruyama	72	68	68	69	277	2,320,000
Toru Suzuki	68	69	69	71	277	2,320,000
Paul Sheehan	68	72	71	67	278	1,720,000
Takashi Kamiyama	72	67	73	66	278	1,720,000
Katsunori Kuwabara	70	68	71	69	278	1,720,000
David Smail	68	71	68	72	279	1,426,666
Thammanoon Srirot	71	65	74	69	279	1,426,666
Satoru Hirota	69	68	72	70	279	1,426,666
Tsuyoshi Yoneyama	71	68	69	72	280	1,140,000
Takashi Kanemoto	65	70	73	72	280	1,140,000
Jeev Milkha Singh	67	71	71	71	280	1,140,000
Yui Ueda	68	70	68	74	280	1,140,000
Toru Taniguchi	73	69	75	65	282	900,000
Steve Conran	69	72	71	70	282	900,000
Frankie Minoza	71	69	70	72	282	900,000
Hidemasa Hoshino	68	71	74	70	283	780,000
Taichi Teshima	66	73	73	71	283	780,000
Kenichi Kuboya	68	71	77	67	283	780,000
Yusaku Miyazato	69	73	71	71	284	621,666
Yeh Wei-tze	71	70	68	75	284	621,666
Yoshiaki Mano	67	71	73	73	284	621,666
Tadahisa Inoue	70	71	74	69	284	621,666
Tsukasa Watanabe	69	74	70	71	284	621,666
Satoshi Higashi	69	72	72	71	284	621,666

Acom International

Ishioka Golf Club, Ogawa, Ibaragi
Par 36-35–71; 7,046 yards
(Final round cancelled—rain.)

September 30-October 3
purse, ¥120,000,000

	SCORES			TOTAL	MONEY
Toru Suzuki	72	65	63	200	¥18,000,000
Paul Sheehan	68	65	70	203	9,000,000
Steve Conran	70	68	67	205	4,320,000
Yeh Wei-tze	69	66	70	205	4,320,000
Masashi Ozaki	69	67	69	205	4,320,000
Gregory Meyer	68	69	68	205	4,320,000
Jeev Milkha Singh	68	70	68	206	2,857,500
Jyoti Randhawa	68	71	67	206	2,857,500
Dinesh Chand	71	69	67	207	2,358,000
Toshimitsu Izawa	74	66	67	207	2,358,000
Richard Lee	66	69	72	207	2,358,000
Tatsuya Mitsuhashi	69	68	71	208	1,818,000
Takashi Kanemoto	73	66	69	208	1,818,000
Craig Jones	70	69	69	208	1,818,000
Hideto Tanihara	70	69	70	209	1,413,000
Taichi Teshima	68	69	72	209	1,413,000
Yasuharu Imano	70	73	66	209	1,413,000
Yusaku Miyazato	69	70	70	209	1,413,000
Takuya Taniguchi	74	70	66	210	1,098,000
Katsumasa Miyamoto	68	69	73	210	1,098,000
Kiyoshi Murota	70	71	69	210	1,098,000
Liang Wen-chong	69	75	66	210	1,098,000
Azuma Yano	71	69	71	211	918,000

	SCORES			TOTAL	MONEY
Keiichiro Fukabori	70	73	69	212	686,700
Takashi Kamiyama	70	69	73	212	686,700
Shinichi Yokota	68	72	72	212	686,700
Kiyoshi Maita	73	70	69	212	686,700
Hiroshi Goda	74	68	70	212	686,700
Naomichi Ozaki	74	70	68	212	686,700
Eiji Mizoguchi	70	73	69	212	686,700
Christian Pena	72	73	67	212	686,700
Yoshikazu Haku	73	69	70	212	686,700
Tatsuhiko Takahashi	71	70	71	212	686,700

Coca-Cola Tokai Classic

Miyoshi Country Club, West Course, Miyoshi, Aichi
Par 36-36–72; 7,180 yards
(Event shortened to 54 holes—rain.)

October 7-10
purse, ¥120,000,000

	SCORES			TOTAL	MONEY
Katsumune Imai	70	68	72	210	¥18,000,000
Kazuhiko Hosokawa	71	70	69	210	9,000,000
(Imai defeated Hosokawa on first playoff hole.)					
Kiyoshi Maita	69	73	70	212	6,120,000
Tatsuya Mitsuhashi	70	72	71	213	3,960,000
Tsuneyuki Nakajima	72	70	71	213	3,960,000
Toru Suzuki	74	67	73	214	3,240,000
Shingo Katayama	71	75	69	215	2,751,000
Paul Sheehan	67	80	68	215	2,751,000
Dinesh Chand	74	71	70	215	2,751,000
Daisuke Maruyama	71	74	71	216	2,088,000
Takenori Hiraishi	68	76	72	216	2,088,000
Toshimitsu Izawa	73	70	73	216	2,088,000
Katsufumi Okino	70	72	74	216	2,088,000
Toru Taniguchi	74	73	70	217	1,336,500
Tsuyoshi Yoneyama	72	72	73	217	1,336,500
Kiyoshi Murota	73	71	73	217	1,336,500
Satoru Hirota	75	73	69	217	1,336,500
Shigeru Nonaka	68	80	69	217	1,336,500
Kazuhiro Takami	70	74	73	217	1,336,500
Kiyoshi Miyazato	72	74	71	217	1,336,500
Tsukasa Watanabe	76	73	68	217	1,336,500
Hideto Tanihara	72	73	73	218	825,428
Tomohiro Kondo	70	75	73	218	825,428
Katsunori Kuwabara	72	70	76	218	825,428
Charlie Wi	68	78	72	218	825,428
Shigemasa Higaki	68	77	73	218	825,428
Kazuhiro Fukunaga	71	74	73	218	825,428
Yoshinobu Tsukada	73	73	72	218	825,428
Hideki Kase	68	75	76	219	574,714
Lin Keng-chi	72	73	74	219	574,714
Gregory Meyer	71	74	74	219	574,714
Christian Pena	72	75	72	219	574,714
Makoto Inoue	71	75	73	219	574,714
Satoshi Higashi	73	72	74	219	574,714
Kenichi Kuboya	71	77	71	219	574,714

Japan Open

Katayamazu Golf Club, Ishikawa
Par 36-36–72; 7,104 yards

October 14-17
purse, ¥120,000,000

	SCORES				TOTAL	MONEY
Toru Taniguchi	68	68	75	74	285	¥24,000,000
David Smail	73	71	69	76	289	9,540,000
Yeh Wei-tze	70	77	70	72	289	9,540,000
Toshimitsu Izawa	71	70	73	75	289	9,540,000
Dinesh Chand	69	71	77	73	290	5,040,000
Keiichiro Fukabori	74	69	73	75	291	4,080,000
Shingo Katayama	73	72	73	74	292	3,444,000
Steve Conran	72	72	73	77	294	2,913,000
Nobuhiro Masuda	74	66	74	80	294	2,913,000
Hideki Kase	71	74	74	76	295	2,376,000
Hideto Tanihara	79	70	74	73	296	1,800,000
Hisayuki Sasaki	74	74	75	73	296	1,800,000
Katsunori Kuwabara	71	78	74	73	296	1,800,000
Ryoken Kawagishi	72	73	73	78	296	1,800,000
Takashi Kamiyama	70	75	75	77	297	1,404,000
Tsuneyuki Nakajima	70	78	74	75	297	1,404,000
Katsuya Nakagawa	73	75	72	77	297	1,404,000
S.K. Ho	72	75	73	78	298	1,284,000
Toru Suzuki	74	74	74	77	299	1,143,200
Tsuyoshi Yoneyama	76	73	77	73	299	1,143,200
Katsumasa Miyamoto	74	72	75	78	299	1,143,200
Taichi Teshima	72	75	75	77	299	1,143,200
Tatsuo Takasaki	72	73	80	74	299	1,143,200
Naomichi Ozaki	75	74	72	79	300	1,040,666
Nozomi Kawahara	74	73	76	77	300	1,040,666
Yoshiaki Kimura	73	72	77	78	300	1,040,666
Takashi Kanemoto	74	74	77	76	301	972,000
Koumei Oda	72	78	72	79	301	972,000
Scott Gardiner	71	77	78	75	301	972,000
Kim Jong-duck	71	74	77	80	302	912,000
Takenori Hiraishi	73	76	77	76	302	912,000

Bridgestone Open

Sodegaura Country Club, Chiba
Par 36-36–72; 7,138 yards

October 21-24
purse, ¥110,000,000

	SCORES				TOTAL	MONEY
Toru Taniguchi	66	71	69	66	272	¥22,000,000
Shinichi Yokota	69	70	70	64	273	9,240,000
Shigeki Maruyama	74	68	67	64	273	9,240,000
Tadahiro Takayama	69	65	69	71	274	4,840,000
Liang Wen-chong	67	70	67	70	274	4,840,000
David Smail	68	69	66	72	275	3,960,000
Dinesh Chand	66	75	67	68	276	3,630,000
Shingo Katayama	70	69	69	69	277	2,888,600
Steve Conran	67	71	71	68	277	2,888,600
Keiichiro Fukabori	68	72	71	66	277	2,888,600
Nobuhiro Masuda	72	68	68	69	277	2,888,600
Yasuharu Imano	72	70	65	70	277	2,888,600
Katsumune Imai	69	66	68	75	278	2,222,000

	SCORES				TOTAL	MONEY
Hideto Tanihara	68	70	70	71	279	1,633,500
Brendan Jones	71	69	67	72	279	1,633,500
Hiroyuki Fujita	68	72	69	70	279	1,633,500
Tomohiro Kondo	66	70	71	72	279	1,633,500
Taichi Teshima	68	72	73	66	279	1,633,500
Prayad Marksaeng	75	67	70	67	279	1,633,500
Jyoti Randhawa	70	72	68	69	279	1,633,500
Brandt Jobe	69	70	70	70	279	1,633,500
Hisayuki Sasaki	74	66	67	73	280	1,034,000
Shigemasa Higaki	71	66	68	75	280	1,034,000
Nozomi Kawahara	70	68	71	71	280	1,034,000
Azuma Yano	72	71	66	71	280	1,034,000
Makoto Inoue	70	71	71	68	280	1,034,000
Katsunari Takahashi	71	70	68	71	280	1,034,000
Paul Sheehan	70	68	72	71	281	737,000
Mamoru Osanai	71	70	72	68	281	737,000
Daisuke Maruyama	71	69	70	71	281	737,000
Nobuo Serizawa	73	69	69	70	281	737,000
Craig Jones	77	65	68	71	281	737,000
Katsuya Nakagawa	67	70	71	73	281	737,000
David Ishii	70	71	72	68	281	737,000

ABC Championship

ABC Golf Club, Tojo, Hyogo
Par 36-36–72; 7,176 yards

October 28-31
purse, ¥120,000,000

	SCORES				TOTAL	MONEY
Makoto Inoue	69	67	66	71	273	¥24,000,000
Toru Suzuki	71	65	68	70	274	10,080,000
Ryoken Kawagishi	71	69	64	70	274	10,080,000
Takashi Kamiyama	68	66	70	71	275	5,760,000
Toru Taniguchi	68	69	71	68	276	4,360,000
Daisuke Maruyama	71	69	68	68	276	4,360,000
Dinesh Chand	72	70	66	68	276	4,360,000
Hideki Kase	72	68	68	71	279	3,396,000
Satoru Hirota	69	74	65	71	279	3,396,000
Christian Pena	71	67	74	67	279	3,396,000
Hisayuki Sasaki	66	69	73	72	280	2,448,000
Toshimitsu Izawa	67	75	67	71	280	2,448,000
Taichi Teshima	68	68	75	69	280	2,448,000
Shigeru Nonaka	71	66	74	69	280	2,448,000
Y.E. Yang	72	69	71	68	280	2,448,000
Naomichi Ozaki	72	69	68	72	281	1,718,400
Kiyoshi Maita	74	65	72	70	281	1,718,400
Hiroyuki Fujita	69	70	69	73	281	1,718,400
Jeev Milkha Singh	70	70	71	70	281	1,718,400
Katsuya Nakagawa	71	70	73	67	281	1,718,400
Kim Jong-duck	71	68	71	72	282	1,320,000
Zhang Lian-wei	76	66	72	68	282	1,320,000
Yasuharu Imano	72	70	69	71	282	1,320,000
Gregory Meyer	74	70	67	72	283	1,080,000
Prayad Marksaeng	68	70	74	71	283	1,080,000
Tomohiro Kondo	70	71	69	73	283	1,080,000
Tsuyoshi Yoneyama	70	73	70	71	284	826,500
Kiyoshi Murota	73	69	73	69	284	826,500
Keiichiro Fukabori	70	73	70	71	284	826,500

	SCORES				TOTAL	MONEY
Brandt Jobe	75	68	71	70	284	826,500
Hidemasa Hoshino	71	68	72	73	284	826,500
Katsumasa Miyamoto	71	70	71	72	284	826,500
Thammanoon Srirot	70	68	74	72	284	826,500
Ippei Sadanobu	71	72	72	69	284	826,500

Asahi-Ryokuken Yomiuri Aso-Iizuka Memorial Open

Aso-Iizuka Golf Club, Fukuoka   November 4-7
Par 36-36–72; 7,106 yards   purse, ¥100,000,000

	SCORES				TOTAL	MONEY
Y.E. Yang	69	68	69	65	271	¥20,000,000
Shingo Katayama	72	66	67	68	273	10,000,000
Hideto Tanihara	69	68	72	66	275	5,200,000
Katsumasa Miyamoto	68	67	67	73	275	5,200,000
Toshimitsu Izawa	65	67	68	75	275	5,200,000
Tetsuji Hiratsuka	70	70	73	63	276	3,316,666
Katsuyoshi Tomori	69	69	71	67	276	3,316,666
Komei Oda	70	72	67	67	276	3,316,666
Hideki Kase	73	69	69	66	277	2,520,000
Kaname Yokoo	66	72	72	67	277	2,520,000
Yusaku Miyazato	69	69	70	69	277	2,520,000
Azuma Yano	70	67	72	68	277	2,520,000
Tatsuya Mitsuhashi	71	65	72	70	278	1,686,666
Hisayuki Sasaki	69	69	72	68	278	1,686,666
Ryoken Kawagishi	65	71	72	70	278	1,686,666
Katsunori Kuwabara	67	72	70	69	278	1,686,666
Yoshiaki Mano	70	72	69	67	278	1,686,666
Christian Pena	69	70	70	69	278	1,686,666
Toru Suzuki	68	70	69	72	279	1,220,000
Yeh Wei-tze	71	69	72	67	279	1,220,000
Ryuichi Oda	69	70	69	71	279	1,220,000
Yui Ueda	69	72	69	69	279	1,220,000
Shinichi Yokota	69	67	69	75	280	886,666
Mitsuhiro Tateyama	68	69	71	72	280	886,666
Nozomi Kawahara	68	70	73	69	280	886,666
Yudai Maeda	72	69	72	67	280	886,666
Zhang Lian-wei	71	69	68	72	280	886,666
Taichiro Kiyota	71	65	74	70	280	886,666
Nobuhiro Masuda	73	71	70	67	281	700,000
Shigemasa Higaki	69	68	75	69	281	700,000
Yoshikazu Haku	74	70	69	68	281	700,000

Mitsui Sumitomo Visa Taiheiyo Masters

Taiheiyo Club, Gotemba Course, Shizuoka   November 11-14
Par 36-36–72; 7,246 yards   purse, ¥150,000,000

	SCORES				TOTAL	MONEY
Darren Clarke	66	65	67	68	266	¥30,000,000
Nozomi Kawahara	67	69	66	70	272	12,600,000
Lee Westwood	68	69	67	68	272	12,600,000
Hideki Kase	67	70	68	69	274	6,600,000
Hidemasa Hoshino	69	70	67	68	274	6,600,000

	SCORES				TOTAL	MONEY
Shingo Katayama	68	65	72	70	275	4,975,000
Nobuhiro Masuda	73	68	71	63	275	4,975,000
Graeme McDowell	69	69	68	69	275	4,975,000
Toru Taniguchi	67	70	71	68	276	3,780,000
Y.E. Yang	71	67	69	69	276 .	3,780,000
Christian Pena	75	68	68	65	276	3,780,000
Azuma Yano	69	69	70	68	276	3,780,000
Ryoken Kawagishi	66	70	72	69	277	2,610,000
Naomichi Ozaki	70	70	67	70	277	2,610,000
Koki Idoki	68	69	71	69	277	2,610,000
Kiyoshi Miyazato	70	67	71	69	277	2,610,000
Kenichi Kuboya	68	69	71	69	277	2,610,000
David Smail	69	71	70	68	278	2,130,000
Takashi Kamiyama	70	72	68	69	279	1,830,000
Steve Conran	71	71	67	70	279	1,830,000
Toshimitsu Izawa	71	72	65	71	279	1,830,000
Shinichi Yokota	71	71	69	68	279	1,830,000
Tsuyoshi Yoneyama	73	68	68	71	280	1,362,000
Kiyoshi Maita	68	71	71	70	280	1,362,000
Kiyoshi Murota	68	73	68	71	280	1,362,000
Shigemasa Higaki	69	73	70	68	280	1,362,000
Zhang Lian-wei	72	67	68	73	280	1,362,000
Hideto Tanihara	68	71	72	70	281	1,027,500
Keiichiro Fukabori	75	68	72	66	281	1,027,500
Tatsuya Mitsuhashi	69	70	72	70	281	1,027,500
Yeh Wei-tze	67	68	69	77	281	1,027,500
Kazuhiko Hosokawa	71	73	70	67	281	1,027,500
Yoshiaki Mano	69	70	73	69	281	1,027,500

Dunlop Phoenix

Phoenix Country Club, Miyazaki
Par 35-35–70; 6,901 yards

November 18-21
purse, ¥200,000,000

	SCORES				TOTAL	MONEY
Tiger Woods	65	67	65	67	264	¥40,000,000
Ryoken Kawagishi	71	67	69	65	272	20,000,000
K.J. Choi	72	66	71	65	274	13,600,000
Steve Conran	73	68	69	65	275	9,600,000
Hideto Tanihara	69	70	69	68	276	7,600,000
Daniel Chopra	71	68	68	69	276	7,600,000
Thomas Bjorn	75	69	69	64	277	6,600,000
Toru Taniguchi	73	70	71	64	278	5,870,000
Kaname Yokoo	68	67	73	70	278	5,870,000
Christian Pena	73	63	73	70	279	5,040,000
Robert Allenby	71	69	69	70	279	5,040,000
Kiyoshi Maita	74	66	71	70	281	3,760,000
Kiyoshi Murota	73	67	70	71	281	3,760,000
Naomichi Ozaki	74	65	68	74	281	3,760,000
Jyoti Randhawa	72	70	70	69	281	3,760,000
Craig Parry	69	74	71	67	281	3,760,000
Shingo Katayama	75	70	70	67	282	2,770,000
Hidemasa Hoshino	74	72	69	67	282	2,770,000
Taichi Teshima	70	72	69	71	282	2,770,000
Yasuharu Imano	73	70	69	70	282	2,770,000
Takuya Taniguchi	71	70	68	74	283	2,280,000
Kazuhiro Takami	72	73	70	68	283	2,280,000

	SCORES			TOTAL	MONEY
Brendan Jones	76	67	72	69	284	1,860,000
Katsumasa Miyamoto	70	70	69	75	284	1,860,000
Kim Jong-duck	69	74	68	73	284	1,860,000
Carlos Franco	72	70	72	70	284	1,860,000
Shinichi Yokota	73	72	65	75	285	1,520,000
Katsunori Kuwabara	70	72	72	71	285	1,520,000
Tsuneyuki Nakajima	78	67	68	72	285	1,520,000
Koki Idoki	75	69	73	68	285	1,520,000

Casio World Open

Ibusuki Golf Club, Kaimon Course, Kagoshima
Par 36-36–72; 7,151 yards

November 25-28
purse, ¥140,000,000

	SCORES			TOTAL	MONEY
David Smail	70	66	69	71	276	¥28,000,000
Hunter Mahan	66	70	71	70	277	14,000,000
Hisayuki Sasaki	68	68	73	70	279	6,720,000
Ryoken Kawagishi	69	70	72	68	279	6,720,000
Takashi Kamiyama	71	69	68	71	279	6,720,000
Charl Schwartzel	68	67	73	71	279	6,720,000
Katsunori Kuwabara	66	71	75	68	280	4,445,000
Shingo Katayama	72	70	70	68	280	4,445,000
Justin Rose	69	71	70	71	281	3,948,000
Tomohiro Kondo	74	66	72	71	283	3,528,000
Yeh Wei-tze	72	70	68	73	283	3,528,000
Kiyoshi Maita	70	70	72	72	284	2,828,000
Colin Montgomerie	74	71	70	69	284	2,828,000
Kaname Yokoo	69	70	73	72	284	2,828,000
Hiroshi Goda	72	71	71	71	285	2,198,000
Keiichiro Fukabori	74	68	70	73	285	2,198,000
Yasuharu Imano	70	75	71	69	285	2,198,000
Tadahiro Takayama	70	66	77	72	285	2,198,000
Daisuke Maruyama	71	73	71	71	286	1,652,000
Jeev Milkha Singh	73	71	71	71	286	1,652,000
Yusaku Miyazato	73	68	76	69	286	1,652,000
Masanori Kobayashi	70	68	76	72	286	1,652,000
Craig Jones	68	73	74	71	286	1,652,000
Naomichi Ozaki	73	69	73	72	287	1,176,000
Toru Suzuki	70	70	75	72	287	1,176,000
Toru Taniguchi	74	69	71	73	287	1,176,000
Go Higaki	74	69	71	73	287	1,176,000
David Ishii	70	71	73	73	287	1,176,000
Masaya Tomida	70	73	74	70	287	1,176,000
Hirofumi Miyase	71	71	74	72	288	870,333
Kazuhiro Takami	70	74	73	71	288	870,333
Taichi Teshima	69	74	76	69	288	870,333
Shinichi Yokota	70	69	74	75	288	870,333
Yui Ueda	69	69	77	73	288	870,333
Christian Pena	69	71	73	75	288	870,333

Golf Nippon Series JT Cup

Tokyo Yomiuri Country Club, Tokyo
Par 35-35–70; 6,961 yards

December 2-5
purse, ¥100,000,000

	SCORES				TOTAL	MONEY
Paul Sheehan	69	65	66	66	266	¥30,000,000
Y.E. Yang	67	68	67	68	270	10,550,000
Katsumasa Miyamoto	69	66	66	69	270	10,550,000
Keiichiro Fukabori	69	65	65	72	271	4,700,000
David Smail	67	67	67	70	271	4,700,000
Hideki Kase	66	66	68	72	272	3,700,000
Brendan Jones	65	67	70	73	275	3,300,000
Takashi Kamiyama	69	74	66	67	276	2,900,000
Kaname Yokoo	71	72	66	67	276	2,900,000
Tomohiro Kondo	71	65	70	70	276	2,900,000
Katsumune Imai	70	67	69	71	277	2,300,000
Yeh Wei-tze	68	72	66	71	277	2,300,000
Toru Suzuki	68	67	68	74	277	2,300,000
Steve Conran	67	69	70	72	278	1,900,000
Ryoken Kawagishi	71	68	73	67	279	1,587,500
Dinash Chand	70	70	70	69	279	1,587,500
Shingo Katayama	73	71	65	70	279	1,587,500
Toru Taniguchi	70	71	67	71	279	1,587,500
Takuya Taniguchi	72	68	73	67	280	1,350,000
Hidemasa Hoshino	76	69	70	66	281	1,300,000
Kim Jong-duck	74	73	70	65	282	1,200,000
Tatsuya Mitsuhashi	75	70	70	68	283	1,100,000
Tetsuji Hiratsuka	77	68	71	68	284	970,000
Chawalit Plaphol	71	68	75	70	284	970,000
Makoto Inoue	72	68	66	79	285	900,000
Andre Stolz	75	73	69	70	287	860,000

Asia/Japan Okinawa Open

Naha Golf Club, Okinawa
Par 36-35–71, 6,789 yards

December 16-19
purse, ¥100,000,000

	SCORES				TOTAL	MONEY
Kiyoshi Miyazato	68	70	68	64	270	¥20,000,000
Masahiro Kuramoto	68	69	67	67	271	5,416,666
Mamoru Osanai	68	70	66	67	271	5,416,666
Charlie Wi	65	69	69	68	271	5,416,666
Scott Barr	67	68	68	68	271	5,416,666
Hideki Kase	68	68	66	69	271	5,416,666
Jeev Milkha Singh	67	62	69	73	271	5,416,666
Scott Laycock	69	67	68	68	272	2,727,500
Kaname Yokoo	71	66	69	66	272	2,727,500
Katsuyoshi Tomori	71	68	66	67	272	2,727,500
Kim Jong-duck	67	72	65	68	272	2,727,500
Lin Wen-tang	70	68	69	66	273	2,020,000
Makoto Inoue	68	67	71	67	273	2,020,000
Nobuhiro Masuda	68	73	63	69	273	2,020,000
Mo Joong-kyung	70	70	68	66	274	1,437,142
Ryuichi Oda	71	67	70	66	274	1,437,142
Wang Ter-chang	67	68	71	68	274	1,437,142
Ted Oh	71	68	67	68	274	1,437,142

	SCORES				TOTAL	MONEY
Ryoken Kawagishi	68	67	70	69	274	1,437,142
Toru Taniguchi	68	72	65	69	274	1,437,142
Dinesh Chand	66	71	67	70	274	1,437,142
Shigemasa Higaki	69	68	70	68	275	1,020,000
Hisayuki Sasaki	70	67	70	68	275	1,020,000
Soshi Tajima	69	68	66	72	275	1,020,000
Kang Wook-soon	69	70	68	69	276	820,000
Angelo Que	72	66	74	64	276	820,000
Y.E. Yang	73	68	71	64	276	820,000
Prayad Marksaeng	71	66	73	66	276	820,000
Terry Pilkadaris	71	68	67	70	276	820,000
Kazuhiro Takami	72	68	71	66	277	598,750
Koki Idoki	71	67	72	67	277	598,750
Shinichi Yokota	72	69	69	67	277	598,750
Ty Tryon	67	72	70	68	277	598,750
Lin Chie-hsiang	66	67	74	70	277	598,750
Yasuharu Imano	70	69	67	71	277	598,750
S.K. Ho	68	69	68	72	277	598,750
Mitsuhiro Tateyama	70	69	65	73	277	598,750

Australasian Tour

Holden New Zealand Open

Grange Golf Club, Auckland, New Zealand
Par 35-35–70; 6,535 yards

January 15-18
purse, NZ$700,000

	SCORES				TOTAL	MONEY
Terry Price	69	65	67	70	271	A$109,491.30
*Brad Heaven	64	66	72	70	272	
Peter Senior	67	72	70	65	274	51,552.15
David Smail	67	68	73	66	274	51,552.15
David Bransdon	66	71	70	68	275	26,764.54
Andrew Buckle	68	70	68	69	275	26,764.54
Adrian Percey	66	71	70	69	276	18,856.83
Wade Ormsby	64	73	68	71	276	18,856.83
Richard Best	68	72	64	72	276	18,856.83
Chris Downes	66	67	69	74	276	18,856.83
Wayne Grady	69	67	72	69	277	14,294.70
Martin Doyle	70	64	73	70	277	14,294.70
Peter O'Malley	64	68	76	70	278	11,557.41
John Inman	68	71	66	73	278	11,557.41
Leigh McKechnie	72	67	76	64	279	8,480.50
Stuart Bouvier	68	69	74	68	279	8,480.50
*Bradley Iles	68	71	71	69	279	
David Diaz	66	69	74	70	279	8,480.50
Matthew Millar	65	70	73	71	279	8,480.50
Eddie Lee	66	73	68	72	279	8,480.50
Euan Walters	66	69	69	75	279	8,480.50
Michael Long	69	71	68	72	280	6,204.50
Scott Laycock	69	67	71	73	280	6,204.50
Chris Campbell	67	70	70	73	280	6,204.50
Peter Fowler	67	69	70	74	280	6,204.50
Ricky Schmidt	65	72	66	77	280	6,204.50
Craig Carmichael	70	69	74	68	281	4,724.34
Ed Stedman	69	67	76	69	281	4,724.34
Steven Jeffress	73	65	71	72	281	4,724.34
Gary Simpson	69	67	72	73	281	4,724.34
Kurt Barnes	66	69	70	76	281	4,724.34
David McKenzie	73	67	65	76	281	4,724.34

Johnnie Walker Classic

See Asia/Japan Tours chapter.

Heineken Classic

Royal Melbourne Golf Club, Melbourne, Victoria
Par 36-36–72; 6,981 yards

February 5-8
purse, A$2,000,000

	SCORES				TOTAL	MONEY
Ernie Els	60	66	68	74	268	A$360,000
Adam Scott	66	68	68	67	269	204,000

	SCORES			TOTAL	MONEY
Peter Fowler	66	68	69	70	273	135,000
Peter Hanson	67	70	66	71	274	96,000
Michael Campbell	64	72	69	70	275	76,000
Stephen Gallacher	68	68	69	70	275	76,000
Greg Owen	68	72	70	66	276	56,500
Paul Sheehan	66	74	65	71	276	56,500
Gareth Paddison	67	68	67	74	276	56,500
Mahal Pearce	65	70	69	72	276	56,500
Peter Senior	70	67	70	70	277	42,000
Peter O'Malley	66	69	68	74	277	42,000
Richard Green	66	67	76	69	278	35,000
Ian Poulter	68	68	73	69	278	35,000
Joakim Haeggman	71	68	68	72	279	32,000
Stuart Appleby	69	73	68	70	280	23,950
Nick O'Hern	70	69	71	70	280	23,950
Thomas Levet	71	68	72	69	280	23,950
Robert Karlsson	72	69	73	66	280	23,950
James Kingston	71	67	69	73	280	23,950
Scott Gardiner	69	67	70	74	280	23,950
Gary Murphy	71	70	67	73	281	19,600
Terry Price	72	68	72	69	281	19,600
David Howell	68	69	73	72	282	15,600
Craig Jones	72	70	69	71	282	15,600
Grant Dodd	68	72	70	72	282	15,600
Matthew Ecob	68	73	68	73	282	15,600
Trevor Immelman	70	70	73	69	282	15,600
Peter Baker	69	71	65	77	282	15,600
Craig Spence	67	72	69	74	282	15,600
Gary Evans	67	72	72	71	282	15,600
Jean Van de Velde	69	72	68	74	283	11,400
Craig Parry	67	73	70	73	283	11,400
Bradley Hughes	70	70	71	72	283	11,400
John Bickerton	70	72	71	70	283	11,400
Nick Dougherty	70	70	70	73	283	11,400
Euan Walters	70	73	69	71	283	11,400
*Nick Flanagan	67	71	71	74	283	
Nick Faldo	68	73	70	73	284	7,200
Klas Eriksson	72	69	71	72	284	7,200
Barry Lane	70	69	71	74	284	7,200
Soren Kjeldsen	69	72	73	70	284	7,200
Steve Collins	68	75	69	72	284	7,200
David McKenzie	69	68	76	71	284	7,200
Michael Long	68	72	70	74	284	7,200
Henrik Stenson	74	69	66	75	284	7,200
Peter Hedblom	67	73	70	74	284	7,200
Miles Tunnicliff	69	68	75	72	284	7,200
Gary Orr	71	71	72	70	284	7,200
Paul Lawrie	73	70	65	76	284	7,200
Simon Khan	70	68	75	71	284	7,200
Paul Casey	68	71	71	74	284	7,200
Jamie Donaldson	72	67	75	70	284	7,200
Steve Conran	71	72	69	73	285	3,468.57
Julien Clement	71	72	68	74	285	3,468.57
Christian Cevaer	69	72	72	72	285	3,468.57
Adrian Percey	74	68	70	73	285	3,468.57
Mikko Ilonen	71	70	70	74	285	3,468.57
Brett Rumford	69	74	68	74	285	3,468.57
Adam Groom	69	71	72	73	285	3,468.57
Wayne Grady	72	69	71	74	286	3,100
Jarrod Moseley	73	69	71	73	286	3,100

	SCORES				TOTAL	MONEY
Raymond Russell	69	72	71	74	286	3,100
Nathan Green	68	70	77	71	286	3,100
Wade Ormsby	65	75	72	74	286	3,100
Simon Wakefield	70	73	71	73	287	2,960
Martin Maritz	70	71	75	71	287	2,960
Greg Norman	71	72	70	75	288	2,753.33
Mark Foster	69	73	71	75	288	2,753.33
Gavin Coles	71	72	74	71	288	2,753.33
Tobias Dier	65	75	73	75	288	2,753.33
Martin LeMesurier	72	67	72	77	288	2,753.33
Eddie Lee	70	73	71	74	288	2,753.33
Sandy Lyle	70	73	67	79	289	2,580
Scott Laycock	70	73	73	73	289	2,580
Marcus Cain	70	71	76	73	290	2,500
Iain Pyman	69	74	77	70	290	2,500
Craig Carmichael	65	73	75	78	291	2,440
Andrew Buckle	71	68	73	80	292	2,400
Scott Drummond	69	72	74	78	293	2,320
David Diaz	71	70	73	79	293	2,320
Simon Nash	74	69	72	78	293	2,320
Stuart Bouvier	72	71	73	78	294	2,240
Paul Marantz	70	73	79	74	296	2,200

ANZ Championship

Horizons Golf Resort, Port Stephens, New South Wales   February 12-15
Par 36-36–72; 6,764 yards   purse, A$1,750,000

	POINTS				TOTAL	MONEY
Brian Davis	7	8	12	17	44	A$315,000
Paul Casey	4	19	6	14	43	178,500
Thomas Levet	9	14	7	9	39	101,062.50
Scott Gardiner	7	14	11	7	39	101,062.50
*Nick Flanagan	14	4	13	8	39	
Steve Webster	14	13	12	(-2)	37	66,500
Nick O'Hern	18	8	8	3	37	66,500
Peter Fowler	7	8	14	6	35	49,437.50
Bradley Hughes	0	19	7	9	35	49,437.50
Brett Rumford	2	7	13	13	35	49,437.50
Ricky Barnes	5	9	16	5	35	49,437.50
Jose Manuel Lara	1	8	13	12	34	32,550
David McKenzie	2	11	16	5	34	32,550
Joakim Haeggman	12	7	10	5	34	32,550
Michael Campbell	11	11	5	7	34	32,550
Martin LeMesurier	5	8	10	11	34	32,550
Zhang Lian-wei	(-2)	15	16	4	33	22,159.37
Barry Lane	2	12	8	11	33	22,159.37
Brendan Jones	(-3)	13	10	13	33	22,159.37
Chris Downes	7	10	6	10	33	22,159.37
Toru Suzuki	5	10	14	3	32	18,200
Andrew Tschudin	11	1	14	6	32	18,200
Martin Maritz	5	6	9	12	32	18,200
Mark Foster	12	(-2)	5	16	31	14,700
Peter Hanson	3	9	7	12	31	14,700
Henrik Stenson	11	1	15	4	31	14,700
Peter O'Malley	12	10	3	6	31	14,700
Gary Evans	4	9	15	3	31	14,700

	POINTS			TOTAL	MONEY
Fredrik Andersson Hed	3	12	13	3	31	14,700
Brad Kennedy	7	2	12	10	31	14,700
Peter Lawrie	0	9	11	10	30	11,316.66
Robert Coles	6	3	10	11	30	11,316.66
John Bickerton	16	1	2	11	30	11,316.66
Michael Long	10	6	4	9	29	9,625
Mathew Goggin	9	8	8	4	29	9,625
Kenneth Ferrie	3	11	4	11	29	9,625
Jonathan Lomas	6	3	15	5	29	9,625
Graeme McDowell	3	9	8	9	29	9,625
Craig Carmichael	4	10	6	9	29	9,625
Peter Hedblom	13	5	7	3	28	8,225
Gareth Paddison	8	7	7	6	28	8,225
Santiago Luna	5	10	8	4	27	7,175
Jens Nilsson	5	5	14	3	27	7,175
Steve Conran	5	4	8	10	27	7,175
Paul Gow	6	7	10	4	27	7,175
Robert Karlsson	3	7	8	8	26	5,950
Stephen Gallacher	8	5	8	5	26	5,950
Alastair Forsyth	3	10	3	10	26	5,950
Gavin Coles	6	6	4	9	25	4,900
Craig Parry	(-1)	12	7	7	25	4,900
Euan Walters	6	6	10	3	25	4,900
Gregory Havret	7	3	13	1	24	3,675
Ricardo Gonzalez	5	4	9	6	24	3,675
Stuart Bouvier	1	8	18	(-3)	24	3,675
Greg Owen	4	12	9	(-1)	24	3,675
Jose Manuel Carriles	5	4	10	4	23	2,896.25
David Smail	8	4	7	4	23	2,896.25
Simon Khan	1	16	(-1)	7	23	2,896.25
Marcus Fraser	5	7	8	3	23	2,896.25
Michael Pearson	5	4	10	4	23	2,896.25
Shannon Jones	(-2)	11	11	3	23	2,896.25
Soren Kjeldsen	5	7	0	10	22	2,660
Steve Collins	4	5	10	3	22	2,660
Pierre Fulke	5	11	4	2	22	2,660
Lucas Parsons	1	8	9	4	22	2,660
Jamie Elson	3	9	(-6)	16	22	2,660
Richard McEvoy	6	4	0	12	22	2,660
Aaron Townsend	2	10	3	6	21	2,537.50
Tony Carolan	4	9	7	0	20	2,467.50
Johan Edfors	6	5	12	(-4)	19	2,415
Richard Green	10	(-1)	7	2	18	2,345
Nathan Green	10	3	4	1	18	2,345
David Diaz	(-3)	12	5	4	18	2,345
Grant Dodd	1	8	3	4	16	2,240
Matthew Ecob	7	4	8	(-3)	16	2,240
Henrik Bjornstad	10	3	(-1)	4	16	2,240
Anthony Gilligan	6	3	3	3	15	2,170
Nick Dougherty	7	3	3	(-1)	12	2,135
Eddie Lee	8	1	1	1	11	2,100
Sandy Lyle	2	7	6	(-6)	9	2,047.50
Stuart Little	2	7	5	(-5)	9	2,047.50
Richard Swift	3	9	(-3)	(-3)	6	1,995

Jacob's Creek Open

Kooyonga Golf Club, Adelaide, South Australia
Par 36-35–71; 6,711 yards

February 19-22
purse, A$1,050,000

	SCORES				TOTAL	MONEY
Euan Walters	66	71	70	68	275	A$189,000
Wayne Grady	67	71	71	71	280	76,125
Anthony Painter	65	71	72	72	280	76,125
Brendan Jones	69	68	72	71	280	76,125
Mathew Goggin	72	70	66	73	281	37,800
Nick O'Hern	66	72	73	70	281	37,800
Scott Gutschewski	70	73	67	71	281	37,800
Craig Parry	68	74	70	70	282	23,700
Michael Long	71	71	72	68	282	23,700
Craig Jones	71	71	72	68	282	23,700
Stephen Collins	68	73	73	68	282	23,700
Scott Gardiner	72	69	70	71	282	23,700
Martin Doyle	69	74	67	72	282	23,700
Jimmy Walker	71	71	72	68	282	23,700
Mike Sposa	69	70	72	72	283	15,960
Adam Groom	66	69	74	74	283	15,960
David Bransdon	72	71	72	69	284	12,350.62
Matthew Ecob	68	71	69	76	284	12,350.62
James Driscoll	69	70	74	71	284	12,350.62
Jason Caron	71	71	75	67	284	12,350.62
Paul Gow	71	65	78	71	285	10,815
David Diaz	70	73	73	69	285	10,815
Fran Quinn	72	69	70	75	286	8,910
David McKenzie	71	70	73	72	286	8,910
Marcus Cain	68	74	73	71	286	8,910
Doug LaBelle	67	74	77	68	286	8,910
Paul Sheehan	68	70	76	72	286	8,910
Jens Nilsson	67	69	73	77	286	8,910
Troy Matteson	74	68	74	70	286	8,910
Gary Simpson	72	72	74	69	287	6,573
Richie Coughlan	71	71	75	70	287	6,573
Wayne Perske	72	67	71	77	287	6,573
Craig Carmichael	68	75	70	74	287	6,573
Jeremy Wilkinson	71	72	74	70	287	6,573

New Zealand PGA Championship

Clearwater Resort, Christchurch, New Zealand
Par 36-36–72; 7,137 yards

February 26-29
purse, A$1,000,000

	SCORES				TOTAL	MONEY
Gavin Coles	70	72	72	68	282	A$180,000
Bradley Hughes	68	73	73	71	285	72,500
Bill Lunde	69	70	73	73	285	72,500
Brendan Jones	67	73	74	71	285	72,500
Peter Senior	71	72	69	74	286	36,000
Franklin Langham	72	69	73	72	286	36,000
Euan Walters	73	68	72	73	286	36,000
Barry Cheesman	69	75	73	70	287	28,000
Scott Sterling	70	69	74	74	287	28,000
Doug Barron	69	72	72	75	288	23,500

	SCORES			TOTAL	MONEY
Richard Best	71 69 75 73			288	23,500
Shane Bertsch	70 72 73 74			289	15,206.25
Vance Veazey	72 72 74 71			289	15,206.25
Lucas Parsons	71 68 79 71			289	15,206.25
Tony Carolan	70 73 74 72			289	15,206.25
Paul Sheehan	70 72 73 74			289	15,206.25
Jess Daley	73 71 72 73			289	15,206.25
D.A. Points	72 70 77 70			289	15,206.25
Jon Mills	67 71 80 71			289	15,206.25
Stephen Collins	72 72 72 74			290	10,200
Steve Conran	70 71 77 72			290	10,200
Doug LaBelle	70 71 76 73			290	10,200
Jason Enloe	71 69 77 73			290	10,200
Andy Doeden	70 72 77 71			290	10,200
Tom Scherrer	67 76 74 74			291	8,175
Ahmad Bateman	69 74 74 74			291	8,175
Paul Claxton	70 72 74 75			291	8,175
Dean Alaban	66 74 77 74			291	8,175
Ryan Armour	73 66 79 74			292	6,175
Toru Suzuki	72 69 76 75			292	6,175
Gabriel Hjertstedt	71 72 76 73			292	6,175
Richie Coughlan	71 72 74 75			292	6,175
David Diaz	70 67 78 77			292	6,175
Nick O'Hern	71 72 78 71			292	6,175
D.J. Trahan	70 72 78 72			292	6,175
Justin Bolli	70 74 77 71			292	6,175

Hillross Centenary Australian Open

Australian Golf Club, Sydney, New South Wales
Par 35-36–71; 7,229 yards

November 25-28
purse, A$1,500,000

	SCORES			TOTAL	MONEY
Peter Lonard	71 71 71 68			281	A$270,000
Stuart Appleby	69 70 72 71			282	153,000
Steven Bowditch	73 70 71 69			283	86,625
Rod Pampling	67 67 74 75			283	86,625
Alistair Presnell	71 71 74 68			284	54,000
Kurt Barnes	65 73 72 74			284	54,000
Richard Green	67 75 67 75			284	54,000
Gavin Coles	70 73 72 70			285	36,900
Rodger Davis	71 73 71 70			285	36,900
Martin Doyle	70 73 70 72			285	36,900
Robert Allenby	74 70 69 72			285	36,900
Paul Gow	71 69 71 74			285	36,900
Stephen Leaney	70 71 72 73			286	26,250
Camilo Villegas	69 74 69 74			286	26,250
Greg Chalmers	67 74 77 69			287	20,775
Anthony Painter	70 70 77 70			287	20,775
Steve Conran	73 72 69 73			287	20,775
Bob Estes	73 70 70 74			287	20,775
Craig Parry	71 76 70 71			288	16,537.50
David Bransdon	70 71 75 72			288	16,537.50
John Senden	70 74 72 74			290	15,600
Ricky Schmidt	78 71 72 70			291	13,392.86
Brad Kennedy	76 73 71 71			291	13,392.86
Nick O'Hern	70 74 75 72			291	13,392.86

	SCORES				TOTAL	MONEY
*Jason Day	72	76	71	72	291	
Aaron Baddeley	69	74	75	73	291	13,392.86
Bradley Hughes	70	77	71	73	291	13,392.86
Brett Rumford	69	70	75	77	291	13,392.86
Paul Sheehan	70	77	67	77	291	13,392.86
Terry Price	70	74	74	74	292	9,975
Geoff Ogilvy	71	72	73	76	292	9,975
Peter Senior	71	74	71	76	292	9,975
Nathan Green	72	70	72	78	292	9,975

Cadbury Schweppes Australian PGA Championship

Hyatt Regency Coolum Resort, Coolum, Queensland   December 2-5
Par 36-36–72; 6,749 yards   purse, A$1,000,000

	SCORES				TOTAL	MONEY
Peter Lonard	69	65	71	65	270	A$180,000
James Nitties	67	65	70	70	272	102,000
Bob Estes	63	70	70	70	273	67,500
Nick O'Hern	71	66	70	67	274	44,000
Corey Pavin	67	70	67	70	274	44,000
Adam Crawford	67	74	68	66	275	32,333.33
John Senden	68	68	71	68	275	32,333.33
Peter Senior	69	67	68	71	275	32,333.33
Craig Parry	68	67	74	67	276	23,500
Wayne Perske	67	69	72	68	276	23,500
Rod Pampling	72	68	68	68	276	23,500
Peter O'Malley	68	67	69	72	276	23,500
Stephen Leaney	70	67	73	67	277	16,350
Daniel Chopra	75	66	68	68	277	16,350
Peter Fowler	70	70	68	69	277	16,350
Gavin Coles	72	70	66	69	277	16,350
Simon Nash	72	67	71	68	278	12,500
Greg Norman	68	72	68	70	278	12,500
Paul Gow	74	66	72	68	280	11,250
Ricky Barnes	72	69	72	68	281	10,000
Brad Kennedy	70	72	71	68	281	10,000
Greg Chalmers	67	72	72	70	281	10,000
Richard Lee	69	72	70	70	281	10,000
Jarrod Lyle	72	71	68	70	281	10,000
Richard Green	75	69	67	70	281	10,000
Dean Alaban	67	69	74	72	282	8,150
Nathan Green	69	72	68	73	282	8,150
Bradley Hughes	74	70	71	68	283	7,100
Paul Marantz	69	76	69	69	283	7,100
Andrew Duffin	73	68	70	72	283	7,100

MasterCard Masters

Huntingdale Golf Club, Melbourne, Victoria
Par 36-36–72; 7,040 yards

December 9-12
purse, A$1,250,000

	SCORES				TOTAL	MONEY
Richard Green	69	67	68	67	271	A$225,000
Greg Chalmers	66	71	69	65	271	105,937.50
David McKenzie	67	68	64	72	271	105,937.50
(Green defeated Chalmers and McKenzie on first playoff hole.)						
Steven Bowditch	68	69	67	68	272	51,666.66
Brad Kennedy	67	70	66	69	272	51,666.66
Bradley Hughes	64	66	71	71	272	51,666.66
Corey Pavin	68	70	68	67	273	40,000
Peter Senior	70	67	68	70	275	33,750
Nick O'Hern	70	68	67	70	275	33,750
Peter Lonard	68	67	68	72	275	33,750
Geoff Ogilvy	69	67	73	67	276	25,000
Shane Tait	71	70	68	67	276	25,000
Gary Simpson	72	66	70	68	276	25,000
Peter Fowler	69	70	71	67	277	16,866.07
Craig Jones	68	69	72	68	277	16,866.07
John Senden	72	70	67	68	277	16,866.07
Stuart Appleby	69	69	70	69	277	16,866.07
Chris Downes	71	69	68	69	277	16,866.07
Marcus Cain	72	67	68	70	277	16,866.07
Michael Long	69	68	68	72	277	16,866.07
Michael Campbell	70	67	72	69	278	11,390.62
Simon Nash	70	69	70	69	278	11,390.62
Paul Sheehan	72	67	70	69	278	11,390.62
David Smail	69	71	69	69	278	11,390.62
Adam Scott	71	68	69	70	278	11,390.62
Dean Alaban	68	72	68	70	278	11,390.62
Hunter Mahan	69	68	68	73	278	11,390.62
Robert Allenby	66	68	68	76	278	11,390.62
Craig Parry	67	70	69	73	279	8,875
Brett Rumford	73	68	71	68	280	7,968.75
Gavin Coles	72	71	69	68	280	7,968.75
Camilo Villegas	69	72	70	69	280	7,968.75
Adam Crawford	70	70	70	70	280	7,968.75

African Tours

South African Airways Open

Erinvale Golf Club, Somerset West, South Africa
Par 36-36–72; 7,090 yards

January 15-18
purse, £500,000

	SCORES				TOTAL	MONEY
Trevor Immelman	71	69	69	67	276	R978,825.80
Alastair Forsyth	68	69	74	68	279	570,878.46
Steve Webster	66	75	67	71	279	570,878.46
Darren Fichardt	69	75	67	70	281	304,798.92
David Carter	74	69	71	68	282	202,734.64
Miles Tunnicliff	70	71	72	69	282	202,734.64
Marcus Fraser	74	71	67	70	282	202,734.64
Raphael Jacquelin	68	71	70	73	282	202,734.64
Sven Struver	70	72	74	67	283	106,555.72
Titch Moore	71	69	75	68	283	106,555.72
Stephen Scahill	67	72	75	69	283	106,555.72
Nico van Rensburg	67	70	75	71	283	106,555.72
Brett Rumford	64	74	73	72	283	106,555.72
Stephen Dodd	65	73	72	73	283	106,555.72
Anders Hansen	70	69	68	76	283	106,555.72
Hennie Otto	66	74	79	65	284	76,199.73
Brad Kennedy	73	71	75	65	284	76,199.73
Colin Montgomerie	68	78	69	69	284	76,199.73
Lee Westwood	71	72	70	71	284	76,199.73
James Kingston	70	73	70	71	284	76,199.73
Nic Henning	75	70	67	72	284	76,199.73
Craig Lile	69	68	70	77	284	76,199.73
Martin Maritz	70	75	75	65	285	64,119.28
Simon Wakefield	70	69	75	71	285	64,119.28
Ian Poulter	71	71	71	72	285	64,119.28
Justin Rose	73	72	68	72	285	64,119.28
Miguel Angel Jimenez	68	79	72	67	286	55,879.80
Jonathan Lomas	73	74	70	69	286	55,879.80
Paul McGinley	76	68	71	71	286	55,879.80
Andrew Marshall	73	74	68	71	286	55,879.80
David Lynn	76	70	68	72	286	55,879.80
Deane Pappas	71	76	70	70	287	48,321.78
Louis Oosthuizen	75	72	69	71	287	48,321.78
Jose Manuel Carriles	70	70	75	72	287	48,321.78
Alan Michell	68	73	74	72	287	48,321.78
Scott Dunlap	72	70	73	72	287	48,321.78
Charl Schwartzel	77	70	65	75	287	48,321.78
Thabang Simon	74	71	72	71	288	40,268.15
Trevor Dodds	70	76	71	71	288	40,268.15
Jarrod Moseley	69	74	73	72	288	40,268.15
Jose Manuel Lara	70	76	70	72	288	40,268.15
David Howell	71	74	70	73	288	40,268.15
Desvonde Botes	69	71	73	75	288	40,268.15
Philip Golding	72	73	68	75	288	40,268.15
Joakim Haeggman	72	75	74	68	289	32,214.52
Maarten Lafeber	71	72	76	70	289	32,214.52
Mads Vibe-Hastrup	69	76	73	71	289	32,214.52
Hendrik Buhrmann	66	78	73	72	289	32,214.52

	SCORES			TOTAL	MONEY
Carlos Rodiles	71	74	72	72	289	32,214.52
Peter Baker	69	77	71	72	289	32,214.52
Chris Gane	73	72	75	70	290	25,399.91
Paul Lawrie	72	73	73	72	290	25,399.91
Peter Lawrie	71	74	72	73	290	25,399.91
Albert Kruger	71	75	70	74	290	25,399.91
Shaun Norris	70	73	71	76	290	25,399.91
Ulrich van den Berg	76	69	78	68	291	20,650.33
Nicholas Lawrence	75	72	74	70	291	20,650.33
Andrew Coltart	71	72	76	72	291	20,650.33
Adilson da Silva	73	74	71	74	292	18,895.05
Jamie Spence	71	76	71	74	292	18,895.05
Sean Farrell	72	75	75	71	293	16,417.01
Andre Cruse	73	73	74	73	293	16,417.01
Wayne Westner	76	71	73	73	293	16,417.01
Raymond Russell	75	72	72	74	293	16,417.01
Marcel Siem	68	75	74	76	293	16,417.01
Kenneth Ferrie	70	74	73	76	293	16,417.01
Tyrol Auret	68	74	81	71	294	13,629.22
Simon Hurd	75	70	77	72	294	13,629.22
Johan Edfors	73	74	73	74	294	13,629.22
Bafana Hlophe	72	74	76	73	295	10,047.64
Michiel Bothma	70	73	77	75	295	10,047.64
Mike Lamb	74	69	75	77	295	10,047.64
Roger Chapman	72	74	70	79	295	10,047.64
Des Terblanche	74	72	78	72	296	9,215.06
Eugen Marugi	75	72	73	78	298	9,189.20
Justin Walters	74	72	77	76	299	9,163.33

Dunhill Championship

Houghton Golf Club, Johannesburg, South Africa
Par 36-36–72; 7,087 yards

January 22-25
purse, £500,000

	SCORES				TOTAL	MONEY
Marcel Siem	65	67	68	66	266	R1,023,373.90
Raphael Jacquelin	66	65	68	67	266	596,860.16
Gregory Havret	66	69	64	67	266	596,860.16
(Siem defeated Havret on second and Jacquelin on third playoff hole.)						
Soren Hansen	66	67	65	69	267	318,670.86
Maarten Lafeber	68	69	68	65	270	268,149.87
James Kingston	72	67	71	62	272	160,414.94
Anders Hansen	65	70	71	66	272	160,414.94
Jarrod Moseley	71	66	68	67	272	160,414.94
Lee Westwood	68	70	66	68	272	160,414.94
Trevor Immelman	70	69	64	69	272	160,414.94
Craig Lile	72	64	66	70	272	160,414.94
Robert Coles	72	67	68	66	273	104,928.21
Alan McLean	65	68	69	71	273	104,928.21
Marc Cayeux	68	68	70	68	274	93,593.37
Keith Horne	73	67	63	71	274	93,593.37
Stuart Manley	71	69	69	66	275	83,877.80
David Lynn	68	71	68	68	275	83,877.80
Scott Drummond	72	65	68	70	275	83,877.80
Peter Lawrie	68	64	72	71	275	83,877.80
Titch Moore	68	66	75	67	276	69,061.54
Andrew McLardy	73	67	69	67	276	69,061.54

	SCORES				TOTAL	MONEY
Bruce Vaughan	72	67	69	68	276	69,061.54
Mads Vibe-Hastrup	67	68	71	70	276	69,061.54
Andrew Butterfield	68	71	67	70	276	69,061.54
Markus Brier	70	70	66	70	276	69,061.54
David Park	67	72	65	72	276	69,061.54
Joachim Backstrom	70	70	64	72	276	69,061.54
Chris Davison	71	69	70	67	277	56,738.96
Matthew Blackey	68	72	68	69	277	56,738.96
Robert-Jan Derksen	69	67	71	70	277	56,738.96
Des Terblanche	72	68	66	71	277	56,738.96
Bradley Dredge	72	66	63	76	277	56,738.96
Mark Foster	72	69	71	66	278	48,577.88
Brian Davis	69	71	70	68	278	48,577.88
Francois Delamontagne	69	72	69	68	278	48,577.88
Ben Mason	71	70	69	68	278	48,577.88
Stuart Little	71	67	70	70	278	48,577.88
Jonathan Lomas	72	66	68	72	278	48,577.88
Hendrik Buhrmann	71	66	67	74	278	48,577.88
David Carter	70	67	71	71	279	42,100.83
Mark McNulty	72	68	68	71	279	42,100.83
Jean-Francois Remesy	72	69	66	72	279	42,100.83
Marten Olander	69	69	74	68	280	35,623.78
Roger Chapman	71	70	71	68	280	35,623.78
Dean van Staden	70	70	70	70	280	35,623.78
Wade Ormsby	71	69	70	70	280	35,623.78
James Hepworth	70	69	70	71	280	35,623.78
Andre Bossert	71	67	70	72	280	35,623.78
Raymond Russell	70	71	66	73	280	35,623.78
Jose Manuel Carriles	70	68	74	69	281	28,499.02
Kenneth Ferrie	69	69	74	69	281	28,499.02
Simon Wakefield	73	66	73	69	281	28,499.02
Sebastian Fernandez	73	68	67	73	281	28,499.02
Jose Manuel Lara	69	70	74	69	282	22,345.82
Scott Dunlap	71	70	71	70	282	22,345.82
Nick Dougherty	70	70	71	71	282	22,345.82
Jeppe Huldahl	70	68	72	72	282	22,345.82
Warren Bennett	73	66	71	72	282	22,345.82
Darren Fichardt	70	71	69	72	282	22,345.82
Klas Eriksson	73	66	74	70	283	18,459.59
Peter Hanson	71	70	71	71	283	18,459.59
Damien McGrane	71	70	71	71	283	18,459.59
Richard Sterne	69	68	74	72	283	18,459.59
Johan Edfors	67	70	73	74	284	16,516.48
Hennie Otto	69	71	70	74	284	16,516.48
Stephen Scahill	68	71	79	68	286	14,897.21
Steve van Vuuren	68	73	74	71	286	14,897.21
Martin Maritz	70	70	73	73	286	14,897.21
Steven Waltman	72	68	72	75	287	13,601.81
Brett Liddle	71	70	79	68	288	11,334.84
Jamie Elson	72	67	72	77	288	11,334.84

Dimension Data Pro-Am

Gary Player Country Club: Par 36-36–72; 6,958 yards
Lost City Golf Course: Par 36-36–72; 6,983 yards
Sun City, South Africa

January 29-February 1
purse, R2,000,000

	SCORES				TOTAL	MONEY
Darren Fichardt	72	69	69	68	278	R317,000
Nick Price	70	69	73	68	280	184,100
Ulrich van den Berg	75	69	67	69	280	184,100
Chris Williams	69	72	72	69	282	90,200
Titch Moore	73	68	70	71	282	90,200
Johan Edfors	74	71	71	69	285	58,867
Adilson da Silva	71	70	72	72	285	58,867
Andrew McLardy	72	71	70	72	285	58,867
Grant Muller	70	71	74	72	287	42,200
Omar Sandys	71	78	70	70	289	34,450
Brett Liddle	70	74	70	75	289	34,450
Keith Horne	72	70	72	75	289	34,450
Callie Swart	70	71	72	76	289	34,450
Richard Sterne	76	70	71	73	290	28,200
Albert Kruger	70	72	73	75	290	28,200
David Frost	71	73	69	77	290	28,200
Mark Mouland	72	76	73	70	291	24,750
Chris Davison	68	76	73	74	291	24,750
Sean Ludgater	73	71	71	76	291	24,750
Bobby Lincoln	73	72	69	77	291	24,750
Craig Lile	74	74	72	72	292	22,000
David Carter	76	73	71	72	292	22,000
Desvonde Botes	76	71	72	73	292	22,000
Ben Mason	73	72	75	73	293	18,220
Bruce Vaughan	73	71	75	74	293	18,220
Ian Kennedy	77	73	69	74	293	18,220
Andre Bossert	72	77	70	74	293	18,220
Thomas Aiken	75	74	69	75	293	18,220
Warrick Druian	71	73	74	75	293	18,220
James Hepworth	74	72	72	75	293	18,220
Simon Hurd	75	73	69	76	293	18,220
Scott Dunlap	73	74	70	76	293	18,220
Kevin Stone	74	73	68	78	293	18,220

Nashua Masters

Wild Coast Country Club, Port Edward, Natal
Par 35-35–70; 5,807 yards

February 5-8
purse, R1,000,000

	SCORES				TOTAL	MONEY
Andrew McLardy	63	69	65	67	264	R158,500
Desvonde Botes	66	65	69	67	267	115,000
Titch Moore	65	69	68	66	268	59,100
Keith Horne	68	68	64	68	268	59,100
Michael Archer	67	69	69	64	269	32,350
Andre Cruse	65	70	68	66	269	32,350
Scott Dunlap	63	71	68	67	269	32,350
Marc Cayeux	70	66	66	67	269	32,350
Michiel Bothma	69	70	66	65	270	21,100
Nic Henning	68	70	66	67	271	19,100

		SCORES			TOTAL	MONEY
Barry Painting	71	69	67	65	272	15,350
Peter Jespersen	65	73	68	66	272	15,350
Brett Liddle	65	73	68	66	272	15,350
Darren Fichardt	67	71	67	67	272	15,350
Thomas Aiken	65	74	66	67	272	15,350
Doug McGuigan	66	71	67	68	272	15,350
Roger Wessels	68	68	73	64	273	12,160
Michael Hoey	66	74	69	64	273	12,160
Adilson da Silva	68	67	70	68	273	12,160
Grant Muller	66	74	64	69	273	12,160
Louis Oosthuizen	65	70	68	70	273	12,160
Craig Lile	64	73	67	70	274	10,850
Warrick Druian	67	67	67	73	274	10,850
Bradford Vaughan	68	72	72	63	275	9,363
Tyrol Auret	70	67	71	67	275	9,363
Mark Murless	71	69	68	67	275	9,363
Paul Eales	69	68	69	69	275	9,363
Lee Slattery	68	70	68	69	275	9,363
David Frost	66	71	68	70	275	9,363
Hendrik Buhrmann	66	71	68	70	275	9,363
Gerry Coetzee	71	68	63	73	275	9,363

Telkom PGA Championship

Woodhill Country Club, Pretoria, South Africa
Par 36-36–72; 7,417 yards

February 12-15
purse, R1,500,000

		SCORES			TOTAL	MONEY
Warrick Druian	67	66	68	66	267	R237,750
Mark Murless	68	67	70	67	272	116,600
Michiel Bothma	68	66	69	69	272	116,600
Desvonde Botes	68	66	68	70	272	116,600
Darren Fichardt	64	73	69	67	273	52,650
Dion Fourie	69	71	66	67	273	52,650
Craig Lile	66	67	67	73	273	52,650
Louis Oosthuizen	66	73	67	68	274	33,900
Garth Mulroy	69	68	67	70	274	33,900
Tyrol Auret	65	71	69	71	276	27,525
Paul Eales	68	70	67	71	276	27,525
Cody Freeman	69	71	69	68	277	23,400
Shaun Norris	69	69	67	72	277	23,400
Jean Hugo	69	64	70	74	277	23,400
Marc Cayeux	70	71	71	66	278	19,300
Raphael de Sousa	68	72	69	69	278	19,300
Bruce Vaughan	66	71	70	71	278	19,300
Roger Wessels	63	76	68	71	278	19,300
Sandeep Grewal	68	68	68	74	278	19,300
Thomas Aiken	64	71	68	75	278	19,300
Richard Sterne	69	72	69	69	279	16,500
Simon Hurd	69	68	71	71	279	16,500
Bradford Vaughan	69	67	70	73	279	16,500
Steve Basson	71	71	72	66	280	13,850
James Kingston	70	70	71	69	280	13,850
Sean Ludgater	72	68	71	69	280	13,850
Ashley Roestoff	67	70	73	70	280	13,850
Adilson da Silva	70	68	72	70	280	13,850
Ulrich van den Berg	69	72	68	71	280	13,850

	SCORES			TOTAL	MONEY
Andrew McLardy	70	68	71	71	280	13,850
Steve van Vuuren	72	67	70	71	280	13,850
Mike Lamb	71	69	68	72	280	13,850

Southern Africa Tour Championship

Leopard Creek Country Club, Malelane, South Africa
Par 36-36–72; 7,352 yards

February 19-22
purse, R2,000,000

	SCORES				TOTAL	MONEY
Andrew McLardy	69	66	66	72	273	R317,000
Louis Oosthuizen	74	68	68	66	276	230,000
Keith Horne	68	74	70	68	280	138,200
Alan McLean	72	70	70	69	281	98,200
Nic Henning	73	66	73	70	282	76,200
Desvonde Botes	68	72	68	74	282	76,200
Marc Cayeux	70	74	69	70	283	44,400
James Kingston	74	70	68	71	283	44,400
Craig Lile	68	68	75	72	283	44,400
Thomas Aiken	71	73	67	72	283	44,400
Barry Painting	71	70	67	75	283	44,400
Mark Murless	73	71	71	69	284	33,200
Richard Sterne	78	67	74	67	286	28,400
Des Terblanche	78	67	72	69	286	28,400
Simon Hurd	71	69	74	72	286	28,400
Titch Moore	68	74	72	72	286	28,400
Mark Mouland	73	69	71	73	286	28,400
Ashley Roestoff	73	71	71	72	287	25,200
Charl Schwartzel	76	69	76	67	288	22,720
Ciaran McMonagle	77	70	74	67	288	22,720
Warrick Druian	74	75	72	67	288	22,720
Paul Eales	75	70	71	72	288	22,720
Lee Slattery	72	71	72	73	288	22,720
Alan Michell	75	68	75	71	289	19,900
Andrew Butterfield	71	71	75	72	289	19,900
Grant Muller	72	71	72	74	289	19,900
Jean Hugo	73	73	67	76	289	19,900
*Anton Haig	76	69	67	77	289	
Chris Davison	73	74	72	71	290	16,675
Ulrich van den Berg	73	72	73	72	290	16,675
Joachim Backstrom	71	70	76	73	290	16,675
Thabang Simon	72	70	74	74	290	16,675
Nico van Rensburg	70	74	72	74	290	16,675
Bruce Vaughan	75	72	69	74	290	16,675
Roger Wessels	72	73	70	75	290	16,675
John Bele	71	67	76	76	290	16,675

Stanbic Zambia Open

Lusaka Golf Club, Lusaka, Zambia
Par 35-38–73; 7,226 yards

March 11-14
purse, €100,000

	SCORES				TOTAL	MONEY
Michael Kirk	68	71	67	68	274	R136,930.61
Leonard Loxton	69	67	67	74	277	97,427.99

	SCORES				TOTAL	MONEY
Hernan Rey	69	69	73	68	279	70,856.72
Michael Hoey	73	71	71	66	281	53,142.54
Benn Barham	72	69	71	70	282	35,428.36
Ariel Canete	70	69	71	72	282	35,428.36
Scott Dunlap	66	71	71	74	282	35,428.36
Leif Westerberg	71	69	75	68	283	21,257.01
Marc Cayeux	74	68	73	68	283	21,257.01
Greig Hutcheon	71	70	72	70	283	21,257.01
Gustavo Rojas	70	75	70	69	284	17,714.18
Titch Moore	68	74	73	70	285	15,057.05
Stuart Davis	70	69	75	71	285	15,057.05
Thomas Aiken	73	67	72	73	285	15,057.05
Stuart Manley	70	74	68	73	285	15,057.05
Simon Katembenuka	72	71	67	75	285	15,057.05
Anil Shah	73	73	70	70	286	11,514.22
Warrick Druian	71	71	73	71	286	11,514.22
Omar Sandys	70	69	75	72	286	11,514.22
Ian Kennedy	74	70	77	66	287	9,299.94
Van Phillips	70	72	75	70	287	9,299.94
Michael Archer	72	71	75	70	288	8,502.80
Ryan Reid	73	71	72	72	288	8,502.80
Ulrich van den Berg	72	70	73	73	288	8,502.80
Dion Fourie	75	71	74	69	289	7,705.66
Colm Moriarty	72	73	73	71	289	7,705.66
Andre Cruse	67	76	73	73	289	7,705.66
Johan Kok	75	69	72	73	289	7,705.66
Kariem Baraka	69	74	72	74	289	7,705.66
Albert Kruger	71	71	72	75	289	7,705.66

Kenya Open

Karen Golf Club, Nairobi, Kenya
Par 35-35–70; 6,901 yards

March 18-21
purse, €110,000

	SCORES				TOTAL	MONEY
Marc Cayeux	65	63	75	67	270	€17,600
Leif Westerberg	71	66	67	66	270	12,100
(Cayeux defeated Westerberg on first playoff hole.)						
Michael Hoey	68	70	69	66	273	7,150
Paul Dwyer	65	71	68	69	273	7,150
Johan Skold	69	69	72	65	275	5,500
Titch Moore	63	68	71	74	276	3,410
Ryan Reid	64	69	74	69	276	3,410
Van Phillips	70	71	68	67	276	3,410
Michael Kirk	70	69	67	70	276	3,410
Gary Clark	69	65	73	70	277	2,112
Erol Simsek	68	67	73	69	277	2,112
Lee Slattery	70	69	70	68	277	2,112
Marco Ruiz	69	69	73	66	277	2,112
Philippe Lima	69	70	70	68	277	2,112
Mark Smith	71	72	73	62	278	1,705
Albert Kruger	70	70	69	69	278	1,705
Mark Mouland	68	67	71	73	279	1,485
Mark Pilkington	69	71	69	70	279	1,485
Alvaro Salto	69	71	74	66	280	1,163.80
Stuart Cohen	68	71	71	70	280	1,163.80
Marco Soffietti	67	71	71	71	280	1,163.80

	SCORES				TOTAL	MONEY
Benoit Teilleria	68	70	74	68	280	1,163.80
Colm Moriarty	71	70	69	70	280	1,163.80
Fredrik Orest	74	68	68	71	281	1,001
Kariem Baraka	70	65	73	73	281	1,001
Ian Kennedy	69	63	78	71	281	1,001
Justin Walters	69	68	68	76	281	1,001
Michael Archer	69	72	71	70	282	924
Gustavo Rojas	69	74	72	67	282	924
Edward Rush	72	68	68	74	282	924

FNB Botswana Open

Gaborone Golf Club, Gaborone, Botswana
Par 36-35–71; 6,814 yards

March 25-27
purse, R250,000

	SCORES			TOTAL	MONEY
Barry Painting	62	65	68	195	R39,250
Omar Sandys	63	67	68	198	28,750
Mark Murless	65	64	70	199	20,000
Thomas Aiken	65	71	64	200	14,750
James Kamte	68	66	68	202	9,166.66
Nic Henning	65	69	68	202	9,166.66
Wallie Coetsee	67	65	70	202	9,166.66
Des Terblanche	68	69	66	203	5,420
Sean Farrell	69	66	68	203	5,420
Alan Michell	67	68	68	203	5,420
Ashley Roestoff	68	66	69	203	5,420
Gary Thain	72	62	69	203	5,420
Callie Swart	67	69	68	204	4,175
David Ryan	65	70	69	204	4,175
Anil Shah	68	67	69	204	4,175
Josef Fourie	69	65	70	204	4,175
Shane Pringle	64	71	70	205	3,633.33
Steve Basson	65	69	71	205	3,633.33
Patrick O'Brien	70	63	72	205	3,633.33
Steve van Vuuren	68	70	68	206	3,187.50
Schalk van der Merwe	70	68	68	206	3,187.50
Justin Walters	69	68	69	206	3,187.50
Grant Muller	66	69	71	206	3,187.50
Adilson da Silva	71	70	66	207	2,800
Andre Cruse	70	69	68	207	2,800
Ulrich van den Berg	69	69	69	207	2,800
Tyrol Auret	73	68	67	208	2,353.57
Lindani Ndwandwe	73	68	67	208	2,353.57
Bobby Lincoln	73	67	68	208	2,353.57
Trevor Fisher, Jr.	67	72	69	208	2,353.57
Teboho Sefatsa	70	68	70	208	2,353.57
Peter Banda	69	69	70	208	2,353.57
Shaun Norris	68	65	75	208	2,353.57

Parmalat Classic

De Zalze Golf Club, Stellenbosch, South Africa
Par 36-36–72; 6,291 yards

March 31-April 2
purse, R200,000

	SCORES			TOTAL	MONEY
Justin Walters	68	72	65	205	R31,400
Nicholas Lawrence	72	66	69	207	23,000
Keith Horne	66	74	68	208	16,000
Steve Basson	70	71	68	209	8,450
Michael Scholz	70	70	69	209	8,450
Jean Hugo	72	67	70	209	8,450
Ian Kennedy	69	67	73	209	8,450
Sammy Daniels	70	72	68	210	5,200
Ulrich van den Berg	70	68	73	211	4,600
Chris Davison	72	70	70	212	4,070
Leon Trenerry	68	73	71	212	4,070
Hendrik Buhrmann	74	69	70	213	3,566.66
Ryan Dreyer	73	68	72	213	3,566.66
Alan Michell	69	71	73	213	3,566.66
John Bele	72	71	71	214	3,140
Albert Kruger	72	72	70	214	3,140
Nico Le Grange	73	72	69	214	3,140
Steve van Vuuren	73	70	72	215	2,557.50
Grant Muller	70	74	71	215	2,557.50
Tyrol Auret	71	72	72	215	2,557.50
Walter Badenhorst-Schnetler	74	69	72	215	2,557.50
Lindani Ndwandwe	70	71	74	215	2,557.50
Schalk van der Merwe	75	70	70	215	2,557.50
Patrick O'Brien	71	74	70	215	2,557.50
Wallie Coetsee	75	70	70	215	2,557.50
Ben Kleynhans	73	70	73	216	2,120
Hennie Walters	69	75	72	216	2,120
Jason Lipshitz	72	71	74	217	1,940
Ian Hutchings	70	73	74	217	1,940
Trevor Fisher, Jr.	71	70	76	217	1,940

Capital Alliance Royal Swazi Sun Open

Royal Swazi Sun Country Club, Mbabane, Swaziland
Par 36-36–72; 6,003 yards

May 5-8
purse, R400,000

	POINTS				TOTAL	MONEY
Nic Henning	10	4	9	19	42	R63,200
Titch Moore	8	16	12	5	41	46,000
Wallie Coetsee	5	15	12	8	40	27,680
Sean Ludgater	5	7	13	14	39	19,640
Hennie Otto	16	10	2	8	36	16,520
Steve van Vuuren	6	8	9	10	33	14,160
Jaco Van Zyl	7	4	10	11	32	10,093.33
Ross Wellington	9	8	10	5	32	10,093.33
Andre Cruse	6	6	13	7	32	10,093.33
Mawonga Nomwa	7	9	5	10	31	7,840
Ashley Roestoff	8	1	11	10	30	7,160
Thomas Aiken	-2	8	11	11	28	6,480
Michael Scholz	3	3	10	12	28	6,480
Chris Davison	3	11	9	4	27	5,880

	POINTS				TOTAL	MONEY
Ulrich van den Berg	0	6	11	9	26	5,580
James du Plessis	8	5	1	12	26	5,580
Trevor Fisher, Jr.	6	4	1	14	25	5,080
Justin Hobday	9	3	6	7	25	5,080
Bradford Vaughan	5	2	7	11	25	5,080
Bafana Hlophe	1	6	3	14	24	4,640
Grant Muller	6	9	3	6	24	4,640
Ian Hutchings	1	-2	18	6	23	4,380
Alex Baillie	2	1	16	4	23	4,380
Jason Lipshitz	8	-1	8	7	22	4,140
Ryan Dreyer	4	6	2	10	22	4,140
Gary Thain	5	9	7	0	21	3,960
Warrick Druian	11	1	-1	9	20	3,660
Mark Murless	10	4	5	1	20	3,660
Adilson da Silva	7	1	7	5	20	3,660
Lindani Ndwandwe	3	7	12	-2	20	3,660

Vodacom Origins of Golf Tour at Pezula

Pezula Championship Course, Knysna, South Africa
Par 36-36–72; 7,006 yards

May 27-29
purse, R300,000

	SCORES			TOTAL	MONEY
Patrick O'Brien	73	71	66	210	R47,100
Ulrich van den Berg	68	73	70	211	34,500
Grant Muller	70	75	67	212	24,000
Des Terblanche	69	76	68	213	17,700
Jaco Van Zyl	72	67	75	214	13,500
Bradford Vaughan	75	69	72	216	10,500
Andre Cruse	70	76	71	217	8,400
Dijon Tintinger	72	71	74	217	8,400
Ashley Roestoff	77	72	69	218	6,370
Chris Davison	75	73	70	218	6,370
Gary Thain	76	72	70	218	6,370
Thomas Aiken	74	74	71	219	5,610
Adilson da Silva	75	76	69	220	5,010
Bafana Hlophe	74	74	72	220	5,010
Keith Horne	74	73	73	220	5,010
Ian Hutchings	72	75	73	220	5,010
Josef Fourie	73	70	78	221	4,530
Steve Basson	74	77	72	223	4,050
Hendrik Buhrmann	81	72	70	223	4,050
Wallie Coetsee	76	78	69	223	4,050
Ryan Dreyer	75	73	75	223	4,050
Elmar van den Berg	73	83	67	223	4,050
Don Gammon	76	75	73	224	3,540
Michael Scholz	79	77	68	224	3,540
Nico van Rensburg	80	73	72	225	3,300
Chris Williams	75	75	75	225	3,300
Mike Lamb	81	76	69	226	3,120
Lindani Ndwandwe	80	72	75	227	2,910
Charles Erasmus	79	79	69	227	2,910
Warren Abery	79	79	69	227	2,910

Vodacom Origins of Golf Tour at Schoeman Park

Schoeman Park Golf Course, Bloemfontein, South Africa   June 10-12
Par 36-36–72; 7,152 yards   purse, R300,000

	SCORES			TOTAL	MONEY
Steve van Vuuren	66	65	69	200	R47,100
Ulrich van den Berg	69	65	70	204	34,500
Adilson da Silva	65	70	70	205	24,000
Chris Davison	70	68	68	206	13,900
Trevor Fisher, Jr.	68	69	69	206	13,900
Nico van Rensburg	66	69	71	206	13,900
Jaco Van Zyl	72	67	68	207	8,400
Mark Murless	70	67	70	207	8,400
Andre Cruse	72	68	68	208	6,180
Keith Horne	73	67	68	208	6,180
Gary Thain	70	70	68	208	6,180
Grant Muller	69	67	72	208	6,180
Patrick O'Brien	67	69	73	209	5,340
Ashley Roestoff	73	67	70	210	4,807.50
Brett Liddle	70	70	70	210	4,807.50
James Kamte	70	68	72	210	4,807.50
Chris Williams	67	70	73	210	4,807.50
Peter Msiza	71	69	71	211	3,975
Bafana Hlophe	69	69	73	211	3,975
Warren Abery	69	73	69	211	3,975
Barry Painting	74	69	68	211	3,975
Des Terblanche	70	68	73	211	3,975
Michael Scholz	72	71	68	211	3,975
Jaco Rall	71	69	72	212	3,185
Thomas Aiken	71	70	71	212	3,185
Kevin Stone	71	71	70	212	3,185
Craig Kamps	71	71	70	212	3,185
Eugen Marugi	72	67	73	212	3,185
Michael McGill	71	74	67	212	3,185
Josef Fourie	70	70	73	213	2,640
David Ryan	71	70	72	213	2,640
Eddie Lombard	70	72	71	213	2,640
Omar Sandys	69	70	74	213	2,640
Sean Ludgater	74	71	68	213	2,640

Royal Swazi Sun Classic

Royal Swazi Sun Country Club, Mbabane, Swaziland   June 18-20
Par 36-36–72; 5,983 yards   purse, R250,000

	SCORES			TOTAL	MONEY
Bradford Vaughan	68	67	64	199	R39,250
Ashley Roestoff	67	68	68	203	28,750
Mark Murless	68	68	69	205	17,375
Ulrich van den Berg	66	68	71	205	17,375
Patrick O'Brien	66	67	73	206	10,000
Dijon Tintinger	66	67	73	206	10,000
David Ryan	72	68	67	207	7,500
Keith Horne	66	71	71	208	6,500
Hendrik Buhrmann	79	65	65	209	5,750
Thomas Aiken	70	69	71	210	4,950

	SCORES			TOTAL	MONEY
Adilson da Silva	70	68	72	210	4,950
Callie Swart	70	68	72	210	4,950
Brett Liddle	69	74	68	211	4,350
Mike Lamb	67	73	71	211	4,350
Warren Abery	69	73	70	212	3,925
Steve van Vuuren	71	68	73	212	3,925
Alan Michell	73	65	74	212	3,925
Henk Alberts	73	72	69	214	3,500
Irvin Mosate	72	70	72	214	3,500
Dean van Staden	72	70	72	214	3,500
Andre Cruse	74	70	71	215	3,125
Bafana Hlophe	68	76	71	215	3,125
Michael Scholz	70	73	72	215	3,125
Eugen Marugi	74	73	69	216	2,610.71
Trevor Fisher, Jr.	73	73	70	216	2,610.71
Wallie Coetsee	72	73	71	216	2,610.71
James Kamte	75	70	71	216	2,610.71
Des Terblanche	70	74	72	216	2,610.71
Jaco Van Zyl	72	71	73	216	2,610.71
Sean Farrell	73	69	74	216	2,610.71

Vodacom Origins of Golf Tour at Zimbali

Zimbali Lodge & Country Club, South Africa
Par 36-36–72; 7,136 yards

June 30-July 2
purse, R292,650

	SCORES			TOTAL	MONEY
Thomas Aiken	66	72	66	204	R47,100
Keith Horne	68	67	69	204	34,500
(Aiken defeated Horne on first playoff hole.)					
James Kamte	66	70	71	207	24,000
Des Terblanche	69	71	68	208	15,600
Adilson da Silva	72	68	68	208	15,600
Callie Swart	70	70	69	209	9,100
Jaco Van Zyl	68	71	70	209	9,100
Ulrich van den Berg	68	70	71	209	9,100
Steve van Vuuren	71	70	70	211	6,600
Shane Pringle	73	73	65	211	6,600
Brett Liddle	71	71	70	212	5,760
Warren Abery	68	71	73	212	5,760
Ashley Roestoff	73	72	68	213	5,010
Craig Kamps	67	76	70	213	5,010
Grant Muller	69	72	72	213	5,010
Mark Murless	71	70	72	213	5,010
Joachim Backstrom	71	69	74	214	4,440
Ryan Dreyer	75	72	67	214	4,440
Wallie Coetsee	71	74	70	215	3,830
Chris Davison	69	73	73	215	3,830
Patrick O'Brien	74	72	69	215	3,830
Omar Sandys	74	72	69	215	3,830
Kevin Stone	69	77	69	215	3,830
Danny Poulter	70	69	76	215	3,830
Sean Farrell	71	71	74	216	3,240
Gary Thain	70	72	74	216	3,240
Nico van Rensburg	72	74	70	216	3,240
Barry Painting	67	77	73	217	2,730
Michael Scholz	73	72	72	217	2,730

	SCORES			TOTAL	MONEY
Bradford Vaughan	76	70	71	217	2,730
Chris Williams	74	72	71	217	2,730
Trevor Fisher, Jr.	74	72	71	217	2,730
Dean van Staden	72	74	71	217	2,730
Alan Michell	74	74	69	217	2,730

Vodacom Origins of Golf Tour at Sun City

Lost City Golf Course, Sun City, South Africa   July 21-23
Par 36-36–72; 7,637 yards   purse, R294,330

	SCORES			TOTAL	MONEY
Thomas Aiken	67	66	71	204	R47,100
Des Terblanche	68	70	69	207	34,500
Grant Muller	71	68	70	209	24,000
Jaco Van Zyl	68	74	68	210	17,700
Adilson da Silva	72	72	67	211	11,000
Keith Horne	69	74	68	211	11,000
Barry Painting	70	73	68	211	11,000
Michael Scholz	71	73	69	213	6,727.50
Hendrik Buhrmann	77	67	69	213	6,727.50
Chris Davison	72	71	70	213	6,727.50
Ulrich van den Berg	74	69	70	213	6,727.50
Brett Liddle	73	73	68	214	5,350
Michael du Toit	74	70	70	214	5,350
Ryan Dreyer	70	70	74	214	5,350
Michael Green	73	72	70	215	4,890
Mike Michell	71	75	70	216	4,447.50
Bradford Vaughan	74	71	71	216	4,447.50
Wallie Coetsee	73	71	72	216	4,447.50
Warren Abery	70	73	73	216	4,447.50
Mark Murless	72	74	71	217	3,975
Ashley Roestoff	74	73	70	217	3,975
Dean van Staden	74	72	72	218	3,610
Desvonde Botes	76	70	72	218	3,610
Alan Michell	74	72	72	218	3,610
Henk Alberts	72	74	73	219	3,180
Lindani Ndwandwe	71	75	73	219	3,180
Andre Cruse	77	72	70	219	3,180
Vaughn Groenewald	71	69	79	219	3,180
Don Gammon	75	71	74	220	2,570
Bafana Hlophe	74	72	74	220	2,570
Trevor Fisher, Jr.	73	73	74	220	2,570
Shane Pringle	77	70	73	220	2,570
Sean Farrell	73	74	73	220	2,570
Omar Sandys	72	76	72	220	2,570
Werner Geyer	71	72	77	220	2,570
Eugen Marugi	74	75	71	220	2,570
Sammy Daniels	74	75	71	220	2,570

Vodacom Origins of Golf Tour at Arabella

Arabella Country Club, Hermanus, South Africa
Par 36-36–72; 6,976 yards

September 17-19
purse, R300,000

	SCORES			TOTAL	MONEY
Louis Oosthuizen	74	70	71	215	R47,100
Keith Horne	68	74	74	216	34,500
Titch Moore	74	73	70	217	18,400
Desvonde Botes	75	71	71	217	18,400
Adilson da Silva	76	69	72	217	18,400
James du Plessis	74	76	68	218	10,500
James Kamte	73	76	70	219	7,500
Lindani Ndwandwe	74	75	70	219	7,500
Nic Henning	74	74	71	219	7,500
Mike Lamb	74	73	72	219	7,500
Mike Michell	74	77	69	220	5,760
Michiel Bothma	73	75	72	220	5,760
Hennie Walters	72	77	72	221	5,220
Ulrich van den Berg	78	70	73	221	5,220
Gerlou Roux	75	72	75	222	4,800
Dijon Tintinger	69	77	76	222	4,800
Jaco Van Zyl	75	75	73	223	4,360
Michael du Toit	76	73	74	223	4,360
Mark Murless	81	74	68	223	4,360
Alan Michell	78	73	73	224	3,900
Divan van den Heever	76	74	74	224	3,900
David Ryan	76	79	69	224	3,900
Sammy Daniels	72	78	75	225	3,540
Bradford Vaughan	77	71	77	225	3,540
Ryan Dreyer	78	74	74	226	3,300
Sean Farrell	77	75	74	226	3,300
Grant Muller	74	77	76	227	3,060
Don Gammon	76	76	75	227	3,060
Patrick O'Brien	80	71	77	228	2,775
Michael Green	78	72	78	228	2,775
Kevin Stone	76	76	76	228	2,775
Steve van Vuuren	76	77	75	228	2,775

Bearingman Highveld Classic

Witbank Golf Club, Witbank, South Africa
Par 36-36–72; 6,702 yards

October 8-10
purse, R220,000

	SCORES			TOTAL	MONEY
Divan van den Heever	67	67	64	198	R39,250
Leonard Loxton	70	66	67	203	28,750
Jaco Van Zyl	68	70	67	205	20,000
Gary Thain	70	67	69	206	13,000
Adilson da Silva	67	67	72	206	13,000
Gavan Levenson	68	72	67	207	6,750
Nico van Rensburg	70	70	67	207	6,750
Hendrik Buhrmann	74	65	68	207	6,750
Thomas Aiken	69	69	69	207	6,750
Bafana Hlophe	69	69	69	207	6,750
Barry Painting	71	70	67	208	4,383.33
Omar Sandys	68	72	68	208	4,383.33

	SCORES			TOTAL	MONEY
Michael Scholz	68	72	68	208	4,383.33
Michiel Bothma	68	71	69	208	4,383.33
Waylon Kukard	70	67	71	208	4,383.33
Chris Williams	67	70	71	208	4,383.33
John Mashego	69	75	65	209	3,700
Sean Farrell	68	73	68	209	3,700
Hennie Walters	71	73	66	210	3,191.66
Steve van Vuuren	70	74	66	210	3,191.66
Andre Cruse	74	68	68	210	3,191.66
Jean Hugo	70	69	71	210	3,191.66
Andrew Odoh	71	68	71	210	3,191.66
Grant Muller	70	68	72	210	3,191.66
Dijon Tintinger	71	70	70	211	2,750
Jaco Rall	67	73	71	211	2,750
Danny Poulter	69	73	70	212	2,550
Peter Banda	67	73	72	212	2,550
Des Terblanche	76	68	69	213	2,425
Shaun Norris	71	73	70	214	2,275
Doug McGuigan	72	71	71	214	2,275
Werner Geyer	69	73	72	214	2,275

Limpopo Eskom Classic

Polokwane Golf Club, Pietersburg, South Africa
Par 36-36–72; 7,090 yards

October 14-16
purse, R500,000

	SCORES			TOTAL	MONEY
Bradford Vaughan	68	63	67	198	R79,000
Kevin Stone	69	65	65	199	46,050
Omar Sandys	64	65	70	199	46,050
Warren Abery	70	67	64	201	22,600
Leonard Loxton	67	65	69	201	22,600
Desvonde Botes	68	69	65	202	14,916.66
Titch Moore	67	66	69	202	14,916.66
James Kamte	68	63	71	202	14,916.66
Jean Hugo	69	67	67	203	9,475
Ashley Roestoff	71	65	67	203	9,475
Alan Michell	64	70	69	203	9,475
Callie Swart	65	67	71	203	9,475
Waylon Kukard	68	71	65	204	7,433.33
Thomas Aiken	70	70	64	204	7,433.33
Hennie Otto	67	69	68	204	7,433.33
Michiel Bothma	70	69	66	205	6,600
Grant Muller	75	66	64	205	6,600
Mawonga Nomwa	67	70	68	205	6,600
Henk Alberts	68	69	69	206	6,000
Sean Farrell	67	74	65	206	6,000
Shaun Norris	68	71	68	207	5,475
Brett Liddle	72	67	68	207	5,475
Bobby Lincoln	72	67	68	207	5,475
Steve van Vuuren	70	68	69	207	5,475
Anil Shah	68	71	69	208	4,725
Shane Pringle	69	69	70	208	4,725
Jaco Van Zyl	66	72	70	208	4,725
Adilson da Silva	69	67	72	208	4,725
Chris Swanepoel, Jr.	70	66	72	208	4,725
Mark Williams	67	67	74	208	4,725

Vodacom Origins of Golf Championship

The Links at Fancourt, George, South Africa
Par 36-37–73; 7,576 yards

October 19-21
purse, R300,000

	SCORES			TOTAL	MONEY
Thomas Aiken	68	73	73	214	R47,100
Jean Hugo	71	71	79	221	34,500
Andre Cruse	71	77	75	223	24,000
Thabang Simon	74	77	73	224	12,675
Ryan Dreyer	75	74	75	224	12,675
Warren Abery	75	71	78	224	12,675
Hennie Otto	74	68	82	224	12,675
Brett Liddle	79	72	74	225	7,350
James Kamte	72	77	76	225	7,350
Lindani Ndwandwe	79	73	76	228	5,652
Grant Muller	75	77	76	228	5,652
Bobby Lincoln	74	77	77	228	5,652
Ian Hutchings	76	74	78	228	5,652
Steve Basson	79	69	80	228	5,652
Jaco Van Zyl	74	81	74	229	4,710
Anton Haig	76	76	77	229	4,710
Doug McGuigan	78	74	77	229	4,710
Jaco Rall	79	78	73	230	4,275
Patrick O'Brien	77	75	78	230	4,275
Andrew Odoh	76	79	76	231	3,756
Bradford Vaughan	82	73	76	231	3,756
Kevin Stone	79	76	76	231	3,756
Warrick Druian	77	75	79	231	3,756
Chris Davison	78	74	79	231	3,756
Ryan Tipping	78	80	74	232	3,126
Sammy Daniels	79	76	77	232	3,126
Steve van Vuuren	77	77	78	232	3,126
Alan Michell	74	80	78	232	3,126
Leonard Loxton	78	72	82	232	3,126
Wickus Myburgh	74	83	76	233	2,685
John Bele	74	81	78	233	2,685
Adilson da Silva	80	73	80	233	2,685
Divan van den Heever	74	78	81	233	2,685

Platinum Classic

Mooi Nooi Golf Club, Rustenburg, South Africa
Par 36-36–72; 6,962 yards

October 28-30
purse, R550,000

	SCORES			TOTAL	MONEY
Titch Moore	64	70	66	200	R86,900
Hennie Otto	69	67	67	203	63,250
Nic Henning	67	68	69	204	29,260
Thomas Aiken	67	66	71	204	29,260
Charl Schwartzel	66	67	71	204	29,260
Ashley Roestoff	67	67	71	205	17,847.50
Ulrich van den Berg	65	67	73	205	17,847.50
Brett Liddle	70	69	67	206	13,530
Bradford Vaughan	69	70	68	207	11,330
Alan Michell	68	68	71	207	11,330
John Mashego	68	67	73	208	9,845
Tjaart van der Walt	72	70	68	210	8,910

	SCORES			TOTAL	MONEY
Marc Cayeux	70	71	69	210	8,910
Sean Farrell	71	71	69	211	7,397.50
Omar Sandys	71	71	69	211	7,397.50
Ian Hutchings	66	76	69	211	7,397.50
Johan Kok	69	71	71	211	7,397.50
Albert Kruger	68	72	71	211	7,397.50
Andre Cruse	66	72	73	211	7,397.50
Jaco Van Zyl	71	73	68	212	5,864.37
Derek Crawford	71	72	69	212	5,864.37
Jean Hugo	70	72	70	212	5,864.37
Andrew McLardy	72	70	70	212	5,864.37
Chris Davison	68	73	71	212	5,864.37
John Bele	68	73	71	212	5,864.37
Warren Abery	68	72	72	212	5,864.37
Richard Sterne	71	68	73	212	5,864.37
Roger Wessels	70	71	72	213	4,950
Mark Murless	71	68	74	213	4,950
Bafana Hlophe	68	71	74	213	4,950

MTC Namibian PGA Championship

Windhoek Country Club, Namibia
Par 35-36–71; 7,106 yards

November 4-6
purse, R500,000

	SCORES			TOTAL	MONEY
Mark Murless	69	68	65	202	R79,000
Bradley Davison	68	69	67	204	46,050
Sean Farrell	69	67	68	204	46,050
James Kamte	71	68	66	205	20,966.66
Des Terblanche	71	65	69	205	20,966.66
Rudy Whitfield	65	70	70	205	20,966.66
Jaco Rall	68	69	69	206	14,750
Leonard Loxton	66	73	68	207	10,462.50
Brett Liddle	71	66	70	207	10,462.50
Steve Basson	67	70	70	207	10,462.50
Anton Haig	71	64	72	207	10,462.50
Werner Geyer	69	70	69	208	7,850
Kevin Stone	71	67	70	208	7,850
Hennie Otto	68	69	71	208	7,850
Chris Swanepoel, Jr.	73	68	68	209	6,600
Patrick O'Brien	68	72	69	209	6,600
Michael du Toit	68	72	69	209	6,600
Bobby Lincoln	72	66	71	209	6,600
Derek Crawford	68	68	73	209	6,600
Albert Kruger	73	68	69	210	5,407.14
Joe Nawanga	74	69	67	210	5,407.14
Grant Muller	69	71	70	210	5,407.14
Bradford Vaughan	71	69	70	210	5,407.14
Ryan Reid	67	72	71	210	5,407.14
Barry Painting	69	69	72	210	5,407.14
John Mashego	68	67	75	210	5,407.14
Marc Cayeux	73	69	69	211	4,392.85
Divan van den Heever	73	68	70	211	4,392.85
Warren Abery	73	70	68	211	4,392.85
Nic Henning	71	68	72	211	4,392.85
Jean Hugo	69	69	73	211	4,392.85
Ross Wellington	69	69	73	211	4,392.85
Omar Sandys	70	66	75	211	4,392.85

Seekers Travel Pro-Am

Dainfern Country Club, Johannesburg, South Africa
Par 36-36–72; 7,258 yards

November 11-13
purse, R230,000

	SCORES			TOTAL	MONEY
Ulrich van den Berg	69	67	67	203	R36,110
Mark Murless	68	69	66	203	22,425
Patrick O'Brien	73	64	66	203	22,425
(Van den Berg defeated Murless and O'Brien on second playoff hole.)					
Des Terblanche	69	69	66	204	13,570
James Kingston	70	67	68	205	9,200
Callie Swart	68	67	70	205	9,200
Michael du Toit	70	69	67	206	6,056.66
Wallie Coetsee	70	68	68	206	6,056.66
Nicholas Lawrence	67	66	73	206	6,056.66
Charl Schwartzel	72	69	66	207	4,439
Steve Basson	71	67	69	207	4,439
Werner Geyer	67	69	71	207	4,439
Leonard Loxton	69	65	73	207	4,439
Grant Muller	70	71	67	208	3,615.60
Ashley Roestoff	71	69	68	208	3,615.60
Chris Swanepoel, Jr.	71	68	69	208	3,615.60
Kevin Stone	71	67	70	208	3,615.60
Warren Abery	69	65	74	208	3,615.60
Tyrol Auret	72	69	68	209	2,990
Steve van Vuuren	72	69	68	209	2,990
Divan van den Heever	68	70	71	209	2,990
John Mashego	72	66	71	209	2,990
John Bele	69	66	74	209	2,990
Richard Sterne	69	70	71	210	2,622
Anton Haig	68	70	72	210	2,622
Chris Williams	71	70	70	211	2,277
Ryan Reid	71	70	70	211	2,277
Waylon Kukard	70	70	71	211	2,277
Roger Wessels	68	71	72	211	2,277
Nic Henning	70	68	73	211	2,277
Barry Painting	69	69	73	211	2,277

Nelson Mandela Invitational

Arabella Country Club, Hermanus, South Africa
Par 36-36–72; 6,976 yards

November 27-28
purse, R125,000

	SCORES		TOTAL	MONEY (Team)
Ernie Els/Vincent Tshabalala	64	66	130	R125,000
Simon Hobday/Lee Westwood	67	64	131	
Tim Clark/Bobby Lincoln	65	67	132	
Andrew McLardy/Gary Player	65	67	132	
John Bland/Andrew Coltart	69	65	134	
Hugh Baiocchi/Thabang Simon	65	70	135	
Omar Sandys/Sam Torrance	67	69	136	
John Mashego/Ian Poulter	67	72	139	

Nedbank Golf Challenge

Gary Player Country Club, Sun City, South Africa
Par 36-36–72; 7,590 yards

December 2-5
purse, US$4,060,000

	SCORES				TOTAL	MONEY
Retief Goosen	70	71	71	69	281	$1,200,000
Ernie Els	70	74	72	71	287	500,000
Stuart Appleby	70	69	74	74	287	500,000
Chris DiMarco	71	74	69	74	288	275,000
Jim Furyk	74	76	66	72	288	275,000
Lee Westwood	70	70	71	80	291	217,500
Jay Haas	75	74	70	72	291	217,500
Todd Hamilton	74	72	71	75	292	195,000
Nick Price	71	70	74	78	293	185,000
Fredrik Jacobson	75	78	72	72	297	175,000
Chad Campbell	80	75	72	72	299	165,000
Sergio Garcia	75	76	74	78	303	155,000

Dunhill Championship

Leopard Creek Country Club, Malelane, South Africa
Par 35-37–72; 7,316 yards

December 9-12
purse, £500,000

	SCORES				TOTAL	MONEY
Charl Schwartzel	71	69	70	71	281	R881,987.60
Neil Cheetham	68	71	69	73	281	641,953
(Schwartzel defeated Cheetham on first playoff hole.)						
Warren Abery	69	70	73	70	282	297,531.26
Ernie Els	67	75	70	70	282	297,531.26
Oliver Whiteley	72	67	72	71	282	297,531.26
Marcel Siem	76	69	71	67	283	181,142.39
David Frost	70	70	69	74	283	181,142.39
Graeme Storm	73	68	75	68	284	122,436.25
Damien McGrane	74	68	72	70	284	122,436.25
Euan Little	71	69	72	72	284	122,436.25
Tim Clark	77	68	73	67	285	96,572.06
Michael Kirk	71	72	69	73	285	96,572.06
Richard Finch	72	69	72	73	286	87,640.54
Des Terblanche	69	70	76	72	287	79,267.24
Johan Edfors	70	74	71	72	287	79,267.24
Martin Maritz	75	72	68	72	287	79,267.24
Darren Fichardt	70	71	78	69	288	67,358.54
Ian Garbutt	71	72	76	69	288	67,358.54
Iain Steel	70	73	75	70	288	67,358.54
Mark Murless	76	69	73	70	288	67,358.54
Garry Houston	80	68	69	71	288	67,358.54
Leif Westerberg	70	70	76	72	288	67,358.54
Anton Haig	77	69	74	69	289	57,775.77
Manuel Quiros	69	72	78	70	289	57,775.77
Lee Slattery	73	69	77	70	289	57,775.77
Matthew Morris	72	72	73	72	289	57,775.77
Ulrich van den Berg	72	75	72	71	290	50,351.44
Andre Bossert	74	72	72	72	290	50,351.44
Gregory Bourdy	74	73	70	73	290	50,351.44
Bruce McDonald	66	76	73	75	290	50,351.44
Mark Davis	70	72	72	76	290	50,351.44

	SCORES			TOTAL	MONEY
Roope Kakko	73	74	75	69	291	42,982.94
Mike Lamb	72	70	78	71	291	42,982.94
Phillip Archer	73	71	75	72	291	42,982.94
Grant Muller	76	71	72	72	291	42,982.94
Joachim Backstrom	71	77	71	72	291	42,982.94
Peter Lawrie	75	67	75	74	291	42,982.94
Peter Gustafsson	69	68	79	75	291	42,982.94
Sam Little	72	71	80	69	292	34,051.42
Stephen Browne	76	71	76	69	292	34,051.42
Titch Moore	72	76	73	71	292	34,051.42
Matthew King	75	73	72	72	292	34,051.42
Louis Oosthuizen	72	69	78	73	292	34,051.42
Hennie Otto	73	71	75	73	292	34,051.42
Alan Michell	72	76	70	74	292	34,051.42
Keith Horne	71	72	72	77	292	34,051.42
Alessandro Tadini	71	70	73	78	292	34,051.42
Matthew Blackey	77	71	74	71	293	25,119.90
Johan Skold	74	74	73	72	293	25,119.90
Francesco Molinari	73	71	76	73	293	25,119.90
Paul Bradshaw	73	71	76	73	293	25,119.90
Mathias Gronberg	70	71	77	75	293	25,119.90
Andrew McLardy	72	72	72	77	293	25,119.90
Lindani Ndwandwe	70	71	73	79	293	25,119.90
Liam Bond	78	70	74	72	294	18,756.19
Chris Davison	72	73	76	73	294	18,756.19
Raphael Eyraud	68	78	75	73	294	18,756.19
Bertrand Cornut	74	71	75	74	294	18,756.19
Sammy Daniels	76	71	72	75	294	18,756.19
Bobby Lincoln	71	74	77	73	295	16,188.38
Omar Sandys	79	68	73	75	295	16,188.38
Andre Cruse	70	72	76	77	295	16,188.38
Benoit Teilleria	68	78	77	73	296	13,955.50
Nico Le Grange	71	74	76	75	296	13,955.50
Jan-Are Larsen	74	74	73	75	296	13,955.50
Sarel Son-Houi	69	73	78	76	296	13,955.50
Johan Axgren	73	72	74	77	296	13,955.50
David Patrick	75	72	75	75	297	12,001.73
Oliver Wilson	69	73	76	79	297	12,001.73
Stuart Manley	74	72	75	77	298	11,164.40
Julien Clement	73	73	80	73	299	8,339.80
Martin Erlandsson	72	75	78	74	299	8,339.80
Callie Swart	71	76	77	75	299	8,339.80
Ryan Tipping	72	74	75	78	299	8,339.80
Steve Basson	74	72	76	78	300	8,283.98
Ryan Reid	75	69	82	75	301	8,250.49
Brett Liddle	74	74	77	76	301	8,250.49
James Kamte	68	76	84	84	312	8,217

Senior Tours

MasterCard Championship

Hualalai Golf Club, Kaupulehu-Kona, Hawaii

January 23-25

Par 36-36–72; 6,850 yards

purse, $1,600,000

	SCORES			TOTAL	MONEY
Fuzzy Zoeller	67	65	64	196	$268,000
Dana Quigley	67	65	65	197	161,000
Craig Stadler	69	66	63	198	108,000
Doug Tewell	64	65	69	198	108,000
Tom Purtzer	67	67	66	200	82,000
Jack Nicklaus	68	66	67	201	71,000
Dave Eichelberger	66	65	71	202	59,500
Allen Doyle	69	67	66	202	59,500
Bruce Fleisher	69	65	69	203	39,071.42
Gil Morgan	67	67	69	203	39,071.43
Jim Thorpe	66	70	67	203	39,071.43
John Jacobs	72	67	64	203	39,071.43
Stewart Ginn	66	69	68	203	39,071.43
Jim Ahern	69	68	66	203	39,071.43
Vicente Fernandez	71	66	66	203	39,071.43
Tom Jenkins	67	68	69	204	29,000
James Mason	65	72	68	205	26,000
Jay Sigel	66	70	69	205	26,000
Hale Irwin	69	68	69	206	23,000
Larry Nelson	71	68	67	206	23,000
Don Pooley	71	65	70	206	23,000
Isao Aoki	71	68	68	207	20,500
Tom Kite	70	68	69	207	20,500
Dave Barr	67	73	68	208	18,000
Wayne Levi	73	67	68	208	18,000
J.C. Snead	68	69	71	208	18,000
David Eger	69	70	70	209	14,625
Bob Gilder	70	71	68	209	14,625
Morris Hatalsky	71	70	68	209	14,625
Graham Marsh	71	68	70	209	14,625
Rodger Davis	71	69	70	210	13,000
D.A. Weibring	68	72	71	211	12,500
Tom Watson	74	72	66	212	12,250
Gary Player	77	69	68	214	11,875
Sammy Rachels	70	74	70	214	11,875
Lee Trevino	74	70	72	216	11,500
Hubert Green	71	73	74	218	11,250
Bruce Lietzke	77	71	73	221	11,000
Arnold Palmer	77	75	75	227	10,750

Royal Caribbean Golf Classic

Crandon Park Golf Course, Key Biscayne, Florida

February 6-8

Par 35-37–72; 6,824 yards

purse, $1,450,000

	SCORES			TOTAL	MONEY
Bruce Fleisher	69	70	71	210	$217,500
Dana Quigley	71	72	68	211	127,600

	SCORES			TOTAL	MONEY
Gil Morgan	72	70	70	212	95,700
John Bland	72	67	73	212	95,700
Wayne Levi	70	68	75	213	56,550
Mark McCumber	72	71	70	213	56,550
Jim Thorpe	72	73	68	213	56,550
John Jacobs	72	69	72	213	56,550
Ed Fiori	71	69	74	214	36,250
Morris Hatalsky	71	69	74	214	36,250
Tom Jenkins	72	70	72	214	36,250
Tom Kite	68	73	73	214	36,250
Bob Gilder	72	70	73	215	26,100
Larry Nelson	73	69	73	215	26,100
Don Pooley	69	69	77	215	26,100
Bruce Summerhays	69	70	76	215	26,100
Allen Doyle	72	73	70	215	26,100
Mark James	73	73	70	216	20,445
Dick Mast	73	68	75	216	20,445
Vicente Fernandez	72	69	75	216	20,445
Jim Dent	72	70	75	217	17,400
Dave Stockton	72	68	77	217	17,400
Rodger Davis	74	71	73	218	14,210
Graham Marsh	74	69	75	218	14,210
Bob Murphy	74	69	75	218	14,210
Lonnie Nielsen	71	72	75	218	14,210
Jerry Pate	79	67	72	218	14,210
J.C. Snead	69	70	79	218	14,210
Bob Eastwood	72	73	74	219	10,730
Doug Tewell	75	70	74	219	10,730
Sam Torrance	73	73	73	219	10,730
Fuzzy Zoeller	76	70	73	219	10,730
John Harris	74	67	78	219	10,730
Rick Rhoden	75	71	73	219	10,730
Andy Bean	71	73	76	220	8,700
Mike San Filippo	76	70	74	220	8,700
Walter Hall	73	74	73	220	8,700
Isao Aoki	74	72	75	221	7,540
Mike McCullough	75	74	72	221	7,540
D.A. Weibring	73	73	75	221	7,540
Hugh Baiocchi	75	72	74	221	7,540

ACE Group Classic

TwinEagles Golf Club, Naples, Florida
Par 36-36–72; 7,102 yards

February 13-15
purse, $1,600,000

	SCORES			TOTAL	MONEY
Craig Stadler	67	67	72	206	$240,000
Gary Koch	62	73	71	206	128,000
Tom Watson	70	69	67	206	128,000
Stadler defeated Koch and Watson on first playoff hole.)					
Gil Morgan	66	72	69	207	86,400
Larry Nelson	65	75	67	207	86,400
Wayne Levi	68	71	69	208	64,000
Morris Hatalsky	66	73	70	209	51,200
Don Pooley	66	75	68	209	51,200
D.A. Weibring	67	73	69	209	51,200
Dave Barr	71	70	70	211	36,800

	SCORES			TOTAL	MONEY
Lonnie Nielsen	63	77	71	211	36,800
J.C. Snead	71	70	70	211	36,800
Bobby Wadkins	68	74	69	211	36,800
Hale Irwin	65	77	70	212	30,400
Jose Maria Canizares	71	73	69	213	25,632
Tom Kite	71	74	68	213	25,632
Jack Nicklaus	68	74	71	213	25,632
Fuzzy Zoeller	70	72	71	213	25,632
John Jacobs	70	76	67	213	25,632
Graham Marsh	69	75	70	214	19,280
Sammy Rachels	73	69	72	214	19,280
Des Smyth	72	71	71	214	19,280
John Harris	67	77	70	214	19,280
David Eger	69	75	71	215	14,960
Mike McCullough	67	74	74	215	14,960
Dave Stockton	70	74	71	215	14,960
Jim Thorpe	70	72	73	215	14,960
Jim Holtgrieve	68	79	68	215	14,960
Jay Sigel	68	77	70	215	14,960
Bob Eastwood	71	75	70	216	11,552
Tom Jenkins	66	79	71	216	11,552
Tom Purtzer	70	73	73	216	11,552
Allen Doyle	68	75	73	216	11,552
Walter Hall	76	70	70	216	11,552
Isao Aoki	70	71	76	217	9,600
Bruce Fleisher	72	76	69	217	9,600
Tom Wargo	71	75	71	217	9,600
Bob Gilder	73	73	72	218	7,840
Joe Inman	71	75	72	218	7,840
Mike Smith	74	75	69	218	7,840
Lee Trevino	71	73	74	218	7,840
Bruce Summerhays	72	75	71	218	7,840
John Bland	69	74	75	218	7,840
Stewart Ginn	69	75	74	218	7,840

Outback Steakhouse Pro-Am

TPC of Tampa Bay, Lutz, Florida
Par 35-36–71; 6,783 yards

February 20-22
purse, $1,600,000

	SCORES			TOTAL	MONEY
Mark McNulty	67	65	68	200	$241,000
Larry Nelson	64	69	68	201	142,000
Tom Purtzer	67	67	68	202	106,250
Fuzzy Zoeller	69	72	61	202	106,250
D.A. Weibring	68	65	70	203	77,000
Tom Jenkins	67	67	70	204	64,700
Gil Morgan	66	69	70	205	48,950
Jim Thorpe	70	67	68	205	48,950
John Bland	65	71	69	205	48,950
Vicente Fernandez	67	67	71	205	48,950
Bruce Fleisher	67	74	65	206	36,800
Tom Kite	63	74	69	206	36,800
Hale Irwin	70	68	69	207	27,200
Graham Marsh	69	67	71	207	27,200
Mike McCullough	64	70	73	207	27,200
Bob Murphy	67	74	66	207	27,200

	SCORES			TOTAL	MONEY
J.C. Snead	69	72	66	207	27,200
Craig Stadler	69	69	69	207	27,200
Jay Sigel	69	69	69	207	27,200
Ed Fiori	69	70	69	208	19,200
Bob Gilder	71	68	69	208	19,200
Gary McCord	68	74	66	208	19,200
Dana Quigley	66	69	73	208	19,200
David Eger	65	72	72	209	16,000
Gary Player	73	70	66	209	16,000
Allen Doyle	67	75	67	209	16,000
Morris Hatalsky	72	70	68	210	14,020
Wayne Levi	69	72	69	210	14,020
Jerry Pate	69	73	68	210	14,020
Dave Barr	72	71	68	211	11,900
Joe Inman	68	72	71	211	11,900
Sammy Rachels	69	73	69	211	11,900
John Jacobs	72	70	69	211	11,900
Isao Aoki	68	75	69	212	8,951.11
Jose Maria Canizares	71	72	69	212	8,951.11
Jerry McGee	72	70	70	212	8,951.12
Don Pooley	71	73	68	212	8,951.11
Doug Tewell	72	71	69	212	8,951.11
Sam Torrance	72	70	70	212	8,951.11
Bobby Wadkins	75	71	66	212	8,951.11
Tom Wargo	72	67	73	212	8,951.11
Walter Hall	69	74	69	212	8,951.11

MasterCard Classic

Bosque Real Country Club, Col. Lomas Altas, Mexico
Par 36-36–72; 7,227 yards

March 5-7
purse, $2,000,000

	SCORES			TOTAL	MONEY
Ed Fiori	72	71	67	210	$300,000
Graham Marsh	70	66	74	210	176,000
(Fiori defeated Marsh on third playoff hole.)					
Hugh Baiocchi	71	66	74	211	144,000
Jack Spradlin	70	71	72	213	98,666.67
Jay Sigel	69	69	75	213	98,666.66
Jim Ahern	70	70	73	213	98,666.67
Andy Bean	67	74	73	214	61,000
Hale Irwin	70	71	73	214	61,000
Tom Jenkins	76	68	70	214	61,000
Sam Torrance	71	71	72	214	61,000
Tom Kite	72	68	75	215	48,000
Mark McNulty	72	75	69	216	44,000
Mark James	72	70	75	217	37,000
Darrell Kestner	69	73	75	217	37,000
Jay Overton	75	69	73	217	37,000
Bobby Wadkins	77	70	70	217	37,000
Jerry Pate	76	70	72	218	32,000
David Eger	72	71	76	219	29,100
Bobby Lincoln	72	71	76	219	29,100
John Schroeder	74	70	76	220	24,800
John Bland	74	73	73	220	24,800
Eamonn Darcy	74	73	73	220	24,800
Jim Colbert	68	78	75	221	17,940

	SCORES			TOTAL	MONEY
Terry Dill	73	72	76	221	17,940
R.W. Eaks	72	74	75	221	17,940
Danny Edwards	74	73	74	221	17,940
Bob Gilder	76	71	74	221	17,940
Joe Inman	75	75	71	221	17,940
Dana Quigley	74	73	74	221	17,940
John Jacobs	71	72	78	221	17,940
Stewart Ginn	68	79	74	221	17,940
John Harris	70	74	77	221	17,940
Bob Eastwood	75	72	75	222	12,900
Jerry McGee	75	74	73	222	12,900
Sammy Rachels	75	72	75	222	12,900
Des Smyth	74	72	76	222	12,900
Butch Baird	75	75	73	223	11,200
Tom Wargo	74	74	75	223	11,200
Dave Barr	73	75	76	224	9,600
Bob Dickson	75	74	75	224	9,600
Keith Fergus	76	71	77	224	9,600
Fred Gibson	75	71	78	224	9,600
James Mason	75	75	74	224	9,600
Rafael Navarro	73	77	74	224	9,600

SBC Classic

Valencia Country Club, Valencia, California
Par 36-36–72; 6,905 yards

March 12-14
purse, $1,500,000

	SCORES			TOTAL	MONEY
Gil Morgan	67	66	69	202	$225,000
Larry Nelson	68	68	68	204	132,000
Peter Jacobsen	67	71	67	205	108,000
Joe Inman	72	70	64	206	81,000
Graham Marsh	72	69	65	206	81,000
Tom Purtzer	68	71	68	207	60,000
Bruce Fleisher	73	67	68	208	42,000
Hale Irwin	69	70	69	208	42,000
Mark James	68	70	70	208	42,000
Gary McCord	71	70	67	208	42,000
Craig Stadler	67	72	69	208	42,000
Allen Doyle	69	70	69	208	42,000
Doug Tewell	70	70	70	210	29,250
John Bland	71	71	68	210	29,250
Sam Torrance	71	67	73	211	25,500
Des Smyth	69	69	73	211	25,500
Hugh Baiocchi	70	71	70	211	25,500
Jim Colbert	70	70	72	212	18,814.28
David Eger	70	75	67	212	18,814.29
Darrell Kestner	72	73	67	212	18,814.29
Tom Kite	69	74	69	212	18,814.29
Mike McCullough	67	70	75	212	18,814.28
Mark McNulty	71	71	70	212	18,814.29
John Jacobs	69	71	72	212	18,814.28
Dave Barr	73	70	70	213	14,625
Morris Hatalsky	74	67	72	213	14,625
Andy Bean	73	70	71	214	12,450
Ben Crenshaw	71	73	70	214	12,450
Keith Fergus	73	71	70	214	12,450

	SCORES			TOTAL	MONEY
Wayne Levi	70	75	69	214	12,450
Lonnie Nielsen	74	69	71	214	12,450
Tom Wargo	74	76	65	215	10,800
Jose Maria Canizares	68	73	75	216	9,250
Bob Gilder	73	72	71	216	9,250
Bruce Lietzke	72	73	71	216	9,250
Jerry Pate	71	76	69	216	9,250
Don Pooley	67	71	78	216	9,250
Jay Sigel	72	68	76	216	9,250
Ed Fiori	75	71	71	217	7,500
John Mahaffey	74	70	73	217	7,500
J.C. Snead	71	70	76	217	7,500
D.A. Weibring	72	75	70	217	7,500

Toshiba Senior Classic

Newport Beach Country Club, Newport Beach, California   March 19-21
Par 35-36–71; 6,571 yards   purse, $1,600,000

	SCORES			TOTAL	MONEY
Tom Purtzer	60	71	67	198	$240,000
Morris Hatalsky	65	66	68	199	140,800
John Jacobs	67	65	68	200	115,200
Keith Fergus	66	66	69	201	96,000
Bruce Fleisher	68	67	67	202	76,800
David Eger	66	69	68	203	57,600
Lonnie Nielsen	67	69	67	203	57,600
D.A. Weibring	69	65	69	203	57,600
Dana Quigley	70	67	67	204	41,600
Leonard Thompson	67	70	67	204	41,600
John Bland	66	73	65	204	41,600
Bob Eastwood	67	70	68	205	30,720
Wayne Levi	70	67	68	205	30,720
Gil Morgan	71	68	66	205	30,720
Craig Stadler	69	67	69	205	30,720
Dave Stockton	68	70	67	205	30,720
John Harris	70	68	68	206	25,600
Joe Inman	64	72	71	207	21,216
Mike McCullough	71	68	68	207	21,216
Doug Tewell	69	70	68	207	21,216
Sam Torrance	69	66	72	207	21,216
Vicente Fernandez	69	67	71	207	21,216
Andy Bean	68	70	70	208	16,400
Jose Maria Canizares	71	69	68	208	16,400
Ben Crenshaw	71	68	69	208	16,400
Gary McCord	72	67	69	208	16,400
Dave Barr	74	66	69	209	12,177.78
Fred Gibson	72	70	67	209	12,177.78
Bob Gilder	69	69	71	209	12,177.77
Tom Kite	72	69	68	209	12,177.78
Don Pooley	69	71	69	209	12,177.78
Mike Smith	72	68	69	209	12,177.78
Fuzzy Zoeller	66	71	72	209	12,177.77
Hugh Baiocchi	70	69	70	209	12,177.78
Walter Hall	70	70	69	209	12,177.78
Graham Marsh	73	68	69	210	8,832
Larry Nelson	70	72	68	210	8,832

	SCORES			TOTAL	MONEY
Jack Nicklaus	71	70	69	210	8,832
Jerry Pate	71	70	69	210	8,832
Allen Doyle	75	67	68	210	8,832

Blue Angels Classic

The Moors Golf Club, Milton, Florida
Par 35-35–70; 6,832 yards

April 16-18
purse, $1,500,000

	SCORES			TOTAL	MONEY
Tom Jenkins	68	65	63	196	$225,000
Rodger Davis	68	68	65	201	132,000
Wayne Levi	68	67	67	202	90,000
Gil Morgan	66	66	70	202	90,000
Jim Ahern	67	70	65	202	90,000
Dave Eichelberger	68	69	67	204	48,600
Tom Purtzer	68	68	68	204	48,600
D.A. Weibring	70	68	66	204	48,600
Fuzzy Zoeller	65	71	68	204	48,600
Des Smyth	69	71	64	204	48,600
Lonnie Nielsen	69	69	67	205	36,000
Jerry Pate	68	69	69	206	29,625
Dana Quigley	69	67	70	206	29,625
John Harris	68	69	69	206	29,625
Walter Hall	67	70	69	206	29,625
Jim Dent	72	67	68	207	23,287.50
Keith Fergus	69	68	70	207	23,287.50
Mark Lye	70	66	71	207	23,287.50
Mike Smith	71	66	70	207	23,287.50
Joe Inman	68	70	70	208	16,757.14
Mark James	73	65	70	208	16,757.14
Doug Tewell	67	71	70	208	16,757.15
Bobby Wadkins	70	68	70	208	16,757.14
James Mason	70	67	71	208	16,757.14
Vicente Fernandez	69	68	71	208	16,757.14
Bobby Lincoln	67	72	69	208	16,757.15
Morris Hatalsky	71	68	70	209	12,450
Hajime Meshiai	68	70	71	209	12,450
Larry Nelson	73	66	70	209	12,450
Leonard Thompson	74	68	67	209	12,450
Bruce Summerhays	68	72	69	209	12,450
Bob Gilder	66	73	71	210	9,471.43
Gary Koch	68	67	75	210	9,471.42
Mike McCullough	68	68	74	210	9,471.43
Mark McNulty	72	68	70	210	9,471.43
Howard Twitty	68	68	74	210	9,471.43
John Jacobs	72	67	71	210	9,471.43
Rafael Navarro	69	69	72	210	9,471.43
Dave Barr	70	72	69	211	7,350
Bob Duval	69	70	72	211	7,350
Ed Fiori	69	72	70	211	7,350
Bruce Fleisher	73	71	67	211	7,350
J.C. Snead	68	71	72	211	7,350

Liberty Mutual Legends of Golf

Westin Savannah Harbor Golf Resort & Spa,
Savannah, Georgia
Par 36-36–72; 6,967 yards

April 23-25
purse, $2,300,000

	SCORES			TOTAL	MONEY
Hale Irwin	66	68	71	205	$364,000
Gary Koch	68	67	71	206	195,000
Gil Morgan	65	68	73	206	195,000
Don Pooley	71	66	70	207	129,500
Craig Stadler	67	68	72	207	129,500
Bruce Fleisher	68	69	71	208	86,333.33
Larry Nelson	69	69	70	208	86,333.34
Tom Purtzer	71	67	70	208	86,333.33
Dave Barr	66	68	75	209	56,000
Andy Bean	69	70	70	209	56,000
Ed Fiori	69	72	68	209	56,000
Wayne Levi	70	70	69	209	56,000
Dana Quigley	68	72	69	209	56,000
John Jacobs	71	67	71	209	56,000
Rodger Davis	71	69	70	210	40,750
Bob Gilder	70	69	71	210	40,750
Bruce Lietzke	70	72	69	211	36,500
Allen Doyle	73	70	68	211	36,500
Charles Coody	70	72	70	212	27,928.57
Bob Eastwood	71	68	73	212	27,928.57
David Eger	71	72	69	212	27,928.57
Dave Stockton	68	72	72	212	27,928.57
Doug Tewell	71	72	69	212	27,928.57
Des Smyth	72	73	67	212	27,928.58
Vicente Fernandez	71	71	70	212	27,928.57
Mark McNulty	69	70	74	213	19,625
Leonard Thompson	68	70	75	213	19,625
Jim Thorpe	72	71	70	213	19,625
D.A. Weibring	71	71	71	213	19,625
Morris Hatalsky	69	74	71	214	15,933.33
Jay Sigel	70	77	67	214	15,933.34
Jim Ahern	73	72	69	214	15,933.33
Jose Maria Canizares	70	73	72	215	14,200
Tom Jenkins	70	75	70	215	14,200
Isao Aoki	75	72	69	216	12,550
Graham Marsh	73	73	70	216	12,550
Jerry Pate	74	72	70	216	12,550
Bobby Wadkins	75	71	70	216	12,550
Ben Crenshaw	75	70	72	217	10,625
Mike McCullough	72	75	70	217	10,625
Mark McCumber	73	70	74	217	10,625
J.C. Snead	71	71	75	217	10,625

Bruno's Memorial Classic

Greystone Golf & Country Club, Founder's Course,
Hoover, Alabama
Par 36-36–72; 6,672 yards

April 30-May 2
purse, $1,500,000

	SCORES			TOTAL	MONEY
Bruce Fleisher	64	68	68	200	$225,000
Bruce Lietzke	69	71	67	207	120,000
D.A. Weibring	68	68	71	207	120,000
Tom Jenkins	71	66	71	208	90,000
Morris Hatalsky	70	71	68	209	62,000
Tom Kite	70	71	68	209	62,000
Larry Nelson	68	70	71	209	62,000
Mike Hill	70	71	69	210	43,000
Jay Sigel	70	67	73	210	43,000
Walter Hall	68	75	67	210	43,000
Dave Eichelberger	68	70	73	211	27,516.66
Mark James	74	68	69	211	27,516.67
Graham Marsh	74	65	72	211	27,516.66
Lonnie Nielsen	66	75	70	211	27,516.67
Dana Quigley	71	69	71	211	27,516.67
Doug Tewell	69	71	71	211	27,516.67
Lee Trevino	68	71	72	211	27,516.67
Des Smyth	68	71	72	211	27,516.66
John Bland	69	72	70	211	27,516.67
Ben Crenshaw	73	69	70	212	18,075
Hale Irwin	70	67	75	212	18,075
Bobby Wadkins	70	72	70	212	18,075
Tom Wargo	74	70	68	212	18,075
Mark McCumber	72	69	72	213	15,750
Andy Bean	72	73	69	214	13,680
Wayne Levi	73	67	74	214	13,680
Jerry Pate	70	73	71	214	13,680
Tom Purtzer	71	72	71	214	13,680
Bruce Summerhays	72	69	73	214	13,680
George Archer	75	70	70	215	11,300
Dave Barr	73	71	71	215	11,300
Stewart Ginn	72	72	71	215	11,300
Jose Maria Canizares	70	75	71	216	8,716.67
Rodger Davis	74	72	70	216	8,716.67
Raymond Floyd	70	70	76	216	8,716.66
Mike McCullough	74	72	70	216	8,716.67
Bob Murphy	70	70	76	216	8,716.66
Jim Thorpe	72	69	75	216	8,716.66
Tom Watson	71	73	72	216	8,716.67
Allen Doyle	71	73	72	216	8,716.67
John Harris	72	71	73	216	8,716.67

FedEx Kinko's Classic

The Hills Country Club, Austin, Texas
Par 36-36–72; 6,879 yards

May 7-9
purse, $1,600,000

	SCORES			TOTAL	MONEY
Larry Nelson	73	69	67	209	$240,000
Bruce Lietzke	69	72	69	210	140,800

	SCORES			TOTAL	MONEY
Bob Gilder	70	76	65	211	96,000
Morris Hatalsky	71	69	71	211	96,000
Wayne Levi	70	69	72	211	96,000
Isao Aoki	69	71	72	212	57,600
Jose Maria Canizares	71	70	71	212	57,600
Gil Morgan	76	69	67	212	57,600
Hajime Meshiai	70	76	67	213	38,400
Dave Stockton	71	74	68	213	38,400
Tom Watson	68	73	72	213	38,400
D.A. Weibring	69	73	71	213	38,400
Jay Sigel	72	75	66	213	38,400
Andy Bean	70	77	67	214	21,821.54
Ed Fiori	73	70	71	214	21,821.54
Graham Marsh	69	74	71	214	21,821.54
Mark McNulty	68	71	75	214	21,821.53
Dana Quigley	74	69	71	214	21,821.54
Bill Rogers	72	72	70	214	21,821.54
Craig Stadler	70	71	73	214	21,821.53
Doug Tewell	77	68	69	214	21,821.54
Sam Torrance	67	76	71	214	21,821.54
Bobby Wadkins	70	73	71	214	21,821.54
Allen Doyle	68	76	70	214	21,821.54
John Bland	72	72	70	214	21,821.54
John Harris	73	70	71	214	21,821.54
Bob Charles	69	70	76	215	12,440
Bruce Fleisher	71	73	71	215	12,440
Raymond Floyd	67	73	75	215	12,440
Joe Inman	73	70	72	215	12,440
Tom Kite	69	73	73	215	12,440
Jerry Pate	71	77	67	215	12,440
Bruce Summerhays	72	76	67	215	12,440
Walter Hall	70	74	71	215	12,440
Dave Barr	73	73	70	216	9,216
R.W. Eaks	70	74	72	216	9,216
Tom Jenkins	73	74	69	216	9,216
Gary Koch	75	73	68	216	9,216
Vicente Fernandez	68	77	71	216	9,216
Hale Irwin	75	71	71	217	7,520
Tom Purtzer	74	71	72	217	7,520
Lee Trevino	72	73	72	217	7,520
Des Smyth	76	70	71	217	7,520
Jim Ahern	73	72	72	217	7,520

Allianz Championship

Glen Oaks Country Club, West Des Moines, Iowa
Par 35-36–71; 6,864 yards

May 21-23
purse, $1,500,000

	SCORES			TOTAL	MONEY
D.A. Weibring	65	68	71	204	$225,000
Tom Jenkins	70	67	70	207	132,000
Tom Watson	69	68	71	208	108,000
Raymond Floyd	73	70	66	209	69,000
Tom Kite	68	69	72	209	69,000
Jim Thorpe	76	65	68	209	69,000
Jay Sigel	69	72	68	209	69,000
Dana Quigley	71	68	71	210	48,000

	SCORES				TOTAL	MONEY
Joe Inman	70	68	73		211	37,500
Doug Johnson	72	67	72		211	37,500
Allen Doyle	69	74	68		211	37,500
Bobby Lincoln	69	69	73		211	37,500
Jose Maria Canizares	75	67	70		212	27,000
Doug Tewell	72	69	71		212	27,000
Fuzzy Zoeller	75	67	70		212	27,000
Bruce Summerhays	69	72	71		212	27,000
Walter Hall	71	72	69		212	27,000
Gil Morgan	73	71	69		213	22,500
Dave Eichelberger	71	69	74		214	17,306.25
Bruce Fleisher	73	68	73		214	17,306.25
Wayne Levi	72	71	71		214	17,306.25
Jerry Pate	75	68	71		214	17,306.25
Bobby Walzel	68	66	80		214	17,306.25
James Mason	73	73	68		214	17,306.25
Stewart Ginn	73	69	72		214	17,306.25
John Harris	73	72	69		214	17,306.25
Bob Gilder	76	69	70		215	12,175
Mark Lye	74	69	72		215	12,175
Mike McCullough	74	69	72		215	12,175
Mark McNulty	71	72	72		215	12,175
Tom Wargo	67	72	76		215	12,175
Rafael Navarro	70	74	71		215	12,175
Keith Fergus	68	75	73		216	9,064.29
Ed Fiori	70	72	74		216	9,064.28
Hajime Meshiai	73	71	72		216	9,064.29
Sammy Rachels	75	70	71		216	9,064.29
Rocky Thompson	71	75	70		216	9,064.29
John Jacobs	72	72	72		216	9,064.29
Roy Vucinich	76	69	71		216	9,064.28
Rodger Davis	72	71	74		217	7,350
J.C. Snead	72	69	76		217	7,350
Bobby Wadkins	72	71	74		217	7,350

Senior PGA Championship

Valhalla Golf Club, Louisville, Kentucky
Par 35-36–71; 6,990 yards
(Event finished on Monday—rain.)

May 27-31
purse, $2,000,000

	SCORES				TOTAL	MONEY
Hale Irwin	67	69	69	71	276	$360,000
Jay Haas	67	71	69	70	277	216,000
Craig Stadler	69	71	70	69	279	136,000
Dave Barr	69	70	69	74	282	79,333.34
Mark James	69	71	73	69	282	79,333.34
Tom Watson	67	72	70	73	282	79,333.34
Mark McNulty	70	71	71	71	283	60,000
Gil Morgan	67	71	74	71	283	60,000
John Harris	70	67	71	76	284	54,000
Raymond Floyd	73	72	69	71	285	46,000
Wayne Levi	69	68	76	72	285	46,000
Jerry Pate	73	72	68	72	285	46,000
Andy Bean	74	70	68	74	286	35,250
Allen Doyle	72	71	71	72	286	35,250
R.W. Eaks	71	71	73	71	286	35,250

	SCORES				TOTAL	MONEY
Tom Jenkins	70	70	73	73	286	35,250
D.A. Weibring	69	75	67	76	287	29,000
Jim White	75	72	69	71	287	29,000
Dave Eichelberger	71	70	75	72	288	25,000
Vicente Fernandez	74	69	68	77	288	25,000
Keith Fergus	73	70	72	74	289	19,250
Tom Kite	76	71	70	72	289	19,250
Mark McCumber	71	70	75	73	289	19,250
Roy Vucinich	74	70	70	75	289	19,250
Doug Tewell	70	74	71	75	290	15,500
Bobby Wadkins	72	70	73	75	290	15,500
Isao Aoki	74	75	71	71	291	13,250
Joe Inman	73	73	72	73	291	13,250
Jay Sigel	69	76	73	73	291	13,250
Fuzzy Zoeller	73	69	69	80	291	13,250
Ed Fiori	70	74	72	76	292	10,500
Walter Hall	71	69	72	80	292	10,500
Hajime Meshiai	72	74	70	76	292	10,500
Lonnie Nielsen	74	70	72	76	292	10,500
Mike San Filippo	76	70	73	73	292	10,500
Bruce Summerhays	77	71	72	72	292	10,500
Bobby Walzel	70	71	75	76	292	10,500
Morris Hatalsky	75	73	74	71	293	8,200
Graham Marsh	72	70	74	77	293	8,200
Sam Torrance	76	71	72	74	293	8,200

Farmers Charity Classic

Egypt Valley Country Club, Ada, Michigan
Par 36-36–72; 6,960 yards

June 4-6
purse, $1,600,000

	SCORES			TOTAL	MONEY
Jim Thorpe	67	70	66	203	$240,000
Fred Gibson	66	72	66	204	140,800
Bob Gilder	66	68	71	205	96,000
Gil Morgan	72	68	65	205	96,000
Dave Stockton	69	70	66	205	96,000
Hale Irwin	71	67	68	206	60,800
Mark McNulty	70	68	68	206	60,800
Graham Marsh	72	67	68	207	48,000
Allen Doyle	72	67	68	207	48,000
Stewart Ginn	66	71	71	208	40,000
Eamonn Darcy	73	65	70	208	40,000
Ed Fiori	68	74	67	209	32,533.34
Vicente Fernandez	66	71	72	209	32,533.33
Mark Johnson	68	71	70	209	32,533.33
Joe Inman	71	69	70	210	25,632
Mike McCullough	72	70	68	210	25,632
Jerry Pate	72	66	72	210	25,632
James Mason	69	69	72	210	25,632
John Bland	72	68	70	210	25,632
Jose Maria Canizares	70	71	70	211	18,320
Dave Eichelberger	66	73	72	211	18,320
Mark James	74	69	68	211	18,320
Bobby Wadkins	70	71	70	211	18,320
Bruce Summerhays	75	65	71	211	18,320
Walter Hall	68	72	71	211	18,320

	SCORES			TOTAL	MONEY
Rodger Davis	70	70	72	212	13,920
David Eger	70	69	73	212	13,920
Keith Fergus	74	71	67	212	13,920
Lonnie Nielsen	73	68	71	212	13,920
Dana Quigley	69	74	69	212	13,920
Isao Aoki	69	72	72	213	10,560
Jim Dent	69	75	69	213	10,560
Morris Hatalsky	69	72	72	213	10,560
Tom Purtzer	68	69	76	213	10,560
Sammy Rachels	64	73	76	213	10,560
John Harris	68	76	69	213	10,560
Bobby Lincoln	71	71	71	213	10,560
Bruce Fleisher	74	72	68	214	7,840
Mike Hill	69	70	75	214	7,840
Doug Johnson	72	69	73	214	7,840
Hajime Meshiai	72	70	72	214	7,840
Doug Tewell	77	68	69	214	7,840
Bobby Walzel	72	68	74	214	7,840
Hugh Baiocchi	71	71	72	214	7,840

Bayer Advantage Celebrity Pro-Am

National Golf Club of Kansas City, Parkville, Missouri
Par 36-36–72; 6,875 yards
(Third round cancelled—rain.)

June 11-13
purse, $1,650,000

	SCORES		TOTAL	MONEY
Allen Doyle	65	66	131	$247,500
Jerry Pate	67	65	132	146,437
Andy Bean	65	70	135	91,007.50
David Eger	67	68	135	91,007.50
Bob Gilder	67	68	135	91,007.50
Mark James	66	69	135	91,007.50
John Harris	65	71	136	59,606
Bruce Summerhays	72	65	137	53,006
Jose Maria Canizares	68	70	138	44,653
Dana Quigley	69	69	138	44,653
Bruce Fleisher	67	72	139	33,990
Morris Hatalsky	66	73	139	33,990
Bruce Lietzke	69	70	139	33,990
Gil Morgan	72	67	139	33,990
Lonnie Nielsen	69	70	139	33,990
Mark McNulty	72	68	140	25,575
Stewart Ginn	70	70	140	25,575
Jim Ahern	67	73	140	25,575
Vicente Fernandez	67	73	140	25,575
Isao Aoki	70	71	141	17,977.25
Dave Barr	73	68	141	17,977.25
Jim Dent	75	66	141	17,977.25
Tom Kite	70	71	141	17,977.25
Gary McCord	69	72	141	17,977.25
Mike Smith	73	68	141	17,977.25
Craig Stadler	71	70	141	17,977.25
James Mason	68	73	141	17,977.25
Bob Ford	70	72	142	13,468
Graham Marsh	70	72	142	13,468
Hajime Meshiai	73	69	142	13,468

	SCORES			TOTAL	MONEY
Jim Thorpe	71	71		142	13,468
Bob Eastwood	71	72		143	10,286.62
Keith Fergus	73	70		143	10,286.62
Hale Irwin	70	73		143	10,286.62
D.A. Weibring	69	74		143	10,286.63
Fuzzy Zoeller	71	72		143	10,286.63
Jay Sigel	71	72		143	10,286.63
Des Smyth	71	72		143	10,286.62
John Bland	69	74		143	10,286.63
Tom Jenkins	69	75		144	7,590
Jay Overton	73	71		144	7,590
Dave Stockton	69	75		144	7,590
Sam Torrance	73	71		144	7,590
Bobby Wadkins	76	68		144	7,590
Walter Hall	71	73		144	7,590

Bank of America Championship

Nashawtuc Country Club, Concord, Massachusetts   June 25-27
Par 35-36–71; 6,729 yards   purse, $1,550,000

	SCORES			TOTAL	MONEY
Craig Stadler	68	69	64	201	$232,500
Tom Kite	67	69	69	205	113,666.67
Tom Purtzer	65	68	72	205	113,666.66
D.A. Weibring	70	70	65	205	113,666.67
Dana Quigley	68	70	68	206	64,066.67
Doug Tewell	69	68	69	206	64,066.67
John Jacobs	68	67	71	206	64,066.66
Jerry Pate	68	68	71	207	49,600
Tom Jenkins	70	69	70	209	37,200
Mike McCullough	67	71	71	209	37,200
Bruce Summerhays	74	68	67	209	37,200
Jay Sigel	68	69	72	209	37,200
Des Smyth	70	69	70	209	37,200
Isao Aoki	72	67	71	210	24,866.42
Andy Bean	72	68	70	210	24,866.43
Keith Fergus	72	68	70	210	24,866.43
Ed Fiori	70	69	71	210	24,866.43
Sammy Rachels	69	70	71	210	24,866.43
Mike Smith	69	71	70	210	24,866.43
Allen Doyle	71	67	72	210	24,866.43
Jim Thorpe	70	71	70	211	18,083.34
John Harris	66	70	75	211	18,083.33
Eamonn Darcy	68	71	72	211	18,083.33
Morris Hatalsky	70	71	71	212	14,492.50
Graham Marsh	69	69	74	212	14,492.50
Bob Murphy	71	72	69	212	14,492.50
Bill Rogers	68	73	71	212	14,492.50
John Bland	69	70	73	212	14,492.50
Walter Hall	67	68	77	212	14,492.50
Bruce Fleisher	73	70	70	213	11,676.67
Stewart Ginn	72	69	72	213	11,676.67
Hugh Baiocchi	72	68	73	213	11,676.66
Gary McCord	69	71	74	214	9,997.50
Dave Stockton	70	74	70	214	9,997.50
Sam Torrance	73	67	74	214	9,997.50
Mark Johnson	73	69	72	214	9,997.50

	SCORES			TOTAL	MONEY
Bob Charles	76	66	73	215	7,905
Ben Crenshaw	72	71	72	215	7,905
Jim Dent	71	74	70	215	7,905
Dave Eichelberger	74	72	69	215	7,905
Wayne Levi	72	69	74	215	7,905
Mike San Filippo	74	72	69	215	7,905
Rafael Navarro	71	70	74	215	7,905

Commerce Bank Long Island Classic

Eisenhower Park, Red Course, East Meadow, New York   July 2-4
Par 35-35–70; 6,914 yards   purse, $1,500,000

	SCORES			TOTAL	MONEY
Jim Thorpe	65	69	67	201	$225,000
Andy Bean	70	65	67	202	110,000
Wayne Levi	67	67	68	202	110,000
Bobby Wadkins	64	68	70	202	110,000
Jerry Pate	64	66	73	203	72,000
Dave Barr	72	66	67	205	51,000
Mike Hill	66	67	72	205	51,000
Bobby Walzel	71	68	66	205	51,000
Walter Hall	69	67	69	205	51,000
Bruce Fleisher	70	69	67	206	34,500
Hale Irwin	69	66	71	206	34,500
Allen Doyle	68	71	67	206	34,500
Bobby Lincoln	68	67	71	206	34,500
Tom Jenkins	67	66	74	207	25,500
Mark McNulty	71	66	70	207	25,500
Gil Morgan	69	70	68	207	25,500
Dave Stockton	67	72	68	207	25,500
Vicente Fernandez	67	71	69	207	25,500
Bob Gilder	67	70	71	208	17,742.85
Morris Hatalsky	70	67	71	208	17,742.86
Mark James	69	69	70	208	17,742.86
Bruce Lietzke	70	72	66	208	17,742.86
Mike McCullough	71	69	68	208	17,742.86
Jay Sigel	69	72	67	208	17,742.86
Jim Ahern	70	67	71	208	17,742.85
Jose Maria Canizares	70	70	69	209	11,700
Peter Jacobsen	64	74	71	209	11,700
Darrell Kestner	68	72	69	209	11,700
Tom Kite	70	66	73	209	11,700
Hajime Meshiai	68	72	69	209	11,700
Dana Quigley	72	68	69	209	11,700
J.C. Snead	70	69	70	209	11,700
Howard Twitty	68	69	72	209	11,700
Bruce Summerhays	70	72	67	209	11,700
James Mason	70	70	69	209	11,700
Dave Eichelberger	68	72	70	210	8,600
Keith Fergus	69	73	68	210	8,600
John Bland	71	67	72	210	8,600
Lonnie Nielsen	68	69	74	211	7,200
Doug Tewell	72	70	69	211	7,200
Leonard Thompson	72	72	67	211	7,200
Tom Wargo	70	70	71	211	7,200
Stewart Ginn	71	70	70	211	7,200
Eamonn Darcy	72	73	66	211	7,200

Ford Senior Players Championship

TPC of Michigan, Dearborn, Michigan
Par 36-36–72; 7,069 yards

July 8-11
purse, $2,500,000

	SCORES				TOTAL	MONEY
Mark James	68	67	67	73	275	$375,000
Jose Maria Canizares	68	66	71	71	276	219,000
Bruce Fleisher	68	69	69	71	277	180,000
Bruce Lietzke	70	67	70	71	278	150,000
Gary McCord	70	64	71	74	279	110,000
Dana Quigley	68	67	72	72	279	110,000
Tom Kite	72	68	69	71	280	85,000
Jim Thorpe	70	69	68	73	280	85,000
Hale Irwin	69	74	66	72	281	62,500
Mark McNulty	69	72	69	71	281	62,500
Gil Morgan	65	70	75	71	281	62,500
Allen Doyle	68	70	70	73	281	62,500
Ed Fiori	69	67	71	75	282	47,500
Don Pooley	72	70	68	72	282	47,500
D.A. Weibring	70	69	73	70	282	47,500
Morris Hatalsky	72	67	72	73	284	41,250
Walter Hall	71	68	73	72	284	41,250
Andy Bean	72	71	74	68	285	34,150
Craig Stadler	70	67	73	75	285	34,150
Bobby Walzel	69	72	72	72	285	34,150
Bruce Summerhays	72	72	70	71	285	34,150
Tom Jenkins	74	72	68	72	286	25,708.33
Graham Marsh	71	70	73	72	286	25,708.34
Mark McCumber	69	72	73	72	286	25,708.34
Doug Tewell	69	67	74	76	286	25,708.33
Leonard Thompson	69	72	72	73	286	25,708.33
Tom Wargo	72	69	70	75	286	25,708.33
Isao Aoki	68	71	72	76	287	19,375
Wayne Levi	73	70	72	72	287	19,375
Hajime Meshiai	73	69	73	72	287	19,375
Mike Smith	72	70	69	76	287	19,375
James Mason	74	67	68	78	287	19,375
Hugh Baiocchi	71	67	74	75	287	19,375
Mike McCullough	73	71	71	73	288	15,050
Jerry Pate	75	68	74	71	288	15,050
Bobby Wadkins	77	69	70	72	288	15,050
Jay Sigel	70	70	74	74	288	15,050
Vicente Fernandez	72	74	70	72	288	15,050
Bob Gilder	78	69	68	74	289	12,000
Gary Koch	70	76	69	74	289	12,000
Jerry McGee	72	72	72	73	289	12,000
Stewart Ginn	74	72	73	70	289	12,000
Jim Ahern	72	65	69	83	289	12,000
Eamonn Darcy	70	70	74	75	289	12,000

Senior British Open

See European Seniors Tour section.

U.S. Senior Open

Bellerive Country Club, Creve Coeur, Missouri
Par 36-35–71; 7,117 yards

July 29-August 1
purse, $2,600,000

	SCORES				TOTAL	MONEY
Peter Jacobsen	65	70	69	68	272	$470,000
Hale Irwin	71	67	67	68	273	280,000
Jay Haas	67	70	69	68	274	149,919.50
Tom Kite	69	68	65	72	274	149,919.50
Bob Gilder	68	69	67	71	275	99,702
D.A. Weibring	71	66	73	67	277	88,402
Doug Tewell	70	70	71	67	278	70,557.25
Walter Hall	69	71	69	69	278	70,557.25
Fuzzy Zoeller	71	66	70	71	278	70,557.25
Craig Stadler	66	69	73	70	278	70,557.25
John Harris	72	70	68	69	279	58,194
Bruce Fleisher	69	71	69	71	280	51,352
Gil Morgan	68	70	72	70	280	51,352
Jose Maria Canizares	68	68	72	72	280	51,352
Wayne Levi	68	74	71	68	281	43,250.33
Don Pooley	68	73	71	69	281	43,250.33
Mark James	70	70	71	70	281	43,250.33
Morris Hatalsky	70	69	70	73	282	38,710
Larry Nelson	72	70	70	71	283	32,625
Jim Thorpe	74	68	71	70	283	32,625
Mark McNulty	68	73	74	68	283	32,625
Bruce Lietzke	75	69	70	69	283	32,625
Mike McCullough	73	73	66	71	283	32,625
Dana Quigley	77	69	69	69	284	27,111
Mike Reid	71	72	70	72	285	23,121.50
Graham Marsh	71	71	69	74	285	23,121.50
Andy Bean	69	71	71	74	285	23,121.50
Tom Watson	74	70	69	72	285	23,121.50
Des Smyth	74	69	73	70	286	18,493.33
Tom Purtzer	70	74	73	69	286	18,493.33
Dave Stockton	72	68	69	77	286	18,493.33
Bruce Summerhays	73	70	75	70	288	16,859.33
Tom Jenkins	69	74	74	71	288	16,859.33
Darrell Kestner	69	72	72	75	288	16,859.33
Gary Sowinski	70	71	73	75	289	15,574.50
Doug Johnson	70	70	73	76	289	15,574.50
Pete Oakley	76	66	74	74	290	13,782.40
David Eger	68	73	77	72	290	13,782.40
Dave Eichelberger	74	69	73	74	290	13,782.40
Dan Halldorson	69	71	78	72	290	13,782.40
Steven Veriato	77	68	73	72	290	13,782.40

3M Championship

TPC of the Twin Cities, Blaine, Minnesota
Par 36-36–72; 7,100 yards

August 6-8
purse, $1,750,000

	SCORES			TOTAL	MONEY
Tom Kite	65	69	69	203	$262,500
Craig Stadler	64	71	69	204	154,000
Larry Nelson	70	70	66	206	105,000

	SCORES			TOTAL	MONEY
Vicente Fernandez	68	70	68	206	105,000
Tom Purtzer	64	68	74	206	105,000
Bruce Lietzke	69	72	66	207	63,000
David Eger	69	71	67	207	63,000
Sammy Rachels	65	71	71	207	63,000
Jay Sigel	69	70	69	208	49,000
Andy Bean	69	71	69	209	42,000
Don Pooley	68	72	69	209	42,000
Jim Thorpe	67	72	70	209	42,000
Bobby Wadkins	71	69	70	210	31,500
Gil Morgan	71	69	70	210	31,500
Doug Tewell	68	71	71	210	31,500
Morris Hatalsky	68	71	71	210	31,500
Dana Quigley	69	70	71	210	31,500
Howard Twitty	69	74	68	211	23,931.25
Bob Eastwood	69	73	69	211	23,931.25
Mike Reid	72	69	70	211	23,931.25
Des Smyth	68	70	73	211	23,931.25
Mark McNulty	67	73	72	212	19,308.34
Hale Irwin	67	73	72	212	19,308.33
Wayne Levi	66	72	74	212	19,308.33
Mike McCullough	71	76	66	213	15,604.17
Jim Ahern	69	75	69	213	15,604.17
Joe Inman	74	68	71	213	15,604.17
Bob Gilder	73	69	71	213	15,604.17
Fuzzy Zoeller	67	74	72	213	15,604.16
Walter Hall	70	70	73	213	15,604.16
John Harris	72	68	74	214	13,125
Bill Rogers	72	72	71	215	11,812.50
Bobby Walzel	71	73	71	215	11,812.50
Gary Koch	69	74	72	215	11,812.50
Jim Albus	67	74	74	215	11,812.50
Lonnie Nielsen	74	74	68	216	9,121.88
Dave Barr	70	77	69	216	9,121.88
Ron Streck	74	72	70	216	9,121.88
Jose Maria Canizares	71	74	71	216	9,121.88
Eamonn Darcy	67	78	71	216	9,121.87
John Jacobs	68	74	74	216	9,121.87
Bruce Summerhays	69	73	74	216	9,121.87
Allen Doyle	73	69	74	216	9,121.87

Greater Hickory Classic at Rock Barn

Rock Barn Golf & Country Club, Jones Course,
Conover, North Carolina
Par 36-36–72; 7,023 yards

August 20-22
purse, $1,600,000

	SCORES			TOTAL	MONEY
Doug Tewell	69	69	64	202	$240,000
Bruce Fleisher	70	65	68	203	140,800
Morris Hatalsky	73	67	66	206	115,200
Jerry Pate	72	67	68	207	96,000
Joe Inman	73	67	68	208	70,400
Bobby Wadkins	67	73	68	208	70,400
Larry Nelson	70	69	70	209	54,400
Eduardo Romero	72	69	68	209	54,400
Mark Lye	66	72	72	210	44,800

	SCORES			TOTAL	MONEY
Bob Charles	71	69	71	211	36,800
Allen Doyle	69	73	69	211	36,800
Gil Morgan	71	70	70	211	36,800
Lonnie Nielsen	72	70	69	211	36,800
Tom Jenkins	74	68	71	213	28,800
Dana Quigley	73	72	68	213	28,800
Sammy Rachels	74	67	72	213	28,800
Keith Fergus	72	73	69	214	20,760
Walter Hall	73	72	69	214	20,760
Don Pooley	73	70	71	214	20,760
Jay Sigel	70	70	74	214	20,760
Des Smyth	71	73	70	214	20,760
Jim Thorpe	69	71	74	214	20,760
Bobby Walzel	75	69	70	214	20,760
D.A. Weibring	73	70	71	214	20,760
Hugh Baiocchi	72	71	72	215	13,640
Andy Bean	74	72	69	215	13,640
Bob Eastwood	76	69	70	215	13,640
John Jacobs	75	69	71	215	13,640
Bobby Lincoln	79	67	69	215	13,640
Mike McCullough	73	74	68	215	13,640
Bob Ralston	72	70	73	215	13,640
Craig Stadler	71	73	71	215	13,640
Graham Marsh	76	72	68	216	9,668.58
Dave Barr	71	75	70	216	9,668.57
R.W. Eaks	74	68	74	216	9,668.57
Ed Fiori	71	73	72	216	9,668.57
Jay Overton	68	77	71	216	9,668.57
Leonard Thompson	73	70	73	216	9,668.57
Larry Ziegler	72	71	73	216	9,668.57
Pete Oakley	72	72	73	217	8,000
J.C. Snead	74	73	70	217	8,000

JELD-WEN Tradition

Reserve Vineyards & Golf Club, Aloha, Oregon
Par 36-36–72; 7,212 yards

August 26-29
purse, $2,300,000

	SCORES				TOTAL	MONEY
Craig Stadler	70	70	68	67	275	$345,000
Allen Doyle	69	72	64	71	276	183,540
Jerry Pate	73	71	66	66	276	183,540
Andy Bean	69	69	72	67	277	88,714.29
Bruce Fleisher	71	70	70	66	277	88,714.29
Tom Kite	72	71	65	69	277	88,714.29
Doug Tewell	69	70	69	69	277	88,714.29
Vicente Fernandez	67	71	66	73	277	88,714.28
Peter Jacobsen	69	66	69	73	277	88,714.28
D.A. Weibring	69	69	69	70	277	88,714.28
Bruce Lietzke	69	67	73	70	279	52,900
Gil Morgan	71	68	69	71	279	52,900
Hale Irwin	69	73	69	69	280	46,000
Morris Hatalsky	73	71	69	68	281	39,100
Gary McCord	72	70	71	68	281	39,100
Sammy Rachels	71	70	70	70	281	39,100
Dave Stockton	72	71	67	71	281	39,100
Jim Thorpe	70	70	73	68	281	39,100

	SCORES			TOTAL	MONEY
Dave Eichelberger	75	70 66	71	282	28,630.40
Walter Hall	75	69 69	69	282	28,630.40
Mark James	69	72 70	71	282	28,630.40
Tom Jenkins	69	69 72	72	282	28,630.40
Wayne Levi	73	68 73	68	282	28,630.40
John Bland	71	71 68	74	284	21,988
Jose Maria Canizares	67	71 72	74	284	21,988
Bob Gilder	72	72 70	70	284	21,988
John Harris	71	70 72	71	284	21,988
Bobby Wadkins	73	69 71	71	284	21,988
Ed Fiori	75	65 73	72	285	17,767.50
Tom Purtzer	71	70 71	73	285	17,767.50
Mike Smith	73	71 71	70	285	17,767.50
Leonard Thompson	71	75 69	70	285	17,767.50
Eamonn Darcy	72	72 71	71	286	15,180
Dana Quigley	71	74 71	70	286	15,180
Fuzzy Zoeller	68	75 71	72	286	15,180
Jim Ahern	71	75 69	72	287	12,937.50
Keith Fergus	74	69 72	72	287	12,937.50
Gary Koch	74	72 71	70	287	12,937.50
Bobby Walzel	74	70 69	74	287	12,937.50
James Mason	71	74 70	73	288	11,500
Des Smyth	73	72 72	71	288	11,500

The First Tee Open at Pebble Beach

Pebble Beach Golf Links, Pebble Beach, California
Par 36-36–72; 6,791 yards
Bayonet Golf Course, Seaside, California
Par 36-36–72; 7,117 yards

September 3-5
purse, $2,000,000

	SCORES			TOTAL	MONEY
Craig Stadler	72	63	66	201	$300,000
Jay Haas	70	66	68	204	176,000
Hale Irwin	73	66	70	209	132,000
Tom Kite	73	66	70	209	132,000
David Eger	67	73	70	210	88,000
D.A. Weibring	68	71	71	210	88,000
Ed Dougherty	71	69	71	211	68,000
Bruce Lietzke	70	74	67	211	68,000
Peter Jacobsen	70	73	69	212	52,000
Lonnie Nielsen	73	70	69	212	52,000
Doug Tewell	73	69	70	212	52,000
Bobby Wadkins	73	73	67	213	42,000
Fuzzy Zoeller	72	70	71	213	42,000
Gary Koch	70	71	73	214	35,000
Tom Purtzer	70	75	69	214	35,000
Bruce Summerhays	70	75	69	214	35,000
Jim Ahern	72	72	70	214	35,000
Bob Gilder	72	69	74	215	24,450
Morris Hatalsky	76	69	70	215	24,450
Gary McCord	71	68	76	215	24,450
Mark McCumber	71	72	72	215	24,450
Gil Morgan	72	73	70	215	24,450
Leonard Thompson	74	71	70	215	24,450
Lanny Wadkins	72	69	74	215	24,450
John Bland	74	68	73	215	24,450

	SCORES			TOTAL	MONEY
Hubert Green	73	69	74	216	18,200
Mark Lye	72	72	72	216	18,200
Dana Quigley	73	71	72	216	18,200
Jose Maria Canizares	70	72	75	217	16,200
Wayne Levi	71	74	72	217	16,200
Isao Aoki	72	75	71	218	13,500
Andy Bean	77	69	72	218	13,500
Jim Colbert	73	76	69	218	13,500
Rodger Davis	70	75	73	218	13,500
Bruce Fleisher	71	75	72	218	13,500
J.C. Snead	72	76	70	218	13,500
Mike McCullough	72	73	74	219	10,000
Jerry Pate	73	71	75	219	10,000
Mike Reid	70	75	74	219	10,000
Jim Thorpe	79	72	68	219	10,000
Tom Watson	70	76	73	219	10,000
Allen Doyle	74	71	74	219	10,000
Pete Oakley	73	74	72	219	10,000
Vicente Fernandez	73	72	74	219	10,000

Kroger Classic

TPC at River's Bend, Maineville, Ohio
Par 36-36–72; 7,063 yards

September 10-12
purse, $1,500,000

	SCORES			TOTAL	MONEY
Bruce Summerhays	67	70	64	201	$225,000
Gil Morgan	69	67	66	202	110,000
Doug Tewell	66	65	71	202	110,000
Jim Thorpe	68	68	66	202	110,000
Mike Reid	67	70	67	204	66,000
Des Smyth	65	67	72	204	66,000
David Eger	66	71	68	205	48,000
Fred Gibson	70	65	70	205	48,000
Hale Irwin	69	67	69	205	48,000
Rodger Davis	69	69	68	206	34,500
John Harris	69	70	67	206	34,500
Gary McCord	65	69	72	206	34,500
D.A. Weibring	70	68	68	206	34,500
Stewart Ginn	70	69	68	207	24,775
Walter Hall	71	68	68	207	24,775
Mark Johnson	74	64	69	207	24,775
Mike McCullough	71	70	66	207	24,775
Jack Spradlin	69	69	69	207	24,775
Fuzzy Zoeller	69	70	68	207	24,775
Jose Maria Canizares	69	68	71	208	18,600
Gary Koch	71	71	66	208	18,600
Bobby Lincoln	69	69	70	208	18,600
Dave Barr	71	70	68	209	14,700
Tom Kite	66	72	71	209	14,700
Graham Marsh	72	67	70	209	14,700
James Mason	69	70	70	209	14,700
Bob Murphy	67	69	73	209	14,700
Jay Overton	77	67	65	209	14,700
R.W. Eaks	70	70	70	210	11,340
Wayne Levi	71	68	71	210	11,340
Jerry McGee	69	73	68	210	11,340

	SCORES			TOTAL	MONEY
Sammy Rachels	72	70	68	210	11,340
Mike Smith	67	70	73	210	11,340
Andy Bean	70	70	71	211	9,030
Mark James	69	69	73	211	9,030
Lonnie Nielsen	67	74	70	211	9,030
Jerry Pate	68	71	72	211	9,030
Dana Quigley	70	75	66	211	9,030
John Bland	71	71	70	212	7,950
Jim Albus	70	70	73	213	7,350
Bob Gilder	68	69	76	213	7,350
Tom Wargo	68	71	74	213	7,350

SAS Championship

Prestonwood Country Club, Cary, North Carolina
Par 36-36–72; 7,129 yards

September 24-26
purse, $1,800,000

	SCORES			TOTAL	MONEY
Craig Stadler	65	68	66	199	$270,000
Tom Jenkins	72	65	68	205	158,400
Jose Maria Canizares	71	71	66	208	118,800
Doug Tewell	68	73	67	208	118,800
John Harris	69	70	70	209	74,400
Larry Nelson	69	71	69	209	74,400
Lonnie Nielsen	72	68	69	209	74,400
Walter Hall	71	70	69	210	51,600
Wayne Levi	67	73	70	210	51,600
D.A. Weibring	67	72	71	210	51,600
Allen Doyle	71	70	70	211	41,400
Mike Reid	72	69	70	211	41,400
Des Smyth	69	72	71	212	36,000
Vicente Fernandez	72	72	69	213	31,500
Tom Kite	70	71	72	213	31,500
James Mason	71	71	71	213	31,500
Gary McCord	69	73	71	213	31,500
Andy Bean	71	71	72	214	23,868
David Eger	70	73	71	214	23,868
Stewart Ginn	69	70	75	214	23,868
Joe Inman	70	75	69	214	23,868
Jim Thorpe	72	74	68	214	23,868
John Bland	72	75	68	215	18,036
Ed Dougherty	73	73	69	215	18,036
Ed Fiori	72	74	69	215	18,036
Mike McCullough	72	73	70	215	18,036
Gil Morgan	71	71	73	215	18,036
Keith Fergus	75	70	71	216	13,950
Bruce Fleisher	72	73	71	216	13,950
Raymond Floyd	70	72	74	216	13,950
Jay Sigel	70	74	72	216	13,950
Leonard Thompson	73	72	71	216	13,950
Lanny Wadkins	72	73	71	216	13,950
Dave Barr	70	74	73	217	10,836
Fred Gibson	74	73	70	217	10,836
Pete Oakley	74	72	71	217	10,836
J.C. Snead	75	70	72	217	10,836
Bobby Walzel	79	70	68	217	10,836
Jim Ahern	71	75	72	218	8,640

	SCORES			TOTAL	MONEY
Terry Dill	71	75	72	218	8,640
Morris Hatalsky	74	73	71	218	8,640
Don Pooley	72	74	72	218	8,640
Dana Quigley	74	73	71	218	8,640
Bruce Summerhays	74	71	73	218	8,640

Constellation Energy Classic

Hayfields Country Club, Hunt Valley, Maryland
Par 36-36–72; 7,060 yards

October 1-3
purse, $1,600,000

	SCORES			TOTAL	MONEY
Wayne Levi	64	68	68	200	$240,000
Hale Irwin	68	70	64	202	140,800
Rodger Davis	65	71	67	203	115,200
Graham Marsh	68	66	70	204	86,400
Jim Thorpe	71	69	64	204	86,400
Jerry Pate	70	66	69	205	60,800
D.A. Weibring	72	67	66	205	60,800
Jose Maria Canizares	68	66	72	206	48,000
Jay Overton	69	70	67	206	48,000
Gil Morgan	68	67	72	207	40,000
Tom Watson	68	68	71	207	40,000
R.W. Eaks	70	69	69	208	30,720
Bruce Fleisher	73	66	69	208	30,720
Bob Gilder	68	67	73	208	30,720
Tom Kite	68	71	69	208	30,720
Tom McKnight	70	68	70	208	30,720
David Eger	71	69	69	209	21,325.72
Peter Jacobsen	72	69	68	209	21,325.72
Lonnie Nielsen	71	69	69	209	21,325.72
Jim Ahern	69	68	72	209	21,325.71
Vicente Fernandez	71	66	72	209	21,325.71
John Harris	70	69	70	209	21,325.71
Eduardo Romero	67	71	71	209	21,325.71
Jim Albus	69	72	69	210	14,960
Joe Inman	67	73	70	210	14,960
Tom Jenkins	69	71	70	210	14,960
Mark McNulty	68	68	74	210	14,960
Dana Quigley	70	70	70	210	14,960
Des Smyth	68	69	73	210	14,960
Hugh Baiocchi	72	69	70	211	11,306.67
Andy Bean	69	72	70	211	11,306.67
Allen Doyle	70	71	70	211	11,306.67
Dave Eichelberger	70	72	69	211	11,306.67
Bruce Lietzke	68	70	73	211	11,306.66
Bobby Lincoln	71	68	72	211	11,306.66
Dave Barr	72	72	68	212	9,000
Keith Fergus	70	71	71	212	9,000
Jay Sigel	72	70	70	212	9,000
Lanny Wadkins	70	70	72	212	9,000
Mark Lye	74	68	71	213	7,520
Mike McCullough	70	71	72	213	7,520
Sammy Rachels	72	70	71	213	7,520
Mike Reid	71	71	71	213	7,520
Rocky Thompson	74	69	70	213	7,520

Administaff Small Business Classic

Augusta Pines Golf Club, Spring, Texas
Par 36-36–72; 7,060 yards

October 8-10
purse, $1,600,000

	SCORES			TOTAL	MONEY
Larry Nelson	68	70	64	202	$240,000
Hale Irwin	67	68	67	202	140,800
(Nelson defeated Irwin on first playoff hole.)					
Peter Jacobsen	69	67	67	203	105,600
Wayne Levi	64	67	72	203	105,600
Morris Hatalsky	68	69	68	205	66,133.34
Jim Dent	66	70	69	205	66,133.33
Jim Thorpe	67	69	69	205	66,133.33
David Eger	68	70	68	206	44,000
Mark Johnson	70	67	69	206	44,000
Tom Kite	67	70	69	206	44,000
Des Smyth	68	70	68	206	44,000
Vicente Fernandez	69	70	68	207	31,600
Walter Hall	64	72	71	207	31,600
Bill Rogers	68	71	68	207	31,600
Bobby Walzel	69	69	69	207	31,600
Allen Doyle	69	70	69	208	25,600
Bob Gilder	68	69	71	208	25,600
D.A. Weibring	68	65	75	208	25,600
Rodger Davis	71	68	70	209	20,520
Keith Fergus	73	65	71	209	20,520
Tom Jenkins	69	72	68	209	20,520
Doug Tewell	72	73	64	209	20,520
Jim Ahern	68	70	72	210	16,032
Bruce Lietzke	72	68	70	210	16,032
James Mason	70	68	72	210	16,032
Mark McNulty	69	71	70	210	16,032
Bruce Summerhays	71	70	69	210	16,032
John Bland	71	68	72	211	12,400
Graham Marsh	73	69	69	211	12,400
Gary McCord	69	72	70	211	12,400
Mark McCumber	70	71	70	211	12,400
Jerry Pate	69	70	72	211	12,400
Craig Stadler	69	71	71	211	12,400
Jose Maria Canizares	72	72	68	212	9,632
Mark James	71	68	73	212	9,632
Gary Koch	73	68	71	212	9,632
Lanny Wadkins	69	71	72	212	9,632
Fuzzy Zoeller	69	70	73	212	9,632
Jim Colbert	69	73	71	213	7,840
Dale Douglass	71	69	73	213	7,840
Lonnie Nielsen	74	69	70	213	7,840
Jay Sigel	68	77	68	213	7,840
Dave Stockton	69	70	74	213	7,840

SBC Championship

Oak Hills Country Club, San Antonio, Texas
Par 35-36–71; 6,671 yards

October 15-17
purse, $1,500,000

	SCORES			TOTAL	MONEY
Mark McNulty	67	63	65	195	$225,000
Gary McCord	68	66	69	203	132,000
Bobby Wadkins	70	67	67	204	108,000
Bruce Fleisher	69	66	70	205	74,000
Tom Kite	66	71	68	205	74,000
Dave Stockton	66	71	68	205	74,000
Morris Hatalsky	68	66	72	206	48,000
Larry Nelson	70	69	67	206	48,000
Dana Quigley	68	66	72	206	48,000
Hale Irwin	68	70	69	207	37,500
Darrell Kestner	70	67	70	207	37,500
Allen Doyle	68	67	73	208	28,800
Mike Hill	71	70	67	208	28,800
Tom Jenkins	66	73	69	208	28,800
Wayne Levi	73	67	68	208	28,800
Craig Stadler	74	64	70	208	28,800
John Bland	71	68	70	209	19,462.50
Bob Gilder	69	68	72	209	19,462.50
Bruce Lietzke	72	67	70	209	19,462.50
Jay Sigel	68	72	69	209	19,462.50
Des Smyth	68	71	70	209	19,462.50
J.C. Snead	71	70	68	209	19,462.50
Doug Tewell	70	68	71	209	19,462.50
Jim Thorpe	67	76	66	209	19,462.50
Gil Morgan	77	62	71	210	14,300
Lonnie Nielsen	68	72	70	210	14,300
Fuzzy Zoeller	70	73	67	210	14,300
Vicente Fernandez	69	70	72	211	12,150
Walter Hall	71	70	70	211	12,150
Bob Murphy	70	69	72	211	12,150
Ron Streck	69	69	73	211	12,150
Dave Barr	68	72	72	212	9,900
Joe Inman	68	73	71	212	9,900
Gary Koch	71	70	71	212	9,900
James Mason	66	73	73	212	9,900
Mike Smith	71	72	69	212	9,900
Isao Aoki	71	70	72	213	7,350
Bob Charles	69	76	68	213	7,350
Ben Crenshaw	70	69	74	213	7,350
Ed Dougherty	73	68	72	213	7,350
Ed Fiori	74	70	69	213	7,350
Peter Jacobsen	70	70	73	213	7,350
Jerry Pate	68	76	69	213	7,350
Bill Rogers	75	72	66	213	7,350
Leonard Thompson	71	70	72	213	7,350

Charles Schwab Cup Championship

Sonoma Golf Club, Sonoma, California
Par 36-36–72; 7,069 yards

October 21-24
purse, $2,500,000

	SCORES				TOTAL	MONEY
Mark McNulty	69	74	68	66	277	$440,000
Tom Kite	64	70	72	72	278	254,000
Allen Doyle	71	73	67	69	280	213,000
Peter Jacobsen	69	70	76	67	282	176,000
Jose Maria Canizares	68	70	70	75	283	128,500
David Eger	74	67	73	69	283	128,500
Morris Hatalsky	68	67	77	72	284	85,200
Hale Irwin	66	69	74	75	284	85,200
Craig Stadler	68	73	73	70	284	85,200
Jim Thorpe	76	67	72	69	284	85,200
D.A. Weibring	71	75	73	65	284	85,200
Dana Quigley	65	70	77	73	285	64,000
Bruce Fleisher	78	72	70	66	286	55,333.34
Gil Morgan	73	70	75	68	286	55,333.33
Bobby Wadkins	73	71	71	71	286	55,333.33
Bruce Lietzke	70	76	74	67	287	47,500
Fuzzy Zoeller	75	68	72	72	287	47,500
Bob Gilder	74	72	72	70	288	41,750
Jerry Pate	69	71	77	71	288	41,750
Vicente Fernandez	78	72	73	66	289	37,000
Wayne Levi	71	74	72	72	289	37,000
Mark James	71	73	73	73	290	31,250
Graham Marsh	72	70	76	72	290	31,250
Tom Purtzer	73	76	71	70	290	31,250
Bruce Summerhays	72	71	70	77	290	31,250
Larry Nelson	77	72	72	70	291	27,000
Ed Fiori	72	75	73	77	297	26,000
Andy Bean	77	73	74	74	298	25,000
Tom Jenkins	71	72	78	78	299	24,500
Doug Tewell	74	78			WD	

European Seniors Tour

Tobago Plantations Seniors Classic

Tobago Plantations Beach & Golf Resort, Tobago
Par 36-36–72; 6,752 yards

March 19-21
purse, €183,980

	SCORES			TOTAL	MONEY
Carl Mason	71	64	72	207	€27,596.63
David Good	72	71	67	210	18,397.75
Jeff Hawkes	73	70	69	212	11,498.59
Terry Gale	75	68	69	212	11,498.59
John Chillas	70	70	73	213	7,837.44
Horacio Carbonetti	71	71	71	213	7,837.44
Ian Mosey	77	70	67	214	5,887.28
Luis Carbonetti	71	74	69	214	5,887.28
Hank Woodrome	72	70	72	214	5,887.28
Manuel Pinero	71	72	72	215	4,415.46
Craig Defoy	71	72	72	215	4,415.46
Jeff Van Wagenen	77	70	68	215	4,415.46
Denis Durnian	71	72	73	216	3,495.57
John Benda	73	73	70	216	3,495.57
Delroy Cambridge	74	70	72	216	3,495.57
Nick Job	71	73	73	217	2,856.25
John Morgan	77	73	67	217	2,856.25
Martin Foster	71	73	73	217	2,856.25
Priscillo Diniz	73	70	74	217	2,856.25
Giuseppe Cali	72	76	70	218	2,354.91
John Grace	69	74	75	218	2,354.91
Bill Longmuir	71	72	76	219	1,850.29
Craig Maltman	74	71	74	219	1,850.29
Mike Miller	71	76	72	219	1,850.29
Bob Larratt	71	75	73	219	1,850.29
David Oakley	71	75	73	219	1,850.29
Mike Ferguson	72	73	74	219	1,850.29
Pete Oakley	75	72	72	219	1,850.29
Denis O'Sullivan	73	78	69	220	1,453.42
John Irwin	73	74	73	220	1,453.42
Alan Mew	72	74	74	220	1,453.42

DGM Barbados Open

Royal Westmoreland Golf Club, St. James, Barbados
Par 36-36–72; 6,745 yards

March 26-28
purse, €187,393

	SCORES			TOTAL	MONEY
Gavan Levenson	69	64	71	204	€29,231.43
Denis Durnian	69	67	70	206	16,562.74
Carl Mason	69	69	68	206	16,562.74
Bill Longmuir	71	68	69	208	9,763.01
Noel Ratcliffe	68	71	69	208	9,763.01
Luis Carbonetti	70	70	69	209	7,405.07

	SCORES			TOTAL	MONEY
Horacio Carbonetti	68	69	72	209	7,405.07
Tommy Horton	71	71	68	210	5,586.29
Nick Job	75	68	67	210	5,586.29
Martin Gray	71	67	72	210	5,586.29
Giuseppe Cali	70	70	71	211	3,897.41
Alan Tapie	72	71	68	211	3,897.41
Guillermo Encina	70	69	72	211	3,897.41
Jim Rhodes	70	68	73	211	3,897.41
Jerry Bruner	74	65	72	211	3,897.41
Brian Jones	71	71	69	211	3,897.41
Mike Miller	71	72	70	213	2,840.24
Ray Carrasco	68	70	75	213	2,840.24
David Good	68	71	74	213	2,840.24
Delroy Cambridge	75	71	67	213	2,840.24
John Morgan	66	72	76	214	2,338.45
John Grace	72	70	72	214	2,338.45
Terry Gale	71	69	76	216	2,046.14
Jeff Van Wagenen	76	70	70	216	2,046.14
Steve Stull	79	69	68	216	2,046.14
Antonio Garrido	72	70	75	217	1,851.27
Manuel Pinero	73	73	72	218	1,656.40
David Oakley	74	70	74	218	1,656.40
Dragon Taki	72	72	74	218	1,656.40
Gary Wintz	72	73	73	218	1,656.40
John Chillas	74	72	73	219	1,432.30
Bob Cameron	76	71	72	219	1,432.30

Open de France Seniors

Omaha Beach Golf Club, Normandy, France
Par 36-36–72; 6,738 yards

May 7-9
purse, €200,000

	SCORES			TOTAL	MONEY
Bob Cameron	70	73	67	210	€30,000
David J. Russell	69	76	68	213	20,000
Manuel Pinero	71	75	68	214	12,500
John Chillas	72	71	71	214	12,500
Denis Durnian	73	73	69	215	8,080
Brian Jones	71	72	72	215	8,080
David Good	70	74	71	215	8,080
Neil Coles	71	74	71	216	5,500
Nick Job	72	74	70	216	5,500
Eddie Polland	71	73	72	216	5,500
Pete Oakley	73	74	69	216	5,500
Tommy Horton	73	73	72	218	3,840
Martin Gray	72	75	71	218	3,840
Denis O'Sullivan	76	75	67	218	3,840
Jeff Van Wagenen	71	75	72	218	3,840
John Benda	73	75	70	218	3,840
Mike Miller	72	74	73	219	3,007
Gery Watine	73	71	75	219	3,007
Malcolm Gregson	73	79	67	219	3,007
Bill Longmuir	72	76	72	220	2,410
Chris Moody	71	77	72	220	2,410
Jim Rhodes	74	74	72	220	2,410
Seiji Ebihara	71	75	74	220	2,410
Maurice Bembridge	71	80	70	221	1,955

	SCORES			TOTAL	MONEY
Terry Gale	73	77	71	221	1,955
Jerry Bruner	78	74	69	221	1,955
Mike Ferguson	75	74	72	221	1,955
Noel Ratcliffe	70	80	72	222	1,584
Giuseppe Cali	75	75	72	222	1,584
Luis Carbonetti	75	72	75	222	1,584
Horacio Carbonetti	73	77	72	222	1,584
Steve Stull	70	75	77	222	1,584

Bosch Italian Seniors Open

Golf Club Venezia, Venezia, Italy
Par 35-37–72; 6,604 yards

May 14-16
purse, €160,152

	SCORES			TOTAL	MONEY
Terry Gale	69	74	68	211	€24,000
David J. Russell	74	67	71	212	16,000
Gavan Levenson	69	72	72	213	10,000
John Chillas	73	70	70	213	10,000
Alan Tapie	73	71	71	215	7,232
David Oakley	75	71	70	216	5,760
Brian Jones	74	72	70	216	5,760
David Good	74	70	72	216	5,760
Denis Durnian	75	71	71	217	4,320
Mike Ferguson	73	73	71	217	4,320
Jerry Bruner	73	76	69	218	3,296
Horacio Carbonetti	70	74	74	218	3,296
John Grace	75	74	69	218	3,296
Gary Wintz	71	74	73	218	3,296
Pete Oakley	75	73	70	218	3,296
Nick Job	77	74	68	219	2,560
John Morgan	71	76	72	219	2,560
Giuseppe Cali	73	75	71	219	2,560
Eamonn Darcy	71	73	76	220	1,892.57
Tommy Horton	75	71	74	220	1,892.57
Noel Ratcliffe	71	75	74	220	1,892.57
Alberto Croce	73	73	74	220	1,892.57
Bob Cameron	75	73	72	220	1,892.57
Priscillo Diniz	75	70	75	220	1,892.57
Alan Mew	75	72	73	220	1,892.57
Maurice Bembridge	74	70	77	221	1,456
Jim Rhodes	73	74	74	221	1,456
Hank Woodrome	70	71	80	221	1,456
Bill Hardwick	73	73	76	222	1,236
Stephen Chadwick	75	76	71	222	1,236
Delroy Cambridge	72	74	76	222	1,236
Bruce Heuchan	72	80	70	222	1,236

Digicel Jamaica Classic

Half Moon Golf Club, Montego Bay, Jamaica
Par 36-36–72; 6,738 yards

May 21-23
purse, €233,030

	SCORES			TOTAL	MONEY
Luis Carbonetti	63	75	70	208	€34,954.59
Terry Gale	68	69	71	208	23,303.06
(Carbonetti defeated Gale on first playoff hole.)					
Delroy Cambridge	69	69	71	209	16,312.14
Carl Mason	73	70	67	210	10,890.30
Bob Cameron	69	74	67	210	10,890.30
David Good	73	69	68	210	10,890.30
Jerry Bruner	68	71	72	211	7,923.04
Philippe Dugeny	70	66	75	211	7,923.04
Nick Job	72	70	71	213	6,524.86
Paul Reed	73	70	71	214	6,058.80
Ian Mosey	71	69	75	215	5,592.73
Gery Watine	70	74	72	216	4,474.19
Alan Tapie	70	73	73	216	4,474.19
Jay Dolan	71	75	70	216	4,474.19
Neville Clarke	72	71	73	216	4,474.19
Pete Oakley	69	73	74	216	4,474.19
Denis Durnian	71	73	73	217	3,295.05
Martin Gray	72	75	70	217	3,295.05
Giuseppe Cali	76	70	71	217	3,295.05
Simon Owen	71	74	72	217	3,295.05
Barry Vivian	69	75	73	217	3,295.05
Noel Ratcliffe	72	70	76	218	2,703.16
Bill Longmuir	72	74	73	219	2,334.97
Mike Miller	76	72	71	219	2,334.97
Gavan Levenson	74	70	75	219	2,334.97
Denis O'Sullivan	73	76	70	219	2,334.97
John Grace	72	77	70	219	2,334.97
Antonio Garrido	75	72	73	220	1,656.85
Ray Carrasco	76	72	72	220	1,656.85
Bill Hardwick	75	71	74	220	1,656.85
David Oakley	73	70	77	220	1,656.85
Horacio Carbonetti	73	73	74	220	1,656.85
John Mashego	73	74	73	220	1,656.85
Mike Ferguson	73	75	72	220	1,656.85
Gary Wintz	77	71	72	220	1,656.85
Steve Stull	77	77	66	220	1,656.85
Alan Mew	73	72	75	220	1,656.85

AIB Irish Seniors Open

Adare Manor Hotel & Golf Resort, Adare, Ireland
Par 36-36–72; 6,762 yards

June 4-6
purse, €330,930

	SCORES			TOTAL	MONEY
Carl Mason	68	69	69	206	€49,500
Nick Job	69	68	70	207	33,000
Noel Ratcliffe	70	67	74	211	20,625
Gery Watine	72	70	69	211	20,625
Seiji Ebihara	70	73	69	212	14,057.50
David Good	67	73	72	212	14,057.50

	SCORES			TOTAL	MONEY
Bill Longmuir	72	71	70	213	11,220
Giuseppe Cali	72	71	70	213	11,220
Simon Owen	74	73	67	214	8,910
Delroy Cambridge	70	74	70	214	8,910
John Morgan	70	73	72	215	7,260
Luis Carbonetti	71	73	71	215	7,260
Jerry Bruner	73	70	72	215	7,260
Craig Maltman	73	71	72	216	5,775
Mike Miller	71	73	72	216	5,775
Gavan Levenson	72	76	68	216	5,775
Bob Lendzion	73	73	70	216	5,775
Terry Gale	73	77	67	217	4,375.80
Guillermo Encina	75	70	72	217	4,375.80
Priscillo Diniz	73	73	71	217	4,375.80
Pete Oakley	71	71	75	217	4,375.80
Bruce Heuchan	72	74	71	217	4,375.80
Denis Durnian	72	76	70	218	3,465
John Grace	74	71	73	218	3,465
Dragon Taki	73	73	72	218	3,465
Alan Tapie	70	75	75	220	2,870.80
Bill Hardwick	72	76	72	220	2,870.80
David Oakley	74	73	73	220	2,870.80
Jay Dolan	74	72	74	220	2,870.80
Barry Vivian	75	72	73	220	2,870.80

Irvine Whitlock Jersey Seniors Classic

La Moye Golf Club, Jersey, England
Par 36-36–72; 6,581 yards

June 11-13
purse, €179,804

	SCORES			TOTAL	MONEY
Jim Rhodes	66	67	72	205	€27,397.70
John Chillas	68	67	73	208	18,265.13
Ray Carrasco	69	71	69	209	12,788.59
Maurice Bembridge	70	72	69	211	10,045.97
Bob Cameron	69	73	70	212	7,781.06
Delroy Cambridge	70	70	72	212	7,781.06
Nick Job	74	64	76	214	5,844.93
Simon Owen	72	66	76	214	5,844.93
Pip Elson	74	73	67	214	5,844.93
Bill Longmuir	68	69	78	215	4,054.92
Craig Maltman	74	72	69	215	4,054.92
David J. Russell	69	73	73	215	4,054.92
Luis Carbonetti	74	72	69	215	4,054.92
David Oakley	73	71	71	215	4,054.92
Craig Defoy	71	74	71	216	3,105.12
Noboru Sugai	72	70	74	216	3,105.12
Steve Stull	69	69	78	216	3,105.12
Denis Durnian	74	70	73	217	2,497.80
Gavan Levenson	75	70	72	217	2,497.80
Bill Hardwick	76	71	70	217	2,497.80
Eddie Polland	68	72	77	217	2,497.80
Giuseppe Cali	70	76	72	218	1,968.10
Malcolm Gregson	75	71	72	218	1,968.10
Priscillo Diniz	72	73	73	218	1,968.10
Hank Woodrome	72	73	73	218	1,968.10
Ian Mosey	70	78	71	219	1,486.36

	SCORES			TOTAL	MONEY
Gery Watine	72	72	75	219	1,486.36
Martin Gray	76	72	71	219	1,486.36
Brian Jones	73	73	73	219	1,486.36
Horacio Carbonetti	70	75	74	219	1,486.36
David Creamer	67	77	75	219	1,486.36
Mike Ferguson	71	72	76	219	1,486.36
Pete Oakley	74	69	76	219	1,486.36

The Mobile Cup

Oxfordshire Golf Club, Oxfordshire, England
Par 36-36–72; 6,868 yards

June 18-20
purse, €189,150

	SCORES			TOTAL	MONEY
Bill Longmuir	72	68	67	207	€29,333.38
Seiji Ebihara	70	71	67	208	19,558.11
Mike Miller	71	64	74	209	13,686.89
Giuseppe Cali	72	70	68	210	10,756.05
Martin Gray	73	71	67	211	7,490.13
Luis Carbonetti	68	69	74	211	7,490.13
Bill Hardwick	71	66	74	211	7,490.13
Steve Stull	68	73	70	211	7,490.13
Ian Mosey	71	69	72	212	4,693.56
Simon Owen	71	68	73	212	4,693.56
Denis O'Sullivan	70	69	73	212	4,693.56
Horacio Carbonetti	74	69	69	212	4,693.56
Mike Ferguson	73	71	68	212	4,693.56
Gery Watine	68	74	71	213	3,520.17
John Chillas	72	70	71	213	3,520.17
Bob Cameron	68	72	73	213	3,520.17
Denis Durnian	73	72	69	214	2,765.29
Ray Carrasco	74	68	72	214	2,765.29
Guillermo Encina	71	73	70	214	2,765.29
David Creamer	70	75	69	214	2,765.29
Pete Oakley	73	71	70	214	2,765.29
Jeff Hawkes	72	71	72	215	2,107.21
Noel Ratcliffe	69	73	73	215	2,107.21
Delroy Cambridge	72	72	71	215	2,107.21
Bruce Heuchan	70	72	73	215	2,107.21
Manuel Pinero	69	68	79	216	1,780.07
Gavan Levenson	70	73	73	216	1,780.07
John Benda	77	69	70	216	1,780.07
John Morgan	74	72	71	217	1,584.08
David Oakley	69	74	74	217	1,584.08

De Vere Northumberland Seniors Classic

De Vere Slaley Hall, Hexham, England
Par 36-36–72; 6,838 yards

June 25-27
purse, €227,363

	SCORES			TOTAL	MONEY
Malcolm Gregson	69	68	73	210	€34,104.60
Seiji Ebihara	68	76	68	212	22,736.40
David J. Russell	67	72	74	213	12,899.12
Luis Carbonetti	72	69	72	213	12,899.12

	SCORES			TOTAL	MONEY
Bob Cameron	71	74	68	213	12,899.12
Brian Jones	67	73	74	214	8,639.83
Delroy Cambridge	71	74	69	214	8,639.83
Simon Owen	69	76	70	215	6,820.92
John Grace	71	72	72	215	6,820.92
Noel Ratcliffe	72	73	71	216	5,229.37
David Oakley	73	72	71	216	5,229.37
John Chillas	66	76	74	216	5,229.37
Priscillo Diniz	69	74	73	216	5,229.37
Ian Mosey	71	72	74	217	3,865.19
Martin Gray	74	72	71	217	3,865.19
Guillermo Encina	72	76	69	217	3,865.19
Horacio Carbonetti	73	73	71	217	3,865.19
Steve Stull	73	74	70	217	3,865.19
Denis Durnian	73	70	75	218	2,832.95
Nick Job	76	72	70	218	2,832.95
Mike Miller	72	75	71	218	2,832.95
Jim Rhodes	73	72	73	218	2,832.95
Pete Oakley	73	73	72	218	2,832.95
Maurice Bembridge	73	74	72	219	2,273.64
John Morgan	75	73	71	219	2,273.64
Denis O'Sullivan	76	69	74	219	2,273.64
Tommy Horton	73	72	75	220	1,845.44
Craig Maltman	74	70	76	220	1,845.44
Pip Elson	72	74	74	220	1,845.44
Bill Hardwick	71	75	74	220	1,845.44
Mike Ferguson	75	74	71	220	1,845.44
Bruce Heuchan	72	75	73	220	1,845.44

Ryder Cup Wales Seniors Open

Royal St. David's Golf Club, Harlech, Wales
Par 36-33–69; 6,565 yards

July 2-4
purse, €753,732

	SCORES			TOTAL	MONEY
Ray Carrasco	68	68	67	203	€112,503
David Oakley	70	67	67	204	75,002
Simon Owen	66	71	69	206	46,876.25
Bob Lendzion	72	67	67	206	46,876.25
Jim Rhodes	72	69	66	207	33,900.91
John Grace	73	70	67	210	28,500.76
David Good	68	73	69	210	28,500.76
Maurice Bembridge	71	70	70	211	19,800.53
Nick Job	75	69	67	211	19,800.53
Liam Higgins	73	71	67	211	19,800.53
Terry Gale	72	72	67	211	19,800.53
Pete Oakley	72	68	71	211	19,800.53
Bob Charles	72	70	70	212	14,250.38
Denis Durnian	69	70	73	212	14,250.38
Paul Leonard	71	71	70	212	14,250.38
Bob Cameron	74	76	63	213	12,375.33
David Creamer	74	72	67	213	12,375.33
Bill Longmuir	72	72	70	214	9,945.27
Noel Ratcliffe	66	77	71	214	9,945.27
Denis O'Sullivan	70	74	70	214	9,945.27
John Mashego	73	72	69	214	9,945.27
Bruce Heuchan	75	68	71	214	9,945.27

	SCORES			TOTAL	MONEY
Luis Carbonetti	72	72	71	215	7,875.21
Hank Woodrome	72	74	69	215	7,875.21
Steve Stull	76	74	65	215	7,875.21
Bernard Gallacher	74	71	71	216	6,525.17
Carl Mason	74	71	71	216	6,525.17
Giuseppe Cali	71	73	72	216	6,525.17
Seiji Ebihara	75	73	68	216	6,525.17
Kenjiro Iwama	71	73	72	216	6,525.17

Nigel Mansell Sunseeker International Classic

Woodbury Park Hotel & Country Club, Exeter, England
Par 36-36–72; 6,722 yards

July 9-11
purse, €223,255

	SCORES			TOTAL	MONEY
Seiji Ebihara	70	67	66	203	€33,456.60
David Oakley	67	70	68	205	22,304.40
Tommy Horton	69	69	69	207	13,940.25
Carl Mason	69	68	70	207	13,940.25
Mike Miller	68	71	69	208	10,081.59
Ian Mosey	69	70	70	209	8,921.76
Bob Shearer	67	72	71	210	7,137.41
David Good	71	69	70	210	7,137.41
Dragon Taki	69	69	72	210	7,137.41
Delroy Cambridge	73	69	69	211	5,799.14
Tony Allen	71	69	72	212	5,353.06
Maurice Bembridge	72	69	72	213	4,046.66
Nick Job	73	69	71	213	4,046.66
Craig Maltman	70	71	72	213	4,046.66
Terry Gale	73	69	71	213	4,046.66
Paul Leonard	71	68	74	213	4,046.66
Jim Rhodes	70	74	69	213	4,046.66
Jerry Bruner	72	69	72	213	4,046.66
Denis Durnian	69	74	71	214	2,638.29
John Morgan	68	76	70	214	2,638.29
David J. Russell	69	73	72	214	2,638.29
Hank Woodrome	68	72	74	214	2,638.29
Steve Stull	71	69	74	214	2,638.29
Pete Oakley	74	71	69	214	2,638.29
Bruce Heuchan	71	73	70	214	2,638.29
Jeff Hawkes	78	69	68	215	1,854.45
Noel Ratcliffe	68	73	74	215	1,854.45
Simon Owen	77	67	71	215	1,854.45
Manuel Velasco	72	69	74	215	1,854.45
John Chillas	72	71	72	215	1,854.45
John Mashego	72	74	69	215	1,854.45
Mike Ferguson	74	74	67	215	1,854.45

Senior British Open

Royal Portrush Golf Club, Portrush, N. Ireland
Par 36-36–72; 6,822 yards

July 22-25
purse, €1,504,220

	SCORES				TOTAL	MONEY
Pete Oakley	73	68	73	70	284	€237,365.90
Eduardo Romero	69	75	74	67	285	123,722.10
Tom Kite	71	71	74	69	285	123,722.10
Mark James	72	70	74	70	286	71,224.82
Mark McNulty	72	69	74	72	287	55,099.58
Don Pooley	69	72	74	72	287	55,099.58
Bill Longmuir	71	71	76	72	290	42,719.85
Carl Mason	70	71	81	69	291	35,574.80
Sam Torrance	72	73	78	69	292	27,745.34
Bruce Summerhays	73	73	75	71	292	27,745.34
Graham Marsh	76	73	72	71	292	27,745.34
Bobby Lincoln	78	69	73	72	292	27,745.34
Giuseppe Cali	76	70	76	71	293	21,405.05
Andy Bean	72	75	75	71	293	21,405.05
Des Smyth	74	76	71	72	293	21,405.05
John Grace	72	73	75	73	293	21,405.05
Hugh Baiocchi	71	77	74	72	294	19,073.51
David Good	75	73	75	72	295	17,554.25
Seiji Ebihara	75	72	76	72	295	17,554.25
Bruce Fleisher	71	76	76	72	295	17,554.25
Morris Hatalsky	75	74	74	72	295	17,554.25
Mike Ferguson	72	77	79	69	297	14,624.78
Isao Aoki	76	75	77	69	297	14,624.78
John Chillas	69	75	83	70	297	14,624.78
Lonnie Nielsen	76	76	73	72	297	14,624.78
Dana Quigley	73	71	80	73	297	14,624.78
Jim Rhodes	69	77	77	74	297	14,624.78
Tom Watson	75	74	74	74	297	14,624.78
Bruce Heuchan	72	75	75	75	297	14,624.78
John Bland	75	77	75	71	298	12,134.04
John Jacobs	71	76	78	73	298	12,134.04
Noel Ratcliffe	73	73	78	74	298	12,134.04

Bad Ragaz PGA Seniors Open

Bad Ragaz Golf Club, Zurich, Switzerland
Par 35-35–70; 6,123 yards

July 29-31
purse, €190,000

	SCORES			TOTAL	MONEY
Horacio Carbonetti	66	65	64	195	€28,500
Denis Durnian	62	68	65	195	19,000
(Carbonetti defeated Durnian on first playoff hole.)					
Bill Longmuir	70	66	65	201	11,875
Giuseppe Cali	69	65	67	201	11,875
Luis Carbonetti	69	67	66	202	8,588
David Oakley	70	68	65	203	6,840
John Chillas	66	69	68	203	6,840
Bob Cameron	65	68	70	203	6,840
Tommy Horton	68	67	69	204	4,132.50
Nick Job	66	69	69	204	4,132.50
Ian Mosey	71	67	66	204	4,132.50

	SCORES			TOTAL	MONEY
Noel Ratcliffe	68	68	68	204	4,132.50
Martin Gray	69	65	70	204	4,132.50
John Mashego	66	70	68	204	4,132.50
Seiji Ebihara	70	64	70	204	4,132.50
Dragon Taki	73	64	67	204	4,132.50
Carl Mason	71	65	69	205	2,532.43
Gavan Levenson	71	69	65	205	2,532.43
Guillermo Encina	67	70	68	205	2,532.43
David Good	70	69	66	205	2,532.43
Barry Vivian	68	68	69	205	2,532.43
Delroy Cambridge	68	67	70	205	2,532.43
Steve Stull	67	71	67	205	2,532.43
Simon Owen	67	72	67	206	1,995
Craig Maltman	70	70	67	207	1,732.80
Denis O'Sullivan	71	67	69	207	1,732.80
Neville Clarke	70	69	68	207	1,732.80
Alan Mew	69	73	65	207	1,732.80
John Curtis	69	71	67	207	1,732.80
Bob Charles	69	70	69	208	1,401.25
Malcolm Gregson	69	72	67	208	1,401.25
Jim Rhodes	68	69	71	208	1,401.25
Paul Reed	72	70	66	208	1,401.25

De Vere PGA Seniors Championship

De Vere Carden Park, Cheshire, England
Par 36-36—72; 6,756 yards

August 5-8
purse, €305,852

	SCORES				TOTAL	MONEY
Carl Mason	67	71	69	68	275	€50,368.96
Jim Rhodes	73	65	69	68	275	25,282.71
Seiji Ebihara	66	68	71	70	275	25,282.71
(Mason defeated Rhodes on first and Ebihara on second playoff hole.)						
Giuseppe Cali	67	68	68	73	276	13,752.10
Gery Watine	70	66	66	74	276	13,752.10
Delroy Cambridge	67	68	70	72	277	11,031.91
Guillermo Encina	67	74	65	73	279	9,520.69
Bruce Heuchan	70	71	69	69	279	9,520.69
Sam Torrance	73	70	66	70	279	9,520.69
Martin Gray	69	69	72	70	280	6,894.94
Bill Hardwick	68	70	73	69	280	6,894.94
Noel Ratcliffe	62	72	75	71	280	6,894.94
Dragon Taki	70	69	67	74	280	6,894.94
Horacio Carbonetti	68	70	72	71	281	4,401.43
David Good	71	67	66	77	281	4,401.43
Bill Longmuir	72	73	67	69	281	4,401.43
Bob Shearer	74	71	65	71	281	4,401.43
Luis Carbonetti	68	69	71	74	282	3,234.01
Tommy Horton	72	71	68	71	282	3,234.01
Nick Job	71	71	67	73	282	3,234.01
Alan Mew	65	74	67	76	282	3,234.01
Mike Miller	71	74	70	67	282	3,234.01
Simon Owen	70	68	72	72	282	3,234.01
John Chillas	66	72	72	73	283	2,780.64
Denis Durnian	65	70	72	76	283	2,780.64
Terry Gale	66	73	69	75	283	2,780.64
Craig Maltman	70	71	69	73	283	2,780.64

	SCORES				TOTAL	MONEY
Hank Woodrome	68	73	69	73	283	2,780.64
Maurice Bembridge	70	73	72	69	284	2,327.28
John Grace	67	71	73	73	284	2,327.28
John Mashego	70	72	65	77	284	2,327.28
John Morgan	72	69	72	71	284	2,327.28
Denis O'Sullivan	71	69	72	72	284	2,327.28
David Oakley	68	72	73	71	284	2,327.28
Steve Stull	69	70	70	75	284	2,327.28

Travis Perkins Senior Masters

Wentworth Club, Edinburgh Course, Surrey, England
Par 36-36–72; 6,873 yards

August 13-15
purse, €338,436

	SCORES			TOTAL	MONEY
Sam Torrance	72	69	62	203	€50,765.40
Seiji Ebihara	69	69	67	205	33,843.60
Alan Tapie	71	69	69	209	23,690.52
Carl Mason	70	71	69	210	18,613.98
Denis Durnian	73	70	68	211	13,672.81
Martin Gray	72	69	70	211	13,672.81
Bob Cameron	70	71	70	211	13,672.81
Maurice Bembridge	74	68	70	212	10,153.08
Denis O'Sullivan	73	70	69	212	10,153.08
Jim Rhodes	72	72	69	213	8,460.90
David Good	73	67	73	213	8,460.90
Bob Charles	72	72	70	214	7,107.16
Horacio Carbonetti	75	70	69	214	7,107.16
John Mashego	76	71	68	215	6,430.28
Neil Coles	74	72	70	216	5,262.68
Jeff Hawkes	69	74	73	216	5,262.68
Nick Job	75	74	67	216	5,262.68
Manuel Pinero	73	73	70	216	5,262.68
Malcolm Gregson	74	70	72	216	5,262.68
Bruce Heuchan	70	77	69	216	5,262.68
Bill Longmuir	72	72	73	217	4,061.23
John Grace	72	72	73	217	4,061.23
Mike Miller	74	74	70	218	3,391.13
Gavan Levenson	73	72	73	218	3,391.13
Paul Leonard	71	74	73	218	3,391.13
John Chillas	71	73	74	218	3,391.13
Steve Stull	72	74	72	218	3,391.13
Ray Carrasco	71	74	74	219	2,944.39
Craig Maltman	74	74	72	220	2,558.58
David Oakley	72	78	70	220	2,558.58
Manuel Velasco	74	72	74	220	2,558.58
Hank Woodrome	73	75	72	220	2,558.58
Dragon Taki	75	76	69	220	2,558.58

Charles Church Scottish Seniors Open

The Roxburghe, Kelso, Scotland
Par 36-36–72; 6,875 yards

August 27-29
purse, €221,677

	SCORES			TOTAL	MONEY
Bill Longmuir	69	73	68	210	€33,251.63
Carl Mason	72	71	68	211	18,842.59
John Chillas	68	71	72	211	18,842.59
David Good	75	64	73	212	12,192.26
Nick Job	74	68	71	213	8,955.77
Terry Gale	72	72	69	213	8,955.77
Tony Allen	69	74	70	213	8,955.77
Giuseppe Cali	72	68	75	215	6,650.32
Alan Mew	76	68	71	215	6,650.32
David J. Russell	72	70	74	216	4,623.56
Ray Carrasco	74	71	71	216	4,623.56
Alan Tapie	76	68	72	216	4,623.56
Guillermo Encina	71	71	74	216	4,623.56
David Oakley	73	70	73	216	4,623.56
Denis O'Sullivan	75	69	72	216	4,623.56
Bob Cameron	75	70	71	216	4,623.56
Gavan Levenson	77	72	68	217	3,332.55
Jim Rhodes	73	74	70	217	3,332.55
Steve Stull	74	75	68	217	3,332.55
Paul Leonard	75	73	70	218	2,926.14
Tommy Horton	76	70	73	219	2,521.58
Martin Gray	75	69	75	219	2,521.58
Luis Carbonetti	73	73	73	219	2,521.58
Bob Lendzion	73	75	71	219	2,521.58
Jeff Hawkes	78	72	70	220	1,976.62
Bill Hardwick	75	74	71	220	1,976.62
Craig Defoy	74	74	72	220	1,976.62
Jeff Van Wagenen	78	72	70	220	1,976.62
Delroy Cambridge	77	73	70	220	1,976.62
Bruce Heuchan	74	71	75	220	1,976.62

Bovis Lend Lease European Senior Masters

Woburn Golf & Country Club, Dukes Course,
Milton Keynes, England
Par 35-37–72; 6,796 yards

September 3-5
purse, €335,638

	SCORES			TOTAL	MONEY
Luis Carbonetti	73	65	71	209	€50,297.96
John Chillas	73	69	69	211	33,531.97
Carl Mason	75	69	68	212	23,472.38
Eamonn Darcy	67	76	70	213	14,770.83
Bill Longmuir	72	69	72	213	14,770.83
Terry Gale	70	71	72	213	14,770.83
Jerry Bruner	69	72	72	213	14,770.83
Sam Torrance	70	68	76	214	10,059.59
Alan Tapie	73	68	73	214	10,059.59
Neil Coles	71	70	74	215	8,047.67
Martin Gray	71	71	73	215	8,047.67
David Good	71	70	74	215	8,047.67
Chris Moody	71	72	73	216	6,371.07

	SCORES			TOTAL	MONEY
Noel Ratcliffe	73	71	72	216	6,371.07
Delroy Cambridge	70	69	77	216	6,371.07
Gavan Levenson	74	71	72	217	5,205.84
Denis O'Sullivan	73	71	73	217	5,205.84
John Mashego	74	69	74	217	5,205.84
Seiji Ebihara	71	73	73	217	5,205.84
Maurice Bembridge	70	75	73	218	3,839.41
Jeff Hawkes	71	74	73	218	3,839.41
Tommy Horton	77	69	72	218	3,839.41
Nick Job	71	74	73	218	3,839.41
Simon Owen	70	74	74	218	3,839.41
Bob Cameron	77	69	72	218	3,839.41
Ian Mosey	71	72	76	219	3,051.41
Priscillo Diniz	74	72	73	219	3,051.41
Paul Reed	77	73	69	219	3,051.41
Gery Watine	77	72	71	220	2,649.03
Craig Defoy	75	72	73	220	2,649.03
Hank Woodrome	75	71	74	220	2,649.03

Daily Telegraph Turismo Andaluz Seniors Match Play

Flamingos Golf Club, Marbella, Spain
Par 36-36–72; 6,412 yards

September 8-11
purse, €147,353

FIRST ROUND

Seiji Ebihara defeated Manuel Pinero, 2 and 1
Gery Watine defeated Steve Stull, 4 and 3
Jerry Bruner defeated Mike Miller, 2 and 1
John Chillas defeated Gavan Levenson, 4 and 3
Brian Jones defeated Ray Carrasco, 3 and 2
Martin Gray defeated Mike Ferguson, 3 and 2
Ian Mosey defeated Simon Owen, 2 and 1
Bob Cameron defeated Bill Longmuir, 2 and 1
Luis Carbonetti defeated Bruce Heuchan, 1 up
Nick Job defeated Horacio Carbonetti, 4 and 3
Guillermo Encina defeated Jim Rhodes, 4 and 3
Malcolm Gregson defeated David Good, 2 up
Maurice Bembridge defeated David Oakley, 5 and 4
Giuseppe Cali defeated Denis O'Sullivan, 3 and 2
Noel Ratcliffe defeated Antonio Garrido, 6 and 4
Carl Mason defeated Delroy Cambridge, 1 up

(Each losing player received €1,657.72.)

SECOND ROUND

Ebihara defeated Watine, 1 up
Chillas defeated Bruner, 4 and 2
Gray defeated Jones, 2 and 1
Cameron defeated Mosey, 2 up
Job defeated Carbonetti, 22 holes
Encina defeated Gregson, 21 holes
Cali defeated Bembridge, 2 and 1
Mason defeated Ratcliffe, 2 up

(Each losing player received €3,683.83.)

QUARTER-FINALS

Chillas defeated Ebihara, 3 and 1
Cameron defeated Gray, 2 and 1
Encina defeated Job, 4 and 2
Mason defeated Cali, 19 holes

(Each losing player received €7,367.65.)

SEMI-FINALS

Chillas defeated Cameron, 2 and 1
Mason defeated Encina, 19 holes

(Each losing player received €11,051.48.)

FINAL

Mason defeated Chillas, 3 and 2

(Mason received €23,576.48; Chillas received €16,208.83.)

ADT English Seniors Open

Formby Hall Golf Club, England
Par 36-36–72; 6,799 yards

September 24-26
purse, €221,029

	SCORES			TOTAL	MONEY
Carl Mason	71	67	75	213	€33,154.43
John Chillas	73	72	71	216	18,787.51
Bob Cameron	72	71	73	216	18,787.51
Eamonn Darcy	71	74	73	218	9,203.67
Ian Mosey	72	73	73	218	9,203.67
Terry Gale	72	73	73	218	9,203.67
Luis Carbonetti	71	74	73	218	9,203.67
Bruce Heuchan	74	72	72	218	9,203.67
Bill Longmuir	69	74	76	219	5,525.74
David J. Russell	74	72	73	219	5,525.74
Simon Owen	70	75	74	219	5,525.74
David Good	71	76	72	219	5,525.74
Alan Tapie	75	75	70	220	4,310.07
Jim Rhodes	74	73	73	220	4,310.07
Martin Gray	68	75	78	221	3,868.02
Paul Leonard	71	75	75	221	3,868.02
Nick Job	71	76	75	222	3,221.51
Craig Maltman	73	72	77	222	3,221.51
John Grace	74	76	72	222	3,221.51
Delroy Cambridge	75	77	70	222	3,221.51
Gery Watine	71	75	77	223	2,453.43
Gavan Levenson	76	74	73	223	2,453.43
Guillermo Encina	73	73	77	223	2,453.43
Bob Lendzion	72	75	76	223	2,453.43
Horacio Carbonetti	74	76	73	223	2,453.43
Mike Miller	78	72	74	224	1,878.75
Chris Moody	73	78	73	224	1,878.75
John Morgan	75	73	76	224	1,878.75
Jerry Bruner	76	74	74	224	1,878.75
Tony Allen	77	75	72	224	1,878.75
Alan Mew	75	77	72	224	1,878.75

Sanremo Masters

Sanremo Golf Club, Sanremo, Italy   October 1-3
Par 34-35–69; 5,681 yards   purse, €200,000

	SCORES			TOTAL	MONEY
Bob Cameron	66	66	61	193	€33,333
Giuseppe Cali	68	63	64	195	22,222
Gery Watine	66	64	66	196	15,555
Guillermo Encina	66	63	68	197	12,222
Bill Longmuir	63	69	66	198	8,977.73
Carl Mason	63	70	65	198	8,977.73
David Good	66	63	69	198	8,977.73
Jim Rhodes	67	68	64	199	6,111.18
Horacio Carbonetti	67	67	65	199	6,111.18
John Grace	66	66	67	199	6,111.18
Seiji Ebihara	64	66	69	199	6,111.18
Mike Ferguson	69	67	64	200	4,888.90
Eamonn Darcy	68	66	67	201	4,222.27
Nick Job	69	69	63	201	4,222.27
Gavan Levenson	67	68	66	201	4,222.27
Luis Carbonetti	64	68	70	202	3,777.80
Maurice Bembridge	68	68	67	203	3,444.50
Delroy Cambridge	68	67	68	203	3,444.50
Ray Carrasco	71	66	67	204	2,940.80
Denis O'Sullivan	68	68	68	204	2,940.80
John Chillas	66	73	65	204	2,940.80
Martin Gray	71	67	67	205	2,511.15
Jerry Bruner	71	67	67	205	2,511.15
Simon Owen	72	71	63	206	2,277.85
Terry Gale	72	69	65	206	2,277.85
Ian Mosey	71	68	68	207	2,111.20
Noel Ratcliffe	68	71	69	208	1,977.85
David Oakley	71	71	66	208	1,977.85
Alberto Croce	68	70	71	209	1,844.50
Baldovino Dassu	70	69	71	210	1,674.10
Malcolm Gregson	70	72	68	210	1,674.10
Bruce Heuchan	75	68	67	210	1,674.10

Estoril Seniors Tour Championship

Quinta da Marinha Oitavos Golfe, Algarve, Portugal   October 22-24
Par 36-35–71; 6,617 yards   purse, €240,000

	SCORES			TOTAL	MONEY
John Chillas	69	70	68	207	€37,325
David Good	72	70	67	209	24,883
Carl Mason	73	68	69	210	14,116.67
Martin Gray	68	73	69	210	14,116.67
John Benda	70	71	69	210	14,116.67
Giuseppe Cali	72	67	72	211	9,953
Eamonn Darcy	72	68	72	212	8,958
Alan Mew	70	72	71	213	7,962.50
Jeff Hawkes	72	70	72	214	5,972.06
Tommy Horton	74	71	69	214	5,972.06
Gery Watine	68	71	75	214	5,972.06
Horacio Carbonetti	73	71	70	214	5,972.06

	SCORES			TOTAL	MONEY
Hank Woodrome	72	73	69	214	5,972.06
John Morgan	72	70	73	215	4,727.90
Malcolm Gregson	74	69	73	216	3,986.38
Paul Leonard	73	71	72	216	3,986.38
Guillermo Encina	74	72	70	216	3,986.38
Jim Rhodes	72	69	75	216	3,986.38
Tony Allen	74	73	69	216	3,986.38
Chris Moody	74	68	75	217	3,085.60
Alan Tapie	73	71	73	217	3,085.60
Luis Carbonetti	70	73	74	217	3,085.60
Noel Ratcliffe	73	72	73	218	2,493.36
David Oakley	73	72	73	218	2,493.36
Bob Cameron	75	73	70	218	2,493.36
Keith Ashdown	73	72	73	218	2,493.36
Delroy Cambridge	74	73	71	218	2,493.36
Craig Maltman	73	75	71	219	2,164.90
Nick Job	79	74	67	220	1,965.83
David J. Russell	73	72	75	220	1,965.83
Simon Owen	71	75	74	220	1,965.83

Japan Senior Tour

Castle Hill Open

Castle Hill County Club, Hoi-gun, Aichi
Par 36-36–72; 6,730 yards

May 21-23
purse, ¥30,000,000

	SCORES			TOTAL	MONEY
Katsunari Takahashi	68	70	70	208	¥5,400,000
Yurio Akitomi	75	68	71	214	2,250,000
Hiroshi Ishii	73	69	72	214	2,250,000
Hikaru Emoto	71	72	72	215	1,350,000
Shuichi Sano	76	69	71	216	1,200,000
Koji Nakajima	72	71	74	217	900,000
Yuichi Yokoshima	74	70	73	217	900,000
Teruo Nakamura	77	70	70	217	900,000
Takeru Shibata	70	75	73	218	660,000
Yoshitaka Yamamoto	73	70	75	218	660,000
Seiji Ebihara	73	73	73	219	570,000
Toru Nakamura	75	75	69	219	570,000
Chuen Lu-hsi	73	75	71	219	570,000
Kenjiro Iwama	75	74	71	220	450,000
Dragon Taki	77	71	72	220	450,000
Yukio Noguchi	72	74	74	220	450,000
Eitaro Deguchi	72	73	75	220	450,000
Noboru Fujiike	72	72	76	220	450,000

	SCORES			TOTAL	MONEY
Kikuo Arai	72	77	72	221	315,000
Fujio Kobayashi	82	67	72	221	315,000
Katsuji Hasegawa	76	73	72	221	315,000
Namio Takasu	73	74	74	221	315,000
Yasuzo Hagiwara	72	74	75	221	315,000
Hisao Inoue	73	73	75	221	315,000
Kiyomasa Sugimoto	73	75	73	221	315,000
*Tetsuo Sakata	75	73	73	221	
Hsieh Min-nan	73	73	76	222	230,571
Toru Nakayama	72	78	72	222	230,571
Takaaki Fukuzawa	77	72	73	222	230,571
Hiroshi Oku	75	73	74	222	230,571
Toshiharu Morimoto	74	76	72	222	230,571
Tadao Furuichi	73	75	74	222	230,571
M. Siodina	76	73	73	222	230,571

Aderans Wellness Open

Nakajo Golf Club, Nakajo, Niigata
Par 36-36–72; 6,937 yards

June 11-13
purse, ¥60,000,000

	SCORES			TOTAL	MONEY
Toyotake Nakao	72	69	64	205	¥12,000,000
Yuichi Yokoshima	69	68	71	208	6,000,000
Takashi Miyoshi	71	70	68	209	2,625,000
Takeru Shibata	71	69	69	209	2,625,000
Takaaki Fukuzawa	68	70	71	209	2,625,000
Tateo Ozaki	68	69	72	209	2,625,000
Koichi Uehara	69	70	71	210	1,500,000
Masaru Amano	69	69	73	211	1,350,000
Motomasa Aoki	74	67	71	212	1,233,000
Chen Tze-ming	70	70	72	212	1,233,000
Yurio Akitomi	70	73	71	214	1,110,000
Hiroshi Ishii	72	71	71	214	1,110,000
Norihiko Matsumoto	71	73	71	215	1,020,000
Katsunari Takahashi	72	73	71	216	870,000
Kazuo Kanayama	70	74	72	216	870,000
Toshihiko Kikuichi	73	70	73	216	870,000
Teruo Nakamura	72	70	74	216	870,000
Masahiro Tokunaga	76	70	71	217	705,000
Yukio Noguchi	74	71	72	217	705,000
Kinpachi Yoshimura	72	73	72	217	705,000
Yoshio Fumiyama	70	74	73	217	705,000
Koji Okuno	75	73	70	218	600,000
Tadao Furuichi	72	75	71	218	600,000
Toru Nakamura	75	72	71	218	600,000
Tadanao Takeshita	75	70	74	219	510,000
Kenjiro Iwama	74	75	70	219	510,000
Koji Nakajima	70	74	75	219	510,000
Shuichi Sano	75	72	73	220	435,000
Hisao Inoue	73	73	74	220	435,000
Shigeru Kawamata	74	70	76	220	435,000

PGA Philanthropy Rebornest Senior Open

Biglayzac Country Club, Miyagi
Par 36-36–72; 6,826 yards

July 15-18
purse, ¥30,000,000

	SCORES				TOTAL	MONEY
Shuichi Sano	68	68	73	73	282	¥5,400,000
Takashi Miyoshi	70	67	77	69	283	2,700,000
Shoichi Sato	70	69	73	72	284	1,260,000
Tadami Ueno	69	71	72	72	284	1,260,000
Takaaki Fukuzawa	71	67	73	73	284	1,260,000
Hisao Inoue	67	72	72	73	284	1,260,000
Norihiko Matsumoto	71	68	69	76	284	1,260,000
Chen Tze-ming	70	75	70	70	285	648,000
Yukio Noguchi	72	72	70	71	285	648,000
Motomasa Aoki	71	69	73	72	285	648,000
Dragon Taki	67	72	73	73	285	648,000
Toru Nakayama	72	70	70	73	285	648,000
Teruo Nakamura	69	74	72	71	286	465,000
Junji Hashizoe	70	74	71	71	286	465,000
Hikaru Emoto	70	72	69	75	286	465,000
Kinpachi Yoshimura	71	72	67	76	286	465,000
Katsunari Takahashi	72	73	73	69	287	360,000
Noboru Fujiike	67	73	75	72	287	360,000
Mitsunobu Hatsumi	69	75	71	72	287	360,000
Toyotake Nakao	70	69	76	73	288	300,000
Tokio Kaneko	73	74	73	69	289	256,200
Akira Yabe	73	73	72	71	289	256,200
Toshiharu Morimoto	72	70	75	72	289	256,200
Toru Nakamura	71	74	72	72	289	256,200
Masaru Amano	71	71	74	73	289	256,200
Katsumi Nanjo	68	74	77	71	290	225,000
Takeshi Shibata	71	69	75	75	290	225,000
Koichi Uehara	72	72	76	71	291	204,000
Kazunari Nobuta	74	71	74	72	291	204,000
Shimon Takamatsu	71	72	75	73	291	204,000
Kikuo Arai	72	72	72	75	291	204,000
Tadao Furuichi	67	76	72	76	291	204,000

Fancl Senior Classic

Susono Country Club, Shizuoka
Par 36-36–72; 6,851 yards

August 20-22
purse, ¥60,000,000

	SCORES			TOTAL	MONEY
Yuichi Yokoshima	71	65	71	207	¥15,000,000
Motomasa Aoki	72	68	68	208	6,900,000
Takaaki Fukuzawa	73	69	69	211	2,490,000
Takeru Shibata	71	69	71	211	2,490,000
Teruo Nakamura	67	72	72	211	2,490,000
Noboru Fujiike	69	71	71	211	2,490,000
Koichi Uehara	73	67	72	212	1,620,000
Hikaru Emoto	72	66	75	213	1,282,000
Yoshitaka Yamamoto	73	70	70	213	1,282,000
Kinpachi Yoshimura	71	72	70	213	1,282,000
Katsuji Hasegawa	69	74	71	214	1,047,000
Koji Ōkuno	74	68	72	214	1,047,000

	SCORES			TOTAL	MONEY
Kenjiro Iwama	75	70	70	215	872,000
Yukio Noguchi	70	75	70	215	872,000
Chen Tze-ming	72	70	73	215	872,000
Mikio Ichikawa	74	70	72	216	672,000
Shuichi Sano	71	76	69	216	672,000
Katsunari Takahashi	77	71	68	216	672,000
Hisao Inoue	73	74	69	216	672,000
Norihiko Matsumoto	73	71	72	216	672,000
Toshiharu Morimoto	73	69	74	216	672,000
Tateo Ozaki	75	72	70	217	540,000
Hajime Meshiai	73	73	71	217	540,000
Yurio Akitomi	75	70	72	217	540,000
Fujio Kobayashi	74	71	73	218	442,000
Masaru Sato	75	71	72	218	442,000
Toru Nakayama	78	69	71	218	442,000
Akira Yabe	74	73	71	218	442,000
Hiroaki Uenishi	75	73	70	218	442,000
Mitsuo Iwata	75	74	69	218	442,000

Japan PGA Senior Championship

Yamada Golf Club, Chiba
Par 36-36–72; 6,620 yards

September 29-October 2
purse, ¥40,000,000

	SCORES				TOTAL	MONEY
Takaaki Fukuzawa	63	67	69	71	270	¥8,000,000
Chen Tze-ming	68	64	72	69	273	3,600,000
Katsunari Takahashi	70	69	71	65	275	2,600,000
Teruo Nakamura	69	68	71	69	277	1,640,000
Toyotake Nakao	68	73	70	67	278	1,400,000
Hsieh Min-nan	70	72	70	68	280	1,028,000
Hisao Inoue	69	72	70	69	280	1,028,000
Takeru Shibata	71	68	69	72	280	1,028,000
Kikuo Arai	68	78	68	67	281	840,000
Shuichi Sano	69	71	71	71	282	780,000
Renkyoku Sugiyama	71	67	73	71	282	780,000
Yoshio Fumiyama	71	72	70	72	285	680,000
Takashi Miyoshi	72	72	71	70	285	680,000
Yoshitaka Yamamoto	70	69	73	73	285	680,000
Kenjiro Iwama	67	76	73	70	286	560,000
Toshimoto Mori	73	67	69	77	286	560,000
Tadao Furuichi	73	73	66	74	286	560,000
Motomasa Aoki	72	70	75	70	287	440,000
Yukio Noguchi	71	74	74	68	287	440,000
Yurio Akitomi	72	71	69	75	287	440,000
Tadami Ueno	70	71	73	73	287	440,000
Hiroshi Taninaka	72	70	72	73	287	440,000
Norihiko Matsumoto	70	73	75	69	287	440,000
Kinpachi Yoshimura	71	74	71	71	287	440,000
Hikaru Emoto	70	72	73	73	288	330,000
Katsuji Hasegawa	69	73	73	73	288	330,000
Hiroshi Ishii	69	74	78	67	288	330,000
Koji Okuno	70	74	70	74	288	330,000
Eitaro Deguchi	74	70	77	68	289	290,000
Dragon Taki	72	72	73	73	290	270,000
Toshihiko Kikuichi	70	66	77	77	290	270,000
Noboru Fujiike	70	75	74	71	290	270,000

Japan Senior Open Championship

Ibaragi Golf Club, East Course, Saitama
Par 36-36–72; 6,865 yards

October 28-31
purse, ¥50,000,000

	SCORES				TOTAL	MONEY
Katsunari Takahashi	67	69	70	75	281	¥10,000,000
Bill Longmuir	68	70	72	71	281	4,687,500
Katsuyoshi Tomori	71	69	71	70	281	4,687,500
(Takahashi defeated Tomori on second and Longmuir on third playoff hole.)						
Tateo Ozaki	66	68	76	72	282	2,325,000
Takaaki Fukuzawa	69	68	76	69	282	2,325,000
Tsuneyuki Nakajima	68	72	72	71	283	1,567,500
Chen Tze-ming	71	71	72	69	283	1,567,500
Yukio Noguchi	70	70	72	72	284	1,214,000
Kazuo Kanayama	70	67	77	70	284	1,214,000
Terry Gale	72	71	74	69	286	920,000
Seiji Ebihara	70	72	73	71	286	920,000
Noboru Fujiike	71	71	73	72	287	745,000
Isao Aoki	73	69	74	71	287	745,000
Yuichi Yokoshima	71	70	79	68	288	635,000
Hajime Meshiai	77	69	74	68	288	635,000
Kinpachi Yoshimura	73	69	75	72	289	560,000
Koji Okuno	74	72	76	67	289	560,000
Toshiharu Morimoto	72	72	70	75	289	560,000
Teruo Nakamura	70	73	74	73	290	497,500
Yoshitaka Yamamoto	74	72	69	75	290	497,500
Toshihiko Ohtsuka	71	72	72	76	291	467,500
Akira Yabe	67	78	74	72	291	467,500
Hikaru Emoto	72	72	75	74	293	450,000
Koichi Uehara	71	72	76	75	294	440,000
Shuichi Sano	71	77	76	71	295	415,400
Teiji Sano	74	74	74	73	295	415,400
Masaru Amano	74	75	71	75	295	415,400
Mitsuo Iwata	74	69	75	77	295	415,400
Hiroshi Fujita	69	76	76	74	295	415,400
Masahiro Tokunaga	74	76	70	76	296	375,000
Hiroshi Ishii	73	72	77	74	296	375,000
Motomasa Aoki	73	71	78	74	296	375,000

Women's Tours

Welch's/Fry's Championship

Randolph Park, Dell Urich Course, Tucson, Arizona
Par 35-35–70; 6,176 yards

March 11-14
purse, $800,000

		SCORES			TOTAL	MONEY
Karen Stupples	63	66	66	63	258	$120,000
Jung Yeon Lee	60	70	67	66	263	61,657
Grace Park	69	66	61	67	263	61,657
Stacy Prammanasudh	66	69	63	67	265	40,108
Shi Hyun Ahn	69	69	66	63	267	26,935
Aree Song	71	64	65	67	267	26,935
Laura Davies	65	65	66	71	267	26,935
Mi-Hyun Kim	67	70	65	66	268	17,543
Se Ri Pak	67	70	64	67	268	17,543
Seol-An Jeon	65	67	67	69	268	17,543
Pat Hurst	70	67	67	65	269	14,674
Becky Morgan	70	68	69	64	271	13,265
Eva Dahllof	66	71	68	66	271	13,265
Emilee Klein	71	69	66	66	272	11,074
Michele Redman	68	71	66	67	272	11,074
Wendy Ward	70	67	67	68	272	11,074
Jean Bartholomew	70	66	67	69	272	11,074
Heather Bowie	68	67	71	67	273	9,176
Janice Moodie	70	70	65	68	273	9,176
Sophie Gustafson	69	68	68	68	273	9,176
Karrie Webb	68	68	67	70	273	9,176
Liselotte Neumann	76	66	66	66	274	7,491
Cristie Kerr	68	71	69	66	274	7,491
Candie Kung	72	70	65	67	274	7,491
Nancy Harvey	73	68	66	67	274	7,491
Hee-Won Han	68	72	67	67	274	7,491
Giulia Sergas	68	69	69	68	274	7,491
Jenna Daniels	70	67	68	69	274	7,491
Christina Kim	75	67	67	66	275	5,791
Reilley Rankin	70	72	66	67	275	5,791
Tammie Green	71	69	68	67	275	5,791
Catherine Cartwright	68	71	67	69	275	5,791
Gloria Park	72	66	67	70	275	5,791
Brandie Burton	68	70	66	71	275	5,791

Safeway International

Superstition Mountain Country Club, Superstition, Arizona
Par 36-36–72; 6,620 yards

March 18-21
purse, $1,200,000

		SCORES			TOTAL	MONEY
Annika Sorenstam	67	65	68	70	270	$180,000
Cristie Kerr	70	63	70	71	274	108,109
Grace Park	72	65	68	72	277	69,547
Lorena Ochoa	69	67	69	72	277	69,547
Se Ri Pak	67	68	70	74	279	44,392

	SCORES				TOTAL	MONEY
Shi Hyun Ahn	69	67	66	77	279	44,392
Laura Davies	71	66	68	76	281	33,442
Brandie Burton	69	71	71	72	283	24,504
Wendy Ward	71	71	68	73	283	24,504
Michele Redman	74	67	69	73	283	24,504
Lorie Kane	68	70	72	73	283	24,504
Donna Andrews	67	69	74	73	283	24,504
Vicki Goetze-Ackerman	70	71	72	71	284	18,269
Rosie Jones	70	71	69	74	284	18,269
Heather Bowie	70	67	69	78	284	18,269
Becky Morgan	71	73	72	69	285	15,429
Jung Yeon Lee	72	69	70	74	285	15,429
Catherine Cartwright	68	73	70	74	285	15,429
Aree Song	73	69	71	73	286	14,087
*Michelle Wie	72	67	70	77	286	
Angela Stanford	70	73	71	73	287	12,666
Juli Inkster	70	71	72	74	287	12,666
Jennifer Rosales	67	74	72	74	287	12,666
Silvia Cavalleri	70	73	69	75	287	12,666
Catriona Matthew	68	72	71	76	287	12,666
Carin Koch	72	71	72	73	288	11,305
Jamie Hullett	72	72	71	74	289	10,476
Dottie Pepper	71	72	72	74	289	10,476
Beth Bauer	73	73	68	75	289	10,476
Deb Richard	72	74	69	75	290	9,115
Pat Hurst	71	72	72	75	290	9,115
Isabelle Beisiegel	70	72	72	76	290	9,115
Candie Kung	71	73	69	77	290	9,115

Kraft Nabisco Championship

Mission Hills Country Club, Rancho Mirage, California   March 25-28
Par 36-36–72; 6,542 yards   purse, $1,600,000

	SCORES				TOTAL	MONEY
Grace Park	72	69	67	69	277	$240,000
Aree Song	66	73	69	70	278	146,826
Karrie Webb	68	71	71	69	279	106,512
*Michelle Wie	69	72	69	71	281	
Cristie Kerr	71	71	71	69	282	74,358
Catriona Matthew	67	75	70	70	282	74,358
Mi-Hyun Kim	71	70	71	71	283	54,261
Lorena Ochoa	67	76	74	67	284	36,737
Candie Kung	69	75	71	69	284	36,737
Christina Kim	72	72	70	70	284	36,737
Rosie Jones	67	73	71	73	284	36,737
Jung Yeon Lee	69	69	71	75	284	36,737
Annika Sorenstam	71	76	69	69	285	26,420
Hee-Won Han	72	71	71	71	285	26,420
Stacy Prammanasudh	71	71	69	74	285	26,420
Laura Davies	71	77	70	68	286	20,633
Se Ri Pak	72	73	72	69	286	20,633
Karen Stupples	70	76	68	72	286	20,633
Young Kim	74	72	67	73	286	20,633
Carin Koch	70	72	71	73	286	20,633
Wendy Doolan	70	69	72	75	286	20,633
Michele Redman	73	73	70	71	287	17,846

	SCORES				TOTAL	MONEY
Jeong Jang	76	71	70	72	289	17,203
Tammie Green	71	78	71	70	290	15,944
*Jane Park	71	74	73	72	290	
Brandie Burton	70	76	71	73	290	15,944
Dottie Pepper	68	70	74	78	290	15,944
Danielle Ammaccapane	75	77	73	66	291	13,682
Juli Inkster	74	74	73	70	291	13,682
Tina Barrett	75	70	73	73	291	13,682
Donna Andrews	70	74	73	74	291	13,682
Wendy Ward	72	74	70	75	291	13,682

Office Depot Championship

El Caballero Country Club, Tarzana, California
Par 36-36–72; 6,394 yards

April 1-4
purse, $1,750,000

	SCORES			TOTAL	MONEY
Annika Sorenstam	68	70	69	207	$262,500
Ashli Bunch	70	75	65	210	138,886
Meg Mallon	69	71	70	210	138,886
Lorie Kane	72	73	67	212	81,529
Mi-Hyun Kim	72	71	69	212	81,529
Tina Barrett	72	72	70	214	54,647
Catriona Matthew	72	70	72	214	54,647
Lorena Ochoa	73	71	71	215	39,516
Michelle Ellis	74	68	73	215	39,516
Michele Redman	71	70	74	215	39,516
Isabelle Beisiegel	74	77	65	216	31,951
Betsy King	71	72	73	216	31,951
Sherri Steinhauer	75	72	70	217	26,442
Laura Davies	72	75	70	217	26,442
Pamela Kerrigan	75	69	73	217	26,442
Se Ri Pak	74	70	73	217	26,442
Dorothy Delasin	77	72	69	218	19,655
Jackie Gallagher-Smith	74	75	69	218	19,655
Grace Park	73	76	69	218	19,655
Christina Kim	76	71	71	218	19,655
Becky Morgan	74	73	71	218	19,655
Helen Alfredsson	72	75	71	218	19,655
Karen Stupples	70	76	72	218	19,655
Young Kim	71	74	73	218	19,655
Jennifer Rosales	73	70	75	218	19,655
Cristie Kerr	72	75	72	219	15,001
Stephanie Louden	73	73	73	219	15,001
Juli Inkster	72	74	73	219	15,001
Jill McGill	69	73	77	219	15,001
Rosie Jones	70	70	79	219	15,001

LPGA Takefuji Classic

Las Vegas Country Club, Las Vegas, Nevada
Par 36-36–72; 6,494 yards

April 15-17
purse, $1,100,000

	SCORES			TOTAL	MONEY
Cristie Kerr	69	67	73	209	$165,000
Seol-An Jeon	70	70	69	209	98,070
(Kerr defeated Jeon on seventh playoff hole.)					
Gloria Park	71	72	67	210	71,142
Mi-Hyun Kim	71	70	70	211	55,034
Heather Daly-Donofrio	72	68	72	212	44,296
Cindy Figg-Currier	72	72	69	213	33,290
Stacy Prammanasudh	69	71	73	213	33,290
Karen Stupples	72	74	68	214	25,234
*In-Bee Park	71	72	71	214	
Reilley Rankin	71	71	72	214	25,234
Shi Hyun Ahn	75	70	70	215	19,571
Michele Redman	71	74	70	215	19,571
Soo-Yun Kang	73	70	72	215	19,571
Dorothy Delasin	72	71	72	215	19,571
Laura Diaz	75	71	70	216	14,819
Natalie Gulbis	74	71	71	216	14,819
Jung Yeon Lee	73	71	72	216	14,819
Rachel Teske	74	69	73	216	14,819
Grace Park	72	70	74	216	14,819
Mardi Lunn	73	74	70	217	11,498
Jean Bartholomew	76	68	73	217	11,498
Stephanie Louden	72	72	73	217	11,498
Emilee Klein	71	73	73	217	11,498
Jennifer Rosales	75	68	74	217	11,498
Aree Song	74	69	74	217	11,498
Catriona Matthew	70	73	74	217	11,498
Kate Golden	77	72	69	218	8,798
Helen Alfredsson	78	70	70	218	8,798
Angela Stanford	75	71	72	218	8,798
A.J. Eathorne	74	70	74	218	8,798
Miriam Nagl	71	72	75	218	8,798
Juli Inkster	74	68	76	218	8,798
Danielle Ammaccapane	72	70	76	218	8,798

Chick-Fil-A Charity Championship

Eagle's Landing Country Club, Stockbridge, Georgia
Par 36-36–72; 6,394 yards

April 29-May 2
purse, $1,600,000

	SCORES				TOTAL	MONEY
Jennifer Rosales	70	70	69	65	274	$240,000
Jung Yeon Lee	71	66	73	65	275	96,894
Rosie Jones	72	66	70	67	275	96,894
Becky Morgan	67	72	68	68	275	96,894
Grace Park	66	70	71	68	275	96,894
Mi-Hyun Kim	70	67	69	70	276	52,305
Natalie Gulbis	70	66	72	69	277	38,876
Rachel Teske	70	69	68	70	277	38,876
Se Ri Pak	68	71	68	70	277	38,876
Kate Golden	73	71	70	64	278	28,246

	SCORES				TOTAL	MONEY
Michele Redman	70	68	70	70	278	28,246
Annika Sorenstam	71	69	67	71	278	28,246
Lorena Ochoa	68	71	68	71	278	28,246
Shi Hyun Ahn	73	68	71	67	279	21,387
Christina Kim	65	74	70	70	279	21,387
Reilley Rankin	70	68	71	70	279	21,387
Janice Moodie	69	71	68	71	279	21,387
Lorie Kane	67	68	73	71	279	21,387
Catriona Matthew	68	73	71	68	280	17,823
Pat Hurst	74	69	67	70	280	17,823
Meg Mallon	69	70	70	71	280	17,823
Heather Bowie	71	71	68	72	282	16,583
Karen Stupples	75	70	71	67	283	14,816
Jamie Hullett	72	70	72	69	283	14,816
Stacy Prammanasudh	69	71	72	71	283	14,816
Isabelle Beisiegel	72	66	73	72	283	14,816
Aree Song	69	66	70	78	283	14,816
Soo-Yun Kang	74	72	68	70	284	12,182
Deb Richard	72	73	69	70	284	12,182
Emilee Klein	71	73	69	71	284	12,182
Angela Stanford	70	71	69	74	284	12,182
Jeong Jang	69	70	71	74	284	12,182

Michelob Ultra Open at Kingsmill

Kingsmill Resort & Spa, Williamsburg, Virginia   May 6-9
Par 36-35–71; 6,285 yards   purse, $2,200,000

	SCORES				TOTAL	MONEY
Se Ri Pak	70	71	69	65	275	$330,000
Juli Inkster	68	71	71	67	277	173,333
Lorena Ochoa	70	68	68	71	277	173,333
Hee-Won Han	69	68	77	66	280	101,750
Wendy Doolan	73	65	72	70	280	101,750
Mi-Hyun Kim	69	70	73	69	281	68,200
Cristie Kerr	71	65	70	75	281	68,200
Pat Hurst	70	70	71	71	282	49,317
Annika Sorenstam	69	71	71	71	282	49,317
Helen Alfredsson	66	73	72	71	282	49,317
Karrie Webb	74	67	75	67	283	41,250
Grace Park	72	69	72	71	284	36,153
*Michelle Wie	72	67	73	72	284	
Angela Stanford	73	69	69	73	284	36,153
Kim Williams	68	63	78	75	284	36,153
Siew-Ai Lim	72	68	74	71	285	26,669
Seol-An Jeon	69	69	76	71	285	26,669
Shi Hyun Ahn	72	69	72	72	285	26,669
Suzann Pettersen	69	67	77	72	285	26,669
Dawn Coe-Jones	72	66	74	73	285	26,669
Stacy Prammanasudh	69	69	73	74	285	26,669
Soo-Yun Kang	65	70	76	74	285	26,669
Jennifer Rosales	69	67	73	76	285	26,669
Christina Kim	68	67	73	77	285	26,669
Dorothy Delasin	66	78	74	68	286	19,486
Natalie Gulbis	73	70	75	68	286	19,486
Karen Stupples	75	69	70	72	286	19,486
Betsy King	69	72	72	73	286	19,486

	SCORES			TOTAL	MONEY
Rosie Jones	72	66	75	73	286	19,486
Jung Yeon Lee	71	66	75	74	286	19,486
Michele Redman	68	71	72	75	286	19,486

Franklin American Mortgage Championship

Vanderbilt Legends Club, Franklin, Tennessee
Par 36-36–72; 6,458 yards

May 13-16
purse, $900,000

	SCORES				TOTAL	MONEY
Lorena Ochoa	70	67	67	68	272	$135,000
Wendy Ward	68	70	68	67	273	81,809
Stacy Prammanasudh	67	72	68	67	274	59,347
Pat Hurst	68	69	68	70	275	45,909
Dorothy Delasin	71	67	71	68	277	36,952
Paula Marti	73	72	70	65	280	25,904
Gloria Park	69	71	71	69	280	25,904
Mi-Hyun Kim	68	73	64	75	280	25,904
Wendy Doolan	69	70	73	69	281	19,036
Candie Kung	72	71	68	70	281	19,036
Becky Iverson	71	74	69	68	282	15,240
Hee-Won Han	71	72	71	68	282	15,240
Nancy Scranton	66	72	75	69	282	15,240
Lorie Kane	69	72	71	70	282	15,240
Helen Alfredsson	72	74	68	69	283	11,496
Becky Morgan	73	67	74	69	283	11,496
Laura Diaz	73	71	69	70	283	11,496
Heather Bowie	72	70	71	70	283	11,496
Moira Dunn	75	70	67	71	283	11,496
Jenna Daniels	74	71	66	72	283	11,496
Candy Hannemann	68	75	73	68	284	8,745
Natalie Gulbis	74	72	69	69	284	8,745
Kristi Albers	70	72	73	69	284	8,745
Tammie Green	72	73	69	70	284	8,745
Janice Moodie	74	68	72	70	284	8,745
Brandie Burton	73	69	71	71	284	8,745
Pamela Kerrigan	71	71	70	72	284	8,745
Liselotte Neumann	74	68	68	74	284	8,745
Karen Pearce	71	75	69	70	285	6,898
Tracy Hanson	70	72	72	71	285	6,898
Riko Higashio	74	72	66	73	285	6,898
Karrie Webb	72	70	70	73	285	6,898

Sybase Classic

Wykagyl Country Club, New Rochelle, New York
Par 35-36–71; 6,161 yards

May 20-23
purse, $1,250,000

	SCORES				TOTAL	MONEY
Sherri Steinhauer	67	70	66	69	272	$187,500
Grace Park	69	66	71	68	274	113,364
Becky Morgan	67	64	72	72	275	82,238
Kelli Kuehne	73	70	66	68	277	63,617
Stacy Prammanasudh	73	70	68	68	279	46,550
Young Kim	71	68	70	70	279	46,550

	SCORES				TOTAL	MONEY
Kristi Albers	74	71	67	68	280	29,636
Meg Mallon	72	72	68	68	280	29,636
Nadina Taylor	66	75	68	71	280	29,636
Young-A Yang	66	69	71	74	280	29,636
Silvia Cavalleri	66	72	72	71	281	22,499
Jeong Jang	72	66	69	74	281	22,499
Dottie Pepper	72	69	73	68	282	18,620
Riko Higashio	72	71	69	70	282	18,620
Seol-An Jeon	72	68	71	71	282	18,620
Amy Hung	68	67	74	73	282	18,620
Rachel Teske	69	71	74	69	283	15,144
Deb Richard	73	71	68	71	283	15,144
Carin Koch	72	68	71	72	283	15,144
Karen Stupples	70	73	64	76	283	15,144
Jenna Daniels	76	71	69	68	284	12,342
Mhairi McKay	70	73	73	68	284	12,342
Hee-Won Han	75	71	69	69	284	12,342
Yu Ping Lin	71	76	67	70	284	12,342
Kim Saiki	72	72	70	70	284	12,342
Siew-Ai Lim	70	71	72	71	284	12,342
Michele Redman	69	69	74	72	284	12,342
Catherine Cartwright	70	70	75	70	285	9,756
Jackie Gallagher-Smith	76	65	73	71	285	9,756
Soo-Yun Kang	67	73	74	71	285	9,756
Gloria Park	73	69	71	72	285	9,756
Beth Daniel	72	69	71	73	285	9,756

LPGA Corning Classic

Corning Country Club, Corning, New York
Par 36-36–72; 6,062 yards

May 27-30
purse, $1,000,000

	SCORES				TOTAL	MONEY
Annika Sorenstam	65	67	70	68	270	$150,000
Vicki Goetze-Ackerman	68	70	67	67	272	78,420
Michelle Estill	67	64	70	71	272	78,420
Wendy Ward	69	70	71	65	275	41,887
Soo Young Moon	73	66	70	66	275	41,887
Shi Hyun Ahn	69	71	66	69	275	41,887
Laura Diaz	69	68	71	68	276	28,119
Catriona Matthew	67	74	69	68	278	22,312
Kelli Kuehne	68	70	70	70	278	22,312
Carin Koch	68	68	72	70	278	22,312
Jeong Jang	68	73	68	70	279	17,468
Laura Davies	70	69	70	70	279	17,468
Nadina Taylor	71	67	70	71	279	17,468
Patricia Meunier-Lebouc	71	71	72	66	280	13,735
Rosie Jones	69	74	68	69	280	13,735
Carri Wood	71	71	68	70	280	13,735
Mhairi McKay	71	66	72	71	280	13,735
Denise Killeen	69	68	70	73	280	13,735
Lorena Ochoa	70	71	71	69	281	11,446
Meg Mallon	69	71	71	70	281	11,446
Sherri Steinhauer	67	70	74	70	281	11,446
Joanne Morley	70	72	71	69	282	9,705
Jean Bartholomew	68	74	70	70	282	9,705
Beth Daniel	70	73	68	71	282	9,705

	SCORES			TOTAL	MONEY
Rachel Teske	70	68	73	71	282	9,705
Liselotte Neumann	65	72	72	73	282	9,705
Natalie Gulbis	66	71	70	75	282	9,705
Karrie Webb	70	71	72	70	283	8,129
Juli Inkster	73	67	73	70	283	8,129
Suzanne Strudwick	68	71	73	71	283	8,129

Kellogg-Keebler Classic

Stonebridge Country Club, Aurora, Illinois   June 4-6
Par 36-36–72; 6,413 yards   purse, $1,200,000

	SCORES			TOTAL	MONEY
Karrie Webb	69	64	67	200	$180,000
Siew-Ai Lim	69	70	66	205	83,730
Annika Sorenstam	71	66	68	205	83,730
Jeong Jang	69	67	69	205	83,730
Angela Stanford	68	72	66	206	45,108
Lorena Ochoa	71	67	68	206	45,108
Isabelle Beisiegel	73	66	68	207	30,172
Cristie Kerr	67	72	68	207	30,172
Yu Ping Lin	69	69	69	207	30,172
Candie Kung	70	71	67	208	20,019
Pat Hurst	71	69	68	208	20,019
Jamie Hullett	69	71	68	208	20,019
Lorie Kane	69	71	68	208	20,019
Christina Kim	68	70	70	208	20,019
Audra Burks	72	65	71	208	20,019
Seol-An Jeon	68	67	73	208	20,019
Becky Morgan	74	67	68	209	15,637
Laura Diaz	70	71	69	210	13,613
Natalie Gulbis	68	72	70	210	13,613
Tina Barrett	66	74	70	210	13,613
Grace Park	68	71	71	210	13,613
Catherine Cartwright	67	71	72	210	13,613
Jill McGill	68	67	75	210	13,613
Beth Bader	72	69	70	211	11,066
Ashli Bunch	68	73	70	211	11,066
Betsy King	74	66	71	211	11,066
Hee-Won Han	71	69	71	211	11,066
Jennifer Rosales	73	66	72	211	11,066
Janice Moodie	73	71	68	212	8,729
Kate Golden	72	72	68	212	8,729
Kim Saiki	70	72	70	212	8,729
Katherine Hull	74	67	71	212	8,729
Mhairi McKay	72	69	71	212	8,729
Catriona Matthew	70	71	71	212	8,729
Nancy Scranton	67	71	74	212	8,729

McDonald's LPGA Championship

DuPont Country Club, Wilmington, Delaware
Par 35-36–71; 6,408 yards

June 10-13
purse, $1,600,000

	SCORES				TOTAL	MONEY
Annika Sorenstam	68	67	64	72	271	$240,000
Shi Hyun Ahn	69	70	69	66	274	144,780
Grace Park	68	70	70	68	276	105,028
Angela Stanford	69	71	67	71	278	73,322
Gloria Park	67	72	68	71	278	73,322
Christina Kim	74	69	64	72	279	49,145
Juli Inkster	70	66	70	73	279	49,145
Wendy Doolan	73	70	65	72	280	35,538
Soo-Yun Kang	69	68	71	72	280	35,538
Lorena Ochoa	71	67	67	75	280	35,538
Carin Koch	69	71	68	73	281	28,734
Reilley Rankin	70	67	71	73	281	28,734
Pat Hurst	69	69	75	69	282	24,466
Mhairi McKay	72	69	69	72	282	24,466
Jennifer Rosales	66	70	74	72	282	24,466
Meg Mallon	69	73	70	71	283	21,718
Betsy King	76	70	70	68	284	18,654
Dawn Coe-Jones	72	72	70	70	284	18,654
Kristi Albers	70	74	69	71	284	18,654
Cristie Kerr	69	73	71	71	284	18,654
Se Ri Pak	69	73	70	72	284	18,654
Michelle Ellis	72	70	69	73	284	18,654
Sherri Steinhauer	69	72	74	70	285	14,596
Tina Barrett	75	71	68	71	285	14,596
Stacy Prammanasudh	73	71	69	72	285	14,596
Siew-Ai Lim	72	70	71	72	285	14,596
Jeong Jang	71	71	71	72	285	14,596
Kim Saiki	69	72	72	72	285	14,596
Chiharu Yamaguchi	67	73	70	75	285	14,596
Young Kim	70	73	74	69	286	10,631
Patricia Meunier-Lebouc	71	70	76	69	286	10,631
Janice Moodie	72	71	73	70	286	10,631
Mi-Hyun Kim	72	70	74	70	286	10,631
Wendy Ward	72	72	71	71	286	10,631
Charlotta Sorenstam	74	70	70	72	286	10,631
Moira Dunn	68	74	72	72	286	10,631
Karen Stupples	67	73	73	73	286	10,631
Aree Song	71	72	69	74	286	10,631

ShopRite LPGA Classic

Marriott Seaview Resort & Spa, Bay Course,
Galloway Twp., New Jersey
Par 36-35–71; 6,071 yards

June 18-20
purse, $1,300,000

	SCORES			TOTAL	MONEY
Cristie Kerr	66	68	68	202	$195,000
*Paula Creamer	70	64	69	203	
Giulia Sergas	65	67	71	203	117,117
Juli Inkster	68	69	67	204	75,342
Mi Hyun Kim	69	66	69	204	75,342

	SCORES			TOTAL	MONEY
Jackie Gallagher-Smith	68	73	64	205	38,537
Aree Song	73	65	67	205	38,537
Tammie Green	69	69	67	205	38,537
Karrie Webb	71	66	68	205	38,537
Jennifer Rosales	70	67	68	205	38,537
Hee-Won Han	70	69	67	206	25,007
Joanne Mills	69	67	70	206	25,007
Johanna Head	67	74	66	207	20,455
Riko Higashio	69	70	68	207	20,455
Michele Redman	68	70	69	207	20,455
Kelly Robbins	69	68	70	207	20,455
Carin Koch	71	66	71	208	17,570
Reilley Rankin	73	69	67	209	15,364
Marcy Hart	69	73	67	209	15,364
A.J. Eathorne	70	71	68	209	15,364
Sherri Steinhauer	69	68	72	209	15,364
Denise Killeen	65	65	79	209	15,364
Soo-Yun Kang	73	69	68	210	12,968
Leta Lindley	70	71	69	210	12,968
Stephanie Louden	68	73	69	210	12,968
Brandie Burton	67	72	71	210	12,968
Siew-Ai Lim	72	70	69	211	10,110
Kelly Cap	70	72	69	211	10,110
Jeong Jang	70	70	71	211	10,110
Kate Golden	69	71	71	211	10,110
Kathryn Marshall	69	71	71	211	10,110
Heather Daly-Donofrio	68	71	72	211	10,110
Gloria Park	67	72	72	211	10,110
Jill McGill	68	70	73	211	10,110
Miriam Nagl	70	67	74	211	10,110

Wegmans Rochester LPGA

Locust Hill Country Club, Pittsford, New York
Par 35-37–72; 6,200 yards

June 24-27
purse, $1,500,000

	SCORES				TOTAL	MONEY
Kim Saiki	66	69	68	71	274	$225,000
Mi Hyun Kim	72	67	70	69	278	118,752
Rosie Jones	69	68	67	74	278	118,752
Brandie Burton	73	71	70	66	280	77,246
Jeong Jang	72	68	73	68	281	56,522
Patricia Meunier-Lebouc	73	71	65	72	281	56,522
Suzann Pettersen	72	74	68	68	282	34,441
Laura Davies	70	73	71	68	282	34,441
Paula Marti	72	69	70	71	282	34,441
Annika Sorenstam	72	66	71	73	282	34,441
Candie Kung	67	68	73	74	282	34,441
Catriona Matthew	70	70	70	73	283	26,377
*Paula Creamer	69	71	72	72	284	
Tammie Green	73	69	75	68	285	21,453
Katherine Hull	70	72	73	70	285	21,453
Carin Koch	71	72	71	71	285	21,453
Moira Dunn	73	70	70	72	285	21,453
Rachel Teske	70	70	70	75	285	21,453
Juli Inkster	68	69	73	75	285	21,453
Gloria Park	72	75	71	68	286	17,333

	SCORES				TOTAL	MONEY
Tina Barrett	71	73	72	70	286	17,333
Becky Morgan	69	67	73	77	286	17,333
Pat Hurst	76	71	72	68	287	14,696
Catherine Cartwright	75	72	70	70	287	14,696
Jamie Hullett	73	73	68	73	287	14,696
Shi Hyun Ahn	73	71	70	73	287	14,696
A.J. Eathorne	70	74	68	75	287	14,696
Christina Kim	70	71	71	75	287	14,696
Candy Hannemann	74	71	76	68	289	10,961
Joanne Mills	74	71	74	70	289	10,961
Tonya Gill	75	72	71	71	289	10,961
Meg Mallon	76	70	72	71	289	10,961
Michelle Ellis	71	74	73	71	289	10,961
Michele Redman	74	70	74	71	289	10,961
Jennifer Rosales	71	72	75	71	289	10,961
Deb Richard	71	71	73	74	289	10,961
Allison Finney	70	72	72	75	289	10,961

U.S. Women's Open

Orchards Golf Club, South Hadley, Massachusetts
Par 36-35–71; 6,473 yards

July 1-4
purse, $3,100,000

	SCORES				TOTAL	MONEY
Meg Mallon	73	69	67	65	274	$560,000
Annika Sorenstam	71	68	70	67	276	335,000
Kelly Robbins	74	67	68	69	278	208,863
Jennifer Rosales	70	67	69	75	281	145,547
Michele Redman	70	72	73	67	282	111,173
Candie Kung	70	68	74	70	282	111,173
Jeong Jang	72	74	71	66	283	86,744
Pat Hurst	70	71	71	71	283	86,744
Moira Dunn	73	67	72	71	283	86,744
Carin Koch	72	67	75	70	284	68,813
Michelle Ellis	70	69	72	73	284	68,813
Rachel Teske	71	69	70	74	284	68,813
Patricia Meunier-Lebouc	67	75	74	69	285	60,602
*Paula Creamer	72	69	72	72	285	
*Michelle Wie	71	70	71	73	285	
Suzann Pettersen	74	72	71	69	286	54,052
Mi Hyun Kim	76	68	71	71	286	54,052
Karrie Webb	72	71	71	72	286	54,052
Catriona Matthew	73	71	72	71	287	48,432
Young Kim	71	73	76	68	288	38,660
Rosie Jones	74	72	72	70	288	38,660
Kate Golden	74	71	72	71	288	38,660
Liselotte Neumann	72	72	72	72	288	38,660
Dawn Coe-Jones	71	73	72	72	288	38,660
Johanna Head	76	69	70	73	288	38,660
Kim Saiki	70	68	74	76	288	38,660
Cristie Kerr	73	71	74	71	289	29,195
Beth Daniel	69	74	71	75	289	29,195
Lorie Kane	75	70	72	73	290	24,533
Shi Hyun Ahn	73	71	72	74	290	24,533
Deb Richard	71	73	72	74	290	24,533

BMO Financial Group Canadian Women's Open

Legends on the Niagara, Battlefield Course,
Niagara Falls, Ontario
Par 36-36–72; 6,544 yards

July 8-11
purse, $1,300,000

	SCORES				TOTAL	MONEY
Meg Mallon	65	70	65	70	270	$195,000
Beth Daniel	69	68	67	70	274	117,899
Jean Bartholomew	75	67	65	69	276	75,845
Lorena Ochoa	69	67	70	70	276	75,845
Lorie Kane	72	69	68	68	277	48,412
Dawn Coe-Jones	68	69	69	71	277	48,412
Jamie Hullett	72	69	70	67	278	34,212
Wendy Ward	72	67	70	69	278	34,212
Jennifer Rosales	68	72	68	71	279	27,433
Gloria Park	67	70	70	72	279	27,433
Natalie Gulbis	72	72	68	68	280	21,963
Jeong Jang	72	68	72	68	280	21,963
Kelli Kuehne	71	71	69	69	280	21,963
Janice Moodie	69	74	67	70	280	21,963
Jill McGill	75	67	69	70	281	17,730
Mi Hyun Kim	69	70	70	72	281	17,730
Stacy Prammanasudh	71	69	68	73	281	17,730
Soo Young Moon	73	70	69	70	282	15,686
Christina Kim	70	72	69	71	282	15,686
*Paula Creamer	73	70	67	72	282	
Cristie Kerr	72	73	70	68	283	13,325
Leta Lindley	73	71	69	70	283	13,325
Jung Yeon Lee	73	71	69	70	283	13,325
Nancy Scranton	69	69	75	70	283	13,325
Siew-Ai Lim	72	71	69	71	283	13,325
Johanna Head	67	72	72	72	283	13,325
Aree Song	71	66	70	76	283	13,325
Jackie Gallagher-Smith	71	72	71	70	284	10,973
Joanne Morley	74	69	70	71	284	10,973
Kim Saiki	72	72	68	72	284	10,973

Giant Eagle LPGA Classic

Squaw Creek Country Club, Vienna, Ohio
Par 37-35–72; 6,454 yards

July 16-18
purse, $1,000,000

	SCORES			TOTAL	MONEY
Moira Dunn	70	69	65	204	$150,000
Young-A Yang	67	71	68	206	92,224
Leta Lindley	71	70	66	207	66,902
Laura Diaz	69	70	69	208	51,754
Michelle Estill	71	67	71	209	41,656
Katherine Hull	76	66	68	210	34,082
Catherine Cartwright	74	70	67	211	26,761
Anna Acker-Macosko	72	70	69	211	26,761
Tina Fischer	72	72	69	213	21,459
Donna Andrews	68	75	70	213	21,459
Natalie Gulbis	72	72	70	214	15,761
Yu Ping Lin	71	73	70	214	15,761
Tammie Green	70	74	70	214	15,761

	SCORES			TOTAL	MONEY
Cathy Johnston-Forbes	71	72	71	214	15,761
Amy Hung	73	70	71	214	15,761
Emilee Klein	70	72	72	214	15,761
Jen Hanna	74	68	72	214	15,761
Lee Ann Walker-Cooper	72	72	71	215	10,456
Mardi Lunn	73	71	71	215	10,456
A.J. Eathorne	75	69	71	215	10,456
Marilyn Lovander	69	74	72	215	10,456
Kristi Albers	70	73	72	215	10,456
Heather Daly-Donofrio	71	71	73	215	10,456
Amy Fruhwirth	71	71	73	215	10,456
Nicole Jeray	73	69	73	215	10,456
Dina Ammaccapane	74	68	73	215	10,456
Nadina Taylor	69	71	75	215	10,456
Kate Golden	70	77	68	215	10,456
Carri Wood	71	74	71	216	7,328
Kathryn Marshall	71	74	71	216	7,328
Seol-An Jeon	74	70	72	216	7,328
Jackie Gallagher-Smith	73	73	70	216	7,328
Ji Yeon Lee	73	70	73	216	7,328
Gloria Park	66	76	74	216	7,328
Heather Bowie	72	69	75	216	7,328

Evian Masters

See Ladies European Tour section.

Weetabix Women's British Open

See Ladies European Tour section.

Jamie Farr Owens Corning Classic

Highland Meadows Golf Club, Sylvania, Ohio   August 5-8
Par 34-37–71; 6,365 yards   purse, $1,100,000

	SCORES				TOTAL	MONEY
Meg Mallon	66	69	74	68	277	$165,000
Se Ri Pak	66	72	72	68	278	86,873
Karen Stupples	65	72	68	73	278	86,873
Rachel Teske	72	69	70	68	279	56,510
Lorie Kane	72	71	67	70	280	45,484
Brandie Burton	67	69	74	71	281	31,884
Lorena Ochoa	69	72	69	71	281	31,884
Jeong Jang	71	70	68	72	281	31,884
Marcy Hart	70	73	73	66	282	21,708
Catriona Matthew	67	74	71	70	282	21,708
Leta Lindley	70	69	71	72	282	21,708
Marilyn Lovander	72	67	69	74	282	21,708
Tammie Green	69	72	74	68	283	15,327
Yu Ping Lin	67	74	73	69	283	15,327
Beth Daniel	69	72	73	69	283	15,327
Candie Kung	72	74	68	69	283	15,327
Dorothy Delasin	71	73	69	70	283	15,327
Seol-An Jeon	73	68	71	71	283	15,327
Karrie Webb	69	68	73	73	283	15,327

	SCORES				TOTAL	MONEY
Wendy Ward	71	72	72	69	284	12,460
Emilee Klein	68	76	67	73	284	12,460
Katherine Hull	71	74	71	69	285	10,358
Tina Fischer	73	73	70	69	285	10,358
Joanne Morley	70	69	75	71	285	10,358
Young Kim	70	72	71	72	285	10,358
Pat Hurst	71	72	70	72	285	10,358
Deb Richard	69	76	67	73	285	10,358
Rosie Jones	71	71	70	73	285	10,358
Laura Diaz	71	71	69	74	285	10,358
Aree Song	71	73	72	70	286	7,994
Tracy Hanson	73	70	73	70	286	7,994
Carri Wood	74	69	71	72	286	7,994
Angela Jerman	67	68	78	73	286	7,994

Wendy's Championship for Children

Tartan Fields Golf Club, Dublin, Ohio
Par 37-35–72; 6,517 yards

August 19-22
purse, $1,100,000

	SCORES				TOTAL	MONEY
Catriona Matthew	72	67	71	68	278	$165,000
Hee-Won Han	66	70	72	70	278	101,192
(Matthew defeated Han on first playoff hole.)						
Lorena Ochoa	76	67	69	67	279	73,408
Patricia Meunier-Lebouc	69	72	72	68	281	51,247
Nancy Scranton	69	72	70	70	281	51,247
*Michelle Wie	73	69	71	69	282	
Meg Mallon	73	68	71	70	282	32,041
Mi Hyun Kim	71	68	71	72	282	32,041
Marilyn Lovander	70	69	71	72	282	32,041
Candie Kung	74	71	70	68	283	21,086
Lorie Kane	69	70	73	71	283	21,086
Wendy Ward	70	71	70	72	283	21,086
Laura Diaz	70	72	68	73	283	21,086
Suzann Pettersen	67	68	75	73	283	21,086
Nanci Bowen	73	74	69	68	284	16,566
Kim Williams	73	72	67	72	284	16,566
Soo-Yun Kang	70	73	71	71	285	15,180
*Paula Creamer	72	70	75	69	286	
Marcy Hart	74	70	73	70	287	13,519
Ji Yeon Lee	69	75	70	73	287	13,519
Jeong Jang	71	71	72	73	287	13,519
Kelli Kuehne	72	70	71	74	287	13,519
Jamie Hullett	76	66	75	71	288	11,635
Michele Redman	70	71	75	72	288	11,635
Rosie Jones	71	73	68	76	288	11,635
Brandie Burton	72	66	73	77	288	11,635
Young Kim	75	70	72	72	289	9,442
Laurel Kean	76	68	73	72	289	9,442
Tina Barrett	72	74	70	73	289	9,442
Donna Andrews	71	73	72	73	289	9,442
Eva Dahllof	75	69	71	74	289	9,442
Natalie Gulbis	71	70	73	75	289	9,442
Reilley Rankin	71	65	75	78	289	9,442

Wachovia LPGA Classic

Berkleigh Country Club, Kutztown, Pennsylvania
Par 35-37–72; 6,197 yards

August 26-29
purse, $1,000,000

	SCORES				TOTAL	MONEY
Lorena Ochoa	67	68	69	65	269	$150,000
Grace Park	68	66	65	72	271	91,544
Hee-Won Han	67	72	67	67	273	58,891
Jill McGill	66	64	70	73	273	58,891
Beth Daniel	70	70	66	68	274	41,349
Catriona Matthew	71	69	69	66	275	27,315
Christina Kim	69	69	71	66	275	27,315
Shi Hyun Ahn	67	67	71	70	275	27,315
Nancy Scranton	68	69	67	71	275	27,315
Young-A Yang	73	67	69	67	276	18,878
Marcy Hart	67	72	67	70	276	18,878
Soo-Yun Kang	67	66	68	75	276	18,878
Laura Diaz	66	69	67	75	277	16,439
Kim Saiki	73	68	69	68	278	14,986
Michele Redman	71	71	67	69	278	14,986
Candie Kung	70	69	70	70	279	13,065
Nadina Taylor	70	68	71	70	279	13,065
Joanne Mills	69	69	71	70	279	13,065
Patricia Meunier-Lebouc	71	70	70	69	280	10,926
Meg Mallon	69	72	69	70	280	10,926
Jeong Jang	71	69	70	70	280	10,926
Gloria Park	74	69	65	72	280	10,926
Katherine Hull	70	70	68	72	280	10,926
Janice Moodie	67	70	71	72	280	10,926
Tina Barrett	73	68	71	69	281	8,871
Mi Hyun Kim	71	70	69	71	281	8,871
Jackie Gallagher-Smith	70	68	71	72	281	8,871
Brandie Burton	69	69	71	72	281	8,871
Wendy Ward	70	66	69	76	281	8,871
Pat Hurst	74	70	72	66	282	7,418
Patricia Baxter-Johnson	69	73	70	70	282	7,418
Karrie Webb	70	67	75	70	282	7,418
Hilary Lunke	66	69	71	76	282	7,418

State Farm Classic

Rail Golf Course, Springfield, Illinois
Par 36-36–72; 6,403 yards

September 2-5
purse, $1,200,000

	SCORES				TOTAL	MONEY
Cristie Kerr	69	63	63	69	264	$180,000
Christina Kim	62	66	71	66	265	107,649
Mi Hyun Kim	68	69	66	67	270	78,090
Pat Hurst	68	70	68	67	273	60,410
Kim Saiki	69	69	71	65	274	35,421
Lorena Ochoa	68	67	69	70	274	35,421
Candy Hannemann	68	68	68	70	274	35,421
Suzann Pettersen	67	67	69	71	274	35,421
Nancy Harvey	68	71	64	71	274	35,421
Dorothy Delasin	69	70	67	69	275	23,870
Chris Johnson	70	65	75	66	276	18,909

	SCORES				TOTAL	MONEY
Marcy Hart	68	68	72	68	276	18,909
Shi Hyun Ahn	71	71	66	68	276	18,909
Reilley Rankin	69	69	69	69	276	18,909
Laura Diaz	65	71	68	72	276	18,909
Jennifer Rosales	68	65	68	75	276	18,909
Marisa Baena	69	71	69	68	277	14,381
Carin Koch	71	72	65	69	277	14,381
Maria Hjorth	67	70	70	70	277	14,381
Candie Kung	67	69	70	71	277	14,381
Karen Stupples	72	67	69	70	278	12,612
Kristi Albers	71	68	69	70	278	12,612
Mikaela Parmlid	64	71	69	74	278	12,612
Laura Davies	71	72	67	69	279	10,638
Young-A Yang	69	67	73	70	279	10,638
Tina Barrett	71	66	71	71	279	10,638
Kathryn Marshall	69	73	66	71	279	10,638
Beth Bauer	68	70	69	72	279	10,638
Aree Song	71	72	64	72	279	10,638
Soo-Yun Kang	68	70	70	72	280	9,076

John Q. Hammons Hotel Classic

Cedar Ridge Country Club, Tulsa, Oklahoma
Par 36-35–71; 6,551 yards

September 10-12
purse, $1,000,000

	SCORES			TOTAL	MONEY
Annika Sorenstam	66	68	70	204	$150,000
Shi Hyun Ahn	66	73	69	208	91,110
Candie Kung	72	69	69	210	66,094
Mi Hyun Kim	74	70	67	211	46,141
Heather Bowie	70	72	69	211	46,141
Shani Waugh	73	70	69	212	30,928
Kelli Kuehne	68	72	72	212	30,928
Candy Hannemann	71	70	72	213	21,450
Laura Diaz	71	70	72	213	21,450
Karen Stupples	69	70	74	213	21,450
Joanne Morley	70	67	76	213	21,450
Dorothy Delasin	76	73	65	214	15,464
Tina Barrett	72	74	68	214	15,464
Juli Inkster	74	70	70	214	15,464
Christina Kim	65	75	74	214	15,464
Johanna Head	70	69	75	214	15,464
Moira Dunn	76	70	69	215	11,739
Rachel Teske	73	73	69	215	11,739
Kate Golden	73	70	72	215	11,739
Karrie Webb	73	70	72	215	11,739
Liselotte Neumann	68	74	73	215	11,739
Reilley Rankin	67	74	74	215	11,739
Wendy Ward	75	73	68	216	9,715
Dawn Coe-Jones	73	74	69	216	9,715
Pat Hurst	73	73	70	216	9,715
Helen Alfredsson	73	70	73	216	9,715
Catriona Matthew	74	74	69	217	7,413
Jenna Daniels	74	74	69	217	7,413
Nadina Taylor	74	74	69	217	7,413
Jill McGill	73	73	71	217	7,413
Soo-Yun Kang	78	67	72	217	7,413

	SCORES			TOTAL	MONEY
Kristi Albers	75	70	72	217	7,413
Hee-Won Han	74	71	72	217	7,413
Beth Bader	70	73	74	217	7,413
Jamie Hullett	72	70	75	217	7,413
Mikaela Parmlid	69	71	77	217	7,413

Safeway Classic

Columbia Edgewater Country Club, Portland, Oregon
Par 36-36–72; 6,327 yards

September 17-19
purse, $1,200,000

	SCORES			TOTAL	MONEY
Hee-Won Han	69	71	67	207	$180,000
Lorie Kane	68	69	70	207	107,204
(Han defeated Kane on first playoff hole.)					
Grace Park	71	69	68	208	77,767
Kristal Parker-Manzo	69	75	65	209	49,400
Annika Sorenstam	70	69	70	209	49,400
Candie Kung	69	68	72	209	49,400
Janice Moodie	67	72	71	210	33,162
Brandie Burton	73	71	67	211	27,584
Gloria Park	69	75	67	211	27,584
Nanci Bowen	69	76	67	212	20,730
Lorena Ochoa	73	70	69	212	20,730
Karrie Webb	72	71	69	212	20,730
Patricia Meunier-Lebouc	70	73	69	212	20,730
Natalie Gulbis	69	73	70	212	20,730
Jeong Jang	72	72	69	213	15,377
Marcy Hart	71	73	69	213	15,377
Michelle Ellis	68	73	72	213	15,377
Christina Kim	69	71	73	213	15,377
Angela Stanford	68	72	73	213	15,377
Pat Hurst	68	78	68	214	12,335
Giulia Sergas	69	74	71	214	12,335
Meg Mallon	68	75	71	214	12,335
Young Kim	70	72	72	214	12,335
Karen Stupples	68	73	73	214	12,335
Carin Koch	72	67	75	214	12,335
Tina Barrett	70	75	70	215	9,801
Jung Yeon Lee	70	75	70	215	9,801
Juli Inkster	72	72	71	215	9,801
Jamie Hullett	69	75	71	215	9,801
Jennifer Rosales	67	77	71	215	9,801
Silvia Cavalleri	70	73	72	215	9,801

Longs Drugs Challenge

The Ridge Golf Course, Auburn, California
Par 36-35–71; 6,235 yards

September 23-26
purse, $1,000,000

	SCORES				TOTAL	MONEY
Christina Kim	64	69	68	65	266	$150,000
Karrie Webb	68	66	69	64	267	91,325
Juli Inkster	66	66	68	68	268	66,250
Hee-Won Han	67	67	71	65	270	51,250

	SCORES				TOTAL	MONEY
Anna Acker-Macosko	69	70	72	60	271	37,500
Jeong Jang	70	71	68	62	271	37,500
Mi Hyun Kim	69	69	68	66	272	25,083
Michelle Estill	66	68	70	68	272	25,083
Katherine Hull	72	67	65	68	272	25,083
Liselotte Neumann	73	65	69	66	273	19,500
Donna Andrews	70	68	67	68	273	19,500
Laura Diaz	70	70	67	67	274	17,500
Candie Kung	72	65	71	67	275	15,433
Emilee Klein	68	70	69	68	275	15,433
Leta Lindley	67	67	65	76	275	15,433
Rosie Jones	72	71	66	67	276	13,033
Meg Mallon	70	68	68	70	276	13,033
Angela Stanford	69	65	70	72	276	13,033
Dina Ammaccapane	70	72	71	64	277	11,300
Ashli Bunch	74	69	67	67	277	11,300
Dawn Coe-Jones	68	71	69	69	277	11,300
Kate Golden	69	71	67	70	277	11,300
Candy Hannemann	67	74	69	68	278	10,100
Nadina Taylor	71	68	68	71	278	10,100
Wendy Ward	70	72	69	68	279	8,683
Stacy Prammanasudh	72	69	69	69	279	8,683
Laura Davies	67	70	72	70	279	8,683
Rachel Teske	65	75	69	70	279	8,683
Patricia Meunier-Lebouc	70	72	66	71	279	8,683
Kim Williams	68	72	67	72	279	8,683

Asahi Ryokuken International

Mount Vintage Plantation Golf Club,
North Augusta, South Carolina
Par 36-36–72; 6,366 yards

October 7-10
purse, $1,000,000

	SCORES				TOTAL	MONEY
Liselotte Neumann	68	68	69	68	273	$150,000
Grace Park	66	74	68	68	276	91,993
Silvia Cavalleri	66	76	69	67	278	53,304
Kris Tschetter	69	73	67	69	278	53,304
Laura Davies	69	69	70	70	278	53,304
Jeong Jang	71	67	73	68	279	31,227
Sophie Gustafson	69	73	66	71	279	31,227
Laura Diaz	70	73	66	71	280	23,672
Cristie Kerr	70	68	70	72	280	23,672
Candie Kung	71	73	71	66	281	17,259
Tina Barrett	70	73	68	70	281	17,259
Beth Daniel	71	68	72	70	281	17,259
Candy Hannemann	72	71	67	71	281	17,259
Donna Andrews	68	68	73	72	281	17,259
Becky Morgan	67	69	70	75	281	17,259
Wendy Ward	71	73	72	66	282	12,843
Karen Stupples	71	74	69	68	282	12,843
Angela Stanford	68	73	69	72	282	12,843
Maggie Will	71	69	70	72	282	12,843
Catriona Matthew	71	70	74	68	283	10,980
Shi Hyun Ahn	70	74	70	69	283	10,980
Aree Song	69	75	70	69	283	10,980
Katherine Hull	72	69	73	69	283	10,980

	SCORES				TOTAL	MONEY
Lorena Ochoa	74	70	71	69	284	9,444
Johanna Head	71	71	71	71	284	9,444
Deb Richard	70	72	70	72	284	9,444
Joanne Morley	67	72	72	73	284	9,444
Karrie Webb	70	73	71	71	285	7,917
Stacy Prammanasudh	72	72	69	72	285	7,917
Gloria Park	74	69	68	74	285	7,917
Chris Johnson	71	70	70	74	285	7,917
Kim Saiki	66	74	71	74	285	7,917

Samsung World Championship

Bighorn Golf Course, Canyons Course,
Palm Desert, California
Par 36-36–72; 6,462 yards

October 14-17
purse, $825,000

	SCORES				TOTAL	MONEY
Annika Sorenstam	66	68	69	67	270	$206,250
Grace Park	62	67	71	73	273	131,000
Lorena Ochoa	66	68	71	70	275	88,000
Sophie Gustafson	66	70	70	71	277	52,000
Cristie Kerr	66	68	69	75	278	42,000
Jeong Jang	67	70	70	72	279	29,313
Juli Inkster	67	70	69	73	279	29,313
Shi Hyun Ahn	68	65	78	69	280	23,000
Karen Stupples	68	65	74	73	280	23,000
Mi-Hyun Kim	70	70	71	70	281	20,000
Christina Kim	68	70	71	73	282	17,500
Catriona Matthew	64	70	72	76	282	17,500
*Michelle Wie	74	72	67	70	283	
Jennifer Rosales	68	73	70	72	283	16,000
Hee-Won Han	71	72	72	69	284	15,000
Karrie Webb	71	69	68	77	285	14,000
Wendy Doolan	70	71	76	69	286	13,000
Meg Mallon	73	72	71	71	287	12,000
Laura Davies	76	71	69	72	288	11,500
Se Ri Pak	74	71	80	78	303	11,000

CJ Nine Bridges Classic

The Club at Nine Bridges, Jeju Island, South Korea
Par 36-36–72; 6,299 yards

October 29-31
purse, $1,350,000

	SCORES			TOTAL	MONEY
Grace Park	66	69	65	200	$202,500
Annika Sorenstam	71	67	67	205	108,849
Carin Koch	66	72	67	205	108,849
Lorena Ochoa	68	71	67	206	58,140
Jeong Jang	70	68	68	206	58,140
Shi Hyun Ahn	68	69	69	206	58,140
Young Kim	69	73	65	207	36,611
Jill McGill	67	70	70	207	36,611
Soo-Yun Kang	71	66	71	208	29,359
Kate Golden	71	64	73	208	29,359
Sherri Steinhauer	71	70	68	209	22,809

	SCORES			TOTAL	MONEY
Catriona Matthew	70	71	68	209	22,809
Stacy Prammanasudh	69	70	70	209	22,809
Karen Stupples	67	72	70	209	22,809
Se Ri Pak	72	66	71	209	22,809
Laura Diaz	71	71	68	210	18,927
*Hee Young Park	71	70	69	210	
Angela Stanford	70	75	66	211	17,546
Janice Moodie	72	72	67	211	17,546
*Jane Park	71	69	71	211	
Heather Bowie	75	69	68	212	15,335
Ju Mi Kim	68	76	68	212	15,335
Kim Saiki	72	71	69	212	15,335
Hyun Hee Moon	71	71	70	212	15,335
Mi-Hyun Kim	69	70	73	212	15,335
Natalie Gulbis	75	70	68	213	12,236
Becky Morgan	71	74	68	213	12,236
Gloria Park	73	71	69	213	12,236
Jamie Hullett	71	73	69	213	12,236
Hee-Won Han	72	70	71	213	12,236
Grace Lee	71	71	71	213	12,236
Dorothy Delasin	70	70	73	213	12,236

The Mitchell Company Tournament of Champions

Robert Trent Jones Golf Trail, Magnolia Grove,
Mobile, Alabama
Par 36-36–72; 6,253 yards

November 11-14
purse, $800,000

	SCORES				TOTAL	MONEY
Heather Daly-Donofrio	69	66	64	70	269	$130,000
Laura Diaz	66	67	71	69	273	84,140
Karen Stupples	69	70	64	71	274	48,250
Candie Kung	69	70	64	71	274	48,250
Sophie Gustafson	69	68	65	72	274	48,250
Hee-Won Han	71	68	69	67	275	30,374
Cristie Kerr	67	70	74	69	280	22,382
Karrie Webb	69	71	70	70	280	22,382
Carin Koch	69	70	71	70	280	22,382
Liselotte Neumann	70	73	68	70	281	17,097
Lorie Kane	71	69	68	73	281	17,097
Catriona Matthew	71	70	73	68	282	14,140
Rosie Jones	70	73	69	70	282	14,140
Dorothy Delasin	71	71	67	73	282	14,140
Lorena Ochoa	68	68	71	75	282	14,140
Wendy Ward	73	69	68	73	283	12,026
Juli Inkster	66	71	72	74	283	12,026
Christina Kim	66	70	74	75	285	11,275
Grace Park	66	73	69	77	285	11,275
Laura Davies	74	72	71	69	286	10,417
Angela Stanford	70	72	71	73	286	10,417
Patricia Meunier-Lebouc	69	68	71	78	286	10,417
Kim Saiki	70	73	71	73	287	9,450
Janice Moodie	70	69	70	78	287	9,450
Rachel Teske	68	71	73	76	288	9,060
Beth Daniel	71	73	72	73	289	8,788
Wendy Doolan	68	74	73	75	290	8,498
Jennifer Rosales	71	71	74	75	291	8,231

	SCORES				TOTAL	MONEY
Helen Alfredsson	72	72	76	72	292	7,975
Shi Hyun Ahn	70	78	71	75	294	7,708

ADT Championship

Trump International Golf Club, West Palm Beach, Florida
Par 36-36–72; 6,514 yards

November 18-21
purse, $1,000,000

	SCORES				TOTAL	MONEY
Annika Sorenstam	66	68	72	69	275	$215,000
Cristie Kerr	67	70	70	68	275	115,000
(Sorenstam defeated Kerr on first playoff hole.)						
Carin Koch	73	67	71	69	280	71,500
Karrie Webb	68	69	74	69	280	71,500
Jennifer Rosales	70	68	69	74	281	50,000
Laura Diaz	69	68	75	70	282	43,000
Meg Mallon	74	66	73	71	284	33,000
Rachel Teske	70	69	72	73	284	33,000
Juli Inkster	74	74	70	69	287	25,250
Jeong Jang	68	72	75	72	287	25,250
Becky Morgan	72	74	70	72	288	20,250
Lorie Kane	75	65	75	73	288	20,250
Karen Stupples	76	70	73	70	289	16,750
Wendy Ward	73	69	74	73	289	16,750
Grace Park	71	70	74	75	290	15,250
Rosie Jones	73	71	74	73	291	14,250
Lorena Ochoa	75	68	74	75	292	13,250
Candie Kung	68	72	71	81	292	13,250
Hee-Won Han	75	69	74	75	293	12,250
Pat Hurst	75	70	74	75	294	11,500
Beth Daniel	76	75	72	72	295	10,967
Christina Kim	77	73	68	77	295	10,967
Kim Saiki	70	73	75	77	295	10,967
Aree Song	72	73	79	74	298	10,150
Sherri Steinhauer	75	73	72	78	298	10,150
Michele Redman	76	74	75	76	301	9,333
Catriona Matthew	78	71	76	76	301	9,333
Shi Hyun Ahn	70	71	82	78	301	9,333
Stacy Prammanasudh	78	83	70	73	304	8,850
Gloria Park	75	76	77	77	305	8,700

Ladies European Tour

ANZ Ladies Masters

See Australian Women's Tour.

AAMI Women's Australian Open

See Australian Women's Tour.

Tenerife Ladies Open

Buenavista Golf Club, Tenerife, Canary Islands
Par 36-36–72; 6,012 yards

April 29-May 2
purse, €220,000

	SCORES				TOTAL	MONEY
Diana Luna	71	66	73	69	279	€33,000
Becky Brewerton	74	67	71	69	281	22,330
Georgina Simpson	71	69	72	70	282	15,400
Minea Blomqvist	66	71	77	70	284	11,880
Elisabeth Esterl	73	68	75	69	285	8,514
Nuria Clau	68	71	77	69	285	8,514
Johanna Westerberg	67	74	73	72	286	6,050
Kirsty Taylor	71	73	75	67	286	6,050
Stephanie Arricau	70	68	79	70	287	4,928
Anne-Marie Knight	76	64	78	72	290	4,400
Bettina Hauert	76	70	79	66	291	3,690.50
Sara Beautell	73	71	80	67	291	3,690.50
Sophie Giquel	70	69	83	69	291	3,690.50
Lynnette Brooky	72	72	75	72	291	3,690.50
Laura Cabanillas Gomez	71	74	77	70	292	3,278
Cecilia Ekelundh	75	71	74	73	293	3,124
*Emma Cabrera	68	71	80	74	293	
Karine Icher	73	75	75	70	293	3,124
Asa Gottmo	74	72	77	71	294	2,948
Alison Nicholas	71	76	72	75	294	2,948
Gina Scott	70	77	75	73	295	2,706
Susan Parry	79	69	74	73	295	2,706
Julie Forbes	72	72	77	74	295	2,706
Riikka Hakkarainen	72	73	76	74	295	2,706
Vibeke Stensrud	69	77	77	72	295	2,706
Lora Fairclough	74	71	74	77	296	2,442
Corinne Dibnah	74	72	72	78	296	2,442
Karen Lunn	72	74	77	73	296	2,442
Marta Prieto	75	75	75	72	297	2,244
Martina Eberl	70	77	80	70	297	2,244
Trish Johnson	77	69	73	78	297	2,244

Ladies Open of Portugal

Aroeira Golf Club, Aroeira, Portugal
Par 36-36–72; 6,075 yards

May 7-9
purse, €300,000

	SCORES			TOTAL	MONEY
Cecilia Ekelundh	67	72	67	206	€45,000
Linda Wessberg	69	70	70	209	30,450
Trish Johnson	73	66	72	211	21,000
Asa Gottmo	73	70	70	213	13,140
Ana Larraneta	69	73	71	213	13,140
Karine Icher	70	72	71	213	13,140
Anja Monke	76	68	70	214	8,250
Elisabeth Esterl	72	69	73	214	8,250
Anne-Marie Knight	68	73	74	215	6,720
Virginie Beauchet	75	72	69	216	5,100
Maria Boden	71	75	70	216	5,100
Tullia Calzavara	74	71	71	216	5,100
Diana Luna	72	71	73	216	5,100
Laurette Maritz	69	74	73	216	5,100
Johanna Westerberg	72	71	73	216	5,100
Stephanie Arricau	73	73	71	217	3,937.50
Raquel Carriedo	69	75	73	217	3,937.50
Isabella Maconi	73	71	73	217	3,937.50
Gina Scott	73	71	73	217	3,937.50
Nathalie David	74	69	74	217	3,937.50
Virginie Auffret	71	72	74	217	3,937.50
Stefania Croce	70	72	75	217	3,937.50
Gwladys Nocera	71	70	76	217	3,937.50
Nuria Clau	70	75	73	218	3,375
Amanda Moltke-Leth	74	71	73	218	3,375
Ludivine Kreutz	76	69	73	218	3,375
Georgina Simpson	72	70	76	218	3,375
Sophie Sandolo	75	72	72	219	2,880
Marta Prieto	76	71	72	219	2,880
Sophie Giquel	74	72	73	219	2,880
Ursula Tuutti	76	69	74	219	2,880
Suzanne Dickens	70	75	74	219	2,880
Lynnette Brooky	70	74	75	219	2,880
Ana Belen Sanchez	72	72	75	219	2,880

Union Fenosa Open de Espana Feminino Xacobeo

Club de Golf de la Coruna, La Coruna, Spain
Par 36-36–72; 6,105 yards

May 27-30
purse, €275,000

	SCORES				TOTAL	MONEY
Stephanie Arricau	71	66	71	71	279	€41,250
Gina Scott	71	69	70	69	279	27,913
(Arricau defeated Scott on first playoff hole.)						
Becky Brewerton	68	71	70	71	280	19,250
Lynnette Brooky	75	68	69	70	282	14,850
Ana Belen Sanchez	70	70	72	72	284	11,660
Stefania Croce	75	72	67	71	285	8,937.50
Nuria Clau	68	68	76	73	285	8,937.50
Carina Vagner	71	70	76	69	286	5,898.75
Ana Larraneta	72	72	73	69	286	5,898.75

	SCORES				TOTAL	MONEY
Martina Eberl	69	75	71	71	286	5,898.75
Anja Monke	68	71	73	74	286	5,898.75
Cecilia Ekelundh	72	71	73	71	287	4,730
Sophie Giquel	73	71	75	69	288	4,180
Kirsty Taylor	76	71	71	70	288	4,180
Lora Fairclough	70	72	74	72	288	4,180
Georgina Simpson	71	71	71	75	288	4,180
*Elisa Serramia	71	71	73	74	289	
Suzanne Dickens	77	69	69	74	289	3,795
Virginie Beauchet	69	71	73	76	289	3,795
Sofia Renell	75	72	70	73	290	3,547.50
Julie Forbes	72	72	72	74	290	3,547.50
Minea Blomqvist	73	72	71	74	290	3,547.50
Barbara Paruscio	77	69	76	69	291	3,258.75
Raquel Carriedo	73	73	76	69	291	3,258.75
Nina Karlsson	75	72	72	72	291	3,258.75
Veronica Zorzi	72	72	75	72	291	3,258.75
Nathalie David	72	70	77	73	292	2,970
Karine Icher	75	69	73	75	292	2,970
Rachel Bailey	74	73	69	76	292	2,970
Ursula Tuutti	73	74	75	71	293	2,681.25
Anne-Marie Knight	75	74	71	73	293	2,681.25
Joanna Whalley	74	72	74	73	293	2,681.25
Riikka Hakkarainen	76	73	70	74	293	2,681.25

BMW Ladies Italian Open

Parco di Roma Golf Club, Rome, Italy
Par 36-36–72; 6,220 yards

June 3-6
purse, €275,000

	SCORES				TOTAL	MONEY
Ana Belen Sanchez	71	69	72	69	281	€41,250
Martina Eberl	71	73	71	67	282	27,912.50
Karine Icher	70	76	71	68	285	19,250
Virginie Beauchet	74	68	76	68	286	14,850
Diana Luna	71	73	70	74	288	11,660
Johanna Head	71	74	71	73	289	9,625
Elisabeth Esterl	70	78	75	67	290	6,696.25
Gwladys Nocera	75	71	74	70	290	6,696.25
Alison Nicholas	74	73	73	70	290	6,696.25
Corinne Dibnah	73	75	70	72	290	6,696.25
Asa Gottmo	74	75	70	72	291	4,613.12
Nicola Moult	70	74	74	73	291	4,613.12
Linda Wessberg	70	77	71	73	291	4,613.12
Anja Monke	76	75	67	73	291	4,613.12
Raquel Carriedo	72	76	76	68	292	3,855.50
Maria Boden	74	76	72	70	292	3,855.50
Sara Beautell	79	73	69	71	292	3,855.50
Marina Arruti	71	73	75	73	292	3,855.50
Minea Blomqvist	76	71	72	73	292	3,855.50
Judith Van Hagen	71	74	77	71	293	3,382.50
Becky Brewerton	76	75	71	71	293	3,382.50
Gina Scott	77	74	71	71	293	3,382.50
Lynnette Brooky	74	72	72	75	293	3,382.50
Trish Johnson	71	74	72	76	293	3,382.50
Stephanie Arricau	73	78	70	73	294	3,052.50
Lara Tadiotto	75	75	70	74	294	3,052.50

	SCORES				TOTAL	MONEY
Nicole Stillig	73	74	72	75	294	3,052.50
Riikka Hakkarainen	72	78	74	71	295	2,805
Karen Margrethe Juul	70	76	77	72	295	2,805
Kirsty Taylor	74	71	76	74	295	2,805

Arras Open de France Dames

Le Golf d'Arras, St. Aubin, France
Par 36-36–72; 6,195 yards

June 10-13
purse, €275,000

	SCORES				TOTAL	MONEY
Stephanie Arricau	71	70	73	67	281	€41,250
Natascha Fink	72	70	69	72	283	27,912.50
Jane Leary	72	72	71	70	285	17,050
Linda Wessberg	73	69	71	72	285	17,050
Lora Fairclough	73	69	73	71	286	9,102.50
Laurette Maritz	69	70	74	73	286	9,102.50
Anja Monke	71	72	69	74	286	9,102.50
Asa Gottmo	70	68	72	76	286	9,102.50
Lynnette Brooky	68	73	76	70	287	5,362.50
Gwladys Nocera	67	76	72	72	287	5,362.50
Gina Scott	66	73	74	74	287	5,362.50
Nathalie David	70	74	69	74	287	5,362.50
Emma Zackrisson	70	75	72	71	288	4,114
Virginie Beauchet	71	71	73	73	288	4,114
Lara Tadiotto	73	70	72	73	288	4,114
Cherie Byrnes	73	71	71	73	288	4,114
Helena Alterby	69	73	70	76	288	4,114
Riikka Hakkarainen	71	76	69	73	289	3,639.16
Diana Luna	69	72	74	74	289	3,639.16
Suzanne O'Brien	71	73	70	75	289	3,639.16
Marina Arruti	73	72	70	75	290	3,465
Monica Cosenza	73	71	76	71	291	3,258.75
Ana Larraneta	73	72	75	71	291	3,258.75
Sophie Giquel	74	73	69	75	291	3,258.75
Sophie Sandolo	70	75	70	76	291	3,258.75
Ursula Tuutti	74	73	71	74	292	3,011.25
Cecilia Ekelundh	74	74	68	76	292	3,011.25
Tullia Calzavara	72	73	76	72	293	2,557.50
Virginie Auffret	73	76	72	72	293	2,557.50
Corinne Dibnah	71	74	75	73	293	2,557.50
Lesley Nicholson	74	74	71	74	293	2,557.50
Kirsty Taylor	70	74	74	75	293	2,557.50
Minea Blomqvist	71	73	73	76	293	2,557.50
Bettina Hauert	71	75	71	76	293	2,557.50
Dale Reid	75	72	70	76	293	2,557.50
Sophie Hunter	72	73	71	77	293	2,557.50

KLM Ladies Open

Kennemer Golf & Country Club, Zandvoort, Netherlands
Par 36-36–72; 6,220 yards

June 25-27
purse, €165,000

	SCORES			TOTAL	MONEY
Elisabeth Esterl	71	75	68	214	€24,750
Marta Prieto	76	70	70	216	16,747.50
Becky Brewerton	74	71	72	217	10,230
Georgina Simpson	75	68	74	217	10,230
Linda Wessberg	78	69	71	218	5,907
Kirsty Taylor	73	73	72	218	5,907
Ludivine Kreutz	75	70	73	218	5,907
Marine Monnet	74	73	72	219	3,399
Carlie Butler	74	73	72	219	3,399
Stephanie Arricau	74	73	72	219	3,399
Tullia Calzavara	81	65	73	219	3,399
Lynnette Brooky	73	73	73	219	3,399
Virginie Auffret	78	72	70	220	2,552
Suzanne O'Brien	74	74	72	220	2,552
Asa Gottmo	72	72	76	220	2,552
Jane Leary	74	76	71	221	2,310
Karine Icher	74	74	73	221	2,310
Sophie Giquel	75	72	74	221	2,310
Elin Olsson	76	75	71	222	2,079
Jessica Lindbergh	78	72	72	222	2,079
Raquel Carriedo	72	77	73	222	2,079
Veronica Zorzi	75	72	75	222	2,079
Minea Blomqvist	73	74	75	222	2,079
Maria Boden	80	71	72	223	1,806.75
Ana Larraneta	77	74	72	223	1,806.75
Cecilia Ekelundh	77	74	72	223	1,806.75
Corinne Dibnah	77	73	73	223	1,806.75
Gwladys Nocera	73	76	74	223	1,806.75
Dale Reid	75	73	75	223	1,806.75
Gina Scott	78	76	70	224	1,633.50
*Dewi-Claire Schreefel	68	76	80	224	

Ladies English Open

Chart Hills Golf Club, Kent, England
Par 36-36–72; 5,845 yards

July 9-11
purse, €179,063

	SCORES			TOTAL	MONEY
Maria Hjorth	66	67	64	197	€26,859.45
Joanne Mills	67	68	68	203	18,174.89
Karen Stupples	67	69	68	204	11,101.90
Asa Gottmo	68	67	69	204	11,101.90
Trish Johnson	69	69	67	205	6,929.74
Anja Monke	72	65	68	205	6,929.74
Minea Blomqvist	66	71	69	206	5,371.89
Lora Fairclough	72	71	64	207	4,022.95
Iben Tinning	70	68	69	207	4,022.95
Veronica Zorzi	73	65	69	207	4,022.95
Laurette Maritz	68	71	69	208	3,003.78
Gwladys Nocera	71	66	71	208	3,003.78
Karen Margrethe Juul	70	67	71	208	3,003.78

	SCORES			TOTAL	MONEY
Margherita Rigon	67	68	73	208	3,003.78
Kirsty Taylor	72	69	68	209	2,584.47
Stephanie Arricau	71	70	68	209	2,584.47
*Shelley McKevitt	71	69	69	209	
Becky Brewerton	68	68	73	209	2,584.47
Linda Wessberg	72	72	66	210	2,313.49
Suzanne O'Brien	71	71	68	210	2,313.49
Stefania Croce	71	70	69	210	2,313.49
Karen Lunn	72	68	70	210	2,313.49
Virginie Beauchet	68	71	71	210	2,313.49
Nina Karlsson	70	72	69	211	1,960.74
Johanna Westerberg	70	72	69	211	1,960.74
Cecilia Ekelundh	72	69	70	211	1,960.74
Filippa Helmersson	73	68	70	211	1,960.74
Sophie Giquel	73	68	70	211	1,960.74
Alison Nicholas	68	72	71	211	1,960.74
Cecilie Lundgreen	69	70	72	211	1,960.74

OTP Bank Ladies Central European Open

Old Lake Golf & Country Club, Tata, Hungary
Par 35-36–71; 6,035 yards

July 16-18
purse, €165,000

	SCORES			TOTAL	MONEY
Minea Blomqvist	62	67	70	199	€24,750
Gina Scott	67	69	67	203	14,148.75
Emma Zackrisson	68	65	70	203	14,148.75
Virginie Auffret	68	66	70	204	7,953
Karine Icher	66	67	71	204	7,953
Kirsty Taylor	71	69	65	205	4,950
Anja Monke	67	69	69	205	4,950
Cecilie Lundgreen	66	67	72	205	4,950
Martina Eberl	70	68	68	206	3,498
Laurette Maritz	68	68	70	206	3,498
Kirsty Taylor	67	71	69	207	2,767.87
Ludivine Kreutz	69	69	69	207	2,767.87
Maria Hjorth	69	67	71	207	2,767.87
Jenni Kuosa	68	65	74	207	2,767.87
Alexandra Armas	70	71	67	208	2,417.25
Rebecca Hudson	68	70	70	208	2,417.25
*Stefanie Endstrasser	68	70	70	208	
Sarah Bennett	71	69	69	209	2,135.57
Veronica Zorzi	68	72	69	209	2,135.57
Karen Lunn	71	70	68	209	2,135.57
Nina Reis	71	69	69	209	2,135.57
Helena Svensson	68	70	71	209	2,135.57
Anne-Marie Knight	69	68	72	209	2,135.57
Raquel Carriedo	67	69	73	209	2,135.57
Laura Cabanillas	69	71	70	210	1,782
Nienke Nijenhuis	71	69	70	210	1,782
Stefania Croce	69	72	69	210	1,782
Lara Tadiotto	69	70	71	210	1,782
Alison Nicholas	73	66	71	210	1,782
Federica Piovano	69	69	72	210	1,782
Elisabeth Esterl	67	76	67	210	1,782

Evian Masters

Evian Masters Golf Club, Evians-les-Bains, France
Par 36-36–72; 6,171 yards

July 21-24
purse, €1,977,826

	SCORES				TOTAL	MONEY
Wendy Doolan	68	68	69	65	270	€296,673.90
Annika Sorenstam	66	69	65	71	271	195,121.24
Lorena Ochoa	68	69	67	68	272	141,547.47
Karen Stupples	68	66	69	70	273	109,498.78
Laura Davies	64	71	72	71	278	88,133.51
Meg Mallon	71	69	72	67	279	61,782.27
Hee-Won Han	71	70	69	69	279	61,782.27
Juli Inkster	70	73	67	69	279	61,782.27
Mi Hyun Kim	71	69	70	70	280	42,063.41
Gloria Park	72	67	70	71	280	42,063.41
Suzann Pettersen	70	69	69	72	280	42,063.41
Carin Koch	69	70	69	72	280	42,063.41
Kim Saiki	70	67	75	69	281	35,039.96
Rosie Jones	70	69	69	74	282	32,903.11
Rachel Teske	70	68	74	71	283	29,342.50
Asa Gottmo	69	72	71	71	283	29,342.50
Stephanie Arricau	67	73	71	72	283	29,342.50
Pat Hurst	74	69	72	69	284	25,496.55
Patricia Meunier-Lebouc	69	70	74	71	284	25,496.55
Wendy Ward	72	68	73	71	284	25,496.55
Paula Marti	72	69	74	70	285	21,243.66
Michele Redman	74	71	70	70	285	21,243.66
Catriona Matthew	70	67	77	71	285	21,243.66
Becky Morgan	69	72	72	72	285	21,243.66
Cristie Kerr	72	71	70	72	285	21,243.66
Soo-Yun Kang	69	72	71	73	285	21,243.66
Lynnette Brooky	66	72	73	74	285	21,243.66
Helen Alfredsson	73	71	72	70	286	16,793.16
Hilary Lunke	75	68	72	71	286	16,793.16
Jeong Jang	76	71	68	71	286	16,793.16
Grace Park	72	67	72	75	286	16,793.16
Marta Prieto	66	73	70	77	286	16,793.16

Weetabix Women's British Open

Sunningdale Golf Club, Old Course, Berkshire, England
Par 36-36–72; 6,308 yards

July 29-August 1
purse, €1,050,000

	SCORES				TOTAL	MONEY
Karen Stupples	65	70	70	64	269	€229,200
Rachel Teske	70	69	65	70	274	143,250
Heather Bowie	70	69	65	71	275	100,275
Lorena Ochoa	69	71	66	70	276	78,787.50
Michele Redman	70	71	70	66	277	56,822.50
Giulia Sergas	72	71	67	67	277	56,822.50
Beth Daniel	69	69	71	68	277	56,822.50
Jung Yeon Lee	67	72	70	69	278	41,542.50
Laura Davies	70	69	69	70	278	41,542.50
Minea Blomqvist	68	78	62	70	278	41,542.50
Pat Hurst	72	72	66	69	279	32,947.50
Cristie Kerr	69	73	63	74	279	32,947.50

	SCORES				TOTAL	MONEY
Carin Koch	70	70	70	70	280	22,785.70
Hee-Won Han	72	68	70	70	280	22,785.70
Grace Park	71	70	69	70	280	22,785.70
Laura Diaz	70	69	70	71	280	22,785.70
Annika Sorenstam	68	71	70	71	280	22,785.70
Natalie Gulbis	68	71	70	71	280	22,785.70
Christina Kim	73	68	68	71	280	22,785.70
Paula Marti	73	66	68	73	280	22,785.70
Se Ri Pak	73	70	69	69	281	17,548.12
Michelle Estill	70	72	68	71	281	17,548.12
Aree Song	72	70	70	70	282	16,115.62
Jeong Jang	70	68	73	71	282	16,115.62
Juli Inkster	71	75	69	68	283	14,611.50
Toshimi Kimura	70	75	68	70	283	14,611.50
Seol-An Jeon	69	69	70	75	283	14,611.50
Alison Nicholas	75	71	70	69	285	13,537.13
Candie Kung	73	69	71	73	286	12,785.06
Catriona Matthew	68	74	68	76	286	12,785.06

HP Open

Ullna Golf Club, Stockholm, Sweden
Par 36-36–72; 6,234 yards

August 5-8
purse, €465,563

	SCORES				TOTAL	MONEY
Annika Sorenstam	70	72	69	64	275	€69,834.45
Carin Koch	71	70	68	68	277	47,254.64
Becky Morgan	70	70	69	70	279	32,589.41
Janice Moodie	70	70	72	68	280	25,140.40
Stephanie Arricau	75	70	68	68	281	19,739.87
Shani Waugh	74	71	70	70	285	15,130.80
Silvia Cavalleri	74	70	70	71	285	15,130.80
Liselotte Neumann	74	74	67	71	286	11,639.08
Ana Larraneta	72	76	72	67	287	9,078.47
Laura Davies	77	71	71	68	287	9,078.47
Cecilia Ekelundh	73	76	70	68	287	9,078.47
Karine Icher	71	71	72	73	287	9,078.47
*Louise Stahle	67	75	72	73	287	
Nina Karlsson	73	73	74	68	288	6,859.29
Lora Fairclough	73	74	72	69	288	6,859.29
Suzann Pettersen	72	77	69	70	288	6,859.29
Veronica Zorzi	75	73	69	71	288	6,859.29
Margherita Rigon	72	72	71	73	288	6,859.29
Trish Johnson	74	70	71	73	288	6,859.29
Johanna Head	72	73	74	71	290	6,005.76
Gwladys Nocera	75	72	72	71	290	6,005.76
Samantha Head	73	74	71	72	290	6,005.76
Emelie Svenningsson	68	79	77	67	291	5,586.75
Linda Wessberg	75	73	74	69	291	5,586.75
Helen Alfredsson	78	70	72	71	291	5,586.75
Marlene Hedblom	74	76	72	70	292	4,958.24
Johanna Westerberg	75	75	72	70	292	4,958.24
Georgina Simpson	75	76	70	71	292	4,958.24
Martina Eberl	77	71	72	72	292	4,958.24
Alison Munt	76	75	68	73	292	4,958.24
Iben Tinning	72	75	71	74	292	4,958.24

Wales "Golf as it should be" Ladies Open

Royal Porthcawl Golf Club, Bridgend, Wales
Par 36-37–73; 6,183 yards

August 12-15
purse, €501,375

	SCORES				TOTAL	MONEY
Trish Johnson	73	70	69	65	277	€75,206.25
Iben Tinning	70	73	69	68	280	42,992.90
Laura Davies	67	73	68	72	280	42,992.90
Marta Prieto	69	74	69	70	282	21,960.22
Asa Gottmo	72	67	70	73	282	21,960.22
Helen Alfredsson	76	68	64	74	282	21,960.22
Cecilia Ekelundh	71	68	73	71	283	13,787.81
Nuria Clau	71	69	72	71	283	13,787.81
Sara Beautell	67	76	70	71	284	11,230.80
Ana Belen Sanchez	70	74	69	72	285	10,027.50
Anne-Marie Knight	66	78	75	67	286	8,410.56
Lara Tadiotto	75	76	67	68	286	8,410.56
Johanna Head	69	71	74	72	286	8,410.56
Lynnette Brooky	73	69	72	72	286	8,410.56
Becky Brewerton	71	76	70	70	287	7,236.51
Karine Icher	72	71	71	73	287	7,236.51
Kirsty Taylor	70	74	70	73	287	7,236.51
Lora Fairclough	76	71	72	69	288	6,324.48
Suzanne O'Brien	75	73	70	70	288	6,324.48
Ana Larraneta	75	74	69	70	288	6,324.48
Nadina Taylor	72	70	72	74	288	6,324.48
Gwladys Nocera	70	73	70	75	288	6,324.48
Karen Margrethe Juul	69	70	73	76	288	6,324.48
Sophie Gustafson	71	72	69	76	288	6,324.48
Liselotte Neumann	73	73	72	71	289	5,490.05
Judith Van Hagen	71	73	72	73	289	5,490.05
Julie Forbes	69	76	71	73	289	5,490.05
Linda Wessberg	75	72	69	73	289	5,490.05
Alexandra Armas	72	76	71	71	290	5,038.82
Martina Eberl	76	72	69	73	290	5,038.82

Catalonia Ladies Masters

Club de Golf Sant Cugat, Barcelona, Spain
Par 34-35–69; 5,598 yards

October 1-3
purse, €180,000

	SCORES			TOTAL	MONEY
Karine Icher	62	66	62	190	€31,000
Stephanie Arricau	67	67	65	199	15,000
Paula Marti	67	66	66	199	15,000
Anja Monke	67	69	64	200	9,000
Gwladys Nocera	64	66	71	201	7,000
Kirsty Taylor	68	68	67	203	5,700
Nadina Taylor	66	67	71	204	4,900
Marta Prieto	69	66	70	205	4,350
Helen Alfredsson	64	68	73	205	4,350
Becky Brewerton	70	70	66	206	4,050
Laurette Maritz	66	69	71	206	4,050
Lynnette Brooky	65	73	69	207	3,900
Asa Gottmo	66	71	70	207	3,900
Laura Davies	65	66	76	207	3,900

	SCORES			TOTAL	MONEY
Gina Scott	64	72	72	208	3,775
Sara Beautell	70	71	67	208	3,775
Linda Wessberg	68	68	73	209	3,700
Minea Blomqvist	77	65	68	210	3,650
Diana Luna	69	69	73	211	3,575
Anne-Marie Knight	69	71	71	211	3,575
Marina Arruti	67	77	68	212	3,500
Virginie Auffret	71	69	73	213	3,425
Candy Hannemann	73	71	69	213	3,425
Elisabeth Esterl	73	72	69	214	3,350
Natascha Fink	73	70	72	215	3,300
Trish Johnson	70	76	70	216	3,250
Patricia Sota	73	73	71	217	3,175
Martina Eberl	73	73	71	217	3,175
Marlene Hedblom	79	73	69	221	3,087.50
Ana Belen Sanchez	71	75	75	221	3,087.50

Japan LPGA Tour

Daikin Orchid Ladies

Tamagasuku Golf Club, Okinawa
Par 36-36–72; 6,338 yards

March 5-7
purse, ¥60,000,000

	SCORES			TOTAL	MONEY
Ai Miyazato	70	66	70	206	¥10,800,000
Kaori Higo	69	70	70	209	5,280,000
Mikiyo Nishizuka	67	73	71	211	3,900,000
Toshimi Kimura	68	71	72	211	3,900,000
Aki Takamura	71	70	72	213	3,000,000
*Shinobu Moromizato	67	72	74	213	
Fuki Kido	75	71	68	214	2,400,000
Yu-Chen Huang	68	76	71	215	1,650,000
Kaori Harada	72	72	71	215	1,650,000
Shiho Ohyama	69	75	71	215	1,650,000
Midori Yoneyama	71	74	70	215	1,650,000
*Mika Miyazato	69	73	73	215	
Riko Higashio	70	72	74	216	1,020,000
Yukari Baba	67	77	72	216	1,020,000
Keiko Sasaki	71	71	74	216	1,020,000
Michiko Hattori	72	75	69	216	1,020,000
Junko Omote	72	72	73	217	810,000
Miho Koga	71	76	70	217	810,000
Rui Kitada	71	72	74	217	810,000
Hiroko Yamaguchi	72	74	72	218	630,000
Kyoko Kadokawa	72	73	73	218	630,000
Yuka Shiroto	68	76	74	218	630,000
Seiko Watanabe	74	72	73	219	534,000

	SCORES			TOTAL	MONEY
Yuri Fudoh	69	76	74	219	534,000
Kayo Yamada	74	73	72	219	534,000
Mihoko Takahashi	73	73	73	219	534,000
Yuko Moriguchi	73	72	74	219	534,000
Miyuki Shimabukuro	71	76	73	220	474,000
Woo-Soon Ko	72	76	72	220	474,000
Harumi Sakagami	71	72	77	220	474,000
Mineko Nasu	68	77	75	220	474,000
Chieko Nishida	71	77	72	220	474,000

Saishunkan Ladies Hinokuni Open

Kumamoto Kuukou Country Club, Kikuyo, Kumamoto
Par 36-36–72; 6,433 yards

April 16-18
purse, ¥60,000,000

	SCORES			TOTAL	MONEY
Yuri Fudoh	76	68	73	217	¥10,800,000
Woo-Soon Ko	71	73	73	217	5,280,000
*Sakura Yokomine	71	75	71	217	
(Fudoh defeated Ko on first and Yokomine on second playoff hole.)					
Mitsuko Kawasaki	72	73	73	218	3,060,000
Yuka Sakaguchi	68	73	77	218	3,060,000
Hiromi Mogi	73	72	73	218	3,060,000
Yuka Tonsho	72	76	70	218	3,060,000
Michie Ohba	72	72	74	218	3,060,000
Ji-Hee Lee	71	72	76	219	1,500,000
Chieko Amanuma	72	73	74	219	1,500,000
Shiho Ohyama	71	76	72	219	1,500,000
Nikki Campbell	72	72	77	221	1,062,000
Ayako Uehara	73	75	73	221	1,062,000
Yun-Jye Wei	73	72	76	221	1,062,000
Hsiu-Feng Tseng	71	74	77	222	822,000
Natsuko Noro	74	74	74	222	822,000
Fumiko Muraguchi	71	76	75	222	822,000
Maki Sasayama	73	71	78	222	822,000
Hiromi Takesue	77	69	76	222	822,000
Miho Koga	69	81	73	223	612,000
Michiko Hattori	75	72	76	223	612,000
Keiko Sasaki	75	72	77	224	528,000
Hikaru Kobayashi	72	75	77	224	528,000
Hsiao-Chuan Lu	72	77	75	224	528,000
Mikiyo Nishizuka	75	76	73	224	528,000
Misato Nishikawa	76	74	74	224	528,000
Junko Omote	71	75	78	224	528,000
Takayo Bandoh	73	74	77	224	528,000
Michiko Mitsui	76	72	76	224	528,000
Kuniko Maeda	74	75	76	225	450,000
Shin Sora	78	73	74	225	450,000
Kaori Higo	79	71	75	225	450,000
Kumiko Hiyoshi	73	76	76	225	450,000
Young-Me Lee	75	75	75	225	450,000

Katokichi Queens

Yashima Country Club, Mure, Kagawa
Par 36-36–72; 6,249 yards

April 30-May2
purse, ¥60,000,000

	SCORES			TOTAL	MONEY
Hsiao-Chuan Lu	69	68	71	208	¥10,800,000
Michie Ohba	68	69	71	208	5,280,000
(Lu defeated Ohba on first playoff hole.)					
Yuri Fudoh	72	66	71	209	4,200,000
Junko Omote	70	70	70	210	3,600,000
Yuka Irie	70	73	69	212	3,000,000
Yun-Jye Wei	72	71	70	213	1,687,000
Ai Miyazato	69	73	71	213	1,687,000
Yuko Saitoh	72	71	70	213	1,687,000
Mihoko Takahashi	67	69	77	213	1,687,000
Aki Nakano	71	71	71	213	1,687,000
Kyoko Ono	69	71	73	213	1,687,000
Young-Me Lee	70	71	73	214	1,002,000
Kasumi Fujii	68	68	78	214	1,002,000
Kaori Suzuki	73	68	73	214	1,002,000
Miho Koga	70	72	73	215	732,000
Yuka Tonsho	77	67	71	215	732,000
Kaori Higo	72	74	69	215	732,000
Nikki Campbell	74	68	73	215	732,000
Kaori Harada	72	71	72	215	732,000
Chieko Amanuma	72	70	73	215	732,000
Kayo Yamada	71	73	72	216	528,000
Mitsuko Kawasaki	71	69	76	216	528,000
Keiko Sasaki	73	70	73	216	528,000
Hiromi Mogi	72	70	74	216	528,000
Mari Nishi	71	74	71	216	528,000
Mizuho Ozawa	72	72	72	216	528,000
Fuki Kido	73	71	72	216	528,000
Toshimi Kimura	67	75	74	216	528,000
Mieko Nomura	69	77	71	217	438,000
Mineko Nasu	74	70	73	217	438,000
Mikiyo Nishizuka	74	71	72	217	438,000
Midori Yoneyama	70	74	73	217	438,000
Yuka Sakaguchi	69	71	77	217	438,000
Akane Takagi	74	71	72	217	438,000
Yasuko Satoh	74	72	71	217	438,000

Nichirei Cup World Ladies

Yomiuri Country Club, Tokyo
Par 36-36–72; 6,456 yards

May 6-9
purse, ¥60,000,000

	SCORES				TOTAL	MONEY
Rui Kitada	68	64	67	73	272	¥10,800,000
Yuri Fudoh	64	65	74	71	274	5,280,000
*Shinobu Moromizato	67	69	66	75	277	
Michie Ohba	71	65	70	72	278	4,200,000
Akiko Fukushima	68	72	69	71	280	3,600,000
Woo-Soon Ko	69	73	66	73	281	3,000,000
Noriko Aso	65	68	75	75	283	1,800,000
Ai Miyazato	71	73	69	70	283	1,800,000

	SCORES			TOTAL	MONEY
Hiromi Mogi	73	72	67	71	283	1,800,000
Hsiao-Chuan Lu	69	74	69	71	283	1,800,000
Laura Davies	70	70	71	72	283	1,800,000
Chieko Amanuma	70	72	70	72	284	1,014,000
Toshimi Kimura	67	69	75	73	284	1,014,000
Yun-Jye Wei	73	66	72	73	284	1,014,000
Mari Katayama	70	70	74	71	285	744,000
Kyoko Ono	72	68	70	75	285	744,000
Yuka Sakaguchi	72	70	70	73	285	744,000
Ji-Yeon Han	69	67	75	74	285	744,000
Michiko Hattori	76	68	71	70	285	744,000
Mitsuko Kawasaki	69	70	73	73	285	744,000
Kim Ju Mi	70	68	75	73	286	510,000
Chihiro Nakajima	71	73	70	72	286	510,000
Fumiko Muraguchi	74	69	70	73	286	510,000
Yasuko Satoh	73	69	73	71	286	510,000
Samantha Head	71	71	72	72	286	510,000
Miho Koga	74	69	70	74	287	438,000
Kasumi Fujii	70	71	71	75	287	438,000
Mika Adaniya	72	72	70	73	287	438,000
Young-Me Lee	73	71	69	74	287	438,000
Hiroko Yamaguchi	72	70	72	73	287	438,000
Junko Omote	70	72	71	74	287	438,000
Kayo Yamada	70	70	73	74	287	438,000

Vernal Ladies

Fukuoka Century Golf Club, Amagi, Fukuoka
Par 36-36–72; 6,568 yards

May 14-16
purse, ¥100,000,000

	SCORES			TOTAL	MONEY
Yuri Fudoh	72	72	70	214	¥18,000,000
Toshimi Kimura	73	69	73	215	8,800,000
Akiko Fukushima	74	73	69	216	6,500,000
Ai Miyazato	71	71	74	216	6,500,000
Shiho Ohyama	71	73	73	217	4,500,000
Kaori Higo	73	71	73	217	4,500,000
Yuka Shiroto	73	74	71	218	3,250,000
Midori Yoneyama	69	73	76	218	3,250,000
Kaori Suzuki	77	72	71	220	2,030,000
Mikiyo Nishizuka	73	72	75	220	2,030,000
Ayako Uehara	73	71	76	220	2,030,000
Samantha Head	71	76	73	220	2,030,000
Mayumi Nakajima	75	71	75	221	1,560,000
Junko Yasui	72	75	74	221	1,560,000
Kasumi Fujii	73	69	79	221	1,560,000
Yasuko Satoh	75	73	74	222	1,160,000
Hsiu-Feng Tseng	73	74	75	222	1,160,000
Kayo Yamada	72	71	79	222	1,160,000
Michiko Hattori	72	77	73	222	1,160,000
Woo-Soon Ko	74	74	74	222	1,160,000
Junko Omote	74	75	74	223	890,000
Yuka Irie	74	73	76	223	890,000
Mika Adaniya	71	73	79	223	890,000
Seiko Watanabe	77	69	77	223	890,000
Hiromi Mogi	77	69	77	223	890,000
Chieko Amanuma	73	72	78	223	890,000

	SCORES			TOTAL	MONEY
Rui Kitada	78	71	75	224	800,000
Akane Takagi	76	73	75	224	800,000
Hiromi Takesue	76	74	74	224	800,000
Hsiao-Chuan Lu	79	71	75	225	800,000
Young-Me Lee	78	71	76	225	720,000
Chieko Nishida	76	74	75	225	720,000
Kumi Yamashita	78	73	74	225	720,000
Hiroko Fujishima	74	74	77	225	720,000

Chukyo TV Bridgestone Ladies Open

Chukyo Golf Club, Toyota, Aichi
Par 36-36–72; 6,371 yards

May 21-23
purse, ¥50,000,000

	SCORES			TOTAL	MONEY
Yuko Saitoh	74	65	67	206	¥9,000,000
Kaori Harada	72	69	68	209	4,500,000
Kaori Suzuki	72	67	71	210	3,500,000
Ji-Yeon Han	73	68	70	211	2,312,500
Hsiao-Chuan Lu	71	71	69	211	2,312,500
Shiho Ohyama	73	66	72	211	2,312,500
Keiko Sasaki	71	69	71	211	2,312,500
Yuri Fudoh	71	68	73	212	1,375,000
Aki Takamura	70	68	74	212	1,375,000
Yuriko Ohtsuka	70	74	69	213	904,000
Midori Yoneyama	69	71	73	213	904,000
Kyoko Ono	73	70	70	213	904,000
Seiko Watanabe	72	70	71	213	904,000
Ai Miyazato	71	71	71	213	904,000
Yuka Sakaguchi	74	68	72	214	595,000
Chieko Amanuma	70	73	71	214	595,000
Megumi Higuchi	73	71	70	214	595,000
Junko Yasui	70	71	73	214	595,000
Junko Omote	72	70	72	214	595,000
Toshimi Kimura	71	72	71	214	595,000
Woo-Soon Ko	72	70	72	214	595,000
Kyoko Furuya	71	73	70	214	595,000
Hiromi Mogi	76	68	71	215	465,000
Harumi Sakagami	72	73	70	215	465,000
*Sakura Yokomine	75	67	73	215	
Masaki Maeda	71	71	73	215	465,000
Samantha Head	71	74	71	216	419,166
Noriko Aso	72	72	72	216	419,166
Mika Tajiri	77	67	72	216	419,166
Michie Ohba	74	69	73	216	419,166
Kaori Higo	73	73	70	216	419,166
Yasuko Satoh	70	71	75	216	419,166

Kosaido Ladies Golf Cup

Chiba Kosaido Country Club, Ichihara, Chiba
Par 36-36–72; 6,280 yards

May 28-30
purse, ¥60,000,000

	SCORES			TOTAL	MONEY
Yuri Fudoh	69	68	69	206	¥10,800,000
Hsiu-Feng Tseng	71	68	69	208	5,280,000
Rui Kitada	71	73	66	210	4,200,000
Fumiko Muraguchi	68	71	72	211	3,600,000
Yuka Irie	70	74	68	212	3,000,000
Junko Yoshida	68	78	67	213	1,950,000
Shin Sora	72	70	71	213	1,950,000
Kyoko Ono	74	70	69	213	1,950,000
Midori Yoneyama	73	72	68	213	1,950,000
Toshimi Kimura	71	72	71	214	1,140,000
Michiko Hattori	72	72	70	214	1,140,000
Hsiao-Chuan Lu	70	71	73	214	1,140,000
Kayo Fukumoto	69	74	72	215	1,020,000
Rie Fujiwara	68	76	72	216	780,000
Yuko Saitoh	70	74	72	216	780,000
Kayo Yamada	73	71	72	216	780,000
Yasuko Satoh	76	69	71	216	780,000
Rena Yamazaki	71	74	71	216	780,000
Kuniko Maeda	72	75	69	216	780,000
Miho Koga	71	76	69	216	780,000
Noriko Aso	68	75	74	217	582,000
Shiho Ohyama	68	74	75	217	582,000
Seiko Watanabe	72	74	72	218	546,000
Yuka Sakaguchi	70	76	72	218	546,000
Yun-Jye Wei	71	75	72	218	546,000
Yukari Horikoshi	76	70	72	218	546,000
Fuki Kido	74	72	73	219	492,000
Woo-Soon Ko	73	73	73	219	492,000
Megumi Higuchi	70	78	71	219	492,000
Ikue Asama	67	78	74	219	492,000
Ayumi Shiota	75	71	73	219	492,000

Resort Trust Ladies

Grande Golf Club, Hamanako, Shizuoka
Par 36-36–72; 6,524 yards

June 4-6
purse, ¥50,000,000

	SCORES			TOTAL	MONEY
Hiromi Mogi	71	67	70	208	¥9,000,000
Yuka Sakaguchi	67	71	70	208	4,400,000
(Mogi defeated Sakaguchi on fourth playoff hole.)					
Hsiao-Chuan Lu	67	72	72	211	3,500,000
Ai Miyazato	74	70	68	212	3,000,000
Chihiro Nakajima	67	74	72	213	2,500,000
Yuri Fudoh	73	69	72	214	1,625,000
Shiho Ohyama	69	73	72	214	1,625,000
Toshimi Kimura	73	69	72	214	1,625,000
*Kumiko Kaneda	73	71	70	214	
Woo-Soon Ko	74	70	70	214	1,625,000
Kaori Higo	77	67	73	217	921,250
Harumi Kawano	74	74	69	217	921,250

	SCORES			TOTAL	MONEY
Yun-Jye Wei	71	73	73	217	921,250
Yasuko Satoh	71	72	74	217	921,250
Mayumi Murai	68	76	74	218	695,000
Akane Takagi	73	69	76	218	695,000
Seiko Watanabe	74	69	75	218	695,000
Maki Sasayama	71	73	74	218	695,000
Yukari Horikoshi	72	71	75	218	695,000
Junko Omote	74	73	72	219	493,000
Hikaru Kobayashi	71	74	74	219	493,000
Young-Me Lee	74	72	73	219	493,000
Yuka Shiroto	73	72	74	219	493,000
Michiko Hattori	77	71	71	219	493,000
Shin Sora	74	75	71	220	450,000
Hiroko Yamaguchi	71	76	73	220	450,000
Yuriko Ohtsuka	72	75	74	221	405,000
Nikki Campbell	74	71	76	221	405,000
Aki Takamura	68	76	77	221	405,000
Michiko Mitsui	70	75	76	221	405,000
Ji-Hee Lee	72	74	75	221	405,000
Yoko Yamagishi	75	74	72	221	405,000
Mayumi Nakajima	75	72	74	221	405,000

We Love Kobe Suntory Ladies Open

Japan Memorial Golf Club, Yoshikawa, Hyogo
Par 36-36–72; 6,528 yards

June 10-13
purse, ¥60,000,000

	SCORES				TOTAL	MONEY
Ai Miyazato	69	70	70	68	277	¥10,800,000
Toshimi Kimura	71	69	72	71	283	4,740,000
Hiroko Yamaguchi	68	70	71	74	283	4,740,000
Mikiyo Nishizuka	67	73	75	70	285	3,600,000
Mitsuko Kawasaki	70	72	71	73	286	2,160,000
Yuriko Ohtsuka	71	72	70	73	286	2,160,000
Shiho Ohyama	71	75	67	73	286	2,160,000
Michiko Hattori	71	75	66	74	286	2,160,000
Hsiao-Chuan Lu	68	76	67	75	286	2,160,000
Maki Sasayama	73	71	69	74	287	1,108,000
Young-Me Lee	66	74	71	76	287	1,108,000
Midori Yoneyama	70	73	64	80	287	1,108,000
Woo-Soon Ko	69	75	72	72	288	942,000
Seiko Watanabe	74	69	71	74	288	942,000
Yuka Sakaguchi	69	75	74	71	289	792,000
Chieko Amanuma	66	77	74	72	289	792,000
Mineko Nasu	71	74	72	72	289	792,000
*Sakura Yokomine	72	76	69	73	290	
Kaori Harada	73	73	68	76	290	642,000
Yukari Horikoshi	70	70	73	77	290	642,000
Namika Omata	70	76	71	74	291	540,000
Ji-Yeon Han	72	72	72	75	291	540,000
Naoko Takasaki	72	73	71	75	291	540,000
Masaki Maeda	71	77	74	70	292	516,000
Yuko Saitoh	72	74	76	71	293	462,000
Shin Sora	71	72	75	75	293	462,000
Mayumi Inoue	75	72	71	75	293	462,000
Junko Omote	71	75	72	75	293	462,000
Fuki Kido	73	73	71	76	293	462,000

	SCORES			TOTAL	MONEY
Ai Takinami	71 71 74 77			293	462,000
Takayo Bandoh	70 74 71 78			293	462,000
Rie Fujiwara	70 72 72 79			293	462,000

Apita Circle K Sankus Ladies

U Green Golf Club, Natsugawa, Gifu
Par 36-36–72; 6,344 yards

June 18-20
purse, ¥50,000,000

	SCORES			TOTAL	MONEY
Ai Miyazato	69	69	72	210	¥9,000,000
Yuri Fudoh	71	70	70	211	4,400,000
Chihiro Nakajima	68	75	70	213	3,000,000
Noriko Aso	73	68	72	213	3,000,000
Miho Koga	73	71	69	213	3,000,000
Hiromi Mogi	69	73	72	214	2,000,000
Michiko Hattori	72	73	70	215	1,218,333
Kayo Fukumoto	71	70	74	215	1,218,333
Mikiyo Nishizuka	72	71	72	215	1,218,333
Chieko Amanuma	71	71	73	215	1,218,333
Yun-Jye Wei	73	66	76	215	1,218,333
Ji-Yeon Han	71	70	74	215	1,218,333
Kaori Harada	74	69	73	216	780,000
Yu-Chen Huang	74	71	71	216	780,000
Hikaru Kobayashi	72	72	72	216	780,000
Rie Fujiwara	73	72	72	217	535,000
Aki Nakano	72	68	77	217	535,000
Shin Sora	70	75	72	217	535,000
Yuka Shiroto	70	74	73	217	535,000
Kyoko Ono	72	72	73	217	535,000
Midori Yoneyama	72	73	72	217	535,000
Michiko Mitsui	73	73	71	217	535,000
Yukari Horikoshi	70	72	75	217	535,000
Junko Yasui	72	72	74	218	415,000
Young-Me Lee	74	71	73	218	415,000
Mayumi Murai	71	74	73	218	415,000
Woo-Soon Ko	72	74	72	218	415,000
Mayumi Inoue	73	74	71	218	415,000
Kuniko Maeda	73	72	73	218	415,000
Ai-Yu Tu	73	72	74	219	360,000
Mitsuko Kawasaki	69	78	72	219	360,000
Mihoko Takahashi	75	72	72	219	360,000
Hiroko Yamaguchi	70	73	76	219	360,000
Hiromi Takesue	73	73	73	219	360,000

Promise Ladies

Water Hills Golf Club, Hyogo
Par 36-36–72; 6,425 yards

June 25-27
purse, ¥60,000,000

	SCORES			TOTAL	MONEY
Kasumi Fujii	70	68	69	207	¥10,800,000
Toshimi Kimura	69	70	68	207	5,280,000
(Fujii defeated Kimura on sixth playoff hole.)					
Shiho Ohyama	72	71	67	210	3,060,000

	SCORES			TOTAL	MONEY
Junko Omote	75	71	64	210	3,060,000
Rui Kitada	72	65	73	210	3,060,000
Yasuko Satoh	69	69	72	210	3,060,000
Hiroko Yamaguchi	71	71	68	210	3,060,000
Yuka Shiroto	71	72	68	211	1,650,000
Kaori Higo	71	70	70	211	1,650,000
Kaori Harada	72	72	68	212	989,142
Mineko Nasu	73	71	68	212	989,142
Yun-Jye Wei	69	72	71	212	989,142
Mika Adaniya	75	67	70	212	989,142
Ai Miyazato	75	67	70	212	989,142
Ji-Hee Lee	73	71	68	212	989,142
Noriko Aso	70	74	68	212	989,142
Michie Ohba	68	75	70	213	684,000
Mikiyo Nishizuka	73	70	70	213	684,000
Yuriko Ohtsuka	70	72	71	213	684,000
Young-Me Lee	74	72	68	214	546,000
Harumi Kawano	73	73	68	214	546,000
Chihiro Nakajima	72	71	71	214	546,000
Kuniko Maeda	73	70	71	214	546,000
Mayumi Inoue	72	68	75	215	492,000
Akiko Fukushima	68	73	74	215	492,000
Kaori Suzuki	70	72	73	215	492,000
Hiroko Fujishima	74	69	72	215	492,000
Keiko Sasaki	77	70	68	215	492,000
Hsiu-Feng Tseng	73	70	73	216	426,000
Seiko Watanabe	70	72	74	216	426,000
Megumi Higuchi	74	71	71	216	426,000
Miho Koga	72	74	70	216	426,000
Chieko Amanuma	75	71	70	216	426,000
Yukari Baba	74	70	72	216	426,000

Belluna Ladies Cup

Obatago Golf Club, Kanra, Gunma
Par 36-36–72; 6,362 yards

July 2-4
purse, ¥60,000,000

	SCORES			TOTAL	MONEY
Mitsuko Kawasaki	69	71	67	207	¥10,800,000
Junko Omote	70	68	70	208	5,280,000
Michiko Mitsui	70	67	72	209	4,200,000
Ok-Hee Ku	71	73	66	210	3,600,000
Woo-Soon Ko	72	68	71	211	2,500,000
Jeong-Eun Lee	72	67	72	211	2,500,000
Takayo Bandoh	68	72	71	211	2,500,000
Mikiyo Nishizuka	72	69	71	212	1,650,000
Hiroko Yamaguchi	72	70	70	212	1,650,000
Seiko Watanabe	71	71	71	213	1,124,000
Noriko Aso	72	69	72	213	1,124,000
Midori Yoneyama	70	71	72	213	1,124,000
Mineko Nasu	76	68	70	214	761,333
Miho Koga	69	77	68	214	761,333
Mika Adaniya	69	69	76	214	761,333
Atomi Shiota	72	73	69	214	761,333
Michiko Hattori	70	72	72	214	761,333
Yuka Irie	70	71	73	214	761,333
Kaori Harada	70	70	74	214	761,333

	SCORES			TOTAL	MONEY
Aki Nakano	70	71	73	214	761,333
Chihiro Nakajima	71	71	72	214	761,333
Rie Fujiwara	72	72	71	215	540,000
Yun-Jye Wei	71	69	75	215	540,000
Mika Tateishi	71	72	72	215	540,000
Kaori Suzuki	72	73	71	216	492,000
Rena Yamazaki	70	73	73	216	492,000
Misato Nishikawa	68	73	75	216	492,000
Hsiu-Feng Tseng	70	71	75	216	492,000
Akiko Fukushima	70	72	74	216	492,000
Mieko Takano	73	74	70	217	420,000
Fumiko Muraguchi	74	71	72	217	420,000
Miyuki Shimabukuro	74	71	72	217	420,000
Yoko Yamagishi	74	72	71	217	420,000
Keiko Sasaki	73	72	72	217	420,000
Yukari Baba	74	71	72	217	420,000
Hiromi Mogi	71	72	74	217	420,000

Chateaureze Queens Cup

Chateaureze Country Club, Sapporo, Hokkaido
Par 36-36–72; 6,558 yards

July 9-11
purse, ¥50,000,000

	SCORES			TOTAL	MONEY
Akiko Fukushima	70	66	71	207	¥9,000,000
Midori Yoneyama	73	73	71	217	4,500,000
Ai Miyazato	78	72	68	218	3,250,000
Woo-Soon Ko	76	71	71	218	3,250,000
Keiko Sasaki	79	68	72	219	2,250,000
Kaori Higo	76	70	73	219	2,250,000
Jeong-Eun Lee	77	73	70	220	1,226,666
Mineko Nasu	77	73	70	220	1,226,666
Yuka Shiroto	74	75	71	220	1,226,666
Mitsuko Kawasaki	76	73	71	220	1,226,666
Toshimi Kimura	76	73	71	220	1,226,666
Kasumi Fujii	73	74	73	220	1,226,666
*Sakura Yokomine	78	72	71	221	
Shiho Ohyama	76	72	73	221	830,000
Eriko Moriyama	74	72	75	221	830,000
Mikiyo Nishizuka	76	74	72	222	705,000
Yuriko Ohtsuka	75	72	75	222	705,000
Seiko Watanabe	75	70	77	222	705,000
Nikki Campbell	75	75	73	223	555,000
Yoko Yamagishi	78	74	71	223	555,000
Michie Ohba	75	74	74	223	555,000
Ok-Hee Ku	74	76	74	224	485,000
Kuniko Maeda	77	75	72	224	485,000
Miho Koga	77	75	72	224	485,000
Shiho Katano	79	71	75	225	440,000
Aki Nakano	78	74	73	225	440,000
Rui Kitada	75	74	76	225	440,000
Kaori Suzuki	80	72	73	225	440,000
Mayumi Murai	78	71	76	225	440,000
Samantha Head	75	73	77	225	440,000

Stanley Ladies

Tomei Country Club, Shizuoka
Par 36-36–72; 6,434 yards

July 16-18
purse, ¥60,000,000

	SCORES			TOTAL	MONEY
Yuri Fudoh	67	69	68	204	¥10,800,000
Michiko Hattori	69	67	69	205	5,280,000
Mikiyo Nishizuka	70	69	67	206	3,900,000
Yuko Saitoh	71	67	68	206	3,900,000
Shiho Ohyama	69	73	65	207	2,325,000
Miho Koga	71	70	66	207	2,325,000
Junko Omote	72	69	66	207	2,325,000
Ai Miyazato	68	67	72	207	2,325,000
Mineko Nasu	69	70	69	208	1,350,000
Nikki Campbell	71	68	69	208	1,350,000
Kaori Higo	74	70	65	209	1,026,000
Midori Yoneyama	69	70	70	209	1,026,000
Yuka Shiroto	71	67	71	209	1,026,000
Hsiao-Chuan Lu	70	67	72	209	1,026,000
Rui Kitada	73	70	67	210	846,000
Mitsuko Kawasaki	69	71	70	210	846,000
Yukari Horikoshi	67	73	71	211	696,000
Kumiko Hiyoshi	68	71	72	211	696,000
Toshimi Kimura	69	70	72	211	696,000
*Mika Miyazato	67	71	73	211	
Yasuko Satoh	72	71	69	212	558,000
Kyoko Kadokawa	72	70	70	212	558,000
Mika Tajiri	68	73	71	212	558,000
Kasumi Fujii	72	67	73	212	558,000
Junko Yoshida	74	70	69	213	480,000
Hsiu-Feng Tseng	72	72	69	213	480,000
Naoko Takasaki	76	67	70	213	480,000
Rie Murata	70	73	70	213	480,000
Ai Ogawa	71	72	70	213	480,000
Hisako Takeda	71	71	71	213	480,000
Fuki Kido	69	73	71	213	480,000
Chieko Nishida	69	72	72	213	480,000
Junko Yasui	70	70	73	213	480,000

Golf 5 Ladies

Alpen Golf Club, Hokkaido
Par 36-37–73; 6,445 yards

July 23-25
purse, ¥50,000,000

	SCORES			TOTAL	MONEY
Yuri Fudoh	75	72	74	221	¥9,000,000
Yun-Jye Wei	73	76	75	224	4,400,000
Woo-Soon Ko	78	73	74	225	3,500,000
*Kumiko Kaneda	74	74	77	225	
Michiko Mitsui	77	76	73	226	3,000,000
Shiho Ohyama	73	82	72	227	1,937,500
Kuniko Maeda	77	77	73	227	1,937,500
Yukari Baba	75	78	74	227	1,937,500
Kasumi Fujii	75	78	74	227	1,937,500
Harumi Sakagami	73	80	75	228	1,058,333
Rui Kitada	79	74	75	228	1,058,333

	SCORES			TOTAL	MONEY
Midori Yoneyama	77	76	75	228	1,058,333
Eriko Moriyama	75	79	75	229	825,000
Fumiko Muraguchi	74	79	76	229	825,000
Mari Katayama	76	77	76	229	825,000
Chihiro Nakajima	74	81	75	230	675,000
Yui Kawahara	72	82	76	230	675,000
Miho Koga	78	78	74	230	675,000
Mayumi Murai	75	80	76	231	482,142
Mineko Nasu	77	80	74	231	482,142
Misato Nishikawa	74	79	78	231	482,142
Mitsuko Kawasaki	74	79	78	231	482,142
Yasuko Satoh	79	78	74	231	482,142
Mika Adaniya	75	83	73	231	482,142
Ji-Yeon Han	77	72	82	231	482,142
Ji-Hee Lee	76	79	77	232	400,000
Hsiu-Feng Tseng	75	78	79	232	400,000
Mikiyo Nishizuka	75	78	79	232	400,000
Kyoko Ono	79	79	74	232	400,000
Ok-Hee Ku	79	79	74	232	400,000
*Sakura Yokomine	79	73	80	232	
Yuriko Ohtsuka	80	78	74	232	400,000

NEC Karuizawa 72

Karuizawa 72 Golf Club, Nagano
Par 36-36–72; 6,523 yards

August 13-15
purse, ¥60,000,000

	SCORES			TOTAL	MONEY
Rui Kitada	69	66	67	202	¥10,800,000
Akiko Fukushima	70	65	69	204	4,740,000
Ai Miyazato	70	70	64	204	4,740,000
Woo-Soon Ko	66	73	68	207	3,300,000
Noriko Aso	67	73	67	207	3,300,000
Aki Takamura	69	71	68	208	2,400,000
Yuko Saitoh	73	68	68	209	1,800,000
Michie Ohba	70	69	70	209	1,800,000
Kasumi Fujii	70	69	70	209	1,800,000
Ai-Yu Tu	69	71	70	210	1,136,000
Michiko Hattori	70	69	71	210	1,136,000
Mayumi Murai	68	73	69	210	1,136,000
Yun-Jye Wei	71	70	70	211	954,000
Namika Omata	68	70	73	211	954,000
Yasuko Satoh	71	69	71	211	954,000
Yuka Irie	71	71	70	212	714,000
Miho Koga	72	70	70	212	714,000
Ji-Hee Lee	69	72	71	212	714,000
Yuka Sakaguchi	72	71	69	212	714,000
Yukari Horikoshi	70	71	71	212	714,000
Mineko Nasu	70	72	71	213	564,000
Yuri Fudoh	71	71	71	213	564,000
Shiho Ohyama	71	70	72	213	564,000
Riko Higashio	69	72	72	213	564,000
Yuka Shiroto	74	69	71	214	528,000
Michiko Mitsui	73	70	71	214	528,000
Ae-Sook Kim	72	71	72	215	480,000
Hsiu-Feng Tseng	71	74	70	215	480,000
Chieko Amanuma	70	71	74	215	480,000

	SCORES			TOTAL	MONEY
Mizuho Ozawa	69	74	72	215	480,000
Kyoko Kadokawa	72	70	73	215	480,000
Kuniko Maeda	72	70	73	215	480,000

New Caterpillar Mitsubishi Ladies

Daihakone Country Club, Hakone, Kanagawa
Par 36-37–73; 6,648 yards

August 20-22
purse, ¥60,000,000

	SCORES			TOTAL	MONEY
Toshimi Kimura	70	69	71	210	¥10,800,000
Kasumi Fujii	73	70	70	213	4,740,000
Yuri Fudoh	72	70	71	213	4,740,000
Chieko Amanuma	72	72	70	214	3,300,000
Akiko Fukushima	72	71	71	214	3,300,000
Woo-Soon Ko	72	74	69	215	2,250,000
Michiko Hattori	73	73	69	215	2,250,000
Keiko Sasaki	75	72	70	217	1,339,200
Kyoko Kadokawa	69	77	71	217	1,339,200
Fumiko Muraguchi	73	73	71	217	1,339,200
Junko Omote	73	71	73	217	1,339,200
Jeong-Eun Lee	75	68	74	217	1,339,200
Fuki Kido	76	73	69	218	918,000
Ji-Hee Lee	76	71	71	218	918,000
Yukari Baba	74	71	73	218	918,000
Rui Kitada	72	70	76	218	918,000
Miho Koga	74	76	69	219	629,142
Yuka Shiroto	72	77	70	219	629,142
Mineko Nasu	75	72	72	219	629,142
Aki Nakano	74	72	73	219	629,142
Young-Me Lee	73	72	74	219	629,142
Hikaru Kobayashi	73	71	75	219	629,142
Kyoko Ono	72	68	79	219	629,142
Ai Miyazato	78	73	69	220	516,000
Yui Kawahara	77	73	70	220	516,000
Michie Ohba	76	70	74	220	516,000
Nikki Campbell	73	72	75	220	516,000
Hiroko Yamaguchi	73	71	76	220	516,000
Kozue Azuma	77	73	71	221	474,000
Kaori Higo	76	73	72	221	474,000

Yonex Ladies

Yonex Country Club, Teradomari, Niigata
Par 36-36–72; 6,342 yards

August 27-29
purse, ¥60,000,000

	SCORES			TOTAL	MONEY
Yukari Baba	67	69	70	206	¥10,800,000
Yuri Fudoh	70	70	68	208	5,280,000
Mayumi Inoue	71	69	70	210	3,900,000
Miho Koga	71	66	73	210	3,900,000
Ai Miyazato	71	72	68	211	2,500,000
Noriko Aso	68	74	69	211	2,500,000
Samantha Head	72	68	71	211	2,500,000
Woo-Soon Ko	69	75	69	213	1,402,500

	SCORES			TOTAL	MONEY
Junko Omote	71	75	67	213	1,402,500
Michiko Mitsui	70	73	70	213	1,402,500
Mikiyo Nishizuka	69	70	74	213	1,402,500
Nikki Campbell	73	73	68	214	900,000
Aki Nakano	71	72	71	214	900,000
Yui Kawahara	72	71	71	214	900,000
Mayumi Nakajima	74	69	71	214	900,000
Fumiko Muraguchi	69	73	72	214	900,000
Kasumi Fujii	69	70	75	214	900,000
Midori Yoneyama	69	74	72	215	612,000
Rena Yamazaki	73	69	73	215	612,000
Yun-Jye Wei	69	71	75	215	612,000
Yuriko Ohtsuka	68	71	76	215	612,000
Rui Kitada	74	71	71	216	516,000
Fuki Kido	73	74	69	216	516,000
Naoko Takasaki	72	71	73	216	516,000
Yuka Sakaguchi	69	73	74	216	516,000
Yasuko Satoh	70	72	74	216	516,000
Mieko Takano	74	66	76	216	516,000
Junko Yasui	74	71	72	217	444,000
Young-Me Lee	73	73	71	217	444,000
Jung-Yun Cho	74	70	73	217	444,000
Michie Ohba	71	75	71	217	444,000
Hikaru Kobayashi	74	73	70	217	444,000
Natsuko Noro	70	72	75	217	444,000

Fujisankei Ladies Classic

Fuji Lakeside Country Club, Kawaguchiko, Yamanashi
Par 36-36–72; 6,531 yards
(Third round cancelled — fog.)

September 3-5
purse, ¥60,000,000

	SCORES		TOTAL	MONEY
Kasumi Fujii	68	71	139	¥8,100,000
Junko Omote	72	70	142	3,960,000
Ai Miyazato	74	69	143	3,150,000
Sakura Yokomine	71	73	144	2,700,000
Akiko Fukushima	76	70	146	1,875,000
Toshimi Kimura	76	70	146	1,875,000
Midori Yoneyama	73	73	146	1,875,000
Yun-Jye Wei	76	71	147	1,049,625
*Yuki Fujita	75	72	147	
Mari Katayama	74	73	147	1,049,625
Yasuko Satoh	73	74	147	1,049,625
Yukari Baba	73	74	147	1,049,625
Kyoko Ono	75	73	148	598,500
Michiko Hattori	75	73	148	598,500
Seiko Watanabe	75	73	148	598,500
Jung-Yun Cho	78	70	148	598,500
Kumiko Hiyoshi	78	70	148	598,500
Shiho Ohyama	73	75	148	598,500
Hiroko Yamaguchi	72	76	148	598,500
Yuka Irie	72	76	148	598,500
Mikiyo Nishizuka	70	78	148	598,500
Miho Koga	76	73	149	369,000
Chieko Nishida	76	73	149	369,000
Mihoko Takahashi	76	73	149	369,000

	SCORES		TOTAL	MONEY
Chieko Amanuma	75	74	149	369,000
Maki Sasayama	74	75	149	369,000
Itsumi Okada	73	76	149	369,000
Woo-Soon Ko	73	76	149	369,000
Hsiao-Chuan Lu	73	76	149	369,000
Kaori Suzuki	72	77	149	369,000
Junko Yoshida	70	79	149	369,000

Japan LPGA Championship

Taiheiyo Club, Associates Masuko Course, Tochigi
Par 36-36–72; 6,537 yards

September 9-12
purse, ¥70,000,000

	SCORES				TOTAL	MONEY
Kaori Higo	73	72	69	67	281	¥12,600,000
Junko Omote	74	69	71	72	286	6,160,000
Akiko Fukushima	72	72	71	72	287	4,900,000
Ai Miyazato	77	72	73	68	290	3,850,000
Yuri Fudoh	74	74	69	73	290	3,850,000
Mitsuko Kawasaki	73	73	74	71	291	2,800,000
Kaori Suzuki	79	69	75	69	292	2,100,000
Shiho Ohyama	73	77	71	71	292	2,100,000
Woo-Soon Ko	72	75	72	73	292	2,100,000
Yukari Baba	75	70	77	72	294	1,269,333
Yoko Inoue	70	79	73	72	294	1,269,333
Yun-Jye Wei	69	72	76	77	294	1,269,333
Kayo Fukumoto	75	74	75	71	295	994,000
Ae-Sook Kim	75	72	76	72	295	994,000
Orie Fujino	78	73	71	73	295	994,000
Midori Yoneyama	71	75	75	74	295	994,000
Ok-Hee Ku	76	74	75	71	296	672,000
Masaki Maeda	74	77	74	71	296	672,000
Chieko Amanuma	77	71	74	74	296	672,000
Ji-Yeon Han	74	71	74	77	296	672,000
Kotomi Akiyama	74	72	73	77	296	672,000
Hiroko Fujishima	72	77	66	81	296	672,000
Michiko Hattori	77	74	74	72	297	539,000
Kyoko Ono	74	73	78	72	297	539,000
Miho Koga	80	71	72	74	297	539,000
Toshimi Kimura	76	73	73	75	297	539,000
Misato Nishikawa	70	74	74	79	297	539,000
Nobuko Kizawa	78	73	74	73	298	476,000
Chihiro Nakajima	74	76	76	72	298	476,000
Ayako Uehara	73	73	76	76	298	476,000
Mihoko Takahashi	73	75	73	77	298	476,000

Munsingwear Ladies Tokai Classic

Ryosen Golf Club, Inabe, Mie
Par 36-36–72; 6,477 yards

September 17-19
purse, ¥60,000,000

	SCORES			TOTAL	MONEY
Hiromi Mogi	66	68	68	202	¥10,800,000
Yuri Fudoh	66	70	67	203	5,280,000
Midori Yoneyama	69	68	68	205	4,200,000

	SCORES			TOTAL	MONEY
Ai Miyazato	68	69	70	207	3,600,000
Nikki Campbell	68	69	71	208	2,700,000
Michie Ohba	66	69	73	208	2,700,000
Misato Nishikawa	68	69	72	209	2,100,000
*Shinobu Moromizato	71	71	68	210	
Michiko Hattori	70	72	68	210	1,800,000
Kasumi Fujii	71	70	70	211	1,274,000
Miyuki Shimabukuro	72	70	69	211	1,274,000
Sakura Yokomine	69	70	72	211	1,274,000
Toshimi Kimura	75	70	67	212	882,000
Yuriko Ohtsuka	70	72	70	212	882,000
Kaori Higo	70	70	72	212	882,000
Mihoko Takahashi	71	70	71	212	882,000
*Kumiko Kaneda	73	70	69	212	
Fuki Kido	71	69	72	212	882,000
Fumiko Muraguchi	68	75	69	212	882,000
Junko Omote	73	68	71	212	882,000
Ayako Uehara	71	70	72	213	612,000
Yuka Sakaguchi	73	69	71	213	612,000
*Mika Takushima	71	71	71	213	
Chieko Amanuma	72	71	71	214	558,000
Mineko Nasu	70	69	75	214	558,000
Atomi Shiota	73	71	70	214	558,000
Jung-yun Cho	72	72	71	215	504,000
Shiho Ohyama	71	71	73	215	504,000
Saya Manabe	71	73	71	215	504,000
Mitsuko Kawasaki	71	71	73	215	504,000
Rui Kitada	72	72	71	215	504,000
Yasuko Satoh	71	71	73	215	504,000

Miyagi TV Cup Dunlop Ladies Open

Rifu Golf Club, Miyagi
Par 36-36–72; 6,380 yards

September 24-26
purse, ¥60,000,000

	SCORES			TOTAL	MONEY
Yoko Yamagishi	67	69	71	207	¥10,800,000
Miho Koga	67	71	69	207	5,280,000
(Yamagishi defeated Koga on first playoff hole.)					
Kaori Higo	70	70	68	208	4,200,000
Yuri Fudoh	69	70	71	210	3,000,000
Samantha Head	65	71	74	210	3,000,000
Michie Ohba	71	65	74	210	3,000,000
Misato Nishikawa	69	72	70	211	1,800,000
Yuka Shiroto	69	72	70	211	1,800,000
Shiho Ohyama	69	72	70	211	1,800,000
Toshimi Kimura	69	73	70	212	1,075,200
Kayo Yamada	71	71	70	212	1,075,200
Rui Kitada	69	71	72	212	1,075,200
Keiko Sasaki	69	69	74	212	1,075,200
Woo-Soon Ko	67	70	75	212	1,075,200
Yukari Horikoshi	70	73	70	213	744,000
Hiroko Yamaguchi	73	70	70	213	744,000
Ayako Uehara	71	71	71	213	744,000
Aki Nakano	69	71	73	213	744,000
Mihoko Takahashi	69	71	73	213	744,000
Junko Omote	70	70	73	213	744,000

	SCORES			TOTAL	MONEY
Eriko Moriyama	69	75	70	214	576,000
Ji-Yeon Han	70	70	74	214	576,000
Mikiyo Nishizuka	72	71	72	215	534,000
Mayumi Murai	73	72	70	215	534,000
Ai Miyazato	70	72	73	215	534,000
Fuki Kido	69	72	74	215	534,000
Megumi Higuchi	70	71	74	215	534,000
Hikaru Kobayashi	73	71	72	216	468,000
Yuko Moriguchi	73	70	73	216	468,000
Mizuho Ozawa	71	73	72	216	468,000
Orie Fujino	72	71	73	216	468,000
Hiromi Mogi	74	70	72	216	468,000
Fumiko Muraguchi	70	72	74	216	468,000

Japan Women's Open

Hiroshima Country Club, Hiroshima
Par 36-36–72; 6,448 yards

September 30-October 3
purse, ¥70,000,000

	SCORES				TOTAL	MONEY
Yuri Fudoh	74	70	69	67	280	¥14,000,000
Kaori Higo	79	72	71	69	291	6,562,500
Sakura Yokomine	73	71	74	73	291	6,562,500
Midori Yoneyama	76	72	73	72	293	3,570,000
*Shinobu Moromizato	72	81	69	72	294	
Fuki Kido	70	73	76	76	295	2,940,000
Ok-Hee Ku	75	74	76	72	297	1,875,200
Mikiyo Nishizuka	73	74	77	73	297	1,875,200
Mitsuko Kawasaki	71	77	76	73	297	1,875,200
Kasumi Fujii	76	72	75	74	297	1,875,200
Hsiao-Chuan Lu	74	73	70	80	297	1,875,200
Rui Kitada	78	76	72	72	298	1,150,666
Shiho Ohyama	74	79	71	74	298	1,150,666
Hiromi Mogi	75	71	75	77	298	1,150,666
Yuko Saitoh	73	79	75	72	299	838,000
Woo-Soon Ko	81	69	76	73	299	838,000
Ayako Uehara	77	75	74	73	299	838,000
Miho Koga	73	78	73	75	299	838,000
Junko Yasui	78	69	76	76	299	838,000
Akiko Fukushima	79	72	75	74	300	704,000
Eika Ohtake	75	75	78	73	301	611,285
Yukari Horikoshi	70	81	77	73	301	611,285
Michiko Mitsui	75	76	74	76	301	611,285
Kyoko Ono	75	77	73	76	301	611,285
Nikki Campbell	80	74	71	76	301	611,285
Rie Murata	72	70	77	82	301	611,285
Aki Nakano	75	72	71	83	301	611,285
Misato Nishikawa	75	74	78	76	303	525,000
Yun-Jye Wei	76	77	74	76	303	525,000
Masaki Maeda	75	75	76	77	303	525,000
Michie Ohba	79	73	74	77	303	525,000
Yoko Tsuchiya	77	77	75	74	303	525,000
Michiko Hattori	76	77	75	75	303	525,000

Sankyo Ladies Open

Akagi Country Club, Niisato, Gunma
Par 36-36–72; 6,461 yards
(Event shortened to 36 holes—rain.)

October 8-10
purse, ¥60,000,000

	SCORES		TOTAL	MONEY
Rui Kitada	71	69	140	¥8,100,000
Mikiyo Nishizuka	72	70	142	3,015,000
Junko Omote	73	69	142	3,015,000
Midori Yoneyama	72	70	142	3,015,000
Kasumi Fujii	71	71	142	3,015,000
Shiho Ohyama	74	69	143	1,462,500
Michiko Hattori	73	70	143	1,462,500
Ji-Hee Lee	71	72	143	1,462,500
Toshimi Kimura	70	73	143	1,462,500
Yukari Baba	73	71	144	795,600
Takayo Bandoh	73	71	144	795,600
Yuka Tonsho	73	71	144	795,600
Michiko Mitsui	72	72	144	795,600
Akiko Fukushima	72	72	144	795,600
Aki Nakano	75	70	145	612,000
Mayumi Murai	74	71	145	612,000
Seiko Watanabe	73	72	145	612,000
Hiroko Yamaguchi	75	71	146	426,000
Kyoko Ono	74	72	146	426,000
Misato Nishikawa	73	73	146	426,000
Kaori Suzuki	76	70	146	426,000
Hiromi Mogi	72	74	146	426,000
Nobuko Kizawa	72	74	146	426,000
Chiaki Takahashi	72	74	146	426,000
Masaki Maeda	71	75	146	426,000
Mineko Nasu	71	75	146	426,000
Ayako Uehara	75	72	147	355,500
Ji-Yeon Han	75	72	147	355,500
Junko Yoshida	73	74	147	355,500
Ai-Yu Tu	72	75	147	355,500

Fujitsu Ladies

Tokyu Seven Hundred Club, Chiba
Par 36-36–72; 6,567 yards

October 15-17
purse, ¥60,000,000

	SCORES			TOTAL	MONEY
Michiko Hattori	68	71	71	210	¥10,800,000
Keiko Sasaki	71	70	69	210	5,280,000
(Hattori defeated Sasaki on second playoff hole.)					
Mikiyo Nishizuka	70	69	74	213	3,900,000
Ai Miyazato	73	67	73	213	3,900,000
Kaori Higo	71	71	72	214	2,500,000
Namika Omata	71	74	69	214	2,500,000
Yasuko Satoh	70	71	73	214	2,500,000
Ji-Hee Lee	71	70	74	215	1,650,000
Ji-Yeon Han	70	71	74	215	1,650,000
Woo-Soon Ko	71	74	71	216	1,020,000
Kasumi Fujii	72	70	74	216	1,020,000
Miho Koga	70	72	74	216	1,020,000

	SCORES			TOTAL	MONEY
Shiho Ohyama	72	72	72	216	1,020,000
Junko Omote	73	70	73	216	1,020,000
Kaori Suzuki	71	73	72	216	1,020,000
Noriko Aso	74	69	73	216	1,020,000
Akiko Fukushima	73	73	71	217	750,000
Michiko Mitsui	74	72	71	217	750,000
Yuri Fudoh	72	72	74	218	616,000
Hikaru Kobayashi	74	71	73	218	616,000
Jeong-Eun Lee	73	73	72	218	616,000
Fuki Kido	75	71	73	219	552,000
Hiromi Kobayashi	68	72	79	219	552,000
Midori Yoneyama	72	73	74	219	552,000
Yuriko Ohtsuka	72	73	74	219	552,000
Orie Fujino	76	70	73	219	552,000
Kumiko Hiyoshi	75	70	75	220	492,000
Eika Ohtake	76	68	76	220	492,000
Shin Sora	73	71	76	220	492,000
Eriko Moriyama	74	72	74	220	492,000
Hiromi Mogi	75	69	76	220	492,000

Masters Golf Club Ladies

Masters Golf Club, Hyogo
Par 36-36–72; 6,444 yards

October 22-24
purse, ¥100,000,000

	SCORES			TOTAL	MONEY
Ai Miyazato	69	68	68	205	¥18,000,000
Miho Koga	68	72	66	206	8,800,000
Yuri Fudoh	69	74	67	210	7,000,000
Michie Ohba	72	73	67	212	6,000,000
Junko Omote	69	74	70	213	3,875,000
Rui Kitada	72	76	65	213	3,875,000
Hiromi Mogi	74	70	69	213	3,875,000
Hiroko Yamaguchi	71	72	70	213	3,875,000
Shiho Ohyama	73	69	72	214	2,250,000
Midori Yoneyama	70	71	73	214	2,250,000
Young-Me Lee	70	75	70	215	1,600,000
Yun-Jye Wei	74	69	72	215	1,600,000
Se Ri Pak	69	74	72	215	1,600,000
Michiko Hattori	71	73	71	215	1,600,000
Akiko Fukushima	69	72	74	215	1,600,000
Hsiao-Chuan Lu	73	72	70	215	1,600,000
Ayako Uehara	71	70	75	216	1,100,000
Kelly Robbins	72	72	72	216	1,100,000
Woo-Soon Ko	76	70	70	216	1,100,000
Hikaru Kobayashi	70	74	72	216	1,100,000
Ji-Hee Lee	70	73	74	217	900,000
Karrie Webb	69	74	74	217	900,000
Misato Nishikawa	78	70	69	217	900,000
Kaori Higo	75	69	73	217	900,000
Yuriko Ohtsuka	73	73	72	218	820,000
Toshimi Kimura	70	76	72	218	820,000
Kaori Suzuki	74	73	71	218	820,000
Nikki Campbell	77	70	71	218	820,000
Jeong-Eun Lee	72	72	75	219	700,000
Yuka Irie	73	69	77	219	700,000
Yuka Sakaguchi	72	76	71	219	700,000

	SCORES			TOTAL	MONEY
Yasuko Satoh	75	72	72	219	700,000
Naoko Takasaki	71	70	78	219	700,000
Yukari Baba	73	73	73	219	700,000
Kaori Harada	74	72	73	219	700,000
Orie Fujino	72	76	71	219	700,000

Hisako Higuchi Hall of Fame Commemoration

Musashigoaka Golf Club, Saitama
Par 36-36—72; 6,513 yards

October 29-31
purse, ¥60,000,000

	SCORES			TOTAL	MONEY
Miho Koga	68	71	71	210	¥10,800,000
Yuri Fudoh	77	69	66	212	4,740,000
Sakura Yokomine	70	73	69	212	4,740,000
Kasumi Fujii	74	70	69	213	2,580,000
Nana Akahori	70	73	70	213	2,580,000
Hiroko Yamaguchi	73	70	70	213	2,580,000
Kuniko Maeda	72	72	69	213	2,580,000
Nikki Campbell	71	71	71	213	2,580,000
Chihiro Nakajima	74	72	68	214	1,274,000
Mineko Nasu	74	72	68	214	1,274,000
Ai Miyazato	71	72	71	214	1,274,000
Young-Me Lee	72	70	73	215	972,000
Midori Yoneyama	73	73	69	215	972,000
Shiho Ohyama	71	72	72	215	972,000
Natsu Nagai	73	74	68	215	972,000
Toshimi Kimura	75	70	71	216	732,000
Takayo Bandoh	72	73	71	216	732,000
Michie Ohba	73	72	71	216	732,000
Yukari Baba	72	74	70	216	732,000
Yuka Irie	70	74	73	217	570,000
Maki Sasayama	73	72	72	217	570,000
Yuriko Ohtsuka	69	74	74	217	570,000
Yuko Saitoh	72	77	69	218	540,000
Junko Omote	70	75	73	218	540,000
Seiko Watanabe	71	73	75	219	504,000
Rui Kitada	69	75	75	219	504,000
Yasuko Satoh	70	76	73	219	504,000
Keiko Sasaki	77	72	70	219	504,000
Yuko Moriguchi	73	75	72	220	450,000
Kyoko Ono	74	70	76	220	450,000
Misato Nishikawa	69	75	76	220	450,000
Mika Tajiri	75	74	71	220	450,000
Hikaru Kobayashi	71	73	76	220	450,000

Mizuno Classic

Seta Golf Club, North Course, Otsu, Shiga
Par 36-36—72; 6,450 yards

November 5-7
purse, ¥110,000,000

	SCORES			TOTAL	MONEY
Annika Sorenstam	63	66	65	194	¥16,050,000
Michie Ohba	73	67	63	203	7,448,056
Ai Miyazato	70	70	63	203	7,448,056

	SCORES			TOTAL	MONEY
Grace Park	67	69	67	203	7,448,056
Junko Omote	69	67	68	204	4,012,500
Aree Song	66	70	68	204	4,012,500
Young Kim	68	72	65	205	2,554,625
Karrie Webb	67	72	66	205	2,554,625
Hee-Won Han	67	70	68	205	2,554,625
Chieko Amanuma	69	67	69	205	2,554,625
Jamie Hullett	69	67	70	206	1,877,850
Candie Kung	69	67	70	206	1,877,850
Laura Davies	67	69	70	206	1,877,850
Gloria Park	71	68	68	207	1,555,031
Stacy Prammanasudh	72	66	69	207	1,555,031
Chihiro Nakajima	63	70	74	207	1,555,031
Lorie Kane	68	73	67	208	1,281,860
Natalie Gulbis	69	71	68	208	1,281,860
Becky Morgan	68	72	68	208	1,281,860
Yuko Saitoh	72	66	70	208	1,281,860
Laura Diaz	72	66	70	208	1,281,860
Hsiao-Chuan Lu	72	69	68	209	1,043,250
Mi-Hyun Kim	70	68	71	209	1,043,250
Kim Saiki	70	68	71	209	1,043,250
Catriona Matthew	69	69	71	209	1,043,250
Akiko Fukushima	67	70	72	209	1,043,250
Rachel Teske	66	71	72	209	1,043,250
Sakura Yokomine	68	73	69	210	873,869
Seol-An Jeon	70	70	70	210	873,869
Carin Koch	70	67	73	210	873,869

Itoen Ladies

Great Island Club, Chonan, Chiba
Par 36-36–72; 6,550 yards
(Event shortened to 36 holes—rain.)

November 12-14
purse, ¥60,000,000

	SCORES		TOTAL	MONEY
Yuriko Ohtsuka	72	68	140	¥9,450,000
Michiko Hattori	71	69	140	4,620,000
(Ohtsuka defeated Hattori on fourth playoff hole.)				
Kaori Higo	71	70	141	3,412,500
Hsiao-Chuan Lu	69	72	141	3,412,500
Hiroko Yamaguchi	72	70	142	1,890,000
Jeong-Eun Lee	75	67	142	1,890,000
Yuri Fudoh	70	72	142	1,890,000
Mitsuko Kawasaki	69	73	142	1,890,000
Yun-Jye Wei	69	73	142	1,890,000
Yasuko Satoh	71	72	143	1,015,875
Kasumi Fujii	70	73	143	1,015,875
Akiko Fukushima	73	71	144	798,000
Tomoko Kusakabe	72	72	144	798,000
Seiko Watanabe	72	72	144	798,000
Ok-Hee Ku	75	69	144	798,000
Ji-Hee Lee	71	73	144	798,000
Michie Ohba	70	74	144	798,000
Ai Miyazato	73	72	145	509,250
Miho Koga	73	72	145	509,250
Toshimi Kimura	73	72	145	509,250
Namika Omata	73	72	145	509,250

	SCORES		TOTAL	MONEY
Keiko Sasaki	72	73	145	509,250
Yuko Saitoh	72	73	145	509,250
Michiko Mitsui	71	74	145	509,250
Mihoko Takahashi	71	74	145	509,250
Noriko Aso	74	72	146	414,750
Midori Yoneyama	74	72	146	414,750
Nikki Campbell	75	71	146	414,750
Shiho Ohyama	75	71	146	414,750
Hsiu-Feng Tseng	72	74	146	414,750
Yukari Baba	71	75	146	414,750
Chihiro Nakajima	76	70	146	414,750

Daioseishi Elleair Ladies Open

Elleair Golf Club, Matsuyama, Kagawa
Par 36-36–72; 6,348 yards

November 19-21
purse, ¥80,000,000

	SCORES			TOTAL	MONEY
Ai Miyazato	66	67	69	202	¥14,400,000
Chieko Amanuma	69	70	66	205	6,400,000
Rui Kitada	66	70	69	205	6,400,000
Michie Ohba	70	70	66	206	4,800,000
Chieko Nishida	67	72	68	207	4,000,000
Akiko Fukushima	70	71	67	208	2,640,000
Riko Higashio	72	69	67	208	2,640,000
Woo-Soon Ko	69	69	70	208	2,640,000
Yuko Saitoh	67	68	73	208	2,640,000
Shiho Ohyama	65	74	70	209	1,492,000
Ae-Sook Kim	69	70	70	209	1,492,000
Kasumi Fujii	71	68	70	209	1,492,000
Junko Omote	71	66	72	209	1,492,000
Hiromi Takesue	68	71	71	210	1,216,000
Keiko Sasaki	69	70	71	210	1,216,000
Sakura Yokomine	73	69	68	210	1,216,000
Rie Fujiwara	68	72	71	211	908,800
Mikiyo Nishizuka	70	70	71	211	908,800
Samantha Head	71	69	71	211	908,800
Hiroko Yamaguchi	68	71	72	211	908,800
Hsiu-Feng Tseng	68	71	72	211	908,800
Midori Yoneyama	70	71	71	212	728,000
Fumiko Muraguchi	70	71	71	212	728,000
Toshimi Kimura	73	68	71	212	728,000
Kuniko Maeda	71	71	70	212	728,000
*Shinobu Moromizato	70	70	72	212	
Mayumi Murai	70	72	70	212	728,000
Ok-Hee Ku	69	70	73	212	728,000
Ji-Yeon Han	69	73	70	212	728,000
Hsiao-Chuan Lu	66	70	76	212	728,000

Japan LPGA Tour Championship

Miyazaki Country Club, Sadohara, Miyazaki
Par 36-36–72; 6,438 yards

November 25-28
purse, ¥60,000,000

	SCORES				TOTAL	MONEY
Yuri Fudoh	68	76	71	71	286	¥15,000,000
Michie Ohba	71	72	72	72	287	7,350,000
Ai Miyazato	69	75	69	74	287	7,350,000
Yuriko Ohtsuka	74	77	68	69	288	4,455,000
Hiroko Yamaguchi	70	74	72	72	288	4,455,000
Akiko Fukushima	74	72	72	71	289	3,528,000
Toshimi Kimura	72	71	77	70	290	2,628,000
Miho Koga	73	72	75	70	290	2,628,000
Kaori Higo	72	72	77	70	291	1,446,000
Kasumi Fujii	73	74	74	70	291	1,446,000
Michiko Hattori	70	77	72	75	294	906,000
Shiho Ohyama	78	70	74	72	294	906,000
Hiromi Mogi	72	72	75	75	294	906,000
Hsiao-Chuan Lu	74	75	76	70	295	666,000
Rui Kitada	75	69	75	77	296	552,000
Midori Yoneyama	75	78	71	73	297	492,000
Mikiyo Nishizuka	75	75	76	72	298	402,000
Junko Omote	76	77	74	71	298	402,000
Yuko Saitoh	74	79	74	72	299	318,000
Woo-Soon Ko	77	72	76	76	301	297,000
Mitsuko Kawasaki	74	77	77	73	301	297,000
Yukari Baba	74	79	74	79	306	288,000
Yoko Yamagishi	73	78	77	81	309	282,000

Australian Women's Tour

ABC Learning Centres Ladies Classic

Lakelands Golf Club, Australia
Par 36-36–72; 6,319 yards

February 20-22
purse, A$100,000

	SCORES			TOTAL	MONEY
Mardi Lunn	71	65	67	203	A$15,000
Shani Waugh	68	68	68	204	10,000
Laura Davies	70	66	72	208	6,000
Kylie Pratt	69	69	70	208	6,000
Georgina Simpson	70	69	70	209	4,000
Elisabeth Esterl	69	68	74	211	2,800
Natascha Fink	65	72	74	211	2,800
Laurette Maritz	69	70	72	211	2,800
Karine Icher	71	70	70	211	2,800
Cecilie Lundgreen	69	70	73	212	1,850
Trish Johnson	70	70	72	212	1,850

	SCORES			TOTAL	MONEY
Charlotta Sorenstam	70	71	72	213	1,600
Lindsey Wright	74	71	69	214	1,385
Rachel Teske	68	73	73	214	1,385
Sophie Sandolo	73	70	72	215	1,280
*Katy Jarochowicz	74	72	70	216	
Raquel Carriedo	74	69	73	216	1,187.50
Sarah Carbon	75	69	72	216	1,187.50
Gina Scott	75	71	70	216	1,187.50
Anne-Marie Knight	76	71	69	216	1,187.50
Johanna Westerberg	69	77	71	217	930
Rebecca Coakley	69	74	74	217	930
Nikki Campbell	69	74	74	217	930
Asa Gottmo	70	73	74	217	930
Cecilia Ekelundh	76	68	73	217	930
Anna Becker	71	70	76	217	930
Nuria Clau	70	73	74	217	930
Ana Larraneta	72	73	72	217	930
Nadina Taylor	73	71	73	217	930
Valerie Van Ryckeghem	73	71	73	217	930
Joanne Morley	75	71	71	217	930
Maria Hjorth	72	73	72	217	930
Nicola Moult	72	72	73	217	930

ANZ Ladies Masters

Royal Pines Resort, Gold Coast, Queensland
Par 35-37–72; 6,547 yards

February 26-29
purse, A$800,000

	SCORES				TOTAL	MONEY
Annika Sorenstam	69	70	65	65	269	A$120,000
Karen Stupples	68	67	70	68	273	79,200
Kylie Pratt	73	67	72	65	277	48,000
Jennifer Rosales	72	65	72	68	277	48,000
Anne-Marie Knight	71	66	69	72	278	32,600
Ana Larraneta	71	73	69	66	279	26,800
Nadina Taylor	72	72	66	70	280	24,000
Laura Davies	69	71	73	68	281	18,200
Rachel Teske	67	72	71	71	281	18,200
Silvia Cavalleri	71	71	72	68	282	16,000
Karrie Webb	71	70	70	72	283	14,000
Johanna Head	73	71	72	68	284	10,800
Liselotte Neumann	69	75	70	70	284	10,800
Yuka Shiroto	72	71	69	72	284	10,800
Mhairi McKay	70	70	71	73	284	10,800
Trish Johnson	73	68	69	74	284	10,800
Johanna Westerberg	73	74	71	67	285	9,333.30
Laurette Maritz	72	73	71	69	285	9,333.30
Grace Lee	70	70	69	76	285	9,333.30
Charlotta Sorenstam	72	73	73	68	286	8,280
Shani Waugh	71	75	71	69	286	8,280
Diana Luna	74	71	70	71	286	8,280
Virginie Auffret	71	69	74	72	286	8,280
Becky Brewerton	71	72	71	72	286	8,280
Karine Icher	70	74	70	72	286	8,280
Joanne Mills	72	72	72	71	287	7,440
Samantha Head	72	74	74	68	288	6,573.30
Natascha Fink	71	70	78	69	288	6,573.30

	SCORES				TOTAL	MONEY
Ana Belen Sanchez	75	70	74	69	288	6,573.30
Lynnette Brooky	75	68	74	71	288	6,573.30
Raquel Carriedo	73	72	72	71	288	6,573.30
Sophie Sandolo	71	72	71	74	288	6,573.30

AAMI Women's Australian Open

Concord Golf Club, Concord, New South Wales
Par 37-35–72; 6,346 yards
(Event extended to Monday—rain.)

March 4-8
purse, A$550,000

	SCORES				TOTAL	MONEY
Laura Davies	68	68	77	70	283	A$82,500
Rachel Teske	73	71	71	74	289	54,450
Trish Johnson	72	72	77	70	291	38,500
Michelle Ellis	73	74	72	74	293	24,750
Martina Eberl	72	74	72	75	293	24,750
Johanna Head	78	71	76	69	294	15,950
Carina Vagner	73	72	79	70	294	15,950
Karrie Webb	75	73	73	73	294	15,950
Sophie Sandolo	71	69	77	78	295	11,825
Stefania Croce	73	71	79	73	296	9,258.30
*Sarah-Jane Kenyon	76	70	77	73	296	
Karen Pearce	74	74	75	73	296	9,258.30
Charlotta Sorenstam	74	71	74	77	296	9,258.30
Liselotte Neumann	73	81	72	71	297	7,241.70
Christina Kuld	68	76	80	73	297	7,241.70
Paula Marti	76	74	74	73	297	7,241.70
Asa Gottmo	77	76	73	72	298	6,462.50
Hilary Lunke	74	71	79	74	298	6,462.50
Lynnette Brooky	76	71	75	76	298	6,462.50
Nadina Taylor	72	70	76	80	298	6,462.50
Shani Waugh	76	78	73	72	299	5,995
Becky Brewerton	75	74	76	74	299	5,995
Mi Jung Jeon	76	75	75	74	300	5,401
Marlene Hedblom	76	76	73	75	300	5,401
Alison Nicholas	77	76	71	76	300	5,401
Raquel Carriedo	76	75	72	77	300	5,401
Virginie Auffret	73	78	72	77	300	5,401
Elisabeth Esterl	75	70	84	72	301	4,331.20
Samantha Head	74	78	77	72	301	4,331.20
Gwladys Nocera	79	72	77	73	301	4,331.20
Mhairi McKay	74	75	78	74	301	4,331.20
Joanne Mills	70	77	78	76	301	4,331.20
Cherie Byrnes	76	75	74	76	301	4,331.20
Ana Belen Sanchez	76	76	73	76	301	4,331.20
Sophie Gustafson	76	78	70	77	301	4,331.20

Nedbank Women's Tour of South Africa

Acer Women's South African Open

Royal Johannesburg & Kensington Golf Clubs, Johannesburg
Par 37-35–72; 6,410 yards

March 17-19
purse, R250,000

	SCORES			TOTAL	MONEY
*Ashleigh Simon	71	74	63	208	
Carina Vagner	70	67	72	209	R32,500
Johanna Westerberg	68	73	68	209	32,500
Cecilia Ekelundh	67	72	73	212	20,000
Gwladys Nocera	69	72	72	213	12,375
Laurette Maritz	69	72	72	213	12,375
Virginie Beauchet	74	70	69	213	12,375
Mandy Adamson	75	69	70	214	8,625
Julie Forbes	74	73	69	216	6,458.33
Minea Blomqvist	70	75	71	216	6,458.33
Cecilie Lundgreen	73	72	71	216	6,458.33
Andrea Hirschhorn	71	74	73	218	5,125
Antonella Cvitan	73	71	75	219	4,625
*Sandra Winter	74	74	71	219	
Ludivine Kreutz	72	76	71	219	4,625
Anna Becker	75	73	72	220	4,212.50
Caryn Louw	74	74	72	220	4,212.50
Peggy Fraysse	75	73	73	221	4,000
Anna Tybring	79	74	70	223	3,687.50
Nina Reis	72	73	78	223	3,687.50
Emma Zackrisson	73	77	73	223	3,687.50
Annerie Wessels	76	76	71	223	3,687.50
Charlaine Coetzee-Hirst	71	77	76	224	3,062.50
Carlie Butler	71	77	76	224	3,062.50
Kirsty Fisher	74	74	76	224	3,062.50
Helena Alterby	70	77	77	224	3,062.50
Lisa Holm Sorensen	80	73	71	224	3,062.50
Josefine Skold	77	75	72	224	3,062.50
*Nikki Garret	77	73	74	224	
*Stacy Bregman	76	78	71	225	
*Kelli Shean	76	76	73	225	
Jehanne Jail	76	75	74	225	2,562.50
Nicole James	78	73	74	225	2,562.50

Pam Golding Ladies International

Glendower Golf Club, Cape Town
Par 37-36–73; 6,155 yards

March 24-26
purse, R250,000

	SCORES			TOTAL	MONEY
Minea Blomqvist	71	73	69	213	R37,500
*Ashleigh Simon	68	76	70	214	
Lisa Holm Sorensen	72	73	70	215	27,500
Christina Kuld	73	73	70	216	17,500

	SCORES			TOTAL	MONEY
Julie Forbes	73	72	71	216	17,500
Nathalie David	75	72	70	217	12,000
Martina Eberl	75	75	68	218	10,125
Mara Larrauri	69	76	74	219	6,625
Maria Boden	72	74	73	219	6,625
Andrea Hirschhorn	75	70	74	219	6,625
Mandy Adamson	74	73	72	219	6,625
Asa Gottmo	71	76	72	219	6,625
Sarah Heath	73	74	73	220	4,625
Ludivine Kreutz	67	74	79	220	4,625
Anna Becker	69	77	75	221	4,300
Cecilia Ekelundh	73	75	74	222	3,750
Nina Reis	73	75	74	222	3,750
Carlie Butler	75	79	68	222	3,750
Laurette Maritz	75	70	77	222	3,750
Tullia Calzavara	74	73	75	222	3,750
Fany Schaeffer	76	70	76	222	3,750
Nicole James	71	75	76	222	3,750
Rikke Rasmussen	75	76	72	223	3,250
Anna Tybring	75	78	71	224	3,000
Ursula Tuutti	74	76	74	224	3,000
Amanda Moltke-Leth	75	72	77	224	3,000
Cecilie Lundgreen	79	71	75	225	2,687.50
Linda Wessberg	79	77	69	225	2,687.50
Helena Alterby	76	78	72	226	2,375
Annerie Wessels	76	73	77	226	2,375
Bettina Hauert	71	81	74	226	2,375

Telkom Women's Classic

Randpark Golf Club, Johannesburg
Par 36-36–72; 6,277 yards

March 31-April 2
purse, R250,000

	SCORES			TOTAL	MONEY
Minea Blomqvist	73	63	68	204	R37,500
Laurette Maritz	70	71	70	211	27,500
*Ashleigh Simon	72	69	70	211	
Johanna Westerberg	69	71	73	213	20,000
Gwladys Nocera	69	71	75	215	12,375
Anna Becker	80	66	69	215	12,375
Ursula Tuutti	71	68	76	215	12,375
Mandy Adamson	72	76	68	216	8,625
Maria Boden	69	76	72	217	7,375
Kelly Hutcherson	71	72	75	218	6,375
Carlie Butler	69	77	73	219	5,375
Nina Reis	74	71	74	219	5,375
Helena Svensson	76	71	73	220	4,258.33
Sofia Renell	74	71	75	220	4,258.33
Amanda Moltke-Leth	71	79	70	220	4,258.33
Lisa Holm Sorensen	73	75	72	220	4,258.33
Cecilie Lundgreen	67	79	74	220	4,258.33
Charlaine Coetzee-Hirst	73	73	74	220	4,258.33
Andrea Hirschhorn	76	70	75	221	3,437.50
Martina Eberl	77	71	73	221	3,437.50
Ludivine Kreutz	74	74	73	221	2,875
Tullia Calzavara	77	72	72	221	3,437.50
Bettina Hauert	74	79	68	221	3,437.50

	SCORES			TOTAL	MONEY
*Nikki Garrett	69	74	78	221	
Sarah Heath	74	74	73	221	3,437.50
Linda Wessberg	71	75	75	221	3,437.50
Mara Larrauri	72	77	73	222	2,875
Anna Tybring	76	74	72	222	2,875
Costanza Trussoni	72	78	73	223	2,625
Jehanne Jail	75	77	73	225	2,437.50
Carina Vagner	81	74	70	225	2,437.50

Nedbank Women's South African Masters

Johannesburg Country Club, Johannesburg
Par 36-36–72; 6,219 yards

April 5-7
purse, R250,000

	SCORES			TOTAL	MONEY
Helena Alterby	69	67	68	204	R37,500
Asa Gottmo	69	69	68	206	27,500
Lisa Holm Sorensen	74	68	65	207	17,500
Laurette Maritz	70	69	68	207	17,500
Minea Blomqvist	70	71	68	209	10,250
Ursula Tuutti	68	69	72	209	10,250
Bettina Hauert	71	69	69	209	10,250
Johanna Westerberg	68	73	69	210	6,875
Carlie Butler	68	69	73	210	6,875
Maria Boden	72	71	69	212	5,625
Anna Tybring	71	69	73	213	5,125
Nina Reis	71	73	70	214	4,750
Peggy Fraysse	68	75	72	215	4,308.33
Caryn Louw	69	72	74	215	4,308.33
Emma Zackrisson	72	74	69	215	4,308.33
*Stacy Bregman	72	72	72	216	
Martina Eberl	72	70	74	216	3,937.50
Cecilie Lundgreen	74	70	72	216	3,937.50
*Ashleigh Simon	74	72	71	217	
Christina Kuld	70	73	74	217	3,500
Amanda Moltke-Leth	72	71	74	217	3,500
Andrea Hirschhorn	76	70	71	217	3,500
Sarah Heath	72	71	74	217	3,500
Linda Wessberg	75	71	71	217	3,500
Julie Forbes	76	73	69	218	3,062.50
Mandy Adamson	72	69	77	218	3,062.50
Sofia Renell	71	73	75	219	2,750
Tullia Calzavara	77	71	71	219	2,750
Emma Weeks	77	71	71	219	2,750
Eva Bjarvall	75	72	73	220	2,437.50
Costanza Trussoni	73	75	72	220	2,437.50